Tower Hamlets College
Learning Centre

128324

KT-482

TENTH EDITION

economics

David Begg, Gianluigi Vernasca, Stanley Fischer, Rudiger Dornbusch

economics

TENTH EDITION

David Begg, Gianluigi Vernasca, Stanley Fischer, Rudiger Dornbusch

THE LEARNING CENTRE
TOWER HAMLETS COLLEGE
ARBOUR SQUARE
LONDON E1 0PS

**McGraw-Hill
Higher Education**

London Boston Burr Ridge, IL Dubuque, IA Madison, WI New York San Francisco
St. Louis Bangkok Bogotá Caracas Kuala Lumpur Lisbon Madrid Mexico City Milan
Montreal New Delhi Santiago Seoul Singapore Sydney Taipei Toronto

Economics 10th Edition
David Begg, Gianluigi Vernasca, Stanley Fischer and Rudiger Dornbusch
ISBN-13 9780077129521
ISBN-10 0077129520

Published by McGraw-Hill Education
Shoppenhangers Road
Maidenhead
Berkshire
SL6 2QL
Telephone: 44 (0) 1628 502 500
Fax: 44 (0) 1628 770 224
Website: www.mcgraw-hill.co.uk

Order No:
Class: 330 BEG
Accession No: 128314
Type: 7 DAYS

British Library Cataloguing in Publication Data
A catalogue record for this book is available from the British Library

Library of Congress Cataloging in Publication Data
The Library of Congress data for this book has been applied for from the Library of Congress

Acquisitions Editor: Natalie Jacobs
Development Editor: Tom Hill
Marketing Manager: Vanessa Boddington
Head of Production: Beverley Shields

Text design by Hard Lines
Cover design by Adam Renvoize
Printed and bound in Spain by Grafo, S.A.

Published by McGraw-Hill Education (UK) Limited an imprint of The McGraw-Hill Companies, Inc., 1221 Avenue of the Americas, New York, NY 10020. Copyright © 2011 by McGraw-Hill Education (UK) Limited. All rights reserved. No part of this publication may be reproduced or distributed in any form or by any means, or stored in a database or retrieval system, without the prior written consent of The McGraw-Hill Companies, Inc., including, but not limited to, in any network or other electronic storage or transmission, or broadcast for distance learning.

Fictitious names of companies, products, people, characters and/or data that may be used herein (in case studies or examples) are not intended to represent any real individual, company, product or event.

ISBN-13 9780077129521
ISBN-10 0077129520

© 2011. Exclusive rights by The McGraw-Hill Companies, Inc. for manufacture and export. This book cannot be re-exported from the country to which it is sold by McGraw-Hill.

The *McGraw·Hill* Companies

Dedication

For Honora, Mary and Robin – DB

To my family and to my beloved Vitalba – GV

TOWER HAMLETS COLLEGE
Learning Centre
Poplar High Street
LONDON
E14 0AF

Brief Table of Contents

Detailed Table of Contents

Detailed Table of Contents

Continued

Detailed Table of Contents

Continued

Detailed Table of Contents

Preface

Economics is much too interesting to be left to professional economists. It affects almost everything we do, not merely at work or at the shops but also in the home and the voting booth. It influences how well we look after our planet, the future we leave for our children, the extent to which we can care for the poor and the disadvantaged, and the resources we have for enjoying ourselves.

These issues are discussed daily, in bars and on buses as well as in cabinet meetings and boardrooms. The formal study of economics is exciting because it introduces a toolkit that allows a better understanding of the problems we face. Everyone knows a smoky engine is a bad sign, but sometimes only a trained mechanic can give the right advice on how to fix it.

This book is designed to teach you the toolkit and give you practice in using it. Nobody carries an enormous toolbox very far. Useful toolkits are small enough to be portable but contain enough proven tools to deal with both routine problems and unforeseen circumstances. With practice, you will be surprised at how much light this analysis can shed on daily living. This book is designed to make economics seem as useful as it really is.

How much do economists disagree?

There is an old complaint that economists never agree about anything. This is simply wrong. The media, taxi-drivers and politicians love to talk about topics on which there is disagreement; it would be boring TV if all participants in a panel discussion held identical views. But economics is not a subject in which there is always an argument for everything. There are answers to many questions.

We aim to show where economists agree – on what and for what reason – and why they sometimes disagree.

Economics in the twenty-first century

Our aim is to allow students to understand today's economic environment. This requires mastering the theory and practising its application. Just as the theory of genetics or of information technology is slowly progressing, so the theory of economics continues to make progress, sometimes in dramatic and exciting ways. Sometimes this is prompted by theoretical reasoning, sometimes it is a response to a dramatic new event, such as the banking crash and subsequent financial meltdown around the world.

We believe in introducing students immediately to the latest ideas in economics. If these can be conveyed simply, why force students to use older approaches that work less well? Two recent developments in economics underlie much of what we do. One is the role of information, the other is globalization.

How information is transmitted and manipulated is central to many issues in incentives and competition, including the recent booming e-commerce. Ease of information, coupled with lower transport costs, also explains trends towards globalization, and associated reductions in national sovereignty, especially in smaller countries. Modern economics helps us make sense of our changing world, think about where it may go next, and evaluate choices that we currently face.

Preface

Changes to the tenth edition

After 25 years at the top, we wanted to ensure that the book remains as relevant for the next 25 years as it has been in the past. Those familiar with previous editions will continue to recognize the underlying structure and approach, a window on the latest thinking about our evolving world and the way in which economics can make sense of it.

The most important change to the tenth edition is the addition of a new co-author, Gianluigi Vernasca, an expert in microeconomics who teaches at the University of Essex. By expanding the writing team, we have been able to undertake a comprehensive updating of the entire book.

The tenth edition has been thoroughly revised like no other edition. Over 40 reviews and two detailed surveys were commissioned over the writing period, each giving useful feedback on how we could better cater for students and lecturers. All this market feedback helped us constantly assess what we were writing, how it could be improved and how it could be best presented. More material has been added to some chapters while others have been deleted almost entirely. A lot has changed in the last three years and it is all reflected in the text. Specific changes to the new edition include:

- A more detailed analysis of welfare assessment of market outcomes, starting from the concepts of consumer and producer surplus.
- A substantial revision of the analysis of consumer choice and demand decisions.
- A comprehensive analysis of the financial crash – its causes, consequences, and possible policy responses, from fiscal stimulus to quantitative easing.
- An updated and expanded assessment of the risks of debt deflation.
- Full updates throughout to include 2009/2010 data in graphs and tables.
- 141 contemporary example boxes, over 80 of which are new, which illustrate key ideas with relevance to the real world.
- Important new pedagogical features, including topical new case studies, boxes on economic concepts and activity applications, and optional maths boxes for the technically minded.
- A revised and larger set of graded review questions, to create flexibility in the level and pace at which you learn and apply economic principles.
- More electronic resources for both students and lecturers.

With all this change, the book's structure is a bit different from the last edition and there are now only 29 chapters instead of 36. The main changes are listed below:

- Chapter 11 (Different types of labour) from the ninth edition has been merged with Chapter 10 (The labour market) to provide one robust chapter covering all the key issues.
- Part Three (Welfare economics) from the ninth edition has been restructured. The four chapters have been reduced to two and the remaining material added to Part Two. Material on natural monopoly and regulation has been placed in Chapter 8 while coverage of competition policy is now in Chapter 9.

- Research showed Chapter 32 (Macroeconomics: taking stock) from the ninth edition was not widely used so it has been removed from the book. For those who found the material beneficial, it is still available on the Online Learning Centre (OLC).

- Part Five (The world economy) has been restructured and made more concise. The four chapters from the ninth edition are now two in this edition.

Learning by doing

Few people practise for a driving test just by reading a book. Even when you think you understand how to do a hill start, it takes a lot of practice to master the finer points. In the same way, we give you lots of examples and real-world applications not just to emphasize the relevance of economics but also to help you master it for yourself. We start at square one and take you slowly through the tools of theoretical reasoning and how to apply them. We use algebra and equations sparingly, more often than not in separate boxes so they can be skipped or used depending on how technically minded you are. The best ideas are simple and robust, and can usually be explained quite easily.

How to study

Don't just read about economics, try to do it! It is easy, but mistaken, to read on cruise control, highlighting the odd sentence and gliding through paragraphs we have worked hard to simplify. Active learning needs to be interactive. When the text says 'clearly', ask yourself 'why' is it clear? See if you can construct the diagram before you look at it. As soon as you don't follow something, go back and read it again. Try to think of other examples to which the theory could be applied. The only way to check you really understand things is to test yourself. There are opportunities to do this in the book through activity questions and review questions, as well as multiple-choice quizzes on the OLC.

To assist you in working through this text, we have developed a number of distinctive study and design features. To familiarize yourself with these features, please turn to the Guided Tour on pages xvi–xviii.

Supplementary resources

Economics tenth edition offers a comprehensive package of resources for the teaching and learning of economics. The resources offered with the new edition have been developed in response to feedback from current users in order to provide lecturers with a variety of teaching resources for class teaching, lectures and assessment. Students are also offered a range of extra materials to assist in learning, revising and applying the principles of economics.

Connect

Connect Economics is McGraw-Hill's new web-based assignment and assessment platform. It gives lecturers and tutors the power to create assignments, tests and quizzes online. Easily accessible grade reports allow you to track your students' progress. Students get feedback on each individual question and immediate grading which makes it the perfect platform to test your knowledge.

Online Learning Centre

An accompanying Online Learning Centre website has been developed to provide an unrivalled package of flexible, high quality resources for both lecturer and student. To access all of the free Online Learning Centre resources and to find out about enhanced options, simply visit the website at **www.mcgraw-hill.co.uk/textbooks/begg**.

To learn more about the resources available to lecturers and students online, go to our tour of the resources on pages xxviii–xxxi (Additional technology to enhance learning and teaching).

Guided tour

In addition to illustrating pertinent concepts and presenting up-to-date coverage, *Economics, 10th edition* strives to present the material in a way that makes it coherent and easy to understand. To meet the varied needs of its intended audience, *Economics, 10th edition* is rich in valuable learning tools and support:

Practice and Testing

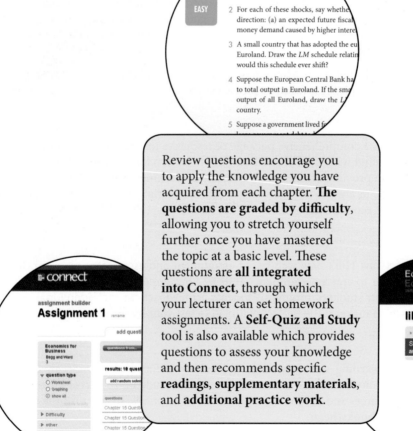

Review questions

EASY

1 Why do people usually save a 'once

2 For each of these shocks, say whethe direction: (a) an expected future fisca money demand caused by higher intere

3 A small country that has adopted the eu Euroland. Draw the *LM* schedule relatir would this schedule ever shift?

4 Suppose the European Central Bank ha to total output in Euroland. If the sma output of all Euroland, draw the *L* country.

5 Suppose a government lived f

Review questions encourage you to apply the knowledge you have acquired from each chapter. **The questions are graded by difficulty,** allowing you to stretch yourself further once you have mastered the topic at a basic level. These questions are **all integrated into Connect**, through which your lecturer can set homework assignments. A **Self-Quiz and Study** tool is also available which provides questions to assess your knowledge and then recommends specific **readings, supplementary materials,** and **additional practice work.**

Continued

Application

CASE **10.1** **Boosting UK labour**

New Labour's labour market policie
Making Work Pay. Both were based o
new opportunities: work is a ladder allowing people
UK labour supply?

Welfare to Work had two elements: more help in find
little effort to find work. The budget line in diagram (a
lower benefits for those out of work, and the rise from
ment helps. In diagram (a) we show the choice of son

Making Work Pay dealt with the part of the budge
Tax Credit gave money to workers with childr
hours a week. Diagram (b) shows the discontin
a person who would not work facing *CAD*
EGJKM. Or so the government hoped!

CONCEPT **9.1** **It's not what it loo**

An investor seeking to hold assets i
there were 8307 US mutual funds
been growing robustly over time: while there
quadrupled to 3100 by 1990, and almost tripled a
the US is a market with many firms, most of w
reasonably free entry. Is the market for mutual fu

The answer appears to be no. The fees that investe
they differ even for mutual funds that are almost
different for goods that are almost homogeneous
performance of the funds, that can affect inves
consulting a financial adviser before purchase, i
element in investor choice. Funds can have
clearly, investors prefer less tax exposure,

ll those facts can explain why produ
ve some sort of product di

ACTIVITY **17.1** **Fiscal stability a**

As Chancellor of the Exchequer,
control of interest rates but also i

The Code for Fiscal Stability committed the gov
government spending out of current revenues.

Borrowing-financed deficits are allowed only to fi
for itself by raising future output and hence future
the actual deficit fluctuates with output over the b
'golden rule' means that government debt accu
investment) should be accompanied by higher o

Because tax revenues fall when the economy
about whether the emergence of a tax reve
whether it is the start of an adverse tren

Having begun with a tight fiscal polic
pending especially on the Natio
l be afforded and wheth

Each chapter includes a number of **boxed examples**. These aim to show how a particular economic example can be applied in practice. They are listed, and explained in more detail, on pages xix–xxiv. Connect also provides helpful tools to relate what is learnt in the book to real life. Captain Consumer (below) explains all about consumer choice in one of the many **videos** available.

Guided tour

Aiding Understanding

to try to hit the
...nent change in demand, whic...
...*hock*, Figure 21.12 showed that it mak...
order to mitigate the shock to output.

The *ii* schedule in Figure 21.1 reflects the average...
Deviations of inflation from target are not all imm...
the policy of raising (lowering) real interest rates wh...
of inflation from target are the price to be paid for...

Flexible inflation targeting commits a central bank to hit inflation targets in the medium run, but gives it some discretion about how quickly to hit its inflation target.

The key to successful **flexibl**...
from target should be *tempor*...
rates until inflation is restore...
reduce interest to boost dem...
increased, and there is no r...
rise in inflation.

In contrast, weak central banks that lack credibil...
People worry that they will not be tough enou...
sustained expansion, inflation gets going. Thi...
Chapter 22 examines the economics of credi...

Learning Outcomes

By the end of this chapter, you should und...

1. perfect competition
2. why a perfectly competitive firm equ...
3. how profits and losses lead to entry a...
4. the industry supply curve
5. comparative static analysis of a comp...
6. pure monopoly
7. why a monopolist's output equates *M*...
8. how output compares under mon...
   how price discrimination...

...to the Phil...
...sed to fit the facts.

Each chapter offers **extensive pedagogy** to help aid your **understanding of the topics** being taught. This includes Learning Outcomes, Key Terms, Summaries and extensive Tables and Figures. **Further tools** such as summaries and videos are available in Connect.

Summary

- Government revenues come mainly from...
  taxes on purchases of goods and servic...
  Government spending comprises governm...

- Governments intervene in a market econom...
  A progressive tax-and-transfer system take...
  system is mildly progressive. The less well of...
  rates. Although some necessities, notably foo...
  by the poor, notably cigarettes and alcohol,...

- Externalities are cases of market failure...
  subsidizing goods that involve externali...
  if it takes account of the externality, el...
  induced by the externality distorti...

- A public good is a good for...
  ...nsumption by other...

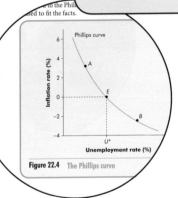

Figure 22.4 The Phillips curve

Boxed material

The text offers a wealth of boxed material to help explain how a particular economic principle can be applied in practice. There are four different types of box:

- Case: These draw on real-life companies and topical events to help illustrate economics in action.
- Concept: These contain content which is slightly more complex and provide some additional, more challenging, topics for you to explore.
- Activity: Similar to those in the last edition, these illustrate key economic concepts and then ask you to apply them to the real world. There are questions at the end of each activity and you can find the answers at the back of the book.
- Maths: These boxes highlight key mathematical formulae and present them in a digestible format. They can easily be skipped without interrupting the flow of the chapter, if necessary.

The majority of boxes are new to this edition (new material is indicated by a * on the chart below) and most of the others have been updated. With over 140 in total, there is plenty of opportunity to delve deeper into the content of each chapter.

Chapter	Title	Type
1	Most output is service	Case
	The oil price shocks	Case
	Scarcely a hospital bed!	Activity
	Poor Marx for central planners	Case
	Green piece	Case
2	The British Household Panel Survey (BHPS)*	Concept
	Hyperinflation	Concept
	Money illusion*	Concept
	Landing the big job	Activity
	Get a Becker view: use an economist's spectacles	Case
3	Market equilibrium with linear demand and supply*	Maths
	One little piggy went to market	Case
	The demand for mobile voice calls in the UK*	Case
	Movement along a curve vs shifts of the curve	Activity
	Graphical derivation of consumer and producer surplus*	Concept

Boxed material

Boxed material

13	General vs partial equilibrium: an example from school policy*	Concept
	Externalities and the London 2012 Olympic Games*	Case
	Internalizing a negative externality using property rights*	Maths
	Stern view of discount rates	Activity
14	The paradox of open source software*	Case
	Do you mind if I smoke? The smoking ban in the UK*	Case
	Using a tax to internalize the negative externality*	Maths
	Hunting the median voter	Activity
15	Emerging markets act as a locomotive for the world economy	Case
	Easily measured but not the whole story*	Concept
	Tax evasion, crime and the mismeasurement of GNP*	Case
	Pollution could make economic growth negative	Activity
16	Exogenous and endogenous variables*	Concept
	The *AD* schedule: moving along it or shifting it?	Activity
	Investment during the crash of 2009*	Case
	Autonomous demand and equilibrium output*	Maths
	How stable is the saving rate?*	Case
17	Fiscal policy under pressure: lessons from Japan	Case
	Budget effects of demand fluctuations*	Case
	The limits to fiscal policy	Concept
	Fiscal stability and responsibility	Activity
	Equilibrium output revisited*	Maths
18	Barter economy vs monetary economy*	Concept
	A beginner's guide to financial markets	Activity
	The sub-prime crisis and its aftermath*	Case
	The money multiplier	Maths
	The collapse of bank lending*	Concept

Boxed material

ECONOMICS

 STUDENTS...

Want to get **better grades**? *(Who doesn't?)*

Prefer to do your **homework online**? *(After all, you are online anyway...)*

Need **a better way** to **study** before the big test?

(A little peace of mind is a good thing...)

 With **McGraw-Hill's** *Connect™ Plus Economics*,

STUDENTS GET:

- **Easy online access** to homework, tests, and quizzes assigned by your instructor.

- **Immediate feedback** on how you're doing. (No more wishing you could call your instructor at 1 a.m.)

- **Quick access** to lectures, practice materials, eBook, and more. (All the material you need to be successful is right at your fingertips.)

- A Self-Quiz and Study tool that **assesses your knowledge** and **recommends** specific readings, supplemental study materials, and additional practice work.*

*Available with select McGraw-Hill titles.

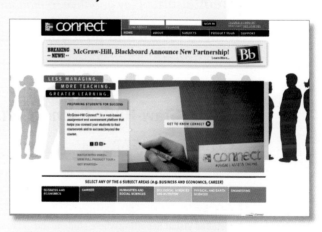

Less managing. More teaching. Greater learning.

 INSTRUCTORS...

Would you like your **students** to show up for class **more prepared**?
(Let's face it, class is much more fun if everyone is engaged and prepared...)

Want an **easy way to assign** homework online and track student **progress**?
(Less time grading means more time teaching...)

Want an **instant view** of student or class performance? *(No more wondering if students understand...)*

Need to **collect data and generate reports** required for administration or accreditation? *(Say goodbye to manually tracking student learning outcomes...)*

Want to **record and post your lectures** for students to view online?

 With **McGraw-Hill's *Connect*™ *Plus Economics*,**

INSTRUCTORS GET:

- Simple **assignment management**, allowing you to spend more time teaching.

- **Auto-graded** assignments, quizzes, and tests.

- **Detailed Visual Reporting** where student and section results can be viewed and analysed.

- Sophisticated **online testing** capability.

- A **filtering and reporting** function that allows you to easily assign and report on materials that are correlated to accreditation standards, learning outcomes, and Bloom's taxonomy.

- An easy-to-use **lecture capture** tool.

- The option to **upload course documents** for student access.

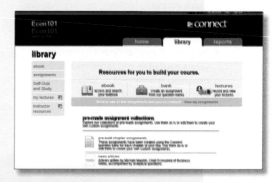

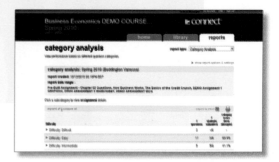

Want an online, **searchable version** of your textbook?

Wish your textbook could be **available online** while you're doing your assignments?

 ### Connect™ Plus Economics eBook

If you choose to use *Connect™ Plus Economics*, you have an affordable and searchable online version of your book integrated with your other online tools.

Connect™ Plus Economics eBook offers features like:

- Topic search
- Direct links from assignments
- Adjustable text size
- Jump to page number
- Print by section

 Want to get more **value** from your textbook purchase?

Think learning economics should be a bit more **interesting**?

 ### Check out the STUDENT RESOURCES section under the *Connect™* Library tab.

Here you'll find a wealth of resources designed to help you achieve your goals in the course. Every student has different needs, so explore the STUDENT RESOURCES to find the materials best suited to you.

Additional technology to enhance learning and teaching

Online Learning Centre (OLC)

Visit www.mcgraw-hill.co.uk/textbooks/begg today

There is a wealth of resources on the Online Learning Centre website to help with your teaching. Be sure to visit the link below and browse through the following materials:

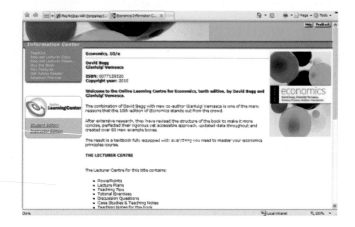

Available for lecturers:

- PowerPoint slides
- Lecture plans
- Teaching tips
- Tutorial exercises
- Discussion questions
- Case study teaching notes
- Lecture-only case studies
- Solutions manual
- Suggested course structures

EZTest

Test Bank available in McGraw-Hill EZ Test Online

A test bank of hundreds of questions is available to lecturers adopting this book for their module. A range of questions is provided for each chapter, including multiple choice, true or false, and short-answer or essay questions. The questions are identified by type, difficulty and topic to help you to select questions that best suit your needs, and are accessible through an easy-to-use online testing tool, **McGraw-Hill EZ Test Online.**

McGraw-Hill EZ Test Online is accessible to busy academics virtually anywhere – in their office, at home or while travelling – and eliminates the need for software installation. Lecturers can choose from question banks associated with their adopted textbook or easily create their own questions. They also have access to hundreds of banks and thousands of questions created for other McGraw-Hill titles. Multiple versions of tests can be saved for delivery on paper or online through WebCT, Blackboard and other course management systems. When created and delivered though EZ Test Online, students' tests can be immediately marked, saving lecturers time and providing prompt results to students.

To register for this FREE resource, visit www.eztestonline.com

Custom Publishing Solutions

Let us help make our **content** your **solution**

At McGraw-Hill Education our aim is to help lecturers to find the most suitable content for their needs delivered to their students in the most appropriate way. Our Custom Publishing Solutions offer the ideal combination of content delivered in the way which best suits lecturer and students.

Our custom publishing programme offers lecturers the opportunity to select just the chapters or sections of material they wish to deliver to their students from a database called CREATE™ at www. mcgrawhillcreate.co.uk

CREATE™ contains over two million pages of content from:

- textbooks
- professional books
- case books – Harvard Articles, Insead, Ivey, Darden, Thunderbird and BusinessWeek
- Taking Sides – debate materials

across the following imprints:

- McGraw-Hill Education
- Open University Press
- Harvard Business Publishing
- US and European material

There is also the option to include additional material authored by lecturers in the custom product – this does not necessarily have to be in English.

We will take care of everything from start to finish in the process of developing and delivering a custom product to ensure that lecturers and students receive exactly the material needed in the most suitable way.

With a Custom Publishing Solution, students enjoy the best selection of material deemed to be the most suitable for learning everything they need for their courses – something of real value to support their learning. Teachers are able to use exactly the material they want, in the way they want, to support their teaching on the course.

Please contact your Local McGraw-Hill representative with any questions or alternatively contact Warren Eels **e:** warren_eels@mcgraw-hill.com.

Improve Your Grades!
20% off any Study Skills book!

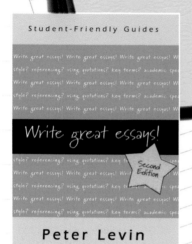

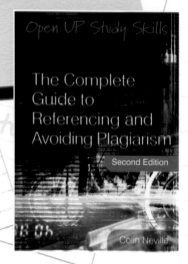

Our Study Skills books are packed with practical advice and tips that are easy to put into practice and will really improve the way you study. Our books will help you:

- Improve your grades
- Avoid plagiarism
- Save time
- Develop new skills
- Write confidently
- Undertake research projects
- Sail through exams
- Find the perfect job

Visit our website to read helpful hints about essays, exams, dissertations and find out about our offers.

www.openup.co.uk/studyskills

Special offer!
As a valued customer, buy online and receive 20% off any of our Study Skills books by entering the promo code *BRILLIANT!*

Acknowledgements for the tenth edition

Firstly, we would like to thank Tom Hill, Natalie Jacobs and all the other people at McGraw-Hill. A special thanks goes to our students at Imperial College London and the University of Essex for the useful feedback they have given us over the years.

We would like to thank the following reviewers who provided helpful suggestions and comments on the book as it progressed through its revision:

John Ball, University of Swansea

Francesco Bravo, University of York

Michael Brookes, Middlesex University

Simeon Coleman, Nottingham Trent University

Graham Cookson, University of London, King's College

William Dixon, London Metropolitan University

Ralf Eriksson, Åbo Akademi University

John Gathergood, Nottingham University

Walter Heering, University of Brighton

Martin Jensen, Birmingham University

Paul Kearney, Regents College

Ben Knight, University of Warwick

Pamela Lenton, University of Sheffield

Mikael Lindback, Umeå University

Jan Peter Madson, Copenhagen Business School

Walter Nonneman, University of Antwerp

Keith Pilbeam, City University, London

Jorn Rattso, Norwegian University of Science and Technology

Jenny Roberts, University of Sheffield

John Salter, University of Manchester

Rob Simmons, Lancaster University

Rauli Svento, Oulu University

Dimitrios Syrrakos, Manchester Metropolitan University

Continued

Gonzalo Varela, University of Sussex

Ian Walker, Lancaster University

Pamela Whisker, Plymouth University

Michael Wood, London South Bank University

We would also like to thank the following academics who participated in one of our many surveys that aided the development of this edition:

Mark Bailey, University of Ulster

Roy Bailey, University of Essex

Rob Branston, University of Bath

Alan Carruth, University of Kent

Steve Cook, Swansea University

Craig Duckworth, London Metropolitan University

Peter Feindt, Cardiff University

Timo Goeschl, University of Heidelberg

Jon Guest, Coventry University

Bersant Hobdari, Copenhagen Business School

Piotr Jaworski, Edinburgh Napier University

Geriant Johnes, Lancaster University

James Johnston, University of the West of Scotland

William Kelly, Dublin City University

Young-Chan Kim, University of Greenwich

David Kraithman, University of Hertfordshire

Paul Andrew Lewis, King's College London

Yioryos Makedonis, Queen Mary, University of London

Alan Matthews, Trinity College Dublin

Robert Mayer, University of Huddersfield

Shaista Naheed Minhas, Canterbury Christchurch University

Shampa Roy-Mukherjee, University of East London

Frank van der Salm, Utrecht University

Yontem Sonmez, University of Central Lancaster

Martin van Tuijl, Tilburg University

Andrey Yukhanaev, Northumbria University

Acknowledgements for the tenth edition

Finally, special thanks to the following academics that helped produce some of the many online resources available with this text:

Bersant Hobdari, Copenhagen Business School

John Hudson, University of Bath

Matthew Olczak, University of Aston

Gerry Wright

Peter Wrigley

David Begg and Gianluigi Vernasca

October 2010

Every effort has been made to trace and acknowledge ownership of copyright and to clear permission for material reproduced in this book. The publishers will be pleased to make suitable arrangements to clear permission with any copyright holders whom it has not been possible to contact.

About the authors

Professor David Begg is Principal of the business school at Imperial College London, currently ranked the world's ninth best university (*Times Higher Education Supplement*, 2010).

Born in Glasgow, David went to Cambridge in the hope of playing cricket but became fascinated with economics. After also studying at Oxford, he won a Kennedy Scholarship to the Massachusetts Institute of Technology, where Stanley Fischer and Rudiger Dornbusch were his PhD supervisors.

David returned to jobs at Oxford then London universities. In 1983 he got together with Stan and Rudi to write what has become Europe's most successful economics textbook, featured by BBC Radio 4 in its series 'Student Bibles' along with other such classics as *Gray's Anatomy*.

Gianluigi Vernasca is a lecturer in economics at the University of Essex. Since October 2009 he has also been Director of Undergraduate Studies in the Department of Economics.

Gianluigi received his PhD in 2006 from the University of Warwick. His research is mainly in the field of industrial economics. He has taught economics at both undergraduate and postgraduate levels in various institutions. Gianluigi has also worked as an economic consultant on competition and antitrust issues.

For those of you wondering about David and Gianluigi's co-authors: after leaving MIT **Stanley Fischer** became Chief Economist of the World Bank, Deputy Head of the IMF, Vice Chairman of Citigroup and Governor of the Bank of Israel. Until his untimely death, **Rudiger Dornbusch** remained a professor at MIT; his analysis and recommendations were sought by countless governments and corporations. Stan and Rudi taught a generation of students – including Ben Bernanke, current Chairman of the US Federal Reserve.

PART ONE Introduction

Economics is all around you. It is about how society deals with the problem of scarcity. We cannot have everything we want, whether this refers to continuous holidays or perfectly clean air. We have to make choices. Economics is the study of how society makes these choices. Economics is not just about incomes, prices and money. Sometimes it makes sense to use markets, sometimes we need other solutions. Economic analysis helps us decide when to leave things to the market and when to override the market.

Chapter 1 introduces the central issues of scarcity and choice, and the extent of government involvement in these decisions. Chapter 2 outlines economic reasoning, discussing how our understanding is advanced by the interaction of theories and evidence. Chapter 3 illustrates markets in action.

Contents

PART
ONE

Introduction

Economics and the economy

Learning Outcomes

By the end of this chapter, you should understand:

1. that economics is the study of how society resolves the problem of scarcity
2. ways in which society decides what, how and for whom to produce
3. the concept of opportunity cost
4. positive and normative economics
5. microeconomics and macroeconomics

Every group of people must solve three basic problems of daily living: *what* goods and services to produce, *how* to produce them and *for whom* to produce them.

Goods are physical commodities, such as steel or strawberries. Services are activities such as massages or live concerts, consumed or enjoyed only at the instant they are produced. In rare cases some of the questions about what, how and for whom to produce have already been answered: until the arrival of Man Friday, Robinson Crusoe can ignore the 'for whom' question. Normally, society must answer all three questions.

By emphasizing the role of society, our definition places **economics** within the social sciences that study and explain human behaviour. Economics studies behaviour in the production, exchange and use of goods and services. The key economic problem for society is how to reconcile the conflict between people's virtually limitless desires for goods and services, and the **scarcity of resources** (labour, machinery and raw materials) with which these goods and services can be produced.

> **Economics** is the study of how society decides what, how and for whom to produce.
>
> A **resource** is **scarce** if the demand of that resource at a zero price would exceed the available supply.

In answering what, how and for whom to produce, economics explains how scarce resources are allocated among competing claims on their use.

Although economics is about human behaviour, we describe it as a science. This reflects the method of analysis, not the subject matter, of economics. Economists develop theories of human behaviour and test them against the facts. Chapter 2 discusses the tools that economists use and explains the sense in which this approach is scientific. This does not mean that economics ignores people as individuals. Moreover, good economics retains an element of art. Only by having a feel for how people actually behave can economists focus their analysis on the right issues.

Most output is service

At the start of the twenty-first century, in advanced countries, agriculture comprises about 1 per cent of national output and industry less than 25 per cent. The rest is services, which include banking, transport, entertainment, communications, tourism, and public services (defence, police, education, health). In countries such as China and India, agriculture remains a higher share of GDP and services are not yet fully developed. Everywhere, services are the fastest growing part of output and of exports. Success in exporting banking, fashion and entertainment helps make the UK the second-largest exporter of services in the world.

In developed countries, services have for a long time been the largest component of national output. But until recently most international trade was trade in goods. The internet has changed all that. Accounting services can be outsourced to India and the advice of Indian accountants is as rapidly received by email in the UK as face to face in India.

% of national output	UK	USA	France	China	India
Agriculture	1	1	2	13	19
Industry	26	22	22	46	28
Services	73	77	76	41	54

Source: World Bank, *World Development Indicators*. © 2010 The World Bank Group. All rights reserved.

1.1 Economic issues

Trying to understand what economics is about by studying definitions is like trying to learn to swim by reading an instruction manual. Formal analysis makes sense only once you have some practical experience. In this section we discuss two examples of how society allocates scarce resources between competing uses. In each case we see the importance of the questions what, how and for whom to produce.

The 2007 financial crisis

The crisis that started in the United States in 2007 is considered the worst economic crisis since the 1929 Great Depression. Because of the crisis many economies entered a recession. A recession is a period of time in which the amount of goods and services produced by an economy (called the gross domestic product or GDP) declines. Recessions are not uncommon; indeed, economies over time experience cyclical periods of recession followed by periods in which economic activity rises.

Figure 1.1 reports the growth rate of the GDP for the US economy from 1985 to 2010. It shows that in the last 15 years there have been several periods in which the US economy faced a negative growth rate of output; however, none to the extent of the recession that began in 2007.

The situation started with a financial crisis in the US market for sub-prime mortgages. Sub-prime mortgages are those given to people who want to buy a house but have a poor credit record and a relatively high probability of eventually not being able to repay their loan.

Why lend money to people who are such a high credit risk? The reason was the constantly increasing price of houses before 2007, as shown in Figure 1.2. With the price of houses increasing, the risk of losing on a

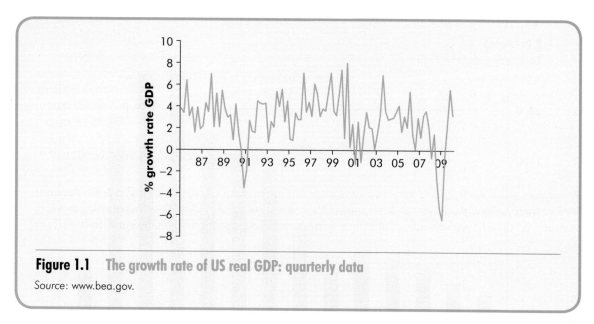

Figure 1.1 The growth rate of US real GDP: quarterly data

Source: www.bea.gov.

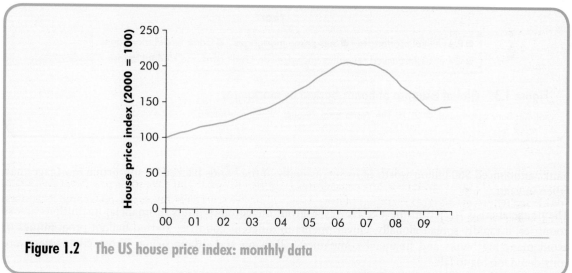

Figure 1.2 The US house price index: monthly data

sub-prime mortgage was limited. In the case of default on a mortgage by a sub-prime borrower, the lender could repossess their house and sell it at a high price. To make those sub-prime mortgages more profitable, mortgage companies started to bundle them into bonds and sell them to other financial companies. By doing so, the mortgage companies were in effect borrowing to lend mortgages.

The sub-prime mortgage market in the US is relatively small, comprising around 10 per cent of the entire market. How can such a small market create such a huge effect? After 2002, bond issuance increased substantially, as shown in Figure 1.3.

The problem started when more and more sub-prime borrowers started to default on their mortgages and repossessions increased. The wave of repossessions had a dramatic effect on house prices. More houses were available in the market, which caused of the house price boom of the previous few years to reverse.

With decreasing house prices, the sub-prime mortgages started losing value. Those financial investors who had bonds with sub-prime mortgages started experiencing big financial losses. At the end of 2007 many

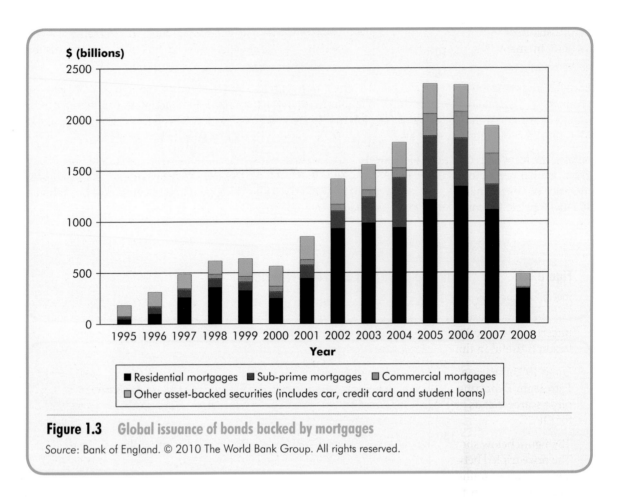

Figure 1.3 Global issuance of bonds backed by mortgages

Source: Bank of England. © 2010 The World Bank Group. All rights reserved.

banks announced $60 billion worth of losses, as many of the bonds backed by sub-prime mortgages had fallen in value.

The financial crisis started in the US. However, given the connectedness of financial institutions across countries, it rapidly spread globally. Governments in different countries started bailout programmes to avoid many big banks and financial companies collapsing and disappearing. Those companies were considered too big to fall.

The losses made by the financial and banking sectors resulted in what is called a *credit crunch*. A credit crunch is a reduction in the availability of credit from the banking sector. Banks become more reluctant to lend to borrowers and, more importantly, to each other. Credit becomes a scarce resource. The contraction of credit affected economic activity in all sectors of various economies and this had the effect of worsening the crisis.

Many firms rely on borrowing for running their usual business. The scarcity of credit available caused those firms to reduce their activity. Many closed down; others reduced their activity by cutting jobs. Unemployment started to rise. Consumers' confidence started to decrease. People started to save more and to spend less.

For many economies the recession caused by the financial crisis started at the end of 2007/beginning of 2008. The first signs of a slight recovery appeared at the end of 2009.

In the case of the financial crisis, we can try to answer the questions what, how and for whom to produce. What is produced? Production decreased in the recession. Some sectors were more affected than others. The building sector suffered big losses as a result of falling house prices. The number of new houses built fell substantially during the crisis. Expensive and non-essential goods also suffered. Demand for cars fell and in many cases governments intervened by providing incentives to buy new cars to sustain demand.

Looking at how things are produced, the crisis has created a reallocation of input resources used in production. This reallocation has affected labour input most dramatically. Reduction in economic activity implies a reduction in employment. The job market contracts and so more people become unemployed. Moreover, finding jobs becomes even more difficult, causing unemployment to last longer.

Finally, the for whom question. As a result of the crisis the banking and financial sector suffered big losses. The same happened to many investors because of the fall in stock values in financial markets. The fall in the price of houses made first-time buyers better off, especially young people who could now buy a house at a lower price. Discount supermarkets' sales figures also rose.

CASE 1.2 The oil price shocks

Oil provides fuel for heating, transport and machinery and is an input for petrochemicals and household products ranging from plastic plates to polyester clothes. What happens if continuing uncertainty in the Middle East or the ravages of climate change lead to very high oil prices? A little history lesson is useful in thinking about the likely results.

Up to 1973 the use of oil increased steadily. It was cheap and abundant. In 1973 OPEC – the Organization of Petroleum Exporting Countries (www.opec.org) – organized a production cutback by its members, making oil so scarce that its price tripled. Users could not quickly do without oil. Making oil scarce was very profitable for OPEC members.

The figure below shows the real (inflation-adjusted) price of oil, measured in US dollars, from 1970 to 2009. The price tripled between 1973 and 1977, doubled between 1979 and 1980, but then fell steadily until the mid-1990s. Markets found ways to overcome the oil shortage that OPEC had created. High oil prices did not last indefinitely. Given time, the higher price induced consumers to use less oil and non-OPEC producers to sell more. These responses, guided by prices, are part of the way many societies determine what, how and for whom to produce.

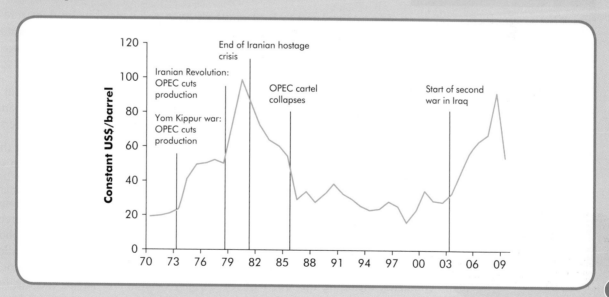

Consider first *how* things are produced. When the price of oil jumps, firms cut their use of oil-based products. Chemical firms develop artificial substitutes for petroleum inputs, airlines order more fuel-efficient aircraft, and electricity is produced from more wind farms. Higher oil prices make the economy produce in a way that uses less oil.

How about *what* is being produced? Households install better insulation to economize on expensive central heating and they buy smaller cars. Commuters form car-pools or move to the city centre. High prices choke off the demand for oil-related commodities but also encourage consumers to purchase substitute commodities. Higher demand for these commodities bids up their price and encourages their production. Designers produce smaller cars, architects use solar energy, and research laboratories develop alternatives to petroleum in chemical production.

The *for whom* question in this example has a clear answer. The revenues of oil producers increased sharply.

Much of their increased revenue was spent on goods produced in the industrialized Western nations. By contrast, oil-importing nations had to give up more of their own production in exchange for oil imports. In terms of goods as a whole, the rise in oil prices raised the buying power of OPEC and reduced the buying power of oil-importing countries such as Germany and Japan. The world economy was producing more for OPEC and less for Germany and Japan.

After 1982, OPEC's power diminished as other oil supplies came on stream and users developed adequate substitutes. However, OPEC got its act together again in 1999, cut supply, forced up oil prices and prompted another fuel crisis in 2000.

Since 1999 some of the cause of sharp rises in oil prices must also be attributed not merely to a restriction of oil supply but also to a surge in energy demand by emerging economies, particularly China and India.

The oil price shocks show how society allocates scarce resources between competing uses. The higher oil price reflected its greater scarcity when OPEC reduced production levels.

Picture: © Instinia | Dreamstime.com

Source: Adapted from *The Economist*, 21 July 2007.

Income distribution

You and your family have an annual income that lets you enjoy various goods and services and live in a particular place. Your standard of living includes the necessities of life – food, shelter, health, education – and something beyond, such as recreation. Your income is lower than some people's but higher than that of others.

Nations also have different levels of income. A nation's income, or national income, is the sum of the incomes of all its citizens. World income is the sum of all countries' incomes, hence also the sum of the incomes earned by all the people in the world.

> The **income distribution** (in a country or in the world) tells us how total income is divided between different groups or individuals.

Income distribution is closely linked to the what, how and for whom questions. Table 1.1 shows the percentage of the world population that lives in different groups of countries. Twenty-one per cent of the world's population live in poor countries, such as Bangladesh and Indonesia. Seventy per cent live in middle-income countries, a group including Thailand, Brazil, Mexico and China. The rich countries, including the US, Western Europe, Canada and Japan, account for 9 per cent of the world population.

Table 1.1   World population and income

	Country group		
	Poor	Middle	Rich
Income per head (£)	300	3900	17 700
% of world population	21	70	9
% of world income	3	19	78

Source: World Bank, *World Development Indicator*. © 2010 The World Bank Group. All rights reserved.

Income per person indicates the average standard of living. Table 1.1 shows that in poor countries the average income per person is only £300 a year. In the rich industrial countries annual income is £17 700 per person, nearly 60 times larger. These are big differences.

Table 1.1 also shows that poor countries account for one-fifth of the world's population but only 3 per cent of world income. Rich countries have 9 per cent of the world's population but 78 per cent of world income.

For whom does the world economy produce? Mainly for the 9 per cent of its population living in the rich industrial countries. This answer also helps answer what is produced. World output is directed mainly to the goods and services consumed in the rich countries. These inequalities are part of what anti-capitalist protesters wish to highlight.

Why is inequality so great? This reflects how goods are produced. Poor countries have little machinery and few people with professional and technical training. One American worker uses power-driven earth-moving equipment to complete a task undertaken in Africa by many more workers equipped only with shovels. Workers in poor countries are less productive because they work under adverse conditions.

Income is unequally distributed within each country as well as between countries. In Brazil, the richest 10 per cent of families get 48 per cent of national income, but in the UK the richest 10 per cent get only 27 per cent of national income and, in Denmark, only 20 per cent.

These differences partly reflect things we have already discussed. For example, state education increases access to education and training. However, in looking at income distribution within a country, we must include two extra things that are often less important when discussing differences in income per person between countries.

First, individual incomes come not just from working but also from owning assets (land, buildings, corporate equity) that earn rent, interest and dividends. In Brazil, ownership of land and factories is concentrated in the hands of a small group; in Denmark, it is not.

Second, societies may decide whether to change their distribution of income. A pure socialist economy aims to achieve considerable equality of income and wealth. In contrast, in an economy of private ownership, wealth and power become concentrated in the hands of a few people. Between these extremes, the government may levy taxes to alter the income distribution that would otherwise emerge in a private ownership economy. One reason why Denmark has a more equal income distribution than Brazil is that Denmark levies high taxes on high incomes to reduce the buying power of the rich, and levies high taxes on inheritance to reduce the concentration of wealth in the hands of a few families.

The degree to which income is unequally distributed within a country affects not only for whom goods and services are produced, but also which goods are produced. In Brazil, where income is unequally distributed, the rich employ poor people as maids, cooks and chauffeurs. In Denmark, where equality is much greater, few people can afford to hire servants.

1.2 Scarcity and the competing use of resources

Consider an economy with workers who can make food or films. Table 1.2 shows how much of each good can be made. The answer depends on how workers are allocated between the two industries. In each industry, more workers means more output of the good.

> The **law of diminishing returns** says each extra worker adds less to output than the previous extra worker added.

The **law of diminishing returns** applies when one input (such as labour) is varied but other inputs (such as equipment and land) remain fixed. Suppose workers in the film industry can use a fixed number of cameras and studios. The first worker has sole use of these facilities. With more workers, these facilities must be shared. Adding extra workers dilutes equipment per worker. Output per film worker falls as employment rises. A similar story applies in the food industry. Each industry faces diminishing returns to extra workers.

Table 1.2 shows combinations of food and films made if all workers have jobs. By moving workers from one industry to the other, the economy can make more of one good but only by making less of the other good. There is a trade-off between food output and film output.

> The **production possibility frontier** (PPF) shows, for each output of one good, the maximum amount of the other good that can be produced.

Figure 1.4 shows the maximum combinations of food and film output that the economy can produce. Point A plots the first row in Table 1.2, where food output is 25 and film output is 0. Points B, C, D and E correspond to the other rows of Table 1.2. The curve joining points A to E in Figure 1.4 is the **production possibility frontier** or PPF.

The frontier curves around the point given by zero output of both goods. This reflects the law of diminishing returns. Movements from A to B to C each transfer a worker from the food industry to the film industry. Each transfer reduces output per person in films but raises output per person in food. Each transfer yields less additional film output and gives up increasing amounts of food output.

> The **opportunity cost of a good** is the quantity of other goods that must be sacrificed to get another unit of that good.

In Figure 1.4 suppose we begin at point A with 25 units of food but no films. Moving from A to B, we gain 9 films but lose 3 units of food. Thus, 3 units of food is the **opportunity cost** of producing the first 9 films. The slope of the PPF tells us the opportunity cost of a good: how much of one good we have to sacrifice to make more of another.

To see why the curve is a 'frontier', think about point G in Figure 1.4. Society makes 10 units of food and 17 films. This is feasible. From Table 1.2, it needs 1 worker in the food industry and 2 in the film

Table 1.2 Production possibilities

Food workers	Output	Film workers	Output
4	25	0	0
3	22	1	9
2	17	2	17
1	10	3	24
0	0	4	30

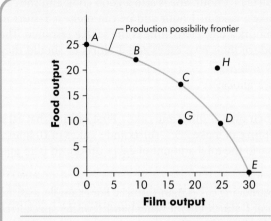

The frontier shows the maximum combinations of output that the economy can produce using all the available resources. The frontier displays a trade-off: more of one commodity implies less of the other. Points above the frontier need more inputs than the economy has available. Points inside the frontier are inefficient. By fully using available inputs the economy could expand output to the frontier.

Figure 1.4   The production possibility frontier

industry. Society has spare resources. The fourth person is not employed. *G* is not a point on the PPF because we can make more of one good without sacrificing output of the other good. Employing the extra person in the food industry takes us to point *C*, with 7 extra units of food for the same film output. Employing the extra person to work in films takes us to point *D*, with 7 extra units of films but no less food output.

The PPF shows the points at which society is producing efficiently. Points such as *G* inside the frontier are inefficient because society is wasting resources. More output of one good would not require less output of the other. There would be no opportunity cost of expanding output of one good a bit.

Points outside the production possibility frontier, such as *H* in Figure 1.4, are unattainable. Given the inputs available, this output combination cannot be made. Scarce resources limit society to a choice of points inside or on the production possibility frontier. Society must choose how to allocate these scarce resources between competing uses.

Since people like food and films, society wants to **produce efficiently**. Points inside the PPF sacrifice output unnecessarily. Society chooses between the different points *on* the production possibility frontier. In so doing, it decides not only what to produce but how to produce. Table 1.2 shows how many workers must be allocated to each industry to make a particular output combination. As yet, our example is too simple to show for whom society produces.

> **Production efficiency** means more output of one good can be obtained only by sacrificing output of other goods.

How does society decide where to produce on the production possibility frontier? The government may decide. However, in most Western economies, the most important process that determines what, how and for whom goods are produced is the operation of markets.

Opportunity cost, absolute and comparative advantage

The concept of opportunity cost introduced above is particularly important in economics. The reason is that, when two individuals (or firms, or nations) have different opportunity costs of performing various tasks, they can always increase the total value of available goods and services by trading with one another. Therefore, the idea of opportunity cost can provide a reason why individuals trade and why trade can be mutually beneficial.

To see how the idea of opportunity cost is related to gains from trade, we consider a simple example. Consider two individuals: Jennifer and John. Both can produce two different goods, cakes and T-shirts.

11

Jennifer is very good at sewing and she can make 4 T-shirts in 1 hour. She is also a good cook and she can bake 2 cakes in 1 hour. On the other hand, John can bake 1 cake in 1 hour and he can make a T-shirt in 2 hours. Suppose that both cannot work more than 10 hours a day. Here, time is the scarce resource. The problem is the following: should John and Jennifer produce their own cakes and T-shirts or should they trade with each other?

We are going to look at two possible scenarios.

First scenario: suppose that John and Jennifer produce their own T-shirts and cakes. First assume that each splits the 10 hours equally in producing the two goods. John can make 2.5 T-shirts and 5 cakes in 10 hours. Jennifer can make 20 T-shirts and 10 cakes. In this scenario the total amount of cakes produced is 15 and the total amount of T-shirts is 22.5.

Second scenario: suppose that John specializes more in producing cakes than T-shirts. For example, assume he spends 8 hours in preparing cakes and 2 hours in making T-shirts. On the other hand, Jennifer specializes more in making T-shirts than cakes. She spends 6 hours in making T-shirts and 4 hours in preparing cakes. In this case, John can make 8 cakes and 1 T-shirt while Jennifer can make 24 T-shirts and 8 cakes. Now the total amount of cakes produced is 16 and we have 25 T-shirts. Compared to the first scenario, the total amount of both goods has increased. Why?

The reason is that in our example John and Jennifer have different opportunity costs in producing the two goods. John is more efficient than Jennifer in producing cakes in terms of T-shirts. On the other hand, Jennifer is more efficient in producing T-shirts in terms of cakes than John.

What is John's opportunity cost of cakes in terms of T-shirts? Suppose that John wants to bake more cakes. He needs to spend less time on making T-shirts. How many T-shirts should he forgo? Suppose that John increases the production of cakes by 1 unit. How much time does he need to do that? He needs 1 hour to bake a cake. In that hour he could have made half a T-shirt ($^1/_2$). So John's opportunity cost of cakes in terms of T-shirts is half a T-shirt.

> An individual has a **comparative advantage** compared to another in the production of a good if she has a lower opportunity cost in producing it.

What about Jennifer? If she wants to bake one more cake she needs an extra half hour. In that half hour she could have made 2 T-shirts. So Jennifer's opportunity of cakes in terms of T-shirts is 2 T-shirts.

Therefore, John has a lower opportunity cost of cakes in terms of T-shirts than Jennifer. In this case, we say that John has a **comparative advantage** in making cakes compared to Jennifer. You can check that Jennifer has a comparative advantage in producing T-shirts compared to John.

Therefore, from our example we can say that if each individual specializes more in producing the good in which he or she has a comparative advantage, then it is possible to increase the total production of goods, and so trade can be beneficial.

Compared to the first scenario, in the second scenario Jennifer can trade 8 T-shirts with John in exchange for 8 cakes. Jennifer ends up with 12 T-shirts and 8 cakes, while John has 8 T-shirts and 8 cakes. Both gain from this trading in goods compared to the first scenario.

> **Absolute advantage** means that that person is the lowest-cost producer of that good.

In contrast to the concept of comparative advantage is that of **absolute advantage**. An individual has an absolute advantage in producing a good if he or she is more efficient at producing that good compared to someone else. In our example, Jennifer has an absolute advantage in producing both goods compared to John. In the same time she can make more T-shirts and cakes compared to John.

Nevertheless, in determining possible benefits from trade the concept of comparative advantage is what matters, not absolute advantage.

1.3   The role of the market

Markets bring together buyers and sellers of goods and services. In some cases, such as a local fruit stall, buyers and sellers meet physically. In other cases, such as the stock market, business can be transacted by computer. We use a general definition of markets.

Prices of goods and of resources (labour, machinery, land, energy) adjust to ensure that scarce resources are used to make the goods and services that society wants. You buy a hamburger for lunch because it is fast, convenient and cheap. You prefer steak but it is more expensive. The price of steak is high enough to ensure that society answers the 'for whom' question about lunchtime steaks in favour of someone else.

> A **market** is a process by which households' decisions about consumption of alternative goods, firms' decisions about what and how to produce, and workers' decisions about how much and for whom to work are all reconciled by adjustment of prices.

McDonald's is in the business because, given the price of beefburger meat, the rent and the wages for staff, it can still sell beefburgers at a profit. If rents were higher, it might sell beefburgers in a cheaper area or switch to luxury lunches for rich executives. The student behind the counter works there because a part-time job helps meet his tuition fees. If the wage were lower, he might not work at all. Conversely, the job is unskilled and there are plenty of students looking for such work, so McDonald's does not have to offer high wages.

ACTIVITY 1.1

Scarcely a hospital bed!

Are we spending more on health, or are hospitals in decline? Real (inflation-adjusted) government spending on health is 60 per cent higher than in 1990. So why do people think health services are being cut? First, we are living longer. Of the UK population, the over-65s will rise from 23 per cent in 1980 to 31 per cent by 2030. Older people need more health care. The same total spending means lower standards per person. Second, medical advances have made available successful but very expensive treatments. We all want them.

Health spending is rising a little faster than national output as a whole. However, with an ageing population, health spending must rise *faster* if people are to get the same standard of care as in the past. And to get any new treatment, however costly, health spending has to rise *much faster* still.

The real issue is *scarcity*: on what to spend our limited resources? Do we have fewer teachers and televisions in order to divert more resources to health? If not, we have to ration health care. Rationing can be done through markets (charging for health care so people choose to have less) or through rules (limiting access to treatment). Society's decision affects what is produced, how it is produced and, dramatically in this example, for whom it is produced.

Better health services do not come free. The *opportunity cost* of having more nurses and doctors is the quantity of education, entertainment and other outputs we have to sacrifice in order to divert more of our scarce resources into health care.

Questions

(a) A century ago, do you think health care was rationed? Explain why or why not.

(b) When the National Health Service made health care 'free at the point of delivery', did this mean everyone could have as much health care as they wished? If not, how did the NHS ration health care?

To check your answers to these questions, go to page 683.

Prices guide your decision to buy a beefburger, McDonald's decision to sell beefburgers, and the student's decision to take the job. Society allocates resources – meat, buildings and labour – into beefburger production through the price system. If people hated beefburgers, McDonald's sales revenue would not cover its cost. Society would devote no resources to beefburger production. People's desire to eat beefburgers guides resources into beefburger production.

However, when cattle contract BSE, consumers shun beefburgers in favour of bacon sandwiches, and the price of BLTs rises. As the fast-food industry scrambles to get enough pork, the price of pigs rises but the price of beef falls. Adjustments in prices encourage society to reallocate land from beef to pig farming. At the height of the British beef crisis, caused by fears about 'mad cow' disease, pork prices rose 2 per cent but beef prices fell. Quite an incentive to reallocate!

The command economy

> In a **command economy** a government planning office decides what will be produced, how it will be produced, and for whom it will be produced. Detailed instructions are then issued to households, firms and workers.

How would resources be allocated if markets did not exist? Such planning is very complicated. There is no complete command economy where all allocation decisions are undertaken in this way. However, in many countries, for example China, Cuba and those formerly in the Soviet bloc, there was a large measure of central direction and planning. The state owned factories and land, and made the most important decisions about what people should consume, how goods should be produced, and how people should work.

This is a huge task. Imagine that you had to run by command the city or town in which you live. Think of the food, clothing and housing allocation decisions you would have to make. How would you decide who should get what and the process by which goods are made and services delivered? These decisions are being made every day, mainly by the allocative mechanism of markets and prices.

CASE 1.3 Poor Marx for central planners

During the Cold War, economists used to argue about the relative merits of capitalism and communism. But the Soviet bloc, falling increasingly behind the living standards of the West, abandoned Marxist central planning after 1990 and began transition to a market economy. By 2003 fans of Chelsea Football Club were celebrating their new owner Roman Abramovich, who had made his fortune in the market economy, initially as an oil trader and then as chairman of one of Russia's leading oil companies.

The Berlin Wall fell because the Soviet bloc had fallen far behind market economies in the West. Key difficulties that had emerged were:

● *Information overload* Planners could not keep track of the details of economic activity. Machinery rusted because nobody came to install it after delivery, crops rotted because storage and distribution were not co-ordinated.

● *Bad incentives* Complete job security undermined work incentives. Factory managers ordered excess raw materials to ensure they got materials again the next year. Since planners could monitor quantity more easily than quality, firms met output targets by skimping on quality. Without environmental standards, firms polluted at will. Central planning led to low-quality goods and an environmental disaster.

● *Insufficient competition* Planners believed big was beautiful. One tractor factory served the Soviets from Latvia in the west to Vladivostok in the east. But large scale deprived planners of information from competing firms, making it hard to assess efficiency. Managers got away with inefficiency. Similarly, without electoral competition, it was impossible to sack governments making economic mistakes.

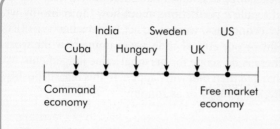

The role of the market in allocating resources differs vastly between countries. In the command economy resources are allocated by central government planning. In the free market economy there is virtually no government regulation of the consumption, production and exchange of goods. In between lies the mixed economy, where market forces play a large role but the government intervenes extensively.

Figure 1.5 *Market orientation*

The 'invisible hand'

Individuals in **free markets** pursue their own self-interest without government direction or interference. The idea that such a system could solve the what, how and for whom problems is one of the oldest themes in economics, dating back to the Scottish economist Adam Smith, whose book *The Wealth of Nations* (1776) remains a classic. Smith argued that individuals pursuing their self-interest would be led 'as by an invisible hand' to do things that are in the interests of society as a whole.

> Markets in which governments do not intervene are called **free markets**.

Suppose you wish to become a billionaire. You play around with new ideas and invent something, perhaps the DVD. Although motivated by self-interest, you make society better off by creating new jobs and opportunities. You move society's production possibility frontier outwards – the same resources now make more or better goods – and become a billionaire in the process. Smith argued that the pursuit of self-interest, without any central direction, could produce a coherent society making sensible allocative decisions.

This remarkable insight has been studied at length by modern economists. In later chapters, we explain when the **invisible hand** works well and when it works badly. Some government intervention may then be justified.

> The **invisible hand** is the assertion that the individual pursuit of self-interest within free markets may allocate resources efficiently from society's viewpoint.

The mixed economy

The free market allows individuals to pursue their self-interest without government restrictions. The command economy allows little scope for individual economic freedom. Decisions are taken centrally by the government. Between these extremes lies the mixed economy.

Most countries are mixed economies, though some are close to command economies and others are much nearer the free market economy. Figure 1.5 illustrates this point. Even Cuba allows consumers some choice over the goods they buy. Conversely, even countries such as the United States, which espouse more enthusiastically the free market approach, still have substantial levels of government activity in the provision of public goods and services, the redistribution of income through taxes and transfer payments, and the regulation of markets.

> In a **mixed economy** the government and private sector jointly solve economic problems. The government influences decisions through taxation, subsidies, and provision of free services such as defence and the police. It also regulates the extent to which individuals may pursue their own self-interest.

Positive and normative

In studying economics it is important to distinguish 'positive' and 'normative' economics.

Positive economics studies objective or scientific explanations of how the economy works.

The aim of **positive economics** is to analyse how society makes decisions about consumption, production and exchange of goods. It aims both to explain why the economy works as it does, and to allow predictions about how the economy will respond to changes. In positive economics, we aim to act as detached scientists. Whatever our political sympathy or our ethical code, we examine how the world actually works. At this stage, there is no scope for personal value judgements. We are concerned with propositions of the form: if *this* is changed then *that* will happen. In this regard, positive economics is similar to the natural sciences such as physics, geology or astronomy.

CASE 1.4

Green piece

Our planet is running out of rainforests and fish stocks, and climate change is threatening to destroy the planet completely. Why do we manage the environment so badly? An economist's response is 'because we do not price it like other commodities'. The market 'solved' the problem of scarcity when OPEC restricted oil supplies in the 1970s. High prices encouraged more supply and less demand. Why not price the environment, encouraging people to look after it?

Until now, the reason has been technology. Anyone can walk in a field, dump rubbish after dark, pump chemicals into a river, or drive down a public street. Gradually, however, electronic monitoring of usage is getting easier and cheaper. It is then possible to treat the environment as another commodity to be marketed. This prompts a vigorous debate about the 'what, how and for whom' questions.

We know how to charge cars for using a particular street at a particular time. A smart card in the car picks up signals as it passes each charge point. The driver gets a monthly bill like a credit card bill. Rush-hour traffic pays more when congestion is severe. The 'for whom' question can also be addressed. Residents can get a flat-rate annual payment, in exchange for supporting road pricing. Pricing the environment has a big advantage. It introduces a feedback mechanism. When society makes mistakes, an alarm bell rings *automatically*. The price of scarce things rises.

This is one reason why so many economists think that establishing a comprehensive global market for carbon, the key component of emissions that lead to a build-up of greenhouse gases, is a necessary part of the solution to global warming.

Economists of widely differing political persuasions would agree that when the government imposes a tax on a good, the price of that good will rise. The normative question of whether this price rise is desirable is entirely distinct.

As in any other science, there are unresolved questions where disagreement remains. These disagreements are at the frontiers of positive economics. Research in progress will resolve some of these issues but new issues will arise, providing scope for further research.

Normative economics offers recommendations based on personal value judgements.

Competent and comprehensive research can in principle resolve many of the outstanding issues in positive economics; no such claim can be made about the resolution of issues in **normative economics**. Normative economics is based on subjective value judgements, not on the search for any objective truth. The following statement combines positive and normative economics: 'The elderly have very high medical expenses, and the government should subsidize their health bills.' The first part of the proposition is a statement in positive economics. It is a statement about how the world works. We can imagine a research programme that could determine whether or not it is correct. (Broadly speaking, it is.)

The second part of the proposition – the recommendation about what the government should do – could never be 'proved' true or false by any scientific research investigation. It is a subjective value judgement based on the feelings of the person making the statement. Many people might share this subjective judgement. Others might reasonably disagree. You might believe that it is more important to devote society's scarce resources to improving the environment not the health of the aged.

Economics cannot be used to show that one of these normative judgements is correct and the other is wrong. It all depends on the preferences or priorities of the individual or the society that has to make this choice. But we can use positive economics to clarify the menu of options from which society must eventually make its normative choice.

Most economists have normative views. Some economists are vociferous champions of particular normative recommendations. However, this advocacy role about what society should do must be distinguished from the role of the economist as an expert on the likely consequences of pursuing any course of action. In the latter case, the professional economist is offering expert advice on positive economics. Scrupulous economists distinguish their role as an expert adviser on positive economics from their status as involved private citizens arguing for particular normative choices.

1.5   Micro and macro

Many economists specialize in a particular branch of the subject. Labour economics deals with jobs and wages. Urban economics deals with land use, transport, congestion and housing. However, we need not classify branches of economics by subject area. We can also classify branches of economics according to the approach used. The division of approaches into **microeconomic** and **macroeconomic** cuts across the subject groupings cited above.

> **Microeconomics** offers a detailed treatment of individual decisions about particular commodities.
>
> **Macroeconomics** emphasizes interactions in the economy as a whole. It deliberately simplifies the individual building blocks of the analysis in order to retain a manageable analysis of the complete interaction of the economy.

For example, we can study why individuals prefer cars to bicycles and how producers decide whether to produce cars or bicycles. We can then aggregate the behaviour of all households and all firms to discuss total car purchases and total car production. We can examine the market for cars. Comparing this with the market for bicycles, we can explain the relative price of cars and bicycles and the relative output of these two goods. The sophisticated branch of microeconomics known as general equilibrium theory extends this approach to its logical conclusion. It studies simultaneously every market for every commodity. From this it is hoped to understand the complete pattern of consumption, production and exchange in the whole economy at a point in time.

But this is very complicated. It is easy to lose track of the phenomena in which we were interested. The interesting task, which retains an element of art in economic science, is to devise judicious simplifications that keep the analysis manageable without distorting reality too much. Here, microeconomists and macroeconomists proceed down different avenues.

Microeconomists tend to study one aspect of economic behaviour but ignore interactions with the rest of the economy in order to preserve the simplicity of the analysis. A microeconomic analysis of footballers' wages would emphasize the characteristics of footballers and the ability of football clubs to pay. It would largely neglect the chain of indirect effects to which an increase in footballers' wages might give rise (such as higher prices for luxury houses, leading to a boom in swimming pool manufacture). When microeconomic analysis ignores indirectly induced effects, it is 'partial' rather than 'general' analysis.

In some instances, indirect effects may not be important and it will make sense for economists to examine particular industries or activities in great detail. When indirect effects are too important to ignore, an alternative simplification must be found.

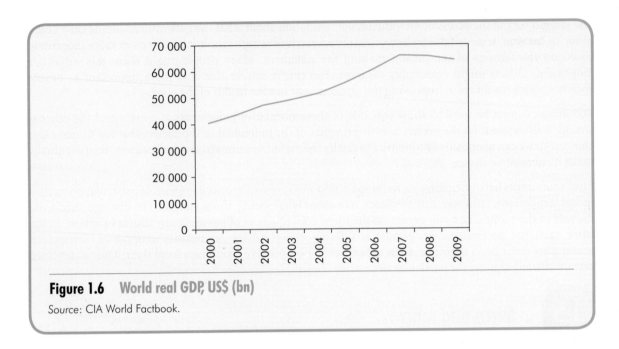

Figure 1.6 World real GDP, US$ (bn)

Source: CIA World Factbook.

Macroeconomists rarely worry about the division of consumer goods into cars, bicycles and videos. Instead, they treat them as a single bundle called 'consumer goods' because they want to study the interaction between household purchases of consumer goods and firms' decisions about purchases of machinery and buildings.

Because macroeconomic concepts refer to the whole economy, they get more media coverage than microeconomic concepts, which are chiefly of interest to those in a specific group. Here are three macroeconomic concepts you have probably encountered.

Gross domestic product (GDP)

> **Gross domestic product (GDP)** is the value of total output of an economy in a given period.

After the credit crunch in 2007 the global economy entered a recession. Figure 1.6 shows world real **gross domestic product (GDP)** (inflation adjusted). We can see that, after 2007, world real GDP started to decrease compared to previous years. During a recession, GDP is falling or is growing only very slowly.

Aggregate price level

> The **aggregate price level** measures the average price of goods and services.

The prices of different goods may move differently. The **aggregate price level** tells us what is happening to prices on average. When this price level is rising, we say there is inflation.

Unemployment rate

> The **unemployment rate** is the fraction of the labour force without a job.

The labour force is people of working age who have a job or want one. Some of the rich, the sick and the lazy are of working age but not looking for work. They are not in the labour force and not counted within the **unemployment rate**.

People dislike both inflation and unemployment. In the 1970s, oil price shocks and excessive money creation led to high inflation. Then, inflation fell but unemployment increased. By 2000 both inflation and unemployment had finally fallen back to low levels. Yet by 2007 inflation was beginning to increase again.

However, after the credit crunch took place, in many economies inflation started to fall. In some cases, inflation became negative; in those we say that there was a *deflation*. Macroeconomists want to understand what generates these fluctuations.

Getting the most out of each chapter

There is a summary of the main points at the end of each chapter. Like learning to drive, the best way to check your progress is not to read more and more but to try to do it for yourself. Attempt the review questions that follow the summary (answers are provided on the Online Learning Centre website: www. mcgraw-hill-co.uk/textbooks/begg). Connect has many more problems, also with answers: a self-contained driving instructor.

Summary

- **Economics** analyses what, how and for whom society produces. The key economic problem is to reconcile the conflict between people's virtually unlimited demands and society's limited ability to produce goods and services to fulfil these demands.

- The **production possibility frontier** (PPF) shows the maximum amount of one good that can be produced given the output of the other good. It depicts the trade-off or menu of choices for society in deciding what to produce. Resources are **scarce** and points outside the frontier are unattainable. It is inefficient to produce within the frontier.

- The **opportunity cost** of a good is the quantity of other goods sacrificed to make an additional unit of the good. It is the slope of the PPF.

- If individuals, firms or countries have different opportunity costs of producing a good compared to others, they have a **comparative advantage**. The fact that individuals have comparative advantages in producing different goods creates the possibility for gains from trading.

- Industrial countries rely extensively on **markets** to allocate resources. The market resolves production and consumption decisions by adjustments in prices.

- In a **command economy**, decisions on what, how and for whom are made in a central planning office. No economy relies entirely on command.

- A **free market economy** has no government intervention. Resources are allocated entirely through markets in which individuals pursue their own self-interest. Adam Smith argued that an '**invisible hand**' would nevertheless allocate resources efficiently.

- Modern economies are **mixed**, relying mainly on the market but with a large dose of government intervention. The optimal level of intervention is hotly debated.

- **Positive economics** studies how the economy actually behaves. **Normative economics** recommends what should be done. The two should be kept separate. Given sufficient research, economists could agree on issues in positive economics. Normative economics involves subjective value judgements. There is no reason why people should agree about normative statements.

- Microeconomics offers a detailed analysis of particular activities in the economy. For simplicity, it may neglect some interactions with the rest of the economy. Macroeconomics emphasizes these interactions at the cost of simplifying the individual building blocks.

Review questions

connect

EASY

1 An economy has workers. Each worker can make 4 cakes or 3 shirts however many others work in the same industry. (a) Draw the production possibility frontier. (b) How many cakes can society get if it does without shirts? (c) What points in your diagram are inefficient? (d) What is the opportunity cost of making a shirt? (e) Does the law of diminishing returns hold in this economy?

2 Communist Russia used prices to allocate production among different consumers. Central planners set production targets but then put output in shops, fixed prices and gave workers money to spend. Why not plan the allocation of particular goods to particular people as well?

3 Society abolishes higher education. Students have to find jobs immediately. If there are no jobs available, how do wages and prices adjust so those who want jobs can find them?

4 Which of the following statements are positive, and which are normative? (a) Annual inflation is below 2 per cent. (b) Because inflation is low the government should cut taxes. (c) Income is higher in the UK than in Poland. (d) The British are happier than the Poles.

5 Which of the following statements refer to microeconomics, and which to macroeconomics? (a) Inflation is lower than in the 1980s. (b) Food prices fell this month. (c) Good weather means a good harvest. (d) Unemployment in London is below the UK average.

6 Common fallacies   Why are these statements wrong? (a) Since some economists are Conservative but others Labour, economics can justify anything. (b) There is no such thing as a free lunch. To get more of one thing, you have to give up something else. (c) Economics is about people, and thus cannot be a science.

MEDIUM

7 Suppose that a country can produce two goods: food and clothing. To produce one unit of food it requires one worker. To produce one unit of clothing it requires two workers. The total amount of workers available in the economy is fixed and is equal to 100. Denote by L the total amount of workers, F the units of food produced, and C the units of clothing produced. Denote by a_F the amount of workers needed to produce one unit of food and by a_C the amount of workers needed to produce one unit of clothing. The resource constraint for this economy can be written as: $L = a_F F + a_C C$. Show how to construct the production possibility frontier from that resource constraint. On a graph with C on the vertical axis and F on the horizontal axis, plot the PPF of this economy. What is the slope of the PPF?

8 OPEC made a fortune for its members by organizing production cutbacks and forcing up prices. (a) Why have coffee producers not managed to do the same? (b) Could UK textile firms force up textile prices by cutting back UK textile production?

9 Suppose it becomes possible in 5 years' time to make as much energy as we want from biofuels provided the price is the equivalent of at least $50/barrel for oil. (a) What does this imply about the

eventual price of oil in, say, 10 years' time? (b) Is it possible for oil prices to be substantially above $50/barrel for the next few years? (c) Do higher oil prices in the short run increase or reduce the incentive to look for alternative energy technologies?

10 **Essay question**   Two similar countries take the decision to try to increase the health of their poorest people. One country raises taxes on the rich and gives more money to the poor. The other country raises taxes on the rich and provides more health care, free to patients, through its national health service. Which country do you think is more likely to meet its objective? Why?

For solutions to these questions contact your lecturer.

Tools of economic analysis

Learning Outcomes

By the end of this chapter, you should understand:

1. why theories deliberately simplify reality

2. time-series, cross-section and panel data

3. how to construct index numbers

4. nominal and real variables

5. how to build a simple theoretical model

6. how to plot data and interpret scatter diagrams

7. how to use 'other things equal' to ignore, but not forget, important influences

It is more fun to play tennis if you know how to serve, and cutting trees is much easier with a chainsaw. Every activity or academic discipline has a basic set of tools. Tools may be tangible, like the dentist's drill, or intangible, like the ability to serve in tennis. This chapter is about the tools of the trade. To analyse economic issues we use both *models* and *data*.

> A **model** or **theory** makes assumptions from which it deduces how people will behave. It is a deliberate simplification of reality.

Models or **theories** – we use these terms interchangeably – are frameworks to organize how we think about a problem. They simplify by omitting some details of the real world to concentrate on the essentials. From this manageable picture of reality we develop an analysis of how the economy works.

An economist uses a model as a tourist uses a map. A map of Glasgow misses out many features of the real world – traffic lights, roundabouts, speed bumps – but with careful study you get a good idea of how the traffic flows and the best route to take. The simplified picture is easy to follow, but helps you understand actual behaviour when you must drive through the city in the rush hour.

The data or facts interact with models in two ways. First, the data help us quantify the relationships to which our theoretical models draw attention. It is not enough to know that all bridges across the Clyde are likely to be congested. To choose the best route we need to know how long we have to queue at each bridge. We need some facts. The model is useful because it tells us which facts are likely to be the most important.

Second, the **data** help us to test our models. Like all careful scientists, economists must check that their theories square with the *relevant* facts. For example, for a while the number of Scottish dysentery deaths was closely related to UK inflation. Is this a factual coincidence or the key to a theory of inflation? The facts alert us to the need to ponder this question, but we can decide only by logical reasoning.

> **Data** are pieces of evidence about economic behaviour.

In this instance, we can find no theoretical connection. Hence, we view the close factual relationship between Scottish dysentery deaths and UK inflation as a coincidence that should be ignored. Without a logical underpinning, the empirical connection will break down sooner or later. Paying attention to a freak relationship in the data increases neither our understanding of the economy nor our confidence in predicting the future.

The blend of models and data is subtle. The data alert us to logical relationships we had overlooked. And whatever theory we wish to maintain should certainly be checked against the facts. But only theoretical reasoning can guide an intelligent assessment of what evidence has reasonable relevance.

When a theory that makes sense has for a long time survived exposure to the relevant economic data, we sometimes accord it the status of a **behavioural law**, such as the law of diminishing returns.

> A **behavioural law** is a sensible theoretical relationship not rejected by evidence over a long period.

Next, we turn to the representation of economic data. Then we show how an economist might develop a theoretical model of an economic relationship. Finally, we discuss how actual data might be used to test the theory that has been developed.

2.1 Economic data

How might we present data to help us think about an economic problem? There are different ways in which real-world data can be presented. We distinguish between time-series data, cross-section data and panel data.

Time-series data

The first two columns of Table 2.1 report a **time series** of monthly copper prices. It shows how the price changes over time. This information may be presented in tables or charts.

> A **time series** is a sequence of measurements of the same variable at different points in time.

Figure 2.1 *plots*, or *graphs*, these data. Each point in the figure corresponds to an entry in the table. Point *A* shows that in January 2010 the price of copper was $7385 per tonne. The series of points or dots in Figure 2.1, in whichever colour, contains the same information as the first two columns of Table 2.1.

Table 2.1 The price of copper, 2010 (US$/tonne)

Monthly	$/tonne	Quarterly	$/tonne
Jan	7385	IV	6696
Feb	6847		
Mar	7462		
Apr	7744	I	7231

Source: London Metal Exchange (www.lme.co.uk).

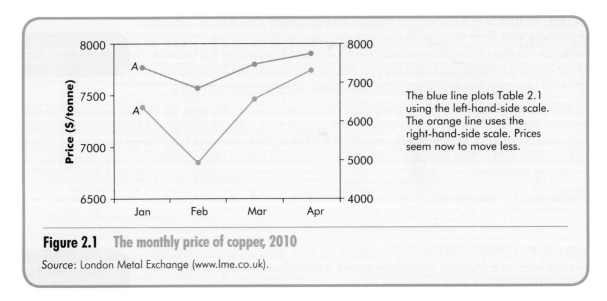

Figure 2.1 The monthly price of copper, 2010

Source: London Metal Exchange (www.lme.co.uk).

Charts or diagrams must be interpreted with care. The eye is easily misled by simple changes in presentation of the data. In Figure 2.1 the blue line corresponds to the left-hand scale and the orange line corresponds to the enlarged scale on the right. Both graphs plot the same data but the blue graph seems to move more. Diagrams can be manipulated in suggestive ways, a point well understood in advertising and politics.

Daily data usually contain too much detail. Imagine studying daily prices over 10 or 20 years![1] Averages over a month, a quarter (three months) or a year may be the best way to present data. The last two columns of Table 2.1 show quarterly averages for copper prices. The four quarters of the year are the periods January–March, April–June, July–September and October–December. For the fourth quarter of 2009 the quarterly average is $6696. In the first quarter of 2010 the price of copper was on average $7231. It can be seen as one-third of the sum of the monthly numbers for January, February and March.

Cross-section data record at a point in time the way an economic variable differs across different individuals or groups of individuals.

Panel data record observations over multiple time periods for the same individuals or groups of individuals.

Cross-section data

Time-series data record how a particular variable changes over time. Economists also use **cross-section data**. Table 2.2 shows a cross-section of unemployment rates in February 2010.

Panel data

Panel data are a mix between time-series and cross-section data. See also Concept 2.1.

Table 2.2 Unemployment by country, March 2010 (% of labour force)

US	Japan	Germany	France	UK
9.7	4.9	8.7	10.1	8.0

Sources: OECD and IMF.

---

1   For financial variables, like stock prices, data are available even in real time, minute by minute.

Table 2.3   Unemployment by country, 2006–09 (% of labour force)

	US	Japan	Germany	France	UK
2006	4.6	4.1	9.8	9.2	5.4
2007	4.6	3.9	8.4	8.4	5.3
2008	5.8	4.0	7.4	7.9	5.7
2009	9.3	5.4	8.1	9.5	7.7

Sources: OECD and IMF.

Table 2.3 shows a panel data example in which the same variable (unemployment rate) is recorded over time for the same group of countries.

CONCEPT 2.1

The British Household Panel Survey (BHPS)

Panel data, also called longitudinal data, are becoming increasingly important in economic analysis. Panel data contain two kinds of information: the cross-sectional information reflected in the differences between individuals or groups of individuals, and the time-series information reflected in the changes within individuals or groups of individuals over time. Another important feature of panel datasets is that often they involve a very large number of observations.

The British Household Panel Survey (BHPS) is an example of a panel data set. It is carried out by the Institute for Social and Economic Research (ISER) at the University of Essex. A sample of British households was drawn and first interviewed in 1991. The sample comprised 5500 households and 10 300 individuals drawn from 250 areas of Great Britain. The members of these original households have since been followed and annually interviewed. The BHPS provides information on household organization, employment, accommodation, tenancy, income and wealth, housing, health, socio-economic values, residential mobility, marital and relationship history, social support, and individual and household demographics. Therefore, the BHPS represents a very detailed dataset containing a lot of economic information about each individual in the sample. Moreover, for each individual, we can track how this economic information changes over time. This is very useful for economic purposes.

Another famous example of a panel data set is the Panel Study of Income Dynamics (PSID), which is the world's longest running household panel survey. The PSID is a longitudinal panel survey of US families that measures economic, social and health factors over the life course and across generations. Data have been collected from the same families and their descendants since 1968. The PSID is conducted by the Survey Research Center at the Institute for Social Research, at the University of Michigan.

2.2   Index numbers

To compare numbers without emphasizing units of measurement, we use index numbers.

Table 2.4   Prices of aluminium and copper (US$/tonne)

	2004	2007	2010
Aluminium price	1758	2644	2232
Copper price	2766	6710	7234
Aluminium Index (2004 = 100)	100	150	127
Copper Index (2004 = 100)	100	242	261
Metals Index (2004 = 100)	100	163	327

Source: London Metal Exchange (www.lme.co.uk).

Table 2.4 shows annual averages for aluminium and copper prices. We could choose 2004 as the base year and assign the value 100 to both the aluminium and the copper price index in this base year.

By 2007 the aluminium price of $2644 per tonne was around 1.5 times its price in 2004. If the aluminium prices had been 100 in 2004, this index must be 150 by 2007. To get the 2010 value, we divide the 2010 aluminium price of $2232 by the 2004 price of $1758 to get 1.27. Multiplying this by the starting value of 100 for the index in 2004 yields 127 for the aluminium index in 2010, as in Table 2.4. The price index for copper is calculated in the same way, dividing each price by the 2004 price, then multiplying by 100.

Now check that you understand this procedure. In 2001 average aluminium prices were $1482 per tonne and average copper prices were $1660. What were the values of the aluminium and copper price indices? (Answer: 84 and 60.)

Index numbers as averages

> An **index number** expresses data relative to a given base value.

Now think about the price of metals as a whole. The prices of different metals change differently. To derive a single measure of metal prices we *average* different metal prices.

Suppose aluminium and copper are the only metals. An index of metal prices in the fifth row of Table 2.4 makes a single time series by combining the time series in the third and fourth rows. In the metal index, each metal has a weight or share that reflects the purpose for which the index is constructed. If it summarizes what firms pay for metal inputs, the weights should reflect the relative use of aluminium and copper as industrial inputs. Copper is much more widely used than aluminium. We might choose a weight of 0.8 for copper and 0.2 for aluminium. The weights always add up to 1.

The last row of Table 2.4 shows changes over time in the metal price index, the *weighted average* of the indices for aluminium and copper. In the base year 2004, the metals index is 100, being $(0.2 \times 100) + (0.8 \times 100)$. By 2007 the index is 163, which is $(0.8 \times 173) + (0.2 \times 113)$. In 2010 the index was 327.

The metals index, a weighted average of aluminium and copper prices, must lie between the indices for the two separate metals. The weights determine whether the metals index more closely resembles the behaviour of copper prices or aluminium prices.

The CPI and other indices

To keep track of the prices faced by consumers, countries construct a *consumer price index* (CPI). The CPI is used to measure changes in the cost of living, that is, the money that must be spent to purchase the

Table 2.5 CPI weights in the UK, 2009

Item	Weights
Food and non-alcoholic beverages	0.118
Alcoholic beverages and tobacco	0.044
Clothing and footwear	0.057
Housing and household services	0.126
Furniture and household goods	0.066
Health	0.022
Transport	0.151
Recreation and culture	0.145
Education	0.021
Restaurants and hotels	0.128
Miscellaneous goods and services	0.099

Source: ONS, *Focus on Consumer Price Index*, 2009.

typical bundle of goods consumed by a representative household. In the UK the CPI forms the basis for the government's inflation target which the Bank of England's Monetary Policy Committee is required to achieve. The CPI is constructed in two stages. First, index numbers are calculated for each category of commodity purchased by households. Then the CPI is constructed by taking a weighted average of the different commodity groupings. Table 2.5 shows the weights used and the main commodity groupings. The weights sum up to 1. The 'shopping basket' described in Table 2.5 is reviewed every year to make sure that it is up to date and representative of consumers' spending.

A 10 per cent rise in food prices will change the CPI more than a 10 per cent rise in the price of alcoholic beverages and tobacco. This is because food has a much larger weight than alcohol and tobacco in consumers' expenditure.

Another price index that is particularly important is the *retail price index* (RPI), which is also used to measure changes in the cost of living. The RPI is similar to the CPI, the main differences being in terms of the items included in one index and not in the other. For example, the RPI includes mortgage interest payments by households while the CPI does not. In the past, the RPI used to be the index used to calculate inflation in the UK. More recently, the CPI has been adopted as the main measure for UK inflation, as it is in other European countries.

In Figure 2.2 we plot the **inflation rate** in the UK for the period 1989–2009 as measured by CPI and RPI indices. While there are differences between the two inflation measures, the behaviour of inflation over time looks pretty similar in both indices.

> The **inflation rate** is the annual rate of change of the consumer price index.

Other examples of indices include the index of wages in manufacturing, a weighted average of wages in different manufacturing industries. The FTSE, or 'footsie', is the *Financial Times–Stock Exchange* index of share prices quoted on the London Stock Exchange. The *index of industrial production* is a weighted average of the *quantity* of goods produced by industry.

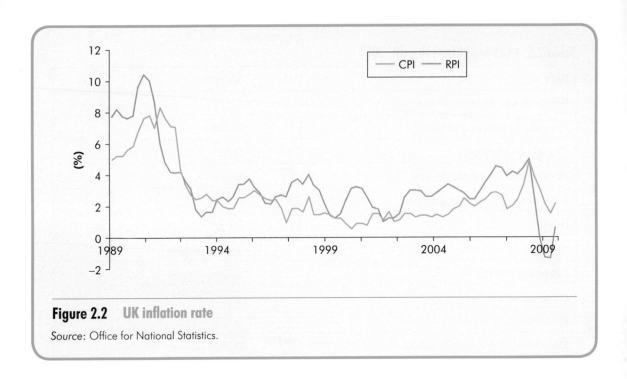

Figure 2.2   UK inflation rate

Source: Office for National Statistics.

The process by which index numbers are calculated is always the same. We choose a base date at which to set the index equal to 100, then calculate other values relative to this baseline. Where the index refers to more than one commodity, we have to choose weights by which to average across the different commodities that the index describes.

CONCEPT 2.2 Hyperinflation

In developed countries over the last few decades inflation has been moderate. However, there are cases in which inflation explodes over time. When prices start to increase very rapidly over time and inflation becomes particularly large, we have a case of hyperinflation. A typical example is what happened in Germany after the First World War. In 1918 the Allied victors demanded that Germany make reparations for the damage done and pay the pensions of Allied armed forces engaged in the war. By 1922, in economic ruin, Germany suspended reparations. In January 1923 French and Belgian troops occupied the Ruhr coalfields. German workers began a general strike and the government rolled the presses to print money to pay the 2 million workers involved.

This was the last straw for the German economy. Prices spiralled out of control. Monthly inflation reached the equivalent of 1 million per cent a year. Paper money became almost worthless.

Hyperinflation is not particularly rare. In the 1980s it occurred in several Latin American countries (Bolivia, Argentina, Brazil). More recently, Zimbabwe experienced extreme hyperinflation. To give an idea of the magnitude of price level increases, in 2008 the inflation rate in Zimbabwe was 231 150 888.87 per cent. This means that if a good had a price of 1 Zimbabwean dollar in 2007, the same good would have a price of 231 150 888.87 Zimbabwean dollars in 2008! During hyperinflation, national currency becomes worthless and people simply do not want to use it. In 2009 Zimbabwe abandoned printing of the Zimbabwean dollar, and the South African rand and US dollar became the standard currencies for exchange.

2.3 Nominal and real variables

The first row of Table 2.6 shows the average price of a new house, which rose from £3100 in 1963 to £161 000 in 2009.[2] Are houses really 52 times as expensive as in 1963? Not when we allow for inflation, which also raised incomes and the ability to buy houses.

The second row of Table 2.6 shows the retail price index, using 2009 as the base year.[3] Inflation led to substantial increases in the RPI during 1963–2009. The third row of Table 2.6 calculates an index of real house prices, expressed in 2009 prices. The value of house prices is the same in 2009 in the top and bottom rows.

To calculate the real price of houses in 1963, by expressing them at 2009 prices, we take the nominal price of £3100 and multiply by [(100)/(6.3)] to allow for subsequent inflation, yielding £49 200. Real prices have roughly tripled since 1963 (from £49 200 to £161 000). Most of the 52-fold increase in nominal house prices in the top row of Table 2.5 was due to inflation.

Real or relative prices

The distinction between **nominal and real values** applies to all variables measured in money values. It does not apply to units of output, such as 4000 carpets per annum, which relate to physical quantities. Whatever the inflation rate, 4000 carpets is 4000 carpets. However, we do not know whether £100 is a large or a small amount until we know the general price level for goods.

> **Nominal values** are measured in the prices ruling at the time of measurement. **Real values** adjust nominal values for changes in the price level.

The argument carries over to prices themselves. The nominal price of silver has risen a lot since 1970. To calculate an index of the *real price of silver*, divide an index of nominal silver prices by the RPI or the CPI and multiply by 100. Real prices indicate economic scarcity. They show whether the price of a commodity rose faster than prices in general. Hence, real prices are sometimes called *relative prices*.

Consider the price of televisions over the past 20 years. TV prices, measured in pounds, have hardly changed. The RPI and the CPI have risen a lot. The real price of TVs has fallen. Advances in technology have reduced the cost of producing televisions. Because the real price has fallen, many households now have several TVs. It is misleading to base our analysis on nominal values of variables.

Table 2.6   UK house prices (average price of a new house)

	1963	1983	2009
House price (£000s)	3.1	35.6	161
RPI (2009 = 100)	6.3	39.7	100
Real price of houses (2009 £000s)	49.2	90	161

Sources: ONS *Economic Trends* and Nationwide.

---

2   The price of new houses in the UK reached a peak in 2007, at around £190 000. In 2008 and 2009 the price of new houses decreased quite substantially due to the credit crunch.

3   Here, we use the RPI instead of the CPI because in the UK the RPI used to be the main index used to measure inflation and therefore we have a longer series of data for the RPI than for the CPI.

The purchasing power of money

> The **purchasing power of money** is an index of the quantity of goods that can be bought for £1.

When the price of goods rises, the **purchasing power of money** falls because £1 buys fewer goods. To distinguish between real and nominal variables, we say that real variables measure nominal variables as if the purchasing power of money had been constant. Another way to express this idea is to distinguish nominal variables in *current* pounds and real variables in *constant* pounds.

Table 2.6 described real prices of houses measured in 2009 pounds. We could of course have used 1960 pounds instead. Although the level of the real price index for houses would have been different, it would have grown at exactly the same rate as in the final row of Table 2.6.

CONCEPT 2.3

Money illusion

The distinction between nominal and real variables is a key concept in economics. Money illusion refers to a tendency to think in terms of nominal rather than real monetary values. This means that the nominal value of money can be mistaken for its purchasing power. Suppose you work and you get a wage of £1000. With that wage you buy only bread and the price of bread is £1 per kg. This means your wage in real terms has a value of 1000 kg of bread (meaning that the purchasing power of your wage is 1000 kg of bread).

Now suppose you are asked to choose between the following two cases:

(1)   You can get an increase to £1600 in your wage while the price of bread is £2.

(2)   You can get a reduction in your wage to £800 while the price of bread is £1.

Which one should you choose? The two situations are equivalent in 'real terms', therefore you should not prefer one to another since, for you, the two cases are the same. In both cases you buy the same amount of bread (800 kg). People who perceive these situations differently are said to be prone to money illusion.

Do people suffer from money illusion? Some evidence suggests that they do. Indeed, if we asked many individuals the same question as above, we would probably see some individuals choosing case (1). The reason is that some individuals will think that an increase in the nominal wage is better than a decrease in the nominal wage, even if in real terms nothing has changed.

Source: Shafir, E. et al. (1997) On money illusion, *Quarterly Journal of Economics*, 112 (2): 341–374.

2.4 Measuring changes in economic variables

> The **percentage change** is the absolute change divided by the original number, then multiplied by 100.

During the BSE crisis in 1996, UK beef production fell from 90 000 tonnes in January to 50 000 tonnes in April. The *absolute change* was −40 000. The minus sign tells us it fell. The **percentage change** in UK beef output was $(100) \times (-40\,000)/(90\,000) = -44\%$. Absolute changes specify units (e.g. tonnes), but percentage changes are *unit-free*. Data are often shown this way.

> The **growth rate** is the percentage change per period (usually a year).

When we study time-series data over long periods such as a decade, we do not want to know just the percentage or absolute change between the initial date and the final date. Negative growth rates show percentage falls. Economists usually take economic growth to mean the percentage annual change in the national income.

Economic models

Now for an example of economics in action. The London Underground, known locally as the tube, usually loses money and needs government subsidies. Might different policies help? You have to set the tube fare that will raise most revenue. How do you analyse the problem?

To organize our thinking, or build a model, we need to simplify reality, picking out the key elements of the problem. We begin with the simple equation

$$\text{Revenue} = [\text{fare}] \times [\text{number of passengers}] \qquad (1)$$

London Underground can set the fare, but influences the number of passengers only through the fare that is set. (Cleaner stations and better service may help. We neglect these for the moment.)

The number of passengers may reflect habit, convenience and tradition, and be completely unresponsive to changes in fares. This is *not* the view an economist would adopt. It is possible to travel by car, bus, taxi or tube. Decisions about how to travel will depend on the relative costs of different modes of transport. Equation (1) requires a 'theory' or 'model' of what determines the number of passengers. We must model the *demand* for tube journeys.

First, the tube fare matters. Other things equal, higher tube fares reduce the number of tube journeys demanded. Second, if there are price rises for competing modes of taxis and buses, more people will use the tube at any given tube fare. Third, if passengers have higher income, they can afford more tube journeys at any given fare. We now have a bare-bones model of the number of tube passengers:

$$\text{Number of passengers} = f(\text{tube fare, taxi fare, petrol price, bus fare, passenger incomes} \ldots) \qquad (2)$$

The number of passengers 'depends on' or 'is a function of' the tube fare, the taxi fare, petrol prices, bus fares, incomes and some other things. The notation $f(\ldots)$ is shorthand for 'depends on all the things listed inside the brackets'. The row of dots reminds us that we have omitted some possible determinants of demand to simplify our analysis. Tube demand probably depends on the weather. It is uncomfortable in the tube when it is hot. If the purpose of our model is to study *annual changes* in the number of tube passengers, we can neglect the weather provided weather conditions are broadly the same every year.

Writing down a model forces us to look for all the relevant effects, to worry about which effects must be taken into account and which can be ignored in answering the question we have set ourselves. Combining equations (1) and (2),

$$\begin{aligned}\text{Tube revenue} &= \text{tube fare} \times \text{number of passengers} \\ &= \text{tube fare} \times f(\text{tube fare, taxi fare, petrol price, bus fare, incomes} \ldots) \end{aligned} \qquad (3)$$

Why all the fuss? You would have organized your approach along similar lines. That is the right reaction. Models are simply devices to ensure we think clearly about a problem. Clear thinking requires simplification. The real world is too complicated for us to think about everything at once. Learning to use models is more an art than a science. Too much simplicity will omit a crucial factor from the analysis. Too much complexity and we lose any feeling for why the answer turns out as it does.

Sometimes data guide us about which factors are crucial and which are not. At other times, as with tube fares, it is not enough to understand the forces at work. We need to quantify them. For both reasons, we turn now to the interaction of economic models and economic data.

2.6   Models and data

Equation (3) is our model of determinants of tube revenue. Higher fares give *more* revenue per passenger, but *reduce* the number of passengers. Theory cannot tell us which effect dominates. This is an *empirical* or factual issue: how many passengers are put off by higher fares?

Empirical evidence

We need some empirical research to establish the facts. *Experimental* sciences, including many branches of physics and chemistry, conduct controlled experiments in a laboratory, varying one factor at a time while holding constant all the other relevant factors. Like astronomy, economics is primarily a *non-experimental* science. Astronomers cannot suspend planetary motion to examine the relation between the earth and the sun in isolation; economists cannot suspend the laws of economic activity to conduct controlled experiments.

Most empirical research in economics must deal with data collected over periods in which many of the relevant factors were simultaneously changing. The problem is how to disentangle the separate influences on observed behaviour. We approach this in two stages. First, we proceed by examining the relationship of interest – the dependence of revenue on fares – neglecting the possibility that other relevant factors were changing. Then we indicate how economists deal with the harder problem in which variations in other factors are also included in the analysis.

Table 2.7 shows data on tube fares and passengers. When annual data are measured over overlapping calendar years – say from April 1999 to March 2000 – we show the year as 1999/00. Column (1) shows the real tube fare per passenger kilometre, column (2) shows tube demand, in billions of passenger kilometres a year, and column (3) shows real revenue.

Table 2.7   The tube, 1999/00–2008/09

	(1) Real fare (08/09 pence)	(2) No. of trips (bn pass. km)	(3) Real revenue (08/09 £m)
1999/00	18.4	7171	1319
2000/01	18.6	7470	1389
2001/02	18.6	7451	1386
2002/03	18.0	7367	1326
2003/04	17.9	7340	1314
2004/05	18.1	7606	1377
2005/06	18.7	7586	1419
2006/07	18.8	7947	1494
2007/08	18.7	8352	1562
2008/09	18.7	8646	1617

Source: Department of Transport (www.dft.gov.uk). © Crown copyright 2010.

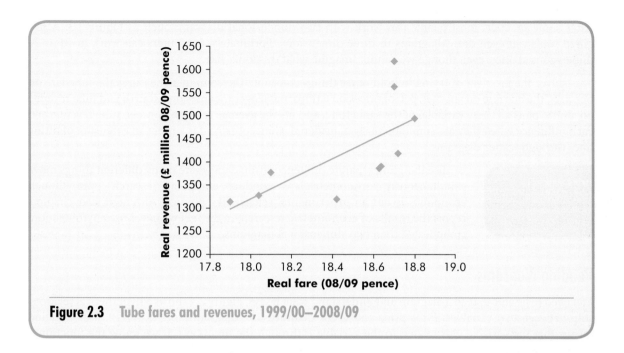

Figure 2.3 Tube fares and revenues, 1999/00–2008/09

It is useful to present evidence such as that in Table 2.7 in a **scatter diagram** such as Figure 2.3. The horizontal axis measures column (3), the real fare per passenger kilometre. The vertical axis measures column (1), real revenue in constant million pounds. Real revenue is the real fare per passenger kilometre multiplied by the number of passenger kilometres travelled.

> A **scatter diagram** plots pairs of values simultaneously observed for two different variables.

From Figure 2.3 we can see a positive relationship between real fare and real revenue. Other things equal, higher fares reduce the number of tube journeys, but if quantity demanded falls only a little, overall revenue may rise when fares are increased. Certainly, in some years, passenger use rose strongly despite higher fares. But we have not yet got to the bottom of things. We return to this issue in Section 2.8.

2.7 Diagrams, lines and equations

If we can draw a line or curve through all these points, this suggests, but does not prove, an underlying relationship between the two variables. If, when the points are plotted, they lie all over the place, this suggests, but does not prove, no underlying relationship between the two variables. Only if economics were an experimental science, in which we could conduct controlled experiments guaranteeing that all other relevant factors had been held constant, could we interpret scatter diagrams unambiguously. Nevertheless, they often provide helpful clues.

Fitting lines through scatter diagrams

In Figure 2.3 we did draw a line through the scatter of points we plotted. The line shows the average relation between fares and revenue between 1999/00 and 2008/09. We can quantify the average relation between fares and usage.

Given a particular scatter of points, how do we decide where to draw the line, given that it cannot fit all the points exactly? The details need not concern us here, but the idea is simple. Having plotted the points describing the data, a computer works out where to draw the line to minimize the dispersion of points around the line.

After some practice, most people can work with two-dimensional diagrams such as Figure 2.3. A few gifted souls can even draw diagrams in three dimensions. Fortunately, computers can work in 10 or 20 dimensions at once, even though we cannot imagine what this looks like.

This solves the problem of trying to hold other things constant. The computer measures the tube fare on one axis, the bus fare on another, petrol prices on a third, passenger incomes on a fourth and tube revenue on a fifth, plots all these variables at the same time, and fits the average relation between tube revenue and each influence when they are simultaneously considered. Conceptually, it is simply an extension of fitting lines through scatter diagrams.

Econometrics uses mathematical statistics to measure relationships in economic data.

By disentangling separate influences from data where many different things move simultaneously, econometricians conduct empirical research even though economics is not an experimental science like physics. Although later chapters report the results of **econometric** research, in the text we never use anything more complicated than two-dimensional diagrams.

Reading diagrams

You need to be able to read a diagram and understand what it says. Figure 2.4 shows a hypothetical relationship between two variables: P for price and Q for quantity. The diagram plots $Q = f(P)$. This notation means that the variable Q is related to the variable P through the function f. If we know the function f, knowing the value of P tells us the corresponding value of Q. We need to know values of P to make statements about Q. In Figure 2.4, Q is a *positive* function of P. Higher values of P imply higher values of Q.

When, as in Figure 2.4, the function is a straight line, only two pieces of information are needed to draw in the entire relationship between Q and P. We need the *intercept* and the *slope*. The intercept is the height of the line when the variable on the horizontal axis is zero. In Figure 2.4, the intercept is 100, the value of Q when $P = 0$.

Lots of different lines could pass through the point at which $Q = 100$ and $P = 0$. The other characteristic is the *slope* of the line, measuring its steepness. The slope tells us how much Q (the variable on the vertical axis) changes each time we increase P (the variable on the horizontal axis) by one unit. In Figure 2.4, the slope is 100. By definition, a straight line has a constant slope. Q rises by 100 whether we move from a price of 1 to 2, or from 2 to 3, or from 3 to 4. The equation of the straight line plotted in Figure 2.4 is

$$Q = 100 + 100P$$

Therefore in this case we have: $f(P) = 100 + 100P$.

Figure 2.4 shows a *positive* relation between Q and P. Since higher P values are associated with higher Q values, the line slopes *up* as we increase P and moves to the right. The line has a positive slope. Figure 2.5 shows a case where Q depends *negatively* on P. Higher P values now imply smaller Q values. The line has a negative slope.

The equation of the straight line plotted in Figure 2.5 is

$$Q = 300 - 100P$$

Economic relationships need not be straight lines or linear relationships. Figure 2.6 shows a non-linear relationship between two variables, Y and X. The slope

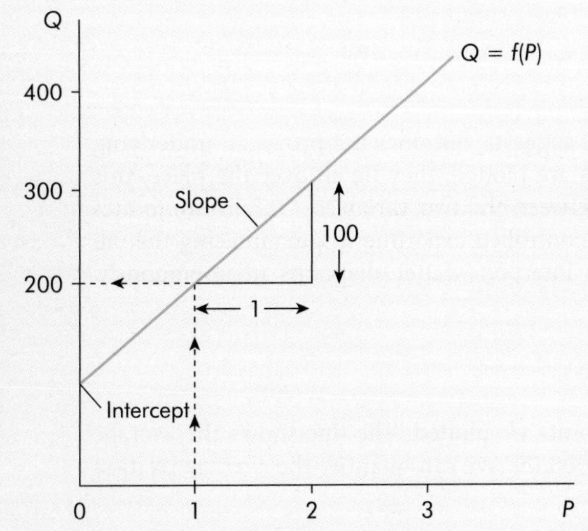

Figure 2.4 A positive linear relationship

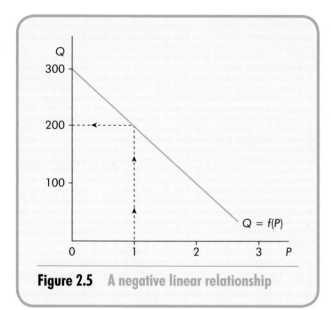

Figure 2.5 A negative linear relationship

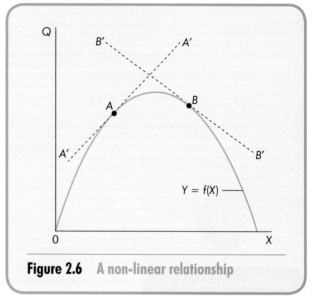

Figure 2.6 A non-linear relationship

keeps changing. Each time we raise X by one unit we get a different rise (or fall) in Y. Consider the relationship between the income tax rate X and income tax revenue Y. When the tax rate is zero, no revenue is raised. When the tax rate is 100 per cent, nobody bothers to work and revenue is again zero. Beginning from a zero tax rate, rises in tax rates initially raise total tax revenue. Beyond some tax rate, further rises in tax rates then reduce tax revenue, which becomes zero by the time the tax rate is 100 per cent. Diagrams display the essence of real-life problems.

An equation that can give rise to the graph in Figure 2.6 is given by

$$Q = 100x - x^2$$

The equation above is non-linear since, on the right-hand side, there is a variable with an exponent different from 1.

ACTIVITY 2.1

Landing the big job

Two students, David and Samantha, have to decide how hard to work for the final exam.

They need a mark of 70 to get the job with Greenpeace that they want. Their tutor has promised them that the exam will be just as hard (or easy) as previous exams. David and Samantha have all the marks from their previous exams, and also know how hard they worked (minimum effort is 1, maximum effort is 5, and neither student worked all that hard in the exams leading up to their finals). From past experience, they know there is a linear relationship between effort and exam results.

| | Effort level | | |
Exam marks	1	2	3
David	20	40	60
Samantha	30	60	90

Questions

(a) What effort level must David make in order to land his job with Greenpeace?

(b) What effort level does Samantha have to make?

(c) Which student is better at exams?

(d) Give three possible reasons for the different exam performance of David and Samantha.

To check your answers to these questions, go to page 683.

 Another look at 'other things equal'

> **Other things equal** is a device for looking at the relationship between two variables, but remembering other variables also matter.

A diagram might help London Underground think about tube fares. Apart from tube fares, the key determinants of passenger use are probably the incomes that passengers have available to spend, and the introduction of the congestion charge in 2003, which induced some Londoners to abandon their cars in favour of public transport.

In the period 1999/00–2008/09, Britain's national income, adjusted for inflation, grew substantially, with the exception of the year 2009 because of the economic recession. Look again at Table 2.7. Even if tube fares had been constant, rising incomes should have led to (and did lead to) rising tube use and rising tube revenues.

Once we allow for movements in *both* tube fares *and* incomes of passengers, our analysis makes more sense. Imagine two sub-periods, one in which incomes were low and one in which incomes were high. Figure 2.7 shows the relationship between tube fare and tube revenue in each period separately. The orange line corresponds to low incomes and hence low passenger demand for tube journeys. The blue line shows greater demand for the tube at each and every potential level of tube fares.

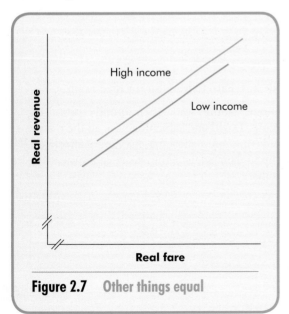

Figure 2.7 Other things equal

During 1999/00–2008/09 we moved from points near the bottom of the blue line to points near the top of the orange line. Tube revenue increased not merely because fares rose but also because incomes rose. Similarly, the introduction of the congestion charge for car use in London increased the demand for tube journeys at any particular level of fares and income.

The axes of Figure 2.7 encourage us to think about the relationship between fares and revenue. Other things equal, higher fares yield higher revenue and we move *along* the upward-sloping line. When one of these other things (like income or congestion charging) changes, we show this as a *shift* in the line. Now we can draw two-dimensional diagrams without neglecting other determinants. When things not drawn on the axes change, lines (or curves) shift.

The same reasoning applies to the introduction of the congestion charge on vehicle use after 2003. Other things equal, fewer people drove cars and more people used the tube. As with the rise in income in Figure 2.7, the consequence of greater tube use is to generate more revenue at any particular level of tube fares. That is why, in Figure 2.3, the data after 2003/04 show much higher tube use than before at each level of tube fares.

2.9 Theories and evidence

Economists analyse a problem in three distinct stages. First, a phenomenon is observed or contemplated and the problem is formulated. By armchair reasoning or a cursory inspection of the data, we decide tube fares have something to do with tube revenues. We want to understand what this relationship is and why it exists.

Second, we develop a theory or model to capture the essence of the phenomenon. By thinking about incomes and the decision about which type of transport to use, we identify the things relevant to tube usage and hence tube revenue.

Third, we *test* the predictions of the theory by confronting it with economic data. An econometric examination of the data can quantify the things the model identifies. We can see if, on average, they work in the direction our model suggests. Indeed, by including in our econometric investigation some extra factors deliberately left out of our model in the quest for simplicity, we can check that the extra influences were sufficiently unimportant that it made sense to omit them from the analysis.

Suppose we confront our theory with the data and the two seem compatible. We *do not reject* our theory. If our model is rejected, we have to start again. If our model is not rejected by the data, this does not guarantee that we have found the correct model. There may be a better model that has escaped our attention but would also be compatible with our particular data. As time passes, we acquire new data. We can also use data from other countries. The more we confront our model with different data and find that it is still not rejected, the more confident we become that we have found the true explanation of the behaviour in which we are interested. Relationships in which we have become very confident are sometimes called economic laws.

2.10 Some popular criticisms of economics and economists

This chapter has introduced the economist's toolkit. You may have some nagging doubts about it. We end the chapter by discussing some of the popular criticisms of economics and economists.

CASE 2.1 Get a Becker view: use an economist's spectacles

Most people accept that the economic analysis of markets – thinking about how incentives affect resource allocation – helps us understand things like inflation or unemployment. Can the same tools be applied to other social behaviour? To crime? To marriage? To drug use?

Since much of economic analysis supposes that people are driven by self-interest, rather than by an altruistic concern for others, some economists doubt whether economics can shed light on highly interactive 'social' situations. Other economists have no such fears. In 1992 Chicago economist Gary Becker was awarded the Nobel Prize for Economics for applying the logic of economic incentives to almost every facet of human behaviour. Some examples of Becker in action . . .

Marriage and divorce

'The courtroom is not a good place to make judgements about the unique circumstances of each marriage or relationship. We should replace judicial determination with marriage contracts that specify, among other things, the financial and child custodial terms of a divorce. Marriage contracts would become much more common if we set aside the legal tradition that they are not unenforceable.'

Picture: **Gary Becker**, © www.nutquote.com

Drugs

Prohibition of alcohol gave the US Al Capone but failed to stop drinking. The end of Prohibition 'was a confession that the US experiment in banning drinking had failed dismally. It was not an expression of support for heavy drinking or alcoholism.' Becker's solution for drugs is to legalize, boost government tax revenue, protect minors and cut out organized crime's monopoly on supply.

Becker's proposals have some merit. For example, in 2001 the police in Brixton were told not to arrest people smoking cannabis in public, part of a gradual policy switch to target hard drugs like cocaine and heroin. UK cannabis seizures in 2000 were only half those of 1997. As supply increased, the price on the street slumped.

Some people argue that implicit toleration of soft drugs should give way to decriminalization, allowing legal sales. With 1500 tonnes consumed annually in the UK, an excise duty of £3 a gramme would raise up to £5 billion a year in tax revenue. Gains to the wider economy would be even greater. There would probably be cuts both in the £1.4 billion currently spent enforcing anti-drugs laws and in the £1.5 billion estimated as the cost of drug-related crime.

Sources: Becker, G. S. and Becker, G. N. (1997) *The Economics of Life*, McGraw-Hill; *The Observer*, 8 July 2001.

No two economists ever agree

You need to distinguish between positive economics and normative economics. Even if all economists agree on the positive economics of how the world works, there is huge scope to disagree on normative recommendations based on different value judgements. Many disagreements between economists fall under this heading.

There *are* disagreements in positive economics. Economics is only rarely an experimental science. It is prohibitively costly to make half of the population unemployed just to find out how the economy then works. Without controlled experiments, we have to disentangle different influences in past data to overcome the problem of other things equal. Using data over many years makes it easier to do this unravelling but introduces a new problem. Since attitudes and institutions are slowly changing, data from many years ago may no longer be relevant to current behaviour. The problems we confront are difficult ones and we have to do the best we can.

Finally, it is wrong to think that there are not serious disagreements between physicists or doctors or engineers. Most people do not pretend to know much about physics; everybody claims to know a bit about the problems that economists study.

Models in economics are so simple they have little to do with reality

A model is a deliberate simplification to help us think more clearly. A good model simplifies a lot but does not distort reality too much. It captures the main features of the problem. The test of a good model is not how simple it is, but how much of observed behaviour it can explain.

Sometimes we can get a long way with a simple model. You will see examples in later chapters. On other occasions, the behaviour we are studying is complex and a simple model may not suffice. Where a more realistic model would take us beyond the scope of this book, we still introduce a simple model to let you begin to see the elements of the problem.

People are not as mercenary as economists make out

Economists believe that most of the phenomena they study, such as whether to travel by bus or by tube, are mainly determined by economic incentives. This does not mean economic incentives are all that matter.

A successful advertising campaign by the tube would change tube usage. So would a change in social attitudes: it might become chic to take the tube. Knowledge of politics, sociology and psychology is needed for a more complete description of human behaviour. These are factors that economists subsume under the heading of 'other things equal'. Economics emphasizes the effect of economic incentives. Social attitudes change slowly and for many purposes may be treated as being held constant. However, if an economist discovered an important change in social attitudes, it would be easy to include this in the analysis.

Actions of human beings cannot be reduced to scientific laws

Physicists accept that individual molecules behave randomly but that we can construct and test theories based on their average or systematic behaviour. Economists take the same view about people. We shall never explain actions based on whim or because you got out of bed on the wrong side. However, random differences in behaviour tend to cancel out, on average. We can describe average behaviour with a lot more certainty.

If behaviour shows no systematic tendencies – tendencies to do the same thing when confronted by the same situation – there is little to discuss. The past is no guide to the future. Every decision is a one-off decision. Not only is this view unhelpful, it is not supported by the data. The economic theories that survive are those consistently compatible with the data. The more random is human behaviour, the less is the systematic element about which we can form theories and use to make predictions. It is better to be able to say something about behaviour than nothing at all. Often, as you will shortly discover, we can say rather a lot.

Summary

- There is a continuing interplay between models and data in the study of economic relationships. A **model** is a simplified framework to organize how we think about a problem.

- **Data** or facts are essential for two reasons. They suggest relationships which we should aim to explain and they allow us to test our hypotheses and to quantify the effects that they imply.

- Tables present data in a form easily understood. **Time-series data** are values of a given variable at different points in time. **Cross-section data** refer to the same point in time but to different values of the same variable across different people. **Panel data** are a mix between time-series and cross-section data.

- **Index numbers** express data relative to some given base value.

- Many index numbers refer to averages of many variables. The **retail price index** summarizes changes in the prices of all goods bought by households. It weights the price of each good by its importance in the budget of a typical household.

- The annual percentage change in the retail price index is the usual measure of **inflation**, the rate at which prices in general are changing.

- **Nominal or current price variables** refer to values at the prices ruling when the variable was measured. **Real or constant price variables** adjust nominal variables for changes in the general level of prices. They are inflation-adjusted measures.

- **Scatter diagrams** show the relationship between two variables plotted in the diagram. By fitting a line through these points we summarize the average relationship between the two variables. **Econometrics** uses computers to fit average relationships between many variables simultaneously. In principle this allows us to get round the 'other things equal' problem, which always applies in two dimensions.

- Analytical diagrams are often useful in building a model. They show relationships between two variables holding other things equal. If we wish to change one of these other things, we have to shift the line or curve we have shown in our diagram.

- To understand how the economy works we need both theory and facts. We need theory to know what facts to look for: there are too many facts for the facts alone to tell us the correct answer. Facts without theory are useless, but theory without facts is unsupported assertion. We need both.

Review questions

connect

EASY

1 The police research department wants to study whether the level of crime is affected by the unemployment rate. (a) How would you test this idea? What data would you want? (b) What 'other things equal' problems would you bear in mind?

2 Use the data in Table 2.6 to plot a scatter diagram of the relationship between nominal house prices and the retail price index. Does this diagram plot time-series data or cross-section data?

3 The table shows consumer spending by households and income from 1999 to 2009, both in £ billion. (a) Plot a scatter diagram with consumption on the vertical axis and income on the horizontal axis. (b) Fit a line through these points. (c) Are consumption and income related?

UK	1999	2000	2001	2002	2003	2004	2005	2006	2007	2008	2009
Income	1067	1109	1136	1160	1192	1227	1254	1290	1323	1330	1265
Consumption	644	673	695	720	743	767	784	796	815	822	796

4 The table below shows unemployment rates in the capital and the rest of the country. One-third of the national population lives in the capital. Construct an index of national unemployment, treating 2005 as 100. What weights did you use for the two unemployment rates? Why?

Unemployment (%)	2001	2002	2003	2004	2005	2006	2007	2008	2009	2010
London	7	6	5	4	6	5	4	6	8	9
Rest of country	10	9	8	8	9	8	8	7	7	8

5 Plot a scatter diagram with variable Y on the vertical axis and variable X on the horizontal axis. Is the relationship between X and Y positive or negative? Is it better to fit a straight line or a curve through these points?

Y	40	33	29	56	81	19	20
X	5	7	9	3	1	11	10

6 Common fallacies   Why are these statements wrong? (a) The purpose of a theory is to let you ignore the facts. (b) Economics cannot be a science since it cannot conduct controlled laboratory experiments. (c) People have feelings and act haphazardly. It is misguided to reduce their actions to scientific laws.

7 The data in Question 3 confirm a very close relationship between household income and consumer spending. Why do other influences, particularly the changing level of interest rates, have only a small effect on household decisions about how much of their income to spend or save?

8 When we use economic data to test an economic theory, we must choose how high to set the bar in our test. If we decide to reject a theory whenever the data depart at all from the prediction of the theory, then we will reject most of our theories, which were only approximations in the first place. Conversely, if we only reject theories when the data are a long way away from the prediction of the theory, we will hardly ever reject any theory. Which of these two possible mistakes is more dangerous?

9 Essay question   Following the introduction of the congestion charge for driving into central London, traffic levels initially fell by 20 per cent. Over the next few years, traffic increased back towards its original level. Does this show the congestion charge failed to reduce congestion? Even if it did fail, might it still be a good idea?

For solutions to these questions contact your lecturer.

Demand, supply and the market

Learning Outcomes

By the end of this chapter, you should understand:

1. the concept of a market
2. demand and supply curves
3. equilibrium price and equilibrium quantity
4. how price adjustment reconciles demand and supply in a market
5. what shifts demand and supply curves
6. free markets and markets with price controls
7. how markets answer what, how and for whom to produce

Society has to find *some* way to decide what, how and for whom to produce. Modern economies rely heavily on markets and prices to allocate resources between competing uses. The interplay of *demand* (representing the behaviour of buyers) and *supply* (representing the behaviour of sellers) determines the quantity produced of a given good or service and the price at which it is bought and sold.

3.1 The market

A **market** is a set of arrangements by which buyers and sellers exchange goods and services.

Shops and fruit stalls physically bring together the buyer and seller. The stock exchange uses intermediaries (stockbrokers), who transact business on behalf of clients. E-commerce is conducted on the internet. In supermarkets, sellers choose the price and let customers choose whether or not to buy. Antique auctions force buyers to bid against each other, with the seller taking a passive role.

Although superficially different, these markets perform the same economic function. They determine prices that ensure that the quantity buyers wish to buy equals the quantity sellers wish to sell. Price and quantity cannot be considered separately. In fixing the price of a Bentley at 20 times the price of a Fiat, the market for motor cars ensures that production and sales of Fiats greatly exceed the production and sales of Bentleys. These prices guide society in choosing what, how and for whom to produce.

To understand this process more fully, we need to model a typical market. We concentrate the analysis on markets where each participant is small as a fraction of the number of buyers and sellers. The ingredients are demand (the behaviour of buyers) and supply (the behaviour of sellers). We can then study how these interact to see how a market works.

3.2 Demand, supply and equilibrium

Demand is not a particular quantity, such as six bars of chocolate, but rather a full description of the quantity of chocolate buyers would purchase at each and every price that might be charged. Suppose we could ask consumers who want to buy chocolate how much they are willing to pay for some different quantities of chocolate bars. The first column of Table 3.1 shows possible prices of chocolate

> **Demand** is the quantity that buyers wish to purchase at each conceivable price.

bars. The second column shows the quantities consumers are willing to buy at these prices. Even if chocolate is free – so the price is zero – only a finite amount is demanded. This is plausible since people may become sick from eating too much chocolate. As the price of chocolate rises, chocolate becomes more and more expensive and therefore the quantity demanded falls, *other things equal*. The fact that, as the price of a good or service increases, the quantity demanded of that good or service decreases (other things equal) holds for almost every good or service and is known as the *law of demand*.[1]

A typical demand curve for a given good is displayed in Figure 3.1. On the vertical axis we plot the price of a good and on the horizontal axis the quantity demanded of that good. As the price of the good increases, say from P_0 to P_1, the quantity demanded of that good decreases from Q_0 to Q_1. Notice that in Figure 3.1 the demand curve is not a straight line. In the rest of the book we will consider mainly linear demand curves. Linear demand curves are simpler to analyse than non-linear ones.

Let's consider Table 3.1 in more detail. Suppose that nobody buys any chocolate if the price exceeds £0.40. Together, columns (1) and (2) describe the demand for chocolate as a function of its price.

Supply is not a particular quantity but a complete description of the quantity that sellers want to sell at each possible price. Suppose that we can ask all suppliers of chocolate in the market how much they wish to sell at different prices. The third column of Table 3.1 summarizes the possible behaviour of the sellers. Chocolate cannot be produced for nothing. Nobody would supply at a zero price. In our

> **Supply** is the quantity of a good that sellers wish to sell at each possible price.

Table 3.1 Demand and supply of chocolate

(1) Price (£/bar)	(2) Demand (no. of bars)	(3) Supply (no. of bars)
0.00	200	0
0.10	160	0
0.20	120	40
0.30	80	80
0.40	40	120
0.50	0	160

---

1   There are goods and services for which the law of demand does not hold. Nevertheless, those cases are rare. In Chapter 5 we discuss in more detail such cases, known as Giffen goods.

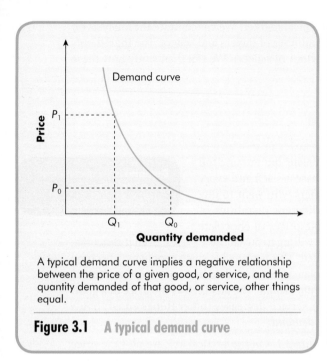

A typical demand curve implies a negative relationship between the price of a given good, or service, and the quantity demanded of that good, or service, other things equal.

Figure 3.1 A typical demand curve

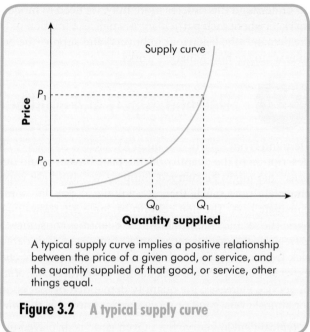

A typical supply curve implies a positive relationship between the price of a given good, or service, and the quantity supplied of that good, or service, other things equal.

Figure 3.2 A typical supply curve

example, it takes a price of £0.20 before there is an incentive to supply chocolate. At higher prices it is more lucrative to supply chocolate bars and there is a rise in the quantity supplied. This positive relationship between the quantity supplied of a given good or service and the price of that good or service (other things equal) is a regularity that holds for almost every good or service. We call this positive relationship between the price and the quantity supplied of a good or service, the *law of supply*. Together, columns (1) and (3) describe the supply of chocolate bars as a function of their price.

An example of a typical supply curve is given in Figure 3.2. As the price of a good increases, say from P_0 to P_1, the quantity supplied of that good increases from Q_0 to Q_1. We plot a supply curve that is not a straight line; however, in the rest of the book we will deal mainly with linear supply curves.

Note the distinction between *demand* and the *quantity demanded*. Demand describes the behaviour of buyers at every price. At a particular price there is a particular quantity demanded. The term 'quantity demanded' makes sense only in relation to a particular price. The same applies to *supply* and *quantity supplied*.

In everyday language, we say that when the demand for football tickets exceeds their supply some people do not get into the ground. Economists must be more precise. At the price charged for tickets, the quantity demanded exceeded the quantity supplied. Now suppose that the ticket price increases. The quantity demanded will be reduced. Here there is no change in demand, the schedule describing how many people want admission at each possible ticket price. What has changed is the quantity demanded because the price changed.

The demand and supply schedules are each constructed as a relationship between the quantity demanded and supplied and the price only, keeping 'other things equal'. In the demand for football tickets, one of the 'other things' is whether the game is televised. If it is, the quantity of tickets demanded at each possible price can be lower than if the game is not televised.

Think again about the market for chocolate in Table 3.1. Other things equal, the lower the price of chocolate, the higher the quantity demanded. Other things equal, the higher the price of chocolate, the higher the quantity supplied. A campaign by dentists warning of the effect of chocolate on tooth decay, or a fall in household incomes, would change the 'other things' relevant to the demand for chocolate. Either of these changes would reduce the demand for chocolate, reducing the quantities demanded at each price. Cheaper cocoa beans, or technical advances in packaging chocolate bars, would change the 'other things' relevant to the supply of chocolate bars. They would tend to increase the supply of chocolate bars, increasing the quantity supplied at each possible price.

The equilibrium price

Assume, initially, that all these other things remain constant. We combine the behaviour of buyers and sellers to model the market for chocolate bars. At low prices, the quantity demanded exceeds the quantity supplied but the reverse is true at high prices. At some intermediate price, which we call the **equilibrium price**, the quantity demanded just equals the quantity supplied.

In Table 3.1 the equilibrium price is £0.30, at which 80 bars is the *equilibrium quantity*, the quantity buyers wish to buy and sellers wish to sell. At prices below £0.30, the quantity demanded exceeds the quantity supplied and some buyers are frustrated. There is a shortage. When economists say there is **excess demand** they are using a shorthand for the more accurate expression: the quantity demanded exceeds the quantity supplied *at this price*.

> The **equilibrium price** is the price at which the quantity supplied equals the quantity demanded.
>
> **Excess demand** exists when the quantity demanded exceeds the quantity supplied at the ruling price.
>
> **Excess supply** exists when the quantity supplied exceeds the quantity demanded at the ruling price.

Conversely, at any price above £0.30, the quantity supplied exceeds the quantity demanded. Sellers have unsold stock. Economists describe this surplus as **excess supply**, shorthand for an excess quantity supplied *at this price*. Only at £0.30, the equilibrium price, are quantity demanded and quantity supplied equal. The market clears. People's wishes are fulfilled at the equilibrium price.

Is a market automatically in equilibrium? What could bring this about? Suppose the price is initially £0.50, above the equilibrium price. Suppliers offer 160 bars but nobody buys at this price. Sellers cut the price to clear their stock. Cutting the price to £0.40 has two effects. It raises the quantity demanded to 40 bars and cuts the quantity producers wish to make and sell to 120 bars. Both effects reduce excess supply. Price-cutting continues until the equilibrium price of £0.30 is reached and excess supply disappears. At this price, the market clears.

If the price is below the equilibrium price the process works in reverse. At a price of £0.20, 120 bars are demanded but only 40 supplied. Sellers run out of stock and charge higher prices. This incentive to raise prices continues until the equilibrium price is reached, excess demand is eliminated and the market clears.

At a particular time, the price may not be the equilibrium price. If not, there is either excess supply or excess demand, depending on whether the price lies above or below the equilibrium price. But these imbalances provide the incentive to change prices towards the equilibrium price. Markets are self-correcting. Some of the key issues in economics turn on how quickly prices adjust to restore equilibrium in particular markets.

 ## Demand and supply curves

Table 3.1 shows demand and supply conditions in the chocolate market and allows us to find the equilibrium price and quantity. It is useful to analyse the same problem diagrammatically.

Figure 3.3 measures chocolate prices on the vertical axis and chocolate quantities on the horizontal axis. The **demand curve** *DD* plots the data in the first two columns of Table 3.1 and joins up the points. This demand curve happens to be a straight line, though it need not be. Our straight line has a negative slope. Larger quantities are demanded at lower prices.

> The **demand curve** shows the relationship between price and quantity demanded, other things equal.
>
> The **supply curve** shows the relationship between price and quantity supplied, other things equal.

Figure 3.3 plots columns (1) and (3) of Table 3.1. Joining up the different points yields the **supply curve** *SS*. Again, this happens to be a straight line but it need not be. It slopes up because suppliers only wish to increase the quantity supplied if they get a higher price.

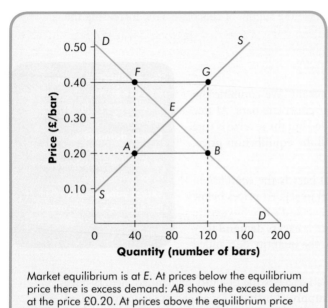

Market equilibrium is at *E*. At prices below the equilibrium price there is excess demand: *AB* shows the excess demand at the price £0.20. At prices above the equilibrium price there is excess supply: *FG* shows the excess supply at the price £0.40.

Figure 3.3   **The market for chocolate**

We can now re-examine excess supply, excess demand and equilibrium. A particular price is shown by a height on the vertical axis, a particular quantity by a length on the horizontal axis. Equilibrium is at point *E*. As in Table 3.1, this entails a price of £0.30 and a quantity of 80 bars. At any price below the equilibrium price, the horizontal distance between the supply curve and the demand curve is the excess demand at that price. At £0.20, 40 bars are supplied but 120 bars are demanded. The distance *AB* is the excess demand of 80 bars. Conversely, above the equilibrium price there is excess supply. At £0.40, 40 bars are demanded, 120 bars are supplied and the horizontal distance *FG* is the excess supply of 80 bars at this price.

Suppose the price is £0.40. Only 40 bars are sold, even though sellers would like to sell 120 bars. Why are sellers – not buyers – frustrated when their wishes differ? Participation in a market is voluntary. Buyers are not *forced* to buy nor sellers *forced* to sell. When markets are not in equilibrium, the quantity transacted is the *smaller* of the quantity supplied and the quantity demanded. Any quantity above 40 bars at a price of £0.40 would force buyers into purchases they do not want. Similarly, at a price of £0.20, any quantity greater than 40 bars involves sellers in forced sales.

We can now reconsider *price determination* in the chocolate market. Figure 3.3 implies that there is excess supply at all prices above the equilibrium price of £0.30. Sellers react to unsold stocks by cutting prices. The existence of an excess of supply creates a downward pressure on the price, therefore the price falls. Once the price falls to the equilibrium price, excess supply is eliminated. Equilibrium is at point *E*. Conversely, at prices below £0.30 there is excess demand. The existence of an excess of demand creates an upward pressure on the price, therefore the price increases. The increase in the price eliminates the excess of demand until the equilibrium point *E* is reached. In equilibrium, buyers and sellers can trade as much as they wish at the equilibrium price. There is no incentive for any further price changes.

MATHS 3.1   Market equilibrium with linear demand and supply

We can describe the equilibrium in a given market in a simple mathematical way. First, we introduce the *direct demand function* as a relationship between the quantity demanded and the price of a given good or service, keeping 'other things constant'. Suppose that the direct demand function is linear; it can be written as

$$Q^D = a - bP \tag{1}$$

where Q^D denotes the quantity demanded, P the price while a and b are two positive constants. Using letters instead of numbers makes the analysis a bit more general. Equation (1) implies a negative relationship between the quantity demanded and the price of a given good or service.

Next, we introduce a linear *direct supply function*:

$$Q^S = c + dP \tag{2}$$

where Q^S is the quantity supplied, while c and d are two constants. We assume that the constant d is positive. This implies that there is a positive relationship between the quantity supplied and the price. The constant c can be positive or negative.

The market equilibrium is where quantity demanded equals quantity supplied, meaning

$$Q^D = Q^S$$

This fact implies that

$$a - bP = c + dP \tag{3}$$

Solving equation (3) for the price P gives us:

$$dP + bP = a - c$$

$$\Rightarrow P(b + d) = a - c$$

$$\Rightarrow P^\star = \frac{(a - c)}{(b + d)}$$

$P^\star$ is the equilibrium price that equates quantity demanded and quantity supplied.

To find the corresponding equilibrium quantity we can substitute the expression of $P^\star$ into the original demand function or into the supply function. Here we use the demand function:

$$Q^D = a - b\frac{(a - c)}{(b + d)}$$

$$\Rightarrow Q^D = \frac{a(b + d) - b(a - c)}{(b + d)}$$

$$\Rightarrow Q^D = \frac{ba + da - ba + bc}{(b + d)}$$

$$\Rightarrow Q^\star = \frac{bc + da}{(b + d)}$$

Therefore the market equilibrium in our example is given by:

$$P^\star = \frac{(a - c)}{(b + d)} \quad \text{and} \quad Q^\star = \frac{bc + da}{(b + d)}$$

From the direct demand function we can always find the *inverse demand function* (and vice versa). The inverse demand function is a relationship between the price and the quantity demanded of a given good. The inverse demand function associated with equation (1) is given by

$$P = \frac{a}{b} - \frac{1}{b}Q^D \tag{4}$$

Why do we need an inverse demand? Because when we plot a demand function on a graph we put the price on the vertical axis and the quantity on the horizontal axis. Therefore, we normally plot the inverse demand. This is what we have called the demand curve. The same applies for the supply function. The *inverse supply function* associated with equation (2) is given by

$$P = -\frac{c}{d} + \frac{1}{d}Q^S \tag{5}$$

3.4 Behind the demand curve

The demand curve depicts the relationship between price and quantity demanded *holding other things constant*. What are those 'other things'? The other things relevant to demand curves can usually be grouped under three headings: the price of related goods, the income of consumers (buyers) and consumer tastes or preferences. We look at each of these in turn.

The price of related goods

In Chapter 2 we discussed the demand for tube travel. A rise in bus fares or petrol prices would increase the quantity of tube travel demanded at each possible tube price. In everyday language, buses and cars are *substitutes* for the tube. Similarly, petrol and cars are *complements* because you cannot use a car without also using fuel. A rise in the price of petrol tends to reduce the demand for cars.

> A price increase for one good raises the demand for **substitutes** for this good but reduces the demand for **complements** of the good.

How do substitutes and complements relate to the demand for chocolate bars? Clearly, other sweets (jelly babies, say) are **substitutes** for chocolate. An increase in the price of other sweets increases the quantity of chocolate demanded at each possible chocolate price, as people substitute away from other sweets towards chocolate. If people buy chocolate to eat at the cinema, films would be a **complement** of bars of chocolate. A rise in the price of cinema tickets would reduce the demand for chocolate since fewer people would go to the cinema. Nevertheless, it is difficult to think of many goods that are complements of chocolate. Complementarity is indeed a more specific feature than substitutability (CD players and CDs, coffee and milk, shoes and shoelaces).

Consumer incomes

> For a **normal good**, demand increases when incomes rise. For an **inferior good**, demand falls when incomes rise.

The second category of 'other things equal' when we draw a particular demand curve is consumer income. When incomes rise, the demand for most goods increases. Typically, consumers buy more of everything. However, there are exceptions.

As their name suggests, most goods are **normal goods**. **Inferior goods** are typically cheap but low-quality goods that people prefer not to buy if they can afford to spend a little more.

Tastes

The third category of things held constant along a particular demand curve is consumer tastes or preferences. In part, these are shaped by convenience, custom and social attitudes. The fashion for the mini-skirt reduced the demand for fabric. The emphasis on health and fitness has increased the demand for jogging equipment, health foods and sports facilities while reducing the demand for cream cakes, butter and cigarettes.

CASE 3.1

One little piggy went to market

The 1996 BSE crisis led to a collapse in the demand for British beef. We can think of the BSE crisis as a shock (at least temporarily) on consumers' tastes. Consumers started to switch to pork and chicken since they were perceived as more secure than beef. With a lower demand curve, given the supply, the equilibrium price of beef fell. On the other hand, the demand for pork increased. The price of pork rose sharply between 1995 and 1996. Many farmers switched from rearing cows to pigs. The result was an increase in the market supply of pork. By 1998 the market was flooded with pork and pig prices collapsed! By 2001 many fewer piggies were being reared for the market.

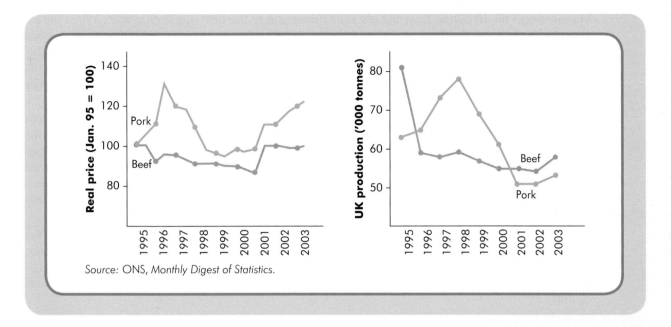

Source: ONS, *Monthly Digest of Statistics.*

3.5   Shifts in the demand curve

We can now distinguish between movements along a given demand curve and shifts in the demand curve itself. In Figure 3.3 we drew the demand curve for chocolate bars for a given level of the three underlying factors: the price of related goods, incomes and tastes. Movements along the demand curve isolate the effects of chocolate prices on quantity demanded, holding other things equal. Changes in any of these three factors will change the demand for chocolate. In particular any change in those three factors will *shift* the demand for chocolate.

Figure 3.4 shows a rise in the price of a substitute for chocolate, say ice cream, which leads people to demand more chocolate and less ice cream. At each chocolate price there is a larger quantity of chocolate demanded when ice cream prices are high. People substitute chocolate for ice cream. This *shifts* the demand curve for chocolate from *DD* to *D'D'*. The entire demand curve shifts to the right. At each price on the vertical axis, a larger horizontal distance indicates a higher quantity demanded.

Changes in the price of ice cream have no effect on the incentives to supply chocolate bars: at each price of chocolate, suppliers wish to supply the same quantity of chocolate as before. The increase in demand, or rightward shift in the demand curve, changes the equilibrium price and quantity in the chocolate market. Equilibrium has changed from *E* to *E'*. The new equilibrium price is £0.40 and the new equilibrium quantity is 120 bars.

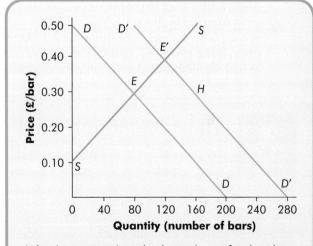

At low ice cream prices, the demand curve for chocolate is *DD* and the market equilibrium occurs at the point *E*. Higher ice cream prices raise the demand for chocolate, shifting the demand curve to *D'D'*. At the former equilibrium price there is now excess demand *EH*, which gradually bids up the price of chocolate until the new equilibrium is reached in *E'*.

Figure 3.4   An increase in chocolate demand

We can sketch the transition from the old equilibrium at E to the new equilibrium at E'. When the ice cream prices first rise, the demand curve for chocolate shifts from DD to $D'D'$. With the chocolate price still at £0.30, there is an excess demand EH: 160 bars are demanded but only 80 bars are supplied. This excess demand bids up prices, which gradually rise to the new equilibrium price of £0.40, choking the quantity demanded back from 160 bars to 120 bars and providing the incentive to raise the quantity supplied from 80 bars to 120 bars.

We draw two lessons from this example. First, the quantity demanded depends on four things: its own price, prices of related goods, incomes and tastes. We could draw a two-dimensional diagram showing the relation between quantity of chocolate demanded and any one of these four things. The other three things would then be the 'other things equal' for this diagram. In drawing demand curves, we single out the price of the commodity itself (here, the price of chocolate bars) to put in the diagram with quantity demanded. The other three factors are the 'other things equal' for drawing a particular demand curve. Changes in any of these other three things shift the position of demand curves.

Why single out the price of the commodity itself to plot against quantity demanded? We want to study the market for chocolate. Prices of related goods, incomes and tastes are determined elsewhere in the economy. By focusing on the price of chocolate, we see the self-correcting mechanism by which the market reacts to excess demand or excess supply: inducing changes in chocolate prices within the chocolate market restores equilibrium.

Comparative static analysis changes one of the 'other things equal' and examines the effect on equilibrium price and quantity.

Second, our example illustrates analysis by *comparative statics*. The analysis is comparative because it compares the old and new equilibria, and static because it compares only the equilibrium positions. In each equilibrium, prices and quantities are constant. **Comparative static analysis** is not interested in the dynamic path by which the economy moves from one equilibrium to the other; it is interested only in the point from which it began and the point at which it ends.

Using Figure 3.4 we can also analyse a change in one of the 'other things equal'. Suppose the demand curve is initially $D'E'$ and the market begins in equilibrium at E'. Then the demand for chocolate falls to DD. This might reflect a fall in the price of a chocolate substitute, a fall in consumer incomes or a change in tastes away from liking chocolate. When the demand curve shifts left to DD, showing less chocolate demanded at each price, the new equilibrium is at E. At the original price of £0.40 there is excess supply, which bids prices down to the new equilibrium price of £0.30. When the demand curve shifts to the left, there is a fall in both equilibrium price and equilibrium quantity.

CASE 3.2 The demand for mobile voice calls in the UK

We have defined demand as quantity that buyers are willing to buy at each conceivable price. To construct a market demand for a given good using our definition, we should be able to ask each consumer in the market how much she wishes to buy of the good at each possible price. As you can guess, it is very impractical to obtain such information. Instead we can use other information that is easily available to us to obtain market demand data. We observe the quantity purchased of a good in a given period of time and the price of the good when the purchase was made. We can observe the income of consumers, the prices of other goods that we think are substitutes for or complements of the good we are analysing, and so on. We can use those data to *estimate* the market demand for a given good. Estimating economic relationships using economic data is the main objective of an important branch of economics known as *econometrics*. We are not interested in explaining how econometrics works, we just want to outline that, from available economic data, it is possible to obtain a numerical expression for a market demand. Here we present an example of an estimated demand for mobile voice calls in the UK using quarterly data from 1999 to 2006. Estimated demand is:

$$Q_t = 11.31 - 1.03P_t + 1.39Y_t + 0.28PFC_t + 0.15PSMS_t + 0.014T \qquad (1)$$

where Q_t is the quantity of mobile voice calls made in period t, P_t is the price of mobile voice calls per minute in period t, Y_t is the consumers' income (measured as disposable income per head) in period t, PFC_t is the price of fixed voice calls per minute in period t, $PSMS_t$ is the price of SMS (short message service) in period t and T denotes a time trend ($T = 1$ in the third quarter of 1999 represents the first observation; $T = 2$ in the fourth quarter of 1999 represents the second observation, and so on).

From equation (1) we can see some interesting results. An increase in the price of mobile voice calls (everything else equal) decreases the quantity of mobile calls made as we should expect from market demand. An increase in the income of consumers (everything else equal) will increase the quantity of mobile calls made, implying that mobile voice calls are a normal good.

From equation (1) we can also obtain the usual demand curve that relates quantity and price, other things equal, in a given period of time. Suppose that in the second quarter of 2005, the level of consumers' income was £2000, the price of fixed voice calls was 10p, the price of SMS was 5p and the time trend was 24. Using those numbers in equation (1) we obtain the demand curve for the second quarter of 2005:

$$Q_{2005q2} = 2795.2 - 1.03 P_{2005q2} \tag{2}$$

A word of caution about the estimated demand in (1): econometrics uses statistical techniques to estimate a relationship between variables using data. Therefore equation (1) is not the exact market demand and the predictions we obtain from it may not be totally reliable.

Source: Adapted from Alpetkin, A. et al. (2007) *Estimating spectrum demand for the cellular services in the UK*, working paper, University of Surrey.

3.6 Behind the supply curve

At low prices, only the most efficient chocolate producers make profits. As prices rise, producers previously unable to compete can now make a profit in the chocolate business and wish to supply. Moreover, previously existing firms may be able to expand output by working overtime, or buying fancy equipment unjustified when selling chocolate at lower prices. In general, higher prices are needed to induce firms to produce more chocolate. Other things equal, supply curves slope up as we move to the right.

Just as we studied the 'other things equal' along a demand curve, we now examine three categories of 'other things equal' along a supply curve: the technology available to producers, the cost of inputs (labour, machines, fuel, raw materials) and government regulation. Along a particular supply curve, all of these are held constant. A change in any of these categories shifts the supply curve, changing the amount producers wish to supply at each price.

Technology

A supply curve is drawn for a given technology. Better technology shifts the supply curve to the right. Producers supply more than previously at each price. Better cocoa refining reduces the cost of making chocolate. Faster shipping and better refrigeration lead to less wastage in spoiled cocoa beans. Technological advance enables firms to supply more at each price.

As a determinant of supply, technology must be interpreted broadly. It embraces all know-how about production methods, not merely the state of available machinery. In agriculture, the development of disease-resistant seeds is a technological advance. Improved weather forecasting might enable better timing of planting and harvesting. A technological advance is any idea that allows more output from the same inputs as before. In the terminology of Chapter 1, a technological advance shifts the production possibility frontier outwards.

Input costs

A particular supply curve is drawn for a given level of input prices. Lower input prices (lower wages, lower fuel costs) induce firms to supply more output at each price, shifting the supply curve to the right. Higher input prices make production less attractive and shift the supply curve to the left. If a late frost destroys much of the cocoa crop, scarcity will bid up the price of cocoa beans. Chocolate producers supply less chocolate at each price than previously.

ACTIVITY 3.1

Movement along a curve vs shifts of the curve

From the initial point A, the figure below shows two quite different 'increases in demand'. One is an increase in the quantity demanded, from Q_0 to Q_1, moving along the curve from A to B. This is the effect of a price cut but *not* an increase in demand since the demand curve DD is unaffected.

By an increase in demand, we mean a shift in the demand curve, say from DD to $D'D'$, which also increases quantity demanded from Q_0 to Q_1 at the going price P_0. This shift in demand reflects an increase in the price of a substitute good (decrease in the price of a complementary good), an increase in income or a change in taste.

Similarly, sellers adjust to higher prices by moving up a given supply curve. But an increase in supply means an upward shift in the whole supply curve, caused by lower input prices, new technology or less regulation.

Other things equal, changes in price move us *along* demand and supply curves. When other determinants change, they shift these schedules.

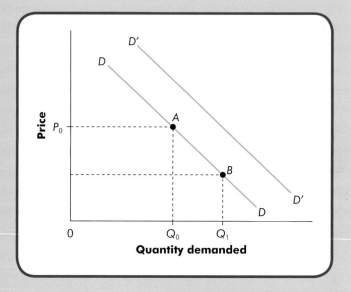

Questions

Classify each of the following as an upward or downward shift in the supply or demand curve:

(a) New interactions between Europe and China make wages of unskilled European workers fall.

(b) New interactions between Europe and China make the price of European coal increase.

(c) The government ban on city parking by large cars reduces the price of Bentleys.

To check your answers to these questions, go to page 683.

Government regulation

In discussing technology, we spoke only of technological advances. Once people have discovered a better production method they are unlikely subsequently to forget it.

Government regulations can sometimes be viewed as imposing a technological change that is *adverse* for producers. If so, the effect of regulations will be to shift the supply curve to the left, reducing quantity supplied at each price.

More stringent safety regulations prevent chocolate producers using the most productive process because it is quite dangerous to workers. Anti-pollution devices may raise the cost of making cars, and regulations to protect the environment may make it unprofitable for firms to extract surface mineral deposits which could have been cheaply quarried but whose extraction now requires expensive landscaping. Whenever regulations prevent producers from selecting the production methods they would otherwise have chosen, the effect of regulations is to shift the supply curve to the left.

 ## 3.7 Shifts in the supply curve

Along a given supply curve, we hold constant technology, the prices of inputs and the extent of government regulation. Any change in those factors will *shift* the supply curve. We now undertake a comparative static analysis of what happens when a change in one of these

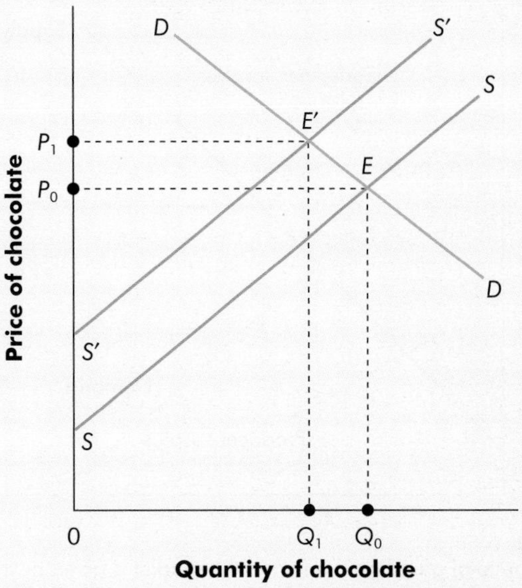

The supply curve initially is SS and market equilibrium is at E. A reduction in the supply of chocolate shifts the supply curve to the left to S'S'. The new equilibrium at E' has a higher equilibrium price and a lower equilibrium quantity than the old equilibrium at E.

Figure 3.5 **A fall in supply**

'other things equal' leads to a fall in supply. Suppose tougher safety legislation makes it more expensive to make chocolate bars in mechanized factories. Figure 3.5 shows a shift to the left in the supply curve, from SS to S'S'. Equilibrium shifts from E to E'.

The equilibrium price *rises* but equilibrium quantity *falls* when the supply curve shifts to the left. Conversely, a rise in supply shifts the supply curve from S'S' to SS. Equilibrium shifts from E' to E. A rise in supply induces a *higher* equilibrium quantity and *lower* equilibrium price.

 ## 3.8 Consumer and producer surplus

In previous sections we defined the market equilibrium. Can we say something about how 'good' a market equilibrium is? In practice, we want to find a possible measure for the gains that consumers and sellers obtain from trading at the equilibrium price. For the consumers, this measure of trade gain is called *consumer surplus*.

For a single consumer, the consumer surplus is the difference between the maximum price (also called the *reservation price*) that she is willing to pay for a given amount of a good or service and the price she actually pays.

Suppose that you want to buy the latest CD of your favourite artist. You are willing to pay a maximum £15 for it. If the price of the CD at the shop is £8, you buy it, and you can say that from buying it you have obtained a surplus of £7. This surplus is a measure of your gain from buying the CD.

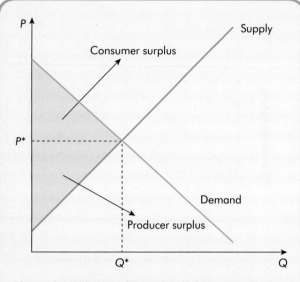

The total gain from trading in the market is given by the sum of the consumer and producer surplus. Here, the gain from trading at the equilibrium price is depicted.

Figure 3.6 Consumer and producer surplus at the market equilibrium

We can extend the idea of consumer surplus to all consumers in a market. In particular, the consumer surplus is measured by the area below the market demand curve and above the equilibrium price.

Similarly we can define a measure for the gain sellers obtain from selling a given quantity of a good or service at the equilibrium price. We call this gain for sellers the *producer surplus*. The producer surplus for sellers is the amount that sellers benefit by selling at a market price that is higher than they would be willing to sell for.

Suppose you want to sell an old record of yours on eBay. You are willing to sell it at a minimum price of £10. Suppose you end up selling it for £30. Your surplus from this transaction is £20. Graphically, the producer surplus is given by the area above the market supply and below the equilibrium price.

The sum of the consumer and producer surplus in a market is a measure of the economic surplus that the participants obtain by trading in the market. This is shown in Figure 3.6. It should be noticed that the economic surplus is highest at the equilibrium price. At any price that is not the equilibrium price, the economic surplus will be lower.

Graphical derivation of consumer and producer surplus

CONCEPT 3.1

Consider a linear market demand for a given good. Suppose that the equilibrium price that consumers pay is £10 for each unit of the good and the equilibrium quantity is 10 units. Suppose that consumers are willing to buy one unit of the good at a price of £19.50. They are willing to buy two units of the good if the price of each unit is £19. They are willing to buy three units if the unit price if £18.50, and so on. In the figure on the right we plot market demand with the information just described.

The consumers are willing to buy 1 unit of the good at the price of £19.50; however, they actually pay £10 for each unit of the good.

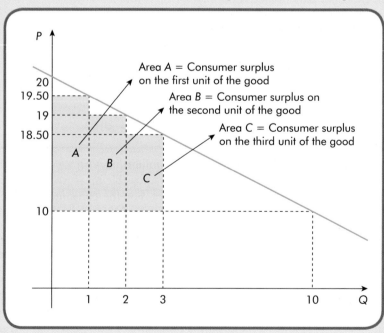

Therefore their gain from trading at the equilibrium price is £9.50 on the first unit of the good. This is given by area *A* in the figure above. The consumers are willing to buy two units of the good if the price is £19 for each unit. Since they pay £10 for each unit, their gain is £9 on the second unit of the good. This is given by area *B* in the figure above. Therefore, the surplus obtained by the consumers from buying the first two units of the good is given by the sum of area *A* and area *B*. We can continue this process until we arrive at the equilibrium quantity 10. The total consumer surplus will be approximately given by the area below the market demand and above the equilibrium price.

We have an approximation because we have considered a good that can be traded only in discrete units (1, 2, 3, and so on). If we assume that the good can be sold in any possible amount (not only discrete), then the consumer surplus is exactly the entire area below the market demand and above the equilibrium price.

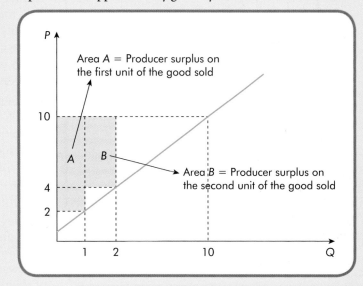

For the producer surplus, we can use similar reasoning. Suppose that the equilibrium price is £10 and the quantity sold in equilibrium is ten. At a price of £2, the sellers are willing to supply one unit of the good. At a price of £4, they are willing to supply two units of the good. In the figure on the right we show the market supply for this case.

By selling ten units of the good, on the first unit the sellers obtain a surplus of £8 (£10 − £2). This is represented by area *A* in the figure. On the second unit sold, the surplus obtained by the sellers is £6 (£10 − £4). This is represented by area *B*. Therefore the surplus obtained by selling two units of the good is given by area *A* plus area *B*. We can continue this process until we reach the equilibrium quantity. The producer surplus is approximately given by the area above the market supply and below the equilibrium price. Again, if we allow the good to be sold in any possible amount the approximation will be exact.

3.9 Free markets and price controls

Government actions may shift demand and supply curves, as when changes in safety legislation shift the supply curve, but the government makes no attempt to regulate prices directly. If prices are sufficiently flexible, the pressure of excess supply or excess demand will quickly bid prices in a free market to their equilibrium level. Markets will not be free when effective **price controls** exist. When price controls are in place in a market, the economic surplus of the participants in that market will also change. Price controls may be *floor* prices (minimum prices) or *ceiling* prices (maximum prices).

> **Free markets** allow prices to be determined purely by the forces of supply and demand.
>
> **Price controls** are government rules or laws setting price floors or ceilings that forbid the adjustment of prices to clear markets.

Price ceilings make it illegal for sellers to charge more than a specific maximum price. Ceilings may be introduced when a shortage of a commodity threatens to raise its price a lot (such as food prices during a war). High prices are the way a free market rations goods in scarce supply. This solves the allocation problem, ensuring that only a small quantity of the scarce commodity is demanded, but may be thought unfair, a normative value judgement. High food prices mean hardship for the poor.

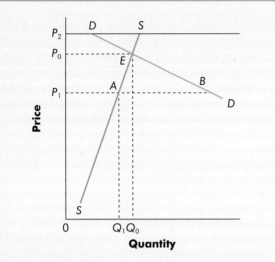

Free market equilibrium occurs at the point *E*. The high price P_0 chokes off quantity demanded to ration scarce supply. A price ceiling at P_1 succeeds in holding down the price but leads to excess demand *AB*. It also reduces quantity supplied from Q_0 to Q_1. A price ceiling at P_2 is irrelevant since the free market equilibrium at *E* can still be attained.

Figure 3.7   The effect of a price ceiling

Faced with a national food shortage, a government may impose a price ceiling on food so that poor people can afford food.

Figure 3.7 shows the market for food. Suppose a war has disrupted imports of food. The supply curve is far to the left and the free market equilibrium price P_0 is very high. Instead of allowing free market equilibrium at *E*, the government imposes a price ceiling P_1. The quantity sold is then Q_1 and excess demand is the distance *AB*. The price ceiling creates a shortage of supply relative to demand by holding food prices below their equilibrium level.[2]

The ceiling price P_1 allows the poor to afford food but it reduces total food supplied from Q_0 to Q_1. With excess demand *AB* at the ceiling price, rationing must be used to decide which potential buyers are actually supplied. This rationing system could be arbitrary. Food suppliers may sell supplies to their friends, not necessarily the poor, or may take bribes from the rich who jump the queue.

Holding down the price of food may not help the poor after all. Ceiling prices are often accompanied by government-organized rationing by quota to ensure that available supply is shared out fairly, independent of ability to pay.

CASE 3.3 Rent ceiling in Sweden

The main justification for introducing a rent ceiling is the right to housing.

A low rent price is believed to make housing affordable for poor people. Unfortunately, as outlined in the analysis above, the introduction of a rent ceiling may have perverse effects and poor people may not be able to get a cheap house anyway. Sweden provides a very interesting example of a rent control policy. In Sweden, rent price is kept particularly low. A study made by the European University Institute (EUI) showed that:

(a) To make a 5 per cent return on investment, a Swedish developer would need to set rents 70 per cent higher than allowed by the rent control.

(b) Rents are little influenced by location, so that metropolitan units are especially underpriced.

The result of this rent control system in Sweden was a reduction in the supply of new properties intended for rental in the market. Of the approximately 30 000 dwellings completed in 2006, only 36 per cent were intended for rental. In comparison, from 1990 to 1996 more than 50 per cent of new dwellings completed were intended for rental. This result is consistent with the analysis we have just made. A price ceiling below the market equilibrium price has the effect of reducing the market supply. This creates a shortage of rental units.

---

2   A price ceiling above the equilibrium price is irrelevant. The free market equilibrium at *E* is still to be attained.

Furthermore, a rent ceiling may have even more perverse effects. Rent control may discourage landlords from maintaining and repairing units during the tenancy. In some cases, landlords collect key money to offset the losses associated with a low rent. This implies that those willing to pay more will get the rental unit, thus eliminating the positive effect of rent control on poor people.

Source: Adapted from Prince Christian Cruz, *The pros and cons of rent control* (http://www.globalpropertyguide.com/investment-analysis/The-pros-and-cons-of-rent-control).

Whereas the aim of a price ceiling is to reduce the price for consumers, the aim of a floor price is to raise the price for suppliers. One example of a floor price is a national minimum wage. In the UK a minimum hourly wage rate was introduced in 1999. Figure 3.8 shows the demand curve and supply curve for labour. The demand for labour tells us for each possible wage rate how many working hours firms demand. The labour supply tells us for each possible wage how many hours workers are willing to work.

The free market equilibrium is at E, where the wage is W_0. A minimum wage below W_0 is irrelevant since the free market equilibrium can still be attained. Suppose, in an effort to help workers, the government imposes a minimum wage at W_1. Firms demand a quantity of labour Q_1 and there is excess supply AB. The lucky workers who manage to get work are better off than before but some workers are worse off since total hours worked fall from Q_0 to Q_1.

Many countries set floor prices for agricultural products. Figure 3.9 shows a floor price P_1 for butter. In previous examples we assumed that the quantity traded would be the smaller of quantity supplied and quantity demanded at the controlled price, since private individuals cannot be forced to participate in a market. There is another possibility: the government may intervene not only to set the control price but also to buy or sell quantities of the good to supplement private purchases and sales.

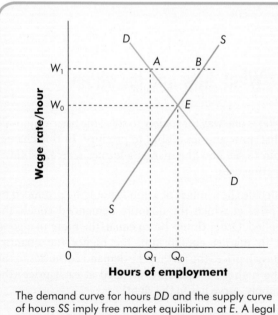

The demand curve for hours DD and the supply curve of hours SS imply free market equilibrium at E. A legal minimum wage at W_1 raises hourly wages for those who remain employed but reduces the quantity of hours of employment available from Q_0 to Q_1.

Figure 3.8 A minimum wage

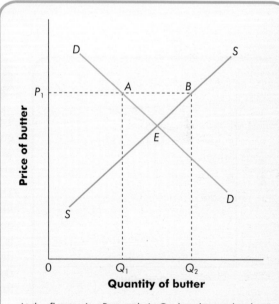

At the floor price P_1 supply is Q_2, but demand only Q_1. Only Q_1 will be traded. By buying up the excess supply AB, the government can satisfy both suppliers and consumers at the price P_1.

Figure 3.9 A price floor for butter

CASE
3.4
More on price controls

California, home of Silicon Valley and Hollywood, is one of the richest places on earth. Yet in 2001 California suffered blackouts as electricity supplies ran out. Since poverty cannot be blamed, it must have been the result of poor policies. California privatized state electricity companies but then capped the price they could charge for electricity. However, the level of the price cap was far too low. Local electricity suppliers haemorrhaged money. This low cap caused the bankruptcy of Pacific Gas and Electric Company (PG&E) and the near bankruptcy of Southern California Edison in early 2001. Not only does an artificially low price lead sooner or later to a lower quantity supplied, it also raises the quantity demanded. Those two effects together were the basis of the electrical blackouts in California. It was estimated that the cost of that electricity crisis was between $40 billion and $45 billion.

Another example of a price control policy is the minimum price (a price floor) that the European Commission imposed on Chinese frozen strawberries in 2007.

Why impose such a price floor? Frozen strawberries from China were too cheap compared to the ones produced in Europe. The price floor aimed to punish Chinese exporters for selling the frozen fruit, used in jam and yoghurt, in Europe below domestic prices or below the production cost, a practice known as *dumping*. In this case, the price floor aimed to protect the European producers of frozen strawberries from Chinese competition.

Here, European producers gained from this policy while Chinese exporters probably lost. What about consumers? A price floor, as shown in Figure 3.9, increases the final price paid by the consumer. Therefore consumers were probably worse off as a result of this policy. Nevertheless, the European Commission decided to impose such a price floor, since it believed that the adverse effects on European producers and farmers would be of a substantial and lasting nature should the price floor not be imposed.

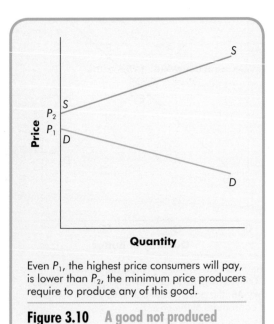

Even P_1, the highest price consumers will pay, is lower than P_2, the minimum price producers require to produce any of this good.

Figure 3.10   A good not produced

3.10 What, how and for whom

The free market is one way for society to solve the basic economic questions what, how and for whom to produce. In this chapter we have begun to see how the market allocates scarce resources among competing uses.

The market decides how much of a good should be produced by finding the price at which the quantity demanded equals the quantity supplied. Other things being equal, the more of a good is produced in market equilibrium, the higher the quantity demanded at each price (the further the demand curve lies to the right) and the higher the quantity supplied at each price (the further the supply curve lies to the right).

The market tells us for whom the goods are produced: the good is purchased by all those consumers willing to pay at least the equilibrium price for it. The market also tells us who is producing: all those willing to supply at the equilibrium price. Later in this book we shall see that the market also tells us how goods are produced.

Finally, the market determines what goods are being produced. Nature supplies goods free of charge. People engage in costly production activities only if they are paid. The supply curve tells us how much has to be paid to bring supply. Figure 3.10 shows a good that will not be produced. The highest price P_1 that consumers are prepared to pay is still insufficient to persuade producers to produce.

Society may not like the answers the market provides. Free markets *do not* provide enough food to remove hunger or enough medical care to treat all the sick. They provide food and medical care for those willing and *able to pay* the equilibrium price. Society may adopt the normative judgement that the poor should get more food and medical care than they get in a free market. Society may also adopt the normative judgement that, although people are willing and able to pay for pornography, it is socially better to ban some of these activities. Few societies allow unrestricted free markets for all commodities. Governments intervene widely to alter market outcomes, through direct regulation, taxation and transfer payments such as unemployment benefit.

CASE 3.5 Anatomy of price and quantity changes

How should we interpret the figure below showing data for the UK housing industry? What was happening? Was it a shift in demand, in supply, or in both that caused this pattern during 1985–2008?

Suppose all the observations represent *equilibrium* prices and quantities in each year. Thus each point reflects the intersection of the demand and supply curve that year. What changes in the 'other things equal' determinants of supply and demand led to shifts in supply and demand curves and hence changed the location of the data points? Try drawing a diagram with a *given* demand curve and a *shifting* supply curve (do it now!). The equilibrium points you will trace out all lie on the *given* demand curve. If only supply shifts, we expect a *negative* relationship between price and quantity as we pick off different points on the same demand curve, which slopes downwards. Now, suppose the supply curve is *fixed* but the demand curve *shifts*. The equilibrium points then all lie on the *given* supply curve and exhibit a positive relation between price and quantity. The data in our example show a positive relationship between the price of houses and the quantity of new private houses built. Indeed, the two series of data move in a similar direction over time and hence principally correspond to a fixed supply curve for construction. It was demand for houses that must have been shifting around. House demand increased steadily during 1985–89, fell back in 1990–93, then grew again thereafter, until 2007/08 when the credit crunch took place.

Having made a diagnosis, we now gather corroborating evidence. Economy-wide activity is an important determinant of the demand for houses. UK real income grew strongly during 1985–89, fell sharply during 1990–93, grew fairly steadily thereafter and then fell again after 2007 because of the credit crunch. These changes in income nicely fit our theory that demand shifts are the main cause of the data pattern in the figure.

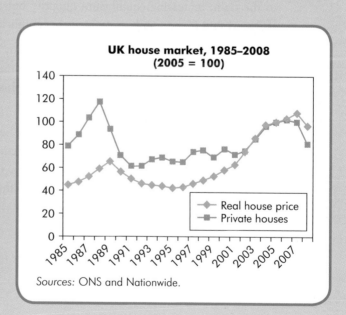

Sources: ONS and Nationwide.

Summary

- **Demand** is the quantity that buyers wish to buy at each price. Other things equal, the lower the price, the higher the quantity demanded. Demand curves slope downwards.

- **Supply** is the quantity of a good sellers wish to sell at each price. Other things equal, the higher the price, the higher the quantity. Supply curves slope upwards.

- **The market clears, or is in equilibrium**, when the price equates the quantity supplied and the quantity demanded. At this point, supply and demand curves intersect. At prices below the equilibrium price there is **excess demand** (shortage), which itself tends to raise the price. At prices above the equilibrium price there is **excess supply** (surplus), which itself tends to reduce the price. In a **free market**, deviations from the equilibrium price tend to be self-correcting.

- Along a given demand curve, the other things assumed equal are the prices of related goods, consumer incomes and tastes or habits.

- An increase in the price of a **substitute** good (or decrease in the price of a **complementary** good) will raise the quantity demanded at each price. An increase in consumer income will increase demand for the good if the good is a **normal good** but decrease demand for the good if it is an **inferior good**.

- Along a given supply curve the other things assumed constant are technology, the price of inputs and the degree of government regulation. An improvement in technology, or a reduction in input prices, will increase the quantity supplied at each price.

- Any factor inducing an increase in demand shifts the demand curve to the right, increasing equilibrium price and equilibrium quantity. A decrease in demand (downward shift of the demand curve) reduces both equilibrium price and equilibrium quantity. Any factor increasing supply shifts the supply curve to the right, increasing equilibrium quantity but reducing equilibrium price. Reductions in supply (leftward shift of the supply curve) reduce equilibrium quantity but increase equilibrium price.

- We can measure the **economic surplus** created by a market transaction by the sum of the consumer and producer surplus. The **consumer surplus** is measured by the area below the market demand and above the equilibrium price. The **producer surplus** is measured by the area above the market supply and below the equilibrium price.

- To be effective, a **price ceiling** must be imposed below the free market equilibrium price. It will then reduce the quantity supplied and lead to excess demand unless the government itself provides the extra quantity required. An effective **price floor** must be imposed above the free market equilibrium price. It will then reduce the quantity demanded unless the government adds its own demand to that of the private sector.

Review questions

1 Supply and demand data for toasters are shown below. Plot the supply curve and demand curve and find the equilibrium price and quantity.

EASY

	Price					
Quantity	10	12	14	16	18	20
Demanded	10	9	8	7	6	5
Supplied	3	4	5	6	7	8

2 What is the excess supply or demand when the price is (a) 12; (b) 20? Describe the price movements induced by positions (a) and (b).

3 What happens to the demand curve for toasters if the price of bread rises? Show in a supply–demand diagram how the equilibrium price and quantity of toasters change.

4 How is the demand curve for toasters affected by the invention of the toaster oven if people prefer this new way of toasting? What happens to the equilibrium quantity and price of toasters?

5 You are a sheep farmer. Give three examples of a change that would reduce your supply of wool. Did you use a fall in the price of wool as one of your examples? Is it a valid example?

6 Goods with snob value are demanded because they are expensive. Does the demand curve for such goods slope upwards?

7 Common fallacies   Why are these statements wrong? (a) Manchester United is a more famous football club than Wrexham, therefore Manchester United will always find it easier to fill its stadium. (b) Holding down rents ensures plenty of cheap housing for the poor.

8 The market demand for milk is $Q^D = 16 - 2P$, while the market supply is $Q^S = -2 + P$. Find the equilibrium quantity and price in the market for milk. Show your solution graphically.

MEDIUM

9 Consider the following market demand: $Q^D = 50 - 2P + Y$, where Y denotes consumers' income. Suppose that $Y = 10$, plot the market demand using the following price levels:

P					
3	5	7	9	12	15

Now suppose that consumers' income increases to $Y = 20$. Plot the market demand using the price levels in the table above. How has the rise in income affected the market demand?

10 The market data for butter are shown below.

	Price				
Quantity	2	7	11	13	15
Demanded	105	80	60	50	40
Supplied	5	30	50	60	70

Suppose that the government introduces a price floor for butter at $P = 14$. In a graph, show the effect on the market for butter of such a price floor. What if the price floor were $P = 8$?

11 Given the following market demand: $Q^D = 120 - 2P$, find the consumer's surplus when $P = 20$ and when $P = 15$.

12 Given the following market supply: $Q^S = 10 + 5P$, find the producer's surplus when $P = 6$ and when $P = 8$.

13 Consider the market for safe cities. Someone knocks on your door and asks if you wish to purchase a reduction in crime by subscribing to an enhanced city-wide police force. Your city has 1 million residents. (a) What happens if you do not subscribe but all your fellow city dwellers do? (b) What happens if you subscribe but nobody else does? (c) What does this tell you about the possibility of a market for public goods such as safe cities? (d) How might society ensure that desirably safe cities are provided?

14 Profitable speculation should stabilize financial markets – successful speculators are those who buy when the price is below the equilibrium price and sell when it has risen, or sell when the price is above the equilibrium price and buy when it has fallen. Why, then, are financial market prices so volatile?

15 Essay question   The UK government is discussing a change in the planning laws to allow the building of 3 million new homes by 2020. Discuss what this is likely to mean for (a) the price of houses for first-time buyers and (b) the demand for country houses in areas adjacent to new housing developments. (c) Does your answer to (b) depend upon whether new houses are accompanied by new infrastructure (better roads, shops, train services, flood protection)?

For solutions to these questions contact your lecturer.

PART TWO

Positive microeconomics

Positive economics looks at how the economy functions. Microeconomics takes a detailed look at particular decisions without worrying about all the induced effects elsewhere. Part Two studies in detail the demand behaviour of consumers and the supply behaviour of producers, showing how markets work and why different markets exhibit different forms of behaviour. By applying similar tools to the analysis of input markets, we can also understand why some people earn so much more than others.

Chapter 4 examines the responsiveness of demand and supply behaviour. Chapter 5 develops a theory of demand based on self-interested choice by consumers. Chapter 6 introduces different types of firm and considers motives behind production decisions. Chapter 7 analyses how costs of production influence the output that firms choose to supply. Chapters 8 and 9 explore how differences in market structure affect competition and the output decision of firms. Chapters 10 and 11 analyse input markets for labour, capital and land, which determine the distribution of income. Chapter 12 explains why people dislike risk, how institutions develop to shift risk on to those who can bear it more cheaply, and why informational problems can inhibit the development of markets for some commodities.

Contents

Elasticities of demand and supply

Learning Outcomes

By the end of this chapter, you should understand:

1. how elasticities measure responsiveness of demand or supply

2. the price elasticity of demand

3. how it affects the revenue effect of a price change

4. why bad harvests may help farmers

5. the fallacy of composition

6. how cross-price elasticity relates to complements and substitutes

7. income elasticity of demand

8. inferior, normal and luxury goods

9. elasticity of supply

10. how supply and demand elasticities affect tax incidence

In Chapter 3 we examined how the price of a good affects the quantity demanded. We saw also that changes in income, or in the price of related goods, shift demand curves, altering the quantity demanded at each price. We now study these effects in more detail.

4.1 The price responsiveness of demand

A downward-sloping demand curve shows that lower prices increase quantity demanded. Often, we need to know by how much quantity will increase. Table 4.1 presents some hypothetical numbers relating ticket price and quantity demanded, other things equal. From columns (1) and (2), Figure 4.1 plots the demand curve, which happens to be a straight line.

How do we measure the responsiveness of the quantity of tickets demanded to the price of tickets? An obvious measure is the slope of the demand curve. Each price cut of £1 leads to 8000 extra ticket sales.

The **price elasticity of demand** (PED) is the percentage change in the quantity demanded divided by the corresponding percentage change in its price.

PED = (% change in quantity)/(% change in price)

Suppose we want to compare the price responsiveness of football ticket sales with that of cars. Using only the slopes of the demand curves makes this comparison not particularly attractive. £1 is a trivial cut in the price of a car and has a negligible effect on the quantity of cars demanded. We need a way to normalize the slope of the demand function in order to make useful comparisons among different goods.

In Chapter 2 we argued that, when commodities are measured in different units, it is often best to examine the percentage change, which is unit-free.

Table 4.1 The demand for football tickets

(1) Price (£/ticket)	(2) Tickets demanded ('000s)	(3) Price elasticity of demand
12.50	0	$-\infty$
10.00	20	-4
7.50	40	-1.5
5.00	60	-0.67
2.50	80	-0.25
0	100	0

Although we later introduce other demand elasticities – the cross-price and the income elasticities – the (own-)price elasticity is the most often used of the three. If economists speak of the *demand elasticity*, they mean the **price elasticity of demand**.

Suppose a 1 per cent price rise reduces the quantity demanded by 2 per cent. The demand elasticity is the percentage change in quantity (−2) divided by the percentage change in price (+1) and is thus given by −2. The minus sign tells us that quantity *falls* when price rises. If a price fall of 4 per cent increases the quantity demanded by 2 per cent, the demand elasticity is $-\frac{1}{2}$ since the quantity change (+2 per cent) is divided by the price change (−4 per cent). Since demand curves slope down, price and quantity changes always have opposite signs. The price elasticity of demand tells us about movements along a demand curve. The demand elasticity is a negative number.

For further brevity, economists often omit the minus sign. It is easier to say the demand elasticity is 2 than to say it is −2. When the price elasticity of demand is expressed as a positive number, it is implicit that a minus sign must be added (unless there is an explicit warning to the contrary). Otherwise, it implies that demand curves slope up, a rare but not unknown phenomenon.

The price elasticity of demand for football tickets is shown in column (3) of Table 4.1. Examining the effect of price cuts of £2.50, we calculate the price elasticity of demand at each price. Beginning at £10 and 20 000 tickets demanded, consider a price cut to £7.50. The price change is −25 per cent, from £10 to £7.50, the change in quantity demanded is +100 per cent, from 20 000 to 40 000 tickets.

The demand elasticity at £10 is (100/−25) = −4. Other elasticities are calculated in the same way, dividing the percentage change in quantity by the corresponding percentage change in price. When we begin from the price of £12.50, the demand elasticity is minus infinity. The percentage change in quantity demanded

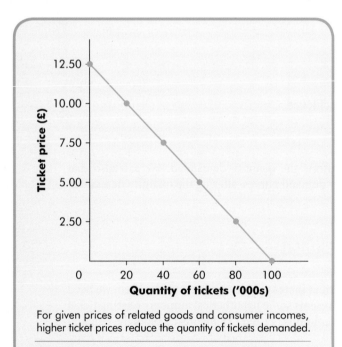

For given prices of related goods and consumer incomes, higher ticket prices reduce the quantity of tickets demanded.

Figure 4.1 The demand for football tickets

is +20/0. Any positive number divided by zero is infinity. Dividing by the −20 per cent change in price, from £12.50 to £10, the demand elasticity is minus infinity at this price.

Price elasticity of demand = [% change in quantity]/[% change in price]

We say that the demand elasticity is *high* if it is a large negative number. The quantity demanded is sensitive to the price. The demand elasticity is *low* if it is a small negative number and the quantity demanded is insensitive to the price. 'High' or 'low' refer to the size of the elasticity, ignoring the minus sign. The demand elasticity falls when it becomes a smaller negative number and quantity demanded becomes less sensitive to the price.[1]

MATHS 4.1 — Practising calculation of price elasticity of demand (PED) and the arc elasticity of demand

P = price (£)	1	2	3	4	5	6
Q = quantity demanded	10	8	6	4	2	1

The rows in the table above give price and quantity data for a particular demand curve. The table below shows five columns, labelled A–E, each corresponding to a situation in which the price changes by £1 and there is a corresponding change in the quantity demanded.

In column A, a 100 per cent price rise (from £1 to £2) induces a 20 per cent fall in quantity demanded (from 10 to 8), implying a price elasticity of demand of (−20/100) = −0.2. Similarly, in column C, a 50 per cent price reduction (from £2 to £1) induces a 25 per cent rise in quantity demanded (from 8 to 10), implying a price elasticity of (25)/(−50) = −0.5.

	A	B	C	D	E
(1) Initial P and Q	P = 1 Q = 10	P = 2 Q = 8	P = 2 Q = 8	P = 4 Q = 4	P = 5 Q = 2
(2) New P and Q	P = 2 Q = 8	P = 3 Q = 6	P = 1 Q = 10	P = 3 Q = 6	P = 6 Q = 1
(3) % change in P	100 * (2 − 1)/1 = 100		100 * (1 − 2)/2 = −50		
(4) % change in Q thus induced	100 * (8 − 10)/10 = −20		100 * (10 − 8)/8 = 25		
(5) PED = (4)/(3)	−0.2		−0.5		

---

1 Notice the difference between the price elasticity of demand and the slope of the demand. The slope of a demand curve is the ratio of the change in price to the change in quantity between two points on the curve. The price elasticity of demand is the ratio of the percentage change in quantity to the percentage change in price. You will see that for a linear demand curve the elasticity changes along the demand curve, even if the slope remains constant. See Maths 4.2.

▶ Notice the asymmetry in the calculation of the elasticity of demand using our definition. If we consider an increase in the price from £1 to £2 (and a corresponding decrease in quantity from 10 to 8), we obtain a given value for the PED (−0.2). If we consider the opposite case (a decrease in the price from £2 to £1 and a corresponding increase in the quantity from 8 to 10), we obtain a different value for the PED (−0.5). To avoid this asymmetry, it is possible to create a refinement in the calculation of the elasticity of demand. We can calculate the arc elasticity of demand. The arc elasticity of demand can be calculated using the following formula:

$$PED_{arc} = \frac{(Q_1 - Q_0)}{(Q_1 + Q_0)/2} \bigg/ \frac{(P_1 - P_0)}{(P_1 + P_0)/2}$$

where Q_1 and P_1 are the new values of quantity and price, respectively, while Q_0 and P_0 are the initial values. In practice, we express the change in price as a percentage of the average price minus the midpoint between the initial and new price. Similarly we express the change in the quantity demanded as a percentage of the average quantity demanded minus the average of the initial and new quantity. The advantage of using the average price and the average quantity is that the value of the elasticity is the same whether the price rises or falls.

Consider the case in column A: $P_0 = 1$, $Q_0 = 10$, $P_1 = 2$, $Q_1 = 8$. The arc elasticity of demand in this case is:

$$PED_{arc} = \frac{(8 - 10)}{(8 + 10)/2} \bigg/ \frac{(2 - 1)}{(2 + 1)/2} = -0.148$$

Now consider the case in column C: $P_0 = 2$, $Q_0 = 8$, $P_1 = 1$, $Q_1 = 10$. The arc elasticity of demand is:

$$PED_{arc} = \frac{(10 - 8)}{(10 + 8)/2} \bigg/ \frac{(1 - 2)}{(1 + 2)/2} = -0.148$$

Using the arc elasticity of demand the result is the same whether we consider a price cut of a given amount or a price increase by the same amount. This is true regardless of whether the demand is linear or non-linear.

Which method should we use to calculate the elasticity of demand? In general, it is better to use the arc elasticity of demand if the form of the demand is unknown.

Applying the normal definition of the PED or the arc elasticity version to a given set of observations on prices and quantities may lead to different numerical results. Nevertheless, in general, the main properties of the elasticity (meaning if a demand is elastic or inelastic between two different points) would be similar independently of the way we calculate the elasticity.

Questions

(a) Try to complete columns B, D and E for yourself.

(b) Complete columns B, D and E using the arc elasticity of demand.

To check your answers to these questions, go to page 683.

The demand curve for football tickets is a straight line with a constant slope: along its entire length a £1 cut in price always leads to 8000 extra ticket sales. Yet Table 4.1 shows that demand elasticity falls as we move down the demand curve from higher prices to lower prices. At high prices, £1 is a small percentage change in the price but 8000 tickets is a large percentage change in the quantity demanded. Conversely, at low prices £1 is a large percentage change in the price but 8000 is a small percentage change in the quantity. When the demand curve is a straight line, the price elasticity falls steadily as we move down the demand curve.[2]

---

2   Except in two special cases: a *horizontal*, or infinitely elastic, demand curve has an elasticity of minus infinity at all points since the *price* change is always zero. A *vertical*, or completely inelastic, demand curve has an elasticity of zero at all points since the *quantity* never changes.

It is possible to construct curved demand schedules (still, of course, sloping downwards) along which the price elasticity of demand remains constant. Generally, however, the price elasticity changes as we move along demand curves, and we expect the elasticity to be high at high prices and low at low prices.

If the demand curve is a straight line, we get the same size of quantity response (20 000 tickets) whether we raise or lower the price by £2.50. It does not matter whether we use price rises or price cuts to calculate the demand elasticity.

When, as in Figure 4.2, the demand curve is not a straight line, we meet a minor difficulty. Beginning at point A where the price is P_0, moves to points B and C are percentage price changes of equal magnitude but opposite sign. Figure 4.2 shows that the quantity response (from Q_0 to either Q_1 or Q_2) differs for price rises and price falls when the demand curve is not a straight line.

For non-linear demand curves, economists resolve this ambiguity about the definition of price elasticity of demand by defining it with respect to *very small* changes in price (see Maths 4.2). If we move only a short distance either side of point A, the demand

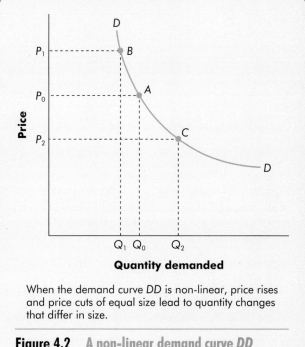

When the demand curve DD is non-linear, price rises and price cuts of equal size lead to quantity changes that differ in size.

Figure 4.2   A non-linear demand curve DD

curve hardly has time to bend round. Over the very short distance corresponding to a small percentage price rise or fall, the demand curve is as near a straight line as makes no difference. With this amendment we can use the old definition.

Elastic and inelastic demand

Although elasticity typically falls as we move down the demand curve, an important dividing line occurs at the demand elasticity of −1. In Table 4.1 demand is **elastic** at all prices of £7.50 and above and **inelastic** at all prices of £5 and below.

> Demand is **elastic** if the price elasticity is more negative than −1.
>
> Demand is **inelastic** if the price elasticity lies between −1 and 0.

Although the price elasticity of demand typically changes as we move along demand curves, economists frequently talk of goods with high or low demand elasticities. For example, the demand for oil is price inelastic (price changes have only a small effect on quantity demanded) but the demand for foreign holidays is price elastic (price changes have a big effect on quantity demanded). Such statements implicitly refer to parts of the demand curve corresponding to prices usually charged for these goods or services.

MATHS 4.2

The point elasticity of demand

We have defined the price elasticity of demand as:

$$PED = \frac{\%\Delta Q^D}{\%\Delta P} \tag{1}$$

where the Greek letter delta (Δ) stands for 'change' and $\%\Delta Q^D$ denotes the percentage change in the quantity demanded, while $\%\Delta P$ denotes the percentage change in the price. Mathematically, the percentage change in the quantity demanded can be written as:

$$\%\Delta Q^D = \frac{\Delta Q^D}{Q^D} \times 100$$

similarly, the percentage change in the price can be written as:

$$\%\Delta P = \frac{\Delta P}{P} \times 100$$

Using those facts in relation to the definition of PED in equation (1) and after some algebra we have:

$$PED = \frac{\Delta Q^D}{\Delta P}\frac{P}{Q^D} \qquad (2)$$

Equation (2) is another way to write the price elasticity of demand. We can use the formula in (1) or the idea of arc elasticity of demand to find the elasticity between two different points of a demand curve. However, in many cases we are interested in calculating the elasticity of demand at a given point of a specific demand function.

Suppose we face the following linear direct demand function for a given good:

$$Q^D = 100 - 2P \qquad (3)$$

where Q^D is the quantity demanded and P is the price.

When the price is $P = 10$, according to the demand in equation (3), the quantity demanded is $Q^D = 80$. Is the demand elastic, or inelastic, at $P = 10$?

To answer that question we use the concept of point elasticity of demand, since we want to measure the elasticity at a particular point of a demand function.

The point elasticity of demand is defined as:

$$PED = \frac{dQ^D}{dP}\frac{P}{Q^D} \qquad (4)$$

where dP is now a very small (close to zero) change in the price and dQ^D is the corresponding change in the quantity demanded. The term dQ^D/dP is the *derivative* of the direct demand function with respect to the price. It measures the slope of the direct demand function at a given point. In the case of a linear direct demand function, the slope is constant along the demand curve. In our case, the slope of the direct demand curve is $dQ^D/dP = -2$.

Using equation (4), we have that at $P = 10$ and $Q^D = 80$ the point elasticity of demand is:

$$PED = -2\frac{10}{80} = -0.25$$

The demand is therefore inelastic when $P = 10$.

From equation (4) we can see why, along a linear demand curve, the elasticity of demand is not constant. While the slope is constant the term P/Q changes along the demand curve. This is summarized in the figure on the right.

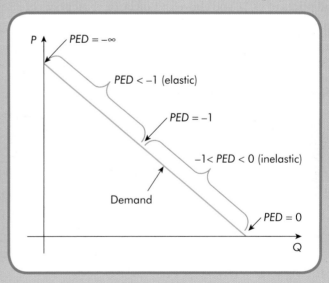

Using (4) you can find the elasticity at any point of a demand curve, linear or non-linear. There are special cases in which the elasticity is constant along a demand curve. Consider the following direct demand function:

$$Q^D = \frac{100}{P} \tag{5}$$

The demand function in (5) is non-linear (try to plot it!). In this case, the derivative of the direct demand is:

$$\frac{dQ^D}{dP} = -\frac{100}{P^2}$$

Suppose we want to know the elasticity of demand at $P = 5$. At that price the quantity demanded according to (5) is $Q^D = 20$. In this case, we have $dQ^D/dp = -[100/(5)^2] = -4$. Applying equation (4) we have:

$$PED = -4\frac{5}{20} = -1$$

at $P = 5$ the demand is **unit elastic**. What about at $P = 10$? In this case, the quantity demanded is $Q^D = 100/10 = 10$ and then $dQ^D/dp = -[100/(10)^2] = -1$. The PED is:

> If the demand elasticity is −1, demand is **unit elastic**.

$$PED = -1\frac{10}{10} = -1$$

the PED is still −1. Indeed, any demand function of the form $Q^D = A/P$, where A is any positive constant, has the property that the elasticity of demand is constant along the demand curve.

Determinants of price elasticity

Why is the price elasticity of demand for a good high (−5) or low (−0.5)? The answer lies in consumer tastes. If it is a social necessity to own a television, higher TV prices have little effect on quantity demanded. If TVs are considered a frivolous luxury, the demand elasticity is much higher. Psychologists and sociologists can explain why tastes are as they are. As economists, we can identify some considerations likely to affect consumer responses to changes in the price of a good. *The most important consideration is the ease with which consumers can substitute another good that fulfils approximately the same function.*

Consider two extreme cases. Suppose the price of all cigarettes rises by 1 per cent. The quantity of cigarettes demanded will hardly respond. People who can easily quit smoking have already done so. In contrast, suppose the price of a particular brand of cigarettes rises by 1 per cent, all other brand prices remaining unchanged. We expect a much larger quantity response. Consumers switch from the dearer brand to other brands that also satisfy the nicotine habit. For a particular cigarette brand the demand elasticity is quite high.

Our example suggests a general rule. The more narrowly we define a commodity (a particular brand of cigarette rather than cigarettes in general), the higher will be the price elasticity of demand.

Measuring price elasticities

Table 4.2 confirms that the demand for broad categories of basic commodities, such as fuel, food or even services to household, is inelastic. As a category, only alcohol seems to have an elastic demand. Households simply do not have much scope to alter the broad pattern of their purchases.

Table 4.2 UK price elasticities of demand

Good (broad type)	Demand elasticity	Good (narrow type)	Demand elasticity
Fuel and light	−0.52	Bread	−0.4
Food	−0.56	Fish	−0.8
Clothing	−0.62	Beer	−0.2
Services	−0.72	Expenditure abroad	−1.6
Alcohol	−1.73	Catering	−2.6

Sources: Blundell, R., Pashardes, P. and Weber, G. (1993) What do we learn about consumer demand patterns from micro data?, *American Economic Review*, 83 (3): 570–597; National Food Survey 2000.

In contrast, there is a much wider variation in the demand elasticities for narrower definitions of commodities. Even then, the demand for some commodities, such as dairy produce, is very inelastic. However, particular kinds of services such as catering have much more elastic demand.

Using price elasticities

Price elasticities of demand are useful in calculating the price rise required to eliminate a shortage (excess demand) or the price fall to eliminate a surplus (excess supply). One important source of surpluses and shortages is shifts in the supply curve. Harvest failures (and bumper crops) are a feature of agricultural markets. Because the demand elasticity for many agricultural products is very low, harvest failures produce large increases in the price of food. Conversely, bumper crops induce very large falls in food prices. When demand is very inelastic, shifts in the supply curve lead to large fluctuations in price but have little effect on equilibrium quantities.

Figure 4.3(a) illustrates this. *SS* is the supply curve in an agricultural market when there is a harvest failure and *S′S′* the supply curve when there is a bumper crop. The equilibrium price fluctuates between P_1 (harvest failure) and P_2 (bumper crop) but induces little fluctuation in the corresponding equilibrium quantities. Contrast this with Figure 4.3(b), which shows the effect of similar supply shifts in a market with very elastic demand. Price fluctuations are much smaller but quantity fluctuations are now much larger. Knowing the demand elasticity helps us understand why some markets exhibit volatile quantities but stable prices, while other markets exhibit volatile prices but stable quantities.

 4.2 Price, quantity demanded and total expenditure

Other things equal, the demand curve shows how much consumers of a good wish to purchase at each price. At each price, total spending by consumers is the price multiplied by the quantity demanded. We now discuss the relationship between total spending and price and show the relevance of the price elasticity of demand.

Figure 4.4 shows how total spending changes with price changes. In case A, we begin at A with price P_A and quantity demanded Q_A. Total spending is $P_A Q_A$, the area of the rectangle $OP_A A Q_A$. At the lower price P_B, consumers demand Q_B and total spending is $P_B Q_B$, the area of the rectangle $OP_B B Q_B$. How does total spending change when prices fall from P_A to P_B? Spending falls by the area marked (−) but rises by the area marked (+). In case A, the (+) area exceeds the (−) area and total spending rises. In the elastic range of the demand curve (towards the upper end), a lower price raises the quantity demanded by more than enough to offset the lower price. Total spending rises.

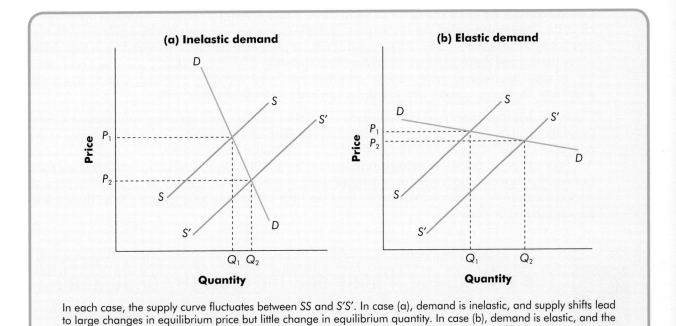

In each case, the supply curve fluctuates between SS and S'S'. In case (a), demand is inelastic, and supply shifts lead to large changes in equilibrium price but little change in equilibrium quantity. In case (b), demand is elastic, and the same supply shift now leads to large changes in equilibrium quantity but little change in equilibrium price.

Figure 4.3   The effect of demand elasticity on equilibrium price and quantity fluctuations

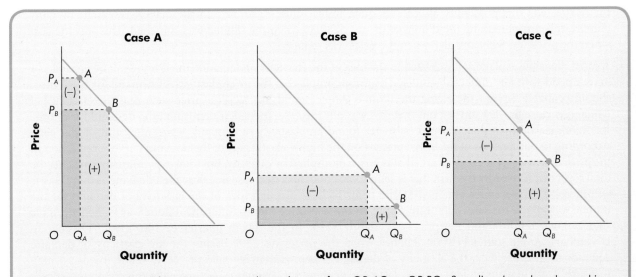

When the price is reduced from P_A to P_B, expenditure changes from OP_AAQ_A to OP_BBQ_B. Spending rises when demand is elastic (case A), falls when demand is inelastic (case B), and is unchanged when demand is unit elastic (case C).

Figure 4.4   Elasticity of demand and the effect of price changes on expenditure

Case B examines the lower end of the demand curve, where demand is inelastic. Although the price cut raises the quantity demanded, the rise in quantity is insufficient to compensate for the lower price. The (+) area is smaller than the (−) area. Total spending falls. If price cuts increase total spending at high prices where the demand elasticity is high and reduce total spending at low prices where the demand elasticity is low, at some intermediate price a fall in price will leave total spending unaltered. Case C shows this possibility. The higher quantity demanded exactly compensates for the lower price.

If quantity demanded rises 1 per cent when the price falls 1 per cent, total spending is unchanged. Case C shows the point on the demand curve at which the price elasticity of demand is −1 (quantity change −1 per cent, price change −1 per cent). If demand is elastic, a demand elasticity more negative than 1, as in case A, a 1 per cent price cut leads to an increase in quantity by *more* than 1 per cent. Hence total spending rises. Conversely, when demand is inelastic, a demand elasticity lying between 0 and 1, as in case B, a 1 per cent price cut leads to an increase in quantity by *less* than 1 per cent. Hence total spending falls. These results are summarized in Table 4.3.

CASE 4.1

The price of the iPhone and the elasticity of demand

The iPhone 8GB, an internet and multimedia smart phone created by Apple, was launched in the US market in June 2007. The launch price was $599. In early September of the same year Apple announced a reduction in the price of the iPhone 8GB of 33 per cent, from $599 to $399. Why such a big reduction in the price a mere two months after the launch?

One possibility is that Apple overestimated its demand for the iPhone and not many customers were willing to buy at that price. In this case, a price cut may be justified. This possibility, however, seems implausible. Demand for iPhones was high; customers were queuing outside Apple stores for hours in order to buy one. Maybe the price cut was due to the fact that Apple discovered that the cost of making the iPhone was lower than expected. This possibility also seems quite implausible. According to the market research company iSupply, the cost of making the iPhone 8GB was $280.83 when the iPhone was launched. This was the cost when the price was $599 and also when the price was reduced.

A more plausible explanation is related to the idea of the elasticity of demand. The iPhone can be viewed as a luxury good with few direct substitutes. This would imply that the price elasticity of demand for the iPhone should probably be low. In pricing the iPhone, Apple would like to set a price such that the elasticity of demand is close to −1. It turned out that this was not the case. Indeed, it seems that the demand for iPhone was more elastic than that. Various estimates found an elasticity of demand between −3 and −5 per cent. According to our analysis, if the initial price is on the highly elastic part of the demand curve, a reduction in the price increases total expenditure, that is, price multiplied by quantity. But total expenditure represents the total revenue received by the firm that is selling the good. So a decrease in price when demand is quite elastic will increase the revenues obtained by the firm. To have a rough idea of the elasticity of demand for the iPhone we can use the sales data from Apple. In the first three months after the iPhone was launched, Apple sold 270 000 iPhones and the price was mainly $599. In the fourth quarter of 2007 (from October to December), Apple sold 1 119 000 iPhones when the price was $399. Using the arc elasticity of demand equation with those data, the elasticity of demand is approximately −3.06 per cent. While this is a rough measure, it still gives us an idea of how elastic the demand for iPhones is. According to this rough measure, a decrease in the price by 1 per cent will increase quantity demanded (and so sold) by 3 per cent.

Obviously the cut in the price made the customers who bought the iPhone at $599 quite unhappy. A $100 discount voucher to be spent in Apple stores was given to those customers to partially compensate them.

Source: Compiled by the authors.

Table 4.3 Demand elasticities and changes in spending

Change in total spending caused by	Price elasticity of demand		
	Elastic (e.g. −3)	Unit-elastic (−1)	Inelastic (e.g. −0.3)
Price rise	Fall	Unchanged	Rise
Price cut	Rise	Unchanged	Fall

The price of football tickets

Think again about revenue from ticket sales. Table 4.4 shows the demand data of Table 4.1, but also shows the tickets demanded at a price of £6.25 per ticket. At this price the demand elasticity is −1. A 20 per cent price cut (−£1.25) induces a 20 per cent rise in the quantity demanded (10 000 tickets). Column (4) shows total spending on tickets at each price.

Beginning from the highest price of £12.50, successive price cuts first increase total spending on tickets, then reduce it. Table 4.4 explains why. When the price is high, demand is elastic: price reductions increase total spending. When demand is unit elastic, at price £6.25, we reach a turning point. Above this price, price cuts have steadily increased total spending. Below this price, further price cuts reduce total spending because demand is then inelastic.

We can thus draw two conclusions. First, as we imagine moving down the demand curve, total spending is instantaneously unchanging as we move through the price £6.25 at which demand is unit elastic. Second, *spending and revenue reach a maximum at the point of unit-elastic demand*. This idea, and the empirical knowledge that this occurs at the price of £6.25 per ticket, are the pieces of information the football club owner needs to know.

Table 4.4 Ticket demand and revenue

(1) Ticket price (£)	(2) Quantity demanded ('000s)	(3) Price elasticity of demand	(4) Total spending (£000s)
12.50	0	−∞	0
10.00	20	−4	200
7.50	40	−1.5	300
6.25	50	−1	312.5
5.00	60	−0.67	300
2.50	80	−0.25	200
0	100	0	0

4.3 Further applications of the price elasticity of demand

The coffee frost

There's an awful lot of coffee in Brazil – the country supplies a large share of the world market. In 1994 people first realized that a frost in Brazil would cause havoc with the 1995 harvest. *The Economist* magazine (30 July 1994: www.economist.co.uk) reported estimates that the 1995 crop would not be the 26.5 million bags previously thought, but only 15.7 million bags. Obviously, coffee was going to be scarce in 1995. Anticipating this, speculators bought coffee in 1994, bidding up its price even before the supply fell.

Table 4.5 shows the effect on Brazilian exports during 1993–95. The first row shows that, even after adjusting for general inflation, coffee prices more than doubled in US dollars. The second row shows an index of the volume of Brazilian coffee exports. The final row shows Brazilian export revenue from coffee. Real revenue rose sharply in 1994: prices had risen *before* production had fallen too much. The interesting comparison is between 1993 and 1995. Brazilian export revenue from coffee *increased* despite the 'bad' harvest.

The demand for coffee is inelastic, despite an abundance of substitutes – tea, soft drinks and beer. This example emphasizes the importance of consumer tastes. If buyers refuse to abandon coffee drinking it is useless to point out that a blend of tea and Coca-Cola has as much caffeine as the average cup of coffee.

Farmers and bad harvests

This example illustrates a general result. When demand is inelastic farmers earn more revenue from a bad harvest than from a good one. When the supply curve shifts to the left it takes a big rise in price to eliminate excess demand when demand is inelastic. And price increases *raise* consumer spending and producer revenues when demand is inelastic. Demand elasticities are low for many commodities such as coffee, milk and wheat. They are part of our staple diet. Eating habits are slow to change, even when prices rise.

If bad harvests raise farmers' revenues and good harvests lead to a fall in agricultural prices and farmers' revenues, why don't farmers get together like OPEC to restrict their supply and increase revenues in the face of inelastic demand? If it were easy to organize such collusion between farmers, it would occur more frequently. Later we discuss the difficulties that arise in trying to maintain a co-operative policy to restrict supply.

> The **fallacy of composition** means that what is true for the individual may not be true for everyone together, and what is true for everyone together may not hold for the individual.

When demand is inelastic, suppliers *taken together* are better off if supply can be reduced. However, if one farmer loses part of the crop but all other farmers' crops are unaffected, the unlucky farmer is worse off – the **fallacy of composition**. The fall in a single farmer's output, unlike the reduction of all farmers' outputs

Table 4.5 Brazilian coffee exports

	1993	1994	1995
Price (US$/lb)	0.9	2.0	2.1
Export quantity (1990 = 100)	113	102	85
Price × quantity	102	204	179

Note: Prices are in 1995 US$.
Source: IMF, *International Financial Statistics.*

simultaneously, has a negligible effect on supply. Market price is unaffected and the unlucky farmer simply sells less output at the price that would have prevailed in any case. This illustrates an important lesson in economics. The individual producer faces a demand that is very elastic – consumers can easily switch to the output of similar farmers – even if the demand for the crop as a whole is very inelastic.

Easy profits

CASE 4.2

Low-cost airline pioneer Sir Stelios Haji-Ioannou, founder of easyJet and then the EasyGroup, credits two things with his success. The first, which he says only half in jest, is coming from a rich family, which made it easier to get through the early years. The second, which he also proudly cites, is his economics degree, where the lecture on elasticity of demand helped underpin his conviction that low prices could generate large revenues by creating high sales volume. A recent estimate of the fare elasticity of demand for air travel in Europe is −1.40, meaning that the demand is indeed elastic.* When he launched easyJet, conventional airlines were happy to fill 70 per cent of their seats on an average flight. EasyJet now runs regularly at 85 per cent capacity on its 600 flights a day, which is a lot of extra revenue without any additional costs.

Picture: © Ice962 | Dreamstime.com

* IATA (2007) *Estimating Air Travel Demand Elasticities: Final Report.*

Source: www.easyJet.com.

4.4 Short run and long run

The price elasticity of demand varies according to the length of time in which consumers can adjust their spending patterns when prices change. The most dramatic price change of the past 50 years, the oil price rise of 1973–74, caught many households with a new but fuel-inefficient car. At first, they may not have expected the higher oil price to last. Then they may have *planned* to buy a smaller car with greater fuel efficiency. But in countries like the US, few small cars were yet available. In the short run, households were stuck. Unless they could rearrange their lifestyles to reduce car use, they had to pay the higher petrol prices. Demand for petrol was inelastic.

> The **short run** is the period after prices change but before quantity adjustment can occur.
>
> The **long run** is the period needed for complete adjustment to a price change. Its length depends on the type of adjustments consumers wish to make.

Over the long run, consumers had time to sell their big cars and buy cars with better fuel efficiency, or to move from the distant suburbs closer to their place of work. Over this longer period, they could reduce the quantity of petrol demanded much more than they could initially.

The price elasticity of demand is lower in the short run than in the long run when there is more scope to substitute other goods. This result is very general. Even if addicted smokers cannot adjust to a rise in the price of cigarettes, fewer young people start smoking and gradually the number of smokers falls.

Table 4.6 reports estimates of the short- and long-run elasticities of demand for various goods in the UK. Those results show that the long-run elasticity tends to be larger than the short-run one.

Table 4.6 *Short- and long-run elasticities in UK*

	Short run	Long run
Bus service	−0.43	−1.25
Underground service	−0.31	−0.57
Mobile calls	−0.78	−1.04

Sources: Alpetkin, A. et al. (2007) *Estimating spectrum demand for the cellular services in the UK*, working paper, University of Surrey; Wardman, M. and Shires, J. (2003) *Review of fares elasticities in Great Britain*, ITS working paper.

How long is the long run?

There is no definite answer to this question. Demand responses to a change in the price of chocolate should be completed within a few months, but full adjustment to changes in the price of oil or cigarettes may take years.

4.5 The cross-price elasticity of demand

> The **cross-price elasticity of demand** for good *i* with respect to changes in the price of good *j* is the percentage change in the quantity of good *i* demanded, divided by the corresponding percentage change in the price of good *j*.

The price elasticity of demand tells us about movements along a given demand curve holding constant all determinants of demand except the price of the good itself. We now hold constant the own-price of the good and examine changes in the prices of *related* goods. The **cross-price elasticity** tells us the effect on the quantity demanded of the good *i* when the price of good *j* is changed. As before, we use percentage changes.

The cross-price elasticity may be positive or negative. It is positive if a rise in the price of good *j* increases the quantity demanded of good *i*. Suppose good *i* is tea and good *j* is coffee. An increase in the price of coffee raises the demand for tea. The cross-price elasticity of tea with respect to coffee is positive. Cross-price elasticities tend to be positive when two goods are substitutes and negative when two goods are complements. We expect a rise in the price of petrol to reduce the demand for cars because petrol and cars are complements.

Table 4.7 shows estimates for the UK for three different goods. Own-price elasticities for food, clothing and travel are given down the diagonal of the table, from top left (the own-price elasticity of demand for food) to bottom right (the own-price elasticity of demand for travel). Off-diagonal entries in the table show cross-price elasticities of demand. Thus, 0.1 is the cross-price elasticity of demand for food with respect to transport. A 1 per cent increase in the price of travel increases the quantity of food demanded by 0.1 per cent.

The own-price elasticities for the three goods lie between −0.4 and −0.5. For all three goods, the quantity demanded is more sensitive to changes in its own price than to changes in the price of any other good.

4.6 The effect of income on demand

Finally, holding constant the own-price of a good and the prices of related goods, we examine the response of the quantity demanded to changes in consumer incomes. For the moment, we neglect the possibility of

Table 4.7 Cross-price and own-price elasticities of demand in the UK

% change in quantity	Caused by a 1% price change in demand for		
	Food	Clothing	Travel
Food	−0.4	0	0.1
Clothing	0.1	−0.5	−0.1
Travel	0.3	−0.1	−0.5

Source: Blundell, R. et al. (1993) What do we learn about consumer demand patterns from micro data?, American Economic Review, 83 (3): 570–597.

Table 4.8 Budget shares, 1997–2005

	Real consumer spending (2003 £bn)	% budget share	
		Food and drink	Recreation and cultural goods
1997	558	10	3
2005	731	9	7

Source: ONS, UK National Accounts.

saving. Thus a rise in the income of consumers will typically be matched by an equivalent increase in total consumer spending.

Chapter 3 pointed out that higher consumer incomes tend to increase the quantity demanded. However, demand quantities increase by different amounts as incomes rise. Thus the pattern of consumer spending on different goods depends on the level of consumer incomes. The **budget share** of a good is the fraction of total consumer spending for which it accounts.

Table 4.8 reports the share of consumer spending in the UK devoted to food and drink and to recreation and cultural goods between 1997 and 2005. Real consumer spending (and incomes) rose during 1997–2005. Even though real spending on food and drink increased, its budget share fell. Spending on recreation and cultural goods rose so much that its budget share increased substantially. These changes in budget share mainly reflect changes in real consumer incomes and different income elasticities of demand.

> The **budget share** of a good is its price times the quantity demanded, divided by total consumer spending or income.
>
> The **income elasticity of demand** for a good is the percentage change in quantity demanded divided by the corresponding percentage change in income.

Normal, inferior and luxury goods

The income elasticity of demand measures how far the demand curve shifts horizontally when incomes change. Figure 4.5 shows two possible shifts caused by a given percentage increase in income. The income elasticity is larger if the given rise in income shifts the demand curve from DD to $D''D''$ than if the same income rise shifts the demand curve only from DD to $D'D'$. When an income rise shifts the demand curve to the left, the income elasticity of demand is a negative number, indicating that higher incomes are associated with smaller quantities demanded at any given prices.

A **normal good** has a positive income elasticity of demand.

An **inferior good** has a negative income elasticity of demand.

A **luxury good** has an income elasticity above unity.

A **necessity** has an income elasticity below unity.

In Chapter 3 we distinguished **normal goods**, for which demand increases as income rises, and **inferior goods**, for which demand falls as income rises. We also distinguish between **luxury goods** and **necessities**. All inferior goods are necessities, since their income elasticities of demand are negative. However, necessities also include normal goods whose income elasticity of demand lies between zero and 1.

These definitions tell us what happens to budget shares when incomes are changed but prices remain unaltered. The budget share of inferior goods falls as incomes rise. Higher incomes and household budgets are associated with lower quantities demanded at constant prices. Conversely, the budget share of luxuries rises when income rises. Because the income elasticity of demand for luxuries exceeds 1, a 1 per cent rise in income increases quantity demanded (and hence total spending on luxury goods) by more than 1 per cent. Rises in income *reduce* the budget share of normal goods that are necessities. A 1 per cent income rise leads to a rise in quantity demanded but of less than 1 per cent, so the budget share must fall.

Inferior goods tend to be goods for which there exist more expensive substitutes. Poor people satisfy their needs for meat and clothing by buying fatty meat and polyester shirts. As their incomes rise, they switch to better cuts of meat (steak) and more comfortable shirts (cotton). Rising incomes lead to an absolute decline in the demand for fatty meat and polyester shirts.

Luxury goods tend to be high-quality goods for which there exist lower-quality, barely adequate, substitutes: BMWs rather than small Fords, foreign rather than domestic holidays. **Necessities** that are normal goods lie between these two extremes. As incomes rise, the quantity of food demanded will rise but only a little. Most people still enjoy fairly simple home cooking even when their incomes rise.

Looking back at Table 4.7, recreation and cultural goods are luxuries whose budget share increased from 3 to 7 per cent as UK incomes rose during 1997–2005. Food and drink cannot be a luxury, since its budget share fell as incomes rose, but it is not an inferior good either. At constant prices which adjust for the effects of inflation, during 1997–2007 real food spending *increased* from £56 billion (10 per cent of £558 billion) to £66 billion (9 per cent of £731 billion).

Table 4.9 summarizes the demand responses to changes in income holding constant the prices of all goods. The table shows the effect of income increases. Reductions in income have the opposite effect on quantity demanded and budget share.

Table 4.10 reports income elasticities of demand in the UK, for broad categories of goods in the first two columns and narrower categories in the last two columns. Again, the variation in elasticities is larger for narrower definitions of goods. Higher incomes have much more effect on the way in which households eat (more prawns, less bread) than on the amount they eat in total. Food is a normal good but not a luxury. Its income elasticity is 0.5.

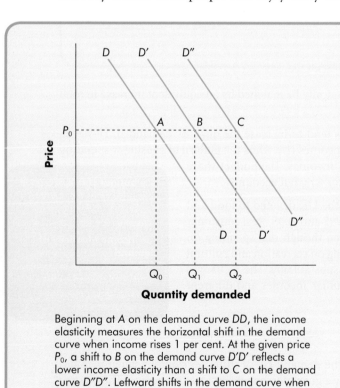

Beginning at *A* on the demand curve *DD*, the income elasticity measures the horizontal shift in the demand curve when income rises 1 per cent. At the given price P_0, a shift to *B* on the demand curve *D'D'* reflects a lower income elasticity than a shift to *C* on the demand curve *D"D"*. Leftward shifts in the demand curve when income rises indicate a negative income elasticity.

Figure 4.5   Income elasticity and shifts in demand

Table 4.9 Demand responses to a 1% rise in income

Good	Income elasticity	Quantity demanded	Budget share	Example
Normal	Positive	Rises		
Luxury	Above 1	Rises more than 1%	Rises	BMW
Necessity	Between 0 and 1	Rises less than 1%	Falls	Food
Inferior	Negative	Falls	Falls	Bread

Table 4.10 UK income elasticities of demand

Broad categories	Income elasticity	Narrower categories	Income elasticity
Tobacco	0.5	Coal	2.0
Fuel	0.3	Bread and cereals	0.1
Food	0.5	Margarine	−0.37
Alcohol	1.1	Liquid wholemilk	−0.17
Clothing	1.2	Vegetables	0.9
Durables	1.5	Leisure goods	2.0
Services	1.8	Wines and spirits	2.6

Sources: Muellbauer, J. (1977) Testing the Barten model of household composition effects, *Economic Journal*, 87: 460–487; Deaton, A. (1975) The measurement of income and price elasticities, *European Economic Review*, 7: 261–273; National Food Survey 2000.

The last column indicates that, within the food budget, higher income leads to a switch towards vegetables (whose income elasticity is higher than that for food as a whole) and away from bread. Rich households can afford to eat expensive salads to avoid getting fat. Poor people need large quantities of bread to ward off the pangs of hunger. Notice that margarine and liquid wholemilk are inferior goods according to the results in Table 4.10.

CASE 4.3

Car crazy

As countries develop and get richer, one of the first things people want is a car. The income elasticity of demand for cars has been estimated at around 2. China, one of the fastest-growing economies in the world, now has an insatiable appetite for cars. With rapidly rising incomes, the once common bicycle is fast giving way to the car. In 1949 the world's most populous economy had a mere 1800 cars. By 2005 that figure was 24 million, making China second only to the US in the size of its car market. In 2009 China became the biggest market in the world in terms of cars. In that year, the number of cars sold in China increased by 49 per cent compared to 2008.

Whereas in the 1970s a worker had to save for a year to buy a bicycle, incomes are now so high that workers only have to save for a year to buy a car. With the financial sector also booming, it is anticipated that by 2015 almost half new car purchases will be financed by car loans.

Income elasticities of demand help us make confident predictions that rapidly rising living standards in countries such as China and India will lead to massive increases in the demand for cars, mobile phones, energy, air travel, and many other goods and services enjoyed in the affluent West. Since many of these are the source of emissions that lead to global warming, the very success of emerging economies adds new urgency to the need to find ways to reduce emissions, either by finding new, cleaner technologies or by co-ordinated government policies to discourage the activities with which harmful emissions are associated.

Source: Adapted from http://news.bbc.co.uk/1/hi/business/6364195.stm. © bbc.co.uk/news

Using income elasticities of demand

Income elasticities help us forecast the pattern of consumer demand as the economy grows and people get richer. Suppose real incomes grow by 15 per cent over the next five years. The estimates of Table 4.10 imply that margarine demand will fall by 5.55 (= 15 × (−0.37)) per cent, while the demand for wines and spirits will rise by 39 per cent. The growth prospects of these two industries are very different. These forecasts will affect decisions by firms about whether to build new factories and government projections of tax revenue from margarine and alcohol.

4.7 Inflation and demand

Elasticities measure the response of quantity demanded to separate variations in three factors: the own-price, the price of related goods and income. Chapter 2 distinguished *nominal* variables, measured in the prices of the day, and *real* variables, which adjust for inflation when comparing measurements at different dates. We end this chapter by examining the effect of inflation on demand behaviour.

Suppose all nominal variables double. Every good costs twice as much, wage rates are twice as high, rents charged by landlords and dividends paid by firms double in money terms. Whatever bundle of goods was previously affordable is still affordable. Goods cost twice as much but incomes are twice as high. If meat costs twice as much as bread, it still costs twice as much. Nothing has really changed. Demand behaviour will be unaltered by a doubling of the nominal value of *all* prices and *all* forms of income.

How do we reconcile this with the idea that own-price elasticities measure changes in quantity demanded as prices change? Each of the elasticities (own-price, cross-price and income) measures the effect of changing that variable *holding constant all other determinants of demand*. When all prices and all incomes are simultaneously changing, the definitions of elasticities warn us that it is incorrect to examine the effect of one variable, such as the own-price, on quantity demanded. We can decompose the change in quantity demanded into three components: the effect of changes in the own-price alone, plus the effect of changes in price of other goods alone, plus the effect of changing incomes. When all nominal variables change by the same proportion, the sum of these three effects is exactly zero.

4.8 Elasticity of supply

Whereas the analysis of demand elasticities is quite tricky, the analysis of supply elasticities is refreshingly simple. We really need only keep track of the supply response to an increase in the own-price of a good or service.

The elasticity of supply measures the responsiveness of the quantity supplied to a change in the price of that commodity.

Supply elasticity = (% change in quantity supplied)/(% change in price)

Because supply curves slope upwards, the elasticity of supply is *always positive*. As we move along a supply curve, positive price changes are associated with positive output changes. The more elastic is supply, the larger the percentage increase in quantity supplied in response to a given percentage change in price. Thus, elastic supply curves are relatively flat and inelastic supply curves relatively steep.

Figure 4.6 shows a typical supply curve *SS* with a positive supply elasticity. If the supply curve is a straight line, the supply elasticity will change as we move along it. As we learned in relation to demand curves, a constant slope implies equal absolute changes in quantity as we successively increase price by one unit; however, these equal absolute changes imply different percentage changes, depending on the point from which we begin.

Figure 4.6 also shows two extreme cases. The vertical supply curve *S′S′* has a zero supply elasticity. A given percentage change in price is associated with a zero percentage change in quantity supplied. The horizontal supply curve *S″S″* has an infinite supply elasticity. Any price increase above the price *P** leads to an infinite increase in quantity supplied.

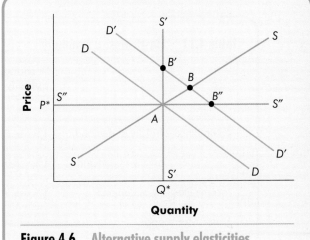

Figure 4.6 Alternative supply elasticities

MATHS 4.3 — The point elasticity of supply

Just as we can for the elasticity of demand, we can also calculate the elasticity of supply at a given point of a specific supply function.

The price elasticity of supply (PES) is defined as:

$$PES = \frac{\%\Delta Q^S}{\% P} \qquad (1)$$

The formula in (1) will measure the elasticity of supply between two different points on a given supply function. The point elasticity of supply is defined as:

$$PES = \frac{dQ^S}{dP}\frac{P}{Q^S} \qquad (2)$$

where the term dQ^S/dP measures the slope of the supply function at a given point.

Consider the following linear direct supply function:

$$Q^S = 2 + 5P \qquad (3)$$

where Q^S denotes the quantity supplied and P the price.

Suppose we want to find the elasticity of supply when $P = 10$. According to (3), at that price $Q^S = 52$. In this case the slope of the supply function is constant and equal to 5. The point elasticity of supply when $P = 10$ and $Q^S = 52$ is therefore:

$$PES = 5 \times \frac{10}{52} = 0.96$$

The point elasticity of demand is less than 1. This means that a 1 per cent increase in the price will increase less than proportionally (by 0.96 per cent) to the quantity supplied.

Table 4.11 **Elasticities: a summary**

	% change in quantity demanded	% change in quantity supplied
	induced by	
(Own-)Price elasticity of demand	1% rise in own price	
Cross-price elasticity of demand	1% rise in price of related good	
Income elasticity of demand	1% rise in income	
Elasticity of supply		1% rise in own price

The elasticity of supply tells us how the equilibrium price and quantity will change when there is a shift in demand. Figure 4.6 shows a demand shift from DD to $D'D'$. Beginning from equilibrium at A, a demand shift from DD to $D'D'$ leads to a new equilibrium at B', B or B'' depending on the elasticity of supply. The more inelastic is supply, the more the demand increase leads to higher prices rather than higher quantities. In the extreme cases, the move from A to B' reflects only a price increase and the move from A to B'' reflects only a quantity increase. Table 4.11 provides a summary.

 4.9   Who really pays the tax?

By spending and taxing, the government affects resource allocation in the economy. By taxing cigarettes, the government can reduce the number of cigarettes smoked and thereby improve health.

By taxing fuel, it can discourage pollution, though it may incur the wrath of lorry drivers and motorists. By taxing income earned from work, the government affects the amount of time people want to work. Taxes loom large in the workings of a mixed economy and have a profound effect on the way society allocates its scarce resources.

Initially we discuss what are called *specific* taxes, those that specify a particular amount, such as £5 per bottle of vodka. We show how the effect of a specific tax is related to the slope of supply and demand curves. We then extend the argument to *ad valorem* taxes, which are measured as a percentage of the commodity's value. For example, VAT is usually levied at 17.5 per cent of the value of the good or service.

Just as specific taxes, in particular units, are related to slopes of supply and demand curves in particular units, so *ad valorem* or percentage taxes are related to *elasticities* of supply and demand, which are already expressed in percentages.

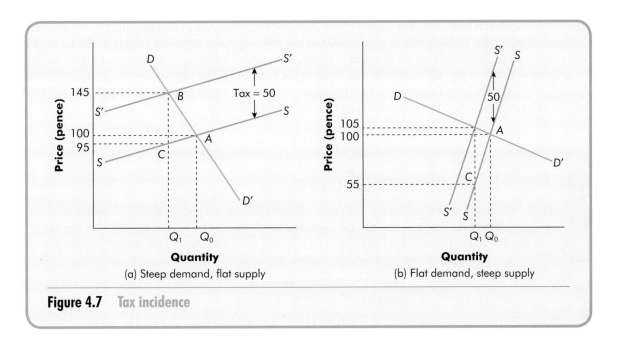

Figure 4.7 Tax incidence

Either way, what we want to know is who ends up paying the tax. Suppose for simplicity we imagine a packet of cigarettes costs £1 and the government imposes a specific tax of 50p per packet. Do smokers end up paying the tax, or is it borne by cigarette producers? How much of the tax can producers pass on to the consumer? We now show that this depends on the slopes of the supply and demand curves.

Figures 4.7(a) and 4.7(b) plot the (after-tax) price to the consumer on the vertical axis. DD' shows the demand curve, which depends on the price to smokers (consumers). Since the price received by the producer is the consumer price minus the 50p tax per packet, the effect of the tax is to shift the supply curve from SS to $S'S'$ in both diagrams. Each possible quantity supplied depends on the price received by the producer, which will be the same as before only if consumer prices are 50p higher: that is why we must shift the supply curve up by 50p.

In Figure 4.7(a), with a flat supply curve and steep demand curve, the tax is borne mainly by cigarette consumers. Point B is nearly 50p higher than point A. Since demand is insensitive to price, producers can pass on most of the tax in higher prices. Supply is price-sensitive, so the price received by producers cannot fall much. Consumers pay £1.45 and producers get £0.95 a packet.

In Figure 4.7(b), with a flat demand curve and a steep supply curve, most of the tax is borne by cigarette producers. Demand is price-sensitive, so attempts to pass on the tax in higher prices quickly lead to a drop in sales. Supply is price-insensitive and producers hardly cut back even though the price they receive has fallen nearly 50p. Consumers pay £1.05 and producers get £0.55 a packet.

The key implication is thus that the **incidence of a tax** – who eventually bears the burden – has nothing to do with who initially hands over money to the government. The existence of the tax changes behaviour. This has induced effects on equilibrium price and quantity. These induced effects may be large or small, depending on the slopes of supply and demand curves.

> The **incidence of a tax** describes who eventually bears the burden of that tax.

Now that we understand the general principle, it is obvious that the same argument will carry over to the more commonly used *ad valorem* taxes. We simply need to remember to confront the change in the percentage tax rate with the relevant percentage measures of price responsiveness of supply and demand, namely the (own-price) supply and demand elasticities.

Hence, when demand is inelastic but supply elastic, the case for percentages corresponding to the absolute change case in Figure 4.7(a), a rise in an *ad valorem* tax will largely be borne by buyers in the form of a higher price paid. Conversely, when demand is elastic, but supply inelastic, the analogue of Figure 4.7(b), a higher *ad valorem* tax will fall mainly on suppliers, in the form of a lower price received. Thus, supply and demand elasticities help us think about the incidence of the commonest taxes, such as income tax, VAT and the corporation tax paid by companies, all of which are *ad valorem*.

MATHS 4.4 — The effects of a specific tax

Here, we derive mathematically the effect of introducing a specific tax in a competitive market. With a specific tax, the tax bill depends on the quantity sold of a good and not on its price. Suppose that the market demand is linear and given by: $Q^D = a - bP$. The market supply is given by: $Q^S = c + dP$. Without any government intervention, the market outcome is:

$$P^\star = \frac{(a-c)}{(b+d)} \quad \text{and} \quad Q^\star = \frac{bc+da}{(b+d)}$$

Now suppose that the government introduces a specific tax in the market that has to be paid by the suppliers. This creates a wedge between the price the consumers pay and that which the suppliers receive. In particular, when the specific tax is charged to the suppliers we have:

$$P^S = P^D - t$$

where t is the tax rate, P^S is the price received by the suppliers and P^D is the price paid by the consumers. In order to see the effects of this new tax we modify the market demand and supply in the following way:

$$Q^D = a - bP^D \quad \text{and} \quad Q^S = c + dP^S$$

Now we take into account the fact that the price that affects the demand (the price consumers pay) can be different from the price that affects supply (the price the suppliers receive). Applying the knowledge that $P^S = P^D - t$ to the market supply, we have: $Q^S = c + d(P^D - t)$.

Notice that the introduction of the tax has the effect of shifting the market supply to the left by an amount given by t.

The market equilibrium is always where demand is equal to supply: $Q^D = Q^S$.

This implies: $a - bP^D = c + d(P^D - t)$. Solving that equation for P^D, we get:

$$P^{\star D} = \frac{(a-c)}{b+d} + \frac{dt}{b+d} \tag{1}$$

This is the price paid in equilibrium by the consumers after the specific tax has been introduced in the market. The price received by suppliers is therefore: $P^S = p^D - t \Rightarrow [(a-c) + dt]/(d+b) - t$. Simplifying that expression, we obtain:

$$P^{\star S} = \frac{(a-c)}{d+b} - \frac{bt}{b+d} \tag{2}$$

To find the equilibrium quantity, substitute equation (1) into the demand function (or equation (2) into the supply function):

$$Q^{\star D} = \frac{ad+cb}{b+d} - \frac{bdt}{b+d}$$

What are the effects of the specific tax introduction? We can evaluate those effects by comparing the market equilibrium without the tax with the one once the tax is introduced (a comparative statics exercise).

Notice that:

$$P^{\star D} = P^{\star} + \frac{dt}{b+d}$$

$$P^{\star S} = P^{\star} - \frac{bt}{b+d}$$

$$Q^{\star D} = Q^{\star} - \frac{bdt}{b+d}$$

where $P^{\star}$ and $Q^{\star}$ were the equilibrium values before the tax introduction.

Therefore the tax introduction has the following effects on equilibrium:

(1) It increases the price paid by consumers.

(2) It decreases the price received by the suppliers.

(3) It reduces the equilibrium quantity in the market.

Notice an important thing: it does not matter if the government charges the suppliers or the consumers, the results will be the same: $P^S = P^D - t$ implies that $P^D = P^S + t$. Using one expression instead of the other in our model will not change the final result.

Summary

- Unless otherwise specified, the **elasticity of demand** refers to the **own-price elasticity**. It measures the sensitivity of quantity demanded to changes in the own-price of a good, holding constant the prices of other goods and income. Demand elasticities are negative since demand curves slope down. In general, the demand elasticity changes as we move along a given demand curve. Along a straight-line demand curve, elasticity falls as price falls.

- **Demand is elastic** if the price elasticity is more negative than −1 (for example −2). Price cuts then increase total spending on the good. **Demand is inelastic** if the demand elasticity lies between −1 and 0. Price cuts then reduce total spending on the good. **Demand is unit-elastic** if the demand elasticity is −1. Price changes then have no effect on total spending on the good.

- The demand elasticity depends on how long customers have to adjust to a price change. In the short run, substitution possibilities may be limited. Demand elasticities will typically rise (become more negative) with the length of time allowed for adjustment. The time required for complete adjustment varies from good to good.

- The **cross-price elasticity of demand** measures the sensitivity of quantity demanded of one good to changes in the price of a related good. Positive cross-price elasticities tend to imply that goods are **substitutes**, negative cross-price elasticities that goods are **complements**.

- The **income elasticity of demand** measures the sensitivity of quantity demanded to changes in income, holding constant the prices of all goods.

- **Inferior goods** have negative income elasticities of demand. Higher incomes reduce the quantity demanded and the budget share of such goods. **Luxury goods** have income elasticities larger than 1. Higher incomes raise the quantity demanded and the budget share of such goods.

- Goods that are not inferior are called **normal goods** and have positive income elasticities of demand. Goods that are not luxuries are called **necessities** and have income elasticities less than 1. All inferior goods are necessities but normal goods are necessities only if they are not luxuries.

- Doubling all nominal variables should have no effect on demand since it alters neither the real value (purchasing power) of incomes nor the relative prices of goods. In examining data from economies experiencing inflation, it is often best to look at real prices and real incomes, adjusting prices and incomes for the effect of inflation.

- The **supply elasticity** measures the percentage response of quantity supplied to a 1 per cent increase in the price of the commodity. Since supply curves slope up, the supply elasticity is positive.

- **Tax incidence** measures who eventually pays the tax. Since taxes induce changes in equilibrium prices and quantities, this can be very different from the people from whom the government appears to collect the money.

- For **specific taxes**, slopes of supply and demand curves are relevant. For **ad valorem taxes**, elasticities of supply and demand are relevant. In either case, it is the more price-insensitive side of the market that bears more of the burden of a tax.

Review questions

connect

1 Your fruit stall has 100 ripe peaches that must be sold at once. Your supply curve of peaches is vertical. From past experience, 100 peaches are demanded if the price is £1. (a) Draw a supply and demand diagram, showing market equilibrium. (b) The demand elasticity is −0.5. You discover ten of your peaches are rotten and cannot be sold. Draw the new supply curve. What is the new equilibrium price?

2 (a) Milk, dental services, beer; (b) chocolate, chickens, train journeys; (c) theatre trips, tennis clubs, films. For each of categories (a), (b) and (c), do you expect demand to be elastic or inelastic? Then rank the elasticities within each category. Explain your answer.

3 Where along a straight-line demand curve does consumer spending reach a maximum? Explain why. What use is this information to the owner of a football club?

4 The following table shows price and income elasticities for vegetables and catering services. For each good, explain whether it is a luxury or a necessity, and whether demand is elastic or inelastic.

	Price elasticity	Income elasticity
Vegetables	0.17	0.87
Catering services	2.61	1.64

5 Common fallacies   Why are these statements wrong? (a) Because cigarettes are a necessity, tax revenues from cigarettes will always increase when the tax rate is raised. (b) Farmers should take out insurance against bad weather that might destroy half of all their crops. (c) Higher consumer incomes always benefit producers.

6 Suppose that the market demand for beef is given by $Q^D = 200 - 6P + 2Y$, where P is the price of meat per kg and Y is consumers' income. Suppose that consumers' income is £100. If the price of beef decreases from £10 to £8 per kg, find the corresponding elasticity of demand. Now suppose that the price is fixed to £8 while consumers' income increases from £100 to £150; find the corresponding income elasticity of demand. Is beef a normal good?

7 The data below refer to the quantity demanded of good A and the price of A as a result of the changes to the price of good B and good C:

Q_A (kg)	P_A (pence)	P_B (pence)	P_C (pence)
3	52	32	64
1.3	82	26	71

Are goods A and B substitutes or complements? What about goods A and C?

8 The data below refer to the market for cheese:

Quantity	Price
130	10
110	20
80	35
70	40
58	46
50	50

Plot the demand for cheese. For which prices is the demand for cheese elastic? For which prices is the demand for cheese inelastic?

9 The market demand for a given good is $Q^D = 26 - 4P$, while the market supply is $Q^S = 2P - 4$. Find the equilibrium price and quantity in the market. Now assume that the government introduces a specific tax $t = 3$ on the suppliers. Find the new equilibrium price and the new equilibrium quantity. Compare the pre-tax equilibrium with the after-tax equilibrium. What are the main differences?

10 Consider the following demand function: $Q^D = 25/P^2$. Show that the point elasticity of demand for that function is always equal to -2.

11 (a) If the government wants to maximize revenue from cigarette tax, should it simply set a very high tax rate on cigarettes? (b) If the government achieves its objective, what is the elasticity of demand for cigarettes at the price corresponding to this tax rate? You may assume that cigarettes

89

are essentially free to produce and the entire price reflects the tax. (c) A research company measures elasticity and concludes that the demand for cigarettes is price-elastic. Should you raise or lower the tax rate? (d) If you want not merely to get tax revenue but also to make people healthier, should you set a tax rate above or below that which maximizes revenue from cigarette taxation?

12 Air conditioners are a luxury good. (a) What does this imply, about which elasticity? (b) Which two countries would you guess have the highest per capita demand for air conditioners at present? (c) If people continue to get richer and global warming continues to increase, what is likely to happen to the quantity of air conditioners demanded? And what will this do to global warming? And hence to the demand for air conditioners? (d) Could this process spiral out of control?

13 Essay question   Suppose climate change causes flooding that wipes out much of the UK's agriculture. Discuss what happens to the price of food in the UK (a) in the short run and (b) in the long run. Did you assume that the UK made and consumed all food itself or did you allow for international trade? How does the outcome differ in these two cases?

For solutions to these questions contact your lecturer.

Consumer choice and demand decisions

CHAPTER 5

Learning Outcomes

By the end of this chapter, you should understand:

1. the relationship between utility and tastes for a consumer
2. the concept of diminishing marginal utility
3. the concept of diminishing marginal rate of substitution
4. how to represent tastes as indifference curves
5. how to derive a budget line
6. how indifference curves and budget lines explain consumer choice
7. how consumer income affects quantity demanded
8. how a price change affects quantity demanded
9. income and substitution effects
10. the market demand curve

In previous chapters we introduced demand curves to represent consumer behaviour. In this chapter we will build a formal theory of consumer choice to explain where those demand curves come from. This theory will help us to explain how consumers reconcile what they would like to consume, as described by their tastes or preferences, with what the market will allow them to do, as described by their incomes and the prices of various goods. We will then use this theory to predict how consumers will respond to changes in market conditions. Furthermore, we will relate the theory developed in this chapter to the price and income elasticities examined in Chapter 4.

 ## 5.1 Demand by a single consumer

In order to build a theory of consumer choice, first we need to specify what the main objective of such a theory is: we want to explain how a consumer chooses how much to consume of different goods given her resources (income) and given the market conditions (the prices of the different goods). If we are able to identify the basic mechanism behind the decision process for a consumer, then we are able to understand how the quantity of goods bought (and so consumed) by that consumer can change if prices change. But this relationship between the quantity bought of a good and its price is what we call a demand function. Therefore our theory of consumer choice will provide a foundation for the demand curves we have studied in previous chapters.

The main ingredients of this theory are:

- *The consumer's tastes and utility*   Tastes, or preferences, are the driving force behind what a consumer chooses to consume. Some prefer coca-cola to orange juice, some prefer beef to chicken, and so on. Utility is what economists call the satisfaction consumers get from consuming goods.

- *The behavioural assumption that consumers are rational*   By rational, we mean that consumers will try to obtain the best they can from their consumption decisions. In particular, of the affordable consumption bundles, a rational consumer picks the bundle that maximizes her own satisfaction.

- *The consumer's income*   This represents the resource available to the consumer for the consumption activity. A consumer cannot consume more than her available income.

- *The prices at which goods can be bought.*

Each element listed above is explained in detail in the following sections.

Tastes and utility

Consumers have tastes, or preferences, about the goods they consume. In building our theory of consumer choice we need to make some assumptions about those tastes. Before doing that we introduce the idea of a *consumption bundle*. This represents what a consumer would like to consume. A consumption bundle contains different quantities of various goods. In the following we make the simplifying assumption that a consumption bundle contains different quantities of only two goods: films and meals. For example, suppose that a consumer faces the following three bundles: bundle *a* contains 6 films and 5 meals, bundle *b* contains 4 films and 2 meals and bundle *c* contains 2 films and 1 meal. The problem for our consumer is how to choose between those bundles. If she likes both films and meals a lot, she would probably go for bundle *a*, which contains more of both goods compared to the other bundles. However, without making any assumptions regarding how the consumer can rank different consumption bundles according to her tastes, we cannot say much. Before turning to the problem of tastes, however, we introduce the concept of *utility*.

Consumers obtain utility from consuming goods. Therefore utility is the final objective of consumption. It represents what a consumer achieves by consuming a particular consumption bundle. For example, suppose you much prefer Italian food to French food. Then you would probably be *happier* going to eat in an Italian restaurant than in a French restaurant. Or to put it another way: you would probably get more *utility* from consuming the Italian food rather than the French food. From this simple example you can probably see that there is a link between the concept of utility and the tastes of a consumer. A consumer prefers one bundle of goods to another if the utility she gets from the former is greater than the utility she gets from the latter.

Given the concepts of consumption bundles and utility just defined, we now make the following plausible assumptions regarding the tastes of a consumer:

- *Completeness*   The consumer can always rank alternative bundles of goods according to the satisfaction or utility they provide. It is unnecessary to quantify this utility,[1] for example to say that one bundle yields twice as much utility as another bundle. We only require that the consumer can decide that one bundle

---

1   We say that utility is an *ordinal* measure. The case of measurable utility, or *cardinal* utility, is considered in the Appendix to this chapter. This is a special case, but easier to master.

is better than, worse than or exactly as good as another. This assumption rules out the possibility that a consumer facing different bundles cannot decide which one she prefers.

- *Transitivity* We assume that the ranking of possible bundles is internally consistent: if bundle *a* is preferred to bundle *b* and bundle *b* is preferred to bundle *c*, then bundle *a* must be preferred to bundle *c*.

- *Consumers prefer more to less* If bundle *b* offers more films but as many meals as bundle *c*, we assume bundle *b* is preferred. The same applies if bundle *b* offers more meals but as many films as bundle *c*. What about things like pollution, which are not goods but 'bads'? Consumers do not prefer more pollution to less. We get round this problem by redefining commodities so that our assumption is satisfied. We analyse clean water rather than polluted water. More clean water is better than less.

Figure 5.1 examines the implications of these three assumptions about taste. Each point shows a consumption bundle of films and meals. Now it is clear why we assumed that a consumption bundle contains only two goods. This assumption allows us to represent our analysis using nice and simple graphs, since a consumption bundle can be depicted as a point where the co-ordinates are the quantities of the two goods. For example, in Figure 5.1 point *a*

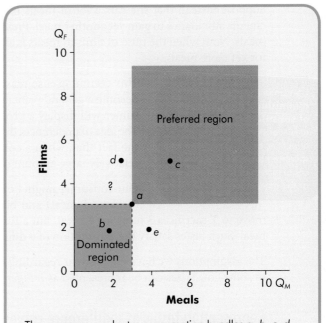

The consumer evaluates consumption bundles *a*, *b*, *c*, *d* and *e*. With respect to point *a*, any point to the north-east is preferred and any point to the south-west is dominated by *c*. Points such as *d* or *e* in the other two regions may or may not be preferred to *a*, depending on the consumer's tastes.

Figure 5.1 **Ranking alternative consumption bundles**

represents a bundle containing 3 films and 3 CDs.[2] We begin at bundle *a*. Since more is preferred to less, any point such as *c* to the north-east of *a* is preferred to *a*. Point *c* offers more of *both* goods than *a*. Conversely, points to the south-west of *a* offer less of both goods than *a*. Point *a* is preferred to points such as *b*. By transitivity, since bundle *c* is preferred to bundle *a* and bundle *a* is preferred to bundle *b*, then it must be that bundle *c* is preferred to bundle *b*. Notice that, given the assumptions made about the tastes of our consumer, we cannot be sure how points in the other two regions (north-west, south-east) compare with *a*. At *d* or *e*, the consumer has more of one good but less of the other good than at *a*. Someone who really likes food might prefer *e* to *a*, but an avid film buff would prefer *d* to *a*.

Consumers prefer more to less. An extra meal increases utility. To hold utility constant when a meal is added, the consumer must sacrifice some of the other good (films). The **marginal rate of substitution** tells us how many films the consumer could exchange for an additional meal without changing total utility.

Suppose the student has 5 films and no meals. Having already seen 4 films, she does not enjoy the fifth film much. With no meals, she is *very* hungry. The utility of this bundle (5 films and zero meals) is low: being so hungry, she cannot enjoy films anyway. For the same low amount of utility she could give up a lot of films for a little food.

> The **marginal rate of substitution** of meals for films is the quantity of films the consumer must sacrifice to increase the quantity of meals by one unit *without changing total utility*.

---

2 The main results we get from our analysis will not change if we allow consumption bundles to contain more than two goods. However, in that case, the analysis will be slightly more complicated.

Suppose instead that she eats a lot of meals but sees few films. She is then reluctant to sacrifice much cinema attendance to gain yet another meal. Previously, it made sense to sacrifice abundant films for scarce meals. Now, when the ratio of films to meals is already low, it does not make sense to sacrifice scarce films for yet more meals.

> Consumer tastes exhibit a **diminishing marginal rate of substitution** when, to hold utility constant, diminishing quantities of one good must be sacrificed to obtain successive equal increases in the quantity of the other good.

This commonsense reasoning about tastes or preferences is very robust. It can become a general principle about consumer tastes. In general, the tastes of a consumer will display a property called **diminishing marginal rate of substitution**. The idea of preferences displaying diminishing marginal rate of substitution captures the fact that, when a consumer has a lot of one good, she is willing to give up a relatively large amount of it to get a good of which she has relatively little.

Our consumer might be equally happy with bundle X (6 films, 0 meals), bundle Y (3 films, 1 meal) and bundle Z (2 films, 2 meals). Beginning from bundle X, a move to Y sacrifices 3 films for 1 meal, but a further move from Y to Z sacrifices only 1 film for 1 extra meal. Such tastes satisfy the assumption of a diminishing marginal rate of substitution.

The assumptions we have made so far regarding consumers' tastes are all we require. It is now convenient to show how tastes can be represented as *indifference curves*.

Representing tastes as indifference curves

> An **indifference curve** shows all the consumption bundles yielding a particular level of utility.

Indifference curves are a graphical representation of the tastes of a consumer. An **indifference curve** is defined as the curve representing all the combinations of consumption bundles that provide the same level of utility for a consumer. Therefore a consumer is indifferent between consuming any of the bundles that lie on a given indifference curve.

Figure 5.2 illustrates how an indifference curve should look. Start at bundle a. Bundles in the preferred region of Figure 5.2 (like bundle c) are preferred to a and therefore they provide a higher utility to our consumer. Therefore those bundles cannot be on the same indifference curve as bundle a. Bundles that are on the dominated region (like bundle b) are worse than bundle a and therefore they provide lower utility to our consumer. Those bundles cannot be on the same indifference curve as bundle a. The only possible bundles that can provide the same utility to our consumer as bundle a are bundles that lie on the north-west and south-east regions compared with a.

An indifference curve is therefore a downward-sloping curve connecting all the bundles that our consumer considers as equally desirable in terms of the utility they provide.

Obviously, since the consumer can face many different bundles, we can have many different indifference curves on the same graph to represent the tastes of our consumer. Figure 5.3 shows three possible indifference curves, U_1U_1, U_2U_2 and U_3U_3.

Why do indifference curves represent graphically the tastes of a consumer? We show that the indifference curves displayed in Figure 5.3 satisfy all the assumptions we have made about consumers' tastes.

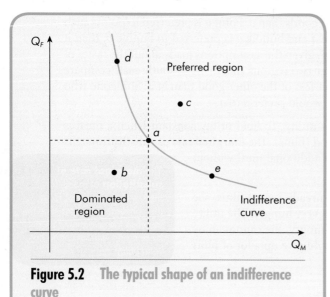

Figure 5.2 The typical shape of an indifference curve

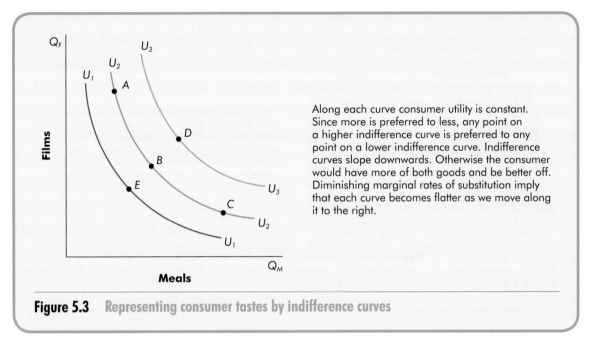

Along each curve consumer utility is constant. Since more is preferred to less, any point on a higher indifference curve is preferred to any point on a lower indifference curve. Indifference curves slope downwards. Otherwise the consumer would have more of both goods and be better off. Diminishing marginal rates of substitution imply that each curve becomes flatter as we move along it to the right.

Figure 5.3   Representing consumer tastes by indifference curves

Consider the indifference curve denoted by U_2U_2. By definition, every point on U_2U_2 yields the same utility for our consumer. Another way to say that is: our consumer is indifferent among all points on that indifference curve. Point C has many meals and few films, and point A offers many films but few meals. Because a consumer prefers more to less, *indifference curves must slope downwards*. Since more meals tend to increase utility, some films must simultaneously be sacrificed to hold utility constant.

The slope of a typical indifference curve gets steadily flatter as we move to the right. This reflects a diminishing marginal rate of substitution. At A, where films are relatively abundant compared with meals, the consumer will sacrifice a lot of films to gain a little more food. At B, where films are less abundant relative to meals, she will sacrifice fewer films to gain the same extra quantity of meals. And at C, she has so many meals that hardly any films will be sacrificed for extra meals. The marginal rate of substitution of meals for films is simply the slope of the indifference curve at the point from which we began. These two properties of a single indifference curve – its downward slope and its steady flattening as we move to the right – follow directly from the assumption that consumers prefer more to less and from the fact that tastes generally display the property of diminishing marginal rates of substitution.

Now consider point D on indifference curve U_3U_3. D offers more of both goods than B. Since consumers prefer more to less, utility at D is higher than utility at B. But all points on U_3U_3 yield the same utility as each other. Thus, every point on U_3U_3 yields more utility than every point on U_2U_2. Conversely, E must yield less utility than B since it offers less of both goods. Every point on U_1U_1 yields less utility than every point on U_2U_2.

Although Figure 5.3 shows only three indifference curves, we can draw in other indifference curves as well. In particular, there is an indifference curve passing through every possible bundle faced by our consumer. This comes from the assumption of completeness of tastes.

Higher indifference curves are associated with higher levels of utility because the consumer prefers more to less.

Indifference curves cannot cross. Figure 5.4 shows why. Suppose UU and $U'U'$ cross. Since X and Y lie on the indifference curve UU, the consumer is indifferent between these points. But Y and Z lie on the indifference curve $U'U'$. Hence the consumer is indifferent between Y and Z. Hence, the consumer is indifferent between X and Z. This is impossible, since the consumer gets more of both goods at Z than at X. Intersecting indifference curves would violate our assumption that consumers prefer more to less.

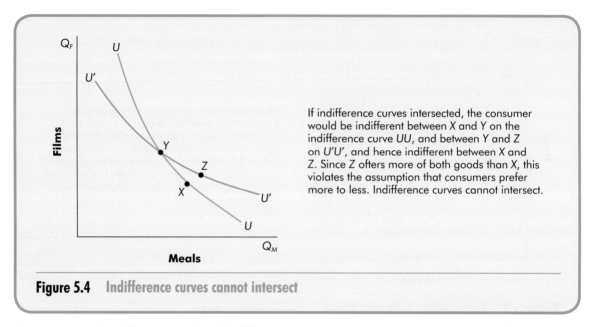

If indifference curves intersected, the consumer would be indifferent between X and Y on the indifference curve UU, and between Y and Z on U'U', and hence indifferent between X and Z. Since Z offers more of both goods than X, this violates the assumption that consumers prefer more to less. Indifference curves cannot intersect.

Figure 5.4 Indifference curves cannot intersect

Furthermore it should be noticed that, if indifference curves cross, the assumption regarding the transitivity of tastes will not hold. If X is indifferent to Y and Y is indifferent to Z, then by the logical consistency of tastes we should have that X is indifferent to Z. However, we know that Z should be preferred to X because of the assumption that consumers prefer more to less.

Our assumptions about consumer tastes rule out intersecting indifference curves.

CONCEPT 5.1 Other contour maps

When you look at a good map, you will see concentric rings or contours, each showing points of equal height. They are like indifference curves but do not have to obey the law of diminishing marginal rate of substitution and hence have stranger shapes. But they never intersect. Different contours are different heights.

As you rise through successive contours, you reach a dot marking the top of the mountain. In economics, we hardly ever reach the top. People are rarely satiated. But an indifference map for champagne and lobster might look like a mountain. Too much of either, and you are sick. The dot for the absolute best, or bliss, point, equivalent to the top of the mountain, then shows the finite combination of champagne and lobster preferred above all others, however much is available. We are now violating our assumption that the consumer always prefers more to less. The part of the contour sloping up corresponds to the range in which more is no longer better.

For broad categories of commodities, we are never satiated. It is as if we are confined to the shaded area of the diagram.

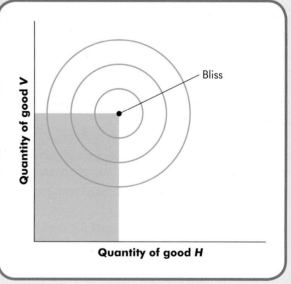

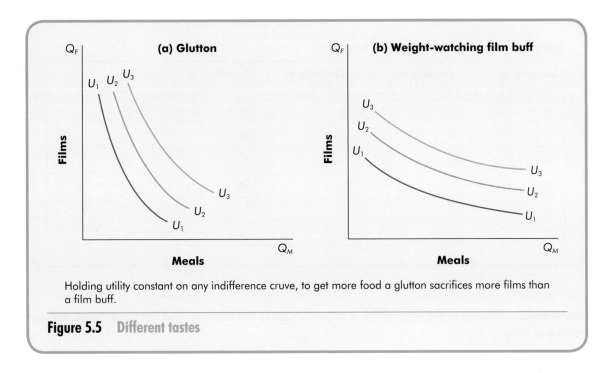

Holding utility constant on any indifference cruve, to get more food a glutton sacrifices more films than a film buff.

Figure 5.5 Different tastes

We can represent the tastes of any consumer by drawing the complete *map* of her indifference curves. Figure 5.5 shows two consumers with different tastes. In each case, moves to a higher indifference curve imply an increase in utility. Figure 5.5(a) shows the indifference map for a glutton prepared to give up a lot of films to gain a little extra food. Figure 5.5(b) shows the indifference map for a weight-watching film buff, who will give up large quantities of food to see more films. Both indifference maps are valid: they satisfy our basic assumptions about consumer tastes. Our theory can cope with extreme preferences as well as with more typical preferences in-between.

The budget constraint

A consumer's income and the market prices of goods define her budget constraint. The budget constraint introduces the problem of scarcity into our analysis.

> The **budget constraint** describes the different bundles that the consumer can afford.

Consider a student with a weekly budget (income, allowance or grant) of £50 to be spent on meals or films. Each meal costs £5 and each film £10. Those are the market prices of the two goods. We assume that the consumer takes those prices as given. What combination of meals and films can she afford? Going without films, she can spend £50 on 10 meals at £5 each. Going without meals, she can buy 5 cinema tickets at £10 each. Between these two extremes lie many combinations of meals and films that together cost exactly £50. These combinations are called the budget constraint.

The budget constraint shows the *maximum* affordable quantity of one good given the quantity of the other good being purchased.[3] Table 5.1 shows her budget constraint. Each row shows a bundle whose total value of £50 just exhausts her income.

Table 5.1 shows the *trade-off* between meals and films. Higher quantities of meals require lower quantities of films. For a given income, the budget constraint shows how much of one good must be sacrificed to

---

3   We assume that all income is spent. There is no saving. In chapter 11 we discuss the important choice between spending and saving.

Table 5.1 Affordable consumption baskets

Quantity of meals Q_M	Spending on meals £5 × Q_M	Quantity of films Q_F	Spending on films £10 × Q_F	Total spending £
0	0	5	50	50
2	10	4	40	50
4	20	3	30	50
6	30	2	20	50
8	40	1	10	50
10	50	0	0	50

obtain larger quantities of the other good. It is because there is a trade-off that she must *choose between* meals and films.

When the price of meals and films is fixed, independently of how many she buys, her budget constraint is a straight line, sometimes called the budget line. Figure 5.6 plots this budget line using the budget constraint data of Table 5.1.

The position of the budget line is determined by its end-points A and F, which have a simple interpretation. Point A is the most films the budget will buy if the student has no meals: £50 buys at most 5 film tickets at £10 each. Point F shows that £50 buys at most 10 meals at £5 each if she has no films. The budget line joins up points A and F. Intermediate points such as B and C show more balanced purchases of meals and films.

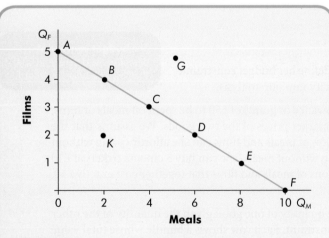

The budget line shows the maximum combinations of goods that the consumer can afford, given income and the prevailing prices. Points on the budget line use up the entire consumer budget. Points above the budget line are unaffordable. Points inside the budget line would allow additional spending.

Figure 5.6 The budget line

The slope of the budget line shows how many meals must be sacrificed to get another film. Moving from point F to point E reduces the quantity of meals from 10 to 8 but raises the quantity of films from 0 to 1. This trade-off between meals and films is constant along this budget line. Giving up 2 meals always yields the extra £10 to buy 1 extra film.

Since films cost twice as much as meals, 2 meals must be sacrificed to buy 1 more film ticket. *The slope of the budget line depends only on the ratio of the prices of the two goods.* The slope of a line is the change in the vertical distance divided by the corresponding change in the horizontal distance. In Figure 5.5 the slope of the budget line is $-1/2$. The (+1) change in films is divided by the (−2) change in meals. This example illustrates the general rule

$$\text{Slope of the budget line} = -P_H/P_V$$

where P_H is the price of the good on the horizontal axis and P_V is the price of the good on the vertical axis. In our example, the price of meals P_H = £5 and the price of films P_V = £10. The formula confirms that the slope of the budget line is $-^1/_2$. The minus sign reminds us that there is a trade-off. We have to *give up* one good to get more of the other good.

The two end-points of the budget line (here, A and F) show how much of each good the budget buys if the other good is not bought at all. The slope of the budget line joining these end-points depends only on the relative prices of the two goods.

Any point above the budget line (such as G in Figure 5.1) is unaffordable. The budget line shows the maximum quantity of one good that is affordable, given the quantity of the other good purchased and the budget available to spend. With an income of £50, G is out of reach: it would need £25 to buy 5 meals and £50 to buy 5 cinema tickets. Points such as K, which lie inside the budget line, leave some income unspent. Only on the budget line is there a trade-off where the student must choose *between* films and meals.

MATHS 5.1

The budget constraint and the budget line

It is helpful to see how we can express the budget constraint in a mathematical way. A consumer faces different bundles containing different quantities of two goods, call them X and Y. The consumer takes the prices of the two goods as given. Define by p_X the price of good X and by p_Y the price of good Y. Define by x the quantity of good X and by y the quantity of good Y. Define by M the income available to the consumer. Then the budget constraint of the consumer can be written as:

$$p_X x + p_Y y = M \qquad (1)$$

The left-hand side of the expression above is the total expenditure of the consumer who buys quantities x and y of the two goods at the given prices. The expenditure of the consumer must be equal to her income M.

From the budget constraint in (1) we can derive the corresponding budget line using simple algebra:

$$y = \frac{M}{p_Y} - \frac{p_X}{p_Y} x \qquad (2)$$

Equation (2) is the budget line. The slope of the budget line is given by $-p_X/p_Y$, that is, the price ratio.

Since the budget line is a straight line, the slope is constant along the line. The term M/p_Y is the vertical intercept of the budget line. It tells you how much the consumer can buy of good Y when she spends all her income on good Y.

The term M/p_X is the horizontal intercept of the budget line; it tells you the amount of good X that the consumer can buy if she spends all the income on good X. Bundle a on the graph contains an amount x_a of good X and an amount y_a of good Y. In moving

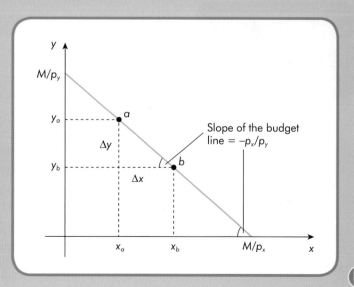

from bundle a to bundle b, the consumer increases her consumption of good X, from x_a to x_b, but she has to reduce the consumption of good Y from y_a to y_b. This shows the trade-off between the two goods implied by the budget constraint. Since the budget line is linear, we can find the slope of the budget line analytically in a simple way. Notice that both bundles (a and b) satisfy the budget constraint, therefore it must be true that:

$$y_a = \frac{M}{p_Y} - \frac{p_X}{p_Y} x_a \tag{3}$$

and

$$y_b = \frac{M}{p_Y} - \frac{p_X}{p_Y} x_b \tag{4}$$

By taking the difference between (4) and (3), we obtain:

$$y_b - y_a = \frac{M}{p_Y} - \frac{M}{p_Y} - \frac{p_X}{p_Y} x_b + \frac{p_X}{p_Y} x_a \tag{5}$$

Call $\Delta y = y_b - y_a$ the change in the quantity of Y between bundle b and bundle a, and similarly for good X define $\Delta x = x_b - x_a$. Then (5) can be written as:

$$\Delta y = -\frac{p_X}{p_Y} \Delta x$$

Or, written differently:

$$\frac{\Delta y}{\Delta x} = -\frac{p_X}{p_Y}$$

that is, exactly the slope of the budget line.

Utility maximization and choice

The budget line shows affordable bundles given a consumer's market environment (her budget and the price of different goods). The indifference map shows her tastes. We put the two concepts together in order to see how the consumer chooses among different bundles. We assume that the consumer is *rational*, implying that she *chooses the affordable bundle that maximizes her utility*. She cannot afford points above the budget line and will never choose points below the budget line (it is then possible to buy more of one good without sacrificing any of the other good). She will select a point on the budget line – her **chosen bundle**.

> The **chosen bundle** will be the point at which an indifference curve just touches the budget line. The budget line is a tangent to the indifference curve at this point.

To find which point on the budget line maximizes utility, we examine the consumer's tastes. Our glutton should pick a point with more meals and fewer films than the point our film buff selects. We first show how to use indifference curves to find the bundle the consumer chooses. Then we confirm that our model of consumer choice captures the different behaviour of the glutton and the film buff.

Figure 5.7 shows the budget line AF for the student who had £50 to spend on films (£10 each) and meals (£5 each). The indifference curves U_1U_1, U_2U_2 and U_3U_3 are part of the indifference map describing her tastes.

All points on U_3U_3 are unattainable since it lies entirely above the budget line AF. The student would like this high level of utility but cannot afford it. Next, suppose she considers the attainable point B on the indifference curve U_1U_1. She prefers this to point A, which must lie on a lower indifference curve (since indifference curves cannot intersect, the indifference curve through A lies entirely below the indifference curve U_1U_1). Similarly, F must lie on a lower indifference curve than E and she prefers E to F.

However, she will choose neither *B* nor *E*. By moving to *C*, she reaches a higher indifference curve and gets more utility and we have assumed that the consumer chooses in order to obtain the highest utility. *C* is the point she chooses. Any other affordable point on the budget line is on a lower indifference curve. The budget line never crosses a higher indifference curve, such as U_3U_3, and crosses twice every lower indifference curve, such as U_1U_1. Point *C* is the point of maximum utility given the budget constraint.

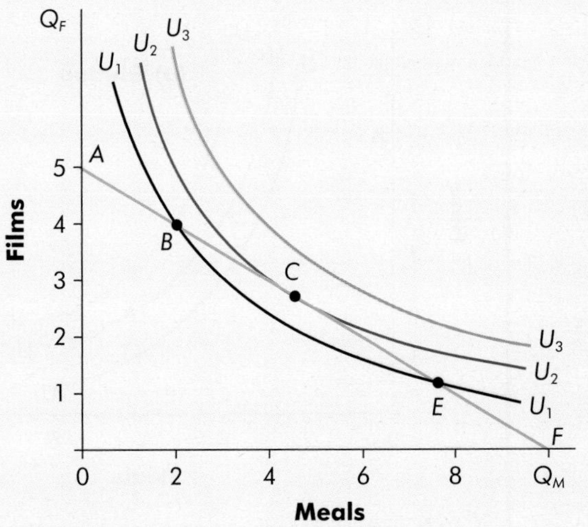

We can reach the same answer by different means. Consider again point *B* in Figure 5.7. The slope of the budget line shows the trade-off between affordable quantities of films and meals that the market environment will allow. When films cost £10 and meals £5, two meals can be traded for one film. The slope of the indifference curve at *B* (the marginal rate of substitution of meals for films) shows how the consumer would trade meals for films to maintain a constant level of utility. At point *B*, the budget line is flatter than the indifference curve. Moves to the left would take the student on to a lower indifference curve because the market trade-off is less than the required utility trade-off.

Similarly, beginning at point *E* it makes no sense to move to the right along the budget line. The market trade-off of meals for films is less than the utility trade-off needed to hold utility constant. Moves from *E* to the right reduce utility and take the consumer to a lower indifference curve.

Points above the budget line *AF* are unaffordable. The consumer cannot reach the indifference curve U_3U_3. Points such as *B* and *E* are affordable but only allow the consumer to reach the indifference curve U_1U_1. The consumer will choose the point *C* to reach the highest possible indifference curve U_2U_2. At point *C*, the indifference curve and the budget line just touch and their slopes are equal.

Figure 5.7 *Consumer choice in action*

However, it makes sense to move from *B* to the right. The market trade-off of affordable meals for films exceeds the utility trade-off required to maintain constant utility. The student reaches a higher indifference curve and increases her utility. Similarly, it makes sense to move from *E* to the left. Again, the market trade-off, this time increasing the quantity of affordable films in exchange for fewer meals, more than compensates for the utility trade-off, the slope of the indifference curve to keep utility constant. Moves from *E* leftwards along the budget line increase utility and allow her to reach a higher indifference curve.

We can make a general principle out of these examples. Wherever the budget line crosses an indifference curve, a move along the budget line in the smart direction will increase utility. Viewed in these terms, *point C, which maximizes utility, is the point at which the slope of the budget line and the slope of the indifference curve coincide*. Only at point *C* is there no feasible move along the budget line that increases utility. The student will choose point *C* since it maximizes utility.

To check that our model of consumer choice makes sense, consider what it implies for the observable behaviour of our glutton and film buff whose tastes between meals and films differ. Figure 5.5 represented the indifference curves of the glutton as steep and those of the film buff as flat.

Figure 5.8 assumes these two people have the *same* budget line. They have the same income and face the same prices for food and films. Only their tastes differ. Figure 5.8(a) shows the chosen point *C* for the glutton, with a lot of meals but few films. Figure 5.8(b) confirms that the film buff will choose point *C*, with many more films but much less food. Our theory of consumer choice successfully translates differences in taste into observable differences in demand for the two goods.

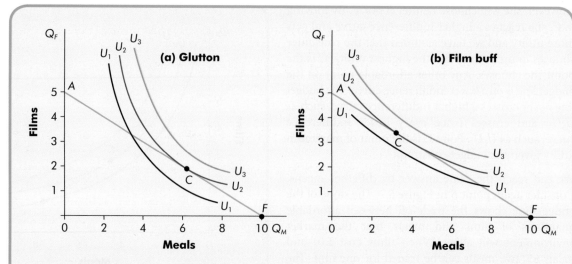

Both students face the same budget line *AF* and choose the point *C*, maximizing utility where the indifference curve is tangent to the budget line. The glutton has steep indifference curves and eats a lot of meals before the diminishing marginal rate of substitution flattens the indifference curve sufficiently. The film buff has flat indifference curves and the point of tangency is much further to the left. The glutton chooses more meals but fewer films than the film buff.

Figure 5.8   The effect of tastes on consumer choice

The optimal choice of each person is a point at which their *marginal rate of substitution* (the slope of the indifference curve) equals the *slope of the budget line*, which depends only on the relative price of films and meals. The glutton has a strong preference for food (steep indifference curves): her chosen point is far to the right to give the indifference curve a long time to flatten out. The film buff has flat indifference curves: her chosen point is far to the left before indifference curves can become flatter than the budget line.

CONCEPT 5.2 Do consumers really behave as utility-maximizing agents?

Our model of consumer choice says that consumers, in deciding what to consume, maximize their utility subject to budget constraint. At the chosen consumption bundle, the marginal rate of substitution between the two goods must be equal to their relative price.

This is fine from a theoretical point of view. What about reality? When we go to shops we probably do not write down our indifference curves, calculate our marginal rate of substitution among goods and try to equalize that to relative prices. Probably we do not even know our indifference curves. How can we test our theory, then?

Fortunately, even if we cannot see indifference curves directly, we can indirectly get information about them. Indeed, we can observe consumers' choices. So, can we infer anything about the preferences of a consumer by looking at her consumption choices? The answer is yes. This is the basis of the approach called *revealed preferences*. While a detailed analysis of the revealed preferences approach is beyond the scope of our analysis, we can introduce the basic principle behind it.

The basic idea is to determine consumers' preferences from observing consumers' behaviour. To briefly illustrate this point, suppose that a consumer faces two bundles, *X* and *Y*. If she chooses *X* when *Y* was also affordable, then we may say that bundle *X* is revealed as preferred to *Y*. If our consumer behaves according to our theory, then we should expect her always to choose X instead of Y when both bundles are affordable. If we see our consumer choosing Y instead of X, it should be the case that X has become unaffordable, otherwise our consumer does not behave according to our theory. The important aspect of revealed preferences is that, if consumer behaviour satisfies some properties (known as the axioms of revealed preferences), then the consumer is indeed a utility-maximizing agent.

The best way to test our theory using revealed preferences is to use experimental data.

We can gather some consumers into a room and ask them to choose among different bundles at given prices. Then we can change the prices and ask them to choose again, and so on. Recent research did just that. One hundred and twenty consumers (randomly selected) from Dijon in France were asked to participate in an experiment in which they had to choose between different bundles in different price/budget configurations. The result of that experiment is that 71 per cent of the consumers indeed behaved as utility maximizers.

Therefore those consumers, in deciding what bundles to choose, were indeed choosing in such a way that the marginal rate of substitution among goods was equalized to the relative prices, even though they may not have been aware of it.

Source: Fevrier, P. and Visser, M. (2004) A study of consumer behavior using laboratory data, *Experimental Economics*, 7 (1): 39–114.

5.2 Adjustment to income changes

Chapter 4 introduced the income elasticity of demand to describe, other things equal, the response of quantity demanded to changes in consumer incomes. Now we can use our model of consumer choice to analyse this response in greater detail.

For given tastes and prices, Figure 5.9 shows the effect of a higher income. The student had an income of £50, faced the budget line AF, and chose point C to maximize utility. Suppose her income rises from £50 to £80. Prices of meals and films remain £5 and £10, respectively. With higher income, she can afford to consume more of one or both of the goods. The budget line shifts outwards from AF to $A'F'$.

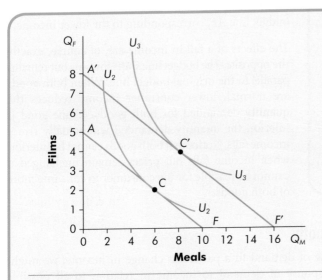

An increase in income from £50 to £80 induces a parallel shift in budget line from AF to $A'F'$. The new end-points A' and F' reflect the increase in purchasing power if only one good is purchased. The slope remains unaltered since prices have not changed. At the higher income the consumer chooses C'. Since both goods are normal, higher income raises the quantity of each good demanded but the percentage increase in film quantity is larger since its income elasticity is higher.

Figure 5.9 An increase in consumer income

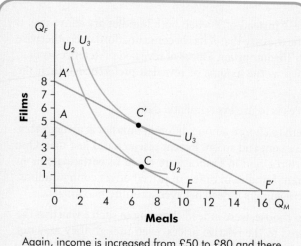

Again, income is increased from £50 to £80 and there is a parallel shift in the budget line from AF to A'F'. If meals were an inferior good, the quantity demanded would fall as income rises. The consumer then moves from C to C' when income rises.

Figure 5.10 **An increase in income reduces demand for the inferior good**

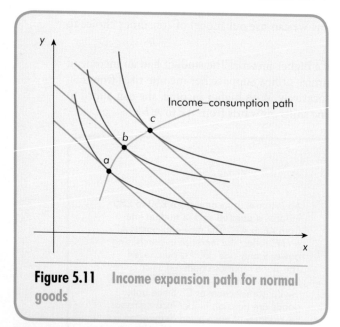

Figure 5.11 **Income expansion path for normal goods**

> The **income expansion path** shows how the chosen bundle of goods varies with consumer income levels, keeping constant everything else.

To find the exact position of this new line, we again calculate the end-points at which all income is spent on a single good. Point A shows that £80 buys at most 8 films at £10 each. Point F shows that £80 buys at most 16 meals at £5 each. Joining these points yields the new budget line A'F'. Since the slope of a budget line depends only on the relative price of the two goods, which is unchanged, the new budget line A'F' is parallel to the old budget line AF. Which point on A'F' will the student choose? She chooses C', at which the new budget line is tangent to the highest attainable indifference curve. However, the position of C' depends on the map of indifference curves that describe her tastes.

For most consumers, food is a normal good but a necessity, whereas films are a luxury. Figure 5.9 shows the case in which her tastes have these properties. A rise in income from £50 to £80 moves her from C (2 films, 6 meals) to C' (4 films, 8 meals). Thus, a 60 per cent rise in income induces a 100 per cent increase in the quantity of films demanded, confirming that films are a luxury good with income elasticity in excess of unity. Similarly, the 60 per cent rise in income induces a 33 per cent increase in the quantity of meals demanded. The income elasticity of demand for food is $(0.33/0.6) = 0.55$, confirming that food is a normal good (income elasticity greater than zero) but a necessity (income elasticity less than unity).

In contrast, in Figure 5.10 her tastes make food an inferior good, for which the quantity demanded declines as income rises. At point C' on the budget line A'F', fewer meals are demanded than at point C on the budget line AF, corresponding to the lower income.

The effects of a fall in income are, of course, exactly the opposite. The budget line shifts inwards but remains parallel to the original budget line. When both goods are normal, lower consumer income reduces the quantity demanded for both goods. If one good is inferior, the quantity demanded will actually rise if income falls. Notice that both goods cannot be inferior: when income falls but prices remain unchanged it cannot be feasible for the consumer to consume more of both goods.

Income expansion paths

Instead of the response of demand to a particular change in income, we might want to know the response of demand to income in relation to all possible variations in income. To study this, we trace out the income expansion path. Look again at Figure 5.9. The budget lines AF and A'F' correspond to incomes of £50 and £80, respectively. With yet higher incomes we could draw more budget lines, parallel to *AF* and *A'F'* but higher up. We could then find the points on these new budget lines that the consumer would choose at these higher income levels. Joining up the chosen points (*C* and *C'* in Figure 5.9) and these new points (say, *C'''* and *C'''*), we get the income expansion path. An example of the income expansion path for the case in which both goods are normal is given in Figure 5.11.

5.3 Adjustment to price changes

Having studied changes in tastes and in income, we now isolate the effect of a price change. Chapter 4 argued that a rise in price reduces the quantity demanded, other things equal. The own-price elasticity of demand measures this response, and is larger the easier it is to substitute towards goods whose prices have not risen.

We also introduced the cross-price elasticity of demand to measure the response of the quantity demanded of one good to a change in the price of another good. An increase in the price of good *j* tends to increase the quantity demanded of good *i* when the two goods are substitutes, but tends to reduce the quantity demanded of good *i* when the two are complements. The empirical evidence was presented in Tables 4.2 and 4.6.

Are those propositions invariably true, or did the evidence we examined just happen to confirm our commonsense reasoning? We now offer a more formal analysis based on the model of consumer choice developed above.

Price changes and the budget line

Figure 5.12 draws the budget line *AF* for a consumer with an income of £50 facing prices of £10 and £5 for films and meals, respectively. Suppose meal prices increase to £10. Since the price of films remains unaltered, £50 still buys 10 films when all income is spent on films. Point *A* must lie on the new budget line as well as the old budget line. But when all income is spent on meals, £50 buys only 5 meals at £10 each, instead of the 10 meals it used to buy at £5 each. Thus the other extreme point on the budget line shifts from *F* to *F'* when meal prices double. As usual, we join up these end-points to obtain the new budget line *AF'*. The effect of a rise in meal prices is to *rotate* the budget line inwards around the point *A* at which no meals are bought and higher meal prices are irrelevant.

Except at *A* itself, higher meal prices mean the consumer can now afford fewer meals for any given number of films, or fewer films for any given number of meals. The new budget line *AF'* lies inside the old budget line *AF*. The consumption bundles between *AF* and *AF'* are no longer affordable at the higher price of meals. In particular, the chosen point on the old budget line is no longer affordable unless it happens to be the end-point *A*. A price increase makes the consumer worse off by reducing consumption opportunities out of a fixed money income. The consumer's standard of living falls.

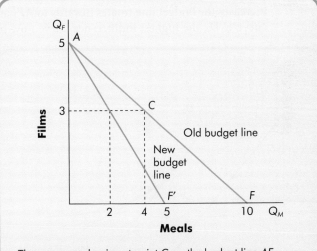

The consumer begins at point *C* on the budget line *AF*. Doubling meal prices halves the amount that can be spent on meals when no films are bought. The point *F* shifts to *F'*. The budget line rotates around the point *A* at which no meals are bought. Along the new budget line the consumer can no longer afford the original consumption bundle *C*. Consumption of one or both commodities must be reduced.

Figure 5.12   An increase in meal prices

To check that you understand, try drawing diagrams to illustrate the effect on the budget line of: (1) a reduction in the price of meals (*hint*: Figure 5.12 can be used – how?); (2) an increase in the price of films (*hint*: around which point does the budget line rotate?).

> The **substitution effect** of a price change is the adjustment of demand to the relative price change alone.
>
> The **income effect** of a price change is the adjustment of demand to the change in real income alone.

Substitution and income effects

Our model of consumer choice is based on the interaction of affordable opportunities (the budget line) and tastes (indifference curves). To analyse the effect of price changes on the actual quantity of goods demanded, we must study how rotations of the budget line affect the highest indifference curve that the consumer can reach.

A higher price of meals has two distinct effects on the budget line in Figure 5.12. First, the budget line becomes steeper, reflecting the rise in the relative price of meals. To get an extra meal, more films must now be sacrificed. Second, the budget line AF' lies inside the original budget line AF. The purchasing power of a given money income is reduced by the price increase. If you have £20 and you used to buy chocolate that cost £2 a bar, then your purchasing power is 10 bars of chocolate (£20/£2). Now suppose that the price of a bar of chocolate rises to £5. Your money now can buy only 4 bars of chocolate.

Economists therefore break up the effect of a price increase into these two distinct effects: the change in the relative price of the two goods and the fall in the purchasing power of the given money income. This is merely a thought experiment but it turns out to be useful to characterize some properties of the goods that consumers choose.

Figure 5.13 shows the response of demand quantities to a higher meal price. At the original prices, the consumer faced the budget line AF and chose C to reach the highest possible indifference curve $U_2 U_2$. At that point, the consumer demands an amount M_C of meals and an amount F_C of films. If the price of meals increases the budget line rotates inwards to AF' and the new optimal bundle will be E on the indifference curve $U_1 U_1$, the highest indifference curve now possible. In this example, higher meal prices reduce the quantity demanded of meals from M_C to M_E, while increasing the quantity demanded of films from F_C to F_E.

The substitution effect

To isolate the effect of relative prices alone, imagine a *hypothetical* budget line HH, parallel to the new budget line (the one after the price of meals has increased, that is, AF') and tangent to the original indifference curve (that is, $U_2 U_2$). Because HH is parallel to the new budget line AF', its slope reflects the new relative prices of films and meals after the price of meals has risen. Because HH is tangent to the old indifference curve $U_2 U_2$, it restores the consumer to the original utility and standard of living shown by all points on $U_2 U_2$. In constructing this new hypothetical budget line, we are doing the following thought experiment: after the price of meals has increased, how much income should we give to our consumer in order for her to have the same level of utility as before?

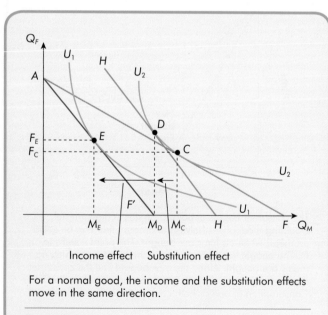

For a normal good, the income and the substitution effects move in the same direction.

Figure 5.13   **Income and substitution effects**

This hypothetical income that we can give to our consumer in order to make her as well off as before a price change is what economists call *compensating variation*.[4]

If confronted with the hypothetical budget line *HH*, the consumer would choose bundle *D*. Why do we need to do all of this? Because we can now decompose graphically the movement from *C* to *E* into two different steps: the movement from *C* to *D* and then from *D* to *E*.

The movement from *C* to *D* depends only on the price change, and we call that the *substitution effect*. The movement from *D* to *E* depends only on the fact that the real income has changed, and we call that the *income effect*.

The move from *C* to *D* is the pure substitution effect that is the adjustment of demand to relative prices when income is adjusted to maintain the old standard of living in the face of the new higher prices. *The substitution effect of an increase in the price of meals unambiguously reduces the quantity of meals demanded.* This result is perfectly general.[5] As meals become relatively more expensive, the consumer switches towards films, which have become relatively cheaper. Therefore, in moving from *C* to *D*, the quantity demanded of meals decreases while the quantity demanded of films increases. In general, the substitution effect is always negative for the good whose price has changed. This means that the consumer will always substitute the good that is now relatively expensive with the good that is now relatively cheap.

The income effect

To isolate the effect of the reduction in real income, holding relative prices constant, consider now the parallel shift in the budget line from the hypothetical position *HH* to the actual new position *AF′*. The consumer moves from *D* to *E*. When both goods are normal goods, a reduction in real income will reduce the quantity demanded of both goods. This is the case considered in Figure 5.13, where *E* lies to the south-west of *D*. From Figure 5.13 we see that, for meals, the income and substitution effects go in the same direction, meaning they reinforce each other in reducing the quantity consumed of meals. This is a general feature of normal goods. When the price of a normal good changes, the substitution and income effects for that good reinforce each other.

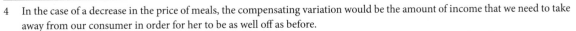

| CASE 5.1 | Income and substitution effects in practice: the effects of petrol prices on grocery expenditure |

Many consumers use cars to go shopping at grocery shops. Recent research tried to understand how changes in the price of petrol can affect the consumption of grocery products for consumers in California. In order to do that, the researchers used data from the Consumer Expenditure Survey and from detailed scanner data from grocery shops about food products. The research explored the following: suppose that consumers can choose between different bundles containing the following two goods: *food away from home* (like eating out in a restaurant) and *food at home* (like grocery shop food). If the price of petrol increases, eating out and going to the grocery shop using a car become more expensive. How do petrol price increases affect expenditure on those two goods?

The researchers found that, if the price of petrol doubles, the expenditure (and so the consumption) of food away from home decreases by 56 per cent. On the other hand, when the petrol price doubles, the expenditure on grocery food increases by around 19 per cent. This means that, when petrol price increases, food away

---

4 In the case of a decrease in the price of meals, the compensating variation would be the amount of income that we need to take away from our consumer in order for her to be as well off as before.

5 With only two goods, substitution away from meals must imply substitution towards films. However, when there are more than two goods, we cannot be sure that the substitution effects will tend to increase the quantity demanded for all other goods. We discuss this shortly in Section 5.5.

from home becomes relatively more expensive than food at home, and so the consumers substitute the former with the latter. So the substitution effect works in the same way as we have seen in our analysis.

Another interesting result of this research is that consumers tend to substitute further within their grocery shop purchases when the petrol price increases. In particular, consumers substitute towards items that are on special offer and away from full-price items when petrol price increases substantially.

Source: Gicheva, D. et al. (2008) *Revisiting the income effect: gasoline price and grocery purchases*, NBER working paper.

The net effect of a price increase on the quantity demanded

The consumer moves directly from the original point C to the new point E. We can interpret this as a pure substitution effect from C to the hypothetical point D, plus a pure income effect from D to E. If the goodwhose price has risen is a normal good, demand curves slope downwards, as asserted in Chapter 4.

The substitution effect from C to D must reduce the quantity of meals demanded. When the price of meals rises, the budget line becomes steeper and we must move along U_2U_2 to the left to find the point at which it is tangent to HH. Similarly, the income effect must further reduce the quantity of meals demanded if meals are a normal good. E must lie to the left of D.

The individual demand curve

Now we have all the tools we need to derive demand by a single consumer for a given good. In Figure 5.14 we show how to derive graphically the individual demand for a normal good. The top part shows how the optimal choice of our consumer changes as the price of meals increases, everything else constant. Suppose we start at point C, where the price of meals is P_C. At that price, the consumer demands an amount of meals given by M_C. Now suppose that the price increases to P_D. The budget constraint rotates inwards to AF'; at the new price of meals, the optimal choice of the consumer is now bundle D. So at price P_D our consumer demands an amount M_D of meals.

Then suppose that the price of meals increases even further, say to P_E. At this new price the optimal choice is point E and our consumer demands an amount M_E of meals. The line joining all the optimal bundles is called the *price–consumption curve*.

The bottom part of Figure 5.14 shows a graph with the price of meals on the vertical axis and the quantity consumed (and so demanded) of meals on the horizontal axis. Using the information in the top graph we can derive a possible negative relationship between the price of meals and the quantity demanded of meals. This is the individual demand for meals of our consumer. In the case where the good is normal, the demand curve

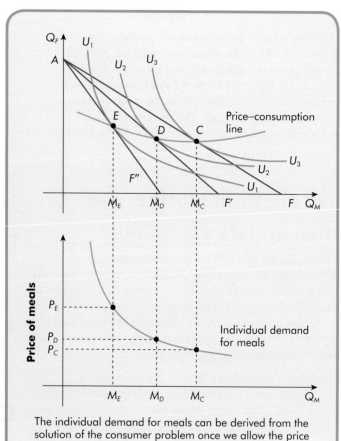

The individual demand for meals can be derived from the solution of the consumer problem once we allow the price of meals to vary keeping constant everything else.

Figure 5.14 **The individual demand curve for a normal good**

implies a negative relationship between the quantity demanded of that good and its market price.

Inferior goods

Although the substitution effect must reduce the quantity of meals demanded when the price of meals increases, the income effect goes in the opposite direction if the good is inferior: reductions in real income increase the quantity demanded. We can even imagine a perverse case in which this effect is so strong that price rises actually increase the quantity of that good demanded. Demand curves then slope *upwards*! We can use our analysis to explain how such a paradoxical case can arise.

Consider the case of two different goods, X and Y. This is represented in Figure 5.15. Suppose that the price of good X *decreases*. As usual after a price change we can decompose the effect of this price change into substitution and income effects. Suppose that before the decrease in the price of X the optimal choice of the consumer was bundle C on the indifference curve $U_1 U_1$. After the price of X decreases, the

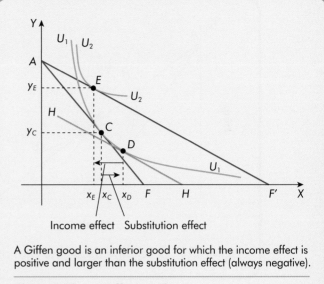

A Giffen good is an inferior good for which the income effect is positive and larger than the substitution effect (always negative).

Figure 5.15   A Giffen good

budget constraint rotates outwards from AF to AF'. The new choice of the consumer is bundle E on the indifference curve $U_2 U_2$. To show the income and substitution effects, we draw a new budget line HH parallel to AF' and tangent to the original indifference curve ($U_1 U_1$). By doing this, we identify bundle D. The movement from C to D is due to the substitution effect. Since the price of X decreased, good X is now relatively cheaper than good Y and so the consumer substitutes Y with X. The movement from D to E is due to the income effect. As income increases, the quantity demanded of good X decreases (from x_D to x_E). In this case, X is an inferior good. For an inferior good, it is always true that income and substitution effects go in opposite directions. In the particular case considered in Figure 5.15, the income effect is larger than the substitution effect and the final result is that, after the price of X has decreased, the quantity demanded of X has decreased (from x_C to x_E). In this case, the demand curve of good X is upward sloping.

A good that has such a property (the income effect is bigger than the substitution effect) is called a Giffen good, after a nineteenth-century economist who examined whether higher potato prices raised the quantity of potatoes demanded by the poor.

Notice in Figure 5.15 that, while good X is a Giffen good, Y is instead a normal good. As income increases, the quantity demanded of Y increases.

An inferior good need not be a Giffen good. It requires a very strong income effect – here, an increase in demand in response to real income reductions – to offset the substitution effect that is always negative. When goods are inferior, theoretical reasoning cannot establish which effect dominates. We must look at the empirical evidence. After decades of empirical research, economists are convinced that Giffen goods are rare. In practice, goods are rarely so inferior that the income effect can reverse the substitution effect. This means that, apart from the rare cases given by Giffen goods, for almost all goods we should have a negative demand curve.

Cross-price elasticities of demand

How does a rise in the price of one good affect demand for other goods? Chapter 4 showed that cross-price elasticities may be negative or positive. We now illustrate these possibilities, highlighting the roles played by substitution and income effects.

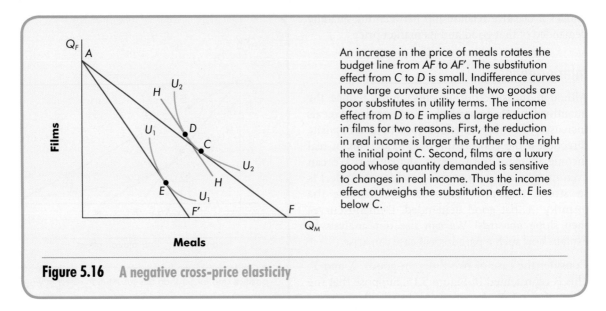

An increase in the price of meals rotates the budget line from AF to AF'. The substitution effect from C to D is small. Indifference curves have large curvature since the two goods are poor substitutes in utility terms. The income effect from D to E implies a large reduction in films for two reasons. First, the reduction in real income is larger the further to the right the initial point C. Second, films are a luxury good whose quantity demanded is sensitive to changes in real income. Thus the income effect outweighs the substitution effect. E lies below C.

Figure 5.16 A negative cross-price elasticity

Figure 5.16 shows a negative cross-price elasticity. A higher price of meals reduces the quantity of films demanded. Figure 5.16 has three properties. First, the two goods are poor substitutes. Indifference curves are very curved. Moving away from balanced combinations of the two goods requires large extra quantities of one good to compensate for small losses of the other good if a constant level of utility is to be preserved. When the price of meals is increased, the substitution effect towards films is small. Moving leftwards along U_2U_2, we quickly attain the slope required to match the new relative prices of the two goods. The substitution effect from C to D adds little to the quantity of films demanded.

Second, films have a high income elasticity of demand. They are a luxury good. Hence the income effect, the move from D to E in response to the parallel downward shift in the budget line from HH to AF', leads to a lot fewer films demanded.

Finally, point C is well to the right on the original budget line AF. Meal expenditure is a large part of consumer budgets. Hence changes in meal prices lead to big changes in the purchasing power of consumer income. Not only is the number of films demanded very responsive to given changes in consumer real income, but also a given rise in meal prices has a large effect on consumer real income because meals are a large part of consumer budgets.

These last two effects lead to a large income effect, which reduces the quantity of films demanded. Because the substitution effect in favour of films is small, the net effect is a reduction in the quantity of films demanded. An increase in meal prices reduces the quantity of films demanded. The cross-price elasticity of demand is negative.

Figure 5.17 shows the opposite case, a positive cross-price elasticity of demand. Suppose the consumer is choosing between bread and other food. If the price of bread rises, potatoes are a good substitute for bread. To maintain a given utility, consumers can substitute lots of cheap potatoes for expensive bread. Indifference curves are less curved than in Figure 5.16.

Suppose also that other food has a small income elasticity of demand. Although higher bread prices reduce real consumer income, this has a small income effect that reduces the quantity of other food demanded. Finally, if bread is a relatively small share in consumer budgets, higher bread prices have a small effect in reducing consumer purchasing power. Comparing Figures 5.16 and 5.17, the parallel shift from HH to AF' is smaller in the latter.

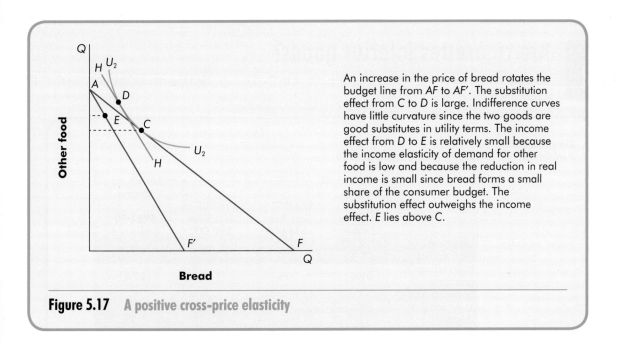

An increase in the price of bread rotates the budget line from AF to AF'. The substitution effect from C to D is large. Indifference curves have little curvature since the two goods are good substitutes in utility terms. The income effect from D to E is relatively small because the income elasticity of demand for other food is low and because the reduction in real income is small since bread forms a small share of the consumer budget. The substitution effect outweighs the income effect. E lies above C.

Figure 5.17   A positive cross-price elasticity

These last two effects imply that there is only a small income effect reducing the quantity of other food demanded. In contrast, the substitution effect towards other food is big. Hence higher bread prices raise the quantity of other food demanded. The cross-price elasticity is positive. This positive effect is even stronger if 'other food' is an inferior good. The income effect then raises the quantity of other food demanded, reinforcing the substitution effect. Table 5.2 summarizes the implications of our model of consumer choice for the demand response to a price change.

For example, suppose good I and good J are both normal. If the price of good I increases, we know that the consumer will substitute good I with good J, which is now relatively cheaper. So the substitution effect has a negative impact on the demand for good I, while it has a positive impact on the quantity demanded of good J. The increase in the price of good I decreases the real income of the consumer and, since goods are normal, the income effect has a negative impact on the quantity demanded of both goods.

Table 5.2   The effect of an increase in the price of good I on the quantity demanded of goods I and J

Good	Type	Substitution effect	Income effect	Total effect
I	Normal	Negative	Negative	Negative
	Inferior	Negative	Positive	Ambiguous
J	Normal	Positive	Negative	Ambiguous
	Inferior	Positive	Positive	Positive

CASE
5.2

Are cigarettes inferior goods?

A recent phone survey about smoking behaviour in the US provided the results displayed in the following table.

Do you smoke?
Percentage 'yes' among Americans aged 30 to 64

		Lower household income ⟶			Higher household income
		Less than $24 000	$24 000 to less than $36 000	$36 000 to less than $90 000	$90 000 and more
Lower education	Less than high school	42%	36%	40%	40%
	High school graduate	39%	32%	26%	23%
	Some college/ Vocational school	38%	29%	21%	18%
Higher education	College graduate/ Postgrad	22%	15%	10%	7%

Americans aged from 30 to 64 were asked whether or not they smoke, their income and their level of education. If we look at the results of the survey, we see that people with lower incomes (less than $24 000) make up the majority (42 per cent) of smokers. Moreover, as income increases, fewer and fewer

Picture: © Konstantin Tavrov | Dreamstime.com

people tend to smoke. This is true for any level of education. The relationship between number of smokers and income level seems to suggest that cigarettes are inferior goods. We know that the demand for cigarettes tends to be negatively sloped, so cigarettes are inferior but not a Giffen good. Why is that?

One possible reason is related to level of education. Better-educated people have greater access to information on the severe health problems resulting from smoking. They are also more likely to accept the truth of such information. Moreover, level of education is normally positively related to income. Those two facts together can explain why cigarettes may be an inferior good.

Source: Smoking is an inferior good (sometimes), *The Economist*, 29 April 2010. © The Economist Newspaper Limited, London 2010.

5.4 The market demand curve

We have now established that individual demand curves (almost always) slope downwards. For the rest of this book we assume that this is the case. Once we have the individual demand for each consumer demanding a given good, we can find the market demand for that good. We get the market demand by aggregating the demand curves of every individual consumer buying a particular good.

Consider the simplest case where there are only two consumers buying a given good. At each price, we find out how much each consumer demands. Adding the quantities demanded by all consumers at that price, we get the total quantity demanded at each price – the market demand curve. Since, as price is reduced, each person increases the quantity demanded, the total quantity demanded must also increase as price falls. The market demand curve also slopes downwards.

The **market demand curve** is the *horizontal addition of individual demand curves*. With prices on the vertical axis and quantities on the horizontal axis, we must add together individual quantities demanded at the same price. Figure 5.18 illustrates this idea.

> The **market demand curve** is the sum of the demand curves of all individuals in a particular market.

Suppose that, when the price is £3, consumer 1 demands 4, while consumer 2 demands 12. Then, at a price of £3, the market quantity demanded is 4 + 12 = 16. This is one point of the market demand. Suppose that, when the price is £5, consumer 1 demands 0, while consumer 2 demands 10, then at p = £5, the market quantity is 10. This is a second point on the market demand. Notice that in the particular example in Figure 5.18, when the price is above £5, consumer 1 always demands 0. Therefore the market demand coincides with the demand of consumer 2 at prices above £5. At prices below £5, the market demand is the horizontal sum of the quantities demanded by each consumer at the same price.

5.5 Complements and substitutes

Income and substitution effects are used to understand the effects of a price change. Whatever the direction of the income effect, with only two goods the substitution effect is always negative. The pure relative price effect leads the consumer to substitute away from the good whose relative price has risen towards the good

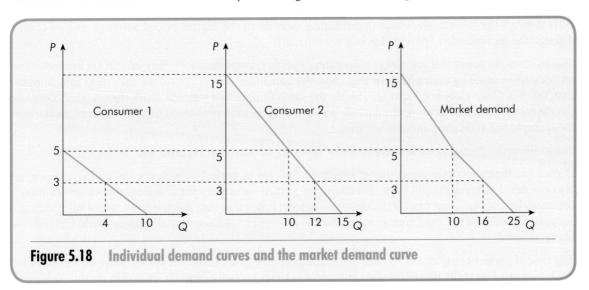

Figure 5.18   *Individual demand curves and the market demand curve*

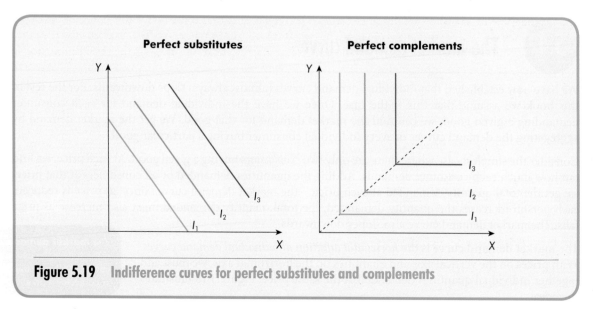

Figure 5.19 Indifference curves for perfect substitutes and complements

whose relative price has fallen. Abstracting from income effects, goods are necessarily substitutes for one another in a two-good world.

With more than two goods, some goods may be consumed jointly – pipes and pipe tobacco, bread and cheese, electric cookers and electricity. These goods are *complements*.

Even with many goods, there is always a substitution effect *away* from goods whose relative price has risen. However, substitution may not be *towards* all other goods. Consumers substitute *away* from goods consumed jointly with the good whose price has risen.

Suppose the price of pipes rises. What will happen to the demand for pipe tobacco? (Ignore the income effect, since expenditure on pipes is a tiny fraction of household budgets, so real incomes are only slightly reduced.) Since pipes and pipe tobacco are used jointly, we expect the demand for pipe tobacco to fall along with the number of pipes demanded. The demand curve for pipe tobacco shifts to the left in response to the increase in pipe prices. Notice that this implies that the cross-price elasticity between those two goods should be negative.

When goods are complements, a rise in the price of one good will reduce the demand for the complement, both through the substitution effect (substituting away from the higher-priced activity) and, of course, through the income effect (provided goods are normal).

Special cases are goods that are *perfect substitutes* or *perfect complements*. Perfect substitutes are goods that are viewed as equal by consumers. In that case, the consumer always consumes the cheap one. Suppose that, for you, Coca-Cola and Pepsi are exactly the same thing. Then you will drink the one that costs less. On the other hand, perfect complements are goods that are always consumed together in fixed proportion, for example one right shoe and one left shoe.

The indifference curves in these two particular cases are displayed in Figure 5.19.

Higher indifference curves imply higher utility. In the case of perfect substitutes, the indifference curves are downward-sloping straight lines. Therefore, for perfect substitutes the marginal rate of substitution is constant. In this particular case, at the optimal choice it is not true that the marginal rate of substitution is equal to the slope of the indifference curve. We have a corner solution. Our consumer consumes only the cheapest good.

The case of perfect complements is one where the property that consumers prefer 'more to less' does not hold. Suppose you really like to eat your chocolate cake with a ball of vanilla ice cream on top. You prefer that to the same cake with two balls of ice cream. Having more of one of the two goods does not make you happier, since you always prefer to consume the two goods in fixed proportion. This explains the L-shaped indifference curves. The slope of the dashed straight line starting from the origin is the fixed proportion in which the two goods are consumed.

5.6 Transfers in kind

Social security payments are a monetary **transfer**. Wages are not: the recipient provides labour services in exchange for wages. An example of a **transfer in kind** is food stamps, given to the poor to buy food. The stamps must be spent on food, not beer, films or petrol. We now use our model of consumer choice to ask whether an in-kind transfer payment is preferred by the consumer to a cash transfer payment of the same monetary value.

> A **transfer payment** is a payment, usually by the government, for which no corresponding service is provided by the recipient. A **transfer in kind** is the gift of a good or service.

The consumer has £100 to spend on food or films, each costing £10 per unit. Figure 5.20 shows the budget line *AF*. Suppose the government issues the consumer with stamps worth 4 food units. For any point on the old budget line *AF*, the consumer can have 4 more units of food from the food stamps. Moving horizontally to the right by 4 food units, the new budget line is *BF'*. Since food stamps cannot buy films, the new budget line is *ABF'*. The consumer can still get at most 10 films.

Suppose the consumer originally chose *e* on the budget line *AF*. Since both goods are normal, the shift in the budget line to *ABF'* – effectively a rise in income – makes the consumer choose a point to the north-east of *e*, as she would have done had the transfer been in cash.

When food costs £10 per unit, the cash equivalent of 4 food units is £40, shifting the budget line to *A'F'*. Thus, if the consumer begins at *e*, it makes no difference if the transfer is in cash or in kind.

Suppose, however, that the consumer begins at *e'*. With a cash payment, the consumer might move to point *c* on the budget line *A'F'*. The transfer in kind, by restricting the consumer to the budget line *ABF'*, prevents her reaching the preferred point *c*. Instead she moves, say, to the feasible point *B*. *B* must yield the consumer less utility than *c*: when she got a cash payment and could choose either point, *c* was preferred to *B*.

Cash transfers let consumers spend the extra income in any way that they wish. Transfers in kind may limit a consumer's options. Where they do, the increase in consumer utility is less than under a cash transfer of the same monetary value.

Yet transfers in kind are politically popular. The electorate wants to know that taxes are being wisely spent. Some people argue that the poor really do not know how to spend their money wisely and may spend cash transfers on 'undesirable' goods such as alcohol or gambling rather than on 'desirable' goods such as food or housing.

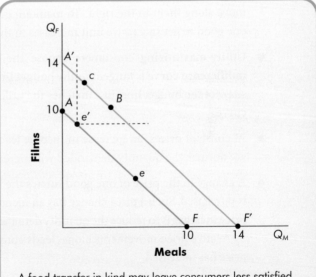

A food transfer in kind may leave consumers less satisfied than a cash transfer of the same value. A consumer at *e'* might wish to spend less than the full allowance on food, moving to *c*. The budget line is *A'BF'* under a cash transfer. The in-kind transfer restricts the budget line to *ABF'*.

Figure 5.20 *Transfers in cash and in kind*

Do people act in their own best interests? This issue is not merely one of economics but also of philosophy, involving wider questions such as liberty and paternalism. In so far as people can judge their own self-interest, economic analysis is clear: people are better off, or at least no worse off, if they get transfers in cash rather than in kind.

Summary

- Given the **budget constraint**, the theory of demand assumes a consumer seeks to reach the **maximum possible level of utility**.

- The **budget line** shows the maximum affordable quantity of one good for each given quantity of the other good. The position of the budget line is determined by income and prices alone. Its slope reflects only relative prices.

- Because the **consumer prefers more to less**, she will always select a point on the budget line. The consumer has a problem of choice. Along the budget line, more of one good can be obtained only by sacrificing some of the other good.

- **Consumer tastes** can be represented by a map of non-intersecting **indifference curves**. Along each indifference curve, utility is constant. Higher indifference curves are preferred to lower indifference curves. Since the consumer prefers more to less, indifference curves must slope downwards. To preserve a given level of utility, increases in the quantity of one good must be offset by reductions in the quantity of the other good.

- Indifference curves exhibit a **diminishing marginal rate of substitution**. Their slope is flatter as we move along them to the right. To maintain given utility, consumers sacrifice ever-smaller amounts of one good to get successive unit increases in the amount of the other good.

- **Utility-maximizing** consumers choose the consumption bundle at which the highest reachable **indifference curve is tangent to the budget line**. At this point, the market trade-off between goods, the slope of the budget line, just matches the utility trade-off between goods, the slope of the indifference curve.

- At constant prices, an increase in income leads to a parallel outward shift in the budget line. If goods are normal, the quantity demanded will increase.

- A change in the price of one good rotates the budget line around the point at which none of that good is purchased. Such a price change has an income effect and a substitution effect. The **income effect of a price increase** is to reduce the quantity demanded for all normal goods. The **substitution effect**, induced by relative price movements alone, leads consumers to substitute away from the good whose relative price has increased.

- In a two-good world, goods must be substitutes. The substitution effect is unambiguous. With many goods, the pure substitution effect of a price increase also reduces demand for goods that are complementary to the good whose price has risen.

- A rise in the price of a normal good must lower its quantity demanded. For inferior goods, the income effect operates in the opposite direction but rarely seems to dominate the substitution effect. Demand curves slope downwards.

- The **market demand curve** is the horizontal sum of individual demand curves, at each price adding together the individual quantities demanded.

- **Consumers prefer to receive transfers in cash** rather than in kind, if the two transfers have the same monetary value. A transfer in kind may restrict the choices a consumer can make.

Review questions

connect

1. A consumer's income is £50. Food costs £5 per unit and films cost £2 per unit. (a) Draw the budget line. Pick a point *e* as the chosen initial consumption bundle. (b) The price of food falls to £2.50. Draw the new budget line. What can be said about the new consumption point *e'* if both goods are normal? (c) The price of films also falls to £1. Draw the new budget line and show the chosen point *e'*. (d) How does *e'* differ from *e*? Why?

EASY

2. The own-price elasticity of demand for food is negative. The demand for food is inelastic. A higher food price raises spending on food. Higher food prices imply less is spent on all other goods. The quantity demanded of each of these other goods falls. Discuss each statement. Are they all correct?

3. Suppose films are normal goods but transport is an inferior good. How do the quantities demanded for the two goods change when income increases? Draw the old and new budget lines and illustrate the change in demand.

4. Suppose Glaswegians have a given income and like weekend trips to the Highlands, a three-hour drive. (a) If the price of petrol doubles, what is the effect on the demand for trips to the Highlands? Discuss both income and substitution effects. (b) Use a demand and supply diagram to show what happens to the price of Highland hotel rooms.

5. *True or false* On a given indifference curve, the marginal rate of substitution is *always* decreasing.

6. *Common fallacies* Why are these statements wrong? (a) Since consumers do not know about indifference curves or budget lines, they cannot choose the point on the budget line tangent to the highest possible indifference curve. (b) Inflation must reduce demand since prices are higher and goods are more expensive.

7. Frank derives utility from two goods, X and Y, that is given by $U = XY$. Find the indifference curves of Frank, when utility is 10, 20 and 30. Plot those indifference curves. How should Frank compare the following two bundles: $(X = 1, Y = 10)$ and $(X = 5, Y = 2)$?

8. Suppose that Frank has an income of £50, the unit price of X is $p_X = £2$ and the unit price of Y is $p_Y = £1$. Write down the budget constraint for Frank. Knowing that the marginal rate of substitution (in absolute value) between X and Y is $MRS = X/Y$, find the optimal bundle that Frank should consume. (*Hint:* in the optimal bundle the absolute value of the MRS must be equal to the absolute value of the slope of the budget constraint. Moreover, the budget constraint must be satisfied. You need to solve a system of two equations in two variables, X and Y.)

MEDIUM

9. Consider a consumer who consumes only two goods: peas and beans. She has an income of £10, the price of beans is 20p (= £0.2) while the price of peas is 40p (= £0.4).

(a) Suppose that the consumer consumes 30 kg of beans. Assuming that she spends all her income, how many kg of peas is she going to consume?

(b) Assume that the price of peas falls from 40p to 20p. Assuming that the consumer still consumes 30 kg of beans, find the new quantity of peas.

(c) After the decrease in the price of peas to 20p, assume that the consumer is just as well off as she was in (a) if she has an income of £7.60. However, with that income and the new price of peas, she would have consumed 20 kg of beans. Find the quantity of peas she would have consumed in this case.

(d) Find the substitution effect due to the decrease in the price of peas that is the difference between The solution in (c) and the solution in (a).

(e) Find the income effect that is the difference between the solution in (b) and the solution in (c).

10 Suppose that Carl cannot tell the differences between a pack of British and a pack of Danish bacon. In a graph with British bacon on the vertical axis, plot some of Carl's indifference curves for British and Danish bacon. Suppose that Carl has an income of £20. The price of Danish bacon is £2 per pack, while the price of British bacon is £4 per pack. In the same graph where you drew the indifference curves, draw Carl's budget constraint and show his optimal bundle choice.

11 You begin with 5 coconuts and 5 fish. You can get extra fish by sacrificing 2 coconuts for each extra fish, or get extra coconuts by sacrificing 1 fish for each extra coconut. (a) Draw your budget line. (b) Draw an indifference map. (c) Where is it likely that you will choose to be? (d) Suppose there is a small change in the number of fish you can swap for an extra coconut – is your behaviour likely to change?

12 You can invest in a safe asset or in a risky asset or in both. The safe asset has a guaranteed return of 3 per cent a year. The risky asset has an expected return of 4 per cent but it could be as much as 8 per cent or as little as 0 per cent. You decide to have some of your wealth in each asset. Now the expected return on the risky asset rises to 5 per cent; it could be as high as 9 per cent or as low as 1 per cent. Given the increase in the expected return on the risky asset, do you invest more of your wealth in the risky asset?

13 Essay question   We observe a person behaving differently in apparently similar situations. Either the situations were not similar or the person is 'irrational'. Which approach would an economist take? Why? Is it realistic to think that we account for rational behaviour in every situation?

For solutions to these questions contact your lecturer.

Consumer choice with measurable utility

Our theory of consumer choice assumed that consumers can rank different bundles according to the utility or satisfaction they give. Saying bundle *A* gives more utility than bundle *B* just means the consumer prefers *A* to *B*. We do not need to know *by how much A* is preferred to *B*. Higher indifference curves are better. We do not need to know how much better.

Nineteenth-century economists believed utility levels could actually be measured, as if each consumer had a *utility meter* measuring his happiness. The further to the right the needle on his utility meter, the happier he was. The units on this meter were traditionally marked off in *utils*. Nowadays, this seems a bit strange: are you 2.9 times as happy if you get an extra week's holiday?

Even so, analysis of consumer choice when utility *is* measurable is quite interesting, even though we derived all the main propositions in the text without this extra assumption. The (robot-like) individual whose utility is exactly calibrated in utils we shall call Fred.

Fred goes to rock concerts and eats hamburgers. For a given consumption of one of these goods, he prefers more of the other to less. His utility goes up. If Fred gets 67 utils of utility from consuming 10 hamburgers and 1 rock concert, and 70 utils from 11 hamburgers but still 1 rock concert, his **marginal utility** from the eleventh hamburger is (70 − 67 =) 3 utils.

> The **marginal utility** of a good is the increase in total utility obtained by consuming one more unit of that good, for given consumption of other goods.
>
> A consumer has **diminishing marginal utility** from a good if each extra unit consumed, holding constant consumption of other goods, adds successively less to total utility.

Fred was not very hungry. He had 10 hamburgers at his only concert. He didn't get much from an eleventh hamburger, only an extra 3 utils. In contrast, if Fred had only 2 hamburgers at one concert (giving him, say, 20 utils), he might rather have enjoyed a third hamburger (taking his utils to, say, 27). The marginal utility of that extra hamburger is (27 − 20 =) 7 utils. Fred's tastes obey the law of **diminishing marginal utility**.

Figure 5.A1 plots Fred's marginal utility of hamburgers. He gets fewer *extra* utils from extra consumption of hamburgers, the more he is already consuming: his marginal utility schedule *MU* slopes down.

Fred has a given income to spend. Once we know the prices of rock concerts and hamburgers, we can work out his budget line. How does Fred choose the affordable point on this line at which to consume? He maximizes his utility.

The price of hamburgers in pounds is P_H and the price of concerts is P_C. If MU_H is Fred's marginal utility from another hamburger, he gets an extra MU_H/P_H utils for each extra pound spent on hamburgers and an extra MU_C/P_C utils for each extra pound spent on concerts.

Suppose MU_H/P_H exceeds MU_C/P_C. An extra pound spent on hamburgers raises Fred's utility more than does an extra pound spent on concerts. If Fred spends £1 more on hamburgers but £1 less on concerts, his total utils rise: he gains more from hamburgers than he loses from concerts. He can increase utility *without spending more*. He will always want to transfer spending towards the good that yields more marginal utility

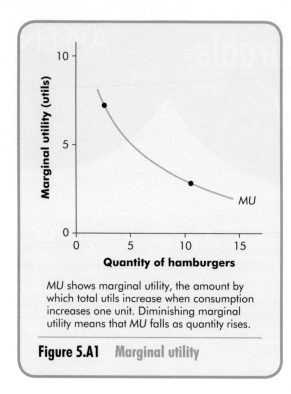

MU shows marginal utility, the amount by which total utils increase when consumption increases one unit. Diminishing marginal utility means that MU falls as quantity rises.

Figure 5.A1   *Marginal utility*

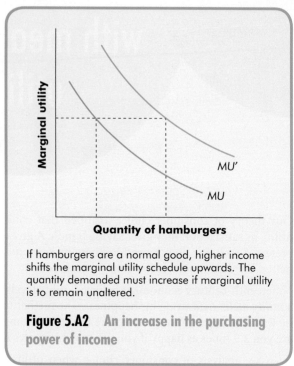

If hamburgers are a normal good, higher income shifts the marginal utility schedule upwards. The quantity demanded must increase if marginal utility is to remain unaltered.

Figure 5.A2   *An increase in the purchasing power of income*

per pound spent. To maximize utility, Fred spends all his income (he is on, not inside, his budget line) and adjusts his spending between hamburgers and concerts until

$$MU_H/P_H = MU_C/P_C \tag{A1}$$

When this holds, Fred cannot rearrange the division of his total spending to increase his utility.[6] Fred maximizes utility by choosing the consumption bundle, on the budget line, at which the ratio of marginal utility to price is the same for every good.

Deriving demand curves

Suppose the price of hamburgers P_H falls. For given hamburger consumption, MU_H/P_H rises, and now exceeds MU_C/P_C for concerts, violating equation (A1). To maximize utility, Fred changes the quantities he demands.

If Fred buys *more* hamburgers when the price *falls*, the law of diminishing marginal utility means that MU_H falls as Fred buys more hamburgers. MU_H/P_H moves towards MU_C/P_C, as required by equation (A1). This is the *substitution effect* of the relative change in the price of hamburgers and concerts. On its own, the substitution effect suggests that *demand curves slope down*: when the price of hamburgers falls, the quantity demanded increases.

However, cheaper hamburger prices also raise the purchasing power of Fred's money income. This affects Fred's marginal utility. If hamburgers are a normal good, Fred buys more when the purchasing power of his income rises. Higher income shifts Fred's marginal utility schedule up in Figure 5.A2.

---

6   Equation (A1) implies $MU_H/MU_C = P_H/P_C$. Multiplying both sides by −1, the right-hand side is the slope of the budget line, which depends only on relative prices. The left-hand side is the marginal rate of substitution: if the marginal utility of one hamburger is 2 and of one concert is 4, then $-MU_H/MU_C = -1/2$. One hamburger can be swapped for 1/2 a concert without altering total utility, precisely what the marginal rate of substitution measures. Equation (A1) implies that the slope of the indifference curve, the marginal rate of substitution, equals the slope of the budget line. This is the tangency condition of the test, derived without using measurable utility!

> ### CONCEPT 5.3 — Marginal utility and the water–diamond paradox
>
> Nineteenth-century economists wondered why the price of water, essential for survival, was so much lower than that for decorative diamonds. One answer is that diamonds are scarcer than water. Yet consumers clearly get more total utility from water (without it, they die) than from diamonds. The concept of marginal utility solves the problem.
>
> Equation (A1) tells us that consumers keep buying a good until the ratio of its *marginal* utility to price equals that for other goods. *At the margin*, the last litre of water we drink or use in the shower gives very little extra utility. At the margin, the last diamond still makes a big difference. People are willing to pay more for extra diamonds than for extra water.
>
> In terms of a figure like Figure 5.A1, the marginal utility schedule *MU* is *very* high for the first few drops of water. Not dying is worth lots of utils. But most of us are a long way down this schedule, using lots of water to the point where its marginal value to us is low.

This *income effect* means that Fred finds that MU_H/P_H rises not only because P_H falls but also because MU_H rises at any particular level of hamburger consumption. Fred buys even more hamburgers, sliding down the higher marginal utility schedule, thereby reducing the marginal utility of hamburgers MU_H, until MU_H/P_H again equals MU_C/P_C. Thus for normal goods the income effect reinforces the substitution effect. Demand curves must slope down.

Suppose hamburgers are an inferior good. Figure 5.A2 then shows a downward shift in the MU_H schedule when the purchasing power of Fred's income increases. At his original consumption bundle, MU_H may fall by more than the fall in P_H, the price of hamburgers. If so, Fred has to *reduce* his hamburger consumption to increase its marginal utility and restore MU_H/P_H to equality with MU_C/P_C as utility maximization requires.

For inferior goods, the income effect goes in the opposite direction to the substitution effect. If the income effect is big enough, it could win out. Lower hamburger prices then reduce the quantity of hamburgers demanded. Demand curves slope upwards. As we discuss in the text, such Giffen goods are rare. It is safe to assume that demand curves slope down in practice.

Modern economists are pretty sniffy about measurable utility, preferring the more general indifference curve analysis used in the text. But indifference curves are tricky the first time you meet them. You need to practise using them to become comfortable with them. Measurable utility, and the simple idea of diminishing marginal utility, allows an easier introduction to the basic properties of demand curves and consumer choice developed in this chapter.

CHAPTER 6

Introducing supply decisions

Learning Outcomes

By the end of this chapter, you should understand:

1. the legal forms in which businesses are owned and run
2. revenue, cost, profit and cash flow
3. accounts for flows and for stocks
4. economic and accounting definitions of cost
5. whether a firm chooses output to maximize profits
6. how this choice reflects marginal cost and marginal revenue

Having analysed demand, we turn now to supply. How do firms decide how much to produce and offer for sale? Can a single theory of supply describe the behaviour of different producers, from giant companies such as Microsoft to the self-employed ice cream vendor with a van?

For each possible output level a firm needs to calculate what it *costs* to make this output and how much *revenue* is earned by selling it. At each output, production costs depend on technology, which in turn determines the inputs needed, and on the input prices that the firm faces. Sales revenue depends on the demand curve faced by the firm. The demand curve determines the price for which any output quantity can be sold and thus the revenue the firm earns.

Profits are the excess of revenues over costs. The key to the theory of supply is the assumption that all firms are rational and so they aim to make as much profit as possible. By examining how revenues and costs change with the level of output produced and sold, the firm chooses the output that maximizes its profits. To understand supply decisions, we then need to analyse what determines revenues and costs.

The assumption of profit maximization is the cornerstone of the theory of supply. We conclude by discussing its plausibility and examine alternative views of what firms' aims might be.

6.1 Business organization

Businesses are self-employed sole traders, partnerships or companies. Sole traders, the commonest type of business organization, operate on a small scale. Partnerships are larger scale; companies are larger still.

A **sole trader** gets the revenue of the business and is responsible for any losses it makes. If he cannot meet these losses, he becomes personally bankrupt. His remaining assets, such as his house, are sold and the money shared out among the creditors.

> A **sole trader** is a business owned by a single individual.
>
> A **partnership** is a business jointly owned by two or more people, sharing the profits and jointly responsible for any losses.

If the business prospers, a sole trader may need money to expand. One way is to bring in new partners, who inject money in exchange for a share of the subsequent profits. **Partnerships** usually have *unlimited liability*. Like sole traders, partners are personally liable for the firm's losses, however large. Firms where trust is involved – solicitors or accountants – are often partnerships. Customers see that the people running the business are willing to put their own wealth behind the firm's obligations.

Any business needs money to start it up and finance its growth. Firms of lawyers, doctors or accountants, businesses relying on human expertise, need relatively little money for such purposes. The necessary funds can be raised from the partners and, possibly, by a bank loan. Businesses requiring large initial expenditure on machinery need much larger initial funds. It is too complicated to have a huge number of partners. Instead, it makes sense to form a company.

Unlike a partnership, a **company** has a legal existence distinct from that of its owners. Ownership is divided among shareholders. The original shareholders may now have sold shares of the profits to outsiders. By selling entitlements to share in the profits, the business can raise new funds.

> A **company** is an organization legally allowed to produce and trade.
>
> Shareholders of a company have **limited liability**. The most they can lose is the money they spent buying shares.

Shareholders earn a return in two ways. First, the company makes regular *dividend* payments, paying out to shareholders that part of the profits that the firm does not wish to reinvest in the business. Second, the shareholders may make *capital gains* (or losses). If you buy Microsoft shares for a value of £1000 but then people decide Microsoft profits and dividends will be unexpectedly high, the Microsoft shares will increase their market value and you may be able to resell the shares for £1200 for example, making a capital gain of £200. Unlike sole traders and partners, shareholders cannot be forced to sell their personal possessions if the business goes bust – they have **limited liability**. At worst, the shares become worthless.

Companies are run by boards of directors who submit an annual report to the shareholders, who can vote to sack the directors if it seems that other directors could do better. Companies are the main form of organization of big businesses.

6.2 A firm's accounts

Firms report two sets of accounts, one for **stocks** and one for **flows**.

The water *flowing* out of a tap is different per second and per minute. The measure needs a time interval to make sense of it. The *stock* of water in the basin at any instant is a number of litres, with no time dimension. A firm reports profit-and-loss accounts per year (*flow* accounts) and a balance sheet showing assets and liabilities at a point in time (*stock* accounts). The two are related, as they are for the basin of water. The inflow from the tap changes the stock of water over time, even though the stock is in litres at each point in time. We begin with flow accounts.

> **Stocks** are measured at a given point in time; **flows** are corresponding measures during a period of time.

Flow accounts

These ideas are simple, but the calculation of **revenue**, **cost** and **profit** for a large firm is tricky. Otherwise we would not need so many accountants. Here is a simple example.

Rent-a-Person (R-a-P) is a firm that hires people whom it then rents out to other firms that need temporary workers. R-a-P charges £10 an hour per worker but

> **Revenue** is what the firm earns from selling goods or services in a given period, **cost** is the expense incurred in production in that period and **profit** is revenue minus cost.

pays its workers only £7 an hour. During 2009 it rented 100 000 hours of labour. Business expenses, including leasing an office, buying advertising space and paying telephone bills, were £200 000. Table 6.1 shows the *income statement* or *profit-and-loss account* for 2009. Profits before tax were £100 000. Tax was £25 000. R-a-P's after-tax profits were £75 000. Now for the complications.

Unpaid bills

People do not always pay bills on time. At the end of 2009, R-a-P has unpaid bills for workers hired to other firms during the year. Nor has it yet paid its own telephone bill for December. From an economic viewpoint, the right definition of revenues and costs relates to the activities during the year whether or not payments have yet been made.

Actual receipts and payments thus may differ from economic revenue and cost. Profitable firms may still have a poor **cash flow**, for example when customers are slow to pay.

Table 6.1   R-a-P income statement, year to 31 December 2009

Revenue		
100 000 hours @ £10		£1 000 000
Cost		
Wages	£700 000	
Adverts	£50 000	
Office rent	£50 000	
Other expenses	£100 000	
		–£900 000
Pre-tax profit		£100 000
Tax		£25 000
Post-tax profit		£75 000

> A firm's **cash flow** is the net amount of money actually received during the period.
>
> **Physical capital** is machinery, equipment and buildings used in production.

Capital and depreciation

R-a-P owns little **physical capital**. Instead, it leases office space, typewriters and desks. However, many firms do buy physical capital. Economists use 'capital' to denote goods not entirely used up in the production process during the period. Buildings and lorries are capital, to be used again in the next year. Electricity is not capital: purchases in 2009 do not survive into 2010. Economists also use 'durable goods' or 'physical assets' to describe capital goods.

How is the cost of a capital good treated in calculating profit and cost? It is the cost of *using* rather than *buying* capital equipment that is part of the firm's costs within the year. If R-a-P leases all its capital equipment, its costs include merely the rentals paid in leasing capital goods.

Suppose R-a-P buys 8 computers in January for £1000 each. £8000 is not the cost of computers in calculating costs and profits for that year. Rather, the cost is the fall in value of the computers over the year. Suppose wear-and-tear and obsolescence reduce the value of a computer by £300 during the year. Part of the economic cost using 8 computers over the year is the £2400 by which they depreciate during the year.

> **Depreciation** is the loss in value of a capital good during the period.

Depreciation makes economic profit and cash flow differ. When a capital good is first bought there is a large cash outflow, much larger than the depreciation cost of using the good in the first year. Profits may be high but cash flow low. In later years, the firm makes no further cash outlay, having already paid for the capital goods, but must still calculate depreciation as an economic cost since the resale value of goods falls steadily. Cash flow is now higher than economic profit.

Treating depreciation, not the purchase price, as the true economic cost spreads the initial cost over the life of the capital goods but that is not why we calculate cost in this way. R-a-P could have sold its computers for £5600 after a year, restricting its costs to £2400. Since it chose to keep them for reuse in the next year, the latter strategy is even more profitable. Hence the true economic cost of using the computers in the first year is at most £2400.

Inventories

> **Inventories** are goods held in stock by the firm for future sales.

If production is instantaneous, firms can produce to meet orders as they arise. In fact, production takes time. Firms hold inventories to meet future demand.

Suppose at the start of 2009 Ford has a stock of 50 000 cars completed and available for sale. In 2009 it makes 1 million new cars and sells 950 000. By December its stock of finished cars is 100 000. What about profit? Revenue arises from selling 950 000 cars. Should cost reflect sales of 950 000 cars or the 1 million actually made?

Economic costs relate to the 950 000 cars actually sold. The 50 000 cars added to stocks are capital the firm made for itself, available for sale in the next period. There was a cash outflow to pay for the manufacture of 1 million cars but part of this cash outflow was used to buy inventories that will provide cash revenue the following year without any new cash outlay on production.

Borrowing

Firms usually borrow to finance their set-up and expansion costs, buying capital goods, solicitors' fees for the paperwork in registering the company, and so on. There is interest to be paid on the money borrowed. This interest is part of the cost of doing business and should be counted as part of the costs.

Stock accounts: the balance sheet

The income statement in Table 6.1 shows flows *in a given year*. We can also examine the firm at *a point in time*, the result of all its past trading operations. The *balance sheet* lists the assets the firm owns and the liabilities for which it is responsible at a point in time. Table 6.2 shows the balance sheet for Snark International on 31 December 2009.

Snark's assets are cash in the bank, money owed by its customers (accounts receivable), inventories in its warehouses and its factory (original cost £500 000, now worth only £330 000 because of depreciation). The total value of Snark assets is £540 000.

> A firm's **net worth** is the assets it owns minus the liabilities it owes.

Snark's liabilities are bills it has yet to pay, the mortgage on its factory and a bank loan for short-term cash needs. Its total liabilities (debts) are £300 000. The **net worth** of Snark International is £240 000, its assets minus its liabilities.

You make a takeover bid for Snark. Should you bid £240 000, its net worth? Probably more. Snark is a live company with good prospects and a proven record. You get not merely its physical and financial assets

Table 6.2 Snark's balance sheet at 31 December 2009

Assets	£000s	Liabilities	£000s
Cash	40	Accounts payable	90
Accounts receivable	70	Mortgage	150
Inventories	100	Bank loan	60
Factory (bought for 500)	330	**Total liabilities**	**300**
		Net worth	240
Total	540		540

minus liabilities but also its reputation, customer loyalty and a host of intangibles that economists call *goodwill*. If Snark is a sound company, bid more than £240 000. Alternatively, you may think Snark's accountants undervalued the resale value of its assets. If you can buy Snark for £240 000, you may make a profit by selling off the separate pieces of capital, a practice known as 'asset-stripping'.

CASE 6.1

The anatomy of a crisis: reading the balance sheet of Northern Rock

Looking carefully at the balance sheet of companies is a job for accountants and not for economists. Nevertheless, we can obtain some interesting economic insights by looking at the balance sheet of particular companies. Consider the case of Nothern Rock. Northern Rock became famous in September 2007 as the first bank in the UK to be heavily hit by the credit crunch. Northern Rock specialized in property finance activities, especially residential mortgage.

In the table we report a simplified version (where some of the categories have been combined together and figures rounded to the nearest billion pounds) of the balance sheet of Northern Rock at the end of two different years, 2006 and 2007.

		2006	2007
Assets	Loans and advances to banks	6	1
	Loans and advances to customers	87	99
	Investment securities	6	6
	Other assets	2	3
	Total assets	**101**	**109**
Liabilities	Loans from central bank	0	28
	Customer accounts	27	12
	Mortgage-backed securities	40	43
	Other securities	24	19
	Other liabilities	7	4
	Equity	3	3
	Total liabilities	**101**	**109**

Without going into detail, we can say that between 2006 and 2007 Northern Rock issued about 12 billion loans and advances to customers (mortgages). How could Northern Rock provide these loans to borrowers? By borrowing from other institutions and from the market in the following forms: by using customer accounts, by issuing mortgage-backed securities and by other securities. However, in 2007, Northern Rock was not able to obtain the resources necessary to finance the loans it made. The credit crunch hit the US in the summer of 2007 and spread rapidly to other economies. Raising money became more difficult for Northern Rock and, on 12 September 2007, it asked for an emergency loan from the Bank of England

Picture: Cate Gillon | Getty Images

(the central bank of the UK) for £28 million. This was the signal that things were going pretty poorly for Northern Rock, and indeed, on 14 September 2007 we witnessed the first bank run in the UK for over 100 years, with bank customers queuing in front of the branches to close their accounts.

Source: Northern Rock plc Annual Report and Accounts 2007.

Earnings

When a firm makes profits after tax, it can pay them out to shareholders as dividends, or keep them in the firm as retained earnings. **Retained earnings** affect the balance sheet. If kept as cash or used to purchase new equipment, they increase assets. Alternatively, they may reduce the firm's liabilities, by repaying the bank loan. Either way, the firm's net worth increases.

> **Retained earnings** are the part of after-tax profits ploughed back into the business.

Opportunity cost and accounting costs

The income statement and the balance sheet of a company provide two useful guides to how a firm is doing. But economists and accountants take different views of cost and profit. An accountant is interested in tracking the actual receipts and payments of a company. An economist is interested in how revenue and cost affect the firm's supply decision, the allocation of resources to particular activities. Accounting methods can mislead in two ways.

Economists identify the cost of using a resource not as the payment actually made but as its **opportunity cost**. To show that this is the right measure of costs, given the questions economists study, we provide two examples.

> **Opportunity cost** is the amount lost by not using a resource (labour, capital) in its best alternative use.

If you run your own firm you should take into account the cost of your labour time in the firm. You might draw up an income statement such as Table 6.1, find that profits are £20 000 a year and conclude that the firm is a good thing. This conclusion neglects the opportunity cost of your time. If you could have earned £25 000 a year working for someone else, being self-employed is losing you £5000 a year despite an accounting profit of £20 000. To understand the incentives that the market provides to guide people towards particular jobs, we must use the economic concept of opportunity cost, not the accounting concept of actual payments.

The second place where opportunity cost must be counted is with respect to capital. You put up the money to start the business. Accounting profits ignore the use of owned (as opposed to borrowed) financial capital. But this money could have been deposited in an interest-bearing bank account or used to buy shares in other firms. The opportunity cost of that money is part of the *economic* costs of the business but not its accounting costs. If it could earn 5 per cent elsewhere, the opportunity cost of your funds is 5 per cent times the money you put in. If, after deducting this cost and the true cost of your time, the business still makes a profit, economists call this **supernormal profit**.

> **Supernormal profit** is pure economic profit and measures all economic costs properly.

Supernormal profits are the true indicator of how well you are doing by tying up your time and funds in the business. Supernormal profits (or losses), not accounting profits (or losses), are the incentive to shift resources into (or out of) a business.

CONCEPT 6.1

Economic vs accounting profits

The inclusion of opportunity costs in economic profits creates an important distinction from the concept of accounting profits. To stress this distinction further, suppose you start your own firm. Suppose that your total revenues are £60 000 and you have explicit costs of £40 000 (for example, wage payments to your workers, the cost of raw materials, etc.). According to those numbers, you should obtain an accounting profit of £20 000.

However, suppose that your best alternative was to work for someone else and receive a wage of £25 000. Then your firm, according to an economist, is running at a loss of £5000.

The £25 000 you could have earned somewhere else represents the opportunity cost of your time working in your firm and should be included in the total costs. This opportunity cost enters the economic profits but not the accounting profits.

According to accounting profits, your firm is profitable. According to economic profits, your firm is not profitable. So, in our definition of economic profits we also include in the total costs the remuneration that the owner of the firm obtains by running the firm.

This remuneration is called *normal profit* and it is included in the total cost of our economic profit definition. This is very important because, in many cases, we will say that firms earn zero profits. Zero profit for us will mean zero economic profits. It means that remuneration of the owner is exactly equal to the opportunity cost of running the firm. In our example, suppose that the total revenues were £65 000. The opportunity cost is still £25 000 and the explicit costs are £40 000. In this case, the economic profits are zero.

This does not mean that the owner of the firm gets nothing from his business. He will get a positive remuneration (£25 000) but that remuneration is exactly equal to remuneration he could have obtained from his best alternative.

6.3 Firms and profit maximization

Economists assume that firms choose how much to produce in order to *maximize profits*. Some economists and business executives question this assumption. For example, a sole owner may prefer to work for himself even if he could earn more in total by working somewhere else. His business decisions reflect maximization of his total job satisfaction not merely his monetary profit.

Ownership and control

A more significant reason to question profit maximization comes from considering the case of large firms. A large firm is run not by its owners but by a salaried board of directors. The directors are the experts with the relevant information on whether the firm is well managed or not. At the annual meeting, shareholders may dismiss the board; doing so is rare, however.

Economists call this a separation of ownership and control. Although shareholders want the maximum possible profit from the firm's activity, the directors who actually make the decisions can pursue different objectives. Do directors have an incentive to act other than in the interests of the shareholders?

Directors' salaries are usually higher, the larger the firm. Directors may aim for size and growth rather than the maximum possible profit, spending large sums on costly advertisements to boost sales.

> A principal or owner may delegate decisions to an agent. If it is costly for the principal to monitor the agent, the agent has inside information about its own performance, causing a **principal–agent problem**.

The separation of ownership and control in companies leads to what economists call a **principal–agent problem**. The agents (here, the directors) are tempted to act in their own interests rather than those of their principals (the shareholders).

Nevertheless, there are two reasons why the aim of profit maximization is a good place to start, including for large firms. Even if the shareholders cannot recognize that profits are lower than they might be, other firms with experience in the industry may catch on faster. If profits are low, share prices will be low. By mounting a takeover, another company can buy the shares cheaply, sack the existing managers, restore profit-maximizing policies and make a handsome capital gain as the share price rises once the stock market sees the improvement in profits. Fear of takeover may induce directors to try to maximize profits.

Moreover, aware of the scope for directors' discretion, shareholders try to ensure that the interests of directors and shareholders coincide. By giving senior directors big bonuses tied to profitability or share performance – a small cost when spread over many shareholders but a major incentive for the existing management – shareholders try to make senior management care about profits as much as shareholders do.

The assumption that firms try to maximize profits is more robust than might first be imagined. Before using it to develop the theory of supply, we discuss the stock market in more detail.

6.4 Corporate finance and corporate control

Sources of finance include (a) borrowing from banks, (b) borrowing by selling pieces of paper (corporate bonds) whereby the firm promises to pay interest for a specified period and then repay the debt, and (c) using the stock market for selling new shares in the firm. Different countries have very different systems of **corporate finance**.

> **Corporate finance** refers to how firms finance their activities.

The US and the UK have market-based or outsider systems, relying on active stock markets trading existing shares and debt, and available to issue new shares and debt. Japan and much of continental Europe, notably Germany, have traditionally had an insider system, in which financial markets play only a small role. German companies got long-term loans from banks, who then sat on company boards with access to inside information about how the firm was doing.

Finance or control?

Large firms finance most of their new investment from their own retained profits. Roughly 90 per cent of UK corporate investment is financed in this way; less than 7 per cent comes from sales of new shares on the stock market. The key difference in the two systems of corporate finance lies not in the ease with which they provide firms with finance but in the way they award control rights to those providing that finance.

In the bank-based insider system, representatives of the bank sit on the firm's board, using this inside position to press for changes when mistakes are made. The market-based system entails a smaller role for banks and a larger role for stock markets and debt markets. Failure to meet interest payments on debt usually gives

> **Corporate control** refers to who controls the firm in different situations.

debt-holders the right to make the firm bankrupt, a radical transfer of **corporate control** in which the existing management rarely survives. Similarly, the existence of publicly quoted shares raises the possibility of a stock market takeover in which a new management team effectively buys control on the open market. Outsider market-based systems of corporate finance thus become markets for corporate control itself.

Hostile takeovers

CONCEPT 6.2

A hostile takeover is an acquisition in which the firm being purchased does not want to be purchased, or does not want to be purchased by the particular buyer making the bid. How is it possible to buy something that is not for sale? Hostile takeovers only work with publicly traded firms. Those are firms that have issued stock that can be bought and sold on public stock markets. The stock of a firm is divided into shares. If a firm has issued 100 shares and you buy 51 of them, then you own a majority and in many respects you now control that firm. This is a possible way for a hostile takeover to take place. The buyer can gain control by acquiring in the market the majority of shares from the existing shareholders of the target firm.

In Germany, hostile takeovers have traditionally been rare. In contrast, many UK takeovers are hostile bids uninvited by existing managers. Some economists see hostile bids as a vital force for efficiency. The threat of hostile takeovers deters managers from departing too far from the profit-maximizing policies that shareholders want. Slack management leads to low profits, depressed share prices and opportunities for takeover raiders to buy the company cheaply. The threat of takeover provides a discipline that helps overcome the principal–agent problem.

Obviously not all hostile takeovers end successfully, since the existing shareholders may refuse the offer made by the buyer. An example of an unsuccessful takeover is the recent attempt by Microsoft to gain control of Yahoo! On 1 February 2008, Microsoft made an unsolicited bid to purchase Yahoo! This offer was rejected on 10 February and on 3 May Microsoft finally withdrew the offer.

6.5 The firm's supply decision

Firms produce goods and services that are sold in markets. We want to understand how a firm decides how much to produce of a given good or service.

Suppose a firm makes spoons. The firm needs to decide how many spoons to produce and sell. The first thing that the firm should consider is how costly it is to produce the spoons. Some ways to make spoons use lots of labour and few machines, other ways use many machines but little labour. The firm knows different techniques for making spoons and the cost of hiring inputs – the wage rate for workers and rental for leasing a machine. The second thing that the firm must consider is the demand condition. The firm knows its demand curve. This is the demand curve derived from all the customers who want to buy the spoons made by that particular firm. If the firm knows the demand curve it faces, then it knows its revenue from selling different quantities of spoons at different prices.

Knowing costs and revenues generated by different amounts of spoons produced, the firm is able to find the profit generated by those amounts, since profit is simply revenues minus costs.

The firm chooses the level of output (here, the number of spoons produced and then sold in the market) in order to maximize its profits. Changing the level of output produced affects both the costs of production and the revenues from sales. Costs and demand conditions jointly determine the output choice of a profit-maximizing firm.

Cost minimization

Closely related to the idea of profit maximization is the concept of cost minimization. Indeed, profit maximization and cost minimization can be seen as two equivalent concepts. A profit-maximizing firm certainly wants to make its chosen output level at the minimum cost possible. By producing the same output at lower cost, it could increase profits. Thus a profit-maximizing firm must produce its chosen output as cheaply as possible.

Total cost

Knowing the available production methods and the costs of hiring workers and machines, the firm calculates the least cost at which each output can be made. It is not worth using many machines to make only a few spoons; to make more spoons, it makes sense to use more machines.

Table 6.3 shows various outputs in column (1). Column (2) shows the minimum cost at which each output can be made. The firm incurs a cost of £10 even when output is zero. This is the cost of being in business

Table 6.3   Cost, revenue, profit (weekly)

(1) Output	(2) Total cost (£)	(3) Price (£)	(4) Total revenue (1) × (3) (£)	(5) Profit (4) − (2) (£)
0	10	–	0	−10
1	25	21	21	−4
2	36	20	40	4
3	44	19	57	13
4	51	18	72	21
5	59	17	85	26
6	**69**	**16**	**96**	**27**
7	81	15	105	24
8	95	14	112	17
9	111	13	117	6
10	129	12	120	−9

at all – running an office, renting a telephone line and so on. Thereafter, costs rise with output. Costs include the opportunity costs of all resources used in production. Total cost is higher, the more is produced. At high levels of output, cost rises sharply as output increases: the firm has to pay the workers overtime to work weekends and nights.

Total revenue

The total revenue the firm obtains from an output depends on price and hence demand. Column (3) of Table 6.3 summarizes the demand curve faced by the firm; it shows the price at which each output can be sold. Column (4) calculates sales revenue (or total revenue), that is, price times quantity. At a price of £21 the firm sells only one spoon, while at a price of £12 the firm is able to sell 10 spoons. The lower the price, the greater the sales: its demand curve slopes down.

Profit

Column (5) of Table 6.3 shows profit, the difference between total revenue and total cost. At low output, profit is negative. At the highest output of 10, profit is again negative. At intermediate outputs, the firm makes positive profit.

The highest profit is £27 a week, at an output of 6 spoons. At £16 each, total revenue is £96. Production cost, properly calculated, is £69, leaving a profit of £27 a week. Therefore we can say that our firm should produce 6 spoons a week, since, at that level of output, profits are the highest possible and thus maximized. This chosen output, or supply decision, is the highlighted row in Table 6.3.

Notice that maximizing profit is not the same as maximizing revenue. By selling 10 spoons a week the firm could earn £120, but it would cost £129 to make them. Making the last few spoons is expensive and brings in little extra revenue. It is more profitable to make fewer.

6.6   Marginal cost and marginal revenue

It is helpful to view the same problem of profit maximization from a different angle. At each output level, we now ask whether the firm should increase output still further. Suppose the firm makes 3 spoons and considers making 4 spoons. Table 6.3 shows this raises total cost from £44 to £51, a £7 increase in total cost. Revenue rises from £57 to £72, a rise of £15. Raising output from 3 to 4 spoons adds more to revenue than to cost. Profit rises by £8 (£15 more revenue minus £7 more cost). The firm then checks if it is also profitable to increase production from 4 to 5, and so on.

> **Marginal cost** is the rise in total cost when output rises 1 unit. **Marginal revenue** is the rise in total revenue when output rises 1 unit.

This approach – examining how 1 more unit of output affects profit – focuses on the **marginal cost** and **marginal revenue** of producing 1 more unit.

If marginal revenue exceeds marginal cost, the firm should raise output. Producing and selling an extra unit adds more to total revenue than to total cost, raising total profit. If marginal cost exceeds marginal revenue, the extra unit of output reduces total profit.

Thus we can use marginal cost and marginal revenue to calculate the output that maximizes profit. As long as marginal revenue exceeds marginal cost, keep increasing output. As soon as marginal revenue falls short of marginal cost, stop increasing output.

Marginal cost

Table 6.4 uses Table 6.3 to calculate the marginal cost of producing each extra unit of output. Increasing output from 0 to 1 raises total cost from £10 to £25. The marginal cost of the first unit is £15. Increasing production from 1 to 2 spoons raises total cost from £25 to £36, meaning that the marginal cost of the second unit produced is £11. Table 6.4 shows this marginal cost of each output level, the extra total cost of raising output by the last unit.

Table 6.4   Total and marginal cost

Output	Total cost (£)	Marginal cost (£)
0	10	–
1	25	15
2	36	11
3	44	8
4	51	7
5	59	8
6	69	10
7	81	12
8	95	14
9	111	16
10	129	18

Marginal cost is large when output is low, but also when output is high. Marginal cost is lowest when making the fourth unit, which adds only £7 to total costs.

As output increases, why do marginal costs start high, then fall, then rise again? The answer reflects different production techniques. At low output, the firm uses simple techniques. As output rises, more sophisticated machines are used, making extra output quite cheap. As output rises still further, the difficulties of managing a large firm emerge. Raising output gets hard and marginal costs rise.

Figure 6.1 plots this relation between output and marginal cost. The marginal cost curve can be different from firm to firm. In a coal mine that is nearly worked out, marginal cost rises steeply with extra output. In mass-production industries, as output increases marginal cost may decline and then become constant (see Figure 6.1 again).

CASE 6.2

Marginal costs in practice: the case of the water industry in the UK

In reality, calculating marginal costs for a firm is not that straightforward. To do so, we need to have an idea of what the firm's total costs look like and of how that total cost is related to the output produced. In practice, we need to estimate how the total costs change and output is increased or decreased.

Water suppliers are normally large and complicated firms. Working out the relationship between output produced (water supply and services) and total costs is not straightforward. In the UK, water companies are regulated by Ofwat, the water service regulation authority.*

Ofwat needs to control the behaviour of water companies and to try to ensure that those companies behave as efficiently as possible. More efficient firms should have lower marginal costs of production. Therefore, getting estimates of marginal costs for those companies is important for Ofwat.

The main costs that water companies incur are related to the use of resources (the inputs used in production), treatment of water, bulk transportation and local distribution. The following table lists estimates for the marginal costs of different water companies made by Ofwat. All the marginal costs are measured as prices (as measured in November 2002) per cubic metre.

Company	Resources (p/m³)	Treatment (p/m³)	Bulk transport (p/m³)	Local distribution (p/m³)	Total marginal cost (p/m³)
Anglian	16	12	15	1	45
Northumbrian	11	5	28	13	58
Severn Trent	13	15	15	15	58
Thames	42	3	2	1	49
Wessex	12	12	25	75	125

Source: Ofwat, Tariff Structure and Charges: 2003–2004 Report (www.ofwat.gov.uk/regulating/reporting/rpt_tar2003-04.pdf).

Separate estimates of marginal costs are made by increment: 'resources', 'treatment', 'bulk transport' and 'local distribution'. The sum of these increment costs yields the total marginal cost. Total marginal cost figures may not add up due to rounding. The table tells us that, if Anglian wants to increase its production by 1 cubic metre of water, the change in its total cost is going to be £45. Notice that, even if water companies produce a similar good (water and related services), there is some variation in the marginal costs they face.

* Regulation will be discussed in more detail in Chapter 8.

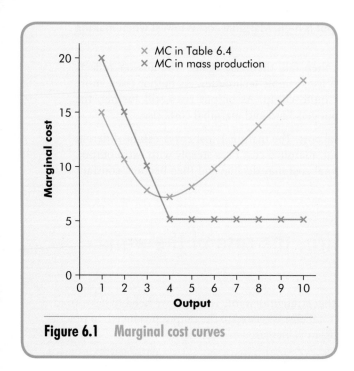

Figure 6.1 Marginal cost curves

Marginal revenue

Still based on Table 6.3, Table 6.5 shows marginal revenue, the extra total revenue when an extra unit of output is made and sold. Raising output from 0 to 1 raises revenue from £0 to £21. The marginal revenue of the first unit is £21. Raising output from 7 to 8 units raises revenue from £105 to £112, so marginal revenue is £7. Total revenue and marginal revenue depend on the demand curve for the firm's product.

Marginal revenue, also shown in Figure 6.2, falls steadily as output rises and can be negative at high output levels. To sell 11 spoons, the price must be cut to £10 each. Total revenue is £110. Since 10 spoons earn £120 in Table 6.5, the marginal revenue from moving from 10 to 11 spoons is £110 − £120, that is, −£10.

Marginal revenue = extra revenue from making and selling 1 more unit of output

The shape of the marginal revenue curve reflects the shape of the firm's demand curve. Demand curves slope down. To sell more output, the price must be cut. Selling an extra unit of output at this lower price is the first component of marginal revenue. However, to sell that extra unit the firm has to cut the price for which *all* previous units of output can be sold. This effect reduces the marginal revenue obtained from selling an extra unit of output.

Table 6.5 Price, total revenue and marginal revenue

Output	Price (£)	Total revenue (£)	Marginal revenue (£)
0	–	0	–
1	21	21	21
2	20	40	19
3	19	57	17
4	18	72	15
5	17	85	13
6	16	96	11
7	15	105	9
8	14	112	7
9	13	117	5
10	12	120	3

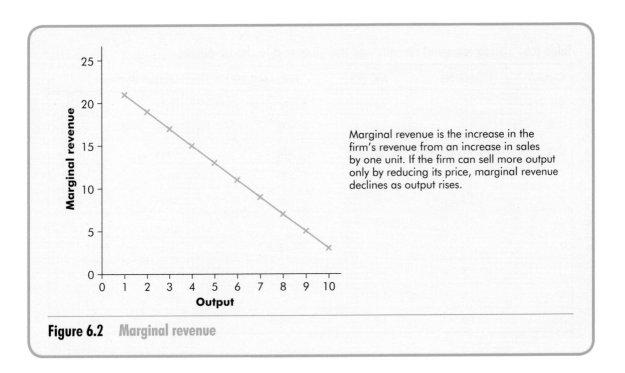

Marginal revenue is the increase in the firm's revenue from an increase in sales by one unit. If the firm can sell more output only by reducing its price, marginal revenue declines as output rises.

Figure 6.2 Marginal revenue

Marginal revenue falls steadily for two reasons. First, because demand curves slope down, the extra unit must be sold at a lower price. Second, successive price reductions reduce the revenue earned from *existing* units of output, and at larger output there are more existing units on which revenue is lost when prices fall further. To sum up, (a) marginal revenue falls as output rises and (b) marginal revenue is less than the price for which the last unit is sold, because a lower price reduces revenue earned from existing output (see Maths 6.1).

MR, MC and the output choice

Combining marginal cost (*MC*) and marginal revenue (*MR*), Table 6.6 examines the output that maximizes the firm's profits. If *MR* exceeds *MC*, a 1-unit increase in output will increase profits. The last column shows that this reasoning leads the firm to make at least 6 units of output. The firm now considers increasing output from 6 to 7 units. Marginal revenue is £9 and marginal cost £12. Profits fall by £3. Output should *not* be expanded to 7 units, or to any level above this.

The firm should expand up to 6 units of output but no further. This output maximizes profits, as we know already from Table 6.5.

Table 6.3, based on total cost and total revenue, and Table 6.6, based on marginal cost and marginal revenue, are different ways to study the same problem. Economists frequently use marginal analysis. Is there a small change that could make the firm better off? If so, the current position cannot be the best possible one and changes should be made.

Marginal analysis should be subjected to one very important check. It may miss an all-or-nothing choice. For example, suppose that *MR* exceeds *MC* up to an output level of 6 units but thereafter *MR* is less than *MC*. Six units is the best positive output level. However, if the firm incurs large costs whether or not it produces (for example, a vastly overpaid managing director), the profit earned from producing 6 units may not cover these fixed costs. Conditional on paying these fixed costs, an output level of 6 units is then the loss-minimizing output level. Shareholders might do better to shut the firm and fire the fat cat boss. We examine this issue in the next chapter.

Table 6.6 Using marginal revenue and marginal cost to choose output

Output	MR (£)	MC (£)	MR – MC (£)	Output decision
1	21	15	6	Raise
2	19	11	8	Raise
3	17	8	9	Raise
4	15	7	8	Raise
5	13	8	5	Raise
6	11	10	1	
7	9	12	–3	Lower
8	7	14	–7	Lower
9	5	16	–11	Lower
10	3	18	–15	Lower

To sum up, a profit-maximizing firm should expand output so long as marginal revenue exceeds marginal cost but stop expansion as soon as marginal cost exceeds marginal revenue. This rule guides the firm to the best positive level of output. If the firm is not making profits even in this position, it may do better to close down altogether.

MATHS 6.1 Total and marginal revenue with a linear demand

Consider a firm that faces a downward-sloping linear inverse demand for its produced good. Suppose the inverse demand function is $P = a - bQ$, where P is the price, Q is the quantity produced by the firm, $a > 0$ is the intercept and $b > 0$ is the slope of the inverse demand.

The total revenue function for the firm is given by

$$TR(Q) = P \times Q \tag{1}$$

where $TR(Q)$ stands for total revenue and the Q in brackets means that the total revenue depends on the quantity produced. As the quantity produced changes, so the total revenue changes. Using the inverse demand to substitute P into the total revenue function gives us:

$$TR(Q) \equiv (a - bQ) \times Q = -bQ^2 + aQ \tag{2}$$

From the total revenue function in (2) we can see that total revenue is zero when the firm does not produce ($Q = 0$) and when the firm produces an amount $Q = a/b$. You should notice that $Q = a/b$ represents the horizontal intercept of the inverse demand. At that quantity the price is going to be zero and so total revenue is zero as well. Between $Q = 0$ and $Q = a/b$ total revenue first increases and then decreases as Q increases.

Once we know the total revenue function, we use calculus to find the marginal revenue function. The marginal revenue tells us by how much the total revenue will change if we increase the quantity by 1 unit.

The marginal revenue function can be found by taking the derivative of the total revenue function with respect to Q:

$$MR(Q) = \frac{dTR(Q)}{dQ} \tag{3}$$

Equation (3) tells us by how much the total revenue changes ($dTR(Q)$) if we change the quantity produced by a very small amount (close to zero) dQ. This is not exactly the definition of marginal revenue we use. A small change close to zero is not the same as a change of 1 unit. However, we can consider equation (3) as an 'approximation' of the true definition of the marginal revenue function.

The marginal revenue function associated with the total revenue function in (2) is:

$$MR(Q) = a - 2bQ \tag{4}$$

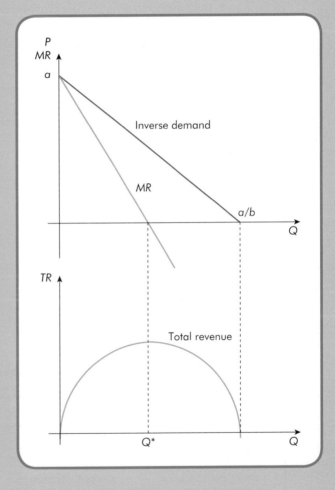

Equation (4) is particularly interesting. First, it is linear in Q. Second, it looks like exactly the inverse demand function but with a slope that is twice as steep. Indeed, this is a general result. When a firm faces a linear inverse demand function, the marginal revenue function of that firm is the inverse demand function with a slope that is twice as steep. In the figure on the right we plot the inverse demand, the total revenue function generated by that demand and the marginal revenue function when the inverse demand is linear.

In the top graph, we plot the inverse linear demand and the marginal revenue function. The marginal revenue function has the same vertical intercept as the inverse demand but the slope is twice as steep and so it is steeper than the inverse demand slope. In the bottom graph we plot the total revenue function. Total revenue is zero when $Q = 0$ and then it increases as Q increases. It reaches a maximum at Q^* and then, as Q increases above Q^*, it decreases and becomes zero when $Q = a/b$. Between $Q = 0$ and Q^*, TR increases as Q increases and so MR is positive.

Between Q^* and $Q = a/b$, TR decreases as Q increases and MR becomes negative. For each level of output Q, the marginal revenue is lower than the price and it decreases steadily as Q increases.*

* By looking at this figure demonstrating demand and total revenue, you may think again of Case 4.1 on the elasticity of demand of the iPhone.

6.7 Marginal cost and marginal revenue curves

Thus far we have assumed the firm produces an integer number of goods, such as 0, 1 or 2, rather than a quantity such as 1.5 or 6.7. Output is not usually confined to integer levels. For goods such as wheat or milk, the firm can sell in odd amounts. Even for goods such as cars, sold in whole units, the firm may be selling 75 cars every four weeks, or 18.75 cars a week. It is convenient to imagine that firms can vary output and sales levels continuously.

We can then draw smooth schedules for marginal cost MC and marginal revenue MR as in Figure 6.3. Profits are maximized where the schedules cross, at point E. The output Q_1 maximizes profits (or minimizes losses). At smaller outputs, MR exceeds MC and expansion increases profits (or reduces losses).

To the right of Q_1, MC exceeds MR. Expansion adds more to costs than revenue, and contraction saves more in costs than it loses in revenue. The profit incentive to increase output to the left of Q_1 and to reduce output to the right of Q_1 is shown by the arrows in Figure 6.3. This incentive guides the firm to choose Q_1, provided the firm should be in business at all. At Q_1, marginal revenue is exactly equal to marginal cost. Table 6.7 summarizes the conditions for determining the output that maximizes profits.

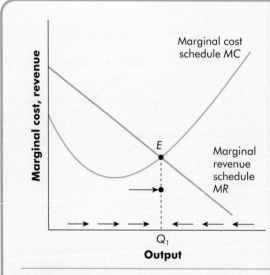

The marginal cost and marginal revenue schedules are shown changing smoothly. The firm's optimal output is Q_1, at which marginal revenue is equal to marginal cost. Anywhere to the left of Q_1, marginal revenue is larger than marginal cost and the firm should increase output, as shown by the arrows. Where output is greater than Q_1, marginal revenue is less than marginal cost and profits are increased by reducing output. If the firm is losing money at Q_1 it has to check whether it might be better not to produce at all than to produce Q_1.

Figure 6.3 Marginal cost and marginal revenue

Table 6.7 The firm's output choice

Marginal condition	Output decision	Check
$MR > MC$	Raise	
$MR < MC$	Cut	
$MR = MC$	Stay	If profits > 0, make this output. If not, quit.

Changes in cost

Suppose the firm faces a price rise for a raw material. At each output, marginal cost is higher than before. Figure 6.4 shows this upward shift from MC to MC'. The firm now produces at E'. Higher marginal costs reduce profit-maximizing output from Q_1 to Q_2.

A demand shift

Suppose the firm's demand curve shifts up, for example because the good produced by the firm becomes more popular and so more consumers want to buy it. If the demand shifts up, the marginal revenue curve must also shift up. At each output, price and marginal revenue are higher than before. In Figure 6.5 the MR curve shifts up to MR', inducing the firm to move from E to E'. Higher demand makes the firm expand output from Q_1 to Q_3. Notice that, as the demand increases, so too does the price at which the firm can sell each level of output. Figure 6.4 shows us that a profit-maximizing firm will respond to this increase in the price by increasing the output produced, a result that is consistent with the idea that a supply curve should be positively sloped, as discussed in Chapter 3.

Do firms know their marginal cost and marginal revenue curves?

Do firms in the real world know their marginal cost and marginal revenue curves, let alone go through some sophisticated calculations to make sure output is chosen to equate the two?

Such thought experiments by firms are not necessary for the relevance of our model of supply. If, by luck, hunch or judgement, a firm succeeds in maximizing profits, marginal cost and marginal revenue *must* be equal. Our formal analysis merely tracks the hunches of smart managers who get things right and survive in a tough business world.

In this chapter we introduced cost and revenue conditions and the idea of profit maximization. Later chapters fill in the details but we now have the basis for a theory of how much output firms choose to supply. Firms choose the level of output that maximizes profits. At this level of output, marginal cost equals marginal revenue.

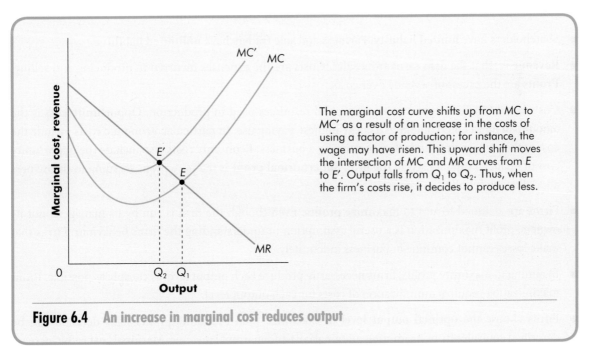

The marginal cost curve shifts up from MC to MC' as a result of an increase in the costs of using a factor of production; for instance, the wage may have risen. This upward shift moves the intersection of MC and MR curves from E to E'. Output falls from Q_1 to Q_2. Thus, when the firm's costs rise, it decides to produce less.

Figure 6.4 **An increase in marginal cost reduces output**

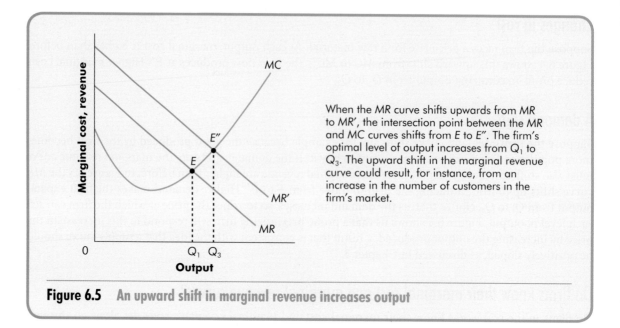

When the MR curve shifts upwards from MR to MR', the intersection point between the MR and MC curves shifts from E to E". The firm's optimal level of output increases from Q_1 to Q_3. The upward shift in the marginal revenue curve could result, for instance, from an increase in the number of customers in the firm's market.

Figure 6.5   An upward shift in marginal revenue increases output

Summary

- The **theory of supply** is the theory of how much output firms choose to produce.

- There are three types of firm: self-employed **sole traders**, **partnerships** and **companies**. Sole traders are the most numerous but are often very small businesses. The large firms are companies.

- Companies are owned by their shareholders but run by the board of directors.

- Shareholders have **limited liability**. Partners and sole traders have **unlimited liability**.

- **Revenue** is what the firm earns from sales. **Costs** are the expenses incurred in producing and selling. **Profits** are the excess of revenue over costs.

- Costs should include opportunity costs of all resources used in production. **Opportunity cost** is the amount an input could obtain in its next-highest-paying use. In particular, economic costs include the cost of the owner's time and effort in running a business. **Economic costs** also include the opportunity cost of financial capital used in the firm. **Supernormal profit** is the pure profit accruing to the owners after allowing for all these costs.

- Firms are assumed to aim to **maximize profits**. Even though the firm is run by its managers, not its owners, profit maximization is a useful assumption in understanding the firm's behaviour. Firms that make losses cannot continue in business indefinitely.

- In aiming to maximize profits, firms necessarily produce each output level as cheaply as possible. Profit maximization requires minimization of costs for each output level.

- Firms choose the **optimal output level** to maximize total economic profits. This decision can be described equivalently by examining marginal cost and marginal revenue. **Marginal cost** is the increase in total cost when one more unit is produced. **Marginal revenue** is the corresponding change in total revenue and depends on the demand curve for the firm's product. **Profits are maximized at the output at which marginal cost equals marginal revenue.** If profits are negative at this output, the firm should close down if doing so reduces losses.

● An upward shift in the marginal cost curve reduces output. An upward shift in the marginal revenue curve increases output.

● It is unnecessary for firms to calculate their marginal cost and marginal revenue curves. Setting MC equal to MR is merely a device that economists use to mimic the hunches of smart firms who correctly judge, by whatever means, the profit-maximizing level of output.

Review questions

---

1 How do the following affect the income statement for R-a-P in Table 6.1? (a) R-a-P owes £70 000 to its workers for work done in the year. (b) Instead of renting an office, R-a-P owns its office. (c) During the year R-a-P was paid by a creditor owing money from the year before.

EASY

2 R-a-P is run by an owner, who can earn £40 000 a year to manage another firm. She has also invested £200 000 in R-a-P that could be earning 12 per cent elsewhere. What are the economic profits of R-a-P? (Use Table 6.1.)

3 (a) Snark International borrows another £50 000 from the bank and increases its inventories. How is its balance sheet affected (Table 6.2)? (b) How would interest on the loan appear in the income statement of Snark International?

4 (a) Do firms aim to maximize profits? (b) Should firms support charities, the arts and political campaigns? Is there any conflict with (a)?

5 In Table 6.3, assume total costs of making each output are higher by £40 than the costs in the second column of the table. What level of output should the firm produce? Explain.

6 A firm with the costs shown in Table 6.4 can now sell as much output as it wants at a price of £13. (a) Draw MR and MC curves. (b) What output will it produce?

7 True or false   If $MR < MC$ at a given level of output, a firm should increase production.

8 Common fallacies   Why are these statements wrong? (a) Firms with an accounting profit must be thriving. (b) Firms do not know their marginal costs. A theory of supply cannot assume that firms set marginal revenue equal to marginal cost. (c) To maximize profit, maximize sales.

9 A firm faces the following linear inverse demand for its product $P = 60 - 2Q$. Find the firm's total revenue function $TR(Q)$. Plot the total revenue function. Find the expression for the firm's marginal revenue.

MEDIUM

10 The firm in Question 9 has a marginal cost of production given by $MC = 8$. What is the amount of output that the firm should produce? What is the price at which the output is sold?

11 The following table reports the total revenue and the total cost of Keinko International, a firm producing coffee. Keinko has no fixed costs.

Quantity	TR	TC	MR	MC
1	48	5	–	–
2	92	20		
3	132	45		
4	168	80		
5	200	125		
6	228	180		
7	252	245		
8	272	320		
9	288	405		
10	300	500		

Complete the columns for the marginal revenue (*MR*) and the marginal cost (*MC*). In a graph, plot the *MR* and the *MC* curves and show the profit-maximizing level of output.

12 Now suppose that Keinko faces an increase in demand for its coffee. For *each unit* of coffee, total revenues increase by 20. Find the new total revenue for each level of output and the corresponding new marginal revenue. In a graph, plot the new *MR* and *MC* curves. How has the increase in demand affected the output choice of Keinko?

13 Airbus makes 50 planes a year, which sell for $50 million each. If Airbus raises its price, Boeing will leave its prices unaltered, so Airbus loses market share. It faces an elastic demand curve. However, if Airbus cuts its price below $50 million, Boeing is forced to match the price cut, so quantity demanded increases only to the extent that additional plane orders are placed when planes are cheaper. Each company faces inelastic demand when it cuts the price. (a) Draw the demand curve that Airbus thinks it faces. (b) Can you deduce what its marginal revenue schedule looks like?

14 Essay question 'The industrial revolution was built on the ability of entrepreneurs to float companies and obtain funding. Today, it is often argued that stock exchanges force firms to be focused too much on the short term, making it hard to raise long-term funds. Private equity firms see themselves as addressing this shortcoming of stock markets. The amazing thing about private equity is not its recent appearance but that it took so long to appear.' Discuss.

HARD

For solutions to these questions contact your lecturer.

CHAPTER

Costs and supply

7

Learning Outcomes

By the end of this chapter, you should understand:

1. a production function

2. technology and a technique of production

3. how the choice of technique depends on input prices

4. total, average and marginal cost, in the long run and short run

5. returns to scale, and their relation to average cost curves

6. fixed and variable factors in the short run

7. the law of diminishing returns

8. how a firm chooses output, in the long run and short run

Chapter 6 introduced the theory of supply. Firms choose the output at which marginal cost equals marginal revenue. This maximizes profits (or minimizes losses). If profits are positive, the firm produces this output. If profits are negative, it checks whether losses are reduced by shutting down. This chapter develops the theory of supply in more detail. In particular, we want to understand how the firm can produce the output that maximizes profits (or minimizes losses). To do that, we need to better understand what the production activity of a firm is.

We distinguish between the *short-run* and the *long-run* output decisions of firms. No firm stays in business if it expects to make losses for ever. We show how and why cost curves differ in the short run, when the firm cannot fully react to changes in conditions, and the long run in which the firm can fully adjust to changes in demand or cost conditions.

Figure 7.1 summarizes the material of this chapter. The new material is all on the cost side. Because there are so many cost curves, you may find it useful to check back to Figure 6.1. We start by introducing the *production function*, which describes the firm's technology.

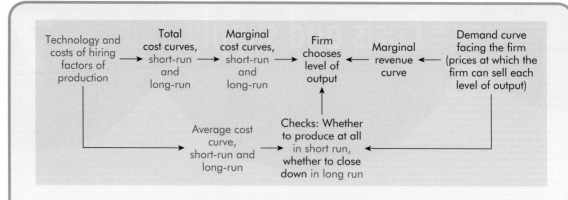

This diagram extends the analysis of Chapter 6 in two ways. First, short- and long-run cost curves and output decisions are carefully distinguished. Second, we go behind the total cost curve to show how the firm chooses the lowest-cost way of producing each level of output, given the technology available to it and the costs of hiring factors of production.

Figure 7.1   The complete theory of supply

7.1   Inputs and output: the production function

An **input** (or **factor of production**) is a good or service used to produce output.

Suppose you want to start a farm to produce tomatoes. You need land, tomato seeds, water for irrigation, workers to work on the farm, a tractor and possibly some other machinery. All those are **inputs** that are going to be used to produce tomatoes (output). Inputs include labour, machinery, buildings, raw materials and energy. The relationship between the quantity of inputs a firm uses and the output it produces is called a production function. We restrict the analysis to the case where only two inputs are used to produce a good or service. Those two inputs will be called capital (e.g. machinery, buildings, etc.) and labour (e.g. number of workers or number of worked hours).

A production technique is **technically efficient** if there is no other way to make a given output using less of one input and no more of the other inputs. The **production function** is the set of all technically efficient techniques.

A production function is a way to summarize the technology available to the firm for its production activity in a given period of time. Suppose a firm uses inputs to make mobile phones. This is an engineering and management problem. Making mobile phones is largely a matter of technology and on-the-job experience. The **production function** summarizes **technically efficient** ways to combine inputs to produce output. Since profit-maximizing firms are not interested in wasteful production methods, we restrict our attention to those that are technically efficient.

Suppose our firm can use two different methods to produce the same number of mobile phones. To make 1 mobile phone, method A needs 2 workers and 1 machine, but method B needs 2 workers and 2 machines. Method B is less efficient than method A; it uses more machines but the same labour to make the same output. Method B is not in the production function.

Short run vs long run

A firm's decisions about production activity depend on the time horizon. We distinguish between short run and long run. The short run is the period in which the firm cannot fully adjust to a change in conditions. In particular, we define the *short-run* as a period of time in which the quantity of at least one input of production is fixed. A fixed input is a factor of production that cannot be increased or decreased in a given period of time.

> A **fixed factor of production** is an input that cannot be varied. A **variable factor** can be varied, even in the short run.

On the other hand, the *long-run* is a period of time sufficiently long such that all inputs can be **varied**.

Consider a firm manufacturing cars. It has a production plant, which represents its capital input, and some workers, which represent its labour input. Suppose demand for the cars produced by the firm increases. This represents a change in the conditions faced by the firm. In the short run, the firm can increase production by increasing the number of workers in the existing production plant. In the long run, the firm has the possibility of building another production plant. However, such a change in its capital input requires time. The long run will be the period of time necessary for the firm to create a new production plant.

How long are the short and the long run? The answer depends on the specific industry. It might take ten years to build a new power station but only a few months to open new restaurant premises if an existing building can be bought, converted and decorated.

What really matters is that production decisions of firms can be different depending upon whether we take a short-run or long-run perspective.

7.2 Production in the short run: diminishing marginal returns

In the short run, the quantity of at least one input is fixed and cannot be varied. Capital will be the *fixed input* while labour will be the *variable input*.

In Table 7.1 we report the short-run production function for a hypothetical firm. In particular, the first two columns tell us how output produced rises as variable labour input is added to a fixed quantity of capital. When no workers are employed, given the existing fixed level of capital, output cannot be produced. When only 1 worker is employed, 2 units of output are produced. When 2 workers are employed, 6 units of output are produced and so on.

Table 7.1   Total and marginal product of labour

Labour input (workers)	Output (total product per week)	Marginal product of labour
0	0	–
1	2	2
2	6	4
3	14	8
4	24	10
5	32	8
6	37	5
7	40	3
8	40	0
9	38	−2

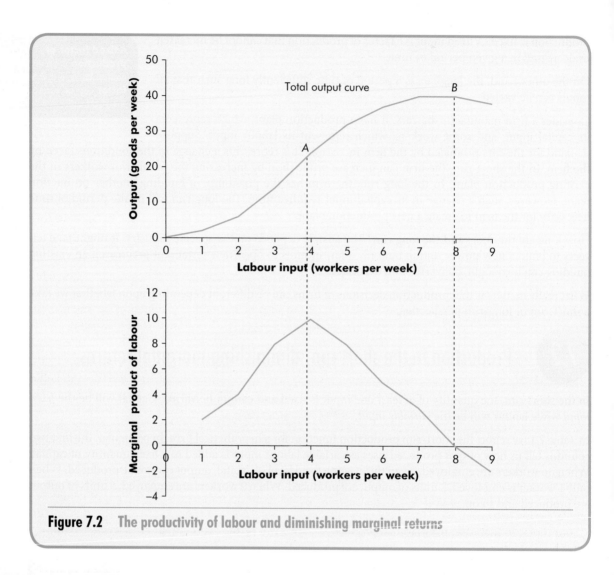

Figure 7.2 **The productivity of labour and diminishing marginal returns**

> The **marginal product** of a variable factor is the extra output from an extra unit of that input, holding constant all other inputs.

In the third column of Table 7.1 we have the **marginal product** of labour. This tells us how much an extra worker employed in the production process adds to the production activity, holding constant the level of capital. The first worker raises output by 2 units. We say that the first worker has a marginal product of 2 units. The second worker has a marginal product of 4 units. This is because, by adding that worker, the output produced rises from 2 to 6 units. The third worker has a marginal product of 8 units, since 2 workers produce 6 units but 3 workers produce 14 units.

The short-run production function outlined in Table 7.1, together with the marginal product of labour, is shown in Figure 7.2.

The top panel of Figure 7.2 shows total output as a function of labour input, keeping constant the level of capital. This is the total output curve.

By looking at that graph we can see some important features. First, when few workers are employed, adding extra workers will increase the output produced more than proportionally. By increasing the number of workers, they can specialize more in what they do and the efficiency of the workers increases. This is the part of the graph between 0 and point *A*.

Second, after point *A*, adding extra workers will continue to increase the output produced but less than proportionally. When 4 workers are employed, total output is 24. Adding an extra worker will increase output to 32, but this extra worker is adding less to the production than the previous worker (8 compared to 10). The efficiency of the workers starts to decrease. This is because, in the short run, the level of capital (the other input of production) is fixed and cannot be changed.

Suppose the factory has 4 machines and there are 4 workers each specializing in fully running one of the factory's machines. If we add a fifth worker, her marginal product is lower. With only four machines, the fifth worker gets to use one only when another worker is having a rest. There is even less useful machine work for the sixth worker to do. In fact, beyond 4 workers, the marginal product of each additional worker decreases steadily as the number of workers is increased. We say that there are **diminishing marginal returns** to labour.

> Holding all factors constant except one, **the law of diminishing marginal returns** says that, beyond some level of the variable input, further increases in the variable input lead to a steadily decreasing marginal product of that input.

The results behind Figure 7.2 are very general. Indeed, the idea of diminishing marginal returns from a variable input is a general law about short-run technology. Adding ever more workers to a fixed quantity of machinery becomes less and less useful. The eighth worker's main role in production is to get coffee for the others. This does not contribute to output and we are at point *B* in Figure 7.2. Adding a ninth worker may also be harmful to production. In practice, the place is so crowded that the ninth worker is in the way of the others, disrupting them and so reducing the total output produced.

The diminishing marginal returns to labour are described by the bottom graph in Figure 7.2. The relationship between the short-run total output curve and the marginal product of labour is the following: between 0 and point *A* on the total output curve, there are no diminishing marginal returns of labour. The marginal product of labour is increasing with the number of workers. After point *A* in the total output curve, diminishing marginal returns take place and the marginal product of labour is decreasing with the number of workers. It must be stressed that the law of decreasing marginal returns of a variable input is a short-run phenomenon.[1]

Notice that we have defined the marginal product of labour as the extra output obtained by employing an extra *unit* of labour, keeping constant the level of capital. So far we have considered a unit of labour as a single worker. However, we could have done the same analysis using an hour of work as a unit for the labour input. In that case, the marginal product of labour will be the extra output produced by adding an extra hour of labour.

If capital was the variable factor and labour the fixed factor, the result would be the same. Adding more and more machines to a given labour force might initially lead to large increases in output but would quickly encounter diminishing returns as machines become under-utilized. Thus the bottom graph in Figure 7.2, showing the marginal product of labour when labour is the variable factor, might also describe the behaviour of the marginal product of capital when capital is the variable factor.

Marginal product is *not* the everyday meaning of 'productivity', which refers to the *average* product. The average product of labour, what is most commonly meant by 'productivity', is total output divided by total labour input. The higher is the productivity of labour, the higher is the output per worker produced.

If the marginal product of labour lies above the average product, adding another worker will raise the average product and 'productivity'. When diminishing returns set in, the marginal product will quickly fall below the average product and the latter will fall if further workers are added. If you do not see why this must be true, try calculating output per unit of labour input as an extra column in Table 7.1.

As usual, we must distinguish between movements along a curve and shifts in a curve. The marginal product curve is drawn for given levels of the other factors. For a higher given level of the fixed factors,

---

1 Economists use *diminishing* returns to describe the addition of one variable factor to other fixed factors in the short run, but *decreasing* returns to describe diseconomies of scale when *all* factors are freely varied in the long run.

the marginal product curve would be higher. With more machinery to work with, an extra worker will generally be able to produce more extra output than previously. The numbers in Table 7.1 and the height of the marginal product curve in Figure 7.2 depend on the number of fixed factors with which the firm began.

MATHS 7.1 **The short-run production function: the average and marginal product of labour**

The short-run production function can be written as:

$$Q = f(K_0, L) \tag{1}$$

where Q is the total output produced, K_0 is the fixed level of capital in the short run and L is the number of workers employed. Equation (1) simply says that the two inputs of production are combined through the function f in order to produce the output Q.

The function f describes mathematically the technology available to the firm in the short run.

The average product of labour is defined as the average output produced by each worker.

Mathematically, the average product of labour is defined as follows:

$$AP_L \equiv \frac{Q}{L} = \frac{f(K_0, L)}{L} \tag{2}$$

By now you should be familiar with the idea that marginal functions are defined using derivatives. Therefore the marginal product of labour is given by:

$$MP_L \equiv \frac{dQ}{dL} = \frac{df(K_0, L)}{dL} \tag{3}$$

Consider the following example for a short-run production function:

$$Q = K_0(L)^{0.5} \tag{4}$$

Equation (4) is a possible specification for the function f defined above.

Suppose that $K_0 = 10$ and $L = 4$. The production function in (4) implies that the output produced by those 4 workers using 10 units of capital is 20.

The average product of labour implied by (4) is given by:

$$AP_L = \frac{K_0 L^{0.5}}{L} = \frac{K_0}{L^{0.5}} \tag{5}$$

If $K_0 = 10$ and $L = 4$, then the average product of labour according to (5) is 5. Each worker produces 5 units of output. The same result is obtained if you divide the total output produced when $K_0 = 10$ and $L = 4$ by the number of workers ($20/4 = 5$).

Now suppose that $K_0 = 20$ instead. In this case, and with $L = 4$, the average product of labour is now 10. The workers are now more productive and each worker produces 10 units of output.

The marginal product of labour implied by (4) is given by:

$$MP_L = \frac{d(K_0, L^{0.5})}{dL} = 0.5 \frac{K_0}{L^{0.5}} \tag{6}$$

As you can see from equation (6), as labour increases, given the amount of capital K_0, the marginal product of labour decreases, as suggested by the idea of diminishing returns to labour.

Equation (4) is an example of a short-run production function displaying decreasing marginal returns. We can think of other possible short-run production functions that do not have such a property. An example is given by the following linear short-run production function:

$$Q = K_0 L$$

In this case, the marginal product of labour is constant for any level of labour. Moreover, the marginal product of labour is always equal to the average product of labour.

7.3   Short-run costs

The short-run production function of a firm tells us the relationship between variable and fixed inputs and output produced. We can translate that information into a relationship between cost of production and output. The cost of production will depend on two elements. First, it depends on the price of inputs. A firm must pay a wage to the workers it employs and it must pay the price of machinery that it wants to buy. The higher the prices of inputs, the higher will be the cost of production. Second, the cost of production will depend on the productivity of the inputs. The higher is the productivity of inputs and the lower is the amount of inputs needed to produce a given level of output, the lower is thus the cost of producing that output.

The existence of fixed factors in the short run has two implications. First, in the short run the firm has some **fixed costs**. These fixed costs must be borne even if output is zero. If the firm cannot quickly add to or dispose of its existing factory, it must still pay depreciation on the building and meet the interest cost of the money it originally borrowed to buy the factory.

> **Fixed costs** do not vary with output.

Second, because in the short run the firm cannot make all the adjustments it would like, its short-run costs must exceed its long-run costs. We now study these short-run costs in more detail. Long-run costs will be discussed later in the chapter.

Short-run fixed and variable costs

Table 7.2 presents data on short-run costs. The second column shows the fixed costs, which are independent of the output level. Those will be costs associated with the level of capital. The third column shows the variable costs. Output and all costs are measured per week.

Variable costs are the costs of hiring variable inputs, in our case labour. Firms may have long-term contracts with workers which reduce the speed at which these inputs can be adjusted. Yet most firms retain some flexibility through overtime and short time hiring or non-hiring of casual and part-time workers.

> **Variable costs** change as output changes.

The fourth column of Table 7.2 shows short-run total costs:

Short-run total cost (STC) = short-run fixed cost (SFC) + short-run variable cost (SVC)   (1)

The short-run total, fixed and variable cost curves are shown in Figure 7.3 using the data of Table 7.2. Notice that the shape of the short-run total cost curve is almost the mirror image of the shape of the short-run production function in Figure 7.2. This is not by accident but is a general result that comes from the relationship between costs of production and the productivity of inputs.

Table 7.2 Short-run costs of production

(1) Output	(2) *SFC* Short-run fixed cost	(3) *SVC* Short-run variable cost	(4) *STC* Short-run total cost	(5) *SMC* Short-run marginal cost
0	30	0	30	–
1	30	22	52	22
2	30	38	68	16
3	30	48	78	10
4	30	61	91	13
5	30	79	109	18
6	30	102	132	23
7	30	131	161	29
8	30	166	196	35
9	30	207	237	41
10	30	255	285	48

Short-run marginal costs

> **Short-run marginal cost** is the extra cost of making an extra unit of output in the short run while some inputs remain fixed.

The final column of Table 7.2 shows the **short-run marginal cost** *SMC*. Since fixed costs do not rise with output, *SMC* is the rise both in short-run total costs and in short-run variable costs as output is increased by 1 unit.

Whatever the output, fixed costs are £30 per week. Marginal costs are always positive. Short-run total costs rise steadily as output rises. Extra output adds to total cost, and adds more the higher the marginal cost. In the last column of Table 7.2, as output increases, marginal costs first fall then rise again.

The short-run marginal cost curve is shown in Figure 7.4. As we can see, the shape in Figure 7.4 is almost the mirror image of the marginal product curve in Figure 7.2. Indeed, there is a close relationship between these two curves.

The short-run marginal cost is related to the variable input, in our case labour. Every worker costs the firm the same wage. While the marginal product of labour is increasing, each worker adds more to output than the previous workers. Hence the extra cost of making extra output is falling. *SMC* is falling as long as the marginal product of labour is rising.

Once diminishing returns to labour set in, the marginal product of labour falls and *SMC* starts

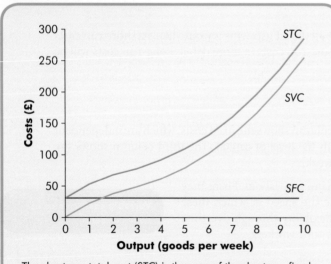

The short-run total cost (*STC*) is the sum of the short-run fixed cost (*SFC*) and the short-run variable cost (*SVC*). The short-run fixed cost does not depend on the level of output and therefore its curve is a horizontal line.

Figure 7.3 Short-run total, fixed and variable cost curves

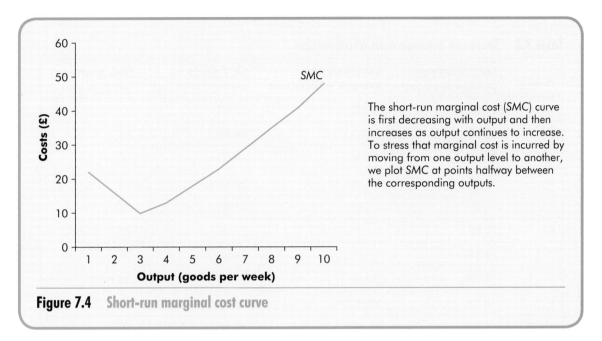

Figure 7.4 Short-run marginal cost curve

The short-run marginal cost (SMC) curve is first decreasing with output and then increases as output continues to increase. To stress that marginal cost is incurred by moving from one output level to another, we plot SMC at points halfway between the corresponding outputs.

to rise again. It takes successively more workers to make each extra unit of output. So, the shape of the short-run marginal cost curve is determined by the shape of the marginal product curve in Figure 7.2, which in turn depends on the technology facing the firm.

Short-run average costs

Another important cost measure is represented by the average cost. The average cost is defined as the total cost divided by the quantity produced. Therefore, the average cost measures the total cost per unit of output.

The short-run average cost is given by:

$$\text{Short-run average total cost } (SATC) = \text{short-run total cost } (STC)/\text{Quantity of output} \qquad (2)$$

In the short run, the total cost is given by the sum of variable and fixed costs. Therefore, together with the short-run total average cost, we can also define the short-run variable cost and the short-run fixed cost.

$$\text{Short-run average variable cost } (SAVC) = \text{short-run variable cost } (SVC)/\text{Quantity of output}$$

$$\text{Short-run average fixed cost } (SAFC) = \text{short-run fixed cost } (SFC)/\text{Quantity of output}$$

Using those two average cost measures, we can define the short-run average total cost in the following way, equivalent to expression (2):

$$\text{Short-run average total cost } (SATC) = \text{short-run average fixed cost } (SAFC)$$
$$+ \text{ short-run average variable cost } (SAVC) \qquad (3)$$

This follows from dividing each term in equation (1) by the output level.

Table 7.3 shows short-run *average* cost data corresponding to Table 7.2. Each number in Table 7.3 is obtained by dividing the corresponding number in Table 7.2 by the output level. The table also shows short-run marginal costs, taken from Table 7.2.

Figure 7.5 plots the three short-run average cost measures from Table 7.3.

In Figure 7.5 SAFC falls steadily because total fixed cost ('overheads') is spread over ever larger output levels, thus reducing average fixed cost. The SATC and SAVC curves are such that, at each output level, SATC = SAVC + SAFC, as in equation (3).

Short-run average fixed cost (SAFC) equals short-run fixed cost (SFC) divided by output.

Short-run average variable cost (SAVC) equals SVC divided by output, and **short-run average total cost** (SATC) equals STC divided by output.

Table 7.3 Short-run average costs of production

Output	SAFC Short-run average fixed cost	SAVC Short-run average variable cost	SATC Short-run average total cost	SMC Short-run marginal cost
1	30.00	22.00	52.00	22
2	15.00	19.00	34.00	16
3	10.00	16.00	26.00	10
4	7.50	15.25	22.75	13
5	6.00	15.80	21.80	18
6	5.00	17.00	22.00	23
7	4.29	18.71	23.00	29
8	3.75	20.75	24.50	35
9	3.33	23.00	26.33	41
10	3.00	25.50	28.50	48

On the relationship between short-run marginal and average costs

In Figure 7.6 we plot the short-run marginal and average costs. Two facts stand out from this figure:

1 *SATC* is falling when *SMC* is less than *SATC*, while it is rising when *SMC* is greater than *SATC*. The same applies for the relationship between *SMC* and *SAVC*.

2 *SATC* is at a minimum at the output at which the *SMC* curve and the *SATC* curve cross (point *A* in Figure 7.6). The *SAVC* is at its minimum at the output at which the *SMC* curve and the *SAVC* curve cross (point *B* in Figure 7.6).

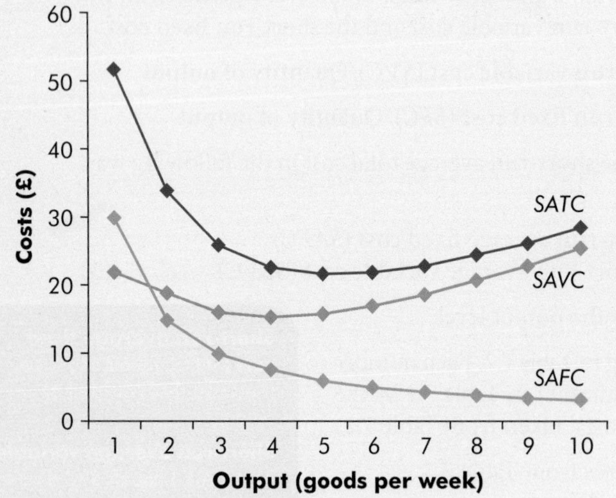

Neither fact is an accident. The relationship between average and marginal is a matter of arithmetic, as relevant for football as for production costs. A footballer with 3 goals in 3 games averages 1 goal per game. Two goals in the next game, implying 5 goals from 4 games, raise the average to 1.25 goals a game. In the fourth game, the marginal goals were 2, raising total goals from 3 to 5. Because the marginal score exceeds the average score in previous games, the extra game must drag up the average.

The same holds for production costs. When the marginal cost of the next unit exceeds the average cost of the existing units, making the next unit must raise average cost. If the marginal cost of the next unit lies below the average cost of existing units, an extra unit of production drags

Figure 7.5 Short-run average cost curves

down average costs. When marginal and average cost are equal, adding a unit leaves average cost unchanged. This explains fact 1.

Fact 2 follows from fact 1. In Figure 7.6 the short-run total average and marginal cost curves cross at point A, which must be the minimum point for *SATC*. To the left of A, *SMC* is below *SATC* so the short-run average total cost is still falling. To the right of A, *SMC* is above *SATC* so the short-run average total cost is rising. The short-run average total cost is lowest at A. The short-run marginal cost curve crosses the *SATC* curve from below, at the point where *SATC* is at the minimum. As in the football example, this rests purely on arithmetic. The same reasoning can be applied to the relationship between *SMC* and *SAVC*.

Table 7.4 summarizes this important relationship. It is true for the relationship between marginal and average costs both in the short run and in the long run.

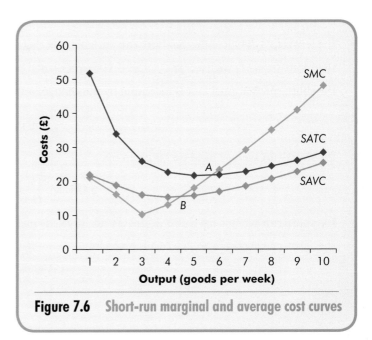

Figure 7.6 *Short-run marginal and average cost curves*

The shape of the *SMC* curve in Figure 7.6 follows from the behaviour of marginal labour productivity. The *SMC* curve passes through the lowest point, A, on the short-run average total cost curve. To the left of this point, *SMC* lies below *SATC* and is dragging it down as output expands. To the right of A, the converse holds. That explains the shape of the *SATC* curve in Figure 7.6 and in Figure 7.5 as well.

Variable cost is total cost minus fixed cost. Fixed cost does not change with output. Hence marginal cost also shows how much total *variable* cost is changing. The *SMC* curve goes through the lowest point B on *SAVC*. To the left of B, *SMC* is below *SAVC* and *SAVC* is falling. To the right of B, *SAVC* is rising. Finally, since average total cost exceeds average variable cost by average fixed cost, *SAVC* lies below *SATC*. Point B must lie to the left of point A. That explains the shape of *SAVC* and its relation to *SATC* in Figure 7.6 and in Figure 7.5 as well.

Table 7.4 Marginal and average cost

	MC < AC	MC = AC	MC > AC
AC is:	Falling	Minimum	Rising

MATHS 7.2	Short-run cost functions

An example of a short-run total cost function is given by:

$$STC = F + cQ + dQ^2 \qquad (1)$$

The term *F* is a constant and denotes the short-run fixed cost that does not depend on output *Q*.

The term $cQ + dQ^2$ denotes the short-run variable cost that varies with output Q.

Therefore, from (1) we have: $SFC = F$ and $SVC = cQ + dQ^2$

The short-run marginal cost is measured by the change in the STC as Q changes:

$$SMC \equiv \frac{dSTC}{dQ} = c + 2dQ \qquad (2)$$

The short-run average fixed cost is given by:

$$SAFC \equiv \frac{SFC}{Q} = \frac{F}{Q} \qquad (3)$$

The short-run average fixed cost decreases steadily as Q increases.

The short-run average variable cost is given by:

$$SAVC \equiv \frac{SVC}{Q} = c + dQ \qquad (4)$$

The short-run average total cost is given by:

$$SATC \equiv \frac{STC}{Q} = \frac{F}{Q} + c + dQ \qquad (5)$$

 ## 7.4   A firm's output decision in the short run

> The firm's **short-run output decision** is to supply Q_1, the output at which $MR = SMC$, if the price covers short-run average variable cost $SAVC_1$ at that output. If not, the firm supplies zero.

Figure 7.7 illustrates the firm's **short-run output decision**. Short-run marginal cost is set equal to marginal revenue to determine the output Q_1 that maximizes profits or minimizes losses.

Next, the firm decides whether or not to produce in the short run. Profit is positive at the output Q_1 if the price p at which this output is sold covers average total cost. It is the short-run measure $SATC_1$ at output Q_1 that is relevant. If p exceeds $SATC_1$, the firm makes profits in the short run and produces Q_1.

Suppose p is less than $SATC_1$. The firm is losing money because p does not cover costs. In the long run the firm closes down if it keeps losing money. In the short run, even at zero output the firm must pay its fixed costs. The firm needs to know whether losses are bigger if it produces at Q_1 or produces zero.

If revenue exceeds *variable cost* the firm is earning something towards its overheads. It produces Q_1 if revenue exceeds variable cost even though Q_1 may involve losses. The firm produces Q_1 if p exceeds $SAVC_1$. If not, it produces zero. Table 7.5 summarizes the short-run output decisions of a firm.

Table 7.5   The firm's output decision in the short-run

	Marginal condition	Check whether to produce
Short run	Choose the output at which $MR = SMC$	Produce this output if $p > SAVC$. Otherwise, produce zero.

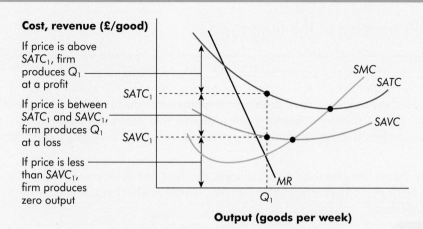

Cost, revenue (£/good)

If price is above $SATC_1$, firm produces Q_1 at a profit

If price is between $SATC_1$ and $SAVC_1$, firm produces Q_1 at a loss

If price is less than $SAVC_1$, firm produces zero output

$SATC_1$

$SAVC_1$

SMC

$SATC$

$SAVC$

MR

Q_1

Output (goods per week)

The firm sets output at Q_1, where short-run marginal costs equal marginal revenue. Then it checks whether it should produce at all. If price is above $SATC_1$, the level of short-run average total cost at output Q_1, the firm is making a profit and should certainly produce Q_1. If price is between $SATC_1$ and $SAVC_1$, the firm partly covers its fixed costs, even though it is losing money. It should still produce output Q_1. Only if the price is below $SAVC_1$ should the firm produce zero. At those prices, the firm is not even covering its variable costs.

Figure 7.7 The firm's short-run output decision

ACTIVITY 7.1

Marginal conditions and sunk costs

The theory of supply obeys two principles of good decision making in life. The first is the *marginal principle*. Once the best position is reached, no feasible change can improve things. To climb a hill, take small steps in an upwards direction. If you cannot move upwards, you are at the top.

There is also the big picture. Having equated marginal cost and marginal revenue, a firm checks it is not better to close down completely. Similarly, the marginal principle guides you to a local peak but, looking around, you may see a higher hill a mile away, but you have to go down a bit before you can scale it.

The second principle is that *sunk costs are sunk*. Costs already incurred should not affect new decisions. In choosing short-run output, the firm ignores fixed costs that are paid anyway. It is no use crying over spilt milk. Having read seven chapters of this book, should you read on? It depends on the costs and benefits you get from the rest of the book, not on the time already spent.

Questions

(a) A firm lasts for two periods and then dies. In the first period, it can choose to buy a very special piece of equipment that will be no use to any other firm and will have no resale value. It will, however, help the firm to make output in each of the two periods. When the second period arrives, should the cost of the machine be included in the marginal cost of the firm? In the first period, should it be included in the marginal cost of producing output? What is the smart way for the firm to think about this problem?

(b) Playing poker, you bet most of your chips on a single hand before getting a sinking feeling that you are going to lose the hand. Should you bet on? Why or why not?

To check your answers to these questions, go to page 684.

7.5   Production in the long run

In the long run all factors of production are variable. Table 7.6 shows some technically efficient methods in the production function. The first two rows show two ways to make 100 mobile phones: 4 machines and 4 workers, or 2 machines and 6 workers. Beginning from the latter, the third row shows the effect of adding an extra worker. Output rises by 6 mobile phones. The last row shows that doubling both inputs in the second row also doubles the output, though this need not be so: overcrowding a small factory can slow people down.

In the long run, the problem for the firm is to choose the right mix of inputs to produce the quantity that maximizes the firm's profit. In practice, among all the possible available efficient techniques the firm must choose the cheapest one.

> **Technical progress** is a new technique allowing a given output to be made with fewer inputs than before.

A method previously technically efficient may become inefficient after a technical advance allows a better production technique. **Technical progress** alters the production function. For now, we assume a given technology and a given production function. Chapter 28 discusses growth and technical progress.

Costs and the choice of technique

Consider the lowest-cost way to make 100 mobile phones.[2] Assume there are two technically efficient techniques: the first two rows of Table 7.6, reproduced as the second and third columns of Table 7.7 and labelled techniques A and B. It costs £320 to rent a machine and £300 to hire a worker.

Table 7.6   A production function

Output	Capital input	Labour input
100	4	4
100	2	6
106	2	7
200	4	12

Table 7.7   Choosing the lowest-cost production technique

Technique	Capital input	Labour input	Rental per machine (£)	Wage per worker (£)	Capital cost (£)	Labour cost (£)	Total cost (£)
A	4	4	320	300	1280	1200	2480
B	2	6	320	300	640	1800	2440

---

2   Since output, revenue and cost are all flows, these should be measured per week or per year. We omit time units for brevity but do not forget they are flows not stocks!

Table 7.8 The effect of a higher wage rate

Technique	Capital input	Labour input	Rental per machine (£)	Wage per worker (£)	Capital cost (£)	Labour cost (£)	Total cost (£)
A	4	4	320	340	1280	1360	2640
B	2	6	320	340	640	2040	2680

To make 100 mobile phones, Table 7.7 shows that the total cost is £2480 with technique A and £2440 with technique B. The firm chooses B. One hundred mobile phones at a total cost of £2440 is one point on the total cost curve for mobile phones. It is the *economically efficient* (lowest-cost) production method at the rental and wage rates in Table 7.7.

To get the whole total cost curve, we repeat the calculation for each output. The production function tells us the inputs needed by each technique. Using input prices, we calculate the cost using each technique and choose the lowest-cost production method. Joining up these points we get the total cost curve, which may switch from one production technique to another at different outputs. From the total cost curve we calculate the marginal cost curve – the rise in total cost at each output when output is increased by one more unit.

Factor intensity

A technique using a lot of capital and little labour is 'capital intensive'. One using a lot of labour but relatively little capital is 'labour intensive'. In Table 7.7, technique A is more capital intensive and less labour intensive than technique B. The ratio of capital input to labour input is 1 in technique A but only $1/_3$ in technique B.

Factor prices and the choice of technique

At the factor prices (prices per unit input) in Table 7.7, the more labour-intensive technique is cheaper. Suppose the wage rises from £300 to £340: labour is dearer but the rental on capital is unchanged. The *relative price* of labour has risen.

We ask two questions. First, what happens to the total cost of making 100 mobile phones? Second, is there any change in the preferred technique? Table 7.8 recalculates production costs at the new factor prices. Because both techniques use some labour, the total cost of making 100 mobile phones by each technique rises. Repeating this argument at all output, the total cost curve must shift *upwards* when the wage rate (or the price of any other input) rises.

In this example, the rise in the relative price of labour leads the firm to switch techniques: it switches to the more capital-intensive technique A.

7.6   Long-run total, marginal and average costs

Faced with an upward shift in its demand and marginal revenue curves, a firm will expand output, as we explained in Chapter 6. However, adjustment takes time. Initially, the firm can get its existing workforce to do overtime. In the long run, the firm can vary its factory size, switch techniques of production, hire new workers and negotiate new contracts with suppliers of raw materials.

Table 7.9 Long-run costs

(1) Output	(2) Total cost (£)	(3) Marginal cost (£)	(4) Average cost (£)
0	0	–	–
1	30	30	30
2	54	24	27
3	74	20	24.67
4	91	17	22.75
5	107	16	21.40
6	126	19	21.00
7	149	23	21.29
8	176	27	22.00
9	207	31	23.00
10	243	36	24.30

The firm may be able to alter the shift length at once. Hiring or firing workers takes longer and it might be years before a new factory is designed, built and operational. In this section we deal with long-run cost curves, when the firm can make all the adjustments it desires.

Long-run total cost is the minimum cost of producing each output level when the firm can adjust all inputs.

Long-run marginal cost is the rise in long-run total cost if output rises permanently by one unit.

Long-run average cost is the total cost *LTC* divided by the level of output *Q*.

Table 7.9 shows the **long-run total cost** *LTC* and **long-run marginal cost** *LMC* of making each output. Since there is always an option to close down entirely, the *LTC* of producing zero output is zero. *LTC* describes the eventual cost after all adjustments have been made.

Table 7.9 also shows long-run marginal cost *LMC*. *LTC* must rise with output: higher output always costs more to produce. *LMC* shows how much total cost is involved in making the last unit of output.

Can large firms produce goods at a lower unit cost than small firms? Might it be a disadvantage to be large? To answer these questions, we need to think about average cost per unit of output.

Table 7.9 shows **long-run average cost** *LAC* (column 2 divided by column 1). These *LAC* data are plotted in Figure 7.8. Average cost starts out high, then falls, then rises again. This is a similar shape to the short-run average cost function previously considered. This common pattern of average costs is called the U-shaped average cost curve. To see why the U-shaped average cost curve is common in practice, we examine 'returns to scale'.

The last two columns of Table 7.9 are plotted in Figure 7.9. At each output, *LAC* is total cost divided by output. To stress that marginal cost is incurred by moving from one output level to another, we plot *LMC* at points halfway between the corresponding outputs. The *LMC* of £30 for the first unit of output is plotted at the output halfway between 0 and 1.

The relationship between *LMC* and *LAC* is exactly the same as the one discussed for the short-run case. When *LMC* is below *LAC*, *LAC* decreases. When *LMC* is above *LAC*, *LAC* increases. Furthermore, *LMC* and *LAC* cross at the point where *LAC* reaches a minimum.

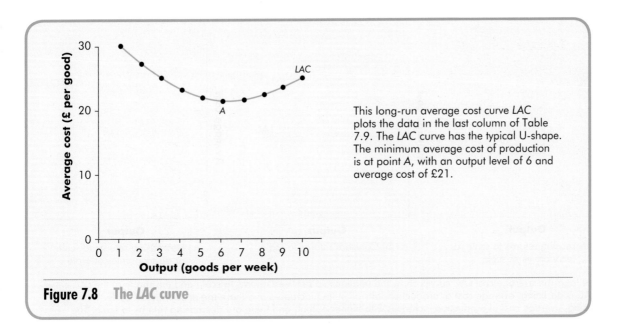

This long-run average cost curve *LAC* plots the data in the last column of Table 7.9. The *LAC* curve has the typical U-shape. The minimum average cost of production is at point *A*, with an output level of 6 and average cost of £21.

Figure 7.8 **The *LAC* curve**

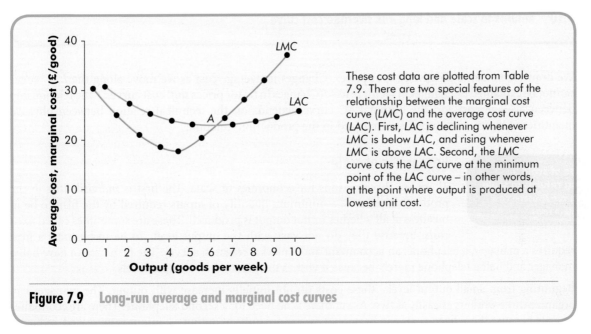

These cost data are plotted from Table 7.9. There are two special features of the relationship between the marginal cost curve (*LMC*) and the average cost curve (*LAC*). First, *LAC* is declining whenever *LMC* is below *LAC*, and rising whenever *LMC* is above *LAC*. Second, the *LMC* curve cuts the *LAC* curve at the minimum point of the *LAC* curve – in other words, at the point where output is produced at lowest unit cost.

Figure 7.9 *Long-run average and marginal cost curves*

7.7 Returns to scale

Scale refers to the output of the firm when all inputs can be varied. Therefore it is a long-run concept. The three cases are shown in Figure 7.10.

In Figure 7.8 the U-shaped average cost curve had scale economies up to point *A*, where average cost was lowest. At higher outputs there were diseconomies of scale. Why are there scale economies at low output levels but diseconomies of scale at high output levels?

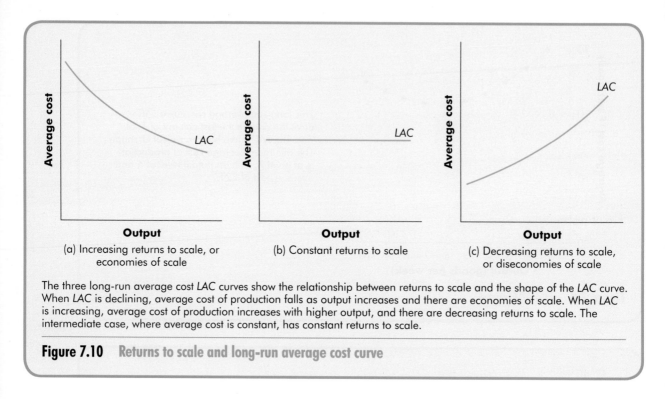

The three long-run average cost *LAC* curves show the relationship between returns to scale and the shape of the *LAC* curve. When *LAC* is declining, average cost of production falls as output increases and there are economies of scale. When *LAC* is increasing, average cost of production increases with higher output, and there are decreasing returns to scale. The intermediate case, where average cost is constant, has constant returns to scale.

Figure 7.10 Returns to scale and long-run average cost curve

We draw a cost curve for given input prices. Changes in average cost as we move along the *LAC* curve cannot be explained by changes in factor prices. (Changes in factor prices *shift* cost curves.) The relationship between average cost and the output *LAC* curve depends on the technical relation between physical quantities of inputs and output, summarized in the production function.

Economies of scale

> **Economies of scale** (or **increasing returns to scale**) mean long-run average cost falls as output rises.

There are three reasons for economies of scale. The first is *indivisibilities* in the production process, a minimum quantity of inputs required by the firm to be in business at all whether or not output is produced. These are sometimes called *fixed costs*, because they do not vary with the output level. To be in business a firm requires a manager, a telephone, an accountant and a market research survey. The firm cannot have half a manager and half a telephone merely because it wishes to operate at low output levels.

Beginning from small output levels, these costs do not initially increase with output. The manager can organize three workers as easily as two. As yet there is no need for a second telephone. There are economies of scale because these fixed costs can be spread over more units of output as output is increased, reducing average cost per unit of output. However, as the firm expands further, it has to hire more managers and telephones and these economies of scale die away. The average cost curve stops falling.

The second reason for economies of scale is *specialization*. A sole trader must undertake all the different tasks of the business. As the firm expands and takes on more workers, each worker can concentrate on a single task and handle it more efficiently.

The third reason for economies of scale is closely related. Large scale is often needed to take advantage of better machinery. No matter how productive a robot assembly line is, it is pointless to install one to make five cars a week. Average costs would be enormous. However, at high output levels the machinery cost can be spread over a large number of units of output and this production technique may produce so many cars that average costs are low.

CASE 7.1
Scale economies and the internet

Producing information products such as films, music and news programmes has a high fixed cost, but distributing these products digitally has almost a zero marginal cost and no capacity constraint. Scale economies are vast. Moreover, if marginal cost is close to zero, smart suppliers will price their products so that marginal revenue is also tiny.

EMI, a legend of the music industry, was formed in 1931. Its Abbey Road studios in London hosted giants such as the Beatles. Moving with the times, EMI has steadily withdrawn from the business of supplying records and CDs, and now operates largely online. In April 2007, EMI announced it would begin releasing its music as superior-quality tracks available exclusively on the iTunes Store. Costing £0.99, the tracks were to be free of restrictions on access and distribution, and no longer utilized anti-copying software. Lower-quality tracks with restrictions were to be sold for £0.79.

Diseconomies of scale

Beyond some output, the U-shaped average cost curve turns up again as diseconomies of scale begin. Management is harder as the firm gets larger: there are *managerial diseconomies of scale*. Large companies need many layers of management, themselves needing to be managed. The company becomes bureaucratic, co-ordination problems arise and average costs begin to rise.

> **Diseconomies of scale** (or **decreasing returns to scale**) mean long-run average cost rises as output rises.

Geography may also explain diseconomies of scale. If the first factory is located in the best site, to minimize the cost of transporting goods to the market, the site of a second factory must be less advantageous. To take a different example, in extracting coal from a mine, a firm will extract the easiest coal first. To increase output, deeper coal seams have to be worked and these will be more expensive.

As output increases, the shape of the average cost curve thus depends on two things: how long economies of scale persist and how quickly the diseconomies of scale set in. The balance of these two forces varies from industry to industry and from firm to firm.

MATHS 7.3
The long-run production function and the returns to scale

We defined the returns to scale in terms of the relationship between the long-run average cost and the level of output. We can define the same concepts using the relationship between inputs and output implied by a long-run production function.

We say that a production function displays increasing, constant or decreasing returns to scale if the following definitions hold:

(a) *Increasing returns to scale (or economies of scale)*: when all the inputs of production are increased by the same factor and the output produced increases more than proportionally.

(b) *Constant returns to scale*: when all the inputs of production are increased by the same factor and the output produced increases by the same factor.

> **Constant returns to scale** mean long-run average costs are constant as output rises.

(c) *Decreasing returns to scale (or diseconomies of scale)*: when all the inputs of production are increased by the same factor and the output produced increases less than proportionally.

161

▶ Definition (a) is equivalent to saying that the long-run average cost is decreasing with output. Suppose we double the amount of inputs used in production. The long-run total cost will double as well. Output produced increases by more than double according to definition (a). Since the long-run average cost is the long-run total cost divided by the output, it implies that the *LAC* must decrease after we double all the inputs. Similar reasoning can be used to explain why definitions in (b) and in (c) are equivalent to the ones given in the text.

Mathematically, consider the following long-run production function, known as a Cobb–Douglas production function:

$$Q = K^\alpha L^\beta \qquad (1)$$

where $\alpha > 0$ and $\beta > 0$ are two constants.

To apply the definitions written above, we need to increase all the inputs of production by the same factor. Suppose we increase all inputs by $\lambda > 0$. What happens to the output produced?

The long-run production function in (1) becomes:

$$Q_1 = (\lambda K)^\alpha (\lambda L)^\beta \qquad (2)$$

where Q_1 denotes the output produced when all inputs are increased by the same factor $\lambda > 0$. A bit of algebra to simplify equation (2) gives us:

$$Q_1 = \lambda^\alpha K^\alpha \lambda^\beta L^\beta = \lambda^{\alpha+\beta} K^\alpha L^\beta$$

Using the fact that $Q = K^\alpha L^\beta$, this can be rewritten as:

$$Q_1 = \lambda^{\alpha+\beta} Q \qquad (3)$$

Equation (3) tells us that, when we increase inputs by the same factor $\lambda > 0$, the output produced increases by a factor $\lambda^{\alpha+\beta}$.

Then we have the following:

(1) If $\alpha + \beta > 1$, the Cobb–Douglas production function displays increasing returns to scale.

(2) If $\alpha + \beta = 1$, the Cobb–Douglas production function displays constant returns to scale.

(3) If $\alpha + \beta < 1$, the Cobb–Douglas production function displays decreasing returns to scale.

If a firm is using a production function that displays increasing returns to scale, then the long-run average cost of that firm will decrease with output.

Returns to scale in practice

To gather evidence on returns to scale, we can talk to design engineers to see how production costs vary with output. It is much harder to quantify managerial diseconomies. Most empirical research focuses only on direct production costs. Because it ignores managerial diseconomies of scale, it overestimates scale economies.

Many such studies of manufacturing industry confirm that scale economies continue over a wide range of output.[3] The long-run average cost curve slopes down, albeit at an ever-decreasing rate. Economists have tried to measure the output at which all scale economies are first achieved: the point at which the average cost curve first becomes horizontal.

---

3   See Scherer, F. M. and Ross, D. (1990) *Industrial Market Sructure and Economic Performance* (3rd edn), Houghton Mifflin.

Table 7.10 Minimum efficient scale, selected industries, UK and US

Industry	% increase in LAC at $\frac{1}{3}$ MES	MES as % of market in	
		UK	US
Cement	26	6	2
Steel	11	15	3
Glass bottles	11	9	2
Bearings	8	4	1
Fabrics	7	2	1
Refrigerators	6	83	14
Petroleum	5	12	2
Paints	4	10	1
Cigarettes	2	30	6
Shoes	2	1	1

Source: Scherer, F. M. et al. (1975) *The Economics of Multiplant Operation*, Harvard University Press, tables 3.11 and 3.15.

Table 7.10 contains some traditional estimates of the **minimum efficient scale** (*MES*) for firms in different industries in the UK and the US. The second column gives an idea of how steeply average costs fall before minimum efficient scale is reached. It shows how much average costs are higher if output is one-third the output of minimum efficient scale. The third and fourth columns show the *MES* output relative to the output of the industry as a whole. This provides a benchmark for the importance of economies of scale to firms in each industry. Since firms in the UK and the US have access to essentially the same technical know-how, differences between the third and fourth columns primarily reflect differences in the size of the industry in the two countries rather than differences in the *MES* output level for an individual firm.

> **Minimum efficient scale** (MES) is the lowest output at which the *LAC* curve reaches its minimum.

Scale economies in manufacturing industries are substantial. At low outputs, average costs are much higher than at minimum efficient scale. We would expect similar effects in aircraft and motor car manufacture, which have huge fixed costs for research and development of new models and which can utilize highly automated assembly lines once output is large. Yet in a large country such as the US, minimum efficient scale for an individual firm occurs at an output that is small relative to the industry as a whole. Most firms are producing on a relatively flat part of their average cost curve, with few scale economies unexploited. In smaller countries such as the UK, the point of minimum efficient scale is larger relative to the industry as a whole.

However, Table 7.10 suggests that there are many industries, even in the manufacturing sector, where minimum efficient scale for a firm is small relative to the whole market and average costs are only a little higher if output is below minimum efficient scale. These firms will be producing in an output range where the *LAC* curve is almost horizontal.

Finally, there are many firms, especially outside the manufacturing sector, whose cost conditions are well represented by a U-shaped average cost curve. With only limited opportunities for economies of scale, these firms run into rising average costs even at quite moderate levels of output. Many service-sector industries – hairdressers, doctors, decorators – have very modest scope for scale economies.

Globalization, technical change and scale economies

We described the estimates in Table 7.10 as 'traditional' rather than 'modern'. The data are more than a decade old. Some things have changed since then. Technical progress in transport has reduced the cost of shipping goods over vast distances. Technical progress in information technology has made it much easier to manage companies with global activities. Computers at courier companies such as Federal Express and DHL can track packages across the world. In 2001 the global activities of FedEx were temporarily halted not by a pilots' strike but by a computer virus.

CASE 7.2 The Rolls-Royce treatment

Rolls-Royce cars, once the badge of Britishness, are now made by BMW. But the Rolls-Royce aero engine business is booming and the company's market share has risen from 20 per cent to over 30 per cent within the past decade, making it the second-largest aero engine manufacturer in the world. How was this success achieved? By recognizing the crucial role of scale economies.

Aircraft engines have huge costs in research and development, requiring large production runs to recover this initial investment. The company's change in strategy reflected two key insights.

First, it extended its initial investment so that its engines could service a wide range of aircraft, thereby increasing the chances of building up long-term relationships with particular aircraft manufacturers and the airlines that they supply. Second, by signing fixed-price agreements for the subsequent repair and maintenance of their engines, Rolls-Royce effectively insured the user against defective quality, thereby signalling their commitment to excellence and safety.

As a result, companies ordered Rolls-Royce engines in greater numbers and over longer time periods, creating the volume of business necessary to recoup the large costs of research and development.

Picture: © Hannu Viitanen | Dreamstime.com

Source: Adapted from http://news.bbc.co.uk. © bbc.co.uk/news

Globalization is partly a matter of policy – countries are abandoning restrictions to keep out foreign businesses – but it is chiefly being driven by cost changes caused by technical progress. New technology and lower transport costs not merely enhance market size, they also reduce managerial diseconomies of scale. It gets easier to run big companies. The output of minimum efficient scale is rising. Global companies like Microsoft, Shell, Nike and Nokia keep popping up successfully in more and more countries: scale economies let them undercut the domestic competition.

> **Globalization** is the increasing integration of national markets that were previously much more segmented from one another.

The second sense in which the presentation of Table 7.10 is 'traditional' is that its final column presumes that the domestic market size is the relevant market size against which to assess minimum efficient scale. That would make sense if firms produced only for the home market. Globalization is making this obsolete too. Of course, the larger the potential market, the easier it is to justify large scale, and the more firms may seek mergers in order to achieve that scale quickly.

For example, when Barclays bank announced in 2007 its proposed £45 billion takeover of Dutch counterpart ABN Amro, it hoped to cut 12 800 jobs from the combined workforce, with another 10 800 positions likely to be transferred to lower-cost locations. The two companies would then have a joint workforce of 217 000 worldwide, including 62 400 staff who work for Barclays in the UK.

Having discussed scale economies, we begin putting flesh on the bare-bones theory of supply we developed in Chapter 6. Despite the growing importance of scale economies, we begin by discussing the output decision of a firm with a U-shaped average cost curve. Then we show how this analysis must be amended when firms face significant economies of scale.

7.8 The firm's long-run output decision

Figure 7.11 shows smooth *LAC* and *LMC* curves for a firm not restricted to producing integer units of output. It also shows the marginal revenue *MR* curve. From Chapter 6 we know that the output of maximum profit, or minimum loss, is at *B*, the output at which marginal revenue equals marginal cost. The firm then checks whether it makes profits or losses at this output. It should not stay in business if it makes losses for ever.

Total profit is average profit per unit of output, multiplied by output. Total profit is positive only if average profit is positive. Average profit is average revenue minus average cost. But average revenue is simply the price for which each output unit is sold. Hence *if long-run average costs at B exceed the price for which the output Q_1 is sold*, the firm makes losses in the long run and should close down. If, at this output, price equals *LAC*, the firm just breaks even. If price exceeds *LAC* at this output, the firm makes long-run profits and happily remains in business.

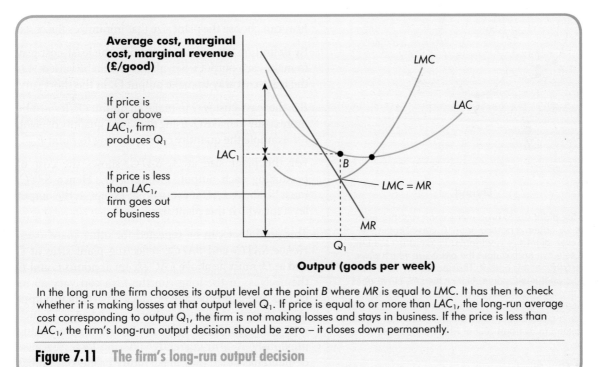

In the long run the firm chooses its output level at the point *B* where *MR* is equal to *LMC*. It has then to check whether it is making losses at that output level Q_1. If price is equal to or more than LAC_1, the long-run average cost corresponding to output Q_1, the firm is not making losses and stays in business. If the price is less than LAC_1, the firm's long-run output decision should be zero – it closes down permanently.

Figure 7.11   The firm's long-run output decision

Table 7.11 The firm's output decision in the long-run

	Marginal condition	Check whether to produce
Long run	Choose the output at which $MR = LMC$	Produce this output if $p > LAC$. Otherwise, produce zero.

First, we use the *marginal condition* ($LMC = MR$) to find the best output provided the firm stays in business. Then, we use the *average condition* (comparing LAC at this output with the price or average revenue received) to see if the best positive output yields a profit or a loss.

This is summarized in Table 7.11.

7.9 The relationship between short-run and long-run average costs

There is a close relationship between short-run and long-run average costs. This relationship is shown in Figure 7.12.

Suppose that in the short-run the fixed input of production of a firm is the number of plants (or plant size). Suppose that the firm produces using one plant in the short run. The short-run average cost of the firm is $SATC_1$. Now suppose instead that the firm produces using two plants in the short run. Its short-run average cost will be different and it will be $SATC_2$, and so on.

In the long run the plant size will be variable and so the firm can choose the plant size that minimizes the costs.

By definition, the LAC curve shows the least-cost way to make each output when all factors can be varied. A is the least-cost way to make output Q_1 in the short run.

B is the least-cost way to make an output Q_2. It *must* be more costly to make Q_2 using the wrong quantity of plant, for example the quantity corresponding to point E.

For the plant size at A, $SATC_1$ shows the cost of producing each output, including Q_2. Hence $SATC_1$ must lie above LAC at every point except A, the output level for which this plant size is best.

This argument can be repeated for other plant sizes. Hence $SATC_3$ and $SATC_4$, reflecting plant sizes at C and at D, must lie above LAC except at points C and D themselves. In the long run the firm can vary all its factors and can generally produce a particular output more cheaply than in the short run, when it is stuck with the quantities of fixed factors it was using previously. A firm currently suffering losses because demand has fallen may make future profits once it has had time to build a plant more suitable to its new output.

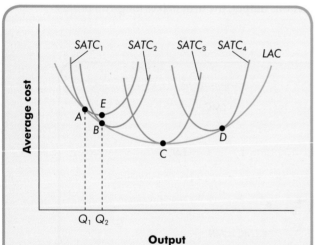

Suppose the plant size is fixed in the short run. For each plant size we obtain a particular $SATC$ curve. But in the long run even plant size is variable. To construct the LAC curve we select at each output the plant size which gives the lowest $SATC$ at this output. Thus points such as A, B, C and D lie on the LAC curve. Notice the LAC curve does not pass through the lowest point on each $SATC$ curve. Thus the LAC curve shows the minimum average cost way to produce a given output when all factors can be varied, not the minimum average cost at which a given plant can produce.

Figure 7.12 The long-run average cost curve *LAC*

Summary

- This chapter discusses short-run and long-run decisions, based on the corresponding cost curves. In the **long run**, a firm can fully adjust all its inputs. In the **short run**, some inputs are fixed. The length of the short run varies from industry to industry.

- The **production function** shows the maximum output that can be produced using given quantities of inputs. The inputs are machines, raw materials, labour and any other factors of production. The production function summarizes the technical possibilities faced by a firm.

- The **total cost curve** is derived from the production function, for given wages and rental rates of factors of production.

- In the short run the firm cannot adjust some of its inputs. But it still has to pay for them. It has short-run fixed costs (*SFC*) of production. The cost of using the variable factors is short-run variable cost (*SVC*). Short-run total cost (*STC*) is equal to *SFC* plus *SVC*.

- Short-run average total cost (*SATC*) is equal to short-run total cost (*STC*) divided by output. *SATC* is **equal to short-run average fixed cost (*SAFC*) plus short-run average variable cost (*SAVC*).** The *SATC* curve is U-shaped. The falling part of the U results both from declining *SAFC* as the fixed costs are spread over more units of output and from declining *SAVC* at low levels of output. The *SATC* continues to fall after *SAVC* begins to increase, but eventually increasing *SAVC* outweighs declining *SAFC* and the *SATC* curve slopes up.

- The **short-run marginal cost curve (*SMC*)** reflects the marginal product of the variable factor holding other factors fixed. Usually we think of labour as variable but capital as fixed in the short run. When very little labour is used, the plant is too big for labour to produce much. Increasing labour input leads to large rises in output and *SMC* falls. Once machinery is fully manned, extra workers add progressively less to output. *SMC* begins to rise.

- The *SMC* curve cuts both the *SATC* and *SAVC* curves at their minimum points.

- In the short run the firm supplies the output at which *SMC* is equal to *MR*, provided price is not less than short-run average variable cost. In the short run the firm is willing to produce at a loss provided it is recovering at least part of its fixed costs.

- The **long-run total cost curve** is obtained by finding, for each output, the least-cost method of production when all inputs can be varied. If the relative price of using a factor of production rises, the firm substitutes away from that factor in its choice of production techniques.

- **Average cost** is total cost divided by output. The **long-run average cost curve (*LAC*)** is derived from the long-run total cost curve.

- *LAC* is typically U-shaped. As output rises, at first average costs fall because of indivisibilities in production, the benefits of specialization and engineering advantages of large scale. There are increasing returns to scale on the falling part of the U. The rising part of the U reflects diseconomies of scale.

- Much of manufacturing has **economies of scale**. For some industries, particularly personal services, economies of scale run out at quite low output levels.

- When **marginal cost** is below average cost, average cost is falling. When marginal cost is above average cost, average cost is rising. Average and marginal cost are equal only at the lowest point on the average cost curve.

- In the long run the firm supplies the output at which **long-run marginal cost (*LMC*)** equals *MR* provided price is not less than the level of long-run average cost at that level of output. If price is less than long-run average cost, the firm goes out of business.

- The *LAC* curve is always below the *SATC* curve, except at the point where the two coincide. This implies that a firm is certain to have higher profits in the long run than in the short run if it is currently producing with a plant size that is not best from the viewpoint of the long run.

Review questions

connect

EASY

1 (a) What information does the production function provide? (b) Explain why the production function does not provide enough information for anyone actually to run a firm.

2 (a) What are economies of scale and why might they exist? (b) The table shows how output changes as inputs change. The wage rate is £5 and the rental rate of capital is £2. Calculate the lowest-cost method of making 4, 8 and 12 units of output. (c) Are there increasing, constant or decreasing returns to scale between those outputs? Which applies where?

Capital input	4	2	7	4	11	8
Labour input	5	6	10	12	15	16
Output	4	4	8	8	12	12

3 (a) For each output in the above table, say which technique is more capital intensive. (b) Does the firm switch towards or away from more capital-intensive techniques as output rises?

4 Suppose the rental rate of capital in Question 2 rose to £3. (a) Would the firm change its method of production for any levels of output? Say which, if any. (b) How do the firm's total and average costs change when the rental rate of capital rises?

5 (a) Calculate the marginal and average costs for each level of output from the following total cost data. (b) Show how marginal and average costs are related. (c) Are these short-run or long-run cost curves? Explain how you can tell.

Output	0	1	2	3	4	5	6	7	8	9
TC (£)	12	27	40	51	60	70	80	91	104	120

6 (a) Explain why it might make sense for a firm to produce goods that it can only sell at a loss. (b) Can it keep on doing this for ever? Explain.

7 Common fallacies Why are these statements wrong? (a) Firms making losses should quit at once. (b) Big firms can always produce more cheaply than smaller firms. (c) Small is always beautiful.

8 Suppose that firm A has the following short-run production function: $Q = K_0\sqrt{L}$, where K denotes capital and L labour. Suppose that the level of capital is fixed at $K_0 = 10$. The total cost of firm A in the short run is: $STC = 10 + wL$, where w is the wage paid to each worker. Assume that the wage is £20. Using the production function, show how the short-run total cost depends on the quantity produced Q. Plot the short-run total cost on a graph where you put Q on the horizontal axis.

MEDIUM

9 For each of the following cases, explain how long you think the short run is:

(a) An electric power station; (b) a superstore hypermarket; (c) a small grocery retail business.

In explaining your answer, specify any assumptions you need to make. For each case, do you expect the law of diminishing marginal returns to hold?

10 The following table shows the data for quantity produced and the total cost of production in the long run for a given firm.

Q	LTC
1	102
2	112
3	136
4	180
5	250
6	352
7	492
8	676
9	910
10	1200

Find the long-run marginal cost and the long-run average cost faced by the firm. In a graph, plot the *LMC* and the *LAC* curves. Why does the *LMC* curve cut the *LAC* curve from below?

11 What kind of return to scale is displayed by the following production functions?

(a) $Q = \sqrt{KL}$; (b) $Q = K^{0.3}L^{0.2}$; (c) $Q = K + L$

12 The 'big three' car makers used to be Ford, General Motors (GM) and Chrysler. Now they are Toyota, Nissan and Honda. In 2007 Ford, GM and Chrysler announced record losses (again). Why do they remain in the industry? Who is financing their losses? What would you need to believe to be prepared to lend these companies more money at this point?

13 The marginal cost of supplying another unit of output of an electronic product on the internet is almost zero. If long-run equilibrium has price equals marginal cost, internet firms will all go broke. Can you resolve the puzzle?

14 Essay question   We choose between couriers such as DHL and Federal Express based on the quality, convenience and reliability of service that they offer, not just on the price that they quote. Once we recognize that service matters, the inevitability of scale economies is greatly reduced. Even Amazon has to organize the distribution of the products it sells. Do you agree?

HARD

Perfect competition and pure monopoly

Learning Outcomes

By the end of this chapter, you should understand:

1. perfect competition

2. why a perfectly competitive firm equates marginal cost and price

3. how profits and losses lead to entry and exit

4. the industry supply curve

5. comparative static analysis of a competitive industry

6. pure monopoly

7. why a monopolist's output equates MC and MR

8. how output compares under monopoly and perfect competition

9. how price discrimination affects a monopolist's output and profits

An industry is the set of all firms making the same product. The output of an industry is the sum of the outputs of its firms. Yet different industries have very different numbers of firms. Eurostar is the only supplier of train journeys from London to Paris. In contrast, the UK has 150 000 farms and 20 000 grocers.

Why do some industries have many firms but others only one? Chapter 9 develops a general theory of market structure, showing how demand and cost conditions together determine the number of firms and their behaviour.

In a **perfectly competitive** market, both buyers and sellers believe that their own actions have no effect on the market price. In contrast, a **monopolist**, the only seller or potential seller in the industry, sets the price.

First it is useful to establish two benchmark cases, extremes between which all other types of market structure must lie. These limiting cases are **perfect competition** and **monopoly**.

We focus on how the number of sellers affects the behaviour of sellers. Buyers are in the background. We simply assume there are many buyers whose individual downward-sloping demand curves can be aggregated into the market demand curve. Thus, we assume that the demand side of the market is competitive but contrast the different cases on the supply side.

Perfect competition means that each firm or household, recognizing that its quantities supplied or demanded are trivial relative to the whole market, assumes its actions have no effect on the market price. This assumption was built into our model of consumer choice in Chapter 5. Each consumer's budget line took market prices as given, unaffected by the quantities then chosen. Changes in *market* conditions, applying to all firms and consumers, change the equilibrium price and hence individual quantities demanded, but each consumer neglects any feedback to market price by his own actions.

This concept of competition, which we now extend to firms and supply, differs from everyday usage. Ford and VW are fighting each other vigorously for the European car market but an economist would not call them perfectly competitive. Each has such a big share of the market that changes in the quantity supplied by either firm affect the market price. Ford and VW each take account of this in deciding how much to supply. They are not *price-takers*. Only under perfect competition can individuals make decisions that treat the price as independent of their own actions.

8.1 Perfect competition

If an individual's action does not affect the price, a perfectly competitive industry must have many buyers and many sellers. Each firm in a perfectly competitive industry faces a horizontal demand curve, as shown in Figure 8.1. However much the firm sells, it gets the market price. If it charges a price above P_0 it will not sell any output: buyers will go to other firms whose product is just as good. Since the firm can sell as much as it wants at P_0, it will not charge less than P_0. The individual firm's demand curve is DD.

A *horizontal* demand curve, along which the price is fixed, is the key feature of a perfectly competitive firm. To be a plausible description of the demand curve facing the firm, the industry must have four attributes. First, there must be many firms, each trivial relative to the entire industry. Second, the product must be standardized. Even if the car industry had many firms it would not be a competitive

industry. A Ford Mondeo is not a perfect substitute for a Vauxhall Vectra. The more imperfect they are as substitutes, the more it makes sense to view Ford as the sole supplier of Mondeos and Vauxhall as the sole supplier of Vectras. Each producer ceases to be trivial relative to the relevant market and cannot act as a price-taker. In a perfectly competitive industry, all firms must be making the same product, *for which they all charge the same price.*

Even if all firms in an industry made *homogeneous* or identical goods, each firm may have some discretion over the price it charges if buyers have imperfect information about the quality or characteristics of products. To rule this out in a competitive industry, we must assume that buyers have almost perfect information about the products being sold. They know the products of different firms in a competitive industry really are identical.

The fourth crucial characteristic of a perfectly competitive industry is *free entry and exit*. Even if existing firms could organize themselves to restrict total supply

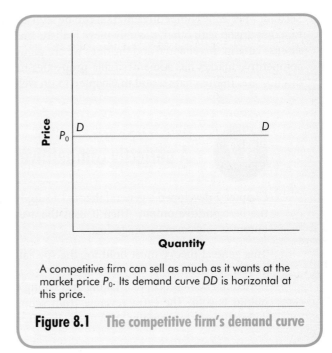

A competitive firm can sell as much as it wants at the market price P_0. Its demand curve DD is horizontal at this price.

Figure 8.1 The competitive firm's demand curve

and drive up the market price, the consequent rise in revenues and profits would simply attract new firms into the industry, thereby increasing total supply again and driving the price back down.

Conversely, as we shall shortly see, when firms in a competitive industry are losing money, some firms will close down and, by reducing the number of firms remaining in the industry, reduce the total supply and drive the price up, thereby allowing the remaining firms to survive.

To sum up, each firm in a competitive industry faces a horizontal demand curve at the going market price. To be a plausible description of the demand conditions facing a firm, the industry must have: (1) many firms, each trivial relative to the industry; (2) a homogeneous product, so that buyers would switch between firms if their prices differed; (3) perfect customer information about product quality, so that buyers know that the products of different firms really are the same; and (4) free entry and exit, to remove any incentive for existing firms to collude.

Why do we need to study perfectly competitive markets?

CONCEPT 8.1

A perfectly competitive market is characterized by many firms producing an identical product and so each firm is a price-taker, firms have freedom of entry and exit, and buyers are perfectly informed about the product sold in the market. All those assumptions rarely hold together in a given market, and therefore we rarely see a perfectly competitive market in reality.

Why do we need to study something that may not exist in the real world?

The answer is that we need to study perfectly competitive markets, for two main reasons. First, a perfectly competitive market may be considered a good approximation for many markets. For example, markets such as those for agricultural products or houses, the stock market and so on, can be reasonably well described by using the theory we are going to build in this chapter (together with the one built in Chapter 3).

Second, a perfectly competitive market can be seen as a benchmark, an almost ideal situation, that we can use for comparison with other, possibly more realistic, market structures (like the monopoly that we are going to discuss later in this chapter, and the ones we are going to analyse in Chapter 9). The reason is that a perfectly competitive market has some desirable properties in terms of efficiency of the market outcome, as we will discuss later in this chapter and in Chapter 13 on welfare economics.

8.2 ## A perfectly competitive firm's supply decision

Chapter 7 developed a general theory of supply. The firm uses the marginal condition ($MC = MR$) to find the best positive output. Then it uses the average condition to check whether the price for which this output is sold covers average cost.

This general theory must hold for the special case of perfectly competitive firms. *The special feature of perfect competition is the relationship between marginal revenue and price.* A competitive firm faces a horizontal demand curve. Making and selling extra output does *not* bid down the price for which existing output is sold. The extra revenue from selling an extra unit is simply the price received. A perfectly competitive firm's marginal revenue is its output price:

$$MR = P \tag{1}$$

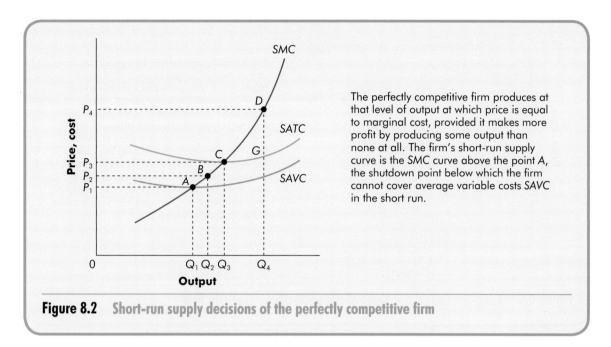

The perfectly competitive firm produces at that level of output at which price is equal to marginal cost, provided it makes more profit by producing some output than none at all. The firm's short-run supply curve is the SMC curve above the point A, the shutdown point below which the firm cannot cover average variable costs SAVC in the short run.

Figure 8.2 **Short-run supply decisions of the perfectly competitive firm**

A firm's short-run supply curve

Figure 8.2 shows again the short-run cost curves – marginal cost *SMC*, average total cost *SATC* and average variable cost *SAVC* – from Chapter 7. Any firm chooses the output at which marginal cost equals marginal revenue. Equation (1) means that a perfectly competitive firm chooses the output at which

$$SMC = MR = P \tag{2}$$

Suppose the firm faces a horizontal demand curve at the price P_4 in Figure 8.2. From equation (2) the firm chooses the output Q_4 to reach point *D*, at which price equals marginal cost.

Next, the firm checks whether it would rather shut down in the short run. It shuts down if the price P_4 fails to cover short-run variable cost at this output. In Figure 8.2 P_4 exceeds *SAVC* at the output Q_4. The firm supplies Q_4 and makes profits. Point *D* lies above point *G*, the short-run average total cost (including overheads) of producing Q_4. Hence profits are the rectangle obtained by multiplying the vertical distance *DG* (average profit per unit produced) by the horizontal distance OQ_4 (number of units produced).

In the short run, the firm supplies positive output for any price above P_1. At a price P_2, the firm makes Q_2, the output at which price equals marginal cost. Any price below P_1 is below the minimum point on the *SAVC* curve. The firm cannot find an output at which price covers *SAVC*. Between points *A* and *C* the firm is making short-run losses but recouping some of its overheads. At any price above P_3, at which the *SMC* curve crosses the lowest point on the *SATC* curve, the firm is making short-run profits.

Remember that these are economic or supernormal profits after allowing for the economic costs, including the opportunity costs of the owner's financial capital and work effort, summarized in the *SAVC* and *SATC* curves.

A firm's long-run supply curve

Figure 8.3 shows the firm's average and marginal costs in the long run. The long-run marginal cost curve *LMC* is flatter than the *SMC* curve since the firm can adjust all inputs in the long run.

The **short-run supply curve** is the SMC curve above the point at which the SMC curve crosses the lowest point on the SAVC curve.

A firm's **long-run supply curve**, relating output supplied to price in the long run, is that part of its LMC curve above its LAC curve.

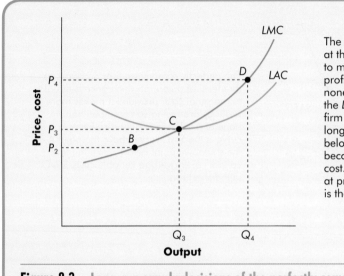

The perfectly competitive firm produces at that level of output at which P is equal to marginal cost, provided it makes more profit by producing some output than none at all. It therefore chooses points on the LMC curve. At any price above P_3 the firm makes profits because price is above long-run average cost (LAC). At any price below P_3, such as P_2, the firm makes losses because price is below long-run average cost. It therefore will not produce any output at prices below P_3. The long-run supply curve is the LMC curve above point C.

Figure 8.3   **Long-run supply decisions of the perfectly competitive firm**

Facing a price P_4, the firm chooses the long-run output Q_4 at point D, then checks if it is better to shut down than to produce this output. In the long run, shutting down means leaving the industry altogether.

> When economic profits are zero the firm makes **normal profits**. Its accounting profits just cover the opportunity cost of the owner's money and time.

The firm exits the industry if price fails to cover long-run average cost LAC at the best positive output. At the price P_2, the best positive output is at point B in Figure 8.3 but the firm makes a loss and should exit the industry in the long run. At any price below P_3, the firm exits the industry. At the price P_3, the firm produces Q_3 and just breaks even after paying all its economic costs. It makes only **normal profits**.

Entry and exit

> **Entry** is when new firms join an industry.
>
> **Exit** is when existing firms leave.

The price P_3 corresponding to the lowest point on the LAC curve in Figure 8.3 is the entry or exit price. Firms make only normal profits. There is no incentive to enter or leave the industry. The resources tied up in the firm are earning just as much as their opportunity costs, that is, what they could earn elsewhere. Any price below P_3 induces the firm to exit the industry in the long run. P_3 is the minimum price required to keep the firm in the industry.

We can also interpret Figure 8.3 as the decision facing a potential entrant to the industry. The cost curves now describe the post-entry costs. P_3 is the price at which entry becomes attractive. Any price above P_3 yields supernormal profits and encourages entry of new firms.

The marginal firm

In the short run the number of firms in a perfectly competitive market is fixed. In the long run the number of firms is determined by entry and exit. If in the long run firms in the market are making supernormal profits, then other firms may find it profitable to enter the market. Assume that all firms in the market and the potential entrants are equal, meaning they have the same cost curves.

Consider Figure 8.4. Suppose that the market demand and the market supply are such that the market price is P_1. Given the long-run average cost curve depicted in Figure 8.4, when the price is P_1, a firm in the market makes supernormal profits. New firms may then enter the market. The main effect of this entry is that more firms will produce in the market and so the market supply will shift to the right. This is represented

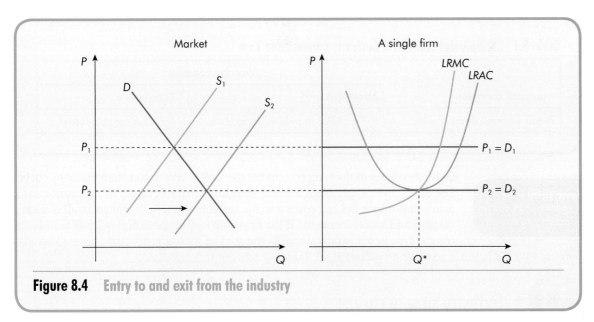

Figure 8.4 Entry to and exit from the industry

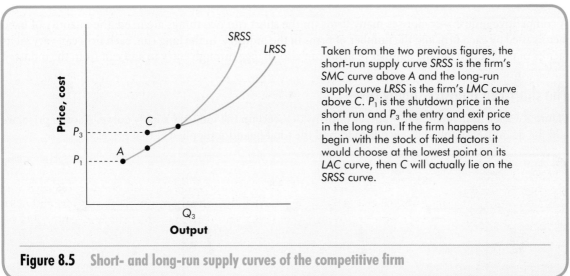

Taken from the two previous figures, the short-run supply curve *SRSS* is the firm's *SMC* curve above A and the long-run supply curve *LRSS* is the firm's *LMC* curve above C. P_1 is the shutdown price in the short run and P_3 the entry and exit price in the long run. If the firm happens to begin with the stock of fixed factors it would choose at the lowest point on its *LAC* curve, then C will actually lie on the *SRSS* curve.

Figure 8.5 Short- and long-run supply curves of the competitive firm

by the shift from S_1 to S_2 in Figure 8.4. Since the supply has increased, for a given market demand, the market price will decrease. This will reduce the profits that firms in the market can make.

When will entry into the market stop? When the last firm to enter makes zero profits. This last firm to enter is called the **marginal firm**. In Figure 8.4, entry stops when the market price is P_2. That price will be equal to the minimum *LRAC* for all firms and so each firm will make zero profit. No other firm will find entry profitable since there are no profits to steal. When the market price is above P_2, entry is profitable. At P_2, entry stops and the market is in long-run equilibrium.

> The **marginal firm** is the last firm to enter the market; it makes zero long-run profits.

Supply decisions of a competitive firm

Figure 8.5 summarizes the preceding discussion. For each level of fixed factors there is a different *SMC* curve and short-run supply curve *SRSS*. The long-run supply curve *LRSS* is flatter than *SRSS* because extra

Table 8.1 Supply decisions of a perfectly competitive firm

Marginal condition	Average condition	
	Short-run	Long-run
Produce output where $P = MC$	If $P < SAVC$, shut down temporarily.	If $P < LAC$, exit industry.

The **shutdown price** is the price below which the firm cuts its losses by making no output.

factor flexibility in the long run makes the *LMC* curve flatter than the *SMC* curve. The *SRSS* curve starts from a lower **shutdown price** because, in the short run, a firm will produce if it can cover average variable costs. In the long run all costs are variable and must be covered if the firm is to stay in the industry. In either case, a competitive firm's supply curve is the part of its marginal cost curve above the point at which it is better to make no output at all. Table 8.1 sets out this principle.

8.3 Industry supply curves

A competitive industry comprises many firms. In the short run two things are fixed: the quantity of fixed factors used by each firm and the number of firms in the industry. In the long run, each firm can vary all its factors of production but the number of firms can also change through entry to and exit from the industry.

The short-run industry supply curve

Figure 8.6 adds individual supply curves of firms to ascertain the industry supply curve. At each price, we add the quantities supplied by each firm to find the total quantity supplied at that price.

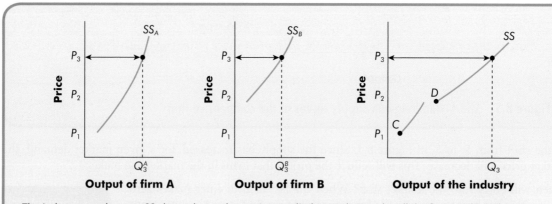

The industry supply curve *SS* shows the total quantity supplied at each price by all the firms in the industry. It is obtained by adding at each price the quantity supplied by each firm in the industry. With only two firms, A and B, the figure shows how, at a price such as P_3, we add Q_3^A and Q_3^B to obtain Q_3 on the industry supply curve. Since firms can have different shutdown prices or entry and exit prices, the industry supply curve can have step jumps at points such as *C* and *D* where an extra firm starts production. However, with many firms in the industry, each trivial relative to the industry as a whole, the step jumps in the industry supply curve when another starts production are so small that we can effectively think of the upward-sloping industry supply curve as smooth.

Figure 8.6 Deriving the industry supply curve

In the short run, the number of firms in the industry is given. Suppose there are two firms, A and B. Each firm's short-run supply curve is the part of its *SMC* curve above its shutdown price. In Figure 8.6, firm A has a lower shutdown price than firm B. Firm A has a lower *SAVC* curve. It may have a better location or better technical know-how. Each firm's supply curve is horizontal at the shutdown price. At a lower price, no output is supplied.

At each price, the industry supply Q is the sum of Q^A, the supply of firm A, and Q^B, the supply of firm B. Thus if P_3 is the price, $Q_3 = Q_3^A + Q_3^B$. The industry supply curve is the horizontal sum of the separate supply curves. The industry supply curve is discontinuous at the price P_2. Between P_1 and P_2 only the lower-cost firm A is producing. At P_2, firm B starts to produce as well.

With many firms, each with a different shutdown price, there are many tiny discontinuities as we move up the industry supply curve. Since each firm in a competitive industry is trivial relative to the total, the industry supply curve is effectively smooth.

Comparing short-run and long-run industry supply curves

Figure 8.6 may also be used to derive the long-run industry supply curve. For each firm, the individual supply curve is the part of its *LMC* curve above its entry and exit price. Unlike the short run, the number of firms in the industry is no longer fixed. Existing firms can leave the industry and new firms can enter. Instead of horizontally aggregating at each price the quantities supplied by the existing firms in the industry, we must horizontally aggregate the quantities supplied by existing firms *and firms that might potentially enter the industry*.

At a price below P_2 in Figure 8.6, firm B is not in the industry in the long run. At prices above P_2, firm B is in the industry. As the market price rises, total industry supply rises in the long run, not just because each existing firm moves up its long-run supply curve but also because new firms join the industry.

Conversely, at low prices, high-cost firms lose money and leave the industry. Entry and exit in the long run are analogous to shutdown in the short run. In the long run, entry and exit affect the number of producing firms whose output is horizontally aggregated to get the industry supply. In the short run, the number of firms in the industry is given but some are producing while others are temporarily shut down. Again, the industry supply curve is the horizontal sum of those outputs produced at the given market price.

The long-run supply curve is flatter than its short-run counterpart. Each firm can vary its factors more appropriately in the long run and has a flatter supply curve. Moreover, higher prices attract extra firms into the industry. Industry output rises by more than the extra output supplied by the firms already in the industry.

Conversely, if the price falls, firms initially move down their (relatively steep) short-run supply curves. If short-run average variable costs are covered, firms may not reduce output very much. In the long run each firm reduces output further since all factors of production can now be varied. In addition, some firms exit the industry since they are no longer covering long-run average costs. A price cut reduces industry output by more in the long run than in the short run.

A horizontal long-run industry supply curve

Each firm has a rising *LMC* curve and thus a rising long-run supply curve. The industry supply curve is a bit flatter. Higher prices do not merely induce existing firms to produce more but also induce new firms to enter. In the extreme case, the industry long-run supply curve is horizontal if all existing firms and potential entrants have *identical cost* curves (Figure 8.7). Below P^*, no firm wants to supply. It takes a price P^* to induce each individual firm to make Q_1.

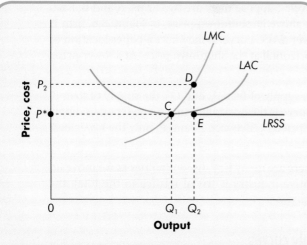

When all existing firms and potential entrants have identical costs, industry output can be expanded without offering a price higher than P^*. The long-run industry curve is the horizontal line *LRSS* at P^*. Industry output can be indefinitely expanded at this price by increasing the number of firms that each produce Q_1.

Figure 8.7 The horizontal long-run industry supply curve

At a price P_2 above P^*, each firm makes Q_2 and earns supernormal profits. Point D is above point E. Since potential entrants face the same cost curves, new firms flood into the industry. The industry supply curve is horizontal in the long run at P^*. It is not necessary to bribe existing firms to move up their individual supply curves. Industry output is expanded by the entry of new firms alone. Figure 8.7 shows the long-run industry supply curve *LRSS*, horizontal at the price P^*.

There are two reasons why a rising long-run industry supply curve is much more likely than a horizontal long-run supply curve for a competitive industry. First, it is unlikely that every firm and potential firm in the industry has identical cost curves. Second, even if all firms face the same cost curves, we draw a cost curve for given technology *and* given input prices. Although each small firm affects neither output prices nor input prices, collective expansion of output by all firms may bid up input prices. It then needs a higher output price to induce industry output to rise. In general, the long-run industry supply curve slopes up.

8.4 Comparative statics for a competitive industry

Having discussed the industry supply curve, we can now examine how supply and demand interact to determine equilibrium price in the short run and the long run.

We now examine equilibrium in a competitive industry and apply the method of **comparative static** analysis introduced in Chapter 3.

Comparative statics examines how equilibrium changes when demand or cost conditions shift.

In **short-run equilibrium** the price equates the quantity demanded to the total quantity supplied by the given number of firms in the industry when each firm is on its short-run supply curve.

In **long-run equilibrium** the price equates the quantity demanded to the total quantity supplied by the number of firms in the industry when each firm is on its long-run supply curve and firms can freely enter or exit the industry.

An increase in costs

Consider a rise in costs, such as a higher input price, that hits all firms in the industry. For simplicity, suppose all firms have the same cost curves and the long-run industry supply curve is horizontal.

In Figure 8.8 the competitive industry faces a downward-sloping demand curve DD. Initially, the long-run supply curve is $LRSS_1$. The market clears at the price P_1^* and the total output Q_1^*. The short-run industry supply curve is $SRSS_1$. The market is in **short-run** and **long-run equilibrium**.

The left-hand figure shows that each firm makes q_1^* at the lowest point on its average cost curve LAC_1. This is also the lowest point on its $SATC$ curve and hence also lies on its SMC curve, though the initial position of these two curves is not shown in Figure 8.8. N_1 firms in the industry each make output q_1^*. Total output is $Q_1^* = N_1 q_1^*$.

A rise in input prices raises costs for all firms. LAC_2 is the new long-run average cost curve for a firm. In the short run, a firm has some fixed factors. $SATC_2$ and

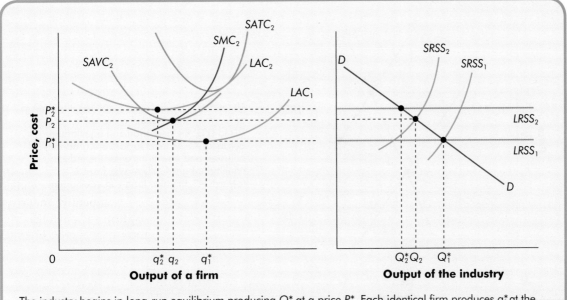

The industry begins in long-run equilibrium producing Q_1^* at a price P_1^*. Each identical firm produces q_1^* at the lowest point on LAC_1. The long-run supply curve $LRSS_1$ is horizontal at P_1^*. When costs increase, firms have fixed factors and the number of firms is given in the short run. Each firm produces q_2 where the short-run equilibrium price P_2 equals SMC_2. Together, these firms produce Q_2. Since firms are losing money, in the long run some firms leave the industry. The new long-run supply curve $LRSS_2$ for the industry is horizontal at P_2^*, the minimum point on each firms's new long-run average cost curve LAC_2. Each firm produces q_2^*. Industry output is Q_2^*.

Figure 8.8   A cost increase in a competitive industry

$SAVC_2$ are average total and average variable costs given these fixed factors. Short-run marginal cost SMC_2 goes through the lowest point of both these curves. The part of SMC_2 above $SAVC_2$ is the firm's short-run supply curve. In the short run the number of firms remains fixed.

Horizontally adding these short-run supply curves for N_1 firms, we get the new industry short-run supply curve $SRSS_2$. The new short-run equilibrium is at P_2, where $SRSS_2$ crosses the demand curve. Each firm has $P_2 = SMC_2$ and supplies q_2. Together, the N_1 firms supply Q_2. Firms cover variable costs, but not fixed costs, at the price P_2. They are losing money.

As time elapses, fixed factors are varied, and firms leave the industry. Long-run equilibrium is at the price P_2^* since the new long-run industry supply curve $LRSS_2$ is horizontal at P_2^*, which just covers minimum long-run average costs. Each firm supplies q_2^*. The number of firms N_2 is such that $Q_2^* = N_2 q_2^*$.

Figure 8.8 makes two points about the change in the long-run equilibrium. First, the rise in average costs is eventually passed on to the consumer in higher prices. In long-run equilibrium the marginal firm (here all firms, since they are identical) breaks even, so there is no incentive for further entry or exit. Hence, price rises to cover the increase in minimum average costs.

Second, since higher prices reduce the total quantity demanded, industry output must fall.

A shift in the market demand curve

Figure 8.9 shows the effect of a shift up in the market demand curve from DD to $D'D'$. We show the effects at the industry level. Try to draw your own diagram showing what is happening for the individual firm, as we did in Figure 8.8.

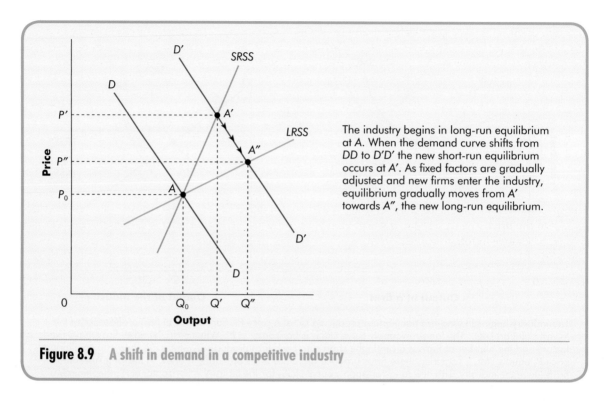

Figure 8.9 **A shift in demand in a competitive industry**

The industry starts in long-run equilibrium at point *A*. Overnight, each firm has fixed factors and the number of firms is fixed. Horizontally adding their short-run supply curves, we get the industry supply curve *SRSS*. The new short-run equilibrium is at *A'*. When demand first rises, it takes a big price rise to induce individual firms to move up their steep short-run supply curves with given fixed factors.

In the long run, firms can adjust all factors and their long-run supply curves are flatter. Moreover, supernormal profits attract extra firms into the industry. Figure 8.9 assumes that the long-run industry supply curve is rising. Either it takes higher prices to attract higher-cost firms into the industry, or the collective expansion bids up some input prices, or both. The new long-run equilibrium is at *A'*. Relative to short-run equilibrium at *A'*, there is another rise in total output. However, a better choice of inputs and the entry of new firms raise supply and reduce the market-clearing price.

8.5 Pure monopoly: the opposite limiting case

A perfectly competitive firm is too small to worry about any effect of its output decision on industry supply and hence price. It can sell as much as it wants at the market price. We next discuss the opposite limiting case of market structure, the case of pure monopoly.

A **monopolist** is the sole supplier and potential supplier of the industry's product.

The firm and the industry coincide. The sole national supplier may not be a monopolist if the good or service is internationally traded. The Royal Mail is the sole supplier of UK stamps and a **monopolist** in them. Airbus is the only large plane maker in Europe but is not a monopolist since it faces cut-throat international competition from Boeing. Sole suppliers may also face invisible competition from potential entrants. If so, they are not monopolists.

First, we study the decisions of a private profit-maximizing monopolist who has no fear of entry or foreign competition. Some monopolies are state-owned and not necessarily run for private profit. However, in the past two decades many countries have been 'privatizing' these state-run monopolies. The analysis in the rest of this chapter is relevant both to existing private monopolies and to how state-run monopolies might behave if restored to private ownership.

8.6 Profit-maximizing output for a monopolist

To maximize profits any firm chooses the output at which marginal revenue *MR* equals marginal cost (*SMC* in the short run and *LMC* in the long run). It then checks it is covering average costs (*SAVC* in the short run and *LAC* in the long run).

The special feature of a competitive firm is that *MR* equals price. Selling an extra unit of output does not bid down the price and reduce the revenue earned on previous units. The price at which the extra unit is sold is the change in total revenue.

In contrast, a monopolist's demand curve *is* the industry demand curve, which slopes down. Hence *MR* is less than the price at which the extra output is sold. The monopolist knows that extra output reduces revenue from *existing* units. To sell more, the price on all units must be cut.

In Chapter 6, and in particular Maths 6.1, we explained how, for a downward-sloping demand curve, price, marginal revenue and total revenue are related. Figure 8.10 reminds you of those relationships. The more inelastic the demand curve, the more an extra unit of output bids down the price, reducing revenue from existing units. At any output, *MR* is further below the demand curve the more inelastic is demand. Also,

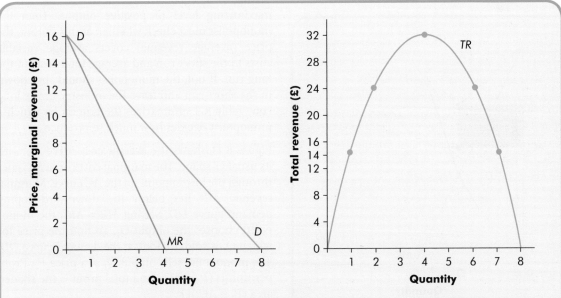

Total revenue (*TR*) equals price times quantity. From the demand curve *DD* we can plot the *TR* curve at each quantity. Maximum *TR* occurs at £32, when 4 units are sold for £8 each. Marginal revenue (*MR*) shows how *TR* changes when quantity is increased a small amount. *MR* lies below the demand curve *DD*. From the price of the extra unit we must subtract the loss in revenue from existing units as the price is bid down. This effect is larger the higher is existing output and the more inelastic is the demand curve. The *MR* curve lies further below *DD* the larger is output and the more inelastic the demand curve. Beyond an output of 4 units, *MR* is negative and further expansion reduces total revenue.

Figure 8.10 *Demand, total revenue and marginal revenue*

Table 8.2 Profit-maximizing monopoly

| | Marginal condition | | | Average condition | | | |
| | | | | Short-run | | Long-run | |
	MR > MC	MR = MC	MR < MC	P > SAVC	P < SAVC	P > LAC	P < LAC
Output decision	Raise	Optimal	Lower	Produce	Shut down	Stay	Exit

the larger the existing output, the larger the revenue loss from existing units when the price is reduced to sell another unit. For a given demand curve, *MR* falls increasingly below price the higher the output from which we begin.

Beyond a certain output (4 in Figure 8.10), the revenue loss on existing output exceeds the revenue gain from the extra unit itself. Marginal revenue is negative. Further expansion reduces total revenue.

On the cost side, with only one producer, the cost curves for a single firm in Chapter 7 carry over directly. The monopolist has the usual cost curves, average and marginal, short run and long run. For simplicity, we discuss only the long-run curves.

Profit-maximizing output

Setting *MR* equal to *MC* leads to the profit-maximizing level of positive output. Then the monopolist must check whether, at this output, the price (average revenue) covers average variable costs in the short run and average total costs in the long run. If not, the monopolist should shut down in the short run and leave the industry in the long run. Table 8.2 summarizes the criteria by which a monopolist decides how much to produce.

Figure 8.11 shows the average cost curve *AC* with its usual U-shape. The marginal cost curve *MC* goes through the lowest point on the *AC* curve. Marginal revenue *MR* lies below the downward-sloping demand curve *DD*. Setting *MR = MC*, the monopolist chooses the output Q_1. To find the price for which Q_1 is sold, we look at the demand curve *DD*. The monopolist sells output Q_1 at a price P_1. Profit per unit is $(P_1 - AC_1)$ and total profit is the shaded area $(P_1 - AC_1)Q_1$.

Even in the long run, the monopolist makes *supernormal profits*, sometimes called *monopoly profits*. Unlike the case in competitive industry, supernormal profits of a monopolist are not eliminated by the entry of more firms and a fall in the price. A monopoly has no fear of possible entry. By ruling out entry, we remove the mechanism by which supernormal profits disappear in the long run.

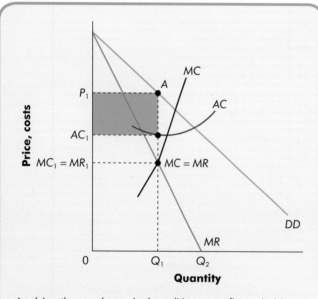

Applying the usual marginal condition, a profit-maximizing monopolist produces the output level Q_1 at which marginal cost MC equals marginal revenue MR. Then it must check that price covers average cost. In this figure, Q_1 can be sold at a price P_1 in excess of average costs AC_1. Monopoly profits are the shaded area $(P_1 - AC_1) \times Q_1$.

Figure 8.11 The monopoly equilibrium: *MC = MR*

Price setting

Whereas a competitive firm is a *price-taker*, a monopolist sets prices and is a *price-setter*. Having decided to produce Q_1 in Figure 8.11, the monopolist quotes a price P_1 knowing that customers will then demand the output Q_1.

Elasticity and marginal revenue

When the elasticity of demand is between 0 and −1, demand is inelastic and a rise in output reduces total revenue. Marginal revenue is negative. In percentage terms, the fall in price exceeds the rise in quantity. All outputs to the right of Q_2 in Figure 8.11 have negative *MR*. The demand curve is inelastic at quantities above Q_2. At quantities below Q_2 the demand curve is elastic. Higher output leads to higher revenue. Marginal revenue is positive.

The monopolist sets $MC = MR$. Since *MC* must be positive, so must *MR*. The chosen output must lie to the left of Q_2. *A monopolist never produces on the inelastic part of the demand curve.*

Price, marginal cost and monopoly power

At any output, price exceeds the monopolist's marginal revenue since the demand curve slopes down. Hence, in setting $MR = MC$ the monopolist sets a price that exceeds marginal cost. In contrast, a competitive firm always equates price and marginal cost, since its price is also its marginal revenue. A competitive firm cannot raise price above marginal cost and has no **monopoly power**.[1] The more inelastic the demand curve of a monopolist, the more marginal revenue is below price, the greater is the excess of price over marginal cost, and the more monopoly power it has.

> The excess of price over marginal cost is a measure of **monopoly power**.

Comparative statics for a monopolist

Figure 8.11 may also be used to analyse changes in costs or demand. Suppose a rise in costs shifts the *MC* and *AC* curves upwards. The higher *MC* curve must cross the *MR* curve at a lower output. If the monopolist can sell this output at a price that covers average costs, the effect of the cost increase must be to reduce output. Since the demand curve slopes down, lower output means a higher equilibrium price.

Similarly, for the original cost curves shown in Figure 8.11, suppose there is an outward shift in demand and marginal revenue curves. *MR* must now cross *MC* at a higher output. Thus a rise in demand leads the monopolist to increase output.

MATHS 8.1

Profit maximization and monopoly power

Consider a monopoly that faces the following linear inverse demand function for its product: $P = a − bQ$, where a and b are positive constants. In order to produce, the monopoly faces the following total cost function: $TC(Q) = cQ + dQ^2$, where c and d are positive constants. The profit function of the monopoly is given by total revenues minus total costs. Total revenues are $TR(Q) = P \times Q$. In our case, the price P is given by the inverse demand function, therefore the total revenues are: $TR(Q) = (a − bQ)Q = −bQ^2 + aQ$.

---

1   A synonym of monopoly power is market power, so those terms can be used interchangeably. Here we use the expression monopoly power since we are dealing with a monopolist. However, there may be firms that are not monopolists in their market that may still have the ability to set a price above their marginal cost. In those cases, we say that those firms have market power. This will be discussed in detail in the next chapter.

▶ The profit function of the monopoly is then:

$$\pi(Q) = -bQ^2 + aQ - cQ - dQ^2 \tag{1}$$

Expression (1) tells us how the profit of the monopolist (π) depends on the quantity produced (Q). The monopolist should choose the quantity to produce in order to maximize the profit function in (1). We know that at the quantity that maximizes profits it must be true that $MR = MC$. In our case, we have that:

$$MR(Q) \equiv \frac{dTR(Q)}{dQ} = -2bQ + a \qquad \text{and} \qquad MC(Q) \equiv \frac{dTC(Q)}{dQ} = c + 2dQ$$

Therefore the quantity that maximizes profits must solve the equation $MR = MC$:

$$-2bQ + a = c + 2dQ \tag{2}$$

Solving equation (2) for Q gives us:

$$Q^\star = \frac{a-c}{2(b+d)} \tag{3}$$

This is the quantity that the monopolist chooses to produce. Notice that we need to assume $a > c$ in order to have a positive quantity produced. Once we know the quantity chosen by the monopolist, we can find the market price. Substitute expression (3) into the inverse demand function:

$$P^\star = a - b\left(\frac{a-c}{2(b+d)}\right) \tag{4}$$

A bit of algebra and expression (4) can be written as:

$$P^\star = \frac{b(a+c) + 2ad}{2(b+d)}$$

Notice that we have assumed that the monopolist chooses the quantity that maximizes the profit and then we found the price charged using the inverse demand. Obviously, we could have done the reverse. We could have found the price that maximizes the profits (since the monopolist is a price-setter) and then applied that information to the demand function to find the quantity the monopolist should sell. The result would be exactly the same.

Here is a numerical example. Suppose that the demand is $P = 100 - 2Q$, while the total cost function is $TC = 10Q + Q^2$. Compared to our previous analysis we now have: $a = 100$, $b = 2$, $c = 10$ and $d = 1$. Using those data in (3), we have that the profit-maximizing quantity chosen by the monopolist is $Q^\star = 15$, while the price charged by the monopolist is $P^\star = 70$. The marginal cost when $Q^\star = 15$ is $MC = 40$. As we can see, the price charged by the monopolist is higher than the marginal cost.

Monopoly power measures the ability of the monopolist to set a price higher than marginal cost. The monopoly power crucially depends on the elasticity of demand. To see this more formally, we first relate the marginal revenue to the elasticity of demand. Consider a generic inverse demand function $P(Q)$. The total revenue function is $TR = P(Q) \times Q$. By taking the derivative with respect to Q of TR, we get that the marginal revenue can be written as:

$$MR(Q) = \frac{dP}{dQ}Q + P \tag{5}$$

where dP/dQ is the derivative of the inverse demand function with respect to Q.

Rearrange equation (5) in the following way:

$$MR(Q) = P\left[\frac{dP}{dQ}\frac{Q}{P} + 1\right] \tag{6}$$

The term $(dP/dQ)(Q/P)$ looks familiar. From Chapter 4 we know that the point elasticity of demand is given by $PED = (dP/dQ)(Q/P)$. Therefore $1/PED = (dP/dQ)(Q/P)$ is the inverse of the elasticity of demand. Using this fact in equation (6), we have:

$$MR(Q) = P\left[1 + \frac{1}{PED}\right] \tag{7}$$

Since the elasticity of demand is a negative number, we can use its absolute value in (7) and we have:

$$MR(Q) = P\left[1 - \frac{1}{|PED|}\right] \tag{8}$$

Equation (8) gives us the relationship between the marginal revenue.

The profit-maximization condition of the monopolist, $MR = MC$, can be written as:

$$P\left[1 - \frac{1}{|PED|}\right] = MC(Q) \tag{9}$$

If demand is inelastic (meaning $|PED|$ between 0 and 1), the term in brackets is negative. There is no way for the left-hand side to be equal to the right-hand side since the marginal cost of production is normally positive. This explains why a monopolist never produces on the inelastic part of the demand curve. Moreover, from equation (9) we can say that the higher is the elasticity of demand (meaning $|PED|$ is a very large positive number), the closer to 1 is the term in brackets. In this case, the price charged by the monopolist will be very close to the marginal cost. Another way to say this is, the more elastic is the demand faced by the monopolist, the lower is its monopoly power.

8.7 Output and price under monopoly and competition

We now compare a perfectly competitive industry with a monopoly. For this comparison to be of interest, the two industries must face the same demand and cost conditions. How would the *same* industry change if it were organized first as a competitive industry then as a monopoly?

Chapter 9 explains why some industries are competitive but others are monopolies. If this theory is right, can the same industry be both competitive and a monopoly? Only in some special cases.

Comparing a competitive industry and a multi-plant monopolist

Consider a competitive industry in which all firms and potential entrants have the same cost curves. The horizontal *LRSS* curve for this competitive industry is shown in Figure 8.12. Facing the demand curve *DD*, the industry is in long-run equilibrium at *A* at a price P_1 and total output Q_1. The industry *LRSS* curve is horizontal at P_1, the lowest point on the *LAC* curve of each firm. Any other price leads eventually to infinite

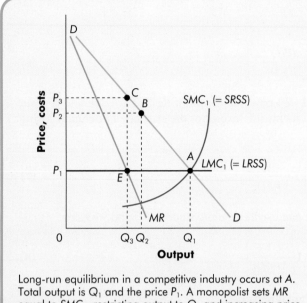

Long-run equilibrium in a competitive industry occurs at A. Total output is Q_1 and the price P_1. A monopolist sets MR equal to SMC_1, restricting output to Q_2 and increasing price to P_2. In the long run the monopolist sets MR equal to LMC_1, reducing output to Q_3 and increasing the price again to P_3. There are no entrants to compete away supernormal profits P_3CEP_1 by increasing the industry output.

Figure 8.12 A monopolist produces a lower output at a higher price

entry to or exit from the industry. *LRSS* is the industry's long-run marginal cost curve LMC_1 of expanding output by enticing new firms into the industry.

Each firm produces at the lowest point on its *LAC* curve, breaking even. The marginal cost curves pass through the point of minimum average costs. Hence, each firm is also on its *SMC* and *LMC* curves. Horizontally adding the *SMC* curves of each firm, we get *SRSS*, the short-run industry supply curve. This is the industry's short-run marginal cost curve SMC_1 of expanding output from existing firms with temporarily fixed factors. Since *SRSS* crosses the demand curve at P_1, the industry is in both short-run and long-run equilibrium.

Beginning from this position, the competitive industry becomes a monopoly. The monopolist takes over each plant (firm) but makes central pricing and output decisions. Overnight, the monopolist still has the same number of factories (ex-firms) as in the competitive industry. Since the firm and the industry now coincide, SMC_1 remains the short-run marginal cost curve for the monopolist taking all plants together.[2] However, the monopolist knows that higher total output bids down the price.

In the short run the monopolist equates SMC_1 and *MR*, reaching equilibrium at *B*. Output is Q_2 and the price is P_2. Relative to competitive equilibrium at *A*, *the monopolist raises price and reduces quantity*.

In the long run the monopolist can enter (set up new factories) or exit (close down existing factories). Whether making short-run profits or losses at *B* (we need to draw the *SATC* curve to see which), a monopolist will now exit the industry or close down some factories in the long run.

The monopolist cuts back output to force up the price. In the long run it makes sense to operate each factory at the lowest point on its *LAC* curve. To reduce total output some factories are closed. In the long run, the monopolist sets $LMC_1 = MR$ and reaches equilibrium at *C*. *Price has risen yet further to P_3 and output has fallen to Q_3*. Long-run profits are given by the area P_3CEP_1 since P_1 remains the long-run average cost when all plants are at the lowest point on their *LAC* curve.

Because *MR* is less than price, a monopolist produces less than a competitive industry and charges a higher price. However, in this example it is a legal prohibition on entry by competitors that allows the monopolist to succeed in the long run. Otherwise, with identical cost curves, other firms would set up in competition, expand industry output and compete away these supernormal profits. Absence of entry is intrinsic to the model of monopoly.

---

2   In a competitive industry each firm equates the price to its own marginal cost. Hence firms produce at the same marginal cost. We horizontally add individual *SMC* curves (at the same price) to get the industry *SMC* curve. A multi-plant monopolist need not equate *MC* across all plants but always finds it profitable to do so. If marginal costs in two plants differ, a monopolist can produce the same total output more cheaply by producing an extra unit in the low *MC* plant and one less unit in the high *MC* plant. Thus *SMC* for the monopolist across all plants remains the horizontal sum of the *SMC* curves for individual plants, as in a competitive industry.

The social cost of monopoly

We know that a monopoly tends to produce less and at a higher price than a perfectly competitive industry. This may be seen as a bad thing, since we should prefer more production at a lower price than less production at a high price (unless of course you are the monopolist). Another way to see why a monopoly may be bad compared to perfect competition is to look at the total surplus in the market, defined as the sum of the consumers' and producers' surplus. From Chapter 3 we know that the total surplus, or social surplus, in the market is a measure of the gain that the participants get from participating in the market.

Consider for simplicity an industry with a constant long-run marginal cost equal to the long-run average cost. An example of a cost function with such a property is $TC = cQ$, where c is a positive constant. In Figure 8.13, under perfect competition LMC is both the industry's long-run marginal cost curve and its supply curve. With constant returns to scale, LMC is also the long-run average cost curve of the industry. Given the demand curve DD, competitive equilibrium is at B. The competitive industry produces an output Q_C at a price P_C.

Now the industry becomes a monopolist, producing output Q_M at a price P_M, thus equating marginal cost and marginal revenue. Under a perfectly competitive industry, the producer's surplus is zero and the total surplus coincides with the consumers' surplus; this is given by area $P_C BD$ in Figure 8.13.

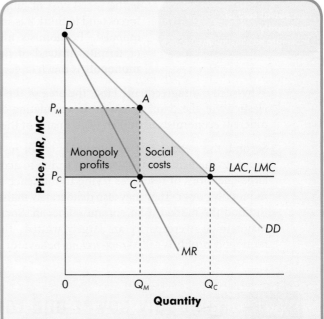

The industry has horizontal long-run average and marginal costs. A perfectly competitive industry produces at B, but a monopolist sets $MR = MC$ to produce only Q_M at a price P_M. The monopolist earns excess profits $P_M P_C CA$, but there is a social cost or deadweight burden equal to the triangle ACB. Between Q_M and Q_C social marginal benefit exceeds social marginal cost and society would gain by expanding output to Q_C. The triangle ACB shows how much society would gain by this expansion.

Figure 8.13   The social cost of monopoly

Under a monopoly industry, the producer's surplus is given by area $P_M P_C AC$, which represents the monopolist's profits. On the other hand, the consumers' surplus is now given by area $P_M AD$. The total surplus under a monopoly is therefore area $P_C CAD$.

By comparing the case of a competitive industry with the monopoly, we can see that under a monopoly the total surplus is lower than under a perfectly competitive industry.

In particular, the difference between the two cases is represented by the triangle ACB in Figure 8.13. That triangle represents the **deadweight loss** in social surplus caused by the fact that the monopolist restricts output to Q_M. Notice that this deadweight loss is just a waste in social surplus. By increasing the level of competition in the industry, it is possible to increase the quantity produced and to reduce that loss. When the industry becomes perfectly competitive, in the sense that output will be sold at a price equal to the long-run marginal cost, the social surplus is maximized, meaning that it cannot be increased further.

> At an output below the efficient level, the **deadweight loss** shows the loss of social surplus.

For the economy, the social cost of monopoly is found by adding together the deadweight loss triangles such as ACB for all industries.

> The **social cost of monopoly** is the failure to maximize social surplus.

Is the social cost of monopoly power large? Economists who believe in market forces tend to think it is small. Professor George Stigler, a Nobel Prize winner, once quipped, 'Economists might serve a more useful purpose if they fought fires or termites instead of monopoly.' Other economists believe the **social cost of monopoly** is much larger.

Why such a disagreement? First, the area of the deadweight loss triangle in Figure 8.13 depends on the elasticity of the demand curve. In calculating the size of deadweight loss triangles under monopoly, different economists use different estimates of the demand elasticity.

Second, the welfare cost of monopoly is not just the deadweight loss. Since monopoly may yield high profits to the firm, firms spend a lot trying to acquire and secure monopoly positions. Firms may devote large quantities of resources trying to influence the government in ways that enhance or preserve their monopoly power. They may also deliberately maintain extra production capacity to create a credible threat to flood the market if an entrant comes in. Socially, resources devoted to lobbying the government or maintaining overcapacity are largely wasted. This kind of behaviour by firms to acquire and protect monopoly profits is called *rent-seeking* behaviour and it may be socially wasteful.

CASE 8.1 Monopoly power and competition policy

We have seen that a monopoly creates a social loss compared to a perfectly competitive market. If it is possible to increase the level of competition in a monopolized market, then society is better off since social surplus increases. Competition policy (also known as antitrust policy) deals with markets where competition can arise; however, given the behaviour of some firms in those markets, competition is restricted. There are markets in which increasing the level of competition is not feasible, so competition policy does not apply. This is the case of a natural monopoly, which will be discussed at the end of this chapter.

Broadly speaking, competition policy can be divided into policies to deal with monopoly power that already exists, and policies to deal with mergers that may increase monopoly power. While mergers will be discussed in the next chapter, here we discuss policies to address existing monopoly power. Since the UK belongs to the European Union, EU competition law takes precedence where it is relevant, essentially in the case of larger businesses with significant European or global activities.

The original Common Market was created by the 1956 Treaty of Rome. The modern and enlarged EU is largely underpinned by the 1999 Treaty of Amsterdam.

Article 81 of this treaty prohibits anti-competitive agreements that have an appreciable effect on trade between EU member states and which prevent or distort competition within the EU. Article 82 prohibits the abuse of any existing dominant position.

Responsibility for enforcement of these articles lies with the European Commission.

Although global businesses are increasingly subject to transnational competition law, many businesses still operate primarily within one country; national decisions are then appropriate. Within the UK, these are governed by the Competition Act 1998 and the Enterprise Act 2002. The latter made it a criminal offence, punishable by a jail sentence, to engage in a dishonest cartel.

Two key institutions of UK competition policy are the Office of Fair Trading (OFT) and the Competition Commission. In particular, the OFT has the power to refer cases in which existing monopoly power may be leading to a 'substantial lessening of competition' to the Competition Commission for detailed investigation.

Prior to the Enterprise Act 2002, the Competition Commission was asked instead to evaluate whether or not a monopoly was acting 'in the public interest', without any presumption that monopoly was bad, and many previous judgements of the Commission concluded that companies were acting in the public interest, for example because they had an excellent record of innovation, *despite* having a monopoly position.

The change in 2002 therefore emphasized competition more strongly and made the Competition Commission more accountable by defining its objectives more clearly. This also brought UK law more clearly into line with EU competition law, by placing measures of competition at the centre of the evaluation of competition policy.

8.8 A monopoly has no supply curve

A competitive firm sets price equal to marginal cost if it supplies at all. If we know its marginal cost curve, we know how much it supplies at each price. Aggregating across firms, we also know how much the industry supplies at each price. We can draw the supply curve without knowing anything about the market demand curve. We then analyse how supply and demand interact to determine equilibrium price and quantity.

A monopolist's output affects marginal cost and marginal revenue simultaneously. Figure 8.14 shows a given LMC curve. How much will the monopolist produce at the price P_1? It all depends on demand and marginal revenue. When demand is DD, marginal revenue is MR and the monopolist produces Q_1 at a price P_1. If demand is $D'D'$, marginal revenue is MR', and the monopolist produces Q_2 but still charges P_1.

A monopolist does not have a supply curve independent of demand conditions. Rather, a monopolist simultaneously examines demand (hence marginal revenue) and cost (hence marginal cost) to decide how much to produce and what to charge.

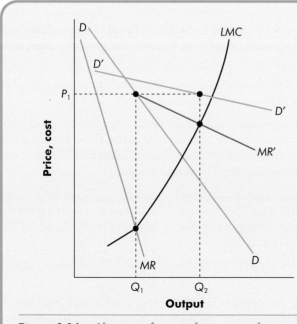

Given the demand curve DD and the corresponding marginal revenue curve MR, the monopolist produces Q_1 at a price P_1. However, lacking DD and MR, the monopolist produces Q_2 at a price P_1. Knowing the price, we cannot uniquely infer the quantity supplied unless we also know demand and marginal revenue. Because the monopolist knows that output affects both marginal cost and marginal revenue, the two must be considered simultaneously.

Figure 8.14   Absence of a supply curve under monopoly

A **discriminating monopoly** charges different prices to different people.

Discriminating monopoly

Thus far we have assumed that all consumers are charged the same price. Unlike a competitive industry, where competition prevents any firm charging more than its competitors, a monopolist may be able to charge different prices to different customers.

Consider an airline monopolizing flights between London and Rome. It has business customers whose demand curve is very inelastic. They have to fly. Their demand and marginal revenue curves are very steep. The airline also carries tourists whose demand curve is much more elastic. If flights to Rome get too expensive, tourists visit Athens instead. Tourists have much flatter demand and marginal revenue curves.

The more inelastic is the demand curve, the more the marginal revenue curve lies below the demand curve. To sell another output unit requires a bigger price cut that hits existing revenue. Since demand elasticity determines the gap between marginal revenue and price, charging the same price to purchasers with different demand elasticities means that the marginal revenue from the last business traveller is less than the marginal revenue from the last tourist.

Whatever the total number of passengers (and total cost of carrying them), the airline then has the wrong *mix* between tourists and business travellers. Since the marginal revenue from the last tourist exceeds the marginal revenue from the last business traveller, the airline gains revenue with no extra cost by carrying one more tourist and one fewer business traveller. It pays to keep changing the mix until the marginal revenue from the types is equal.

To do this, the airline must charge the two groups *different* prices. Since tourist demand is elastic, the airline charges tourists a low fare to raise tourist revenue. Since business demand is inelastic, the airline charges business travellers a high fare to increase business revenue. This kind of price discrimination is called *third-degree price discrimination*. In this case, the monopoly can divide its customers into different groups according to some characteristics of those groups (for example, business travellers versus tourist travellers, old customers versus young customers, and so on).

Profit-maximizing output satisfies two separate conditions. First, business travellers with inelastic demand pay sufficiently more than tourists with elastic demand so that the marginal revenue from the two types is equal. There is thus no incentive to rearrange the mix by altering the price differential between the two groups. Second, the level of prices and the total number of passengers is determined to equate marginal cost to each of these marginal revenues. The airline operates at the most profitable scale as well as with the most profitable mix.

When a producer charges different customers different prices, we say that the producer *price discriminates*. There are many examples of this in the real world. Rail companies charge rush-hour commuters a higher fare than midday shoppers whose demand for trips to the city is much more elastic.

Most examples of price discrimination refer to services consumed on the spot rather than to goods that can be resold. Price discrimination in a standardized commodity is unlikely to work. Those buying at the low price resell to those paying the high price, undercutting price discrimination. Effective price discrimination requires that the sub-markets can be quarantined to prevent resale.

Price discrimination illustrates again the absence of a supply curve under monopoly. Figure 8.15 shows *perfect price discrimination*, also known as *first-degree price discrimination*. Each customer pays a different price for the same product. In particular, each customer pays according to his willingness to pay for the good, which is the maximum price at which he is willing to buy.

If a monopolist charges every customer the same price, profit-maximizing output is Q_1 where MR equals MC and the price is P_1.

If the monopolist can perfectly price discriminate, the very first unit of output can be sold at a price E. Having sold the first unit to the highest bidder most desperate for the good, the next unit can be sold to the next-highest bidder, and so on. Moving down the demand curve DD, we can read off the price for which each extra unit is sold. In reducing the price to sell extra output, the monopolist no longer reduces revenue from previously sold units. *Hence the demand curve is the marginal revenue curve under perfect price discrimination.* The marginal revenue of the last unit is simply the *price* for which it is sold.

Treating *DD* as the marginal revenue curve, a perfectly price-discriminating monopolist produces at point *C*, where marginal revenue and marginal cost are equal. Two points follow immediately. First, if price discrimination is possible, it is profitable to use it. Moving from the uniform pricing point *A* to the price discriminating point *C*, the monopolist adds the area *ABC* to profits. This is the excess of extra revenue over extra cost when output is increased.

The monopolist makes a second gain from price discrimination. Even the output Q_1 now earns more revenue than under uniform pricing. The monopolist also gains the area EP_1A by charging different prices on the first Q_1 units of output rather than the single price P_1. In practice, one of the main ways management consultants raise the profits of firms that they advise is by devising new ways in which the firm can price discriminate.

Second, whether or not the firm can price discriminate affects its output choice. Uniform pricing leads to an output Q_1. Perfect price discrimination leads to an output Q_2. Uniform and discriminatory pricing lead to different outputs because they affect the marginal revenue obtained by a monopolist from a given demand curve.

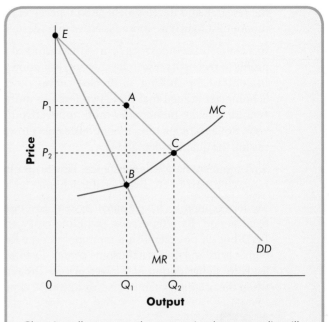

Charging all customers the same price the monopolist will produce at *B* where *MC = MR*. If each output unit can be sold for a different price the revenue from existing units is not reduced by cutting the price to sell another unit. The demand curve *DD* is the marginal revenue curve and the perfectly discriminating monopolist will produce at *C*. Output is higher and profits are higher. By price discrimination the monopolist gains an extra revenue EP_1A from selling Q_1 but also increases output beyond this level making a marginal profit of *ABC* in expanding from Q_1 to Q_2.

Figure 8.15 *Perfect price discrimination*

Perfect price discrimination is normally not feasible in reality. In order to perfectly discriminate, the monopolist should know the willingness to pay of each consumer, information that is impractical to obtain. Nevertheless, perfect discrimination gives an interesting result. If the monopolist can perfectly discriminate, the social loss associated with a monopoly disappears. The social surplus under a monopoly that perfectly discriminates is the same as under perfect competition. However, the distribution of the social surplus is completely different in the two cases. Under perfect competition the producer surplus is zero, while the social surplus coincides with the consumers' surplus. For a perfectly discriminating monopolist, the reverse is true. The perfectly discriminating monopolist extracts the entire consumers' surplus, and so the social surplus coincides with the producer surplus (the profits of the monopolist).

8.9 Monopoly and technical change

Section 8.7 compared a monopoly and a perfectly competitive industry. When such a comparison was meaningful, we discovered: (1) a monopoly will restrict output and drive up prices, and (2) a monopoly may make economic profits permanently.

Joseph Schumpeter (1883–1950) argued that this comparison ignores technical advances that reduce costs, allowing price cuts and output expansion. A large monopolist with steady profits may find it easier to *fund* the research and development (R&D) necessary to make cost-saving breakthroughs. More importantly, a monopolist may have more *incentive* to undertake R&D.

In a competitive industry a firm with a technical advantage has only a temporary opportunity to earn high profits to recoup its research expenses. Imitation by existing firms and new entrants competes away profits. In contrast, by shifting all its cost curves downwards, a monopoly can enjoy higher profits for ever. Schumpeter argued that these two forces – more resources for R&D and a higher return on a successful venture – make monopolies more innovative than competitive industries. Taking a dynamic long-run view, not a static picture, monopolists enjoy lower cost curves. As a result, they charge lower prices, thus raising the quantity demanded.

This argument has some substance. Tiny firms often do little R&D. Many of the largest firms have excellent research departments. Even so, the Schumpeter argument may overstate the case.

Modern economies have a *patent* system. Inventors of new processes get a temporary legal monopoly for a fixed period. By temporarily excluding entry and imitation, patent laws raise the incentive to conduct R&D but do not establish a monopoly in the long run. Over the life of the patent, the inventor charges a higher price and makes handsome profits. Eventually, the patent expires and competition from other firms leads to higher output and lower prices. The real price of copiers and microcomputers fell significantly when the original patents of Xerox and IBM expired.

8.10 Natural monopoly

> A **natural monopoly**'s average costs keep falling as its output rises. It undercuts all smaller competitors.

Consider a monopolist meeting the entire industry demand from a single plant. This is most plausible when scale economies are big. There are huge costs in setting up a national telephone network, for example. Yet the cost of connecting a marginal subscriber is low once the network has been set up.

Monopolies enjoying huge economies of scale – falling *LAC* curves over the entire range of output and always above the *LMC* curve – are *natural monopolies*. Large-scale economies may explain why there is a sole supplier with no fear of entry by others. Smaller new entrants would be at a prohibitive cost disadvantage.

Figure 8.16 shows an industry with steadily falling long-run average costs as output rises. Only one private firm can survive in such an industry. Any firm that expands output can cut costs and undercut its rivals. Facing a demand curve *DD* and marginal revenue curve *MR*, the resulting monopolist produces Q_M and earns profits $P_M CBE$. The monopolist makes too little and it creates a deadweight burden *AEE'*.

In the case of a natural monopoly, competition cannot be increased in the market. It is better to have a single firm producing in the market. The reason is that, if you split up the firm to create competition, a lot of small firms each produce at higher average cost and this is a waste of society's resources.

You could order the firm to produce at the efficient point *E'*. You will get the desired output *Q'*, but the price P_C is below the firm's average costs at *Q'*. It makes losses. Since marginal cost always lies below average cost when average cost is falling, forcing a natural monopolist to price at marginal cost is always loss-making. You cannot force a private firm to make losses. It will shut down.

> A **two-part tariff** charges a fixed sum for access to the service and then a price per unit that reflects the marginal cost of production.

One solution is the use of *regulation* (see also Concept 8.2). In the UK for example, Ofgem is the regulatory body for the gas and electricity markets. It aims to get close to the efficient allocation *E'* while letting the monopolist break even after allowing a proper deduction for all economic costs. By making the monopolist produce *Q* at the price corresponding to average cost at this output, the deadweight burden is cut from *AEE'* to *GHE'*.

An even better solution is to allow the monopolist to charge a **two-part tariff**.

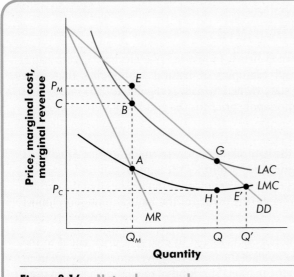

The efficient point E′ equates long-run marginal cost LMC and marginal benefit DD. A private monopolist sets MR = MC, produces Q_M and earns profits $P_M CBE$. The deadweight loss under private monopoly is AEE′. If by law the monopolist was forced to charge a fixed price P_C, the monopolist would face a horizontal demand curve $P_C E′$ up to the output Q′. Since P_C would then also be marginal revenue, the monopolist would produce at E′ where the marginal revenue and marginal cost coincide. Although efficient, society cannot force the monopolist to produce here in the long run. Since E′ lies below LAC the monopolist is making a loss and would rather go out of business.

Figure 8.16   Natural monopoly

A two-part tariff uses fixed charges to pay for fixed costs, and marginal charges to cover marginal costs. In Figure 8.16 the monopolist is told to charge P_C for each unit of the good. Consumers demand the socially efficient quantity Q′. Since the monopolist is now a price-taker at the controlled price P_C, it is loss-minimizing for the monopolist to produce Q′, at which both price and marginal revenue equal marginal cost. The regulator then allows the monopolist to levy the minimum fixed charge necessary to ensure that it breaks even after allowing for all relevant economic costs.

A third solution to the natural monopoly problem is to order the monopolist to produce at the efficient point E′ at the price P_C, and for the government to provide a subsidy to cover the losses entailed. It is socially desirable to make the efficient output Q′ in the cost-minimizing way. If the subsidy solution is adopted, there is pressure for the government to get involved in the entire running of the industry so that operations can be carefully monitored.

Three problems recur with all these solutions to the problem of natural monopoly. First, information is costly for monitors to acquire. It is hard to ensure that the industry strives to keep its cost curves at their lowest possible positions. Unnecessarily high costs can be passed on under average cost pricing (solution 1), can result in a higher fixed charge to ensure break-even under a two-part tariff (solution 2), or can require a larger subsidy (solution 3). In each case, the regulatory body has the difficult task of trying to make the natural monopoly as efficient as possible.

The second problem is **regulatory capture**. Regulated companies devote considerable time, effort and money to lobbying the regulator. Of necessity, regulators build up contacts with the regulated. Eventually, the regulator can come to sympathize with the problems of the regulated.

Third, regulators find it hard to make credible commitments regarding their future behaviour. For example, the regulator may encourage the monopolist to invest by promising 'light' regulation in the future. Once the investment is made and the cost sunk, the regulator then faces temptations to change the ground rules, toughening requirements. Foreseeing all this, the monopolist does not invest in the first place. There is underinvestment if the regulator faces commitment problems.

> **Regulatory capture**
> implies that the regulator gradually comes to identify with the interests of the firm it regulates, becoming its champion not its watchdog.

During 1945–80, many European governments concluded that the least-bad solution to these problems was nationalization.

CONCEPT
8.2

Regulation of natural monopolies

Natural monopolies were normally state-owned firms. Industries like electricity, gas, water, telecommunications and the railways are all examples of natural monopolies that were nationalized. In those industries, the price charged by the state-owned firms was regulated. This means that those natural monopolies were not allowed to charge the monopoly price for the good they were selling.

There are various ways in which a price can be regulated.

First best solution: $P = MC$. The first possibility is to force the natural monopoly to charge a price equal to its marginal cost. This possibility represents a first best solution since it mimics the same result under perfect competition and so no deadweight loss will arise in the market. However, this solution implies that the natural monopoly faces a loss all the time. In this case, the government (the owner of the natural monopoly) must subsidize the natural monopoly.

Second best solution: $P = AC$. In this case, the natural monopoly is forced to charge a price equal to the average cost (like point G in Figure 8.16), and faces zero profits all of the time. The government does not need to subsidize the firm but a deadweight loss is still present in the market. This kind of regulation has been used extensively in real-world cases and is known as *rate of return regulation*.

The main problem with this kind of regulation is that a natural monopoly has no incentive to be efficient. This regulation is a low-power incentive mechanism. Even if the natural monopoly is efficient and can effectively reduce its costs, the price charged will always reflect the average cost and so the natural monopoly will always get zero profits.

Price cap regulation: the regulator sets the maximum price (price cap) that the firm can set. The firm is free to charge any price equal to or below the maximum price. In contrast to the average cost pricing regulation, a price cap regulation is a high-power incentive mechanism since it provides incentives for the regulated firm to reduce its costs. The regulated firm can charge the maximum price allowed and, by reducing its costs, can increase its profits.

In the UK the price cap was defined according to the formula '*RPI – X*'. *Nominal* prices could rise by the same percentage as the retail price index (*RPI*), minus X per cent. X is the annual cut in *real* prices. For example, this kind of regulation was used when British Telecom (BT) was privatized in 1984. Since telecommunications enjoy rapid technical progress, BT could reduce costs year on year in real terms. Initially, the regulator set X at 3 per cent a year, but later raised it to 4.5 per cent and then 6.25 per cent. During its first ten years as a private company, BT cut its real price by 43 per cent.

Summary

- In a **competitive industry** each buyer and seller is a **price-taker**, believing individual actions have no effect on the market price. Competitive supply is most plausible when many firms make a standard product, with free entry and exit, and easy verification by buyers that the products of different firms really are the same.

- For a **competitive firm**, the price is its marginal revenue. Output equates price to marginal cost. The firm's supply curve is its *SMC* curve above *SAVC*. At a lower price, the firm temporarily shuts down. In the long run, the firm's supply curve is its *LMC* curve above its *LAC* curve. At a lower price, the firm eventually exits the industry.

- Adding at each price the quantities supplied by each firm, we obtain the **industry supply curve**. It is flatter in the long run both because each firm can fully adjust all factors and because the number of firms in the industry can vary. In the extreme case where all potential and existing firms have identical costs, the long-run industry supply curve is horizontal at the price corresponding to the lowest point on each firm's *LAC* curve.

- An increase in demand leads to a large price increase but only a small increase in quantity. The existing firms move up their steep *SMC* curves. Price exceeds average costs and the ensuing profits attract new entrants. In the long run output increases still further but the price falls back. In the long-run equilibrium the **marginal firm** makes only normal profits and there is no further change in the number of firms in the industry.

- An increase in costs for all firms reduces the industry's output and increases the price. In the long run the marginal firm must break even. A higher price is required to match the increase in its average costs.

- A **pure monopoly** is the only seller or potential seller of a good and need not worry about entry, even in the long run. Though rare in practice, this case offers an important benchmark against which to compare less extreme forms of monopoly power.

- A **profit-maximizing monopolist has a supply rule** – choose output to set *MC* equal to *MR* – but not a supply curve uniquely relating price and output. The relationship between price and *MR* depends on the demand curve.

- Where a monopoly and a competitive industry can meaningfully be compared, the monopolist produces a smaller output at a higher price. Compared to a perfectly competitive market, a monopoly creates a **deadweight loss**. This is the loss in social surplus caused by the monopolist restriction of output compared to perfect competition.

- A **discriminating monopolist** charges different prices to different customers. To equate the marginal revenue from different groups, groups with an inelastic demand must pay a higher price. Successful price discrimination requires that customers cannot trade the product among themselves.

- Monopolies may have more internal resources available for research and may have a higher incentive for cost-saving research because the profits from technical advances will not be eroded by entry. Although small firms do not undertake a great deal of expensive research, it appears that the **patent laws** provide adequate incentives for medium- and larger-sized firms. There is no evidence that an industry has to be a monopoly to undertake cost-saving research.

Review questions

connect

1 Draw a diagram showing the positions of a competitive firm and of the industry in long-run equilibrium. Suppose this is the wool industry. The development of artificial fibres reduces the demand for wool. (a) Show what happens in the short run and the long run if all sheep farmers have identical costs. (b) What happens if there are high-cost and low-cost sheep farmers?

EASY

2 The table shows the demand curve facing a monopolist who produces at a constant marginal cost of £5. Calculate the monopolist's marginal revenue curve. What is the equilibrium output? Equilibrium price? What would be the equilibrium price and output for a competitive industry?

Price (£)	8	7	6	5	4	3	2	1	0
Quantity	1	2	3	4	5	6	7	8	9

3 Now suppose that, in addition to the constant marginal cost of £5, the monopolist has a fixed cost of £2. How does this affect the monopolist's output, price and profits? Why?

4 **True or false** In a monopoly market social welfare is always lower than in a competitive market.

5 **Common fallacies** Why are these statements wrong? (a) Since competitive firms break even in the long run, there is no incentive to be a competitive firm. (b) By breaking up monopolies we always get more output at a lower price.

6 Consider a perfectly competitive firm that has a total cost of producing output given by $TC = 10Q + 2Q^2$. The market price is $P = 54$. Find the profit-maximizing quantity produced by the firm.

7 Suppose that the total output produced in a competitive market is 200 units. Suppose there are n identical firms in the market. Each firm then produces an amount $200/n$. The total cost of a single firm in the market is $TC = (200/n)^2$. If the market price is $P = 10$, find the number of firms active in the market.

8 A monopolist faces the following inverse market demand: $P = 50 - Q$. Suppose that the total cost faced by the monopolist is $TC = 10Q$. Find the profit-maximizing quantity produced by the monopolist. What about the price charged by the monopolist? Find the deadweight loss in the market. Illustrate your answer in a diagram.

9 The following table reports the data on total costs of a competitive firm. We know that the market price is $P = 44$.

Q	1	2	3	4	5	6	7	8	9
TC	4	16	36	64	100	144	196	256	324

Find the marginal cost curve. In a graph, plot the marginal revenue and marginal cost curves and show the amount of output that the firm should produce.

10 The following table reports the total cost for a natural monopoly.

Q	1	2	3	4	5	6	7	8	9
TC	22	24	26	28	30	32	34	36	38

Find the average cost curve and plot it in a graph? What about the marginal cost curve? What is the relationship between the two curves?

11 A competitive industry has free entry and exit. Why does free exit matter? How would the analysis change if it was costly to exit?

12 A firm's market power can be measured by its ability to raise price above marginal cost. Relative to the level of marginal cost, this measure is $(P - MC)/MC$. How do you expect this to be related to the elasticity of demand for the monopolist's output?

Market structure and imperfect competition

Learning Outcomes

By the end of this chapter, you should understand:

1. imperfect competition, oligopoly and monopolistic competition

2. how cost and demand affect market structure

3. how globalization changes domestic market structure

4. equilibrium in monopolistic competition

5. the tension between collusion and competition in a cartel

6. game theory and strategic behaviour

7. the concepts of commitment and credibility

8. reaction functions and Nash equilibrium

9. Cournot and Bertrand competition

10. Stackelberg leadership

11. why there is no market power in a contestable market

12. innocent and strategic entry barriers

Perfect competition and pure monopoly are useful benchmarks of the extremes of market structure. Most markets are between the extremes. What determines the structure of a particular market? Why are there 10 000 florists but only a few chemical producers? How does the structure of an industry affect the behaviour of its constituent firms?

A perfectly competitive firm faces a horizontal demand curve at the market price. It is a price-taker. Any other type of firm faces a downward-sloping demand curve for its product and is **imperfectly competitive**.

> An **imperfectly competitive firm** faces a downward-sloping demand curve. Its output price reflects the quantity of goods it makes and sells.

For a pure monopoly, the demand curve for the firm and the industry coincide. We now distinguish between two intermediate cases of an imperfectly competitive market structure.

Table 9.1 Market structure

Competition	Number of firms	Ability to affect price	Entry barriers	Example
Perfect	Lots	Nil	None	Fruit stall
Imperfect: Monopolistic	Many	Little	Small	Corner shop
Oligopoly	Few	Medium	Bigger	Cars
Monopoly	One	Large	Huge	Post Office

> An **oligopoly** is an industry with few producers, each recognizing their interdependence.
>
> An industry with **monopolistic competition** has many sellers of products that are close substitutes for one another. Each firm has only a limited ability to affect its output price.

The car industry is an **oligopoly**. The price of Rover cars depends not only on Rover's own output and sales but also the output of Ford and Toyota. The corner grocer's shop is a **monopolistic competitor**. Its output is a subtle package of physical goods, personal service and convenience for local customers. It can charge a slightly higher price than an out-of-town supermarket. But, if its prices are too high, even local shoppers travel to the supermarket.

As with most definitions, the lines between different market structures can get blurred. One reason is ambiguity about the relevant definition of the market. Is Eurostar a monopoly in cross-channel trains or an oligopolist in cross-channel travel? Similarly, when a country trades in a competitive world market, even the sole domestic producer may have little influence on market price. We can never fully remove these ambiguities, but Table 9.1 shows some things to bear in mind as we proceed through this chapter. The table includes the ease with which new firms can enter the industry, which affects the ability of existing firms to maintain high prices and supernormal profits in the long run.

9.1 Why market structures differ

Some industries are legal monopolies, the sole licensed producers. Patent laws may confer temporary monopoly on producers of a new process. Ownership of a raw material may confer monopoly status on a single firm. We now develop a general theory of how demand and cost interact to determine the likely structure of each industry.

The car industry is not an oligopoly one day but perfectly competitive the next. Long-run influences determine market structures. Eventually, one firm can hire another's workers and learn its technical secrets.

Figure 9.1 shows the demand curve DD for the output of an industry in the long run. Suppose all firms and potential entrants face the average cost curve LAC_1. At the price P_1, free entry and exit means that each firm produces q_1. With the demand curve DD, industry output is Q_1. The number of firms in the industry is $N_1 = (Q_1/q_1)$. If at q_1, the minimum average cost output on LAC_1, is small relative to DD, N_1 will be large. Each firm has a tiny effect on industry supply and market price. We have found a perfectly competitive industry.

Next, suppose that each firm has the cost curve LAC_3. Scale economies are vast relative to the market size. At the lowest point on LAC_3, output is big relative to the demand curve DD. Suppose initially two firms each make q_2. Industry output is Q_2. The market clears at P_2 and both firms break even. If one firm expands a bit, its average costs fall. Its higher output also bids the price down. With lower average costs, that firm survives but the other firm loses money. The firm that expands undercuts its competitor and drives it out of business.

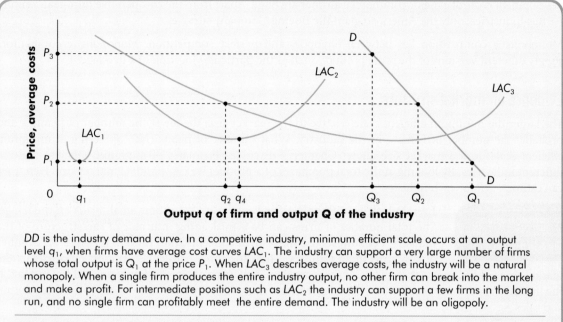

DD is the industry demand curve. In a competitive industry, minimum efficient scale occurs at an output level q_1, when firms have average cost curves LAC_1. The industry can support a very large number of firms whose total output is Q_1 at the price P_1. When LAC_3 describes average costs, the industry will be a natural monopoly. When a single firm produces the entire industry output, no other firm can break into the market and make a profit. For intermediate positions such as LAC_2 the industry can support a few firms in the long run, and no single firm can profitably meet the entire demand. The industry will be an oligopoly.

Figure 9.1   Demand, costs, and market structure

Table 9.2   Demand, cost and market structure

Minimum efficient scale relative to market size		
Tiny	Intermediate	Large
Perfect competition	Oligopoly	Natural monopoly

This industry is a **natural monopoly**. Suppose Q_3 is the output at which its marginal cost and marginal revenue coincide. The price is P_3 and the natural monopoly makes supernormal profits. There is no room in the industry for other firms with access to the same LAC_3 curve.

> A **natural monopoly** enjoys such scale economies that it has no fear of entry by others.

A new entrant needs a big output to get average costs down. Extra output on this scale so depresses the price that both firms make losses. The potential entrant cannot break in.

Finally, we show the LAC_2 curve with more economies of scale than a competitive industry but fewer than a natural monopoly. This industry supports at least two firms enjoying scale economies near the bottom of their LAC_2 curves. It is an oligopoly. Attempts to expand either firm's output beyond q_4 quickly meet decreasing returns to scale and prevent a firm driving competitors out of business.

The crucial determinant of market structure is **minimum efficient scale** relative to the size of the total market as shown by the demand curve. Table 9.2 summarizes our analysis of the interaction of market size and minimum efficient scale. When the demand curve shifts to the left, an industry previously with many firms may have room for only a few. Similarly, a rise in fixed costs, raising the minimum efficient scale, reduces the number of firms. In the 1950s there were many European aircraft makers. Today, the research and

> **Minimum efficient scale** is the lowest output at which a firm's LAC curve stops falling.

development costs of a major commercial airliner are huge. Apart from the co-operative European venture Airbus Industries, only the American giant the Boeing Company survives.

Monopolistic competition lies between oligopoly and perfect competition. Monopolistic competitors supply different versions of the same product, such as the particular location of a newsagent.

Evidence on market structure

The larger the minimum efficient scale relative to the market size, the fewer the number of plants – and probably the number of firms – in the industry. What number of plants (*NP*) operating at minimum efficient scale does a market size allow? Chapter 7 discussed estimates of minimum efficient scale in different industries. By looking at the total purchases of a product we can estimate market size. Hence we can estimate *NP* for each industry.

> The **N-firm concentration ratio** is the market share of the largest N firms in the industry.

Even industries with only a few key players have some small firms on the fringe. The total number of firms can be a misleading indicator of the structure of the industry. Economists use the *N*-firm concentration ratio to measure the number of key firms in an industry. Thus, the three-firm concentration ratio tells us the market share of the largest three firms. If there are three key firms, they will supply most of the market. If the industry is perfectly competitive, the largest three firms will only have a tiny share of industry output and sales.

It would be nice to look at cross-country evidence to see if market structures always obey our theory. If this is to be an independent check, we really need national data before globalization and European integration became important. Table 9.3 examines evidence for the UK, France and Germany for the mid-1970s.

CR is the three-firm concentration ratio, the market share of the top three firms. *NP* is the number of plants at minimum efficient scale that the market size allows. If our theory of market structure is correct, industries with large-scale economies relative to market size, and thus few plants *NP*, should have a large concentration ratio *CR*. Such industries should have few key firms. Conversely, where *NP* is very high, economies of scale are relatively unimportant and the largest three firms should have a much smaller market share. *CR* should be low.

Table 9.3 Concentration and scale economies

Industry	UK		France		Germany	
	CR	NP	CR	NP	CR	NP
Refrigerators	65	1	100	2	72	3
Cigarettes	94	3	100	2	94	3
Refineries	79	8	60	7	47	9
Brewing	47	11	63	5	17	16
Fabrics	28	57	23	57	16	52
Shoes	17	165	13	128	20	197

Note: Concentration ratio CR is % market share of three largest firms; number of plants NP is market size divided by minimum efficient scale.

Sources: Scherer, F. M. et al. (1975) *The Economics of Multiplant Operation*, Harvard University Press; Scherer, F. M. (1980) *Industrial Market Structure and Economic Performance*, Rand McNally.

Table 9.3 confirms that this theory of market structure fits these facts. Industries such as refrigerator and cigarette manufacture had room for few plants operating at minimum efficient scale: these industries had high degrees of concentration. The largest three firms controlled almost the whole market. Scale economies still mattered in industries such as brewing and petroleum refining: the top three firms had about half the market. Industries such as shoemaking quickly met rising average cost curves, had room for many factories operating at minimum efficient scale and thus were much closer to competitive industries. The top three firms in shoemaking had under one-fifth of the market.

Globalization and multinationals

Table 9.3 showed data before the rise of globalization and multinationals. Globalization reflects cheaper transport costs, better information technology and a deliberate policy of reducing cross-country barriers in order to get efficiency gains from large scale and specialization. Multinationals sell in many countries at the same time. They may, or may not, also produce in many countries.

> **Globalization** is the closer integration of markets across countries.
>
> **Multinationals** are firms operating in many countries simultaneously.

CASE 9.1

Facing the music

Recorded music, from albums to digital, is now a global business. According to 2005 data, the industry was owned by Sony–Bertelsmann (21.5 per cent), Universal Music Group (25.5 per cent), EMI Group (13.4 per cent), Warner Music Group (11.3 per cent) and independent labels (28.4 per cent). The market structure of the music industry was, then, characterized by four giant firms that together accounted for 71.6 per cent of the total market. However, the value of the global recorded music market is falling every year because of price competition and endemic internet piracy. In 1999 the total value of the music industry (defined as total sales) was \$14 585 million, while in 2006 it was \$12 297 million.

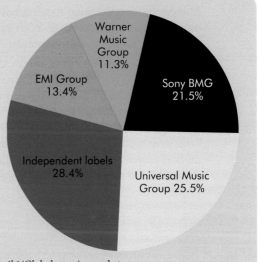

Source: Compiled from a number of sources including http://en.wikipedia.org/wiki/Global_music_market.

Multinationals affect the analysis implied by Figure 9.1 and Table 9.3. To what market size should we compare minimum efficient scale to estimate the number of plants that can survive in the long run? Multinationals can produce on a large scale somewhere in the world, where production is cheapest, enjoy all the benefits of scale economies, but still sell small quantities in many different markets.

This has three effects. First, it reduces entry barriers in a particular country. A foreign multinational entrant need not achieve a large market share, and therefore need not bid down the price a lot, to achieve scale economies. These now arise because of success in selling globally. Second, small domestic firms, previously sheltered by entry barriers, now face greater international competition and may not survive. Third, greater competition by low-cost producers leads *initially* to lower profit margins and lower prices.

However, if there are only a few multinationals, they may drive the higher-cost domestic firms out of business but then collude among themselves to raise prices again. Some of the debate about globalization hinges on which of these two outcomes dominates: the initial price fall or a possible subsequent price increase. We return shortly to the analysis of collusion. First, we study a simpler case.

9.2 Monopolistic competition

The theory of monopolistic competition envisages a large number of quite small firms so that each firm can neglect the possibility that its own decisions provoke any adjustment in other firms' behaviour. We also assume free entry to and exit from the industry in the long run. In these respects, the industry resembles *perfect* competition. What distinguishes *monopolistic* competition is that each firm faces a *downward*-sloping demand curve.

Monopolistic competition describes an industry in which each firm can influence its market share to some extent by changing its price relative to its competitors. Its demand curve is not horizontal because different firms' products are only limited substitutes, as in the location of local shops. A lower price attracts some customers from another shop but each shop always has some local customers for whom convenience is more important than a few pence off the price of a jar of coffee.

Monopolistically competitive industries exhibit *product differentiation*. Corner grocers differentiate by location, hairdressers by customer loyalty. The special feature of a particular restaurant or hairdresser lets it charge a slightly different price from other firms in the industry without losing all its customers.

Monopolistic competition requires not merely product differentiation but also limited opportunities for economies of scale. Firms are small. With lots of producers, each can neglect its interdependence with any particular rival. Many examples of monopolistic competition are service industries where economies of scale are small.

The industry demand curve shows the total output demanded at each price if all firms in the industry charge that price. The market share of each firm depends on the price it charges and on the number of firms in the industry. For a given number of firms, a shift in the industry demand curve shifts the demand curve for the output of each firm. For a given industry demand curve, having more (fewer) firms in the industry shifts the demand curve of each firm to the left (right) as its market share falls (rises). But each firm faces a downward-sloping demand curve. This implies that firms in monopolistic competition have market power and they are price-setters. For a given industry demand curve, number of firms and price charged by all other firms, a particular firm can raise its market share a bit by charging a lower price.

CONCEPT 9.1

It's not what it looks like

An investor seeking to hold assets in a mutual fund is a consumer with many choices: in 2001, there were 8307 US mutual funds in operation. A mutual fund investor's choice set has also been growing robustly over time: while there were 834 mutual funds in operation in 1980, this nearly quadrupled to 3100 by 1990, and almost tripled again by 2001. So it appears that the mutual fund market in the US is a market with many firms, most of whose mutual funds are pretty homogeneous, and there is reasonably free entry. Is the market for mutual funds a competitive market?

The answer appears to be no. The fees that investors pay to hold assets in funds are really dispersed, meaning they differ even for mutual funds that are almost homogeneous in their performance. Why should prices be different for goods that are almost homogeneous? The reason is that there are other elements, apart from pure performance of the funds, that can affect investor choice. For example, 60 per cent of investors reported consulting a financial adviser before purchase, implying that the ability of the financial adviser is an important element in investor choice. Funds can have divergent taxable distribution rates for a given return pattern; clearly, investors prefer less tax exposure, all else being equal.

All those facts can explain why products that may appear homogeneous in their physical characteristics can still have some sort of product differentiation that can explain their different prices.

Source: Hortaçsu, A. and Syverson, C. (2003) *Product differentiation, search costs and competition in the mutual fund industry: a case study of S&P index funds*, NBER working paper 9728.

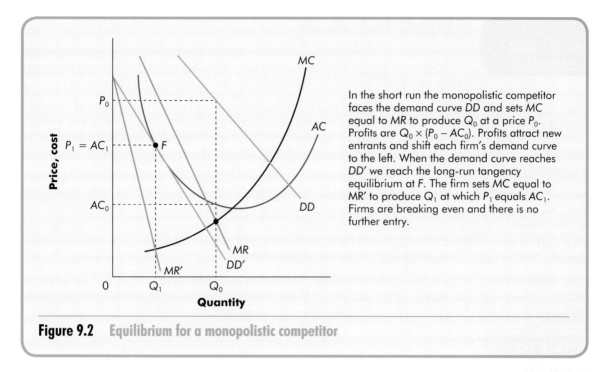

In the short run the monopolistic competitor faces the demand curve DD and sets MC equal to MR to produce Q_0 at a price P_0. Profits are $Q_0 \times (P_0 - AC_0)$. Profits attract new entrants and shift each firm's demand curve to the left. When the demand curve reaches DD' we reach the long-run tangency equilibrium at F. The firm sets MC equal to MR' to produce Q_1 at which P_1 equals AC_1. Firms are breaking even and there is no further entry.

Figure 9.2 **Equilibrium for a monopolistic competitor**

Figure 9.2 shows a firm's supply decision. Given its demand curve DD and marginal revenue curve MR, the firm makes Q_0 at a price P_0, making short-run profits $Q_0(P_0 - AC_0)$. In the long run, these profits attract new entrants, diluting the market share of each firm in the industry, shifting their demand curves to the left. Entry stops when each firm's demand curve shifts so far left that price equals average cost and firms just break even. In Figure 9.2 this occurs when demand is DD'. The firm makes Q_1 at a price P_1 in the **tangency equilibrium** at F.

Note two things about the firm's long-run equilibrium at F. First, the firm is *not* producing at minimum average cost. It has excess capacity. It could reduce average costs by further expansion. However, its marginal revenue would be so low that this is unprofitable. Second, the firm has some monopoly power because of the special feature of its particular brand or location. Price exceeds marginal cost.

> In monopolistic competition, in the long-run **tangency equilibrium** each firm's demand curve just touches its AC curve at the output level at which MC equals MR. Each firm maximizes profits but just breaks even. There is no more entry or exit.

This explains why firms are usually eager for new customers prepared to buy additional output at the *existing* price. We are a race of eager sellers and coy buyers. It is purchasing agents who get Christmas presents from sales reps, not the other way round. In contrast, a perfectly competitive firm does not care if another buyer shows up at the existing price. With price equal to marginal cost, the firm is already selling as much as it wants to sell.

9.3 Oligopoly and interdependence

Under perfect competition or monopolistic competition, there are many firms in the industry. Each firm can ignore the effect of its own actions on rival firms. However, the key to an oligopolistic industry is the need for each firm to consider how its own actions affect the decisions of its relatively few competitors. Each firm has to guess how its rivals will react. Before discussing what constitutes a smart guess, we introduce the basic tension between competition and collusion when firms know that they are interdependent. Initially, for simplicity, we neglect the possibility of entry and focus on existing firms.

> **Collusion** is an explicit or implicit agreement to avoid competition.

The profits from collusion

As sole decision maker in the industry, a monopolist would choose industry output to maximize total profits. Hence, the few producers in an industry can maximize their total profit by setting their total output as if they were monopolists.

Figure 9.3 shows an industry where each firm, and the whole industry, has constant average and marginal costs at the level P_C. Chapter 8 showed that a competitive industry produces Q_C at a price P_C but a multi-plant monopolist maximizes profits by making Q_M at a price P_M. If the oligopolists collude to produce Q_M they act as a *collusive monopolist*. Having decided industry output, the firms agree how to share total output and profits among themselves.

However, it is hard to stop firms cheating on the collective agreement. In Figure 9.3 joint profit is maximized at a total output Q_M and price P_M. Yet each firm can expand output at a marginal cost P_C. Any firm can expand output, selling at a little below the agreed price P_M, and make extra profit since its marginal revenue exceeds its marginal cost. This firm gains at the expense of its collusive partners. Industry output is higher than the best output Q_M, so total profits fall and other firms suffer.

Oligopolists are torn between the desire to collude, in order to maximize joint profits, and the desire to compete, in order to raise market share and profits at the expense of rivals. Yet if all firms compete, joint profits are low and no firm does very well. Therein lies the dilemma.

Cartels

Collusion between firms is easiest if formal agreements are legal. Such arrangements, called *cartels*, were common in the late nineteenth century, agreeing market shares and prices in many industries. Cartels are now outlawed in Europe, the US and many other countries. There are big penalties for being caught, but informal agreements and secret deals are sometimes discovered even today.

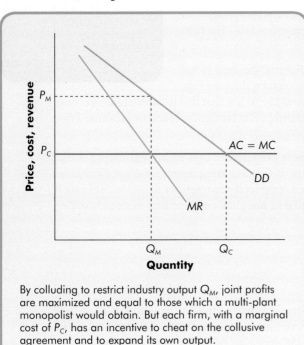

By colluding to restrict industry output Q_M, joint profits are maximized and equal to those which a multi-plant monopolist would obtain. But each firm, with a marginal cost of P_C, has an incentive to cheat on the collusive agreement and to expand its own output.

Figure 9.3 **Collusion versus competition**

Cartels across continents are harder to outlaw. The most famous cartel is OPEC, the Organization of Petroleum Exporting Countries. Its members meet regularly to set price and output. Initially, OPEC succeeded in organizing quantity reductions to force up the price of oil. Real OPEC revenues rose 500 per cent between 1973 and 1980. Yet many economists predicted that OPEC, like most cartels, would quickly collapse. Usually, the incentive to cheat is too strong to resist and once somebody breaks ranks others tend to follow. One reason that OPEC was successful for so long was the willingness of Saudi Arabia, the largest oil producer, to restrict its output further when smaller members insisted on expansion.

By 1986 Saudi Arabia was no longer prepared to play by these rules and refused to prop up the price any longer. The oil price collapsed from just under $30 to $9 a barrel. During 1987–98, apart from a brief period during the First Gulf War, oil prices fluctuated between $8 and $20 a barrel. Only after 1998 did OPEC recover the cohesion it displayed during 1973–85. The Second Gulf War and continuing uncertainty in the Middle East has continued to restrict supply in any case, also underpinning the high oil prices since 2003.

The kinked demand curve

Collusion is much harder if there are many firms in the industry, if the product is not standardized and if demand and cost conditions are changing rapidly. In the absence of collusion, each firm's demand curve depends on how competitors react. Firms must guess how their rivals will behave.

Suppose that each firm believes that its own price cut will be matched by all other firms in the industry, but that a rise in its own price will not induce a price response from competitors. Figure 9.4 shows the demand curve DD that each firm then believes that it faces. At the current price P_0, the firm makes Q_0. If competitors do not follow suit, a price rise by one firm alone leads to a large loss of market share to other firms. The firm's demand curve is elastic above A at prices above the current price P_0. However, if each firm believes that if it cuts prices this will be matched by other firms, market shares are unchanged. Lower prices then induce extra sales rises only because the whole industry moves down the market demand curve as prices fall. The demand curve DD is much less elastic for price cuts from the initial price P_0.

In Figure 9.4 we have to draw marginal revenue MR for each of the separate sections of the kinked demand curve. The firm jumps discontinuously from one part of MR to the other when it reaches the output Q_0. Below Q_0, the elastic part of the demand curve is relevant, and marginal revenue is high since additional output does not depress the price much for existing sales. At the output Q_0 the firm hits the inelastic portion of its kinked demand curve and marginal revenue becomes much lower: now that demand is less elastic, further output increases require much lower prices to sell the extra output, hitting revenue from existing sales. Q_0 is the profit-maximizing output for the firm, given its belief about how competitors respond.

Suppose the MC curve of a single firm shifts up or down by a small amount. Since the MR curve has a discontinuous vertical segment at Q_0, it remains optimal to make Q_0 and charge the price P_0. In contrast, a monopolist facing a continuously downward-sloping MR curve would adjust quantity and price when the MC curve shifted. The kinked demand curve model may explain the empirical finding that firms do not always adjust prices when costs change.

It does not explain what determines the initial price P_0. One interpretation is that it is the collusive monopoly price. Each firm believes that an attempt to undercut its rivals will provoke them to co-operate among themselves and retaliate in full. However, its rivals will be happy for it to charge a higher price and see it lose market share.

If we interpret P_0 as the collusive monopoly price, we can contrast the effect of a cost change for a single firm and a cost change for all firms. The latter shifts the marginal cost curve up for the entire industry, raising the collusive monopoly price. Each firm's kinked demand curve shifts up since the monopoly price P_0 has risen. Hence, we can reconcile the stickiness of a firm's price with respect to changes in its own costs alone, and the speed with which the entire industry marks up prices when all firms' costs increase. Examples of the latter are higher taxes on the industry's product, or a union wage increase across the whole industry.

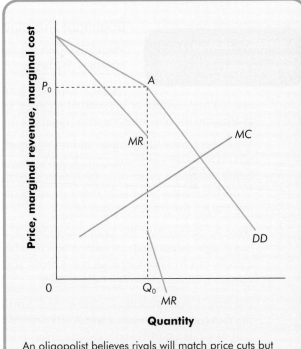

An oligopolist believes rivals will match price cuts but not price rises. The oligopolist's demand curve is kinked at A. Price rises lead to a large loss of market share, but price cuts increase quantity only by increasing industry sales. Marginal revenue is discontinuous at Q_0. The oligopolist produces Q_0, the output at which MC crosses the MR schedule.

Figure 9.4   The kinked demand curve

9.4 Game theory and interdependent decisions

A good poker player sometimes bluffs. You can win with a bad hand if your opponents misread it for a good hand. Similarly, by having bluffed in the past and been caught, you may persuade opponents to bet a lot when you have a terrific hand.

> A **game** is a situation in which intelligent decisions are necessarily interdependent.
>
> A **strategy** is a game plan describing how a player acts, or moves, in each possible situation.
>
> In **Nash equilibrium**, each player chooses the best strategy, *given* the strategies being followed by other players.

Like poker players, oligopolists try to anticipate their rivals' moves to determine their own best action. To study interdependent decision making, we use *game theory*. The *players* in the **game** try to maximize their own *payoffs*. In an oligopoly, the firms are the players and their payoffs are their profits in the long run. Each player must choose a strategy. Being a pickpocket is a strategy. Lifting a particular wallet is a move.

As usual, we are interested in equilibrium. In most games, each player's best strategy depends on the strategies chosen by other players. It is silly to be a pickpocket when the police have CCTV cameras or to play four centre backs when the opponents have no proven goal-scorers.

Nobody, then, wants to change strategy, since other people's strategies are already figured into assessing each player's best strategy. This definition of equilibrium, and its application to game theory, was invented by a Princeton University mathematician **John Nash**.[1]

Dominant strategies

> A **dominant strategy** is a player's best strategy *whatever* the strategies adopted by rivals.

Sometimes (but not usually) a player's best strategy is independent of those chosen by others. We begin with an example in which each player has a **dominant strategy**.

Figure 9.5 shows a game[2] between the only two members of a cartel. Each firm can select a high-output or low-output strategy. In each box of Figure 9.5 the orange number shows firm A's profits and the blue number firm B's profits for that output combination.

When both have high output, industry output is high, the price is low and each firm makes a small profit of 1. When each has low output, the outcome is like collusive monopoly. Prices are high and each firm does better, making a profit of 2. Each firm does best (a profit of 3) when it alone has high output: the other firm's low output helps hold down industry output and keep up the price. In this situation we assume the low-output firm makes a profit of 0.

Now we can see how the game will unfold. Consider firm A's decision. It first thinks what to do if firm B has a high-output strategy. Firm A will thus be in one of the two left-hand boxes of Figure 9.5. Firm A gets a profit of 1 by choosing high but a profit of 0 by choosing low. If firm A thinks firm B will choose high output, firm A prefers high output itself.

But firm A must also think what to do if firm B chooses a low-output strategy. This puts firm A in one of the two right-hand boxes. Firm A *still* prefers high output for itself, which yields a profit of 3 whereas low output yields a profit of only 2. Firm A has a dominant strategy. Whichever strategy B adopts, A does better to choose a high-output strategy.

---

1 Nash, who battled schizophrenia, won the Nobel Prize in Economics for his work on game theory. A film about his life, *A Beautiful Mind* (dir. Ron Howard), was released in 2001 and starred Russell Crowe.

2 The game, called the Prisoner's Dilemma, was first used to analyse the choice facing two people arrested and in different cells, each of whom could plead guilty or not guilty to the only crime that had been committed. Each prisoner would plead innocent if only she knew the other would plead guilty. For more information go to www.mcgraw-hill.co.uk/textbooks/begg where there is a video fully explaining the Prisoner's Dilemma.

Firm B also has a dominant strategy to choose high output. If firm B anticipates that firm A will go high, facing a choice of the two boxes in the top row, firm B prefers to go high. If B thinks A will go low, B faces a choice from the two boxes in the bottom row of Figure 9.5, but B still wants to go high. Firm B does better to go high whichever strategy A selects. Both firm A and firm B have a dominant strategy to go high. Equilibrium is the top left-hand box. Each firm gets a profit of 1.

Yet both firms would do better, getting a profit of 2, if they colluded to form a cartel and both produced low – the bottom right-hand box. But neither can risk going low. Suppose firm A goes low. Firm B, comparing the two boxes in the bottom row, will then go high, preferring a profit of 3 to a profit of 2. And firm A will be in trouble; earning a profit of 0 in that event. Firm A can figure all this out in advance, which is why its dominant strategy is to go high.

		Firm B output	
		High	Low
Firm A output	High	1 1	3 0
	Low	0 3	2 2

The orange and blue numbers in each box indicate profits to firms A and B, respectively. Whether B pursues high or low output, A makes more profit going high; so does B, whichever strategy A adopts. In equilibrium both go high. Yet both would make greater profits if both went low!

Figure 9.5 *The Prisoner's Dilemma game*

This shows vividly the tension between collusion and competition. In this example, it appears that the output-restricting cartel will never be formed, since each player can already foresee the overwhelming incentive for the other to cheat on such an arrangement. How, then, can cartels ever be sustained? One possibility is that there exist binding **commitments**.

> **Commitment** is an arrangement, entered into voluntarily, that restricts future actions.

If both players in Figure 9.5 could simultaneously sign an enforceable contract to produce low output they could achieve the co-operative outcome in the bottom right-hand box, each earning profits of 2. This beats the top left-hand box, which shows the Nash equilibrium of the game when collusion cannot be enforced. Without a binding commitment, neither player can go low because then the other player goes high. Binding commitments, by removing this temptation, let both players go low. Both players gain.

This idea of commitment is important and we shall encounter it many times. Just think of all the human activities that are the subject of legal contracts, a simple commitment simultaneously undertaken by two parties or players.

Although this insight is powerful, its application to oligopoly requires care. Cartels within a country are usually illegal and OPEC is not held together by a contract enforceable in international law. Is there a less formal way in which oligopolists can avoid cheating on the collusive low-output solution to the game? If the game is played only once, this is difficult.

Repeated games

In the real world, the game is repeated many times: firms choose output levels day after day. Suppose two players try to collude on low output: each announces a *punishment strategy*. If firm A ever cheats on the low-output agreement, firm B says that it will subsequently react by raising its output. Firm A makes a similar promise.

Suppose the agreement has been in force for some time and both firms have stuck to their low-output deal. Firm A assumes that firm B will go low as usual. Figure 9.5 shows that firm A makes a *temporary* gain today if it cheats and goes high. Instead of staying in the bottom right-hand box with a profit of 2, it can move to the top right-hand box and make 3. However, from tomorrow onwards, firm B will also go high and firm A can then do no better than continue to go high too, making a profit of 1 for ever more. But if A refuses to cheat today, it can continue to stay in the bottom right-hand box and make 2 for ever. In cheating,

> A **credible threat** is one that, after the fact, is still optimal to carry out.

A swaps a temporary gain for a permanent reduction in future profits. Thus, punishment strategies can sustain an explicit cartel or implicit collusion even if no formal commitment exists.

It is all very well to promise punishment if the other player cheats. But this will affect the other player's behaviour only if the **threat is credible**.

In the preceding example, once firm A has cheated and gone high, it is then in firm B's interest to go high anyway. Hence a threat to go high if A ever cheats is a credible threat.

These insights shed light on the actual behaviour of OPEC in 1986, when Saudi Arabia dramatically raised its output, leading to a collapse of oil prices. In the 1980s, other members of OPEC had gradually cheated on the low-output agreement, trusting that Saudi Arabia would still produce low to sustain a high price and the cartel's prestige. They hoped Saudi threats to adopt a punishment strategy were empty threats. They were wrong. Figure 9.5 shows that, once the others went high, Saudi Arabia had to go high too.

9.5 Reaction functions

In the previous example, in a one-off game each player had a dominant strategy, to produce high output whatever its rival did. This led to a poor outcome for both players because they were not co-operating despite being interdependent. When the game is repeated, commitments and punishment strategies help players co-operate to find an outcome that is better for both of them.

In punishing a rival, a player's actions change in response to bad behaviour by the rival. Dominant strategies are rare. More usually, each player's best action depends on the actual or expected actions of other players. How a player reacts depends on what it, assumes about its rivals' behaviour. For simplicity we analyse *duopoly*, in which there are only two players.

Cournot behaviour

In 1838 French economist Augustin Cournot analysed a simple model of duopoly.

Imagine a duopoly in which both firms have the same constant marginal costs *MC*. Figure 9.6 draws the decision problem for firm A. If firm A assumes that firm B produces 0, firm A gets the whole industry

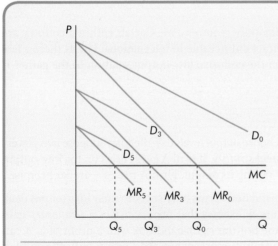

Assuming firm B makes 0, firm A faces the market demand curve D_0 and maximizes profits by producing Q_0 to equate marginal cost and marginal revenue. If firm B is assumed to make 3 units, firm A faces the residual demand curve D_3 lying 3 units left of D_0. Firm A then makes Q_3. If firm B is assumed to make 5 units, firm A faces D_5 and makes Q_5. Optimal output for firm A is lower the higher the output that it assumes firm B will make.

Figure 9.6   Cournot behaviour

demand curve D_0. This shows what output firm A can sell given the prices that it charges. From this, firm A calculates the marginal revenue MR_0, and produces Q_0 to equate its marginal cost and marginal revenue.

If, instead, firm A assumes that firm B makes 3 units, firm A faces a demand curve D_3 obtained by shifting the market demand D_0 to the left by 3 units. Firm B gets 3 units and the residual demand is available for firm A. For this demand curve D_3, firm A computes the marginal revenue curve MR_3 and chooses output Q_3 to equate marginal cost and marginal revenue.

Similarly, if firm A expects firm B to make 5 units, firm A shifts D_0 to the left by 5 units to get D_5, and produces Q_5 in order to equate marginal cost and its marginal revenue MR_5. The larger the output that firm 2 is expected to make and sell, the smaller the optimal output of firm A. Q_5 is smaller than Q_3, which is smaller than Q_0.

Repeating this exercise for every possible belief that firm A has about the output of firm B, yields the **reaction function** of firm A.

> A firm's **reaction function** shows how its optimal output varies with each possible action by its rival.

In the **Cournot model**, a rival's action is its output choice. Figure 9.7 shows the two outputs Q^A and Q^B. From Figure 9.6, firm A makes less the more it thinks that firm B will make. In Figure 9.7, firm A's optimal output choice is the reaction function R^A. If firm B is expected to produce 1 unit less, firm A chooses to raise output by less than 1 unit. This ensures total output falls, raising the price. Because this lets firm A earn more on its previous output units, it is not worth raising its output by as much as it expects the output of B to fall. Equivalently, in Figure 9.6 firm A's demand curve shifts more than its marginal revenue curve, hence its rise in output is smaller than the conjectured fall in the output of firm B.

> In the **Cournot model**, each firm treats the *output* of the other firm as given.

In the duopoly, both firms are the same. Hence firm B faces a similar problem. It makes guesses about the output of firm A, calculates the residual demand curve for firm B, and chooses its best output. Figure 9.7 shows the reaction function R^B for firm B, which also makes less the more that it assumes its rival will produce.

Along each reaction function, each firm makes its best response to the assumed output of the other firm. Only in equilibrium is it optimal for the other firm actually to behave in the way that has been assumed. In **Nash equilibrium**,

> **Nash equilibrium** is where the two reaction functions intersect.

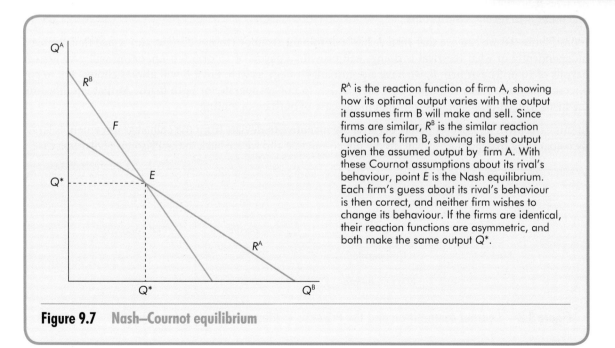

R^A is the reaction function of firm A, showing how its optimal output varies with the output it assumes firm B will make and sell. Since firms are similar, R^B is the similar reaction function for firm B, showing its best output given the assumed output by firm A. With these Cournot assumptions about its rival's behaviour, point E is the Nash equilibrium. Each firm's guess about its rival's behaviour is then correct, and neither firm wishes to change its behaviour. If the firms are identical, their reaction functions are asymmetric, and both make the same output Q^*.

Figure 9.7   **Nash–Cournot equilibrium**

neither firm wishes to alter its behaviour even after its conjecture about the other firm's output is then confirmed.

Since both firms face the same industry demand curve, their reaction functions are symmetric if they also face the same marginal cost curves in Figure 9.6. The two firms then produce the same output Q^* as shown in Figure 9.7. If costs differed, we could still construct (different) reaction functions and their intersection would no longer imply equal market shares.

Suppose the marginal cost curve of firm A now shifts down in Figure 9.6. At each output assumed for firm B, firm A now makes more. It moves further down any MR schedule before meeting MC. Hence, in Figure 9.7 the reaction function R^A shifts up, showing firm A makes more output Q^A at any assumed output Q^B of its rival. The new intersection of the reaction functions, say at point F, shows what happens to Nash equilibrium in the Cournot model.

It is no surprise that the output of firm A rises. Why does the output of firm B fall? With lower marginal costs, firm A is optimally making more. Unless firm B cuts its output, the price will fall a lot. Firm B prefers to cut output a little, in order to prop up the price a bit, preventing a big revenue loss on its existing units.

As in our discussion of the Prisoner's Dilemma game in Section 9.4, the Nash–Cournot equilibrium does not maximize the joint payoffs of the two players. They fail to achieve the total output that maximizes joint profits. By treating the output of the rival as given, each firm expands too much. Higher output bids down prices for everybody. In neglecting the fact that its own expansion hurts its rival, each firm's output is too high.

Each firm's behaviour is correct given its assumption that its rival's output is fixed. But expansion by one firm induces the rival to alter its behaviour. A joint monopolist would take that into account and make more total profit.

This is considered in Figure 9.8. Suppose there are two identical firms producing cars. The firms have two possible strategies: co-operate and form a cartel or do not co-operate and compete in quantities. The game is played simultaneously and only once, so it is a one-shot game. If they co-operate (collude), they can set the monopoly price and both obtain half of the monopoly profits. If they compete, they both obtain the Cournot profits, which are lower than in the case of collusion. If a firm is co-operating while the rival deviates from the collusive agreement, the firm deviating steals most of the market and obtains high profits. The other firm receives low profits.

From Figure 9.8 we can see that firm A has a dominant strategy (to not co-operate), since that strategy, independently of what the rival is doing, will provide a payoff of 15 or 5 (co-operating will give firm A payoffs of 10 or 2). For firm B, we have a dominant strategy as well. Firm B will always choose not to co-operate. The only Nash equilibrium of the game is to not co-operate for both firms. At that equilibrium, the firms will get profits of 5, lower than in the case of both co-operating.

In this case, firms do not co-operate because the incentive to deviate from the collusive agreement is large. By recognizing that, both firms will simply not co-operate and we are back to the Prisoner's Dilemma case.

		Firm B	
		Co-operate	Not co-operate
Firm A	Co-operate	10, 10	2, 15
	Not co-operate	15, 2	5, 5

Figure 9.8 Cournot competition and the Prisoner's Dilemma

MATHS 9.1 Deriving the reaction functions in a Cournot duopoly

Consider a market in which there are two firms, A and B, competing in quantities. The inverse market demand is given by $P = a - bQ$, where $Q = Q_A + Q_B$ is the total quantity produced in the market and is simply the sum of what is produced by firm A and firm B. Assume that the cost functions of the two firms are the same, meaning that the two firms are equal (the case of unequal cost function can be handled easily too).

The cost function of firm A is $TC_A = cQ_A$, while for firm B it is $TC_B = cQ_B$, where $c > 0$ is the marginal cost.

The reaction function (or best response) of firm A tells us how the output produced by firm A depends on the output produced by firm B. The reaction function for firm B is defined in a similar way.

Each firm maximizes profits. This means that each firm chooses a level of output such that the marginal revenue of selling that output is equal to the marginal cost of producing it. The total revenue for firm A is given by $TR_A = P \times Q_A$. Using the inverse demand for substituting for P, we get $TR_A = [a - b(Q_A + Q_B)] \times Q_A = aQ_A - bQ_A^2 - bQ_AQ_B$. As we can see, the total revenue of firm A now depends on the output chosen by firm B as well (Q_B). For firm B, using a similar argument, the total revenue is $TR_B = aQ_B - bQ_B^2 - bQ_BQ_A$.

The marginal revenue functions for the two firms are:

$$MR_A \equiv \frac{dTR_A}{dQ_A} = a - 2bQ_A - bQ_B \quad \text{and} \quad MR_B \equiv \frac{dTR_B}{dQ_B} = a - 2bQ_B - bQ_A$$

The marginal costs of the firms are the same:

$$MC_A \equiv \frac{dTC_A}{dQ_A} = c \quad \text{and} \quad MC_B \equiv \frac{dTC_B}{dQ_B} = c$$

The reaction function of each firm is found for the profit-maximization conditions:

$$MR_A = MC_A \quad \text{and} \quad MR_B = MC_B.$$

Using our data to express those two conditions we have:

$$a - 2bQ_A - bQ_B = c \quad \text{and} \quad a - 2bQ_B - bQ_A = c$$

From those two conditions we can find the reaction functions of each firm. For firm A, the reaction function is:

$$Q_A = \frac{a-c}{2b} - \frac{Q_B}{2} \tag{1}$$

For firm B we have:

$$Q_B = \frac{a-c}{2b} - \frac{Q_A}{2} \tag{2}$$

Notice that the reaction function of each firm depends negatively on the output produced by the rival. If firm B increases its output level, the best response by firm A is to reduce its output level. Reaction function (1) tells us the output that maximizes the profits of firm A, given the output chosen by firm B.

The Nash equilibrium of the Cournot model is where the two reaction functions above are mutually consistent, meaning they cross.

Therefore, we just need to solve a system of two equations in two variables Q_A, Q_B.

By solving the system of equations (1) and (2), we have:

$$Q_A = \frac{a-c}{3b} \quad \text{and} \quad Q_B = \frac{a-c}{3b}$$

Since the two firms are identical by assumption, they must produce the same level of output. The total output produced in the market is therefore: $Q_A + Q_B = 2[(a-c)/3b]$. The equilibrium price is found through the inverse demand function:

$$P = \frac{a+2c}{3}$$

Bertrand behaviour

To show how the assumption about rivals' behaviour affects reaction functions and hence Nash equilibrium, consider a different model suggested by another French economist, Joseph Bertrand.

> In the **Bertrand model** of oligopoly, each firm treats the prices of rivals as given.

Each firm decides a price (and hence an output) reflecting the price it expects its rival to set. We could go through a similar analysis to the Cournot model, find reaction curves showing how the *price* set by each firm depends on the *price* set by its rival, and hence find the Nash equilibrium in prices for the Bertrand model. Knowing the equilibrium price, we could work out equilibrium quantity. If the firms are identical, again they divide the market equally. However, in the Bertrand model, it is easy to see what the Nash equilibrium must be. It is the perfectly competitive outcome: price equals marginal cost. How do we know?

Suppose firm B sets a price above its marginal cost. Firm A can grab the whole market by setting a price a little below that of firm B. Since firm B can anticipate this, it must set a lower price. This argument keeps working until, in Nash equilibrium, both firms price at marginal cost and split the market between them. There is then no incentive to alter behaviour.

Comparing Bertrand and Cournot

Under Bertrand behaviour, Nash equilibrium entails price equal to marginal cost, so industry output is high. Under Cournot behaviour, Nash equilibrium entails lower industry output and a higher price. Because marginal and average costs are constant, each firm makes profits since the price is higher. But the firms do not co-operate. A joint monopolist would make more profit by co-ordinating output decisions. Industry output would be even lower and the price even higher.

Thus, Nash equilibrium depends on the *particular* assumption each firm makes about its rival's behaviour. Generally, economists prefer the Cournot model. In practice, few oligopolies behave like a perfectly competitive industry, as the Bertrand model predicts.

Moreover, since prices can be changed rapidly, treating a rival's *price* as fixed does not seem plausible. In contrast, we can interpret the Cournot model as saying that firms first choose *output capacity* and then set price. Since capacity takes time to alter, this makes more sense.

<table>
<tr><td>CONCEPT
9.2</td><td></td></tr>
</table>

Mergers and competition policy

Two firms can unite in two different ways: via a takeover bid or a merger. When a firm makes a takeover bid, managers of the 'victim' firm usually resist since they are likely to lose their jobs, but the shareholders will accept if the offer is sufficiently attractive.

From now on we use mergers as shorthand for both forms of union. Mergers can be distinguished in the following way: a *horizontal merger* is the union of two firms at the same production stage in the same industry. A *vertical merger* is the union of two firms at different production stages in the same industry. In a *conglomerate merger*, the production activities of the two firms are unrelated.

Are mergers in the public interest, or do they just create private monopolies?

On the one hand, a merger reduces the number of competitors in a market. Consider a market with six main competitors. If two of them merge, the number of competitors is reduced to five. This reduction in competition is beneficial for all the remaining firms in the market, but it may be detrimental for consumers. Less competition may result in higher prices. The merger of two large firms gives them market power from a large market share. The merged company is likely to restrict output and increase prices – a deadweight burden for society as a whole.

On the other hand, two firms may merge for efficiency reasons. The new firm may be more efficient than the two separate firms; there may be gains to co-ordination and planning and in managerial and financial aspects. If companies achieve any of these benefits, they will increase productivity and lower costs. Competition policy related to mergers must compare the gains (potential cost reduction) with the costs (larger market power).

The table below shows annual averages of takeovers and mergers involving UK firms. It shows dramatic merger booms in the late 1980s and late 1990s, which coincided with high stock market values, which raised the value of both firms involved in the merger.

The proliferation of large companies through merger would not have been possible if there had been a tough anti-merger policy.

There are currently two grounds for referring a prospective merger to an investigation by the Competition Commission: (1) that the merger will promote a new monopoly as defined by the 25 per cent market share used in deciding references for existing monopoly positions, or (2) that the company taken over has an annual UK turnover of at least £70 million.

UK takeovers and mergers, 1972–2006 (annual averages)

	Number	Value (1998 £bn)
1972–85	560	3
1986–89	1300	43
1990–98	585	20
1999–00	540	61
2001–06	600	30

Sources: British Business Trends, 1989; Business Trends, 1997; ONS, First Release.

213

▶ Since the merger legislation was introduced in 1965, only 4 per cent of all merger proposals have been referred to the Competition Commission. For much of the period, government policy has been to consent to, or actively encourage, mergers. In believing that the benefits would outweigh the costs, UK merger policy reflected two assumptions. The first was that the cost savings from economies of scale and more intensive use of scarce management talent could be quite large. The second was that the UK was part of an increasingly competitive world market so that the monopoly power of the merged firms, and the corresponding social cost of the deadweight burden, would be small. Large as they were, the merged firms were small in relation to European or world markets, and would face relatively elastic demand curves, giving little scope to raise price above marginal cost.

Finally, as with competition policy, EU legislation takes precedence where this is appropriate. It is not appropriate in assessing whether a merger of two UK supermarkets should be allowed, since this predominantly affects only UK consumers. However, the European Commission will investigate mergers involving enterprises with an aggregate worldwide annual turnover of over €5 billion and where the aggregate EU-wide turnover of each of the enterprises exceeds €250 million.

First-mover advantage and the Stackelberg model

In the **Stackelberg model**, firm B can observe the output already fixed by firm A. In choosing output, firm A must thus anticipate the subsequent reaction of firm B.

So far we have assumed that the two duopolists make decisions simultaneously. Suppose one firm can choose output before the other. This means that we move from a simultaneous game to a sequential game structure. Does it help to move first?

To anticipate how firm B behaves once the output of firm A is fixed, firm A examines the reaction function of firm B as derived in Figures 9.6 and 9.7. In setting output, firm A then takes account of how its own output decisions *affect* output by firm B.

Firm A thus has a different reaction function. Figure 9.7 showed the Cournot reaction function R^A treating Q^B as chosen independently of Q^A. Now firm A uses the reaction function R^B to deduce that a higher output Q^A induces a *lower* output Q^B. Hence, firm A expects its own output expansion to bid the price down *less* than under Cournot behaviour. Its marginal revenue schedule is higher up. Firm A knows that firm B will help prop up the price by cutting Q^B in response to a rise in Q^A.

A **first-mover advantage** means that the player moving first achieves higher payoffs than when decisions are simultaneous.

Facing a higher *MR* schedule as a *Stackelberg leader* than under Cournot behaviour, firm A produces more than under Cournot behaviour. Firm B makes less because it must react to the fact that a high output Q^A is already a done deal. Firm A ends up with higher output and profits than under Cournot behaviour but firm B has lower output and lower profit. Firm A has a **first-mover advantage**.

Moving first acts like a commitment that prevents your subsequent manipulation by the other player. Once firm A has built a large output capacity, firm B has to live with the reality that firm A will produce large output. The best response of firm B is then low output. Propping up the output price helps firm A. Being smart, firm A had already figured all that out.

In some industries, firms are fairly symmetric and Cournot behaviour is a good description of how these oligopolists behave. Other industries have a dominant firm, perhaps because of a technical edge or privileged location. That firm may be able to act as a Stackelberg leader and anticipate how its smaller rivals will then react.

<table>
<tr><td>MATHS
9.2</td><td># The Stackelberg model</td></tr>
</table>

The Stackelberg model

Consider a market in which operate two firms, A and B. Firm A is the leader while firm B is the follower.

The market inverse demand function is $P = a - b(Q_A + Q_B)$. Assume that the total cost of firm A is $TC_A = c_A Q_A$, while for firm B it is $TC_B = c_B Q_B$. The marginal cost of firm A is therefore c_A and for firm B is c_B.

The follower (firm B) takes the output produced by the leader (firm A) as given. Let's look at the behaviour of the follower first. The total revenue function of firm B is $TR_B = aQ_B - bQ_A Q_B - bQ_B^2$. The marginal revenue of the follower is $MR_B = a - bQ_A - 2bQ_B$. The reaction function of the follower comes from the profit-maximizing condition of firm B $MR_B = MC_B$. Using our data, that condition implies $a - bQ_A - 2bQ_B = c_B$. Solve for Q_B:

$$Q_B = \frac{a - c_B}{2b} - \frac{Q_A}{2} \tag{1}$$

This is the reaction function of firm B. Firm A is the leader and takes into account that the follower has the reaction function given by (1).

The total revenue function of the leader is therefore:

$$TR_A = \left[a - b\left(Q_A + \frac{a - c_B}{2b} - \frac{Q_A}{2} \right) \right] \times Q_A \tag{2}$$

The term in the square brackets is just the inverse demand (and so the price) once we take into account the reaction function of the follower. Equation (2) becomes:

$$TR_A = aQ_A - bQ_A^2 - \frac{a - c_B}{2}Q_A + \frac{b}{2}Q_A^2$$

The marginal revenue of the leader is therefore:

$$MR_A \equiv \frac{dTR_A}{dQ_A} = a - 2bQ_A + bQ_A - \frac{a - c_B}{2}$$

The output that maximizes the profits of firm A comes from the condition $MR_A = MC_A$, that is: $a - 2bQ_A + bQ_A - (a - c_B)/2 = c_A$. Solve for Q_A:

$$Q_A = \frac{a + c_B - 2c_A}{2b}$$

Once we know the optimal choice for the leader, we can go back to the reaction function of the follower and substitute for the Q_A we just found:

$$Q_B = \frac{a - c_B}{2b} - \left(\frac{a + c_B - 2c_A}{4b} \right)$$

Simplifying that expression we obtain:

$$Q_B = \frac{a - 3c_B + 2c_A}{4b}$$

9.6 Entry and potential competition

So far we have discussed imperfect competition between existing firms. To complete our understanding of such markets, we must also think about the effect of potential competition from new entrants to the industry on the behaviour of existing or incumbent firms. Three cases must be distinguished: where entry is completely easy, where it is difficult by accident and where it is difficult by design.

Contestable markets

> A **contestable market** has free entry and free exit.

Free entry to, and exit from, the industry is a key feature of perfect competition, a market structure in which each firm is tiny relative to the industry. Suppose, however, that we observe an industry with few incumbent firms. Before assuming that our previous analysis of oligopoly is needed, we must think hard about entry and exit. The industry may be a contestable market.

By free entry, we mean that all firms, including both incumbents and potential entrants, have access to the same technology and hence have the same cost curves. By free exit, we mean that there are no *sunk* or irrecoverable costs: on leaving the industry, a firm can fully recoup its previous investment expenditure, including money spent on building up knowledge and goodwill.

A contestable market allows *hit-and-run* entry. If the incumbent firms, however few, do not behave as if they were a perfectly competitive industry ($p = MC = $ minimum LAC), an entrant can step in, undercut them and make a temporary profit before quitting again.

As globalization proceeds, we should remember that foreign suppliers are important potential entrants. This can take two forms. First, if monopoly profits are too high in the domestic market, competition from imports may augment supply, bidding down prices and profits in the domestic market. In the extreme case, in which imports surge in whenever domestic prices rise above the world price, we are back in the competitive world analysed in Chapter 8.

Globalization also raises the likelihood that foreign firms will set up production facilities in the home market, a tangible form of entry. By raising the supply of potential entrants, globalization increases the relevance of contestable markets as a description of market structure. Moreover, we normally think of an entrant as having to start from scratch. When an existing foreign firm enters the domestic market, its production and marketing expertise may already be highly developed.

Globalization may be a two-edged sword. On the one hand, it raises the size of the relevant market and makes entry easier. On the other hand, by allowing multinationals to become vast by operating in many countries simultaneously, globalization may encourage the formation of large firms that then have substantial market power wherever they operate. Coke and Pepsi are slugging it out for global dominance and Virgin Cola provides only limited competition, even in the UK.

The theory of contestable markets remains controversial. There are many industries in which sunk costs are hard to recover or where the initial expertise may take an entrant some time to acquire, placing it at a temporary disadvantage against incumbent firms. Nor, as we shall shortly see, is it safe to assume that incumbents will not change their behaviour when threatened by entry. But the theory does vividly illustrate that market structure and incumbent behaviour cannot be deduced simply by counting the number of firms in the industry.

In the previous chapter, we were careful to stress that a monopolist is a sole producer *who can completely discount fear of entry*. We now refine the classification of Table 9.1 by discussing entry in more detail.

Innocent entry barriers

Our discussion of entry barriers distinguishes those that occur anyway and those that are deliberately erected by incumbent firms.

> An **innocent entry barrier** is one not deliberately erected by incumbent firms.

The American economist Joe Bain distinguished three types of entry barrier: product differentiation, absolute cost advantages and scale economies. The first of these is not an innocent barrier, as we shall shortly explain. Absolute cost advantages, where incumbent firms have lower cost curves than those that entrants will face, may be innocent. If it takes time to learn the business, incumbents will face lower costs, at least in the short run. If they are smart, they may already have located in the most advantageous site. In contrast, if incumbents have undertaken investment or R&D specifically with a view to deterring entrants, this is not an innocent barrier. We take up this issue shortly.

Figure 9.1 showed the role of scale economies as an innocent entry barrier. If minimum efficient scale is large relative to the industry demand curve, an entrant cannot get into the industry without considerably depressing the market price, and it may prove simply impossible to break in at a profit.

The greater such innocent entry barriers, the more appropriate it is to neglect potential competition from entrants. The oligopoly game then comes down to competition between incumbent firms along the lines we discussed in the previous section. Where innocent entry barriers are low, one of two things may happen. Either incumbent firms accept this situation, in which case competition from potential entrants will prevent incumbent firms from exercising much market power – the outcome will be closer to that of perfect competition – or else incumbent firms will try to design some entry barriers of their own.

9.7 Strategic entry deterrence

A *strategy* is a game plan where decision making is interdependent. The word 'strategic' is used in everyday language but it has a precise meaning in economics.

In Figure 9.9 a single incumbent firm plays a game against a potential entrant. The entrant can come in or stay out. If the entrant comes in, the incumbent can opt for the easy life, accept the new rival and agree to share the market – or it can fight. Each party undertakes a series of **strategic moves**. Fighting entry means producing at least as much as before, and perhaps considerably more than before, so that the industry price collapses. In this *price war*, sometimes called *predatory pricing* by the incumbent, both firms do badly and make losses. The top row of boxes in Figure 9.9 shows the profits to the incumbent (in blue) and the entrant (in orange) in each of the three possible outcomes.

> A **strategic move** is one that influences the other person's choice, in a manner favourable to oneself, by affecting the other person's expectations of how one will behave.

If the incumbent is unchallenged it does very well, making profits of 5. The entrant of course makes nothing. If they share the market, both make small profits of 1. In a price war, both make losses. How should the game go?

Suppose the entrant comes in. Comparing the left and middle boxes of the top row, the incumbent does better to cave in than to fight. The entrant can figure this out. Any threat by the incumbent to resist entry is not a credible threat – when it comes to the crunch, it will be better to cave in. Much as the incumbent would like the entrant to stay out, in which case the incumbent would make profits of 5, the equilibrium of the game is that the entrant will come in and the incumbent will not resist. Both make profits of 1, the top left-hand box.

The incumbent, however, may have got its act together before the potential entrant appears on the scene. It may be able to invent a binding pre-commitment, forcing itself to resist entry and thereby scare off a future challenge. The incumbent would be ecstatic if a Martian appeared and guaranteed to shoot the

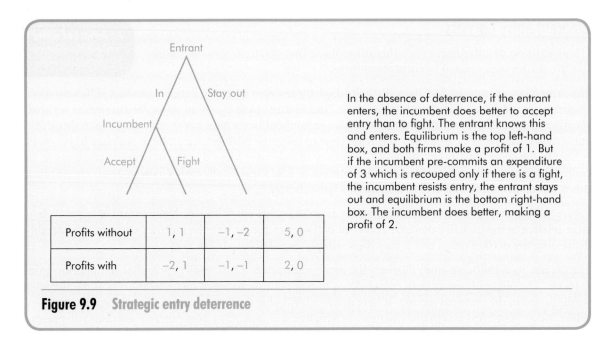

In the absence of deterrence, if the entrant enters, the incumbent does better to accept entry than to fight. The entrant knows this and enters. Equilibrium is the top left-hand box, and both firms make a profit of 1. But if the incumbent pre-commits an expenditure of 3 which is recouped only if there is a fight, the incumbent resists entry, the entrant stays out and equilibrium is the bottom right-hand box. The incumbent does better, making a profit of 2.

Profits without	1, 1	−1, −2	5, 0
Profits with	−2, 1	−1, −1	2, 0

Figure 9.9 Strategic entry deterrence

incumbent's directors if they ever allowed an entry to be unchallenged. Entrants would expect a fight, would anticipate a loss of 1, and would stay out, leaving the incumbent with a permanent profit of 5.

In the absence of Martians, the incumbent can achieve the same effect by economic means. Suppose the incumbent invests in expensive spare capacity that is unused at low output. The incumbent has low output in the absence of entry or if an entrant is accommodated without a fight. Suppose in these situations the incumbent loses 3 by carrying this excess capacity. The second row of boxes in Figure 9.9 reduces the incumbent's profits by 3 in these two outcomes. In a price war, however, the incumbent's output is high and the spare capacity is no longer wasted; hence we do not need to reduce the incumbent's profit in the middle column of boxes in Figure 9.9. Now consider the game again.

> **Strategic entry deterrence** is behaviour by incumbent firms to make entry less likely.

If the entrant comes in, the incumbent loses 2 by caving in but only 1 by fighting. Hence entry is resisted. Foreseeing this, the entrant does not enter, since the entrant loses money in a price war. Hence the equilibrium of the game is the bottom right-hand box and no entry takes place. **Strategic entry deterrence** has been successful.

It has also been profitable. Even allowing for the cost of 3 of carrying the spare capacity, the incumbent still makes a profit of 2, which is better than the profit of 1 in the top left-hand box when no deterrence was attempted and the entrant came in.

Does deterrence always work? No. Suppose in Figure 9.9 we change the right-hand column. In the top row the incumbent gets a profit of 3 if no entry occurs. Without the pre-commitment, the equilibrium is the top left-hand box, as before. But if the incumbent has to spend 3 on a spare capacity pre-commitment, it now makes a profit of 0 in the bottom right-hand box when entry is deterred. The entrant is still deterred but the incumbent would have done better not to invest in spare capacity and to let the entrant in.

This model suggests that price wars should never happen. If the incumbent really is going to fight, then the entrant should not have entered. This of course requires the entrant to know accurately the profits of the incumbent in the different boxes and therefore correctly predict its behaviour. In the real world, entrants sometimes get it wrong. Moreover, if the entrant has much better financial backing than the incumbent, a price war may be a good investment for the entrant. The incumbent will exit first and thereafter the entrant will be able to cash in and get its losses back with interest.

CASE
9.2

Barriers at the checkout

In 2004 the Morrisons supermarket chain finally completed its takeover of rival Safeway. At a stroke, Morrisons was catapulted from the supermarket minnow, with a 6 per cent market share, to a big league player with 17 per cent of the UK market, only marginally less than Sainsbury's, one-time leader of the supermarket industry.

The takeover of Safeway was contested, with Tesco, Asda and Sainsbury's all mounting rival bids to Morrisons'. At one stage, Philip Green, the owner of high-street retailer British Home Stores (Bhs), also registered an interest in Safeway. Safeway was such an attractive target because it provided the last chance to enter the supermarket industry. Without access to land, and facing difficulty getting planning permission for new supermarkets, the only entry mode was a takeover. With Safeway now in the hands of Morrisons, and the industry consolidated into large players, the next takeover will be even more difficult.

Photo: Morrisons supermarket in Newport, Isle of Wight. © Editor5807

Is spare capacity the only pre-commitment available to incumbents? Pre-commitments must be irreversible, otherwise they are an empty threat, and they must increase the chances that the incumbent will fight. Anything with the character of fixed and sunk costs may work: fixed costs artificially increase scale economies and make the incumbent more keen on high output, and sunk costs cannot be reversed. Advertising to invest in goodwill and brand loyalty is a good example. So is product proliferation. If the incumbent has only one brand, an entrant may hope to break in with a different brand. But if the incumbent has a complete range of brands or models, an entrant will have to compete across the whole product range.

9.8 Summing up

Few industries in the real world are like the textbook extremes of perfect competition and pure monopoly. Most are imperfectly competitive. This chapter introduced you to types of imperfect competition. Game theory in general, and concepts such as commitment, credibility and deterrence, allow economists to analyse many of the practical concerns of big business.

What have we learned? First, market structure and the behaviour of incumbent firms are determined *simultaneously*. Economists used to start with a market structure, determined by the extent of scale economies relative to the industry demand curve, then deduce how the incumbent firms would behave (monopoly, oligopoly, perfect competition), then check out these predictions against performance indicators, such as the extent to which prices exceeded marginal cost. Now we realize that strategic behaviour by incumbent firms can affect entry, and hence market structure, except where entry is almost trivially easy.

Second, and related, we have learned the importance of *potential* competition, which may come from domestic firms considering entry, or from imports from abroad. The number of firms observed in the industry today conveys little information about the extent of the market power they truly exercise. If entry is easy, even a single incumbent or apparent monopolist may find it unprofitable to depart significantly from perfectly competitive behaviour.

Finally, we have seen how many business practices of the real world – price wars, advertising, brand proliferation, excess capacity or excessive research and development – can be understood as strategic competition in which, to be effective, threats must be made credible by prior commitments.

Summary

- **Imperfect competition** exists when individual firms believe they face downward-sloping demand curves. The most important forms are monopolistic competition, oligopoly and pure monopoly.

- **Pure monopoly** status can be conferred by legislation, as when an industry is nationalized or a temporary patent is awarded. When **minimum efficient scale** is very large relative to the industry demand curve, this innocent entry barrier may be sufficiently high to produce a natural monopoly in which all threat of entry can be ignored.

- At the opposite extreme, entry and exit may be costless. The market is **contestable**, and incumbent firms must mimic perfectly competitive behaviour to avoid being flooded by entrants. With an intermediate size of entry barrier, the industry may be an oligopoly.

- **Monopolistic competitors** face free entry to and exit from the industry but are individually small and make similar though not identical products. Each has limited monopoly power in its special brand. In long-run equilibrium, price equals average cost but exceeds marginal revenue and marginal cost at the tangency equilibrium.

- **Oligopolists** face tension between collusion to maximize joint profits and competition for a larger share of smaller joint profits. **Collusion** may be formal, as in a cartel, or informal. Without **credible threats** of punishment by its partners, each firm faces a temptation to cheat.

- **Game theory** analyses interdependent decisions in which each player chooses a strategy. In the Prisoner's Dilemma game, each firm has a dominant strategy. With binding commitments, both players could do better by guaranteeing not to cheat on the collusive solution.

- A **reaction function** shows one player's best response to the actions of other players. In **Nash equilibrium** reaction functions intersect. No player then wishes to change her decision.

- In **Cournot behaviour** each firm treats the output of its rival as given. In **Bertrand behaviour** each firm treats the price of its rival as given. Nash–Bertrand equilibrium entails pricing at marginal cost. Nash–Cournot equilibrium entails lower output, higher prices and profits. However, firms still fail to maximize joint profits because each neglects the fact that its output expansion hurts its rivals.

- A firm with a **first-mover advantage** acts as a **Stackelberg leader**. By deducing the subsequent reaction of its rival, it produces higher output, knowing the rival will then have to produce lower output. Moving first is a useful commitment.

- **Innocent entry barriers** are made by nature, and arise from scale economies or absolute cost advantages of incumbent firms. **Strategic entry barriers** are made in boardrooms and arise from credible commitments to resist entry if challenged. Only in certain circumstances is strategic entry deterrence profitable for incumbents.

Review questions

connect

1 An industry faces the demand curve:

EASY

Q	1	2	3	4	5	6	7	8	9	10
P	10	9	8	7	6	5	4	3	2	1

(a) Suppose it is a monopolist whose constant $MC = 3$: what price and output are chosen? (b) Now suppose there are two firms, each with $MC = AC = 3$: what price and output maximize joint profits if they collude? (c) Why might each firm be tempted to cheat if it can avoid retaliation by the other?

2 With the above industry demand curve, two firms, A and Z, begin with half the market each when charging the monopoly price. Z decides to cheat and believes A will stick to its old output level. (a) Show the demand curve Z believes it faces. (b) What price and output would Z then choose?

3 Vehicle repairers sometimes suggest that mechanics should be licensed so that repairs are done only by qualified people. Some economists argue that customers can always ask whether a mechanic was trained at a reputable institution without needing to see any licence. (a) Evaluate the arguments for and against licensing car mechanics. (b) Are the arguments the same for licensing doctors?

4 Think of five adverts on television. Is their function primarily informative, or to erect entry barriers to the industry?

5 A good-natured parent knows that children sometimes need to be punished but also knows that, when it comes to the crunch, the child will be let off with a warning. Can the parent undertake any pre-commitment to make the threat of punishment credible?

6 True or false   A firm in a monopolistically competitive market faces a downward-sloping demand curve for its product.

7 Common fallacies   Why are these statements wrong? (a) Competitive firms should get together to restrict output and drive up the price. (b) Firms would not advertise unless they expected advertising to increase sales.

8 Consider a market with two firms, 1 and 2, producing a homogeneous good. The market demand is $P = 130 - 2(Q_1 + Q_2)$, where Q_1 is the quantity produced by firm 1 and Q_2 is the quantity produced by firm 2. The total cost of firm 1 is $TC_1 = 10Q_1$, the one of firm 2 is $TC_2 = 10Q_2$. Therefore, we have that $MC_1 = 10$ and $MC_2 = 10$. The marginal revenue of firm 1 is $MR_1 = 130 - 4Q_1 - 2Q_2$, while the marginal revenue of firm 2 is $MR_2 = 130 - 2Q_1 - 4Q_2$. Each firm chooses its quantity to maximize profits.

MEDIUM

(a) From the condition $MR_1 = MC_1$, find the reaction function of firm 1, and from $MR_2 = MC_2$, find the reaction function of firm 2.

(b) Find the equilibrium quantity produced by each firm by solving the system of the two reaction functions you found in (a). Sketch your solution graphically.

(c) Find the equilibrium price. Find the profits of each firm.

9 Suppose that the two firms in Question 8 behave as competitive firms. What will be the quantity they produce and what will be the equilibrium price? (*Hint:* use the fact that both firms are equal, so they must produce the same amount.)

10 Consider two firms, A and B. They have two possible strategies, pricing low or pricing high. The possible outcomes from those strategies are reported in the following table:

		Firm B	
		P high	P low
Firm A	P high	3, 3	1, 6
	P low	6, 1	5, 5

Find the Nash equilibrium of the game.

11 Two identical firms, 1 and 2, compete in quantities. The reaction function of firm 1 is $Q_1 = 15 - \frac{1}{2}Q_2$, while for firm 2 we have $Q_2 = 15 - \frac{1}{2}Q_1$. In the table below we have the total quantity produced in the market:

$Q_1 + Q_2$	2	6	10	14	18	22	26	30	34

Using the fact that both firms must produce the same quantity, plot the reaction functions of the two firms in a graph. Explain why the equilibrium quantity produced is where the two reaction functions intersect.

12 'Since a firm's optimal behaviour depends on how it believes that its rival(s) will react, there are as many output decisions, and hence equilibria, as there are guesses about what rivals will do.' How do economists try to narrow down the assumptions that firms make about their rivals?

13 Many of the interesting games are games against the government. Think of a European airline, until recently state-owned, now private but losing money under the pressure of high oil prices and the growth of low-cost airlines. Believing that the government will bail it out if the worst comes to the worst, the airline has no incentive to take the tough measures today needed to make its business profitable. How can the government signal that it will not bail out the airline, forcing the airline to improve or go bust?

14 **Essay question** 'Globalization, by increasing the size of the market, reduces market power of individual firms and the need to address strategic interactions.' 'Globalization increases the payoff to scooping the pool, making mergers more attractive and enhancing worries about market power.' Are either of these views correct? Both of them?

For solutions to these questions contact your lecturer.

The labour market

Learning Outcomes

By the end of this chapter, you should understand:

1. a firm's demand for inputs in the long run and short run

2. marginal value product, marginal revenue product and marginal cost of a factor

3. the industry demand for labour

4. labour supply decisions

5. transfer earnings and economic rent

6. labour market equilibrium and disequilibrium

7. how minimum wages affect employment

8. isoquants and the choice of production technique

In winning a golf tournament, a top professional earns more in a weekend than a professor earns in a year. Students studying economics can expect higher career earnings than those of equally smart students studying philosophy. An unskilled worker in the EU earns more than an unskilled worker in India. Few market economies provide jobs for all their citizens wanting to work. How can we explain these aspects of the real world?

In each case the answer depends on the supply and demand for that type of labour, the subject of the next two chapters. We begin our analysis of the markets for the factors of production – labour, capital and land. We discuss what determines the equilibrium prices and quantities of these inputs in different industries and in the whole economy. We begin with the factor called 'labour'. Chapter 11 applies the same principles to the markets for other production inputs.

We have already studied the market for goods. There is nothing intrinsically different about our approach to factor markets. You should be able to guess the structure of this chapter: demand, supply, equilibrium, problems of disequilibrium and adjustment.

Table 10.1 gives data on UK earnings (full-time males) in 2009 and compares these with inflation-adjusted data for 1997. By 2009, workers in financial services earned £268 a week more than the national average. Workers in energy and water were also doing well in their high-tech industry. The house market boom experienced until 2007 benefited the wages of construction workers.

Table 10.1 Weekly real earnings, UK (full-time male, 2009 £)

	1997	2009
Whole economy	484	531
Financial services	701	799
Construction	456	550
Energy and water	578	636

Source: ONS, *Annual Survey of Hours and Earnings.*

The demand for inputs is a **derived demand**, reflecting demand for the firm's output.

Although the economics of factor markets still focus on supply and demand, there is something special about demand in factor markets. It is not a direct or final demand, but a **derived demand**. Firms demand inputs only because they want to produce output. Each firm simultaneously decides how many outputs to supply and how many inputs to demand. The two are inextricably linked.

On the supply side we distinguish between the supply of factors to the economy and to an individual firm or industry. A firm can gain factors by attracting them away from other firms. However, the economy as a whole may be able to expand particular inputs only slowly. It takes time to build factories or train skilled workers.

In the short run, the supply of pilots to the economy may be fixed. Any rise in the total demand for pilots raises their equilibrium wage. In the longer run, high wages for pilots then act as a signal for school-leavers to abandon plans to become train drivers and go to flying school instead. Thus, we need to distinguish labour supply in the short run and long run.

Combining demand and supply leads to equilibrium prices and quantities in the labour market. How quickly does the labour market return to equilibrium? Whereas some output markets may return to equilibrium relatively quickly, labour market adjustment is often more sluggish. We examine reasons why the labour market may be slow to adjust.

10.1 The firm's demand for factors in the long run

In the long run all inputs can be adjusted. Chapter 7 studied a firm's long-run costs. Chapters 8 and 9 considered various descriptions of the demand curve facing a firm and showed how a firm would choose output supplied to maximize profits. Although part of the same decision, we now focus not on the firm's supply of output but on its corresponding demand for inputs.

The firm thinks about the least-cost way of making each possible output and then selects the output that maximizes profit. In producing any particular output by the cheapest available technique, a rise in the price of labour relative to capital makes the firm switch to a more capital-intensive technique. Conversely, if capital becomes relatively more expensive, the least-cost technique for a given output is now more labour-intensive. The firm substitutes away from the factor of production that has become relatively more expensive.

This principle helps explain cross-country differences in capital–labour ratios in the same industry. European farmers face high wages relative to the rental of a combine harvester. Mechanized farming economizes on expensive workers. Indian farmers, facing cheap and abundant labour but scarce and expensive capital, use labour-intensive techniques. Workers with scythes and shovels do the jobs done by combine harvesters and bulldozers in the UK.

A higher wage makes the firm substitute capital for labour in making a given output. But it also raises the total cost of producing any output. Firms still use *some* labour, for which they now pay more than before. With higher marginal costs, but unchanged demand and marginal revenue curves, the firm chooses to make less output.

Thus a rise in the price of one factor not merely changes factor intensity at a given output, but also changes the profit-maximizing level of output. Studying consumer decisions in Chapter 5, we saw that a change in the price of a good has both a substitution effect and an income effect. The substitution effect reflects the change in relative prices of different goods and the income effect reflects changes in real income as a result of the price change. The demand for production inputs works in exactly the same way.

There is a pure substitution effect at a given level of output. A higher relative price of labour compared with capital leads firms to substitute capital for labour. But there is also an output effect, the analogue of the income effect in consumer demand theory. By raising the marginal cost of producing output, a rise in the price of labour leads to a lower output.

In the long run a rise in the wage *will* reduce the quantity of labour demanded. The substitution effect leads to less demand for labour and each output, and the output effect reduces the demand for all inputs.

A rise in the wage also affects the long-run demand for capital and other inputs. At any particular output, the firm substitutes capital for labour. However, with lower output it needs less capital input. The overall effect could go either way. The easier it is to substitute capital for labour, the more likely is the substitution effect to dominate. Firms will substitute a lot of capital for labour. The quantity of capital demanded will rise.

The demand for factors of production is a derived demand. It depends on demand for the firm's output. The output demand curve affects the output effect on the demand for inputs when an input price changes.

In Figure 10.1 at the original wage, the long-run marginal cost curve *LMC* of output is LMC_0. A rise in the wage shifts this up to LMC_1. The original profit-maximizing point is *A*. If the firm faces a horizontal demand curve *DD*, output falls from Q_0 to Q_1. With the less elastic demand curve *D'D'*, the firm still begins at *A* where LMC_0 equals *MR*, the marginal revenue curve corresponding to *D'D'*. Now the shift to LMC_1 leads to a much smaller fall in output. The new output is Q_2 and the firm is at *C*.

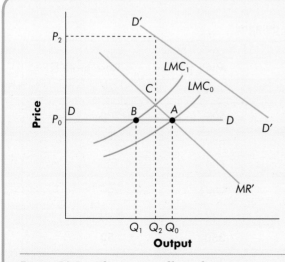

A wage increase will have a substitution effect leading firms to substitute relatively more capital-intensive techniques. Nevertheless, total costs and marginal costs of producing output will be greater than before. Facing the horizontal demand curve *DD*, a shift from LMC_0 to LMC_1 will lead the firm to move from *A* to *B* and output will fall from Q_0 to Q_1. This tends to reduce the demand for all factors of production. Facing the demand curve *D'D'* and corresponding marginal revenue curve *MR'*, the upward shift from LMC_0 to LMC_1 leads the firm to move from *A* to *C* at which marginal cost and marginal revenue are again equal. The output effect reduces output only from Q_0 to Q_2.

Figure 10.1 The output effect of a wage increase

The more elastic the demand curve for the firm's output, the more a given rise in the price of an input, and a given shift in the *LMC* curve for output, leads to a big fall in output. The larger the output effect, the greater the fall in the quantity of all factors demanded.

The Appendix at the end of this chapter shows that we can also analyse factor demands using techniques such as the indifference curves and budget lines used to study household demands for goods in Chapter 5.

10.2 The firm's demand for labour in the short run

In the short run the firm has some fixed factors of production. We now consider the firm's short-run demand for labour when its capital input is fixed.

> The **marginal product of labour** is the extra total output when an extra worker is added, with other input quantities unaltered.

Table 10.2 shows a firm's variable labour input and corresponding output, holding capital input fixed. Column (3) shows the **marginal product of labour** (*MPL*). This marginal product rises as the first workers are added. It is hard for the first and second worker to carry all the tools. After the third worker has been added, the *diminishing marginal productivity* of labour sets in. With existing machines fully utilized, there is less and less for each new worker to do.

As in our discussion of output, we use the *marginal principle*. Does the cost of a new worker exceed the benefit of a new worker? Table 10.2 shows a competitive firm hiring workers at a wage of £300 and selling output at a price of £500. Column (4) shows the extra revenue from taking on another worker.

Since the firm is perfectly competitive, the marginal value product of another worker is the marginal product in physical goods multiplied by the (constant) price for which the extra goods are sold. From this extra revenue from the extra worker, the firm subtracts the extra wage cost. The last column of Table 10.2 shows the extra profit from an extra worker.

> The **marginal value product of labour** is the extra revenue from selling the output made by an extra worker.

The firm hires more workers if the **marginal value product** of another worker exceeds the wage cost. It is profitable to hire 7 workers. The seventh worker has a marginal value product of £350, just above the cost of £300 for this extra worker.

Table 10.2 Short-run output supply and labour demand

(1) Workers	(2) Output	(3) MPL	(4) MVPL (£)	(5) Extra profit (£)
1	0.8	0.8	400	100
2	1.8	1.0	500	200
3	3.1	1.3	650	350
4	4.3	1.2	600	300
5	5.4	1.1	550	250
6	6.3	0.9	450	150
7	7.0	0.7	350	50
8	7.5	0.5	250	−50

An eighth worker's marginal value product is only £250, below the £300 another worker costs. The firm hires 7 workers.

In so doing, the firm chooses both labour input and goods output: the highlighted row shows that 7 workers make 7 units of output. The firm gets the same answer, namely maximum profit, whether it compares the marginal revenue from another output unit with the marginal cost of making that output unit, or compares the marginal revenue from hiring another unit of the variable factor with the marginal cost of hiring that variable factor.

The firm's employment rule is thus: expand (contract) employment if the marginal value product of labour is greater than (less than) the wage of an extra worker. If labour can be smoothly adjusted, for example if labour input is measured in [hours] × [workers], the firm's demand for labour must satisfy the condition

$$\text{Wage} = \text{marginal value product of labour } (MVPL) \tag{1}$$

Figure 10.2 illustrates this principle. If we assume diminishing marginal productivity at all employment levels, the marginal value product of labour ($MVPL$) slopes down. A competitive firm can hire labour at the constant wage rate W_0. It is a price-taker in the labour market. Below L^* profits are increased by raising employment, since $MVPL$ exceeds the wage rate or marginal cost of hiring extra labour. Above L^* it is profitable to shrink employment, since the wage exceeds the $MVPL$. Thus L^* is the profit-maximizing level of employment.

Changes in the firm's demand for labour

Consider a rise in the wage W_0 faced by a competitive firm. Using Figure 10.1 or 10.2, the firm hires fewer workers than before. The marginal cost of labour has risen. Diminishing labour productivity makes the $MVPL$ schedule slope down. Hence lower employment is needed to raise the marginal value product of labour in line with its higher marginal cost.

Suppose that a competitive firm faces a higher output price. The MPL remains unaltered in physical goods, but this output now earns more money. The $MVPL$ schedule shifts up at each level of employment. Hence in Figure 10.1 or 10.2 the horizontal line through the wage W_0 crosses the new $MVPL$ schedule at a higher employment level. With the marginal cost of labour unaltered and the marginal revenue from labour increased, output and employment expand until diminishing marginal productivity drives $MVPL$ back down to the wage W_0.

Finally, suppose the firm had begun with a higher capital stock. Each worker has more machinery with which to work and makes more output. Although wages and prices are unchanged, there is a rise in MPL in physical goods at each employment level. The $MVPL$ schedule shifts up, since $MVPL$ equals MPL times output price. As with a higher output price, this upward shift in the $MVPL$ schedule leads the firm to expand employment and output.

For a competitive firm there is a neat way to combine our first two results. Noting that $MVPL$ equals the

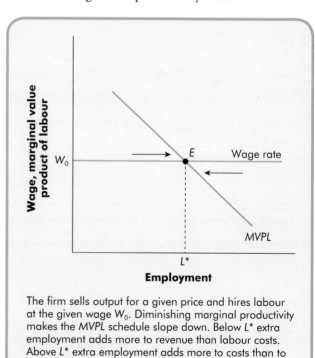

The firm sells output for a given price and hires labour at the given wage W_0. Diminishing marginal productivity makes the $MVPL$ schedule slope down. Below L^* extra employment adds more to revenue than labour costs. Above L^* extra employment adds more to costs than to revenue. L^* is the profit-maximizing employment level where the wage rate equals the $MVPL$.

Figure 10.2 The firm's choice of employment

output price P times MPL, the extra physical product of another worker, the firm's profit-maximizing condition is wage $W = P \times MPL$. Dividing both sides of this equation by P gives:

$$W/P = MPL \qquad (2)$$

A profit-maximizing competitive firm demands labour up to the point at which the marginal physical product of labour equals its *real* wage, the nominal wage divided by the output price.

The position of the MPL schedule depends on technology and the existing capital stock. Since these are fixed in the short run, we can alter MPL only by moving along the schedule. Diminishing returns imply that, with more workers, the marginal physical product of the last worker is lower. From the particular level of the marginal physical product of labour, we can deduce how many workers are being employed.

Equation (2) tells us that if nominal wages and output prices both double, real wages and employment are unaffected. But changes in either the nominal wage or the output price, if not matched by a change in the other, alter employment by affecting the real wage. Lower real wages move the firm down its MPL schedule, taking on more workers until the marginal physical product of labour equals the real wage.

Having studied the firm's demand for labour in the short run, we now turn to the demand by the industry as a whole. Although each competitive firm regards itself as a price-taker in both its output and input markets, an expansion by the whole industry will change output prices and wages. In moving from the firm's demand curve to the industry demand curve for labour, we take account of these effects.

MATHS 10.1 — The demand for inputs and profit maximization

Here we see how to derive the inputs demand from profit maximization in competitive markets. We consider both labour and capital, even though capital will be discussed in more detail in Chapter 11.

Consider a perfectly competitive firm that faces competitive markets for capital and labour. The firm is producing output according to the following production function:

$$Q = f(K, L)$$

where K is the amount of capital and L is the amount of labour.

The prices of inputs are r for capital (the rental rate) and w for labour (the wage) and they are taken as given by the firm. The profit function of the firm is:

$$\pi = pf(K, L) - wL - rK$$

where p is the price (taken as given) at which the firm sells its output Q. The firm chooses the amounts of capital and labour to employ in order to maximize profits.

We know that this implies that the firm chooses K and L, such that the marginal value product of the two inputs equals the prices of the two inputs:

$$p\frac{\partial f(K, L)}{\partial K} = r \qquad p\frac{\partial f(K, L)}{\partial L} = w$$

The term $(\partial f(K, L))/\partial L$ is the *partial derivative* of the production function with respect to labour. It tells us how the quantity produced (remember that $Q = f(K, L)$) changes if we change the level of labour by a small amount, *keeping constant* the level of capital. If labour increases by 1 unit, for a given amount of capital, the extra output we obtain is $(\partial f(K, L))/\partial L$. We can sell this extra output at a price p. Therefore the term $p((\partial f(K, L))/\partial L)$ is the marginal value product of labour. A similar interpretation is given for the term $p((\partial f(K, L))/\partial K)$, which represents the marginal value product of capital.

10.3 The industry demand curve for labour

For a given price P_0 and wage W_0, each firm in a competitive industry chooses employment to equate the wage and the $MVPL$. Figure 10.3 horizontally adds the marginal value product of labour curves for each firm to obtain the $MVPL_0$ schedule for the industry. At the wage W_0 and the price P_0, the industry is at E_0. This is a point on the industry demand curve for labour.

However, $MVPL_0$ is *not* the industry demand curve for labour. It is drawn for a particular output price P_0. Suppose the wage is cut from W_0 to W_1. At the output price P_0, each firm wants to move down its $MVPL$ schedule and the industry expand output and employ labour to point E_1 in Figure 10.3. In terms of the supply and demand for output, the cut in wages has shifted the industry supply curve to the right.

At the given price P_0, there is now an excess supply of goods. This bids down the price for the industry's product to a lower price P_1. The lower price shifts each firm's $MVPL$ schedule to the left. $MVPL_1$ is thus the new $MVPL$ schedule for the industry at the new price P_1. The industry chooses the point E_1' at the new wage W_1.

Connecting points such as E_0 and E_1', we get the *industry demand for labour schedule $D_L D_L$* in Figure 10.3. Each firm constructs its $MVPL$ schedule as if it were a price-taker but the industry demand curve has a steeper slope, since a lower wage shifts the industry output supply curve to the right and reduces the equilibrium price.

The slope of the $MVPL$ schedule reflects the production technology. The more MPL diminishes as labour input rises, the steeper is the $MVPL$ schedule of the firm and of the industry. The slope of the industry demand curve for labour also depends on the elasticity of the market demand curve for the industry's product. The more inelastic output demand is, the more a wage cut – by raising the supply of output – bids down the output price and shifts $MVPL$ schedules to the left, and the steeper is the industry demand curve $D_L D_L$ for labour.

The demand for factors of production is a *derived* demand. Firms want factors only because they see a demand for their output that it is profitable to supply. The elasticity of input demand reflects the elasticity of output demand.

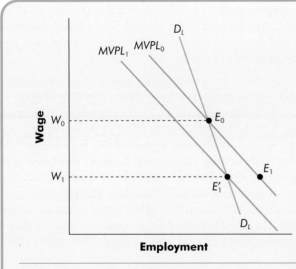

$MVPL_0$ is the horizontal sum of each firm's $MVPL$ schedule at the price P_0. Each firm and the industry as a whole sets $MVPL$ equal to W_0. Hence E_0 is a point on the industry demand curve for labour. A lower wage W_1 leads each firm and the industry as a whole to move down their $MVPL$ schedules to a point E_1. Extra employment and output by the whole industry (a shift to the right in the industry supply curve of goods) leads to excess goods supply at the original price P_0. To clear the output market the price must fall, and this shifts to the left each firm's $MVPL$ schedule. The new industry schedule is $MVPL_1$ and the chosen point is E_1'. Joining all the points such as E_0 and E_1', we obtain the industry demand curve $D_L D_L$.

Figure 10.3 The industry demand for labour

10.4 The supply of labour

We now discuss the supply of labour, for the individual, the industry and the whole of the economy. We can then combine labour demand and labour supply to determine the equilibrium level of wages and employment.

Individual labour supply: hours of work

> The **labour force** is all individuals in work or looking for work.

We analyse labour supply in two stages: how many hours people work once in the labour force and whether people join the labour force at all.

Once in the labour force, how many hours will a person wish to work? This depends on the *real* wage, W/P, the nominal wage divided by the price of goods, which shows the quantity of goods that labour effort will purchase. It is the real wage that affects labour supply decisions.

Figure 10.4 shows two possible labour supply curves, relating hours of work supplied to the real wage. The curve SS_1 slopes up. Higher real wages make people want to work more. The labour supply curve SS_2 is *backward-bending*. Beyond A, further real wage rises make people want to work fewer hours.

The alternative to working another hour is staying at home and having fun. Each of us has 24 hours a day to divide between work and leisure. More leisure is nice but by working longer we can get more real income with which to buy consumer goods. How should an individual trade off leisure against consumer goods in deciding how much to work?

This is an application of the model of consumer choice in Chapter 5. The choice is now between goods as a whole and leisure. An individual will want to work until the marginal utility derived from the goods that an extra hour of work will provide is just equal to the marginal utility from the last hour of leisure.

A higher real wage increases the quantity of goods an extra hour of work will purchase. This makes working more attractive than before and tends to increase the supply of hours worked. But there is a second effect. Suppose you work to get a target bundle of goods. You work to get enough to be able to eat, pay the rent, run a car and have a holiday. With a higher real wage you need to work fewer hours to earn the same target bundle of goods.

These two effects are precisely the *substitution and income effects* introduced in the consumer choice model of Chapter 5. An increase in the real wage increases the relative return on working. It leads to a substitution effect or pure relative price effect that makes people want to work more. But a higher real wage also tends to raise people's real income. This has a pure income effect. Since leisure is probably a luxury good, the quantity of leisure demanded increases sharply when real incomes increase. This income effect tends to make people work less. The overall effect of a real wage rise, and the shape of the supply curve for hours worked, depends on which effect is larger.

To decide whether or not the substitution effect will dominate the income effect, we must look at actual data on what people

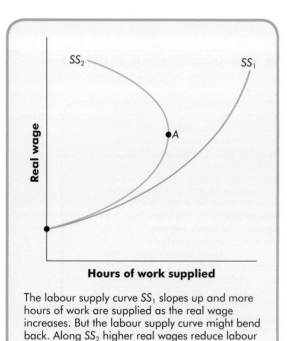

The labour supply curve SS_1 slopes up and more hours of work are supplied as the real wage increases. But the labour supply curve might bend back. Along SS_2 higher real wages reduce labour supply once we reach the point A.

Figure 10.4 Individual labour supply

Table 10.3   Participation rates (%)

	1994		2008	
	Men	Women	Men	Women
UK	85.1	67.1	83.4	70.2
France	74.1	59.3	74.3	65.2
Germany	79.8	60.9	82.1	69.7
US	84.3	69.4	81.4	69.3
EU15	78.4	56.5	79.7	65.3

Note: EU15 refers to the average for the 15 countries that were in the European Union on 1 January 1995.

Source: OECD, *Employment Outlook*, 2009.

do. Economists have tried three techniques in an attempt to discover how people actually behave. Interview studies ask people how they behave. Econometric studies, of the kind discussed in Chapter 2, try to disentangle the separate effects from data on actual behaviour. And experiments have been conducted by giving different people different amounts of take-home pay and recording their behaviour.

The empirical evidence for the UK, the US and most other Western economies is as follows. For adult men, the substitution effect and the income effect almost exactly cancel out. A change in the real wage has almost no effect on the quantity of hours supplied. The supply curve of hours worked is almost vertical.[1]

For women, the substitution effect just about dominates the income effect. The supply curve for hours slopes upward. Higher real wages make women work longer hours.

Workers care about take-home pay after deductions of income tax. Lower income tax rates raise after-tax real wages. The empirical evidence on labour supply implies that lower income tax rates should not be expected to lead to a dramatic increase in the supply of hours worked.

Individual labour supply: participation rates

The effect of real wages on the supply of hours is smaller than often supposed. The more important effect of real wages on labour supply is on the incentive to join the labour force.

Table 10.3 gives data on **participation rates** for different countries in 1994 and in 2008. Most men of working age are in jobs or are seeking employment, but this percentage is gradually falling in some countries like the UK and the US, while in others it is quite stable. On the other hand, there has been a rise in labour force participation by women in the last 15 years. Can our model of choice explain these trends?

> The **participation rate** is the fraction of the population of working age who join the labour force.

We now develop a model in which labour force participation is higher (a) the more their tastes favour the benefits of working (goods or job status) relative to the benefits of leisure, (b) the lower their income from non-work sources, (c) the lower the fixed costs of working, and (d) the higher the real wage rate.

Figure 10.5 plots leisure on the horizontal axis. The maximum leisure a day is 24 hours. The vertical axis plots total real income from work and other sources. This shows the ability to buy consumer goods and

---

1   This conclusion applies to small changes in real wage rates. In most Western countries, the large rise in real wages over the past 100 years has been matched by reductions of ten hours or more in the working week.

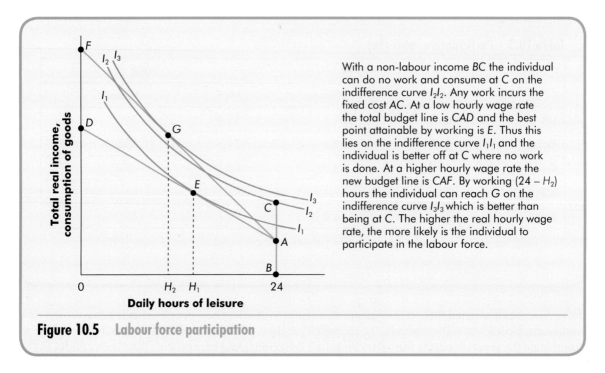

With a non-labour income *BC* the individual can do no work and consume at *C* on the indifference curve I_2I_2. Any work incurs the fixed cost *AC*. At a low hourly wage rate the total budget line is *CAD* and the best point attainable by working is *E*. Thus this lies on the indifference curve I_1I_1 and the individual is better off at *C* where no work is done. At a higher hourly wage rate the new budget line is *CAF*. By working $(24 - H_2)$ hours the individual can reach *G* on the indifference curve I_3I_3 which is better than being at *C*. The higher the real hourly wage rate, the more likely is the individual to participate in the labour force.

Figure 10.5   *Labour force participation*

services. We begin with budget constraint. Suppose the individual has a non-labour income given by the vertical distance *BC*. This may be income earned by a spouse, income from rent or dividends, or welfare payments received from the government.

Someone not working at all can have 24 hours of leisure a day plus a daily income *BC*. He can consume at point *C*. Now suppose he works. There may be fixed costs in working. Unemployment benefit from the government may be lost immediately, the right clothes or uniform must be purchased, travel expenses must be incurred to get to the place of work, childcare must be found for the children. These costs are independent of the number of hours worked provided any work is done. They are a fixed cost of working.

Figure 10.5 shows these costs as the vertical distance *AC*. Instead of being able to consume at *C*, the net non-labour income *BC* is reduced to *BA* after these fixed costs of working are incurred. Having decided to work, he can then move along the budget line *AD*, sacrificing leisure to gain wage income. The higher the real wage, the steeper the budget line *AD*.

Fixed costs of working lead to a kinked budget line *CAD*. Working a few hours reduces total real income. The small wage income does not cover the fixed costs of working. The lower the real wage rate, the flatter is the *AD* line and the more hours he has to work merely to recoup the fixed costs. This is sometimes called the *poverty trap*. Unskilled workers face such a low wage that they actually lose out by working.

To complete the model of consumer choice, we superimpose an indifference map on the kinked budget line *CAD*. Individuals like both leisure and goods. Each indifference curve has the usual slope and curvature. A higher indifference curve means the individual is better off. We can now analyse the participation decision and establish the four effects we cited above.

The indifference curve I_2I_2 shows how well off he is by not participating. He can start to consume at *C*. Given the budget line *CAD*, the best he can do by working is to work $(24 - H_1)$ hours, consume H_1 hours of leisure and choose point *E*, reaching the indifference curve I_1I_1. But he can reach the higher indifference curve I_2I_2 by not working. He chooses not to work.

Now suppose the real wage rises. Each hour of leisure could now earn a higher real wage. *AD* rotates to *AF* and the complete budget line is now *CAF*. By choosing point *G*, he can reach the indifference curve I_3I_3 and is better off than at *C*. Hence higher real wages raise the number of people wishing to join the labour force.

A reduction in *AC*, the fixed cost of working, also raises participation. Point *C* is fixed but point *A* shifts up. There is a parallel upward shift in the sloping part of the budget line such as *AD* or *AF*. It is more likely that the highest indifference curve attainable by working will lie above the zero-work indifference curve I_2I_2.

Although not shown in Figure 10.5, lower non-labour income *BC* also raises labour force participation. Changes in non-labour income have no effect on the relative return of an hour's work and an hour's leisure. There is no substitution effect but there is an income effect. Lower non-labour income reduces the quantity demanded of all normal goods, including leisure. People are more likely to work.

Finally, consider a change in tastes. People decide leisure is less important and work more important. Each indifference curve in Figure 10.5 is flatter: people are prepared to sacrifice more leisure for the direct and indirect benefits of extra work. Consider again the budget line *CAD*. The flatter the indifference curves are, the more likely it is that the indifference curve through *C* will cross the portion of the budget line *AD* on which work is done. But if it crosses *AD* there must be another point on *AD* yielding even higher utility. In Figure 10.5 it is possible to attain a higher indifference curve by choosing point *G* on *AF*. Exactly the same argument applies if the flatter indifference curve through *C* crosses the line *AD*.

CASE 10.1

Boosting UK labour supply

New Labour's labour market policies fell under two main headings, Welfare to Work and Making Work Pay. Both were based on the belief that work allows people to acquire skills and new opportunities: work is a ladder allowing people gradually to climb out of poverty. Did the policy boost UK labour supply?

Welfare to Work had two elements: more help in finding a job and possible loss of benefits for those making little effort to find work. The budget line in diagram (a) changes from *CAD* to *FGH*. The fall from *C* to *F* reflects lower benefits for those out of work, and the rise from *A* to *G* the lower fixed cost of working once the government helps. In diagram (a) we show the choice of someone drawn into the labour force by the change in policy.

Making Work Pay dealt with the part of the budget line once some work is being done. The Working Families Tax Credit gave money to workers with children, provided the parent is working a minimum number of hours a week. Diagram (b) shows the discontinuity *JK* when the benefit kicks in. The indifference map shows a person who would not work facing *CAD* but for whom *K* is better than *F* once the budget line becomes *FGJKM*. Or so the government hoped!

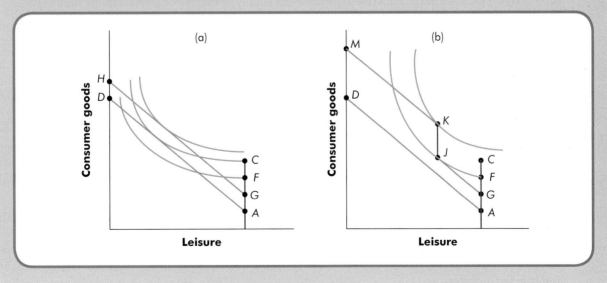

Thus labour force participation rises with (a) a higher real hourly wage rate, (b) lower fixed costs of working, (c) lower income from non-labour sources, and (d) changes in tastes in favour of more work and less leisure. Is this why participation by married women increased?

First, there was a change in social attitudes to work, especially to work by married women. Indifference curves became flatter. Second, pressure for equal opportunities for women raised women's real wages. The budget line for women working rotated from AD to AF in Figure 10.5. Finally, the fixed costs of working fell. Automatic ovens, labour-saving devices for housework, a second family car and many other changes, not least in the attitude of husbands, reduced the cost of work, especially for married women.

We have reached two conclusions. First, a higher real wage rate raises total labour supply but perhaps by less than is commonly thought. Second, this operates more by sucking people into the labour force than by greatly raising the supply hours of those already in the labour force. This analysis relates best to the supply of unskilled workers.

The supply of labour to an industry

Now we discuss an individual industry. Suppose it is small relative to the economy and wishes to employ workers with common skills. It has to pay the going rate for the job. Jobs in different industries have different non-monetary characteristics, such as risk, comfort or anti-social hours like night shifts. The going rate must be adjusted industry by industry to allow for the *equilibrium wage differential* that offsets these non-monetary characteristics and makes workers indifferent to where they work. Dangerous, nasty industries have to pay more than pleasant, safe industries if they are to attract workers.

Adjusted in this way, this determines the wage at which a small industry can hire as many workers as it wants from the economy-wide labour pool. At this wage, the industry faces a horizontal labour supply curve.

Many industries are not this small relative to all the skills they wish to employ. The steel industry is a big user of welders, the freight industry a big user of lorry drivers. When an industry is a significant user of a particular skill, higher employment in the industry bids up the wages of that particular skill in the whole economy. In the short run, the industry's labour supply curve slopes upwards.

In the long run, the industry's labour supply curve may be flatter. When short-run expansion bids up the wages of computer programmers, more school-leavers train in this skill. In the long run, the economy-wide supply rises and the wages of these workers fall back a bit. An individual industry does not have to offer such a high wage in the long run to increase the supply of that type of labour to the industry.

In the short run, the supply of a given skill may be nearly fixed. To get a larger share of the total pool, an individual industry has to offer higher relative wages than other industries to bid workers away from them.

 ## 10.5 Industry labour market equilibrium

Figure 10.6 shows equilibrium in the labour market for an industry. Its labour demand curve $D_L D_L$ slopes down and crosses the upward-sloping labour supply curve $S_L S_L$ at the equilibrium point E. Employment is L_0 and the wage W_0. We do not distinguish long-run and short-run supply curves, though this is easily done.

We draw the industry labour demand curve $D_1 D_1$ for a given output demand curve. A recession in the building industry would shift the demand curve for cement to the left. The equilibrium price of cement falls. This shifts to the left the marginal value product of labour curve $MVPL$ for each cement manufacturer. Hence $D_1 D_1$ shifts to $D_1' D_1'$ for the cement industry. At the new equilibrium E_1, wages and employment are lower in the industry.

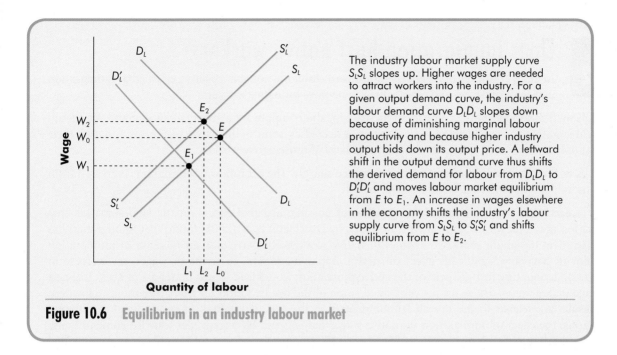

The industry labour market supply curve S_LS_L slopes up. Higher wages are needed to attract workers into the industry. For a given output demand curve, the industry's labour demand curve D_LD_L slopes down because of diminishing marginal labour productivity and because higher industry output bids down its output price. A leftward shift in the output demand curve thus shifts the derived demand for labour from D_LD_L to $D_L'D_L'$ and moves labour market equilibrium from E to E_1. An increase in wages elsewhere in the economy shifts the industry's labour supply curve from S_LS_L to $S_L'S_L'$ and shifts equilibrium from E to E_2.

Figure 10.6 Equilibrium in an industry labour market

Conversely, suppose there is a spurt of investment in new machinery in every industry except cement. With more capital to work with, labour is more productive in other industries. Setting wages equal to the *MVPL*, these industries pay higher wages. This shifts up the supply curve of labour to the cement industry to $S_L'S_L'$. At each wage in the cement industry, the industry attracts fewer workers from the general pool.

The new equilibrium for cement workers is at E_2. Employment falls from L_0 to L_2. Since the remaining workers have more capital to work with, they have a higher marginal product. In addition, the contraction in cement output shifts the output supply curve to the left and bids up the cement price. Together, these effects move the industry up its demand curve D_LD_L and allow it to pay a higher wage rate to its remaining workers.

Thus wage increases in one industry spill over into other industries. The crucial link between industries is labour mobility. It is because cement workers are lured away from the industry by wage rises elsewhere that the cement industry's labour supply curve shifts to the left in Figure 10.6. The degree of labour mobility between industries affects not only how much an industry's labour supply curve shifts when conditions change elsewhere, but also the slope of the industry's labour supply curve. Consider two extreme cases.

Suppose first that workers can move effortlessly between similar jobs in different industries. If each industry is small relative to the economy, it will face a completely elastic (horizontal) labour supply curve at the going wage rate (adjusted for non-monetary advantages). When all other industries pay higher wages, the horizontal supply curve of labour to the cement industry shifts up by the full amount of the wage increase elsewhere. Unless the cement industry matches the going rate, it loses all its workers.

At the opposite extreme, consider the market for concert pianists. Suppose they can do no other job. The supply curve of concert pianists is vertical. If all other industries pay higher wages, this has no effect on the market for concert pianists. There is no possible entry into or exit from the occupation of concert pianists.

The general case of Figure 10.6 is between these extremes. With limited mobility between industries, the cement industry can attract more workers by offering higher wages. But its labour supply curve shifts when wages change elsewhere.

CASE 10.2 Does immigration hurt native workers?

In many countries there is a rising concern about the possible negative effects that immigration may have on wages and employment outcomes for native workers.

Indeed, if we think about immigration as an increase in labour supply, for a given labour demand, we should expect a decrease in the equilibrium wage. If the wage decreases, some of the native workers may reduce their labour supply and this may reduce the employment level of those native workers.

In the UK in the last decade immigration has increased sharply. The net inflow of immigrants increased from 50 000 individuals in 1995 to 220 000 in 2005.

Recent research has tried to address the question of possible negative effects on the labour market that immigration may have for native residents. Research by Dustmann et al. (2005) found that immigration has very little effect on labour market outcomes of native workers. In particular, an increase in immigration seems not to have any significant effect on native employment rate. In terms of wages, an increase in immigration amounting to 1 per cent of the native population would lead to just under a 2 per cent increase in average native wages. Those results confirmed some of the results found for the US economy. However, those results are related to the overall labour market in the UK. If we look in more detail at different occupations, the effect of immigration on native wages may instead be negative, at least for some of them. This is the result of research by Nickell and Saleheen (2008). They found that for jobs like managers, skilled production workers (engineers, IT technicians, and so on) and semi/unskilled service workers (cleaners, labourers, and so on), an increase in immigration has a small, but negative effect on average wages of native workers in those occupations. Therefore, while overall the impact of immigration seems negligible, for some specific occupations immigration may have a negative effect on native workers.

Sources: Dustmann, C., Fabbri, F. and Preston, I. (2005) The impact of immigration on the British labour market, *Economic Journal*, 115 (507): 324–341; Nickell, S. and Saleheen, J. (2008) *The impact of immigration on occupational wages: British evidence*, SERC Discussion Paper, No. 34.

Monopsony power

The theory discussed so far can be amended to consider the case when the firm has **monopsony power** in its input markets (an upward-sloping supply curve for its inputs: the firm must then offer a higher factor price to attract a larger quantity of that input). Consider a big factory located close to a small town. It is likely that most of the workers of the small town will work for that big factory.

> A firm with **monopsony power** faces an upward-sloping factor supply curve and must offer a higher factor price to attract more factors. The marginal cost of the input exceeds the factor price. In expanding inputs, the firm bids up the price paid on all inputs already employed.
>
> The **marginal revenue product of labour (MRPL)** is the change in total output revenue when a firm sells the extra goods that an extra unit of labour input allows it to produce.

For a perfectly competitive firm, the *MVPL* schedule is its marginal revenue from an extra worker. We use the term *marginal value product of labour* (*MVPL*) for competitive firms who are price-takers in their output markets. *MVPL* is simply the marginal product of labour in physical goods *MPL* multiplied by the output price. We reserve the term **marginal revenue product of labour** (*MRPL*) for firms with a downward-sloping demand curve for their output.

To find *MRPL*, we use the marginal physical product of labour *MPL* to work out the extra quantity of output when an extra worker is hired, then calculate the change in the firm's total revenue when it sells these extra goods.

Figure 10.7 shows the *MRPL* schedules for a monopsony. The *MRPL* schedule slopes down more because the firm faces a downward-sloping demand curve for its output and recognizes that additional output reduces the price and hence the revenue earned on previous units of output.

The monopsony, in contrast to a competitive firm in the labour market, does not take the wage as given. The wage is now upward sloping since the monopsonist faces an upward-sloping labour supply. The higher the wage, the higher is the number of workers willing to work. The average cost of the monopsonist is just the wage and it is increasing with the number of workers.

The marginal cost of a monopsony is upward sloping. A monopsonist recognizes that expanding employment bids up the wage. If all workers are paid the same wage, the marginal cost of an extra worker is not just the wage paid to that worker but also the rise in the wage bill for previously employed workers. The monopsonist's marginal cost of labour exceeds the wage, and rises with the level of employment. This implies that the marginal cost is always above the average cost (ACL). This is shown in Figure 10.7.

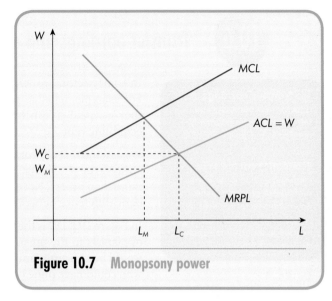

Figure 10.7 **Monopsony power**

The monopsonist chooses the level of employment that maximizes profits. This happens where $MCL = MRPL$. So the monopsonist chooses a level of employment L_M. The wage paid by the monopsonist is found by looking at the wage curve. The monopsonist pays a wage given by W_M. If, instead of a monopsonist, we have a perfectly competitive labour market, the equilibrium wage will be given by the intersection of the labour supply (the ACL curve) and labour demand (the $MRPL$ curve). In that case, the level of employment will be L_C and the equilibrium wage will be W_C.

A monopsonist, as we should expect from a firm with market power, employs fewer workers compared with perfect competition. Moreover, the wage paid by the monopsonist is lower than the wage that would be paid in a perfectly competitive labour market.

<table>
<tr><td>CONCEPT
10.1</td><td></td></tr>
</table>

How common is monopsony?

Economists have often assumed that small firms probably face a pretty horizontal labour supply curve – they can attract extra workers without bidding the wage up much. If so, monopsony is more of a special case for textbook writers than something to worry about much in the real world.

However, in the past decade this view has been increasingly challenged. Even small firms not requiring very many extra workers may have difficulty in attracting the workers they need without bidding up the wage they have to offer.

For example, Professors Alan Manning and Steve Machin (2002) studied residential care homes in southern England. Towns like Bournemouth and Eastbourne are famous as places in which the elderly cluster in their retirement. Manning and Machin collected data on the wages paid to individual care workers in individual retirement homes and discovered a surprising fact. There is a very large wage dispersion across care homes, even after controlling for identifiable differences in their workers. This is difficult to reconcile with a labour market in which each firm is a price-taker for labour. Monopsony may be more relevant than you first thought.

Source: Adapted from Machin, S. and Manning, A. (2002) *The structure of wages in what should be a competitive labour market*, Centre for Economic Performance, London School of Economics.

10.6   Transfer earnings and economic rents

The **transfer earnings** of a factor in a particular use are the minimum payments needed to induce the input to work in that job.

Economic rent (not to be confused with income from renting out property) is the payment a factor receives in excess of the transfer earnings needed to induce it to supply its services in that use.

In some sectors workers are paid much more, on average, than in other sectors. For example, talented pianists or footballers generally earn high wages.[2] Why do they get paid so much? We need to distinguish between **transfer earnings** and **economic rent**.

We assume that all workers hired by a firm must be paid the same wage. This is not always true. Consider football players. In the same team, some players are paid more than others. Nevertheless, our assumption will help us in understanding the basic difference between transfer earnings and economic rents.

In Figure 10.8 DD is the labour demand curve for concert pianists and SS the supply of pianists to the music industry. Even at a zero wage some dedicated musicians would be concert pianists. Higher wages attract into the industry concert pianists who could have done other things. The supply curve slopes upwards.

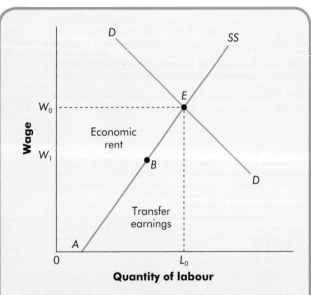

DD is the industry demand curve for labour. A quantity A of labour would work in the industry even at a zero wage. Higher wages attract additional workers to the industry. SS is the industry labour supply curve. If each worker was paid only the transfer earnings required to attract them to the industry (to keep them on their supply curve), the industry need only pay AL_0E in wages. If all workers must be paid the highest wage rate necessary to attract the last worker to the industry, equilibrium at E implies workers as a whole derive economic rent $OAEW_0$. For workers who would work for a zero wage rate, W_0 is economic rent, a pure bonus.

Figure 10.8   Transfer earnings and economic rent

Because all workers are paid the same wage, equilibrium is at E, with a wage W_0 and a number of pianists L_0. W_0 may be a large wage. Each firm in the music industry pays W_0 because their workers are very talented, with a high marginal product. In the output market (concerts), firms earn a large revenue. The derived demand curve DD for concert pianists is very high.

The supply curve SS shows the transfer earnings that the industry pays to attract pianists into the industry. The first A pianists would work for nothing. A wage W_1 is needed to expand the supply of pianists to B, and W_0 must be paid to increase supply to L_0. If the industry can pay each individual pianist a different amount, paying only the minimum required to attract each to the industry, triangle AL_0E is the total transfer earnings paid to attract L_0 pianists.

At the equilibrium E, the last pianist entering the industry has transfer earnings W_0 since E is on the supply curve SS. This last pianist's marginal value product is also W_0, since E is on the demand curve DD. However, when an industry has to pay all workers the same wage, all previous workers are paid W_0 even though the labour supply curve SS implies they would have worked for less than W_0. These workers, with transfer earnings below W_0, earn *economic rent*, a pure surplus arising because W_0 is needed to attract the last pianist. Rent reflects differences in pianists' *supply* decisions, not their *productivity* as musicians.

---

2   According to *The Guardian* newspaper, in 2009 the average Premiership footballer earned £21 000 a week. A staggering £1 092 000 a year!

In Figure 10.8 the industry makes total wage payments equal to the rectangle OW_0EL_0. It pays L_0 workers W_0 each. These payments comprise the total transfer earnings AL_0E and the economic rent $OAEW_0$.

Economic rent arises if the factor supply curve is not horizontal. With a horizontal supply curve, no worker earns more than the going rate required to keep pianists in the industry. All earnings are transfer earnings.

Note the distinction between the firm and the industry. Economic rent is an unnecessary payment as far as the industry is concerned. By colluding in order to wage-discriminate, paying each worker his transfer earnings alone, the industry could retain all its workers without paying them economic rent. But the entire wage W_0 is a transfer earning as far as a single competitive firm is concerned. If it fails to pay the going rate, its workers will go to another firm.

In the UK football industry[3] and the US baseball industry, it is often said that high player salaries are bankrupting the industry. But wages are high because the derived demand is high – crowds at the ground and television rights make it profitable to supply this output – and because the supply of talented players is scarce. The supply curve of good players is steep: even very high wages cannot increase the number of good players by much. There is no simple link between high salaries and the ruin of the game. If supplying the output was not profitable, the derived demand for players would be lower and their wages reduced.

CASE 10.3 — Higher education pays off

Nowadays most students have to contribute to the cost of their higher education. What can we tell them about the financial benefits likely to accrue in the future? The table shows the results of a major empirical study on determinants of people's wages by the time they are 33 years old.

The research suggests that degrees add a lot to future earning power. This is consistent with the idea of human capital. Human capital is the result of past investment in order to raise future income. The cost of investing in another year of school education or a further qualification is the direct cost, such as tuition fees, plus the opportunity cost of the time involved, namely delaying paid employment. The benefit of the investment is a higher future monetary income or a future job yielding more job satisfaction.

The results in the table also outline another important fact. Investing in higher education by students seems to pay off in terms of future earnings, but the subject studied also matters. Economics students can expect to earn much more than history or language students.

	% extra wage in Britain at age 33 for	
	Men	Women
First degree	+15	+32
Postgraduate degree	+15	+35
Extra effect by subject		
Arts	−10	+5
Economics	+10	+24
Chemistry/biology	−17	−11
Maths/physics	+9	+16

Source: Blundell, R. et al. (2000) Returns to higher education in Britain, *Economic Journal*, 110 (461): 82–99.

Picture: © ericsphotography | istockphoto.com

---

3   Football clubs pay transfer fees to another club from whom they wish to take over a player. These transfer fees between clubs should not be confused with the economist's concept of transfer earnings of players, the amount needed to keep them in the industry.

10.7 Do labour markets clear?

So far we have assumed that wages are flexible. The equilibrium wage equates labour supply and labour demand. In Part Four you will see that many questions in macroeconomics turn on whether wage flexibility is sufficient to keep labour markets near their equilibrium positions. It may not be possible to take labour market equilibrium for granted.

Minimum wage agreements

The UK minimum wage is £5.35 an hour. Figure 10.9 shows the demand curve $D_L D_L$ and the supply curve $S_L S_L$ for a particular skill in a particular industry. Free market equilibrium is at E. For skilled workers, the equilibrium wage W_0 exceeds a minimum wage at W_1, which is thus irrelevant.

> Workers are **involuntarily unemployed** if they would work at the going wage but cannot find jobs.

Suppose the minimum wage is W_2, above the free market equilibrium wage W_0. At W_2 there is excess labour supply $L_2 - L_1$. Since firms cannot be forced to hire workers they do not want, employment is L_1 and the quantity of workers $L_2 - L_1$ are involuntarily unemployed.

A national minimum wage may exceed the free market equilibrium wage for low-skill occupations. If so, those workers lucky enough to find jobs get higher wages than before but the total amount of employment is lower than in free market equilibrium. Minimum wages may explain involuntary unemployment among low-skilled workers.

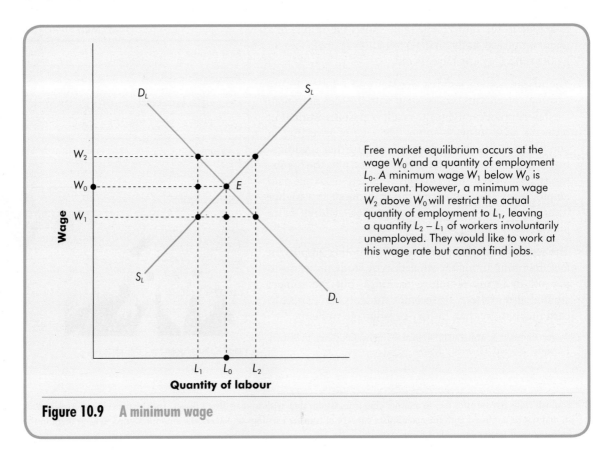

Free market equilibrium occurs at the wage W_0 and a quantity of employment L_0. A minimum wage W_1 below W_0 is irrelevant. However, a minimum wage W_2 above W_0 will restrict the actual quantity of employment to L_1, leaving a quantity $L_2 - L_1$ of workers involuntarily unemployed. They would like to work at this wage rate but cannot find jobs.

Figure 10.9   **A minimum wage**

CONCEPT 10.2

Minimum wages hurt jobs, don't they?

A minimum wage prices some workers out of a job: by raising wages, it slides firms up their demand curves, cutting jobs. Even politicians understand. Right?

The 'proof' relies on a competitive labour market. People's intuition is often based on perfect competition. What happens if there is a sole employer? A monopsonist's new hiring bids up the price of existing workers: the marginal cost of labour exceeds the wage. The diagram shows the marginal revenue product of labour, the labour supply curve facing the firm, and the marginal cost of labour to the monopsonist. In equilibrium, $MRPL = MCL$. Employment is N_1 and a wage W_1 is needed to attract this labour. The vertical gap between LS and $MRPL$ shows workers are paid less than their marginal product. This is called exploitation.

At a minimum wage W_2, the monopsonist faces a horizontal labour supply at W_2, at least until N_2 people are hired. W_2 is now the marginal cost of labour. The firm hires N_2 workers to equate the marginal cost and marginal benefit of hiring. By offsetting exploitation, the minimum wage boosts jobs from N_1 to N_2.

Beginning at free market equilibrium at a wage W_1, successive rises in the minimum wage boost jobs (sliding the firm along the labour supply curve LS) until the minimum wage reaches W_2 at which employment is maximized. Still higher minimum wages now move the firm up its demand curve, reducing jobs thereafter. When firms have some monopsony power, a minimum wage slightly above the free market equilibrium is good for jobs – it offsets the distortion caused by the market power of employers – but a minimum wage substantially above the free market equilibrium is bad for jobs.

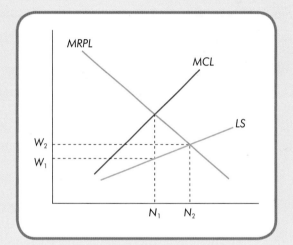

Source: Dolado, J. et al. (1996) The economic impact of minimum wages in Europe, *Economic Policy*, 11 (23): 319–372.

Trade unions

Trade unions are worker organizations set up by workers to affect pay and working conditions. Do unions protect workers from exploitation by powerful employers or do they use their power to secure unjustified pay increases and oppose technical change and productivity improvements that might threaten the jobs of their members?

In 1980 half the civilian labour force in the UK belonged to a trade union. Figure 10.10 shows changes since 1910. After a steady increase in union membership until the late 1920s there was a massive decline during the Depression of the 1930s. After a sharp recovery until 1950, the degree of unionization of the labour force remained

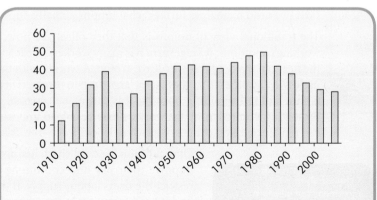

Figure 10.10 Union membership (% of civilian labour force)

Sources: Bain, G. S. and Elsheik, F. (1976) *Union Growth and the Business Cycle*, Basil Blackwell; ONS, *Labour Market Trends*.

Table 10.4 Trade union density rates in selected countries (% of civilian labour force)

Country	1980	1990	1995	2002
Sweden	78.2	80.0	83.1	78.0
Denmark	78.6	75.3	77.0	73.8
Italy	54.5	38.8	38.1	34.0
Ireland	57.4	51.0	47.1	35.9
France	17.1	10.1	9.8	9.7
Germany	34.9	31.2	29.2	23.2

Source: Waddington, J. (2005), *Trade union membership in Europe* (http://library.fes.de/pdf-files/gurn/00287.pdf).

fairly constant until the late 1960s. The 1970s saw a sharp rise in union membership, which peaked in 1979, since when it has been falling sharply.

The trend outlined in Figure 10.10, to different degrees, is common to many other European countries, as we can see in Table 10.4.

Declining unionization reflects several trends. First, as the share of the service sector in national output rises, the share in traditional industry, manual and male, has shrunk. Second, the public sector, in which unions were traditionally well organized, has shrunk as a result of privatization and cuts in its size. Third, computers and other technical advances have made production much more flexible and small scale, circumstances in which it is harder to organize a trade union. Fourth, increased female participation in the labour force has often been in part-time jobs in which union organization is harder. Finally, globalization has had a powerful impact. Globalization is affecting unions. Greater international competition in more and more industries is eliminating pockets of domestic monopoly whose profits were tempting targets for unions. As greater competition makes the derived demand for labour more elastic, unions face an ever-worsening trade-off between wages and employment. Restricting labour supply only raises wages by sacrificing many jobs. As the trade-off gets less attractive, belonging to a union becomes less worthwhile.

First, we need to analyse further what unions actually do.

The traditional view of unions is that they offset the power that a firm enjoys in negotiating wages and working conditions. A single firm has many workers. If each worker must make a separate deal with the firm, the firm can make a take-it-or-leave-it offer. A worker with firm-specific human capital, which will be almost useless in any other firm, may face a large drop in productivity and wages if he rejects the firm's offer. The firm is in a strong bargaining position if it can make separate agreements with each worker. In contrast, by presenting a united front, the workers may be able to impose large costs on the firm if they *all* quit. The firm can replace one worker but not its whole labour force. The existence of unions evens up the bargaining process.

> A **closed shop** is an agreement that all a firm's workers will be members of a trade union.

Once a union is established, it aims not merely to protect its members but also to improve their pay and conditions. To be successful, the union must be able to restrict the firm's labour supply. If the firm can hire non-union labour, unions will find it hard to maintain the wage above the level at which the firm can hire non-union workers. This is one reason why unions are keen on **closed-shop** agreements with individual firms.[4]

---

4   Unions frequently argue that, in the absence of a closed shop, non-union workers will benefit from improvements in pay and conditions achieved through the efforts of the union. Non-union members are getting a 'free ride' without paying their union subscriptions.

How do unions raise wages by restricting supply? Figure 10.11 shows an industry's downward-sloping labour demand curve *DD*. The wage in the rest of the economy is W_0, and we assume the industry faces a perfectly elastic labour supply curve at the wage rate W_0. In the absence of unions, equilibrium is at E_0 with employment N_0.

Now suppose everyone in the industry must belong to a trade union and the union restricts labour in this industry to N_1. The industry faces a vertical labour supply curve at N_1. Equilibrium is at E_1. By sacrificing employment in the industry, the union raises the wage for each employed member from W_0 to W_1. At a higher wage and marginal cost of production, each firm is forced to raise its price. The full effect of the trade union is not merely to raise wages and lower employment in the industry but also to raise the output price and lower equilibrium output of the industry.

This analysis raises two questions. What determines how far the union will trade off lower employment for higher wages in the industry? And what determines how much power unions have to control the supply of labour to particular industries?

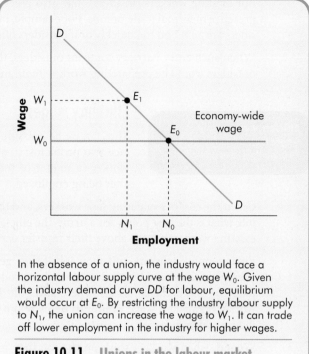

In the absence of a union, the industry would face a horizontal labour supply curve at the wage W_0. Given the industry demand curve *DD* for labour, equilibrium would occur at E_0. By restricting the industry labour supply to N_1, the union can increase the wage to W_1. It can trade off lower employment in the industry for higher wages.

Figure 10.11   **Unions in the labour market**

Assume that the union has full control over the supply of labour to a firm or an industry. It can trade off employment for wage rises. How far it will go depends on the preferences or tastes of the union and its members. It might try to maximize total income (wage times employment) of its members, or it might try to maximize per capita income (wages) of those in employment. A lot depends on the power and decision structure within the union.

The more the union cares about its senior members, the more it is likely to maximize the wage independently of what happens to employment. Senior workers have the most firm-specific human capital and are the least likely to be sacked if total employment in the industry must fall. Conversely, the more the union is democratic, and the more it cares about its potential members as well as those actually in employment, the less likely it is to restrict employment to ensure higher wages for those who remain employed in the industry.

Scale economies

Involuntary unemployment may reflect scale economies and imperfect competition. These create entry barriers and prevent new firms from joining an industry. Entry barriers prevent the unemployed from starting new firms even if unemployed workers would work for a lower wage than that paid in existing firms.

Insiders and outsiders

The previous explanation emphasizes entry barriers in forming new firms. Insider–outsider theories emphasize barriers to entering employment in existing firms.

Entry barriers take many forms. It is costly to advertise for workers, interview them, evaluate what sort of job they should be offered, train them in activities specific to the firm, build up teamwork and allow new employees to master their new jobs. In the terminology of Chapter 9, these are innocent entry barriers.

Insiders have jobs and are represented in wage bargaining.

Outsiders do not have jobs and are unrepresented in wage bargaining.

But existing workers (insiders) may also erect strategic barriers to entry by outsiders, even without the presence of formal trade unions. For example, insiders may threaten industrial disruption if too many outsiders are admitted too quickly or if outsiders offer to work at a lower wage than that being paid to insiders.

When such entry barriers confront outsiders, the insiders can raise their own wage above that for which outsiders would be prepared to work *without* inducing a spate of hiring of outsiders.

Efficiency wages

> **Efficiency wages** are high wages that raise productivity through their incentive effect.

Thus far, we have assumed that information is cheap to come by. In practice, firms face two problems: it is hard to tell whether a job applicant will be a productive worker (a matter of innate ability) and hard to monitor whether workers shirk after being employed.[5]

Given the cost of evaluating new workers, and the subsequent cost of monitoring their performance on the job, what is the best policy for a firm? The efficiency wage theory argues that it is profitable for firms to pay existing workers a wage above their transfer earnings.

First, suppose workers quit their job if they get a better offer elsewhere. If firms pay a wage that is the average of that faced by productive and unproductive workers, it is the productive workers who are more likely to find better offers elsewhere and quit. Eventually, the firm will be left only with the low-quality workers. Paying a wage premium helps retain high-quality workers, even if the firm has some trouble telling which these are.

Second, when workers shirk on the job they may get caught. If caught, they get sacked. How big is the penalty for being caught? It is the difference between the current wage and what the worker gets in unemployment benefit or in a subsequent job. The higher the wage paid by the existing employer, the larger the penalty of being caught shirking. To increase the penalty and reduce the incentive to shirk, firms pay existing workers a higher wage than on average is necessary to get them to supply their labour.

Again, the implication is that some workers may be involuntarily unemployed. They may be happy to work for wages at or below those paid to existing workers but have little practical chance of securing a job at such wages.

Minimum wage agreements, trade union power, scale economies, insider–outsider distinctions and efficiency wages are *possible* explanations for insufficient wage flexibility in the short run to maintain the labour market in continuous equilibrium. Whether the labour market is always in equilibrium, and the length of time for which disequilibrium persists, are questions to which we return repeatedly in Part Four.

UK wages and employment

We began the chapter by looking at real earnings in energy, financial services and construction. By re-examining these industries, we draw together some of the themes of the chapter.

Table 10.5 shows real earnings and employment during 1997–2009. In the economy, real earnings rose 10 per cent. Technical advances, better machinery and better skills raised labour's marginal value product, shifting the labour demand curve to the right. But this process differed in different industries.

In construction, immigration has tended to increase labour supply, in itself putting downward pressure on wages. Nevertheless, total jobs and real earnings in the construction sector have increased more than the national average. Why? Demand must have risen strongly, as the result of the housing boom experienced until 2007, partly caused by lower interest rates and also because higher incomes raised demand.

---

5   Economists refer to these problems as adverse selection and moral hazard. We discuss them in detail in Chapter 12 when we examine the economics of information.

Table 10.5 UK jobs and real earnings, males (% cumulative change)

	Real earnings, 1997–2009	Jobs, 1997–2009
Whole economy	+10	+8
Financial services	+14	+27
Construction	+20	+22
Energy and water	+10	−17

Source: ONS.

In financial services (such as banking and insurance), wages and employment both increased. Demand increases were more than sufficient to offset any tendency for information technology or global outsourcing to reduce the need for workers.

Technical progress and capital investment in the basic utilities – energy and water supply – meant that jobs continued to contract sharply in the sector. With so much capital per worker, workers are very productive and are highly paid. High energy prices – in part caused by global rises in the price of oil – meant that energy companies declared record profits. The competition for workers meant that incomes in the industry rose sharply.

Wage discrimination: wage differences between men and women

Wage discrimination refers to a situation whereby equally productive workers are paid differently. Few women do manufacturing jobs; most have jobs in services. Yet the pattern of employment is not the major cause of the fact that women on average earn 80 per cent as much as men. Sector by sector, women systematically get paid substantially less than men. The main reason that women earn less is that they earn less than men whatever job they do.

The percentage of women in professional or managerial occupations is comparable with that for men but few women are on the boards of major companies. Why do firms promote or train women more slowly? Suppose firms bear some of the cost of training. The firm makes a hard-nosed investment decision. Assuming men and women are of inherently equal ability and educational attainment, it costs the firm the same to train either sex.

Suppose firms believe women are more likely than men to interrupt, or even end, their careers at a young age. As a matter of biology, women have babies. Firms may conclude that the extra productivity benefits in the future are lower for women than men simply because many women work fewer years in the future. It is more profitable to train and promote men.

Some women plan to have a full-time career, either remaining childless or returning to work almost immediately after any children are born. It would make sense for firms to invest in such people. How is a firm to tell which young women are planning to stay? Asking is pointless. There is no incentive for young women to tell the truth.

Suppose firms offer young workers the choice between a relatively flat age–earnings profile and a steep profile that begins at a lower wage but pays a much higher wage later in a worker's career. In this way, firms can make the two profiles of equal value to someone planning a lifetime career. The early sacrifice (low wages) is recouped with interest later (high wages). Someone planning to quit the labour force, say at the age of 30, will never opt for the steeper profile.

Table 10.6 Wage gap between men and women

Country	Gender wage gap (%)	
	1997	2007
Austria	23	22
Denmark	13	9
France	10	12
Germany	24	23
Spain	29	17
Sweden	17	15
UK	26	21

Source: OECD, *Employment Outlook*, 2009.

Age–earnings profiles may induce recruits to reveal their true career plans. If women, or any other group with a high risk of quitting at a young age, accept the steeper profile, the firm can embark on training with some confidence that its investment will not be wasted.

Some firms may still try to pay female workers less than male workers who are identical in every respect, including their risk of quitting. This is overt discrimination.

Society may discriminate against women in more subtle ways. Our analysis suggests that paternity leave for fathers, the provision of crèches for working parents, or a greater acceptance of part-time working by both sexes, would reduce the incentive for hard-nosed firms to decide to favour the training of men. Whether or not society wishes to organize its work and home life on such principles is not just a matter of economics.

In Table 10.6 some data about the wage differential between men and women for some European countries are reported. The wage differential between men and women is measured as a percentage of the difference between the median wages of men and women relative to the median wage of men. In the UK, in 2007, women tended to earn a wage 21 per cent lower than men.

From Table 10.6 we can see that in most of the countries the wage gap between men and women has tended to decrease over time (apart from in France); nevertheless it is still substantial in many cases.

Summary

- In the long run, a firm chooses a **production technique** to minimize the cost of a particular output. By considering each output, it constructs a **total cost curve**.

- In the long run, a **rise in the price of labour** (capital) has a **substitution effect** and an **output effect**. The substitution effect reduces the quantity of labour (capital) demanded as the capital–labour ratio rises (falls) at each output. But total costs and marginal costs of output increase. The more elastic the firm's demand curve and marginal revenue curve, the more the higher marginal cost curve reduces output, reducing demand for both factors. For a higher price of a factor, the substitution and output effects both reduce the quantity demanded.

- In the short run, the firm has **fixed factors**, and probably a **fixed production technique**. The firm can vary short-run output by varying its variable input, labour, which is subject to diminishing returns when other factors are fixed. The **marginal physical product of labour** falls as more labour is hired.

- A profit-maximizing firm produces the output at which marginal output cost equals marginal output revenue. Equivalently, it hires labour until the **marginal cost of labour** equals its **marginal revenue product**. One implies the other. If the firm is a price-taker in its output market, the *MRPL* is its **marginal value product**, the output price times its marginal physical product. If the firm is a price-taker in the labour market, the marginal cost of labour is the wage rate. A perfectly competitive firm equates the real wage to the marginal physical product of labour.

- The downward-sloping marginal physical product of labour schedule is the **short-run demand curve for labour** (in terms of the real wage) for a competitive firm. Equivalently, the marginal value product of labour schedule is the demand curve in terms of the nominal wage. The *MVPL* schedule for a firm shifts up if the output price increases, the capital stock increases or if technical progress makes labour more productive.

- The **industry's labour demand curve** is not merely the horizontal sum of firms' *MVPL* curves. Higher industry output in response to a wage reduction also reduces the output price. The industry labour demand curve is steeper (less elastic) than that of each firm, and more inelastic the more inelastic is the demand curve for the industry's output.

- Labour demand curves are **derived demands**. A shift in the output demand curve for the industry will shift the derived factor demand curve in the same direction.

- For someone already in the labour force, a **rise in the hourly real wage** has both a **substitution effect** tending to increase the supply of hours worked, and an **income effect** tending to reduce the supply of hours worked. For men, the two effects cancel out almost exactly in practice but the empirical evidence suggests that the substitution effect dominates for women. Thus women have a rising labour supply curve; for men it is almost vertical.

- Individuals with non-labour income may prefer not to work. Four things raise the **participation rate in the labour force**: higher real wage rates, lower fixed costs of working, lower non-labour income and changes in tastes in favour of working. These explain the trend for increasing labour force participation by married women over the past few decades.

- The **industry supply curve of labour** depends on the wage paid relative to wages in other industries using similar skills. **Equilibrium wage differentials** are the monetary compensation for differences in non-monetary characteristics of jobs in different industries undertaken by workers with the same skill. Taking monetary and non-monetary rewards together, there is then no incentive to move between industries.

- When the labour supply curve to an industry is less than perfectly elastic, the industry pays higher wages to expand employment. For the marginal worker, the wage is a pure **transfer earning**, required to induce that worker into the industry. For workers prepared to work in the industry at a lower wage, there is an element of **economic rent** (the difference between income received and transfer earnings for that individual).

- In free market equilibrium, some workers choose not to work at the equilibrium wage rate. They are **voluntarily unemployed. Involuntary unemployment** is the difference between desired supply and desired demand at a disequilibrium wage rate. Workers would like to work but cannot find a job.

- There is considerable disagreement about how quickly labour markets can get back to equilibrium if initially in disequilibrium. Possible causes of involuntary unemployment are **minimum wage** agreements, **trade unions, scale economies, insider–outsider** distinctions and **efficiency wages.**

Review questions

connect

EASY

1 (a) Explain why the marginal product of labour eventually declines. (b) Show in a diagram the effect of an increase in the firm's capital stock on its demand curve for labour.

2 (a) Over the past 100 years the real wage has risen but the length of the working week has fallen. Explain this result using income and substitution effects. (b) Explain how an increase in the real wage could cause everyone in employment to work fewer hours but still increase the total amount of work done in the economy.

3 Why should the labour supply curve to an industry slope upwards even if the aggregate labour supply to the economy is fixed?

4 Answer the questions with which we began the chapter. (a) Why can a top golfer earn more in a weekend than a university professor earns in a year? (b) Why can students studying economics expect to earn more than equally smart students studying philosophy?

5 Common fallacies Why are the following statements wrong? (a) There is no economic reason why a sketch that took Picasso one minute to draw should fetch £100 000. (b) Higher wages must raise incentives to work.

MEDIUM

6 In a competitive labour market, the labour supply and the labour demand are reported in the following table:

L	W^D	W^S
1	15.5	5
2	15	6
3	14.5	7
4	14	8
5	13.5	9
6	13	10
7	12.5	11
8	12	12
9	11.5	13

Where W^D is the inverse labour demand and W^S is the inverse labour supply.

In a graph with the wage on the vertical axis and labour on the horizontal axis, show the labour market equilibrium. Suppose that the labour demand comes from many identical perfectly competitive firms. If the price of the output produced by those firms is reduced by half because of a recession, explain what happens to the labour demand. How will the equilibrium of the labour market be affected?

7 A firm is producing chocolate bars using only labour. The production function is $Q = 20L - 0.5L^2$, where L denotes labour. The firm is selling its chocolate bars in a competitive market and the price of a chocolate bar is £1. The firm hires workers in a competitive market. The wage paid to a worker is w. Write down the profit of the firm and find the labour demand function (L as a function of w) of the firm.

8 Suppose that the labour supply of workers is $L^S = w - 5$. Use the labour demand you found in Question 7 to derive the labour market equilibrium.

9 Suppose that the firm in Question 7 is now a monopsony in the labour market and faces the labour supply outlined in Question 8. This means that the wage that the monopsony must pay is $w = L + 5$. Find the labour demand that maximizes the profits of the monopsony. What about the wage? Compare your results with the ones you found in Question 8.

10 In the Appendix to this chapter the concept of isoquant is introduced. Suppose that the long-run production function of a firm is $Q = KL$, where K denotes capital. In a graph with K on the vertical axis and L on the horizontal axis, plot the isoquants associated with $Q = 10$ and $Q = 20$. What is the slope of a given isoquant?

11 'A minimum wage set sufficiently high will always reduce jobs, but whether a modest level of minimum wage reduces or increases employment depends entirely on the degree of competition in the labour market.' Explain.

12 Could a university degree increase your subsequent job prospects even if the subject that you studied at university had no relevance whatsoever for your subsequent career?

13 Essay question   In the past 50 years, there has been a dramatic increase in female participation in the labour force. Three possible explanations are: (a) a change in social attitudes to women working, (b) technological advances that make it easier to accomplish household chores (shopping, cleaning, etc.) without women themselves having to remain at home full time, and (c) the possibility that material goods are a luxury and that people wish to buy disproportionately more of them as living standards rise. What evidence would you gather in order to test these different hypotheses?

HARD

For solutions to these questions contact your lecturer.

Isoquants and the choice of production technique

The choice of technique can be examined with techniques similar to the indifference curve–budget line approach used to study consumer choice in Chapter 5. Figure 10.A1 plots input quantities of capital K and labour L. Points A, B, C and D show the *minimum* input quantities needed to make 1 unit of output using each of four different techniques. Technique A is the most labour intensive, requiring L_A units of labour and K_A units of capital to make 1 unit of output. Technique D is the most capital intensive. Connecting A, B, C and D yields an *isoquant* (iso = the same, quant = quantity).

> An **isoquant** shows minimum combinations of inputs to make a given output. Different points on an isoquant reflect different production techniques.

Figure 10.A1 shows four techniques but we can imagine that there are others. Figure 10.A2 shows smooth **isoquants**. Isoquant I corresponds to a particular output. Each point on isoquant I reflects a different technique, from very capital intensive to very labour intensive.

Higher isoquants, such as I, show higher output levels since more inputs are required. Each isoquant shows different input combinations to make a given output. The isoquants constitute an isoquant map.

Three properties of isoquants are important. First, they cannot cross. Each isoquant refers to a different output. Second, each isoquant slopes down. To make a given output, a technique can use more capital only if it uses less labour and vice versa. Hence isoquants must slope down. Third, each isoquant becomes flatter as we move along it to the right, as Figure 10.A2 shows. Moving down a given isoquant, it takes more and more extra capital input to make equal successive reductions in the labour input required to produce a given output.

In Figure 10.A2 the line L_0K_0 is an *isocost* line. It shows different input combinations with the *same* total cost. For a given cost, the firm can use more units of capital only if it uses fewer units of labour. Facing given prices at which different inputs may be hired, we can say two things about isocost lines.

First, the slope of the isocost line reflects the relative price of the two factors of production. Beginning at K_0, where all the firm's money is spent on capital, the firm can trade off 1 unit of capital for more units of labour the cheaper the wage rate relative to the rental cost of capital. Second, facing given factor

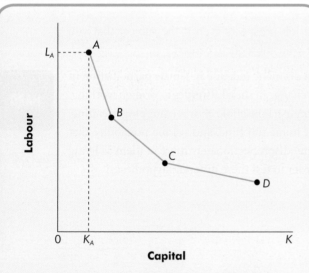

Points A, B, C and D show different input combinations required to produce 1 unit of output. By connecting them we obtain an isoquant that shows the different input combinations which can produce a particular level of output.

Figure 10.A1   An isoquant

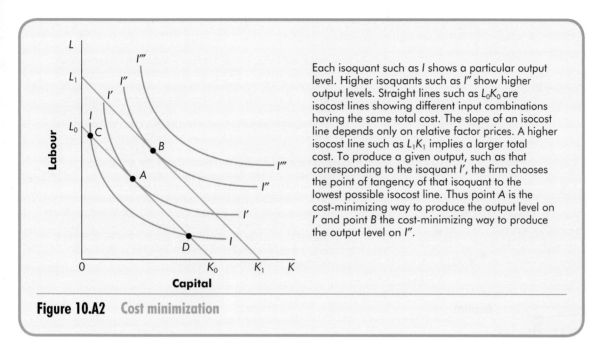

Each isoquant such as I shows a particular output level. Higher isoquants such as I'' show higher output levels. Straight lines such as L_0K_0 are isocost lines showing different input combinations having the same total cost. The slope of an isocost line depends only on relative factor prices. A higher isocost line such as L_1K_1 implies a larger total cost. To produce a given output, such as that corresponding to the isoquant I', the firm chooses the point of tangency of that isoquant to the lowest possible isocost line. Thus point A is the cost-minimizing way to produce the output level on I' and point B the cost-minimizing way to produce the output level on I''.

Figure 10.A2   Cost minimization

prices, by raising spending a firm can have more capital and more labour. A higher isocost line parallel to L_0K_0 shows a higher spending on inputs. Along the isocost line L_1K_1 the firm spends more on inputs than along the isocost line L_0K_0.

To minimize the cost of making a given output, a firm chooses the point of tangency of that isoquant to the lowest possible isocost line. At this point, the (negative) slope of the isocost line equals the (negative) slope of the isoquant. If w is the wage rate and r the rental cost of a unit of capital, the slope of the isocost line is r/w. What about the slope of the isoquant?

With an extra unit of capital, the firm gains MPK units of output, where MPK is the marginal physical product of capital. But along an isoquant line output is constant. By shedding a unit of labour the firm gives up MPL units of output. Lowering labour input by $[-MPK/MPL]$ keeps output constant when capital input is 1 unit higher. The isoquant's slope $[-MPK/MPL]$ tells us by how much labour is changed to keep output constant when capital is 1 unit higher. Hence the tangency condition in Figure 10.A2 implies

$$\text{Slope of isocost line} = r/w = -MPK/MPL = \text{slope of isoquant} \qquad \text{(A1)}$$

Point A in Figure 10.A2 is the least-cost way to make the output shown by isoquant I'. We can repeat this analysis for every other isoquant showing different outputs. That is how we derive the total cost curve discussed in the text.

How does the firm find the profit-maximizing output? Suppose at point A the marginal product of labour exceeds the wage rate w. Equation (A1) tells us that in the long run the marginal product of capital must also exceed the rental rate r. Only then can the factor price ratio r/w equal the ratio of the marginal products MPK/MPL. But if the marginal product of each factor exceeds the price at which the firm can hire that factor, it is profitable to expand output. In the long run, the firm expands output and factor use until the marginal product of each factor equals the price for which that factor can be hired. In Figure 10.A2, long-run profit-maximizing output is at a point such as B, at which

$$MPL = w \qquad \text{and} \qquad MPK = r \qquad \text{(A2)}$$

If equation (A2) holds, equation (A1) is automatically satisfied. Profits are maximized only if the chosen output is produced in the cost-minimizing way.

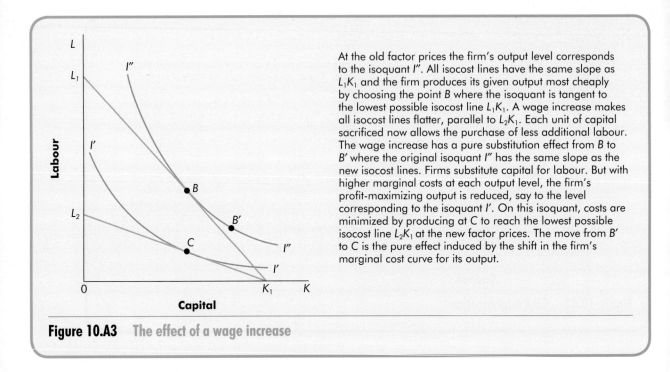

At the old factor prices the firm's output level corresponds to the isoquant I''. All isocost lines have the same slope as L_1K_1 and the firm produces its given output most cheaply by choosing the point B where the isoquant is tangent to the lowest possible isocost line L_1K_1. A wage increase makes all isocost lines flatter, parallel to L_2K_1. Each unit of capital sacrificed now allows the purchase of less additional labour. The wage increase has a pure substitution effect from B to B' where the original isoquant I'' has the same slope as the new isocost lines. Firms substitute capital for labour. But with higher marginal costs at each output level, the firm's profit-maximizing output is reduced, say to the level corresponding to the isoquant I'. On this isoquant, costs are minimized by producing at C to reach the lowest possible isocost line L_2K_1 at the new factor prices. The move from B' to C is the pure effect induced by the shift in the firm's marginal cost curve for its output.

Figure 10.A3   The effect of a wage increase

Finally, we show the effect of a rise in the price of one factor. Figure 10.A3 shows the initial position B where the isocost line L_1K_1 is tangent to the isoquant I''. Suppose the wage rate rises. Each isocost line then becomes less steep. Sacrificing a unit of labour allows more extra capital at any given total cost. At the original output on isoquant I'', this leads to a pure substitution effect from B to B', the point on the old isoquant tangent to an isocost line with the new flatter slope. But a higher wage rate also shifts up the total cost curve and the marginal cost curve for output. Profit-maximizing output falls.

The lower isoquant I shows the new profit-maximizing output. L_2K_1 is the lowest attainable isocost line embodying the flatter slope corresponding to the new relative input prices. The firm now chooses point C. The move from B' to C is the pure output effect of a higher wage rate. The actual move from B to C can be decomposed into a substitution effect from B to B' and an output effect from B' to C. Both effects reduce the quantity of labour demanded.

CHAPTER 11

Factor markets and income distribution

Learning Outcomes

By the end of this chapter, you should understand:

1. the markets for capital and land

2. how incomes of factors are determined

3. functional and personal distributions of income

4. flows over time and stocks at a point in time

5. the markets for capital services and for new capital assets

6. the concept of present value

7. nominal and real interest rates

8. how saving and investment determine the real interest rate

9. how land is allocated between competing uses

The previous two chapters focused on labour. We now examine the other inputs with which labour co-operates in production. Some issues can be dealt with briefly. You already know how a firm chooses a production technique in the long run, when all factors can be freely varied, and you are familiar with the concept of a factor's marginal product.

Apart from investment in human capital, many aspects of labour market behaviour are easily analysed within a short-run time horizon. Labour is a variable input even in the short run. Since it takes much longer to adjust other factor inputs, decisions about their use must take a longer view.

One theme of this chapter is how the future affects the present. We examine how decisions today should value future benefits and costs, and show how to discount future payments or receipts to calculate their *present value*.

Our interest in the markets for capital and land goes beyond the equilibrium quantity of capital or the equilibrium price of land. There are two reasons to study factor markets as a whole. First, firms rarely use a single input. Decisions about inputs of capital and land affect the demand curve for labour and the equilibrium wage, just as decisions about labour inputs affect the demand for other factors of production.

Second, having completed our analysis of factor markets, we can discuss what determines the *income distribution*. The price of a factor, multiplied by the quantity used, tells us its income. We need to know the prices and quantities of all productive factors to understand how the economy's total income is distributed. We end this chapter by examining income distribution in the UK.

> **Physical capital** is the stock of produced goods that are inputs to production of other goods and services.
>
> **Land** is the factor of production that nature supplies.

Apart from labour, the other principal inputs to production are capital and land.

The stock of **physical capital** includes assembly-line machinery used to make cars, railway lines making transport services, school buildings producing education services, dwellings that produce housing services, and consumer durables, such as televisions, that produce entertainment services.

Physical capital is distinguished from **land** by the fact that the former is produced.

Although nature can change the quantity of land – through earthquakes, fires and the deposit of silt – economists treat land as fixed in supply. Its quantity is largely unaffected by economic decisions, whereas capital can be produced. The distinction between land and capital can become blurred. Fertilizer and irrigation can 'produce' better land. Because land and capital may be hard to disentangle, we discuss them in the same chapter. However, the distinction is often useful.

Chapter 6 introduced *depreciation*, the extent to which an asset or durable good is used up within the period of analysis. Capital and land are both assets. Capital depreciates a little every year, though new capital can be produced. In treating land as fixed, we assume it does not depreciate.

> Together, capital and land are the **tangible wealth** of the economy.

Capital and land are wealth or assets because they are durable. They are **tangible** because they are physical and we could touch them. Financial wealth is not tangible, and not a physical input to production, though it can hire such inputs. We distinguish between *physical* capital – plant, machinery and buildings, which henceforth we call 'capital' – and *financial* capital, or money and paper assets.

 ## 11.1 Physical capital

Table 11.1 shows the level and composition of physical capital in the UK in 2005. (Data on capital takes ages to collect!) Dwellings are houses and flats. Productive fixed capital is plant, machinery and buildings. Productive capital that is not fixed is called working capital: inventories or stocks of manufactured goods awaiting sale, partially finished goods (work in progress), and raw materials held for future production. Inventories are capital because they are produced goods that contribute to future production.

Table 11.2 shows productive fixed capital (PFK) used in production in the UK in 1997 and 2005. The final row shows that, at 2003 prices, the quantity of capital per employed worker rose from £77 000 to £90 000 during 1997–2005.

Table 11.1   UK capital stock, 2005

	£bn	%
Dwellings	1558	45
Productive fixed capital	1874	55
Total capital stock	3432	100

Source: ONS, UK National Accounts.

Table 11.2 Capital input to UK production

	1997	2005
PFK	1558	1778
PFK/employed worker	77	90

Note: PFK in £bn. PFK per worker in £000, both at 2003 prices.
Source: ONS, UK National Accounts.

Investment in physical capital increases capital as a production input, not only in absolute terms but also relative to the number of workers employed. Table 11.2 shows that, in less than a decade, production techniques have become more *capital intensive*. Each worker has more capital with which to work.

Because capital depreciates over time, it takes some investment in new capital goods merely to keep the level of capital constant.

If **net investment** is positive, **gross investment** more than offsets depreciation. The capital stock rises. Conversely, if low, gross investment may fail to offset depreciation: the capital stock falls.

> **Gross investment** is the production of new capital goods and the improvement of existing capital goods.
>
> **Net investment** is gross investment minus depreciation of the existing capital stock.

11.2 Rentals, interest rates and asset prices

Table 11.3 distinguishes *stocks* and *flows*, and distinguishes *rental payments* and *asset prices*. The price for hiring labour services is the wage. Rather loosely, we call it the 'price of labour' but the wage is the *rental payment* to hire labour. There is no asset price for buying the physical asset called a 'worker'. We no longer have slavery, that is, ownership of workers by firms.

Capital assets and capital services can be bought and sold. We have to be more careful. Rental payments and asset prices correspond to **flows** and **stocks**.

Tourists rent a car for the weekend. Building contractors pay a **rental rate** to lease earth-moving equipment. Sometimes there is no rental market. It is impossible to rent a power station. When firms make a once-and-for-all purchase of a capital asset or stock they must calculate how much it is implicitly costing them to use their capital. We return to this question in Section 11.4.

> A **stock** is the quantity of an asset at a point in time.
>
> A **flow** is the stream of services an asset provides in a period of time.
>
> The cost of using capital services is the **rental rate** for capital.

Table 11.3 Stock and flow concepts

	Capital	Labour
Flow input to hourly production	Capital services	Labour services
Payment for flow	Rental rate (£/machine hour)	Wage rate (£/labour hour)
Asset price	£/machine	£/slave, if purchase allowed

> The **price of an asset** is the sum for which the asset can be purchased outright. The owner of a capital asset gets the future stream of capital services from this asset.

Unlike labour, capital goods can be bought and have an **asset price**. Buying a car for £9000 entitles you to a stream of future transport services. You might even obtain a stream of future rental payments by letting your friend drive it.

What will a buyer pay for a capital asset? This reflects the value of the future income from capital services that the asset stock provides. However, we cannot simply add the future rental payments over the life of the capital asset to calculate its current asset price or value. We have to pay attention to the role of *time* and *interest payments*.

Interest and present values

A lender makes a loan to a borrower, who agrees to repay the initial sum (the principal) *with interest* at some future date. A loan of £100 for a year at 10 per cent interest must be repaid at £110 by the end of the year. The extra £10 (10 per cent of £100) is the interest cost of borrowing £100 for a year. *Interest rates* are quoted as a percentage per annum.

Suppose we lend £1 and re-lend the interest as it accrues. The first row of Table 11.4 shows what happens if the annual interest rate is 10 per cent. After a year, we have £1 plus an interest payment of £0.10. Re-lending the whole £1.10, we have £1.21 by the end of the second year. Because of *compound interest*, that is, the process of adding interest rate payments to an original sum of money, the absolute amount by which our money grows increases every year. The first year we increase our money by £0.10, which is 10 per cent of £1. Since we re-lend the interest, our money grows by £0.11 in the next year since we earn 10 per cent on £1.10. If we lend for yet another year, our money will grow by £0.121 to £1.331 at the end of the third year.

At 10 per cent interest per annum, £1 in year 0 is worth £1.10 in year 1 and £1.21 in year 2. Now ask the question the other way round. If we offered you £1.21 in two years' time, what sum today would be just as valuable? The answer is £1. If you had £1 today, you could always lend it out to get exactly £1.21 in two years' time. The second row of Table 11.4 extends this idea. If £1.21 in year 2 is worth £1 today, then £1 in year 2 must be worth £[1/1.21] = £0.83 today. £0.83 today could be lent out at 10 per cent interest to accumulate to £1 in year 2. Similarly, £1 in year 1 is worth only £[1/1.10] = £0.91 today.

Compound interest implies that lending £1 today cumulates to ever-larger sums the further into the future we keep the loan and re-lend the interest. Conversely, the present value of £1 earned at some future date becomes smaller the further into the future the date at which the £1 is earned.

Table 11.4   **Interest and present value (*PV*)**

	Year		
	0	1	2
At 10% interest rate:			
Value of £1 lent today in:	£1	£1.10	£1.21
PV of £1 earned in:	£1	£0.91	£0.83
At 5% interest rate:			
Value of £1 lent today in:	£1	£1.05	£1.10
PV of £ earned in:	£1	£0.95	£0.91

The **present value** of a future payment also depends on the interest rate. Table 11.4 shows that a loan of £1 accumulates less rapidly over time if the interest rate is lower. At 5 per cent interest, a loan of £1 cumulates to only £1.10 after two years, compared with £1.21 after two years when the interest rate was 10 per cent in row 1. Hence the bottom row of Table 11.4 shows that the present value of £1 in year 1 or year 2 is larger when the interest rate is only 5 per cent than in the corresponding entry when the interest rate is 10 per cent.

> The **present value** of a future £1 is the sum that, if lent today, would cumulate to £1 by that date.

Figure 11.1 illustrates the same points, showing how lending £1 today cumulates at compound interest rates of 5 and 10 per cent. After 10 years, the loan fund is worth £2.59 at 10 per cent interest but only £1.62 at 5 per cent interest. Higher interest rates imply more rapid accumulation through lending. The same diagram can be used for present values. A payment of £2.59 in 10 years' time has a present value of £1 if the annual interest rate is 10 per cent. The present value of £1 in 10 years' time is thus £1/[2.59] = £0.386. If interest rates are 5 per cent, the value of £1 in 10 years' time is £1/[1.62] = £0.617.

Using interest rates to calculate present values of future payments tells us the right way to add together payments at different points in time. For each payment at each date we calculate its present value. Then we add together the present values of the different payments.

To relate the price of a capital asset to the stream of future payments earned from the capital services it provides, we calculate the present value of the rental payment earned by the asset in each year of its working life, and add these present values together. This is what the asset is worth today. In equilibrium it should be the asset price.

Asset valuation

How much would you bid for a machine that earns £4000 in rental for two years and is then sold for scrap for £10 000? If you bid anything without finding out the interest rate, you misunderstood the previous section! Suppose the annual interest rate is 10 per cent. The first two rows of Table 11.5 show the money received each year. The final column shows the present value

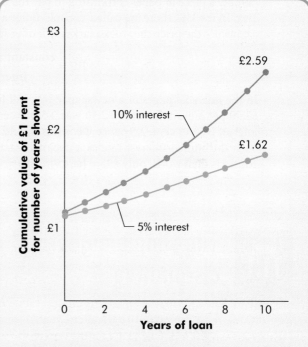

At 10 per cent interest per annum, £1 accumulates £2.59 after 10 years. At the lower interest rate of 5 per cent per annum, the accumulated interest value rises much more slowly, reaching only £1.62 after 10 years.

Figure 11.1   **Accumulation through interest**

Table 11.5   Present values and asset prices (at annual interest rate of 10%)

Year	Rental (£)	Scrap value (£)	Present value (£)
1	4000		3 640
2	4000+	10 000	11 620
Asset price in year 0			15 260

Note: From Table 11.4, the present value of each £1 in year 1 is £0.91 and in year 2 is £0.83 when the interest rate is 10%.

of these receipts. From Table 11.4, £1 next year is worth only £0.91 today, and £1 in year 2 only £0.83 today. The present value *PV* of £4000 in year 1 is £3640 (£4000 × 0.91), and the *PV* of the £14 000 received from rental earnings and sale for scrap in year 2 is £11 620 (£14 000 × 0.83). Adding these present values for years 1 and 2, the asset price should be £15 260.

£15 260 is much smaller than the £18 000 actually earned from two years of rental income and the scrap value. Present values *discount* the future.

These principles can be used to calculate the present value of any future income stream once the interest rate is known. The calculation is very simple in one special case: when the asset lasts for ever and the income stream per time period is constant. Governments sometimes borrow by selling a *perpetuity*, a bond (simply a piece of paper) promising to pay the owner a constant interest payment (called the 'coupon') for ever. In the UK, these are called 'consols' (after a famous bond issue called Consolidated Stock). The *PV* of a consol – the price the stock market will offer for this piece of paper – obeys the formula

$$PV = \frac{\text{constant annual coupon payment}}{\text{interest rate per annum}} \tag{1}$$

In the financial pages of a newspaper you will find 2.5 per cent consols. This perpetuity promises to pay £2.50 per annum for ever. £2.50 was 2.5 per cent of the original sale price of £100. If the current rate of interest is 5 per cent, 2.5 per cent consols should be worth around £50 (the annual coupon £2.5, divided by 0.05, the annual interest rate as a decimal fraction). If interest rates rise to 10 per cent per annum, the consol is then worth only £25 = [(£2.5)/(0.10)].

MATHS 11.1 The simple algebra of present values and discounting

Suppose we lend £*K* today at an annual interest rate *i*. After one year our money has grown to £*K*(1 + *i*). With *K* = 100 and *i* = 0.1, we get £110 back after a year. If we re-lend the money for another year at the same interest rate, we get back £{*K*(1 + *i*)} (1 + *i*) at the end of the second year. For example, our £100 has grown to £121 after two years. If we lend this sum for yet another year we get back £*K*(1 + *i*)^3 at the end of the third year. Hence, after *N* years we get back £*K*(1 + *i*)^N. This process tells you how to calculate the value after *N* years of an amount £*K* that you have today.

Conversely, the present value of £*X* to be received *N* years later is £*X*/(1 + *i*)^N, and we call 1/(1 + *i*)^N the *discount factor*. Since the interest rate *i* is a positive number, the discount factor must be a positive fraction. Higher interest rates imply lower discount factors. The table shows the present value of £1 *N* years from now when the interest rate is 10 per cent a year (*i* = 0.1).

Present value (PV) of £1 N years from now, annual interest rate of 10%						
N	1	5	10	20	30	40
PV	£0.91	£0.62	£0.39	£0.15	£0.06	£0.02

To calculate the present value of a whole stream of future payments, we multiply the face value of each payment by the relevant discount factor.

Assuming that the interest rate remains constant, the present value of a future stream of revenues over *N* years from now is given by:

$$PV = \sum_{t=1}^{N} \frac{R_t}{(1+i)^t}$$

where R_t is the revenue in year t, i is the interest rate and $\sum$ is a symbol that means the sum of each year's discounted earnings $R_t/(1 + i)^t$.

For example, suppose a firm wants to buy today a machine that costs £8000. The machine can give a revenue of £2000 a year for four years. After four years the machine can be sold as scrap for £3000. Assume that the interest rate is 10 per cent in all four years. The present value of this stream of future revenues is:

$$PV = \frac{2000}{(1+0.1)} + \frac{2000}{(1+0.1)^2} + \frac{2000}{(1+0.1)^3} + \frac{5000}{(1+0.1)^4} = £8388.7$$

In this case, the present value of the future revenues from the machine is higher than the cost of buying the machine. The firm should indeed buy the machine in this case.

The difference between the present value of a stream of revenues from a given investment minus the actual cost of that investment is called the *net present value (NPV)*. In our case, the net present value from buying the machine is $NPV = 8388.7 - 8000 = £388.7$.

This provides a rule for investment decisions: you should invest in a particular project if the net present value of that project is non-negative.

An alternative way to assess whether an investment should be undertaken is given by the calculation of the required real rate of return. This is discussed in Section 11.5.

When an asset is a perpetuity, earning £K a year for ever, formula (1) implies that the present value of this stream is £K/i.

Real and nominal interest rates: inflation and present values

Thus far we have discussed future payments valued in nominal terms. The first column of Table 11.5 shows rental receipts in actual pounds. The interest rate of 10 per cent tells us how many actual pounds we earn by lending £1 for a year.

At a **nominal interest rate** of 10 per cent, £100 lent today accumulates to £110 by next year. But we want to know how many goods that £110 will then buy. This is what really matters for the lender.

> The **nominal interest rate** tells us how many actual pounds are earned by lending £1 for a year.

Suppose the nominal interest rate is 10 per cent and inflation is 6 per cent when the lender receives back the money lent. Lending £1 for a year gives £1.10. Since inflation is 6 per cent, it costs £1.06 to buy goods we could have bought for £1 today. With £1.10 to spend next year, our purchasing power rises by only 4 per cent. The **real interest rate** is 4 per cent. Thus

Real interest rate = nominal interest rate − inflation rate (2)

Consider another example: nominal interest rates are 17 per cent and inflation is 20 per cent. Lending £100 for a year, you get £117. But it will cost you £120 to buy goods you could have bought today for £100. You are worse off by 3 per cent by delaying purchases for a year and lending your money at the apparently high rate of 17 per cent. Real interest rates are *negative*. The real interest rate is −3 per cent. In real terms, it *costs* you to be a lender. The nominal interest rate does not compensate for higher prices of goods you ultimately wish to buy. Notice that the nominal interest rate *cannot* be negative whereas the real interest rate can.

> The **real interest rate** on a loan is the extra quantity of goods that can be purchased.

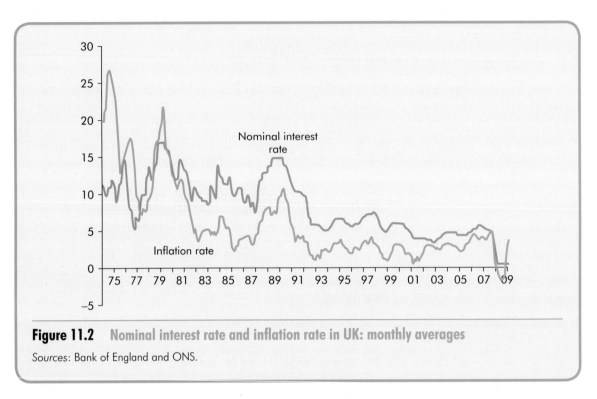

Figure 11.2 Nominal interest rate and inflation rate in UK: monthly averages

Sources: Bank of England and ONS.

Equation (2) is known as the Fisher equation.[1] It implies that the nominal interest rate can be written as the sum of the real interest rate and the inflation rate. Therefore, for a given real interest rate inflation and nominal interest rate should move together. This is shown in Figure 11.2, where we plot the nominal interest rate (as measured by the monthly average official bank rate) and the monthly inflation rate (measured by the change in the retail price index) in the UK.

What determines the real interest rate?

Two forces lead to positive real interest rates. First, people are impatient. Given the choice of an equal number of goods tomorrow or today, we'd rather have them today. To delay spending on goods and services, savers have to be bribed with a positive real interest rate that lets them consume *more* goods in the future if they postpone consumption and lend today.

Second, there must be a way of earning positive real returns, or borrowers would never borrow. Borrowers pay positive real interest rates because they can buy capital goods that provide a stream of returns more than sufficient to meet the interest cost.

Impatience to consume and the productivity of physical capital are the two forces that lead us to expect a positive real interest rate. Real interest rates are usually small and positive. Since real interest rates change little, big changes in nominal interest rates usually occur to offset big changes in inflation rates, keeping real interest rates in their normal range, determined by the forces of impatience and capital productivity. A good rule of thumb is that each percentage point rise in inflation is matched by a percentage point rise in nominal interest rates, leaving real interest rates the same as before.

To calculate present values, we must be consistent. If we wish to calculate the present value of a future payment expressed in nominal terms, we must discount by the nominal interest rate. If the future payment is expressed in real terms, we must discount using the real interest rate.

---

1   From Irving Fisher, the economist who first pointed out that relationship between nominal and real interest rates.

The following is a common mistake. You want to buy a farm whose rental this year is £10 000. Today's interest rate is 10 per cent. You reckon that the farm's output should not change much over time. You use the formula of equation (1) for a perpetuity, divide £10 000 by 0.1, and get £100 000. The farmer wants £150 000 for the farm, so you decide not to buy.

You missed a financial killing. Nominal interest rates are 10 per cent only because the market thinks inflation will be about 7 per cent, leaving a real interest rate of 3 per cent. Doing the calculation in real terms at constant prices, we divide £10 000 for ever by 0.03 to obtain £333 000 as the right price for the farm. Equivalently, to calculate in nominal terms, we can use discount factors based on the 10 per cent nominal interest rate, but remember that the likely inflation rate of around 7 per cent will steadily increase the nominal farm rental over time. If we do this calculation, we shall again conclude that £100 000 for the farm is a bargain.

11.3 Saving, investment and the real interest rate

Figure 11.3 shows the production possibility frontier AA' – feasible combinations of current and future consumption goods that the economy can produce. The way agents can transfer consumption over time is through saving. At A the economy only produces for current consumption, at A' only for future consumption.

The frontier AA' shows different amounts of *investment* in the capital stock. At A not only is no investment undertaken, the existing capital is sold off and entirely consumed today. Future consumption is zero.

At A' all current resources are going in investment to raise the capacity to make consumption goods in the future. Current consumption is zero. Moving down AA', more and more resources are transferred from future to current consumption. As usual, the curvature of the production possibility frontier reflects diminishing returns in this trade-off.

Assume for simplicity that inflation is zero, so that nominal and real interest rates coincide. The slope of the frontier is the extra future consumption from sacrificing a unit of current consumption. The slope has magnitude $-(1 + i)$ where i is the real rate of return on investment. The minus sign reminds us we sacrifice current consumption to add to future consumption.

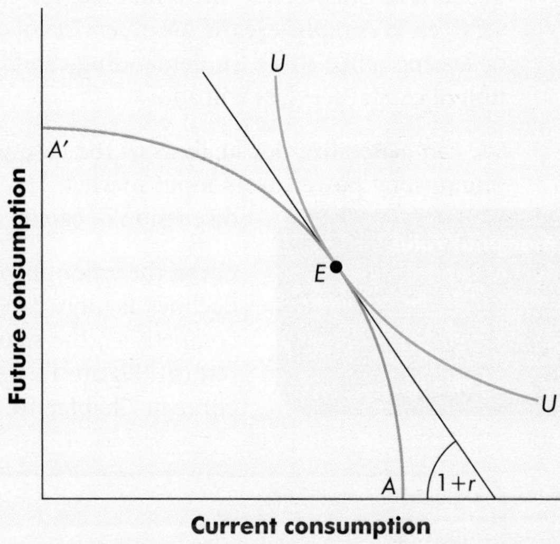

What about consumer tastes? Both current and future consumption are desirable, so we can imagine a standard indifference map. The more impatient are consumers for current consumption, the steeper their indifference curves. Impatient people will give up lots of future consumption to get a bit more today. Thrifty people have flatter indifference curves.

By devoting more current resources to investment, society can trade off current for future consumption, moving up the frontier AA'. The frontier has slope $-(1 + i)$, where i is the rate of return on investment. Facing a real interest rate r, producers will choose E and so will consumers. The equilibrium real interest rate balances the productivity of investment and thriftiness of consumers.

Figure 11.3 The equilibrium real interest rate

In Figure 11.3, UU is the highest indifference curve that can be reached and E is the best allocation of current resources between consumption and investment.

The real interest rate may adjust to accomplish this outcome, even though decisions to add to the capital stock are taken by firms, and decisions about **saving** are taken by households.

> **Saving** is the difference between current income and current consumption.

Firms will invest until the real rate of return i equals the real interest rate r at which they can borrow money. Households face a budget line of slope $-(1 + r)$, since by saving and lending they can exchange £1 of consumption today for £$(1 + r)$ of consumption in the future. Households save up to the point at which their indifference curve is tangent to their budget line with slope $-(1 + r)$.

Equilibrium occurs where saving equals investment. Households and firms are happy with the same transfer of resources from the present to the future. Figure 11.3 shows the equilibrium real interest rate r. Firms wish to be at E, where the rate of return i equals the cost of borrowing r [the slope of the frontier $-(1 + i)$ is tangent to the line $-(1 + r)$]. Households want to be at the *same* point E, where their indifference curve UU is tangent to the line $-(1 + r)$.

11.4 The demand for capital services

The analysis of the demand for capital services by an industry closely parallels the analysis of labour demand in Chapter 10. The rental rate for capital replaces the wage rate. Each is the cost of hiring factor services. We emphasize the *use* of *services* of capital. The example to bear in mind is a firm renting a vehicle or leasing office space. In demanding capital services, a firm considers how much extra output another unit of capital services will add.

We can generalize our analysis to the case where the firm has monopoly power in its output market or monopsony power in its input market. Having discussed that extension in Chapter 10, we confine our discussion of capital services to the simpler case in which the firm is competitive.

> The **marginal value product of capital** is the extra value of the firm's output when another unit of capital services is used, all other inputs being held fixed.

Given the amounts of other inputs, the **marginal value product of capital** $MVPK$ declines as more capital is used. Although the firm's output price is fixed since it is competitive, the marginal physical product of capital is subject to diminishing returns. Figure 11.4 shows a downward-sloping $MVPK$ curve, just like the $MVPL$ curve in Chapter 10.

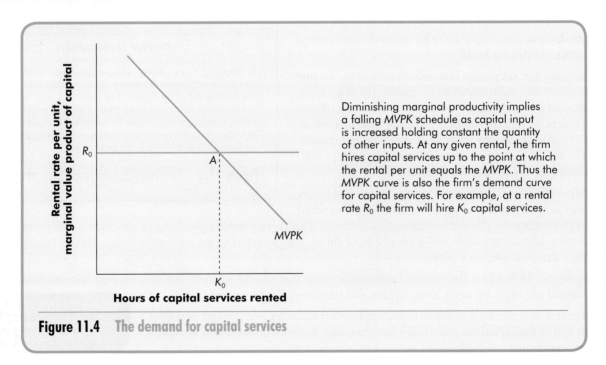

Diminishing marginal productivity implies a falling $MVPK$ schedule as capital input is increased holding constant the quantity of other inputs. At any given rental, the firm hires capital services up to the point at which the rental per unit equals the $MVPK$. Thus the $MVPK$ curve is also the firm's demand curve for capital services. For example, at a rental rate R_0 the firm will hire K_0 capital services.

Figure 11.4 The demand for capital services

A firm rents capital up to the point at which its marginal cost – the rental rate – equals its marginal value product. The firm demands K_0 capital services at the rental rate R_0.

For given rental rates and quantities of other factors of production, $MVPK$ is the firm's demand curve for capital services at each rental rate for capital services. The firm's $MVPK$ curve showing its capital demand curve can be shifted outwards by one of three events: (1) an increase in its output price, which makes the marginal *physical* product of capital more valuable, (2) an increase in the level of other factors (chiefly labour) with which capital works to produce output, making capital more productive, or (3) a technical advance that makes capital more productive.

The industry demand curve for capital services

As with labour, we can move from the firm's demand for capital services to the industry demand curve for capital services by horizontally adding the marginal value product of each firm. Again, we must recognize that, in expanding output, the industry bids down the price of its output.

Thus the industry demand curve for capital services is steeper than the horizontal sum of each firm's $MVPK$ curves. The industry demand curve recognizes that output prices fall as output rises. The more inelastic the demand curve for the industry's output, the more inelastic is the industry's derived demand curve for capital services.

11.5　The supply of capital services

Capital services are produced by capital assets. We analyse the market for capital services, then consider what this implies for the market for capital assets. In so doing, we assume that the flow of capital services is directly determined by the stock of capital assets, such as machines.

This is a simplification. By working overtime shifts, a firm can alter the effective flow of machine services it gets from a given machine bolted to the factory floor. It can also leave machines idle.

Even so, in normal times firms have limited ability to vary the flow of capital services from a given capital stock. We shall grasp the key features of the market for capital if we assume that the flow of capital services is determined by the stock of capital available. Our analysis must distinguish the long run and the short run, and examine both the supply of capital services to the economy and to a particular industry.

The short-run supply of capital services

In the short run, the total supply of capital assets (machines, buildings and vehicles), and thus the services they provide, is fixed to the economy. New factories cannot be built overnight. The supply curve for capital services is vertical at a quantity determined by the existing stock of capital assets. Some types of capital are fixed even for an individual industry. The steel industry cannot change overnight its number of blast furnaces. However, by offering a higher rental rate for delivery vans, the supermarket industry can attract a larger share of the delivery vans that the economy currently has. For such capital services, an industry faces an upward-sloping supply curve. It can bid services away from other industries.

The long-run supply of capital services

In the long run, the quantity of capital in the economy can be varied. New machines and factories can be built. Conversely, without new investment in capital goods the existing capital stock will depreciate and gradually fall. Similarly, individual industries can adjust their stocks of capital.

At what rental rates will owners of capital *assets* be willing to buy or build?

You buy a machine to rent out as a business. The machine costs £10 000, which you borrow. How much must the machine earn if you are to break even? First you have to cover the interest cost. Suppose the *real*, or inflation-adjusted, interest rate is 5 per cent. You have to pay the bank £500 (= £10 000 × 0.05) a year in real terms.

> The **required rental on capital** just covers the opportunity cost of owning the asset.

Then you have spending on maintenance. Also, the resale value of the machine depreciates each year. In real terms, maintenance and depreciation cost you £1000 per annum, 10 per cent of the purchase price. The depreciation rate is 10 per cent a year. The annual cost of renting out a machine is £500 for the opportunity cost of the funds and £1000 for depreciation.

To break even, the **required rental** is £1500 a year at constant prices. The asset cost £10 000. Hence the *required real rate of return* is 15 per cent a year.[2] It is worth borrowing if the real interest rate on the loan is less than 15 per cent a year.[3]

What determines the required rental?

The required rental rate, or cost of using capital, depends on three things: the price of the capital good, the real interest rate and the depreciation rate. Depreciation depends largely on technology; on how fast the machine wears out with use and age. The real interest rate is determined by economy-wide forces and changes only slowly. Treating the depreciation rate and the real interest rate as given, we examine how the purchase price of capital goods affects the required rental on capital.

The long-run supply curve for the economy

In the long run, the quantity of capital services must earn the required rental. If it earns more, people will build extra capital goods. If it earns less, owners of capital will let assets depreciate without building new ones.

Figure 11.5 shows the long-run supply curve of capital services to the economy. Capital services come from capital goods. The construction industry produces buildings and the motor industry produces container lorries. Each industry has an upward-sloping supply curve. The higher the price of the capital good, the more the capital goods producing industry will choose to supply.

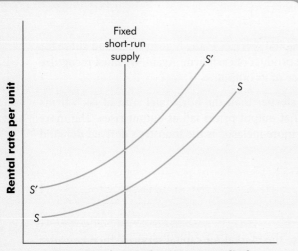

In the short run, the stock of capital goods, and the services they supply, is fixed by past investment decisions; new capital goods cannot be produced overnight. In the long run, the higher rental rate is required to call forth a higher supply of capital services and a permanently higher capital stock. The higher rental rate just offsets the higher price for capital goods required to induce higher output of new capital goods to match the higher total depreciation of a larger capital stock. Thus the required rate of return is met at all points on SS. If real interest rates increase, the required rate of return will also increase to match the opportunity cost of funds tied up in capital goods. Hence the long-run supply curve of capital services shifts up to S'S' providing a higher rental level at each level of the capital stock and its corresponding purchase price. Each point on S'S' matches the new required rate of return.

Figure 11.5   The supply of capital services to the economy

---

2   To simplify the calculation, assume the machine and the bank loan last for ever. We can then use our formula for the present value of a perpetuity. The price p of a perpetuity is the annual payment c divided by the required rate of return r that lenders could get by lending to a bank. If $p = c/r$, then $r = c/p$. When c is the annual cost and p is the initial price of a machine, you need a rate of return $r = c/p$ to make it worth renting out machines.

3   If the firm using the capital services also owns the capital good, the required rental is the cost the firm should charge itself to use the capital when calculating economic costs (see our discussion of accounting versus economic costs in Chapter 6).

In the long run, a larger flow of capital services needs a higher capital stock. But capital depreciates. The higher the capital stock, the larger is total depreciation. Thus, a higher long-run flow of capital services needs a higher capital stock, which needs a higher flow of new capital goods to offset depreciation and maintain the capital stock intact.

Producers need a higher price for capital goods to make more new capital goods. To maintain the required rate of return on assets, we need a higher rental rate for capital services. In the long run a higher flow of capital services is supplied only if the rental rate on capital rises to match the higher price of capital goods needed to induce producers of new capital goods to keep pace with higher absolute levels of depreciation.

Figure 11.5 shows the long-run supply curve for capital services. SS slopes upwards in the long run when plotted against the rental rate on capital. We draw SS for a given real interest rate. If the real interest rate rises, the opportunity cost of holding capital assets rises. For a given purchase price of capital goods, the required rental must rise. Suppliers of capital services need a higher return to offset the higher opportunity cost of the money they tie up in purchasing capital goods.

In Figure 11.5, higher real interest rates shift leftwards the long-run supply curve for capital services, from SS to $S'S'$. Higher rentals at each level of capital services (and hence capital assets) provide the higher real return to match the increase in the real interest rate.

The long-run supply curve for the industry

The preceding analysis determines the supply of capital services to the economy. In the long run, a small industry can get as much of this capital as it wishes, provided it pays the going rental rate. A larger industry may bid up the rental rate as it attracts a large fraction of the economy-wide supply of capital. Such an industry faces an upward-sloping supply curve for capital services.

We analyse the case of a small industry facing a horizontal long-run supply curve for capital services at the going rental rate. The analysis is easily extended to an industry facing an upward-sloping long-run supply curve for capital services.

11.6 Equilibrium and adjustment in the market for capital services

Figure 11.6 shows the market for capital services for a particular industry. Long-run equilibrium is at E, where the horizontal long-run supply curve $S'S'$ crosses the industry demand curve DD derived from firms' $MVPK$ curves. The industry hires K_0 capital services at the going rental R_0.

Adjustments in the market for capital services

Suppose workers in the industry get a wage increase. In the long run this has a *substitution effect* and an *output effect*. The substitution effect makes firms switch to more capital-intensive techniques, raising the demand for capital services. However, by raising costs, a wage increase reduces the quantity of output supplied. This output effect reduces demand for all inputs. The second effect is more likely to dominate, the more elastic is the demand for the industry's output.

Short-run and long-run adjustment

Suppose in Figure 11.6 the wage rise reduces demand for capital services from DD to $D'D'$. The industry begins in equilibrium at E. Initially, the short-run supply of capital services SS is vertical at K_0. When demand shifts from DD to $D'D'$, the industry cannot immediately cut its input of capital services. With a vertical short-run supply curve, the new short-run equilibrium is at E'. The rental on capital falls from R_0 to R_1.

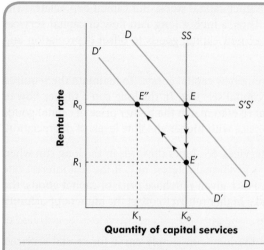

The industry begins in equilibrium at E. Overnight its short-run supply of capital is fixed at K_0, but in the long run it faces the horizontal supply curve $S'S'$ at the going rental, R_0. Suppose a wage increase shifts the demand curve for capital from DD to $D'D'$. The new short-run equilibrium is at E'. Since the rental R_1 fails to provide the required rate of return, owners of capital goods allow these goods slowly to depreciate without buying any new capital goods. The industry's capital stock and the services it provides gradually fall back. Eventually the industry reaches long-run equilibrium at E''. Since capital is again earning the required rate of return, owners of capital goods now replace goods as they depreciate.

Figure 11.6 *Short- and long-run adjustment of capital to a wage rise*

The industry faces a long-run supply curve $S'S'$ for capital services. Eventually it must pay the going rate. At E', owners of capital do not get the required rental for the capital services they supply. They let their capital stock depreciate. Over time, the industry's capital stock and supply of capital services fall until equilibrium is reached at E''. The capital services used by the industry have fallen to K_1. Less capital means a higher marginal product of capital and higher rentals. At E'', users of capital again pay the required rental R_0.

The arrows in Figure 11.6 show the dynamic path that the industry will follow. When demand for capital falls, there is a sharp fall in the rental on capital. Owners of the fixed factor cannot adjust the quantity of capital services supplied. As time elapses, they adjust the quantity, allowing capital goods to depreciate, and the rental gradually recovers.

CONCEPT 11.1 Factor markets: a summary

Chapters 10 and 11 examine markets for production inputs. In the long run, when all inputs can be freely varied, the firm's choice of technique at each output level is determined by technology and relative factor rentals. At a given output, a higher relative price of one factor makes the firm substitute towards techniques using that factor less intensively. The long-run total cost curve shows the cheapest way to produce each output level when production techniques are optimally chosen.

From long-run total cost, we calculate long-run marginal cost and hence the output at which marginal cost and marginal revenue are equal. For each factor, the firm's demand is a derived demand that reflects the factor's marginal physical product in making extra output and the marginal revenue from selling that extra output. A competitive firm's demand curve for a factor is the marginal value product schedule, which assumes a given output price, given quantities of all other inputs, and given technology. Changes in any of these shift the marginal value product schedule. In the short run, a competitive firm demands that quantity of its variable factor which equates its marginal value product and its factor rental. In the long run, every factor can be varied. Each factor is demanded to the point at which its factor rental equals its marginal value product given the quantity of all other factors, *each having been adjusted in the same way*.

What distinguishes labour, capital and land is mainly the speed with which their supply can adjust. The input of casual labour on construction sites or during crop picking is easily variable, even in the short run. The supply of skilled workers with extensive training can be changed less quickly and the supply of capital goods takes even longer to adjust. Land is the factor whose total supply can never be adjusted. The slower the speed of adjustment, and the more irreversible the process, the more current decisions reflect beliefs about the future. The latter, neglected in our discussion of unskilled labour in Chapter 10, are central to our analysis of investment in physical capital (Chapter 11).

11.7 The price of capital assets

We now turn from capital services to capital assets, demanded by firms wishing to supply capital services. Think of Hertz renting out cars, or property companies renting out office space. Anticipating a stream of rentals, suppliers of capital services work out the present value of this stream of rentals at the going interest rate. This tells us how much they should be prepared to pay to buy a capital asset. The price of capital assets is higher when (a) the anticipated rental stream is higher, or (b) the interest rate is lower. Both raise the present value of the future rental stream.

People anticipating a higher stream of rental earnings pay a high purchase price for capital assets. At a lower price, people with lower anticipated streams then find it profitable to demand capital goods. There is a downward-sloping demand curve for capital goods. The lower the price, the higher the quantity demanded. The upward-sloping supply curve and downward-sloping demand curve together determine the equilibrium price and quantity of capital goods for the economy. This determines the flow supply of capital services that this stock will provide.

What happens when an individual industry faces a fall in its derived demand for capital services, as in Figure 11.6? In the short run, the rental on capital services falls to R_1. Moreover, everyone can work out that it will take some time before the rental rate climbs back to R_0. At the going interest rate, the present value of rental earnings on new capital goods in this industry falls.

Now the industry is no longer willing to pay the economy-wide equilibrium price for capital assets. It makes no new investment, and its capital stock depreciates. Its capital stock falls until capital services become so scarce that the rental rate returns to its original level. The present value of future rentals then matches the price of capital goods in the whole economy. The industry now buys capital goods to replace goods as they depreciate. The capital stock is constant, and the industry is in its new long-run equilibrium.

The long-run equilibrium price of a capital asset is both the price that induces suppliers to make enough new assets to offset depreciation and keep the capital stock constant, and the price that buyers of capital goods are prepared to pay for that quantity. That price is the present value of the anticipated rental stream for capital services discounted at the going rate of interest.

11.8 Land and rents

Land is essentially a capital good in fixed supply to the economy, even in the long run. This is not literally true. The Dutch reclaimed from the sea some areas of low-lying land, and fertilizers enhance the effective input of land for farming. Nevertheless, it makes sense to think about a factor whose total long-run supply is fixed.

<table>
<tr><td colspan="2">CASE 11.1</td></tr>
</table>

The best address

Since land is in fixed supply, land prices are highest where demand is greatest. We should expect that the demand for land is higher in places like major cities where many people live. The table below shows the ten most expensive places according to the average prices of residential apartments in 2008. The price is for square metres and expressed in US dollars.

Top 10 most expensive cities	
1. London ($24.250)	6. Tokyo ($11.870)
2. New York ($15.933)	7. Singapore ($11.800)
3. Moscow ($15.531)	8. Mumbai ($10.222)
4. Paris ($13.826)	9. Barcelona ($9.871)
5. Hong Kong ($12.599)	10. Geneva ($7.532)

Source: www.globalpropertyguide.com.

Picture: A row of classic Edwardian houses in the area of Kensington & Chelsea, London. © David Palmer | istockphoto.com

Figure 11.7 shows the derived demand curve *DD* for land services. With a fixed supply *SS*, the equilibrium rental per acre is R_0. A rise in the derived demand, for example because wheat prices rise, raises the rental to R_1. The quantity of land services is fixed by assumption.

Consider a tenant farmer who rents land. Wheat prices have risen but so have rents. Not only may the farmer be no better off, but the connection between the two rises may also be unrecognized. The farmer complains that high rents make it hard to earn a decent living. As in our discussion of footballers' wages in Chapter 10, it is the high derived demand combined with the inelastic factor supply that causes the high payments for factor services.[4]

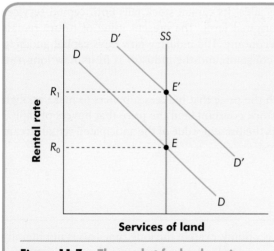

The total supply of land is fixed to the economy. The supply curve is vertical. The derived demand curve for land services reflects the marginal value product of land. Its derivation is exactly the same as the demand curves for labour and capital from the *MVPL* and *MVPK* schedules. The demand curve *DD* for land services determines the equilibrium land rental rate R_0. If the derived demand curve for land services shifts up to *D'D'*, the equilibrium land rental will increase to R_1.

Figure 11.7   The market for land services

---

4   If most farmers rent their land, agricultural subsidies, such as the EU Common Agricultural Policy, increase land rentals as well as the price farmers get from crops. It is the landowners who really benefit!

Because land is *the* asset in fixed supply, economists have taken over the word 'rent', the payment for land services, to the concept of *economic rent*, the excess of actual payments over transfer earnings, introduced in Chapter 10. Economic rent is large when supply is inelastic.

11.9 Income distribution in the UK

The income of a factor is its rental rate multiplied by the quantity of the factor employed. We pull together our discussion of factor markets to examine the distribution of income in the UK.

The functional distribution of income

Table 11.6 shows the total earnings of the different factors of production in the UK in 2006 and compares their shares of national income with the shares they received during 1981–89. There have been only small changes in the shares of different factors of production. As the real incomes increased, the real incomes of the different production inputs broadly kept pace.

Aggregate labour supply to the economy is relatively inelastic. Hence, the total number of employed workers was little higher in 2006 than in 1981. Table 11.6 shows that the UK capital per worker increased. Technical progress also boosted productivity. For both reasons, labour's marginal product schedule shifted outwards. Confronted with an almost vertical labour supply curve, this steady rise in the demand for labour raised the equilibrium real wage. Labour income from employment rose as national income rose.

Table 11.6 shows that the share of income from profits and rents fell slightly during 1989–2006, with a slight rise in income from self-employment. The quantity of capital employed rose steadily, at about the same rate as national output. Since the ratio of capital to output has been fairly constant, a declining real return on capital has accounted for the evolution of the share of capital earnings in national output.

If the quantity of capital rose substantially without a substantial fall in its rate of return, the economy cannot simply have moved down a given marginal product of capital schedule; otherwise, the rental on capital and its rate of return would have been reduced. Rather, the marginal product schedule must have shifted outwards. This outward shift is mainly reflected by technical progress.

The supply of land is very inelastic. As national income increased, the derived demand curve for land shifted upwards. Property rentals have risen at least in line with national income.

> The **functional income distribution** is the division of national income among different factors of production.
>
> The **personal income distribution** is the division of national income across individuals, regardless of the factor services from which these individuals earn their income.

The personal income distribution

The personal income distribution is relevant to issues such as equality and poverty. Table 11.7 excludes the very poor, whose income is so low that the Inland Revenue

Table 11.6 UK functional income distribution, 1981–2006 (% of national income)

Source (factor of production)	1981–89 average	2006
Employment	64	64
Self-employment	7	10
Profits and property rents	29	26

Source: ONS, UK National Accounts.

Table 11.7 UK personal income distribution, 2006/07

Taxable income band (£000 per annum)	Million taxpayers
< 7.5	2.7
7.5–10	3.4
10–15	6.0
15–20	4.9
20–30	6.4
30–50	4.4
50–100	1.4
100–200	0.4
200+	0.1

Source: ONS, Social Trends.

does not record what they earn. Even confining attention to people who pay income tax, pre-tax income is unequal in the UK. Based on 29.7 million taxpayers, the top row of Table 11.7 shows that the poorest 2.7 million households had an average taxable income of less than £7500 in 2006/07, whereas the bottom three rows show that the richest 1.9 million households all had taxable incomes in excess of £50 000.

Why do some people earn so much while others earn so little? Chapter 10 discussed some reasons why people earn different wages and salaries. Unskilled workers have little training and low productivity. Workers with high levels of training and education earn much more. Some jobs, such as coal mining, pay high compensating differentials to offset unpleasant working conditions. Pleasant, but unskilled, jobs pay much less since many people are prepared to do them. Talented superstars in scarce supply but strong demand earn very high economic rents.

CASE 11.2 Income inequality in the UK

Britain is becoming an ever-more segregated society, with the gap between rich and poor reaching its highest level for 40 years, a report from the Rowntree Foundation concluded in 2007. In the past 15 years, there has been a rise in the number of households living below the poverty line, while the wealthy have become even more wealthy. In this move to the extremes, fewer UK households are now classed as neither rich nor poor.

The increase in inequality, especially after 1997, was due to the fact that the income of the very wealthy people (the top 10 per cent of the richest) has increased at an annual rate of 3.1 per cent compared to the 2.3 per cent for the UK population as a whole.

In 2007, the top 10 per cent of individuals in UK received 40 per cent of all personal income, while the remaining 90 per cent received 60 per cent.

Although inequality has increased, the number of people living in extreme poverty has fallen. Why the discrepancy? Because in most developed countries the poverty line is a relative concept, a certain percentage of average earnings. As living standards rise, the poverty line rises too. In Britain, when we say more people live in poverty, this is really the same thing as saying that inequality has increased.

In contrast, in looking at the poorest areas of the world, international agencies such as the World Bank often use measures of absolute poverty, such as the number of people living on less than $1 a day. If this number rises, the poorest are getting absolutely poorer. Given that the world as a whole is getting richer, an increase in absolute poverty means an increase in relative poverty. The UK shows that the converse need not always be true – relative poverty has increased in the UK but absolute poverty has declined.

We should also be interested in the social consequences arising from income inequality. Different income groups were also becoming geographically more segregated. If the rich retreat into affluent areas where they meet only other rich people, and travel only in their luxury cars rather than on public transport, their awareness of the problems of the poor may diminish. The Rowntree report concluded that urban clustering of poverty had increased, while wealthy households were becoming concentrated on the outskirts of major cities.

Table 11.8 UK distribution of marketable wealth, 1991–2003

	1991	2003
Percentage of wealth owned by:		
Most wealthy 1%	17	21
Most wealthy 25%	71	72
Most wealthy 50%	92	93
Total marketable wealth (£bn)	1711	3783

Note: Table applies to adults aged 18 and over.

Source: ONS, *Social Trends*.

Table 11.7 refers not just to income from the supply of labour services. One reason why the distribution of personal income is so unequal is that the ownership of wealth, which provides income from profits and rents, is even more unequal. Table 11.8 gives details for 1991–2003.

The most wealthy 1 per cent of the population owns 21 per cent of UK marketable wealth and the most wealthy 25 per cent of the population own 72 per cent of UK marketable wealth. The stream of profit and rent income to which such wealth gives rise plays a large part in determining the personal distribution of pre-tax *income*.

Summary

- **Physical capital** comprises real assets yielding services to producing firms or consuming households. The main categories of physical capital are plant and machinery, residential structures, other buildings, consumer durables and inventories. **Tangible wealth** is physical capital plus land.

- **Present values** convert future receipts or payments into current values. Because lenders can earn – and borrowers must pay – interest over time, a pound tomorrow is worth less than a pound today. How much less depends on the interest rate. The higher the interest rate, the lower the present value of any future payment.

- Since lending or borrowing cumulates at compound interest, for any given annual interest rate the present value of a given sum is smaller the further into the future that sum is earned or paid.

- The present value of a **perpetuity** is the constant annual payment divided by the rate of interest (expressed as a decimal fraction).

- **Nominal interest rates** measure the monetary interest payments on a loan. The inflation-adjusted **real interest rate** measures the extra goods a lender can buy by lending for a year and delaying purchases of goods. The real rate of interest is the nominal interest rate minus the inflation rate over the same period.

- In the long run, the real interest rate adjusts to make investment equal to saving, and is determined by the return on firms' investments and the degree of impatience of households.

- The demand for capital services is a derived demand. The **firm's demand for capital services** is its marginal value product of capital curve. Higher levels of the other factors of production and higher output prices shift the derived demand curve up. The **industry demand for capital services** is less elastic than the horizontal sum of each firm's curve because it also allows for the effect of an industry expansion in bidding down the output price.

- In the short run the supply of capital services is fixed. In the long run it can be adjusted by producing new capital goods or allowing the existing capital stock to depreciate.

- The **required rental** is the rental that allows a supplier of capital services to break even on the decision to purchase the capital asset. The required rental is higher, the higher is the interest rate, the depreciation rate or the purchase price of the capital good.

- A rise in the industry wage has two effects on the derived demand curve for capital services. By reducing labour input it reduces the marginal physical product of capital. By reducing the industry output it increases the output price. When output demand is very inelastic the latter effect will dominate. When output demand is very elastic the former effect dominates.

- The **asset price** is the price at which a capital good is bought and sold outright. In long-run equilibrium it is both the price at which suppliers of capital goods are willing to produce and the price at which buyers are willing to purchase. The latter is merely the present value of anticipated future rentals earned from the capital services that the good provides in the future.

- **Land** is the special capital good whose supply is fixed even in the long run. However, land and capital can move between industries in the long run until rentals on land or on capital are equalized in different industries.

- Technology and the ease of factor substitution dictate the very different capital intensity of different industries. Most industries are becoming more capital intensive over time, but at different rates. This reflects the ease with which industries can substitute capital for labour, the rise in wage rates relative to capital rentals, and technical advances in different industries.

- The **functional distribution of income** shows how national income is divided between the factors of production. The share of each factor has remained fairly constant over time. This conceals a rise in the quantity of capital relative to labour, and a corresponding fall in the ratio of capital rentals to labour wages.

- The **personal distribution of income** shows how national income is divided between different individuals regardless of the factor services from which income is earned. A major cause of income inequality in the UK is a very unequal distribution of income-earning wealth.

Review questions

1 (a) Consumer durables such as washing machines are part of the capital stock but do not generate any financial income for their owners. Why do we include consumer durables in the capital stock? (b) To wash your clothes you can take them to a launderette and spend £2 per week indefinitely or buy a washing machine for £400. It costs £1 per week (including depreciation) to run a washing machine, and the interest rate is 10 per cent per annum. Does it make sense to buy the washing machine? Does this help you answer part (a)?

EASY

2 A bank offers you £1.10 next year for every £0.90 you give it today. What is the implicit interest rate?

3 A firm buys a machine for £10 000, earns rentals of £3600 for each of the next two years, and then sells it for scrap for £9000. Use the data of Table 11.4 to determine if the machine is worth buying when the interest rate is 10 per cent per annum.

4 The interest rate falls from 10 per cent to 5 per cent. Discuss in detail how this affects the rental on capital services and the level of the capital stock in an industry in the short and the long run.

5 Suppose a plot of land is suitable only for agriculture. Can the farming industry experience financial distress if there is an increase in the price of land? Is your answer affected if the land can also be used for housing?

6 Common fallacies Why are these statements wrong? (a) Inflation leads to high nominal interest rates. This reduces the present value of future income. (b) If the economy continues to become more capital intensive, eventually there will be no jobs left for workers to do. (c) Since the economy's supply of land is fixed, it would be supplied even at a zero rental, which should therefore be the equilibrium rental in the long run.

7 Suppose you face the following two investment opportunities: (i) You can invest £3000 and after five years you are going to get £4500. (ii) You can invest your £3000 at the annual market interest rate of 10 per cent for five years. Which investment will you make? Demonstrate your answer by comparing the present values of the two investment opportunities.

MEDIUM

8 Suppose that the demand for capital is given by $K = 20 - 2r$, where K denotes capital and r is the rental rate. In a graph with r on the vertical axis and K on the horizontal axis, plot the demand for capital. Suppose that in the short run the supply of capital is fixed at 6. In a graph show how the rental rate is determined in equilibrium. An earthquake destroys part of the capital available in the economy. The supply of capital shrinks to 4 in the short run. What happens to the equilibrium rental rate?

9 Suppose that the *real* interest rate in the economy is 4 per cent, while the inflation rate one year from now is known to be 2 per cent. Use the Fisher equation to find the nominal interest rate. Use the nominal interest rate to find the present value of £100 one year from now. Now suppose that inflation in one year from now is known to be 4 per cent. How is the present value calculated previously going to change? Why?

10 A firm is producing output using only capital. Its production function is $Q = 10K - K^2$. The firm sells its product in a competitive market at a price of £2 and it rents capital from a competitive market at a rental rate r per unit of capital. Write down the profit function of the firm and find its capital demand function (K as a function of r).

11 What should be the impact of globalization on assets in fixed supply, particularly land? Can you think of an example in which globalization might induce a fall in land prices?

12 Some pension funds work as follows. Young workers pay a fraction of their salary into the scheme and retired workers withdraw money from the scheme. The scheme does not invest contributions into any fund. Year by year, it simply calculates what to charge young workers in order to meet obligations that year to old workers. (a) In a country that had a baby boom a couple of decades ago, is it easy or difficult to run such a scheme? (b) Suppose babies dry up and life expectancy increases. What happens to such pension schemes? (c) You are the government. What are your options now?

For solutions to these questions contact your lecturer.

Risk and information

Learning Outcomes

By the end of this chapter, you should understand:

1. risk aversion and diminishing marginal utility

2. risk pooling and risk spreading

3. how inside information leads to moral hazard and adverse selection

4. how an asset return reflects its cash income and its capital gain (loss)

5. how correlation of asset returns affects risk pooling

6. asset market efficiency

7. spot and forward markets

8. information products and network externalities

Every action today has a future outcome that is not certain. It is risky. When you start studying economics, you have only a rough idea of what is involved, and even less idea about how it will be used once the skill is acquired. This chapter examines how risk affects our actions, and how economic institutions have evolved to help us deal with the risky environment in which we live. The role of risk in our lives has been magnified by the recent credit crunch. A global economic crisis has been created by, in particular, the excessive risks taken by large international investors.

Some activities reduce risk, but others increase it. We spend billions of pounds on insurance, but also on the lottery and on risky assets in the stock market. People generally dislike risk and are prepared to pay to have their risks reduced. This explains the existence of many economic institutions that, at a price, allow people who dislike risk most to pass on their risks to others more willing or more able to bear them.

 12.1 Individual attitudes to risk

A risky activity has two characteristics: the likely outcome, and the degree of variation in the possible outcomes. Suppose you are offered a 50 per cent chance of making £100 and a 50 per cent chance of losing £100. On average, you make no money by taking such gambles.

In contrast, a 30 per cent chance of making £100 and a 70 per cent chance of losing £100 is an *unfair* gamble. On average, you lose money. With the probabilities of winning and losing reversed, the gamble would on average be profitable. The odds are then *favourable*.

Compare a gamble with a 50 per cent chance of making or losing £100 and a gamble with the same chances of winning or losing £500. Both are **fair gambles**, but the second is *riskier*. The range of possible outcomes is greater.

> A **fair gamble** on average yields zero monetary profit.

We turn now to individual tastes. Economists classify people as risk-averse, risk-neutral or risk-loving. The key issue is whether or not a person would accept a fair gamble. A **risk-neutral** person ignores the dispersion of possible outcomes, betting if and only if the odds on a monetary profit are favourable.

> A **risk-neutral** person is interested only in whether the odds yield a profit *on average*.
>
> A **risk-averse** person will refuse a fair gamble.
>
> A **risk-lover** bets even when the odds are unfavourable.

A **risk-averse** person may bet if the odds are very favourable. The probable monetary profit overcomes the inherent dislike of risk. The more risk-averse the individual, the more favourable must be the odds before he takes the bet.

The more **risk-loving** the individual, the more unfavourable must be the odds before the individual will not bet.

Insurance is the opposite of gambling. Suppose you own a £100 000 house. There is a 10 per cent chance it burns down by accident. You have a 90 per cent chance of continuing to have £100 000 but a 10 per cent chance of having nothing. Our risky world forces you to take this bet. On average, you end up with £90 000, which is 90 per cent of £100 000 plus 10 per cent of nothing.

An insurance company offers to insure the full value of your house for a premium of £15 000. Whether or not your house burns down, you pay the insurance company the £15 000 premium. It pays you £100 000 if it burns down. Whatever happens, you will end up with £85 000.

Would you insure? The insurance company is offering unfavourable odds, which is how it makes its money. Uninsured, on average you are worth £90 000, insured only £85 000. A risk-neutral person would not insure on these terms. The mathematical calculation in monetary terms says it is on average better to stand the risk of a fire. The risk-lover will also decline insurance. Not only are the odds poor, there is also the added enjoyment of standing the risk. But a person who is sufficiently risk-averse will accept the offer, happy to give up £5000 on average to avoid the possibility of catastrophe. Table 12.1 summarizes this discussion of attitudes to risk.

Diminishing marginal utility

Decisions about gambling or insurance depend on two considerations. First, there is the thrill of the activity. The thrill of a flutter on the Grand National is a pleasure, like seeing a good film. Having a lottery ticket provides excitement. In part it is pure entertainment. Gambling for fun is a legitimate form of consumption. We are prepared to pay for this modest form of entertainment. Unfair odds are the implicit price of our fun.

Table 12.1 Behaviour towards risk

Tastes	Betting	Insurance at unfair premium
Risk-averse	Needs favourable odds	May buy
Risk-neutral	Except at unfavourable odds	Won't buy
Risk-lover	Even if odds against	Won't buy

Such leisure activities form only a trivial part of the risk that we face in our everyday lives. This approach is unhelpful in thinking about the risk of our house burning down, or the risk a firm takes in building a new factory. These are not leisure pursuits. Serious money is at stake.

Suppose you are starving and broke. Getting £1000 would yield you a lot of utility or happiness, by allowing you some basic food. If you got another £1000, there are still things to spend it on that you really need. Clothes and shelter, for example. Having dealt with your immediate needs, the next £1000 is still helpful, but of less extra value than when you were desperate.

Thus, the marginal utility of the first £1000 is very high. You really needed it. The marginal utility of the next £1000 is not quite so high. As you get more, the marginal utility of the extra consumption tends to **diminish**.

> People's tastes exhibit a **diminishing marginal utility**. Successive equal rises in consumption quantities add less and less to total utility.

Of course, there are exceptions to this general rule. Some people *really* want a yacht, and their utility takes a huge jump when they can finally afford one. But most of us first spend our money on the things we most need, and get less and less extra satisfaction out of successive equal increases in our spending power.

You have £11 000 and are offered an equal chance of winning or losing £10 000. This is a fair bet in money terms since the average profit is £0. But it is not a fair bet in utility terms. Diminishing marginal utility implies that the extra utility you enjoy if the bet wins, taking your total wealth from £11 000 to £21 000, is much smaller than the utility you sacrifice if the bet loses, taking your wealth from £11 000 to £1000. You get a few extra luxuries with the £10 000 you might win, but you have to give up almost everything if you lose and have to survive on only £1000.

A risk-averse person declines a fair bet in money terms. The hypothesis of diminishing marginal utility implies that, except for the occasional gamble for pure entertainment, people should generally be risk-averse. They should refuse fair money gambles because they are not fair utility gambles. As we shall see, this story fits many of the facts.

Two implications of this analysis recur throughout the chapter. First, *risk-averse people devote resources to finding ways to reduce risk*. As the booming insurance industry confirms, people will pay to get out of some of the risks that the environment otherwise forces them to bear. Second, *individuals who take over the risk have to be rewarded for doing so*. Many economic activities consist of the more risk-averse bribing the less risk-averse to take over the risk.

CASE 12.1

Why play a losing game? The case of the National Lottery

The UK's original National Lottery game, first introduced in 1994, is based on drawing six balls without replacement from a stock of 49 balls. The odds on matching all six balls are about 1 in 14 million. Only 45 per cent of sales revenue is returned as prizes, worse odds than received by a blind punter at a horse race. Nevertheless, the National Lottery is very popular and represents an important source of revenue for the government. Moreover, the poorest 20 per cent of the population in the UK account for over a third of all spending on the National Lottery.

Why do many low-income people buy lottery tickets even though the return from them is so poor? Recent research has shown that poor people see playing the lottery as their best opportunity for improving their financial situation, albeit wrongly so. The hope of getting out of poverty encourages people to continue to buy tickets, even though their chances of stumbling upon a life-changing windfall are nearly impossibly slim and buying lottery tickets in fact exacerbates the very poverty that purchasers are hoping to escape. In practice, lottery tickets are an *inferior good*.

According to this research, lotteries set off a vicious cycle that not only exploits low-income individuals' desire to escape poverty but also directly prevents them from improving upon their financial situation. This raises concern on behalf of the government that it should try to explore strategies that balance the economic burdens faced by low-income households with the need to maintain important funding streams.

Source: Haisley, E. et al. (2008) Subjective relative income and lottery ticket purchases, *Journal of Behavioral Decision Making*, 21 (3): 283–295.

Picture: © Sean Gladwell | Dreamstime.com

12.2 Insurance and risk

A farmer and an actress have risky incomes. Each gets 10 in a good month, 0 in a bad month. But the risks are *independent*. Whether the farmer has a good month is not connected to whether the actress has a good month. Individually, their incomes are very risky. Collectively, they are less so.

In Table 12.2 they *pool* their incomes and their risk, each getting half of their joint income. If they both have a good month (top left entry) or both have a bad month (bottom right entry), the pooling arrangement makes no difference. They each get what they would have got on their own. In the other two cases, the success of one partner offsets the failure of the other. Together, their income is more *stable* than as individuals. If the farmer and the actress are risk-averse, they gain by pooling their risky incomes. If it were not so hard to set up such deals (lawyers' fees, the problem of cheating, tax problems), we would see more of them.

Pooling independent risks is the key to insurance. Suppose mortality tables show that on average 1 per cent of people aged 55 will die during the next year. Deaths result from heart disease, cancer, road accidents and other causes, in predictable proportions.

Now randomly choose any 100 people aged 55 knowing nothing about their health. Throughout the nation, 1 per cent of such people will die in the next year. In our sample of 100 people, it could be 0, 1 or 2 per cent, or even more. The larger the sample, the more likely it is that around 1 per cent will die in the next year. With 1 million 55-year-olds we could be pretty confident that around 10 000 will die, though we could not of course say which ones. By putting together more and more people we reduce the risk or dispersion of the aggregate outcome.[1]

Table 12.2 Risk-pooling of incomes: sharing joint incomes

	Farmer	
Actress	Good month, 10	Bad month, 0
Good month, 10	10	5
Bad month, 0	5	0

---

1 This is 'law of large numbers'. Proof of this law can be found in most statistics textbooks.

Life assurance companies take in premium payments in exchange for a promise to pay a large amount to the family if the insured person dies. The company can make this promise with great certainty because it pools risks over many clients. Since the company cannot guarantee that exactly 1 per cent of its many 55-year-olds will die in any one year, there is a small element of residual risk for the company to bear, and it makes a small charge for this in calculating its premiums. However, the company's ability to pool the risk means that it will make only a small charge. If life assurance companies try to charge more, new entrants join the industry knowing that the profits more than compensate for the small residual risk to be borne.

Risk pooling does not work when all individuals face the same risk. Suppose there is a 10 per cent risk of a nuclear war in Europe in the next ten years. If it happens, everyone in Europe dies, leaving money to their nearest surviving relative in the rest of the world. Ten million people in Western Europe offer to buy insurance from an American company.

> **Risk pooling** aggregates independent risks to make the aggregate more certain.

Despite the number of people, the risk cannot be pooled. If everybody in Europe dies, if anybody dies, the insurance company either pays out to everybody's relatives or it pays nothing. In the aggregate there is still a 10 per cent chance of having to pay out, just as individual Europeans face a 10 per cent chance of disaster. When the same thing happens to everybody, if it happens at all, the aggregate behaves like the individual. There is no risk reduction from pooling.

Many insurance companies do not insure against what they call 'acts of God' – floods, earthquakes, epidemics. Such disasters are no more natural or unnatural than a heart attack. But they affect large numbers of the insurance company's clients if they happen at all. The risk cannot be reduced by pooling. Companies cannot quote the low premium rates that apply for heart attacks, where risks are independent and the aggregate outcome is fairly certain.

There is another way to reduce the cost of risk bearing. This is known as **risk sharing**, and the most famous example is the Lloyd's insurance market in London. Risk sharing is necessary when it has proved impossible to reduce the risk by pooling. Lloyd's offers insurance on earthquakes in California, and insurance of a film star's legs.

> **Risk sharing** works by reducing the stake.

To understand risk sharing we return to diminishing marginal utility. We argued that the utility benefit from an extra £10 000 is less than the utility sacrificed when £10 000 is given up. However, this difference in marginal utility for equivalent monetary gains and losses is tiny if the size of the stake is tiny. The marginal utility from an extra £1 is only fractionally less than the utility lost by sacrificing £1. For small stakes, people are almost risk-neutral. You would probably toss a coin with us to win or lose £0.10, but not to win or lose £10 000. The larger the stake, the more diminishing marginal utility bites.

You go to Lloyd's to insure the US space shuttle launch for £20 billion – a big risk. Only part of this risk can be pooled as part of a larger portfolio of risks. It is too big for anyone to take on at a reasonable premium.

The Lloyd's market in London has hundreds of 'syndicates', each a group of 20 or so individuals who have each put up £100 000. Each syndicate takes perhaps 1 per cent of the £20 billion deal and then resells the risk to yet other people in the insurance industry. By the time the deal has been subdivided and subdivided again, each syndicate or insurance company holds a tiny share of the total. And each syndicate risk is further subdivided among its 20 members. The risk is shared out until each individual's stake is so small that there is a tiny difference between the marginal utility from a gain and the marginal loss of utility in the event of a disaster. It now takes only a small premium to cover this risk. The package can be sold to the client at a premium low enough to attract the business.

By pooling and sharing risks, insurance allows individuals to deal with many risks at affordable premiums. But two things inhibit the operation of insurance markets, reducing the extent to which individuals can use insurance to buy their way out of risky situations.

MATHS 12.1

Choice under uncertainty: expected utility of income and attitude to risk

We can describe an individual's attitude to risk using the concept of total utility of Income. This is a way to link the idea developed in Chapter 5 about consumer choice to the case of uncertainty.

Suppose that a consumer has an initial income of £5. He can invest his initial income in a stock asset today (assume that the stock today costs exactly £5). Next month the value of the stock can either increase or decrease. If it increases, then the consumer increases his income to £7.50. If the value of the stock decreases, the consumer ends up with an income of £2.50. Our consumer believes that there is a 50 per cent chance that the stock increases its value in the next month. The expected value from buying the stock asset is the probability weighted average of the value from each possible outcome: $EV = 0.5(£7.50) + 0.5(£2.50) = £5$. Buying the asset is, for our consumer, a *fair gamble*; on average, he does not gain or lose. Should the consumer buy the stock asset?

The answer depends on our consumer's attitude to risk. To understand preferences in relation to risk, we introduce the idea of utility of income for our consumer.

The consumer obtains utility from income.[2] Suppose that his utility of income is such that he obtains 120 in terms of utility if his income is £5, while he gets a utility of 150 if his income is £7.50 and a utility of 50 if his income is £2.50. More formally, we can write his utility as a function of income as: $U(£5) = 120$, $U(£7.50) = 150$ and $U(£2.50) = 50$. What is the expected utility level for the uncertain event faced by the consumer? The *expected utility* is the probability weighted average of the utility from each possible outcome. The expected utility of buying the stock is:

$$EU = 0.5[U(£7.50)] + 0.5[U(£2.50)] = 0.5(150) + 0.5(50) = 100$$

where *EU* denotes expected utility. For our consumer, the expected utility from buying the asset (100) is lower than the utility of not buying the asset and keeping £5 in his pocket with certainty (120). This implies that our consumer *prefers* having £5 with certainty (not buying the stock asset) to buying the asset, even if the asset gives him the same income on average. He does not like to take the risk. In this case, we say that our consumer is *risk-averse*. If we plot the total utility of income for a risk-averse consumer, the graph looks like the one in the following figure.

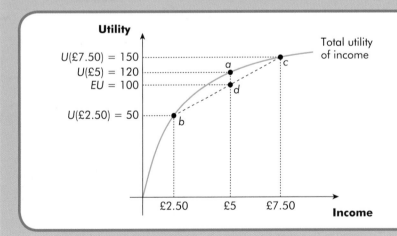

The utility of having £5 with certainty (point *a*) is higher than the expected utility from buying the asset (point *d*). The consumer is risk-averse. Point *d* lies on the chord connecting points *b* and *c*. This is because expected utility is given by: $EU = 0.5U(£2.50) + 0.5U(£7.50)$. Point *b* is associated with $U(£2.50)$, while point *c* is associated with $U(£7.50)$.

---

2   In Chapter 5 we discussed the case in which utility depends only on consumption. Here you can consider the case where utility depends on income, since income is ultimately used for consumption. Notice that in Chapter 5 utility was ordinal. Here, instead, utility of income is cardinal (see the Appendix to Chapter 5).

The utility from having £5 with certainty is point *a*, which is above point *d*, which represents the expected utility from buying the asset. Our consumer will not buy the asset in this case. The utility of income displayed in the figure has the property of diminishing marginal utility of income. As income increases, total utility increases by less and less.

A consumer who is *risk-neutral* will have a total utility of income that will look like a straight line.

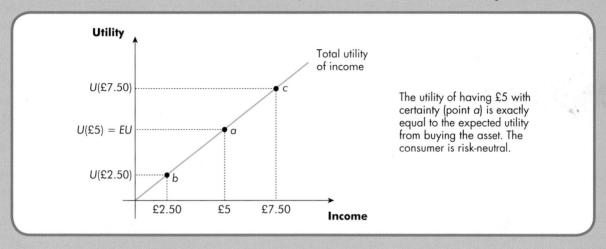

The utility of having £5 with certainty (point *a*) is exactly equal to the expected utility from buying the asset. The consumer is risk-neutral.

In the case of a consumer who is risk-neutral, the utility of having £5 with certainty is equal to the expected utility of buying the asset. Here, the consumer is indifferent between buying and not buying the asset. In the case of a risk-neutral consumer, his total utility of income displays constant marginal utility of income.

Finally, in the following figure we plot the utility of income for a *risk-loving* consumer.

A risk-lover prefers the fair gamble (in this case, buying the asset).

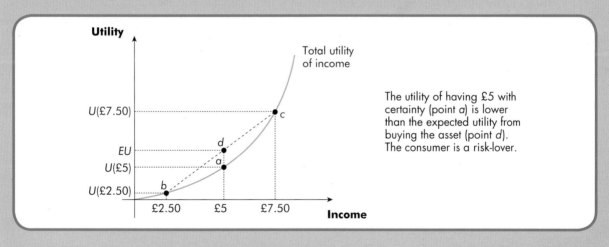

The utility of having £5 with certainty (point *a*) is lower than the expected utility from buying the asset (point *d*). The consumer is a risk-lover.

12.3 Asymmetric information

A concept that is related to risk and uncertainty is asymmetric information. Suppose you have a company and you want to hire a new worker. You would like to hire someone who is productive since you do not want to pay for a lazy worker. However, you do not know with certainty if the worker you are hiring is going to be productive or not. On the other hand, the worker knows himself and knows if he is productive or not. In this case, there is asymmetric information, since one party (the worker) has more information about an important characteristic of the transaction (his productivity) than the other party (you, as the owner of the company). Why is this related to risk and uncertainty?

You are uncertain about the productivity of the worker and in the case of them being unproductive you face the risk of paying someone who does not contribute to the profits of the company. The existence of asymmetric information creates the possibility of *opportunistic behaviour*: the informed individual benefits at the expense of the less-informed individual.

In the case of asymmetric information we distinguish between two possible cases:

1   *Moral hazard (or hidden action)*   In this case the uninformed agent cannot observe a particular *action* of the informed individual. For example, a worker may put little effort into performing his job if it is difficult for the employer to monitor him. The problem of moral hazard is also known as the *principal–agent problem*, where the principal is the name we give to the uninformed individual and the agent is the informed one.

2   *Adverse selection (or hidden information)*   This is the case where the uninformed individual does not know about an *unobservable characteristic* of the informed individual. For example, a person who wants to buy life insurance has more information about his own health than does the insurance company.

In the following sections we discuss the two cases in the context of the insurance market.

Moral hazard

Insurance companies calculate the statistical chances of particular events. They work out how many cars are stolen each year. Since different thefts are largely independent risks, we expect insurance firms to pool the risk over many clients and charge low premiums for car theft.

Sitting in a restaurant, you remember that your car is unlocked. Do you abandon your nice meal and rush outside to lock it? Not if you know the car is *fully* insured against theft. If the act of insuring changes the odds, then we have the problem of *moral hazard*. The informed individual (the insured) has an incentive to engage in risky behaviour; in this case, by not making the effort to minimize the chance of having his car stolen.

Statistical averages for the whole population, some of whom are uninsured and take greater care, are no longer a reliable guide to the risks the insurance company faces and the premiums it should charge. Moral hazard makes it harder to get insurance and more expensive when you do get it.

Insurance companies insure your car or house only up to a certain percentage of its replacement cost. They take over a big part of the risk, but you are worse off if the bad thing happens. The company gives you an incentive to minimize the chance of the bad thing happening. By limiting moral hazard, the insurance company pays out less frequently and can charge a lower premium.

CASE 12.2

Why are CEOs paid so much?

The compensation received by chief executive officers (CEOs) of large banks has featured prominently in the news in the past couple of years. As a result of the credit crunch some troubled large banks were rescued using taxpayers' money. Nevertheless, those large banks continued to provide large bonuses to their CEOs. US President Barak Obama once described such large bonuses as 'shameful' and the public appears outraged each time one is announced in the news.

Executive compensation is a classic moral hazard or principal–agent problem. The principals (the shareholders) need to structure rewards for agents (managers) so that they make decisions that are in the long-term interests of the principals when the strategies of the agents are hardly discernible.

Lots of research shows that the best way to align interests is to give managers significant stakes in the future value of the company they are running, in the form of restricted stock and option grants. The problem with the current bonus system is that it rewards short-term targets at the cost of jeopardizing long-run objectives.

Clementi and Cooley (2009) compared the compensation of Wall Street CEOs in the finance, insurance and real-estate sector (FIRE) with pay packages in other sectors. There are two features that stand out. First, executives in the FIRE sector really do make considerably more than their counterparts in other industries. Second, CEOs in the FIRE sector tend to receive a larger part of their compensation as stock (usually restricted stock). In actuality, that structure helps wed executives' interests to those of shareholders.

Problems do, however, emerge when one looks at how companies compute and allocate their bonus pools. Normally, the pools are divided among participating employees according to how much each contributed to the success of the firm. The intent: to reward good past performance and motivate effort in the future.

But all too often the profits that determine the size of the bonus pool are based on trades that produce short-term returns from taking on more risk. For example, in many firms it was enough to book profits on the short-term difference between the yield on AAA-rated mortgage-related securities and the internal cost of funds. This seemed like free money at the time – until these securities turned out to be extremely toxic. Bonuses were based on assets that were not correctly assessed and on profits that were not real. As it turns out, it is not actually possible to tell what 'profits' are, except over a longer time horizon.

Source: Adapted from: Clementi, G. C. and Cooley, T. F. (2009) Are CEOs paid too much? How to fix Wall Street's bonus system, *Newsweek*, 5 March (http://www.newsweek.com/id/187632).

Adverse selection

Some people smoke cigarettes but others do not. People who smoke reduce their life expectancy. Individuals know whether they themselves smoke, but suppose the insurance company cannot tell the difference and must charge all clients the same premium rate for life assurance.

Suppose the premium is based on mortality rates for the nation as a whole. People who do not smoke know they have an above-average life expectancy and find the premium too expensive. Smokers know their life expectancy is low and realize that the premium is a bargain. Even though the insurance company cannot tell the difference between the two groups, it knows a premium based on the national average will attract only the high-risk people.

One solution is to assume that all clients smoke and charge the correspondingly high premium to all clients. Non-smokers cannot get insurance at what they believe is a reasonable price. They might pay for a medical examination to try to prove they are low-risk clients who should be charged a lower price. Medical examinations are now compulsory for many insurance contracts.

To check that you understand the difference between moral hazard and adverse selection, say which is which in the following examples. (1) A person with a fatal disease signs up for life insurance. (2) Reassured by the fact that he took out life assurance to protect his dependants, a person who has unexpectedly become depressed decides to commit suicide. (The first was adverse selection, the second moral hazard.)

Education and signalling

In Chapter 10 (Case 10.3) we showed that higher education pays off in terms of future earnings. This represents a good reason why students want to invest in degrees. An alternative theory that explains why individuals want to invest in education is the theory of *signalling*. This theory says it could be rational to invest in costly education *even if education adds nothing directly to a worker's marginal product*.

The theory assumes that people are born with different innate ability. Some people are good at most things, other people are less smart and less productive. Not all smart people have blue eyes. The problem for firms is to tell which applicants are the smart ones with high productivity. Looking at their eyes is not enough. There is a problem of asymmetric information.

Suppose higher education contributes nothing to productivity. Signalling theory says that, in going on to higher education, people who know that they are smart send a signal to firms that they are the high-productivity workers of the future. Higher education *screens out* the smart high-productivity workers.[3] Firms can pay university graduates more because they know that they are the high-ability workers.

To be effective, the screening process must separate the high-ability workers from the others. Why don't lower-ability workers go to university and fool firms into offering them high wages? Lower-ability workers could not be confident of passing the necessary exams. If studying adds to productivity, firms should offer higher wages to people who *attend* university, whether or not they pass the final exams. If university screens out the good people, firms will care not about attendance but *academic performance*.

Some firms hire university students before they sit their final exams. Is this evidence refuting signalling theory? Not necessarily. Screening works in a second way. Since most people know their own ability, firms may take it on trust that people who have stuck it out until their final year at university believe themselves to be at the high end of the ability range.

It seems probable that education (even at the highest level) contributes something to productivity. But there may also be an element of screening. Engineering, law and business degrees presumably contribute more to productivity than philosophy, history or medieval French.

12.4   Uncertainty and asset returns

There are many ways to carry wealth from the present to the future. People can hold money, government bills or bonds, company shares, housing, gold, and so on. We now compare the rates of return on shares and Treasury bills, two particular ways of holding wealth.

Treasury bills are issued usually for a period of three months. The Treasury sells a bill for, say, £99 and simultaneously promises to buy back the bill for £100 in three months' time. People who buy the bill, and later resell it to the government, earn around 1 per cent on their money in three months. By reinvesting the proceeds to buy three more bills in the course of the year, they will earn around 4 per cent a year. Each time an individual buys a bill, the implicit nominal interest rate over the three-month period is known for certain since the government has guaranteed the price at which the bill will be repurchased.

The *real return* is the nominal return minus the inflation rate over the period the bill is held. People have a pretty good idea about what inflation is *likely* to be in the next three months. The real return on Treasury bills is not very risky.

---

3   Screening is the process of learning inside information by observing differences in behaviour.

Table 12.3 Average annual real rates of return, 1900–2005 (% per annum)

	2005	1985–2005	1900–2005
Equities	18.9	5.0	5.2
Gilts	6.0	5.6	1.2
Short-term liquid assets	2.7	2.9	1.0

Source: Barclays Capital, *Equity Gilt Study*.

Company shares offer a return in two different ways. If a share is bought at a low price and later sold at a high price, this contributes to the return earned while holding the share. The *rate of return* is the return as a percentage of the money initially invested. Hence

$$\text{Rate of return} = \frac{[\text{dividend} + \text{capital gain}]}{\text{initial purchase price}}$$

To compute the real rate of return, we subtract the inflation rate from the nominal rate of return. For 1900–2005, Table 12.3 compares the average annual real rate of return on company shares (equities) with that on government bonds (gilts) and on short-term assets, such as Treasury bills or interest-bearing liquid loans, and on company shares in the UK during 1900–2005. It shows that, on average, equities yield substantially higher returns.

Dividends are the regular payments of profit to shareholders.

The **capital gain** (loss) is the rise (fall) in the share price while the share is held.

However, the real rate of return on company shares is much more variable than that on Treasury bills. The latter varied little, but the annual real return on shares was as high as 130 per cent during 1975 and as low as –70 per cent in 1974. There are many years when the real return on shares exceeded 20 per cent or fell below –10 per cent. Shares are much riskier than Treasury bills.[4] This larger risk is compensated *on average* by a higher return. Since the risk is big – people recently lost fortunes as shares in dotcom companies plummeted – it needs a large real return on average to induce people to take this risk.

CASE 12.3 Stock market volatility

The chart overleaf shows an index of corporate share prices, the Financial Times Stock Exchange (FTSE) index of 100 top companies from 1996 and 2010. The graph shows that, even for a broad average over 100 individual companies, the index showed many variations over time. Between 1996 and 2000, the index showed an upward trend. In the period 2001–03 the index moved downwards. This downward trend was created by the 11 September terrorist attack in New York and the bursting of the dotcom 'bubble'. After 2003 the FTSE index started improving, and then came the credit crunch.

The returns from the shares of the companies in the index have varied quite a lot over the last 14 years. In those years inflation in the UK was low and stable, thus implying that *real returns* were very volatile.

---

4 Large positive or negative returns on shares were probably not forecast by the market. If people had foreseen a real return of 30 per cent they would have bought shares earlier, bidding up share prices earlier. If large capital losses had been foreseen, share prices would already have been lower, as people tried to dump these shares before they fell.

Why such wild swings? Largely because the market is having to extrapolate current information to make guesses about the entire stream of future earnings of these companies. In volatile sectors, small changes in current information can lead to rapid reassessments about future earnings. Since the share price embodies the future earnings that a company will earn, share prices can change dramatically when uncertainty about a sector is great.

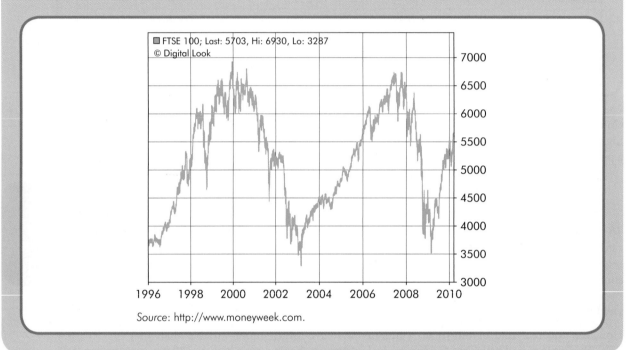

Source: http://www.moneyweek.com.

Shares are riskier for two reasons. First, nobody is sure what dividend the firm will pay. It depends what profit the firm makes and how confident it is about the future. When firms anticipate tough times, they cut dividends in order to keep a contingency reserve within the firm.

Second, views about the likely capital gains change radically. Stock market investors paid high prices for dotcom companies in the late 1990s, even though profits were still years away. People thought the present value of distant dividends was big. Discounting reduces the value of future dividends, but people were projecting spectacular growth and eventually huge dividends. Growth projections were slashed as reality crept in, and estimated present values changed a lot. Share prices in Amazon and Yahoo! fell by 80 per cent or more during 2000–01. Case 12.3 gives details over a longer period. Thus, revisions in belief about capital gains are what cause volatile share prices and share returns.

 ## 12.5 Portfolio selection

The *portfolio* of a financial investor is the bundle of financial and real assets – bank deposits, Treasury bills, government bonds, shares in industrial companies, gold, works of art – in which wealth is held. How does a risk-averse investor select his portfolio or wealth composition?

Chapter 5 set out the basic model of consumer choice. The budget line summarized the market opportunities – the goods that a given income would buy. Indifference curves showed individual tastes, and the consumer chose the bundle on the highest possible indifference curve given the budget constraint describing which bundles were affordable.

We use the same approach for the choice of a portfolio. Instead of a choice between different goods, we now focus on the choice between the average or expected return on the portfolio and the risk that the portfolio embodies.

The risk–return choice

Tastes

The risk-averse consumer (or financial investor) prefers a higher average return on the portfolio but dislikes higher risk. To take more risk, he needs to think he will get a higher average return. By 'risk' we mean the variability of returns on the *whole portfolio*. From the previous section, we know that a portfolio composed exclusively of industrial shares is much riskier than a portfolio composed only of Treasury bills.

Opportunities

To highlight the problem of portfolio selection, assume there are only two assets in which to invest. Bank deposits are quite a safe asset. Their return is predictable. The other asset is company shares, which are much riskier since their return is more variable.

The investor has a given amount of money to invest. Putting it all in bank deposits, the whole portfolio would earn a small but riskless return. The higher the fraction of the portfolio held in shares, the larger the average return on the whole portfolio but the greater its risk.

Portfolio choice

A very risk-averse investor will put the whole portfolio into the safe asset. To consider buying the risky asset, he must believe the average return on the risky asset is much higher than on the safe asset. Suppose this is the case. How much of the portfolio will he put into the risky asset? Generally, the fraction of the portfolio held in the risky asset will be higher (1) the higher the average return on the risky asset compared with the safe asset, (2) the less risky is the risky asset, and (3) the less risk-averse is the investor.

Diversification

When there are several risky assets the investor may be able to reduce the risk on the whole portfolio *without* having to accept a lower average return on the portfolio. We illustrate using Table 12.4, whose structure resembles the problem of the actress and the farmer in Table 12.2. There are two risky assets: oil shares and bank shares. Each has two possible returns: £4 if things go well and £2 if things go badly. Each industry has a 50 per cent chance of good times and a 50 per cent chance of bad times. Finally, we assume that returns in the two industries are independent. Good times in the oil industry tell us nothing about whether the banking industry is having good or bad times.

You have £2 to invest, and oil and bank shares each cost £1. Which portfolio gives the best risk–return combination? A bank share and an oil share have the same risk and expected return. You are indifferent between buying only oil shares and buying only bank shares. But a superior strategy is to buy one of each and *diversify* the portfolio.

Diversification means not putting all your eggs in one basket. If you put your eggs in one basket, buying, say, two oil shares for your £2, you have a 50 per cent chance of earning £8 and a 50 per cent chance of earning £4. It depends on whether the oil industry has good times or bad times. The average return is £6, but the actual return will either be £4 or £8.

> **Diversification** pools risk across several assets whose individual returns behave differently from one another.

Table 12.4 shows a diversified portfolio with one bank share and one oil share. If both industries do well, you will make £8, but this is only a 25 per cent chance. There is a 50 per cent chance of oil doing well; since

TOWER HAMLETS COLLEGE
Learning Centre
Poplar High Street
LONDON
E14 0AF

Table 12.4 A diversified portfolio

Oil	Banking	
	Good	Bad
Good	£8	£6
Bad	£6	£4

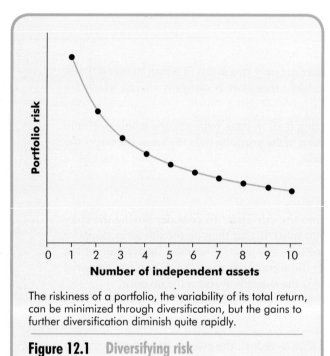

The riskiness of a portfolio, the variability of its total return, can be minimized through diversification, but the gains to further diversification diminish quite rapidly.

Figure 12.1 Diversifying risk

returns in the two industries are independent, on only half of those occasions will banking also be doing well. Similarly, there is a 25 per cent chance of both industries doing badly at the same time. There is also a 25 per cent chance that one industry does well while the other one does badly. Each of the four portfolio returns shown in Table 12.4 is a 25 per cent chance.

The average return on the portfolio is still £6, as if you put your £2 in one basket, but the variability of returns is smaller. Instead of a 50/50 chance of £4 or £8, you now have only a 25 per cent chance of each extreme, and a 50 per cent chance of earning the average return of £6.

Diversification reduces the risk by pooling it without altering the average rate of return. It offers you a better deal. As in our earlier discussion of risk-pooling by insurance companies, the greater the number of risky assets with independent returns across which the portfolio pools the risk, the lower will be the total risk of the portfolio.

Figure 12.1 shows the typical relationship between total portfolio risk and the number of independent assets in the portfolio. Portfolio risk declines as the number of independent risky assets is increased. However, most of the risk reduction through diversification comes very quickly. Even a few assets cut the total risk a lot. Your car has one spare tyre, not five.

Because it is more expensive to buy in small quantities, small investors typically hold a dozen different shares rather than a hundred. They get most of the benefit of diversifying without needing lots of small packages of shares. People who are more risk-averse and want a large number of shares can buy shares in a mutual fund or unit trust, a professional fund that buys large quantities of shares in many firms, and then retails stakes in the fund to small investors.

Diversification when asset returns are correlated

Risk pooling works because asset returns are independent of each other. When asset returns move together, we say that they are *correlated*. When returns on two assets tend to move in the same direction we say they are *positively correlated*. For example, a boom in the whole economy will tend to be good for bank shares and shares in TV companies. If returns tend to move in opposite directions, we say they are *negatively correlated*. For example, if people buy gold shares during financial crises, gold shares will tend to rise when other shares are falling, and vice versa.

Positive and negative correlations affect the way in which diversification changes risk. Suppose bank shares and oil shares always rise or fall together. Buying one of each is like putting all your money in either share. Diversification achieves nothing. When returns are perfectly positively correlated, risk pooling does not work, just as it fails for 'acts of God' in the insurance industry.

Conversely, diversification is a spectacular success when returns are negatively correlated. Suppose bank shares do well only when gold shares do badly, and vice versa. Buying one of each, you earn either £4 from oil and £2 from gold or £2 from oil and £4 from gold. With the diversified portfolio, you earn £6 for certain. You have diversified away all the risk, even though each share is individually risky.

In practice, returns on different shares are never perfectly correlated. Some *tend* to vary together and some *tend* to vary in opposite directions, but over any particular period actual returns on two shares may not exhibit their usual correlation. Thus it is impossible to completely diversify away all portfolio risk. But smart fund managers are always on the lookout for an asset that tends to have a negative correlation with the assets in the existing portfolio. On average, extending the portfolio to include that asset will improve the risk–return characteristics of the portfolio.

Beta

> **Beta** measures how much an asset's return moves with the return on the whole stock market.

Table 12.5 gives some examples. The first row shows returns on the market as a whole in booms, normal times and slumps. A share with beta = 1 moves the same way as the whole market. A high beta share does even better when the market is up, even worse when the market is down. A low beta share moves in the same general direction as the market but more sluggishly than the market. Negative beta shares move against the market.

Most shares move pretty much with the market and have a beta close to unity. There are not too many negative beta shares, but some gold shares have betas close to zero. Most people should have some gold shares in their portfolios.

Bankers and stockbrokers calculate betas from the past behaviour of individual shares and the whole stock market. Ideally, they are looking for negative beta shares that greatly reduce the risk of a portfolio whose other components vary with the market as a whole. Even low beta shares are partly independent of the rest of the market and allow some risk to be pooled. High beta shares are undesirable. Including them in the portfolio adds to its total risk.

A share with a low (or even negative) beta will be in high demand. Risk-averse purchasers are anxious to buy low beta shares whose inclusion in their portfolios reduces the total portfolio risk. High demand bids up the share price and reduces the average return: since it costs more to buy the shares, people get fewer per pound invested. However, investors are happy to trade off a lower return for the fact that low beta shares reduce the total risk of their portfolios.

In stock market equilibrium, low beta shares have high prices and low rates of return on average. Conversely, high beta shares add to investors' portfolio risk and are purchased only because they have low prices and

Table 12.5 Share returns and beta

Asset	Return (%)		
	Boom	Normal	Slump
Whole market	14	6	22
High beta	20	10	28
Beta = 1	14	6	22
Low beta	5	4	3
Negative beta	2	3	5

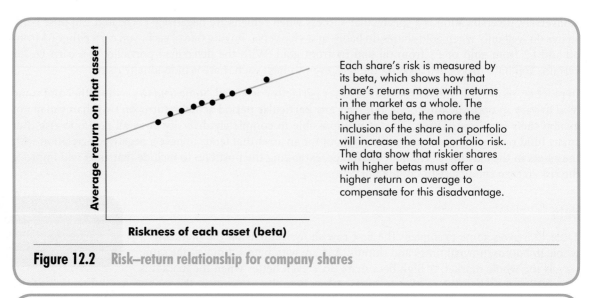

Figure 12.2 Risk–return relationship for company shares

Table 12.6 Beta for selected sectors

Retailing	0.96	Media	1.2
Cosmetics	0.66	Defence	1.14
Banks	1.27	Paper	0.99
Chemicals	0.81	Mining	1.19
Energy	0.82	Textiles	0.27
Brewing	0.66	Personal products	0.63
Tobacco	0.59	Clothing	0.71

Source: Risk Management Services, 2003.

on average offer high rates of return that compensate for their undesirable risk characteristics. Figure 12.2 shows the results of a pioneering study by Professors Black, Jensen and Scholes[5] using stock market data from 1931 to 1965. Average returns on individual shares rise steadily with the shares' beta as the theory predicts. Table 12.6 shows recent estimates of beta for selected sectors of the FTSE index.

To sum up, individual share prices depend both on expected or average returns and on risk characteristics. The risk characteristics of a firm's shares determine the expected return its shares must offer to compete with other shares. For a given required return, higher anticipated income (dividends or capital gains) means a higher current share price.

The riskiness of a firm's shares refers not to variability of the share's return in isolation from the rest of the market. This is why beta matters. Adding a risky asset to the portfolio reduces the risk of the portfolio provided the share's beta is less than 1. Low beta shares can be individually risky; nevertheless, taken with other shares they reduce portfolio risk and are therefore desirable. Low beta shares have an above-average price and a below-average rate of return to offset this advantage; high beta shares must offer an above-average expected return to be competitive.

---

5 Black, F., Jensen, M. C. and Scholes, M. (1972) The capital asset pricing model: some empirical tests, in M. C. Jensen (ed.), *Studies in the Theory of Capital Markets*, Praeger, pp. 79–121.

Beta in action

ACTIVITY 12.1

The table below shows three possible outcomes – boom, slump and normal times – and three possible assets – the FTSE index, an asset with negative beta that moves against the general stock market trend, and a high beta asset that moves in the same direction as the stock market but even more so.

Outcome	Asset price			Portfolio value		
	(a) FTSE index	(b) Low beta asset	(c) High beta asset	A ½ of (a) + ½ of (b)	B ⅓ of (a) + ⅔ of (b)	C ½% of (a) + ½ of (c)
Boom	120	90	150			
Normal	100	100	100			
Slump	80	110	50			

Question

(a) Complete the table by showing for each outcome (boom, normal, slump) the level of portfolios A, B and C, respectively (for example in portfolio A, half your money is invested in the FTSE index and half in the low beta asset).

To check your answers to this question, go to page 684.

Diversification in other situations

Risk is all around us, and diversification happens all the time. Countries diversify their sources of raw materials, otherwise, if anything disrupts the sole supplier's ability or willingness to sell, the country may face a disaster. Similarly, a farmer is reluctant to rely on a single crop. It may be better for a navy to have two small aircraft carriers than one large one. If the only aircraft carrier sinks, there is no air cover.

12.6 Efficient asset markets

There are two basic images of the stock market. One is that of a casino, without any rational basis for speculation; it is all a matter of luck. The other view – the theory of *efficient markets* – is that the stock market is a sensitive processor of information, quickly responding to new information to adjust share prices correctly.

> An **efficient asset market** already incorporates existing information properly in asset prices.

The second view recognizes that share prices fluctuate a lot but argues that these fluctuations are the appropriate response to new information as it becomes available.

Companies with high average returns and low betas should be valued both by society and by the stock market. The higher the share price, the more money a company raises from a new share issue, and the more likely is the company to invest in plant and machinery financed by this new share issue. High share prices are guiding the right firms to invest. Companies with low average returns and high betas are valued neither by financial investors nor by society. Low share prices make it harder for them to finance new plant and equipment, and they will tend to contract.

It matters which of the two views of the stock market is correct. If share prices correctly reflect prospective dividends and risk characteristics – the efficient market view – a free market in industrial shares is guiding society's scarce resources towards the right firms. But if share prices are purely pot luck, as in a casino, the wrong firms may expand just because their share prices are high.

Testing for efficiency

Suppose everybody has all the information available today about the likely risks and returns on different shares. Equilibrium share prices should equate the likely return on all shares with the same risk characteristics. Otherwise there would be an obvious opportunity to switch from the low return shares to higher return shares with equivalent risk characteristics. If the market has got it right, it does not matter which share you buy in any risk class. They are all expected to yield the same return. The efficient market view says there is no way of beating the market to earn an above-average return on a share of a given risk class.

If the market neglects some available information, you could use this information to beat the market. If the market failed to spot that hot weather increases ice cream sales, it would never mark up share prices in ice cream companies when good weather occurred. By buying ice cream shares when the sun shone you would make money and beat the market. The market would be surprised by high dividends from ice cream companies. But you bought them, having figured all this out by using extra information. You knew ice cream shares would pay a higher rate of return than the market thought. You spotted an inefficiency in the market.

In contrast, the efficient market view says all the relevant available information is immediately incorporated in the share price. Given the long-range weather forecast, the market makes the best guess about profits and dividends in the ice cream industry and sets the current price to give the required rate of return for shares with the same risk characteristics as ice cream shares. If the weather forecast is correct, the return will be as predicted. If there is an unexpected hot spell, the market will immediately mark up ice cream shares to reflect the new information that ice cream profits will be higher than previously expected. How high are ice cream shares marked up? To the price that reduces the expected rate of return back to the average for that risk class.

The crucial implication of the efficient market theory is that asset prices correctly reflect all existing information. It is unforeseen new information that changes share prices as the market quickly incorporates this unanticipated development to restore expected returns to the required level. Existing information cannot systematically be used to get above-average returns for that risk class of asset.

The theory of efficient markets has been tested extensively to see whether there is any *currently available* information that would allow an investor systematically to earn an above-average return for that risk class. The vast majority of all empirical studies conclude that there is no readily available information that the market neglects. Rules of the form 'buy shares when the price has risen two days in a row' do not work. Nor do rules that use existing information about how the economy or the industry is doing. Smart investors have taken this information on board as it became available. It is already in the price.

The empirical literature usually concludes that you may as well stick a pin in the financial pages of a newspaper as employ an expensive financial adviser. Paradoxically, it is because the market has *already* used all the relevant economic information correctly that there are no bargains around. The theory of efficient markets does not say share prices and returns are unaffected by economics; it says that, because the economics has been correctly used to set the price, there are no easy pickings left.

Financial newspapers and stock market institutions run competitions for the investor of the year. If the theory of efficient markets is right, why do some portfolios do better than others? Why, indeed, are financial portfolio advisers in business at all? The world is uncertain, and there will always be surprises that could not have been forecast. As this new information is incorporated in share prices, some lucky investors will find they happen to have already invested in shares whose price has unexpectedly risen. Others are unlucky, holding shares whose price unexpectedly falls.

Behavioural finance

Behavioural finance is the study of the influence of psychology on the behaviour of financial practitioners and the subsequent effect on markets.

'People make barmy decisions about the future. The evidence is all around, from their investments in the stockmarkets to the way their run their businesses. In fact, people are consistently bad at dealing with uncertainty, underestimating some kinds of risk and overestimating others.

Daniel Kahneman, now a professor at Princeton, noticed as a young research psychologist in the 1960s that the logic of decision science was hard for people to accept. [. . .] In the past decade the fields of behavioural finance and behavioural economics have blossomed, and in 2002 Mr Kahneman shared a Nobel prize in economics for his work.'

(*The Economist*, 22 January 2004)

So far, the economics that we have examined assumes that people are completely rational and that the cost of acquiring information is either free or can be modelled in simple ways. This leads to an incredibly powerful set of economic tools that help us understand many complicated situations. But it is not the whole story. Here is a glimpse of how we could complicate our analysis.

Suppose there is a fixed cost of either acquiring information or of taking the time to make a decision. This leads to 'bounded rationality'. It is no longer optimal to examine every possible decision in great detail – you would incur too many fixed costs – so instead you incur costs once, have a good think, and then come up with a simple decision rule that you implement automatically until it no longer fits the facts, at which point you incur some more thinking costs and try to improve your rule. Simple rules may explain why people extrapolate the recent past rather than conduct extensive research all the time.

Such behavioural rules are a large part of the concern of psychologists, who have conducted a lot of empirical research on how accurate these rules are. Often, people err in systematic ways, over time because they have not updated their old rules, and across people because they are using similar short cuts that are making the same mistake. For example, most people's optimism rises the longer the time horizon. Forty per cent of Americans think they will some day be in the top 1 per cent of income earners! Recently, economists have applied these ideas to financial markets, in the search for systematic mistakes in asset pricing.

One reason that economists have been sceptical about applications that make use of departures from full rationality is that there is only one way to be rational but a million ways in which to be irrational. Anyone can explain a particular event by invoking a particular kind of irrationality – it then takes a lot of data to establish whether there is anything systematic in this irrationality or whether it was just a coincidence invoked by someone trying to be wise after the event.

Thus one interpretation of why some investors do better than others is pure chance. This story could even explain why some investors have above-average returns for several years in a row. Even with a fair coin there is roughly one chance in a thousand of tossing ten consecutive heads. Even if there is no systematic way to beat the market, there are thousands of investors, and someone is going to have a lucky streak for ten years.

But there is also a more subtle interpretation. When a piece of new information first becomes available, someone has to decide *how* share prices should be adjusted. The price does not change by magic. And there is an incentive to be quick off the mark. The first person to get the information, or to calculate correctly where the market will soon be setting the price, may be able to buy a share just before everyone else catches on and the share's price rises.

The non-specialist investor cannot use *past* information to make above-average profits. But specialist investors, by reacting very quickly, can make capital gains or avoid capital losses within the first few hours of new information becoming available. It is their actions that help to change the price, and the profits that they make from fast dealing are what pay for City salaries. It is the economic return on their time and effort in gathering and processing information.

Speculative bubbles

Consider the market for gold. Unlike shares or bonds, gold pays no dividend or interest payment. Its return accrues entirely through the capital gain. Today's prices depend on the anticipated capital gain, which in turn depends on expectations of tomorrow's price. But tomorrow's price will depend on the capital gain then expected, which will depend on expectations of the price the day after; and so on.

In such markets there is no way for the *fundamentals*, the economic calculations about future dividends or interest payments, to influence the price. It all depends on what people today think people tomorrow will expect people the next day to expect. Such a market is vulnerable to *speculative bubbles*. If everyone believes the price will rise tomorrow, it makes sense to purchase the asset today. So long as people expect the price to keep rising, it makes sense to keep buying even though the price may already have risen a lot.

A famous example of a speculative bubble is the South Sea Bubble of 1720. A company was set up to sell British goods to people in the South Seas and to bring home the wonderful and exotic goods produced there. The shares were issued long before any attempt was made to actually trade these goods. It sounded a great idea and people bought the shares. The price rose quickly, and soon people were buying not in anticipation of eventual dividends but purely to resell the shares at a profit once the price had gone even higher. The price rose even faster, until one day it became apparent that the company's proposal was a fiasco with no chance of success and the bubble burst. Sir Isaac Newton lost £2000 (over half a million pounds at today's prices).

The great English economist John Maynard Keynes argued that the stock market is like a casino, dominated by short-term speculators who buy not in anticipation of future dividends but purely to resell at a quick profit. Since next period's share price depends on what people then think the following period's share price will be, Keynes compared the stock market to a beauty competition in a newspaper, where the winner is the reader who guesses the beauty receiving most votes from all readers. Share prices reflect what average opinion expects average opinion to be.

Undoubtedly, financial markets sometimes exhibit temporary bubbles. The overpricing of shares in dotcom companies was a recent example. Nevertheless, bubbles *are* usually temporary. Eventually it is obvious that the share price cannot be justified by fundamentals. Bubbles are less likely for assets whose income is mainly from dividends or interest rather than capital gains.

 12.7   ## More on risk

Risk is central to economic life. Every topic in this book could be extended to include risk. Individual applications differ, but two features recur: individuals try to find ways to reduce risk, and those who take over the bearing of risk have to be compensated for so doing.

Hedging and forward markets

> A **forward market** deals in contracts made today for delivery of goods at a specified future date at a price agreed today.
> A **spot market** deals in contracts for immediate delivery and payment.

There are **forward markets** for many commodities and assets, including corn, coffee, sugar, copper, gold and foreign currencies.

Suppose the current price of copper is £800 a tonne and people expect the price to rise to £880 a tonne after 12 months. Some people will hold copper in their portfolios. The expected capital gain is 10 per cent of the purchase price, and it may be interesting to diversify a portfolio by including copper. However, that is not our concern at present.

You own a copper mine and will have 1 tonne of copper to sell in 12 months' time. The **spot** price of copper is the price for immediate delivery. Today's spot price is £800 and people expect the spot price to be £880 at this time next year. One option is for you simply to sell your copper at the spot price at this time next year. You expect that to be £880 but you cannot be sure today what the price next year will actually be. It is risky.

Alternatively, you can **hedge** against this risk in the forward market for copper. Suppose today you can sell 1 tonne of copper for delivery in 12 months' time at a price of £860 agreed today. You have hedged against the risky future spot price. You know for certain what you will receive when your copper is available for delivery. But you have sold your copper for only £860, even though you expect copper then to sell for £880 on the spot market. You regard this as an insurance premium to remove the risk associated with the future spot price.

> **Hedging** is the use of forward markets to shift risk on to somebody else.

To whom do you sell your copper in the forward market? You sell it to a trader whom we can call a **speculator**. The speculator has no interest in 1 tonne of copper *per se*. But the speculator, having promised you £860 for copper to be delivered in one year's time, currently expects to resell that copper immediately it is delivered. The speculator expects to get £880 for that copper in the spot market next year. He expects to make £20 as compensation for bearing your risk. If spot copper prices turn out to be less than £860 next year, the speculator will lose money. £20 is the risk premium necessary to attract enough speculators into the forward market to take up the risky positions that hedgers wish to avoid.

> A **speculator** temporarily holds an asset in the hope of making a capital gain.

Someone buying spot copper today at £800 for possible resale next year at £880 must compare the expected capital gain of 10 per cent with returns and interest rates on offer in other assets. Copper must cover the opportunity cost of the returns that could have been earned by using this money elsewhere. The speculator in the forward market need not make this comparison. No money is currently tied up in the forward contract. Although the price has been agreed today at £860, the money is handed over only next year when the copper is delivered. Provided the speculator then resells in next year's spot market, no money is actually tied up. All the speculator has to think about is the likely spot price in 12 months' time and how much it could vary either side of this estimate. The riskier the future spot price, the larger premium the speculator will need and the more the current forward price will lie below the expected future spot price. All the information is summarized in Table 12.7.

This speculator had an open position, having taken forward delivery of copper without yet having a purchaser to whom to resell. However, other firms use copper as an input to production, and may wish to *buy* copper for delivery in 12 months' time at a price agreed today. They too wish to hedge against the risky future spot price. A speculator who can make two forward contracts, one to take delivery of copper from the copper miner, the other to sell copper to a copper user, does not have an open position. The speculator's book is balanced, without any residual risk. The risky future spot price is irrelevant.

In forward markets with roughly equal numbers of people wishing to hedge by buying and by selling, speculators' books roughly balance and residual risk is small. Speculators need only a little compensation to cover this residual risk and the administration costs. The current price of forward copper is close to the expected future spot price.

However, speculation is a risky business if buyers and sellers cannot be matched up in the forward market. In practice, the spot prices that subsequently transpire can vary by a large amount on either side of the estimate implicitly contained in the current forward price.

Why do forward markets exist for copper and silver but not for BMWs? The answer again is moral hazard and adverse selection. Suppose today you contract for delivery of a new car model in 12 months' time. You thought you were buying a luxury car, but the company brings out a low-quality car and says 'This is our new model'. By making all these forward contracts, the car maker affects its own quality incentives.

Table 12.7 Summary of the spot and forward market for copper

Today's spot price	Price of copper today for delivery and payment today	£800
Future spot price	Spot market price of copper in a year's time	£900
Expected future spot price	The best guess today about spot price in a year's time	£880
Forward price	Price today in forward market at which copper is being traded for delivery and payment in a year's time	£860
Risk premium	Expected future spot price minus the current forward price. The sum a hedger expects on average to lose by making a forward contract rather than by taking a chance on the future spot price. Hence, what the hedger expects to pay, and the speculator expects to make, by transferring the risk from hedger to speculator	£880 – £860 = £20

Forward markets do not exist for most goods because it is impossible to write legally binding and cheaply enforceable contracts that adequately specify the characteristics of the commodity being traded. Where forward markets exist they are for very standardized commodities – 18-carat gold, Japanese yen – that are easily defined. Forward markets are an important way in which individuals can reduce the risks they face, but there are only a limited number of risks that can be hedged in this way.

Compensating differentials in the return to labour

Since people are risk-averse, we expect those with risky jobs to earn more on average than people whose jobs are safe. Broadly speaking, this is confirmed by the facts. Divers who inspect North Sea oil pipelines earn high hourly rates because the death rate in this activity is high. University academics earn relatively low wages in the UK because many of them have secure jobs, unlike industrial managers who face the sack if their company has a bad spell.

Profits are often seen as a reward to entrepreneurs, individuals who set up and run firms, for taking big risks. The average person who starts a business works long hours for small rewards initially. In the early stages there is the continual threat of failure, and most small firms never get off the ground. The possibility of becoming a millionaire, like Richard Branson of Virgin or Bill Gates of Microsoft, is the carrot needed to persuade people to embark on this risky activity.

 ## 12.8 E-products

An **e-product** can be digitally encoded then transmitted rapidly, accurately and cheaply.

Information is relevant not only because it is related to uncertainty and risk. It is also related to an important and constantly growing economic sector.

A century ago, fortunes were made in railways, steel and oil. John D. Rockefeller (1839–1937), founder of Standard Oil, amassed a fortune worth $200 billion if

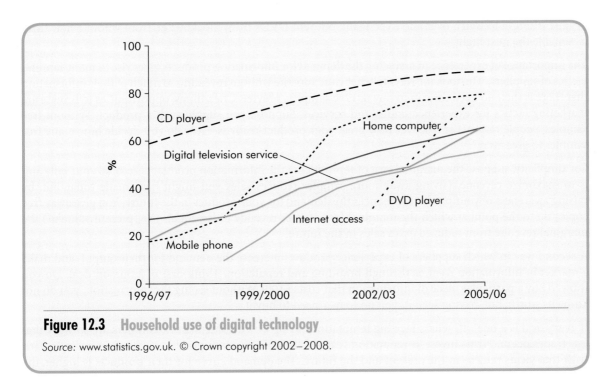

Figure 12.3 Household use of digital technology

Source: www.statistics.gov.uk. © Crown copyright 2002–2008.

valued at 2004 prices. Today, the richest people on the planet are in the information business. Bill Gates of Microsoft (www.microsoft.com) is currently worth about $55 billion. The information revolution is here. It is big business and it is changing people's lives.

Figure 12.3 shows the rapid rise in digital technology in UK households, for entertainment, communication and information. The same applies in the corporate world, where 93 per cent of UK businesses had information and communications technology by 2006 and 70 per cent had a website. UK sales over the internet – from last-minute plane tickets to used car sales – topped £100 billion for the first time in 2005. The use of email has led to a collapse in the use of letters and the sale of stamps.

Examples of e-products include music, films, magazines, news, books and sport. Information is expensive to assemble and produce but very cheap to distribute. The fixed cost of creating a usable product is large; the marginal cost of distributing it is tiny. This cost structure implies vast scale economies in production. We discuss the key attributes of information products as viewed by users. These users or consumers of information are not merely households but businesses themselves.

Consuming information

From the viewpoint of users, e-products have four key features: experience, overload, switching costs and network externalities.

Experience

Information is an **experience product**. The first time we try something we find out how useful it is to us. Most goods and services that we buy are repeat purchases. We no longer buy them just to find out what they are like. What is different about information is that it is nearly always new. If we already had the information, we would not need to buy it. We say 'nearly always' because we all have a DVD that we like to watch more than once. People buy DVDs of Manchester United's Champions'

> An **experience good or service** must be sampled before the user knows its value.

League triumph to watch over and over again, but rent DVDs from Blockbuster, from whom a new thrill is rentable the next night.

The importance of experience in assessing the demand for information products gives rise to many familiar tactics of suppliers, who look for ways to whet your appetite without revealing so much of their information that there is then no need for you to buy it. Free samples, previews, headlines, opportunities to browse are marketing tactics for experience goods and services. Suppose you supply such a product. Without free samples, people may never discover how great your product really is. How do you decide how many free samples to give away?

For simplicity, suppose the marginal cost of reproducing the information product is zero, so your only aim is to maximize revenue. Giving away more samples reduces sales you might have made today but, by raising awareness of your product, enhances the demand for your product in the future. You give away free copies up to the point at which the marginal loss of sales revenue today equals the (present value of) the marginal revenue from induced extra sales in the future.

A second way in which suppliers of experience products increase the demand for their output, and make a market in information itself, is through branding and reputation. Think first of a one-off deal. Do you want to buy a particular piece of information that costs £100? Without seeing the information, you do not know its worth; but, having seen it, you no longer need to buy it.

If every deal is a one-off, sellers face big temptations to rip off customers and customers are so wary that few trades occur. Firms invest in reputation (earned through previous good behaviour) in order to earn trust that yields returns in the present and the future. The demand curve for their products is higher, the better the reputation they have previously established.

Information overload

Information overload arises when the volume of available information is large but the cost of processing it is high. Screening devices are then very valuable.

Families with two Sunday newspapers rarely read the six sections in each paper. On the internet, the problem is compounded many times. There is so much information, it is hard to know where to start. Search is much easier after someone else narrows down your options. Rich people looking for a house do not spend weeks driving round Belgravia. They hire an agent to narrow things down, and look only at the agent's shortlist. Similarly, a firm seeking a new director often employs a specialist 'headhunter' to produce a shortlist of suitable candidates.

Just as the agent charges a fee for the screening service, suppliers of internet screening have a valuable product that they can sell. Search engines such as Yahoo! are among the most visited websites on the internet, and hence offer valuable opportunities to advertisers.

Pre-screening explains why makers of yachts advertise in yachting magazines not football club fanzines. The internet allows the yacht producer to target customers even more accurately. One reason why internet firms may supply services without charge is that their register of customers, with customers' permission, can be retailed not just to advertisers but also to others doing internet business. Similarly, the next time you buy a TV and complete your personal details on the 'free' guarantee form, remember that the guarantor is 'buying' information about TV customers – where they live, and what they spend. This information helps other businesses target their sales more accurately. It is a valuable commodity.

Switching costs

Switching costs arise when existing costs are sunk. Changing supplier then incurs extra costs.

Whereas compiling an ever-better customer database may provide a permanent reason to subsidize an information product, a second motive is strictly temporary. Suppliers may provide free services during an initial period to lock users into a particular supplier. Such users then face switching costs.

If Britain had to start from scratch, it might decide to drive not on the left but on the right. British cars would no longer be different from those in continental Europe. Car makers would find it much harder to charge British people premium prices for cars if similar cars were easily imported across the Channel. However, the UK has made many investments in driving on the left. Any switch would entail changing street signs and motorway slip roads, scrapping most of the existing stock of left-hand-drive cars, and teaching drivers to do things the other way round. During the transition there would be accidents and expense. Even though Britons would benefit from cheaper right-hand-drive cars, switching costs may be so high that it is better to leave things unaltered.

Table 12.8 Switching costs

	Supplier A	Supplier B
User benefit	£500	£700
Switching cost = £300		
Net benefit		
If began with A	£500	£400
If began with B	£200	£700

Similarly, the cost of switching out of nicotine dependence is large. Someone who has never smoked and someone smoking 20 cigarettes a day make different decisions. The past matters. So does the future. Switching costs force users and suppliers to take a long-run view in the first place. Do not start smoking on the assumption it is easy to quit. You get locked in.

Table 12.8 illustrates this. A service can be bought from supplier A or supplier B. The latter is now a better supplier. Its service yields a benefit (net of any charges to consumers) of £700. The former yields a benefit of only £500. Without any switching costs, everyone would use supplier B.

However, if switching costs are £300, people who began using supplier A will not switch. The gain is £200 but the cost is £300. So they stay with supplier A and get benefits of £400. People who began with supplier B are delighted to stay with that supplier and get benefits of £700.

Why did anyone start out with supplier A? Perhaps, previously, this supplier had offered a great deal that tempted some customers who believed that the good deal would last, or were too short-sighted to realize that a long-run decision was needed. In Table 12.8 it is best to interpret the benefits as present values of the benefits over all the future time that the user needs the service. It is the difference in these present values that must be compared with the one-off switching cost.

In Chapter 9 we distinguished innocent and strategic entry barriers, one made by nature, the other planned in boardrooms. Switching costs have both aspects. Smart suppliers devise strategies to lock in users. Air miles and reward points are obvious examples made possible by the information economy. Previously, it was too costly to keep track of individual retail customers.

Modern computing changed all that. Once individuals can be distinguished, they can be 'incentivized'. Reward points offer customers a small reward for staying with a particular supplier. The customer may care little whether he flies with BA or Virgin, or shops at Tesco or Sainsbury's, but to the airline or supermarket it makes a big difference. Yahoo! and Freeserve were initially free. Once you are familiar with their systems they can charge you for the same services in the future, just as leading football clubs used satellite TV to reach wide audiences but then set up their own pay-TV stations.

The information economy did not invent these practices but is pushing to the limit things done more crudely for years. For decades, high street banks have known that today's students are tomorrow's profitable customers. Banks compete for space on campus and offer students subsidized banking, relying on the later cost of switching banks to lock in the customer, offering a future opportunity to get back their original investment with interest. Banks could always distinguish between students and non-students. The information economy takes this principle to the limit, distinguishing between individual customers and working out when early subsidies earn later returns.

Network externalities

> A **network externality** arises when an additional network member conveys benefits to those already on the network.

From the user viewpoint, the final attribute of information products is that they have network externalities.

There is no point having a phone if nobody else has one, nor any reason to master Esperanto if this new language does not catch on. The fax was invented in 1843 and the first email was sent in 1969. It was not until other people adopted the technologies that they became popular.[6]

Figure 12.4 shows how usage affects demand for a product exhibiting network externalities. It parallels our discussion of costs in Chapter 7. There, we saw that firms have different cost curves in the short run and long run. Even when short-run cost curves are U-shaped, long-run average costs may fall for a long time, exhibiting scale economies in production. Producing more can lower average costs.

Network externalities give rise to a similar phenomenon on the demand side: cutting prices can boost demand a lot, especially in the long run. Figure 12.4 shows the initial short-run demand curve D_1D_1, the demand for the product for a *given* number of users already on the network. Suppose A is the point at which the number of people using the network is the same as in the previous period. There is no reason for the demand curve to shift.

Now, however, suppose the supplier cut the price and induced extra customers today, moving down the demand curve D_1D_1 from A to B. With more people on the network, the product is now more valuable to everyone and the demand curve shifts up next period to D_2D_2. At the price p_2, the quantity demanded then rises to q_2. Further reductions in the price will shift the short-run demand curve even further to the right. The long-run demand curve DD, formed by joining up points such as A and C, is more elastic than the short-run demand curve.

Even without switching costs, network externalities may justify a price subsidy – even free provision – early in the life of a product. The supplier is investing in enhancing the network. Once customers build up, the price can be raised.

Network externalities explain why users herd together, are slow to take up the new product and then cross over all at once. Even if you know email is wonderful, it is no use until your friends (and customers) are connected. When everyone thinks everyone else is ready, people all switch within a very short time.

These four characteristics – experience, overload, switching costs and network externalities – are key features of information products from the users' viewpoint. We turn now to the special features of costs, production and competition between suppliers.

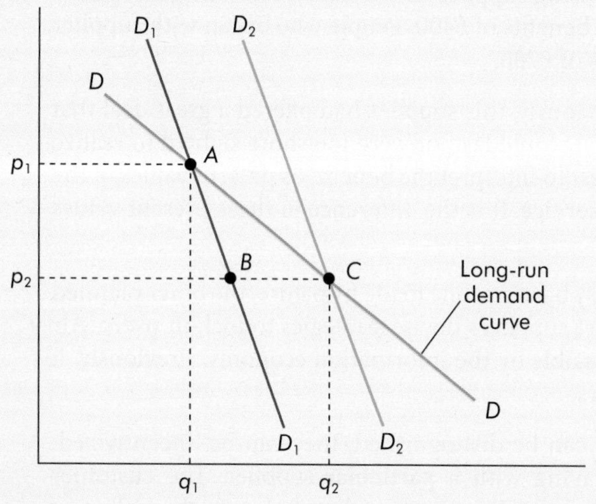

Each short-run demand curve reflects the number of people already using the network. Reducing the price from p_1 to p_2 not only causes a move from A to B it also induces a shift in demand curve since the network is more valuable. The long-run demand curve, joining points such as A and C, is more elastic.

Figure 12.4 A demand curve with network externalities

---

6   These, and many other, fascinating examples are quoted in Carl Shapiro and Hal Varian's *Information Rules* (Harvard University Press, 1999).

CASE 12.4	*Britannica* shelved

Serious parents used to purchase their children a bookshelf of *Encyclopaedia Britannica* (www.britannica.co.uk). This prestige reference work was the market leader for two centuries after its launch in 1768, despite commanding a premium price, which peaked at £1000. Annual sales reached £450 million in 1990. Since 1990, sales revenue has collapsed. The CD-ROM destroyed the printed encyclopaedia. The marginal cost of making a CD-ROM is about £1. The marginal cost of *Encyclopaedia Britannica* had been about £150 for the books, plus several hundred pounds in commission for the doorstep salesforce.

The first challenge came when Microsoft decided to produce software for an encyclopaedia, called Encarta, at a thirtieth of the price of *Britannica*. Encarta was not only cheaper but also easier to carry around. Being shorter, it fitted on a single CD-ROM. *Britannica* was not brought down by a new entrant to the 24-volume book business but by a new technology that changed the nature of the niche.

During the 1990s, Britannica gradually figured out how best to respond to Encarta's entry. It produced its own CD-ROM. The door-to-door salesforce got fired. Those using computers pay more attention to website advertising than doorstep sales patter. Britannica has tried to emphasize that; now with similar technology to Encarta, *Encyclopaedia Brittanica* remains longer and therefore more informative. Encarta is trying to get bigger to undermine the new niche that Britannica is hoping to create. Nowadays, a hardback set of *Britannica* costs almost £1000 but you can buy a DVD for £60, and Encarta for around £40.

Alternatively, you can visit the free online encyclopaedia Wikipedia at www.wikipedia.org, which has 75 000 active volunteers working on over 5 million articles in 100 languages.

Sources: Evans, P. and Wurster, T. (1999) *Blown to Bits*, Harvard Business School Press; Melcher, R. (1997) Dusting off the Britannica, *Business Week*, 20 October.

Summary

- **Risk** pervades economic life. Some people gamble for fun; some addicts gamble in spite of themselves. Most people are **risk-averse**. They volunteer to take risks only if offered favourable odds that on average yield a profit. Conversely, most people **insure**, despite less than fair odds, to reduce the risks they otherwise face.

- **Risk-aversion** reflects the **diminishing marginal utility of wealth**. A fair gamble in monetary terms yields less extra utility when it succeeds than it sacrifices when it fails. Hence people refuse fair gambles, except for very small stakes. The prevalence of risk aversion means that people look for ways to reduce risk, and must pay others to take over their risk-bearing.

- Insurance **pools** risks that are substantially independent to reduce the aggregate risk, and **spreads** any residual risk across many people so that each has a small stake in the risk that cannot be pooled away.

- Insurance markets are inhibited by **adverse selection** and **moral hazard**. The former means that high-risk clients are more likely to take out insurance; the latter means that the act of insuring increases the likelihood that the undesired outcome will occur.

- Company shares have a higher average return but a much more variable return than that on Treasury bills or bank deposits.

- Portfolio choices depend on the investor's tastes – the trade-offs between risk and average return that yield equal utility – and on the opportunities that the market provides – the risk and return combinations on existing assets.

- When risks on different asset returns are independent, the risk of the whole portfolio can be reduced by diversification across assets.

- The risk that an asset contributes to a portfolio is not measured by the variability of that asset's own return but by the correlation of its return with the return on other assets. An asset that is negatively correlated with other assets will actually reduce the risk of the whole portfolio even though its own return is risky. Conversely, assets with a strong positive correlation with the rest of the portfolio increase the overall risk. The value of beta for an asset measures its correlation with other assets.

- In equilibrium risky assets earn higher rates of return on average to compensate portfolio holders for bearing this extra risk. High beta assets have high returns. If an asset is offering too high an expected return for its risk class, people will buy the asset, bidding up its price until the expected return is forced back to its equilibrium level.

- In an efficient market assets are priced to reflect the latest available information about their risk and return. There are no easy systematic investment opportunities to beat the market unless you systematically get or use new information faster than other people. Evidence from share prices is compatible with stock market efficiency, but speculative bubbles sometimes occur.

- Forward markets set a price today for future delivery of and payment for goods. They allow people to hedge against risky spot prices in the future by making a contract today. Speculators take over this risk and require a premium unless they can match buyers and sellers.

- Information is expensive to produce but very cheap to copy and distribute. From the users' viewpoint, e-products have four key attributes: experience, overload, switching costs and network externalities. Experience explains why sellers allow sampling and browsing. Sellers also invest in a good reputation to reduce the need for buyers to sample. Potential information overload explains why specialist agents develop to pre-screen material. Switching costs make future opportunities depend on current choices. Network externalities arise when the value of a network depends on how densely it is populated.

Review questions

EASY

1 A fair coin is to be tossed. If it comes down heads, the player wins £1. If it comes down tails, the player loses £1. Person A doesn't mind whether or not he takes the bet. Person B will pay £0.02 to play the game. Person C demands £0.05 before being willing to play. Characterize the three people's attitude to risk. Which is most likely to take out insurance against car theft?

2 You see an advert for life insurance for anyone over 45 years old. No medical examination is required. Do you expect the premium rates to be high, low or average? Why?

3 In which of the following are the risks being pooled: (a) life insurance, (b) insurance against the Thames flooding, (c) insurance for a pop star's voice?

4 You set up a firm to advise the unemployed on the best way to use their time to earn money. Your firm issues shares on the stock market. In equilibrium, will your shares be expected to earn a higher or lower return than the stock market average? Why?

5 Why are stock markets regulated to prevent 'insider trading', where a firm's managers use inside information about the firm to buy and sell its shares?

6 True or false   Your lecturer says that the exam in economics will be so easy that no students will fail. Given that, no students prepare for it and they all fail. This is an example of an adverse selection problem.

7 Common fallacies   Why are the following statements wrong? (a) Economists cannot predict changes in the stock market. This proves that economics is useless in thinking about share prices. (b) It is silly to take out insurance. If the insurance company is making money, its clients are losing money. (c) Prudent investors should not buy shares whose returns are volatile.

8 Suppose that George has a total utility of income given by $U(I) = I$, where I denotes income. In a graph with utility on the vertical axis and income on the horizontal axis, plot George's total utility of income. What is George's attitude towards risk? Explain.

9 Suppose that George from Question 8 can have two income levels this year: if he keeps his job, he earns £30 000; if he loses the job, he must live on a subsistence payment from the government of £10 000. George thinks he has a 50/50 chance of losing the job when he talks to his boss tomorrow. So he is considering purchasing employment insurance today. The insurance will pay him £20 000 in the case of him losing his job; otherwise, it will pay nothing. The insurance payment does not affect the subsistence payment from the government. The insurance costs £10 000, which he must pay now. In the graph of George's utility of income, show the possible income levels George faces. Should George buy the insurance? Explain.

10 In the following table the total utility of income of an individual is reported.

Income	Utility
1	1.00
2	1.26
3	1.44
4	1.59
5	1.71
6	1.82
7	1.91
8	2.00
9	2.08
10	2.15

In a graph with utility on the vertical axis and income on the horizontal axis, plot the total utility of income of the individual. Suppose our individual has an initial income of £4. He can use this money in a fair gamble that gives him with probability 0.5 an income of £6 and with probability 0.5 an income of £2. Should the individual put his income into this fair gamble? Use the graph of the total utility of income to illustrate your answer.

11 We know from many situations that people will pay to avoid risk. Name three risky products that you choose to buy. In each case, explain the motive.

12 Suppose the stock exchange is expected to yield a return of 5 per cent next year, but this is risky and could be several percentage points either side of the central forecast. You are also aware that it is possible to hold gold as an asset and that gold is known to have a small negative beta. People buy gold in a panic so the gold price rises when the stock market is doing badly. Today's price of gold is £500. (a) If people are risk-neutral, what is the best estimate of next year's gold price? (b) If people are risk-averse, what do you think is the best estimate of next year's gold price?

HARD

13 Essay question You run a pension fund and know that in 20 years' time you need to make a lot of payments to people who will then have retired. Should you (a) invest in bonds that mature in 20 years' time so you know exactly how much you will then have, (b) invest in equities because historically their average return has been greater than that of bonds in the long run, or (c) begin mainly in equities but switch gradually into bonds as the 20-year period elapses?

For solutions to these questions contact your lecturer.

Welfare economics

Normative or welfare economics is concerned with making value judgements and using these to recommend which policies are desirable. Much of economics is about reconciling the goals of efficiency and fairness. Part Three discusses reasons for market failures that give rise to inefficiencies, then investigates how government might intervene to improve the market. Such intervention may itself be subject to failures: well-meaning intervention can sometimes make things worse. As globalization begins to undermine the economic sovereignty of nation states, it is also necessary to think about when national policies will suffice and when cross-border co-operation is beneficial.

Chapter 13 introduces welfare economics, defines efficiency and equity (fairness), and examines reasons for market failure. Chapter 14 focuses on direct government intervention through taxes and public spending.

Contents

PART
THREE
Welfare economics

Welfare economics

Learning Outcomes

By the end of this chapter, you should understand:

1. what we mean by welfare economics
2. horizontal and vertical equity
3. the concept of Pareto efficiency
4. how the 'invisible hand' may achieve efficiency
5. the concept of market failure
6. why partial removal of distortions may be harmful
7. the problem of externalities and possible solutions
8. how monopoly power causes market failure
9. distortions from pollution and congestion
10. why missing markets create distortions
11. the economics of climate change

Normative or welfare economics is concerned with making value judgements and using these to recommend which policies are desirable. Much of economics is about reconciling the goals of efficiency and fairness. In this chapter we define efficiency and equity (fairness), and examine reasons for market failure.

Chapter 1 noted that markets are not the only way society can resolve what, how and for whom to produce. Communist economies relied heavily on central direction or command. Are markets a good way to allocate scarce resources? What is a 'good' way? Is it fair that some people earn much more than others in a market economy? These are not positive issues about how the economy works but normative issues about how well it works. They are normative because the assessment depends on the value judgements adopted by the assessor.

Left- and right-wing parties disagree about how well a market economy works. The right believes the market fosters choice, incentives and efficiency. The left emphasizes the market's failings and the need for

Welfare economics deals with normative issues. It does not describe how the economy works but assesses how well it works.

government intervention. What lies behind the disagreement? Two themes recur in the analysis of **welfare economics**. The first is *allocative efficiency*. Is the economy getting the most out of its scarce resources or are they being squandered? The second is *equity*. How fair is the *distribution* of goods and services among different members of society?

13.1 Equity and efficiency

Horizontal equity is the identical treatment of identical people.

Vertical equity is the different treatment of different people in order to reduce the consequences of these innate differences.

Whether or not either concept of equity – horizontal or vertical – is desirable is a pure value judgement. **Horizontal equity** rules out discrimination between people whose economic characteristics and performance are identical. **Vertical equity** is the Robin Hood principle of taking from the rich to give to the poor.

Many people agree that horizontal equity is a good thing. In contrast, although few people believe that the poor should starve, the extent to which resources should be redistributed from the 'haves' to the 'have-nots' to increase vertical equity is an issue on which people disagree.

Efficient resource allocation

A **resource allocation** is a complete description of who does what and who gets what.

Suppose that allocations are made by a central dictator. Feasible allocations depend on the technology and resources available to the economy. The ultimate worth of any allocation depends on consumer tastes – how people value what they are given.

Figure 13.1 shows an economy with only two people, David and Susie. The initial allocation at *A* gives David a quantity of goods Q_D and Susie a quantity Q_S. Are society's resources being wasted? By reorganizing things, suppose society can produce at *B*, to the north-east of *A*. If David and Susie assess utility by the quantity of goods they get themselves, and if they would each rather have more goods than less, *B* is a better allocation than *A*. Both David and Susie get more. It is inefficient to produce at *A* if production at *B* is possible. Similarly, a move from *A* to *C* makes both David and Susie worse off. If it is possible to be at *A*, it is inefficient to be at *C*.

What about a move from *A* to *E* or *F*? One person gains; the other person loses. Whether this change is desirable depends on how we value David's utility relative to Susie's. If we think David's utility is very important we might prefer *F* to *A*, even though Susie's utility is reduced.

Value judgements about equity or fairness get mixed up with our attempt to make statements about waste or inefficiency. Since different people will make different value judgements, there is no unambiguous answer to the question of whether a move from *A* to *D*, *E* or *F* is desirable. It depends on who makes the assessment.

For a given set of consumer tastes, resources and technology, an allocation is **Pareto-efficient** if there is no other feasible allocation that makes some people better off and nobody worse off.

To try to separate the discussion of equity from the discussion of efficiency, modern welfare economics uses the idea of **Pareto efficiency**, named after the economist Vilfredo Pareto.

In Figure 13.1 a move from *A* to *B* or *A* to *G* is a *Pareto gain*. Susie is better off; David is no worse off. If *B* or *G* is feasible, *A* is *Pareto-inefficient*. A free lunch is available.

A move from *A* to *D* makes David better off but Susie worse off. The Pareto criterion has nothing to say about this change. To evaluate it, we need a judgement about the relative value of David and Susie's utility. The Pareto principle is of limited use in comparing allocations on efficiency grounds. It only allows us to evaluate moves to the north-east or the south-west in Figure 13.1. Yet it is the most we can say about efficiency without making value judgements about equity.

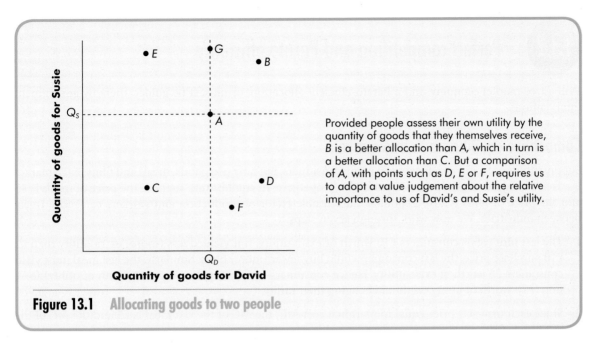

Figure 13.1 shows points plotted with Quantity of goods for Susie on the vertical axis and Quantity of goods for David on the horizontal axis.

Provided people assess their own utility by the quantity of goods that they themselves receive, B is a better allocation than A, which in turn is a better allocation than C. But a comparison of A, with points such as D, E or F, requires us to adopt a value judgement about the relative importance to us of David's and Susie's utility.

Figure 13.1　Allocating goods to two people

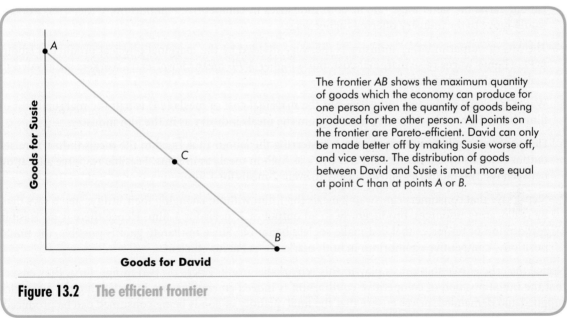

The frontier AB shows the maximum quantity of goods which the economy can produce for one person given the quantity of goods being produced for the other person. All points on the frontier are Pareto-efficient. David can only be made better off by making Susie worse off, and vice versa. The distribution of goods between David and Susie is much more equal at point C than at points A or B.

Figure 13.2　The efficient frontier

Figure 13.2 takes the argument a stage further. By reorganizing production, we can make the economy produce anywhere inside or on the frontier AB. From inside the frontier, a Pareto gain can be achieved by moving to the north-east on to the frontier. Any point inside the frontier is Pareto-inefficient. One person can be made better off without making the other worse off. But *all* points on the frontier are Pareto-efficient. One person can get more only by giving the other person less. Since no Pareto gain is possible, every point on the frontier is Pareto-efficient.

Thus society should never choose an inefficient allocation inside the frontier. Which of the efficient points on the frontier is most desirable will depend on the value judgement of the relative value of David and Susie's utility, a judgement about equity.

13.2 Perfect competition and Pareto efficiency

Will a free market economy find a Pareto-efficient allocation, or must it be guided there by government intervention?

Competitive equilibrium in free markets

Suppose there are many producers and many consumers, but only two goods, meals and films. Each market is a free, unregulated market and is perfectly competitive. In equilibrium, suppose the price of meals is £5 and the price of films is £10. Labour is the variable factor of production and workers can move freely between industries. We now work through seven steps:

1   The last film yields consumers £10 worth of extra utility. If it yielded less (more) extra utility than its £10 purchase price, the last consumer would buy fewer (more) films. Similarly, the last meal must yield consumers £5 worth of extra utility. Hence consumers could swap 2 meals (£10 worth of utility) for 1 film (£10 worth of utility) without changing their utility.

2   Since each firm sets price equal to marginal cost MC, the MC of the last meal is £5 and the MC of the last film is £10.

3   Labour earns the same wage rate in both industries in competitive equilibrium. Otherwise, workers would move to the industry offering higher wages.

4   The MC of output in either industry is the wage divided by the marginal physical product of labour MPL. Higher wages raise marginal cost, but a higher MPL means fewer extra workers are needed to make an extra unit of output.

5   Wages are equal in the two industries but the marginal cost of meals (£5) is half the marginal cost of films (£10). Hence, the MPL is twice as high in the meals industry as in the film industry.

6   Hence reducing film output by 1 unit, transferring the labour thus freed to the meals industry, raises output of meals by 2 units. The MPL is twice as high in meals as in films. Feasible resource allocation between the two industries allows society to swap 2 meals for 1 film.

7   Step 1 says that consumers can swap 2 meals for 1 film without changing their utility. Step 6 says that, by reallocating resources, producers swap an output of 2 meals for 1 film. Hence there is no feasible reallocation of resources that can make society better off. Since no Pareto gain is possible, the initial position – competitive equilibrium in both markets – is Pareto-efficient.

Notice the crucial role that prices play in this remarkable result. Prices do two things. First, they ensure that the initial position of competitive equilibrium is indeed an *equilibrium*. By balancing the quantities supplied and demanded, prices ensure that the final quantity of goods being consumed can be produced. They ensure that it is a feasible allocation.

But in *competitive* equilibrium prices perform a second role. Each consumer and each producer is a price-taker and cannot affect market prices. In our example, each consumer knows that the equilibrium price of meals is £5 and the equilibrium price of films is £10. Knowing nothing about the actions of other consumers and producers, each consumer automatically ensures that the last film purchased yields twice as much utility as the last meal purchased. Otherwise that consumer could rearrange purchases out of a given income to increase her utility.

Thus by her individual actions facing given prices, each consumer arranges that 1 film could be swapped for 2 meals with no change in utility. Similarly, every producer, merely by setting its own marginal cost equal to the price of its output, ensures that the marginal cost of films is twice the marginal cost of meals.

Thus it takes society twice as many resources to make an extra film as it does to make an extra meal. By rearranging production, transferring labour between industries, society can swap 2 meals for 1 film, exactly the trade-off that leaves consumer utility unaffected.

Thus, as if by an 'invisible hand', prices are guiding individual consumers and producers, each pursuing only self-interest, to an allocation of the economy's resources that is Pareto-efficient. Nobody can be made better off without someone else becoming worse off.

Figure 13.3 makes the same point. *DD* is the market demand curve for one of the goods, say films. At a price P_1, a quantity of films Q_1 is demanded. The last film demanded yields consumers P_1 pounds worth of utility; otherwise they would buy a different quantity. Hence *DD* shows also the marginal utility of the last unit of films which consumers purchase. When Q_1 films are purchased, the last film yields exactly P_1 pounds worth of extra utility to consumers.

In a competitive industry, the supply curve for films *SS* is also the marginal cost of films. The variable factor, labour, is paid its marginal value product in each industry. Labour mobility ensures wage rates are equal in the two industries. Hence the marginal cost of making the last film is the value of the meals sacrificed by using the last worker to make films not meals.

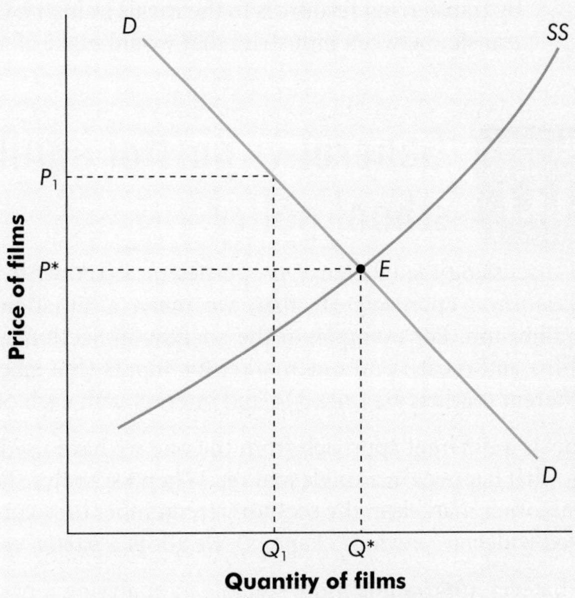

Prices ensure that both industries are in equilibrium. Figure 13.3 shows that, in equilibrium at *E*, the marginal utility of the last film equals its marginal cost. But the marginal cost of the last film is the value of meals sacrificed; the price of meals multiplied by the meals forgone by using labour to make that last film. However, the meals industry is also in equilibrium. An equivalent diagram for the meals industry shows that the equilibrium price of meals is also the marginal utility of the last meal purchased. Hence the value of meals sacrificed to make the last film is also the marginal utility of the last meal times the number of meals sacrificed.

At any output such as Q_1 the last film must yield consumers P_1 pounds worth of extra utility; otherwise they would not demand Q_1. The supply curve *SS* for the competitive film industry is also the marginal cost of films. If the meals industry is in competitive equilibrium, the price of a meal is also the value of its marginal utility to consumers. Thus the marginal cost of a film is not only its opportunity cost in meals but also the value of the marginal utility consumers would have derived from those meals. Hence at any film output below Q^* the marginal utility of films exceeds the marginal utility of meals sacrificed to produce an extra film. Above Q^* the marginal utility of films is less than the marginal utility of meals sacrificed. The equilibrium point *E* for films and the corresponding equilibrium point in the market for meals thus ensure that resources are efficiently allocated between the two industries. No reallocation could make all consumers better off.

Figure 13.3   Competitive equilibrium and Pareto efficiency

Thus, provided the *meals* industry is in competitive equilibrium, the marginal cost curve for the *film* industry is the extra pounds worth of utility sacrificed by using scarce resources to make another film instead of extra meals. It is the opportunity cost in utility terms of the resources being used in the film industry. And equilibrium in the film industry, by equating the marginal utility of films to the marginal utility of the meals sacrificed to make the last film, guarantees that society's resources are allocated efficiently.

At any output of films below the equilibrium quantity Q^*, the marginal consumer benefit of another film exceeds the marginal consumer valuation of the meals that would have to be sacrificed to produce that extra film. At any output of films above Q^*, society is devoting too many resources to the film industry. The marginal value of the last film is less than the marginal value of the meals that could have been produced by transferring resources to the meals industry. Competitive equilibrium ensures that there is no resource transfer between industries that would make all consumers better off.

CONCEPT 13.1 General vs partial equilibrium: an example from school policy

In discussing the efficiency properties of a competitive equilibrium we have implicitly followed a *general equilibrium* approach. By that, we mean a situation whereby multiple markets are simultaneously in equilibrium. For example, in the analysis in Section 13.2 we have considered two markets for final goods (films and meals) and one market for inputs (the labour market). In general equilibrium we analyse how different markets are linked to and interact with each other.

This is a different approach from the one we have used in previous chapters where we have focused mainly on what happens in a single market. When we analyse just a single market, without looking at any interaction with other markets in the economy (remember the expression 'keeping constant everything else' that we have used widely in previous chapters), we adopt a *partial equilibrium* approach.

Whatever approach is more suitable in analysing a particular case depends on the objective of the analysis itself. In many cases, a partial equilibrium analysis of a particular market is fine if the objective is to understand that particular market only.

When we are interested in analysing how different markets are linked together, a general equilibrium approach is preferred.

The differences between a partial equilibrium and a general equilibrium approach are more evident when we evaluate government policies. Here is an example on school policy.

Heckman* et al. (1998) studied the partial and general equilibrium effects of a particular school policy: a $500 tuition subsidy to college students. The partial equilibrium effect will focus on the effect that such a policy has on the college students, everything else constant. They found that a $500 tuition subsidy leads to an increase of 5.3 per cent in college attendance. This is quite intuitive; with such a subsidy college fees become less expensive and more students can go to college.

However, this is the partial equilibrium effect only.

To get the general equilibrium we need to understand how the effect of the policy is linked to other markets. In particular, Heckman et al. focused on the labour market for college graduates. Now there are two markets linked together: the market for colleges and the labour market for college graduates.

They found that, once we take into account the link between the two markets, the result of the policy is an increase in college students of only 0.49 per cent. Why is that?

In response to the tuition subsidy more people go to college. This makes high school graduates more scarce in the labour market and college graduates more common.

As a result, wages of college graduates will fall (higher labour supply of college graduates in the labour market), while wages of high school graduates will increase. Rational students will anticipate this effect and so the result of the policy will be mitigated.

*   James J. Heckman shared the Nobel Prize in Economics in 2000 with Daniel McFadden.

Source: Heckman J., Lochner, L. and Taber, C. (1998) General equilibrium treatment effects: a study of tuition policy, *American Economic Review*, 88 (2): 381–386. © 1998 James J. Heckman, Lance Lochner and Christopher Taber.

Equity and efficiency

The previous section showed that there are many Pareto-efficient allocations, each with a different distribution of utility between different members of society. A competitive equilibrium in all markets generates a particular Pareto-efficient allocation. What determines each one?

People have different innate abilities, human capital and wealth. These differences mean people earn different incomes in a market economy. They also affect the pattern of consumer demand. Brazil, with a very unequal distribution of income and wealth, has a high demand for luxuries such as servants. In more egalitarian Denmark, nobody can afford servants.

Different inheritances of ability, capital and wealth thus imply different demand curves and determine different equilibrium prices and quantities. In principle, by varying the distribution of initial income-earning potential, we could make the economy pick out each possible Pareto-efficient allocation as its competitive equilibrium.

Here is an attractive idea. The government is elected to express the value judgements of the majority. If the market gets the economy to the Pareto-efficient frontier, the government can make the value judgement about which point on this frontier the economy should attain. Every competitive equilibrium is Pareto-efficient. Different efficient allocations correspond to different initial distributions of income-earning potential in a competitive economy. Can the government confine itself to redistributing income and wealth through taxation and welfare benefits *without having to intervene to ensure that resources are allocated efficiently*?

This seems a powerful case for the free enterprise ideal. The government should let markets get on with the job of allocating resources efficiently. We do not need regulations, investigatory bodies or state-run enterprises. Nor need the free enterprise ideal be uncompassionate. The government can redistribute income without impairing the efficient functioning of a free market economy. The right-wing case can be backed up by rigorous economic arguments.

However, the left-wing case can also be made. Remember the qualifications in the above argument. *Under certain conditions* free markets lead to a Pareto-efficient allocation. These conditions explain the difference between the two views of how a market economy works. The right believes that they are *minor* qualifications that do not seriously challenge the case for a free market economy. The left believes that the qualifications are so serious that substantial government intervention is necessary to *improve* the way the economy works.

13.3   Distortions and the second-best

Competitive equilibrium is efficient because the independent actions of producers setting marginal cost equal to price, and consumers setting marginal benefits equal to price, ensure that the marginal cost of producing a good just equals its marginal benefit to consumers.

> A **distortion** exists if society's marginal cost of producing a good does not equal society's marginal benefit from consuming that good.

Taxation as a distortion

To finance subsidies to the poor, a government must tax the incomes of rich people or the goods rich people buy. Suppose everyone buys meals, but only the rich can afford to go to the cinema. A subsidy for the poor can be financed by a tax on films.

In Figure 13.4 the pre-tax price of films to consumers exceeds the post-tax price received by makers of films. The difference between the two prices is the tax on each film. Consumers equate the tax-inclusive price to the value of the marginal benefit they receive from the last film, but suppliers equate the marginal cost of films to the lower net-of-tax price of films.

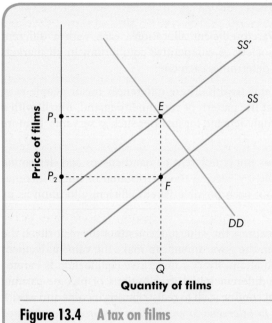

DD shows the demand for films and the marginal benefit of the last film to consumers. SS shows the quantity of films supplied at each price received by producers and is also the marginal social cost of producing films. Suppose each unit of films bears a tax equal to the vertical distance EF. To show the tax-inclusive price required to induce producers to produce each output, we must draw the new supply curve SS' that is a constant vertical distance EF above SS. The equilibrium quantity of films is Q. Consumers pay a price P_1, producers receive a price P_2 and the tax per film is the distance EF. At the equilibrium quantity Q the marginal benefit is P_1 but the marginal social cost is P_2. Society would make a net gain by producing more films. Hence the equilibrium quantity.

Figure 13.4   **A tax on films**

In competitive equilibrium, the price system no longer equates the social marginal cost of making films with the social marginal benefit of consuming films. The marginal benefit of another film exceeds its marginal cost. The tax on films induces too few films. Making another film adds more to social benefit than to social cost.

Earlier, we showed that the marginal cost of a film equals the value of the extra meals that society could have had instead. When films are taxed, the marginal social benefit of another film exceeds its marginal cost, and hence exceeds the marginal social benefit of the extra meals that society could have had by using resources differently. By transferring labour from meals into films, society could make some people better off without making anyone else worse off.

A similar argument holds for any other commodity we tax. A tax causes a discrepancy between the price the purchaser pays and the price the seller receives. The 'invisible hand' no longer equates marginal social benefits of resources in different uses.

The choice between efficiency and equity is now clear. If the economy is perfectly competitive, and if the government is happy with the current income distribution, competitive free market equilibrium is efficient and the income distribution desirable.

However if, as a pure value judgement, the government dislikes this income distribution, it has to tax some people to provide subsidies for others. Yet the very act of raising taxes *introduces a distortion*. The resulting equilibrium has a more desirable distribution but is less efficient. Governments may have to make trade-offs between efficiency and equity.

One explanation for differing political attitudes to the market economy is a difference in value judgements about equity. Later, we will see that there may also be disagreements in positive economics. We consider other distortions in the next section. Before leaving our tax example, there is one final point to make.

> The **first-best allocation** has no distortions and is fully efficient.

The second-best

When there is no distortion in the market for *meals*, a tax on *films* leads to an inefficient allocation. If we could abolish the tax on films neither industry would be distorted and we get the **first-best allocation**.

Suppose, however, that we cannot get rid of the tax on films. The government needs tax revenue to pay for national defence or its EU budget contribution. Given an unavoidable tax on films, at least it should not tax meals as well.

This plausible view is in fact *quite wrong*. Suppose both industries are in equilibrium but there is a tax on films. Above, we saw that too few films are produced and consumed. By implication, too many meals are therefore produced and consumed. Given an inevitable tax on films, a tax on meals would help not hinder.

A suitable tax on meals could restore the original relative price of meals and films. With only two goods, this would restore the first-best. However, there is always a third good – leisure. Households reduce consumption of leisure in order to supply labour for work. Taxing meals and films gets the right balance between meals and films, but makes the price of both wrong relative to the price of leisure. With higher taxes, the net wage falls, changing the implicit price of leisure.

In contrast to the first-best allocation, when we achieve full efficiency by removing all distortions, we have now developed the principle of the *second-best*. Suppose we care only about efficiency but there is an inevitable distortion somewhere else in the economy that we cannot remove. It is inefficient to treat other markets as if that distortion did not exist. In the meals industry, it is inefficient to equate private marginal cost and private marginal benefit, the efficient outcome in the absence of a film tax. Rather, it is efficient to deliberately introduce a new distortion in meals to help counterbalance the unavoidable distortion in the meals industry.

The theory of the **second-best** says that, if there must be a distortion, it is a mistake to concentrate the distortion in one market. It is more efficient to spread its effect more thinly over a wide range of markets.

> The **second-best** is the most efficient outcome that can be achieved conditional on being unable to remove some distortions.

Several applications of this general principle are found in the ensuing chapters. The real world in which we live provides several inevitable distortions. Given their existence, the argument of this section implies that the government may *increase* the overall efficiency of the whole economy by introducing *new* distortions to offset those that already exist. By now you will want to know the source of these inevitable distortions that the government could take action to offset.

13.4 Market failure

In the absence of any distortions, competitive equilibrium is efficient. We use the term *market failure* to cover all the circumstances in which market equilibrium is inefficient. Distortions then prevent the 'invisible hand' from allocating resources efficiently. We now list the possible sources of distortions that lead to market failure.

Imperfect competition

Only perfect competition makes firms equate marginal cost to price and thus to marginal consumer benefit. Under imperfect competition, producers set a price above the marginal cost. Since consumers equate price to marginal benefit, marginal benefit exceeds marginal cost in imperfectly competitive industries. Such industries produce too little compared to the efficient level. Increasing the level of competition in an imperfectly competitive market would result in higher output produced. This would add more to consumer benefit than to production costs (or the opportunity cost) of the resources used.

Equity, taxation and public goods

Redistributive taxation induces allocative distortions by driving a wedge between the price the consumer pays and the price the producer receives. So far, when we discussed the goods produced in the market we have considered private goods. Private goods are those that can be consumed only by the buyer. For example, if you buy a can of Coke, you pay for it and you drink it. Other consumers cannot drink the same can of Coke. In contrast to private goods, public goods are those that, if consumed by one person, must be consumed by others in exactly the same quantity. For example, national defence. Since you get the same quantity of national defence as everyone else, *whether or not you pay for it*, you never buy national defence in a private market. Therefore, in the case of public goods, we have goods that society would like to consume but the private market mechanism cannot provide (or will underprovide). Taxes and public goods are analysed in detail in Chapter 14.

Externalities

Externalities are things like pollution, noise and congestion. One person's actions have direct costs or benefits for other people, but the individual does not take these into account. Much of the rest of this chapter examines this distortion. The problem arises because there is no market for things like noise. Hence markets and prices cannot ensure that the marginal benefit you get from making a noise equals the marginal cost of that noise to other people.

Asymmetric information

In Chapter 12 we saw how moral hazard and adverse selection inhibit the setting up of insurance markets to deal with risk. The fact that there exists imperfect information in certain markets may lead to a failure in such markets.

Under asymmetric information, one party in a market transaction has more information than the other party. For example, a seller may know the true quality of the good she is selling while the buyer does not.

Suppose that buyers want to buy used cars. There are various sellers in the market, some selling high-quality used cars some selling low-quality cars. If the buyers cannot tell the difference between low and high quality, they will probably be unwilling to pay much for a used car (they always face the possibility of getting a low-quality used car). As a result, the sellers with high-quality used cars may end up selling them at a price that is lower than their value, meaning it is unprofitable for those sellers to stay in the market. In practice, under asymmetric information, the existence of the low-quality product drives the high-quality product out of the market. This is a market failure since the market for the high-quality product is eliminated even if the buyers value it at more than the cost of producing it.

The case of used cars is known as the market for 'lemons' (whereby lemons means the low-quality used cars) – a typical example of adverse selection.

13.5 Externalities

> An **externality** arises if one person's production or consumption physically affects the production or consumption of others.

A chemical firm discharges waste into a lake, polluting the water. It affects the production of anglers (fewer fish, harder to catch) or the consumption of swimmers (dirty water). Without a 'market' for pollution, the firm can pollute the lake without cost. Its self-interest leads it to pollute until the marginal benefit of polluting (cheaper production of chemicals) equals its own marginal cost of polluting, which is zero. It ignores the marginal cost that pollution imposed on anglers and swimmers.

Conversely, by painting your house you make the whole street look nicer and give consumption benefits to your neighbour. But you paint only up to the point on which your own marginal benefit equals the marginal cost of the paint you buy and the time you spend. Your marginal costs are also society's marginal costs, but society's marginal benefits exceed your own. Hence, there is too little house painting.

In both cases there is a divergence between the individual's comparison of marginal costs and benefits and society's comparison of marginal costs and benefits. Free markets cannot induce people to take account of indirect effects if there is no market in these indirect effects.

Divergences between private and social costs and benefits

Suppose a chemical firm pollutes a river, the quantity of pollution rising with output. Downstream, companies use river water as an input in making sauce for baked beans. At low chemical output, pollution is negligible. The river dilutes the small amounts of pollutant discharged by the chemical producer. As the discharge rises, the costs of pollution rise sharply. Food processors must worry about water purity, and build expensive purification plants. Still higher levels of pollution start to corrode their pipes.

Figure 13.5 shows the marginal private cost *MPC* of producing chemicals. For simplicity, we treat *MPC* as constant.[1] It also shows the marginal *social cost MSC* of chemical production. At any output, the divergence between marginal private cost and marginal social cost is the marginal *production externality*. The demand curve *DD* shows how much consumers will pay for the output of the chemical producer. If that firm is a price-taker, equilibrium is at *E* and the chemical producer's output is *Q*, at which the marginal private cost equals the price of the firm's output.

At this output *Q*, the marginal social cost *MSC* exceeds the marginal social benefit of chemicals,

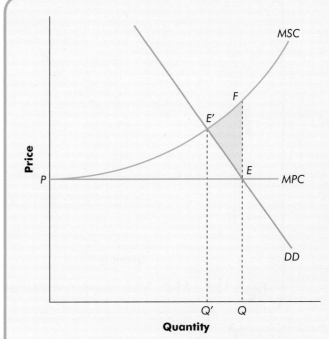

Competitive equilibrium occurs at *E*. The market clears at a price *P*, which producers equate to marginal private cost *MPC*. But pollution causes a production externality which makes the marginal social cost *MSC* exceed the marginal private cost. The socially efficient output is at *E'*, where marginal social cost and marginal social benefit are equal. The demand curve *DD* measures the marginal social benefit because consumers equate the value of the marginal utility of the last unit to the price. By inducing an output *Q* in excess of the efficient output *Q'* free market equilibrium leads to a social cost equal to the area *E'FE*. This shows the excess of social cost over social benefit in moving from *Q'* to *Q*.

Figure 13.5   The social cost of a production externality

given by the height of the demand curve *DD*. The market for chemicals ignores the production externality inflicted on other firms. At *Q*, the marginal social benefit of the last output unit is less than the marginal social cost inclusive of the production externality. Output *Q* is inefficient. By reducing the output of chemicals, society saves more in social cost than it loses in social benefit. Society could make some people better off without making anyone worse off.

The efficient output is *Q'*, at which the marginal social benefit equals the marginal social cost. *E'* is the efficient point. How much does society lose by producing at the free market equilibrium *E* not the efficient point *E'*? The vertical distance between the marginal social cost *MSC* and the marginal social benefit shows the marginal social loss of producing the last output unit. By over-expanding from *Q'* to *Q*, society loses

---

1   The results of the analysis will not change if we consider a positively-sloped *MPC* curve. What matters is that marginal private costs lie below the marginal social costs.

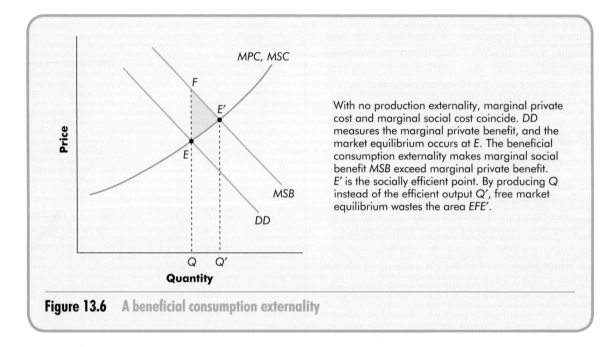

With no production externality, marginal private cost and marginal social cost coincide. DD measures the marginal private benefit, and the market equilibrium occurs at E. The beneficial consumption externality makes marginal social benefit MSB exceed marginal private benefit. E' is the socially efficient point. By producing Q instead of the efficient output Q', free market equilibrium wastes the area EFE'.

Figure 13.6   A beneficial consumption externality

the area E'FE in Figure 13.5. This is the social cost of the market failure caused by the production externality of pollution.[2]

Production externalities make social and private marginal costs diverge. A consumption externality makes private and social marginal benefits diverge. Figure 13.6 shows a beneficial consumption externality. Planting roses in your front garden also makes your neighbours happy.

With no production externality, MPC is both the private and social marginal cost of planting roses. It is the cost of the plants and the opportunity cost of your time. DD is the marginal private benefit. Comparing your own costs and benefits, you plant a quantity Q of roses.

But you ignore the consumption benefit to your neighbours. The marginal social benefit MSB exceeds your marginal private benefit. The free market equilibrium is at E, but the efficient output is Q' since marginal social benefit and marginal social cost are equated at E'.

Society could gain the area EFE', the excess of social benefits over social costs, by increasing the quantity of roses from Q to Q'. This triangle measures the social cost of the market failure that makes equilibrium output too low.

CASE 13.1

Externalities and the London 2012 Olympic Games

The summer Olympic Games are among the most important sporting events in the world. Moreover, such events provide the possibility for environmental and economic improvements in the host city. In 2012 London will host the Olympic Games.

---

2   Conversely, a farmer who spends money on pest control reduces pests on nearby farms. If production externalities are beneficial, the marginal social cost is below the marginal private cost. Suppose we swap the labels MSC and MPC in Figure 13.5. Free market equilibrium is at E' but E is now the efficient allocation.

There are many costs involved in preparing for such a massive sporting event and, hopefully, there will also be many benefits accruing from it. Some of those costs and benefits can be easily measured in monetary terms. For example, it is expected that the Olympic Games will boost tourism in London and in general all over the UK. We can measure such a benefit because we have a market for tourism. However, many other benefits and costs associated with the Olympic Games will be intangible.

By intangible we mean costs and benefits that will impact the well-being of many people but that will not in general have market prices. Or in other words: intangible benefits are positive externalities and intangible costs are negative externalities. Therefore, the Olympic Games is a source of externalities.

For example, hosting the Olympic Games normally boosts the national pride of the hosting country. This can be seen as a positive externality (a sort of 'feelgood' effect) but there is no market for national pride. Another possible positive externality that may be produced is related to environmental improvements through creation of new green spaces and recreational areas. The Olympic Games will probably create a sport and cultural legacy in the UK. This will enhance and accelerate investment in sporting facilities not only within the Olympic zone (and the areas immediately surrounding it) but also in other parts of the UK. It may contribute to increased participation in sport, and this will be expected to promote healthy living.

Cultural and social events may also improve during and after the Olympic Games.

Obviously there are also negative externalities that will arise from London 2012. During the Games, in some parts of London congestion will probably be very high. There may be local disruption during the construction of the Olympic site. As a result of building all the facilities, pollution may increase in the Olympic zone.

Another possible negative effect is that, as more people come for the Olympic Games, petty theft may increase. Moreover the risk of terrorist attack during the Games may also increase.

All those intangible benefits and costs are difficult to measure in monetary terms. In 2005 the UK Department for Culture, Media and Sport commissioned PricewaterhouseCoopers to study the possible costs and benefits of the London 2012 Games. An interesting finding of that study is the estimated willingness of London households to pay for the intangible benefits of the Olympic Games. On average, London households are willing to pay £22 each per annum for ten years in order to host the Olympic Games. Therefore, there is a positive valuation of the intangible benefits that London 2012 can bring to Londoners.

Source: PricewaterhouseCoopers, *Olympic Games Impact Study: Final Report*, December 2005.

Picture: Wenlock and Mandeville, the London 2012 Mascots. © LOCOG

Property rights and externalities

Your neighbour's tree obscures your light – a harmful consumption externality. If the law says that you must be compensated for any damage suffered, your neighbour has to pay up or cut back the tree.

She likes the tree and wants to know how much it would take to compensate you to leave it at its current size. Figure 13.7 shows the marginal benefit MB that she gets from the last inch of tree and the marginal cost MC to you of that last inch. At the tree's current size S_1, the total cost to you is the area $OABS_1$. This is the marginal cost OA of the first inch, plus the marginal cost of the second inch, and so on to the existing size S_1. The area $OABS_1$ is what you need in compensation if the tree size is S_1.

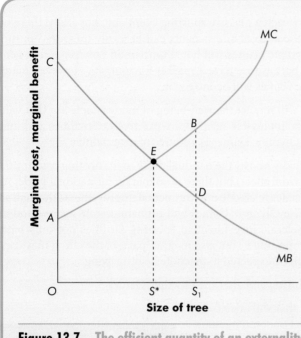

MB and MC measure the marginal benefit to your neighbour and marginal cost to you of a tree of size S. The efficient size is S^*, where the marginal cost and benefit are equal. Beginning from a size S_1, you might bribe your neighbour the value S^*EDS_1, to cut back to S^*. Below S^* you would have to pay more than it is worth to you to have the tree cut back further. Alternatively, your neighbour might pay you the value $OAES^*$ to have a tree of size S^*. Property rights, in this case whether you are legally entitled to compensation for loss of light to your garden, determine who compensates whom but not the outcome S^* of the bargain.

Figure 13.7 The efficient quantity of an externality

Your neighbour is about to pay up when her daughter, an economics student, points out that, at size S_1, the marginal benefit of the last inch to her is less than the marginal cost to you, the amount you must be compensated for that last inch of the tree. It is not worth her mother having a tree this big. Nor, she points out, is it worth cutting the tree down altogether. The first inch yields a higher marginal benefit to her than the amount that you need in compensation to offset your marginal cost of that first inch. A tiny tree has little effect on your light.

At the efficient tree size S^*, the marginal benefit to your neighbour equals the marginal cost to you. Above S^*, she cuts back the tree, since the marginal cost (and compensation) exceeds her marginal benefit. Below S^*, she increases the tree size, and pays you marginal compensation that is less than her marginal benefit. At the efficient size S^*, your total cost is the area $OAES^*$. This is the compensation you are paid.

Since a larger tree benefits one party but hurts the other, *the efficient tree size, and therefore the efficient quantity of the externality, is not zero*. It is where the marginal benefit equals the marginal cost.

> **Property rights** are the power of residual control, including the right to be compensated for externalities.

Property rights affect who compensates whom, a distributional implication. Suppose there is no law requiring compensation. Instead of letting her tree grow to S_1, inflicting a huge cost on you, you bribe your neighbour to cut it back. You compensate her for the loss of her marginal benefit. You would pay to have the tree cut back as far as S^* but no further. Beyond that size, you pay more in compensation for loss of marginal benefit than you save yourself in lower cost of the externality. So you pay a *total* of S^*EDS_1 to compensate for the loss of benefit in cutting the tree back from S_1 to S^*. Who has the property rights determines who pays whom, but does not affect the efficient quantity that the bargain determines. It is always worth reaching the point at which the marginal benefit to one of you equals the marginal cost to the other.

Property rights have a distributional implication – who compensates whom – but also achieve the efficient allocation. They set up the 'missing market' for the externality. The market ensures that the price equals the marginal benefit and the marginal cost, and hence equates the two.

Economists say that property rights 'internalize' the externality. The relationship between property rights, efficiency and externalities is known as the *Coase theorem*.[3]

This theorem says that, when there are no transaction costs and trading externalities is possible, then the trading mechanism will lead to an efficient outcome independent of the initial allocation of the property rights. For example, consider two firms: one is polluting and doing so negatively affects the other firm. In this case, it does not matter if we assign the right to pollute to the polluting firm or, alternatively, the right not to be polluted to the other firm. Once the property rights are assigned, the externality will be internalized.

The basic idea behind the Coase theorem is: if people must pay for it they will take its effects into account in making private decisions and there will no longer be market failure. Why, then, do externalities, like congestion and pollution, remain a problem? Why don't private individuals establish the missing market through a system of bribes or compensation?

There are two reasons why it is hard to set up this market. The first is the cost of organizing the market. A factory chimney dumps smoke on a thousand gardens nearby, but it is costly to collect £1 from each household to bribe the factory to cut back to the efficient amount. Second, there is a **free-rider** problem.

Someone knocks on your door and says: 'I'm collecting bribes from people who mind the factory smoke falling on their gardens. The money will be used to bribe the factory to cut back. Do you wish to contribute? I am going round 1000 houses nearby.' Whether you mind or not, you say: 'I don't mind, and won't contribute.' If everybody else pays, the factory will cut back and you cannot be prevented from getting the benefits. The smoke will not fall exclusively on your garden just because

> A **free-rider**, unable to be excluded from consuming a good, has no incentive to buy it.

you alone did not pay. Regardless of what other people contribute, your dominant strategy is to be a free-rider. Everyone else reasons similarly; hence no one pays, even though you are all better off paying and getting the smoke cut back.

MATHS 13.1 — Internalizing a negative externality using property rights

Consider a firm that is polluting a lake in order to produce. This is called firm A. There is another firm, B, which uses the fish in the lake. All markets for outputs are competitive. The total cost function of the polluting firm (firm A) is:

$$TC_A = TC_A(Q_A, P_A)$$

That is a function of the quantity produced (Q_A) and the level of pollution (P_A).

We assume that the total cost of firm A is increasing with the output produced:

$$\frac{\partial TC_A}{\partial Q_A} > 0$$

This means that if we increase by a small amount (∂Q_A) the quantity produced, the total cost increases. We assume that the total cost of firm A is decreasing with the pollution level: $\partial TC_A / \partial P_A \leq 0$.

More pollution implies lower costs for the firm. Think about the case in which, to pollute less, the firm must invest in an expensive cleaner technology. Denote by p the market price of output for firm A, then the profit function of that firm is $\pi_A = pQ_A - TC_A(Q_A, P_A)$.

---

3 From Ronald Harry Coase, Nobel Prize winner in Economics in 1991, who first pointed out the relationship between property rights and efficiency in the presence of externalities.

Firm A chooses the optimal quantity to produce (Q_A) at which the marginal revenue is equal to the marginal cost of producing that quantity: $p = \partial TC_A/\partial Q_A$.

Similarly, the optimal quantity of pollution that maximizes profits is where marginal revenue of pollution (in this case, zero) is equal to the marginal cost of pollution:

$$-\frac{\partial TC_A}{\partial P_A} = 0$$

The firm chooses a level of pollution such that the cost of an extra unit of pollution is zero. Since higher is the pollution, lower is the total cost of the firm, we should expect that the level of pollution that solves that condition to be quite high.

Firm B has the following total cost function: $TC_B = TC_B(Q_B, P_A)$ with the following properties: $\partial TC_B/\partial Q_B > 0$ and $\partial TC_B/\partial P_A > 0$.

This means that the total cost of firm B increases with output produced and with the pollution made by firm A. The externality problem is the following: firm A in deciding how much to pollute does not take into account the effects that its decision has on firm B. Denote by f the market price of fish for firm B. The profit of firm B is given by: $\pi_B = fQ_B - TC_B(Q_B, P_A)$.

Suppose we give the right to pollute to firm A. Firm A can sell its right to firm B.

The profit function of firm A becomes $\pi_A = pQ_A - TC_A(Q_A, P_A) + qP_A$, where q is now the price that firm A can get by selling its right to pollute to firm B.

For firm B, the profit function is now $\pi_B = fQ_B - TC_B(Q_B, P_A) - qP_A$.

For firm A, the optimal level of pollution that maximizes profits is given by the condition:

$$-\frac{\partial TC_A}{\partial P_A} + q = 0 \Rightarrow \frac{\partial TC_A}{\partial P_A} = q \tag{1}$$

That condition simply says marginal cost is equal to marginal revenue from polluting (now equal to q).

For firm B, the quantity of pollution that maximizes its profit is given by the condition:

$$-\frac{\partial TC_B}{\partial P_A} - q = 0 \Rightarrow -\frac{\partial TC_B}{\partial P_A} = q \tag{2}$$

Equations (1) and (2) imply that the price q should satisfy the following: $-\partial TC_A/\partial P_A = \partial TC_B/\partial P_A$.

In deciding the optimal level of P_A, firm A now takes into account the effect that its decision has on firm B. In particular, it must set a level of pollution such that the marginal private cost of polluting ($-\partial TC_A/\partial P_A$) is equal to the marginal social cost of polluting ($\partial TC_B/\partial P_A$). So, by assigning the property rights we can obtain the efficient level of pollution. You can try to work out the case in which firm B has the right not to be polluted and can sell this right to firm A; does the result above still hold?

13.6 Environmental issues and the economics of climate change

When there is no implicit market for pollution, pollutants are overproduced. Private producers ignore the costs they impose on others. In equilibrium, social marginal cost exceeds social marginal benefit.

The most topical environmental externality we are currently facing is global warming, or climate change; that is, the rise in global temperature due to human activity. In particular, global warming is an externality in two main dimensions:

1 An intergenerational dimension: what humans are currently doing will affect future generations not yet born.

2 An international dimension: what a country does in terms of emissions will affect other countries.

The problem with externalities such as those affecting the environment is that the private sector cannot organize charges for the marginal externalities pollution creates. However, a government may be able to do it. By charging (through taxes) for the divergence between marginal private and social cost, the government can induce private producers to take account of the costs inflicted on others. This argument for pollution taxes or congestion charges is examined in the next chapter.

Pollution taxes, especially for water pollution, are used in many countries. But most policy takes a different approach: imposing pollution standards to regulate the quantities of pollution allowed.

For global warming, given its international dimension, things are more complicated, since an effective policy should be agreed on and implemented by a coalition of governments.

We now begin to discuss UK government policy in relation to pollution, followed by an analysis of the problem of global warming in more detail.

Air pollution

Since the Clean Air Act 1956, UK governments have designated clean air zones in which certain pollutants, notably smoke caused by burning coal, are illegal. The number of designated clean air zones has risen steadily. Table 13.1 shows a big fall in smoke pollution in the UK.

Adding lead to petrol improves the fuel efficiency of cars. However, lead emissions from car exhausts are an atmospheric pollutant harmful to people's health. Since 1972 the UK government has steadily reduced the quantity of lead permitted in petrol. Lead emission into the UK atmosphere has fallen from over 8000 tonnes a year in 1975 to only 1000 tonnes a year, even though consumption of petrol has risen dramatically.

Water pollution

Since 1951, governments in the UK have also imposed controls on discharges into inland waterways. Although we think of *industrial* effluent, sewage is a more important source of pollution. Since 1970, regional water authorities in England and Wales have spent (at 2000 prices) over £3 billion a year on water purification and sewage treatment. Another key source of water pollution is nitrates used to fertilize agricultural land. The EU has laid down tough standards for water purity that will take many years to achieve.

Evaluating UK pollution policy

Direct regulation of pollution has been a mixed success. Cutting smoke pollution, which used to mix with winter fog to create dense 'smog', has been a big success. Many rivers are also cleaner, and fish have reappeared. In other cases, regulation was less successful. It is hard to enforce regulations such as those that prevent ships discharging oil at sea. UK beaches still feature on the EU blacklist. Coal-fired power stations still emit large quantities of sulphur dioxide.

Table 13.1 Smoke emission, UK (million tonnes per annum)

1958	1974	2003
2.0	0.8	0.1

Sources: Digest of Environmental Protection and Water Statistics; ONS, Social Trends.

Was the government tough enough on polluters? Recall that the efficient quantity of pollution is not zero. The fact that pollution still exists does itself not prove that policy has been too feeble.

Pollution control has often been crude and simple. Calculations of social marginal costs and benefits of cutting back pollution are rare. Measuring costs and benefits is difficult. In deciding how much to cut lead emissions from cars, we can estimate the marginal social cost of producing cars with antipollution exhaust systems and the marginal social cost of cars that use more fuel per mile. But even if doctors were unanimous on the effects of lead emission on health, how should society value a marginal increase in the health of current and future generations?

This is not merely a question of efficiency but also of equity, both within the current generation – poor inner-city children are more vulnerable to arrested development caused by inhaling lead-polluted air – and across generations. Today's consumers bear the cost of the clean-up, but its benefits accrue largely to future consumers.

Prices vs quantities

If free markets tend to overpollute, society can cut pollution either by regulating the quantity of pollution or by using the price system to discourage such activities by taxing them. Is it more sensible to intervene through the tax system than to regulate quantities directly?

Many economists prefer taxes to quantity restrictions. If each firm is charged the same price or tax for a marginal unit of pollution, each firm equates the marginal cost of reducing pollution to the price of pollution. Any allocation in which different firms have different marginal costs of reducing pollution is inefficient. If firms with low marginal reduction costs contract further and firms with high marginal reduction costs contract less, lower pollution is achieved at less cost.

The main problem with using taxes not quantity restrictions is uncertainty about the outcome. Suppose pollution beyond a critical level has disastrous consequences, for example irreversibly damaging the ozone layer. By regulating the quantity directly, society can ensure a disaster is avoided. Indirect control, through taxes or charges, runs the risk that the government does its sums wrong and sets the tax too low. Pollution is then higher than intended, and may be disastrous.

Regulating the total quantity of pollution, with spot checks on compliance by individual producers, is a simple policy that avoids the worst outcomes. However, by ignoring differences in the marginal cost of reducing pollution across different polluters, it does not reduce pollution in a way that is cost-minimizing to society.

Lessons from the United States

The US has gone furthest in trying to use property rights and the price mechanism to cut back pollution efficiently. The US Clean Air Acts established an environmental policy that includes an *emissions trading programme* and *bubble policy*.

The Acts lay down a minimum standard for air quality, and impose pollution emission controls on particular polluters. Any polluter emitting less than their specified amount gets an *emission reduction credit* (ERC), which can be sold to another polluter wanting to exceed its allocated pollution limit. Thus, the total quantity of pollution is regulated, but firms that can cheaply reduce pollution have an incentive to do so, and sell off the ERC to firms for which pollution reduction is more expensive. We get closer to the efficient solution in which the marginal cost of pollution reduction is equalized across firms.

When a firm has many factories, the bubble policy applies pollution controls to the firm as a whole. The firm can cut back most at the plants in which pollution reduction is cheapest.

Thus, the US policy combines 'control over quantities' for aggregate pollution, where the risks and uncertainties are greatest, with 'control through the price system' for allocating efficiently the way these overall targets are achieved.

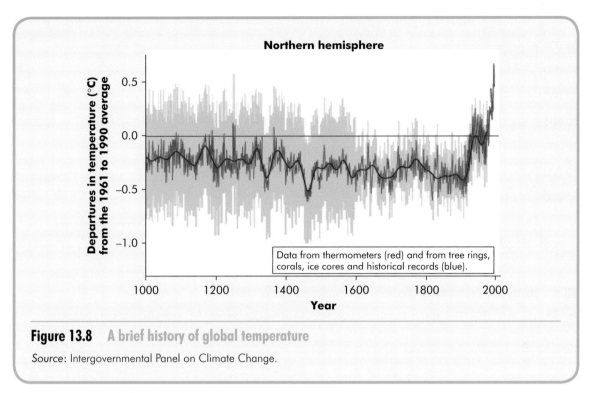

Figure 13.8 A brief history of global temperature

Source: Intergovernmental Panel on Climate Change.

The economics of climate change

There is increasing evidence that global temperatures are rising. The science of climate change means that we are also likely to see greater fluctuations in climate as well. Hence, extreme events will become much more frequent. Large parts of Bangladesh may disappear under water for ever; and English villages, from Yorkshire to Cornwall, have already experienced flash flooding. Conversely, regions of the world that are currently temperate may become arid and uninhabitable. Figure 13.8 shows the dramatic change in global temperatures in recent years.

The science of climate change

The earth's climate is affected by many things, from solar radiation to the consequences of human behaviour. The ebb and flow of previous ice ages reminds us that human behaviour is not the only cause of climate change. Even so, there is increasing evidence that we must look to ourselves as a major cause of recent global warming.

In the same period in which we experienced an increase in global temperature, there was a significant increase in global CO_2 emissions due to human activity. This is shown in Figure 13.9.

Greenhouse gases – including carbon dioxide and methane – shield the earth from solar radiation, but also trap the heat underneath. Without them, all heat would escape and we would freeze to death. But we need just the right amount. Too much greenhouse gas and the earth overheats, causing global warming.

The recent build-up of greenhouse gases reflects large emissions of carbon dioxide from households, power stations and transport. This may cause ice to melt and water to expand, causing sea levels to rise. A catastrophic eventual consequence would be melting of permafrost in Siberia, releasing such volumes of methane that a large rise in temperature would then be inevitable, perhaps threatening human survival.

Carbon, a key constituent of all greenhouse gases, is a useful common denominator. Slowing, let alone reversing, global warming requires the emission of much less carbon.

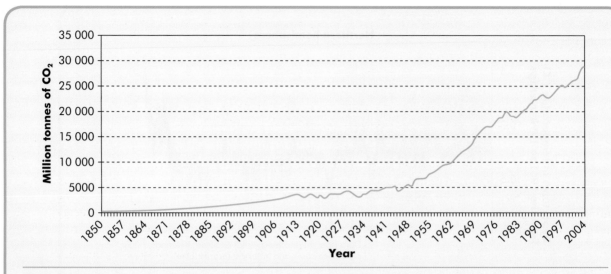

Figure 13.9 Historical evolution of global CO_2 emissions, 1850–2004

Source: Marland, G. et al. (2007) Global, regional, and national CO_2 emissions, *Trends: A Compendium of Data on Global Change*, CDIAC, USA.

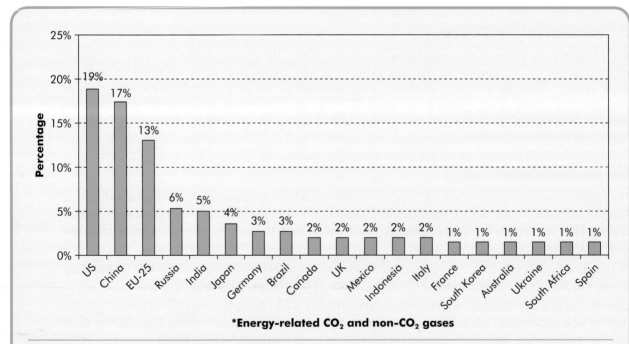

Figure 13.10 Annual greenhouse gas emissions per country, 2004

Sources: IEA (2006) CO_2 emissions from fossil fuel combustion; EPA (2006) Global anthropogenic non-CO_2 greenhouse gas emissions 1990–2020.

Figure 13.10 shows greenhouse gas emissions per country in 2004 (CO_2 is an important greenhouse gas but it is not the only one). As we can see, the US is the country that produces the largest amount of greenhouse gases, followed by China and then the European Union as a whole.

The Kyoto Protocol

In 1997 a group of countries signed an amendment to the UN International Treaty on Climate Change, committing themselves to cut greenhouse gas emissions. By 2006, 169 countries (though not the US) had signed.

Developed countries accept the obligation to reduce emissions by 2012 to 5 per cent below the level of their emissions in 1990. Developing countries have not yet made a commitment but can take part in the Clean Development Mechanism. Thus, China and India ratified the protocol but are not yet bound by the commitment to reduce emissions: given their population size, rate of economic growth and future energy demands, China and India will have a huge impact on what happens with greenhouse gases.

Within the EU's overall targets, individual members can buy and sell obligations within the EU Emissions Trading Scheme (which resembles the US pollution scheme discussed earlier). The Clean Development Mechanism allows India or China to invest in emissions reduction, such as by building a cleaner power station, and sell the emissions credit to a UK or German company so that Europe then meets its overall emissions obligations.

Thus the projected total cutbacks can be achieved efficiently – those most easily able to reduce emissions cheaply do so; those for whom emissions reduction is expensive can instead purchase a credit from someone else better placed to cut back emissions cheaply.

If you think about it this is an application of the property rights argument we have previously discussed.

Cost–benefit analysis

Even if we accept the science, what should we do, and how quickly? This gets to the core of the what, how and for whom questions of Chapter 1. The for whom question is particularly acute. How much pain should the current generation take in order to make life nicer for future generations? Can we expect China and India to slow their economic development to make life nicer for citizens in Europe and the US who begin with many more economic advantages?

The Kyoto targets are modest, and as yet fail to include the key economies of the US, China and India, on whom much will actually depend. Kyoto supporters see these targets as the thin end of the wedge, creating a political dynamic that will create tougher targets soon; which is precisely why they are opposed by those who would potentially lose out (for example, the air-conditioned affluent citizens of the US and Australia whose current energy consumption is enormous).

In 2006 the UK government published a report on the economics of climate change written by Sir Nicholas Stern, a London School of Economics professor, and ex-Chief Economist of both the World Bank and the European Bank for Reconstruction and Development. The Stern Review (details of which are available at www.hm-treasury.gov.uk) concluded that 1 per cent of global GDP must be invested from now on if we are to head off the worst effects of climate change; and that failure to act now risks a future cost of up to 20 per cent of global GDP.

Many of the world's leading economists – including economics Nobel Prize winners Sir James Mirrlees, Amartya Sen, Joe Stiglitz and Bob Solow, and Professor Jeffrey Sachs, Director of the Earth Institute at Columbia University in New York – have come out strongly in support of the Stern Review. The principal point of subsequent debate has been the appropriate interest rate at which to discount future costs and benefits, a topic we discuss in Activity 13.1. The decision about how much to discount the welfare of future generations affects the present value of the benefits of tackling climate change today, and hence both the optimal pace of action and estimates of the cost of inaction. Although the quantitative conclusions change, the qualitative conclusions do not.

Stern view of discount rates

ACTIVITY 13.1

Figure 13.8 showed a 1000-year history of temperatures on the planet. Suppose we could all agree on the science of global warming. This would allow statements of the form, 'if we continue producing emissions at the current rate, global temperatures will rise according to the following profile, with the following consequences in terms of flooding, volatile weather, drought, and so on.'

Suppose too that there was only one country in the world, so we did not have to worry about whether the US or India participated in trying to slow down climate change. The central issue then would be, 'how much pain should we inflict on today's generation in order to mitigate the problem for future generations?'

The lower the discount rate we use in this calculation, the greater the present value of the benefits of helping future generations; the lower the discount rate we use, the less today we care about helping future generations. The Stern Review's recommendation that we should take urgent action to reduce emissions substantially follows inexorably from its analysis provided we agree with its assumption that we should not discount the welfare of future generations in making this policy decision today.

Others, such as Professor William Nordhaus of Yale University, have argued that today's decision makers should discount the welfare of future generations – not least because they are still likely to be richer than us and have better options than we face – in which case, the optimal policy response to climate change is a slower mitigation of emissions today, albeit then requiring that future generations will have to take much more drastic action.

The discount rate is not an academic abstraction. It affects key valuations and decisions, whether in the stock market or in the politics of controlling global warming.

Questions

(a) If we wish to weight equally the utility of current and future generations, what discount rate should we apply to future utility?

(b) Still weighting utility equally, suppose future generations are richer than us and we believe in the principle of diminishing marginal utility of consumption. Will a unit of consumption be worth more today when we are poor, or tomorrow when we are rich?

(c) Suppose, by sacrificing consumption today, we invest in physical capital that would make future generations richer. Say, on average, this investment has a rate of return of 5 per cent a year in real terms. What return would an environmental investment (e.g. preventing climate change) have to yield in order for future generations to be pleased with the decisions we made today?

To check your answers to these questions, go to page 684.

13.7 Other missing markets: time and risk

The previous two sections were devoted to a single idea. When externalities exist, free market equilibrium is inefficient because the externality itself does not have a market or a price. People take no account of the costs and benefits their actions inflict on others. Without a market for externalities the price system cannot bring marginal costs and marginal benefits of these externalities into line. We now discuss other 'missing markets' – those for time and for risk.

The present and the future are linked. People save, or refrain from consumption, today in order to consume more tomorrow. Firms invest, reducing current output by devoting resources to training or building, in order to produce more tomorrow. How should society make plans today for the quantities of goods produced and consumed in the future? Ideally, everyone makes plans such that the social marginal cost of goods in the future just equals their social marginal benefit.

Chapter 12 discussed a *forward market*, in which buyers and sellers make contracts today for goods delivered in the future at a price agreed today. Suppose there is a forward market for copper in 2010. Consumers equate the marginal benefit of copper in 2010 to the forward price, which producers equate to the marginal cost of producing copper for 2010. With a complete set of forward markets for all commodities for all future dates, producers and consumers today make consistent plans for future production and consumption of all goods, and the social marginal benefit of every future good equals its social marginal cost.

Chapter 12 explained why few forward markets exist. You can trade gold but not cars or washing machines. Since nobody knows the characteristics of next year's model of car or washing machine, we cannot write legally binding contracts to be easily enforced when the goods are delivered. Without these forward markets, the price system cannot equate the marginal cost and marginal benefits of planned future goods.

There are also few *contingent* or insurance markets for dealing with risk. People usually dislike risk. It reduces their utility. Does society undertake the efficient amount of risky activities?

A complete set of insurance markets lets risk be transferred from those who dislike risk to those who will bear risk at a price. The equilibrium price equates social marginal costs and benefits of risky activities. However, adverse selection and moral hazard inhibit the organization of private insurance markets. If some risky activities are uninsurable at any price, the price system cannot guide society to equate social marginal costs and benefits.

Future goods and risky goods are examples of commodities with missing markets. Like externalities, these are market failures. Free market equilibrium is generally efficient. And the theory of the second-best tells us that, when some markets are distorted, we probably do not want other markets to be completely distortion free.

13.8 Quality, health and safety

Information is incomplete because gathering information is costly. This leads to inefficiency. A worker unaware that exposure to benzene may cause cancer may work for a lower wage than if this information is widely available. The firm's production cost understates the true social cost and the good is overproduced. Governments regulate health, safety and quality standards because they recognize the danger of market failure.

UK examples include the Health and Safety at Work Acts, legislation to control food and drugs production, the Fair Trading Act governing consumer protection, and various traffic and motoring regulations. Such legislation aims to encourage the provision of information that lets individuals more accurately judge costs and benefits, and aims to set and enforce standards designed to reduce the risk of injury or death.

Providing information

Figure 13.11 shows the supply curve *SS* for a drug that is potentially harmful. *DD* is the demand curve if consumers do not know the danger. In equilibrium at *E*, the quantity *Q* is produced and consumed. With full information about the dangers, people would buy less of the drug. The demand curve *DD'* shows the marginal consumer benefit with full information. The new equilibrium at *E'* avoids the deadweight burden *E'EF* from overproduction of the drug.

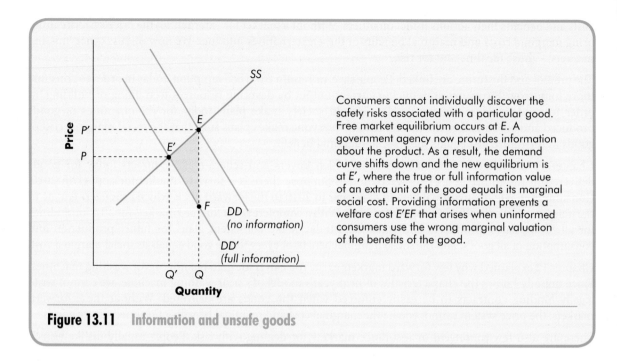

Consumers cannot individually discover the safety risks associated with a particular good. Free market equilibrium occurs at E. A government agency now provides information about the product. As a result, the demand curve shifts down and the new equilibrium is at E', where the true or full information value of an extra unit of the good equals its marginal social cost. Providing information prevents a welfare cost E'EF that arises when uninformed consumers use the wrong marginal valuation of the benefits of the good.

Figure 13.11   Information and unsafe goods

If information were free to collect, everyone would know the true risks. From the social gain E'EF we should subtract the resources needed to discover this information. Free market equilibrium is at E because it is not worth each individual checking up privately on each drug on the market. It makes sense for society to have a single regulatory body to check drugs, and a law whose enforcement entitles individuals to assume that drugs have been checked out as safe.

Certification of safety or quality need not be carried out by the government. Sotheby's certify Rembrandts, the AA will check out a used car for you, and drunk drivers may send half their blood sample to a private certification agency to corroborate the results of the police analysis.

Two factors inhibit the use of private certification in many areas of health and safety. First, the public perceives a conflict between the profit motive and the incentive to tell the truth. Public officials may be less easily swayed.

Second, a private certification agency might have to decide standards. What margin of error should be built into safety regulations? How safe must a drug be to get a certificate? These are issues of public policy. They involve externalities and have distributional implications. Even if society uses private agencies to *monitor* regulations, it usually sets the standards itself.

Imposing standards

The public interest is important when little is known about a product and where the consequences of any error may be catastrophic. Few believe that safety standards for nuclear power stations can be adequately determined by the private sector.

In imposing standards, governments raise the private cost of production by preventing firms from adopting the cost-minimizing techniques they otherwise would use. Sometimes the government has better information than the private sector. Sometimes standards compensate for externalities neglected by the private firm. Sometimes standards reflect a pure value judgement based on distributional considerations. One contentious area is the value of human life itself.

Politicians often claim, ridiculously, that human life is beyond economic calculation and must be given absolute priority at any cost. The UK government repeated this assurance after the Paddington rail disaster in October 1999. An economist will make two points in reply. First, it is *impossible* to implement such an objective. It is too costly in resources to try to eliminate *all* risks of premature death. Sensibly, we do not go this far. Second, in occupational and recreational choices, for example driving racing cars or going climbing, people take risks. Society must ask how much more risk-averse it should be than the people it is trying to protect.

Beyond some point, the marginal social cost of further risk reduction exceeds the marginal social benefit. It takes a huge effort to make the world just a little safer, and the resources might have been used elsewhere to greater effect. Zero risk does not make economic sense. We need to know the costs of making the world a little safer, and we need to encourage society to decide how much it values the benefits. By shying away from the 'unpleasant' task of spelling out the costs and benefits, society induces an inefficient allocation in which marginal costs and marginal benefits of saving life are very different for different activities.

Summary

- **Welfare economics** deals with normative issues or value judgements. Its purpose is not to describe how the economy works but to assess how well it works.

- **Horizontal equity** is the equal treatment of equals, and **vertical equity** the unequal treatment of unequals. Equity is concerned with the distribution of welfare across people. The desirable degree of equity is a pure value judgement.

- A **resource allocation** is a complete description of what, how and for whom goods are produced. To separate as far as possible the concepts of equity and efficiency, economists use Pareto efficiency. An allocation is **Pareto-efficient** if no reallocation of resources would make some people better off without making others worse off. If an allocation is inefficient it is possible to achieve a Pareto gain, making some people better off and none worse off. Many reallocations make some people better off and others worse off. We cannot say whether such changes are good or bad without making value judgements to compare different people's welfare.

- For a given level of resources and a given technology, the economy has an infinite number of Pareto-efficient allocations that differ in the distribution of welfare across people. For example, every allocation that gives all output to one individual is Pareto-efficient. But there are many more allocations that are inefficient.

- Under strict conditions, competitive equilibrium is Pareto-efficient. Different initial distributions of human and physical capital across people generate different competitive equilibria corresponding to each possible Pareto-efficient allocation. When price-taking producers and consumers face the same prices, marginal costs and marginal benefits are equated to prices (by the individual actions of producers and consumers).

- In practice, governments face a conflict between equity and efficiency. Redistributive taxation drives a wedge between prices paid by consumers (to which marginal benefits are equated) and prices received by producers (to which marginal costs are equated). Free market equilibrium will not equate marginal cost and marginal benefit and there will be inefficiency.

- **Distortions** occur whenever free market equilibrium does not equate **marginal social cost** and **marginal social benefit**. Distortions lead to inefficiency or **market failure**. Apart from taxes, there are three other important sources of distortion: imperfect competition (failure to set price equal to marginal cost), externalities (divergence between private and social costs or benefits), and other missing markets in connection with future goods, risky goods or other informational problems.

- When only one market is distorted the **first-best** solution is to remove the distortion, thus achieving full efficiency. The first-best criterion relates only to efficiency. Governments caring sufficiently about redistribution might still prefer inefficient allocations with more vertical equity. However, when a distortion cannot be removed from one market, it is not generally efficient to ensure that all other markets are distortion-free. The theory of the **second-best** says that it is more efficient to spread inevitable distortions thinly over many markets than to concentrate their effects in a few markets.

- **Production externalities** occur when actions by one producer directly affect the production costs of another producer, as when one firm pollutes another's water supply. **Consumption externalities** mean one person's decisions affect another consumer's utility directly, as when a garden gives pleasure to neighbours. Externalities shift indifference curves or production functions.

- Externalities lead to divergence between private and social costs or benefits because there is no implicit market for the externality itself. When only a few people are involved, a system of **property rights** may establish the missing market. The direction of compensation will depend on who has the property rights. Either way, it achieves the efficient quantity of the externality at which marginal cost and marginal benefit are equated. The efficient solution is rarely a zero quantity of the externality. **Transaction costs** and the **free-rider problem** may prevent implicit markets being established. Equilibrium will then be inefficient.

- When externalities lead to market failure, the government could set up the missing market by pricing the externality through taxes or subsidies. If it were straightforward to assess the efficient quantity of the externality and hence the correct tax or subsidy, and straightforward to monitor the quantities produced and consumed, such taxes or subsidies would allow the market to achieve an efficient resource allocation.

- In practice, governments often regulate externalities such as **pollution** or **congestion** by imposing standards that affect quantities directly rather than by using the tax system to affect production and consumption indirectly. Overall quantity standards may fail to equate the marginal cost of pollution reduction across different polluters, in which case the allocation will not be efficient. However, simple standards may use up fewer resources in monitoring and enforcement and may prevent disastrous outcomes when there is uncertainty.

- **Global warming** represents a negative environmental externality that is believed to be caused by human activity and is posing a serious threat to the global economy. As an externality, it has two main dimensions: an intergenerational dimension and an international dimension. To assess the possible effects of global warming on our economies, we employ cost–benefit analysis.

- **Moral hazard, adverse selection** and **other informational problems** prevent the development of a complete set of **forward markets** and **contingent markets**. Without these markets the price system cannot equate social marginal cost and benefit for future goods or risky activities.

- Incomplete information may lead to inefficient private choices. Health, quality and safety regulations are designed both to provide information and to express society's value judgements about intangibles, such as life itself. By avoiding explicit consideration of social costs and benefits, government policy may be inconsistent in its implicit valuation of health or safety in different activities under regulation.

Review questions

connect

1 An economy has ten units of goods to share out between two people. [x, y] means that the first person gets a quantity x, the second person a quantity y. For each of the allocations (a) to (e), say whether they are (i) efficient and (ii) equitable: (a) [10, 0], (b) [7, 2], (c) [5, 5], (d) [3, 6], (e) [0, 10]. What does 'equitable' mean? Would you prefer allocation (d) to allocation (e)?

EASY

2 The price of meals is £1 and of films £5. There is perfect competition and no externality. What can we say about (a) the relative benefit to consumers of a marginal film and a marginal meal, (b) the relative marginal production cost of films and meals, or (c) the relative marginal product of variable factors in the film and meal industries? Why is this equilibrium efficient?

3 In deciding to drive a car in the rush hour, you think about the cost of petrol and the time of the journey. Do you slow other people down by driving? Is this an externality? Will too many or too few people drive cars in the rush hour? Should commuter parking in cities be restricted?

4 In 1885, 200 people died when the steam boiler exploded on a Mississippi river boat. Jeremiah Allen and three friends formed a private company offering to insure any boiler that they had inspected for safety. Boiler inspections caught on, and explosion rates plummeted. Would Jeremiah Allen's company have been successful if it had certified boilers but not insured them as well? Explain.

5 (a) Why might society ban drugs that neither help nor harm the diseases they are claimed to cure? (b) If regulatory bodies are blamed for bad things that happen despite regulations (a train crash) but not blamed for preventing good things through too much regulation (rapid availability of a safe and useful drug), will regulatory bodies over-regulate activities under their scrutiny?

6 John and Jennifer need to decide how to divide a chocolate cake. Putting the quantity of the cake that John can get on the vertical axis and the quantity of the cake that Jennifer can get on the horizontal axis, plot the Pareto frontier of this cake allocation problem. What does a point below the Pareto frontier represent? Is an allocation whereby John gets the entire cake and Jennifer nothing Pareto-efficient?

7 Common fallacies Why are these statements wrong? (a) Society should ban all toxic discharges. (b) Anything the government can do, the market can do better. (c) Anything the market can do, the government can do better.

8 A firm producing plastic bags is polluting the air of the neighborhood. In the following table the marginal private costs (MPC) of the firm for different quantities of plastic bags are reported, together with the inverse demand for plastic bags.

MEDIUM

Q	MPC (£)	Selling Price (£)
1	11	28
2	12	26
3	13	24
4	14	22
5	15	20
6	16	18
7	17	16
8	18	14
9	19	12

Polluting the air creates an externality. We know that the value of the externality is £20 for each quantity level. On a graph with Q on the horizontal axis, plot the MPC, the marginal social costs and the demand. Show the equilibrium in the market. Why is the equilibrium inefficient?

9   A honey firm is located next to an apple field owned by a farmer. The bees go into the apple field and help make all the trees more productive. This in turn reduces the farmer's costs. We have a positive externality. The total cost of the honey firm is $TC_H = H^2$, where H denotes the amount of honey. For the farmer, the total cost is $TC_A = A^2 - H$, where A denotes the amount of apples. Assume that the price of honey is fixed at £2, while the price of an apple is fixed at £4. Write down the profit functions for the honey firm and for the farmer. What is the profit-maximizing level of honey produced by the honey firm? What is the profit-maximizing level of apples produced? Find the profits earned by the honey firm and the farmer.

10 Now suppose that the honey firm and the farmer in Question 9 merge to become a single firm that produces honey and apples. The total cost faced by the merged firm is $TC_M = H^2 + A^2 - H$. The prices of the two goods are the same as in Question 9. Write down the profit function of the merged firm. Find the profit-maximizing levels of honey and apples produced. What is the total profit obtained by the merged firm? Compare your answer with your results in Question 9. Is the externality internalized?

11 Much of the economics of efficiency is about ensuring that we equate the marginal cost of producing the last unit with the marginal benefit of that unit to the last consumer. Suppose the marginal cost of preventing the planet overheating is £10 000 billion. How would you attempt to assess the marginal benefit?

12 A government needs to raise £10 billion from taxes. It knows that taxes create deadweight burden triangles, and it taxes a number of activities and products. In the most efficient outcome possible, say whether the tax rate on each of the following should be low, average or high: (a) mobile international capital, (b) unskilled domestic labour, (c) food, (d) tobacco.

13 **Essay question**   Why do politicians pretend that trains can be made perfectly safe and hospitals can supply all the health care that we know how to supply, when it is perfectly obvious that we do not have the resources to do these things and that it would be highly wasteful to try?

CHAPTER 14

Government spending and revenue

Learning Outcomes

By the end of this chapter, you should understand:

1. different kinds of government spending

2. why public goods cannot be provided by a market

3. average and marginal tax rates

4. how taxes can compensate for externalities

5. supply-side economics

6. why tax revenue cannot be raised without limit

7. how cross-border flows limit national economic sovereignty

8. the political economy of how governments set policy

The scale of government rose steadily until the 1970s. Then many people felt it had become too big, using resources better employed in the private sector. High taxes were thought to be stifling private enterprise. Electorates in many countries turned to the political leaders who promised to reduce the scale of government.

Now the pendulum is swinging back. In the US, even a Republican president, George W. Bush, promised massive government resources to rebuild New York after the terrorist attacks of 2001. In the UK the tax burden rose in the 1990s, after falling under Mrs Thatcher. Labour won the 2001 election on a promise of higher government spending on health, education and transport.

For historical perspective, Table 14.1 shows how government grew everywhere in the last century.

Most government spending is financed by tax revenue. However, just as you may overspend your student income by borrowing now and repaying later, the government need not balance its spending and revenue in any particular period. When the difference between total revenues and total spending is negative, we then have a budget deficit. When that difference is positive, the government is running a **budget surplus**. Table 14.2 shows that, by 2009, after two years of the credit crunch, the US and the UK had budget deficits higher than those in France and Germany.

After this broad background, we now examine microeconomic issues. First, we distinguish **marginal and average tax rates**.

> The **budget surplus** (deficit) is the excess (shortfall) of government's spending over its revenue.
>
> The **marginal tax rate** is the fraction of the last pound of income paid in tax.
>
> The **average tax rate** is the fraction of total income paid in tax.

Table 14.1 Government spending (% of GDP)

	1880	1960	2009
Japan	11	18	39.3
US	8	28	36.1
Germany	10	32	47.6
UK	10	32	51.7
France	15	35	55.6
Sweden	6	31	55.8

Sources: World Bank, *World Development Report*. © 2010 The World Bank Group. All rights reserved.

Table 14.2 Government activity in 2009 (% of GDP)

	UK	US	France	Germany
Spending	51.7	36.1	55.6	47.6
Total revenue	40.3	24.8	48.1	44.3
Budget surplus	−11.4	−11.3	−7.5	−3.3

Sources: EUROSTAT; www.bea.gov.

Table 14.3 UK income tax rates, 1978–2008

Taxable income (2004 £000s)	Marginal tax rate (%)	
	1978/79	2008/09
2020	34	20
5000	34	20
10 000	34	20
20 000	45	20
31 400	50	20
40 000	70	40
70 000	83	40

Note: Taxable income after deducting allowances. In 2008/09 a single person's allowance was almost £5500.

Sources: HMSO, *Financial Statement and Budget Report*; ONS, Budget 2007.

In a *progressive* tax structure, the average tax rate rises with an individual's income. The government takes proportionately more from the rich than from the poor. In a *regressive* tax structure, the average tax rate falls as income level rises, taking proportionately less from the rich.

Table 14.3 shows that the UK, like most countries, has a progressive income tax structure. Figure 14.1 explains why. We plot pre-tax income on the horizontal axis and post-tax income on the vertical axis. The line *OG*, with a slope of 45 degrees, implies no taxes. A pre-tax income *OA* on the horizontal axis matches the same post-tax income *OA* on the vertical axis. Now suppose there is an income tax, but the first *OA* of income is untaxed. If the marginal tax rate on taxable income is constant, individuals face a schedule *OBCD*, keeping a constant fraction of each pound of pre-tax income above *OA*. The higher the marginal tax rate, the flatter is *BC*.

To calculate the average tax rate at a point such as *D*, we join up *OD*. The flatter the slope of this line, the

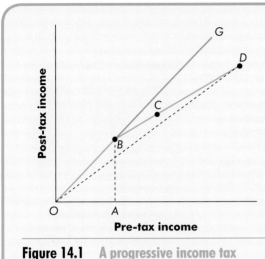

G

D

C

B

Post-tax income

O   A

Pre-tax income

The 45° line *OG* shows zero taxes or transfers so that pre-tax and post-tax income coincide. With an allowance *OA*, then a constant marginal tax rate *t*, the post-tax income schedule is *OBCD*. The slope depends only on the marginal tax rate [on *BCD* it is (1 − *t*)]. The average tax rate at any point *D* is the slope of *OD*. A tax is progressive if the average tax rate rises with pre-tax income.

Figure 14.1   A progressive income tax

higher is the average tax rate. Even with a constant marginal tax rate, and a constant slope along *BC*, the initial tax allowance makes the tax structure progressive. The higher an individual's gross income, the smaller is the tax allowance as a percentage of gross income, so the larger is the fraction of total income on which tax is paid.

But Table 14.3 shows that *marginal* tax rates may also rise with income. As individuals move into higher tax bands they pay higher marginal tax rates, moving on to even flatter portions of the tax schedule. The average tax rate now rises sharply with income.

Table 14.3 shows that UK marginal tax rates have fallen a lot in the past two decades, especially for the very rich. A millionaire paying an 83 per cent tax rate on all taxable income except the first £70 000 in 1978 paid only 40 per cent in 2008/09.

The UK was not alone in cutting tax rates. There was a worldwide move to cut tax rates, especially for the very rich. In part, this reflected the belief that tax rates were previously so high that distortions had been large. However, it also reflected increasing competition between governments to attract mobile resources (physical and human capital) to their country. At the end of the chapter we discuss how cross-border mobility undermines national sovereignty.

14.1   Taxation and government spending

Government spending, and the taxes that finance it, are now about 45 per cent of national output. Figure 14.2 shows the composition of government spending and revenue in 2007/08.

Nearly a third of total government spending went on **transfer payments** such as social protection of pensions, jobseeker's allowance (formerly unemployment benefit) and debt interest. Of the remaining spending directly on goods and services, the most important spending categories are health, defence and education. Figure 14.2 also shows how this government spending is financed. The most important **direct taxes** are income tax, and corporation tax on company profits.

The most important **indirect taxes** are value added tax (VAT) and customs duties. Note that, since state provision of retirement pensions is included on the expenditure side as a transfer payment, pension contributions under the national insurance scheme are included on the revenue side.

A **transfer payment** requires no good or service in return during the period in which it is paid.

Direct taxes are taxes on income and wealth.

Indirect taxes are taxes on spending and output.

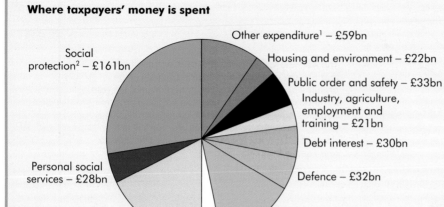

Where taxpayers' money is spent

Social protection[2] – £161bn

Other expenditure[1] – £59bn

Housing and environment – £22bn

Public order and safety – £33bn

Industry, agriculture, employment and training – £21bn

Debt interest – £30bn

Defence – £32bn

Personal social services – £28bn

Education – £77bn

Health – £104bn

Transport – £20bn

Total managed expenditure – £587 billion

[1]Other expenditure includes spending on general public services; recreation, culture, media and sport, international co-operation and development; public service pensions; plus spending yet to be allocated and some accounting adjustments.

[2]Social protection includes tax credit payments in excess of an individual's tax liability.

Source: HM Treasury. 2007–08 near cash projections. Figures may not sum to total due to rounding.

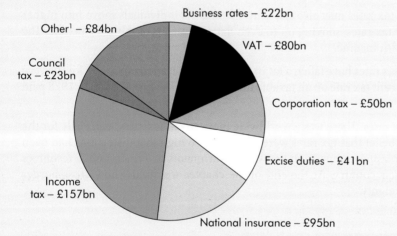

Where taxes come from

Other[1] – £84bn

Council tax – £23bn

Income tax – £157bn

Business rates – £22bn

VAT – £80bn

Corporation tax – £50bn

Excise duties – £41bn

National insurance – £95bn

Total receipts – £553 billion

[1]Other includes capital taxes, stamp duties, vehicle excise duties, and some other tax and non-tax receipts (e.g. interest and dividends).

Source: HM Treasury. 2007–08 projections. Figures may not sum to total due to rounding.

Figure 14.2 UK government expenditure and revenue, 2007/08

14.2 The government in the market economy

How do we justify government spending in a market economy?

> A **public good**, if consumed by one person, must be consumed by others in exactly the same quantity.

Public goods

In Chapter 13 we introduced the idea of **public good** as market failure. Here, we discuss this issue in more detail.

Ice cream is a **private good**. If you eat an ice cream nobody else can eat that particular ice cream. For any given supply, your consumption reduces the quantity available for others to consume. Most goods are private goods.

> A **private good**, if consumed by one person, cannot be consumed by others.

Clean air and defence are examples of public goods. If the air is pollution-free, your consumption of it does not interfere with our consumption of it. If the navy is patrolling coastal waters, your consumption of national defence does not affect our quantity of national defence. We all consume the same quantity; namely, the quantity is supplied in the aggregate. We may get different amounts of utility if our tastes differ, but we all consume the same quantity.

The key aspects of public goods are (1) that it is technically possible for one person to consume without reducing the amount available for others, and (2) that it is impossible to exclude anyone from consumption except at a prohibitive cost. A football match can be watched by many people, especially if it is on TV, without reducing the quantity consumed by other viewers; but *exclusion* is possible. The ground holds only so many, and some Premier League clubs now charge to watch their games live on their own TV stations. The interesting issues arise when, as with national defence, exclusion of certain individuals from consumption is impossible.

Free-riders

Chapter 13 introduced the *free-rider problem* when discussing why bribes and compensation for externalities might not occur. Public goods are wide open to the free-rider problem if they are supplied by the private sector. Since you get the same quantity of national defence as everyone else, *whether or not you pay for it*, you never buy national defence in a private market. Nor does anyone else. No defence is demanded, even though we all want it.

Public goods are like a strong externality. If you buy defence, everyone else also gets the benefits. Since marginal private and social benefits diverge, private markets will not produce the socially efficient quantity. Government intervention is needed.

The marginal social benefit

Suppose the public good is a pure public water supply. The more infected the water, the more people are likely to get cholera. Figure 14.3 supposes there are two people. The first person's demand curve for water purity is D_1D_1. Each point on the demand curve shows what she would pay for the last unit of purer water, her marginal benefit. D_2D_2 shows the marginal benefit of purer water to the second person.

Curve DD is the marginal social benefit of purer water. At each level of the public good, we *vertically* sum the marginal benefit of each individual to get the marginal social benefit. At the output Q, the marginal social benefit is $P = P_1 + P_2$. We sum vertically at *a given quantity* because everyone consumes the same quantity of a public good.

Figure 14.3 also shows the marginal cost of the public good. If there are no production externalities the marginal private cost and marginal social cost coincide. The socially efficient output of the public good is Q^*, where the marginal social benefit equals the marginal social cost.

What happens if the good is privately produced and marketed? Person 1 might pay P_1 to have a quantity Q produced by a competitive supplier pricing at marginal cost. At the output Q, the price P_1 just equals the marginal private benefit that person 1 gets from the last unit of the public good. Person 2 will not pay to have the output of the public good increased beyond Q. Person 2 cannot be excluded from consuming the output Q that person 1 has commissioned. At the output Q, person 2's marginal private benefit is only P_2, less than the current price P_1. Person 2 will not pay the higher price needed to induce a competitive supplier to expand output beyond Q. Person 2 free rides on person 1's purchase of Q. This quantity privately produced and consumed in a competitive market is below the efficient quantity Q^*.

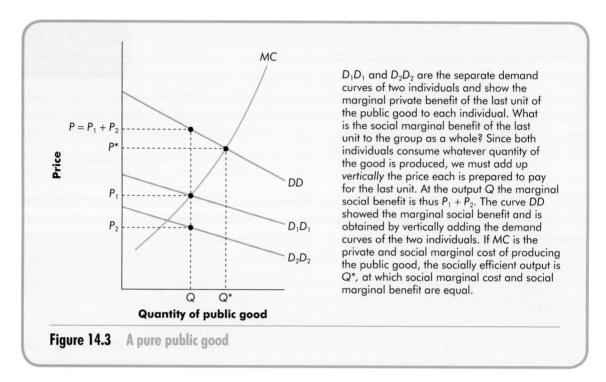

D_1D_1 and D_2D_2 are the separate demand curves of two individuals and show the marginal private benefit of the last unit of the public good to each individual. What is the social marginal benefit of the last unit to the group as a whole? Since both individuals consume whatever quantity of the good is produced, we must add up *vertically* the price each is prepared to pay for the last unit. At the output Q the marginal social benefit is thus $P_1 + P_2$. The curve DD showed the marginal social benefit and is obtained by vertically adding the demand curves of the two individuals. If MC is the private and social marginal cost of producing the public good, the socially efficient output is Q^*, at which social marginal cost and social marginal benefit are equal.

Figure 14.3 A pure public good

Revelation of preferences

If it knows the marginal social benefit curve *DD*, the government can decide the efficient output of the public good. How does the government discover the individual demand curves that must be vertically added to get *DD*? If people's payments for the good are related to their individual demand curves, everyone will lie. People will understate how much they value the good in order to reduce their own payments, just as in a private market. Conversely, we are all for safer streets if we do not have to contribute to the cost.

In practice, democracies try to resolve this problem through elections of governments. Politics lets society get closer to the efficient answer than the market can. Different parties offer different quantities of public goods, together with statements on how they will be financed by taxes. By asking 'How much would you like, given that everyone is charged for the cost of providing public goods?', society comes closer to providing the efficient quantities of public goods. However, with only a few parties competing in an election and many policies on which they offer a position, this remains a crude way to decide the quantities of public goods provided.

Government production

The output of public goods must be *decided* by the government, not the market. This need not mean government must produce the goods itself. Public goods need not be produced by the public sector.

National defence is a public good largely produced in the public or government sector. We have few private armies. Street-sweeping, though a public good, can be subcontracted to private producers, even if local government determines its quantity and pays for it out of local tax revenue. Conversely, state hospitals involve public sector production of private goods. One person's hip replacement operation prevents the busy surgeon from operating on someone else.

In the next chapter we examine why the public sector may wish to produce private goods. Whether public goods need be produced by the public sector depends not on their consumption characteristics, on which our definition of public good relies, but on their production characteristics. There is nothing special about street-sweeping. In contrast, armies rely on discipline and secrecy. Generals and admirals may believe, and society may agree, that offences against these regulations should receive unusual penalties not generally sanctioned in private firms. Few people believe that insubordination is an important offence for street-sweepers.

CASE 14.1

The paradox of open source software

Open source software, developed by volunteers, represents a case of a public good that is somehow paradoxical. It is a public good since the 'source code' used to generate the programs is freely available – hence 'open source'.

According to the theory of public goods, without government intervention, a public good will not be provided at the efficient level. However, open source software is now quite popular. Why have private agents, without property rights over the source code, invested effort in developing a public good subject to free-riding?

A possible answer may be that such agents are moved by reputation building and career concerns. A software programmer who is able to prove his skills by programming open source code may have a chance to be employed by important software companies. Therefore, according to this view, private agents have an incentive to provide effort in developing open source software since this will signal their quality as a programmer.

Another possible answer is that open source software is not an alternative to proprietary software (like Microsoft, which has the property right for its software), but instead can be viewed as a complement. Proprietary provision fails to effectively meet the needs of many customers in markets where customers have highly disparate needs and products are complex. Open source software and proprietary provision of pre-packaged software can both exist in a market, recognizing that they mainly serve different groups of customers. Open source will be used most by firms which have their own development capability and which have complex, specialized needs; pre-packaged software will be used by firms with simpler needs and those which lack development capabilities.

Source: Bessen, J. (2005) *Open source software: free provision of complex public goods*, working paper, Boston University School of Law and Research on Innovation.

Transfer payments and income redistribution

Government spending on transfer payments is primarily concerned with *equity* and *income redistribution*. By spending money on the unemployed, the old and the poor, the government alters the distribution of income and welfare that a free market economy would otherwise have produced: there is a minimum standard of living below which no citizen should fall. The specification of this standard is a pure value judgement.

To finance this spending, the government taxes those who can afford to pay. Taken as a whole, the tax and transfer system takes money from the rich and gives it to the poor. The poor get cash transfers but also enjoy the consumption of public goods paid for by income taxes raised from the rich. Figure 14.4 shows estimates of the cumulative effect of government intervention during 1997–2005. The richest 10 per cent of the population lost 4 per cent of their disposable incomes as a result of measures undertaken by the Labour government while

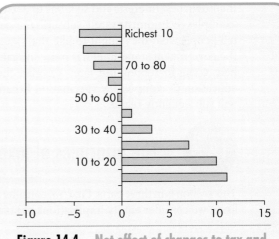

Figure 14.4 Net effect of changes to tax and benefits, 1997–2005 (% of initial disposable income)

Source: Institute for Fiscal Studies.

Gordon Brown was Chancellor. In contrast, the poorest 10 per cent of the population benefited from changes to the tax and benefit system by an amount equal to 11 per cent of their initial disposable income. Labour redistributed spending power significantly.

The desirable amount of redistribution is a value judgement on which people and parties will disagree. There is also the trade-off between efficiency and equity. To redistribute more the government has to raise tax rates, driving a larger wedge between the price paid by the purchaser and the price received by the seller. Since the price system achieves efficiency by inducing each individual to equate marginal cost or marginal benefit to the price received or paid, and hence to one another, taxes are generally distortionary and reduce efficiency.

Merit and demerit goods

> **Merit (demerit) goods** are goods that society thinks everyone should have (not have) regardless of whether an individual wants them.

Merit goods are goods that societies should consume regardless of whether an individual wants them. Those goods are provided by governments despite the fact that they can be consumed and bought individually on the market. The reason is that if we leave to the private market the burden of providing merit goods, those goods will be underprovided. Merit goods include education and health.

On the other hand, there are also demerit goods. Demerit goods include cigarettes and heroin. Since society places a different value on these goods from the value placed on them by the individual, individual choice in a free market leads to a different allocation from the one that society wishes.

There are two reasons for providing merit goods. The first is externalities. Indeed, merit goods generate positive externalities. If more education raises the productivity not merely of an individual worker but also of the workers with whom he co-operates, he ignores this production externality when choosing how much education to acquire. If people demand too little education, society should encourage the provision of education.

Conversely, if people ignore the burden on state hospitals when deciding to smoke and damage their health, society may regard smoking as a demerit to be discouraged. Taxing cigarettes may offset externalities that individuals fail to take into account.

The second reason for providing merit goods is that a society may believe that individuals no longer act in their own best interests and so it has to decide on their behalf. Addiction to drugs, tobacco or gambling are examples. Economists rarely subscribe to paternalism. The function of government intervention is less to tell people what they ought to like than to allow them better to achieve what they already like. However, the government sometimes has more information or is in a better position to take a decision. Many people hate going to school, but later are glad they did. The government may spend money on compulsory education or compulsory vaccination because it recognizes that otherwise individuals act in a way they will subsequently regret.

 ## 14.3 The principles of taxation

This section is in three parts. First, we consider different taxes through which the government can raise revenue. Then we consider equity implications of taxation. Finally, we examine efficiency implications of taxation.

Types of taxes

Governments can collect tax revenue only if they monitor and enforce the activities being taxed. Before sophisticated records of income or sales, governments raised most of their revenue from customs duties and road tolls, places where transactions were easily monitored. Income tax in peacetime was not introduced in the UK until the 1840s, and VAT not until the 1970s.

How to tax fairly

The last chapter gave two notions of equity: *horizontal equity*, or the equal treatment of equals, and *vertical equity*, the redistribution from the 'haves' to the 'have-nots'.

Progressive taxes reflect the principle of *ability to pay*. The principle of ability to pay reflects a concern about vertical equity. Thus, car users should be taxed to finance public roads. However, the **benefits principle** often conflicts with the principle of ability to pay. If those most vulnerable to unemployment pay the highest contributions to a government unemployment insurance scheme, it is hard to redistribute income or welfare. If the main objective is vertical equity, ability to pay must take precedence.

> The **benefits principle** is that people getting most benefit from public spending should pay most for it.

Two factors make the entire tax and benefit structure more progressive than an examination of income tax alone would suggest. First, transfer payments actually give money to the poor. The old receive pensions, the unemployed receive unemployment benefit and, as a final safety net, anyone whose income falls below a certain minimum is entitled to supplementary benefit. Second, the state provides public goods that can be consumed by the poor, even if they have not paid any taxes to finance these goods.

However, the system of tax, transfer and spending has some *regressive* elements that take proportionately more from the poor. Beer and tobacco taxes are huge earners for the government. Yet the poor spend a much higher proportion of their income on these goods than do the rich. Regressive taxes inhibit redistribution from the rich to the poor.

Tax incidence

The ultimate effect of a tax can be very different from its initial effect. Figure 14.5 shows the market for labour. *DD* is the demand curve and *SS* the supply curve. Without an income tax (a tax on wages), labour market equilibrium is at *E*.

> **Tax incidence** is the final tax burden once we allow for all induced effects of a tax.

Now the government imposes an income tax. If we measure the gross wage on the vertical axis, the demand curve *DD* is unaltered. Firms' demand for labour depends on the gross wage that they pay. Workers'

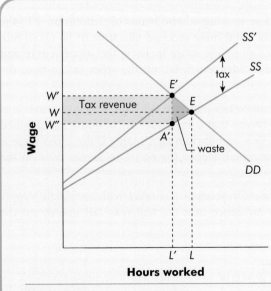

With no tax, equilibrium is at *E* and the wage is *W*. A wage tax raises the gross wage paid by firms above the net wage received by workers. Measuring gross wages on the vertical axis, the demand curve *DD* is unaltered by the imposition of the tax. Firms demand labour to equate the gross wage to the marginal value product of labour. *SS* continues to show labour supply, but as a function of the net wage. To get labour supply in terms of the gross wage we draw the new supply curve *SS'*. *SS'* lies vertically above *SS* by a distance reflecting the tax on earnings from the last hour worked. The new equilibrium is at *E'*. The hourly wage paid by firms is *W'* but the net wage received by workers is *W''*. The vertical distance *A'E'* shows the tax rate. Whether the government collects the tax from firms or from workers, the incidence of the tax is the same. It falls partly on firms, who pay a higher gross wage *W'* and partly on workers, who receive the lower net wage *W''*. The area of pure waste *A'E'E* is discussed in the text.

Figure 14.5 **A tax on wages**

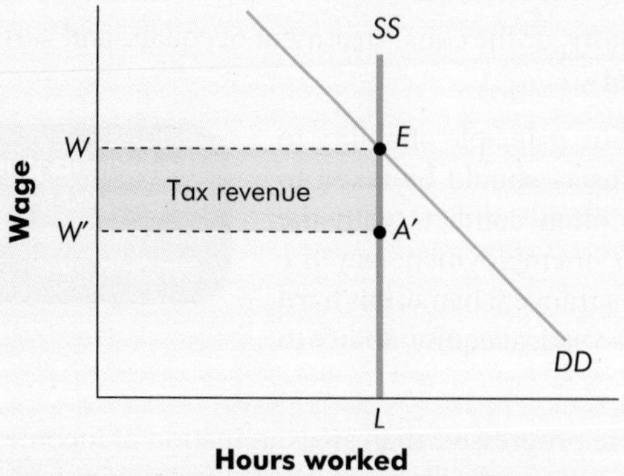

If the supply curve *SS* is vertical, a tax *A'E* per unit leaves the quantity *L* unaffected. Since the demand curve *DD* is unaltered, the tax has no effect on the pre-tax wage rate. The full incidence of the tax falls on workers whose after-tax wage is reduced by the full amount of the tax.

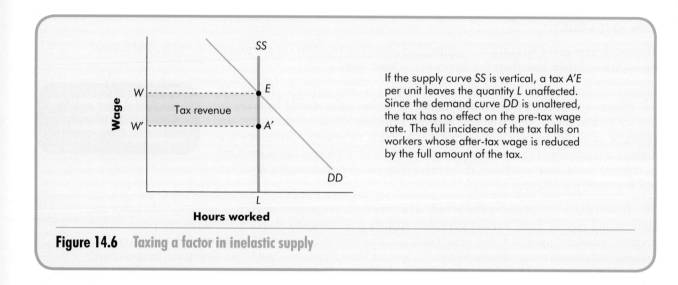

Figure 14.6 Taxing a factor in inelastic supply

The **tax wedge** is the gap between the price paid by the buyer and the price received by the seller.

preferences are unchanged, but it is the wage net-of-tax that workers compare with the marginal value of their leisure in deciding how much labour to supply. *SS* continues to show labour supply in terms of the net-of-tax wage, but we must draw in the higher schedule *SS'* to show the supply of labour in terms of the gross or *tax-inclusive wage*. The vertical distance between *SS'* and *SS* is the tax on earnings from the last hour's work.

DD and *SS'* show the behaviour of firms and workers at any gross wage. At the new equilibrium *E'*, the gross wage is *W'* and firms demand *L'* workers. The vertical distance between *A'* and *E'* is the tax paid on the last hour of work. The net-of-tax wage is *W''*, at which workers supply *L'* hours.

The tax on wages has raised the pre-tax wage to *W'*, but lowered the after-tax wage to *W''*. It has raised the wage that firms pay but lowered the take-home wage for workers. The incidence of the tax falls on *both* firms and workers.

The incidence or burden of a tax cannot be established by looking at who hands over the money to the government. Taxes alter equilibrium prices and quantities and these induced effects must be taken into account. However, we can draw one very general conclusion. The more inelastic the supply curve and the more elastic the demand curve, the more the final incidence will fall on the seller rather than the purchaser.

Figure 14.6 shows the extreme case in which supply is completely inelastic. With no tax, equilibrium is at *E* and the wage is *W*. Since the vertical supply curve *SS* means that a fixed quantity of hours *L* is supplied whatever the after-tax wage, a tax on wages leads to a new equilibrium at *A'*. Only if the gross wage is unchanged will firms demand the quantity *L* that is supplied. Hence the entire incidence falls on the workers.

To check you have grasped the idea of incidence, draw for yourself a market with an elastic supply curve and an inelastic demand curve. Show that the incidence of a tax will now fall mainly on the purchaser.[1]

1 Does a tax always shift the supply curve? Yes, if we measure the gross price on the vertical axis. If we measure the net-of-tax price on the vertical axis, the tax shifts not the supply curve but the demand curve. In Figures 14.5 and 14.6, in terms of the net wage the demand curve shifts down until it passes through *A'*. The distance between *A'* and *E* still measures the tax and we get exactly the same conclusions as before.

Taxation, efficiency and waste

Taxes have efficiency effects as well as equity effects. We can use Figure 14.5 again. Before the tax is imposed, labour market equilibrium is at E. The wage W measures both the marginal social benefit of the last hour of work and its marginal social cost. The demand curve DD tells us the marginal benefit of the extra goods produced. The supply curve SS tells us the marginal value of the leisure being sacrificed in order to work another hour, the marginal social cost of extra work. At E, marginal social cost and benefit are equal, which is socially efficient.

When the tax is imposed, the new equilibrium is at E'. The tax $A'E'$ increases the wage to firms to W' but reduces the after-tax wage for workers to W'''. But there is an additional tax burden or deadweight loss that is pure waste. It is the triangle $A'E'E$. By reducing the quantity of hours from L to L', the tax drives a wedge between marginal benefit, the height of the demand curve DD, and marginal social cost, the height of the supply curve SS. This distortion makes free market equilibrium inefficient.

CASE 14.2

Do you mind if I smoke? The smoking ban in the UK

The smoking ban that took effect in the UK in 2006/07 is an example of a government policy to tackle a negative externality. The ban makes it illegal to smoke in all enclosed public venues and workplaces in the UK.

Smoking is a negative externality since smokers pollute the air for other people but ignore this in deciding how much to smoke. Doing so has negative effects on passive smokers. Doctors estimate that second-hand smoke kills more than 600 people a year.

Moreover it has negative effects on society as a whole. By smoking, smokers have a greater likelihood of suffering from smoking-related diseases and so they are likely to need health care in the future. This will affect health care expenditure in the country. Since the public health care system is financed also by non-smokers, smoking will have a negative effect on non-smokers as well.

Finally, smoking is viewed as a demerit good and therefore governments should do something to discourage people from smoking.

The smoking ban, together with heavy taxation on cigarettes, aims to reduce the number of smokers so that the negative externality created by smoking will decrease.

After the introduction of the smoking ban, cigarettes sales decreased by 7 per cent. By looking at markets linked to the cigarette market, we can also gain a better idea of the general equilibrium effect of the smoking ban. In particular, we can look at the sales figures for public houses. Market researchers Nielsen estimated beer sales in England and Wales could drop by 200 million pints each year as a result of the ban.

Source: Adapted from http://news.bbc.co.uk/1/hi/uk/6258034.stm. © bbc.co.uk/news.

Must taxes distort?

Government needs tax revenue to pay for public goods and make transfer payments. Figure 14.6 shows what happens when a tax is levied but supply is completely inelastic. There is no change in equilibrium quantity. Hence there is no distortionary triangle. The equilibrium quantity remains the efficient quantity.

We can make this into a general principle. When either the supply or the demand curve for a good or service is very inelastic, a tax leads to a small change in equilibrium quantity. Hence the deadweight burden triangle is small. Given that the government must raise some tax revenue, waste is smallest when the goods that are most inelastic in supply or demand are taxed most heavily.

In the UK tax system, the most heavily taxed commodities are alcohol, fuel and tobacco. Alcohol, fuel and tobacco have inelastic demand.

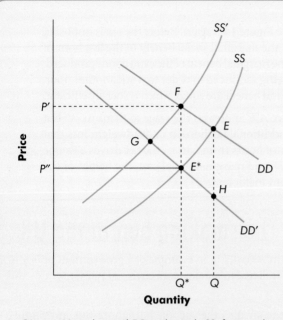

Given private demand *DD* and supply *SS,* free market equilibrium is at *E* with a quantity *Q*. With a negative consumption externality, the social marginal benefit is *DD'* lying below *DD*. *E** is the socially efficient point at which output is *Q**. At this output the marginal externality is *E*F*. By levying a tax of exactly *E*F* per unit, the government can shift the private supply curve from *SS* to *SS'*, leading to a new equilibrium at *F* at which the socially efficient quantity *Q** is produced and the deadweight burden of the externality *E*HE* is eliminated.

Figure 14.7 Taxes to offset externalities

So far, we have discussed the taxes that do least harm to efficiency. Sometimes taxes improve efficiency and reduce waste. The most important example is when externalities exist.

Cigarette smokers pollute the air for other people but ignore this in deciding how much to smoke. They cause a harmful consumption externality as discussed in Maths 14.1. Figure 14.7 shows the supply curve *SS* of cigarette producers. With no production externalities, *SS* is also the marginal social cost curve. *DD* is the private demand curve, the marginal benefit of cigarettes to smokers. Because of the harmful consumption externality, the marginal social benefit *DD'* lies below *DD*.

With no tax, equilibrium is at *E*, but there are too many cigarettes. The efficient quantity is *Q**, which equates marginal social cost and marginal social benefit. Suppose the government levies a tax, equal to the vertical distance *E*F*, on each packet of cigarettes. With the tax-inclusive price on the vertical axis, the demand curve *DD* is unaffected, but the supply curve shifts up to *SS'*. Each point on *SS'* then allows producers to receive the corresponding net-of-tax price on *SS*.

The tax shifts equilibrium to *F*. The efficient quantity *Q** is produced and consumed. Consumers pay *P'* and producers get *P"* after tax is paid at the rate *E*F* per packet.

The tax rate *E*F* guides the free market to the efficient allocation. A lower tax rate (including zero) leads to too much consumption and production of cigarettes. A higher tax rate than *E*F* moves consumers too far up their demand curve, causing too little consumption and production.

A tax rate *E*F* leads to the efficient quantity because this is the size of the marginal externality when the efficient quantity *Q** is produced. A tax at this rate makes consumers behave as if they took account of the externality, though they think only about the tax-inclusive price.

When externalities induce distortions, the government can improve efficiency by levying taxes. The fact that alcohol and tobacco have harmful externalities is another reason to tax them heavily.

MATHS 14.1 Using a tax to internalize the negative externality

Consider the same example as in Maths 13.1 and two firms, A and B. Firm A pollutes the lake used by firm B for fishing. Here, we briefly report the main features of the two firms. The cost function of firm A is $TC_A = TC_A(Q_A, P_A)$, where Q_A is the quantity produced by A and P_A is the level of pollution of firm A. The cost function of firm A has the following properties:

- it increases with the output produced: $\partial TC_A / \partial Q_A > 0$
- it decreases with the level of pollution: $\partial TC_A / \partial P_A \leq 0$

Firm B has the total cost function $TC_B = TC_B(Q_B, P_A)$, with the following properties:

$$\partial TC_B/\partial Q_B > 0 \qquad \text{and} \qquad \partial TC_B/\partial P_A > 0$$

If property rights are not assigned and with no government intervention, the optimal level of pollution chosen by firm A satisfies the condition:

$$-(\partial TC_A/\partial P_A) = 0$$

that is, marginal cost of pollution equals marginal revenue of pollution (zero in this case).

Firm A is polluting more than it should, so we can tax firm A in such a way that the socially efficient level of pollution is reached. Those kinds of taxes are also called Pigouvian taxes.

When firm A has to pay a tax for its polluting activity, the profit function of firm A becomes:

$$\pi_A = pQ_A - TC_A(Q_A, P_A) - tP_A$$

where t is the tax rate and p is the market price for the output of firm A. Now the optimal level of pollution (the one that maximizes firm A's profits) is:

$$-(\partial TC_A/\partial P_A) - t = 0 \Rightarrow -(\partial TC_A/\partial P_A) - t$$

The tax simply increases the marginal cost of polluting. Now the level of pollution that maximizes the profits is lower than before since $-\partial TC_A/\partial P_A$ must be equal to t, that is, greater than zero.

What tax level provides the efficient solution for the externality?

If we set $t = \partial TC_B/\partial P_A$, we obtain the efficient solution. Why? Because by setting $t = \partial TC_B/\partial P_A$, firm A now chooses a level of pollution that satisfies $-\partial TC_A/\partial P_A = \partial TC_B/\partial P_A$. In deciding the optimal level of P_A, firm A now takes into account the effect that its decision has on firm B. In practice, in order to obtain the efficient solution we need to set the tax (paid by the polluting firm) equal to the marginal social cost of pollution.

14.4 Taxation and supply-side economics

Suppose the government cuts spending and tax rates. What are the effects? First, by spending less on goods and services, the government frees some resources for use by the private sector. If the private sector is more productive than the public sector, the transfer of resources may directly raise output. Whether the private sector actually uses resources more productively than the government is unclear. It seems to do many things better but some things worse.

> **Supply-side economics** analyses how taxes and other incentives affect national output when the economy is at full capacity.

What about the effects of lower tax rates? Figure 14.7 suggests that tax distortions cause inefficiency. Lower taxes mean a lower deadweight burden. The size of this gain depends on supply and demand elasticity. If either elasticity is small, the social gain is low.

For example, Chapter 10 argued that labour supply is fairly inelastic for those in employment, but a bit more elastic for those thinking of joining the labour force. Cutting income tax rates *will* increase labour supply, but perhaps by less than many advocates of tax cuts believe.

The Laffer curve

We now discuss the relationship between tax rates and tax revenues. Professor Laffer was an adviser to US President Ronald Reagan.

> The **Laffer curve** shows how much tax revenue is raised at each possible tax rate.

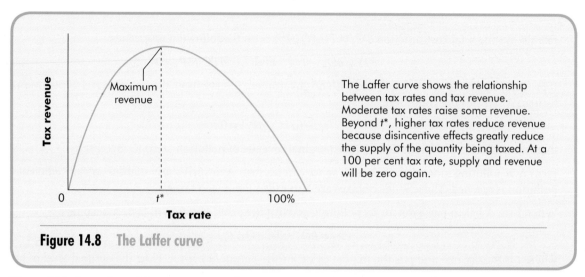

The Laffer curve shows the relationship between tax rates and tax revenue. Moderate tax rates raise some revenue. Beyond t^*, higher tax rates reduce revenue because disincentive effects greatly reduce the supply of the quantity being taxed. At a 100 per cent tax rate, supply and revenue will be zero again.

Figure 14.8   The Laffer curve

Figure 14.8 shows that with a zero tax rate the government gets zero revenue. At the opposite extreme, with a 100 per cent income tax rate, there is no point working and again tax revenue is zero. Beginning from a zero rate, a small increase in the tax rate yields some tax revenue. Initially tax revenue rises with the tax rate, but beyond the tax rate t^* higher taxes have major disincentive effects on work effort, and revenue falls.

Professor Laffer's idea was that 'big government–big tax' countries were at tax rates above t^*. If so, tax cuts were the miracle cure. The government would get *more* revenue by cutting taxes. By reducing the tax distortion and increasing the amount of work *a lot*, lower tax rates would be more than offset by higher incomes to tax.

The shape of the Laffer curve is not in dispute. However, many economists disputed the view that *in fact* tax rates were above t^*. Most economists' reading of the empirical evidence is that our economies were always to the left of t^*. Cutting income tax rates may eliminate some of the deadweight burden of distortionary taxation, but governments should probably expect their tax revenue to fall if tax rates are cut. Governments wishing to avoid borrowing need to cut their spending if they wish to cut the tax rate.

 ## Local government

So much for central government. What about local government? Local government spends on things from sweeping the streets to providing local schooling. This is financed both by local taxes and by money from central government financed by national taxes. Local government is also responsible for some types of regulation, for example land use or *zoning* laws.

Economic principles

Why don't we make central government responsible for everything? First, diversity matters. People are different and do not want to be treated the same. Civic pride is necessarily local. Second, people feel that central government is remote from their particular needs. Even if central government paid attention to local considerations, it would find it hard to do so efficiently.

We examine two important models of local government. The *Tiebout model*[2] emphasizes diversity. Some people want high spending, good public services and high local taxes; others want low local taxes even if this means poor public services. If all local governments are the same, everyone hates the compromise. The

---

2   Tiebout, C. (1956) A pure theory of local expenditures, *Journal of Political Economy*, 64 (5): 416–424.

Tiebout model is sometimes called the *invisible foot*: people cluster in the area providing the package of spending and taxes they want. The 'invisible foot' allocates resources efficiently via competition *between* local governments.

In practice, the 'invisible foot' is a crude incentive structure. First, it is hard to move between local authorities. You may lose your place in the queue for housing provided by that local authority. Second, if much of local authority revenue comes from central government, the levels of spending and taxes may be insensitive to the wishes of local residents.

Even if the 'invisible foot' led to efficiency, it might also lead to inequity. The rich are likely to cluster together in suburbs. Then they pass zoning laws specifying a minimum size for a house and its garden. The poor cannot move into that area. By forming an exclusive club, the rich ensure that their taxes do not go to supporting the poor. The poor get stuck with one another in inner-city areas whose governments face the biggest social needs but have the smallest local tax base.

The Tiebout model assumes that residents consume the public services provided by their own local authority. When each unit of local government has responsibility for a small geographical area, this may be a bad assumption. If a city supplies free art galleries, financed by taxes on city residents, the rich still come in from the suburbs to use these facilities. Conversely, urban trendies spend their Sundays enjoying countryside facilities supported by rural taxes. In both cases, provision of public services in one area confers a beneficial externality on nearby areas.

Economic theory suggests an answer to this problem. Widen the geographical area of each local government until it includes most of the people who use the public services it provides. It may make sense to have an integrated commuter rail service and inner-city subway, and to subsidize it to prevent people driving through congested streets. However, only a local government embracing both the suburbs and the inner city is likely to get close to the efficient policy.

The Tiebout model favours a lot of small local government jurisdictions to maximize choice and competition between areas. However, the presence of externalities across areas suggests larger jurisdictions to 'internalize' externalities that would otherwise occur. The right answer may involve a bit of both.

14.6 Economic sovereignty

Nowadays, no country is an economic island, cut off from the rest of the world. We examine the world economy in Part Five, but some issues cannot be postponed until then. In a democratic country insulated from the rest of the world, the government is sovereign: while it retains democratic support and observes existing laws, it has the final say in policy design. Sometimes central government chooses to delegate powers to local government. Section 14.5 discussed when it is efficient

> **Economic sovereignty** is the power of national governments to make decisions independently of those made by other governments.

to do so. What this account ignores is the existence of other countries. How do interactions with the rest of the world affect the sovereignty of national governments?

Even in a quarantined economy, governments cannot do anything they like. Within market economies they have to work within the forces of supply and demand. For example, in Section 14.3 we argued that it is generally more efficient to have high tax rates on things for which the demand or supply is inelastic. High tax rates on things with elastic supply and demand induces large distortions since equilibrium quantity is very sensitive to the price. We now apply this insight to economies open to interactions with the rest of the world.

International capital is now highly mobile across countries. Suppose the UK government tries to levy a large tax on capital in Britain. Lots of capital will quickly move elsewhere to escape the high taxes. The *tax base*, in this example the quantity of capital available for taxing in Britain, quickly shrinks. So the high tax *rates* may raise little tax *revenue*. In contrast, since people are much less mobile than capital across national boundaries, the tax base for taxing workers' incomes in Britain is much less sensitive to tax rates than the tax base for capital taxes.

Even people are more mobile across national boundaries than they were a few decades ago. Communication is easier, transport costs are lower and satellites pay no attention to national frontiers on a map. Migration affects not just taxation but government spending as well. Suppose a country wishes to implement a generous welfare state. As a closed economy, all it has to worry about is how much of its tax base disappears from work into leisure. If welfare is too generous, people may not work enough. As an open economy, it also has to consider whether more generous welfare provision will lead to more migration into the country as foreigners take advantage, legally or illegally, of the generous welfare provision.

Closer economic integration with other countries – through trade in goods and movement of factors of production – effectively undermines the sovereignty of nation states. If the tax rate was 80 per cent in Liverpool but 20 per cent in Manchester, one would expect big movements of capital and people from Liverpool to Manchester. The tax base in Liverpool would evaporate (even die-hard Everton supporters could commute from Manchester). The local government of Liverpool has limited local sovereignty because it is effectively in competition with Manchester.

As modern technology undermines even barriers between countries, the same process is at work. The economic sovereignty of nation states, their freedom to do what they want, is steadily being constrained by competition from foreign countries. More than one in ten cans of beer now consumed in England was bought by British households in France, hopping across the Channel to take advantage of lower alcohol taxes in France. UK Chancellors, caught between the pressure to raise revenue and support jobs in the UK drinks industry, have been cutting the real value of UK alcohol taxes. They have already lost the sovereignty to set tax rates at the high levels that they would have liked.

National sovereignty is undermined not just by competition between countries for tax bases but also by two other forces. The first is other cross-country spillovers such as acid rain, greenhouse gases or the threat of pollution from a nuclear accident. Banning nuclear power generation in southern England has limited value if northern France is studded with nuclear power stations.

The second is the scope for redistribution. Economics is about equity as well as efficiency. In an important sense, the right jurisdiction for government is the area within which citizens feel sufficient identity with one another that the rich are prepared to pay for the poor, and the fortunate are prepared to assist the unlucky. European nation states have long histories and strong national identities. But these are not always set in stone. Countries such as Belgium, Italy, Spain and the UK have faced strong internal pressures to allow parts of their country to secede. In the opposite direction, some Europeans now feel as much a citizen of Europe as of their own particular nation.

Nation states are not yet obsolete. But they are coming under pressure. Further developments in technology will increase the transnational scope of economic interactions and cultural identity. The proliferation of e-commerce and the internet will only accelerate this process.

 ## 14.7 Political economy: how governments decide

Political economy is the study of how governments make decisions.

Firms are in business to make profits for their owners. Individuals buy affordable combinations of goods that yield them most satisfaction. These simple assumptions let economists explain most consumer and business decision making. What about government decision making?

Government is the most important single player in the economy. It is important to develop theories of how governments behave. There is no point analysing the consequences of a policy that a sane government will never implement.

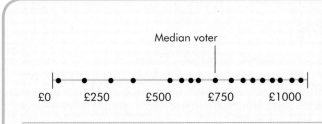

Each dot represents the preferred expenditure of each of 17 voters. The outcome under majortiy voting will be the level preferred by the median voter. Everybody to the left will prefer the median voter's position to any higher spending level. Everybody to the right will prefer it to any lower spending level. The median voter's position is the only position that cannot be outvoted against some alternative. Hence it will be chosen.

Figure 14.9   The median voter

Voters elect governments to set spending and taxing, pass new laws and establish new regulations. The electorate chooses among alternative policy *packages* offered by competing parties, but is rarely allowed a referendum on each issue.

The government does not simply do the bidding of society. Government has its own agenda, which may be to promote what it thinks is good for the public or simply to get re-elected.

> The **median voter** on an issue is the person whose preferences are such that half the population's preferences on the issue lie on one side and half the population's preferences on the other side.

The median voter

If everyone was identical and of one mind, public decision making would be trivial. Through the political process, society tries to reconcile different views and different interests.

Figure 14.9 shows 17 different voters and how much each wants the government to spend on the police. A dot shows each voter's preferred amount. Assume that a voter whose ideal amount is £250 will think that £300 is better than £400 if these are the only choices on offer, and will prefer £200 to £100. Each person has *single-peaked* preferences, being happier with an outcome the closer it is to his peak or preferred level.

There is a vote on how much to spend on the public good called police. A proposal to spend £0 is defeated by 16 votes to 1. Only the voter who is the left-hand dot in Figure 14.9 votes for £0 rather than £100. From either extreme, as we move to the centre more people vote for a particular proposal. With 17 voters, the median voter is the person who wants to spend the ninth-highest amount on the police. Eight voters want to spend more; eight want to spend less.

Any proposal for higher spending than the median voter's preferred amount can be defeated. The median voter, plus the eight voters below him, all vote against. But any proposal for lower spending is also defeated. The median voter, and the eight voters above him, all vote against. Hence, the median voter gets his way by majority voting.

> **Log-rolling** is a vote for another person's preferred outcome on one issue in order to exchange for their vote your preferred outcome on another issue.

Log-rolling

So far we have assumed each issue is voted on independently. Making decisions through legislative compromises is much more complicated when votes can be traded between different issues. Groups of politicians form parties or coalitions within which some vote trading can take place.

For two issues, A and B, and three politicians, Tom, Dick and Harry, Table 14.4 shows the value of each outcome to each politician. Suppose each person votes for a proposal only if the outcome is positive. Tom votes against A and B, Dick votes against A but for B, and Harry votes for A but against B. Both issues are defeated on a majority vote.

Table 14.4   Log-rolling

Politician	Issue A	Issue B
Tom	−4	−1
Dick	−3	4
Harry	6	−1

ACTIVITY 14.1

Hunting the median voter

After Labour lost the 1979 general election it moved to the left. This pleased party activists but took the party too far away from the preferences of the median voter. The Conservatives were in power for the next 17 years. After heavy defeat in 1983, successive Labour leaders slowly moved the party back to the middle ground that the median voter inhabits. Labour focus groups interviewed people directly to clarify the median voter's view on different issues. The result? Labour victories in 1997, 2001 and 2005.

Did Labour abandon its principles to win and keep office? It gave up old traditions of high welfare spending and high, visible taxes. But, when Gordon Brown was the Chancellor of the Exchequer, he helped the poor substantially without frightening the middle classes. As a result of his budgets, the post-tax income of the poorest 20 per cent of people rose by over 10 per cent (see Figure 14.4 again).

How did he do it? Not by raising income tax or VAT. Some of it was financed by stealth taxes, such as the tax treatment of pension funds, which the median voter did not initially notice or understand. Some was financed by making transfer payments more selective. Instead of a universal benefit, scarce resources were concentrated only on those who really needed them. Some of it was financed by economic growth: as incomes grew, given tax rates yielded more tax revenue, which was given mainly to the poor.

Unusually, Labour did not take credit for the extent to which it helped the poor. This kept the median voter sweet (the middle classes were not told repeatedly how they were paying too much to support the poor), but upset some traditional Labour supporters (who probably still voted Labour anyway).

The electoral success of the Labour Party partly ended in May 2010, when the Conservatives won the majority of seats (not the necessary number to have an overall majority though) at the general election and a coalition government between the Conservatives and the Liberal Democrats was formed. Did the median voter change his mind?

Questions

(a) In a country with two parties, suppose both end up with almost identical policies in the centre ground. What does this tell you about (i) the ideology of the party leaders, and (ii) the extent to which party activists trade off the desire for power and their political beliefs?

(b) Suppose we could order voters from left to right with equal numbers of voters holding each possible opinion. If everyone votes for the party nearest their own beliefs, where should the two parties locate to maximize their vote?

(c) Now, however, suppose that people abstain if the party is not close to the voters' ideal positions. Does this change the optimal positioning of party manifestos?

Picture: David Cameron (Conservative), Nick Clegg (Liberal Democrat) and Gordon Brown (Labour) in a live televised debate in May 2010 in the lead-up to the UK general election. © PA Photo.

To check your answers to these questions, go to page 685.

Now suppose Dick and Harry vote together. They vote for A, which Harry really wants, and for B, which Dick really wants. Dick gains 4 since B passes, and loses only 3 when A passes. Harry gains 6 when A passes and loses only 1 when B passes. By forming a coalition that allows them to express the intensity of their preferences, they do better than under independent majority voting, when neither A nor B would have passed.

Many decisions in the European Union reflect log-rolling. Individual countries get favourable decisions on issues they really mind about, but are expected to repay the favour on other issues.

Commitment and credibility

Chapter 9 introduced **credibility** and **commitment** in the context of games between firms. Similar ideas apply to the political economy of policy design. Because expectations about the future affect current decisions, politicians are tempted to make optimistic promises about the future in the hope of influencing people today.

> A **credible** promise about future action is one that is optimal to carry out when the future arrives.
>
> A **commitment** is a current device to restrict future room for manoeuvre to make promises more credible today.

Our discussion of strategic entry deterrence in Chapter 9 gives you all the clues you need to think about political credibility. Project your imagination into the future and consider how politicians will then want to behave. Use this insight to form smart guesses today about which promises are credible and which are not.

For example, most post-war Labour governments were big spenders, which required high taxation. When out of office, Labour promises of low spending and low taxes when next in government were not very credible. Gordon Brown's Code for Fiscal Stability was an attempt to enhance Labour's credibility by openly and repeatedly committing to a tough policy that would then be politically costly to abandon. With so much political capital invested in prudence and the Code for Fiscal Stability, the government would look very stupid if it subsequently abandoned it.

Recently, many countries have adopted a commitment that has been very successful. They have made the central bank operationally independent of government control, as Labour did with the Bank of England in 1997. The government chooses the aim of monetary policy – to keep inflation low – but the Bank alone now decides what interest rates are needed to achieve this. By keeping the government's hands off interest rates, central bank independence removes the temptation for the government to overheat the economy in pursuit of a pre-election boom.

Policy co-ordination

> **Policy co-ordination** is the decision to set policies jointly when two interdependent areas have big cross-border spillovers.

Chapter 9 contained another useful insight for modern political economy. In discussing games between oligopolists, we showed that collectively they make more profit acting as a joint monopolist than by acting without co-ordination. In the language you later learned in Chapter 13, when actions are interdependent and externalities matter, the efficient solution needs to take these spillovers fully into account. Internalizing externalities means stopping free-riding.

The more interdependent different nation states become, the more it may be necessary to co-ordinate national policies rather than formulate them in isolation. Global warming is one example, but many forms of regulation and taxation fall under this heading.

French tax rates on alcohol are so much lower than UK rates that UK Chancellors can no longer set UK alcohol taxes as high as they would like. The UK would like continental tax rates on alcohol to be higher. Conversely, continental Europeans complain about low levels of worker protection in the UK and the competitive edge this may give UK firms.

Pressure for closer policy co-ordination is likely to increase as globalization continues.

Summary

- Government revenues come mainly from **direct taxes** on personal incomes and company profits, **indirect taxes** on purchases of goods and services, and **contributions** to state-run social security schemes. Government spending comprises **government purchases** of goods and services and **transfer payments**.

- Governments intervene in a market economy in pursuit of distributional equity and allocative efficiency. A **progressive tax-and-transfer system** takes most from the rich and gives most to the poor. The UK system is mildly progressive. The less well off receive transfer payments and the rich pay the highest tax rates. Although some necessities, notably food, are exempt from VAT, other goods intensively consumed by the poor, notably cigarettes and alcohol, are heavily taxed.

- **Externalities** are cases of market failure where intervention may improve efficiency. By taxing or subsidizing goods that involve externalities, the government can induce the private sector to behave as if it takes account of the externality, eliminating the **deadweight burden** arising from the misallocation induced by the externality distortion.

- A **public good** is a good for which one person's consumption does not reduce the quantity available for consumption by others. Together with the impossibility of effectively excluding people from consuming it, this implies all individuals consume the same quantity, but they may get different utility if their tastes differ.

- A free market will undersupply a public good because of the **free-rider problem**. Individuals need not offer to pay for a good that they can consume if others pay for it. The socially **efficient** quantity of a public good equates the marginal social cost of production to the sum of the marginal private benefits over all people at this output level. Individual demand curves are vertically added to get the social demand or marginal benefit curves.

- Except for taxes to offset externalities, taxes are **distortionary**. A **wedge** between the sale price and purchase price prevents the price system equating marginal costs and marginal benefits. The size of the **deadweight burden** is higher, the higher is the marginal tax rate and the size of the wedge, but also depends on supply and demand elasticities for the taxed commodity or activity. The more inelastic are supply and demand, the less the tax changes equilibrium quantity and the smaller is the deadweight burden.

- **Tax incidence** describes who ultimately pays the tax. The more inelastic is demand relative to supply, the more incidence falls on buyers not sellers.

- Rising tax rates initially increase tax revenue but eventually lead to such large falls in the equilibrium quantity of the taxed commodity or activity that revenue falls. Cutting tax rates will usually reduce the deadweight tax burden but might increase revenue if taxes were initially very high. Few economies are in this position. Lower tax rates usually reduce tax revenue.

- The **economic sovereignty** of nation states is reduced by cross-border mobility of goods, capital, workers and shoppers. Policy co-ordination may increase efficiency by making decisions reflecting previously neglected policy spillovers.

- **Political economy** examines political equilibrium and incentives to adopt particular policies.

- When all those voting have single-peaked preferences, majority voting achieves what the **median voter** wants.

Review questions

1 Which of the following are public goods? (a) The fire brigade, (b) clean streets, (c) refuse collection, (d) cable television, (e) social tolerance, (f) the postal service.

EASY

2 Why does society try to ensure that every child receives an education? Discuss the different ways this could be done and give reasons for preferring one method of providing such an education.

3 How would you apply the principles of horizontal and vertical equity in deciding how much to tax two people, each capable of doing the same work, but one of whom chooses to devote more time to sunbathing and therefore has a lower income?

4 Classify the following taxes as progressive or regressive: (a) a 10 per cent tax on all luxury goods, (b) taxes in proportion to the value of owner-occupied houses, (c) taxes on beer, (d) taxes on champagne.

5 There is a flat-rate 30 per cent income tax on all income over £2000. Calculate the average tax rate (tax paid divided by income) at income levels of £5000, £10 000 and £50 000. Is the tax progressive? Is it more or less progressive if the exemption is raised from £2000 to £5000?

6 Common fallacies   Why are these statements wrong? (a) If government spends all its revenue, taxes are not a burden on society as a whole. (b) Taxes always distort. (c) Political economy is just an excuse to waffle, and cannot be made rigorous.

7 A firm that produces steel is polluting the air. Assume that the marginal cost of producing steel is constant at £4. The inverse market demand for steel is $P = 44 - 2Q$, where P is the price of steel and Q is the quantity of steel. The air pollution associated with steel production is creating an externality given by $£\frac{1}{2}Q$.

MEDIUM

Assuming that the market for steel is competitive, what is the profit-maximizing level of steel when only marginal private costs are taken into account? The marginal social costs are given by the sum of the marginal private costs plus the externality. What is the social level of steel output? Show your solution graphically. What is the social loss associated with the externality? How can we solve this externality problem using taxation?

8 The lake of Mangrovia is polluted by a firm. A clean water lake is considered a public good by the local community. Two residents, Sam and Ronald, are interested in reducing the level of water pollution in the lake. The following table shows the marginal benefits (or marginal willingness to pay) of the two residents for each unit of pollution reduction.

Units of pollution reduced	MB Sam	MB Ronald
1	£30	£12
2	£20	£9
3	£15	£4
4	£5	£2

Suppose that the cost of reducing pollution is £19 per unit. By how much would you expect pollution to be reduced? What is the efficient amount of pollution reduction?

9 The market demand for milk is $Q^D = 60 - 4p$, while the market supply is $Q^S = p + 10$, where p denotes the milk's price. Suppose that the government imposes a specific tax $t = 5$ on the suppliers of milk. Find the equilibrium in the milk market. Show your solution graphically. Calculate the total revenues generated by the tax. What proportion of the tax revenue is paid by consumers? What proportion is paid by the suppliers? Explain graphically how those proportions may depend on the elasticity of demand.

10 (a) Suppose labour supply is completely inelastic. Show why there is no deadweight burden if wages are taxed. Who bears the incidence of the tax? (b) Now suppose labour supply is quite elastic. Show the area that is the deadweight burden of the tax. How much of the tax is ultimately borne by firms and how much by workers? (c) For any given supply elasticity, show that firms bear more of the tax the more inelastic is the demand for labour.

11 Hypothecation is the promise to use tax revenue from a product to achieve benefits for the group who bear the tax, for example using the London congestion charge to improve London's public transport or using tobacco taxes to build health centres for smokers. (a) Why are politicians attracted by hypothecation? (b) Why are economists not attracted by hypothecation?

12 Essay question   Imagine that a new UK government, to the surprise of everyone, announces that income tax rates will rise by 15 percentage points in order to provide decent schools and hospitals. Describe the good and bad consequences. How did you decide what you meant by good and bad?

For solutions to these questions contact your lecturer.

Macroeconomics

Part Four studies the economy as an interrelated system. Output is demanded by firms, by households, by the government and by foreigners. Since interest rates and bank lending affect the demand for output, the financial sector interacts with the real economy. Price and wage adjustments help restore output to full capacity, but monetary policy and fiscal policy also play a role. Together, all this affects inflation and unemployment. Economies are increasingly open to foreign trade and foreign capital. The balance of payments records transactions with foreigners. The dynamics of the national economy also depend on the exchange rate policy pursued. By the end of Part Four, we can explain business cycles around full capacity and long-run growth in full capacity output.

Chapter 15 introduces the macroeconomy. Chapters 16–17 develop a basic model of output determination in the short run. Chapters 18–19 describe money, banking, and how interest rates are set. Chapter 20 examines monetary and fiscal policy. Chapter 21 introduces aggregate supply and price adjustment. Chapters 22–23 look at inflation and unemployment, and Chapters 24–25 at exchange rates and the balance of payments. Chapter 26 discusses long-run growth and Chapter 27 analyses short-run business cycles.

Contents

Introduction to macroeconomics

Learning Outcomes

By the end of this chapter, you should understand:

1. macroeconomics as the study of the whole economy

2. internally consistent national accounts

3. the circular flow between households and firms

4. why leakages always equal injections

5. more comprehensive measures of national income and output

We now turn to the big issues, such as unemployment, inflation, economic growth and financial crashes. Macroeconomics sacrifices details to study the big picture.

The distinction between microeconomics and **macroeconomics** is more than the difference between economics in the small and economics in the large, which the Greek prefixes *micro* and *macro* suggest. The purpose of their analysis is also different.

> **Macroeconomics** is the study of the economy as a system.

A model simplifies to focus on the key elements of a problem and think about them clearly. We could study the whole economy by piecing together a microeconomic analysis of every market, but it would be hard to keep track of all the economic forces at work. Our brains do not have a big enough Intel chip to make sense of it.

Microeconomics and macroeconomics take different approaches to keep the analysis manageable. Microeconomics stresses a detailed understanding of particular markets. To achieve this detail, many interactions with other markets are suppressed. In saying a tax on cars reduces the equilibrium quantity of cars, we ignore what the government does with the tax revenue. If government debt is reduced, interest rates may fall, making households more willing to borrow to buy new cars.

Microeconomics is like looking at a horse race through a pair of binoculars. It is great for details, but sometimes we get a clearer picture of the whole race by using the naked eye. Because macroeconomics studies the interaction of different parts of the economy, it uses a different simplification to keep the analysis manageable. Macroeconomics simplifies the building blocks in order to focus on how they fit together and influence one another.

Macroeconomics stresses broad aggregates such as the total demand for goods by households or the total spending on machinery and building by firms. As in watching the horse race with the naked eye, our notion of individual details is more blurred but our full attention is on the big picture. We are more likely to notice the horse sneaking up on the rails.

15.1 The big issues

Here are some key questions that form the theme of the analysis in Part 4.

> Real **gross national product (GNP)** measures the income of an economy, the quantity of goods and services the economy can afford to purchase.
>
> The **business cycle** refers to swings in output around an economy's trend rate of growth.
>
> **Economic growth** is a rise in real GNP.
>
> The **labour force** is people at work or looking for work. It excludes people neither working nor looking for work.
>
> The **unemployment rate** is the fraction of the labour force without a job.
>
> The **inflation rate** is the percentage increase in the average price of goods and services.

What determines the total income of a country, which we call its real **GNP**? Why was there a long boom in output and house prices after 1992, but the worst post-war crash in 2009? Are there inevitably **business cycles**, or can output grow smoothly? Taking a longer run view, why do some countries **grow** faster than others over sustained periods? And why, after centuries asleep, have the Chinese and Indian giants finally awoken?

We care not just about the output of goods and services, but also the market for **labour**. Why did unemployment rise during 1960–80 but fall substantially thereafter? How much will **unemployment** increase again in the aftermath of the financial crash? Do workers price themselves out of jobs by greedy wage claims? Does technical progress destroy jobs? Can the government create more jobs? These are questions we need to answer in Part Four.

A third big theme is **inflation**. The price level is a weighted average of the prices households pay for goods and services. Inflation measures rises in the price level. What causes inflation? Money growth, oil price rises or a budget deficit? Have we now learned how to defeat inflation? Could a boom in China cause inflation in Europe? Will the vast money creation deliberately undertaken in 2009 in order to mitigate the recession lead to subsequent inflation? With prices actually falling in some countries in 2010 because of the severity of the recession, could economies experience a death spiral of falling prices?

A fourth big theme is boom and bust. Why can't we arrange for economic growth to be smooth? What caused the spectacular crash of 2008/09? Can we prevent another one? Almost every day the media discuss inflation, unemployment, economic growth and output cycles. These issues help determine elections, and make people interested in macroeconomics.

15.2 Some facts

We begin with some facts. Figure 15.1 puts recent performance in perspective, showing data for the past 50 years.

The decade between 1960 and 1970 was a golden age of low unemployment, rapid growth and low inflation. In the early 1970s, with the world economy booming, OPEC quadrupled the price of oil. The rest of the 1970s saw high inflation, low growth and rising unemployment. After another oil price hike in 1979–80, the 1980s were another tough period. Figure 15.1 shows that it was not until the 1990s that inflation and unemployment fell. The longer the period of economic success lasted during 1991–2008 – steady growth, low unemployment, low inflation – the more confident people became that successful economic policies had finally been discovered. Confidence bred overconfidence, spiralling house prices and rash lending by banks. In 2009 the crash finally came. Figure 15.1 shows the end of output growth and higher unemployment.

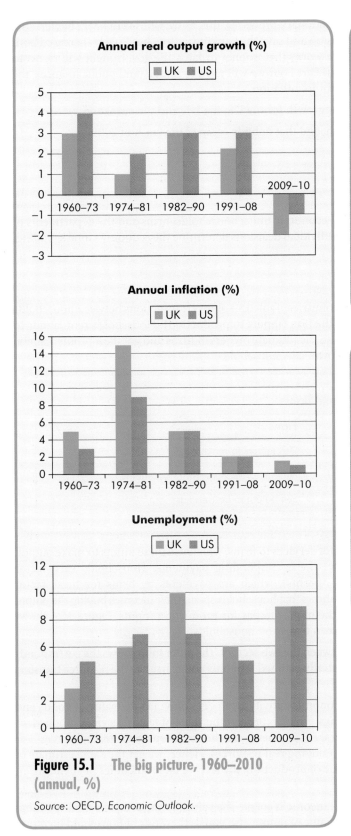

Figure 15.1 The big picture, 1960–2010 (annual, %)

Source: OECD, Economic Outlook.

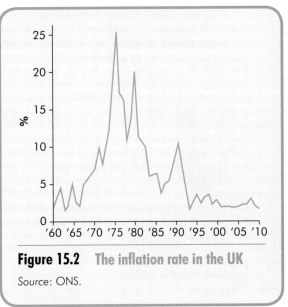

Figure 15.2 The inflation rate in the UK

Source: ONS.

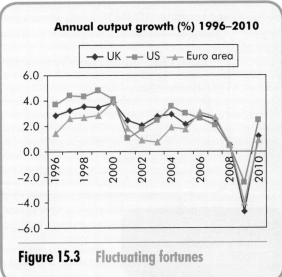

Figure 15.3 Fluctuating fortunes

Figure 15.2 takes a longer look at UK inflation, which soared in the 1970s. The Thatcher government reduced inflation after 1980, but lost control in the late 1980s when it let the economy grow too rapidly, leading to more inflation. Subsequent Chancellors – John Major, Norman Lamont, Kenneth Clarke and Gordon Brown – gradually got the UK back on an even keel, not least by giving the Bank of England much more independence in decisions on monetary policy.

The recent recession has temporarily reduced inflationary pressures. But, as we will see in later chapters, the government's recent attempt to offset the recession and save the banking system has hugely increased both government debt and its budget deficit. People worry that, sooner or later, the government will resort to money creation in order to finance its deficit. In Part Four we will need to understand public finances, the role of money creation, and the prospects for future inflation.

Figure 15.3 shows yearly fluctuations in output growth for the US, the UK and the eurozone.

It confirms that output growth is rarely smooth, and that nobody escaped the crash of 2009.

15.3 An overview

The economy comprises millions of individual economic units: households, firms and the departments of central and local government. Together, their individual decisions determine the economy's total spending, income and output.

The circular flow

Initially, we ignore the government and other countries. Table 15.1 shows transactions between households and firms. Households own the factors of production (inputs to production). Households rent labour to firms in exchange for wages. Households are also the ultimate owners of firms and get their profits. Capital and land, even if held by firms, are ultimately owned by households.

Table 15.1 Transactions by households and firms

Households	Firms
Supply factor services to firms	Use factors to make output
Receive factor incomes from firms	Rent factor services from households
Buy output of firms	Sell output to households

The **circular flow** shows how real resources and financial payments flow between firms and households.

Households supply factor services to firms, which use these inputs to make output. The second row shows the corresponding payments. Households earn factor incomes (wages, rents, profits), which are payments by firms for these factor services. The third row shows that households spend their incomes buying the output of firms, giving firms the money to pay for production inputs. Figure 15.4 shows this **circular flow** between firms and households.

The inner loop shows flows of real resources between the two sectors. The outer loop shows the corresponding flows of money in a market economy. A centrally planned economy could arrange the resource transfers on the inner loop without using the outer loop.

Figure 15.4 suggests three ways to measure economic activity in an economy: (a) the value of goods and services produced, (b) the level of factor earnings, which represent the value of factor services supplied, or (c) the value of spending on goods and services. All payments are the counterparts of real resources. For the moment, we assume all payments are spent buying real resources. Hence, we get the same estimate of total economic activity whether we use the value of production, the level of factor incomes or spending on goods and services.

Factor incomes equal household spending if all income is spent. The value of output equals total spending on goods and services if all goods are sold. The value of output also equals the value of household incomes.

Since profits are residually defined as the value of sales minus the rental of factor inputs, and since profits accrue to the households that own firms, household incomes – from supplying land, labour and capital, or from profits – equal the value of output.

Our model is still very simple. What happens if firms do not sell all their output? What happens if firms sell output not to households but to other firms? What happens if households do not spend all their incomes? The next section answers these questions. Having done so, our conclusion will be unchanged: the level of economic activity can be measured by valuing total spending, total output or total earnings. All three methods give the same answer.

The circular flow diagram in Figure 15.4 lets us keep track of some key interactions in the economy as a whole. But the diagram is too simple. It leaves out important features of the real world: saving and investment, government spending and taxes, transactions between firms and with the rest of the world. We need a comprehensive system of national accounts.

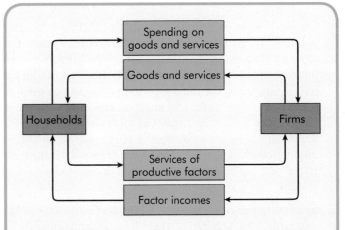

The inner loop shows the flow of real resources. Households supply the services of factors of production to firms who use these factors to produce goods and services for households. The outer loop shows the corresponding flow of payments. Firms pay factor incomes to households but receive revenue from households' spending on goods and services that the firms produce.

Figure 15.4   The circular flow between firms and households

CASE 15.1

Emerging markets act as a locomotive for the world economy

The largest economy in the world often acts as a locomotive, dragging other economies along behind it. In the nineteenth century, the UK acted as the locomotive for the expansion in world trade. During the twentieth century, the US played a similar role. When the locomotive was fired up, other countries benefited. When the US was booming, it acted as a buoyant market into which other countries could export. Conversely, during the few periods of US recession, other countries found it harder to sustain their own growth because their largest export market was stagnating.

During the last 35 years of the twentieth century, the fastest growth was to be found not in the US or in Europe but in Asia. Small countries – such as Singapore, South Korea, Hong Kong and Malaysia – abandoned previous policies of sheltering their economies behind high import tariffs, and made a sustained effort to join the world economy, compete in export markets and use these revenues to import foreign goods that they would make only very inefficiently themselves. The table shows the huge success of this strategy for these 'Asian tigers'.

	Annual real growth, per capita GDP, 1965–2002 (%)	Share of manufactured exports in total exports (%)	
		1965	2002
Indonesia	7	2	89
Malaysia	6	6	85
Singapore	8	34	76
South Korea	8	59	93
Thailand	6	4	78

Source: World Bank, *World Development Report* (various issues).

The tigers were each small enough that their spectacular growth did not cause insuperable economic and political problems for the mature markets into which they were exporting. In terms of global impact, the more important question was whether the world's two most populous economies were going to continue their inward-looking economic isolationism or whether they would emulate the tigers, embrace economic reform, and enjoy the rapid growth that might potentially be theirs once they adopted modern technologies, promoted competition, and engaged seriously with the global economy. After the death of Mao Zedong, China's new leadership embarked on economic reform in the 1980s. A decade later, Indian Prime Minister Rajiv Gandhi began to dismantle state controls and allow greater market competition, both at home and internationally. The results have been dramatic. China has experienced nearly 30 years of real growth close to 10 per cent per annum, and for over a decade India has sustained a real growth rate of around 8 per cent per annum.

In terms of per capita income, China and India have only progressed from poverty to middle-income living standards. But because of their huge populations, their aggregate GDP is already significant by world standards. Combining China, India and the smaller Asian tigers, the emerging Asian market economies are now extremely important for the performance of the world economy. Nor have the benefits of globalization been confined to Asia. Large countries such as Brazil and Russia have also moved from state control and import controls towards greater market competition and greater integration with the world economy.

As a bloc, emerging markets are increasingly the engine of growth in the world economy. Individually, they have been growing much more rapidly than the US, Europe or Japan, and collectively they have now grown to an aggregate size that makes them significant. Emerging markets did not escape the financial crash of 2008/09, but they have recovered more quickly from its adverse effects. In its October 2009 *Economic Outlook*, the International Monetary Fund pronounced that the worst of the global economic crisis was over. The US and Europe were showing signs of coming out of recession, in part as a result of considerable stimulus by their domestic governments, but also because of better export prospects to the emerging markets of Asia, particularly China and India.

Since emerging economies had previously been growing incredibly quickly, a slowdown still meant only a shallow recession. Asia in particular was quick to revert to healthy growth rates after the initial jolt, helped by government stimulus packages, just as in the West, but with less output contraction to reverse. Moreover, very large economies typically trade less with the outside world than do small economies, which have to specialize in order to enjoy economies of scale. Given their vast size, once stimulated by their own monetary and fiscal policies, China and India were able to power ahead whatever was going on elsewhere.

The figure shows how Asian economies were growing fastest before the crash, and were first to recover thereafter. As they grow, they suck in exports from the US and Europe, helping to pull along these more sluggish and mature economies. We study determinants of long-term growth in Chapter 26, where we examine catch-up in more detail.

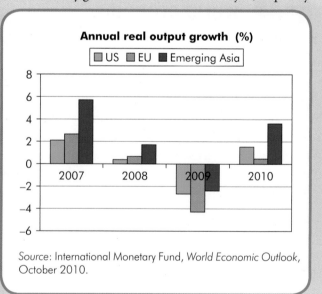

Source: International Monetary Fund, *World Economic Outlook*, October 2010.

15.4 National income accounting

Measuring national income and output

Gross domestic product (GDP) measures the value of output produced in a country. Gross national product (GNP) measures the value of the income that its citizens earn. Initially we discuss a *closed economy*, not linked to the rest of the world, in which output and income are the same.

First, we extend the simple circular flow diagram shown in Figure 15.4. Transactions do not take place exclusively between a single firm and a single household. Firms hire labour services from households but buy raw materials and machinery from *other* firms. To avoid double counting, we use **value added**.

To get value added, we take the firm's output then deduct the cost of the input goods used up to make that output. Closely related is the distinction between final goods and intermediate goods.

Thus, ice cream is a **final good**. Steel is an **intermediate good**, made by one firm but used as an input by another firm. Capital goods are final goods because they are *not* used up in subsequent production. They do not fully depreciate.

An example will clarify these concepts. Study it until you have mastered them. We assume that there are four firms in the economy: a steel maker, a producer of capital goods (machines) for the car industry, a tyre maker and a car producer who sells to the final user, households. Table 15.2 calculates GDP for this simple economy.

The steel firm makes £4000 worth of steel, one-quarter sold to the machine maker and three-quarters sold to the car maker. If the steel producer also mines the iron

> **Gross domestic product** (GDP) measures the output made in the domestic economy, regardless of who owns the production inputs.
>
> **Gross national product** (GNP) measures the income of a country.
>
> **Value added** is the increase in the value of goods as a result of the production process.
>
> **Final goods** are purchased by the ultimate user, either households buying consumer goods or firms buying capital goods such as machinery.
>
> **Intermediate goods** are partly finished goods that form inputs to a subsequent production process that then uses them up.

Table 15.2   Calculating GDP

(1) Good	(2) Seller	(3) Buyer	(4) Transaction value	(5) Value added	(6) Spending on final goods	(7) Factor earnings
Steel	Steel maker	Machine maker	£1000	£1000	–	£1000
Steel	Steel maker	Car maker	£3000	£3000	–	£3000
Machine	Machine maker	Car maker	£2000	£1000	£2000	£1000
Tyres	Tyre maker	Car maker	£500	£500	–	£500
Cars	Car maker	Households	£5000	£1500	£5000	£1500
Total transactions			£11 500			
GDP			£7000	£7000	£7000	£7000

ore from which the steel is produced, all £4000 is value added or net output of the steel firm. This revenue is paid out in wages and rents, or is residual profits that also accrue to households as income. Hence the first two rows of the last column also add up to £4000. Firms have spent £4000 buying this steel output, but it is not expenditure on final goods. Steel is an intermediate good, used up in later stages of the production process.

The machine maker spends £1000 buying steel input, then converts it into a machine sold to the car maker for £2000. The value added by the machine maker is £2000 less the £1000 spent on steel input. This net revenue of £1000 accrues directly or indirectly to households as income or profit. Since the car firm intends to keep the machine, the full value of £2000 is then shown under 'final expenditure'.

Like the steel producer, the tyre manufacturer makes an intermediate output that is not final expenditure. If the tyre manufacturer also owns the rubber trees from which the tyres were made, the entire output of £500 is value added and contributes to household incomes. If the tyre company bought rubber from a domestic rubber producer, we subtract the input value of rubber from the tyre manufacturer's output to get value added or net output, but add another row in the table showing activity of the rubber producer.

The car producer spends £3000 on steel and £500 on tyres. Since both are used up during the period in which cars are made, we subtract £3500 from the car output of £5000 to get the value added of the car maker. This net revenue pays households for factor services supplied, or is paid to them as profits.

Finally, the car producer sells the car for £5000 to the final consumer – households. Only then does the car become a final good. Its full price of £5000 is final expenditure.

Table 15.2 shows that the gross value of all the transactions is £11 500. This overstates the value of the goods the economy has actually produced. For example, the £3000 that the steel producer earned by selling steel to the car producer is already included in the final value of car output. It is double-counting to count this £3000 again as output of the steel producer.

Column (5) shows the value added at each stage in the production process; £7000 is the true net output of the economy. Since each firm pays the corresponding net revenue to households either as direct factor payments or indirectly as profits, household earnings are £7000 in the last column of the table. If we add up payments made to households as income and profits, we get the same measure of GDP.

Table 15.2 confirms that we also get the same answer if we measure spending on *final* goods and services. In this case final users are households buying cars and the car producer buying the (everlasting) machinery used to make cars.

Investment and saving

This example explains value added, and the distinction between intermediate and final goods. It also deals with a second complication. Total output and household incomes are each £7000, but households spend only £5000 on cars. What do they do with the rest of their incomes? And who does the rest of the spending? To resolve these issues, we need **investment** and **saving**.

Investment is the purchase of new capital goods by firms.

Saving is the part of income not spent buying goods and services.

Households spend £5000 on cars. Since their income is £7000, they save £2000. The car maker spends £2000 on investment, buying new machinery. Figure 15.5 shows how to amend the circular flow diagram of Figure 15.4. The bottom half of the figure shows that incomes and factor services are each £7000. But £2000 leaks out from the circular flow when households save. Only £5000 finds its way back to firms as household spending on cars.

The top half of the figure shows that £5000 is the value of output of consumer goods and of household spending on these goods. Since GDP is £7000, where does the other £2000 come from? If not from household spending, it must come from spending by firms themselves. It is the £2000 of investment expenditure made by the car producer buying machinery for car production.

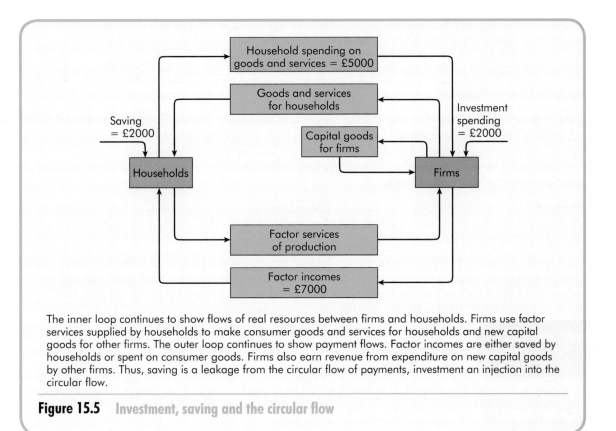

The inner loop continues to show flows of real resources between firms and households. Firms use factor services supplied by households to make consumer goods and services for households and new capital goods for other firms. The outer loop continues to show payment flows. Factor incomes are either saved by households or spent on consumer goods. Firms also earn revenue from expenditure on new capital goods by other firms. Thus, saving is a leakage from the circular flow of payments, investment an injection into the circular flow.

Figure 15.5   Investment, saving and the circular flow

The numbers in Table 15.2 relate to flows of output, expenditure and income in a particular period, such as a year. During this period the economy goes once round the inner and outer loops of Figure 15.5. On the inner loop, firms make an output of £5000 for consumption by households and an output of £2000 of capital goods for investment by firms. On the outer loop, which relates to money payments, saving is a leakage of £2000 from the circular flow and investment spending by firms on new machinery is an injection of £2000 to the circular flow.

> A **leakage** from the circular flow is money no longer recycled from households to firms.
>
> An **injection** is money that flows to firms without being recycled through households.

Two questions immediately arise. First, is it coincidental that household savings of £2000 exactly equal investment expenditure of £2000 by firms? Second, if not, how is the money saved by households transferred to firms to allow them to pay for investment spending?

Suppose Y denotes GDP, which also equals the value of household incomes, C denotes household spending on consumption, and S saving. By definition, saving is unspent income, so $Y = C + S$, where the symbol $=$ means 'is identically equal to, as a matter of definition'. Since one definition of GDP is the sum of final expenditure, $Y = C + I$. Putting these two definitions together,

$$S = I \qquad\qquad (1)$$

since both are identical to $(Y - C)$.

It is thus no accident that saving and investment are each £2000 in our example. Equation (1) tells us that saving and investment are always equal, in the absence of government and foreign sectors.

Look again at the outer loop of Figure 15.5. All household spending in the top half of the figure returns to households as income in the bottom half of the figure. Investment spending by firms is matched by an income flow to households in excess of their consumer spending. Since saving is defined as the excess of income over consumption, investment and savings must always be equal.

These accounting identities follow from our definitions of investment, saving and income. *Actual* saving must equal *actual* investment. This need not mean *desired* saving equals *desired* investment. To study that, we need models of desired saving and investment, a task we begin in the next chapter.[1]

What connects the leakage of saving and the injection of investment? Since firms pay households £7000 but get only £5000 from household spending, they are borrowing £2000 to pay for the new capital goods they are buying. Since households save £2000, they are lending it to firms for investment. In a market economy, financial institutions and financial markets channel household saving to the firms that wish to borrow to invest in new capital goods.

Investment lets us deal with another problem glossed over in our simpler circular flow diagram. What happens if firms cannot sell all the output that they produce? Surely this creates a gap between the output and expenditure measures of GDP?

Final goods are goods not used up in the production process in the period. In Table 15.2 steel was an intermediate good used up in making cars and machines; machines were a final good because the car maker could use them again in the next period. Suppose that car sales are not £5000 but only £4000. The car maker is left with £1000 worth of cars that must be stockpiled.

Inventories or **stocks** are goods currently held by a firm for future production or sale.

The car producer may hold stocks of steel, an input to production of cars in the next period, or **inventories** or **stocks** of finished cars awaiting sale to consumers in the next period.

Stocks are sometimes called *working capital*. Not used up in production and sale during the current period, stocks are classified as capital goods. Adding to stocks is investment in working capital. When stocks are depleted, we treat this as negative investment, or disinvestment.

Now we can keep the national accounts straight. When the car firm sells only £4000 of the £5000 worth of cars made this period, we treat the inventory investment of £1000 by the car producer as final expenditure. As in Table 15.2, the output and expenditure measures of GDP are each £7000, including the output and expenditure on the machinery for making cars. But spending on final goods is now: car firm £2000 on machines, £1000 on stocks; household-consumer £4000 on cars.

This can be confusing. The trick is to distinguish between classification by commodity and classification by economic use. Steel is an intermediate commodity but that is not important. When a steel producer makes *and sells* steel we show this as production of an intermediate good. Since it has been passed on to someone else, our expenditure measure picks it up further up the chain of production and sales. But when a firm adds to its stocks, we must count that as final expenditure because it will not show up anywhere else in the national accounts. The firm is temporarily adding to its capital. When it later uses up these stocks, we treat this as negative investment to keep the record straight.

We now introduce the government and foreign sectors.

The domestic government and foreign countries

Governments raise revenue both through direct taxes on income (wages, rents, interest and profits) and through indirect taxes or expenditures taxes (VAT, petrol duties and cigarette taxes). Taxes finance two kinds of expenditure. Government spending on goods and services G is purchases by the government of

---

1   It helps to draw parallels with microeconomics. The demand curve shows desired purchases at any price, the supply curve desired sales at any price. In equilibrium, desired purchases equal desired sales. When the price is too high, there is excess supply and some desired sales are frustrated. But since every transaction has a buyer and a seller, actual purchases equal actual sales whether or not the market is in equilibrium.

physical goods and services. It includes the wages of civil servants and soldiers, the purchase of computers, tanks and military aircraft, and investment in roads and hospitals.

Governments also spend money on **transfer payments** or benefits, *B*. These include pensions, unemployment benefit and subsidies to firms.

> **Transfer payments** are monetary payments that require no goods or services in return.

Transfer payments do not affect national income or national output. They are not included in GDP. There is no corresponding net physical output. Taxes and transfer payments merely redistribute existing income and spending power away from people being taxed and towards people being subsidized. In contrast, spending *G* on goods and services produces net output, and gives rise to factor earnings in the firms supplying this output and also to additional spending power of the households receiving this income. Hence government spending *G* on goods and services is part of GDP. It is final expenditure since government is now an additional end user of the output.

National income accounts aim to provide a logically coherent set of definitions and measures of national output. However, taxes drive a wedge between the price the purchaser pays and the price the seller receives. We can choose to value national output either at **market prices** inclusive of indirect taxes on goods and services, or at the prices received by producers after indirect taxes have been paid.

> **GDP at market prices** measures domestic output inclusive of indirect taxes on goods and services.

So far we have studied a closed economy not transacting with the rest of the world. We now examine an *open economy* that deals with other countries.

Households, firms and the government may buy imports *Z* that are not part of domestic output and do not give rise to domestic factor incomes. These goods are not in the output measure of GDP, the *value added* by domestic producers. However, imports show up in final expenditure. There are two solutions to this problem. We could subtract the import component separately from *C*, *I*, *G* and *X* and measure only final expenditure on the domestically made bit of consumption, investment, government spending and exports. But it is easier to continue to measure total final expenditure on *C*, *I*, *G* and **exports** *X* and then to subtract from this total expenditure on **imports** *Z*. It comes to exactly the same thing.

> **Exports (X)** are domestically produced but sold abroad.
>
> **Imports (Z)** are produced abroad but purchased for use in the domestic economy.

In the previous section, we saw that our definitions should imply that total income, expenditure and output measures of total activity should coincide. We now explain how this works once we introduce the government and foreign sectors as well. The complete system of national accounts is summarized in Figure 15.6.

We begin on the left with gross national product (or gross national income – same thing) at market prices. The second column is the expenditure measure of GNP, which comprises spending by households on consumption, spending by firms on investment, spending by government goods and services (which we could think of as government contributions to consumption and investment), net exports (the excess of exports over imports) and, finally, net international transfers from abroad.

This last item is sometimes called net international property income, since most transfers arise from the return on assets held abroad (minus the return paid by us to foreigners holding assets in our country). International transfer payments also include aid by the UK when an earthquake hits Haiti, or remittances of cash to their families by foreign workers temporarily resident in the UK.

The third column takes us from GNP to GDP. The latter measures gross output during the period. Whereas net international transfer payments add to our income, they do not add to our physical output of goods and services. Hence, Figure 15.6 deducts these from GNP to get to GDP.

The fourth column shows the difference between gross and net output. Net means deducting depreciation of physical capital as buildings and machinery wear out or become obsolete. Statisticians have to make

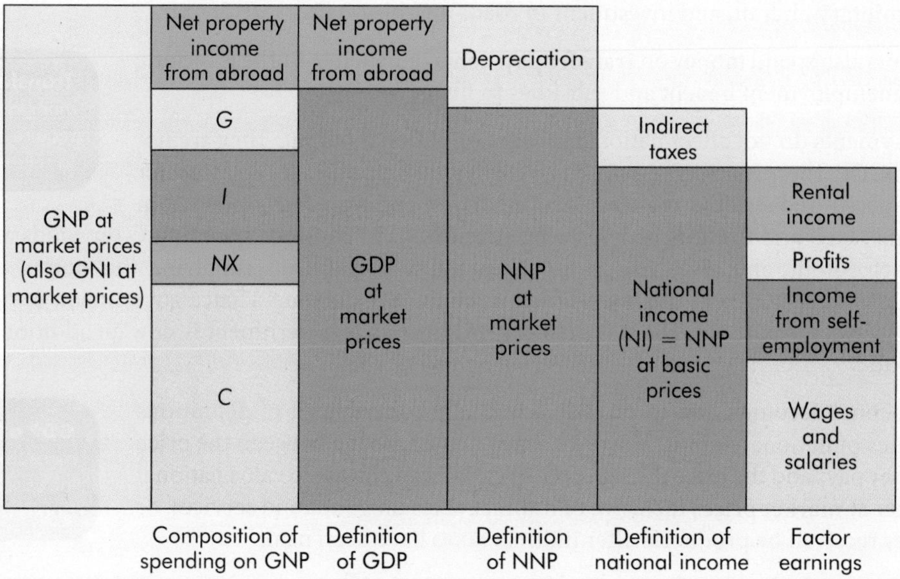

Figure 15.6 Summarizing the national accounts

some fairly heroic guesses sometimes about how much depreciation is going on. So far, our national accounts leave out depreciation of environmental capital. One day, if global warming proceeds enough, it will probably become essential to make explicit estimates for environmental depreciation. An economist's first thought should be that this would then reward governments that took action to reduce environmental depreciation.

> **GDP at basic prices**
> measures domestic output exclusive of indirect taxes on goods and services.

The fifth column shows the role of indirect taxes. Measurements at market prices include indirect taxes in the statistics; measurements at **basic prices** remove them.

The final column shows the net incomes that accrue to the inputs (or factors of production) used in making output. Total factor incomes arise from the supply of labour to earn wages and salaries, self-employe work, the supply of land to earn rent, or the supply of capital to earn profits.

Understanding Figure 15.6 is a key step in mastering the definitions, confirming that they make sense, and checking that we have not left anything out.

Revisiting the circular flow

Using Y to measure GDP at market prices, the value added or net output of the economy is now:

$$Y = \text{GDP at market prices} = C + I + G + NX$$

> **Personal disposable income** is household income after direct taxes and transfer payments. It shows how much households have available for spending and saving.

Household incomes at market prices are supplemented by benefits B less direct taxes T_d. This gives us **personal disposable income** ($Y + B - T_d$).

Assuming for the moment that saving is done only by households, disposable income must be spent on consumption or saving

$$Y + B - T_d = C + S$$

Figure 15.7 shows the extended picture of the circular flow.

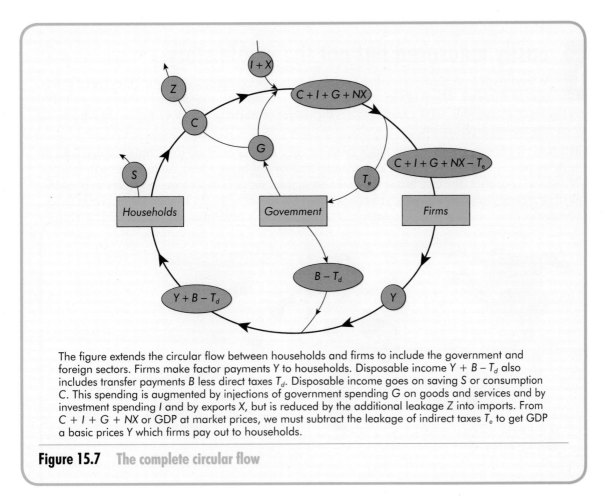

The figure extends the circular flow between households and firms to include the government and foreign sectors. Firms make factor payments Y to households. Disposable income $Y + B - T_d$ also includes transfer payments B less direct taxes T_d. Disposable income goes on saving S or consumption C. This spending is augmented by injections of government spending G on goods and services and by investment spending I and by exports X, but is reduced by the additional leakage Z into imports. From $C + I + G + NX$ or GDP at market prices, we must subtract the leakage of indirect taxes T_e to get GDP a basic prices Y which firms pay out to households.

Figure 15.7   The complete circular flow

Round the top loop of Figure 15.7, consumption C at market prices is now supplemented by injections of investment spending I, net exports NX and government spending G. From $(C + I + G + NX)$ or GDP at market prices, we subtract indirect taxes T_e to get GDP at basic prices.

Since total leakages are always equal to total injections, you can check from the diagram that this implies $S + T_d + T_e - B + Z = I + G + X$. Investment, government spending and exports are all injections to the circular flow that do not originate from households. Conversely, household spending leaks out, directly or indirectly, through saving, taxes (net of benefits) and imports: only the remaining spending flows back to domestic firms and round again as household incomes.

In the special case where $T_d = T_e = G = B = 0$, there is no government sector and this becomes $S = I$, as was the case before we introduced the government and foreign sectors.

Notice too that when net exports are zero,

$$T_d + T_e - B - G = I - S$$

The left-hand side is the financial surplus of the government, total revenue minus its total spending. The right-hand side is the private sector deficit, the excess of investment spending over household saving. As a matter of definition, the private sector can run a deficit only if the government runs a surplus, and vice versa.

More generally, with three sectors – households, firms and government – our accounts imply that if one sector is running a surplus, this must correspond to the aggregate deficit of the other two sectors. Our accounting does not allow things simply to evaporate.

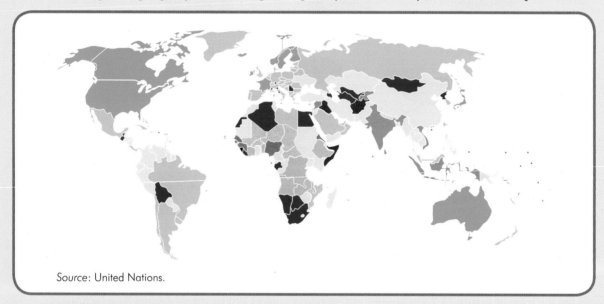

CONCEPT 15.1 Easily measured but not the whole story

When things are traded in a market, or embedded in government tax statistics, they are relatively easy to measure. Many of our difficulties arise precisely because some of the most valuable things are not easily measurable. GDP easily captures the output of washing machines, but not of happiness, health or environmental depreciation.

The United Nations Human Development Index systematically tries to measure three broad dimensions of economic development – health, education and material standard of living – and produces annual statistics for all UN member countries. The map below shows the geographic range of outcomes – no prizes for guessing which colours represent prosperity and which represent poverty as measured by the Human Development Index.

Source: United Nations.

Health is crudely captured by life expectancy at birth, education by the proportion of the children enrolled at school and by the proportion of adults who can read, and material standard of living by per capita GDP.

Some of these indicators are more stable than others. For example, before the financial crash, Iceland came top in the world in the UN measure, and Sierra Leone bottom. But Iceland's banks experienced the biggest crash of all, and so the Icelandic economy is now in serious trouble. This will not immediately affect its adult literacy or the life expectancy of its population, but these will gradually suffer unless economic prosperity can be restored.

Like sausages, economic statistics simply reflect what you put into them. If you care about democracy, equality or environmental sustainability, don't get hung up merely because your country is not doing well on the particular things that GDP does measure.

People who visit France quickly learn that the French have a good quality of life, better than you would expect simply by looking at their GNP. In 2009 President Sarkozy commissioned a panel of economic experts to advise on how to adjust their national statistics better to reflect the benefits of long lunches, long holidays and early retirement.

Think of this as a health warning on GNP and GDP statistics. They measure what they measure. Unless and until electorates want to spend more money collecting more comprehensive statistics, GNP and GDP will use data already being collected annually for other purposes such as taxation.

Source: Adapted from Kay, J. (2009) Do not discount what you cannot measure, *Financial Times*, 22 September.
© The Financial Times Ltd 2010.

Table 15.3 UK national accounts, 2008 (£bn, current prices)

Expenditure measure		Income measure	
At market prices:		Income source:	
		Employment	770
C by households	891	Profits and rents	429
C by government and non-profit organizations	350	Other	83
I by private firms and government	245	GDP at basic prices	1282
NX	−40	Indirect taxes	164
GDP at market prices	1446	GDP at market prices	1446
Net property income from abroad	25		
GNP (GNI) at market prices	1471		

Source: www.statistics.gov.uk.

Table 15.3 shows actual data for UK GDP and GNP in 2008. Official statistics often decompose G, government spending on goods and services, into government consumption and government investment. Table 15.3 therefore shows data on consumption by households, consumption by government (and non-profit organizations) and on combined investment by government and private firms.

15.5 What GNP measures

A firm's accounts show how the company is doing. Our national income accounts let us assess how the economy is doing. Just as a firm's accounts may conceal as much as they reveal, we must interpret the national income accounts with care.

We focus on GNP as a measure of economic performance. Since depreciation is rather difficult to measure, and consequently may be treated differently in different countries or during different time periods, using GNP avoids the need to argue about depreciation.

In this section we make three points. First, we recall the distinction between nominal and real variables. Second, we show how per capita GNP can provide a more accurate picture of the standard of living of an average person in an economy. Finally, we discuss the incompleteness of GNP as a measure of the activities that provide economic welfare to members of society.

CASE 15.2

Tax evasion, crime and the mismeasurement of GNP

Gangster Al Capone, never charged with murder, was eventually convicted of tax evasion. Taxes are evaded by smugglers and drug dealers but also by gardeners, plumbers and everyone else doing things 'for cash'. Since GNP data are based on tax statistics, the 'hidden' economy is unreported. This means that official GNP statistics may substantially understate the true value of GNP.

Economists have various ways to estimate the size of the hidden economy. One way is to count large-denomination banknotes in circulation. People with fistfuls of £50 notes are often engaged in tax evasion.

Indeed, when the euro was first launched as a currency, the decision to make the most valuable note €500 (much more valuable than the largest dollar banknote, the $100 bill) led to fierce discussion as to whether the euro would replace the dollar as the preferred currency of crooks – and in 2010 it was taken out of currency in the UK for precisely that reason.

Another way is to guess people's income by studying what they spend. Maria Lacko has used the stable relationship between household use of electricity and its main determinants – income and weather temperature – to estimate incomes from data on electricity consumption and temperature. She confirms two popularly held views. The hidden economy is large both in former communist economies, where the new private sector is as yet unrecorded, and in several Mediterranean countries with a history of trouble getting their citizens to pay tax. She found that the size of the hidden economy might be around 20–30 per cent of reported GDP in the countries of Eastern Europe and the Mediterranean, but probably only 5–10 per cent of the size of GDP in the US and UK. If we measured this properly, GDP would therefore be much larger.

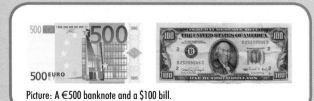

Picture: A €500 banknote and a $100 bill.

Another way to estimate the hidden economy is to conduct surveys and offer people immunity if they tell the truth. Recent work by Friedrich Schneider is quoted by the UK National Audit Office (2008). His estimates are shown in the table below.

The hidden economy (% of national income)

Belgium	Sweden	Canada	Australia	UK	US
22	19	16	14	12	9

Source: National Audit Office (2008) *Tackling the Hidden Economy*, The Stationery Office.

Nominal and real GNP

Nominal GNP measures GNP at the prices prevailing when income was earned.

Real GNP, or GNP at constant prices, adjusts for inflation by measuring GNP in different years at the prices prevailing at some particular date known as the *base year*.

The **GNP deflator** is the ratio of nominal GNP to real GNP expressed as an index.

Since it is physical quantities of output that yield people utility or happiness, it can be misleading to judge the economy's performance by looking at **nominal GNP**.

Table 15.4 presents a simple hypothetical example of a whole economy. Nominal GNP rises from £600 to £1470 between 1980 and 2010. If we take 1980 as the base year, we can measure **real GNP** in 2008 by valuing output quantities in 2010 using 1980 prices. Real GNP rises only from £600 to £860. This rise of 43 per cent in real GNP gives a truer picture of the extra quantity of goods made by the economy as a whole.

The GNP deflator

Chapter 2 introduced the consumer price index (CPI), an index of the average price of goods purchased by consumers. The most common measure of the inflation rate in the UK is the percentage rise in the CPI over its value a year earlier.

However, consumption expenditure is only one part of GNP, which also includes investment, government spending and net exports. To convert nominal GNP to real GNP, we need to use an index showing what is happening to the price of all goods. This index is called the **GNP deflator**.

Table 15.4   Nominal and real GNP

		1980	2010
Quantity	apples	100	150
	chickens	100	140
Price £	apples	2	4
	chickens	4	6
Value in current £	apples	200	600
	chickens	400	840
	Nominal GNP	**600**	**1440**
Value in 1980 £	apples	200	300
	chickens	400	560
	Real GNP	**600**	**860**

Table 15.5   UK GNP, 1960–2008

	1960	1995	2008
Nominal GNP (current £bn)	25	750	1471
GNP deflator (1995 = 100)	8	100	141
Real GNP (£bn, 1995 prices)	316	750	1043

Source: www.statistics.gov.uk.

Table 15.5 gives UK data over four decades. Nominal GNP in the UK rose from £25 billion in 1960 to £1471 billion in 2008. Without knowing what happened to the price of goods in general, we cannot judge what happened to the quantity of output over the period. The second row of Table 15.5 answers this question. On average, prices in 2008 were 41 per cent higher than in 1995. Hence, the change in real GNP was much smaller than the change in nominal GNP in the same period. Whenever inflation is not zero, it is important to distinguish between nominal and real GNP.

The contrast is even more marked if we go back to 1960 since inflation rose steadily in the 1970s. Whereas nominal GNP rose 50-fold between 1960 and 2008, real GNP only tripled. The rest of the growth in nominal GNP simply reflected inflation.

Per capita real GNP

Real GNP is a simple measure of the real income of an economy. The annual percentage rise in real GNP tells us how fast an economy is growing. Table 15.6 shows the average annual growth rate of real GNP in three countries over two decades. The first column shows that the annual growth rate of real GNP during 1980–2008 was highest in Jordan and lowest in Denmark. Although this tells us about the growth of the whole economy, we may be interested in a different question: what was happening to the standard of living

Source: World Bank. © 2010 The World Bank Group. All rights reserved.

Table 15.6 Growth, 1980–2008 (% per annum)

	Real GNP	Per capita real GNP
Denmark	2.3	2.2
UK	2.7	2.3
Jordan	4.1	0.1

of a representative person in each of these countries? To answer this question, we need to examine per capita real GNP.

> **Per capita real GNP** is real GNP divided by the total population. It is real GNP per head.

Table 15.6 also shows growth of **per capita real GNP**. The ranking is reversed. To get a simple measure of the standard of living enjoyed by a person in a particular country, it is better to look at per capita real GNP, which adjusts for population, than to look at total real GNP. On average, GNP per head grew much more quickly in Denmark than in Jordan: despite the growth in real GNP in Jordan, it was barely sufficient to keep pace with population growth.

Even per capita real GNP is only a crude indicator. Table 15.6 does *not* say that every person in Denmark got 2.2 per cent more goods and services each year. It shows what was happening on average. Some people's real incomes increased by a lot more; some people became absolutely poorer. The more the income distribution changes over time, the less reliable is the change in per capita real GNP as an indicator of what is happening to any particular person.

A comprehensive measure of GNP

Because we use GNP to measure the income of the economy, the coverage of GNP should be as comprehensive as possible. In practice, we encounter two problems in including all production in GDP and GNP. First, some outputs, such as noise, pollution and congestion, are 'bads'. We should subtract them from GDP and GNP. This is a sensible suggestion but hard to implement. These nuisance goods are not traded through markets, so it is hard to quantify their output or decide how to value their cost to society.

Similarly, many valuable goods and services are excluded from GNP because they are not marketed and therefore hard to measure accurately. These activities include household chores, DIY activities and unreported jobs.

Deducting the value of nuisance outputs and adding the value of unreported and non-marketed incomes would make GNP a more accurate measure of the economy's production of goods and services. But there is another important adjustment to make before using GNP as the basis for national economic welfare. People enjoy not merely goods and services but also leisure time.

ACTIVITY
15.1

Pollution could make economic growth negative

Well-run firms spend serious money on information systems that let their managers make intelligent decisions. In contrast, governments often have to make do with economic data gathered on the cheap. Many data are simply the by-product of tax records. Published GDP data ignore valuable commodities like leisure, and omit important harmful outputs like environmental pollution.

Citing a study by the Asian Development Bank, the BBC noted that Asian emissions of greenhouse gases would treble in the next 25 years. If so, Asia will overtake the OECD as the world's biggest source of greenhouse gas pollutants. China is currently building a new coal-fired power station every two weeks, and India's microcar – the Tata Nano – will make motoring affordable to tens of millions of new drivers every year. As populations move from villages to the cities, demand for heat and power increases all the time.

Environmental degradation means that almost 40 per cent of Asia's population now lives in areas prone to drought and erosion. With the Asian population set to triple in the next 20 years, and half these people living in cities, air pollution will reach new records. Nor is access to clean water much better.

Case 15.1 documented the sustained success of the Asian tigers, countries such as Thailand, Singapore, Hong Kong, Korea and the Philippines. On measured GDP, they can point to four decades of very rapid growth. But if national accounts had to keep proper account of environmental depreciation – a cost that would be subtracted from gross output when measuring the true net output of an economy – many of these countries would have much less impressive growth records. We would have to call them Asian snails instead of Asian tigers. Their success in making consumer electronics has been offset by extensive pollution and urban congestion. Just ask anyone who has recently visited Bangkok.

Source: Adapted from www.bbc.co.uk. © bbc.co.uk/news.

Questions

(a) How does depreciation of ordinary machinery and buildings enter calculations of GDP or national income?

(b) What measure properly reflects depreciation of physical capital?

(c) How are conventional estimates of depreciation made?

(d) What would be entailed in following the same procedures for environmental capital?

(e) How would environmental capital for the whole planet affect national accounts?

To check your answers to these questions, see page 685.

Suppose Leisurians value leisure more highly than Industrians. Industrians work more and produce more goods. Industria has a higher measured GNP. It is silly to say this proves that Leisurians have lower welfare. By choosing to work less hard they reveal that the extra leisure is worth at least as much as the extra goods they could have made by working more.

Because it is difficult and expensive to collect regular measurements on non-marketed and unreported goods and bads, and to make regular assessments of the implicit value of leisure, real GNP inevitably remains the commonest measure of economic activity. Far from ideal, it is the best measure available on a regular basis.

 ## 15.6   International comparisons

International agencies prefer to compare like with like, which means eliminating measures that are sensitive to large differences in national practices. No country invests much of its resources in collecting accurate data for depreciation. Hence international statistics focus on gross measures rather than net measures, since the latter would entail making allowances for depreciation.

Similarly, it is generally felt that GDP data are more reliable than GNP data, since the latter includes estimates of property income earned abroad. One reason why people hold assets abroad is to avoid declaring the income to national tax authorities. Assessing capital gains (which are really income) on foreign assets is also problematic. Hence, most international comparisons are based on GDP. We have a more reliable idea of gross output than of gross income.

Summary

- **Macroeconomics** examines the economy as a whole.

- Macroeconomics sacrifices individual detail to focus on the interaction of broad sectors of the economy. Households supply production inputs to firms that use them to make output. Firms pay factor incomes to households, who buy the output from firms. This is the **circular flow**.

- **Gross domestic product (GDP)** is the value of net output of the factors of production located in the domestic economy. It can be measured in three equivalent ways: value added in production, factor incomes including profits, or final expenditure.

- **Leakages** from the circular flow are those parts of payment by firms to households that do not automatically return to firms as spending by households on the output of firms. Leakages are saving, taxes net of subsidies and imports. **Injections** are sources of revenue to firms that do not arise from household spending. Investment expenditure by firms, spending on goods and services by the government and exports are injections. By definition, total leakages equal total injections.

- **GDP at market prices** values domestic output at prices inclusive of indirect taxes. **GDP at basic prices** measures domestic output at prices exclusive of indirect taxes. **Gross national product (GNP)**, also called gross national income (GNI), adjusts GDP for net property income from abroad.

- **National income** is net national product (NNP) at basic prices. NNP is GNP minus the **depreciation** of the capital stock during the period. In practice, many assessments of economic performance are based on GNP since it is hard to measure depreciation accurately.

- **Nominal GNP** measures income at current prices. **Real GNP** measures income at constant prices. It adjusts nominal GNP for changes in the **GNP deflator** as a result of inflation.

- **Per capita real GNP** divides real GNP by the population. It is a more reliable indicator of income per person in an economy, but only an average measure of what people get.

- Real GNP and per capita real GNP are crude measures of national and individual welfare. They ignore non-market activities, bads such as pollution, valuable activities such as work in the home, and production unreported by tax evaders. Nor do they measure the value of leisure.

- Because it is expensive, and sometimes impossible, to make regular and accurate measurements of all these activities, in practice GNP is the most widely used measure of national performance.

Review questions

1 Car firms buy in raw materials (steel), intermediate goods (windscreens, tyres) and labour to make cars. Windscreen and tyre companies hire workers and also buy raw materials from other industries. What is the value added of the car industry (the three firms shown below)?

EASY

Producer of	Output	Intermediate goods used	Raw materials used	Labour input
Cars	1000	250	100	100
Windscreens	150		10	50
Tyres	100		10	30

2 GNP at market prices is £300 billion. Depreciation is £30 billion and indirect taxes are £20 billion. (a) What is national income? (b) Why does depreciation cause a discrepancy between GNP and national income? (c) Why do indirect taxes enter the calculation?

3 GNP = 2000, C = 1700, G = 50 and NX = 40. (a) What is investment I? (b) If exports are 350, what are imports? (c) If depreciation is 130, what is national income? (d) In this example net exports are positive. Could they be negative?

4 Given the data below: (a) What is 2010 GNP in 2009 prices? (b) What is the growth rate of real GNP from 2009 to 2010? (c) What is the inflation rate?

Year	Nominal GDP	GNP deflator
2009	2000	100
2010	2400	110

5 Should these be in a comprehensive measure of GNP: (a) time spent by students in lectures; (b) the income of muggers; (c) the wage paid to traffic wardens; (d) dropping litter?

6 Common fallacies Why are these statements wrong? (a) Unemployment benefit props up national income in years when employment is low. (b) A high per capita real GNP is always a good thing. (c) In 2010 *Crummy Movie* earned £1 billion more at the box office than *Gone With the Wind* earned 50 years ago. *Crummy Movie* is already a bigger box office success.

7 Which is correct? (a) Increasing the size of the police force in response to higher crime raises national income because government spending is higher. (b) Increasing the size of the police force reduces national income because society is having to waste resources tackling crime. (c) There is no effect on national income because the benefit of more police is offset by the cost of more crime.

8 Suppose a country is unable to borrow from abroad and must always equate the value of its exports and imports. If the private sector is saving a lot more than it is investing, is the government in surplus or in deficit? Why?

MEDIUM

9 It is the year 2060. Nation states have been abolished and there is a world government whose spending is financed entirely by income tax. Redraw Figure 15.6 explaining how you have changed it.

10 The world government now publishes world economic accounts that estimate the depreciation not only of the stock of physical capital but also of the stock of environmental capital. (a) If pollution and climate change are causing adverse effects, how does your new diagram on world income and output differ from that in Question 8. (b) Suppose environmental depreciation was initially $500 billion and the world government spends $100 billion on pollution control with the consequence that environmental depreciation is now only $300 billion. How is your diagram now affected?

11 You are head of the Leisure Commission that has to recommend to the government how to include the value of leisure in GDP. How do you come up with an estimate?

12 The price of a new television has remained roughly constant for the last 30 years. What does this show?

13 Suppose the injections to the circular flow (investment I, government spending G and exports X) do not depend on the current level of national output Y. In contrast, suppose leakages increase as output increases. Specifically, saving $S = 0.1Y$, imports $Z = 0.4Y$ and taxes $T = 0.5Y$. (a) If total injections equal 100, what is the value of national output? (b) If $G = 40$, is the government budget $(G - T)$ in surplus or deficit?

14 Essay question 'Economists are preoccupied with what they can measure. GDP is so misleading an indicator of welfare that it is almost pointless to gather statistics about it, either for international comparison across countries or to assess how well particular governments are doing.' How useful is GDP? Could we easily have a better indicator?

For solutions to these questions contact your lecturer.

Output and aggregate demand

CHAPTER 16

Learning Outcomes

By the end of this chapter, you should understand:

1. actual output and potential output

2. why output is demand determined in the short run

3. short-run equilibrium output

4. consumption and investment demand

5. how aggregate demand determines short-run equilibrium output

6. the marginal propensity to consume (*MPC*)

7. how the size of the multiplier affects the *MPC*

8. the paradox of thrift

During 1970–2009 UK real output grew on average by 2.3 per cent a year, but fluctuated around this trend. Real output actually fell during 1979–81 and 1989–92, and especially during 2008–09, but grew strongly during 1975–79, 1981–89 and 1995–2007. Words used by economists to describe these fluctuations – recession, recovery, boom and slump – are part of everyday language.

Why does real GDP fluctuate? To construct a simple model, we ignore discrepancies between national income, real GNP and real GDP. We use income and output interchangeably. First, we distinguish *actual* output and *potential* output.

Potential output tends to grow over time as the supply of inputs grows. Population growth adds to the labour force. Investment in education, training and new machinery adds to human and physical capital. Technical advances let given inputs produce more output. Together, these explain UK average growth at 2.3 per cent a year since 1970.

> **Potential output** is the economy's output when inputs are fully employed.

We study the theory of long-run economic growth in potential output in Chapter 26. First, we focus on deviations of actual output from potential output in the short run. Since potential output changes slowly, we begin with a short-run analysis of an economy with a fixed potential output.

381

Potential output is not the maximum an economy can conceivably make. With a gun to our heads, we could all make more. Rather, it is the output when every market in the economy is in long-run equilibrium. Every worker wanting to work at the equilibrium wage can find a job, and every machine that can profitably be used at the equilibrium rental for capital is in use. Thus, potential output includes an allowance for 'equilibrium unemployment'. Some people do not want to work at the equilibrium wage rate. Moreover, in a constantly changing economy, some people are temporarily between jobs. Today, UK potential output probably entails an unemployment rate of about 5 per cent, yet in 2010 it was over 8 per cent.

Suppose actual output falls below potential output. Workers are unemployed and firms have idle machines or spare capacity. A key issue in macroeconomics is how quickly output returns to potential output. In microeconomics, studying one market in isolation, we assumed excess supply would quickly bid the price down, eliminating excess supply to restore equilibrium. In macroeconomics, this cannot be taken for granted. Disturbances in one part of the economy induce changes elsewhere that may feed back again, exacerbating the original disturbance.

We cannot examine this issue by *assuming* that the economy is always at potential output, for then a problem could never arise. We must build a model in which departures from potential output are possible, examine the market forces then set in motion and decide how successfully market forces restore output to potential output. Because we want initially to focus on the possibility of additional unemployment, we start by considering a world in which there might be idle capacity and too little demand.

Thus our initial model has two crucial properties. First, all prices and wages are fixed at a given level. Second, at these prices and wage levels, there are workers without a job who would like to work, and firms with spare capacity they could profitably use. The economy has spare resources. It is then unnecessary to analyse the supply side of the economy in detail. Any rise in demand is happily met by firms and workers until potential output is reached.

> Trade is voluntary, so actual exchange is always the smaller of supply and demand. **Output is demand-determined** when there is excess supply, and wages and prices have yet to adjust to restore long-run equilibrium. Output then depends only on aggregate demand.
>
> Conversely, if excess demand exists, as under rationing in the former Soviet Union, we would have to discuss a model in which output was **supply-determined**.

Below potential output, firms happily supply whatever output is demanded. Total **output is demand-determined**.

Later, we shall relax the assumption that prices and wages are fixed. Not only do we want to study inflation, we also want to examine how quickly market forces, acting through changes in prices and wages, can eliminate unemployment and spare capacity. But first we must learn to walk. We postpone the analysis of price and wage adjustment until Chapter 21.

Until then, we study the demand-determined model of output and employment developed by John Maynard Keynes in *The General Theory of Employment, Interest and Money* (1936). Keynes used the model to explain high unemployment and low output in the Great Depression of the 1930s.

Most young economists soon became *Keynesians*, advocating government intervention to keep output close to potential output. By the 1950s, this approach was challenged by *monetarists*, led by Milton Friedman. They argued that Keynesian analysis, although helpful in studying recession, was a poor tool for studying inflation, which monetarists attribute to money creation. We develop an approach that uses the best insights of both Keynesians and monetarists.

In the 1970s unemployment rose again, despite Keynesian policies. Some economists discarded Keynesian economics completely. Not only did they deny the effectiveness of government policy to stabilize output, they argued that stabilizing output may not even be desirable. This has now prompted a fightback by *New Keynesians*, who believe that the central messages of Keynes, right all along, can be understood better by using modern microeconomics to explain the market failures that justify Keynesian intervention.

After the mid-1990s there appeared to be considerable convergence in ideas about macroeconomics. Central banks were made independent from government interference and asked to stabilize national economies, particularly their inflation rates. For more than a decade, central banks appeared to be succeeding in using interest rate changes to accomplish this task. There was little dispute about the underlying theories on which they were basing their behaviour, and their success in practice reinforced the belief that our understanding of macroeconomics was high.

In some sense, central banks became too successful. In stabilizing economies, they created a climate of safety in which the private sector felt able to take huge 'risks' precisely because they did not think that doing so would be risky. Households borrowed too much and speculated on property, banks borrowed too much and invested in more and more dubious assets in pursuit of ever higher returns. The central banks were so focused on macroeconomic stability of inflation and GDP that nobody blew the whistle on increasingly dangerous private sector behaviour. We all know what happened next.

Mastering modern macroeconomics will take us to great heights. But we will climb slowly, and need to begin at the foothills.

Chapter 15 introduced the circular flow of income and payments between households and firms. Households buy the output of firms. Firms' revenue is ultimately returned to households. We now build a simple model of this interaction of households and firms. The next chapter adds the government and the foreign sector.

16.1 Components of aggregate demand

Without a government or a foreign sector, there are two sources of demand: consumption demand by households and investment demand by firms. Using *AD* to denote aggregate demand, *C* for consumption demand and *I* for investment demand,

$$AD = C + I \qquad (1)$$

Consumption demand and investment demand are chosen by different economic groups and depend on different things.

> **Personal disposable income** is the income households receive from firms, plus transfer payments received from the government, minus direct taxes paid to the government. It is the net income households can spend or save.

Consumption demand

Households buy goods and services from cars to cinema tickets. These consumption purchases account for about 90 per cent of **personal disposable income**.

With no government, disposable income is simply the income received from firms. Given its disposable income, each household plans how much to spend and to save. Deciding one, decides the other. One family may save to buy a bigger house; another may spend more than its income, or 'dissave', taking the round-the-world trip it always wanted.

Many things affect consumption and saving decisions. We examine these in detail in Chapter 20. To get started, one simplification takes us a long way. We assume that, in the aggregate, households' consumption demand rises with aggregate personal disposable income.

Figure 16.1 shows real consumption and real GDP, both corrected for inflation by valuing them throughout at the prices prevailing in 2005, in the UK during 1960–2008. Figure 16.1 confirms that the basic relation between income and consumption

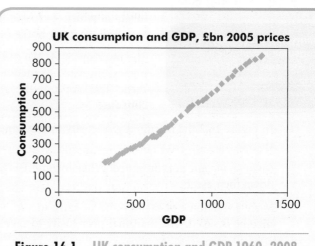

Figure 16.1 UK consumption and GDP, 1960–2008

Source: www.statistics.gov.uk. © Crown copyright 2010.

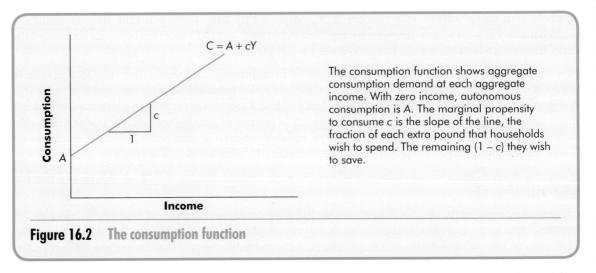

The consumption function shows aggregate consumption demand at each aggregate income. With zero income, autonomous consumption is A. The marginal propensity to consume c is the slope of the line, the fraction of each extra pound that households wish to spend. The remaining (1 – c) they wish to save.

Figure 16.2 **The consumption function**

is strong. The marginal propensity to consume is a positive fraction, as the theory assumes, and this *MPC* is reasonably stable over time. Our simplified consumption function is a good approximation to reality. But it is not a perfect description of what occurs. The points do not lie *exactly* along the line. Our simplification omits some other influences on consumption demand, which we take up in Chapter 20.

> The **consumption function** shows aggregate consumption demand at each level of personal disposable income.

The consumption function

This positive relation between disposable income and consumption demand is shown in Figure 16.2 and is called the **consumption function**.

The consumption function tells us how to go from personal disposable income Y to consumption demand C. If A is a positive constant, and c is a positive fraction between zero and one, then

$$C = A + cY \qquad (2)$$

Our bare-bones model has no government, no transfer payments and no taxes. Personal disposable income equals national income. The consumption function then relates consumption demand to *national* income Y. The consumption function is a straight line. A straight line is completely described by its intercept – the height at which it crosses the vertical axis – and its slope – the amount it rises for each unit we move horizontally to the right.

> **Marginal propensity to consume** is the fraction of each extra pound of disposable income that households wish to consume.

The intercept is A. We call this *autonomous* consumption demand. Autonomous means unrelated to income. Households wish to consume A even if income Y is zero.[1] The slope of the consumption function is the **marginal propensity to consume**

In Figure 16.2 the marginal propensity to consume *MPC* is c. If income rises by £1, desired consumption rises by £c.

Saving is income not consumed. When income Y is zero saving is $-A$. Households are dissaving, or running down their assets.

Since a fraction c of each pound of extra income is consumed, a fraction $(1 - c)$ of each extra pound of income is saved. The marginal propensity to save *MPS* is $(1 - c)$. Since an extra pound of income leads

---

1   *A* is the minimum consumption needed for survival. How do households finance it when their incomes are zero? In the short run they dissave and run down their assets. But they cannot do so for ever. The consumption function may differ in the short run and the long run, an idea we discuss in Chapter 20.

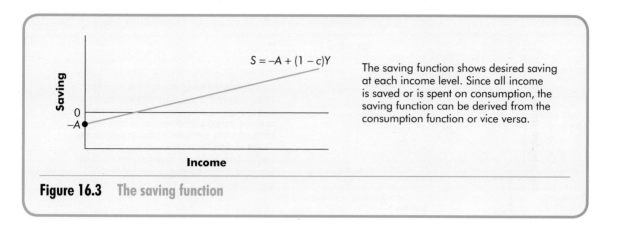

$$S = -A + (1 - c)Y$$

The saving function shows desired saving at each income level. Since all income is saved or is spent on consumption, the saving function can be derived from the consumption function or vice versa.

Figure 16.3   The saving function

either to extra desired consumption or to extra desired saving, $MPC + MPS = 1$. Figure 16.3 shows the **saving function** corresponding to the consumption function in Figure 16.2.

> The **saving function** shows desired saving at each income level.

From the definition of saving

$$Y = C + S \tag{3}$$

we can use the earlier formula for the consumption function to deduce the corresponding saving function shown in Figure 16.3. At an income of zero, autonomous consumption is A. Since desired saving plus desired consumption must equal income, when income Y is zero, desired saving must therefore be $-A$. And since each unit increase in income leads to an extra c of desired consumption, it must also lead to an extra $(1 - c)$ of desired saving. Whatever is not consumed must be saved. Hence the saving function is as shown in Figure 16.3. Planned saving is the part of income not planned to be spent on consumption.

Investment spending

Income is the key determinant of household consumption or spending plans as described by the consumption function. What about the factors determining the investment decision by firms?

Firms' **investment demand** depends chiefly on firms' current guesses about how fast the demand for their output will increase. Sometimes output is high and rising, sometimes it is high and falling. Since there is no close connection between the current *level* of income and firms' guesses about how the demand for their output is going to *change*, we make the simple assumption that investment demand is autonomous. Desired investment I is constant, independent of current output and income. In Chapter 20 we discuss investment demand in more detail.

> **Investment demand** is firms' desired or planned additions to physical capital (factories and machines) and to inventories.
>
> **Aggregate demand** is the amount firms and households plan to spend at each level of income.

 ## 16.2   Aggregate demand

In our simple model, aggregate demand is simply households' consumption demand C plus firms' investment demand I.

Figure 16.4 shows the *aggregate demand schedule*. To the previous consumption function it adds a constant amount I for desired investment. Each extra unit of income adds c to consumption demand but nothing to investment demand: aggregate demand rises by c. The AD schedule is parallel to the consumption function. The slope of both is the marginal propensity to consume.

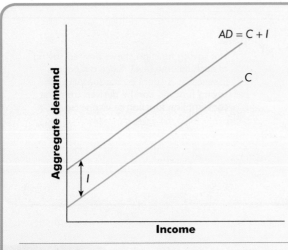

Figure 16.4 Aggregate demand

Aggregate demand is what households plan to spend on consumption and firms plan to spend on investment. Since we assume investment demand is constant, consumption is the only part of aggregate demand that increases with income. Vertically adding the constant investment demand to the consumption function C gives the aggregate demand schedule AD.

CONCEPT 16.1 — Exogenous and endogenous variables

A model is like a sausage machine. Our economic theory is the design of how the machine works, which is deduced from our assumptions about how people behave. Even once it has been built, a sausage machine still needs inputs – raw meat, breadcrumbs, spices, and the butcher's secret ingredients – in order to deliver an output of sausages. In the same way, our economic models require inputs of some economic variables in order then to deliver implications for how other variables will behave.

Exogenous variables are those fed into the model as inputs.

Endogenous variables are those which they model then deliver as outputs, conditional on the values of the exogenous inputs.

In our simple model of aggregate demand, the levels of both investment and autonomous consumption are exogenous, or given from outside the model. Conditional on these inputs to the model, the model then determines the endogenous variables' consumption demand and thus total aggregate demand.

16.3 Equilibrium output

Wages and prices are *fixed*, and output is demand determined. If aggregate demand falls below potential output, firms cannot sell as much as they would like. There is *involuntary* excess capacity. Workers cannot work as much as they would like. There is *involuntary* unemployment.

When prices and wages are fixed, at **short-run equilibrium output** aggregate demand or planned spending equals the output actually produced.

To define **short-run equilibrium** we cannot use the definition used in microeconomics, the output at which both suppliers and demanders are happy with the quantity bought and sold. We wish to study a situation in which firms and workers would like to supply more goods and more labour. Suppliers are frustrated. At least we can require that demanders are happy.

Thus, spending plans are not frustrated by a shortage of goods. Nor do firms make more output than they can sell. In short-run equilibrium, actual output equals the output demanded by households as consumption and by firms as investment.

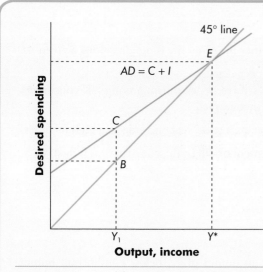

The 45° line reflects any value on the horizontal axis on to the same value on the vertical axis. The point E, at which the AD schedule crosses the 45° line, is the only point at which aggregate demand AD is equal to income. Hence E is the equilibrium point at which planned spending equals actual output and actual income.

Figure 16.5 The 45° diagram and equilibrium output

Figure 16.5 shows income on the horizontal axis and planned spending on the vertical axis. It also includes the 45° line, along which quantities on the horizontal and vertical axes are equal.

We draw in the AD schedule from Figure 16.4. This crosses the 45° line at E. On the 45° line, the value of output (and income) on the horizontal axis equals the value of spending on the vertical axis. Since E is the *only* point on the AD schedule also on the 45° line, it is the only point at which output and desired spending are equal.

Hence Figure 16.5 shows equilibrium output at E. Firms produce Y*. That output is equal to income. At an income Y*, the AD schedule tells us the demand for goods is also Y*. At E, planned spending is exactly equal to the output produced.

At any other output, output is not equal to aggregate demand. Suppose output and income are only Y_1. Aggregate demand exceeds actual output. There is excess demand. Spending plans cannot be realized at this output level.

Figure 16.5 shows that, for all outputs below the equilibrium output Y*, aggregate demand AD exceeds income and output. The AD schedule lies *above* the 45° line along which spending and output are equal. Conversely, at all outputs above the equilibrium output Y*, aggregate demand is less than income and output.

ACTIVITY 16.1

The *AD* schedule: moving along it or shifting it?

The aggregate demand AD schedule is a straight line whose position depends on its intercept and its slope. The intercept, the height of the schedule when income is zero, reflects autonomous demand: part of consumption demand and all of investment demand. The slope of the schedule is the MPC. Changes in income induce movements along a given AD schedule.

Autonomous demand is influenced by many things that we study in Chapter 20. It is not fixed for ever. But it *is* independent of income. The AD schedule separates out the change in demand directly induced by changes in income. All other sources of changes in aggregate demand are shown as shifts in the AD schedule. If firms get more optimistic about future demand and invest more, autonomous demand rises. The new AD schedule is parallel to, but higher than, the old AD schedule.

▶ **Questions**

In each case, decide whether the *AD* schedule is shifting or whether the economy is moving along a given *AD* schedule:

(a) After the US sub-prime mortgage market crisis, there was a wave of pessimism among UK consumers, who decided to play safe and save more, even before their incomes fell.

(b) UK consumer spending has risen because households are having a good year and enjoying high incomes.

(c) The 2012 Olympic Games in London are causing an investment boom in the construction industry.

To check your answers to these questions, go to page 685.

Adjustment towards equilibrium

Suppose in Figure 16.5 that the economy begins with an output of Y_1, below equilibrium output Y^*. Aggregate demand AD_1 exceeds output Y_1. If firms have inventories from the past, they can sell more than they have produced by running down stocks for a while. Note that this destocking is *unplanned*; planned changes of stocks are already included in the total investment demand *I*.

If firms cannot meet aggregate demand by unplanned destocking, they must turn away customers. Either response – unplanned destocking or turning away customers – is a signal to firms to raise output above Y_1. Hence, at *any* output below Y^*, aggregate demand exceeds output and firms get signals to raise output.

Conversely, if output is initially above its equilibrium level, Figure 16.5 shows that output will then exceed aggregate demand. Firms cannot sell all their output, make *unplanned* additions to inventories and respond by cutting output.

Hence, when output is below its equilibrium level, firms raise output. When output is above its equilibrium level, firms reduce output. At the equilibrium output Y^*, firms sell all their output and make no unplanned changes to their stocks. There is no incentive to change output.

In this example, short-run equilibrium output is Y^*. Firms sell all the goods they produce, and households and firms buy all the goods they want. But nothing guarantees Y^* is the level of potential output.

The economy can end up at a short-run equilibrium output below potential output, with no forces then present to move output to potential output. At the given level of prices and wages, a lack of aggregate demand will prevent expansion of output above its short-run equilibrium level.

CASE
16.1
Investment during the crash of 2009

Our simple model of aggregate demand assumes that output is the principal driver of consumption demand but does not directly affect investment demand. This does not mean that investment demand is always constant, merely that it is not well explained by changes in income. In later chapters we return to the question of what does affect investment demand.

Even at this early stage, it is a good idea to check our theory is proceeding along the right lines. How did consumption and investment respond during the crash of 2009? The figure below shows UK data during 2007–10. It shows annual percentage changes in output, consumer spending and investment.

In 2007 output was growing at 2.6 per cent per annum and consumption was growing a little more slowly, at 2.1 per cent. Output growth slowed sharply in 2008 and the growth of consumer spending also slowed down. In 2009 output fell by nearly 5 per cent and consumer spending fell by 3 per cent. By late 2009, the forecasts were that output and consumption would be growing again by 2010. The figure confirms the close correlation between output and consumption, with changes in output typically leading to slightly smaller changes in consumption.

In contrast, there is a much weaker connection between output and investment. In 2007 UK investment grew by nearly 8 per cent, despite output growth of less than 3 per cent. During the crash of 2009, UK investment plummeted by 16 per cent, and was forecast to keep contracting in 2010 even after output growth had resumed.

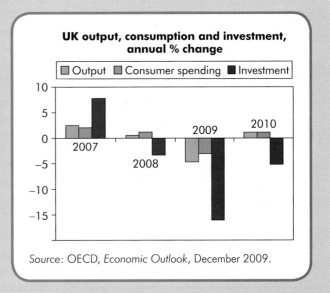

Source: OECD, *Economic Outlook*, December 2009.

Thus the figure supports the basic idea of the consumption function – a close relation between output and consumption demand – but denies any similar relationship will work between output and investment demand. For now, we assume that investment is part of autonomous demand, independent of the level of output. Other things equal, investment is constant. But other things are not always equal, and actual investment can be highly volatile. We return to models of investment demand in later chapters.

16.4   Another approach: planned saving equals planned investment

Equilibrium income equals the demand from investment and consumption. Hence, planned investment equals equilibrium income minus planned consumption: $I = Y - C$. This is not a definition, but holds only when output and income are at the right level to achieve equilibrium output. However, planned saving S is always the part of income Y not devoted to planned consumption C. Thus $S = Y - C$.

Thus $Y - C$ is equal to planned investment but also to planned saving. Since the latter depends on income and output, and since household plans are met only in equilibrium, equilibrium output occurs where planned investment equals planned savings:

$$I = S \qquad (4)$$

In modern economies, firms make investment decisions, and the managers of these firms are not the same decision units as the households making saving and consumption plans. But household plans depend on their income. Since planned saving depends on income but planned investment does not, equilibrium income adjusts to make households plan to save as much as firms are planning to invest. Figure 16.6 illustrates.

Planned investment I is autonomous, and so a horizontal line. It does not depend on the level of income. Planned saving increases with income and output. Hence, equilibrium output must be Y^*, the only output at which planned investment equals planned saving.

Suppose investment demand is 10 and the saving function is $S = -10 + 0.1Y$. Hence, equilibrium output Y is 200. At this Y, planned saving is $[-10 + 20] = 10$. Hence 10 is both planned saving and planned investment.

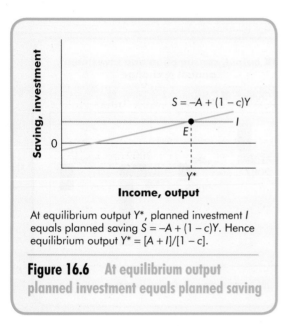

S = –A + (1 – c)Y

I

E

0

Y*

Income, output

At equilibrium output Y*, planned investment I equals planned saving S = –A + (1 – c)Y. Hence equilibrium output Y* = [A + I]/[1 – c].

Figure 16.6 At equilibrium output planned investment equals planned saving

If the saving function is $S = -10 + 0.1Y$, the consumption function must be $C = 10 + 0.9Y$. At an income of 200, consumption demand is 190. Add on 10 for investment demand, and aggregate demand is 200. When output and income are 200, aggregate demand is also 200. Again, this proves that equilibrium output is 200.

If income exceeds 200, households want to save more than firms want to invest. But saving is the part of income not consumed. Households are not planning enough consumption, together with firms' investment plans, to purchase all the output produced. Unplanned inventories pile up and firms cut output. Lower output and income reduces planned saving, which depends on income. When output falls back to 200, planned investment again equals planned saving.

Conversely, when output is below its equilibrium level, planned investment exceeds planned saving. Together, planned consumption and planned investment exceed actual output. Firms make unplanned inventory reductions and raise output until it reverts to its equilibrium level of 200.

MATHS 16.1

Autonomous demand and equilibrium output

In equilibrium, output equals aggregate demand, Hence

$$Y = AD = C + I = [A + cY] + I = [A + I] + cY$$

Hence, in equilibrium

$$Y^* = [A + I]/(1 - c) \qquad (1)$$

Notice that this implies that a unit increase in either A or I then leads to an increase of $[1/(1-c)]$ in equilibrium output Y^*. Since c is a positive fraction, $[1/(1-c)]$ is greater than 1. So a unit increase in either autonomous consumption demand or investment demand leads to a larger increase in equilibrium output because a further increase in consumption demand is then induced. We explain below why this is called the multiplier.

Note too that desired saving is given by $S = Y - C = Y - [A + cY] = -A + (1-c)Y$, which is the saving function corresponding to the consumption function $C = A + cY$. In equilibrium, equation (1) implies

$$I = Y^*(1 - c) - A \qquad (2)$$

But the right-hand side of equation (2) is simply desired saving in equilibrium when output is Y^*. Hence in equilibrium $I = S$. Planned investment equals planned leakages.

Planned versus actual

Equilibrium output and income satisfy two equivalent conditions. Aggregate demand must equal income and output. Equivalently, planned investment must equal planned saving.

In the previous chapter we showed that *actual* investment is *always* equal to *actual* saving, purely as a consequence of our national income accounting definitions. When the economy is not in equilibrium, planned saving and investment are not equal. However, unplanned investment in stocks and/or unplanned saving (frustrated consumers) always ensures that actual investment, planned plus unplanned, equals actual saving, planned plus unplanned.

16.5 A fall in aggregate demand

The *slope* of the *AD* schedule depends only on the marginal propensity to consume (*MPC*). For a given *MPC*, the level of autonomous spending [*A* + *I*] determines the *height* of the *AD* schedule. Autonomous spending is spending unrelated to income.

Changes in autonomous spending lead to parallel shifts in the *AD* schedule. Investment demand depends chiefly on current guesses by firms about future demand for their output. Beliefs about this future demand can fluctuate significantly, influenced by current pessimism or optimism about the future. Similarly, a fall in consumer confidence reduces autonomous consumption demand.

Suppose firms get pessimistic about future demand for their output. Planned investment falls. If autonomous consumption is unaffected, the aggregate demand schedule *AD* is now lower at each income than before. Figure 16.7 shows this downward shift from *AD* to *AD′*.

Before we go into the details, think about what is likely to happen to output. It will fall, but how much? When investment demand falls, firms cut output. Households have lower incomes and cut consumption. Firms cut output again, further reducing household incomes. Consumption demand falls further. What brings the process of falling output and income to an end?

Figure 16.7 shows that a given downward shift of the *AD* schedule reduces equilibrium output by a *finite* amount, but by an amount larger than the vertical fall in the *AD* schedule. This is because the *AD* schedule has a slope flatter than the 45° line: its slope, the marginal propensity to consume, is always smaller than unity.

Equilibrium moves from *E* to *E′*. Equilibrium output falls *more* than the original cut in investment demand, but does not fall all the way to zero.

Table 16.1 explains. Since many students find arithmetic easier than algebra, we illustrate for the particular values [*A* = 10] for autonomous consumption demand and [*c* = 0.9] for the marginal propensity to consume. Thus the particular consumption function is *C* = 10 + 0.9*Y*.

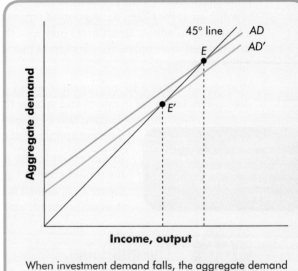

When investment demand falls, the aggregate demand schedule shifts down from *AD* to *AD′* and equilibrium output falls by a larger amount.

Figure 16.7 A fall in investment demand

Table 16.1 Adjustment to a shift in investment demand

	Y	I	C = 10 + 0.9Y	AD = C + I	Y − AD	Unplanned stocks	Output
Step 1	200	10	190	200	0	Zero	Constant
Step 2	200	5	190	195	5	Rising	Falling
Step 3	195	5	185.5	190.5	4.5	Rising	Falling
Step 4	190.5	5	181.5	186.57	4	Rising	Falling
New equilibrium	150	5	145	150	0	Zero	Constant

If original investment demand is also 10, the first row of Table 16.1 shows that the original equilibrium output is 200, since consumption demand is then [10 + 180] and investment demand is 10. Thus aggregate demand just equals actual output.

In step 2, investment demand falls to 5. Firms did not expect demand to change, and still produced 200. Output exceeds aggregate demand by 5. Firms add this 5 to inventories, then cut output.

Step 3 shows firms making 195, the level of demand in step 2. But when firms cut output, income falls. Step 3 shows consumption demand falls from 190 to 185.5. Since the *MPC* is 0.9, a cut in income by 5 causes a fall in consumption demand by 4.5. The induced fall in consumption demand means that output of 195 still exceeds aggregate demand, which is now 190.5. Again inventories pile up, and again firms respond by cutting output.

At step 4, firms make enough to meet demand at step 3. Output is 190.5, but again this induces a further cut in consumption demand. Output still exceeds aggregate demand. The process keeps going, through many steps, until it reaches the new equilibrium, an output of 150. Output and income have fallen by 50, consumption demand has fallen by 45 and investment demand has fallen by 5. Aggregate demand again equals output.

How long it takes for the economy to reach the new equilibrium depends on how well firms figure out what is going on. If they keep setting output targets to meet the level of demand in the previous period, it takes a long time to adjust. Smart firms may spot that, period after period, they are overproducing and adding to unwanted inventories. They anticipate that demand is still falling and cut back output more quickly than Table 16.1 suggests.

Why does a fall of 5 in investment demand cause a fall of 50 in equilibrium output? Lower investment demand induces a cut in output and income that then induces an extra cut in consumption demand. Total demand falls by more than the original fall in investment demand, but the process does not spiral out of control. Equilibrium output is 150.

> The **multiplier** is the ratio of the change in equilibrium output to the change in autonomous spending that caused the change.

In our example, the initial change in autonomous investment demand is 5 and the final change in equilibrium output is 50. The **multiplier** is 10. That is why, in Figure 16.7, a small downward shift in the *AD* schedule leads to a much larger fall in equilibrium income and output.

16.6 The multiplier

The multiplier tells us how much output changes after a shift in aggregate demand. The multiplier exceeds 1 because a change in autonomous demand sets off further changes in consumption demand. The size of the multiplier depends on the marginal propensity to consume. The initial effect of a unit fall in investment demand is to cut output and income by a unit. If the *MPC* is large, this fall in income leads to a large fall in consumption and the multiplier is big. If the *MPC* is small, a given change in investment demand and output induces small changes in consumption demand and the multiplier is small.

Table 16.2 examines a one-unit increase in investment demand. In step 2, firms raise output by 1 unit. Consumption rises by 0.9, the marginal propensity to consume times the one-unit change in income and output. At step 3, firms raise output by 0.9 to meet the increased consumption demand in step 2. In turn, consumption demand is increased by 0.81 (the *MPC* 0.9 times the 0.9 increase in income) leading in step 4 to a rise in output of 0.81. Consumption rises again and the process continues.

To find the multiplier, we add all the increases in output from each step in the table and keep going:

$$\text{Multiplier} = 1 + (0.9) + (0.9)^2 + (0.9)^3 + (0.9)^4 + (0.9)^5 + \dots$$

The dots at the end mean that we keep adding terms such as $(0.9)^6$ and so on. The right-hand side of this equation is called a geometric series. Each term is (0.9) times the previous term. Fortunately, mathematicians have shown that there is a general formula for the sum of all the terms in such a series:

Table 16.2 Calculating the multiplier when the *MPC* equals 0.9

Change in	Step 1	Step 2	Step 3	Step 4	Step 5	*	*	*
I	1	0	0	0	0	*	*	*
Y	0	1	0.9	$(0.9)^2$	$(0.9)^3$	*	*	*
C	0	0.9	$(0.9)^2$	$(0.9)^2$	$(0.9)^3$	*	*	*

$$\text{Multiplier} = 1/(1 - 0.9)$$

The formula applies whatever the (constant) value of *c*, the marginal propensity to consume:

$$\text{Multiplier} = 1/(1 - c) \tag{5}$$

For the particular value of $c = 0.9$, the multiplier is $1/(0.1) = 10$. Hence a cut in investment demand by 5 causes a fall in equilibrium output by 50, as we know from Table 16.1. For those of you who 'did the maths' above, equation (1) implies that equilibrium output is simply autonomous demand multiplied by the multiplier!

The marginal propensity to consume tells how much of each extra unit of income is spent on consumption. Thus the *MPC* is a number between zero and unity. The higher the *MPC*, the lower is $(1 - c)$. Dividing 1 by a smaller number leads to a larger answer. The general formula for the multiplier in equation (5) confirms that a larger *MPC* implies a larger multiplier.

The multiplier and the *MPS*

Any part of an extra unit of income not spent must be saved. Hence $(1 - c)$ equals *MPS*, the marginal propensity to save.

Hence we can also think of the multiplier as $1/MPS$. The higher the **marginal propensity to save**, the more of each extra unit of income leaks out of the circular flow into savings and the less goes back round the circular flow to generate further increases in aggregate demand, output and income. Since the marginal propensity to save is a positive fraction, the multiplier exceeds unity, as we already know.

> The **marginal propensity to save** is the fraction of each extra unit of income that households wish to save.

 16.7 The paradox of thrift

The previous section analysed a parallel shift in the aggregate demand schedule caused by a change in autonomous investment demand. We now examine a parallel shift in the *AD* schedule caused by a change in the autonomous part of planned consumption and saving.

Suppose households increase autonomous consumption demand by 10. There is a parallel upward shift in the consumption function, and hence also in the aggregate demand schedule *AD*. Higher autonomous consumption demand implies an identical fall in autonomous planned saving. There is a parallel downward shift in the saving function.

In equilibrium planned saving always equals planned investment, and the latter is unaltered. Hence planned saving cannot change. Equilibrium income must therefore adjust to restore planned saving to the unchanged level of planned investment. Figure 16.8 illustrates. When a decline in thriftiness, or the desire to save, shifts planned saving from *S* to *S′*, equilibrium income must rise from Y^* to Y^{**} to maintain the equality of planned saving and planned investment.

A change in the amount households wish to save at each income leads to a change in equilibrium income, but no change in equilibrium saving, which must still equal planned investment. This is the **paradox of thrift**.

The **paradox of thrift** helps us to understand an old debate about the virtues of saving and spending. Does society benefit from thriftiness and a high level of desired saving at each income level? The answer depends on whether or not the economy is at full employment.

When aggregate demand is low and the economy has spare resources, the paradox of thrift shows that a *reduction* in the desire to save will increase spending and increase the equilibrium income level. Society benefits from higher output and employment. And since investment demand is autonomous, a change in the desire to save has no effect on the desired level of investment.

Conversely, during the crash of 2009 politicians were worried that the panic might lead to too great a desire to save. At a time when aggregate demand had already fallen, equilibrium output had fallen even with a constant propensity to save: any additional increase in the propensity to save was going to reduce equilibrium output even further. Case 16.2 discusses the saving rate in more detail.

In contrast, think what happens if the economy is at potential output. Chapter 21 discusses how this might happen in the long run once prices and wages have time to adjust. If the economy is at potential output, an *increase* in the desire to save at each income level must increase saving, and reduce consumption, at potential output. However, investment demand *may* increase to restore aggregate demand to its full-employment level. The next few chapters explain why. Hence, in the long run, society may benefit from an *increase* in the desire to save. Investment will rise and the economy's capital stock and potential output may grow more quickly.

In this chapter we have focused on the short run before prices and wages have time to adjust. Saving and investment decisions are made by different people. There is no automatic mechanism to translate higher saving into a corresponding rise in investment demand. Since planned saving depends on the level of income, income adjusts to equate planned saving and planned investment.

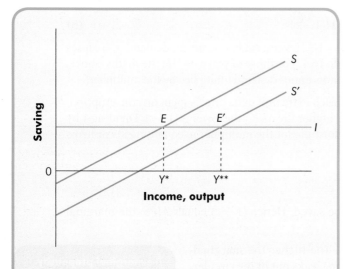

In equilibrium planned saving equals planned investment. A fall in the desire to save induces a rise in equilibrium output to keep planned saving equal to planned investment.

Figure 16.8   The paradox of thrift

CASE 16.2

How stable is the saving rate?

In the last boom of the Thatcher era, in the late 1980s, heady optimism and easy access to credit made UK consumers spend a lot. Personal saving collapsed as people bought champagne, sports cars and houses. The boom years didn't last. As inflation rose, the government raised interest rates to slow down the economy. House prices fell. People's mortgage debt was larger than the value of their houses. To pay off this 'negative equity', households raised saving sharply in the early 1990s.

During 1992–2008, UK households were borrowing again. Low interest rates fuelled a spending boom and a protracted rise in house prices. People saved less and borrowed more in order to spend. TV shows such as *The Property Ladder* showed people how to do up houses for subsequent letting or sale. In a rising market, people made money on buying and selling houses whether or not they were much good at redeveloping them.

The chart shows that household saving, as a percentage of their disposable income, fell steadily during 1992–2008, by the end of which it was lower even than during the boom in the 1980s. Less than 2 per cent of household disposable income was saved in 2008.

What do you think happened as a result of the financial crash in 2009? People got scared. Property prices began to fall and borrowing for house purchase no longer seemed a good idea. Banks became terrified their customers could not repay so the supply of new lending from banks dried up completely. And people who foresaw a deep recession began to cut out unnecessary expenditure. They chose to save a larger fraction of their income. The saving rate rose sharply in 2009, as the chart confirms.

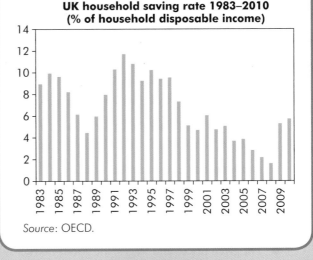

UK household saving rate 1983–2010 (% of household disposable income)

Source: OECD.

Clearly, then, the saving rate can fluctuate a lot. Although in this chapter we assume a constant marginal propensity to save, Chapter 20 discusses more sophisticated theories of consumption and saving.

One final remark. Does it matter whether households borrow in order to buy a foreign holiday or to buy a house for subsequent rental to others? In the former case, no asset is purchased for the future; in the latter case, the household acquires an asset that will give rise to future incomes. Simply measuring today's income and today's spending gives a misleading picture of the long-run economic position of the household. We return to this issue in Chapter 19.

Picture: © Martin Crowdy | Dreamstime.com

16.8 The role of confidence

Shifts in autonomous demand – whether autonomous consumption demand or autonomous investment demand – are often caused by changes in confidence, swings in optimism or pessimism about the future. Our simple model assumes these are independent of current income and output.

This does not mean that they are not important, and not subject to influence by policy and politicians. Rather than spend taxpayers' money trying to boost aggregate demand through a subsidized car scrappage scheme, most governments would rather talk up demand if only they could.

Like the boy who cried wolf once too often, governments who mislead the public soon become distrusted, and their warm words are then ignored. However, where government can provide a clear and credible account of why the future may be rosier than the present, they may indeed be able to stimulate aggregate demand through increasing confidence and thereby inducing households and firms to spend more. Conversely, when they announce bad news that had not previously been foreseen, then at any particular level of current output firms and households will reduce their demand, and aggregate demand will fall.

Summary

- **Aggregate demand** is planned spending on goods (and services). The *AD* schedule shows aggregate demand at each level of income and output.

- This chapter neglects planned spending by foreigners and by the government, studying **consumption demand** by households and **investment demand** by firms (desired additions to physical capital and to inventories). We treat investment demand as constant.

- Consumption demand is closely though not perfectly related to **personal disposable income**. Without taxes or transfers, personal disposable income and total income coincide.

- **Autonomous consumption** is desired consumption at zero income. The **marginal propensity to consume** (*MPC*) is the fraction by which planned consumption rises when income rises by a pound. The **marginal propensity to save** (*MPS*) is the fraction of an extra pound of income that is saved. Since income is consumed or saved, *MPC* + *MPS* = 1.

- For given prices and wages, the goods market is in equilibrium when output equals planned spending or aggregate demand. Equivalently, in equilibrium, planned saving equals planned investment. **Goods market equilibrium** does not mean output equals potential output. It means planned spending equals actual spending and actual output.

- The **equilibrium output is demand-determined** because we assume that prices and wages are fixed at a level that implies an excess supply of goods and labour. Firms and workers are happy to supply whatever output and employment is demanded.

- When aggregate demand exceeds actual output there is either unplanned disinvestment (inventory reductions) or unplanned saving (frustrated customers). Actual investment always equals actual saving, as a matter of definition. Unplanned inventory reductions or frustrated customers act as a signal to firms to raise output when aggregate demand exceeds actual output. Similarly, unplanned additions to stocks occur when aggregate demand is below output.

- A rise in planned investment increases equilibrium output by a larger amount. The initial increase in income to meet investment demand leads to further increases in consumption demand.

- The **multiplier** is the ratio of the change in output to the change in autonomous demand that caused it. In the simple model of this chapter, the multiplier is $1/[(1 - MPC)]$ or $1/MPS$. The multiplier exceeds 1 because *MPC* and *MPS* are positive fractions.

- The **paradox of thrift** shows that a reduced desire to save leads to an increase in output but no change in the equilibrium level of planned saving, which must still equal planned investment.

Review questions

connect

1 Suppose the consumption function is $C = 0.8Y$ and planned investment is 40. (a) Draw a diagram showing the aggregate demand schedule. (b) If actual output is 100, what unplanned actions will occur? (c) What is equilibrium output? (d) Do you get the same answer using planned saving equals planned investment?

2 Suppose the *MPC* is 0.6. Beginning from equilibrium, investment demand rises by 30. (a) How much does equilibrium output increase? (b) How much of that increase is extra consumption demand?

3 Planned investment is 100. People decide to save a higher proportion of their income: the consumption function changes from $C = 0.8Y$ to $C = 0.5Y$. (a) What happens to equilibrium income? (b) What happens to the equilibrium proportion of income saved? Explain.

4 What part of actual investment is not included in aggregate demand?

5 (a) Find equilibrium income when investment demand is 400 and $C = 0.8Y$. (b) Would output be higher or lower if the consumption function were $C = 100 + 0.7Y$?

6 Common fallacies Why are these statements wrong? (a) If people were prepared to save more, investment would increase and we could get the economy moving again. (b) Lower output leads to lower spending and yet lower output. The economy could spiral downwards for ever.

7 Which is correct? (a) Any tax is a tax on jobs because it reduces aggregate demand. (b) Provided the government spends the tax revenue, the impact of higher spending outweighs the adverse demand effect of higher taxes. (c) When autonomous consumption demand is adversely influenced by fears about the future consequences of a large budget deficit, an increase in taxes could stimulate demand by boosting autonomous consumption demand. (d) All of the above statements could be true, depending on the other things assumed equal.

8 Suppose firms are initially surprised by changes in demand. (a) When demand falls, what is the initial effect on stocks of unsold goods held by firms? (b) What do firms plan to do to stocks as soon as they have time to adjust production? Does this reduce or increase the initial fall in demand? (c) Once stocks have been adjusted, what then happens to production and output?

9 (a) Show the answer to Question 2 in a diagram. (b) Draw the corresponding diagram using planned investment and planned saving. (c) Is the answer the same? Why or why not?

10 Planned investment is 100. Initially, the consumption function is $C = 100 + 0.8Y$. There are three ways in which greater pessimism about the future might affect behaviour: (a) planned investment falls from 100 to 50; (b) autonomous consumption falls from 100 to 50; (c) the marginal propensity to consume falls from 0.8 to 0.7 as people save more of each unit of additional income. Draw a graph of each change and its effect on short-run equilibrium output.

11 Suppose confidence depends a little on the current level of output, and the model therefore becomes

$$I = aY + I^* \qquad C = A + cY = [A^* + bY] + cY$$

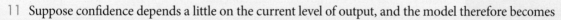

where I^* and A^* remain autonomous and independent of output, but a and b reflect the dependence of confidence on the current level of output. (a) What is the new value of the multiplier? (b) Is this higher or lower than before? (c) Is equilibrium output higher or lower than before?

12 Could the multiplier ever be less than 1?

13 When could the paradox of thrift fail to be true?

14 Essay question 'The remarkably strong relationship between consumption and income confirms that most people want to spend most of their income as soon as they can. We are all material girls and boys at heart.' Is the inference justified?

Fiscal policy and foreign trade

Learning Outcomes

By the end of this chapter, you should understand:

1. how fiscal policy affects aggregate demand
2. short-run equilibrium output in this extended model
3. the balanced budget multiplier
4. automatic stabilizers
5. the structural budget and the inflation-adjusted budget
6. how budget deficits add to national debt
7. the limits to discretionary fiscal policy
8. how foreign trade affects equilibrium output

> **Fiscal policy** is government policy on spending and taxes.
>
> **Stabilization policy** is government action to keep output close to potential output.
>
> The **budget deficit** is the excess of government spending over government receipts.

In most European countries, the government directly buys about a fifth of national output and spends about the same again on transfer payments. This spending is financed mainly by taxes. What is the macroeconomic impact of government **fiscal policy**? And why did governments conclude that a massive fiscal response was required when confronted with the biggest economic crash since 1945?

We show how fiscal policy affects equilibrium output, then study three fiscal issues. We analyse opportunities and limitations in using fiscal policy to **stabilize** output. We then examine the significance of the government's budget deficit. When the government runs a **deficit**, it spends more than it earns. Deficits worry people. How can the government keep spending more than it receives? We examine the size of the deficit and ask if we should worry.

A government deficit is financed mainly by borrowing from the public by selling bonds, promises to pay specified amounts of interest payments at future dates. This borrowing adds to government debts to the public.[1] During 2009, governments around the world had huge budget deficits as they bailed out their

---

1   Government is responsible not merely for its own deficits but also for any losses made by state-owned firms. The public sector net cash requirement (PSNCR) is the government deficit plus net losses of these firms.

banking systems and spent money on car scrappage schemes to try to prevent the car industries imploding. Just as for an individual, when a government spends more than it earns it adds to its debts.

In 2007, UK **national debt** was 38 per cent of GDP, about £540 billion, or £8000 per person. As a result of the massive budget deficits projected during 2009–14, the IMF estimates that by 2014 UK national debt will have risen to 92 per cent of GDP, more than £1300 billion, or about £17 500 per person. We will need to understand how this is likely to affect aggregate demand.

> The **national debt** is the stock of outstanding government debt.

Most of this chapter is about the government's role in aggregate demand, but we complete our model of income determination by also adding foreign trade. Exports X and imports Z are each nearly 30 per cent of UK GDP. The UK is a very open economy, and the effects of foreign trade are too important to ignore.[2]

17.1 Government and the circular flow

Government spending G on goods and services adds directly to aggregate demand. The government also withdraws money from the circular flow through indirect taxes T_e on expenditure and direct taxes T_d on factor incomes, less transfer benefits B that augment factor incomes. However, transfer payments affect aggregate demand only by affecting other components such as consumption or investment demand.

Table 17.1 shows UK government activity in 2009/10. The main components of G are health, education and defence. Social security payments – state pensions, unemployment benefit and child support – and debt interest payments are the main components of transfer payments.

The main direct taxes are income tax, corporation tax and social security contributions to state schemes for pensions and unemployment benefit. Indirect taxes include VAT, specific duties on tobacco, alcohol and fuel, and the property taxes levied by local government.

17.2 Government and aggregate demand

Since it is a pain to keep distinguishing between market prices and basic prices, we assume all taxes are direct taxes. With no indirect taxes, measurements at market prices and at basic prices coincide. For the moment, we still ignore foreign trade.

Aggregate demand AD is consumption demand C, investment demand I and government demand G for goods and services. Transfer payments affect aggregate demand only by affecting C or I. Thus $AD = C + I + G$.

In the short run, government spending G does not vary automatically with output and income. We assume G is fixed, or at least independent of income. Its size reflects how many hospitals the government wants to build and how many teachers it wants to hire. We now have three autonomous components of aggregate demand independent of current income and output: the autonomous consumption demand, investment demand I and government demand G.

The government also levies taxes and pays out transfer benefits.

With no indirect taxes, net taxes NT are simply direct taxes T_d minus transfer benefits B. Net taxes reduce personal disposable income – the amount available for spending or saving by households – relative to

---

2   In contrast, net property income is 1 per cent of GNP. We continue to treat GNP and GDP as equivalent.

Table 17.1 UK public finances, 2009/10

Revenue	£bn	Expenditure	£bn
Direct tax		*Goods and services*	
Income tax	140	Health	119
Corporation tax	34	Education	88
Social security	95	Defence	38
		Law and order	36
Indirect tax		Housing, environment	30
VAT	67	Transport	23
Business rates	24	Industry and agriculture	21
Excise duties	44	Personal social services	29
Council tax	25	*Transfer payments*	
Other receipts	69	Social security	190
		Debt interest	30
		Other spending	72
Total revenue	498	**Total spending**	676
Deficit	178		

Source: www.hm-treasury.gov.uk.

Net taxes are taxes minus transfers.

national income and output. If YD is disposable income, Y national income and t the **net tax** rate (which for simplicity we assume to be a constant proportion of income), then disposable income $YD = (1 - t)Y$.

Suppose taxes net of transfer benefits are about 20 per cent of national income. We can think of the (net) tax rate t as 0.2. If national income Y rises by £1, net tax revenue will rise by 20 pence, so household disposable income will increase only by 80 pence.

We still assume that households' desired consumption is proportional to their disposable income. For simplicity, suppose autonomous consumption is zero but that, as before, the marginal propensity to consume out of disposable income is 0.9. Households plan to spend 90p of each extra pound of disposable income. The consumption function is now $C = 0.9YD$.

With a net tax rate t, disposable income YD is only $(1 - t)$ times national income Y. Thus, to relate consumption demand to *national* income, $C = 0.9YD = 0.9(1 - t)Y$.

If national income rises by £1, consumption demand rises by only $0.9(1 - t)$, which is less than £0.90. If the net tax rate t is 0.2, consumption demand rises by only $£(0.9 \times 0.8) = £0.72$. Each extra pound of national income increases disposable income by only 80 pence, out of which households plan to consume 90 per cent and save 10 per cent.

Clearly, spending £0.72 of each extra pound of national income implies a flatter consumption function, when plotted against national income, than spending £0.90 of each extra pound of national income. The

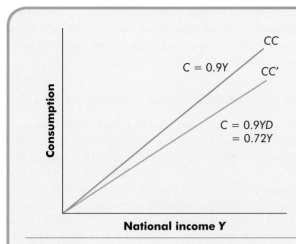

In the absence of taxation, national income Y and disposable income YD are the same. The consumption function CC' shows how much households wish to consume at each level of national income. With a proportional net tax rate of 0.2, households still consume 90p of each pound of disposable income. Since YD is now only 0.8Y, households consume only $0.9 \times 0.8 = 0.72$ of each extra unit of national income. Relating consumption to national income, the effect of net taxes is to rotate the consumption function downwards from CC to CC'.

Figure 17.1 *Net taxes and consumption*

effect of a positive net tax rate *t* therefore acts like a reduction in the marginal propensity to consume. Figure 17.1 illustrates.

Aggregate demand and equilibrium output do not depend on whether the leakage is through saving (as when the *MPC* is low) or through taxes (as when the *MPC* multiplied by $(1 - t)$ is low). Either way, the leakage prevents money being recycled as demand for output of firms.

If *MPC* is the marginal propensity to consume out of *disposable* income, and there is a proportional net tax rate *t*, then *MPC'*, the marginal propensity to consume out of *national* income, is given by $MPC' = MPC \times (1 - t)$.

We now show how the government affects equilibrium national income and output. We start with an example in which autonomous investment demand is *I* and the consumption function in terms of disposable income is $C = 0.9YD$.

The effect of net taxes on output

Suppose initially that government spending is zero. Figure 17.2 illustrates. A rise in the net tax rate from zero to 0.2 makes the consumption function pivot downwards from *CC* to *CC'* in Figure 17.1. We obtain aggregate demand *AD* by adding the constant investment demand *I* to the consumption function. Hence, the rise in the net rate that rotates the consumption function from *CC* to *CC'* in Figure 17.1 causes a similar rotation of aggregate demand from *AD* to *AD'* in Figure 17.2. Hence, aggregate demand equals actual output at a lower output level. The aggregate demand schedule now crosses the 45° line at *E'* not *E*. Equilibrium income and output fall.

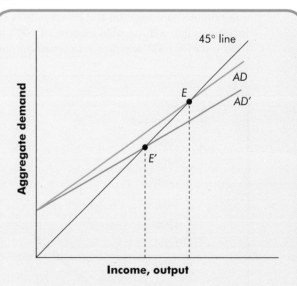

An increase in the income tax rate or a reduction in rate of unemployment benefit will increase the net tax rate *t*. The consumption function rotates from CC to CC' in Figure 17.1. With constant investment demand, the aggregate demand schedule rotates from AD to AD' in Figure 17.2. The equilibrium level of output falls and the equilibrium point moves from E to E'.

Figure 17.2 *A higher net tax rate*

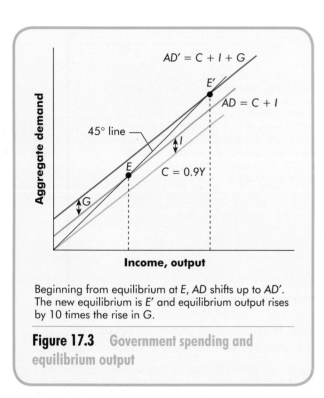

Beginning from equilibrium at E, AD shifts up to AD'. The new equilibrium is E' and equilibrium output rises by 10 times the rise in G.

Figure 17.3 Government spending and equilibrium output

Raising the net tax rate reduces equilibrium output. When aggregate demand and equilibrium output are below potential output, lower tax rates or higher transfer benefits will raise aggregate demand and equilibrium output.

The effect of government spending on output

Now forget taxes and think government spending. Suppose the net tax rate is zero. National income and disposable income coincide. Figure 17.3 shows that higher government spending has an effect similar to that of higher autonomous investment demand studied in Chapter 16. With a marginal propensity to consume of 0.9, the multiplier is again $1/(1 - MPC) = 10$. A rise in government spending G induces a rise in equilibrium output by 10 times that amount. In Figure 17.3 equilibrium moves from E to E' when the aggregate demand schedule shifts from AD to AD'.

The combined effects of government spending and taxation

Suppose an economy begins with an equilibrium output of 1000 but no government. Assume demand from autonomous consumption and investment is 100. With a marginal propensity to consume out of disposable income of 0.9, a disposable income of 1000 induces consumption demand of 900. Aggregate demand is $(900 + 100) = 1000$, which is also actual output.

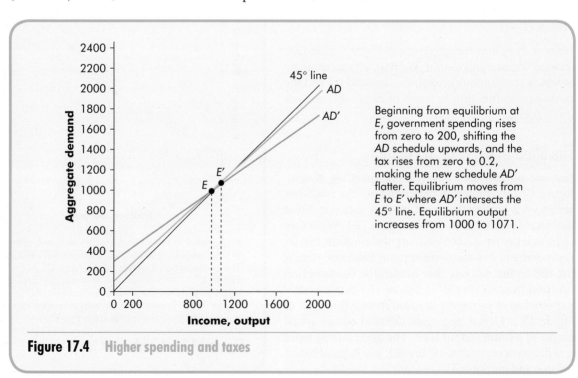

Beginning from equilibrium at E, government spending rises from zero to 200, shifting the AD schedule upwards, and the tax rises from zero to 0.2, making the new schedule AD' flatter. Equilibrium moves from E to E' where AD' intersects the 45° line. Equilibrium output increases from 1000 to 1071.

Figure 17.4 Higher spending and taxes

Now introduce extra autonomous demand of 200 from the government, taking total autonomous demand to 300. Also introduce a net tax rate of 0.2. The marginal propensity to consume out of national income falls from 0.9 to 0.72, and the multiplier becomes $1/(1 - 0.72) = 1/0.28 = 3.57$. Multiplying autonomous demand of 300 by 3.57 yields equilibrium output of 1071, above the original equilibrium output of 1000. Figure 17.4 illustrates.

The balanced budget multiplier

The economy began at an equilibrium output of 1000. With a proportional tax rate of 20 per cent, initial tax revenue was 200, precisely the amount of government spending.

> The **balanced budget multiplier** says that a rise in government spending plus an equal rise in taxes leads to higher output.

This balanced increase in government spending and taxes did not leave demand and output unaltered. Figure 17.4 shows equilibrium output is larger. The new 200 of government spending raises aggregate demand by 200 and the tax increase cuts disposable income by 200. The *MPC* out of disposable income is 0.9, so lower disposable income reduces consumption demand by only $0.9 \times 200 = 180$.

The initial effect of the tax and spending package raises aggregate demand by 200 but reduces it by 180. Aggregate demand rises by 20. Output rises, inducing further rises in consumption demand. When the new equilibrium is reached, output has risen a total of 71, from 1000 to 1071. This is the famous balanced budget multiplier, which gives the government a fiscal tool to boost aggregate demand without adding to the deficit or debt.

To use this tool, the government does, however, have to have the political courage to raise tax revenue in line with higher expenditure. Sometimes governments are unable or unwilling to do this.

CASE 17.1

Fiscal policy under pressure: lessons from Japan

For the last 15 years, this textbook has used the Japanese example both to illustrate what hypothetically might happen to Western economies if they got into a macroeconomic mess, and to draw lessons for what better policy might look like. Suddenly, Western economies are in that mess themselves and the Japanese example is more relevant than ever. What happened in Japan, and how do we avoid making the same mistakes?

After three decades of post-war success, Japanese economic growth came to an abrupt end in the 1990s. A property crash made banks bankrupt. Instead of admitting this and sorting it out, policy makers ignored the problem. Consumers lost confidence, and output fell. To restore confidence, Japan had big fiscal expansions to boost demand – just as Gordon Brown successfully exhorted world leaders to do in 2008/09. But if things are this easy, Japan should have recovered easily from its difficulties in the early 1990s.

Facing fiscal expansion in a severe recession, Japanese households and firms decided aggressively expansionary government policy was being undertaken only because the government knew things were even worse than the private sector had previously thought. The private sector took on board this new information and became even more pessimistic. The autonomous parts of consumption and investment demand fell sufficiently to offset the fiscal expansion injected by the government; and this fall in autonomous demand was therefore caused by the expansionary policy itself. Fiscal expansion failed to boost output. In macroeconomics the induced effects can outweigh the direct effect. Not until 2003 did sustainable growth return: Japan grew by 2 per cent a year between 2003 and 2007, before experiencing the global crash of 2008/09.

Japan's macroeconomic misery

The table below illustrates Japan's economic misery during this period.

	Annual GDP growth (%)	Interest rate (%)	Budget deficit (% of GDP)	Government net debt (% of GDP)
1993	0	3	2	18
1994–95	1.5	1.5	3	23
1996	5	1	4	29
1997–99	−1	1	5	45
2000–02	1.5	0	6	66
2003–07	2	0	6	82
2008–09	−3.3	0	6	90

Source: OECD.

Lessons for Western economies

The Japanese example contains three important lessons. First, when confidence collapses, even fiscal policy may not be able to boost aggregate demand. This means that governments should do all they can to prevent confidence ever collapsing to this extent. In retrospect, Western banks were too loosely regulated and governments had failed to discharge their responsibility to create a stable financial environment in the years leading up to 2008.

Second, cleaning up the banks must be an important priority. The Japanese government's unwillingness to lose face by admitting the extent of the problem meant that suspicion and lack of confidence persisted longer

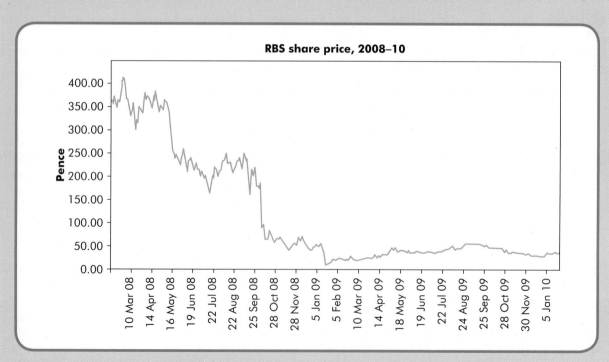

404

than was necessary. When global financial meltdown began in 2008/09, governments thought they had learned this lesson, and threw the kitchen sink at fixing the banks.

By early 2010, many of the banks seemed to have come back from the brink. The chart opposite shows the share price of Royal Bank of Scotland, in which, during 2009, the government had to take an 84 per cent stake in order to avert its collapse. Its share price having fallen from 400 pence to 10 pence, it then seemed to stabilize around 30–50 pence thereafter.

Improved private sector solvency has come at the price of reduced solvency for the government that injected all the money. Whether the government can cope with its high debt burden is a subject to which we return.

This leads to the third lesson from Japan. If pressing the fiscal accelerator is difficult once the government is heavily indebted, the monetary accelerator must be flat on the floor. Japanese monetary policy eventually cut interest rates to zero. Having learned from this experience, central banks in the US, the UK and eurozone slashed interest rates to very low levels in 2009 when aggregate demand and output began to plummet.

The multiplier revisited

The multiplier relates changes in autonomous demand to changes in equilibrium income and output. The formula in Chapter 16 still applies, provided we use MPC', the marginal propensity to consume out of gross, rather than out of disposable, income.

$$\text{Multiplier} = 1/(1 - MPC') \tag{1}$$

With proportional taxes, MPC' equals $MPC \times (1 - t)$. For a given marginal propensity to consume out of disposable income, a higher tax rate t reduces MPC', raises $(1 - MPC')$ and so reduces the multiplier. The more the circular flow leaks out into taxation, the less flows round again to stimulate further expansion of output and income. Table 17.2 illustrates.

In Chapter 16, without government the multiplier was simply $1/(1 - MPC)$ or $1/MPS$. With a larger marginal propensity to save, there was a larger leakage from the circular flow between firms and households, and the multiplier was correspondingly smaller.

Table 17.2 merely extends this insight. Now leakages arise both from saving and from net taxes. When both are large, the multiplier is small. The bottom row of the table has a much smaller multiplier than the top row.

Table 17.2 Values of the multiplier

MPC	T	MPC'	Multiplier
0.9	0	0.90	10.00
0.9	0.2	0.72	3.57
0.7	0	0.70	3.33
0.7	0.2	0.56	2.27
0.7	0.4	0.42	1.72

17.3 The government budget

A **budget** is the spending and revenue plans of an individual, a company or a government.

The government **budget** describes what goods and services the government will buy during the coming year, what transfer payments it will make and how it will pay for them. Most of its spending is financed by taxes. When spending exceeds taxes, there is a budget deficit. When taxes exceed spending, there is a budget surplus. Continuing to use G for government spending on goods and services, and NT for net taxes or taxes minus transfer payments,

$$\text{Government budget deficit} = G - NT \tag{2}$$

Figure 17.5 shows government purchases G and net taxes tY in relation to national income. We assume G is fixed at 200. With a proportional net tax rate of 0.2, net taxes are $0.2Y$. Taxes are zero when output is zero, 100 when output is 500 and 200 when output is 1000. At outputs below 1000, the government budget is in deficit. At an output of 1000 the budget is balanced, and at higher outputs the budget is in surplus. Given G and t, the budget deficit or surplus depends on the level of output and income.

The budget surplus or deficit is determined by three things: the tax rate t, the level of government spending G and the level of output Y. With a given tax rate, an increase in G will raise output and hence tax revenue. Could the budget deficit be *reduced* by higher spending? We now show that this is impossible.

Investment, saving and the budget

By definition, actual leakages from the circular flow always equal actual injections to the circular flow. Payments cannot vanish into thin air. Our model now has two leakages – saving by households and net taxes paid to the government – and two injections – investment spending by firms and government spending on goods and services. Thus *actual* saving plus *actual* net taxes always equal *actual* government spending plus *actual* investment spending.

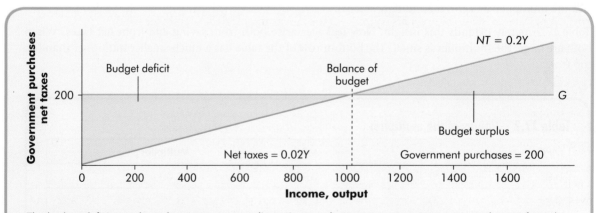

The budget deficit equals total government spending minus total tax revenue or government purchases of goods and services minus net taxes. Government purchases are shown as constant independent of income, while net taxes are proportional to income. Thus at low levels of income the budget is in deficit and at high income levels the budget is in surplus.

Figure 17.5 The government budget

In the last chapter we saw that, when the economy is not at equilibrium income, actual saving and investment differ from *desired* or *planned* saving and investment. Firms make unplanned changes in inventories and households may be forced to make unplanned saving if demand exceeds the output actually available.

The economy is in equilibrium when all quantities demanded or *desired* are equal to *actual* quantities. In equilibrium, planned saving S plus planned net taxes NT must equal planned government purchases G plus planned investment I. Planned leakages equal planned injections:

$$S + NT = G + I$$

Without the government, this reduces to the equilibrium condition of Chapter 16: planned saving equals planned investment. Notice that the above equation implies that in equilibrium desired saving minus desired investment equals the government's desired budget deficit:

$$S - I = G - NT$$

A rise in planned government spending G must *raise* the budget deficit. For a given tax rate, a rise in G increases aggregate demand and raises equilibrium income. Provided the tax rate is less than 100 per cent, disposable income must rise. Households increase both desired consumption and desired saving when disposable income rises. Some of the extra disposable income goes in extra desired saving.

Since desired investment I is independent of income, this rise in desired saving must increase $(S - I)$ and thus raise $(G - NT)$. Hence, net taxes NT cannot rise by as much as G. This proves that the equilibrium budget deficit rises if **government spending increases** but the net tax rate is unaltered.

> **Higher government spending** on goods and services increases equilibrium output. With a given tax rate, tax revenue rises but the budget deficit increases (or the budget surplus falls).
>
> For given government spending G, a **higher tax rate** reduces both equilibrium output and the budget deficit.

We can analyse a tax increase in a similar way. We know from Figure 17.2 that a rise in the tax rate makes the aggregate demand schedule rotate downwards. Equilibrium income must fall. Disposable income falls, both because of lower national income and a **higher tax rate**. With lower disposable income, desired saving must fall. Since $(S - I)$ is now lower, in equilibrium the budget deficit $(G - NT)$ must also be lower.

We can also understand this more intuitively. When one sector runs a deficit, another sector must be running a surplus to compensate. Saving minus investment is the net surplus of the private sector (households plus firms). A private sector surplus equals a public sector (government) deficit, and vice versa.

17.4 Deficits and the fiscal stance

Is the budget deficit a good measure of the government's **fiscal stance**? Does the size of the deficit show whether fiscal policy is *expansionary*, aiming to raise national income, or *contractionary*, trying to reduce national income?

> The **fiscal stance** shows the effect of fiscal policy on demand and output.

In itself, the deficit may be a poor measure of the government's fiscal stance. The deficit can change for reasons unconnected with fiscal policy. Even if G and t are unaltered, a fall in investment demand will reduce output and income. In turn, this reduces net tax revenue and raises the budget deficit.

For given levels of government spending and tax rates, the budget has larger deficits in recessions, when income is low, than in booms, when income is high. Suppose aggregate demand suddenly falls. The budget will go into deficit. Someone looking at the deficit might conclude that fiscal policy was expansionary and that there was no need to expand fiscal policy further. That might be wrong. The deficit may exist because of the recession.

The structural budget

> The **structural budget** shows what the budget will be if output is at potential output.

To use the budget deficit as an indicator of the fiscal stance, we calculate the *structural* or *cyclically adjusted budget.*

Suppose government spending is 200 and the tax rate is 0.2. As in Figure 17.4, the budget is in deficit at any income below 1000 and in surplus at any income above 1000. If, given the other components of aggregate demand, equilibrium output is 800, the actual budget will be in deficit. Net tax revenue will be $0.2 \times 800 = 160$. With government spending at 200, the budget deficit is 40.

Conversely, suppose equilibrium output is 1200. With a tax rate of 0.2, net tax revenue would be 240 but autonomous government spending would still be 200. There would be a budget *surplus* of 40.

Looking at the deficit of 40 when the actual output is 800, we might conclude that fiscal policy is too expansionary and the government should tighten fiscal policy to eliminate the deficit. Once we realize that the main cause of the deficit is low income, we are less likely to reach this conclusion. We may also recognize that tightening fiscal policy during a recession is likely to reduce output further.[3]

CASE 17.2 — Budget effects of demand fluctuations

Public spending and taxes of Germany, the UK and the US tell a surprising story, which largely answers a baffling question about the 2008–09 recession. Why did the US and UK government deficits suffer blowouts of unprecedented proportions, while those of Germany and many other advanced economies, that suffered equal or greater output losses, expand much less?

The answer is suggested by looking separately at public spending and taxes. US public spending rose by 3.2 per cent of GDP in the past eight quarters, compared with 3.4 per cent in Germany and 4.7 per cent in the UK. Incidentally, almost half the increase in all these figures was not caused by an actual expansion of public spending, but simply by the shrinkage of GDP, which resulted in a smaller denominator in these ratios.

The striking difference between the three countries' performance appears on the tax side. The US and UK governments both suffered big drops in revenue: 2.2 per cent of GDP in the UK and 3.2 per cent in the US. In Germany, the revenue-to-GDP ratio fell by 0.9 percentage points.

The main explanation for the big difference between the UK and US experience, on the one hand, and the German, on the other, probably lies in the tax structures of the three countries. The US, surprisingly, has a 'progressive' tax structure that relies heavily on taxing the rich. Germany and most European countries raise most of their revenues through 'regressive' consumption and energy taxes, bearing mainly on the middle class.

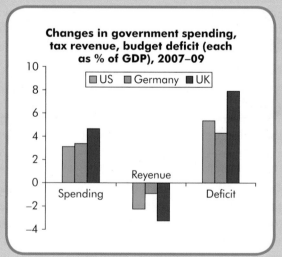

Changes in government spending, tax revenue, budget deficit (each as % of GDP), 2007–09

---

3   In this chapter we are concerned only with the impact of fiscal policy on aggregate demand. There may be other reasons to worry about a deficit. We examine these in Chapter 26.

As a result, the US government's tax take suffers much more in severe recessions, especially when these hit the richest citizens, such as bankers and stock market investors. Britain's system lies somewhere in-between, with more reliance on highly redistributive income and capital tax than Germany but also a much bigger yield than in the US from less progressive taxes on energy and from VAT.

The long-term implication is that US and UK politicians will have to bite the bullet of raising middle-class taxes if they want to preserve middle-class welfare entitlements.

Reading regular economics columns in the newspapers is a great way to learn more macroeconomics, stay up to date and impress your friends. Of the many excellent columnists, three worth following both in print and online are Martin Wolf of the *Financial Times* (http://www.ft.com/comment/columnists/martinwolf), Larry Elliott of the *Guardian* (http://www.guardian.co.uk/profile/larryelliott), and Anatole Kaletsky of *The Times* (http://www.timesonline.co.uk/tol/comment/columnists/anatole_kaletsky/).

Source: Adapted from Kaletsky, A. (2010) Democrat defeat will tighten squeeze on middle class, *The Times*, 25 January. © Times Newspaper Limited 2010.

Inflation-adjusted deficits

A second reason why the actual government deficit may be a poor measure of fiscal stance is the distinction between real and nominal interest rates. Official measures of the deficit treat all nominal interest paid by the government on the national debt as government expenditure. It makes more sense to count only the *real* interest rate times the outstanding government debt as an item of expenditure that contributes to the deficit – the **inflation-adjusted budget**.

Suppose inflation is 10 per cent, nominal interest rates are 12 per cent, and real interest rates are 2 per cent. From the government's viewpoint, the interest burden is only really 2 per cent on each £1 of debt outstanding. Although nominal interest rates are 12 per cent, inflation will inflate future nominal tax revenue at 10 per cent a year, providing most of the revenue needed to pay the high nominal interest rates. The real cost of borrowing is only 2 per cent.

> The **inflation-adjusted budget** uses real not nominal interest rates to calculate government spending on debt interest.

17.5 Automatic stabilizers and discretionary fiscal policy

Table 17.2 showed that a higher net tax rate *t* reduces the multiplier. Suppose investment demand falls by 100. The larger the multiplier, the larger is the fall in equilibrium output. A high net tax rate reduces the multiplier and dampens the output effect of shocks to autonomous aggregate demand. A high net tax rate is a good automatic stabilizer.

> **Automatic stabilizers** reduce the multiplier and thus output response to demand shocks.

Income tax, VAT and unemployment benefit are important automatic stabilizers. At given tax rates and given benefit levels, a fall in income and output raises payments of unemployment benefits and reduces tax revenue. Both effects reduce the multiplier and dampen the output response. A given shift of the aggregate demand schedule has a smaller effect on equilibrium income and output. The automatic reduction in net tax revenue acts as a fiscal stimulus. Conversely, in a boom, net tax revenue rises, which helps dampen the boom.

Automatic stabilizers have a great advantage. They are automatic. Nobody has to decide whether there has been a shock to which policy should respond. By reducing the responsiveness of the economy to shocks, automatic stabilizers reduce output fluctuations.

All leakages are automatic stabilizers. A higher saving rate and lower marginal propensity to consume reduce the multiplier. Later in the chapter, we shall see that a high marginal propensity to import also dampens output fluctuations.

Active or discretionary fiscal policy

> **Discretionary fiscal policy** is decisions about tax rates and levels of government spending.

Although automatic fiscal stabilizers are always at work, governments also use *discretionary* fiscal policies to change spending levels or tax rates to stabilize aggregate demand. When other components of aggregate demand are abnormally low, the government can boost demand by cutting taxes, raising spending, or both. When other components of aggregate demand are abnormally high, the government raises taxes or cuts spending.

By now you should be asking two questions. First, why can fiscal policy not stabilize aggregate demand completely? Surely, by maintaining aggregate demand at its full-employment level, the government could eliminate booms and slumps altogether? Second, why are governments reluctant to expand fiscal policy and aggregate demand to a level that would completely eliminate unemployment? Concept 17.1 provides some of the answers.

CONCEPT 17.1 The limits to fiscal policy

Why can demand shocks not be fully offset by fiscal policy?

1   *Time lags* It takes time to spot that aggregate demand has changed. It may take six months to get reliable statistics on output. Then it takes time to change fiscal policy. Long-term spending plans on hospitals or defence cannot be changed overnight. And once the policy is changed, it takes time to work through the steps of the multiplier process to have its full effect. Where possible, modern economies rely on interest rate changes, not fiscal changes, to make short-term adjustments to aggregate demand.

2   *Uncertainty* The government faces two problems. First, it is unsure of key magnitudes such as the multiplier. It only has estimates from past data. Mistaken estimates induce incorrect decisions about the extent of the fiscal change needed. Second, since fiscal policy takes time to work, the government has to forecast the level that demand will reach by the time fiscal policy has its full effects. If investment is low today but about to rise sharply, a fiscal expansion may not be needed. Mistakes in forecasting non-government sources of demand, such as investment, lead to incorrect decisions about the fiscal changes currently required.

3   *Induced effects on autonomous demand* Our model treats investment demand and the autonomous consumption demand as given. This is only a simplification. Changes in fiscal policy may lead to offsetting changes in other components of autonomous demand, as they did in Japan. These induced effects may offset the direct effect of fiscal stimulus if fiscal expansion causes a collapse of confidence because of worries about government debt. If estimates of these induced effects are wrong, fiscal changes have unexpected effects. To study this issue, we extend our model of aggregate demand in Chapter 20.

Why not expand fiscal policy when unemployment is high?

1   *The budget deficit* When output is low and unemployment high, the budget deficit may be large. Fiscal expansion makes it larger. The government may worry about the size of the deficit itself or worry that a large deficit will lead to inflation.

2   *Maybe we are at full employment!* Our simple model assumes there are spare resources. Output is demand-determined. Fiscal expansion raises demand and output. But we could be at potential output. People are unemployed, and machines idle, only because they do not wish to supply at the going wages or rentals. If so, there are no spare resources to be mopped up raising aggregate demand. If high unemployment and low output reflect not low demand but low supply, fiscal expansion is pointless.

17.6 The national debt and the deficit

Occasionally, the UK government had a budget surplus. Historically, this is rare. Most governments have budget deficits. The flow of deficits is what adds to the stock of debt.

> The government's debts are called the **national debt**.

The UK government had large deficits in the 1970s. The nominal value of its debt soared. Yet inflation was also raising nominal income and nominal tax revenue. Moreover, real growth was also taking place. For both reasons, rising levels of nominal government debt have often taken place without the debt being out of control. When nominal debt rises more slowly than nominal output, the ratio of debt to GDP is falling and the government can meet its debt interest commitments without having to raise tax rates. What must happen to tax rates is a good indicator of how much the debt burden is hurting.

Table 17.3 shows how the UK's debt/GDP ratio has evolved over the last 35 years. Despite a steadily rising level of debt, the ratio fell steadily to a mere 15 per cent in 1989. Thereafter, the debt/GDP ratio rose steadily until 2007, but still remained at levels that were modest by international standards.

This gradually evolving picture came to an abrupt end with the crash of 2008/09 and the dramatic fiscal expansion needed to prop up the banks and provide additional injections to aggregate demand. This raises an obvious question: given increasing confidence that GDP growth had been restored by the start of 2010, why not withdraw the fiscal stimulus more quickly in order to shrink the size of the budget deficit and prevent government debt spiralling to the extent predicted by the IMF?

First, to the extent that the national debt is owed to UK citizens, it is a debt we owe ourselves as a nation. Paying interest entails redistributing income within the UK, from taxpayers to debt-holders, but is a drain on national income only to the extent the UK has previously borrowed abroad and must now pay interest to foreigners.

Second, to the extent that the debt has financed investment in physical or human capital, this will raise *future* output and tax revenue, and help pay off the debt. Prudent businesses sometimes borrow to finance profitable investment. A prudent government may do the same. More investment in rail infrastructure would probably have been good for the UK, even if financed by greater debt.

Third, specifically in relation to the recent surge in debt, some of which has been financed by foreigners, it is vital that financial markets believe that the UK government has a credible plan to reduce the debt before any financial panic about whether or not the government can meet future interest repayments. In an ideal world, this would entail raising tax rates a little and taking a long time to reduce debt/GDP levels. Doing this too quickly would entail drastic cuts in public spending or punitive rates of tax in the short run. Complete financial collapse in 2009 would have scarred the economy for decades – just like the Great Depression of the 1930s. Future generations will benefit from the actions that averted such a collapse, and it is entirely reasonable they should pay a little in order that the current generation does not bear the burden alone.

Table 17.3 UK government net debt, 1973–2014 (% of GDP)

1973	1979	1989	1999	2007	2014
60	48	15	39	44	92

Sources: OECD, Economic Outlook; IMF, World Economic Outlook, 2009.

Table 17.4 Government net debt, 2010 (% of GDP)

Japan	105
Italy	101
Greece	95
Belgium	84
UK	59
Eurozone average	58
Switzerland	11

Source: OECD, Economic Outlook.

Finally, if the government cannot raise tax rates beyond a certain point, a large debt and hence large debt interest payments may cause large deficits that can be financed only by borrowing or printing money. Since borrowing compounds the problem, eventually it is necessary to print money on a huge scale. That is how hyperinflations start. Chapter 22 fills in the details.

Table 17.4 gives current estimates of government net debt in 2010 in a range of countries. High debt levels are especially worrying when real interest rates are also high, for then the government must levy high taxes to meet the burden of paying interest on its debt.

This completes our introduction to fiscal policy, aggregate demand and the economy. We now extend our model of income determination to include the sector we have so far neglected – foreign trade with the rest of the world.

ACTIVITY
17.1

Fiscal stability and responsibility

As Chancellor of the Exchequer, Gordon Brown not only gave the Bank of England independent control of interest rates but also introduced a *Code for Fiscal Stability*.

The Code for Fiscal Stability committed the government to a medium-run objective of financing all current government spending out of current revenues.

Borrowing-financed deficits are allowed only to finance public sector investment (which should eventually pay for itself by raising future output and hence future tax revenues). A medium-run perspective is needed because the actual deficit fluctuates with output over the business cycle if tax rates remain constant. Chancellor Brown's 'golden rule' means that government debt accumulation in the long run (because of borrowing to finance investment) should be accompanied by higher output and tax revenue without requiring a change in tax rates.

Because tax revenues fall when the economy is growing more slowly, there is always some room for dispute about whether the emergence of a tax revenue shortfall can be attributed to temporary cyclical factors or whether it is the start of an adverse trend that requires a change in tax rates to restore stability again.

Having begun with a tight fiscal policy in 1997, Labour embarked on a sustained fiscal expansion after 2002, spending especially on the National Health Service. Unsurprisingly, people began to question whether this could be afforded and whether secretly the government had back-pedalled on the Code for Fiscal Stability. Just before the financial crash occurred, the Treasury in its 2007 Budget Statement was trying to meet this criticism head on:

> The golden rule is being met in this cycle with a surplus of 0.1 per cent of GDP, in contrast to the last cycle's average deficit of 2.0 per cent of GDP. [. . .] Debt has remained at low and sustainable levels, while at the same time public sector net investment is now over three times higher as a share of the economy than it was in 1997–98. [. . .] The IMF noted in March this year, that in the UK 'shocks, such as the global downturn of 2000–03 and the increase in oil prices during 2004–06, were managed with good policy responses', and noted 'the shallowness of the UK growth slowdown during the last global downturn'. The credibility of the framework has been established not only by the performance of the key fiscal aggregates, but also by the enhanced transparency introduced by the Code for Fiscal Stability.

An implicit assumption of the Code for Fiscal Stability had been that a typical business cycle of around seven years was long enough to constitute the medium run in which underlying budget balance should be achieved. The financial crash changed all that, in two ways.

First, in order to prop up the banks and the real economy, the government had to embark on a dramatic fiscal expansion that obviously exceeded all the bounds implied by the Code for Fiscal Stability. Desperate times required desperate measures.

Second, the foreseen doubling of government debt by 2014 was not then going to be unwound within a couple of years thereafter. Thus, the aftershock of the crisis was going to last much longer than a single business cycle. Future generations would be paying for years for the actions that staved off something even worse.

In order to try to reassure voters and investors that the debt would eventually be tackled, in December 2009 the government proposed a longer-term commitment. The *Fiscal Responsibility Bill* set out a *Fiscal Consolidation Plan*, from 2009/10 to 2015/16, that required the government to do three things:

1 Halve its borrowing as a share of GDP within four years of its forecast peak in 2009/10, restoring the deficit to below 5.5 per cent of GDP by 2013/14.

2 Cut borrowing as a share of GDP in each year from 2009/10 to 2015/16.

3 Ensure that public sector net debt is falling as a share of GDP by 2015/16.

Questions

(a) Why is it important to assess the fiscal position in the medium run and not merely at a point in time?

(b) If the government could choose the definition of the cycle's length in order to suit its own purposes, would there be any gain from a report by an independent group of fiscal experts in the same way as the Bank of England publishes an independent *Inflation Report* on monetary policy?

(c) How would you expect financial markets to react if they thought that the Treasury was cooking the books in respect of its assessment of whether the golden rule was being met?

(d) Why does the golden rule apply to current expenditure by the government but exclude spending on physical investment?

(e) Suppose a new government promised to eliminate the large UK budget deficit within a year to 'put the economy on a sounder footing'. (i) Describe some steps it would have to take on spending and taxes. What effect would this have on: (ii) national output; (iii) tax revenue; (iv) the deficit itself; (v) autonomous investment?

To check your answers to these questions, go to page 685.

17.7　Foreign trade and income determination

Adding the government sector to the circular flow provides additional channels of injections and leakages. Adding the foreign sector has similar effects. We now take account of exports X, goods made at home but sold abroad, and imports Z, goods made abroad but bought by domestic residents. Table 17.5 shows UK exports, imports and net exports. Two points should be noted: net exports are small relative to GDP; exports and imports are about equal in size. The UK has fairly balanced trade with the rest of the world.

When a household overspends its income, it dissaves, or is in deficit, and runs down its net assets (selling assets or adding to debt) to meet this deficit. When a country runs a trade deficit with the rest of the world,

Table 17.5 UK foreign trade, 1950–2008 (% of GDP)

	Exports	Imports	Net exports
1950	23	23	0
1960	20	21	1
1970	22	21	1
1980	27	25	2
2008	25	28	−3

Sources: ONS, *Economic Trends*; www.statistics.gov.uk/elmr.

the country as a whole must sell off some assets to foreigners to pay for this deficit. Chapter 24 explains how this occurs.

Table 17.5 shows that the UK is a very open economy. Exports and imports are each over a quarter of GDP. In large countries such as the US and Japan, exports and imports are each less than half of this fraction of GDP. In contrast, in small countries such as Belgium, exports and imports are each close to 80 per cent of GDP. Foreign trade is much more important for most European countries than for a huge country like the US, which largely trades with itself.

Net exports $X - Z$ add to our income and expenditure measures of GDP. Hence, the equilibrium condition for the goods market must now be expanded to[4]

$$Y = AD = C + I + G + X - Z$$

What determines desired exports and imports? Export demand depends mainly on what is happening abroad. Foreign income and foreign demand are largely unrelated to domestic output. Hence we treat the demand for exports as autonomous.

> The **marginal propensity to import (MPZ)** is the fraction of each extra pound of national income that domestic residents wish to spend on extra imports.

Demand for imports rises when domestic income and output rise. Figure 17.6 shows the demand for exports, imports and net exports, as domestic income changes. The export demand schedule is horizontal. Export demand is independent of domestic income. Desired imports are zero when income is zero but rises as income rises. The slope of the import demand schedule is the **marginal propensity to import**.

The import demand schedule in Figure 17.6 assumes a value of 0.2 for the marginal propensity to import. Each additional pound of national income adds 20 pence to desired imports. One of the problems facing the UK is that the marginal propensity to import *MPZ* is much higher than 0.2. Any increase in national income leads to a large increase in the demand for imports.

> The **trade balance** is the value of net exports. If this is positive, the economy has a **trade surplus**. If imports exceed exports, the economy has a **trade deficit**.

At each output, the gap between export demand and import demand is the demand for net exports. At low output, net exports are positive. There is a **trade surplus** with the rest of the world. At high output, there is a **trade deficit** and net exports are negative. By raising import demand while leaving export demand unchanged, higher output worsens the **trade balance**.

---

4   This also implies $Y + Z = C + I + G + X$. Home output Y plus output Z from abroad equals final demand $C + I + G + X$.

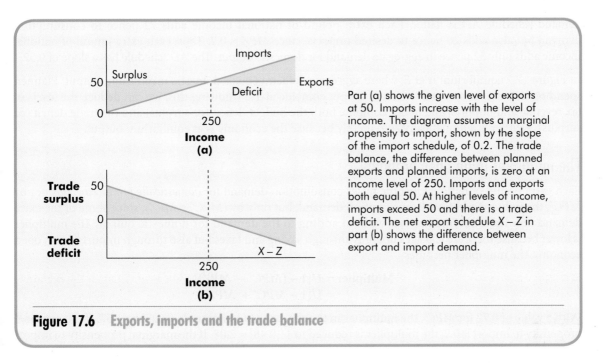

Figure 17.6 Exports, imports and the trade balance

Part (a) shows the given level of exports at 50. Imports increase with the level of income. The diagram assumes a marginal propensity to import, shown by the slope of the import schedule, of 0.2. The trade balance, the difference between planned exports and planned imports, is zero at an income level of 250. Imports and exports both equal 50. At higher levels of income, imports exceed 50 and there is a trade deficit. The net export schedule $X - Z$ in part (b) shows the difference between export and import demand.

Net exports and equilibrium income

Figure 17.7 shows how equilibrium income is determined. We start from the aggregate demand schedule $C + I + G$, described earlier in the chapter, then add net exports NX. At low output, net export demand is positive. Aggregate demand $C + I + G + X - Z$ will then exceed $C + I + G$. As output rises, import demand rises and desired *net* exports fall. At the output of 250, Figure 17.6 tells us that net export demand is zero. Figure 17.7 shows the new aggregate demand schedule AD crossing $C + I + G$ at an output of 250. Beyond this output, net export demand is negative and the aggregate demand schedule is below $C + I + G$.

At a zero income, Figure 17.7 shows autonomous demand $I + G + X$. Suppose the marginal propensity to consume out of national income MPC is still 0.72. The $C + I + G$ schedule has a slope of 0.72, but the aggregate

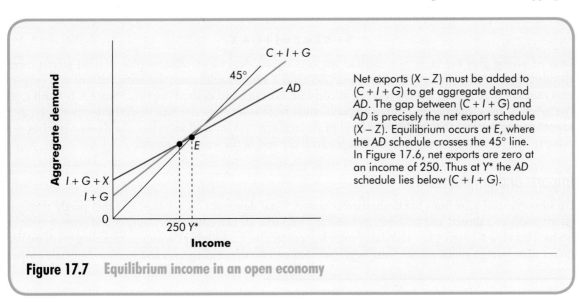

Figure 17.7 Equilibrium income in an open economy

Net exports $(X - Z)$ must be added to $(C + I + G)$ to get aggregate demand AD. The gap between $(C + I + G)$ and AD is precisely the net export schedule $(X - Z)$. Equilibrium occurs at E, where the AD schedule crosses the 45° line. In Figure 17.6, net exports are zero at an income of 250. Thus at Y^* the AD schedule lies below $(C + I + G)$.

demand schedule *AD* is flatter. Each extra pound of national income adds 72 pence to consumption demand but also adds 20 pence to desired imports, since *MPZ* = 0.2. Thus, each extra pound of national income adds only 52 pence to aggregate demand for domestic output. The *AD* schedule has a slope of 0.52.

In Figure 17.7 equilibrium is at *E*, where aggregate demand equals domestic income and output. Planned spending, actual incomes and domestic output coincide at *Y**. Knowing this, we can deduce the levels of tax revenue and imports, and hence compute both the budget deficit (or surplus) and the trade deficit (or surplus). Neither is automatically zero merely because the economy is at equilibrium output.

The multiplier in an open economy

Each extra pound of national income raises consumption demand for *domestically produced goods* not by *MPC′*, the induced additional consumption demand, but only by (*MPC′* − *MPZ*), since some of the extra demand now leaks out into imports without adding to the demand for domestic output. The multiplier is lower because there are leakages not only through saving and taxes but also through imports. In an open economy, the multiplier becomes

$$\text{Multiplier} = 1/[1 - (MPC' - MPZ)]$$
$$= 1/[1 - MPC' + MPZ)]$$

With a value of 0.72 for *MPC′*, the multiplier in the absence of foreign trade would be 3.57. If the marginal propensity to import is 0.2, the multiplier is reduced to 1/[0.48] = 2.08. If the marginal propensity to import was as high as 0.72, the multiplier would be reduced to 1, which is no multiplier at all.

For small economies, very open to international trade, this leakage through import demand is very important. Small economies that are very open thus face powerful automatic stabilizers.

Higher export demand

A rise in export demand leads to a parallel upward shift in the aggregate demand schedule *AD*. Equilibrium income must increase. A higher *AD* schedule crosses the 45° line at a higher level of income. With a higher income, desired imports rise. The analysis of what happens to net exports is very similar to our analysis of the effect of an increase in government spending on the budget deficit. As a matter of national income accounting, total leakages from the circular flow always equal total injections to the circular flow. And in equilibrium, desired spending must coincide with actual income and spending on domestic goods. Hence the amended equilibrium condition for an open economy is

$$S + NT + Z = I + G + X$$

Desired saving plus net taxes plus desired imports equals desired investment plus desired government spending plus desired exports. Higher export demand *X* raises equilibrium domestic income and output. This raises desired saving, net tax revenue at constant tax rates and desired imports.[5] Since *S*, *NT* and *Z* all rise when *X* rises, the rise in desired imports must be smaller than the rise in desired exports. Higher export demand raises the equilibrium level of desired imports but still increases the desired level of net exports. The domestic country's trade balance with the rest of the world improves.

Imports and employment

Do imports steal jobs from the domestic economy? Final demand *C* + *I* + *G* + *X* is met partly through goods produced abroad, not at home. By reducing imports, we can create extra output and employment at home. This view is correct, but also dangerous. It is correct because higher consumer spending on domestic rather than foreign goods *will* increase aggregate demand for domestic goods and so raise domestic output

---

5 Since tax rates remain constant, higher domestic income raises disposable income, desired consumption and saving.

and employment. In Figure 17.7, a lower marginal propensity to import makes the *AD* schedule steeper and raises equilibrium income and output.

There are many ways to restrict import spending at each level of output. In Chapter 24 we begin the analysis of how the exchange rate affects the demand for imports (and exports). However, imports can also be restricted directly through *import quotas* or indirectly through *tariffs*. We explore these further in Chapter 28.

The view that import restrictions help domestic output and employment is dangerous because it ignores the possibility of retaliation by other countries. By reducing our imports, we cut the exports of others. If they retaliate by doing the same thing, the demand for our exports will fall. In the end, nobody gains employment but world trade disappears. If the whole world is in recession, what is needed is a worldwide expansion of fiscal policies, not a collective, and ultimately futile, attempt to steal employment from other countries.

Equilibrium output revisited

MATHS 17.1

Short-run equilibrium is given by

$$Y^* = C + I + G + X - Z$$

where $C = A + c(1 - t)Y$ and $Z = zY$. Hence $Y^* = [A + G + X + I] + c(1 - t)Y - zY$, which implies

$$Y^* = [A + I + G + X] / [1 - c(1 - t) + z] \tag{1}$$

Equilibrium output is the product of autonomous spending – autonomous consumption demand A, plus injections from investment, government spending and exports – and the multiplier $\{1/[1 - c(1 - t) + z]\}$. Because of leakages into saving, taxes and imports, the multiplier may be only a little larger than unity. In a very small open economy, the marginal propensity to import z will be much higher than in a large closed economy such as the US. Hence the multiplier will be lower in Belgium than in the US. In principle, if the tax rate and marginal propensity to import are large enough, the multiplier could be less than 1. Raising injections by £1 would then raise equilibrium income by less than £1.

Summary

- The government buys goods and services, and levies taxes (net of transfer benefits) that reduce disposable income below national income and output.

- **Net taxes**, if related to income levels, lower the marginal propensity to consume out of national income. Households get only part of each extra pound of national income to use as disposable income.

- **Higher government spending on goods and services** raises aggregate demand and equilibrium output. A **higher tax rate** reduces aggregate demand and equilibrium output.

- An equal initial increase in government spending and taxes raises aggregate demand and output. This is the **balanced budget multiplier**.

- The **government budget** is in deficit (surplus) if spending is larger (smaller) than tax revenue. Higher government spending raises the budget deficit. A higher tax rate reduces it.

- In equilibrium in a closed economy, desired saving and taxes equal desired investment and government spending. An excess of desired saving over desired investment must be offset by an excess of government purchases over net tax revenue.

- The budget deficit is a poor indicator of **fiscal stance**. Recessions make the budget go into deficit; booms generate a budget surplus. The **structural budget** calculates whether the budget would be in surplus or deficit if output were at potential output. It is also important to **inflation-adjust** the deficit.

- **Automatic stabilizers** reduce fluctuations in GDP by reducing the multiplier. Leakages act as automatic stabilizers.

- The government may also use **active or discretionary fiscal policy** to try to stabilize output. In practice, active fiscal policy cannot stabilize output perfectly.

- Budget deficits add to the **national debt**. If the debt is mainly owed to citizens of the country, interest payments are merely a transfer within the economy. However, the national debt may be a burden if the government is unable or unwilling to raise taxes to meet high interest payments on a large national debt.

- Deficits are not necessarily bad. Particularly in a recession, a move to cut the deficit may lead output further away from potential output. But huge deficits can create a vicious cycle of extra borrowing, extra interest payments and yet more borrowing.

- In an open economy, **exports** are a source of demand for domestic goods but **imports** are a leakage since they are a demand for goods made abroad.

- Exports are determined mainly by conditions abroad and can be viewed as autonomous demand unrelated to domestic income. Imports are assumed to rise with domestic income. The **marginal propensity to import** *MPZ* tells us the fraction of each extra pound of national income that goes on extra demand for imports.

- Leakages to imports reduce the value of the **multiplier** to $1/[1 - MPC' + MPZ]$.

- Higher export demand raises domestic output and income. A higher marginal propensity to import reduces domestic output and income.

- The **trade surplus**, exports minus imports, is larger the lower is output. Higher export demand raises the trade surplus; a higher marginal propensity to import reduces it.

- In equilibrium, desired leakages $S + NT + Z$ must equal desired injections $G + I + X$. Thus any surplus $S - I$ desired by the private sector must be offset by the sum of the government deficit $(G - NT)$ and the desired trade surplus $(X - Z)$.

Review questions   connect

EASY

1 Equilibrium output in a closed economy is 1000, consumption 800 and investment 80. (a) Deduce *G*. (b) Investment rises by 50. The marginal propensity to consume out of national income is 0.8. What is the new equilibrium level of *Y*, *C*, *I* and *G*? (c) Suppose instead that *G* had risen by 50. What would be the new equilibrium of *Y*, *C*, *I* and *G*? (d) If potential output is 1200, to what must *G* rise to make output equal potential output?

2 The government spends £6 billion on new rail track. The income tax rate is 0.25 and the *MPC* out of disposable income is 0.8. (a) What is the effect on equilibrium income and output? (b) Does the budget deficit rise or fall? Why?

3 In equilibrium, desired saving equals desired investment. True or false? Explain.

4 Why does the government raise taxes when it could borrow to cover its spending?

5 The EU's trade partners have a recession. (a) What happens to the EU's trade balance? (b) What happens to equilibrium EU output? Explain.

6 Common fallacies   Why are these statements wrong? (a) The Chancellor raised taxes and spending by equal amounts. It will be a neutral budget for output. (b) Government policy should balance exports and imports but ensure that the government and private sector spend less than they earn.

7 Which of these is correct? The trade surplus equals: (a) the government surplus plus the private sector surplus; (b) the government deficit plus the private sector surplus; (c) the government deficit plus the private sector deficit.

8 In 2010 the new UK government wanted to reduce the size of the enormous budget deficit, but also pointed out that the structural budget deficit was significantly smaller than the actual deficit. (a) What does this mean? (b) Why does it matter? (c) Why does this make the subsequent growth of the UK economy so important?

9 Suppose the marginal propensity to consume out of disposable income is 0.8, the marginal tax rate is 0.5 and the marginal propensity to import is 0.8. Draw a diagram showing the 45° line and the aggregate demand schedule. (a) How does this diagram differ from those earlier in the chapter? (b) What is the size of the multiplier? (c) Illustrate graphically the effect of a shift in aggregate demand.

10 Repeat your answer to Question 9 using a diagram in which planned injections equal planned leakages.

11 If Y^{**} is the level of long-run equilibrium output, and if short-run equilibrium output Y^* is given by the model in this chapter, deduce the relationship between the marginal tax rate t, the discrepancy between the actual budget and the structural budget, and the power of the automatic stabilizers.

12 Is the ratio of government debt to GDP a useful indicator of a government's indebtedness? When could it be misleading?

13 What values of the marginal propensity to save s, the marginal tax rate t and the marginal propensity to import z would be consistent with a multiplier as low as 0.67?

14 Essay question   'By 2007 the UK had had over 50 consecutive quarters of steady growth. This period coincides with the period in which it was decided to make the Bank of England responsible for macroeconomic stabilization. Because interest rates can be changed easily and quickly, whereas tax rates and spending programmes cannot, this example confirms the superiority of monetary policy over fiscal policy in demand management.' Is this broadly correct? Can you think of examples in which fiscal policy would still be crucial? Did events after 2007 help you answer this question?

For solutions to these questions contact your lecturer.

CHAPTER 18

Money and banking

By the end of this chapter, you should understand:

1. the medium of exchange as the key attribute of money
2. other functions of money
3. how banks create money
4. liquidity crisis and solvency crisis
5. narrow and broad money
6. the money multiplier and bank deposit multiplier
7. different measures of money
8. motives for holding money
9. how money demand depends on output, prices and interest rates

> **Money** is any generally accepted means of payment for delivery of goods or settlement of debt. It is the **medium of exchange**.

Money is a symbol of success, a source of crime, and it makes the world go round.

Dogs' teeth in the Admiralty Islands, sea shells in parts of Africa, gold in the nineteenth century: all are examples of money. What matters is not the commodity used but the social convention that it is accepted *without question* as a means of payment. We now explain how society uses money to economize on scarce resources used in the transacting process.

18.1 Money and its functions

Although the crucial feature of money is its acceptance as the means of payment or **medium of exchange**, money also has three other functions: a unit of account, a store of value and a standard of deferred payment.

The medium of exchange

Money is used in almost half of all exchanges. Workers exchange labour services for money. People buy or sell goods for money. We accept money not to consume it directly but to use it subsequently to buy things we do wish to consume. Money is the medium through which people exchange goods and services.[1]

To see that society benefits from a medium of exchange, imagine a **barter economy**, in which the seller and the buyer *each* must want something the other has to offer. Each person is simultaneously a seller and a buyer. To see a film, you must swap a good or service that the cinema manager wants. There has to be a *double coincidence of wants*.

> A **barter economy** has no medium of exchange. Goods are swapped for other goods.

Trading is very expensive in a barter economy. People spend a lot of time and effort finding others with whom to make mutually satisfactory swaps. Time and effort are scarce resources. A barter economy is wasteful. The use of money – any commodity *generally* accepted in payment for goods, services and debts – makes trading simpler and more efficient. By economizing on time and effort spent in trading, society can use these resources to produce extra goods or leisure, making everyone better off.

Other functions of money

In Britain prices are quoted in pounds sterling; in the US in dollars. It is convenient to use the same units for the medium of exchange and **unit of account**. However, there are exceptions. During the German hyperinflation of 1922–23, when prices in marks changed very quickly, German shopkeepers found it more convenient to use dollars as the unit of account. Prices were quoted in dollars but payment was made in marks, the German medium of exchange. In 2009 Zimbabwe had to legalize the use of foreign currency as money because its domestic currency was almost worthless after years of hyperinflation.

> The **unit of account** is the unit in which prices are quoted and accounts kept.

To be accepted in exchange, money *has* to **store value**. Nobody will accept money in payment for goods supplied today if the money is worthless when they try to buy goods with it later. But money is not the only, nor necessarily the best, store of value. Houses, stamp collections and interest-bearing bank accounts all serve as stores of value. Since money pays no interest and its real purchasing power is eroded by inflation, there are better ways to store value.

> Money is a **store of value** that can be used to make future purchases.

Finally, money is a *standard of deferred payment* or unit of account over time. When you borrow, the amount to be repaid next year is measured in pounds. However, the key feature of money is its use as a medium of exchange. For this, it must act as a store of value as well. And it is usually, though not invariably, convenient to make money the unit of account and standard of deferred payment as well.

Different kinds of money

In prisoner-of-war camps, cigarettes were money. In the nineteenth century money was mainly gold and silver coins. These are examples of *commodity money*, ordinary goods with industrial uses (gold) and consumption uses (cigarettes), which also serve as a medium of exchange. To use a commodity money, society must either cut back on other uses of that commodity or devote scarce resources to additional production of the commodity. There are cheaper ways for society to make money.

A £10 note is worth far more as money than as a 7.5 × 14 cm piece of high-quality paper. Similarly, the monetary value of most coins exceeds what you would get by melting them down and selling off the metal. By collectively agreeing to use token money, society economizes on the scarce resources required to produce a medium of exchange. Since the manufacturing cost is tiny, why doesn't everyone make £10

---

1   For an interesting account of cigarettes as money in prisoner-of-war camps, see Radford, R. A. (1945) The economic organisation of a POW camp, *Economica*, 48: 189–201.

> A **token money** is a means of payment whose value or purchasing power as money greatly exceeds its cost of production or value in uses other than as money.
>
> An **IOU money** is a medium of exchange based on the debt of a private firm or individual.

notes? The survival of **token money** requires a restriction on the right to supply it. Private production is illegal.[2]

Society enforces the use of token money by making it *legal tender*. By law, it must be accepted as a means of payment. However, when prices rise very quickly, domestic token money is a poor store of value. People are reluctant to accept it as a medium of exchange. Shops and firms give discounts to people paying in gold or in foreign currency.

In modern economies, token money is supplemented by **IOU money**, principally bank deposits, which are debts of private banks. When you have a bank deposit, the bank owes you money. The bank is obliged to pay your cheque. Bank deposits are a medium of exchange because they are generally accepted as payment.

CONCEPT 18.1

Barter economy vs monetary economy

Life without money

Some years since, Mademoiselle Zelie, a singer, gave a concert in the Society Islands in exchange for a third part of the receipts. When counted, her share was found to consist of 3 pigs, 23 turkeys, 44 chickens, 5000 cocoa nuts, besides considerable quantities of bananas, lemons and oranges [. . .] as Mademoiselle could not consume any considerable portion of the receipts herself it became necessary in the meantime to feed the pigs and poultry with the fruit.

(W. S. Jevons, 1898)

This vivid example shows just how costly a barter economy can be. The direct exchange of goods and services for other goods and services either leaves one party with a load of stuff in which they have little interest – in which case they then have to go to the further effort of bartering this in turn for something more useful – or else restricts barter opportunities to the rare cases in which there is a 'double coincidence of wants', such that not only does person A want what person B is offering but also person B wants what person A is offering.

The great benefit of a monetary economy is that the medium of exchange can be confidently accepted in the knowledge that it can easily be reused for another transaction. The example below documents the first European to discover paper money. But Europeans did not invent it. As in many other things, the Chinese got there first.

Marco Polo discovers paper money

In this city of Kanbula [Beijing] is the mint of the Great Khan, who may truly be said to possess the secret of the alchemists, as he has the art of producing money. [. . .]

He causes the bark to be stripped from mulberry trees [. . .] made into paper [. . .] cut into pieces of money of different sizes. The act of counterfeiting is punished as a capital offence. This paper currency is circulated in every part of the Great Khan's domain. All his subjects receive it without hesitation because, wherever their business may call them, they can dispose of it again in the purchase of merchandise they may require.

(*The Travels of Marco Polo*, Book II)

Source: World Bank (1989) *World Development Report*.

---

2   The existence of forgers confirms society is economizing on scarce resources by producing money whose value as a medium of exchange exceeds its production cost.

18.2 Modern banking

When you deposit your coat in the theatre cloakroom, you do not expect it to be rented out during the performance. Banks lend out most coats in their cloakroom. A theatre would have to get your particular coat back on time, which might be tricky. A bank finds it easier because one piece of money looks just like another.

Unlike other financial institutions, such as pension funds, the key aspect of banks is that some of their liabilities are used as the medium of exchange: cheques allow their deposits to be used as money.

> **Bank reserves** are the money that the bank has available to meet possible withdrawals by depositors.

At any time, some people are writing cheques on a Barclays account to pay for goods purchased from a shop that banks with Lloyds; others are writing cheques on Lloyds' accounts to finance purchases from shops banking with Barclays. The *clearing system* is the process of interbank settlement of the net flows required between banks as a result. Thus the system of clearing cheques represents another way in which society reduces the cost of making transactions.[3]

Private commercial banks have assets and liabilities. Their assets are mainly loans to firms and households, and purchases of financial securities such as bills and bonds issued by governments and firms. Because many securities are very **liquid**, banks can lend short term and still get their money back in time if depositors withdraw their money.

In contrast, many loans to firms and households are quite illiquid. The bank cannot easily get its money back in a hurry. Modern banks thought they could get by with very few cash reserves in the vault because they thought they had sufficient liquid assets that would fulfil the same function: in an emergency they could be sold easily, quickly, and for a predictable price.

> **Liquidity** is the cheapness, speed and certainty with which asset values can be converted back into money.
>
> The money in **sight deposits** can be withdrawn 'on sight' without prior notice.
>
> **Time deposits**, paying higher interest rates, require the depositor to give notice before withdrawing money.

Liabilities of commercial banks include sight and time deposits. Chequing accounts are **sight deposits**. **Time deposits**, which include some savings accounts, pay higher interest rates because banks have time to organize the sale of some of their high-interest assets in order to have the cash available to meet withdrawals. Certificates of deposit (CDs) are large 'wholesale' time deposits – one-off deals with particular clients for a specified period, paying more generous interest rates. The other liabilities of banks are various 'money market instruments'; short-term and highly liquid borrowing by banks.

The business of banking

A bank makes profits by lending and borrowing. To get money in, the bank offers attractive interest rates to depositors, and offers higher interest rates on time deposits than sight deposits since the latter are subject to the possibility of immediate and unpredictable withdrawal.

Banks have to find profitable ways to lend what has been borrowed. In sterling, most is lent as advances of overdrafts to households and firms, usually at high interest rates. Some is used to buy securities, such as long-term government bonds. Some is more prudently invested in liquid assets. Although these pay a lower interest rate, the bank can get its money back quickly if people withdraw a lot of money from their sight deposits. And some money is held as cash, the most liquid asset of all.

A bank uses its specialist expertise to acquire a diversified portfolio of investments. Without the existence of the bank, depositors would have neither the time nor the expertise to decide which of these loans or investments to make. Before the financial crisis, UK banks held reserves as low as 2 per cent of the sight

---

3 Society continues to find new ways to save scarce resources in producing and using a medium of exchange. Many people use credit cards. Some supermarket tills directly debit customers' bank accounts. And shopping via the TV, telephone and internet is growing rapidly.

deposits that could be withdrawn at any time. This shows the importance of the other liquid assets in which banks had invested. At very short notice, banks could cash in liquid assets easily and for a predictable amount. The skill in running a bank entails being able to judge how much must be held in liquid assets, including cash, and how much can be lent out in less liquid forms that earn higher interest rates.

> **Commercial banks** are financial intermediaries licensed to make loans and issue deposits, including deposits against which cheques can be written.
>
> A **financial intermediary** specializes in bringing lenders and borrowers together.

A **commercial bank** borrows money from the public, crediting them with a deposit. The deposit is a liability of the bank. It is money owed to depositors. In turn, the bank lends money to firms, households or governments wishing to borrow. Banks are not the only **financial intermediaries**. Insurance companies, pension funds and building societies also take in money in order to re-lend it. The crucial feature of banks is that some of their liabilities are used as a means of payment, and are thus part of the money stock.[4]

18.3 How banks create money

> The **reserve ratio** is the ratio of reserves to deposits.

To simplify the arithmetic, assume banks use a **reserve ratio** of 10 per cent. Suppose, initially, the non-bank private sector has wealth of £1000 held in cash, which is a private sector asset but a liability of the government, who issued it, but not a liability of the private banks. The first row of Table 18.1 shows this cash as an asset of the non-bank private sector.

Now people pay this £1000 of cash into the banks by opening bank deposits. Banks have assets of £1000 cash, and liabilities of £1000 of deposits – money owed to depositors. If banks were like cloakrooms, that would be the end of the story. Table 18.1 would end in row 2.

However, banks do not need all deposits to be fully covered by cash reserves. Suppose banks create £9000 of overdrafts. This is a simultaneous loan of £9000, an asset in banks' balance sheets and the granting to customers of £9000 of deposits, against which customers can write cheques. The deposits of £9000 are a liability on banks' balance sheets. Now the banks have £10 000 total deposits – the original £1000 when cash was paid in, plus the new £9000 as counterpart to the overdraft – and £10 000 of total assets, comprising £9000 in loans and £1000 cash in the vaults. The reserve ratio is still 10 per cent in row three of Table 18.1.

> The **interest rate spread** is the excess of the loan interest rate over the deposit interest rate.

It does not even matter whether the 10 per cent reserve ratio is imposed by law or is merely profit-maximizing, smart behaviour by banks that balance risk and reward. The risk is the possibility of being caught short of cash; the reward is the interest rate spread.

Table 18.1 Money creation by the banking system

| | Banks | | Non-bank private sector | |
	Assets	Liabilities	Monetary assets	Liabilities
Initial	Cash 0 Loans 0	Deposits 0	Cash 1000	Loans from banks 0
Intermediate	Cash 1000	Deposits 1000	Cash 0 Deposits 1000	Loans from banks 0
Final	Cash 1000 Loans 9000	Deposits 10 000	Cash 0 Deposits 10 000	Loans from banks 9000

---

4 In fact, building societies now issue cheque books to their depositors, which is why building societies are now included in monetary statistics.

How did banks create money? Originally, there was £1000 of cash in circulation. That was the **money supply**. When paid into bank vaults, it went out of general circulation as the medium of exchange. But the public acquired £1000 of bank deposits against which cheques may be written. The money supply was still £1000. Then banks created overdrafts *not* fully backed by cash reserves. Now the public had £10 000 of deposits against which to write cheques. The money supply rose from £1000 to £10 000. Banks created money.

> The **money supply** is the value of the stock of the medium of exchange in circulation.

ACTIVITY 18.1 — A beginner's guide to financial markets

Financial asset   A piece of paper entitling the owner to a specified stream of interest payments for a specified period. Firms and governments raise money by selling financial assets. Buyers work out how much to bid for them by calculating the present value of the promised stream of payments. Assets are frequently retraded before the date at which the original issuer is committed to repurchase the piece of paper for a specified price.

Cash   Notes and coin, paying zero interest. The most liquid asset.

Bills   Short-term financial assets paying no interest directly but with a known date of repurchase by the original borrower at a known price. Consider a three-month Treasury bill. In April the government sells a piece of paper, promising to repurchase it for £100 in July. If people bid £98.50 in April, they will make 1.5 per cent in three months by holding the bill to July, when it is worth £100. As July gets nearer, the price at which the bill is retraded climbs towards £100. Buying it from someone else in June for £99.50 and reselling to the government in July for £100 still yields 0.5 per cent in a month, or over 6 per cent a year at compound interest. Treasury bills are easily bought and sold. Their price can only fluctuate over a small range (say, between £98 and £99 in May when they expire in July), so they are highly liquid. People can get their money out easily, cheaply and predictably.

Bonds   Longer-term financial assets. Look under UK gilts in the *Financial Times*. You will find a bond listed as 'Treasury 8pc 13'. In the year 2013 the government will buy back this bond for £100 (the usual repurchase price). Until then, the bondholder gets interest payments of £8 a year (8 per cent of the repurchase price). Bonds are less liquid than bills, not because they are hard to sell, but because the price for which they could be sold, and the cash this will generate, is less certain. To see why, we study the most extreme kind of bond.

Perpetuities   Bonds never repurchased by the original issuer, who pays interest for ever. Called Consols (consolidated stock) in the UK. 'Consols 2.5%' pay £2.50 a year for ever. Most were issued when interest rates were low. People originally would have bid around £100 for this Consol. Suppose interest rates on other assets rise to 10 per cent. Consols are retraded between people at around £25 each so that new purchasers of these old bonds get about 10 per cent on their financial investment. The person holding a bond makes a capital loss when other interest rates rise and the price of the bond falls. Moreover, since the price of Consols, once £100, could fall to £25 if interest rates rise a lot, Consol prices are much more volatile than the price of Treasury bills. The longer the remaining life of a bond, the more its current price can move around as existing bondholders try to sell on to new buyers at a rate of return in line with other assets today. Bonds can easily be bought and sold, but are not very liquid. You do not know how much you would get if you had to sell out in six months' time.

Gilt-edged securities   Government bonds in the UK. Gilt-edged because the government will not go bust and refuse to pay interest.

Company shares (equities)   Entitlements to dividends, that is, the part of firms' profits paid out to shareholders rather than retained to buy new machinery and buildings. In good years, dividends are high; in bad years dividends may be zero. Hence a risky asset that is not very liquid. Share prices are volatile. Firms could even go bust, making the shares worthless.

Securitization   The practice of aggregating collections of individual contracts (such as individual mortgages) into bundles of contracts that are then sold and bought by institutions far removed from the original deal. It was thought that this would spread the risk of an individual contract going wrong, thereby reducing risk in total. In practice, many of the buyers of these securities understood little about them and were amazed when the contracts all became worthless together. The most famous example was the securitization of US sub-prime mortgages – dubious loans to poor people who were often duped into taking out mortgages whose repayments they would later be unable to afford. Suddenly, many institutions around the world found themselves holding 'assets' that were revealed to be worth almost nothing, setting up a tsunami of insolvency.

The chart below shows the huge growth of securitization, and corresponding fall in old-fashioned bank loans, in the US in the run up to the financial crash.

Questions

(a) If cash pays no interest, why does anyone hold it?

(b) Since firms could use bills and bonds to raise finance, what advantages do they see in raising money through issuing equities?

(c) If it is good for firms to issue equities, can it simultaneously be good for investors?

(d) While the Treasury is closed and the prime minister is on holiday, the Bank of England announces it has made a loan to a regional bank whose depositors were panicking. Did the Bank of England think this was a liquidity crisis or a solvency crisis? Explain your answer.

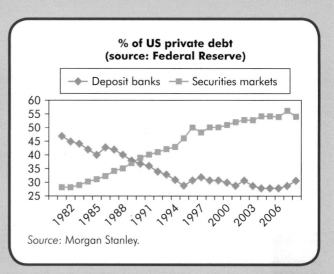

Source: Morgan Stanley.

To check your answers to these questions, go to page 685.

18.4   Financial crises

> A **financial panic** is a self-fulfilling prophecy. Believing a bank will be unable to pay, people rush to get their money out. But this makes the bank go bankrupt.

Everybody knows what the banks are doing. Usually, people do not mind. But if people believe that a bank has lent too much and will be unable to meet depositors' claims, there will be a *run* on the bank – a **financial panic**. If the bank cannot repay all depositors, you try to get your money out first while the bank can still pay. Since everyone does the same thing, they ensure that the bank is unable to pay. Some of its loans will be too illiquid to get back in time.

Notice that there are two kinds of financial crisis. First, a bank may have made loans that turn out to be worthless. They are no longer valuable assets of the bank. Liabilities now exceed assets and the bank is insolvent. Unless rapidly bailed out by injections of new assets by shareholders or the government, the bank will be declared bankrupt and it will be closed down. In such circumstances, depositors are simply being smart in trying to get their money out before this happens.

However, there may also be self-fulfilling panics even when the bank's assets are fine and the bank is not insolvent. If a depositor believes that other depositors will panic and withdraw money, it makes no sense to be last in the queue – the bank may have trouble selling enough liquid assets quickly enough to meet all the withdrawals, and it may be forced into difficulty by the panic itself.

We call this second case a **crisis of liquidity**, whereas the first case is a true crisis of insolvency. The problem for policy makers is to diagnose which is taking place. If the bank is fundamentally sound, lending it some cash or other liquid assets will allow the panic to subside and confidence to be restored. On the other hand, if the bank is truly insolvent, temporary loans will not help it. Its assets are less than its liabilities and more drastic action is required – donate enough government funds to make it solvent again, force shareholders to do the same, or close the bank.

> In a **liquidity crisis**, an institution is temporarily unable to meet immediate requests for payment even though its underlying assets exceed its liabilities.

When the financial crisis first erupted in the UK in 2008, with a panic by depositors of Northern Rock and long queues of people shown on the news, this was initially interpreted as a liquidity crisis that some temporary assistance, or government promises to guarantee depositors' money, could reverse. It soon became apparent that the Rock was in much deeper trouble than that. Its entire solvency was at stake.

Whether it is a liquidity or a **solvency crisis** determines which arm of government might potentially be involved in a solution. The Bank of England can make emergency loans if it expects them to be repaid in full, for there are then no long-term issues for taxpayers. Fixing insolvency, on the other hand, requires permanent injections of taxpayers' money, for which the authority of the Treasury (and ultimately the prime minister) is required. Since crises move quickly once they have begun, co-ordination of the fiscal and monetary authorities is vital if crisis resolution is to be effective.

> In a **solvency crisis**, an institution's assets have become less than its liabilities. It is bankrupt without a rapid new injection of assets from government or shareholders.

CASE 18.1

The sub-prime crisis and its aftermath

Most countries experienced an explosion in house prices around 2005–06. Inflation appeared to have been conquered, interest rates were low and borrowing did not look too risky. Many of those working in the financial sector – whether in banks or in property – were receiving bonuses for doing a large number of deals. There were strong incentives to dream up new products and find new lines of business.

In the US, one of these new products was the sub-prime mortgage, a housing loan to a low-income, high-risk person who had previously been unable to borrow in order to buy a house. Most of these mortgages were at variable interest rates. Although initially low and 'affordable', they could subsequently be raised if either general market interest rates rose or if lots of people started to default and it became necessary to build a larger risk premium into the interest rate. It is unclear how much of this was explained to the low-income people being signed up for first-time mortgages.

US house prices peaked in 2006. As they then fell, lenders got scared and began to raise mortgage interest rates, driving many of the poor to default. Suddenly, these sub-prime mortgages were worth a lot less than had been thought. And the crisis fed upon itself. The more scared people became, the more asset prices fell, validating the initial fears.

If mortgages had simply been issued by a few institutions specializing in loans for house purchase, the damage might have been quarantined. The US government would have had to decide whether to (a) let these particular institutions go bust, or (b) inject taxpayers' money to prop them up.

Securitization transformed a local crisis into a global problem. Smart financiers, driven by the prospect of new business and big personal bonuses, had bundled lots of individual sub-prime mortgages into large bundles and sold them on to new buyers in London, Frankfurt and Mumbai. The market was convinced that this trick was a bit like insurance – although one poor sub-prime household might go bust, they would not all go bust together. Holding a large bundle made them safer, just as an insurance company pools the risk of individual burglary by having large numbers of clients. This was the alchemy of risk reduction. A recipe for profits and bonuses.

Two things went wrong. First, buyers of securitized mortgages had miscalculated. It was quite likely that circumstances could arise in which all sub-prime borrowers would get into trouble at the same time – a fall in house prices, a fall in confidence, a rise in risk perception – especially if they could barely afford the loan in the first place. So smart bankers in London, New York and other financial capitals had mispriced the risk: the securitized bundles were riskier than had been thought.

Second, the perfect storm did indeed arise. As US house prices fell sharply, the chain of events was triggered. Banks found their assets worth much less than they had thought. Worse, the boards of the banks had not even realized the extent to which their bonus-hungry employees had exposed them to such large risks. The left-hand figure below shows annual changes in US house prices, which peaked around 2006. The right-hand side shows the level of UK house prices, which peaked around the end of 2007.

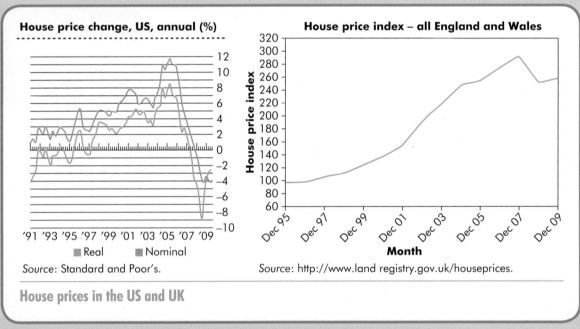

House prices in the US and UK

As the solvency of banks came into question, people became reluctant to lend to banks, and banks themselves became reluctant to lend to anyone else. Aware of the potentially fatal hole in their balance sheets, banks prioritized using resources to rebuild their own reserves. The entire, apparently well-oiled, system of liquidity dried up as banks disappeared from the lending business. One way to see how dramatic this was is to examine interest rate spreads, the difference between the interest rate banks were charging for the few scarce loans they were prepared to make, and the interest rate at which banks could borrow from the Bank of England.

The figure below plots the official bank rate, the interest rate at which commercial banks can borrow from the Bank of England, and LIBOR, the London interbank rate at which they are prepared to lend to other banks. In normal times, competition between banks means that the 'profit margin' between the lending rate and the borrowing rate is very small. Banks charging too much are quickly outcompeted by banks prepared to offer a better deal. For convenience, the right-hand panel calculates the actual spread – the difference between the two graphs in the left-hand panel.

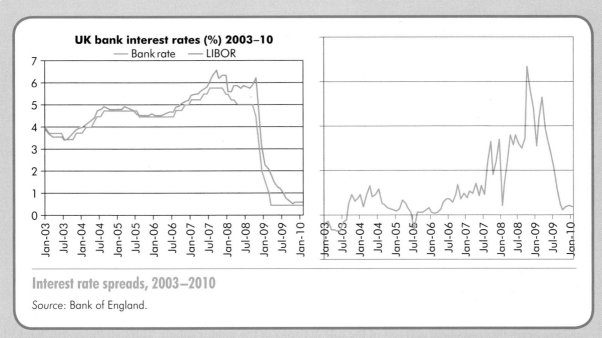

Interest rate spreads, 2003–2010

Source: Bank of England.

This figure is a thermometer with which to monitor the health of the banking system. In a healthy system, banks feel confident, competition prevails and spreads are very small. When a crisis breaks out, spreads shoot up, raising the price to ration loans only to the very safest customers. And the volume of bank lending collapses. The figure shows spreads rising as early as 2006, sharply in 2008, and more sharply still in 2009. Notice that by January 2010 spreads had returned almost to normal levels. Markets believed that, in the absence of a major new shock, they were through the worst of the financial crisis.

The table below presents a run-through of events, from a UK perspective.

2006	US house prices start to fall, the sub-prime crisis begins, interest spreads edge up around the world, bank lending slows down, liquidity begins to evaporate.
2007	UK bank Northern Rock hits a liquidity crisis in September 2007 – not yet because its asset values have fallen (UK house prices still rising) – but because UK credit markets have dried up and the Rock cannot roll over its short-term loans. Borrowing short term to lend long term for housing loans is always a risky business. Crisis temporarily resolved once Bank of England agrees to provide liquidity financing to Northern Rock.
2008	February – with UK house prices now having peaked, the market becomes worried not just about Northern Rock's ability to refinance its loans, but also about the value of its underlying assets. A full-blown insolvency crisis. UK government decides to nationalize the Rock. March – US investment bank Bear Sterns, a pioneer of securitization of mortgage-backed securities, suffers an insolvency crisis. Competitor JP Morgan Chase agrees to buy Bear Sterns for a much reduced price. Getting competitors to take over failing banks is often a good way out, since no bankruptcy or severe dislocation ensues. September – US Treasury has to bail out Freddie Mac and Fannie Mae, the two largest mortgage lenders in the US. US investment bank giant Lehman Brothers is allowed to go bankrupt without US Treasury managing to arrange a satisfactory bailout. Arguably the single event that then triggered financial panic around the world, from which no country was immune. October – Royal Bank of Scotland, having overextended itself buying Dutch bank ABN AMRO at a price that subsequently proved much too high, faces a solvency crisis, temporarily resolved by UK Treasury taking 58 per cent stake in RBS.

| 2009 | January – UK government persuades Lloyds bank to buy the potentially insolvent Halifax Bank of Scotland group. Lloyds' shareholders subsequently discover HBOS worth much less than they paid for it. The outcome appears good for the system but bad for Lloyds.
UK taxpayer eventually has to take an 84 per cent stake in RBS to prevent it going bankrupt. Governments around the world gradually admit to the scale of government injections to bail out their banks. Since taxes are not raised to pay for this, the initial consequence is a huge jump in levels of government deficits and government debt. |
| 2010+ | Where governments have taken large stakes in banks, the key issue will be how much of this money they eventually recover. If the assets are permanently bad, all the injection is needed to restore the banks' solvency. However, if there was an element of liquidity crisis, or if asset prices fell too much in the panic, it is possible that asset values will recover enough to allow substantial repayments by banks (or privatization of those that were nationalized). In the extreme case, governments might even eventually make some profits. Future behaviour of banks likely to be more cautious, and changes in the regulation of banks are now being discussed. |

18.5 The traditional theory of money supply

We begin the traditional account of the role of banks in the money supply. Through the *central bank*, the Bank of England in the UK, the government controls the issue of token money in a modern economy. Private creation of token money must be outlawed when its value as a medium of exchange exceeds the direct cost of its production.

People hold cash for many reasons. It makes transactions easier and cheaper. Moreover, some people do not trust banks; they keep their savings under the bed. Remarkably, only three-quarters of British households have chequing accounts. Some people hold cash in order to make illegal or tax-evading transactions in the 'black economy'. In a modern economy most of the broad measure of money is in bank deposits.

> The **money multiplier** is the ratio of broad money to the monetary base.

Suppose, as was the case a few years ago, UK banks hold cash reserves equal to 1 per cent of their total deposits, and the private sector holds cash in circulation equal to 3 per cent of the value of sight deposits. Maths 18.1 shows that this implies a **money multiplier** of 26. Each £100 rise in the monetary base increases the money supply by £2600.

MATHS 18.1

The money multiplier

Suppose banks wish to hold cash reserves R equal to some fraction c_b of deposits D, and that the private sector holds cash in circulation C equal to a fraction c_p of deposits D:

$$R = c_b D \quad \text{and} \quad C = c_p D$$

The monetary base H is either in circulation or in bank vaults:

$$H = C + R = (c_p + c_b)D$$

Finally, the money supply is circulating currency C plus deposits D:

$$M = C + D = (c_p + 1)D$$

These last two equations give us the money multiplier, the ratio of M to H:

$$M/H = (c_p + 1)/(c_p + c_b) > 1$$

If the public hold cash to the value of 3 per cent of their deposits, $c_p = 0.03$, and if banks hold reserves equal to 1 per cent of deposits, $c_b = 0.01$. Hence the money multiplier is

$$M/H = 1.03/(0.04) = 26$$

the ratio of broad money to the monetary base. The ratio M/R, dividing broad money only by bank reserves but not by cash held outside the banks, is called the **bank deposit multiplier**.

> The **bank deposit multiplier** is the ratio of broad money to bank reserves.

At present, it is more important to remember that a fall in either the banks' desired cash reserve ratio or the private sector's desired ratio of cash to bank deposits raises the money multiplier. For a given monetary base, the money supply rises.

What determines the cash reserve ratio desired by banks? The higher the interest rate spread, the more banks wish to lend and the more they risk a low ratio of cash reserves to deposits. Conversely, the more unpredictable are withdrawals from deposits, or the fewer lending opportunities banks have in very liquid loans, the higher cash reserves they have to maintain for any level of deposits.

The public's desired ratio of cash to deposits partly reflects institutional factors, for example whether firms pay wages by cheque or by cash. It also depends on the incentive to hold cash to make untraceable payments to evade taxes. And credit cards reduce the use of cash. Credit cards are a temporary means of payment, a *money substitute* not money itself. A signed credit card slip cannot be used for *further* purchases. Soon, you have to settle your account using money. Nevertheless, since credit cards allow people to carry less cash in their pocket, their increasing use reduces the desired ratio of cash to bank deposits.

> The **monetary base**, or **narrow money**, is the quantity of notes and coins in private circulation plus the quantity of reserves held by commercial banks.

Figure 18.1 summarizes the traditional account of the **monetary base** and the money supply. The monetary base, or stock of high-powered money, is held either

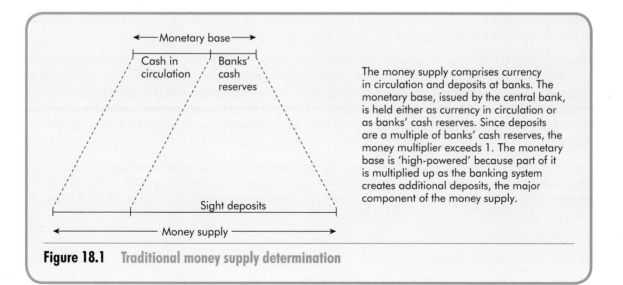

The money supply comprises currency in circulation and deposits at banks. The monetary base, issued by the central bank, is held either as currency in circulation or as banks' cash reserves. Since deposits are a multiple of banks' cash reserves, the money multiplier exceeds 1. The monetary base is 'high-powered' because part of it is multiplied up as the banking system creates additional deposits, the major component of the money supply.

Figure 18.1 Traditional money supply determination

as cash reserves by the banks or as cash in circulation. Since bank deposits are a multiple of banks' cash reserves, the money multiplier exceeds unity. The money multiplier is larger (a) the lower the non-bank public's desired ratio of cash to bank deposits, giving the banks more cash with which to create a multiplied deposit expansion, and (b) the lower is the banks' desired ratio of cash to deposits, leading them to create more deposits for any given cash reserves.

18.6 UK money supply after the 2006 reforms

The key aspect of the traditional account was that bank reserves earned no interest – they were either cash in bank vaults or zero-interest accounts with the central bank. Those running the banks faced a tension between the safety of holding reserves and the risky profits to be made by borrowing in order to lend at even higher interest rates. Many countries still run their banking system this way.

> **Broad money** includes all assets fulfilling the functions of money, and is principally bank deposits.

London has always been at the forefront of financial innovation in order to preserve its status as a global financial centre. Forcing banks to hold zero-interest reserves is partly a tax on bank profits, and may be unnecessary. What matters to the central bank, in thinking how its supply of narrow money will be multiplied into **broad money**, is its ability to predict the size of bank reserves, not the fact that reserves earn zero interest. Moreover, in our modern electronic economy, most of the bank reserves that matter are those credited electronically to banks' reserve accounts at the Bank of England, not those held in old-fashioned physical cash in their bank vaults. Nowadays the Bank of England adds to the monetary base not by printing banknotes but by electronic creation of reserve accounts for banks.

In 2006 the Bank of England therefore introduced a new system in London. Once a month, its Monetary Policy Committee (MPC) would meet to set the bank rate, the interest rate at which the Bank of England would lend to banks in normal circumstances. Commercial banks were then free to *choose* the level of reserves they would hold at the Bank of England during the month to the next MPC meeting. Provided banks did what they said, the Bank of England would pay interest on these reserves. If banks deviated by more than 1 per cent from their promise for the month, the Bank of England would levy heavy penalties.

This new system (a) made London banks more competitive within the global economy, since they no longer had to carry a chunk of their assets as zero-interest bearing reserves, and (b) was therefore expected to lead to healthier financial markets.

However, since the monetary base now comprises zero-interest-bearing cash and interest-bearing reserves with the Bank of England, aggregating these two assets together no longer makes sense. The Bank of England no longer publishes data on the monetary base. What remains the case is that banks' deposits are much, much larger than banks' reserves. The modern theory of money supply recognizes that bank reserves are not simply, nor even mainly, cash. Most bank reserves are interest-bearing accounts held at the Bank of England.

Earlier in this chapter we pointed out that the priority for banks close to insolvency is to restore their solvency by rebuilding their assets and reserves. What do you think happened to the size of the money multiplier during the financial crisis? You know enough to work out the answer, which is shown in Concept 18.2.

The collapse of bank lending

CONCEPT 18.2

The bank deposit multiplier

The money multiplier is $M/(R + C_p)$, the broad money supply M divided by banks' reserves R and cash held by the public C_p. Prior to the financial crisis, it had a value of around 26. The bank deposit multiplier M/R is several times larger, since the denominator is smaller. The figure shows that, just before the crisis, the bank deposit multiplier was around 90. Banks had £90 of deposits for every £1 in reserves.

However, the more bank lending dried up during the credit crunch, the smaller the bank deposit multiplier became. For any given level of reserves, broad money was much smaller. The figure shows that the bank deposit multiplier fell from 90 to around 14.

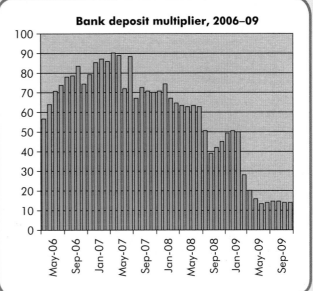

Bank deposit multiplier, 2006–09

This has two implications. First, the theory of monetary control, which we discuss in Chapter 19, cannot assume that financial multipliers are stable over time: they are very sensitive to the level of confidence in banks and the extent of risk-taking they feel able to undertake.

Second, without some additional change in behaviour by the Bank of England, the collapse of the bank deposit multiplier threatened to lead to a corresponding collapse of broad money. The attempt to prevent this, known as quantitative easing, is discussed in Chapter 19.

Measures of money

Money is the medium of exchange available to make transactions. Hence, the money supply is cash in circulation outside banks, plus bank deposits. It sounds simple, but is not. Two issues arise: which bank deposits, and why only bank deposits?

We can think of a spectrum of liquidity. Cash, by definition, is completely liquid. Sight deposits (chequing accounts) are almost as liquid. Time deposits (savings accounts) used to be less liquid, but now many banks offer automatic transfer between savings and chequing accounts when the latter run low. Savings deposits are almost as liquid as chequing accounts.

UK statistics distinguish between *retail* and *wholesale* deposits. Retail deposits are made in high-street branches at the advertised rate of interest. Wholesale deposits, big one-off deals between a corporate depositor and a bank at a negotiated interest rate, are also quite liquid.

Everyone used to be clear about what a bank was, and hence whose deposits counted towards the money supply. Financial deregulation blurred this distinction in the UK and US, and is now doing so in continental Europe. Before 1980, UK banks did not lend for house purchase, and cheques on building society deposits could not be used at the supermarket checkout. Now 'banks' compete vigorously for mortgages, supermarket chains are in the banking business, and building society cheques are widely accepted as a means of payment.

Table 18.2   Narrow and broad money in the UK, December 2009

	£ billion
cash in circulation (outside central bank)	46
+ retail deposits in banks and building societies	1134
+ wholesale deposits	867
= Money supply M4 (broad money)	2047

Source: Bank of England.

There is no longer a reason to exclude building society deposits from measures of the money supply. Since January 2010, UK monetary statistics do not even distinguish between banks and building societies.

Table 18.2 shows the components of broad money in the UK in 2009. Notes and coins in circulation outside the Bank of England are the most liquid form of the medium of exchange. To this we add retail deposits in banks and building societies. Next, we add wholesale deposits. The sum of all these is M4, the most commonly used measure of broad money.

18.7   The demand for money

> The **demand for money** is a demand for *real* money balances.

The quantity of money M4 in the UK was 90 times higher in 2010 than in 1965. Why did UK residents hold so much extra money? We focus on three variables that affect money demand: interest rates, the price level and real income.

Motives for holding money

Money is a stock. It is the quantity of circulating currency and deposits *held* at any given time. Holding money is not the same as *spending* it. We hold money now to spend it later.

Money is the medium of exchange, for which it must also be a store of value. These two functions of money provide the reasons why people wish to hold it. People can hold their wealth in various forms – money, bills, bonds, equities and property. For simplicity, assume that there are only two assets: money, the medium of exchange that pays no interest, and bonds, which we use to stand for all other interest-bearing assets that are not directly a means of payment. As people earn income, they add to their wealth. As they spend, they deplete their wealth. How should people divide their wealth between money and bonds?

> The **cost of holding money** is the interest given up by holding money rather than bonds.
>
> The **transactions motive** for holding money reflects the fact that payments and receipts are *not* synchronized.

People **hold money** only if there is a benefit to offset this cost. What is that benefit?

The transactions motive

Transacting by barter is costly in time and effort. Holding money economizes on these costs. If all transactions were perfectly synchronized, we could be paid at the same instant as we did our spending. Except at that instant, we need hold no money at all.

Must we hold money between being paid and making subsequent purchases? We could put our income into interest-earning assets, to be resold later when we need money for purchases. However, every time we buy and sell assets there are brokerage and bank charges. And it takes an eagle eye to keep track of cash flow and judge the precise moment at which money is needed and assets must be sold. If small sums are involved, the extra interest does not compensate for the brokerage fees, and the time and effort. It is easier to hold some money.

How much money we need to hold depends on the value of the transactions we later wish to make and the degree of synchronization of our payments and receipts. Money is a nominal variable not a real variable. How much £100 buys depends on the price of goods. If all prices double, our receipts and our payments double in nominal terms. To transact as before we need to hold twice as much money.

We need a given amount of real money, nominal money deflated by the price level, to make a given quantity of transactions. When the price level doubles, other things equal, the demand for nominal money balances doubles, leaving the demand for real money balances unaltered. People want money because of its purchasing power in terms of the goods it will buy.

Real GNP is a good proxy for the total real value of transactions. Thus we assume that the transactions motive for holding real money balances rises with real income.

The transactions motive for holding money also depends on the synchronization of payments and receipts. Suppose, instead of shopping throughout the week, households shop only on the day they get paid. Over the week, national income and total transactions are unaltered, but people now *hold* less money over the week.[5]

A nation's habits for making payments usually change only slowly. In our simplified model we assume that the degree of synchronization is constant over time. Thus we focus on real income as *the* measure of the transactions motive for holding *real* money balances.

Of course, the degree of synchronization is not literally constant over time. For example, compared with having to queue up in a bank to withdraw cash from one's account, the introduction of ATMs (cash machines) made it easier to get cash, even when banks were closed. People therefore held less cash on average in their pocket because they could easily get more. Conversely, bank accounts were even more useful than previously.

The precautionary motive

We live in an uncertain world. Uncertainty about the timing of receipts and payments creates a precautionary motive for holding money.

Suppose you buy a lot of interest-earning bonds and get by with a small amount of money. Walking down the street you see a great bargain in a shop window, but have too little money to close the deal. By the time you cash in some bonds, the bargain is gone, snapped up by someone with ready money.

How can we measure the benefits from holding money for precautionary reasons? The payoff grows with the volume of transactions we undertake and with the degree of uncertainty. If uncertainty is roughly constant over time, the level of transactions determines the benefit of real money held for precautionary reasons. As with the transactions motive, we use real GNP to proxy the level of transactions. Thus, other things equal, the higher is real income, the stronger is the **precautionary motive** for holding money.

> In an uncertain world, there is a **precautionary motive** to hold money. In advance, we decide to hold money to meet contingencies that we cannot yet foresee.

The transactions and precautionary motives are the main reasons to hold the medium of exchange, and are most relevant to the benefits from holding a narrow measure of money. The wider measure, M4, includes higher-interest-earning deposits. The wider the definition of money, the less important are the transactions and precautionary motives that relate to money as a medium of exchange, and the more we must take account of money as a store of value.

---

5   By allowing us to pay all at once when the statement arrives monthly, credit cards have this effect.

The asset motive

Forget the need to transact. Think of someone deciding in which assets to hold wealth. At some distant date, wealth may be spent. In the short run, the aim is a good but safe rate of return.

Some assets, such as company shares, on average pay a high return but are risky. Some years their return is *very* high, in other years it is negative. When share prices fall, shareholders make a capital loss that swamps the dividends they receive. Other assets are less risky, but their average rate of return is correspondingly lower.

How should people divide their portfolios between safe and risky assets? You might like to reread Chapter 13. Since people dislike risk, they will not put all their eggs in one basket. As well as holding some risky assets, they will keep some of their wealth in safe assets.

> The **asset motive** for holding money reflects dislike of risk. People sacrifice a high average rate of return to obtain a portfolio with a lower but safer rate of return.

The **asset motive** for holding money is important when we consider why people hold broad measures of money such as M4.

The demand for money: prices, real income and interest rates

The transactions, precautionary and asset motives suggest that there are benefits to holding money. But there is also a cost, the interest forgone by not holding high-interest-earning assets instead. People hold money up to the point at which the marginal benefit of holding another pound just equals its marginal cost. Figure 18.2 illustrates how much money people want to hold.

People want money for its purchasing power over goods. The horizontal axis plots real money holdings; nominal money in current pounds divided by the average price of goods and services. The horizontal line *MC* is the marginal cost of holding money, the interest forgone by not holding bonds. *MC* shifts up if interest rates rise.

The *MB* schedule is the marginal benefit of holding money. We draw *MB* for a given real GNP measuring the transactions undertaken. For this level of transactions, it is possible but difficult to get by with low real money holdings. We have to watch purchases and receipts and be quick to invest money as it comes in and ready to sell off bonds just before we make a purchase. Nor do we have much precautionary money. We may be frustrated or inconvenienced if, unexpectedly, we want to make a purchase or settle a debt.

With low real money holdings, the marginal benefit of another pound is high. We can put less effort into timing our transfers between money and bonds, and we have more money for unforeseen contingencies. For a given real income and level of transactions, the marginal benefit of the last pound of money holdings declines as we hold more real

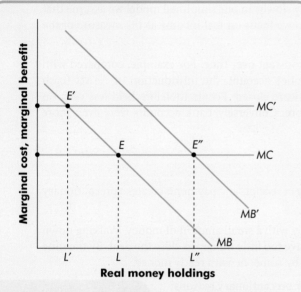

The horizontal axis shows the purchasing power of money in terms of goods. The MC schedule shows the interest sacrificed by putting the last pound into money rather than bonds. The MB schedule is drawn for a given real income and shows the marginal benefits of the last pound of money. The marginal benefit falls as money holdings increase. The desired point is *E*, at which marginal cost and marginal benefit are equal. An increase in interest rates, a rise in the opportunity cost schedule from MC to MC′, reduces desired money holdings from *L* to *L′*. An increase in real income increases the marginal benefit of adding to real balances. The MB schedule shifts up to MB′. Facing the schedule MC, a shift from MB to MB′ increases real money holdings to *L″*.

Figure 18.2 Desired money holdings

Table 18.3 The demand for money

Quantity demanded	Effect of rise in		
	Price level	Real income	Interest rate
Nominal money	Rises in proportion	Rises	Falls
Real money	Unaffected	Rises	Falls

money. With more real money, we have plenty both for precautionary purposes and for transactions purposes. Life is easier. The marginal benefit of yet more money holding is low.

Given our real income and transactions, desired money holdings are at E in Figure 18.2. For any level of real money below L, the marginal benefit of another pound exceeds its marginal cost in interest forgone. We should hold more money. Above L, the marginal cost exceeds the marginal benefit and we should hold less. The optimal level of money holding is L.

To emphasize the effect of prices, real income and interest rates on the quantity of money demanded, we now change each of these variables in turn. If all prices of goods and services double but interest rates and real income are unaltered, neither MC nor MB shifts. The desired point remains E and the desired level of *real* money remains L. Since prices have doubled, people hold twice as much nominal money to preserve their real money balances at L.

If interest rates on bonds rise, the cost of holding money rises. Figure 18.2 shows this upward shift from MC to MC'. The desired point is now E' and the desired real money holding falls from L to L'. Higher interest rates reduce the quantity of real money demanded.[6]

Finally, consider a rise in real income. At each level of real money holdings, the marginal benefit of the last pound is higher than before. With more transactions to undertake and a greater need for precautionary balances, a given quantity of real money does not make life as easy as it did when transactions and real income were lower. The benefit of a bit more money is now greater. Hence we show the MB schedule shifting up to MB' when real income rises.

At the original interest rate and MC schedule, the desired level of money balances is L_0. Thus a rise in real income raises the quantity of real money balances demanded. Table 18.3 summarizes our discussion of the demand for money as a medium of exchange.

So far we have studied the demand for M0, the narrowest measure of money. Wider definitions of money must also recognize the asset motive for holding money. To explain the demand for M4, we interpret MC as the average extra return by putting the last pound into risky assets rather than time deposits, which are safe but yield a lower return. For a given wealth, MB is the marginal benefit of time deposits in reducing the risk of the portfolio. If no wealth is invested in time deposits, the portfolio is very risky. A bad year is a disaster. There is a big benefit in having some time deposits. As the quantity of time deposits increases, the danger of a disaster recedes and the marginal benefit of more time deposits falls.

A rise in the average interest differential between risky assets and time deposits shifts the cost of holding broad money from MC to MC', reducing the quantity of broad money demanded. Higher wealth shifts the marginal benefit from MB to MB'. More time deposits are demanded.

---

6   The cost of holding money is the differential return between bonds and money. If π is the inflation rate and r the nominal interest rate, the real interest rate is $r - \pi$. In financial terms, the real return on money is $-\pi$, the rate at which the purchasing power of money is eroded by inflation. The differential real return between bonds and money is $(r - \pi) - (-\pi) = r$. The *nominal* interest rate is the opportunity cost of holding money.

Table 18.4 Holdings of M4, 1965–2009

	1965	2009
Index of:		
Nominal M4	100	10 100
Real M4	100	800
Real GDP	100	285
Interest rate (%)	6	1–4

Sources: Bank of England; OECD.

Explaining the rise in money holdings from 1965 to 2009

Why were nominal money holdings 90 times higher in 2009 than in 1965? We have identified three explanations: prices, real income and nominal interest rates. Table 18.4 shows how these variables changed over the period.

Although nominal money holdings rose 101-fold, the price level also rose a lot between 1965 and 2009. Table 18.4 shows real money rising eight-fold over the period. Real GDP was almost three times its initial level. Higher real output and income raised the quantity of real money demanded. Nominal interest rates fell substantially, which also added to the demand for money.

Summary

- **Money** has four functions: a **medium of exchange** or means of payment, a **store of value**, a **unit of account** and a **standard of deferred payment**. Its use as a medium of exchange distinguishes money from other assets.

- In a **barter economy**, trading is costly because there must be a double coincidence of wants. Using a medium of exchange reduces the cost of matching buyers and sellers, letting society devote scarce resources to other things. A **token money** has a higher value as a medium of exchange than in any other use. Because its monetary value greatly exceeds its production cost, token money economizes a lot on the resources needed for transacting.

- Token money is accepted either because people believe it can subsequently be used to make payments or because the government makes it legal tender. The government controls the supply of token money.

- **Banks create money** by making loans and creating deposits that are not fully backed by cash reserves. These deposits add to the medium of exchange. Deciding how many reserves to hold involves a trade-off between interest earnings and the danger of insolvency.

- Modern banks attract deposits by acting as **financial intermediaries**. A national system of clearing cheques, a convenient form of payment, attracts funds into sight deposits. Interest-bearing time deposits attract further funds. In turn, banks lend out money as short-term liquid loans, as longer-term less liquid advances, or by purchasing securities.

- Sophisticated financial markets for short-term liquid lending allow modern banks to operate with very low cash reserves relative to deposits. The **money supply** is currency in circulation plus deposits. Most is the latter.

- The **monetary base M0** is currency in circulation plus banks' cash reserves. The **money multiplier**, the ratio of the money supply to the monetary base, is big. The money multiplier is larger (a) the smaller is the desired cash ratio of the banks, and (b) the smaller is the private sector's desired ratio of cash in circulation to deposits.

- **Financial deregulation** has allowed building societies into the banking business. **M4** is a broad measure of money and includes deposits at both banks and building societies.

- The **demand for money** is a demand for real money, for its subsequent purchasing power over goods. The demand for **narrow money** balances the transactions and precautionary benefits of holding another pound with the interest sacrificed by not holding interest-bearing assets instead. The quantity of real money demanded falls as the interest rate rises. Higher real income raises real money demand at each interest rate.

- For **wide money** such as M4, the asset motive for holding money also matters. When other interest-bearing assets are risky, people diversify by holding some safe money. With no immediate need to transact, this leads to an asset demand for holding interest-bearing bank deposits. This demand is larger, the larger the total wealth to be invested and the lower the interest differential between deposits and risky assets.

Review questions

connect

1 (a) A person trades in a car when buying another. Is the used car a medium of exchange? Is this a barter transaction? (b) Could you tell by watching someone buying mints (white discs) with coins (bronze discs) which one is money?

EASY

2 Initially gold coins were used as money but people could melt them down and use the gold for industrial purposes. (a) What must have been the relative value of gold in these two uses? (b) Explain the circumstances in which gold could become a token money. (c) Explain the circumstances in which gold could disappear from monetary circulation completely.

3 How do commercial banks create money?

4 Would it make sense to include (a) travellers' cheques, (b) student rail cards, or (c) credit cards in measures of the money supply?

5 Sight deposits = 30, time deposits = 60, banks' cash reserves = 2, currency in circulation = 12, building society deposits = 20. Calculate M0 and M4.

6 Common fallacies   Why are these statements wrong? (a) Since their liabilities equal their assets, banks cannot create anything. (b) The money supply has risen because of tax evasion. Since cash is untraceable, people are putting less in the banks.

7 Which of these is the correct answer? After the financial crash, bank lending to the private sector slumped because: (a) new regulations were introduced, (b) banks were broken up to prevent another crisis, (c) banks thought prospective borrowers were too risky, (d) the value of bank reserves had fallen, (e) answers a and d, (f) answers c and d.

8 Saying that banks had become too big to fail meant: (a) large banks are safer, (b) large banks are less safe, or (c) managers of large banks realize they can take risks because politicians will have to bail them out if things go wrong?

MEDIUM

9 Suppose banks raise interest rates on time deposits whenever interest rates on bank loans and other assets rise. Does a rise in the general level of interest rates have a big or small effect on the demand for time deposits?

10 Imagine a diagram with the interest rate on the vertical axis and the quantity of money on the horizontal axis. (a) Draw the demand for broad money. (b) Suppose the supply curve is vertical. Show money market equilibrium. (c) Depict the impact effect of the financial crash on supply and demand for broad money. (d) Why did monetary policy create substantial quantities of narrow money in these circumstance?

11 In the previous diagram, what would be the consequence of a sharp increase in confidence regarding the health of the financial sector? How would monetary policy be likely to respond?

12 Suppose banks initially wish to hold reserves R equal to 1 per cent of the deposits D that they provide, and that the general public wish to hold cash C equal to 2 per cent of the deposits that they hold. The monetary base is $H = C + R$, and broad money is cash with the public plus bank reserves. What is the value of the money multiplier?

13 Since credit cards can be used to make payments, why are they not treated as money?

HARD

14 *Essay question* Lots of institutions accept deposits and reissue them on demand – building societies, Christmas savings clubs and theatre cloakrooms. What is the key feature of banks that distinguishes them from other institutions? Why does this matter?

For solutions to these questions contact your lecturer.

Interest rates and monetary transmission

Learning Outcomes

By the end of this chapter, you should understand:

1 how a central bank can affect the money supply

2 quantitative easing

3 the central bank's role in financial regulation

4 money market equilibrium

5 an intermediate target for monetary policy

6 the transmission mechanism of monetary policy

7 how a central bank sets interest rates

8 how interest rates affect consumption and investment demand

Today, every country of any size has a central bank. Originally private firms in business for profit, central banks came under public control as governments placed more emphasis on monetary policy. Founded in 1694, the Bank of England (www.bankofengland.co.uk) was not nationalized until 1947. The Federal Reserve System, the US central bank, was not set up until 1913. Within the eurozone, individual central banks survive, but the European Central Bank is in charge of the single monetary policy.

This chapter examines the role of the central bank, and shows how it influences financial markets. The central bank influences the supply of money. Combining this with the demand for money, examined in the previous chapter, we analyse money market equilibrium. The central bank's monopoly on the supply of cash allows it to control equilibrium interest rates. Finally, we discuss how monetary policy decides what interest rates to set.

> A **central bank** is banker to the government and to the banks. It also conducts monetary policy.

19.1 The Bank of England

The Bank of England, usually known simply as the Bank, is the UK central bank. It is divided into Issue and Banking Departments. Its balance sheet is shown in Table 19.1.

Table 19.1 Bank of England, balance sheet, November 2009

Liabilities	£bn	Assets	£bn
Cash in circulation	49	Reverse repos	28
Banks' reserves	146	Bonds bought in the market	14
Other liabilities	40	Other assets	193
Total liabilities	235	Total assets	235

Source: Bank of England.

Banknotes and coins are liabilities of the Bank. When you hold £1, it is a debt of the Bank of England. When commercial banks have reserves at the Bank of England, these are now owed by the Bank to the commercial banks who are the ultimate owners of these reserves. Cash in circulation, banks' reserves held at the Bank of England, and other liabilities of the Bank came in total to £235 billion in November 2009.

What were the corresponding assets? To introduce cash into circulation, the Issue Department engages in open market operations to buy financial securities issued by the government, commercial firms or local authorities. One particular financial security, shown in Table 19.1, is a reverse repo. We explain below what this means. In 2009 the largest class of assets of the Bank was in fact 'other assets', which were largely explained by the programme of 'quantitative easing' described in Concept 19.1. Together, these assets came to £235 billion.

Table 19.1 resembles the balance sheet of a commercial bank, with one key difference. *A central bank cannot go bankrupt.* You take £50 to the Bank and cash it in for £50. The Bank gives you £50 in cash. It can always create new cash. Hence, it can never run out of money.

> A **repo** is the sale of an asset with a simultaneous agreement to repurchase later.
> A **reverse repo** is a purchase with a simultaneous agreement to resell later.

What are **repos** and **reverse repos**? In American movies, people in arrears on their loans have their cars repossessed by the repo man. In the mid-1990s, London finally established a repo market. Frankfurt and Milan had operated repo markets for years. Was the ultra-cautious German Bundesbank involved in dubious car loans?

A repo is a *sale and repurchase agreement*. A bank sells you a bond, simultaneously agreeing to buy it back at a specified price on a particular future date. You have made the bank a short-term loan secured or 'backed' by the long-term bond temporarily in your ownership. Thus repos use the outstanding stock of *long-term* assets as backing for new and secured *short-term* loans.

One party's repo is the other party's reverse repo. Suppose you get a short-term loan from the bank by initially selling bonds to the bank, plus an agreement for you to repurchase the bonds at a specified date in the near future at a price agreed now. Reverse repos are effectively secured temporary fixed-term loans by the Bank. That is why they appear on the asset side of its balance sheet.

Repos and reverse repos are very like other short-term lending and borrowing. The Bank of England used to alter cash in circulation by buying or selling Treasury bills. Now it follows other central banks in using the repo market to conduct these 'open market operations' in order to alter cash in circulation.

19.2 Traditional means of monetary control

> The **money supply** is currency in circulation *outside* the banking system, plus deposits of commercial banks and building societies.

The **money supply** M4 is partly a liability of the Bank (currency in private circulation) and partly a liability of banks (bank deposits). Henceforth, we talk of 'banks' without distinguishing between banks and building societies.

The central bank can therefore affect broad money M4 either by affecting the cash in circulation or by affecting the number of deposits for any given amount of cash in circulation. We begin with policies that affect the latter.

Reserve requirements

Banks can hold more than the required cash reserves but not less. If their reserves fall below the required amount, they must immediately borrow cash, usually from the central bank, to restore their **required reserve ratio**.

> A **required reserve ratio** is a minimum ratio of cash reserves to deposits that banks are required to hold.

Suppose banks have £1 billion in cash and, for commercial purposes, want cash reserves equal to 5 per cent of deposits. Deposits are 20 times cash reserves. Banks create £20 billion of deposits against their £1 billion cash reserves. However, if there is a reserve requirement of 10 per cent, banks only create £10 billion deposits against cash reserves of £1 billion. The money supply falls from £20 billion to £10 billion.

When the central bank imposes a higher reserve requirement than the reserve ratio that prudent banks would anyway have maintained, the effect is fewer bank deposits and a lower money supply for any amount of cash in circulation. Raising the reserve requirement reduces the money supply.

The discount rate

Suppose banks think the *minimum* safe ratio of cash to deposits is 10 per cent. It does not matter whether this figure is a commercial judgement or a requirement imposed by the Bank. Banks may also hold extra cash. If their cash reserves are 12 per cent of deposits, how far dare they let their cash fall towards the 10 per cent minimum?

> The **discount rate** is the interest rate that the Bank charges when banks want to borrow cash.

Banks balance the interest rate on extra lending against the cost incurred if withdrawals push their cash reserves below the critical 10 per cent. If the central bank lends to banks at market interest rates, there is no penalty incurred from being caught short and having to borrow from the central bank. Banks lend as much as they can and their cash reserves fall to the minimum required.

Suppose the Bank only lends to banks at an interest rate above market interest rates. Now commercial banks will not drive down their reserves to the minimum permitted. They hold extra cash as a cushion, to avoid possibly having to borrow from the central bank at penalty rates.

By setting the discount rate above general interest rates, the Bank can induce banks voluntarily to hold extra cash reserves. Bank deposits are a lower multiple of banks' cash reserves, and the money supply is lower for any given level of cash in circulation. Variations in the discount rate can change the money supply.

Open market operations

Whereas the previous two methods of monetary control alter the amount of deposits created for any given amount of cash in circulation, open market operations alter the amount of cash in circulation. Since this then affects the amount of deposits that banks wish to create, open market operations alter the money supply both directly (via the effect on cash in circulation) and indirectly (via the induced effect on the number of deposits created).

The Bank prints £1 million of new banknotes and buys bonds on the **open market**. There are £1 million fewer bonds in private hands but £1 million more in cash. Some of the extra cash is held in private circulation but most is deposited with the banks, which then expand deposit lending against their higher cash reserves. Conversely, if the Bank sells £1 million of bonds from its existing holdings, the monetary base falls by £1 million. Banks lose cash reserves, have to reduce deposit lending and the money supply falls.

> An **open market operation** occurs when the central bank alters the monetary base by buying or selling financial securities in the open market.

Open market operations are nowadays the principal channel by which the central bank affects the money supply. Having discussed the central bank's role in monetary control, we turn next to its role in financial stability.

19.3 Lender of last resort

Modern fractional reserve banking lets society produce the medium of exchange with tiny inputs of scarce physical resources. But the efficient production of the medium of exchange yields a system of fractional reserve banking vulnerable to financial panics. Since banks have too few reserves to meet a withdrawal of all their deposits, a hint of big withdrawals may become a self-fulfilling prophecy as people scramble to get their money out before the banks go bust.

In Chapter 18 we described how the central bank can create and lend cash to banks to stave off a liquidity crisis. This requires a guarantee that banks can get cash if they really need it. The central bank is the only institution that can manufacture cash in unlimited amounts. The threat of financial panics is greatly diminished if it is known that the central bank will act as **lender of last resort**. As lender of last resort, the Bank can maintain confidence in the banking system, provided the underlying solvency of banks is not threatened. What went wrong in 2008/09 is that some banks acquired assets that turned out to be worthless, and became insolvent. Last resort lending could not save them since it made no difference to their underlying solvency.

> The **lender of last resort** lends to banks when financial panic threatens the financial system.

Prudential regulation

The prospect of insolvency raises two issues: how to respond to a particular insolvency crisis, and how to prevent such a crisis arising in the first place.

> A **capital adequacy ratio** is a required minimum value of bank capital relative to its outstanding loans and investments.

Generally, it is the shareholders of the particular bank that bear the cost of its poor performance. To try to make sure that shareholders have sufficient funds for this purpose, financial regulations require banks to meet **capital adequacy ratios**.[1]

Banks face the liquidity risk that depositors may withdraw money before banks can sell their less liquid assets, and the solvency risk that a downward revaluation of the value of their assets may leave assets worth less than their liabilities. Bank reserves help protect against liquidity risk. Bank capital helps protect against solvency risk. Bank capital is supplied originally by shareholders or represents bank profits ploughed back into the business.

A crisis depletes this capital reserve and thereby reduces the share price of the bank. *Shareholders* suffer, but *depositors* are protected if the bank still has adequate bank reserves to meet the prospect of future withdrawals. Depositors may also have an explicit or implicit guarantee from the government.

If a bank makes larger losses it may go bankrupt. Losses incurred by rogue trader Nick Leeson brought down Barings Bank in the 1990s. Typically, governments then compensate depositors but not shareholders. Barings was actually sold to Dutch bank ING for a notional amount and deposits were honoured in full. The knowledge that depositors are unlikely to suffer helps prevent unjustified financial panics. The knowledge that shareholders *are* likely to suffer helps keep management on its toes.

Three things went wrong in the perfect storm of 2008/09. First, the magnitude of the initial shock was very large. Greedy banks had borrowed billions to speculate on securitized products whose true risk characteristics they did not properly understand, and which subsequently proved a very bad investment.

---

1   Financial regulation is sometimes the responsibility of the central bank, but sometimes the responsibility of a separate financial regulator. In the UK, responsibility was transferred from the Bank of England to the Financial Services Agency in 1997.

Second, capital adequacy regulations had been poorly designed. What was adequate financial backing by shareholders in good times turned out to be grossly inadequate capital reserves in a big crisis. This has led to calls for future capital adequacy requirements to be variable – less onerous when economies are doing well, but increasingly demanding as risks of crises get larger. As the sub-prime crisis got off the ground in 2006, variable capital adequacy requirements would have required banks around the world to retain more profits or ask shareholders for new funds in order to build up capital reserves.

The third lesson is that many banks had become 'too big to fail'. In a capitalist economy, you might have expected insolvent banks to be made bankrupt in the same way as a defunct car company or steel producer. However, as the US discovered when it allowed Lehman Brothers to go bust, if the bank is large enough it causes massive ripples throughout the financial system. Sometimes, the government concludes that injecting taxpayers' money into keeping the bank going is the lesser of two evils, and preferable to letting the bank go under.

This, of course, is what happened in many Western economies in 2008/09. Nor were governments prepared instantly to raise taxes to pay for this huge spike in their spending on bank bailouts. Instead, they borrowed money and acquired debt; as a result they now owe huge amounts that will take years to pay back.

How do we minimize the chances of such an awful dilemma arising in the future? Case 19.1 discusses possible solutions.

CASE 19.1

Structural solutions to prevent a future banking crisis?

In our discussion of microeconomics in Part Two, we examined two important ideas: moral hazard and imperfect commitment. *Moral hazard* arises when the adoption of a set of rules that would be ideal under perfect information then fosters unwelcome behaviour because it is too costly subsequently to monitor individual behaviour. For example, insurance reduces the cost of bearing risk, which is a good thing. However, fully insured people may no longer bother to act prudently to avoid risk , which is the consequence of moral hazard. It is too costly to verify which individuals had acted prudently and which had not. We generally solve this problem by a compromise: we offer partial but not full insurance so that individuals still have an incentive to act prudently.

Bank of England governor Mervyn King has repeatedly drawn attention to the moral hazard problems in bailing out banks. Even if bank bailouts are helpful in preventing a crisis from escalating today, their signal that future bailouts are also likely may increase behaviour that makes future crises more likely. If all bankers know they are going to be bailed out, they might as well take big risks. When these come off, the banks do well and bankers' bonuses are high; when the risks prove disastrous, the government will step in. This is a one-way bet for bankers.

Imperfect commitment is also a problem. Most governments say they will be tough in future – thereby scaring bankers into more prudent behaviour today – but if bankers can deduce that governments will always cave in when it comes to the crunch, tough words today are empty threats that the bankers can ignore.

Either we live with the reality that bailouts are likely, because the financial tsunami caused by allowing Lehman Brothers to go bankrupt can never be repeated, or we have to find a structural solution that prevents such problems recurring in the future.

The first possibility is the separation of *retail banking* – the relatively boring business of taking deposits from the general public and making loans of a traditional nature, a key aspect of which is that these banks are banned from speculating with their own capital – and *investment banking*, in which banks may gamble extensively with their own funds in derivatives and other volatile and fancy products.

▶ We have seen all this before. In response to the Wall Street crash of 1929, after a previous episode of banking irresponsibility, the US passed the Glass–Steagall Act, which prevented retail banks undertaking risky investment banking activities. The intention was to ensure that neither the real economy nor government finances would again be endangered by casino banking. If investment banks got into trouble, they could be allowed to fail and repercussions for the rest of us would be much smaller. In turn, this made it more credible that they would indeed be allowed to fail if necessary.

For 70 years this approach was largely a success. Yet as the financial sector became increasingly competitive, institutions facing legal restrictions on their behaviour pressed to be allowed to join the lucrative investment banking business which had prospered during decades of stability and growth. The UK began liberalizing its financial sector in 1986, the so-called Big Bang that paved the way for building societies to behave like banks, and banks to behave like investment banks. The US finally repealed the Glass–Steagall Act in 1999. President Obama is now considering reintroducing such a measure.

This first structural solution acts by limiting the types of activity that deposit-taking retail banks can undertake. A second possible solution is to allow all banks to undertake all types of transaction, but to place an absolute limit on the size of banks that are eligible for deposit guarantees and fiscal bailouts. If the problem is that some banks became 'too big to fail' – not because they were incapable of making mistakes but because governments were then forced to rescue them – the solution is to keep banks sufficiently small that it becomes credible that their failure will not trigger automatic bailout by government.

> It is impossible for regulators to prevent business failure, and undesirable to pursue that objective. The essential dynamic of the market economy is that good businesses succeed and bad ones do not. There is a sense in which the bankruptcy of Lehman was a triumph of capitalism, not a failure. It was badly run, it employed greedy and overpaid individuals, and the services it provided were of marginal social value at best. It took risks that did not come off and went bust. That is how the market economy works.
>
> The problem now is how to have greater stability while extricating ourselves from the 'too big to fail' commitment, and taking a realistic view of the limits of regulation. 'Too big to fail' exposes taxpayers to unlimited, uncontrolled liabilities. The moral hazard problem is not just that risk-taking within institutions that are too big to fail is encouraged but that private risk-monitoring of those institutions is discouraged.
>
> (John Kay, 'Too big to fail is too dumb an idea to keep', *Financial Times*, 27 October 2009)

The third possibility is to rely on stronger prudential supervision by regulatory agencies, particularly in the enforcement of tougher capital adequacy ratios, so that failures of private banks are much less likely.

Two problems arise in all these approaches. The first is the need to co-ordinate regulation across the different national regulators. When RBS began to take excessive risks, should this have been a concern for the Financial Services Authority (the UK body charged with supervising financial institutions), the Bank of England (the potential lender of last resort in a liquidity crisis) or the Treasury (the government department potentially responsible for injecting taxpayers' money in a solvency crisis)? It may be easier to obtain a once-off agreement for a long-term structural solution, as in Glass–Seagall, than to co-ordinate different agencies on a daily basis to evaluate ongoing performance.

Second, much of this risky financial business is globally footloose. If some financial centres regulate more than others, private business may tend to migrate to the least intrusive location. Competition *between* financial centres was and remains part of the problem. London might have regulated earlier if it had been less frightened of losing business to Frankfurt and New York. This suggests that any reforms that will make an enduring difference may have to be negotiated at the level of the top ten global countries, not merely a country at a time.

19.4 Equilibrium in financial markets

Having discussed the role of the central bank in financial crises, we now revert to its more normal role.

The traditional account of central banking views the central bank as controlling the *nominal* money supply (it has monopoly power to supply narrow money (cash plus banks' reserves at the central bank), and, if the money multiplier is stable, this allows it to control the nominal supply of broad money. When we simplify by assuming that the price of goods is fixed, the central bank also controls the *real* money supply. In later chapters, we allow the price level to change. Changes in nominal money tend to lead to changes in prices. The central bank can still control the **real money supply** M/P in the short run – it can change M faster than prices P respond – but, in the long run, other forces determine real money M/P. For the moment, we treat the price level as fixed.

In the previous chapter, we argued that the quantity of real money demanded rises when real income rises, but falls when the nominal interest rate rises.

> The **real money supply** L is the nominal money supply M divided by the price level P.
>
> In **money market equilibrium** the quantity of real balances demanded and supplied is equal.

Money market equilibrium

Figure 19.1 shows the demand curve LL for real money balances for a given real income. The higher the interest rate and the cost of holding money, the less real money is demanded. With a given price level, the central bank controls the quantity of nominal money and real money. The supply curve is vertical at this quantity of real money L_0. Equilibrium is at E. At the interest rate r_0, the real money people wish to hold just equals the outstanding stock L_0.

Suppose the interest rate is r_1, below the equilibrium level r_0. There is excess demand for money AB in Figure 19.1. How does this excess demand for money bid the interest rate up from r_1 to r_0 to restore equilibrium? The answer is rather subtle. Strictly speaking, there is no market for money. Money is the medium of exchange for payments and receipts in *other* markets. A market for money would exchange pounds for pounds.

The other market relevant to Figure 19.1 is the market for bonds. Since the interest rate is the cost of holding money, people who do not hold money hold bonds. What happens explicitly in the market for bonds determines what is happening in the implicit market for money in Figure 19.1.

Real wealth W is the existing supply of real money L_0 and real bonds B_0. People divide their wealth W between desired real bond holdings B_D and desired real money holdings L_D. Hence

$$B_0 - B_D = L_D - L_0$$

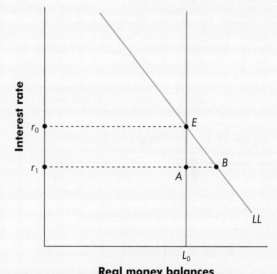

The demand schedule LL is drawn for a given level of real income. The higher the opportunity cost of holding money, the lower the real balances demanded. The real money supply schedule is vertical at L_0. The equilibrium point is E and the equilibrium interest rate r_0. At a lower interest rate r_1 there is excess demand for money AB. There must be a corresponding excess supply of bonds. This reduces bond prices and increases the return on bonds, driving the interest rate up to its equilibrium level at which both markets clear.

Figure 19.1 **Money market equilibrium**

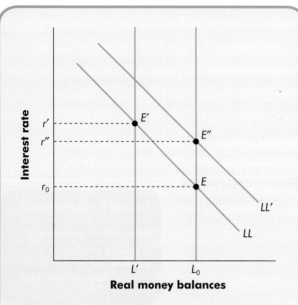

With a given real income, LL is the demand schedule for real money balances. A reduction in the real money supply from L_0 to L' moves the equilibrium interest rates from r_0 to r' to reduce the quantity of money demanded in line with the fall in the quantity supplied. With a given supply of real money L_0, an increase in real income shifts the demand schedule from LL to LL'. The equilibrium interest rates must increase from r_0 to r'. Higher real income tends to increase the quantity of real money demanded and higher interest rates are required to offer this, maintaining the quantity of real money demanded in line with the unchanged real supply.

Figure 19.2   Equilibrium interest rates

An excess demand for money must be exactly matched by an excess supply of bonds. Otherwise people are planning to hold more wealth than they actually possess.

An excess demand for money at the interest rate r_1 in Figure 19.1 bids up the interest rate to its equilibrium level r_0. With excess demand for money, there is an excess supply of bonds. To make people want more bonds, suppliers of bonds offer a higher interest rate.[2] People switch from money to bonds. The higher interest rate reduces both the excess supply of bonds and the excess demand for money. At the interest rate r_0, money supply equals money demand. Bond supply equals bond demand. Both markets are in equilibrium. People wish to divide their wealth in precisely the ratio of the relative supplies of money and bonds.

From now on, we examine the implicit market for money. However, any statement about the money market is also a statement about the bond market.

Changes in equilibrium

A shift in either money supply or money demand changes equilibrium in the money market (and the bond market). These shifts are examined in Figure 19.2.

A fall in the money supply

Suppose the central bank lowers the money supply. For a fixed price level, lower nominal money reduces the real money supply. Figure 19.2 shows this leftward shift in the supply curve. Real money falls from L_0 to L'. The equilibrium interest rate rises from r_0 to r'. A higher interest rate reduces the demand for real money in line with the lower quantity supplied. Hence a lower real money supply raises the equilibrium interest rate. Conversely, a rise in the real money supply reduces the equilibrium interest rate.

A rise in real income

Figure 19.2 shows real money demand LL for a given real income. A rise in real income increases the marginal benefit of holding money at each interest rate, raising real money demand from LL to LL'. The equilibrium interest rate rises to keep real money demand equal to the unchanged real supply L_0. Conversely, a fall in real income shifts LL to the left and reduces the equilibrium interest rate.

More competition in banking

Figure 19.2 also draws money demand LL for a given interest rate paid on bank deposits. Holding this rate constant, a rise in bond interest rates r raises the cost of holding money and reduces the quantity of money demanded. This implies the economy moves up a given demand curve LL.

---

2   A bond is a promise to pay a given stream of interest payments over a given time period. The bond price is the present value of this stream of payments. The higher the interest rate at which the stream is discounted, the lower the price of a bond. With an excess supply of bonds, bond prices fall and the interest rate or rate of return on bonds rises.

However, more competition between banks, reflected in permanently higher interest rates paid on bank deposits, reduces the cost of holding money at each level of r. By raising money demand at each interest rate r, this shifts the demand for money up from LL to LL'. For a given money supply, this equilibrium interest rate on bonds is higher.

To sum up, a higher real money supply reduces the equilibrium interest rate, raising real money demand in line with the higher real money supply. Conversely, higher real income, which tends to raise real money demand, must lead to a rise in the equilibrium interest rate, which tends to reduce real money demand. Only then does real money demand remain equal to the unchanged supply. An increase in banking competition has similar effects to a rise in real income.

19.5 Monetary control

The central bank can control the money supply by using open market operations to affect cash in circulation, or by using reserve requirements and the discount rate to affect the incentive of banks to create deposits. This is easy in theory, but not in practice.

It is hard for the Bank to control cash because it is also lender of last resort. When the banks wish to increase lending and deposits they can *always* get extra cash from the Bank.

Nor, for any given quantity of cash, are deposits easily manipulated. To affect them, reserve requirements must force banks to hold reserves they would not otherwise have held. This is a tax on banks, stopping them conducting profitable business. Modern banks operating in global markets find ways around these controls. UK banks do business with UK borrowers using financial markets in Frankfurt or New York, and London is disadvantaged as a global financial centre.

The UK has given up required reserve ratios on banks for the purpose of monetary control. In the previous chapter, we saw that since 2006 the Bank rewards banks for announcing their reserves at the Bank and sticking to them within the month. In essence, this allows the Bank to forecast the largest part of bank reserves. However, to translate this into a forecast for broad money, the Bank then has to forecast the size of the bank deposit multiplier. The figure in Concept 18.2 showed how volatile this can be, especially in a crisis when it really matters.

Hence precise control of the money supply is difficult. Most central banks no longer try. Instead, they set interest rates. The TV news reports decisions by the Bank on interest rates, not decisions on the money supply.

Control through interest rates

Figure 19.3 shows again the market for money. We draw the money demand schedule LL for a given level of real income. If the central bank can control the money supply, then, for a given level of goods prices, it can fix the real

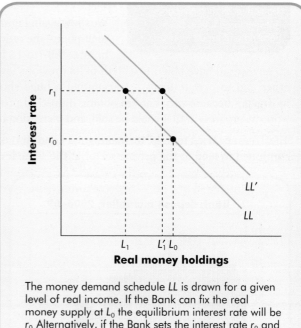

The money demand schedule LL is drawn for a given level of real income. If the Bank can fix the real money supply at L_0 the equilibrium interest rate will be r_0. Alternatively, if the Bank sets the interest rate r_0 and provides whatever money is demanded, the money supply will again be L_0. To control the money supply by using interest rates, the Bank must know the position of the demand schedule. Fixing an interest rate r_1, the resulting money supply will be L_1 if the demand schedule is LL but will be L_1' if the demand schedule is LL'.

Figure 19.3 Interest rates and monetary control

money supply at L_0. The equilibrium interest rate is r_0. Instead, the central bank can fix the interest rate at r_0 and supply the money needed to clear the market at this interest rate. In equilibrium, the central bank supplies L_0.

The central bank can fix the money supply and accept the equilibrium interest rate implied by the money demand equation, or it can fix the interest rate and accept the equilibrium money supply implied by the money demand equation. Central banks now do the latter.

Uncertainty about the exact size of the money multiplier or bank deposit multiplier is now unimportant. When the interest rate starts to fall below the level r_0, either because of too little demand for money or too much supply, the Bank reduces the monetary base, through an open market operation, until the interest rate is r_0 again. Conversely, when the interest rate exceeds r_0, the Bank simply increases the monetary base until the interest rate falls to r_0.

CONCEPT **19.1**	Quantitative easing

In Chapter 18 we saw how banks responded to the financial crisis by prioritizing the rebuilding of their solvency. This had four aspects: (a) holding a much higher percentage of their assets in ultra-safe bank reserves and other very liquid assets; (b) avoiding any new lending that was thought to be risky; (c) raising profit margins throughout the industry in order to build up capital reserves; and, where possible, (d) issuing new shares in order to attract additional capital from shareholders. Here we focus on the implications of (a) and (b).

> **Quantitative easing** is the creation of substantial quantities of bank reserves in order to offset a fall in the bank deposit multiplier and prevent large falls in bank lending and broad money.

We show again Figure 18.4 which documents the collapse of the bank deposit multiplier – the ratio of broad money to bank reserves – which fell from 90 in mid-2007 to 14 by late 2009. If reserves had remained constant, broad money would have fallen to a sixth of its previous level! The complete drying up of bank lending – to each other and to private firms – transmitted a huge shock to the real economy. House prices fell since new mortgages became very hard to obtain, industrial production fell as firms struggled to find loans to finance work-in-progress until it could be sold, and increasing numbers of bankruptcies were reported.

The Treasury tried to help, by making it a condition of government support for banks such as RBS that they continued to lend to the private sector at the same level as in previous years. Unsurprisingly, the banks said they would do so but then did not, and there was little that the government could do.

Bank deposit multiplier, 2006–09

UK and US central banks have usually been run by professional bankers, not world-class economics professors. At the time of the crisis, the governor of the Bank of England was Mervyn King, former professor at the London School of Economics, and the governor of the US Federal Reserve was Ben Bernanke, former economics professor at Princeton University. They understood the problem and adopted a bold solution: quantitative easing.

The chart on the next page shows the evolution of the reserves R of the UK banks and of the M4 measure of broad money, in each case using an index that sets the May 2006 level equal to 100.

The reserves of UK banks rose six-fold between May 2008 and July 2009 as the Bank of England took

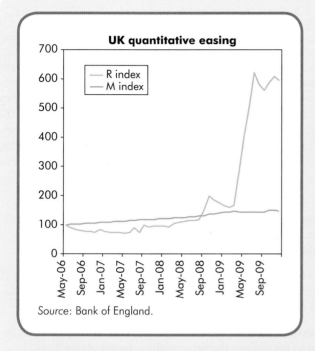

UK quantitative easing

— R index
— M index

Source: Bank of England.

action. The consequence of this action was to achieve steady growth in broad money – notice that there was no spike in broad money growth. Broad money was nevertheless 50 per cent higher at the end of 2009 than it had been in mid-2006.

This raises three obvious questions. (a) How did the Bank achieve this? (b) Why did it want broad money to grow by 50 per cent when real output was stagnating? (c) Is inflation just around the corner?

To accomplish quantitative easing, the Bank announced that it would buy 'safe' bonds from private firms or government, in quantities that made this the mother of all open market operations. This put narrow money into the system. The chart shows that most of this injection of narrow money, having circulated around the system a few times, ended up being held by banks as reserves at the Bank of England. Banks were still afraid of lending very much. But overall lending did increase. From May 2008 to July 2009, banks' reserves increased from £27 billion to £152 billion, whereas broad money increased from £1737 billion to £2001 billion – so the £264 billion increase in broad money was caused not only by the £125 billion in bank reserves. As banks felt a little safer, they lent a little more, thereby raising bank deposits.

Why was broad money allowed to grow so much despite the fact that the real economy was going backwards? The Bank of England was doing everything it could to stimulate economic recovery. Interest rates were reduced to near zero, which in itself raised the demand for money, which the Bank was then happy to see supplied.

Although we defer our discussion of inflation until Chapter 22, we are already in a position to sketch an answer to our third question. If the economy is at full capacity, one might expect a 50 per cent increase in the broad money supply, and the interest rate reductions that presumably accompanied this, to cause a large rise in aggregate demand, well above the economy's capacity to supply – a recipe for a surge in inflation.

However, when the economy is facing its sharpest output downturn since the Great Depression, private firms and households are in no mood to spend. The immediate task is to raise aggregate demand back to acceptable levels. If and when that is accomplished, confidence will return. The proper task for the central bank is then to reverse the quantitative easing, reduce the money supply to more normal levels, and raise interest rates to the levels then required to prevent recovery spilling over into excess demand.

If it is technically possible to inject so much narrow money in such a short time, it is technically possible to do the reverse – the Bank sells the bonds it has recently acquired and receives narrow money in exchange, which is then 'retired' from circulation. Narrow money falls, and broad money falls even more as the normal bank deposit multiplier takes effect.

The key issue concerning financial markets is how the Treasury will then cope. During quantitative easing, it has been a simple matter to sell government debt to cover the budget deficit – if necessary, the Bank of England will buy it. Once the Bank is no longer a buyer but now an active seller of government debt, many private buyers must be found. This could cause a collapse in bond prices or, equivalently, a rise in the interest rates the government must pay to finance its debt.

In deciding to undertake quantitative easing on such a scale, central banks decided that these possible future outcomes were the lesser of two evils – without quantitative easing, the severe cutback in bank lending would have crippled the private sector already.

Targets and instruments of monetary policy

Setting the interest rate not the money supply finesses the question of how the central bank forecasts the bank deposit multiplier. It also has a second advantage. When money demand is uncertain, fixing the money supply makes the interest rate uncertain; whereas fixing the interest rate makes the money supply uncertain. If the *effects* of monetary policy on the rest of the economy operate mainly via the interest rate, it is better to view monetary policy as the choice of interest rates not the money supply. In normal times, this is usually the case. However, if credit is in effect rationed because the banks are too scared to lend, the interest rate is not the whole story. Since we do not live in a permanent crisis – otherwise we would not call it a crisis – we revert to the discussion of monetary policy when the weather is less stormy.

Two other concepts guide our discussion of monetary policy in later chapters. One is the *ultimate objective* of monetary policy. Possible objectives could include price stability, output stabilization, manipulation of the exchange rate and the reduction of swings in house prices.

> The **monetary instrument** is the variable over which the central bank makes day-to-day choices.
>
> An **intermediate target** is a key indicator used to guide interest rate decisions.

To pursue its ultimate objective, what information does a central bank use at its frequent meetings to decide interest rates? It gets up-to-date forecasts of many variables. Sometimes, it concentrates on one or two key indicators.

Interest rates are the **instrument** about which policy decisions are made, but interest rates are chosen to try to keep the **intermediate target** on track.

This shows how interest rates should adjust to the state of the economy. New data on the money supply (largely bank deposits) come out faster than new data on the price level or output. In the heyday of monetarism, central banks changed interest rates to try to meet medium-run targets for the path of nominal growth. In terms of Figure 19.3, it was as if they were fixing the money supply, not interest rates.

Throughout the world, in the past two decades there have been two key changes in the design of monetary policy. First, central banks have been told that their ultimate objectives should concentrate more on price stability.

Second, money has become less important as an intermediate target. The financial revolution reduced its reliability as a leading indicator of future inflation. When structural changes in the financial sector are causing changes in money demand, it is hard to predict how much money will be held and how much will be spent. Increasingly, central banks use *inflation targets* as the intermediate target to which interest rate policy responds.

MATHS
19.1

Quantitative easing revisited

Suppose money demand is given by

$$M = aY - br \qquad a > 0, b > 0$$

where r is the nominal interest rate. Money demand is higher, the higher is output and the lower are interest rates.

Broad money is related to bank reserves R via the bank deposit multiplier m:

$$M = mR \qquad m > 0$$

Aggregate demand AD increases with autonomous demand A but is reduced by higher interest rates:

$$AD = A - hr \qquad A > 0, h > 0$$

Consider a fall in autonomous demand from A to λA, where $0 < \lambda < 1$. Simultaneously, banks get scared and the bank deposit multiplier falls from m to ρm, where $1 < \rho < 1$. By how much does the central bank need to increase bank reserves R in order to maintain aggregate demand at its original level? Originally,

$$mR = M = aY - br$$

However, $r = (A - AD)/h = (A - Y)/h$, and substituting this for r in the above equation

$$R = [aY - b(A - Y)/h]/m = [(ah + b)Y - bA]/hm \qquad (1)$$

Equation (1) tells us that, for a given level of autonomous demand A, aggregate demand and output can be higher only if interest rates are lower, which requires a larger money supply, for which a larger quantity of narrow money is necessary if there is a fixed ratio of broad money to narrow money. Conversely, if autonomous demand A is higher, output and aggregate demand can remain fixed only if interest rates increase to offset the rise in autonomous demand, for which a reduction in the money supply is necessary. Hence, with a fixed bank deposit multiplier, reserves must be lower.

Thus when the deposit multiplier falls from m to ρm, this effect alone induces the central bank to increase R in order to maintain output at its former level. The new level of reserves would be $R/\rho > R$, since $\rho < 1$. Additionally, the fall in autonomous demand from A to λA also raises the level of reserves that the central bank must supply if output and aggregate demand are not to fall. Thus we can interpret quantitative easing as the central bank response to the twin problems – with the same cause – of a fall in aggregate demand and a fall in the bank deposit multiplier.

The transmission mechanism

The central bank sets interest rates. How do interest rates affect the real economy?

In a closed economy, monetary policy affects consumption and investment demand by affecting real interest rates.[3] The central bank chooses the nominal interest rate. If prices are fixed, this is also the real interest rate. Once we allow prices to vary, monetary policy needs to anticipate what inflation will be. Since the real interest rate is simply the nominal interest rate minus the inflation rate, monetary policy then sets the nominal interest rate to get the desired real interest rate.

> The **transmission mechanism** of monetary policy is the channel through which it affects output and employment.

Consumption demand revisited

Chapter 16 used a very simple consumption function, an upward-sloping straight line relating aggregate consumption to the disposable income of households. The slope of this line, the marginal propensity to consume, showed the fraction of each extra pound of disposable income that households wished to spend, not save.

The height of the consumption function showed autonomous consumption demand, the part unrelated to personal disposable income. Changes in disposable income moved households *along* the consumption function. Changes in autonomous demand *shifted* the consumption function. How can monetary policy affect autonomous consumption demand?

---

3   In Chapter 29 we show that, in an open economy, there is also a strong relationship between interest rates, the exchange rate and competitiveness. Monetary transmission then includes effects on export and import demand.

> The **wealth effect** is the shift in the consumption function when household wealth changes.

Household wealth

Suppose real wealth rises because of a stock market boom. Households spend some of their extra wealth on a new car. At each level of disposable income, consumption demand is higher. The entire consumption function shifts up when household wealth increases.

Money and interest rates affect household wealth, and thus consumption and aggregate demand, in two ways. First, since money is a component of household wealth, a higher real money supply adds directly to household wealth. Second, interest rates affect household wealth indirectly. The price of company shares and long-term government bonds is the present value of the expected stream of divided earnings or promised coupon payments. When interest rates fall, future earnings, now discounted at a lower interest rate, are worth more today. Lower interest rates make the price of bonds and corporate shares rise and make households wealthier.[4]

Durables and consumer credit

When spending exceeds disposable income, net wealth falls. People sell off assets or borrow money to finance their dissaving. A lot of borrowing is to finance purchases of *consumer durables*, household capital goods such as televisions, furniture and cars. Splashing out on a new car can cost a whole year's income.

Two aspects of consumer credit or borrowing possibilities affect consumption spending. First, there is the quantity of credit on offer. If banks or retailers make more credit available to customers, people are more likely to buy the car or dream kitchen they have always wanted. An increase in the supply of consumer credit shifts the consumption function upwards. People spend more at any level of disposable income. Second, the cost of credit matters. The higher the interest rate, the lower the quantity that households can borrow while still being able to make repayments out of their future disposable incomes.

Money and interest rates thus affect consumer spending by affecting both the quantity of consumer credit and the interest rates charged on it. An increase in the monetary base increases the cash reserves of the banking system and allows it to extend more consumer credit in the form of overdrafts. And by reducing the cost of consumer credit, lower interest rates allow households to take out bigger loans while still being able to meet the interest and repayments.

Those two forces – wealth effects and changes in consumer credit – explain most of the shifts in the consumption function. They are part of the *transmission mechanism* through which monetary policy affects output and employment. Operating through wealth effects or the supply and cost of consumer credit, changes in the money supply and in interest rates shift the consumption function and the aggregate demand schedule, thus affecting equilibrium income and output.

Two closely related theories of the consumption function reinterpret these phenomena and make some of their subtleties more explicit.

The permanent income hypothesis

Developed by Professor Milton Friedman, this hypothesis assumes that people's incomes fluctuate but that people dislike fluctuating consumption. Because of diminishing marginal utility, a few extra bottles of champagne in the good years does not compensate for hunger in the bad years. Rather than allow fluctuations in income to induce fluctuations in consumption, people smooth out fluctuations in consumption. People go without champagne to avoid being hungry.

---

4   When interest rates are 10 per cent, a bond paying £2.50 for ever is worth £25. New buyers get about 10 per cent a year on their investment. If interest rates fall to 5 per cent, bond prices rise to £50. New buyers still get an annual return in line with interest rates on other assets. A similar argument applies to company shares.

What determines the consumption people can afford on average? Friedman coined the term **permanent income** to describe people's average income in the long run, and argued that consumption depends not on current disposable income but on permanent income.

> The **permanent income hypothesis** says consumption reflects long-run or permanent income.

Suppose people think current income is unusually high. This temporarily high income makes little difference to their permanent income or the consumption they can afford in the long run. Since permanent income has hardly risen, they hardly increase current consumption.

They save most of their temporary extra income and put money aside to see them through the years when income is unusually low. Only if people believe that a rise in today's income will be sustained as higher future incomes will their permanent income rise significantly. Only then is a large rise in current income matched by a large rise in current consumption.

The life-cycle hypothesis

> The **life-cycle hypothesis** assumes people make a lifetime consumption plan (including bequests to their children) that is just affordable out of lifetime income (plus any initial wealth inherited).

Developed by Professors Franco Modigliani and Albert Ando, this theory takes a long-run approach like the permanent income hypothesis, but recognizes that changing tastes over a lifetime may undermine complete consumption smoothing.

Each individual household need not plan a constant consumption level over its lifetime. There may be years of heavy expenditure (a round-the-world cruise, sending the children to private school) and other years when spending is a bit less. However, such individual discrepancies tend to cancel out in the aggregate. Like the permanent income hypothesis, the life-cycle hypothesis suggests that it is average long-run income that determines the total demand for consumer spending.

Figure 19.4 shows a household's actual income over its lifetime. Income rises with career seniority until retirement, then drops to the lower level provided by a pension. The household's permanent income is *OD*. Technically, this is the constant annual income with the same present value as the present value of the actual stream of income. If the household consumed exactly its permanent income, it would consume *OD* each year and die penniless. The two shaded areas labelled *A* show when the household would be spending more than its current income and the area *B* shows when the household would be saving.

The household spends its income over its lifetime, but area *B* is not the sum of the two areas *A* because of compound interest. In the early years of low income, the household borrows. The area *B* shows how much the household has to save to pay back the initial borrowing *with interest* and accumulate sufficient wealth to see it through the final years when it is again dissaving.

Now let's think about wealth effects and consumer credit again. With more initial wealth, a household can spend more in every year of its lifetime without going broke. We can shift the permanent income line in Figure 19.4 upwards and consumption will rise.

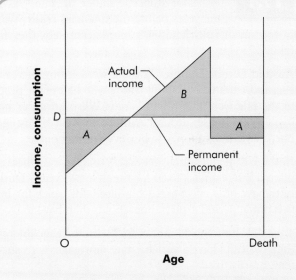

Actual disposable income rises over a household's lifetime until retirement, then falls to the pension level. Permanent income is the constant income level *OD* with the same present value as actual income. Suppose consumption equals permanent income. The two areas *A* show total dissaving and the area *B*, total saving. In the absence of inherited wealth and bequests, *B* must be large enough to repay borrowing with interest and also build up enough wealth to supplement actual income during retirement.

Figure 19.4 *Consumption and the life-cycle*

Although area *B* is now smaller and the areas *A* are now larger, the household can use its extra wealth to meet this shortfall between the years of saving (the area *B*) and the years of dissaving (the two areas *A*).

Again, we conclude that higher wealth leads to more consumption at any current disposable income, but we pick up something we missed earlier. If households believe their *future* income will be higher than previously imagined, this also raises their permanent income. Households can spend more each year and still expect to balance their lifetime budget. They raise *current* consumption as soon as they raise their estimates of future incomes. The present value of future income plays a role very similar to wealth. It is money to be shared out in consumption over the lifetime. Friedman called it 'human wealth', to distinguish it from financial and physical assets. Rises in expected future incomes have wealth effects. They shift up the simple consumption function relating *current* consumption to *current* disposable income.

What about consumer credit? A rise in interest rates reduces the present value of future incomes and makes households worse off. In Figure 19.4, households must enlarge area *B* to meet the extra interest costs of paying back money borrowed in area *A* early in the lifetime. We must shift the permanent income line downwards. A rise in interest rates reduces current consumption not merely by reducing the market value of financial assets, but also by reducing the present value of future *labour* income. By reducing human wealth, it shifts the consumption function downwards.

ACTIVITY 19.1

Transmission lag

Professor Robert Schiller of Yale University accused markets of 'financial exuberance' in the years before the financial crash. We have already discussed how banks became engaged in too much risky lending – more accurately, they failed to appreciate the extent of the risks they were taking.

Around Europe and the US there were strong increases in house prices as households willingly borrowed ever more to make a killing. Those who had many properties became buy-to-let millionaires. In the UK, top of the pile were Judith and Fergus Wilson, former maths teachers who, starting with nothing, eventually owned 600 houses around Ashford in Kent by using the capital appreciation on their existing houses to borrow yet more money to buy even more houses.

In the UK, people rarely get access to fixed-rate mortgages for the entire life of the loan, but are sometimes offered interest rates fixed for the first two years. During this initial period, changes in short-term interest rates have little effect on such households, since the interest rate they care about most is fixed. However, as this initial period expires, households then have to face whatever the new level of interest rate has become.

Thus, UK households cannot fix their mortgage interest rate for an extended period. Taking a 20-year view, they basically have a variable-rate mortgage, with successive small steps in which the interest rate may be temporarily fixed.

In fact, the UK is quite unusual in having such a high proportion of variable-rate mortgages – many continental European countries fix the mortgage interest rate for 20 years or whatever the duration of the mortgage loan. This has important consequences for the transmission mechanism of monetary policy. When most households are immune to the mortgage impact of interest rate changes, then, other things equal, the central bank has to move the interest rate by more in order to have the same effect on aggregate demand. If interest rates do not work through existing mortgages, they have to work more on other determinants of aggregate demand. Conversely, since the UK is so exposed to the effect of interest rate changes in the short run, the Bank of England has a more powerful weapon with which to manage aggregate demand. Since the weapon works more effectively, it requires smaller interest rate changes to achieve the same effect.

In calculating the likely transmission mechanism of UK monetary policy, the Bank of England therefore pays close attention to the particular terms of outstanding mortgage contracts. This is one of many reasons why changes in interest rates may take up to two years to have their full effect on aggregate demand. Overnight, people are locked into old contracts that shield them for a while from the effect of the new interest rate. Even after they feel its effect, it may take time to assess how painful it is and to look for alternative ways to behave.

Questions

(a) Suppose we are creatures of habit – calculating optimal behaviour takes time and effort so we recalculate only rarely when it has become obvious to us that circumstances have changed substantially and previous behaviour cannot possibly be optimal. Could this explain a delay in the transmission mechanism of monetary policy even if there are no long-term contracts in force? Give an example.

(b) Would this justify a transmission lag in responses to fiscal policy too?

(c) Suppose interest rates can be changed frequently whereas fiscal policy changes are infrequent. Would this help explain why people are slower to respond to monetary changes than fiscal changes?

To check your answers to these questions, go to page 686.

Finally, what about a rise in the quantity of consumer credit on offer? Figure 19.4 assumes that people spend more than their incomes early in life. Students run up overdrafts knowing that, as rich economists, they can pay them back later. What if nobody will lend? People without wealth are restricted by their actual incomes, although people with wealth can lend to themselves by running down their wealth. Hence a rise in the availability of consumer credit lets people dissave in the early years. Total consumption rises. More students run up overdrafts and buy cars.

Having discussed how monetary policy affects consumption demand, we conclude our examination of monetary transmission by analysing how interest rates affect investment demand.

Investment demand

In earlier chapters we treated investment demand as autonomous, or independent of current income and output. We now begin to analyse what determines investment demand. Here we focus on interest rates.

Total investment spending is investment in fixed capital and investment in working capital. Fixed capital includes factories, houses, plant and machinery. The share of investment in GDP fluctuates between 10 and 20 per cent.[5] Although the total change in inventories is quite small, this component of total investment is volatile and contributes significantly to changes in the total level of investment.

In a closed economy, aggregate demand is $C + I + G$. Public investment is part of G. We still treat government demand as part of fiscal policy. Thus we assume that G is fixed at a level set by the government. In this section we focus on private investment demand I.

Investment in fixed capital

Firms add to plant and equipment because they foresee profitable opportunities to expand output or because they can reduce costs by using more capital-intensive production methods. BT needs new equipment because it is developing new products for data transmission. Nissan needs new assembly lines to substitute robots for workers in car production.

---

5   These numbers refer to gross investment: the production of new capital goods that contribute to aggregate demand. Since the capital stock is depreciating, or wearing out, some gross investment is needed merely to keep the existing capital stock from falling.

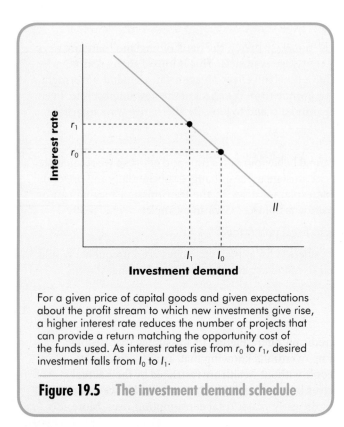

For a given price of capital goods and given expectations about the profit stream to which new investments give rise, a higher interest rate reduces the number of projects that can provide a return matching the opportunity cost of the funds used. As interest rates rise from r_0 to r_1, desired investment falls from I_0 to I_1.

Figure 19.5 **The investment demand schedule**

The **investment demand schedule** shows the desired investment at each interest rate.

The firm weighs the benefits from new capital – the rise in profits – against the cost of investment. The benefit occurs in the future, but the costs are incurred when the plant is built or the machine bought. The firm compares the value of extra future profits with the current cost of the investment.

Will the investment yield enough extra profit to pay back *with interest* the loan used to finance the original investment? Equivalently, if the project is funded out of existing profits, will the new investment yield a return at least as great as the return that could have been earned by lending the money instead? The higher the interest rate, the larger must be the return on a new investment to match the opportunity cost of the funds tied up.

At any moment, there are many investment projects a firm *could* undertake. The firm ranks these projects, from the most profitable to the least profitable. At a high interest rate, only a few projects earn enough to cover the opportunity cost of the funds employed. As the interest rate falls, more and more projects earn a return at least matching the opportunity cost of the funds used to undertake the investment. The firm invests more.

Figure 19.5 plots the **investment demand schedule** *II* relating interest rates and investment demand.

If the interest rate rises from r_0 to r_1, fewer investment projects cover the opportunity cost of the funds tied up, and desired investment falls from I_0 to I_1. The height of the schedule *II* reflects the cost of new capital and the stream of profits to which it gives rise. For a given stream of expected future profits, a higher price of new capital goods reduces the return on the money tied up in investment. Fewer projects match the opportunity cost of any particular interest rate. Since desired investment is then lower at any interest rate, a rise in the cost of new capital goods shifts the investment demand schedule *II* downwards.

Similarly, pessimism about future output demand reduces estimates of the stream of profits earned on possible investment projects. The return on each project falls. At each interest rate, fewer projects match the opportunity cost of the funds. Desired investment falls at any interest rate. Lower expected future demand shifts the investment demand schedule downwards.[6]

The investment demand schedule *II* can be used to analyse both business investment in plant and machinery and residential investment in housing. What about the slope of the schedule? There is a big difference between a machine that wears out in three years and a house or a factory lasting 50 years. The longer the economic life of the capital good, the larger the fraction of its total returns earned in the distant future, and the more the original cost of the goods accumulates at compound interest before the money is repaid.

---

6   We can make the same points another way. Given the stream of future profits and the interest rate, a firm does all projects for which the present value of operating profits exceeds the initial price of the capital goods. A higher interest rate cuts the present value of profits. Some projects no longer cover the initial cost of capital goods. Higher interest rates reduce desired investment. Similarly, a lower expected future profit stream, or higher purchase price of capital goods, cuts the present value of operating profits relative to the initial cost, reducing investment demand.

Hence a change in interest rates has a larger effect the longer the life of the capital good. The investment demand schedule is flatter, and the monetary transmission mechanism more powerful, for long-lived houses and factories than for short-term machinery.[7] A change in interest rates has more effect on long-term projects.

Inventory investment

There are three reasons why firms desire stocks of raw materials, partly finished goods and finished goods awaiting sale. First, the firm may be betting on price changes. Sometimes, firms hold large stocks of oil, believing it cheaper to buy now rather than later. Similarly, firms may hold finished goods off the market hoping to get a better price later.

Second, many production processes take time. A ship cannot be built in a month, or even a year. Some stocks are simply the throughput of inputs on their way to becoming outputs.

Third, stocks help smooth costly adjustments in output. If output demand rises suddenly, plant capacity cannot be changed overnight. A firm has to pay big overtime payments to meet the upsurge in orders. It is cheaper to carry some stocks, available to meet a sudden rise in demand. Similarly, in a temporary downturn, it is cheaper to maintain output and pile up stocks of unsold goods than to incur expensive redundancy payments to cut the workforce and reduce production.

CONCEPT 19.2

The credit channel of monetary policy

Recent research emphasizes that interest rates are not the only channel through which monetary policy affects consumption and investment, and hence aggregate demand.

The credit channel affects the value of collateral for loans, and thus the supply of credit.

A lender usually asks for collateral – assets available for sale if you fail to repay the loan. Collateral is how lenders cope with moral hazard and adverse selection: borrowers who know more about their ability and willingness to repay than lenders know.

Suppose the price of goods falls, raising the real value of nominal assets. People have more collateral to offer lenders, who thus lend more than before at any particular interest rate. The supply of credit rises and aggregate demand for goods increases.

There are really two credit channels, since there are two reasons for changes in the value of collateral. First, changes in goods prices change the real value of nominal assets. Second, and quite distinct, when monetary policy changes the interest rate, this affects the present value of future income from assets and hence the market value of collateral assets themselves.

This theoretical reasoning is supported by evidence from the natural experiment that we have called quantitative easing. The purpose of quantitative easing was not simply to raise the broad money supply to support the desired low level of interest rates. It was also believed that credit rationing by lenders was curtailing private spending and reducing equilibrium asset prices, from houses to the stock market. Injecting more money provided additional liquidity to people who would otherwise have been credit rationed, and the consequent spending helped bid up house prices and share prices on the stock market. In turn, this improved private sector collateral and made banks more willing to lend, causing a second-round beneficial effect.

---

7 Equivalently, a 1 per cent rise in the interest rate has a small effect on the present value of earnings over a three-year period but a large effect on the present value of earnings over the next 50 years. Note that this is the same argument as we used in Chapter 17, in saying that a change in interest rates would have little effect on the price (present value of promised payments) of a short-term bond but a large effect on the price of a long-term bond.

> In this extreme example, raising the money supply has beneficial effects despite the fact that interest rates have already fallen as low as they can go. In effect, interest rates cannot fall below zero.
>
> How can we add to the money supply once interest rates have reached their effective floor? This implies that money demand must be perfectly elastic at this minimum interest rate – what John Maynard Keynes called the *liquidity trap*. In these circumstances, he thought that creating more money was pointless precisely because it could not reduce interest rates any further. Great man that he was, he did not get everything right. Nowadays, we know about the credit channel, and quantitative easing is proof that it can work.

These are benefits of holding inventories. The cost is that, by retaining unsold goods or buying goods not yet inputs to production, a firm ties up money that could have earned interest. The cost of holding inventories is the interest forgone, plus any storage charges for holding stocks.

Thus the investment demand schedule *II* for fixed capital in Figure 19.5 also applies to increases in working capital, or inventories. Other things equal, a higher interest rate reduces desired stockbuilding, an upward move *along* the investment demand schedule. This is part of the monetary transmission mechanism. But a rise in potential speculative profits, or fall in storage costs for inventories, *shifts* the schedule *II* up and raises inventory investment at any interest rate. Not all changes in investment demand are caused by monetary policy.

Summary

- The Bank of England, the UK **central bank**, is banker to the banks. Because it can print money it can never go bust. It acts as **lender of last resort** to the banks.

- The Bank conducts the government's monetary policy. It affects the monetary base through **open market operations**, buying and selling government securities. It can also affect the money multiplier by imposing **reserve requirements** on the banks, or by setting the **discount rate** for loans to banks at a penalty level that encourages banks to hold excess reserves.

- There is no explicit market in money. Because people plan to hold the total supply of assets that they own, any excess supply of bonds is matched by an excess demand for money. Interest rates adjust to clear the market for bonds. In so doing, they clear the money market.

- A rise in the real money supply reduces the equilibrium interest rate. For a given real money supply, a rise in real income raises the equilibrium interest rate.

- In practice, the Bank cannot control the money supply exactly. Imposing artificial regulations drives banking business into unregulated channels. **Monetary base control** is difficult since the Bank acts as lender of last resort, supplying cash when banks need it.

- Thus the Bank sets the interest rate not money supply. The demand for money at this interest rate determines the quantity of money supplied. **Interest rates are the instrument of monetary policy.**

- Interest rates take time to affect the economy. **Intermediate targets** are used as leading indicators when setting the interest rate.

- **Quantitative easing** is the creation of substantial quantities of bank reserves in order to offset a fall in the bank deposit multiplier and prevent large falls in bank lending and broad money.

- A higher interest rate reduces household wealth and makes borrowing dearer. Together, these effects reduce autonomous consumption demand and shift the consumption function downwards.

- **Consumption demand** reflects long-run disposable income and a desire to smooth out short-run fluctuations in consumption. Higher interest rates reduce consumption demand by reducing the present value of expected future labour income.

- Given the cost of new capital goods and expected stream of future profits, a higher interest rate reduces **investment demand**, a movement down a given investment demand schedule *II*. Higher expected future profits, or cheaper capital goods, shift the *II* schedule upwards.

- These effects of interest rates on consumption and investment demand are the **transmission mechanism** of monetary policy.

Review questions
connect™

1 The Bank sells £1 million of securities to Mr Jones, who banks with Barclays. (a) If Mr Jones pays by cheque, show the effect on the balance sheets of the Bank of England and Barclays Bank. (b) What happens to the money supply? (c) Is the answer the same if Mr Jones pays in cash?

EASY

2 Now the Bank requires banks to hold 100 per cent cash reserves against deposits. Repeat your answers to Question 1. What is the money multiplier?

3 What are the desirable properties of a good leading indicator for interest rate decisions?

4 People previously without bank overdrafts get credit cards on which they can borrow up to £500. What happens to the consumption function? Why?

5 Why do higher interest rates reduce investment demand? Be sure to discuss all the different ways in which firms might finance their investment projects.

6 **Common fallacies** Why are these statements wrong? (a) By abolishing reserve requirements the Bank gave up any attempt to control the money supply. (b) When real interest rates are negative, people are being paid to hold cash. (c) Consumers are crazy if their spending is up when their disposable income is lower.

7 Which of these is correct? The purpose of quantitative easing is: (a) to create money in order to create inflation and reduce the real value of government debt; (b) to force banks to create deposits despite having inadequate bank reserves; (c) to make the central bank the purchaser of last resort for government bond issues; (d) to prevent a collapse of broad money when banks are unable or unwilling to lend.

8 Suppose banks begin lending again as confidence is restored. (a) If monetary policy takes no action, what will be the likely outcome? (b) What action by the central bank would then be appropriate?

9 Using a diagram like Figure 19.1, (a) illustrate the initial effects of a recovery in confidence after the financial crash. (b) Did you expect a larger effect on money supply or money demand? (c) What response in monetary policy will then occur?

MEDIUM

10 You live for five periods, during which you earn 100, 200, 300, 200 and 100, respectively. (a) Draw a diagram of your life-cycle income similar to Figure 19.4. (b) If the interest rate is zero, and there

is no inflation, what is your permanent income? (c) Using your diagram, or otherwise, identify your saving or dissaving in each period of your life. (d) If the real interest rate is positive instead of zero, what effect does this have on your initial estimate of your permanent income? Illustrate in your diagram.

11 Consider a simplified vesion of the model in Maths 19.1, in which money demand, the deposit multiplier and aggregate demand are, respectively:

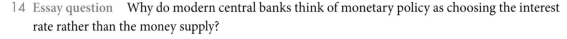

$$M = Y - r \qquad M = mR \qquad Y = 100 - r$$

(a) If output is 90, find the interest rate and bank reserves levels. (b) Suppose autonomous aggregate demand falls from 100 to 95, and the deposit multiplier falls from m to $m/2$. How much must reserves increase to preserve the initial level of output? (c) What is the maximum fall in autonomous aggregate demand that can be offset by quantitative easing?

12 Why might it take up to two years for a change in interest rates fully to affect aggregate demand? What does this imply about decisions to set interest rates?

13 If the permanent income hypothesis is correct, we should expect to see a lower marginal propensity to consume in the short run than in the long run. Why?

14 Essay question   Why do modern central banks think of monetary policy as choosing the interest rate rather than the money supply?

HARD

For solutions to these questions contact your lecturer.

CHAPTER
20

Monetary and fiscal policy

Learning Outcomes

By the end of this chapter, you should understand:

1. different forms of monetary policy

2. a monetary target

3. the *IS* and *LM* schedules

4. equilibrium in both the output and money markets

5. the effect of a fiscal expansion

6. the effect of a monetary expansion

7. the mix of monetary and fiscal policy

8. how expected future taxes affect current demand

Chapters 16 and 17 introduced a simple model of income determination, and studied how fiscal policy affects aggregate demand and equilibrium output. Chapters 18 and 19 examined the demand for money, the supply of money and the determination of interest rates. Interest rates connect the present and the future, affecting spending decisions of both households and firms. We analysed the transmission mechanism by which monetary policy affects aggregate demand.

We now examine the interaction of the markets for goods and for money. Interest rates affect the demand for goods and the level of income and output, but income and output affect the demand for money and the interest rates set by the central bank.

We need to think about both markets at once. In so doing, we explain how equilibrium income and interest rates are simultaneously determined. In this richer model, we study changes in monetary and fiscal policy. Finally, we discuss how the mix of monetary and fiscal policy affects the composition as well as the level of equilibrium output.

This is the last chapter in which we retain the simplifying assumption that prices are fixed. The interest rate is the key variable connecting the markets for money and output. In the next chapter, we allow prices to change, and introduce aggregate supply for the first time.

20.1 Monetary policy

Economists distinguish between rules and discretion. A smoker decides from minute to minute whether to have a cigarette. Once we understand his preferences, the price of cigarettes, his income, and the attitude of his friends, we can model his behaviour and predict pretty accurately how he will behave since this is consistently related to the environment that he faces, even though he has discretion or freedom to decide how much to smoke.

> A **rule** is a commitment describing how behaviour changes when circumstances change.
>
> **Discretion** means free choice without restrictions imposed by prior commitments.

A **rule** is a commitment on how to behave, for example to smoke no more than ten cigarettes a day. This rule is credible only if we understand what prevents the smoker having the eleventh cigarette when he desperately wants one. Being abandoned by his friends if he smokes more than ten might be a commitment mechanism to enforce the rule. A rule constrains his **discretion**, limits his freedom, and precludes the choice he would otherwise have made.

What do we mean by a given monetary policy? This has two aspects. First, to what variable does it refer – the interest rate or the money supply? For the reasons given in the previous two chapters, we prefer to focus on the interest rate.

Second, does a given policy mean the choice of a particular interest rate? Changing the interest rate would then be a change in policy. This is simple, but we can do better. We can usually model *why* that interest rate was chosen: the relationship between the chosen interest rate and other economic variables. A particular monetary policy is then a particular relationship rather than a particular interest rate. This relationship may reflect discretionary choices of the central bank or a commitment to a particular rule. Either way, a change in **monetary policy** is then a change in the relationship between the chosen interest rate and the economic circumstances faced by the central bank.

> A particular **monetary policy** is a relationship between the state of the economy and the interest rate chosen by the central bank.

Thus interest rates change either because economic circumstances change (within a *given* monetary policy) or because the central bank switches to a different preferred relationship between interest rates and the state of the economy (a *change* in monetary policy).

In the heyday of monetarism, central banks used to adjust interest rates to stop the money supply deviating from a given target path of monetary growth. Most central banks have abandoned this policy, preferring to target the inflation rate itself.

> Following a **monetary target**, the central banks adjust interest rates to maintain the quantity of money demanded in line with the given target for money supply.

Inflation targeting makes no sense in a model in which we still assume prices are fixed. We introduce inflation targeting in Chapter 21. In this chapter, we assume instead that the central bank pursues a **monetary target**. This is a good way to introduce many key ideas, and is useful in understanding how monetary policy was set in the 1980s before inflation targeting became popular.

We now combine our analysis of the goods market and money market to examine interest rates and output simultaneously. Chapters 16 and 17 analysed short-run equilibrium output using a diagram with the 45° line and a straight-line aggregate demand line. The height of the aggregate demand line reflected autonomous demand from consumption, investment and government spending; the slope of the line reflected the marginal propensity to spend out of national income.

This diagram is not suitable in our extended model. As output changes, interest rates alter, affecting consumption and investment demand. And changes in monetary policy, by changing interest rates at any output level, can shift the aggregate demand schedule. To keep track of all these effects, it is easier to develop a new diagram.

20.2 The *IS–LM* model

The trick is to consider *combinations* of income and interest rates that lead to equilibrium in each of the two markets – output and money – and thus determine the unique combination of income and interest rates yielding equilibrium in both markets at the same time.

The *IS* schedule: goods market equilibrium

The goods market is in equilibrium when aggregate demand equals actual income. Hence, as shorthand, the combinations of interest rates and income compatible with short-run equilibrium in the goods market is called the *IS* schedule.[1]

Figure 20.1 shows the *IS* schedule. It is drawn for a given level of present and future government spending, a given level of present and future taxes and given present beliefs about future output and income. Holding these constant, lower interest rates increase both investment and consumption demand. At an interest rate r_1, aggregate demand and short-run equilibrium output Y_1 are higher than their level Y_0 when the interest rate is r_0.

> The **IS schedule** shows combinations of income and interest rates at which aggregate demand equals actual output.

Changes in interest rates move the goods market along the *IS* curve. Anything else that affects aggregate demand is shown as a shift in the *IS* schedule.

The slope of the *IS* schedule

The *IS* schedule slopes down. Lower interest rates boost aggregate demand and output. The *slope* of the *IS* schedule reflects the sensitivity of aggregate demand to interest rates. If demand is sensitive to interest rates, the *IS* schedule is flat. Conversely, if output demand is insensitive to interest rates, the *IS* schedule is steep.

Shifts in the *IS* schedule

Movements along the *IS* schedule show how interest rates affect aggregate demand and equilibrium output. Other changes in aggregate demand shift the *IS* schedule. For a *given* interest rate, more optimism about future profits raises investment demand. Higher expected future incomes raise consumption demand. Higher government spending adds directly to aggregate demand. Any of these, by raising aggregate demand at a given interest rate, raises equilibrium output at any interest rate – an *upward shift* in the *IS* schedule.

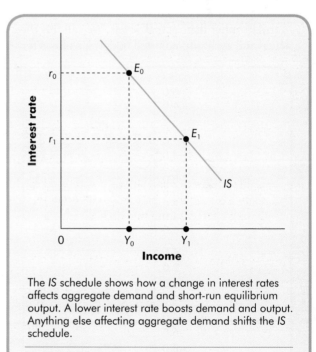

The *IS* schedule shows how a change in interest rates affects aggregate demand and short-run equilibrium output. A lower interest rate boosts demand and output. Anything else affecting aggregate demand shifts the *IS* schedule.

Figure 20.1   The *IS* schedule

---

1   The name *IS* schedule derives from the fact that, in the simplest model without either a government or a foreign sector, equilibrium income is where planned investment I equals planned saving S. However, the *IS* schedule – combinations of income and interest rates consistent with equilibrium income – can be constructed for models including the government and foreign sector as well.

CASE 20.1 PIGS might fly

By 2009 financial markets were concerned about the fiscal solvency of a number of countries. Within Europe, attention focused especially on the PIGS – Portugal, Italy, Greece and Spain – which had three characteristics: high government debt, high budget deficits and membership of the eurozone. Markets wondered if fiscal problems of the PIGS might cause the first real crisis of the eurozone.

Pessimists argued that markets were now penalizing these countries. For example, by the end of January 2010, despite sharing a common currency, interest yields on Greek bonds were nearly 4 percentage points higher than interest yields on German bonds. Future Greek bond issues were going to be expensive for Greek taxpayers.

Optimists, such as Nobel Laureate Professor Joseph Stiglitz, argued that both interest rates and budget deficit indicators were misleading. If the crisis could be solved, risk premia embedded in the PIGS' interest rates would evaporate as quickly as they had arisen. Budget deficits were also misleading because, as we saw in Chapter 17, the size of the budget deficit fluctuates with the level of output – in a slump tax revenue falls but, as output recovery occurs, tax revenue automatically rises again. Focusing on budget deficit data at the bottom of the slump gives a misleading impression of how bad the fiscal situation had become. Stiglitz therefore argued that Germany and France could help PIGS at little risk to themselves. If the speculators could be defeated, the situation would correct itself and the PIGS would survive without having to default.

How sensitive are budget deficits to fluctuations in output? The Organization for Economic Cooperation and Development (OECD) makes estimates of what the budget deficit would have been if output had been at 'normal' rather than 'actual' levels. We call this the cyclically-adjusted budget deficit. The charts below show actual and cyclically-adjusted budget surpluses for the UK and three of the PIGS – Italy, Greece and Spain.

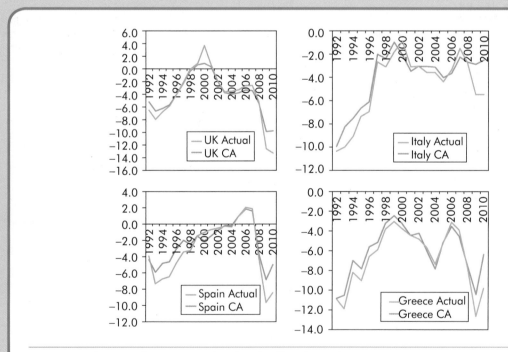

Budget surplus (% of GDP), actual and cyclically adjusted, 1992–2010

Source: OECD, *Economic Outlook*.

Until 2008 monetary policy had successfully stabilized most countries close to the trend level of normal output. There was little discrepancy between actual and cyclically-adjusted budgets, because the business cycle had largely been eliminated. The evolution of the budget position was therefore due to changes in fiscal policy – decisions about tax rates and spending levels – not fluctuations in output.

For example, in the UK, after 2000 the government embarked on a substantial increase in government spending, especially on health care. Since tax rates were not raised in line, both the actual and the cyclically-adjusted budget deficit increased. Chancellor Gordon Brown was finding it harder and harder to live up to his claim of fiscal responsibility.

In the years leading up to 2008, the Spanish budget surplus was steadily increasing, and that of Italy was essentially flat. Italy and Spain were not on a course of fiscal recklessness. Since Greece has subsequently admitted that all of its official statistics were wrong, changes in Greece probably had more to do with changes in reporting than in underlying reality.

All four charts confirm that large falls in output in 2009 had immediate and adverse effects on budget deficits. Not merely did banks require bailouts, but tax revenues fell as activity fell. There are reasons to hope that both may be reversed as output recovers. Tax revenue will improve and governments may recoup some of the bailout funds as banks become healthier.

None of this detracts from the fact that substantial tax rises and spending cuts will still be required. Some of the bank assets are permanently bad, governments have to pay interest on the debts they have issued in the meantime, and projected output paths (and hence tax revenues) are lower than we had previously been projecting.

All of this affects the decision of *when* to tighten fiscal policy. If interest rates could be reduced further, fiscal policy could be tightened immediately without threatening the output recovery. But interest rates are already close to rock bottom, If fiscal policy is tightened too much too soon, output recovery will stall, tax revenues will not materialize, and the desired improvement in government finances will be frustrated. However, if fiscal tightening is postponed too long, government debt will have mushroomed to levels that will then be very hard to repay. Nobody said economic policy was supposed to be easy.

The *LM* schedule: money market equilibrium

Pursuing a monetary target, the central bank endeavours to fix the money supply itself. In Figure 20.2, along the *LM* schedule, the demand for money (or liquidity, hence *L*) equals the given supply of money (hence *M*). Hence the shorthand *LM*.

> The **LM schedule** shows combinations of interest rates and income-yielding money market equilibrium when the central bank pursues a given target for the nominal money supply.

The quantity of money demanded rises with output Y but falls with the interest rate r. In money market equilibrium, money demand equals the given money supply. Hence if output rises from Y_0 to Y_1 – tending to raise the quantity of money demanded – money market equilibrium is restored only if interest rates rise from r_0 to r_1, thereby reducing money demand back to the level of the given money supply. Figure 20.2 shows the upward-sloping schedule *LM* describing money market equilibrium. Higher output and income are accompanied by higher interest rates.

The slope of the schedule

The *LM* schedule slopes up. Following a monetary target, higher output induces a higher interest rate to keep money demand in line with money supply. The more sensitive is money demand to income and output, the more the interest rate must change to maintain money market equilibrium, and the steeper is the *LM* schedule. Similarly, if money demand is not responsive to interest rates, it takes a big change in interest rates to offset output effects on money demand, and the *LM* schedule is steep. Conversely, the more money demand responds to interest rates and the less it responds to income, the flatter is the *LM* schedule.

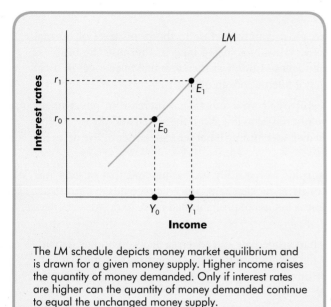

The *LM* schedule depicts money market equilibrium and is drawn for a given money supply. Higher income raises the quantity of money demanded. Only if interest rates are higher can the quantity of money demanded continue to equal the unchanged money supply.

Figure 20.2   The *LM* schedule

Shifts in the *LM* schedule

Movements along the schedule indicate interest rate changes to implement the *existing* policy as output changes. Shifts in the schedule reflect a *change* in monetary policy.

We draw an *LM* schedule for a *given* nominal money target. A rise in the target money supply means that money demand must also be increased to maintain money market equilibrium. This implies a rightward *shift* in the *LM* schedule. Output is higher, or interest rates lower, raising money demand in line with the rise in real money supply.

Conversely, a lower monetary target shifts the *LM* schedule to the left. Since money demand must also be reduced to preserve money market equilibrium, a higher interest rate is required at each income level. To sum up, moving along the *LM* schedule, higher interest rates need higher income to keep real money demand equal to the fixed supply. A higher (lower) target for money supply shifts the *LM* schedule to the right (left).

CONCEPT 20.1

A modern interpretation of the *LM* schedule

The *LM* schedule shows the relationship between interest rates and output implied by the monetary policy in force. Such a policy might be the pursuit of a fixed target for the quantity of money supplied, in which case higher output, by increasing the quantity of money demanded, induces a rise in interest rates in order to restore that quantity demanded to the level compatible with the fixed supply of money.

We could instead interpret the *LM* schedule as a monetary policy in which the central bank deliberately sets higher interest rates when output is higher. This is consistent with a desire to stabilize output around its full capacity level. The steeper the *LM* schedule, the more aggressively the central bank 'leans into the wind' in order to offset deviations of output from full capacity. What is happening to the quantity of money supplied? Whatever is necessary to achieve the interest rate that the central bank wishes, given the level of output that is being produced. A steeper schedule means that interest rates are worked harder as a lever to stabilize output. A vertical *LM* schedule would stabilize output completely.

An upward shift in the *LM* schedule again reflects a tighter monetary policy. At any output level, interest rates are higher under the new policy than under the previous one. The new policy is more restrictive than the old one.

20.3   The *IS*–*LM* model in action

Figure 20.3 shows both the *IS* schedule, depicting combinations of income and interest rates consistent with goods market equilibrium, and the *LM* schedule, depicting combinations of interest rates and income consistent with money market equilibrium when the central bank's monetary policy rule is to pursue a fixed money supply target. Equilibrium in both the money market and the output market is at point *E*, with an interest rate r^* and income level Y^*.

Fiscal policy: shifting the *IS* schedule

Figure 20.4 shows the effect of a fiscal expansion that shifts the *IS* schedule from IS_0 to IS_1. If unchanged monetary policy is shown by LM_0, equilibrium moves from E to E_1. Fiscal expansion leads to higher income but also higher interest rates. Higher output tends to increase the quantity of money demanded. Only higher interest rates prevent this from happening.

Fiscal contraction has the opposite effect. The *IS* schedule shifts to the left and output falls, tending to reduce money demand. Only lower interest rates restore money demand to the unchanged level of money supply, preserving money market equilibrium. In Figure 20.4, this is a move from E_1 to E when the *IS* schedule shifts down from IS_1 to IS_0.

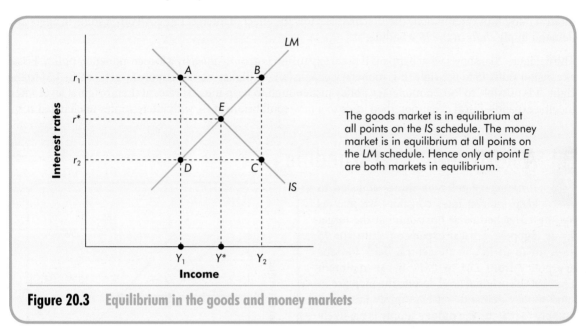

The goods market is in equilibrium at all points on the *IS* schedule. The money market is in equilibrium at all points on the *LM* schedule. Hence only at point E are both markets in equilibrium.

Figure 20.3   Equilibrium in the goods and money markets

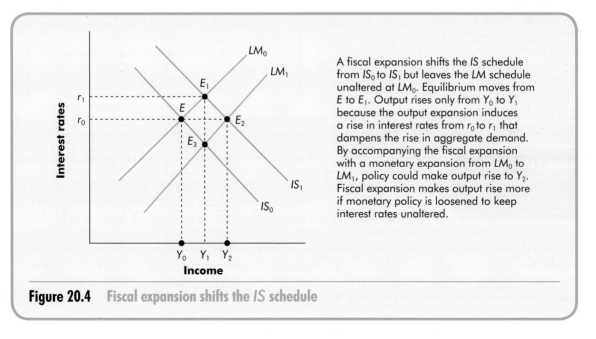

A fiscal expansion shifts the *IS* schedule from IS_0 to IS_1 but leaves the *LM* schedule unaltered at LM_0. Equilibrium moves from E to E_1. Output rises only from Y_0 to Y_1 because the output expansion induces a rise in interest rates from r_0 to r_1 that dampens the rise in aggregate demand. By accompanying the fiscal expansion with a monetary expansion from LM_0 to LM_1, policy could make output rise to Y_2. Fiscal expansion makes output rise more if monetary policy is loosened to keep interest rates unaltered.

Figure 20.4   Fiscal expansion shifts the *IS* schedule

Figure 20.4 makes three other points. First, **crowding out is complete** – extra government spending G leads to an equivalent reduction in consumption and investment $(C + I)$, leaving output unaltered – only if the LM schedule is vertical. Then, an upward shift in the IS schedule raises interest rates but not income.

In practice, the LM schedule is never completely vertical, which would occur only if it took an *infinite* rise in interest rates to offset the effect of slightly higher output on money demand. Since the LM schedule normally has a positive slope, fiscal expansion raises demand and output despite some induced rise in interest rates.

> A fiscal stimulus to aggregate demand **crowds out** some private spending. Higher output induces a rise in interest rates that dampens the expansionary effect on demand by reducing some components of private spending.

Second, fiscal policy is not the only autonomous change that is possible in aggregate demand. An increase in export demand would also shift the IS schedule to the right, again inducing higher output and higher interest rates. Movements *along* the IS schedule show the effect of interest rates. All other shifts in aggregate demand imply *shifts* in the IS schedule.

Third, Figure 20.4 shows what happens if fiscal expansion is *accompanied* by a looser monetary policy. Fiscal expansion shifts IS to the right, but monetary expansion – a higher money supply target – shifts LM to the right. It is possible to loosen monetary policy just enough to keep interest rates at their original level when income expands. Fiscal expansion then leads to a new equilibrium at E_2, with interest rates unchanged at r_0.

CONCEPT
20.2 # A horizontal LM schedule

If monetary policy is always adjusted to keep interest rates constant, we may as well view the LM schedule as horizontal at the target interest rate. Suppose a fiscal expansion shifts the IS schedule from IS to IS'. If the central bank loosens monetary policy from LM to LM', it can maintain interest rates at the original level despite the increase in output and money demand – it has simply increased money supply to match. The money supply is passively adjusted to whatever level of money is demanded at that interest rate. Shifts in the IS schedule no longer lead to crowding out because the money supply is adjusted to prevent interest rates from changing. Instead of depicting monetary policy as a whole potential set of parallel LM schedules, it is easier just to summarize it by the horizontal line at height r^*. Whatever happens to the IS schedule, monetary policy will then be adjusted to maintain the interest rate at a constant level.

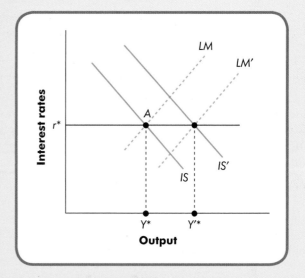

> A **horizontal LM schedule** implies the money supply is adjusted to keep interest rates constant.

In Chapter 24 we show that defending a fixed exchange rate may require a constant interest rate and hence a **horizontal LM schedule**. Hence, small countries within the eurozone face a horizontal LM schedule. The European Central Bank (ECB) sets an interest rate for the whole eurozone, and countries such as Ireland, Portugal or Greece simply have to take this interest rate as given. Germany is a little luckier – as the largest country within the eurozone, German economic conditions tend to affect the ECB's decisions regarding the interest rate within the eurozone. Most of the time, euro interest rates are higher when German output is higher, and Germany enjoys an LM curve that slopes upwards. Upward-sloping LM curves mean that monetary policy is acting to stabilize output fluctuations by raising interest rates when that country's output is higher.

Hence, the output effect of a fiscal expansion depends on the monetary policy in force. The more that monetary policy prevents a rise in interest rates, the more the fiscal expansion will lead to higher output.

Monetary expansion: shifting the *LM* schedule

Similarly, beginning from E in Figure 20.4, an increase in the target money supply shifts the LM schedule from LM_0 to LM_1: for any income, it requires lower interest rates to help raise money demand in line with the new higher money supply. Lower interest rates also boost income, which also helps raise money demand. Equilibrium moves from E to E_3. Conversely, a reduction in the target money supply shifts the LM schedule to the left, leading to higher interest rates but lower output.

 20.4 Shocks to money demand

In the last three decades, competition between banks has increased dramatically, raising interest rates paid on deposits. Since the opportunity cost of holding money in a bank deposit is only the differential between the deposit interest rate and the higher interest rate available on other financial assets, changes in banking competition change the opportunity cost of holding money *at any market interest rate r*. Conversely, since the financial crash, banks have been desperate to increase profit margins in order to rebuild capital reserves. The spread between deposit interest rates and market interest rates has widened sharply.

We draw an LM schedule for a given nominal money target. Greater banking competition raises money demand at every combination of output and interest rates. To keep money demand in line with the unchanged supply, either output must fall or interest rates must rise. The LM schedule *shifts* left. Conversely, if spreads widen and the opportunity cost of holding money increases, the LM schedule shifts to the right.

Figure 20.4 showed how changes in money *supply* shift the LM schedule under monetary targeting. We have now discovered that changes in money *demand*, other than those caused by changes in output and interest rates, also shift the LM schedule under monetary targeting.

In Figure 20.5, LM_1 corresponds to 'low' money demand and LM_2 to 'high' money demand. Suppose money demand increases but the central bank is not yet aware of the change. In choosing what monetary target to set, the central bank is expecting the schedule LM_1, which will place the economy at E_1. In fact, because of the undetected shift in money demand, the actual out-turn is at E_2, not at all what monetary policy intended when it decided what monetary target to set.

In practice, this helps explain why monetary targets were gradually abandoned by many central banks. When money demand was predictable, monetary targets worked fine. As the financial sector has become more sophisticated, more competitive and more volatile, monetary targets were gradually abandoned as the basis for the monetary policy rule.

Moreover, as we saw in Chapter 18, the bank deposit multiplier can be highly unstable. This means that a given

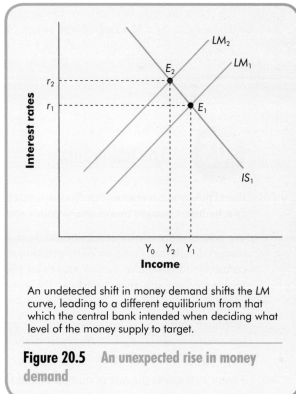

An undetected shift in money demand shifts the *LM* curve, leading to a different equilibrium from that which the central bank intended when deciding what level of the money supply to target.

Figure 20.5   **An unexpected rise in money demand**

quantity of narrow money can imply very different quantities of broad money. It is much simpler for central banks to decide what interest rate they wish to set, and then passively supply whatever narrow money is necessary to get whatever quantity of broad money is needed for money market equilibrium at that interest rate.

The monetary fiscal mix

Consider the model:

$$Y = A - br \qquad \textit{IS schedule} \qquad A, b > 0 \tag{1a}$$

$$Y = D + er \qquad \textit{LM schedule} \qquad e > 0, 0 < D < A \tag{1b}$$

Hence, $Y = A - br = D + er$, so in short-run equilibrium:

$$r = (A - D) / (b + e) \qquad Y = (Ae + bD) / (b + e) \tag{2}$$

Thus, for example, a rise in autonomous aggregate demand will lead to an increase in short-run equilibrium output and interest rates.

To understand the *LM* schedule in more detail, we can use the money market equations:

$$M = fY - hr \qquad \textbf{Money demand} \qquad f, h > 0$$

$$M = mR \qquad \textbf{Deposit multiplier} \qquad m > 0$$

Hence,

$$Y = [mR + hr] / f = [mR/f] + (h/f) r \tag{3}$$

Comparing this with equation (1b), we can see that the constant D in the *LM* schedule, which determines how far to the right the *LM* schedule lies, is just $[mR/f]$ and will increase if the central bank supplies more reserves R, if banks raise the deposit multiplier m, or if money demand becomes more sensitive to income via the parameter f. Moreover, the slope of the schedule, which depends on e in equation (1b), simply depends on the parameters h and f.

20.5 The policy mix

Fiscal policy is government decisions about tax rates and spending levels. Changes in fiscal policy shift the *IS* schedule. Changes in monetary policy shift the *LM* schedule.

We now explore consequences of different *IS* and *LM* schedules (different monetary and fiscal policies). Budget deficits can be financed by printing money or by borrowing. In the latter case, there is no short-run connection between monetary and fiscal policy provided the government is solvent and can borrow any reasonable amount that it wishes. The government can then pursue independent monetary and fiscal policies.

Although both fiscal and monetary policy can alter aggregate demand, the two policies are not interchangeable. They affect aggregate demand through different routes and have different implications for the *composition* of aggregate demand.

Figure 20.6 shows the mix of monetary and fiscal policy. There are two ways to stabilize income at Y^*. First, there is expansionary or *easy* fiscal policy (high government spending or low tax rates). This leads to a high

IS schedule, IS_1. To keep income in check with such an expansionary fiscal policy, *tight* monetary policy is needed. With a low money supply target, the schedule LM_1 is far to the left.

Equilibrium at E_1 achieves an output Y^* but also a high interest rate r_1. With high government spending, private demand must be kept in check. The mix of easy fiscal policy and tight monetary policy implies government spending G is a big share of national income Y^* but private spending $(C + I)$ a small share.

Alternatively, the government can adopt a tight fiscal policy (a low IS_0 schedule) and an easy monetary policy (LM_0 far to the right). The target income Y^* is now attained with a lower interest rate r_2 at the equilibrium E_2. With easy monetary policy and tight fiscal policy, the share of private expenditure $(C + I)$ is higher, and the share of government expenditure is lower, than at E_1. With lower interest rates, there is less crowding out of private expenditure.

Of course, easy monetary policy *and* easy fiscal policy together are highly expansionary. With the schedules IS_1 and LM_0 the equilibrium in Figure 20.6 is at E_4. Income is well above Y^*. Conversely, with tight monetary policy and tight fiscal policy, and schedules LM_1 and IS_0, equilibrium is at E_3, with income well below Y^*.

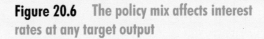

The target income Y can be attained by easy fiscal policy and tight monetary policy. Equilibrium at E_1, the intersection of LM_1 and IS_1, implies high interest rates r_1 and a low share of private sector investment and consumption in GNP. Alternatively, with easy monetary policy and tight fiscal policy, equilibrium at E_2, the intersection of LM_0 and IS_0, still attains the target income but at lower interest rates r_2. The share of private sector investment and consumption in GNP will be higher than at E_1.

Figure 20.6 The policy mix affects interest rates at any target output

What should determine the mix of fiscal and monetary policy? In the long run, the government may care not just about keeping output close to potential output, but also about raising potential output. High investment increases the capital stock more quickly, giving workers more equipment with which to work and raising their productivity. Governments interested in long-run growth may choose a tight fiscal policy and an easy monetary policy. Conversely, if governments are politically weak and unable to resist demands for high government spending to pay off various factions, fiscal policy will be loose and a tight monetary policy is needed to keep aggregate demand in line with potential output.

Solvency concerns also affect the feasible monetary–fiscal mix. In 2010 financial markets panicked when they thought Greece might default on its government debt. In such circumstances, ever greater bond-financed fiscal expansion may not be possible. Nobody will buy the bonds. The more difficult it is to meet aims through one policy, the more desirable it is for the other policy to do the work. The problem for Greece was that, as a member of the eurozone, it had surrendered its ability to use an independent monetary policy which targeted the needs of Greece alone.

One final point about the monetary–fiscal mix: changing fiscal policy takes time whereas monetary policy can be changed very quickly. In effect, the fiscal authorities decide first, and then monetary policy decisions are made subsequently. In the words of Mervyn King, governor of the Bank of England, when launching the February 2010 *Inflation Report*:

> Fiscal policy is an input into monetary policy. It is not the only one. The key thing is that monetary policy is something that can be changed every month, while fiscal policy cannot, so in that sense monetary policy has to bear the burden of steering the economy. And that's the policy we will adopt.

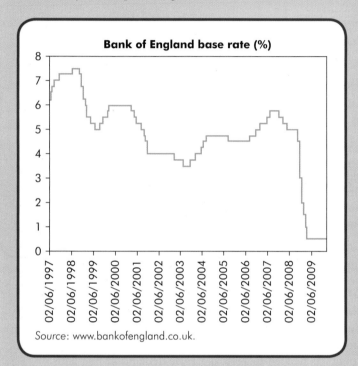

ACTIVITY 20.1

Monetary *or* fiscal policy?

Concept 17.1 noted some reasons why fiscal policy may not be ideal for short-run management of aggregate demand. Some of these reasons – for example, problems in diagnosing where the economy is and forecasting where it might go if policy is left unchanged – apply just as much to monetary policy as to fiscal policy. However, two problems are often thought to make fiscal policy less suitable for short-run variation.

First, fiscal policy is difficult to change quickly. Rapid changes in hospital building or in tax rates are more costly than rapid changes in interest rates. Financial markets are accustomed to asset prices changing quickly. Second, it is politically easy to loosen fiscal policy but politically much more difficult to tighten it again later. For this reason, the most important source of short-term movements in fiscal policy is the operation of automatic stabilizers. Since tax rates are not changing, no visible decisions are being made to which voters could object. Yet tax revenue is varying with output.

It used also to be politically difficult to tighten monetary policy. For example, people (voters!) who have borrowed to buy a house get upset when interest rates rise sharply. The main reason that most countries have made their central banks independent of political control in decisions about interest rates is precisely to take the politics out of monetary policy. Nowadays, interest rates can and do change rapidly, in both directions, though usually by very small amounts. The chart shows data from June 1997 to February 2010.

The figure confirms how aggressively interest rates were reduced in 2008/09 once the magnitude of the financial crisis became apparent.

What does this imply about the monetary fiscal mix? The budget deficit was already high because of the need to bail out banks. Further fiscal expansion threatened to create unsustainable levels of government debt that would be difficult to repay. In these circumstances, monetary policy had to provide as much stimulus as possible, both because a large stimulus was needed and because fiscal policy was already overstretched.

By March 2009 the Bank of England's official rate had been cut to 0.5 per cent and could hardly go much lower. As we saw in Chapter 19, the Bank then embarked on a £200 billion programme of quantitative easing, partly to offset the collapse of the bank deposit multiplier and partly in the hope of providing additional stimulus through the credit channel of monetary policy.

Source: Bank of England.

Questions

(a) During which periods was the Bank of England most worried about inflation?

(b) Was this current inflation at the time or was it the prospect of inflation in a year or two?

(c) Should the Bank worry about changing its mind, raising interest rates only to lower them shortly afterwards if necessary, or should it act more slowly so that it rarely has to reverse its recent decisions?

(d) Suppose an output slump leads to a period of negative inflation. What is the lowest possible nominal interest rate? What would then happen to real interest rates?

To check your answers to these questions, go to page 686.

20.6 The effect of future taxes

Chapter 19 argued that consumption demand reflects both *current* disposable income and expected *future* disposable income. Two hundred years ago, the English economist David Ricardo noticed a striking implication. Suppose the path of government purchases *G* is fixed over time. What path of taxes over time finances this spending?

The government can lend and borrow. In some years, its spending may exceed taxes, in other years taxes must then exceed spending.

For a given planned path of spending, and a suitable planned path of tax revenue, the government cuts taxes this year, and pays for it by borrowing – hence achieving **government solvency**. It sells bonds. The tax cut is a fiscal expansion that boosts aggregate demand. Right?

> **Government solvency**
> requires that the present value of the current and future tax revenue equals the present value of current and future spending plus any initial net debts.

If the tax cut is £1 billion, this is also the value of bonds issued to finance it. The market value of bonds is the present value of future income to bondholders. By assumption, the path of government spending is fixed. Hence, interest payments to bondholders must be financed by higher taxes in the future.

£1 billion is the value of the tax cut, *and* the value of the new bonds, *and* the present value of the extra future taxes. The private sector gets a handout today (a tax cut) offset by a future penalty (higher taxes) of identical present value. The private sector is neither richer nor poorer. Its desired spending should not change. Today's tax cut has no effect on aggregate demand because it is matched by the *prospect* of higher future taxes.

Equivalently, the fall in government saving (larger deficit today) is exactly offset by a rise in private saving: private spending is unaltered, and larger disposable incomes (because of the tax cut) go entirely in extra saving (to pay for the future taxes).

Some people getting tax cuts today will die before future taxes arrive. But suppose these people have children and care about them. After a tax cut today, parents save more to bequeath extra money to their children, or grandchildren, to pay the higher future taxes. The extra disposable income is saved to raise the bequest for future generations.

Ricardian equivalence does not deny that roadbuilding, financed by higher taxes, affects aggregate demand. Government spending always has real effects. Rather, for a *given* path of real government spending, it may not matter *when* people pay for it. Ricardo himself thought the equivalence hypothesis would not hold

> **Ricardian equivalence** says that it does not matter *when* a government finances a given spending programme. Tax cuts today do not affect private spending if, in present value terms, future taxes rise to match.

in the real world. Economists are still arguing about the extent to which Ricardian equivalence should hold.

Why Ricardian equivalence is too strong

There are three reasons why the tax cuts today *do* stimulate demand a bit even if future taxes are correspondingly higher. First, people without children get the benefit of tax cuts without paying the full burden of higher future taxes in the distant future. They spend more at once.

Second, by reducing marginal tax rates and distortions, tax cuts may increase potential output and raise income. Expecting higher incomes, people spend more immediately.

Third, solvent governments can borrow at a low interest rate. Ricardian equivalence holds only if we can borrow as easily as the government. If only! Households and firms are riskier than governments. Private people have no residual power to tax or print money when things go wrong. Hence, lenders charge private borrowers a higher rate of interest, and may refuse to lend at all.

Now do the sums again. £1 billion is the value of the tax cut, the extra government bonds and the present value of extra tax payments *discounted at the interest rate faced by the government*. We face a higher interest rate when we try to borrow. *As viewed by us, the present value of our extra future taxes is less than £1 billion because we discount at a higher interest rate.*

The tax cut is a fiscal expansion because in effect the government borrows on the good terms it enjoys, then lends to us at better terms than the capital market. It gives us a loan, tax cuts today, which we repay later in higher taxes. But we are charged the government's low interest rate for our loan. We are better off and spend more. Aggregate demand increases.

Theory and evidence suggest that complete Ricardian equivalence is too extreme to fit the real world. Tax cuts do boost aggregate demand today (though higher future taxes will reduce demand at some future date). Ricardian equivalence is not completely right, but not completely wrong. Expectations of future conditions affect current behaviour. Private saving rises a bit when public saving falls. The private sector does substitute between present and future, despite obstacles to doing this easily. These obstacles make consumption demand more sensitive to current disposable income than it would be if borrowing were easy and only permanent income mattered.

Current demand by firms and households depends both on current fiscal policy and expected future fiscal policy. Since one does not fully offset the other, for simplicity we can look at current fiscal policy in isolation. We need to remember only that some of its quantitative effects will be smaller if people expect fiscal policy to have to be reversed at some future date.

If Ricardian equivalence held exactly, government efforts to prop up aggregate demand during 2009 by running budget deficits would have been largely a waste of time. But understanding the trade-off between the present and the future allows three insights into the events of 2009/10:

1. It was precisely in 2009 that banks were most scared to lend and the private sector had so much difficulty borrowing. These are the circumstances in which bond-financed tax cuts are most powerful. They increase private sector liquidity at the critical time.

2. Conversely, as governments get closer to the limits of what they can easily borrow and guarantee to repay, the differential between private sector and government creditworthiness narrows. At some future point, deficit-financed tax cuts (or other subsidies to the private sector) may lose most of their power.

3. Two specific measures – the temporary VAT cut and the temporary subsidy to scrappage of old cars – work not by increasing the permanent income of households but by persuading them to bring forward spending from the future to the present. This is great when the measures are first introduced (and

helped explain positive UK output growth by the fourth quarter of 2009), but we should then prepare for a corresponding fall in demand when we get to the future from which the spending has been brought forward. All that has occurred is a retiming of spending, not an increase in the entire path of spending.

Governments wish to bring spending forward because of the effect on confidence. If this can be established, by ending the downward spiral, growth may become strong enough to cope with the future lack of spending for a while.

 20.7 Demand management revisited

In the last five chapters we have studied how aggregate demand determines output and employment. Fiscal and monetary policy can manage aggregate demand, aiming to keep the economy close to its full-employment level. In periods of recession, when aggregate demand is insufficient, monetary and fiscal expansion can boost demand, output and employment.

> **Demand management** uses monetary and fiscal policy to stabilize output near potential output.

Thus far, we have treated the price level as given. If the price level can change, boosting demand may lead not to higher output but to higher prices. In the next chapter, we begin the study of prices and inflation. In so doing, we introduce aggregate supply, and hence the balance between aggregate supply and aggregate demand.

However, you have now completed the first stage of macroeconomics, learning how to analyse the demand side of the economy. Even after mastering the analysis of supply, adjustment and price behaviour, the demand analysis of the last few chapters remains a key part of the story, especially in the short run.

Summary

- A **given fiscal policy** means a given path of government spending and tax rates. A **given monetary policy** must specify the implicit **monetary policy rule** by which interest rates are set. In this chapter, we assume that is to achieve a given **money supply target**.

- The *IS schedule* shows combinations of interest rates and output compatible with short-run equilibrium output in the goods market. Lower interest rates boost demand and output. Other causes of shifts in demand are shown as shifts in the *IS* schedule.

- The *LM schedule* shows combinations of interest rates and output compatible with money market equilibrium when the central bank pursues a money supply target. Higher output is associated with higher interest rates to maintain the equality of money supply and money demand.

- The intersection of *IS* and *LM* schedules shows simultaneous equilibrium in both goods and money markets, jointly determining output and interest rates.

- With a given monetary policy, a **fiscal expansion** increases output, money demand and interest rates, thus **crowding out** or partially displacing private consumption and investment demand.

- For a given fiscal policy, a **monetary expansion** leads to lower interest rates and higher output.

- The **mix of monetary and fiscal policy** affects the equilibrium interest rate as well as the level of output.

- **Ricardian equivalence** says that, for a given present value of government spending, the private sector does not care *when* this is financed by taxes, since the total present value of taxes is the same. A tax cut today has no effect on aggregate demand since people anticipate higher future taxes to finance the extra debt interest.

- Ricardian equivalence is true only under extreme assumptions not generally true in practice. Tax cuts today do have some effect today. This effect is dampened by the knowledge that, unless government spending is also cut, future taxes will have to rise.

- **Demand management** helps stabilize output. Fiscal policy may be difficult to adjust quickly, and may be difficult politically to reverse later: much of its impact on aggregate demand thus arises through **automatic stabilizers** with an unchanged fiscal policy.

Review questions

connect

EASY

1 Why do people usually save a 'once-off income tax rebate'?

2 For each of these shocks, say whether it shifts the *IS* schedule or the *LM* schedule, and in which direction: (a) an expected future fiscal expansion, (b) a higher money supply target, (c) a rise in money demand caused by higher interest rates being paid by banks on bank deposits.

3 A small country that has adopted the euro must accept the single interest rate set for the whole of Euroland. Draw the *LM* schedule relating the interest rate to that country's national output. Why would this schedule ever shift?

4 Suppose the European Central Bank has a monetary policy rule that relates Euroland's interest rate to total output in Euroland. If the small Euroland country's output is perfectly correlated with the output of all Euroland, draw the *LM* schedule (a) for Euroland and (b) for the small member country.

5 Suppose a government lived for ever and never broke its promises. Facing a large budget deficit and large government debt today, should the bond market be confident that any level of initial debt will be repaid provided the government pledges to do so at some time in the future?

6 Common fallacies   Why are the following statements wrong? (a) If tax rates never change, fiscal policy cannot stabilize output. (b) Higher government spending makes interest rates rise, which could cut aggregate demand by more than the rise in government spending. (c) Future policy cannot affect present behaviour.

7 Which is correct? Other things equal, high output and high interest rates imply: (a) loose monetary policy and loose fiscal policy; (b) tight fiscal policy and tight monetary policy; (c) tight fiscal policy and loose monetary policy; (d) none of the above.

MEDIUM

8 Use the *IS–LM* diagram to depict (a) the start of a financial crash in which confidence evaporates in the private sector and the banking system, and (b) a subsequent policy of quantitative easing.

9 In 2010, having accumulated substantial government debt owned by foreigners and having a large budget deficit, Greece lost the confidence of its international creditors and was given a loan on condition that it embarked on substantial fiscal tightening. (a) Illustrate these changes, using the

IS–LM diagram, recognizing that Greece is a eurozone member. (b) Suppose Greece left the eurozone; what, if anything, would be different?

10 Imagine a world of only two periods and zero interest rates. A consumer's income is 100 in each period, taxes are 50 each period, permanent disposable income is therefore 50, and consumption is 50 per period (since the world ends after period 2). The government now offers a tax cut of 10 in period 1, financed by government borrowing that will be repaid in period 2. (a) Since interest rates are zero, by how much must the government raise taxes in period 2 in order to pay off its loan in full? (b) What is disposable income now in each period for the consumer? (c) Since interest rate is zero, what is permanent disposable income? (d) What is the effect on consumption decisions? (e) If the government pays zero interest on loans, but the consumer pays 10 per cent interest, how is permanent income affected? (f) What now is the effect of the temporary tax cut?

11 Suppose mortgage lenders issued 20-year loans at fixed interest rates. (a) How would short-term changes in interest rates impact households with a mortgage? (b) Would the Bank of England have to change interest rates by more or by less to have the same effect on aggregate demand as at present?

12 Suppose monetary policy raises nominal interest rates by 0.8 every time inflation rises by 1. (a) How do you expect the central bank to manage stabilizing inflation around a low level? (b) Suppose inflation is nevertheless low and stable: how might you explain this outcome?

13 Essay question   'If households can lend and borrow easily, their consumption and saving decisions simply offset anticipated future tax changes. The principal power of taxation policy to influence aggregate demand arises because households in practice face difficulties borrowing what would be required to implement Ricardian equivalence.' Discuss.

For solutions to these questions contact your lecturer.

Aggregate supply, prices and adjustment to shocks

Learning Outcomes

By the end of this chapter, you should understand:

1. inflation targets for monetary policy

2. the *ii* schedule

3. how inflation affects aggregate demand

4. aggregate supply in the classical model

5. the equilibrium inflation rate

6. complete crowding out in the classical model

7. why wage adjustment may be slow

8. short-run aggregate supply

9. temporary and permanent supply shocks

10. how monetary policy reacts to demand and supply shocks

11. flexible inflation targets

12. A Taylor rule

Keynesian models suggest that higher aggregate demand always raises output. However, with only finite resources, the economy cannot expand output indefinitely. We now introduce only aggregate supply – firms' willingness and ability to produce – and show how demand and supply together determine output. Aggregate demand reflects the interaction of the markets for goods and money. Aggregate supply reflects the interaction of the markets for goods and labour.

Introducing supply means that we abandon the simplifying assumption that output is determined by demand alone. With both supply and demand, we can also explain what determined prices. We no longer need to assume that prices are given. And since inflation is simply the growth of prices from period to period, a model of prices is also a model of inflation. This allows us to represent monetary policy as inflation targeting, the policy rule actually followed by most central banks today.

To get started, we swap the Keynesian extreme, with fixed wages and prices, for the opposite extreme, full wage and price flexibility.

In the classical model, the economy is *always* at full capacity. Any deviation of output from full capacity causes instant price and wage changes to restore output to potential output. In the classical model, monetary and fiscal policies affect prices but not output, which is always at potential output.

The **classical model** of macroeconomics assumes wages and prices are completely flexible.

In the short run, until prices and wages adjust, the Keynesian model is relevant. In the long run, once all prices and wages have adjusted, the classical model is relevant. We study how the economy evolves from the Keynesian short run to the classical long run.

21.1 Inflation and aggregate demand

If a central bank behaves predictably, its behaviour can be modelled. Chapter 20 explained why the growing instability of money demand led central banks to abandon monetary targeting. Nowadays, most central banks pursue an **inflation target**.

Inflation is the growth rate of the price level of aggregate output.

Target inflation π^* varies from country to country, but is usually around 2 per cent a year. Why not a target of zero inflation? Policy makers are keen to avoid *deflation* (negative inflation), which can become a black hole. Even if the nominal interest rate r is reduced to zero, the real interest rate i, which is simply $(r - \pi)$, can be large if inflation π is large but negative.

With an **inflation target**, the central bank adjusts interest rates to try to keep inflation close to the target inflation rate.

In turn, high real interest rates cause further contraction and make inflation more negative still, making real interest rates even higher. If nominal interest rates have already been reduced to zero, monetary policy can do nothing further to combat shrinking aggregate demand. To avoid this black hole, setting a positive inflation target leaves a margin of error. If inflation today is 2 per cent and an unforeseen shock reduces inflation by 1 per cent, there is still time for the central bank to act to boost the economy before it gets too close to a deflationary spiral.

Under inflation targeting, the *ii* **schedule** shows that at higher inflation rates the central bank will wish to have higher real interest rates.

Figure 21.1 shows how monetary policy works when interest rates are set in pursuit of an inflation target. When inflation is high, the central bank ensures that real interest rates are high, which reduces aggregate demand, putting downward pressure on inflation.

With a vertical *ii* schedule, inflation would be completely stabilized at its target rate π^*. If inflation started to rise, real interest rates would be raised by whatever was necessary to restore inflation to its target level.

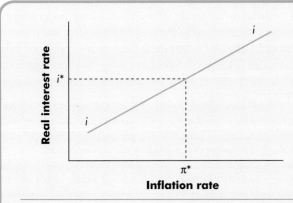

When inflation is above (below) the target π^*, real interest rates are set higher (lower) than normal. Along the schedule *ii*, a given monetary policy is being pursued. If the inflation target is π^*, the corresponding real interest rate will be i^*.

Figure 21.1   Interest rates and inflation targeting

Conversely, if inflation started to fall, real interest rates would be reduced to whatever level it took immediately to restore inflation to target.

Such a monetary policy would be too aggressive. By the end of this chapter, you will understand why some of its side effects would be undesirable. The *ii* schedule shown in Figure 21.1 shows more moderate intervention. When inflation is too high, the central bank raises real interest rates a bit; when inflation is too low, real interest rates are reduced a bit.

> The central bank sets the **nominal interest rate r** not the **real interest rate i**.

Although the central bank is interested in the real interest rate, which affects aggregate demand, the central bank does not directly control the price of output or the inflation rate. Hence, to achieve the *ii* schedule of Figure 21.1, the central bank first forecasts inflation, then sets a **nominal interest rate r** to achieve the **real interest rate i** $(= r - \pi)$ that it desires.

One important implication of Figure 21.1 is that a rise in inflation must lead to a *larger* rise in the nominal interest rate, for only then will the real interest rate be higher when inflation is higher.[1] Merely raising nominal interest rates in line with inflation would mean a constant real interest rate.

We regard a given *ii* schedule as a given monetary policy. Moving along the schedule, the central bank is adjusting interest rates to inflation according to the policy rule already adopted. Changes in monetary policy are shown by *shifts* in the schedule. A looser monetary policy means a downward shift in the *ii* schedule; a lower interest rate at each possible inflation rate. A tighter monetary policy shifts the *ii* schedule upwards; a higher interest rate at each possible inflation rate.

If π^* is the inflation target, the chosen height of the *ii* schedule determines the corresponding real interest rate i^* when the inflation target is being met. A tighter monetary policy (higher *ii* schedule) thus implies either accepting a higher real interest rate i^* at the given inflation target π^*, or a lower inflation target at the same real interest rate i^*.

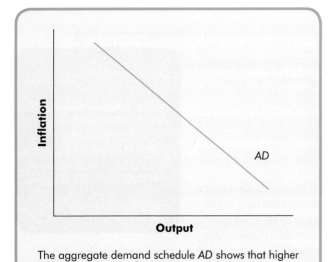

The aggregate demand schedule *AD* shows that higher inflation reduces aggregate demand by inducing the central bank to raise real interest rates.

Figure 21.2 The aggregate demand schedule

> The **aggregate demand schedule AD** shows how inflation affects aggregate demand when the interest rate is set in pursuit of an inflation target.

Figure 21.2 shows the level of aggregate demand for output when interest rates obey the *ii* schedule implied by inflation targeting. Movements *along* the aggregate demand schedule *AD* show how inflation makes the central bank alter real interest rates and thus aggregate demand.[2] The *AD* schedule is flat when (a) interest rate decisions react a lot to inflation and (b) interest rates have a big effect on aggregate

---

1 Across countries, higher inflation is often matched by equally higher nominal interest rates, leaving real interest rates roughly constant. This reflects the relative constancy of i^* in the long run. For short-run data for a single country, nominal interest rates vary more than inflation, reflecting the central bank behaviour embodied in Figure 21.1. Recognizing that interest rates must rise sharply when inflation increases has been a key breakthrough of monetary policy design in the last two decades.

2 A similar *AD* schedule exists if instead the central bank pursues a money supply target. For a given path of nominal money *M*, higher inflation, by raising prices more, reduces the real money supply *M/P* by more. With lower real money supply, interest rates rise to reduce real money demand and maintain money market equilibrium. Higher real interest rates reduce aggregate demand, just as in Figure 21.2. Under a monetary target, interest rates rise because inflation has reduced the real money supply. Under inflation targeting, interest rates rise in direct response to inflation itself, and the real money supply is then reduced to make this an equilibrium. Either way, higher inflation induces higher real interest rates and lower aggregate demand.

demand. The *AD* is steep when (a) interest rate decisions do not respond much to inflation and (b) changes in interest rates have a small effect on aggregate demand.

Shifts in *AD* reflect all other shifts in aggregate demand *not* caused by the effect of inflation on interest rate decisions. Thus, *AD* shifts up if fiscal policy eases, net exports rise or monetary policy eases (a lower *ii* schedule).

The *AD* schedule relates aggregate demand, output and inflation. Next, we turn to aggregate supply.

21.2 Aggregate supply

When prices and wages are completely flexible, output is always at **potential output**.

Potential output depends on the level of technology, the quantities of available inputs (labour, capital, land, energy) in long-run equilibrium, and the efficiency with which resources and technology are exploited. In the long run, investment in physical and human capital raises inputs of labour and capital, technical progress improves technology and supply-side policies reduce distortions and raise efficiency. In the short run, we treat potential output as given; it is long-run **equilibrium output**.

With flexible wages and prices, how does a rise in inflation (and correspondingly faster growth of nominal wages) affect the incentive of firms to supply goods and services?

Thinking in real terms, firms compare the real wage (the nominal wage *W* divided by the price level *P*) with the real benefit of labour, the extra output it makes. Similarly, workers compare real take-home pay (its purchasing power over goods and services) with the disutility of sacrificing more leisure in order to work longer. If wages and prices both double, real wages are unaffected. Neither firms nor workers should change their behaviour. **Aggregate supply** is unaffected by pure inflation since everything nominal rises by the same proportion, as shown in Figure 21.3.

Wage and price flexibility ensures all nominal variables rise together. Without **money illusion**, people see through nominal changes: real variables are unaltered. In the classical model, real things determine real things, and nominal things determine other nominal things. Better technology, more capital or greater labour supply raise potential output, shifting the vertical supply curve from AS_0 to AS_1 in Figure 21.3. However,

> The **aggregate supply schedule** shows the output that firms wish to supply at each inflation rate.
>
> **Equilibrium output** is independent of inflation.
>
> At **potential output** all inputs are fully employed.
>
> In the classical model, the **aggregate supply schedule** is vertical at potential output.
>
> **Money illusion** exists if people confuse nominal and real variables.

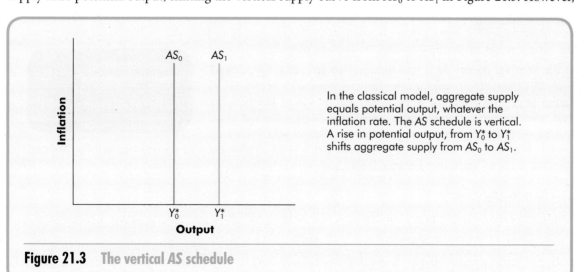

In the classical model, aggregate supply equals potential output, whatever the inflation rate. The AS schedule is vertical. A rise in potential output, from Y_0^* to Y_1^* shifts aggregate supply from AS_0 to AS_1.

Figure 21.3 The vertical *AS* schedule

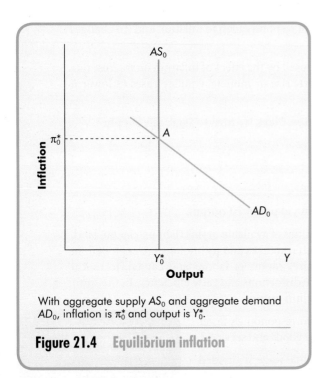

With aggregate supply AS_0 and aggregate demand AD_0, inflation is π_0^* and output is Y_0^*.

Figure 21.4 Equilibrium inflation

for any given level of potential output, lower inflation does *not* reduce the real output that firms wish to supply.

21.3 Equilibrium inflation

For the classical model, Figure 21.4 shows the aggregate demand schedule AD_0 and the vertical aggregate supply schedule AS_0. Output is at potential output and inflation is π_0^*. At point A there is equilibrium in all markets: for output, money and labour.

The labour market is in equilibrium anywhere on the AS_0 schedule, since the economy is at potential output and full employment. A is also on the aggregate demand schedule along which interest rates are adjusted in line with monetary policy and the aggregate demand for goods equals the actual output of goods.

The equilibrium inflation rate π_0^* reflects the positions of the AS and AD schedules. Potential output Y_0^* reflects technology, efficiency and available input supplies. The macroeconomic demand schedule depends on the IS schedule showing how interest rates affect aggregate demand, and on the *ii* schedule of Figure 21.1, showing how interest rates respond to deviations of inflation from its target level.

CONCEPT 21.1

Anchors away!

When prices can change, monetary policy must anchor all nominal variables.

Suppose the interest rate r is simply constant. In the classical model, output is Y^*. Y^* and r determine money demand M/P. Nominal money M is passively supplied to get the right level of real money M/P. If the market imagines prices P will be larger, the central bank supplies more nominal money M to maintain equilibrium M/P. Since prices are completely flexible, *any* price level can be the equilibrium price level! The economy has no nominal anchor, no starting point.

A target for nominal money M is one **nominal anchor**. Money demand determines M/P but, with M now known, the market knows where to set P. An inflation target is an alternative nominal anchor. Given *last* period's price level, now known and unalterable, an inflation target for the price increase between last period and this period is also a target for the current price level P. With money demand M/P and the price level P now known, money market equilibrium determines M. Later we show that a nominal exchange rate can also act as a nominal anchor.

> A **nominal anchor** determines the *level* of other nominal variables. Market forces determine real variables.

Price level or inflation rate?

Since last period's price level is now known, statements about today's inflation π can be converted into statements about today's price level P. All the diagrams in this chapter could be drawn with P rather than π on the vertical axis. We prefer to show inflation for two reasons. First, it fits more easily with inflation targeting, the actual policy of modern central banks. Second, it has a clearer link to the Phillips curve in the next chapter.

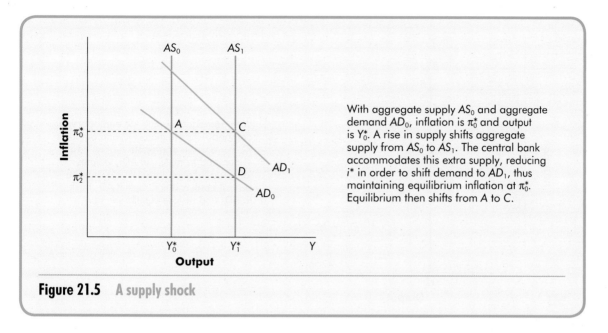

With aggregate supply AS_0 and aggregate demand AD_0, inflation is π_0^* and output is Y_0^*. A rise in supply shifts aggregate supply from AS_0 to AS_1. The central bank accommodates this extra supply, reducing i^* in order to shift demand to AD_1, thus maintaining equilibrium inflation at π_0^*. Equilibrium then shifts from A to C.

Figure 21.5   A supply shock

To ensure that equilibrium inflation π_0^* coincides with the inflation target π^*, the central bank chooses the correct height of the *ii* schedule in Figure 21.1, thereby ensuring the *AD* schedule has the correct height to make equilibrium inflation π_0^* coincide with the target inflation rate π^*. If π_0^* is too low, the central bank loosens monetary policy, shifting the *ii* schedule down and the *AD* schedule up. If π_0^* exceeds the inflation target, a tighter monetary policy shifts the *ii* schedule up and the *AD* schedule down.

A supply shock

Supply shocks may be beneficial, such as technical progress, or may be adverse, such as higher real oil prices or loss of capacity after an earthquake. Suppose potential output rises. In Figure 21.5 the *AS* schedule shifts to the right, from AS_0 to AS_1. For a *given AD* schedule, equilibrium inflation falls to π_2^* with equilibrium at *D*.

However, the central bank still wants a long-run equilibrium inflation rate π_0^*. Hence, in response to the supply shock, the central bank loosens **monetary policy**, shifting the *ii* schedule downwards and the *AD* schedule upwards. Lower real interest rates boost aggregate demand in line with higher potential output Y_1^*. The new equilibrium is at *C*, not *D*. With unchanged inflation, the lower real interest rate also implies a lower nominal interest rate.

> **Monetary policy** accommodates a permanent supply change by altering the real interest rate (shift in the *ii* schedule) to induce a similar change in aggregate demand.

Lower interest rates raise the demand for money. To restore money market equilibrium, the central bank must then supply more money.

Conversely, if high oil prices permanently reduce aggregate supply, this shifts AS_1 to AS_0. Beginning at point *C*, the central bank must then tighten monetary policy, so that higher real interest rates reduce aggregate demand in line with the lower aggregate supply.

A demand shock

Suppose aggregate demand shifts up because of easier fiscal policy or greater private sector optimism about future incomes and profits. Beginning from equilibrium at *A* in Figure 21.6, but keeping supply fixed at AS_0, a demand shift from AD_0 to AD_1 leads to a new equilibrium at *B*.

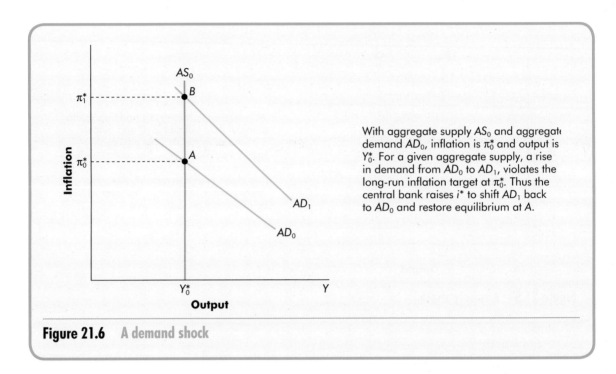

With aggregate supply AS_0 and aggregate demand AD_0, inflation is π_0^* and output is Y_0^*. For a given aggregate supply, a rise in demand from AD_0 to AD_1, violates the long-run inflation target at π_0^*. Thus the central bank raises i^* to shift AD_1 back to AD_0 and restore equilibrium at A.

Figure 21.6   A demand shock

Oil prices and UK inflation

CASE 21.1

The figure below shows the dramatic increase in oil prices after 2003. If oil price shocks lead to inflation, why did so little inflation materialize? Was the Bank of England lulled into a false sense of security? Should we be surprised that, by April 2007, the Bank had to justify why it had allowed UK inflation to exceed the target range to which it is committed. Was it only the financial crash that spared the Bank further embarrassment?

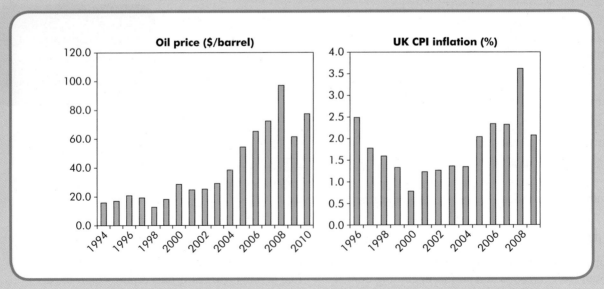

It was certainly true that the early years of inflation targeting were a benevolent environment for monetary policy. Globalization was flooding the West with cheap imports from China that helped keep prices down, and trade unions in Europe and the US were all too aware that they could make domestic firms uncompetitive by pressing too hard for wage increases.

This same globalization put upward pressure not just on oil but on other commodity prices. Once China and India, the world's two most populous economies, were growing at 8–10 per cent a year, their demands for raw materials were substantial by the early years of the twenty-first century.

The Bank was fully aware of what was going on. For example, Monetary Policy Committee member David Walton gave a speech in February 2006 entitled 'Has oil lost the capacity to shock?', concluding:

- *The size and nature of the shock have been different.* Relative to previous episodes, the shock had taken longer to unfold.

- *The UK economy had been better placed to absorb the current oil price shock.* There were few inflationary pressures in the economy when oil prices first began to rise sharply and there had been little sign subsequently of higher wage demands.

- *The monetary policy framework had played an important role.* Inflation targeting had helped to anchor inflation expectations, preventing inflation from spilling over into wage claims, yet had allowed the Bank to respond flexibly to the oil shock.

To these, he might have added the fourth, which we described above:

- *Beneficial supply shocks* (cheaper imports from China and other parts of the global economy had provided downward pressure on prices at precisely the time that adverse supply shocks (oil and commodity price rises) were providing upward pressure on prices.

Even so, by 2007, the balance of these effects had turned clearly towards inflation, and consumer price inflation peaked at 3.8 per cent in 2008. On the retail price index that had previously been used to measure prices, inflation was heading up towards 5 per cent. The honeymoon for Bank of England independence was well and truly over.

We will never know what would have happened in the absence of the financial crash. Presumably world commodity prices would have remained high, and the Bank of England would have had to raise interest rates, possibly quite a bit, to get inflation back on track. Whether price bubbles in housing and other assets could have been gently restrained, or whether the medicine needed to reverse them would then have led to a rapid collapse in prices, remains a fascinating topic for debate.

The financial crash imposed a sharp fall in aggregate demand, and initiated rapid contraction. Even China and India were not immune from the ripples of the crash. World demand and world commodity prices fell for a bit. But by 2009, China had returned to 10 per cent growth, and the price of oil and other commodities was rising again.

The right-hand chart shows that UK inflation was brought under control in 2009. However, it is expected to have a temporary upward blip in 2010. VAT, reduced in 2009 to help boost aggregate demand, was increased again in January 2010. Depreciation of the UK exchange rate during 2009 had also made imports more expensive.

Interestingly, the Bank of England announced in advance that it would regard the inevitable rise in UK inflation during 2010 as temporary, and would not expect to raise interest rates immediately to stave this off. Given the fragility of the economy, it preferred to keep interest rates low for a little longer.

This episode illustrates the flexibility with which a credible central bank can pursue inflation targeting. The more people believe that the Bank will keep a grip on inflation in the long run, the less people will care about blips in the short run.

The central bank can continue to hit its inflation target π_0^* only by tightening monetary policy to offset the demand shock. In full equilibrium, with unchanged supply AS_0, aggregate demand must not change. By raising real interest rates, the central bank can reduce aggregate demand again. The central bank thus tightens monetary policy (an upward shift in the *ii* schedule) until the demand shock is fully offset and AD_1 has shifted down to AD_0 again. Equilibrium remains at A and the inflation target π_0^* is still achieved.

> In the classical model with a vertical AS schedule, **a rise in government spending crowds out an equal amount of private spending.** Aggregate demand remains equal to potential output.

The original rise in demand could have come from the private or the public sector. If it was higher private demand, the higher real interest rate simply reduces private demand back to its original level. If it was higher government spending, the central bank raises interest rates until private spending falls by as much as government spending increased.

Note the distinction between partial crowding out in the Keynesian model and complete crowding out in the classical model. In the Keynesian model, output was demand-determined in the short run. Higher *output* induced the central bank to raise interest rates, which partly offset the expansionary effect of higher government spending.

In the classical model, aggregate supply is the binding constraint. Output does not change. When higher government expenditure raises aggregate demand, higher interest rates must reduce consumption and investment to leave aggregate demand unaltered.

We may draw a second conclusion from Figure 21.6. Suppose monetary policy changes because the inflation target is raised from π_0^* to π_1^*. With a higher target inflation rate, the central bank no longer needs such high real interest rates at any particular level of inflation. Real interest rates fall and the aggregate demand schedule shifts up from AD_0 to AD_1. With an unchanged AS schedule, equilibrium moves from A to B.

In the new equilibrium, inflation is higher but real output is unaltered. Since it is a full equilibrium, all real variables are then constant. One of these variables is the real money stock M/P. Since prices grow at the rate π_1^*, the nominal money supply must also grow at this rate.

> In the classical model, **faster nominal money growth** is accompanied by higher inflation but leaves real output constant at potential output.

The idea that **nominal money growth** is associated with inflation, but not growth of output or employment, is the central tenet of *monetarists*. Figure 21.6 shows this is correct in the classical model with full wage and price flexibility and no money illusion.

How long does all this take?

The classical model studies the economy once all variables have fully adjusted. Instead of thinking of adjustment as instant, we can view the classical model as applying to a long enough time for slower adjustment to be completed. This means not just wage and price adjustment, but time for the central bank to work out what is going on and amend monetary policy if necessary, and time for these interest rate changes to have their full effect on private behaviour. Suppose the economy faces a fall in aggregate demand. What happens next?

The classical model

With aggregate supply unaffected, a fall in aggregate demand leads to lower inflation, to which the central bank immediately responds by easing monetary policy, reducing the real interest rate, boosting private sector demand and thus restoring aggregate demand to the unchanged level of potential output.[3]

---

3   A similar analysis applies under monetary targeting. Suppose this is 2 per cent annual growth in nominal money. Long-run inflation will also be 2 per cent. A fall in aggregate demand bids down wage and price growth *below what they would have been*. With inflation below 2 per cent but an unchanged nominal money growth of 2 per cent, the real money supply expands. This causes a fall in real interest rates and boosts aggregate demand back to potential output. Thereafter, money and prices both grow at 2 per cent. The real money supply is permanently higher and real interest rates permanently lower.

The Keynesian model

Before wages and price adjustment is possible, there is no change in inflation to which the central bank can respond. The initial effect of lower aggregate demand is simply a fall in output. The rest of this chapter studies the adjustment process by which the economy gradually makes the transition from the Keynesian short run to the classical long run. To do so, we introduce the short-run aggregate supply curve.

21.4 The labour market and wage behaviour

Downward shocks cause recessions lasting years not weeks. Why don't changes in prices react faster, allowing changes that restore potential output? Firms relate prices to costs. Wages are the largest part of costs. Sluggish wage adjustment to departures from full employment is the main cause of slow adjustment of prices.

For both firms and workers, a job is often a long-term commitment. For the firm, it is costly to hire and fire workers. Firing entails a redundancy payment and the loss of the expertise the worker had built up on the job. Hiring entails advertising, interviewing and training a new worker in the special features of that firm. Firms are reluctant to hire and fire workers just because of short-term fluctuations in demand.

For the worker, looking for a new job costs time and effort, and throws away experience, seniority and the high wages justified by the high productivity that comes from having mastered a particular job in a particular firm. Like firms, workers care about long-term arrangements. Firms and workers reach an understanding about pay and conditions *in the medium term*, including how to handle fluctuations in the firm's output in the short run.

A firm and its workers have explicit contracts, or implicit agreements, specifying working conditions. These include normal hours, overtime requirements, regular wages and pay schedules for overtime work. The firm then sets the number of hours, within the limits of these conditions, depending on how much output it wishes to make in that week.

When demand falls, the firm initially reduces hours of work. Overtime ends and factories close early. If demand does not recover, or declines further, firms start firing workers. Conversely, in a boom a firm makes its existing workforce work overtime. Then it seeks temporary workers to supplement the existing labour force. Only when the firm is sure that higher sales will be sustained does it hire extra permanent workers.

Wage adjustment

Wages are not set in a daily auction in which the equilibrium wage clears the market for labour. Firms and workers both gain from long-term understandings. This mutual commitment partly insulates a firm and its workforce from temporary conditions in the labour market.

Nor can a firm and its workforce spend every day haggling. Bargaining is costly, using up valuable time that could be used to produce output. Bargaining costs mean wages change only at discrete intervals. Immediate wage adjustment to shocks is ruled out. At best, firms must wait until the next scheduled date for a revision in the wage structure. In practice, complete wage adjustment is unlikely to take place even then. Chapter 10 discussed other reasons why involuntary unemployment is not instantly eliminated by wage adjustment.

Recap

In the short run (the first few months), changes in labour input are largely changes in hours. In the medium run (up to two years), as changes in labour demand persist, the firm begins to alter its permanent workforce. In the long run (perhaps four to six years), adjustment is complete.

In the short run, trends in wages are largely given. The firm has some flexibility over earnings, as distinct from negotiated wage rates, because fluctuations in overtime and short time affect average hourly earnings. But this flexibility is limited. In the medium run, the firm begins to adjust the path of wages. In the long run, the process is complete and the economy is back at potential output.

We now use this analysis to think about the market for output. By distinguishing between supply in the short and long run, our model of output reflects *both* supply and demand, even in the short run. Nevertheless, its short-run behaviour is like the simple Keynesian case in which output is demand-determined. Its long-run behaviour is fully classical.

21.5 Short-run aggregate supply

In Figure 21.7 the economy is at potential output at *A*. In the short run, the firm inherits a given rate of nominal wage growth (not shown in the figure). Previous wage negotiations anticipated remaining in long-run equilibrium at *A* with inflation π_0. By keeping up with inflation, nominal wage growth is expected to maintain the correct real wage for labour market equilibrium.

> The **short-run supply curve SAS** shows how desired output varies with inflation, for a given inherited growth of nominal wages.

If inflation exceeds the expected inflation rate π_0, this helps firms by raising their output prices. The real wage is lower than expected. If this had been foreseen when wages were negotiated, the inherited nominal wage would have been higher; but it was not foreseen. Firms take advantage of their good luck by supplying a lot more output. They can afford to pay overtime to ensure that the workforce co-operates, and may also take on temporary extra staff.

Conversely, if inflation is below π_0, the real wage is now higher than anticipated when the nominal wage was agreed. Since labour is now costly, firms cut back output a lot. They move from *A* to *B* in Figure 21.7. Firms move along the **short-run supply curve SAS** in the short run.

If demand and output remain low, the growth rate of negotiated nominal wages gradually falls. With lower wage growth, firms do not need to raise output prices so quickly. The short-run aggregate supply schedule shifts down from *SAS* to SAS_1 in Figure 21.7. Lower inflation moves the economy down its aggregate demand schedule, increasing the demand for goods. If full employment and potential output are still not restored, negotiated wage growth falls again, leading to a short-run aggregate supply schedule such as SAS_2.

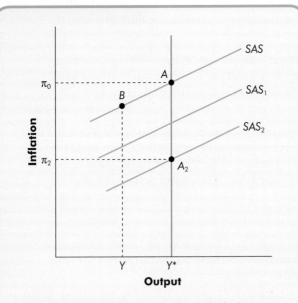

Firms raise prices when wage costs rise. Each short-run aggregate supply schedule reflects a different rate of inherited nominal wage growth. For any given rate, higher inflation moves firms up a given short-run supply schedule. A persisting boom or slump gradually bids nominal wage growth up or down, shifting short-run aggregate supply schedules. When these shift enough to restore to the inflation rate at which *AD* and *AS* intersect, potential output is restored.

Figure 21.7   *Short-run aggregate supply*

These short-run aggregate supply schedules give a realistic picture of adjustment to demand shocks. Because the short-run aggregate supply schedule is flat, a shift in aggregate demand leads mainly to changes in output not prices in the short run. This is the Keynesian feature. But deviations from full employment gradually change wage growth and short-run aggregate supply.

The economy gradually works its way back to potential output. That is the classical feature. We now describe adjustment in more detail.

21.6 The adjustment process

We now combine the aggregate demand schedule with the short-run aggregate supply schedule to show how demand or supply shocks set up an adjustment process. In so doing, we now assume that the goods market clears, even in the short run. Short-run aggregate supply gradually changes over time as wage growth adjusts to the rate that restores full employment and potential output, placing firms eventually on their long-run aggregate supply schedule.

Output is no longer demand-determined when aggregate demand lies below the level of potential output. In the short run, firms are also on their short-run supply schedules producing what they wish, *given the inherited nominal wages*.

However, sluggish wage adjustment prevents immediate restoration of full employment. When aggregate demand for goods falls, firms reduce output and employment. Since wages do not fall at once, there is involuntary unemployment. *Employment* is demand-determined in the short run.

Figure 21.8 shows a downward shift in the aggregate demand schedule from AD to AD' because monetary policy is tightened (a higher ii schedule in Figure 21.1). In the long run, aggregate demand must return to potential output, and the economy will end up at E_3. Hence, the tighter monetary policy can be viewed as a cut in the target inflation rate from π^* to π_3^*.

When monetary policy is first tightened, interest rates are initially raised since actual inflation at E is now above target. Aggregate demand shifts down to AD'. In the classical model there is an instant adjustment of prices and wages to keep the economy at full employment and potential output. Equilibrium inflation immediately falls to π_3^* and the new equilibrium is at E_3. Output remains at potential output Y^*.

These classical results are valid only in the long run. When adjustment of wages and prices is slow, the economy faces the short-run aggregate supply schedule SAS, reflecting the nominal wages recently agreed.

In the short run, the downward shift in AD causes a move from E to E'. Since firms cannot cut costs much, they reduce output to Y'. At E' the goods market clears at the intersection of the aggregate demand schedule AD' and the supply schedule SAS. Inflation has fallen a little because of lower demand, but output has fallen a lot. With lower inflation than the expectation built into nominal wage agreements, *real wages have risen*, despite the fall in output. Once firms can adjust employment, some workers are fired and unemployment rises.

In the medium run, this starts to reduce wage growth. With inherited wages lower than they would have been, firms move on to a lower short-run aggregate

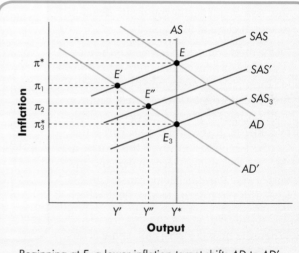

Beginning at E, a lower inflation target shifts AD to AD'. Given inherited wage growth, the new equilibrium is at E'. Output falls from Y^* to Y', and actual inflation is only π_1. Since wages have risen faster than prices despite the fall in output, unemployment rises. In the next wage settlement, nominal wage growth slows, and the short-run supply schedule becomes SAS'. Equilibrium is now at E'', and output recovers to Y''. Once wage growth slows enough to make SAS_3 the supply curve, long-run equilibrium is re-established at E_3.

Figure 21.8 A lower inflation target

supply schedule SAS'. The goods market now clears at E''. Output and employment recover a bit, but some unemployment persists. Since inflation has fallen, the central bank is less worried about the amount by which inflation exceeds its new target and cuts real interest rates, moving the economy down AD' to E''.

In the long run, adjustment is complete. Wage growth and inflation fall to π_3^*. The short-run aggregate supply schedule is SAS_3 in Figure 21.8. The economy is in full equilibrium at E_3, on AS, SAS_3 and AD'. Output is Y^* and the labour market is back at full employment.

The real world lies between the extreme simplifications of the simple Keynesian model and classical models. In practice, prices and wages are neither fully flexible nor fully fixed. A tougher inflation target has real effects in the short run, since output and employment are reduced. But after wages and prices adjust fully, output and employment return to normal. Inflation is permanently lower thereafter.

ACTIVITY 21.1

Output gaps 1998–2010

The output gap $(Y - Y^*)$ is the percentage deviation of actual output Y from potential output Y^*. Each year the Paris-based Organization for Economic Cooperation and Development (OECD) estimates potential output for all its member countries. The diagram below shows estimates for the UK, US and Germany. Positive output gaps are booms; negative gaps indicate slumps.

The diagram shows the relative stability of the period 1998–2006. Central banks were successfully managing aggregate demand to keep it close to full capacity.

Of the three countries, Germany is the most dependent on manufacturing exports. China led the global economy into a boom in the first decade of the twenty-first century, and commodity prices were rising sharply by 2007/08. It should be no surprise that German exporters enjoyed this boom in the world economy. German demand and output were above their long-run sustainable level. This was true to a lesser extent in both the UK and US.

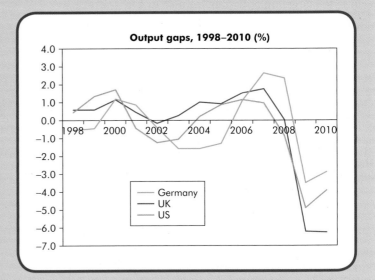

When the financial crisis hit, some economists thought that Germany would be relatively well insulated, since its regulation of banks had been more stringent than in the UK and US. Yet, the diagram shows that Germany, experienced nearly as dramatic a slump in aggregate demand as its Anglo-Saxon competitors. Sub-prime mortgages had found their way even into Stuttgart and Frankfurt. Even China did not escape. When aggregate demand in China fell in 2009, German exports were hard hit. Thus different countries experienced the crash through different channels. It originated in the US, and UK banks were then very exposed, but Germany suffered because all its export markets suffered.

The diagram shows how the upturn is slowly starting to take effect. It also confirms that for the next few years all major economies will have substantial spare capacity – the underlying assumption of the Keynesian perspective.

Finally, the diagram helps identify periods in which simple Keynesian analysis cannot be the whole story. Once the output gap has been eliminated, there is no spare capacity remaining, and the classical model is increasingly relevant.

Questions

There are two ways in which you might try to calculate potential output, and hence the output gap: (i) statistically, by fitting trend lines through previous business cycles, or (ii) economically by trying to get an idea of the balance of aggregate supply and aggregate demand.

(a) If you wanted a quick procedure capable of being replicated across many countries, which of the two would you be inclined to choose?

(b) How might you build up an idea of an empirical economic model of the balance between actual output and potential output?

(c) A central bank reduces interest rates but is disappointed to find that this quickly generates higher inflation not higher output. What can you infer about the initial level of the output gap? Why?

To check your answers to these questions, go to page 686.

Sluggish adjustment to shocks

A permanent supply shock

Suppose a change in attitudes towards women working leads to an increase in labour supply. Potential output rises. In the long run, aggregate demand must rise in line with aggregate supply. Lower real interest rates allow higher aggregate demand at the unchanged inflation target π^*. Provided monetary policy is loosened, the rightward shift in AD can match the rightward shift in aggregate supply. By accommodating the extra supply with looser monetary policy, the inflation rate remains π^*, and the economy moves directly to the new long-run equilibrium, from E_0 to E_1 in Figure 21.9.

Because of lags in diagnosing the shock, and in the response of consumption and investment demand to lower interest rates, Figure 21.9 exaggerates the ease of adjustment to a **permanent supply shock**. In practice, output may not jump all the way to the new level of potential output.

If the aggregate demand schedule does not fully and immediately shift to AD_1, output is below Y_1^*. This reduces inflation and the central bank responds with lower interest rates. Over time, the aggregate demand schedule will drift to the right until it reaches AD_1 in Figure 21.9.

> A **permanent supply shock** changes potential output.

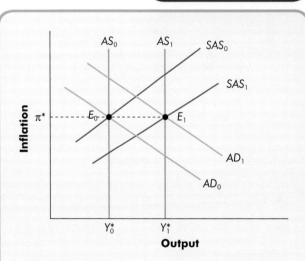

A permanent rise in supply shifts AS_0 and SAS_0 to AS_1 and SAS_1. By permanently reducing interest rates, the central bank shifts AD_0 to AD_1, meeting its inflation target π^* in the new equilibrium at E_1. If the central bank acts quickly, no further shifts in SAS_1 are required.

Figure 21.9   A permanent supply increase

A temporary supply shock

A **temporary supply shock** shifts the short-run aggregate supply schedule, but leaves potential output unaltered.

Monetary policy accommodates a temporary supply shock when monetary policy is altered to help stabilize output. The consequence, however, is higher inflation.

A **temporary supply shock** leaves potential output unaffected in the long run. With the vertical AS schedule unaltered, the short-run supply curve must shift. Although the SAS schedule is *mainly* influenced by inherited nominal wages, it is *also* affected by other input prices. Suppose a temporary oil price rise makes firms charge higher prices at any output level. Figure 21.10 shows a shift upwards in short-run supply, from SAS to SAS'. The new short-run equilibrium is at E'. Inflation rises but output and employment fall because the central bank raises real interest rates in response to higher inflation.

If the central bank maintains its inflation target π^*, lower output and employment at E' gradually reduce inflation and nominal wage growth, shifting SAS' gradually back to SAS. The economy slowly moves down the AD schedule back to the original equilibrium at E.

A different outcome is possible. When the higher oil price shifts SAS to SAS', it is possible to *avoid* the period of low output as the economy moves along AD from E' back to E. A *change* in monetary policy can *shift AD* up enough to pass through E'. Output can quickly return to potential output, but only because the inflation target[4] has been loosened from π^* to $\pi^{*''}$. The new long-run new equilibrium is then at E''.

A central bank caring a lot about output stability may accommodate short-run supply shocks, even if this means higher inflation. A central bank caring more about its inflation target than about output stability will not accommodate temporary supply shocks.

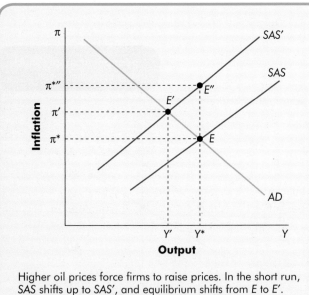

Higher oil prices force firms to raise prices. In the short run, SAS shifts up to SAS', and equilibrium shifts from E to E'. Higher inflation reduces aggregate demand since the central bank raises real interest rates. Once the temporary supply shock disappears, SAS' gradually falls back to SAS, and equilibrium is eventually restored at E.

Figure 21.10   A temporary supply shock

It matters a lot whether the supply shock is temporary or permanent. If potential output is *permanently* affected, aggregate demand *must* eventually rise to match. Once a supply side shock is diagnosed as permanent, it should be accommodated.

Demand shocks

Figure 21.11 explores demand shocks *not* caused by monetary policy. If demand is high, facing AD' the economy moves along its short-run supply curve to point A. If demand is low, facing AD'' the economy moves along the SAS curve to point B.

Suppose the central bank diagnoses that an expansionary demand shock has occurred. It can tighten monetary policy and shift AD' back down to AD again. Similarly, it can loosen monetary policy in response to low aggregate demand AD'', restoring AD again. The economy remains at E. Both inflation *and* output are stabilized.

It is easy for the central bank to tell where inflation is relative to its target rate. It is harder to estimate the level of potential output, which can change over time. This is part of the modern case for using

---

4   Looser monetary policy shifts the *ii* schedule to the right in Figure 21.1. However, once long-run equilibrium is restored i^* must be unaltered: since aggregate supply is eventually unaltered, aggregate demand cannot eventually change. The only way for the central bank to loosen monetary policy without changing i^* is to accept a higher inflation target π^*.

inflation targeting as the intermediate target of monetary policy. When all shocks are **demand shocks**, it works perfectly.

Suppose, instead, that all shocks are supply shocks. Figure 21.12 shows the long-run supply curve AS, vertical at potential output Y^*, and a set of short-run supply curves whose average level is SAS but which fluctuate between SAS' and SAS''.

On average, output is Y^* and inflation is π^*. If interest rates are varied very aggressively to stabilize inflation in the face of supply shocks, the AD schedule is effectively horizontal at π^*. Inflation is stabilized, but output fluctuates between Y' and Y'' when supply fluctuates between SAS' and SAS''. Unlike the case of demand shocks, it is no longer possible to stabilize output *and* inflation.

Similarly, it is possible to stabilize output completely but only at the cost of allowing big fluctuations in inflation. The AD schedule is then vertical at potential output. A rise in short-run supply to SAS' induces a big rise in interest rates to reduce aggregate demand to Y^* again. With high supply but low demand, inflation is temporarily low (relative to inherited wage growth) and firms wish to supply only Y^*. When supply shrinks temporarily to SAS'', firms supply output Y^* only if inflation is high (relative to inherited wage growth), which needs a low interest rate to boost demand.

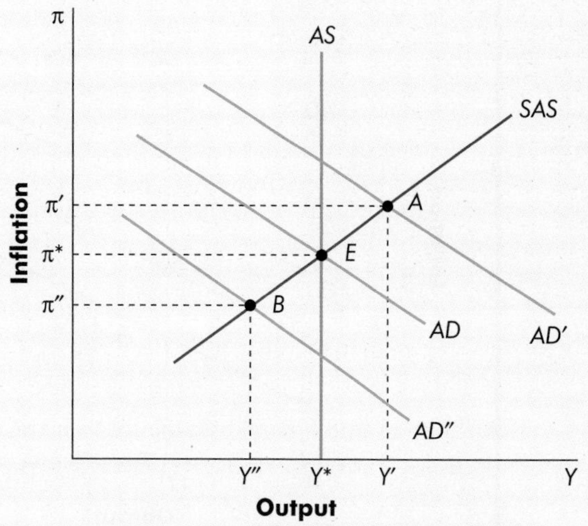

Demand fluctuates between AD' and AD'', causing fluctuations in output and inflation. If the central bank can react quickly, it can offset demand shocks by changing i^* to shift demand back to AD. Stabilizing inflation at π^* has the effect of stabilizing output at Y^*.

Figure 21.11 **Demand shocks**

When all shocks are **demand shocks**, stabilizing inflation also stabilizes output, even in a Keynesian model.

21.8 Trade-offs in monetary objectives

Facing supply shocks, Figure 21.12 implies that it is a bad idea either to stabilize inflation completely at π^* (which induces big fluctuations in output) or to stabilize output at Y^* (which induces big fluctuations in inflation). The aggregate demand schedule AD in Figure 21.12 is a particular compromise in the way interest rates are set.[5]

Any AD schedule through point E achieves the targets π^* and Y^* on average. The particular schedule AD in Figure 21.12 makes the economy fluctuate between A (when supply is SAS'') and B (when supply is SAS'). This achieves acceptable fluctuations in both output and inflation. A steeper AD schedule, still through A, induces lower output fluctuations but larger inflation fluctuations. A flatter schedule has the opposite effect. The steepness of the schedule reflects the relative weight the central bank places on stabilizing inflation and output.

This trade-off does not arise for demand shocks. Figure 21.11 showed that, by fully offsetting demand shocks, the central bank stabilizes both output and prices. In reality, the central bank faces both supply and demand shocks, and cannot always diagnose which is which. It must choose a monetary policy that gives reasonable answers under both kinds of shock.

---

5   And this finally explains why in Figure 21.1 the central bank does not simply choose a vertical *ii* schedule at the target inflation rate. When adjustment is sluggish and supply shocks occur, this would imply big swings in output.

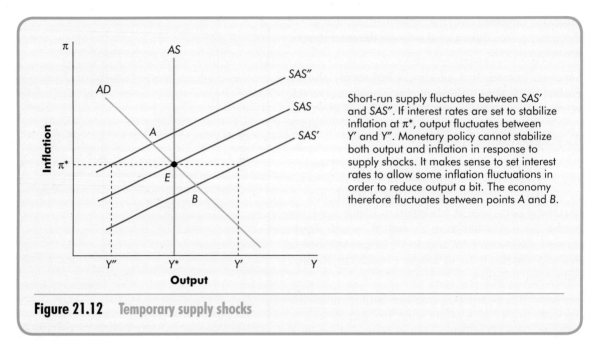

Figure 21.12 Temporary supply shocks

Short-run supply fluctuates between SAS' and SAS". If interest rates are set to stabilize inflation at π*, output fluctuates between Y' and Y". Monetary policy cannot stabilize both output and inflation in response to supply shocks. It makes sense to set interest rates to allow some inflation fluctuations in order to reduce output a bit. The economy therefore fluctuates between points A and B.

There is no conflict between output stability and inflation stability when shocks are demand shocks. It makes sense to try to hit the target as quickly as possible. Similarly, a permanent supply shock requires a permanent change in demand, which there is little reason to postpone. However, facing a *temporary supply shock*, Figure 21.12 showed that it makes sense temporarily to allow inflation to deviate from its target in order to mitigate the shock to output.

The *ii* schedule in Figure 21.1 reflects the average behaviour of the central bank under flexible inflation targeting. Deviations of inflation from target are not all immediately eliminated, but they are eventually eliminated by the policy of raising (lowering) real interest rates whenever inflation is too high (low). Temporary deviations of inflation from target are the price to be paid for ensuring that output fluctuations are not too large.

> **Flexible inflation targeting** commits a central bank to hit inflation targets in the medium run, but gives it some discretion about *how quickly* to hit its inflation target.

The key to successful **flexible inflation targeting** is that any deviation of inflation from target should be *temporary*. Credible central banks persist with high interest rates until inflation is restored to its target rate. And when credible central banks reduce interest to boost demand, nobody fears that the inflation target has been increased, and there is no reason for nominal wage bargains to fear a permanent rise in inflation.

In contrast, weak central banks that lack credibility may cause panic by easing monetary policy today. People worry that they will not be tough enough later to reverse this demand expansion. Foreseeing sustained expansion, inflation gets going. This insight places credibility centre stage, where it belongs. Chapter 22 examines the economics of credibility and its effect on inflation.

CONCEPT 21.2

A Taylor rule for monetary policy

Stanford professor John Taylor suggested that a neat way to describe flexible inflation targeting is to say that interest rates respond to deviations of both inflation and output from their target long-run equilibrium levels. Inflation above target, or output above target, is a signal to raise interest rates; inflation below target or output below target is a signal to reduce interest rates. We can think of the Taylor rule as applying to either nominal or real interest rates. However, a key insight of the Taylor rule is that, if inflation rises by 1 per cent, nominal interest rates must be increased by more than 1 per cent to ensure that real interest rates rise when inflation is higher. In the short run, the central bank – which must deal with a world in which both supply and demand shocks occur, and may not immediately be able to diagnose which – sets higher real interest rates if inflation exceeds the target and/or if real output exceeds potential output. Taylor showed that this formula provides a good empirical description of the behaviour of all major central banks.

Picture: Professor John Taylor

In terms of rules versus discretion, this behaviour is not imposed on the central bank. It is largely the result of its discretionary behaviour, so it is a rule only in the sense of being a stable empirical relationship. But it does not reflect complete discretion. The target inflation rate itself is usually delegated by the government, not freely chosen by the central bank. For example, in the UK the government reserves the right to alter the inflation target during a crisis.

The Taylor rule also provides a way to indicate how rare and extreme an event the financial crash has been. For example, Princeton professor Paul Krugman, himself a Nobel Prize winner, took empirical estimates of the Taylor rule for the US and calculated that by late 2009 'normal' behaviour of the US central bank, given observed levels of inflation and output, would have implied a nominal interest rate of *minus* 5.6 per cent.* In other words, by late 2009 central banks would ideally liked to have cut interest rates way below zero if following their normal behaviour. The fact that they could not drive nominal interest rates below zero was really getting in the way of normal monetary policy.

This had two implications. First, fiscal policy was going to be asked to do 'too much' because monetary policy could not do enough. Second, quantitative easing was adopted not merely because of the need to offset the collapse of the bank deposit multiplier but also in the hope that the credit channel of monetary policy could help boost aggregate demand at a time when further interest rate cuts were not possible.

* Paul Krugman's *New York Times* column of 10 October 2009 is reproduced on his blog at http://krugman.blogs.nytimes.com.

The formula for the Taylor rule

MATHS 21.1

In the long run, the real interest rate is i^*, inflation is π^* and real output is Y^*. Formally, the Taylor rule implies that real interest i obeys

$$i - i^* = a(\pi - \pi^*) + b(Y - Y^*) \qquad a > 0, b > 0 \tag{1}$$

Since the nominal interest rate r is simply the real interest rate i plus the inflation rate π,

$$r - r^* = (1 + a)(\pi - \pi^*) + b(Y - Y^*) \qquad a > 0, b > 0 \tag{2}$$

where

$$r^* = i^* + \pi^* \tag{3}$$

Hence, the long-run target for nominal interest rates depends both on the long-run inflation target and on the desired level of real interest rates in the long run, which may depend, among other things, on the monetary/fiscal mix.

Thus, we can think of the Taylor rule as applying to either nominal or real interest rates, with the key requirement that the nominal interest version in equation (2) insists that any increase in inflation leads to a larger increase in nominal interest rates – by $(1 + a)$ times – in order to ensure that real interest rates move in the right direction to stabilize inflation. The absolute size of the parameters a and b tells us how aggressively monetary policy attempts to stabilize inflation and output. The relative size of the parameters tells us the relative importance of inflation and output to policy makers in the short run.

Many economists have noted that deviations of output from target are an important indicator of future inflation. Hence it is also possible to interpret the empirical success of the Taylor rule as implying central bank concern for current and future inflation, rather than for current output and current inflation.

Finally, as noted in Concept 21.2, empirical estimates of Taylor rules using data for the previous decade would have led to choices of nominal interest rates that were negative, which is not possible in practice. With no danger of inflation and output well below target, central banks would have loved to set negative interest rates if only they could. This led IMF chief economist Olivier Blanchard to note that a temporarily *higher* inflation target might have been one way in which real interest rates could become more negative. Suppose, for example, inflation was 4 per cent and nominal interest rates were still close to zero. Real interest rates would then have been −4 per cent, a powerful stimulus to aggregate demand. Mathematically, the Blanchard proposal achieves the appropriately negative left-hand side of equation (2) not by reducing r below zero but by raising π^* and hence r^* above previous levels. Most central banks were unenthusiastic above this proposal: whatever its short-run attraction, they feared it would then be hard to restore belief in a low inflation target again after the crisis was over.

Summary

- The **classical model** of macroeconomics assumes full flexibility of wages and prices and no money illusion.

- The *ii* **schedule** shows, under a policy of **inflation targeting**, how the central bank achieves high interest rates when inflation is high and low interest rates when inflation is low. Central banks set nominal not real interest rates, and hence must first forecast inflation in order to calculate what nominal interest rate they wish to set.

- The *ii* schedule shifts to the left, a higher real interest rate at each inflation rate, when monetary policy is tightened, and to the right, a lower real interest rate at each inflation rate, when monetary policy is loosened.

- The **aggregate demand schedule** shows how higher inflation reduces aggregate demand by inducing monetary policy to raise real interest rates.

- The classical model always has full employment. The **aggregate supply schedule** is vertical at **potential output**. **Equilibrium inflation** is at the intersection of the aggregate supply schedule and the aggregate demand schedule. The markets for goods, money and labour are all in equilibrium. Monetary policy is set to make the equilibrium inflation rate coincide with the inflation target.

- In the classical model, fiscal expansion cannot increase output. To continue to hit its inflation target, the central bank must raise real interest rates to restore aggregate demand to the level of potential output. **Higher government spending crowds out an equal amount of private spending**, leaving demand and output unaltered.

- Changing the target inflation rate leads to an equivalent change in the growth of wages and nominal money in the classical model, but not to a change in output.

- In practice, wages adjust slowly to shocks since job arrangements are long term. **Wage adjustment** is sluggish not merely because wage bargaining is infrequent, but also because workers prefer their long-term employers to smooth wages.

- Prices reflect mainly labour costs. The **short-run aggregate supply schedule** shows firms' desired output, given the inherited growth of nominal wages. Output is temporarily responsive to inflation, since nominal wages are already determined. As wage adjustment occurs, the short-run supply schedule shifts.

- The **Keynesian model** is a good guide to short-term behaviour but the **classical model** describes behaviour in the long run.

- **Permanent supply shocks** alter potential output. **Temporary supply shocks** merely alter the short-run supply curve for a while.

- If its effects were instant, monetary policy could completely offset **demand shocks**, stabilizing both inflation and output. **Temporary supply shocks** force a trade-off between output stability and inflation stability. The output effect of **permanent supply shocks** cannot be escaped indefinitely.

- **Flexible inflation targeting** implies the central bank need not immediately hit its inflation target, allowing some scope for temporary action to cushion output fluctuations.

- A **Taylor rule** views interest rate decisions as responding to both deviations of output from target and deviations of inflation from target. Except during the financial crash, when interest rates could not be reduced below zero, this fits the data well for most countries over an extended period.

Review questions

connect

1 (a) Define the aggregate demand schedule. (b) How does a fiscal expansion affect the schedule under a flexible inflation target? (c) How would the central bank have to change monetary policy to hit its given inflation target in the long run?

EASY

2 Suppose opportunities for investing in high-tech applications boost aggregate demand in the short run, but aggregate supply in the long run. Using *AS* and *AD* schedules, show why output might rise *without* much inflation.

3 How do the following affect the short-run supply schedule, and hence output and inflation in the short run? (a) A higher tax rate; (b) higher labour productivity.

4 An economy has the choice of having half its workers make annual wage agreements every January, and the other half make annual wage agreements every July, or instead forcing everyone to make their annual agreement on 1 July. Which system is likely to induce greater wage flexibility during a period of a few months and during a period of several years?

5 OPEC raises the price of oil for a year but then a new supply of oil from Russia bids oil prices back down again. Contrast the evolution of the economy if monetary policy follows: (a) a fixed interest rate, (b) flexible inflation targeting, or (c) a nominal money target.

6 Common fallacies Why are these statements wrong? (a) Fiscal expansion can increase output for ever. (b) Higher inflation always reduces output.

7 Which is correct? (a) Inflation targeting implies the central bank can ignore what is happening to output; (b) inflation targeting implies nominal interest rates will typically rise by more than the rise in inflation; (c) inflation targeting was immediately abandoned once the financial crash occurred.

8 'Central banks, by focusing too much on the inflation rate for goods and services, neglected important signals from asset prices that risk taking had become excessive.' Do you agree? What is this likely to imply in future?

9 Use a Figure like 21.8 to explore how the collapse of bank lending to companies affects short-run supply curves, and show how subsequent adjustment occurs.

10 Using the same diagram, distinguish between adjustment in the UK (small open economy, flexible exchange rate) and the US (large economy, international trade a much smaller proportion of its GDP).

11 Using definitions in Maths 21.1, the Taylor rule $r - r^* = (1 + a)(\pi - \pi^*) + b(Y - Y^*)$ and the aggregate demand equation $Y = A - d(r - \pi)$, describe an economy. (a) Provide an interpretation of A. Is d positive or negative? (b) What is the relation between long-run equilibrium output and the central bank targets for inflation and nominal interest rates? (c) If nominal interest rates are to rise by more than inflation when inflation increases, what must be the relation between the sensitivity of aggregate demand to real interest rates and the parameters a and b in the Taylor rule decribing monetary policy?

12 Imagine that the UK adopts the euro, and interest rates are set by the European Central Bank. (a) Are euro interest rates likely to be adjusted to help stabilize either UK inflation or UK output? (b) What automatic mechanisms, if any, can still achieve these outcomes? (c) Would UK fiscal policy be able to help more?

13 In 2007 the Governor of the Bank of England had to write to the Chancellor of the Exchequer to explain why UK inflation had exceeded the target range laid down by the Chancellor. (a) Why were these difficult circumstances? (b) Was the letter proof that the Bank of England had screwed up?

14 *Essay question* 'Climate change is essentially a permanent adverse supply shock. Production costs will rise; potential output will fall. If the private sector fails to adjust, then either monetary or fiscal policy will have to reduce aggregate demand to the required lower level.' Discuss.

For solutions to these questions contact your lecturer.

Inflation, expectations and credibility

Learning Outcomes

By the end of this chapter, you should understand:

1. the quantity theory of money

2. how nominal interest rates reflect inflation

3. seigniorage, the inflation tax and why hyperinflations occur

4. when budget deficits cause money growth

5. the Phillips curve

6. the costs of inflation

7. central bank independence and inflation control

8. how the Monetary Policy Committee sets UK interest rates

On its election in 1997 the Labour government made the Bank of England independent, with a mandate to achieve low inflation.

Sustained inflation is a recent phenomenon. Before 1950, prices rose in some years but fell in others. The UK price level was no higher in 1950 than in 1920. Figure 22.1 shows that the UK price level fell sharply in some interwar years when inflation was negative. The post-war price level has never fallen. Since 1950 the price level has risen 20-fold, more than its rise over the previous three centuries. This story applies in most advanced economies.

The effects of **inflation** depend on what causes inflation. We start with the causes of inflation, then examine its effects, which partly depend on whether inflation was anticipated or took people by surprise. We contrast costs that inflation imposes on individuals and costs it imposes on society as a whole. We conclude by considering what the government can do about inflation.

> **Inflation** is a rise in the price level. **Pure inflation** means that prices of goods and inputs rise at the same rate.

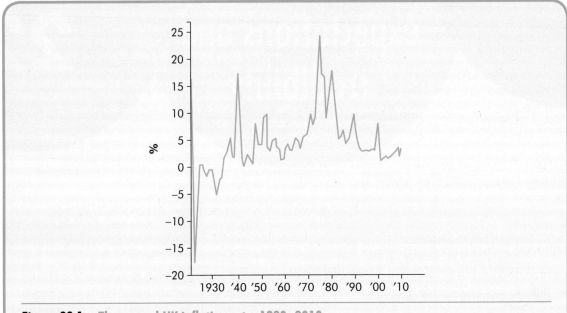

Figure 22.1   The annual UK inflation rate, 1920–2010

Sources: Mitchell, R. B. (1975) *European Historical Statistics, 1750–1970*, Macmillan; OECD, *Economic Outlook.*

Money and inflation

There is a link between nominal money and the price level, and hence between nominal money growth and inflation.

People demand money because of its purchasing power over goods. They demand *real* money. When real income is Y and the interest rate is r, the term $L(Y, r)$ shows the stock of real money demanded. This rises with real income Y, since the benefit of holding money increases. It falls with the interest rate r, since the cost of holding money is higher.

$$M/P = L(Y, r) \tag{1}$$

CONCEPT 22.1 The quantity theory of money: $MV = PY$

The velocity of circulation V is nominal income PY divided by nominal money M. If prices adjust to keep real output at potential output Y^*, assumed constant, M and P must move together, *provided velocity V stays constant.* Velocity is the speed at which the stock of money is passed round the economy as people transact. If everyone holds money for less time and passes it on more quickly, the economy needs less money relative to nominal income. How do we assess whether velocity is constant, as the simple quantity theory requires?

The quantity theory equation implies $M/P = Y/V$. The left-hand side is the **real money supply**. The right-hand side must be real money demand. It rises with real income and falls with velocity. But real money demand rises with real income and falls with nominal interest rates. Hence velocity just measures the effect of interest rates on real money demand. Higher nominal interest rates reduce real money demand. People *hold* less money relative to income. Velocity rises.

> The **real money supply** M/P is the nominal money supply M divided by the price level P.

While inflation and nominal interest rates are rising, velocity is rising. But if inflation and nominal interest rates settle down at a particular level, velocity is then constant. Thereafter, the simple quantity theory once more applies.

This assumes prices are fully flexible. In the short run, if prices are sluggish, changes in nominal money change the real money supply. Changes in nominal money are not matched by changes in prices. The quantity theory of money will fail in the short run.

In money market equilibrium, real money supply and demand are equal. Flexible interest rates maintain continuous money market equilibrium. Equation (1) always holds.

If nominal wages and prices adjust slowly in the short run, higher nominal money supply M leads initially to a higher real money stock M/P since prices P have not yet adjusted. The excess supply of real money bids down interest rates. This boosts the demand for goods. Gradually this bids up goods prices. In the labour market, nominal wages start to rise.

After complete adjustment of wages and prices, a once-off rise in nominal money leads to an equivalent once-off rise in wages and prices. Output, employment, interest rates and real money revert to their original levels. After adjustment is complete, the demand for real balances is unchanged. Hence the price level changes in proportion to the original change in the nominal money supply.

The theory is over 500 years old and may date from Confucius. The **quantity theory** is espoused by monetarists, who argue that *most* changes in prices reflect changes in the nominal money supply.

> The **quantity theory of money** says that changes in nominal money lead to equivalent changes in the price level (and money wages), but have no effect on output and employment.

The theory must be interpreted with care. If the demand for real money is constant, the supply of real money must be constant: changes in nominal money are matched by equivalent changes in prices. This raises two issues: (a) even if the demand for real money is constant, do changes in nominal money cause changes in prices or vice versa; and (b) is the demand for real money constant?

Money, prices and causation

Suppose the demand for real money is constant over time. Money market equilibrium implies that the real money supply M/P is then constant. Monetary policy could fix the nominal money supply M, in which case money M determines prices P to get the required level of M/P implied by money demand.

Conversely, monetary policy may choose a target path for the price level P. Changes in this path then cause changes in the nominal money supply to achieve the required real money supply. Equation (1) says prices and money are correlated, but is agnostic on which causes which. That depends on the form of monetary policy pursued. With an intermediate target for nominal money, the causation flows from money to prices. With a target for prices or inflation, the causation flows the other way.

The leading monetarist Professor Milton Friedman always said that inflation is a monetary phenomenon. Sustained price increases, what we call inflation, are possible only if nominal money is also growing. It is always an option to change monetary policy and stop printing money. Sooner or later prices have to stop rising. Take away the oxygen and the fire goes out.

Is real money demand constant?

We already know that the demand for real money M/P depends on income Y and the cost of holding money (the spread between interest rates on assets and whatever interest if any is earned while holding money).

Hence, countries experiencing sustained income growth will experience a sustained increase in the demand for real money, whereas countries growing more slowly will experience slower growth in money demand.

Second, countries experiencing different degrees of financial competition will face different equilibrium interest rate spreads between market rates and the interest rate on money. Greater banking competition will compress spreads and reduce the cost of holding money, thus boosting money demand. Conversely, countries in which banks become overextended may face large spreads and high costs of holding money as banks try to rebuild their balance sheets.

Third, countries with high inflation are likely to face high nominal interest rates, larger spreads and a higher cost of holding money. Since inflation can become very large, this is potentially the most important reason why real money demand may change. We study this effect in the next section.

To sum up, even after adjustment is complete, changes in real income and interest rates can alter real money demand. However, *if* real income and interest rates were unaltered, changes in nominal money would eventually be accompanied by equivalent changes in nominal wages and prices.

Inflation

So far we have studied levels. Now think about rates of change. Equation (1) implies that the growth in real money demand equals the growth in real money supply, that is, the excess of nominal money growth over the growth in prices. Hence,

Nominal money growth = real money demand growth + inflation rate

Since real income and interest rates *usually* change only a few percentage points a year, real money demand usually changes slowly.[1] The essential insight of the quantity theory of money is that real variables usually change slowly.

Large changes in one nominal variable (money) are accompanied by large changes in other nominal variables (prices, nominal wages) to keep real money (and real wages) at their equilibrium values. This is a useful first look at inflation, but we simplified too much.

22.2   Inflation and interest rates

Figure 22.2 shows interest and inflation rates for selected countries in 2008 before interest rates were driven to abnormal levels during the financial crisis. Countries with high inflation have high interest rates. An extra percentage point of inflation is accompanied on average by a nominal interest rate nearly one percentage point higher, a proposition first suggested by Professor Irving Fisher.

Real interest rate = [nominal interest rate] − [inflation rate]

> The **Fisher hypothesis** says higher inflation leads to similarly higher nominal interest rates.

The Fisher hypothesis says that *real* interest rates do not change much. If they did, there would be large excess supply or demand for loans. Higher inflation is largely offset by higher nominal interest rates to stop the real interest rate changing much. Figure 22.2 shows this is a good rule of thumb in reality.[2]

---

1   An exception is the hyperinflation example of the next section.
2   Chapter 21 argued that this is likely to be a long-run relationship. In the short run, higher inflation must induce a larger rise in nominal interest rates if real interest rates are to push inflation back towards its target.

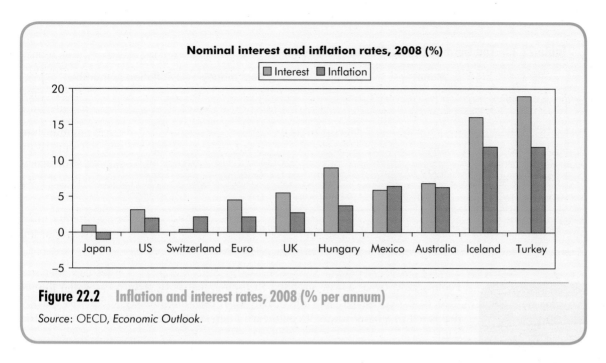

Figure 22.2 Inflation and interest rates, 2008 (% per annum)

Source: OECD, *Economic Outlook.*

Faster nominal money growth leads both to higher inflation and higher nominal interest rates. Hence a rise in the rate of money growth leads to a rise in nominal interest rates. This reduces the demand for real money, requiring money and prices to grow at *different* rates until the real money supply adjusts to the change in real money demand. To show how this works, we study a spectacular example – the German hyperinflation.

Hyperinflation

Bolivian annual inflation reached 11 000 per cent in 1985, Ukraine's inflation topped 10 000 per cent in 1993 and by 2007 inflation in Zimbabwe was heading to what may have exceeded a trillion per cent – certainly in January 2009 its central bank introduced trillion Zimbabwe dollar banknotes worth around US$30 each. The most famous example, however, is still Germany during 1922–23.

> **Hyperinflation** is a period of very high inflation.

Germany lost the First World War. The German government had a big deficit, financed by printing money. Table 22.1 shows what happened. The government had to buy faster printing presses. In the later stages of the hyperinflation, they took in old notes, stamped on another zero, and reissued them as larger-denomination notes in the morning.

Prices rose 75-fold in 1922 and much more in 1923. By October 1923 it took 192 million Reichmarks to buy a drink that had cost 1 Reichmark in January 1922. People carried money in wheelbarrows to go shopping. According to the old joke, thieves stole the barrows but left the near worthless money behind.

If inflation is π and the nominal interest rate is r, the real interest rate is $(r - \pi)$ but the real return on non-interest-bearing cash is $-\pi$, which shows how quickly the real value of cash is being eroded by inflation. The extra real return on holding interest-bearing assets rather than cash is $(r - \pi) - (-\pi) = r$. The *nominal* interest rate measures the *real* cost of holding cash. Nominal interest rates rise with inflation. In the German hyperinflation the cost of holding cash became enormous.

Table 22.1 shows that, by October 1923, real money holdings were only 11 per cent of their level in January 1922. How did people get by with such small holdings of real cash?

Table 22.1   The German hyperinflation, 1922–23

	Money	Prices	Real money	Inflation % monthly
January 1922	1	1	1.00	5
January 1923	16	75	0.21	189
July 1923	354	2021	0.18	386
September 1923	227 777	645 946	0.35	2532
October 1923	20 201 256	191 891 890	0.11	29 720

Source: Data adapted from Holtfrerish, C. L. (1980) *Die Deutsche Inflation 1914–23*, Walter de Gruyter.

> The **flight from cash** is the collapse in the demand for real cash when high inflation and high nominal interest rates make it very expensive to hold cash.

People, paid twice a day, shopped in their lunch hour before the real value of their cash depreciated too much. Any cash not immediately spent was quickly deposited in a bank where it could earn interest. People spent a lot of time at the bank.

What lessons can we draw? First, *rising* inflation and *rising* interest rates significantly reduce the demand for *real* cash. Hyperinflations are a rare example in which a real quantity (real cash) changes quickly and by a lot. Second, and as a result, money and prices can get quite out of line when inflation and nominal interest rates are rising. Table 22.1 shows that prices rose by six times as much as nominal money between January 1922 and July 1923, reducing the real money supply by 82 per cent, in line with the fall in real money demand – a **flight from cash**.

22.3   Inflation, money and deficits

Persistent inflation must be accompanied by continuing nominal money growth. Printing money to finance a large deficit is a source of inflation. Budget deficits may explain why governments have to print money rapidly. If so, tight *fiscal* policy is needed to fight inflation.

The level of GDP affects how much tax revenue the government gets at given tax rates. If government debt is low relative to GDP, the government can finance deficits by borrowing. It has enough tax revenue with which to pay interest and repay the debt. For governments with low debt, there may be no relation between their budget deficit and how much money they print. Sometimes they print money; sometimes they issue bonds. We do not expect a close relationship between deficits and money creation in a country like the UK.

Nevertheless, many years of deficits may make government debt large relative to GDP. The government can no longer finance deficits by more borrowing. It then has to tighten fiscal policy to shrink the deficit, or print money to finance the continuing deficit.

To ensure that the European Central Bank did not face fiscal pressure to print too much money and thus create inflation, members of the eurozone had to obey the Stability and Growth Pact, which restricts their budget deficits to less than 3 per cent of GDP, except in severe recession. Of course, when severe recession arrived in 2009, budget deficits escalated to 10 per cent and beyond. We never quite know how binding a commitment will be until a crisis occurs. Similarly, the UK's Code for Fiscal Stability committed the UK government to not keep running big deficits that steadily raise government debt relative to GDP. When it came to the crunch, this commitment was (wisely) jettisoned.

Deficits, money growth and real revenue

A hyperinflation is a situation in which fiscal policy is out of control. A government with a persistently high deficit, financed by borrowing, now has so much debt that nobody will lend it any more. Instead, it prints money to finance its deficit.

How much real revenue can the government get by printing banknotes? The government has a monopoly on cash. As a token money, its production cost is tiny relative to its value as money. The government prints money for nothing, then uses it to pay nurses and build roads.

Real money demand M/P rises with real income. Long-run growth of real income allows the government some scope to raise M without adding to P. This is **seigniorage**. A second potential source of real revenue is the inflation tax.

> **Seigniorage** is real revenue acquired by the government through its ability to print money.

Suppose real income and output are constant but that a weak government cannot shrink its budget deficit and now has debt so large that nobody will lend to it. It prints money to cover the budget deficit. If ΔM is the amount of new cash created, this finances an amount of real spending $(\Delta M)/P$, which is the same as $(\Delta M/M) \times (M/P)$, the growth rate of cash multiplied by the real demand for cash. The rise in nominal money must feed into prices sooner or later. Suppose the rate of nominal money growth $(\Delta M/M)$ equals the inflation rate π. Thus,

$$\text{Real revenue from inflation} = [\pi] \times [M/P]$$

Inflation helps the government by reducing the real value of the non-interest-bearing part of the government debt, namely cash. Think of inflation as the tax rate and real cash as the tax base for the **inflation tax**.

> The **inflation tax** is the effect of inflation in raising real revenue by reducing the real value of the government's nominal debt.

Now for the part that may be new to you. If money growth and inflation rise, does the government get more *real* revenue from the inflation tax? Higher inflation raises nominal interest rates and hence reduces the real demand for cash.

Figure 22.3 shows the answer. At low inflation, real cash demand is high, but the multiple of inflation and real cash demand is small. Similarly, at high inflation, although the inflation tax rate is high, the tax base – real cash demand – is now tiny because nominal interest rates are so high. The multiple of inflation and real cash is again low. Real revenue raised through the inflation tax cannot be increased indefinitely. After a certain point, faster money growth and higher inflation shrink the tax base more than they raise the tax rate.

The figure has two implications. First, if the government needs to cover a particular *real* deficit d by printing money, there may be two rates of money growth and inflation that do the job. Either is a long-run equilibrium in which inflation is constant.

Second, if for political reasons the government has a real deficit as large as D, printing money cannot do the job. The economy explodes into hyperinflation. At high inflation, real cash demand is already low. Raising inflation further causes such a large percentage fall in the tiny demand for real cash that inflation tax revenue falls, the government prints even more cash and the problem gets even worse.

That is how hyperinflation starts. The only solution is to cut the size of the deficit. Often the government does this by defaulting on its debt, which slashes the burden of interest payments.

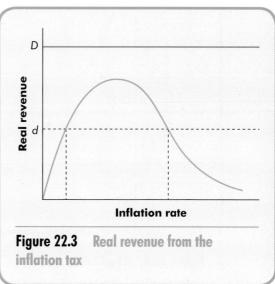

Figure 22.3 Real revenue from the inflation tax

Notice that the inflation tax applies to cash which has no nominal interest rate to increase in line with inflation. For interest-bearing money, in principle interest rates can rise to protect money holders. Then it is only unforeseen inflation, not incorporated in interest rates, that acts as a tax.

This is one reason we tend to see hyperinflation in more primitive economies, in which cash is very important. In modern European economies, cash is much less important and the potential tax base for the inflation tax is a lot lower.

Inflation, unemployment and output

One of the most famous relationships in post-war macroeconomics is the Phillips curve.

The Phillips curve

In 1958 Professor Phillips of the London School of Economics found a strong statistical relationship between annual inflation and annual unemployment in the UK. Similar relationships were found in other countries. The Phillips curve is shown in Figure 22.4.

> The **Phillips curve** shows that a higher inflation rate is accompanied by a lower unemployment rate. It suggests we can trade off more inflation for less unemployment or vice versa.

The **Phillips curve** seemed a useful compass for choosing macroeconomic policy. By its choice of fiscal and monetary policy, the government set aggregate demand and hence unemployment. The Phillips curve showed how much inflation then ensued. Higher aggregate demand bid up wages and prices, causing higher inflation but lower unemployment.

The Phillips curve shows the trade-off that people believed they faced in the 1960s. In those days UK unemployment was rarely over 2 per cent of the labour force. But people believed that, if they did the unthinkable and reduced aggregate demand until unemployment rose to 2.5 per cent, inflation would fall to zero.

Since then there have been years when *both* inflation and unemployment were over 10 per cent. Something happened to the Phillips curve. The next two chapters explain why the simple Phillips curve of Figure 22.4 ceased to fit the facts.

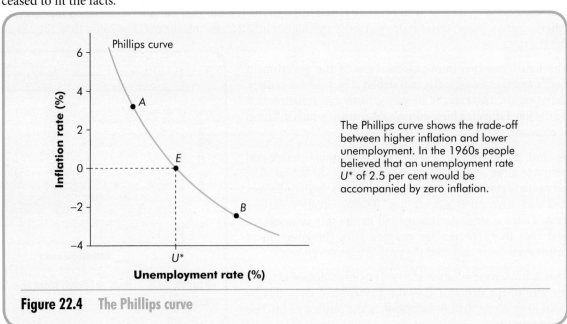

The Phillips curve shows the trade-off between higher inflation and lower unemployment. In the 1960s people believed that an unemployment rate U* of 2.5 per cent would be accompanied by zero inflation.

Figure 22.4 **The Phillips curve**

Equilibrium unemployment is not zero, for reasons that we explore in Chapter 23. Suppose equilibrium employment and potential output are fixed in the long run, but there is sluggish wage and price adjustment. Chapter 21 discussed the vertical long-run aggregate supply curve and sloping short-run supply curve, relating output and the price level. These ideas are easily translated from inflation and output to inflation and unemployment.

The vertical long-run Phillips curve

In long-run equilibrium, the economy is at both potential output and equilibrium unemployment. Sometimes these are referred to as the **natural level of output** and the **natural rate of unemployment**.

> The **natural level of output**, and the **natural rate of unemployment**, are their values in long-run equilibrium.

Both are determined by real things, not nominal things. They depend on the supply of inputs, the level of technology, the level of tax rates and so on. They do not depend on inflation, provided all prices P and nominal wages W are rising together. Equilibrium unemployment depends on the real wage W/P, as we discuss in Chapter 23.

Just as long-run aggregate supply is vertical at potential output – output is unaffected by inflation – so the long-run Phillips curve is vertical at equilibrium unemployment. Equilibrium unemployment is independent of inflation. Plotting inflation and unemployment, Figure 22.5 shows the long-run Phillips curve vertical at equilibrium unemployment U^*.

In long-run equilibrium, inflation is constant. People correctly anticipate inflation, and adjust the growth of nominal wages to keep real wages constant, at the real wage required for long-run equilibrium. Similarly, nominal interest rates are sufficiently high to offset inflation and maintain real interest rates at their equilibrium level. Everyone adjusts to inflation because it can be completely foreseen.

Suppose inflation is 10 per cent a year. This is consistent with many forms of monetary policy. We can think of monetary policy as having either a target of 10 per cent annual money growth, or an inflation target of 10 per cent a year, or as a Taylor rule in which the inflation part aims for 10 per cent annual inflation. In Figure 22.5 long-run equilibrium is at E. Inflation is 10 per cent, as everybody expects. Nominal money grows at 10 per cent a year. Unemployment is at its natural rate.

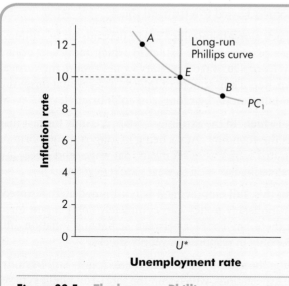

Since people care about real variables not nominal variables, when full adjustment has been completed people will arrange for all nominal variables to keep up with inflation. The vertical long-run Phillips curve shows that eventually the economy gets back to the natural rate of unemployment U^*, whatever the long-run inflation rate. There is no long-run trade-off between inflation and unemployment. The short-run Phillips curve PC_1 shows short-run adjustment as before. The height of the short-run Phillips curve depends on the rate of inflation and nominal money growth in long-run equilibrium, as shown by the position of point E on the long-run Phillips curve.

Figure 22.5   The long-run Phillips curve

The short-run Phillips curve

Beginning from E, suppose something raises aggregate demand. Unemployment falls, inflation rises and the economy is at A. Then the central bank raises interest rates to achieve its targets (in whichever form), and the economy slowly moves back down the short-run Phillips curve PC_1 from A back to E again. Since interest rates take time to affect aggregate demand, this may take one or two years.

Conversely, beginning from E a downward demand shock takes the economy to B in the short run. The central bank alters interest rates to bring the economy steadily back from B to E.

> The **short-run Phillips curve** shows that, in the short run, higher unemployment is associated with lower inflation. The height of the short-run Phillips curve reflects expected inflation. In long-run equilibrium at E, expectations are fulfilled.

The **short-run Phillips curve** corresponds to the short-run supply curve for output. Given inherited wages, higher prices make firms supply more output and demand more workers. For any level of last period's prices, higher prices today imply higher inflation today. In Chapter 21, the height of the short-run aggregate supply curve depended on the inherited growth rate of nominal wages. Similarly, the height of the short-run Phillips curve reflects inherited nominal wage growth.

When workers and firms expect high inflation, they agree a large rise in nominal wages. If inflation turns out as expected, real wages are as forecast and the nominal wage growth was justified. If inflation is higher than expected, real wages are lower than planned. Firms supply more output and demand more labour. High inflation (relative to expectations) goes with lower unemployment. The short-run Phillips curve slopes down. Its height reflects the inflation expectations embodied in the inherited wage agreement.

This explains why most economies had high inflation at each unemployment rate in the 1970s and 1980s: the short-run Phillips curve had shifted upwards. Governments were printing money at a faster rate than before. The long-run equilibrium inflation rate was high, and expected to be so.

The point E lay further up the long-run Phillips curve in Figure 22.5. The short-run Phillips curve through this point was much higher than the short-run Phillips curve in the data originally studied by Professor Phillips. The 1970s and 1980s were a period of high inflation. The original Phillips curve data had been for a period of much lower inflation.

We draw two conclusions. First, it was wrong to interpret the original Phillips curve as a *permanent* trade-off between inflation and unemployment. It was the temporary trade-off, corresponding to a particular short-run aggregate supply schedule, while the economy adjusted to a demand shock.

Second, the speed with which the economy moves back along the Phillips curve depends on two things: the degree of flexibility of nominal wages and hence prices; and the extent to which monetary policy adjusts interest rates to restore demand more quickly. Complete wage flexibility would restore the vertical Phillips curve and the vertical aggregate supply curve. Rapid adjustment of interest rates would offset the demand shock, restoring output, unemployment and inflation to their long-run equilibrium levels.

Extreme monetarists believe that wage flexibility is very high. In the extreme version, it is only the fact that workers make annual wage settlements that prevents the economy always being in long-run equilibrium. Changes in aggregate demand unforeseen when nominal wages were set mean that wages and prices are temporarily at the wrong level. But such mistakes are rectified as soon as wages are renegotiated.

If wage and price adjustment are more sluggish than this, full employment is not immediately restored. However, we know from the previous chapter that monetary policy can completely compensate for a demand shock once it has been diagnosed. Nor is there any conflict between stabilizing inflation and stabilizing output or employment. Such conflicts arise only in response to supply shocks.

We have made considerable progress in understanding the Phillips curve, but there is more still to study. First, we need to analyse changes in long-run inflation expectations, which shift the short-run Phillips curve. Second, we need to examine supply shocks. Temporary supply shocks also shift the short-run Phillips curve. Permanent supply shocks alter equilibrium unemployment and shift the long-run Phillips curve.

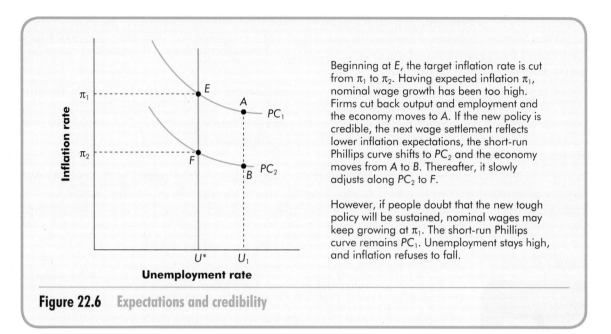

Beginning at *E*, the target inflation rate is cut from π_1 to π_2. Having expected inflation π_1, nominal wage growth has been too high. Firms cut back output and employment and the economy moves to *A*. If the new policy is credible, the next wage settlement reflects lower inflation expectations, the short-run Phillips curve shifts to PC_2 and the economy moves from *A* to *B*. Thereafter, it slowly adjusts along PC_2 to *F*.

However, if people doubt that the new tough policy will be sustained, nominal wages may keep growing at π_1. The short-run Phillips curve remains PC_1. Unemployment stays high, and inflation refuses to fall.

Figure 22.6 Expectations and credibility

Expectations and credibility

Figure 22.6 puts this apparatus to work to discuss what happens when a new government is elected with a commitment to reduce inflation. Think of this as describing the problem faced by Mrs Thatcher. The economy begins in long-run equilibrium at *E*, facing the short-run Phillips curve PC_1. Nominal money, prices and money wages are all rising at the rate π_1.

The government wants to reduce inflation to π_2 to reach point *F*. The day the government is elected it announces a cut in the inflation target from π_1 to π_2.

Overnight, firms inherit nominal wage increases that had anticipated the old inflation rate π_1. They have little scope to reduce inflation. If inflation does fall, real wages are now too high. Firms reduce output and employment. Inflation falls a little and unemployment rises. The economy moves along the short-run Phillips curve PC_1 to *A*.

What happens next? In the good scenario, workers believe the tighter monetary policy will last. The next wage bargain is based on inflation expectations π_2. The short-run Phillips curve shifts down to PC_2 and the economy moves from *A* to *B*. Inflation falls quickly. The economy then moves slowly along PC_2 from *B* to *F*.

Now for the bad scenario. When the economy first reaches *A*, workers do not believe that the tough new monetary policy will last. They think π_1 will remain the inflation rate in the long run. Thinking inflation will remain high, workers do not reduce nominal wage growth. They believe PC_1 not PC_2 will be relevant.

Suppose workers are wrong. Although nominal wages grow at π_1, the tough policy lasts and actual inflation is below π_1. Real wages rise and unemployment gets worse without much fall in inflation. The worse the slump becomes, the more likely is the government to give in, easing monetary policy to boost aggregate demand again. A belief that the government's nerve will crack can become a **self-fulfilling prophecy**.

> A **self-fulfilling prophecy** is an expectation that creates the incentive to make it come true.

The economy stays on PC_1 and the attempt to reduce inflation fails. Gradually the economy moves back along PC_1 to equilibrium at *E*.

This explains why governments go to such lengths to commit to tight monetary policy. The sooner people accept that long-run inflation will be low, the sooner nominal wage growth will slow. Making central banks independent is an institutional reform designed to increase the credibility of monetary policy by insulating it from short-term political expediency.

Figure 22.6 was used to describe a fall in inflation expectations, but the opposite is also possible. By 2010 many people were wondering whether Western governments would indeed curtail government spending and raise taxes in order to bring budget deficits under control. If future governments are weak, they may resort to money creation instead. We could then envisage a shift upwards in the short-run Phillips curve in Figure 22.6 as inflation expectations increase.

In assessing how likely this is, people will look at the independence of the central banks and whether they are prepared to use this to adhere to the monetary targets they have been set. In principle, central banks should be prepared to raise interest rates if they foresee any systematic increase in inflation above its target level.

Supply shocks

> A **permanent supply shock** affects equilibrium unemployment and potential output.
>
> A **temporary supply shock** leaves these long-run values unaffected, but shifts the short-run Phillips curve and the short-run aggregate supply schedule for output.

In the long-run, other things equal, the Phillips curve is vertical at equilibrium unemployment U^*. But other things are unequal, and U^* is not constant. In terms of Figure 22.6, a rise in equilibrium unemployment shifts the vertical long-run Phillips curve to the right. Changes in equilibrium unemployment reflect **permanent supply shocks**.

The short-run Phillips curve can shift for two reasons. Inherited nominal wage growth changes if inflation expectations change, as analysed in Figure 22.6. Alternatively, a change in firms' desired supply of output and demand for workers, for a given rate of inherited nominal wage growth, shifts the short-run Phillips curve. Examples include a change in oil prices, regulations or tax rates.

MATHS 22.1 — Short-run and long-run Phillips curves

Consider the short-run Phillips curve:

$$\pi = \pi^e - b(U - U^*) \qquad b > 0 \tag{1}$$

where U and U^* are, respectively, actual unemployment and equilibrium unemployment, π is inflation and π^e is expected inflation. When actual and equilibrium unemployment coincide, inflation is determined by the inherited level of inflation expectations, which therefore determines the height of the short-run Phillips curve. When expected inflation is higher, the entire short-run Phillips curve is higher. The parameter b determines the slope of the short-run Phillips curve. The larger is b, the steeper is the short-run curve. Because b is a constant, in this example $SRPC$ has a constant negative slope. In the long run, any level of inflation expectations can prevail when U and U^* coincide. All we know is that then actual and expected inflation coincide along the long-run Phillips curve. Any actual inflation rate is compatible eventually with U^*. $LRPC$ is vertical.

Suppose people believe the central bank will try to stabilize inflation at 2 per cent, but that this cannot be achieved overnight. People therefore expect:

$$\pi^e = 0.02 - a(U - U^*) \qquad a > 0 \tag{2}$$

When unemployment exceeds U^*, people expect inflation to be lower than normal; when unemployment is below U^*, people expect a boom to be leading to above normal inflation.

Combining equations (1) and (2):

$$\pi = 0.02 - (a + b)(U - U^*) \tag{3}$$

In this example, when unemployment has reverted to its long-run equilibrium, inflation is then 2 per cent. In the short run, inflation is affected by deviations of unemployment from equilibrium unemployment not only because this affects wages, prices and inflation, but also because it has a second effect on inflation expectations themselves. Exactly how inflation expectations adjust over time in the real world is a subject of continuing controversy.

Figure 22.7 shows an adverse temporary supply shock. The short-run Phillips curve shifts up, from PC_1 to PC_2. If monetary policy accommodates the shock, the target inflation rate rises from π_1 to π_2. The economy moves from E to F with no change in output or unemployment, but at the cost of higher inflation. Eventually the shock wears off, since it is temporary, and the economy reverts to E, with another accommodating change in monetary policy.

Alternatively, monetary policy may *not* fully accommodate the supply shock. In Chapter 21, we showed that this would mean higher inflation *and* lower output. Now, the analogue is higher inflation *and* higher unemployment – stagflation. To prevent inflation shifting up by as much as the vertical shift up in the short-run Phillips curve, monetary policy makes sure that aggregate demand falls a bit. Hence inflation rises a bit and unemployment rises a bit. The economy moves from E to G in Figure 22.7. Output stagnates despite higher inflation.

> **Stagflation** is high inflation and high unemployment, caused by an adverse supply shock.

Again, the credibility of policy is crucial. If workers think the government, frightened of high unemployment, will accommodate any shock, large wage rises buy temporarily higher real wages until prices adjust fully. And in the long run, monetary policy is loosened to maintain aggregate demand at full employment, so there is little danger of extra unemployment.

Once a government proves that it will not accommodate shocks, nominal wage growth slows. Workers then fear that higher wages will reduce demand and price workers out of a job.

Fifty years of inflation and unemployment

The original Phillips curve seemed to offer a permanent trade-off between inflation and unemployment. It also suggested both inflation *and* unemployment could be low.

At that time, governments were committed to full employment even in the short run. Any shock tending to raise inflation – including temporary supply shocks – was accommodated by a higher money supply to prevent a fall in aggregate demand. Money growth and inflation steadily rose. After the mid-1970s, government policy changed in most countries. The emphasis was on keeping

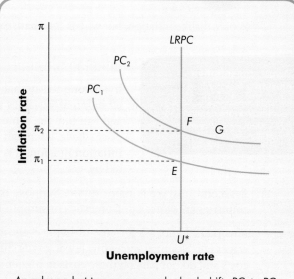

An adverse but temporary supply shock shifts PC_1 to PC_2 without affecting *LRPC*. Beginning from E monetary polic can accommodate the shock, moving to F. If interest rate are raised to prevent inflation rising as high as π_2, the fa in demand raises unemployment. At G the economy experiences stagflation, both high inflation and high unemployment.

Figure 22.7 *Temporary supply shocks*

inflation low. Inflation fell after the early 1980s. Only in 2009 did output and employment once again become the principal focus.

What about unemployment? We now understand that the Phillips curve is vertical in the long run at equilibrium unemployment. The rise and fall of equilibrium unemployment explained much of the rise and fall in actual unemployment. It was not the whole story.

The short-run Phillips curve is the *temporary* trade-off between inflation and unemployment while the economy adjusts to a demand shock and works its way back to long-run equilibrium. The height of the short-run Phillips curve mainly reflects anticipated inflation.

At the start of the 1980s, inflation was high because it had been high in the past. Anti-inflation policies were just beginning to bite. When tight money was first introduced, aggregate demand fell and the economy moved to the right along the short-run Phillips curve. In addition to high equilibrium unemployment, many countries had a short-run Keynesian slump. Unemployment exceeded its equilibrium level.

In the 1990s many European economies reduced inflation to low levels to show they were fit candidates for monetary union. The UK also adopted tight policies to get inflation down. First, it joined the Exchange Rate Mechanism and, when that failed, it made the Bank of England independent of political control.

Once inflation expectations had been brought down, super-tight policies were unnecessary. British unemployment fell a lot after 1993. In part, it was a recovery from the Keynesian recession of 1990–92. In part, supply-side policies reduced equilibrium unemployment. Like other countries, the UK then entered a benign period of low unemployment, low inflation and steady growth.

22.5 The costs of inflation

People dislike inflation, but why is it so bad? Some reasons commonly given are spurious.

Inflation illusion?

People have **inflation illusion** if they confuse nominal and real changes. People's welfare depends on real variables, not nominal variables.

It is wrong to say that inflation is bad because it makes goods more expensive. If *all* nominal variables rise at the same rate, people have larger nominal incomes and can buy the same physical quantity of goods as before. If people realize that prices have risen but forget that nominal incomes have also risen, they have inflation illusion. It is real incomes that tell us how many goods people can afford to buy.

A second mistake is more subtle. Suppose there is a sharp rise in the real price of oil. Oil-importing countries are worse off. Domestic consumption per person has to fall. It can fall in one of two ways.

If workers do not ask for 'cost-of-living' wage increases to cover the higher cost of oil-related products, real wages fall. Nominal wages buy fewer goods. Suppose too that domestic firms absorb higher oil-related fuel costs and do not pass on these costs in higher prices. There is no rise in domestic prices or nominal wages. The domestic economy has adjusted to the adverse supply shock without inflation. People are worse off.

Suppose instead that people try to maintain their old standard of living. Workers claim cost-of-living rises to restore their real wages, and firms protect their profit margins by raising prices in line with higher wage and fuel costs. There is a lot of domestic inflation, which the government accommodates by printing extra money. Eventually the economy settles down in its new long-run equilibrium position.

People must still be worse off. The rise in the real oil price has not disappeared. It still takes more domestic exports, made possible by lower domestic consumption, to pay for the more expensive oil imports. In the new long-run equilibrium, workers find that their wages do not quite keep up with higher prices, and firms find that higher prices do not quite keep up with higher costs. The market has brought about the required fall in real domestic spending, letting resources go into exports to pay for the more expensive oil imports.

People notice (a) rising prices and (b) lower real incomes, but draw the wrong conclusion. It is not the inflation that has made them worse off, but the rise in oil prices. Inflation is a symptom of the initial refusal to accept the new reality.

We now turn to better arguments about the cost of inflation. Our discussion has two themes. First, was the inflation fully expected in advance, or were people surprised? Second, do our institutions, including regulations and the tax system, let people adjust fully to inflation once they expect it? The costs of inflation depend on the answer to these two questions.

Complete adaptation and full anticipation

Imagine an economy with annual inflation of 10 per cent for ever. Everybody anticipates it. Nominal wages grow and nominal interest rates incorporate it. Real wages and real interest rates are unaffected. The economy is at full employment. Government policy is also fully adjusted. Nominal taxes are changed every year to keep real tax revenue constant. Nominal government spending rises at 10 per cent a year to keep real government spending constant. Share prices rise with inflation to maintain the real value of company shares. The tax treatment of interest earnings and capital gains is adjusted to reflect inflation. Pensions and other transfer payments are raised every year, in line with expected inflation.

This economy has no inflation illusion. Everyone has adjusted to it. This explains the long-run vertical Phillips curve in the previous section. But is complete adjustment possible?

Nominal interest rates usually rise with inflation to preserve the real rate of interest. But the nominal interest rate is the opportunity cost of holding cash. When inflation is higher, people hold less real cash.

Society uses money to economize on the time and effort involved in undertaking transactions. High nominal interest rates make people economize on real money – thus incurring **shoe-leather costs**. Using more resources to transact, we have fewer resources for production and consumption of goods and services.

> **Shoe-leather costs of inflation** are the extra time and effort in transacting when we economize on holding real money.

When prices rise, price labels have to be changed. Menus are reprinted to show the higher price of meals.

The faster the rate of price change, the more often menus must be reprinted if real prices are to remain constant. Among the **menu costs of inflation** is the effort of doing mental arithmetic. If inflation is zero, it is easy to see that a beer costs the same as it did three months ago. When inflation is 25 per cent a year, it takes more effort to compare the real price of beer today with that of three months ago. People without inflation illusion try to think in real terms, but the mental arithmetic involves time and effort.

> **Menu costs of inflation** are the physical resources needed for adjustments to keep real things constant when inflation occurs.

How big are menu costs? In supermarkets it is easy to change price tags. The cost of changing parking meters, pay telephones and slot machines is larger. In countries with high inflation, pay phones usually take tokens whose price is easily changed without having physically to alter the machines.

Even when inflation is perfectly anticipated and the economy has fully adjusted to it, we cannot avoid shoe-leather and menu costs. These costs are big when inflation is high, but may not be too big when inflation is moderate. However, if we cannot adjust to expected inflation, the costs are then larger.

Fully anticipated inflation when institutions do not adapt

Assume inflation is fully anticipated but institutions prevent people fully adjusting to expected inflation. Inflation now has extra costs.

Taxes

Tax rates may not be fully inflation-adjusted. One problem is fiscal **drag**.

> **Fiscal drag** is the rise in real tax revenue when inflation raises nominal incomes, pushing people into higher tax brackets in a progressive income tax system.

Suppose income below £4000 is untaxed but you pay income tax at 25 per cent on all income over that amount. Initially, you earn £5000 and pay income tax of £250. After ten years of inflation, all wages and prices double but tax brackets and tax rates remain as before. You now earn £10 000. Paying tax at 25 per cent on the £6000 by which your nominal income exceeds £4000, you pay nominal tax of £1500. Wages and prices only doubled, but your nominal tax payment rose from £250 to £1500. Fiscal drag raised the real tax burden. The government gained from inflation. You lost.

For an inflation-neutral tax system, nominal tax brackets must rise with inflation. The real tax exemption is constant if the nominal limit rises from £4000 to £8000. Everything is then inflation-adjusted. You would pay £500 in tax – double what you paid before.

Percentage taxes on value, such as VAT, automatically raise nominal tax revenue in line with the price level. However, *specific* duties, such as £5 on a bottle of whisky, must be raised as the price level rises. In the UK there is no *automatic* formula for raising such duties. Each year the government decides.

Taxing capital

Income tax on interest income is also affected by inflation. Suppose there is no inflation. Nominal and real interest rates are both 4 per cent. With a 40 per cent tax rate, the after-tax real return on lending is 2.6 per cent. Now suppose inflation is 11 per cent and nominal interest rates are 15 per cent to keep a pre-tax real interest rate of 4 per cent. Suppose lenders must pay income tax on nominal interest income. The after-tax nominal interest rate is 9 per cent (0.6×15). Subtracting 11 per cent inflation, the after-tax *real* interest rate is −2 per cent. This compares with +2.6 per cent when inflation was zero.

> **Inflation accounting** uses fully inflation-adjusted definitions of costs, income and profit.

When inflation was 11 per cent, nominal interest rates were 15 per cent. Eleven per cent of this was not real income, merely a payment to keep up with inflation. Only 4 per cent was the real interest rate providing real income. But income tax applied to all 15 per cent. Higher inflation reduced the real return on lending because the tax system was not properly inflation-adjusted, that is, it did not use **inflation accounting**. The government gained more real tax revenue. You lost.

Capital gains tax is another example. Suppose people pay tax of 40 per cent on any capital gain made when asset prices rise. When inflation is zero, only real gains are taxed. When inflation is 10 per cent, nominal asset prices rise merely to preserve their real value. People pay capital gains tax even though they are not making real capital gains.

Institutional imperfections help explain why inflation has real effects even when inflation is fully anticipated. These effects can be large. Usually, the government is the winner.

Unexpected inflation

Previously, we assumed that inflation was fully anticipated. What if inflation is a surprise?

Redistribution

When prices rise unexpectedly, people with nominal assets lose and people with nominal liabilities gain. Nominal contracts to buy and sell, or lend and borrow, can reflect expected inflation, but cannot reflect surprise inflation.

Expecting inflation of 10 per cent, you lend £100 for a year at 12 per cent, expecting a real interest rate of 2 per cent. Unexpectedly, inflation is 20 per cent. The real interest rate on your loan is $[12 - 20] = -8$ per cent.

You lose by lending. Conversely, borrowers gain 8 per cent. Their nominal income rises 20 per cent with inflation but they repay at 12 per cent interest.

For every borrower, there is a lender. One person's gain is another person's loss. In the aggregate, they cancel out. But unexpected inflation redistributes real income and wealth; in this case from lenders to borrowers. This may lead to economic dislocation. Some people may have to declare bankruptcy, which then affects other people. We also have to make a value judgement about whether we like the redistribution that is taking place.

One redistribution is between the government and the private sector. *Unexpected* inflation reduces the real value of all outstanding nominal government debt. It is as if the government had taxed us in order to repay this debt.[3]

The old and the young

In practice, many savers are the old. Having paid off their mortgages and built up savings during their working life, they put their wealth into nominal bonds to provide income during retirement. These people lose out from surprise inflation.

Nominal debtors are the young and, mainly, those entering middle age with a large mortgage. They gain when surprise inflation raises house prices and nominal incomes without a matching rise in the nominal sum they owe the bank or building society.

Surprise inflation redistributes from the old to the young. We may judge this redistribution undesirable. With technical progress and productivity growth, each generation is richer than the one before. Redistribution from the old to the young raises intergenerational inequality.

Uncertain inflation

Uncertainty about future inflation has two costs. First, it makes planning more complex, raising the real resources society uses to make plans and do business.

Second, people dislike risk. The extra benefits of the champagne years are poor compensation for the years of starvation. People would rather average out these extremes and live comfortably all the time. The psychological costs of worrying about how to cope with the bad years may also be important.

When people make nominal contracts, uncertainty about inflation means uncertainty about the eventual real value of the nominal bargains currently made. This is a true cost of inflation. If a lower average level of inflation also reduces uncertainty about inflation, this may be a reason to aim for low inflation. The institutions that commit the government to low inflation may also reduce the scope for uncertainty about inflation. If so, lower average inflation has a real benefit because it is also more certain.

CASE 22.1

Public enemy number two

For several decades, policy makers convinced themselves that inflation was public enemy number one. Inflation is certainly destructive, for the reasons discussed above. However, when financial crisis erupted, concerns about inflation were temporarily but completely set aside. Saving the banking system was more important, preventing another Great Depression was more important, and getting output on the path to recovery was more important. Several of these judgements reflected a fear that Western economies were about to experience **deflation**.

Deflation is negative inflation, when the price level is falling.

---

3   Why stress unexpected inflation? Because expected inflation is already built into the terms on which bonds were originally issued. Expected inflation affects nominal interest rates.

If inflation is bad, you might be forgiven for thinking that deflation is good. Nothing could be further from the truth. Price stability is good. Low inflation is good. Negative inflation is horrible. Here's why.

Imagine you have borrowed money, and have a nominal debt of £1000. If inflation is foreseen and is 10 per cent, the chances are you had to pay 12 per cent interest in order to provide the lender with a real interest rate of 2 per cent.

Now suppose inflation is −2 per cent. A nominal interest rate of zero will still achieve a real interest rate of 2 per cent. But what happens if inflation is −4 per cent. Nominal interest rates cannot fall below zero, so now the real interest rate is $[(0 − (−4)] = +4$ per cent. This cripples the borrower.

Worse yet, if, as a result of this heavy debt burden, borrowers then spend less, reducing aggregate demand, this puts downward pressure on inflation, taking it to say −5 per cent, which causes a bigger debt burden still, a further reduction in aggregate demand, further deflation, and yet higher real interest rates. This is an economic black hole, a vicious spiral downwards, from which the economy may not easily escape.

Understanding the dangers of deflation then makes sense of two things. First, this is why we normally set inflation targets for monetary policy at 2 per cent not 0 per cent. This provides a margin of safety before any dangers of deflation arise. Aiming on average for zero inflation is a bit too close to the edge of the cliff.

Second, the threat of deflation was one reason why so many governments threw the kitchen sink at the recessionary threat in 2009. They preferred to cope later with the problem of large government debt rather than cope almost immediately with being sucked into the black hole of debt deflation.

Thus, for example, in August 2009, Reuters (London) reported:

> The Bank of England will downgrade its growth forecasts and issue a warning this week that the UK economy risks slumping into a debt deflation trap, the *Telegraph* reported on Monday. The newspaper said Bank Governor Mervyn King will use the Bank's Inflation Report on Wednesday to say the risk of such a slump was one of the main reasons behind the Bank's surprise decision last week to extend its quantitative easing programme.
>
> (http://news.stv.tv/uk/114875-bank-to-warn-that-uk-risks-deflation)

Or, as Yale professor Irving Fisher put it in 1933,

> [I]n the great booms and depressions, […] [there were] two dominant factors, namely over-indebtedness to start with and deflation following soon after; also that where any of the other factors do become conspicuous, they are often merely effects or symptions of these two.
>
> ('Debt-deflation theories of great depressions', *Econometrica*, 1933)

Did any countries actually experience negative inflation during 2009? According to the table below, the list is surprisingly extensive.

Country	Inflation (%)
Canada	−1.9
Denmark	−0.5
Ireland	−3.8
Netherlands	−0.3
Norway	−3.3
Slovakia	−0.6

Without fiscal expansion, the slashing of interest rates and quantitative easing, we might already be stuck in a downward spiral. By early 2010 nobody could yet be sure that we had completely escaped. In the Great Depression of the 1930s, economies appeared to have recovered from the initial crash, only to then enter a renewed recession. Hence, the 'double dip' remains a possibility until recovery is much more securely established.

Notice that there are now two different reasons why inflation might arise as a postscript to the financial crash. First, governments might be unwilling or unable to raise sufficient tax revenue to service the interest on their huge debt levels. They might create money to finance budget deficits. Second, and nothing to do with the fiscal argument, governments might prefer a period of slightly higher inflation to overcome the fact that, when prices are stable, real interest rates cannot be negative even when nominal interest rates have fallen to zero. This second argument for inflation aims to make monetary policy more powerful by allowing negative real interest rates, which requires positive inflation when nominal interest rates are close to zero.

22.6 Controlling inflation

Policy makers are reluctant to sanction higher inflation because they have spent the last 30 years bringing inflation down. We now discuss how they did it and what they might have to do again. Essentially, inflation is low if people expect it to be low. Credibility is vital.

Incomes policy

A freeze on wage increases certainly gets inflation down quickly. Historically, it has not been able to keep inflation down. Why were past incomes policies unsuccessful?

> **Incomes policy** is the direct control of wages and other incomes.

Once governments intervene in the labour market, they often cannot resist pursuing other aims at the same time. For example, they try to compress relative wages across different skills in the name of fairness. Such policies alter real wages for particular skills, causing excess supply in some skills and excess demand in others. Market forces eventually break the policy.

At best, incomes policy is a temporary adjustment device. In the long run, low nominal money growth is essential if low inflation is to be maintained. Some incomes policies failed because governments introduced a wage freeze but kept printing money – a guarantee that excess demand for workers would eventually break the policy.

Long-term incomes policies are also hard to administer because equilibrium real wages for particular skills change over time. Freezing the existing wage structure gradually sets up powerful market forces of excess supply and excess demand.

Institutional reform

This approach is concerned not with the temporary costs of first getting inflation down, but with how to *keep* inflation down. Central bank independence is a useful pre-commitment to tight monetary policy and low inflation. Here are some examples drawn from the past 20 years.

The Maastricht Treaty

Signed in 1991, the treaty set out conditions both for entering the eurozone and after admission to it. The first requirement was to avoid loose fiscal policy: a ceiling of 3 per cent on budget deficits relative to GDP.

High-debt countries were also supposed to initiate actions to bring their debt/GDP levels below 60 per cent to minimize the possibility that member states could get into fiscal difficulties and pressurize the European Central Bank to create money to help them out. Moreover, euro entrants first had to succeed in disinflating to low levels, measured both directly by changes in price indexes and indirectly by nominal interest rates.

Not only did EU governments have to sign up for tight policy in the 1990s and beyond, euro hopefuls had to undertake institutional reform, making their national central banks formally independent. The Maastricht Treaty also made the new European Central Bank independent of government, with a mandate to pursue price stability.

It is easy to make commitments, but harder to stick to them, as the eurozone has discovered in the aftermath of the crisis.

Bank of England independence

In May 1997 the new Chancellor, Gordon Brown, gave the Bank of England 'operational independence' to set interest rates. The Bank aims to achieve an inflation target set by the Chancellor. In an emergency (a very adverse supply shock), the government can temporarily raise the target rather than force the Bank to initiate a drastic recession merely to hit the inflation target quickly. Nevertheless, any change in the target is politically hard except in truly exceptional circumstances. Operational independence is a commitment to policies favouring low inflation.

ACTIVITY 22.1

'Asia's inflation genie leaps out of the bottle'

In early 2010 Asian inflation rose sharply again, after a muted period in the aftermath of the financial crash. Unlike Europe and North America, where fears surrounding renewed recession were keeping the lid on inflation, Asia was experiencing its highest inflation for over a decade.

India, where prices were flat in mid-2009, was experiencing wholesale price inflation of almost 10 per cent; in Vietnam it had risen to 8.5 per cent, in South Korea to 4.2 per cent, and Chinese inflation had almost returned to the 3 per cent target set by the government earlier in 2010. In Australia, with inflation over 2 per cent, the Reserve Bank of Australia became the first central bank to increase interest rates several times since the financial crash, at a time when Europe and the US were still pursuing quantitative easing and keeping interest rates as low as they dared.

'Robert Prior-Wandesforde, HSBC Asia economist in Singapore, says India's inflation index is largely driven by food and oil prices, while Australian inflation, currently at 2.1 per cent, is driven mainly by red-hot demand from China for commodities. The main driver is the speed and breadth of the recovery generated by three quarters of double-digit, quarter-on-quarter annualised growth in GDP in most of Asia outside Japan,' concluded the *Financial Times*.

Not only had rapid growth rates been restored, for emerging Asia as a whole the level of GDP by early 2010 was 4 per cent above its previous peak in the third quarter of 2008, before the output effects of the financial crash then took their toll. Private sector consumption was 7 per cent higher than pre-crisis levels in the ten largest Asian economies, excluding Japan.

Source: Adapted from Brown, K. (2010) Asia's inflation genie leaps out of the bottle, *Financial Times*, 18 March. © Financial Times Limited 2010.

Questions

(a) If Europe, North America and Japan were still stagnating, what must have been the source of aggregate demand for Asian goods?

(b) How much spare capacity – for output and for labour – is likely now to be left in emerging Asian markets?

(c) What does this imply about the likely course of future monetary policy in these countries?

(d) Why was Australia driven to act even more quickly?

(e) If energy, food and commodities prices rise sharply, what dilemma will then face policy makers in Europe, the US and Japan?

To check your answers to these questions, go to page 687.

22.7 The Monetary Policy Committee

Since 1997 UK interest rates have been set by the Bank of England's Monetary Policy Committee (MPC), which meets monthly to set interest rates to try to hit the inflation target laid down by the Chancellor. Initially, the target was 2.5 per cent annual inflation, plus or minus 1 per cent. The target applied to **underlying inflation** (which ignores mortgage interest rates) not **headline inflation**.

> **Underlying inflation** is the growth of the retail price index (RPI), after omitting the effect of mortgage interest rates on the cost of living (hence the abbreviation RPIX).
>
> **Headline inflation** is actual inflation, the growth in the RPI.

Why omit mortgage interest from the price level on which monetary policy should focus? Suppose inflation is too high. To reduce aggregate demand, interest rates are raised. But higher interest rates *raise* the RPI by raising the cost of living for homeowners. Moreover, when temporary changes in interest rates are required to get the economy back on track, it may also be more sensible to target the underlying rate of inflation.

Different countries construct price indexes in slightly different ways. EU countries have each adopted a common procedure for calculating their consumer price index (CPI), making cross-country comparisons of inflation more meaningful. In December 2003, the UK Chancellor, Gordon Brown, instructed the Bank of England to switch from using the RPIX to using the CPI as the basis for inflation targeting.

> **CPI inflation** measures the rate of growth of an index of consumer prices.

For statistical reasons, **CPI inflation** tends to grow less rapidly than RPIX inflation. At the time of the crossover, UK inflation was 2.9 per cent measured by the growth rate of the RPIX but only 1.3 per cent measured by the growth rate of the CPI. Hence, Gordon Brown also changed the target inflation rate from 2.5 per cent growth in the RPI to 2.0 per cent growth in the CPI.

The quarterly *Inflation Report* includes the famous **fan chart** for CPI inflation. Figure 22.8 shows the fan chart for February 2010. The darker is the projected line, the more likely the outcome. Figure 22.8 shows that, in August 2007, the Bank was expecting UK inflation to average around 2.5 per cent in 2007, and then to revert to the 2 per cent target (with most possible outcomes within 1 per cent of this).

> A **fan chart** indicates the probability of different outcomes.

In this section, we discuss three questions. Why was the MPC given a target for inflation? How does it work? How easy was it for the MPC to decide where to set interest rates?

Inflation targets

Without a nominal anchor, nothing ties down the price level or any other nominal variable. Market forces only determine real variables.

Nominal money is a possible nominal anchor and is attractive as an intermediate target because new data on money come out faster than data on prices or output. Monetary targets fell out of favour because large and unpredictable changes in real money demand made it hard to know where to set the nominal money

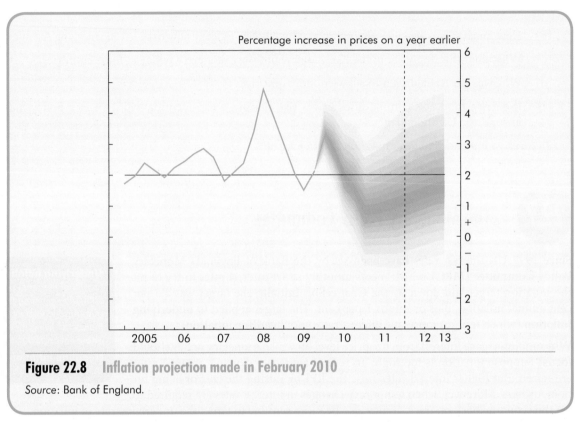

Percentage increase in prices on a year earlier

Figure 22.8 Inflation projection made in February 2010

Source: Bank of England.

target; more recently, broad money supply has also been unpredictable because of changes in the bank deposit multiplier. When it is hard to predict M/P, it is hard to know where to set M in order to get the desired path of P.

As explained in previous chapters, most modern central banks implicitly follow a Taylor rule but their policy is often portrayed and communicated as a flexible inflation target. This is easily understood by the public, and more easily monitored than a Taylor rule, which could lead to disputes about what the (unobservable) level of potential output really is.[4]

Back to the future

Delays in data availability mean that the MPC has to forecast where the economy is today. Moreover, the interest rate medicine takes up to two years to have its full effect on private behaviour. Hence the MPC has to *forecast* the path of prices at least two years into the future merely to know where to set interest rates *today*!

On occasion, the MPC may raise interest rates even though current inflation is under control. This means that, in the absence of any change in interest rates, the MPC is forecasting that inflation will be too high. It then has to act quickly to keep inflation on track.

Good on inflation, shame about the crash

The MPC successfully maintained UK inflation within a much narrower range than previously accomplished. The Bank was prepared to change interest rates even when this was unpopular. But low levels of inflation

---

4   Like central banks deciding where to set interest rates, academic researchers engaged in empirical evaluation of monetary policy have to make estimates of how potential output is evolving. The OECD regularly publishes estimates of output gaps $(Y - Y^*)$ for the major countries.

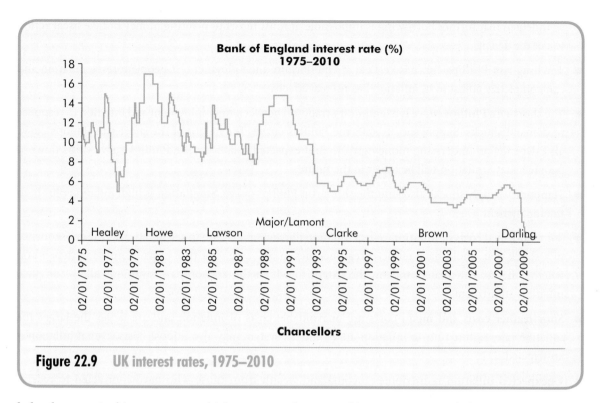

**Bank of England interest rate (%)
1975–2010**

Chancellors: Healey, Howe, Lawson, Major/Lamont, Clarke, Brown, Darling

Figure 22.9 UK interest rates, 1975–2010

led to low nominal interest rates, which encouraged more reckless private sector behaviour. Determining sensible monetary policy was never the entire remit of the Bank of England – it has a *financial stability* wing as well as a *monetary stability* wing – and the Financial Services Authority was explicitly charged with financial regulation. Good monetary policy cannot be held responsible for inadequate financial regulation.

Figure 22.9 shows the history of UK interest rates since 1974; for much of this period these were set directly by the Chancellor, whose names are listed. Although the Bank's operational independence to set interest rates was granted in 1997, Figure 22.9 shows that the decisive break was in 1992 when sterling left the Exchange Rate Mechanism and changed nominal anchors from a pegged exchange rate to an inflation target. Reinforced by formal independence, since 1997 the MPC has built on the earlier success during 1992–97. The low interest rates of 2009/10 are clearly an emergency response to the recession caused by the financial crash.

Summary

- The **quantity theory of money** says changes in prices are caused by equivalent changes in the nominal money supply. In practice, prices cannot adjust at once to changes in nominal money, so interest rates or income alter, changing real money demand. Nevertheless, in the long run, changes in prices are usually associated with changes in nominal money.

- The **Fisher hypothesis** is that a 1 per cent rise in inflation leads to a similar rise in nominal interest rates so real interest rates change little. Since the nominal interest rate is the cost of holding money, higher inflation reduces real money demand. The *flight from cash* during hyperinflation is a vivid example.

- For a solvent government, there need be no close relationship between the budget deficit and nominal money growth. In the long run, persistent borrowing to finance large deficits may leave the government so indebted that further borrowing is impossible. It must resort to printing money or take fiscal action to cut the deficit.

● The **long-run Phillips curve** is vertical at equilibrium unemployment. If people foresee inflation and can completely adjust to it, inflation has no real effects.

● The **short-run Phillips curve** is a temporary trade-off between unemployment and inflation in response to demand shocks. Supply shocks shift the Phillips curve. The height of the short-run Phillips curve also depends on underlying money growth and expected inflation. The Phillips curve shifts down if people believe inflation will be lower in the future.

● Temporary supply shocks also shift the short-run Phillips curve. **Stagflation** is high inflation plus high unemployment.

● Some so-called **costs of inflation** reflect inflation illusion or a failure to see inflation as the consequence of a shock that would have reduced real incomes in any case. The true costs of inflation depend on whether it was anticipated and on the extent to which the economy's institutions allow complete inflation-adjustment.

● **Shoe-leather costs** and **menu costs** are unavoidable costs of inflation and are larger the larger the inflation rate. Failure fully to inflation-adjust the tax system may also impose costs, even if inflation is anticipated.

● **Unexpected inflation** redistributes income and wealth from those who have contracted to receive nominal payments (lenders and workers) to those who have contracted to pay them (firms and borrowers).

● Uncertainty about future inflation rates imposes costs on people who dislike risk. Uncertainty may be greater when inflation is already high.

● **Incomes policy** may accelerate a fall in inflation expectations, allowing disinflation without a large recession. But it is unlikely to succeed in the long run. Only low money growth can deliver low inflation in the long run.

● **Operational independence of central banks** is designed to remove the temptation faced by politicians to print too much money.

Review questions

connect

EASY

1 Your real annual income is constant, and initially is £10 000. You borrow £200 000 for ten years to buy a house, paying interest annually and repaying the £200 000 in a final payment at the end. (a) List your annual incomings and outgoings in the first and ninth year if inflation is 0 and the nominal interest rate is 2 per cent a year. (b) Repeat the exercise if annual inflation is 100 per cent and the nominal interest rate is 102 per cent. Are the two situations the same in real terms?

2 Does this explain why voters mind about high inflation even when nominal interest rates rise in line with inflation?

3 (a) Explain the following data taken from *The Economist* a few years ago (when some countries still had proper inflation!). (b) Is inflation always a monetary phenomenon?

	Money growth (%)	Inflation (%)
Eurozone	3	2
Japan	12	−3
UK	6	2
Australia	15	3
US	8	2

4 Looking at data on inflation and unemployment over ten years, could you tell the difference between supply shocks and demand shocks?

5 Name three groups which lose out during inflation. Does it matter whether this inflation was anticipated?

6 Common fallacies   Why are these statements wrong? (a) Getting inflation down is the only way to cure high unemployment. (b) Inflation stops people saving. (c) Inflation stops people investing.

7 Which is correct? (a) The long-run Phillips curve should really have a positive slope because higher inflation makes firms substitute away from workers who are causing the underlying problem. (b) If inflation leads people to economize on some forms of money, this must make the economy less productive and probably raises long-run unemployment. (c) Compared with all the other things equal assumptions already made, it is a tolerable approximation to view the long-run Phillips curve as vertical.

8 'As jobs migrate to Asia, equilibrium unemployment in Europe may rise and governments will therefore seek higher inflation to make labour temporarily cheap and preserve employment.' Discuss.

MEDIUM

9 Suppose Asia emerges from the financial crisis much more quickly than Europe and North America. As China and India bid up world commodity prices, use a figure resembling Figure 22.7 to illustrate the effect on European unemployment.

10 Draw a curve to illustrate how the real revenue raised by the government through foreseen inflation varies with the inflation rate. What is the name of this curve? If an economy moves from using a lot of cash to using a lot of electronic money on which market interest rates are paid, illustrate how the curve changes.

11 D is real government debt, s is the primary budget surplus $T − G$ (that is, excluding interest payments on debt), i the real interest rate, Y real output and g the rate of output growth. The debt burden D/Y rises with debt but falls with output and the ability to repay debt. Let Δ denote the increase in a variable. (a) Since $\Delta(D/Y) = (\Delta\,D/D) − (\Delta Y\,/\,Y)$, show that the debt/GDP ratio shrinks only if $s/D > i − g$. (b) Suppose all debt is cash, paying no interest. Show how the above relationship becomes $s/D > −(g + \pi)$ where π is the rate of inflation.

12 Professor Milton Friedman argued that money was socially useful but essentially free to create. Society should therefore reduce the opportunity cost of holding money to zero, so that people would demand it up to the point at which its marginal benefit was zero. (a) Suppose the real interest rates on other assets is around 3 per cent. Is there any way society could arrange for cash to earn a similar real return? (b) Why don't governments do this?

13 Inflation in Zimbabwe, high for many years, recently reached hyperinflation levels. (a) President Mugabe blames Western governments for restricting trade and driving up prices. Could a fall in supply have generated sustained high inflation? (b) Why do you think Zimbabwe has such high inflation? (c) Is inflation high enough to raise the maximum possible revenue for the government?

14 Essay question   Does the huge success of central bank independence in so many countries suggest that other decisions should be removed from government? Your answer should include assessments of the case for: (a) an independent health services board, (b) an independent budget deficit commission, and (c) a redistribution commission.

For solutions to these questions contact your lecturer.

Unemployment

Learning Outcomes

By the end of this chapter, you should understand:

1 classical, frictional and structural unemployment

2 voluntary and involuntary unemployment

3 measured unemployment: claimant count and standardized rate

4 determinants of unemployment

5 how supply-side policies reduce equilibrium unemployment

6 private and social costs of unemployment

7 hysteresis

In the early 1930s over a quarter of the UK labour force was unemployed. Society threw away output by failing to put people to work. For the next 40 years macroeconomic policy tried to manage aggregate demand to avoid a rerun of the 1930s. Figure 23.1 shows that until the 1970s the policy succeeded.

In the 1970s high inflation emerged for reasons discussed in the previous chapter. Governments eventually tightened monetary and fiscal policy to get inflation under control. The mix of tighter demand policies and adverse supply shocks led to a big rise in unemployment in the 1980s.

After the economy adjusted, deficient demand was no longer the cause of high unemployment. Equilibrium unemployment remained high because of adverse changes in supply. Better supply-side policies since the mid-1990s have reduced unemployment to levels not seen since before the 1970s.

Table 23.1 shows that the fight against unemployment was even harder to win in other countries. Why did high unemployment persist for so long, especially in continental Europe? What can governments do about unemployment?

 23.1 The labour market

Not everyone wants a job. The people who do are called the labour force.

Table 23.1 Unemployment, 1972–2009 (%)

	1972	1982	1992	2004	2009
UK	4	11	10	5	8
Italy	6	8	9	8	8
France	3	10	10	9	9
Euro area	3	9	9	9	9
US	5	10	8	6	9

Source: OECD, Economic Outlook.

The **labour force** is people with a job or registered as looking for work at the current wage rate. The **participation rate** is the fraction of the population of working age in the labour force. The **unemployment rate** is the fraction of the labour force without a job but registered as looking for work.

Some people looking for work do not register as unemployed. They do not appear in official statistics for the registered **labour force** or the registered unemployed. Yet from an economic viewpoint, such people *are* in the labour force and *are* unemployed. For the moment, our data on the labour force or the unemployed refer only to those registered.

Figure 23.1 shows that UK unemployment was high in the interwar years, especially in the 1930s. By comparison, the post-war unemployment rate was tiny until the late 1970s. In the 1980s it started to get back to pre-war levels, but then fell steadily after 1990.

Stocks and flows

Unemployment is a stock concept measured at a point in time. Like a pool of water, its level rises when inflows (the newly unemployed) exceed outflows (people getting new jobs or quitting the labour force altogether). Figure 23.2 illustrates this important idea.

There are three ways for workers to become unemployed. Some people are sacked or made redundant (job-losers); some are temporarily laid off but expect eventually to be rehired by the same company; and some voluntarily quit their existing jobs. But the inflow to unemployment also comes from people not previously in the labour force: school-leavers (new entrants) and people who, having left the labour force, are now returning to look for a job (re-entrants).

People leave the unemployment pool in the opposite directions. Some get jobs. Others give up looking for jobs and leave the labour force completely. Some of this latter group

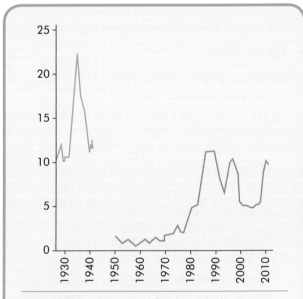

Figure 23.1 UK unemployment (%)

Sources: Mitchell, B. R. (1988) Abstracts of British Historical Statistics, Cambridge University Press; Mitchell, B. R. and Jones, H. G. (1971) Second Abstract of British Historical Statistics, Cambridge University Press; OECD, Economic Outlook.

may simply have reached the retirement age at which they get a pension, but many are **discouraged workers**.

> **Discouraged workers**, pessimistic about finding a job, leave the labour force.

Table 23.2 shows that the pool of unemployment is not stagnant. In October 2009 the stock of unemployed people claiming jobseeker's allowance was 1.7 million. A much larger number, around 4.2 million people, had flowed into and out of unemployment during the previous 12 months.

When unemployment is high, people often have to spend longer in the pool before they find a way out. Table 23.3 gives data on the duration of unemployment. Unemployment is not always a temporary stopover on the way to better things. A higher unemployment rate usually also means that people are spending longer in the pool of unemployment before escaping. Table 23.3 shows the 1.7 million UK unemployed in 2009 divided by the period for which they have already been unemployed.

Even by late 2009 the full labour market consequences of the sharp 2009 output contraction had yet to be felt. Since labour is expensive both to recruit and to dismiss, firms try to ride out a temporary storm by hoarding the workers that they have. Once the recession is evidently going to persist for some time, firms then have little choice but to adjust the number of workers in their employment. In Table 23.3 there are

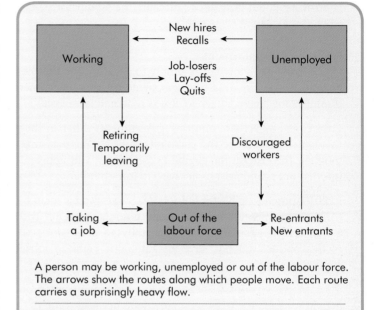

A person may be working, unemployed or out of the labour force. The arrows show the routes along which people move. Each route carries a surprisingly heavy flow.

Figure 23.2 Labour market flows

relatively few 'long-term' unemployed because the previous decade had been a period of economic growth with strong employment opportunities. The longer the recession persists, the more we expect to see a 'drift to the right' in Table 23.3, with larger numbers out of work for longer periods at a stretch.

Table 23.2 UK unemployment, October 2009 (million)

Inflow to unemployment over previous 12 months	4.2
Outflow from unemployment over previous 12 months	4.2
Stock of unemployed at October 2009	1.7

Source: ONS, *Labour Market Trends*.

Table 23.3 Unemployment by duration, October 2009 ('000 people)

< 6 months	6–12 months	12–24 months	24+ months
1093	365	155	25

Source: ONS, *Employment Outlook*.

<table>
<tr><td>CASE
23.1</td><td></td></tr>
</table>

Measuring unemployment

The unemployed are those without a job but willing to work at the prevailing wage rate – the difference between the labour force and those with jobs. Measuring those with jobs is not so controversial, but how do we measure the labour force? How do we know how many people would like to work at the current wage rate?

Claimant unemployment

One convenient short cut is simply to measure the number of people in receipt of unemployment-related benefit. In the UK, this transfer payment from government used to be called unemployment benefit. To diminish any stigma attached, it was renamed jobseeker's allowance.

Over time and across countries, governments differ in the generosity of the eligibility criteria for claiming this benefit. If we use the claimant count as our measure of unemployment, any government attempt to toughen the criteria for eligibility for benefit will appear to have reduced measured unemployment, and international comparisons are hard to interpret because of national differences in eligibility for benefit.

In 2010 those ineligible for UK jobseeker's allowance included: (a) those with savings above a certain amount, (b) those unable to work at least 40 hours a week, (c) those aged 16–17, and (d) those unwilling to sign a 'jobseeker's agreement' systematically to seek work. Those whose previous job terminated because of misconduct did not have an automatic right to jobseeker's allowance. Other countries make other stipulations.

Thus, in every country, measured unemployment based on counting claimants for unemployment-related benefit understates 'true unemployment' because some of those declared ineligible are in fact in the labour force, seeking a job, and unemployed.

Standardized unemployment

Fully aware of this issue, international agencies have endeavoured to produce a more comprehensive definition capable of being compared across countries. Accurate measures of unemployment depend on knowing people's intentions. It would be prohibitively expensive to ask every individual and assess whether their answers were truthful.

Standardized measures use surveys of smaller numbers of people and then extrapolate the answers to an estimate for the entire economy, just as opinion poll surveys try to predict election results and crime surveys try to estimate national crime statistics. Surveys are always subject to a margin of error, but the widespread use of standardized unemployment measures suggests that there is a degree of confidence in this approach.

The surveys ask people of working age, but without work, whether they: (a) are available to work within two weeks and actively job-hunting, (b) are waiting to take up a job already offered, or (c) have no wish to have a job at current wage rates. Those replying yes to (a) and (b) are included in the standardized measure of unemployment.

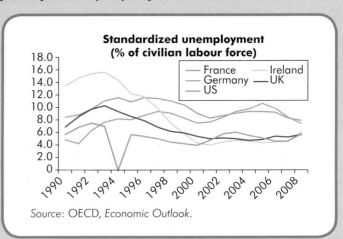

Source: OECD, Economic Outlook.

The figure above shows the evolution of standardized unemployment rates during 1996–2008 reported by the OECD.

The year 2008 may prove to have been a point of low unemployment – as Western economies are driven to fiscal austerity to combat their high levels of government debt, they will be delighted if other sources of aggregate demand increase sufficiently quickly to keep pace with the underlying growth of aggregate supply. The OECD itself was less optimistic:

> Developed countries will lose about 30 million jobs from the end of 2007 through the end of 2010, the Organization for Economic Cooperation and Development said on Tuesday, underscoring concerns the global economy has yet to recover from its worst recession in at least seven decades.
>
> (Reuters, Brasilia)

The job losses were mainly a result of the global financial crisis and the subsequent economic downturn that has pushed most developed economies into recession, Angel Gurria, the OECD's secretary general, said on 14 July 2009.

Table 23.4 Unemployment rates, 2009 (% of relevant group)

Age	Men	Women
16–17	36	29
18–24	21	15
25–49	7	5
50+	6	3

Source: ONS, *Labour Market Trends*.

The composition of unemployment

Table 23.4 gives a recent breakdown of unemployment by gender and age. Young workers find it much harder to get a job. Unlike established workers with accumulated skills and job experience, young workers have to be trained from scratch. Youth unemployment considerably exceeds the national average. The unemployment rate is lower for women than for men, perhaps because more women leave the labour force if they do not succeed in getting jobs. Over the age of 50, both men and women tend to retire or move on to sickness benefit if they have sustained spells of unemployment, and thus disappear from the unemployment statistics.

 ## 23.2 Analysing unemployment

We now develop a theoretical framework in which to analyse unemployment. We can classify unemployment by the source of the problem or by the nature of behaviour in the labour market.

Types of unemployment

Frictional unemployment includes people whose handicaps make them hard to employ. More importantly, it includes people spending short spells in unemployment as they hop between jobs in a dynamic economy.

> **Frictional unemployment** is the irreducible minimum unemployment in a dynamic society.

> **Structural unemployment** arises from the mismatch of skills and job opportunities as the pattern of demand and supply changes.
>
> **Demand-deficient unemployment** occurs when output is below full capacity.
>
> **Classical unemployment** describes the unemployment created when the wage is deliberately maintained above the level at which the labour supply and labour demand schedules intersect.

Structural unemployment reflects the time taken to acquire human capital. A skilled steelworker may have worked for 25 years but is made redundant at age 50 when the industry contracts in the face of foreign competition. That worker may have to retrain in a new skill which is more in demand in today's economy. Firms may be reluctant to take on and train older workers who have only a short remaining working life in which to repay the expensive investment. Such workers become the victims of structural unemployment.

Until wages and prices have adjusted to their new long-run equilibrium level, a fall in aggregate demand reduces output and employment. Some workers want to work at the going real wage rate but cannot find jobs. Only when demand has returned to its long-run level is **demand-deficient unemployment** eliminated.

Since the **classical** model assumes that flexible wages and prices maintain the economy at full employment, classical economists had difficulty explaining high unemployment in the 1930s. They concluded that the wage was prevented from adjusting to its equilibrium level. It can be caused either by the exercise of trade union power or by minimum wage legislation which enforces a wage in excess of the equilibrium wage rate.

The modern analysis of unemployment takes the same types of unemployment but classifies them differently to highlight the behavioural implications and consequences for government policy. Modern analysis stresses the difference between *voluntary* and *involuntary* unemployment.

Equilibrium unemployment

Figure 23.3 shows the labour market. The labour demand schedule *LD* slopes down. Firms demand more workers at a lower real wage because the cost of labour is lower. As in most economic applications, demand curves slope downwards.

The schedule *LF* shows how many people are in the labour force. A higher real wage increases the number of people wishing to work. This is not as obvious as it may at first appear. A higher wage increases the benefit

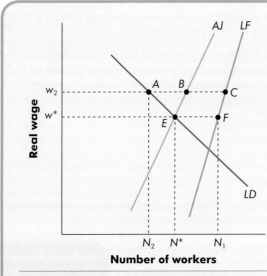

The schedules *LD*, *LF* and *AJ* show, respectively, labour demand, the size of the labour force and the number of workers willing to accept job offers at any real wage. *AJ* lies to the left of *LF* both because some labour force members are between jobs and because optimists are hanging on for an even better job offer. When the labour market clears at *E*, *EF* is the natural rate of unemployment, the people in the labour force not prepared to take job offers at the equilibrium wage w^*. If union power succeeds in maintaining the wage w_2 in the long run, the labour market will be at *A*, and the natural rate of unemployment *AC* now shows the amount of unemployment chosen by the labour force collectively by enforcing the wage w_2.

Figure 23.3 **Equilibrium unemployment**

of an hour of work relative to an hour of leisure. The substitution effect leads to a desire to work more and consume less leisure. But there is also an income effect. A higher wage makes people richer, raising the quantity of goods and leisure demanded. This income effect makes people less interested in working when wages are higher. Figure 23.3 shows what we have learned from considerable empirical research – higher real wages do increase the size of the labour force, but by only a little. The *LF* schedule is pretty steep.

The schedule *AJ* shows how many people accept job offers at each real wage. The schedule is to the left of the *LF* schedule: only people in the labour force can accept a job. How far *AJ* lies to the left of *LF* depends on several things. Some people are inevitably between jobs at any point in time. Also, a particular real wage may tempt some people into the labour force even though they will accept a job offer only if it provides a higher real wage than average.

We draw these schedules for a given level of jobseeker's allowance. When wages are high, jobseekers grab available jobs. The two upward-sloping schedules are close together. When wages are low (relative to unemployment benefit), potential workers are more selective in accepting job offers. People invest in searching for a good job. The two schedules are further apart.

Labour market equilibrium is at *E* in Figure 23.3. *Equilibrium employment* is N^*. The distance *EF* is **equilibrium unemployment**. This unemployment is entirely *voluntary*.

At the equilibrium real wage w^*, N_1 people want to be in the labour force but only N^* accept job offers; the remainder do not want to work at the equilibrium real wage.

> **Equilibrium unemployment** (also called the *natural rate of unemployment*) is the unemployment rate when the labour market is in equilibrium.

Equilibrium unemployment includes frictional and structural unemployment. Suppose a skilled welder earned £500 a week before being made redundant. The issue is not why workers became redundant (the decline of the steel industry), but why these workers will not take a lower wage as a dishwasher to get a job. Their old skills are obsolete. Until new skills are learned, dishwashing may be their only skill valued by the labour market. People not prepared to work at the going wage rate for their skills, but wanting to be in the labour force, are **voluntarily unemployed**.

> A worker is **voluntarily unemployed** if, at the given level of wages, she wishes to be in the labour force but does not yet wish to accept a job.

What about classical unemployment, for example if unions keep wages above their equilibrium level? This is shown in Figure 23.3 as a wage w_2 above w^*. Total unemployment is *AC*. As individuals, *AB* workers want jobs at the wage w_2 but cannot find them. Firms wish to be at point *A*. As individuals, the workers *AB* are **involuntarily unemployed**.

> A worker **involuntarily unemployed** would accept a job offer at the going wage rate.

However, through their unions, workers collectively opt for the wage w_2 above the equilibrium wage, thus reducing employment. For workers as a whole, the extra unemployment is voluntary. We include classical unemployment in equilibrium unemployment. If unions maintain the wage w_2, the economy stays at *A* and *AC* is equilibrium unemployment.

CONCEPT 23.1

The lump-of-labour fallacy

Those without economics training often think there is a simple solution for reducing unemployment: shorten the working week, so that the same amount of total work is shared between more workers, leaving fewer people unemployed. What's wrong with this argument?

It presumes the demand for labour (hours × people) is fixed, whatever the cost of hiring workers or their benefit in goods produced and revenue earned. In practice, both would be affected by the proposal. ▶

▶ You go to work for seven hours a day, but probably have an hour of dead time (visiting Starbucks, tidying your desk, being nice to colleagues, talking about sport, texting friends). This is a fixed cost, say an hour of time. There are probably economies of scale to shift length. Shortening the shift length adds to the cost of labour, making firms less competitive. For any given output demand for their product, from which we can derive the labour demand curve, a higher cost of labour makes firms choose to demand fewer workers. Firms move up their downward-sloping demand curve for labour and offer fewer jobs.

Few economists think compulsory reductions in the length of the working week are a promising solution to the problem of high unemployment.

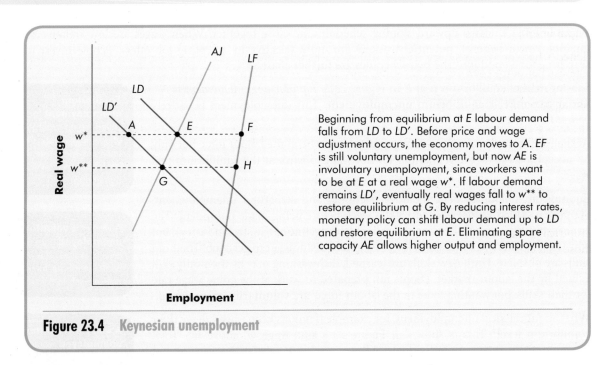

Beginning from equilibrium at E labour demand falls from LD to LD'. Before price and wage adjustment occurs, the economy moves to A. EF is still voluntary unemployment, but now AE is involuntary unemployment, since workers want to be at E at a real wage w*. If labour demand remains LD', eventually real wages fall to w** to restore equilibrium at G. By reducing interest rates, monetary policy can shift labour demand up to LD and restore equilibrium at E. Eliminating spare capacity AE allows higher output and employment.

Figure 23.4   Keynesian unemployment

Figure 23.4 illustrates how Keynesian or demand-deficient unemployment may arise. Initially, labour demand is *LD* and the labour market is in equilibrium at *E*, with equilibrium unemployment *EF*. Then labour demand shifts down to *LD'*. Before wages or prices adjust, the real wage is still *w**. At this wage, workers want to be at *E* but firms want to be at *A*. The distance *AE* is demand-deficient unemployment, involuntary unemployment caused by sluggish adjustment of wages and prices. *EF* remains voluntary unemployment.

If labour demand remains *LD'*, eventually real wages fall to *w*** to restore equilibrium at *G*. However, by reducing interest rates, monetary policy can shift labour demand up to *LD* again and restore equilibrium at *E*. At *A*, output and employment are low. Involuntary unemployment also reduces wage growth and inflation.

Thus, we can divide total unemployment into two parts. The equilibrium or natural rate is the equilibrium unemployment determined by normal labour market turnover, structural mismatch, union power and incentives in the labour market. Keynesian unemployment, also called demand-deficient or cyclical unemployment, is involuntary unemployment in disequilibrium, caused by low aggregate demand and sluggish wage adjustment.

This division helps us think clearly about the policies needed to tackle unemployment. Keynesian unemployment reflects spare capacity and wasted output. By boosting labour demand, policy can mop up this spare capacity and increase output and employment. Wage adjustment could logically accomplish the same outcome, but may take several years to do so. The more sluggish are market forces, the more it makes sense for policy to intervene. Most forms of monetary policy have the consequence that interest rates will adjust to such a situation and help offset the original demand shock. The automatic fiscal stabilizers also act in this direction.

In marked contrast, when the economy is already in long-run equilibrium, further demand expansion is pointless. Even though unemployment is not zero, there is no spare capacity. At points *E* or *G* in Figure 23.4, all remaining unemployment is voluntary.

It is true that, beginning from *G*, shifting labour demand up from *LD′* to *LD* achieves a small reduction in equilibrium unemployment. The distance *EF* is smaller than *GH* because the *AJ* and *LF* schedules are not parallel to one another. However the main effect of raising demand is to bid up wages, not to increase output or employment.

Hence, when the economy begins with only voluntary unemployment, reductions in unemployment and increases in output are mainly accomplished not by demand policies but by supply-side policies. These policies either *shift* the supply schedules *AJ* and *LF* or they reduce distortions that prevented the economy getting to points like *E* or *G*.

The next section presents some evidence on the relative magnitude of unemployment responses to demand and supply, and then analyses these supply-side policies in more detail.

23.3 Explaining changes in unemployment

Empirical research aims to decompose causes of unemployment into those that changed equilibrium and those that caused demand-deficient unemployment. Figure 23.5 compares the actual unemployment rate

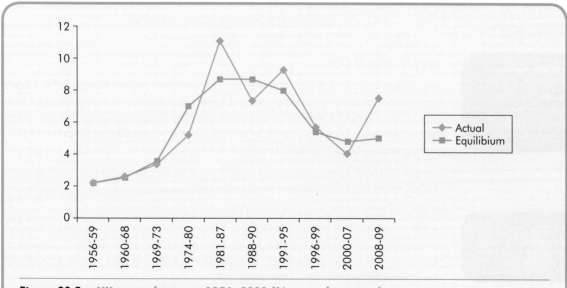

Figure 23.5 UK unemployment, 1956–2009 (% annual average)

Sources: Layard, R., Nickell, S. and Jackman, R. (1991) *Unemployment*, Oxford University Press; Nickell, S. (1996) Inflation and the UK Labour Market, in T. Jenkinson (ed.), *Readings in Macroeconomics*, Oxford University Press; authors' estimates.

with estimates of the equilibrium unemployment rate from 1956 to 2009. Averaging data within sub-periods reduces the influence of short-term fluctuations.

Until the 1970s demand management maintained aggregate demand in line with aggregate supply in the output market. Hence, in the labour market actual and equilibrium unemployment pretty much coincided. As unemployment then rose throughout the 1970s, people initially assumed that this must be due to deficient demand.

In retrospect, we know that the diagnosis was wrong – it was really the supply side that was deteriorating. Equilibrium unemployment was increasing steadily. Misreading the situation, governments tried boosting demand to eliminate spare capacity. Since they had no spare capacity, instead they stoked up inflation.

When Mrs Thatcher came to power in 1979 the Conservative government reduced aggregate demand to try to tackle inflation, and embarked on supply-side reform to reduce equilibrium unemployment. Figure 23.5 shows that demand-deficient unemployment rose sharply when aggregate demand was first reduced, whereas it took longer to obtain reductions in equilibrium unemployment.

Nevertheless, the rise in equilibrium unemployment was slowly reversed. The government became overconfident in its success, allowing aggregate demand to increase sharply during the 'Lawson boom' of the late 1980s. Figure 23.5 shows that actual unemployment had fallen below equilibrium unemployment as the economy overheated and inflation picked up again.

The 1990s saw the restoration of balance between demand and supply, and the continuing benefits of supply-side reform. By the late 1990s the UK was enjoying a period of low inflation, low unemployment and considerable stability. Figure 23.5 shows that actual and equilibrium unemployment were close together until the financial crash, after which aggregate demand plummeted and a new gap has emerged between actual and equilibrium unemployment.

Figure 23.5 confirms three periods in which involuntary unemployment became important – the Thatcher squeeze in the early 1980s, the Major squeeze in the early 1990s, and the aftermath of the financial crash. In the first two examples, sharp reductions in demand were the result of policies to combat inflation.

However, the main message of Figure 23.5 is that longer-term trends in unemployment have been largely caused by supply-side changes and their consequences for equilibrium unemployment.

Supply-side factors

> **Supply-side economics** is the use of microeconomic incentives to alter the level of full employment, the level of potential output and equilibrium unemployment.

Keynesians believe that the economy can deviate from full employment for quite a long time, certainly for several years. Monetarists believe that the classical full-employment model is relevant much more quickly. Everyone agrees that, long run, the performance is changed only by affecting the level of full employment and the corresponding level of potential output.

We now discuss four reasons why equilibrium unemployment rose and then fell during 1970–2010.

First, increasing skill **mismatch** raised equilibrium unemployment after 1970. Recent research emphasizes that the labour market is not very good at processing workers as they step out of one job and hope to step into another. The larger is mismatch, the harder the task is to perform, and the more likely it is that people get stuck in unemployment.

> **Mismatch** occurs if the skills that firms demand differ from the skills the labour force possesses.

When firms no longer want the skills possessed by the existing workforce, the labour demand curve LD shifts leftwards to LD' in Figure 23.6, leading to a lower equilibrium real wage, and an increase in equilibrium unemployment from AB to CD. A rise in mismatch explained some of the rise in unemployment in the 1970s and 1980s.

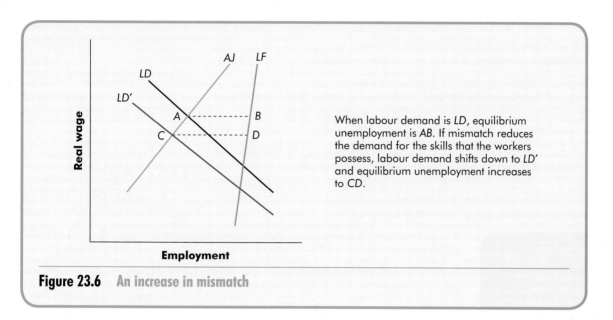

Figure 23.6   An increase in mismatch

When labour demand is *LD*, equilibrium unemployment is *AB*. If mismatch reduces the demand for the skills that the workers possess, labour demand shifts down to *LD'* and equilibrium unemployment increases to *CD*.

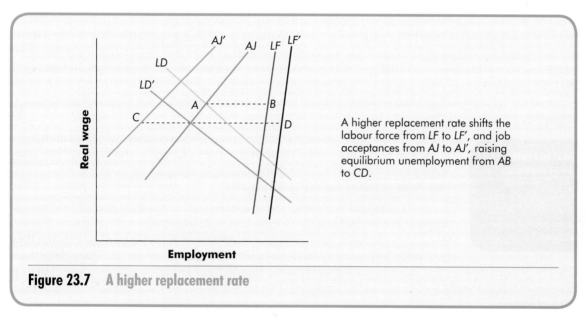

Figure 23.7   A higher replacement rate

A higher replacement rate shifts the labour force from *LF* to *LF'*, and job acceptances from *AJ* to *AJ'*, raising equilibrium unemployment from *AB* to *CD*.

Conversely, since 1990, government policy has stressed reconnecting the unemployed with the labour market rather than leaving them to languish in long-term unemployment. By offering the unemployed advice on how to get back into work quickly, government policy stopped people becoming stigmatized as unemployable. This raised the demand for their labour, reducing equilibrium unemployment. At a higher real wage, *AJ* and *LF* are closer together.

A second potential explanation of a rise in equilibrium unemployment is a rise in the generosity of unemployment benefit relative to wages in work. A higher **replacement rate** may entice more people into the labour force, shifting *LF* to the right. More significantly, it shifts *AJ* to the left. People spend longer in unemployment searching for the right job. For both reasons, equilibrium unemployment increases in Figure 23.7.

> The **replacement rate** is the level of benefits relative to wages in work.

Most empirical research concludes that higher benefits caused some of the increase in equilibrium unemployment, though less than sometimes supposed. In practice, UK unemployment benefit (now jobseeker's allowance) did not rise enough to explain the rise in unemployment.

However, benefits policy probably does explain some of the fall in equilibrium unemployment after 1992. First, as in other countries such as the Netherlands, the UK redefined many of its long-term unemployed as sick. People on sickness benefit are no longer measured as unemployed. This improves statistical unemployment, though of course in economic terms it is entirely cosmetic.

Second, Labour's employment policy viewed getting the unemployed back into work as the best form of social policy. People reacquire the work habit and rebuild their confidence. Accordingly, Labour focused on its *Welfare to Work* and *Making Work Pay* – measures intended, respectively, to actively assist the unemployed to look for work and to incentivize them to want to look for work. Measures of these types are sometimes called *active labour market policy*.

> **Trade union power** is measured by the ability of unions to co-ordinate lower job acceptances, thereby increasing wages but reducing employment.

A third source of changes in equilibrium unemployment has been changes in **trade union power**.

Rises in union power, especially in the 1970s, had a big effect on equilibrium unemployment. Powerful unions made labour scarce and forced up its price. By shifting the *AJ* curve to the left, unions forced up real wages but increased equilibrium unemployment. Conversely, the fall in union power has shifted the *AJ* schedule right, reducing equilibrium unemployment.

Union power increased in the 1970s partly because sympathetic governments passed legislation enhancing worker protection and partly because many nationalized industries were sheltered state monopolies from which unions could extract potential profits as extra wages for their members. Their power declined after the 1980s, partly because a less sympathetic government reduced the legal protection of unions, privatization removed the Treasury as last-resort funder of union wage claims and globalization increased competition in general.

> The **marginal tax rate** is the fraction of each extra pound that the government takes in tax. This creates a **tax wedge** between the price the purchaser pays and the price the seller receives.

The final important source of changes in equilibrium unemployment was changes in the size of the **tax wedge** between the cost of labour to the firm and the take-home pay of the worker. A key theme of supply-side economists is the benefits that stem from reducing the **marginal tax rate**.

A cut in marginal tax rates, and a consequent increase in the take-home pay derived from the last hour's work, make people substitute work for leisure. Against this *substitution effect* must be set an *income effect*. If people pay less in taxes, they have to do less work to reach any given living standard target. Thus, theoretical economics cannot prove that tax cuts raise desired labour supply. Most empirical studies confirm that, at best, tax cuts lead to only a small rise in labour supply. Figure 23.8 shows how tax rates affect equilibrium unemployment.

Suppose the marginal tax rate equals the vertical distance AB. Equilibrium employment is then N_1. The tax drives a wedge between the gross-of-tax wages paid by firms and the net-of-tax wages received by workers. Firms wish to hire N_1 workers at the gross wage w_1. Subtracting the income tax rate AB, N_1 workers want to take job offers at the after-tax wage w_3. Thus N_1 is equilibrium employment, where quantities supplied and demanded are equal. The horizontal distance BC shows equilibrium unemployment: the number of workers in the labour force not wishing to work at the going rate of take-home pay.

Suppose taxes are abolished. The gross wage and the take-home pay now coincide, and the new labour market equilibrium is at E. Two things happen. First, equilibrium employment rises. Second, although more people join the labour force because take-home pay has risen from w_3 to w_2, equilibrium unemployment falls from BC to EF. A rise in take-home pay relative to unemployment benefit reduces voluntary unemployment. If lower tax rates reduce equilibrium unemployment, higher tax rates increase equilibrium unemployment.

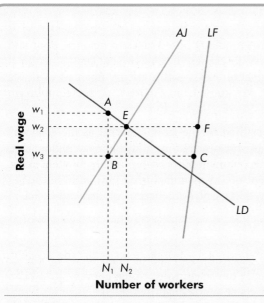

An income tax makes the net-of-tax wage received by households lower than the gross wage paid by firms. *AB* measures the amount each worker pays in income tax, and equilibrium employment is N_1, the quantity that households wish to supply at the after-tax wage w_3 and that firms demand at the gross wage w_1. At the after-tax wage w_2 the natural rate equilibrium would be at *EF*. Employment would rise from N_1 to N_2 and the natural rate of unemployment would fall from BC to *EF*. Relative to the fixed level of unemployment benefit, the rise in take-home pay from w_3 to w_2 reduces voluntary unemployment.

Figure 23.8   **A cut in marginal income tax rates**

ACTIVITY 23.1

Did the tax carrot work?

A lower marginal tax rate makes people substitute work for leisure. But tax cuts also make workers better off. This income effect makes them want to consume more leisure and hence work less. The combined effect on hours of work is small for those already in work. Of more importance is the decision about whether to work at all. Higher take-home pay, for example because of tax cuts, makes more people join the labour force by reducing the significance of the fixed costs of working (commuting, finding cleaners and babysitters, giving up social security).

Over a long period, UK evidence showed that tax cuts had a tiny effect on labour supply by the primary breadwinner in a household. But in households where both partners might consider working, higher take-home pay encouraged labour force participation by encouraging the second partner to work, overcoming the fixed costs of going out to work.

The Thatcher programme

The most dramatic natural experiment with which to assess the effectiveness of tax cuts is the programme of the Thatcher government in the 1980s. The real value of personal allowances – how much you can earn before paying income tax – rose by 25 per cent. The basic rate of income tax fell from 33 to 22 per cent and, for top income-earners, from 83 to 40 per cent. Many politicians anticipated a surge in labour supply. Most economists were pessimistic because of the evidence from the past.

The effect of the Thatcher programme is assessed by C. V. Brown (1988) in 'The 1988 tax cuts, work incentives and revenue' (*Fiscal Studies*, 9 (4): 93–107). Brown finds that the big rise in tax allowances led to less than 0.5 per cent extra hours of labour supply. The cut in the basic rate of income tax had no detectable effect at all. The massive cut in the marginal tax rate of top earners had a small effect in stimulating extra hours of work by the rich. The evidence from the past stood up well to a big change in tax policy.

New Labour after 1997

During 1997–2001 Chancellor of the Exchequer Gordon Brown quietly raised taxes to help the poor and provide funding for public services. In order not to scare the middle classes, the government kept rather quiet about these tax increases, which were sometimes labelled 'stealth taxes'. Neither theory nor past evidence suggests that these had a large and adverse incentive effect. We know from Figure 23.5 that equilibrium unemployment remained low thereafter.

It remains to be seen whether some sharper adjustments required by the labour market as the economy reacts to the financial crash and its austerity aftermath will lead to a renewed rise in equilibrium unemployment; for example, because the composition of demand in the new economy requires substantially different skills, as would be the case if the UK experienced another shakeout of old manufacturing jobs and the further rise of new service industries. We can be fairly sure that there will be a period of demand-deficient unemployment.

Emigrating non-doms and hedge fund managers

A general lesson of tax policy is that, when things are very elastically supplied or demanded (very price sensitive), tax rates can have large effects on the quantity traded. Conversely, when things are very inelastic in supply or demand (very price insensitive), tax rates have little effect on the quantity traded.

Since most workers are reluctant either to emigrate or to give up working, income tax usually has only a small effect on labour supply. But there are exceptions. Investment bankers, hedge fund managers, and the super-rich may sometimes fall into this category. If they have global lifestyles anyway, they may be relatively indifferent as to whether they live in Manhattan, London, Paris or Geneva. If a single country attempts to tax them very differently from other countries, they may move location in order to find a more agreeable tax regime.

Of course, they are likely to threaten to move, whether or not they really will. This may deter a government from trying to tax them more heavily. In 2009 the UK announced both that it was going to raise its top income tax rate from 40 to 50 per cent in 2010, and also proposed eliminating some of the tax breaks enjoyed by rich foreign residents (the so-called non-domiciles or non-doms). In the subsequent outcry, the government backed down on non-doms, but the top marginal income tax rate will increase to 50 per cent as planned. We will then discover how mobile the 'protesters' turned out to be.

Questions

(a) Suppose national insurance contributions by firms – which depend on the value of wages paid to workers – are increased by 1 per cent. Draw a diagram to display the effect on equilibrium unemployment. Does this constitute a 'tax on jobs'?

(b) Now suppose that, instead of higher national insurance contributions by firms, the same additional revenue for the Treasury is raised by asking workers to increase the contributions they make to national insurance. How, if at all, does the outcome differ from that in (a)?

(c) Suppose that the revenue raised is spent entirely on additional nurses for the National Health Service. Is the combined effect of the two policies a tax on jobs?

To check your answers to these questions, go to page 687.

Another possible supply-side policy is to cut unemployment benefit. For a given labour force schedule *LF*, fewer people now wish to be unemployed at any real wage. The schedule *AJ*, showing acceptances of job offers, shifts to the right. This raises equilibrium employment (and hence potential output) and reduces equilibrium unemployment.

What about changes in the national insurance contributions paid both by firms and by workers? These are mandatory contributions to state schemes that provide unemployment and health insurance. They act like an income tax, driving a wedge *AB* between the total cost to a firm of hiring another worker and the net take-home pay of a worker. Figure 23.8 implies that a fall in these contributions will raise equilibrium employment and cut equilibrium unemployment.

Supply-side policies can reduce equilibrium unemployment. Where this involves being tough on those already relatively disadvantaged, there is a conflict between efficiency and fairness, and only through the political process can society express its view.

 ## 23.4 Cyclical fluctuations in unemployment

We discuss business cycles in Chapter 27. Cycles may reflect fluctuations in demand or fluctuations in supply. Since supply usually changes slowly, most of the sharp movements in the short run are caused by changes in demand.

Unless a counter-cyclical demand management policy is deliberately and successfully pursued, there may well be a business cycle. If so, there tends to be a cyclical relationship between demand, output, employment and unemployment. On average, boosting aggregate demand by 1 per cent will not raise employment by 1 per cent or reduce unemployment by 1 per cent, even if the economy begins with spare resources. Table 23.5 shows two periods of demand growth and two of demand decline. In practice, booms lead initially to a sharp increase in shift lengths and hours worked; slumps lead to the abolition of overtime, the introduction of short time and a marked decline in hours worked.

The table confirms that changes in demand and output lead to smaller changes in employment. For example, when output grew by 16.8 per cent between the fourth quarter of 1992 and the second quarter of 1998, employment rose by only 6.8 per cent. Nor do changes in employment lead to corresponding changes in unemployment. The last two rows of the table show that rapid expansion or contraction of employment leads to significantly smaller changes in unemployment.

One reason is the 'discouraged worker effect'. When unemployment is high and rising, some people who would like to work become pessimistic and stop looking for work. No longer registered as looking for work, they are not recorded in the labour force or the unemployed. Conversely, in a boom, people who had previously given up looking for work rejoin the labour force since there is now a good chance of getting a suitable job. Hence in booms and slumps recorded employment data change by more than recorded unemployment data. After 1997, the Monetary Policy Committee kept the UK economy on a more even keel until the recession of 2009.

Table 23.5   *Output, employment and unemployment: evidence from the past*

Cumulative change in	79ii–81ii	86ii–88ii	90ii–91ii	92iv–98ii
Real GDP (%)	−7.8	+9.1	−3.4	+16.8
Employment (%)	−6.3	+2.5	−2.9	+6.8
Employed (million)	−1.7	+0.5	−0.7	+1.5
Unemployed (million)	+1.4	−0.9	+0.6	−1.2

Source: ONS, Economic Trends.

How bad could unemployment become?

The OECD is a club of the most advanced economic nations in the world – living standards and per capita income count more than absolute size. Newer members include Turkey, Mexico and Hungary. China and India are not yet members despite their vast populations. Currently, the OECD has 32 members.

The 2009 OECD *Employment Outlook* discusses prospects for unemployment and possible policy responses. The evolution of unemployment depends on: (a) the size of the shock, (b) the flexibility of the economy to respond, and (c) the extent of support by government. In the worst previous post-war recession of 1973–76, OECD unemployment increased by half. By 2009 the OECD reckoned that unemployment would rise by 80 per cent – from 5.5 to 10 per cent of the labour force – during 2007–10.

This analysis reflected the magnitude of the initial shock. Clearly, this would affect different countries differently. One way in which to assess which economies were most vulnerable is to estimate their capacity to absorb shocks through flexible labour markets that match potential workers and job opportunities more quickly. This is likely to depend on wage flexibility, labour market mobility, attitudes of trade unions and the extent of labour market regulation.

The figure below shows a measure of labour market flexibility based on labour market history during 2000–05. It plots the annual fraction of workers hired in new jobs or leaving existing jobs (by choice or dismissal) during the year. It shows that, in Turkey, Denmark and the US, half of all workers are changing jobs annually. In contrast, the countries with the lowest labour market mobility are Greece, Italy and Austria.

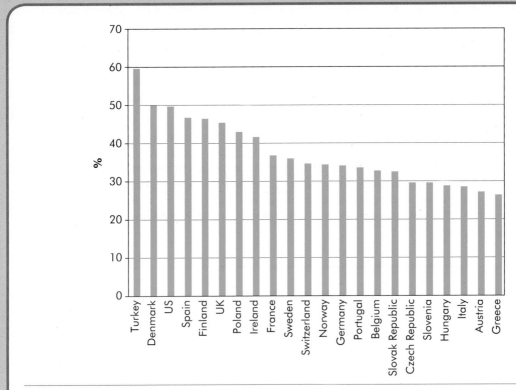

Annual fraction of workers hired or fired, 2000–05 (%)

Source: OECD, Employment Outlook, 2009.

Countries with greater job stability are probably slower to experience initial unemployment but, when unemployment does increase, they are also less successful at helping people out of unemployment back into work. Since there is considerable cross-country evidence that those in longer-term unemployment find it ever more difficult to reconnect with the labour market, in the medium run this fiscal burden of unemployment benefits is likely to be greater in countries with less flexible labour markets.

Governments provide two kinds of support. The first is measurable by the generosity of unemployment benefit, which has two dimensions – the replacement rate (the ratio of benefit to previous wages in work) and the number of years for which benefit is available. The table documents considerable differences across countries.

In Norway and Belgium, with strong traditions of social democracy, unemployment benefit is generous both because it is high relative to wages in work and because it continues for at least five years after a spell of unemployment begins. French unemployment benefit is initially as generous but less so after year two. The UK is considerably less generous in its replacement rate, but entitlement continues undiminished over the five-year period. In countries such as Japan, Greece and the US, unemployment benefit is almost worthless after the first year in unemployment.

The second aspect of state support for the unemployed is active labour market policies that enhance incentives, confidence and the ability of the unemployed to look for jobs. Even if the post-crash recession reflected a sharp fall in demand – for output and then for labour – it is important not to neglect supply-side policies that maintain maximum labour market flexibility.

Duration of unemployment	Year 1	Year 2	Year 5
	Replacement rate (%)		
Norway	72	72	72
Belgium	65	63	63
France	67	64	31
UK	28	28	28
Japan	45	3	3
Greece	33	5	1
US	28	0	0

Source: OECD, *Employment Outlook*, 2009.

Picture: People enter Job Centre Plus in Central London, 2009. © Matt Cardy/Stringer. Getty Images.

23.5 The cost of unemployment

The private cost of unemployment

It is important to distinguish between voluntary and involuntary unemployment. When individuals are voluntarily unemployed, they reveal that they do better by being unemployed than by immediately taking a job offer at the going wage rate. The private cost of unemployment (the wage forgone by not working) is less than the private benefits of being unemployed. What are these benefits?

The first is transfer payments from government. Workers who have contributed to the national insurance scheme get jobseeker's allowance for the first 12 months after becoming unemployed. Thereafter they get income support, the ultimate backstop in the British welfare state.

There are other benefits too. First, there is the value of leisure. By refusing a job, some people reveal that the extra leisure is worth more to them than the extra disposable income if they took a job. Second, some people expect to get a better job by being choosy about accepting offers. These future benefits must be set against the current cost: a lower disposable income as a result of being out of work.

When people are involuntarily unemployed, the cost changes. Involuntary unemployment means that people would like to work at the going wage but cannot find a job because there is excess labour supply at the existing wage rate. These people are worse off by being unemployed.

The distinction between voluntary and involuntary unemployment matters because it may affect our value judgement about how much attention to pay to unemployment. When unemployment is involuntary, people are suffering more and the case for helping them is stronger.

The social cost of unemployment

Again we distinguish between voluntary and involuntary unemployment. When unemployment is voluntary, individuals prefer to be unemployed. Does this unemployment also benefit society?

An individual receives transfer payments during unemployment, but these transfers give no corresponding benefit to society as a whole. They may ease the collective conscience in regard to poverty and income inequality, but they are not payments for the supply of any goods or services that other members of society may consume. Since the private benefit exceeds the social benefit, too many people may be voluntarily unemployed.

CONCEPT 23.2

Hysteresis and high unemployment

Supply and demand curves are supposed to be independent of one another. The labour supply curve or job acceptances schedule *AJ* shows the people willing to work at each real wage whatever the position of the labour demand curve *LD*, and vice versa. But this may be wrong.

In the diagram, the initial equilibrium is at *E*. Something then shifts labour demand down from *LD* to *LD'*. Suppose this causes a permanent fall in labour supply. *JA* shifts to *JA'*. When labour demand reverts to *LD*, the new equilibrium is at *F*, not *E*. The short-run history of the economy has affected its long-run equilibrium.

Hysteresis may explain high and persistent unemployment in much of continental Europe. Here are some channels through which it might work.

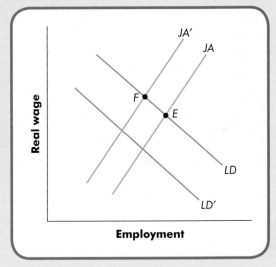

The insider–outsider distinction

Outsiders are those unemployed without jobs. Only insiders with jobs participate in wage bargaining. At the original equilibrium *E*, the numerous insiders in work ensure that real wages are low enough to preserve their

> An economy experiences **hysteresis** when its long-run equilibrium depends on the path it follows in the short run.

own jobs. When a recession occurs, *LD* shifts to *LD'*. Some insiders get fired and become outsiders. Eventually, as explained in Chapter 21, market forces restore labour demand to *LD*. But now there are fewer insiders than originally. They exploit their scarcity by securing higher wages for themselves rather than encouraging firms to rehire. The economy is trapped in the high-wage, low-employment equilibrium at *F* instead of the low-wage, high-employment equilibrium at *E*. Thereafter, only long-run supply-side measures aimed at breaking down insider power can gradually break the economy out of this low-employment equilibrium.

Discouraged workers
Again, the economy begins at *E*. It has a skilled and energetic labour force. A temporary recession leads to unemployment. If the recession is protracted, we see the emergence of long-term unemployed people and a culture in which they stop looking for jobs. Again, when demand picks up, labour supply has been permanently reduced and equilibrium reverts to *F*, not *E*. Only long-term supply-side measures to restore the work culture will succeed.

Search and mismatch
When employment is high at *E*, firms are trying to find scarce workers, and potential workers are searching hard for a job. A recession makes firms advertise fewer vacancies, and workers realize it is a waste of time searching for jobs. When demand picks up again, both firms and workers are accustomed to low levels of search. New jobs are not created.

The capital stock
At *E*, the economy has a lot of capital. Labour productivity is high and firms want lots of workers. During a temporary recession, firms scrap old machines. When demand picks up again, firms have permanently lower capital. The demand for labour, which depends on the marginal product of labour, never rises to its original level. Again, the economy returns to *F*, not *E*.

Policy implications of hysteresis
Hysteresis means that a temporary fall in demand induces permanently lower employment and output, and higher equilibrium unemployment. There are two policy implications. First, once the problem has emerged, it is dangerous to try to break out of it simply by expanding aggregate demand. Before long-run supply can respond, you get major inflation. Supply-side policies, needed to rebuild aggregate supply, take a long time to work.

Second, because the problem is so hard to cure once it occurs, it is vital not to let demand fall in the first place. The payoff to demand management is higher than in an economy with a unique long-run equilibrium where all that is at stake is how quickly the economy reverts to its original point.

These arguments help explain why governments intervened so heavily in 2009–10 to endeavour to offset the worst of the demand effects of the financial crash. They feared that too little action would imply a dramatic fall in aggregate demand from which it would be hard to recover.

This does not mean that society should go to the opposite extreme and eliminate voluntary unemployment completely. First, society is perfectly entitled to adopt the value judgement that it will maintain a reasonable living standard for the unemployed, whatever the cost in resource misallocation. Second, the efficient level of voluntary unemployment is well above zero.

In a changing economy, it is important to match up the right people to the right jobs. Getting this match right lets society make more output. Freezing the existing pattern of employment in a changing economy leads to a mismatch of people and jobs. The flow through the pool of unemployment allows people to be reallocated to more suitable jobs, raising potential output in the long run.

Two points from our earlier discussion are also relevant here. First, even when unemployment is high, flows both into and out of the pool are large relative to the pool itself. Second, people who do not get out of the pool quickly are in danger of stagnating when unemployment is high: the fraction of the unemployed who have been unemployed for over a year was higher in the 1990s than at the end of the 1970s when unemployment was much lower.

Involuntary or Keynesian unemployment has an even higher social cost. Since the economy is producing below capacity, it is literally throwing away output that could have been made by putting these people to work. Moreover, since Keynesian unemployment is involuntary, it may entail more human and psychological suffering than voluntary unemployment. Although hard to quantify, it is also part of the social cost of unemployment.

Summary

- People are either **employed, unemployed** or out of the **labour force.** The level of unemployment rises when inflows to the pool of the unemployed exceed outflows. Inflows and outflows are large relative to the level of unemployment.

- As unemployment has risen, the average duration of unemployment has increased.

- Women face lower unemployment rates than men. The unemployment rates for old workers and, especially, for young workers are well above the national average.

- **Unemployment** can be classified as **frictional, structural, classical** or **demand-deficient.** In modern terminology, the first three types are **voluntary unemployment** and the last is **involuntary unemployment.** The **natural rate of unemployment** is the equilibrium level of voluntary unemployment.

- In the long run, sustained rises in unemployment must reflect increases in the natural rate of unemployment. During temporary recessions, **Keynesian unemployment** is also important.

- **Supply-side economics** aims to increase equilibrium employment and potential output, and to reduce the natural rate of unemployment, by operating on incentives at a microeconomic level. Supply-side policies include reducing mismatch, reducing union power, tax cuts, reductions in unemployment benefit, retraining and relocation grants and investment subsidies.

- A 1 per cent increase in output is likely to lead to a much smaller reduction in Keynesian unemployment. Some of the extra output will be met by longer hours. And as unemployment falls, some people, effectively in the labour force but not registered, look for work again.

- **Hysteresis** means that short-run changes can move the economy to a different long-run equilibrium. It may explain why European recessions have raised the natural rate of unemployment substantially.

- People voluntarily unemployed reveal that the private benefits from unemployment exceed the private cost in wages forgone. Society derives no output from transfer payments to support the unemployed. However, society would not benefit by driving unemployment to zero. Some social gains in higher productivity are derived from improved matching of people and jobs that temporary unemployment allows.

- Keynesian unemployment is involuntary and hurts private individuals who would prefer to be employed. Socially it represents wasted output. Society may also care about the human misery inflicted by involuntary unemployment.

- Most European countries took two decades to reverse the high unemployment of the 1980s. Having brought unemployment down, they now face a new period of higher unemployment as budgets are cut back to cope with the fiscal crises caused by trying to offset the effects of the financial crash.

Review questions

1 What is the discouraged worker effect? Suggest two reasons why it occurs.

2 'The average duration of an individual's unemployment rises in a slump. Hence the problem is a higher inflow to the pool of unemployment, not a lower outflow.' Do you agree?

EASY

3 'The microchip caused a permanent rise in the level of unemployment.' Did it? What about all previous technical advances?

4 How is high unemployment explained by (a) a Keynesian and (b) a classical economist?

5 Explain why boosting demand sometimes fails to reduce unemployment.

6 Common fallacies   Why are these statements wrong? (a) Unemployment is always a bad thing. (b) So long as there is unemployment, there is pressure on wages to fall. (c) Unemployment arises only because greedy workers are pricing themselves out of a job.

7 Which is correct? The fact that unemployment rose in 2009 by less than originally predicted shows: (a) that the fall in output and demand was illusory; (b) that wages were more flexible than in previous recessions; or (c) that firms believed that lower output would be very short-lived?

8 'An increase in national insurance contributions by workers reduces the income per hour that workers take home and therefore reduces the incentive to work.' 'An increase in national insurance contributions, by reducing income per hour, forces people to work longer hours to attain their target take-home income.' Is either statement correct? Are both? What light does this shed on national insurance contributions as a 'jobs tax'?

MEDIUM

9 Draw a diagram to illustrate your answer to Question 8.

10 Most economists forecast a period of protracted unemployment after 2009 as government takes tough measures for a sustained period to bring the budget deficit and national debt under control. (a) Why might such an evolution involve hysteresis? (b) Draw a diagram to illustrate both the initial increase in unemployment and the subsequent developments when demand eventually expands again.

11 Labour supply L, job acceptances J and labour demand D are, respectively, related to the real wage W by

$$L = 10 + W \qquad J = bW, 0 < b < 1 \qquad D = 50 - dW, d > 0$$

(a) Find equilibrium unemployment. (b) If there is now an income tax at rate t on wages, what happens to equilibrium unemployment?

12 Suppose the government wants to encourage lone parents to take part-time jobs and thinks 15 hours a week is consistent with children being in a crèche for three hours a day, Monday to Friday.

Which of the following might achieve the government's aim: (a) an additional lump-sum payment to lone parents, (b) a lower income tax rate for lone parents, or (c) a payment conditional on their taking at least 15 hours of work a week?

13 Why is teenage unemployment so high?

14 **Essay question**   For two decades, unemployment in France has been significantly higher than that in the UK. If you become president of France, should you: (a) blame the European Central Bank for cautious monetary policy; (b) blame the French Treasury for a fiscal policy that has been too tight; or (c) tackle labour market reform in France? Explain your answer.

For solutions to these questions contact your lecturer.

Exchange rates and the balance of payments

Learning Outcomes

By the end of this chapter, you should understand:

1. the foreign exchange market

2. balance of payments accounts

3. determinants of current account flows

4. perfect capital mobility

5. speculative behaviour and capital flows

6. internal and external balance

7. the long-run equilibrium real exchange rate

Exports and imports are each about 10 per cent of the size of GDP in Japan, 15 per cent in the US, around 30 per cent in the UK and France, 40 per cent in Germany, but nearly 80 per cent in small European economies such as Belgium. Even in the US and Japan, the exchange rate, international competitiveness and the trade deficit are major issues. International linkages matter even more in more **open economies** such as the UK, Germany and Belgium.

> An **open economy** has important trade and financial links with other countries.

In this chapter we show how international transactions affect the domestic economy.

24.1   The foreign exchange market

Different countries use different national currencies. In the UK, goods, services and assets are bought and sold for pounds sterling; in France, they are bought and sold for euros.

Measuring exchange rates

Suppose $2 converts to £1. We can say either that the exchange rate is $2/£ or that it is £0.50/$. Both statements contain the same information.

> The **foreign exchange (forex) market** exchanges one national currency for another.
>
> The price at which the two currencies exchange is the **exchange rate**.

> The **international value of the domestic currency** is the quantity of foreign currency per unit of the domestic currency.
>
> The **domestic price of foreign exchange** is the quantity of domestic currency per unit of the foreign currency.

Thus an exchange rate of $1.50/£ is the **international value of the domestic currency** as viewed by a UK resident, but the domestic price of foreign exchange as viewed by a US resident. Conversely, £0.50/$ is the **domestic price of foreign exchange** for a UK resident but the international value of the domestic currency for a US resident.

Whenever you see a table or graph with 'the' exchange rate, you need to work out which way round it has been expressed. There is no short cut. Even after years in the subject, we ourselves go slowly at that bit. For the rest of this book, we will use the international value of domestic currency. For the UK, this means talking about dollars or euros that exchange for £1. If we are discussing Germany, it would mean the number of pounds or dollars that exchange for 1 euro.

On television and at money-changing kiosks, you will rarely see quotes of £/$ – most of the world conventionally quotes $/£ whether they are talking about the US or the UK. This means that if you happen to look at a US textbook, you will find it using the domestic price of foreign exchange as its definition of the exchange rate. When its graph slopes up and the text talks about its exchange rate 'depreciating', this is because it is thinking about the exchange rate the other way round from how someone in the UK would view it. A change from $1/£ to $2/£ is an appreciation of sterling but a depreciation of the dollar. Conversely, a change from $2/£ to $1/£ is a depreciation of sterling but an appreciation of the dollar.

For exchange rates against the euro, it is quite common to see them quoted both ways, either as €/£ or as £/€. Whatever the circumstances, take your time and ask which is the domestic currency of the country you are considering. Foreign currency per unit of domestic currency is the international value of the domestic currency. Domestic currency per unit of the foreign currency is the domestic price of foreign exchange.

Whichever way we express the exchange rate, in practice each currency exchanges for many others, not just one. However, for simplicity our discussion assumes only two countries, the domestic economy (say the UK) and the foreign country (say the US).

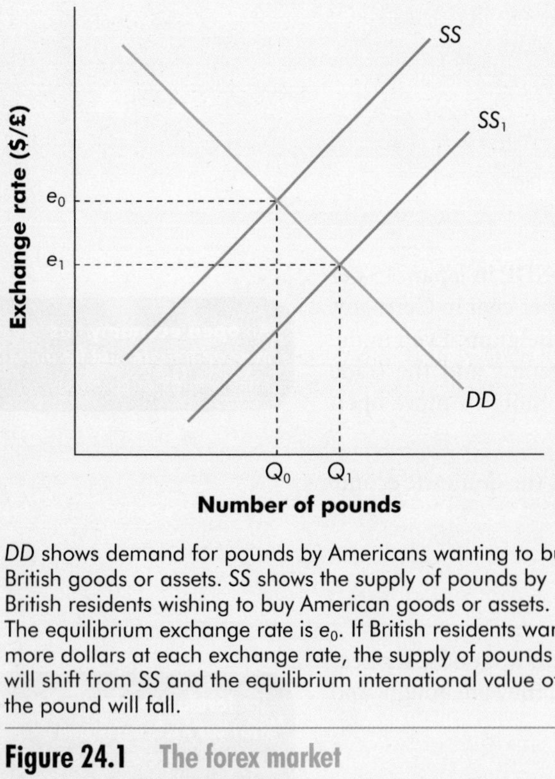

Exchanging currencies

Who supplies dollars to the forex market demanding pounds in exchange? The demand for pounds has two sources. First, US importers pay in dollars but UK exporters want to bring this money home as pounds. Second, US residents buying UK assets (shares in BT or UK bonds) must convert their dollars into pounds to buy these UK assets. Conversely, a supply of pounds reflects UK imports of US goods and UK residents buying assets in the US.

Figure 24.1 shows the supply and demand for pounds in the forex market. We begin with the demand. Suppose UK whisky costs £8 a bottle. At $2/£ it sells in the US for $16, but at $1.50/£ it sells for $12. Hence at a lower exchange rate,[1] and a lower

DD shows demand for pounds by Americans wanting to buy British goods or assets. SS shows the supply of pounds by British residents wishing to buy American goods or assets. The equilibrium exchange rate is e_0. If British residents want more dollars at each exchange rate, the supply of pounds will shift from SS and the equilibrium international value of the pound will fall.

Figure 24.1   The forex market

---

1   We are thus using the 'international value of sterling' as the measure of 'the' UK exchange rate.

dollar price of all UK goods, the UK exports more goods to the US. US residents buy more at a lower dollar price.

If the sterling price of UK goods is constant, a lower exchange rate, by raising the quantity of UK exports, must raise export revenue in pounds. Figure 24.1 shows that the demand schedule for pounds, *DD*, slopes downwards. More pounds are demanded at a lower $/£ exchange rate.

The supply of pounds *SS* depends on the quantity of dollars UK residents need to buy UK imports of goods or to buy dollar assets. Suppose a holiday in Florida costs $600: at $2/£ it costs £300, but at $1.50/£ it costs £400. A lower $/£ exchange rate raises the price in pounds and reduces the quantity of Florida holidays demanded by UK residents. Whether it reduces the number of pounds spent depends on the elasticity of demand for pounds.

Figure 24.1 assumes that the demand for Florida holidays and other UK imports is price-elastic. For a given dollar price of Florida holidays, a lower $/£ exchange rate raises the price in pounds and reduces the sterling value of this spending. The supply of pounds *SS* slopes up. However, if the UK demand for US goods, services and assets is price-inelastic, a lower exchange rate and higher sterling price will raise sterling spending on these things, and the supply schedule of pounds to the forex market slopes down.[2]

At the equilibrium exchange rate e_0, the quantity of pounds supplied and demanded is equal. What would change this equilibrium? Suppose, at each sterling price, US demand for UK goods or assets increases. The demand for pounds *DD* shifts to the right, raising the equilibrium $/£ exchange rate. Similarly, a fall in UK demand for US goods and assets shifts the supply of pounds *SS* to the left, and the equilibrium $/£ exchange rate rises.

When the $/£ exchange rate rises, the pound **appreciates** so the dollar **depreciates**. Conversely, when the exchange rate is measured the other way, a rise in the £/$ exchange rate reflects an appreciation of the dollar but a depreciation of the pound. This reinforces our earlier warning: to know whether a rise in the exchange rate reflects appreciation or depreciation, first you need to know which way round the exchange rate was measured.

> The pound **appreciates** when the $/£ exchange rate rises. The international value of sterling rises.
>
> The pound **depreciates** when the $/£ exchange rate falls. The international value of sterling falls.

CONCEPT 24.1

Effective exchange rates

Each currency has a bilateral exchange rate against each other currency. For example, we can measure the $/£ or €/£. Sometimes it is useful to examine a single exchange rate that summarizes all the bilateral rates.

The **effective exchange rate** (eer) is a weighted average of individual bilateral exchange rates. Usually, we use the share of trade with each country to decide the weights. Important trading partners get more weight in the effective exchange rate index. The figure below shows sterling's effective exchange rate, based on an index whose value is set at 1.60 at end 2000. The figure also shows exchange rates for the UK's two main trading partners, the US and the eurozone. Sterling has fluctuated against both the dollar and

> A country's **effective exchange rate** is an average of its exchange rate against all its trade partners, weighted by the relative size of trade with each country.

---

2   The supply and demand for cars refers to physical quantities supplied or demanded at each price. However, the supply and demand schedules for pounds sterling refer to values of pounds supplied and demanded at each exchange rate. That is why the analysis can be more tricky than the analysis of the market for physical commodities. 'Number of pounds' on the horizontal axis is really a value not a quantity.

the euro, but its average or effective rate is a little smoother than the individual exchange rates. The figure also implies that the weight on the euro is substantially higher than the weight on the dollar: the effective or average exchange rate is more similar to the bilateral rate against the euro than to the bilateral rate against the dollar. Nowadays, the UK trades mainly with other European countries.

Once we have the nominal effective exchange rate, we could also construct a weighted average of foreign price levels and hence compute the real effective exchange rate. Changes in the real eer are a good indication of what is happening to competitiveness.

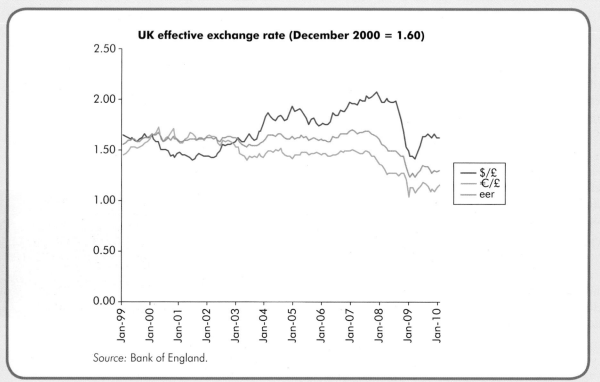

UK effective exchange rate (December 2000 = 1.60)

Source: Bank of England.

24.2 Exchange rate regimes

An **exchange rate regime** describes how governments allow exchange rates to be determined.

In a **fixed exchange rate** regime, governments maintain the convertibility of their currency at a fixed exchange rate. A currency is *convertible* if the central bank will buy or sell as much of the currency as people wish to trade at the fixed exchange rate.

To grasp the basics, we focus on the two extreme forms of exchange rate regime that have been adopted to handle international transactions in the world economy: fixed exchange rates and floating exchange rates.

Fixed exchange rates

In Figure 24.2 suppose the exchange rate is fixed at e_1. This is a free market equilibrium at A if the supply curve for pounds is SS and the demand curve for pounds is DD. Nobody needs to buy or sell pounds to the central bank. The market clears unaided.

Suppose the demand for pounds shifts from DD to DD_1. Americans, addicted to whisky, need more pounds to import more UK whisky. Free market equilibrium is now at B and the pound appreciates against the dollar. However, at a fixed exchange

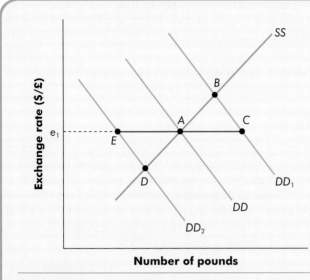

Suppose the exchange rate is fixed at e_1. When demand for pounds is DD_1, there is an excess demand AC. The Bank of England intervenes by supplying AC pounds in exchange for dollars, which are added to the UK foreign exchange reserves. When demand is DD_2, the Bank sells foreign exchange reserves in exchange for pounds. It demands EA pounds to offset the excess supply EA. When damand is DD, the market clears at the exchange rate e_1, and no intervention by the Bank is required.

Figure 24.2   Central bank intervention in the forex market

rate e_1 there is an excess demand for pounds equal to AC. To peg the exchange rate, the central bank meets this excess demand and maintains the peg e_1 by supplying an extra AC pounds to the market.

The Bank prints AC extra pounds and sells them in exchange for $(e_1 \times AC)$ dollars, which are added to the UK **foreign exchange reserves**.

> The **foreign exchange reserves** are foreign currency held by the domestic central bank.

What if the demand for pounds now falls to DD_2? The free market equilibrium is now at D. Pegging the exchange rate at e_1 causes an excess supply of pounds EA. To defend the peg the central bank must demand EA pounds, which it pays for by selling $(EA \times e_1)$ dollars from the foreign exchange reserves.

When the demand schedule is DD_1, the UK is adding to its foreign exchange reserves. When the schedule is DD_2, it is running down its reserves. If the demand for pounds fluctuates between DD_1 and DD_2, the Bank of England can sustain the exchange rate e_1 in the long run.

However, if the demand for pounds on average is DD_2, the Bank is steadily losing foreign exchange reserves to support the pound at e_1. We say that the pound is overvalued, or is at a higher international value than is warranted by its long-run equilibrium position. As reserves start to run out, the government may try to borrow foreign exchange reserves from the International Monetary Fund (IMF), an international body that exists primarily to lend to countries in short-term difficulties.

At best, this is only a temporary solution. Unless the demand for pounds increases in the long run, it is necessary to *devalue* the pound. In a fixed exchange rate regime, a *devaluation* (*revaluation*) is a fall (rise) in the exchange rate governments commit themselves to maintain.

Notice that we say governments, plural. Fixing the $/£ exchange rate is possible only if both the US and UK wish to do so. For simplicity, our discussion of Figure 24.2 supposed that only one central bank intervened. In practice, it might be both central banks.

Floating exchange rates

In a **floating exchange rate regime**, the exchange rate is allowed to find its equilibrium level *without* central bank intervention using the forex reserves. Thus, in Figure 24.2, demand shifts from DD_2 to DD to DD_1 would be allowed to move the equilibrium from D to A to B.

> In a **floating exchange rate regime** regime, the exchange rate is allowed to find its equilibrium level without central bank intervention using the forex reserves.

Of course, it is not necessary to adopt the extreme regimes of pure or clean floating on the one hand and perfectly fixed exchange rates on the other. *Dirty floating* implies intervention is used to offset large and rapid shifts in supply or demand schedules in the short run, but the exchange rate is gradually allowed to find its equilibrium level in the longer run.

Having examined the foreign exchange market, we look next at the balance of payments.

24.3   The balance of payments

> The **balance of payments** records transactions between residents of one country and the rest of the world.

Taking the UK as the domestic country and the US as the 'rest of the world', all international transactions that give rise to an inflow of pounds to the UK are entered as credits in the UK **balance of payments** accounts. Outflows of pounds are debits, entered with a minus sign. Similarly, inflows of dollars to the US are credits in the US balance of payments accounts but outflows are debits. Table 24.1 shows the actual UK balance of payments accounts in 2008.

Visible trade is exports and imports of goods (cars, food, steel). *Invisible trade* refers to exports and imports of services (banking, shipping, tourism). Together, these make up the trade balance or net exports of goods and services.

> The **current account** of the balance of payments records international flows of goods, services and **current transfers**.

Current transfers are transfer payments paid across borders. These include payment by the UK government of EU subsidies for agriculture, social security payments paid abroad, bilateral foreign aid payments and cross-border flows of income, profits and dividends earned on assets or debts held in other countries.

Table 24.1 shows the UK had a trade deficit in goods in 2008, offset partly by surpluses on trade in services and on international transfer payments (mainly income on net foreign assets). Combining trade in goods and services with net income from transfers, the **current account** of the balance of payments was £25 billion in deficit in 2008.

A current account surplus means that a country's foreign income exceeds its foreign spending. A current account deficit means that its foreign spending exceeds its foreign income. These surpluses and deficits are saving and dissaving, and lead to purchases or sales of foreign assets.

The *capital account* of the balance of payments records the international flows of transfer payments relating to capital items. This covers payments received from the EU regional development fund for investment in infrastructure projects, the transfer of capital into or out of the UK by migrants and the forgiveness of international debt by the UK government.

Table 24.1 shows a net financial inflow of £18 billion in 2008. The inflow of money to the UK as foreigners bought UK physical and financial assets exceeded the outflow of money from the UK as residents bought assets abroad.

The balancing item, a statistical adjustment, would be zero if all previous items were correctly measured. It reflects a failure to record all transactions in the official statistics. Estimating implicit changes in the value of foreign investments, which the

Table 24.1   UK balance of payments, 2008 (£bn)

Trade in goods	−92
Trade in services	+54
Current transfers and other income	+13
(1) CURRENT ACCOUNT	−25
(2) CAPITAL ACCOUNT	+4
(3) FINANCIAL ACCOUNT	+18
(4) Balancing item	+3
(5) UK BALANCE OF PAYMENTS (1 + 2 + 3 + 4)	0
(6) Official financing	0

Source: ONS, *Economic Trends*.

statistics treat as money brought home and then reinvested abroad, is particularly tricky. Adding together the current account (1), the capital account (2), the **financial account** (3) and the adjustment (4), we obtain the UK **balance of payments** in 2008. It so happens that it just balanced in 2008.

The balance of payments shows the net inflow of money to the country when individuals, firms and the government make the transactions they wish to undertake under existing market conditions. It is in surplus (deficit) when there is a net inflow of money (outflow of money). It takes account of the transactions that individuals wish to make in importing and exporting and in buying and selling foreign assets, and the number of transactions that governments wish to make in the form of foreign aid (transfer payments to foreigners), military spending (maintaining military bases abroad) and so on.

> The **financial account** of the balance of payments records international purchases and sales of financial assets.
>
> The **balance of payments** is the sum of current account, capital and financial account items.

The final entry in Table 24.1 is *official financing*. This is always of equal magnitude and opposite sign to the balance of payments in the line above, so that the sum of all the entries in Table 24.1 is *always* zero. Official financing measures the international transactions that the government must take to *accommodate* all the other transactions shown in the balance of payments accounts. What is this official financing?

Floating exchange rates

If the exchange rate floats freely, there is *no* government intervention in the forex market. Forex reserves are constant. The exchange rate adjusts to equate the supply of pounds and the demand for pounds in the forex market.

The supply of pounds reflects imports to the UK and UK purchases of foreign assets. These are the outflows in the UK balance of payments accounts. Conversely, the demand for pounds reflects UK exports and sales of UK assets to foreigners. These are the inflows in the UK balance of payments accounts. With a freely floating exchange rate, the quantities of pounds supplied and demanded are equal. Hence inflows equal outflows and the balance of payments is exactly zero. There is no intervention in the forex market and no official financing.

Since the balance of payments is the sum of the current account and the capital and financial accounts, under floating exchange rates a current account surplus must be exactly matched by a deficit on capital and financial accounts, or vice versa. This just says any unspent surplus on goods and services must be spent buying assets. A foreign deficit is financed by running down *net* foreign assets (lower assets or higher debt).

Fixed exchange rates

With a fixed exchange rate, the balance of payments need not be zero. When there is a deficit, total outflows exceed total inflows on the combined current and capital accounts. How is the deficit financed?

Since there is a deficit, the supply of pounds to the foreign exchange market, reflecting imports or purchases of foreign assets, exceeds the demand for pounds, reflecting exports or sales of assets to foreigners. The balance of payments deficit is exactly the same as the excess supply of pounds in the forex market.

To maintain the fixed exchange rate, the central bank offsets this excess supply of pounds by demanding an equivalent quantity of pounds. It runs down the foreign exchange reserves, selling dollars to buy pounds. In the balance of payments accounts this shows up as 'official financing'.

When there is a balance of payments surplus, the government intervenes in the forex market to buy foreign exchange reserves. When there is a balance of payments deficit, reserves must be sold. Table 24.2 summarizes this discussion.

Table 24.2 Balance of payments and exchange rate regimes

Fixed exchange rate	Floating exchange rate
current account	current account
+ capital account	+ capital account
+ financial account	+ financial account
= balance of payments	= balance of payments
= [– official financing]	= 0
= rise in forex reserves	No official financing; no change in forex reserves

24.4   The real exchange rate

The **real exchange rate** is the relative price of goods from different countries when measured in a common currency.

In 1981 the $/£ exchange rate was \$2.03/£; by early 2010 it was only \$1.54/£. A fall in the international value of sterling makes UK goods cheaper in foreign currencies and foreign goods more expensive in pounds. Other things equal, the UK became more competitive as sterling fell.

But other things were not unaltered. The UK had more inflation than the US, so its prices rose more during 1981–2010. UK competitiveness rose because of a lower nominal or actual exchange rate, but fell because the sterling price of UK goods rose more than the dollar price of US goods. As usual, we must distinguish nominal and real variables.

Thus if $E^{\$/£}$ is the nominal exchange rate, measured by $/£ the international value of sterling, and $p_{UK}^{£}$ and $p_{US}^{\$}$ are the domestic sterling price of UK goods and the dollar price of US goods,

$$\text{Real exchange rate} = \{E^{\$/£} \times p_{UK}^{£}\}/p_{US}^{\$} \tag{1}$$

Table 24.3 gives some examples. Pretend the only good is shirts. In row 1, a US shirt costs \$10 and a UK shirt £6. At a nominal exchange rate of \$2/£, the relative price of UK to US shirts, in a common currency, is 1.2, whether we compare the relative dollar price of shirts (\$12/\$10) or the relative price in pounds (£6/£5). Two things can make UK shirts more competitive in relation to US shirts.

Table 24.3 Calculating real exchange rates

Nominal exchange rate ($/£)	UK shirt price (£)	UK shirt price ($)	US shirt price ($)	Real exchange rate
2.0	6	12	10	1.2
1.5	6	9	10	0.9
2.0	4.5	9	10	0.9
2.0	6	12	13.3	0.9

In row 2, a lower nominal exchange rate for sterling of $1.50/£ reduces the relative price of UK to US shirts from 1.2 to 0.9. The UK's real exchange rate depreciated in equation (1) and the UK became more competitive since its shirts became cheaper when measured in a common currency.

In row 3, the nominal exchange rate is $2/£, as in row 1, but now the sterling price of UK shirts has fallen from £6 to £4.50. At a nominal exchange rate of $2/£, a UK shirt costs $9. Since a US shirt costs $10, the UK real exchange rate has again fallen to 0.9. Row 4 shows that a change in US prices can have the same result.

Equation (1) makes clear that the arithmetic of real exchange rates does not care whether the nominal exchange rate E falls, the sterling price of UK shirts falls or the dollar price of US shirts rises. Any one of these changes reduces sterling's real exchange rate and makes the UK more competitive (and the US less competitive). Conversely, a rise in the nominal exchange rate, a rise in UK sterling prices or a fall in US dollar prices increases sterling's real exchange rate and makes the UK less competitive (and the US more competitive).

Table 24.4 shows how this works out in practice. The first row shows the nominal $/£ exchange rate depreciated during 1981–2010. The second and third rows show what happened to the price level in each country. Setting the price index in each country equal to 100 in 1981, US prices rose from 100 to 240 by 2010, whereas UK prices had risen to 312.

The fourth row calculates an index of the real exchange rate, using the formula of equation (1). While the nominal exchange rate depreciated from 2.03 to 1.54 between 1981 and 2010, the real exchange rate only depreciated from 2.03 to 2.00. Almost all the additional competitiveness arising from a lower nominal exchange rate was offset by the rise in UK prices relative to US prices.

Purchasing power parity (PPP)

What hypothetical path would the nominal exchange rate have had to follow to keep the real exchange rate at its initial level? The PPP exchange rate offers a quick check that lets us compare the present with what we know about the past.

> The **purchasing power parity (PPP)** exchange rate path is the path of the nominal exchange rate that maintains a constant real exchange rate.

The final row of Table 24.4 shows what would have had to happen to the nominal exchange rate in order to maintain the real exchange rate at its 1981 level. If the 2010 nominal exchange rate had been $1.56/£, this would exactly have offset the differential evolution of prices in the UK and US, restoring the real exchange rate to its original level.

Table 24.4 Nominal and real exchange rates

	1981	2010
$/£	2.03	1.54
Prices (1981 = 1)		
UK (in £)	1.00	3.12
US (in $)	1.00	2.40
Real $/£ rate index (1981 = 2.03)	2.03	2.00
PPP exchange rate index (1981 = 2.03)	2.03	1.56

Source: IMF, International Financial Statistics.

Frequently asked questions

1 *Does it matter which is the base year in calculating a real exchange rate index?*
As with any index, there are many possible ways in which to construct it. Table 24.4 begins at 1981 and then goes forward. We could instead have chosen 2010 as the base year and worked backwards, asking how real exchange rates were different in 1981.

2 *Does it matter which real exchange rate is used as the basis for computing the PPP path of the nominal exchange rate?*
Same answer. The PPP path plots the path of a nominal exchange rate to accomplish a particular constant real exchange rate. Choosing a different real exchange rate to be held constant would imply a different PPP path for the nominal exchange rate.

24.5 Determinants of the current account

Having defined the real exchange rate and discussed its relationship to competitiveness, we can now study what determines the current and capital accounts of the balance of payments. We begin with the current account.

Exports

Chapter 17 assumed that demand for exports was given. We now recognize that the demand for UK exports depends chiefly on two things. First, since UK exports are imports by the rest of the world, higher income abroad leads to higher UK exports. Second, the lower the UK real exchange rate, the greater is UK competitiveness and the larger are UK exports.

Exports respond quickly to changes in world income, but changes in competitiveness affect exports more slowly. Exporters may be unsure if the change in competitiveness is temporary or permanent. If they believe it to be temporary, they may change their profit margins but leave the price of their goods in foreign currency unaffected.

Even where this means losses in the short run, it may be cheaper in the long run than temporarily withdrawing from those markets and having to spend large sums on advertising and marketing to win back market share when competitiveness improves again. But if competitiveness fails to improve and the real exchange rate remains high, firms will gradually conclude that they should quit the exporting business.

Imports

Import demand is larger the higher is domestic income, as we recognized in Chapter 17 through the marginal propensity to import. But import demand is also larger the higher is the real exchange rate and the cheaper are foreign goods relative to domestic goods when both are measured in the domestic currency. Again, in practice, imports respond more quickly to changes in domestic income than to changes in the real exchange rate. However, if sustained, an appreciation of the real exchange rate eventually raises imports.

Other items on the current account

Foreign aid and spending on military bases abroad are matters of government policy. The net flow of interest, dividend and profit income between countries arises because residents of one country hold assets in another. The size of this net flow of income depends on the pattern of international asset-holding and on the level of interest rates, profits and dividends at home and abroad.

Table 24.5 Lending £100 for a year

| | Interest rate (%) | | Exchange rate ($/£) | | Final wealth | |
£100 lent in:	UK	US	Initial	Final	$	£
UK	10	–	–	–	–	110
US	–	0	2.0	1.8	200	110

24.6 The financial account

We have distinguished between transfer payments on the capital account, for example EU subsidies for roadbuilding, and movements of financial capital to buy and sell assets on the financial account. The former are tiny and henceforth we ignore them completely, implicitly assuming that the capital account is in balance. However, financial flows on the financial account can be huge. These flows of financial capital are often called 'capital flows' even though they relate to the financial account.

Capital inflows and outflows reflect sales and purchases of foreign assets. These flows have become increasingly important. Computers and telecommunications make it as easy for a British resident to transact in the financial markets of New York or Frankfurt as in London. Moreover, controls on international capital flows have gradually been dismantled as a result of globalization and financial integration.

The world's financial markets now have two crucial features. First, restrictions have been abolished for capital flows between the advanced countries. Funds can be freely moved from one country to another in search of the highest rate of return. Second, trillions of pounds are internationally footloose, capable of being switched between countries and currencies when assets in one currency seem to offer a higher rate of return than assets elsewhere.

Since the stock of international funds is now huge, capital flows could swamp the typical current account flows from imports and exports.

In international asset markets, capital gains arise not merely from changes in the domestic price of an asset but also from changes in exchange rates while temporarily holding a foreign asset – **speculation**. In Table 24.5, you can invest £100 for a year. UK interest rates are 10 per cent a year. US interest rates are zero. Keeping your funds in pounds, row 1 shows that you have £110 at the end of the year.

> **Speculation** is the purchase of an asset for subsequent resale, in the belief that the total return – interest plus capital gain – exceeds the total return on other assets.

CASE 24.1 International flows of financial capital

Flows on the financial account of the balance of payments may be short term, such as putting money in a foreign bank account, or long term, such as taking a permanent stake in a foreign company – foreign direct investment.

> **Foreign direct investment (FDI)** is the purchase of foreign firms or the establishment of foreign subsidiaries.

Surely globalization has made capital flows more important recently? The figure below shows the scale of average annual capital flows, relative to GDP, for 12 OECD economies in peacetime years during 1870–1996. The figure confirms that capital flows dried up in the 1930s, during the Great Depression, but today we tend to forget that the late nineteenth century was also a great period of foreign investment.

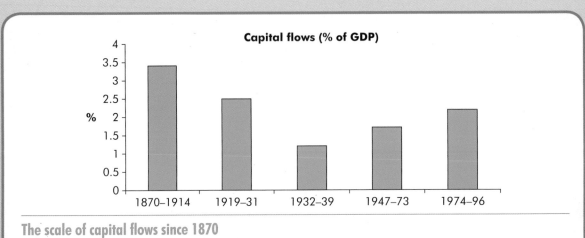

The scale of capital flows since 1870

Source: Obstfeld, M. (1998) The global capital market: benefactor or menace?, *Journal of Economic Perspectives*, 12: 9–30.

Whereas this 100-year view shows no sign of an upward trend, focusing more recently reveals that financial globalization is indeed a new phenomenon, as the next figure illustrates. After 1995 there was a quadrupling of gross financial flows relative to world GDP, which itself was growing quickly. We now live in a world of highly mobile financial capital.

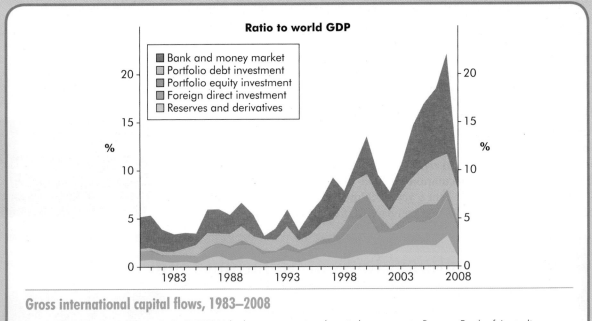

Gross international capital flows, 1983–2008

Source: Becker, C. and Noone, C. (2009) Volatility in international capital movements, Reserve Bank of Australia.

You might have expected this to be one-way traffic: rich, advanced countries investing in emerging markets, such as China, India and the Gulf states. But this was not always the case. China has used its export surpluses to buy debt issued by Western governments, and also to lend to their private sectors; 'sovereign wealth funds' from the oil-rich states of Abu Dhabi, Qatar, Kuwait and Bahrain have done the same. Without capital inflows on this scale, the pre-crash credit binge in Western countries would not have been as extensive.

This second figure also confirms that international capital flows are increasingly volatile. This leads to two questions. First, when countries borrow from foreigners can they rely on this inflow being stable, or do they have to worry about possible outflows again? Second, if international capital is so mobile, would it be feasible and desirable to regulate it to reduce its mobility? These questions lie at the heart of international macroeconomics. We return to them in more detail in subsequent chapters.

The figures in this case need to be interpreted with care. They refer to gross flows – total inflows, total outflows, or the sum of the two. This is not the same as net inflows or outflows. Since official financing is usually small, our balance of payments arithmetic guarantees that the sum of the current and financial accounts must be near zero, especially when averaged over many years. If countries cannot run large current account deficits, they cannot have large net capital inflows either. In equilibrium, the size of the net flow must be of the same order of magnitude as the size of the current account. Since current account balances are rarely in excess of 10 per cent of GDP, we need to understand the market forces or policy responses that ensure that net capital flows are similar in size.

Looking at the *size* of capital flows does not itself tell us about capital mobility, which relates to the *sensitivity* of capital flows to perceived profit opportunities. If exchange rates adjust to *prevent* massive capital flows, we will never see large flows in the data, whatever the degree of capital mobility.

Row 2 of Table 24.5 shows what happens if you convert £100 into dollars at an initial exchange rate of $2/£, then lend this $200 for a year at zero interest, to get $200 by the year end. Suppose sterling depreciates 10 per cent during the year. At the year end, at the exchange rate of $1.80/£, a fall of 10 per cent on the original rate of $2/£, your $200 converts back to £110. You get 10 per cent less interest than staying in the UK, but make a capital gain of 10 per cent by temporarily holding dollars, whose value relative to pounds rises 10 per cent in the year.

In this example you end up with £110 whether you lend in dollars or in pounds for the year. If the pound depreciates more than 10 per cent, the capital gain on holding dollars outweighs the loss of interest, and the total return on lending in dollars is higher than in pounds. Conversely, if the pound depreciates against the dollar by less than the interest rate differential, you earn a higher total return by keeping your money in pounds.

Equation (2), which is called the **interest parity** condition, summarizes this important result. The total return on temporarily lending in a foreign currency is the interest rate paid on assets in that currency plus any capital gain (or minus any capital loss) arising from depreciation (appreciation) of the domestic currency during the period.

> **Interest parity** means that expected exchange rate changes offset the interest differential between domestic and foreign currency assets.

Return on domestic asset = return on foreign asset (2)
= foreign interest rate + % depreciation of exchange rate while funds abroad

With near **perfect capital mobility**, there is a vast capital outflow if the total return on foreign lending exceeds the total return (the domestic interest rate) on domestic lending. There is a huge capital inflow if the return on domestic lending exceeds the return on lending abroad.

> **Perfect capital mobility** means that a vast quantity of funds flow from one currency to another if the expected return on assets differs across currencies.

Net flows on the financial account of the balance of payments are small only when the total return on foreign lending is similar to the return on lending in the domestic currency. With no barriers to capital mobility, expected total returns are the same in assets of different currencies. Expectations about the future determine the capital gains or losses that people expect to make through changes in the exchange rate.

Interest parity conditions

Let r denote the domestic interest rate, r^* the foreign interest rate, s the nominal exchange rate (international value of the domestic currency) and ds/dt the instantaneous rate of change of the exchange rate. $(1/s)ds/dt$ is then the instantaneous percentage capital gain that a foreign investor makes by holding the domestic currency for an instant before repatriating the money, and, under perfect certainty, the interest parity condition implies

$$r^* + (1/s)ds/dt = r \tag{1}$$

The real exchange rate v is given by

$$v = sp/p^* \tag{2}$$

where p is the domestic price level and p^* the foreign price level. The instantaneous change in the real exchange rate obeys

$$(1/v)dv/dt = (1/s)ds/dt + (1/p)dp/dt - (1/p^*)dp^*/dt = (1/s)ds/dt + \pi - \pi^* \tag{3}$$

Real exchange rate appreciation reflects nominal exchange rate appreciation, domestic (π) inflation or foreign deflation ($-\pi^*$).

Combining equations (1) and (3):

$$r^* - \pi^* = r - \pi + (1/s)ds/dt + \pi - \pi^*$$
$$\Rightarrow [r^* - \pi^*] = [r - \pi] + [(1/v)dv/dt] \tag{4}$$

Thus, the interest parity condition expressed in nominal terms in equation (1) – nominal interest differentials must be offset by appropriate capital gains or losses in nominal exchange rates to preserve the equality of return in different currencies under perfect international capital mobility – implies a similar statement in terms of real interest rate differentials being offset by capital gains or losses on the real exchange rate.

Although derived for an instantaneous decision, we can always view a longer horizon as a series of instant decisions. Hence, interest parity conditions also hold over longer horizons, provided the duration of the interest rates matches the period over which exchange rate changes are assessed.

Finally, once uncertainty exists, we have to replace actual exchange rate changes by those expected at the outset of the period. An investor contemplating lending abroad for a year can always obtain a one-year foreign bond with a known interest rate today, but will have to take a view on the likely change in the exchange rate over the year.

24.7 Internal and external balance

Next, we discuss the relationship between the state of the economy – boom or recession – and the current account on the balance of payments.

Figure 24.3 shows the different combinations of boom and recession and current account surpluses and deficits. Think about demand and supply for domestic output. Equation (3) reminds us of the basic equation for goods market equilibrium:

$$Y = C + I + G + (X - Z) \tag{3}$$

Domestic output Y equals aggregate demand that arises from spending on consumption, investment, government purchases and net exports. If aggregate demand for domestic output equals potential output,

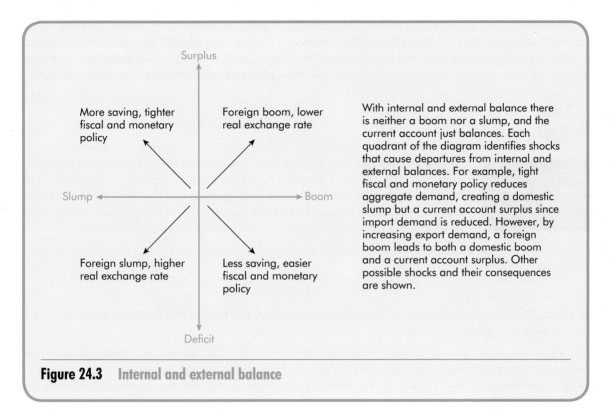

Figure 24.3 Internal and external balance

firms produce the full-employment output level and in the labour market demand as much employment as workers wish to supply.

With sluggish wage and price adjustment, lower aggregate demand causes a recession. Only when aggregate demand returns to potential output is **internal balance** restored.

> A country is in **internal balance** when aggregate demand equals potential output.
>
> A country in **external balance** has a zero current account balance.

For a floating exchange rate, the total balance of payments is always zero. Saying that the current account is in internal balance then also implies financial account balance.

In Figure 24.3 the point of internal *and* **external balance** is the intersection of the two axes, with neither boom nor slump, and with the current account in neither surplus nor deficit.

Internal balance implies aggregate demand equals potential output, and there is full employment in the labour market. External balance means current account balance. The country is neither underspending nor overspending its foreign income. Nor is it augmenting or depleting its foreign assets. Foreigners are not acquiring domestic assets without limit, nor are domestic residents acquiring ever-larger holdings of foreign assets.

Figure 24.3 shows how shocks move the economy away from internal and external balance. For example, the top left-hand quadrant shows a combination of domestic slump and current account surplus. This can be caused by a rise in desired saving (a downward shift in the consumption function) or by the adoption of tight fiscal and monetary policy. These reduce aggregate demand and thereby cause both a domestic slump and a reduction in imports.

Similarly, a higher real exchange rate (lower competitiveness) reduces export demand and raises import demand. The fall in net exports induces both a current account deficit and lower aggregate demand, leading to a domestic slump as shown in the bottom left-hand quadrant. The figure shows other shocks that move the economy into other quadrants, causing departures from both internal and external balance.

A key lesson of Figure 24.3 is that most shocks in an open economy move the economy away from *both* internal *and* external balance. In studying a closed economy, we examined whether the economy could return to internal balance on its own. When adjustment is sluggish, monetary and fiscal policy can speed up adjustment. In a slump, expansionary monetary and fiscal policy hasten the return to full employment.

24.8 The long-run equilibrium real exchange rate

> Simultaneous internal and external balance is the **long-run equilibrium** of the economy.

In **long-run equilibrium**, both internal and external balance must hold. Domestic output Y is at potential output Y^* and the current account is in balance. For countries with large foreign debts or foreign assets, and thus large flows of interest income, the current account can deviate a lot from the trade balance. However, for most countries, the trade balance and the current account balance are similar.

Initially, we focus on this latter case. External balance then requires that net exports $X - Z$ must be zero. Long-run equilibrium then requires

$$Y^* = Y = [C + I + G] + [X - Z] \tag{4}$$

In external balance, net exports $(X - Z) = 0$. Internal balance then requires that domestic demand $(C + I + G)$, the domestic absorption of resources, equals potential output Y^*.

Net exports depend on real income at home, real income abroad and the real exchange rate that determines competitiveness. In long-run equilibrium, both domestic and foreign income are fixed at their respective levels of potential output. Given these income levels, net exports depend only on the real exchange rate.

ACTIVITY 24.1 Changes in equilibrium real exchange rates

Paul Samuelson, one of the fathers of modern economics, won the Nobel Prize for his work on many aspects of economics, including international trade. Empirical research confirms a relation first noticed by Béla Balassa and Paul Samuelson: countries with higher per capita real incomes have a higher real exchange rate.

Typically, there is more technical progress in industries making goods for trade (computers, cars, telecommunications) than in industries making services for the home economy (haircuts, laundry, crèches). Similarly, productivity-enhancing capital accumulation occurs mainly in the traded goods sector. The main difference between a rich country and a poor country is not that hairdressers or childminders are more productive in rich countries, but that industries making exports and competing with imports are more productive.

Countries with high per capita incomes therefore have high real exchange rates because their traded goods sector is more productive. Without real exchange rate appreciation such countries would be too competitive. Why does the Balassa–Samuelson effect matter? Here are some examples.

At what exchange rate should eurozone members be admitted?

The eurozone is a monetary union whose members have permanently fixed exchange rates against one another but a floating exchange rate in relation to the rest of the world. Suppose, just suppose, the eurozone decided to allow Turkey to join their fixed exchange rate club. A country outside the eurozone will typically have a floating exchange rate which will move around a bit. How do negotiators decide on a sensible exchange rate to permanently fix to the currency of a new entrant?

They might look at past data, hoping to find a period of internal and external balance in that country. This would be a starting point for calculating a sensible real exchange rate that would provide just the right amount of competitiveness.

So, from the base date, they would calculate how much relative prices of Turkey and the eurozone had changed up to the date of Turkish entry, and adjust the original nominal exchange rate by this amount to restore the real exchange rate to the level at which it had last appeared correct. This would determine the nominal exchange rate at which Turkey was admitted to the common currency.

Without knowing about the Balassa–Samuelson effect, negotiators might make a mistake in assuming that the past was the perfect guide to the future. More sophisticated negotiators might take the above as a starting point but then ask whether Turkey was still an emerging economy, in relation to the more mature eurozone economies, and therefore make an estimate of the further real appreciation of the Turkish currency that might be compatible in the longer run with achieving a sustainable real exchange rate. This would lead to a different estimate of a suitable initial exchange rate for Turkish entry.

Overcompetitive China

Perhaps the most obvious example in the current global economy is the Chinese exchange rate. For years, China has chosen to fix its exchange rate to the US dollar, and to maintain this peg at a level that keeps the Chinese economy supercompetitive. This explains why China has massive current account surpluses (and an outflow of capital as it invests these abroad again). On 23 February 2010 the *Financial Times* reported an estimate by the US Petersen Institute that the Chinese exchange rate was undervalued by 41 per cent relative to the level consistent with internal and external balance.

Policy makers, from Washington to Paris, complain that China's exchange rate policy is bankrupting their economies, leading to an export of jobs from the West to Asia, and leaving Western economies exposed to the inflows of financial capital from China that might, at some future date, decide to become outflows.

An upward adjustment of China's nominal exchange rate peg would reduce this problem overnight. But it is not the only adjustment mechanism. As China creates domestic money to fuel its incredible economic expansion, it is possible that Chinese domestic prices will rise sufficiently more quickly than those in the West that its real appreciation – or loss of competitiveness – will be achieved not by a nominal exchange rate change but by a change in relative price levels in China and the West.

For the optimists who think such market forces may be an adequate substitute for a proactive change in the nominal exchange rate peg, the Balassa–Samuelson effect comes as bad news. As Chinese economic development continues, rapid productivity growth in its traded goods sector will allow it to cope with some degree of real appreciation without losing competitiveness. So, at a fixed nominal exchange rate, its supercompetitiveness will be reduced only if its domestic inflation (relative to competitors) exceeds its productivity growth (relative to competitors). A large rise in inflation would have that effect; a small rise probably would not.

Questions

(a) Except for footballers, investment bankers and university professors, labour is largely a commodity that is not traded across national frontiers. Does this mean that countries with a high real exchange rate will also be those with a high real wage rate?

(b) Rank the following countries in terms of the current level of their real exchange rate, with the highest first: China, Greece, Italy, Switzerland. Which country should have the least scope for real appreciation in the long run?

(c) Suppose the internet allows extensive international trade in services (for example, legal, accounting, software and entertainment services). Is the Balassa–Samuelson effect then likely to break down? Why, or why not?

To check your answers to these questions, go to page 687.

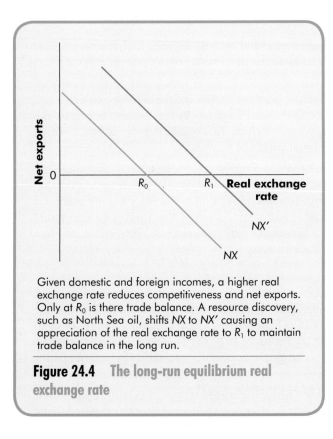

Given domestic and foreign incomes, a higher real exchange rate reduces competitiveness and net exports. Only at R_0 is there trade balance. A resource discovery, such as North Sea oil, shifts NX to NX' causing an appreciation of the real exchange rate to R_1 to maintain trade balance in the long run.

Figure 24.4 The long-run equilibrium real exchange rate

Figure 24.4 shows that there is a unique real exchange rate that makes net exports equal to zero. Given domestic and foreign levels of potential output, a lower real exchange rate raises export demand and reduces import demand. The net export schedule NX slopes down. Only at the real exchange rate R_0 are net exports zero. At a higher real exchange rate, competitiveness is too low and net exports are negative. At a lower real exchange rate, competitiveness is too high and net exports are positive.

Beginning from R_0, suppose the country gets a favourable and lasting supply shock that raises potential output Y^*. For example, the country discovers a natural resource, such as oil or gold, or develops a new high-tech industry, such as computers. Since the marginal propensity to consume is less than unity, if output and income rise by 100, aggregate demand rises by less than 100. The remaining output is exported and net exports rise.

In Figure 24.4 the favourable supply shock shifts the net export schedule to NX' and the long-run equilibrium real exchange rate appreciates from R_0 to R_1. If finding North Sea oil adds to UK net exports, only a fall in the country's manufacturing exports will prevent a permanent trade surplus. A real exchange rate appreciation – a fall in UK competitiveness – is the market mechanism that restores external balance.[3]

Large supply shocks, such as a big resource discovery, are the exception not the norm. If no shocks occur, the real exchange rate is constant in long-run equilibrium. This has two implications. First, if domestic and foreign prices grow at different rates, the nominal exchange rate has to adjust steadily to keep the real exchange rate constant. The nominal exchange rate then follows the purchasing power parity path discussed in Section 24.4.

Second, if the nominal exchange rate is fixed as an act of policy, it is possible to maintain a constant real exchange rate in the long run only if domestic and foreign prices change at the same rate. Otherwise the real exchange rate is changing in the long run, and net exports will not remain zero, as external balance requires.

Foreign debt and foreign assets

Finally, we recognize that some countries have important flows of international income or payments as a result of owning large foreign assets or having large foreign debts. The current account is net exports $(X - Z)$ plus rA the stock of net foreign assets multiplied by the interest rate r. For creditor countries A is positive; for debtor countries A is negative.

Figure 24.5 shows how inherited foreign assets or debts affect the long-run equilibrium real exchange rate. The current account CA is net exports NX, as in Figure 24.4, plus net interest on foreign assets. For current account balance, a debtor country needs a low real exchange rate R_0 to be competitive and have a sufficient trade surplus to pay interest on its foreign debts. A creditor country has a high real exchange rate R_1 to reduce competitiveness and run a trade deficit, financed by interest earned on foreign assets.

---

3 The fact that a resource discovery hurts other sectors, such as manufacturing, is sometimes called Dutch Disease. Holland's real exchange rate appreciated significantly after its discovery of offshore gas fields in the North Sea. Sterling also appreciated after the UK subsequently found North Sea oil.

This figure is helpful in thinking about implications of foreign indebtedness in the aftermath of the financial crisis. Because of greater risk-taking by financial institutions in London, the UK had above-average exposure to the financial crash. The UK government's debts increased sharply as it bailed out failing financial institutions. Figure 24.5 implies that, to the extent that interest payments are made to foreigners such as Chinese investors, we should expect the real sterling exchange rate permanently to depreciate as a result of the crash. To service permanent interest payments to the Chinese, the UK has to run a larger trade surplus than before, which requires greater competitiveness achieved by a depreciated exchange rate.

What about countries such as Greece within the eurozone. With much higher debts than previously recognized, it also requires a real depreciation, for the same reason as the UK. This could be achieved by a nominal depreciation of the euro. But the eurozone also includes some much healthier economies that do not require such a depreciation. The textbook solution therefore includes a reduction of domestic prices in Greece in order to improve its competitiveness by depreciating its real exchange rate.

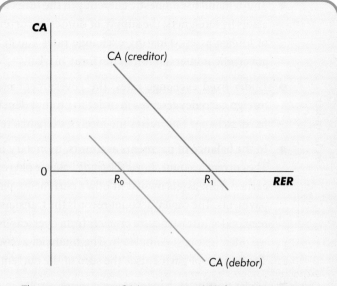

The current account CA is net exports NX plus net interest on foreign assets. For current account balance, a debtor country needs a low real exchange rate R_0 to be competitive and have a sufficient trade surplus to pay interest on its foreign debts. A creditor country has a high real exchange rate R_1 to reduce competitiveness and run a trade deficit, financed by interest earned on foreign assets.

Figure 24.5 Foreign assets and the real exchange rate

In practice, this requires that Greece undertake a greater reduction in aggregate demand than other countries. Thus a fiscal contraction not merely deals with its budget deficit, but also puts downward pressure on prices and wages in Greece. With sluggish wage adjustment in the Greek labour market, this is a recipe for high unemployment while adjustment is taking place. Whether the Greek government is strong enough to administer the medicine is something that bond markets are watching with concern.

This completes our analysis of the long-run equilibrium exchange rate, compatible with both internal and external balance. In the long run, it is thus the current account of the balance of payments that affects the exchange rate. The financial account gets into the story only to the extent that the cumulation of *past* capital flows is what determines the current stock of net foreign assets.

In the short run, the story is very different. Countries can run large current account surpluses and deficits. Short-run changes in the exchange rate then have much more to do with the financial account. The role of capital flows is one theme of the next chapter. The other themes are how the economy adjusts to temporary shocks and returns to internal and external balance, whether macroeconomic policy can ease this adjustment and how choice of exchange rate regime affects these issues.

Summary

- The **exchange rate** is the number of units of foreign currency that exchange for a unit of the domestic currency. A fall (rise) in the exchange rate is called **depreciation** (**appreciation**).

- The **demand for domestic currency in the forex market** arises from exports and purchases of domestic assets by foreigners; the **supply of domestic currency** to the market arises from imports and purchases of foreign assets. **Floating exchange rates** equate supply and demand for currency in the absence of government intervention in the forex market.

- Under **fixed exchange rates**, the government meets an excess supply of pounds by running down foreign currency reserves in order to prompt demand for pounds. An excess demand for pounds, at the fixed exchange rate, raises the foreign exchange reserves as pounds are supplied to the market.

- In the **balance of payments accounts**, monetary inflows are credits and monetary outflows are debits. The **current account** shows the trade balance plus current transfer payments, which largely reflect income earned from assets owned in other currencies, payment of international subsidies and social security payments. The capital account records the transfers of capital by migrants, debt forgiveness and net grant receipts for infrastructure projects from overseas institutions. Typically, this is small and for convenience we often ignore it completely. The **financial account** shows net purchases and sales of foreign assets. The balance of payments is the sum of the current, capital and financial account balances.

- Under floating exchange rates, a current surplus must be offset by a financial account deficit or vice versa. Under fixed exchange rates, a balance of payments surplus or deficit must be matched by an offsetting quantity of official financing. **Official financing** is government intervention in the forex market.

- The **real exchange rate** adjusts the nominal exchange rate for prices at home and abroad, and is the relative price of domestic to foreign goods when measured in a common currency. A rise in the real exchange rate reduces the **competitiveness** of the domestic economy.

- The **purchasing power parity** is the path of the nominal exchange rate that would keep the real exchange rate at its initial level.

- An increase in domestic (foreign) income increases the demand for imports (exports). An increase in the real exchange rate reduces the demand for exports, increases the demand for imports and reduces the demand for net exports.

- Holders of international funds compare the domestic interest rate with the total return from temporary lending abroad. This return is the foreign interest rate plus the depreciation of the international value of the domestic currency during the loan. Perfect international capital mobility means that an enormous quantity of funds shifts between currencies when the perceived rate of return differs across currencies.

- The **interest parity** condition says that, when capital mobility is perfect, interest rate differentials across countries should be offset by expected exchange rate changes, so that the total expected return is equated across currencies.

- **Internal balance** means output is at potential output. **External balance** means the current account equals zero. Long-run equilibrium needs both.

- Given domestic and foreign levels of potential output, there is a unique real exchange rate that achieves trade balance. An increase in domestic potential output, for example from a resource discovery, causes a real exchange rate appreciation to maintain trade balance in the long run.

- Interest flows from foreign assets and debts make the current account differ from the trade balance. The higher are net foreign assets, the higher is the inflow of interest income and the higher is the real exchange rate needed to maintain external balance.

Review questions

1   If $1 exchanges for €1 and $1.40 exchanges for £1, what is the exchange rate between the euro and the pound? Can the dollar appreciate against the euro but not against the pound?

EASY

2   A country has a current account surplus of £6 billion but a financial account deficit of £4 billion. (a) Is its balance of payments in deficit or surplus? (b) Are its foreign exchange reserves rising or falling? (c) Is the central bank buying or selling domestic currency? Explain.

3   For decades, Japan has had a trade surplus. Must countries eventually get back to external balance? Is there more pressure on deficit countries than surplus countries to restore external balance?

4   Newsreaders say that 'the pound had a good day' if the sterling exchange rate rises. When is an appreciation: (a) desirable and (b) undesirable?

5   Suppose the initial exchange rate is $4/£. After ten years, the US price level has risen from 100 to 300 and the UK price level has risen from 100 to 200. What nominal exchange rate would preserve purchasing power parity?

6   Common fallacies   Why are these statements wrong? (a) Countries with lower inflation gain competitiveness. (b) Current and financial accounts are equally important in determining the level of floating exchange rates. (c) UK interest rates are high. This means the pound will appreciate for the next few months.

7   Which is correct? (a) An exchange rate appreciation causes a loss of competitiveness. (b) If a country gained competitiveness for other reasons, such as a technological improvement, the consequence would be an appreciation of its equilibrium real exchange rate. (c) In the short run, exchange rates are driven more by the views of speculators than by the need to balance imports and exports. (d) All of the above. (e) None of the above.

8   Does Manchester have a balance of payments with everyone else? By what mechanism is long-run equilibrium achieved?

9   Suppose Greece has to borrow extensively from foreign countries, thereby acquiring substantial foreign debt. Use Figure 24.5 to show what has to happen to its equilibrium real exchange rate. Why is this change required? If Greece remains within the eurozone, how can such a change be accomplished?

MEDIUM

10 The following table shows country A's bilateral exchange rate against country B and country C. If the countries are equally important trade partners of country A, what is happening to country A's effective exchange rate? If it trades twice as much with country B as with country C, what is the evolution of country A's effective exchange rate?

	2011	2012	2013
Country A exchange rate index against:			
Country B	100	200	400
Country C	100	50	25

11 D is real debt owed to foreigners, s is the trade surplus deficit, i the real interest rate paid on foreign debt, Y real output and g the rate of output growth. The foreign debt burden D/Y rises with debt but falls with output and the ability to repay debt. Let Δ denote the increase in a variable. (a) Since $\Delta(D/Y) = (\Delta D/D) - (\Delta Y/Y)$, show that the debt/GDP ratio shrinks only if $s/D > i - g$. Assuming that the real interest rate exceeds the long-run growth rate, thereby confirm that countries with foreign debts need in the long run to have trade surpluses. Why can a country that is temporarily growing very rapidly sidestep this constraint?

12 A country discovers oil and its real exchange rate appreciates. Manufacturers go bust because their exports are no longer competitive. Could the country be worse off as a result of finding this valuable resource?

13 Suppose Bob Geldof and Bono succeed in getting all the debts of poor countries written off. (a) What happens to the real exchange rate of poor countries? (b) What happens to the real exchange rate of rich countries? (c) What happens to the manufacturing exports of rich countries? (d) If there were single monopoly producers of manufactures in rich countries, how would they have been lobbying their governments? (e) Why did we not see more of this in practice?

14 **Essay question** 'Capitalist firms have no problem prospering despite the volatility of stock markets. Nobody has ever suggested government policies to fix stock market prices. Exchange rates are just another asset price and it is just as silly to fix exchange rates. Let them float.' Why do governments ever want to fix exchange rates?

For solutions to these questions contact your lecturer.

Open economy macroeconomics

Learning Outcomes

By the end of this chapter, you should understand:

1. price and output adjustment under fixed exchange rates
2. monetary and fiscal policy under fixed exchange rates
3. the effects of devaluation
4. what determines floating exchange rates
5. monetary and fiscal policy under floating exchange rates

Chapter 24 introduced fixed and floating exchange rate regimes. We now study how the exchange rate regime affects the way in which an economy operates.

Openness is often measured by the size of exports (or imports) relative to GDP. However, links through financial markets often have more impact. Large outflows of financial capital can provoke acute crises. Such crises may induce austerity measures to reassure foreign investors, devaluation of a pegged exchange rate or adoption of a completely new exchange rate regime.

UK discussions about future exchange rate policy still recall the day in 1992 that the UK was forced off a pegged exchange rate in the Exchange Rate Mechanism; and in 2010 the options for Greece, pegged to its eurozone partners, were very different from those of the UK. Even in the absence of crises, the choice of exchange rate regime affects the transmission mechanism of both monetary and fiscal policy. In this chapter, we study how our analysis for a closed economy must be amended for an **open economy**.

> **Open economy macroeconomics** examines how the economy is affected by links with other countries through trade, the exchange rate and capital flows.

Initially, we examine fixed exchange rate regimes. Then we discuss the determination of floating exchange rates and the consequences for macroeconomic policy.

25.1 Fixed exchange rates

The balance of payments and the money supply

To understand the role of capital mobility, suppose initially that there are no private sector capital flows, perhaps because of controls on capital flows.

> **Capital controls** are regulations preventing private sector capital flows between different currencies.

Most economies had **capital controls** during the period of fixed exchange rates from 1945 to 1973. Subsequent integration of global financial markets made these controls less effective and now they have been scrapped.

With a fixed exchange rate but no private capital flows, suppose the economy has a balance of payments deficit (because it has a current account deficit). To finance the deficit, the forex reserves must fall. The central bank sells foreign exchange and buys domestic currency, demanding the domestic currency that nobody else wants. In consequence, domestic money in circulation falls as pounds disappear back into the Bank of England. The balance of payments deficit reduces the domestic money supply. A balance of payments surplus would increase the money supply.

Under fixed exchange rates, the money supply is not determined exclusively by the original decision about how much domestic money to create. It also depends on the balance of payments surplus or deficit. When there is a payments surplus (deficit), cash flows into (out of) the country, directly changing narrow money, which in turn affects bank deposits and broad money.

> **Unsterilized intervention** uses the forex reserves to offset balance of payments surpluses or deficits. Since foreign reserves are exchanged for domestic cash, this alters the cash in circulation and the domestic money supply.
>
> **Sterilization** is an open market operation between domestic money and domestic bonds, to offset the change in domestic money supply that a balance of payments surplus or deficit otherwise induces.

Allowing the balance of payments to change the money supply is called **unsterilized intervention** in the forex market. For a given money demand schedule, allowing changes in the money supply means then having to change interest rates to make this an equilibrium.

Figure 25.1 illustrates using the *IS–LM* model. Initially, the economy faces the *IS* curve shown, and its monetary policy is reflected in *LM*. Short-run equilibrium is therefore at point *A*. However, the economy has a current account deficit and balance of payments deficit. If it allows this to deplete its domestic money supply, the *LM* curve will shift to *LM′*, causing a rise in interest rates and a domestic recession. The economy moves to point *B*. The recession reduces import demand and eliminates the current account deficit.

Alternatively, the central bank may create additional domestic money to prevent the balance of payments deficit reducing the money supply. The *LM* curve remains in its original position and the economy remains at point *A*.

Although the total money supply is not changing, something important is happening to the balance sheet of the central bank. On the liability side, money supplied is constant. On the asset side, the central bank holds foreign exchange reserves and government bonds.

$$M = R + B$$

To keep *M* constant while *R* is falling, the central bank is effectively selling foreign exchange and buying domestic government bonds. It can keep doing so until *R* becomes zero, at which point it runs out of foreign exchange reserves and can no longer keep financing the balance of payments deficit. If the exchange rate is not to be devalued, thereafter it requires a domestic recession to get imports down. This can be achieved either by allowing the shift in the *LM* schedule shown in Figure 25.1 or by fiscal action, for example higher taxes, that shifts the *IS* schedule to the left. Higher taxes reduce disposable incomes, reduce aggregate demand, and thereby reduce imports.

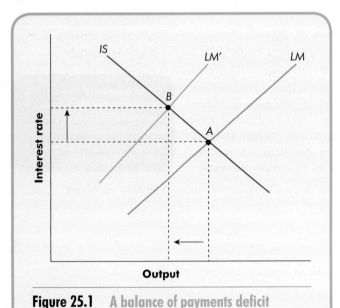

Figure 25.1 A balance of payments deficit reduces the money supply and raises interest rates

So far, we have discussed how changes in aggregate demand and income can act as an adjustment mechanism; later in the chapter we also examine how changes in prices can affect competitiveness and thereby the current account balance.

The role of capital mobility

Now restore highly mobile private capital. If international investors have more funds at their disposal than central banks, central banks no longer defend exchange rates by buying and selling foreign exchange reserves. Instead, central banks set domestic interest rates to provide the correct incentive for speculators.

The interest-rate tail now wags the speculative dog. A change in interest rates manipulates capital flows and hence the financial account of balance of payments. Since these flows can be huge, in the short run this dwarfs the current account of the balance of payments.

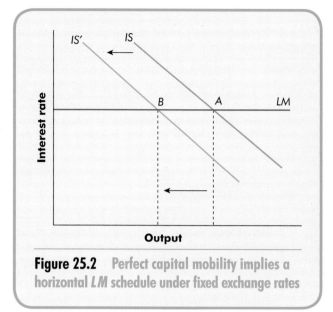

Figure 25.2 Perfect capital mobility implies a horizontal *LM* schedule under fixed exchange rates

Fixing the exchange rate is now a commitment to set the correct interest rate to eliminate one-way capital flows. This interest rate, coupled with the level of domestic income, determines money demand. This must equal real money supply. Given inherited prices, this determines the nominal money supply.

Thus, in the short run, only one level of the nominal money supply will do. Suppose the central bank tries further domestic open market operations between money and bonds. If it boosts the money supply, interest rates fall, capital flows out until the money supply falls back again, and interest rates return to the only level compatible with the pegged exchange rate.

When capital mobility is high, adjustment back to long-run equilibrium no longer occurs through induced changes in the money supply and interest rates.

The important conclusion is that pegging the exchange rate when capital mobility is very high means subordinating domestic interest rates to the single task of defending the exchange rate. There is no scope for any other choice of monetary policy. In the language of earlier chapters, the *LM* schedule is horizontal at the given interest rate necessary to maintain the pegged exchange rate. In such a world, there would be little scope for an independent monetary policy committee.

Figure 25.2 illustrates. With a fixed exchange rate and perfect capital mobility, domestic interest rates must match interest rates abroad. The *LM* curve is horizontal and the supply of money is passively adjusted to maintain this interest rate whatever the level of money demand. Thus, anything that shifts the *IS* curve to *IS'* leads to a fall in short-run equilibrium output as the economy moves from point *A* to point *B*. Of course, this will affect what then happens to domestic prices. We discuss this shortly.

> Sterilized intervention does not work when there is **perfect capital mobility** because offsetting capital flows are immediately induced.

CASE 25.1

Sand in the wheels of international capital flows?

Case 24.1 documented the rise of international capital mobility during the last 20 years. Not only have gross capital inflows and outflows become much larger, they have also become much more sensitive to small perceived differences in the expected return of holding assets in different currencies. In part, this has been driven by changes in information technology that allow the integration of global financial markets, in part by the supposed benefits of large scale that allowed global financial institutions to outcompete small national competitors. In turn, this led national regulators to compete to attract the globally footloose institutions and the assets that they had to invest.

For many years, the International Monetary Fund was at the forefront of championing financial liberalization. Nor was this a difficult argument to make. Cities such as London and New York were evidently booming, and greater competition in financial markets appeared to be a recipe for smaller profit margins in financial services, loans on better terms to customers, and proliferation of financial-sector employment and taxable income.

The financial crash hit the UK so hard precisely because it had previously been doing so well out of the financial services industry.

> At a black-tie event this summer, some of the world's most powerful bankers and business executives gathered for a toast: 'We are the international finance and business capital of the world, the world's greatest global financial centre, without question,' the mayor told the assembled crowd. But that wasn't Michael Bloomberg talking. That's because the city wasn't New York – it was London.
>
> (Heather Timmons, *New York Times*, 26 October 2006)

The subsequent financial crash has led to reconsideration of the desirability of unfettered capital mobility, for several reasons:

- *Volatility of capital flows*   Capital inflows may be an easy way to access funding, but most of this is usually short term, and what comes in, can easily flow out. If international lenders committed to long-term loans, much of this objection would be dissipated. But most international flows are short term, sometimes therefore called 'hot money'.

- *Economic sovereignty*   Adverse capital flows cause huge problems for the government in power. If all lending and borrowing was domestic, the ebb and flow of loans would amount to transfer payments between citizens. The principal effect is on wealth distribution within the country, not on the size of national wealth. When foreign funds exit the country, they can topple government policy itself. For example, the UK had to abandon its exchange rate peg in 1992 after a speculative attack on the currency.

- *Financial contagion*   Once financial markets become concerned about a country with particular attributes (such as Greece in 2010) they tend to look around for other countries with some of the same attributes and immediately attack those (for example, the other PIGS – Portugal, Italy and Spain – are much more likely to face a speculative attack if speculators have already succeeded against Greece. If Greece repels boarders, the other PIGS may escape lightly. Thus, the outcome for Portugal, Italy and Spain may depend not on their own performance but on the performance of another country with which they become identified.

> A **Tobin tax** is a small tax on capital flow transactions.

In November 2009 the UK prime minister, Gordon Brown, resurrected an old idea, the Tobin tax, named after Yale professor James Tobin. Since many financial transactions entail moving huge volumes of money for tiny profit margins, Tobin argued that a tiny 'transactions tax' could seriously inhibit international capital flows; throwing sand in the wheels of this activity would restore a greater degree of national autonomy by limiting international capital mobility. For several decades, economists and bankers took the view that the tax might not be desirable in theory and was certainly impossible to implement in practice: smart financial traders would find other untaxed ways of doing the same business. Notice that such a tax would make little difference to the return on an investment held for ten years but a large difference to the return on holding a foreign asset for ten minutes. It would skew capital flows away from short-term hot money.

Gordon Brown's motive in resurrecting the proposal was not merely, perhaps not principally, to limit international capital flows. He was responding to the conclusion that the financial crisis had been caused by irresponsible lending by financial instititutions, often large in scale but in pursuit of small margins, from institutions that had grown 'too big to fail' and therefore had de facto insurance from the taxpayer. A Tobin tax would reduce the incentive to pursue such transactions, reduce risk in the system, and also shrink the size of the financial sector, mitigating the 'too big to fail' problem.

In highly connected global financial markets, regulation or taxation by a country in isolation risks driving mobile financial business to all the other countries that have not raised taxes or imposed regulations. Even if a Tobin tax is desirable – which remains contentious to some – it would require simultaneous introduction in most important financial centres for it to be effective. As soon as Gordon Brown proposed it, Tim Geithner, the US Treasury Secretary, dismissed the idea. For the moment, it has made no progress.

In February 2010 IMF chief economist Olivier Blanchard, drawing lessons from the financial crisis, observed that perfect international capital mobility is an idealized benchmark against which to compare actual capital mobility, which would differ in different countries. Where countries have a small margin of manoeuvre, they could use this to pursue expected rates of return on assets that might differ slightly from the world average. But when major strains emerge – as in the case of Greece in 2010 – the extent of national autonomy from speculation is quickly revealed to be small.

The figure below shows the additional interest rates, in basis points relative to Germany, that fiscally vulnerable countries must pay to induce international investors to hold their bonds as well as safer German bonds (called bunds); 100 basis points equals 1 percentage point. The additional risk premium paid as higher interest rates is the insurance that international investors require against two risks: outright default, or the possibility that a weak country leaves the euro and devalues its exchange rate, causing a capital loss for foreign investors who have invested in that currency.

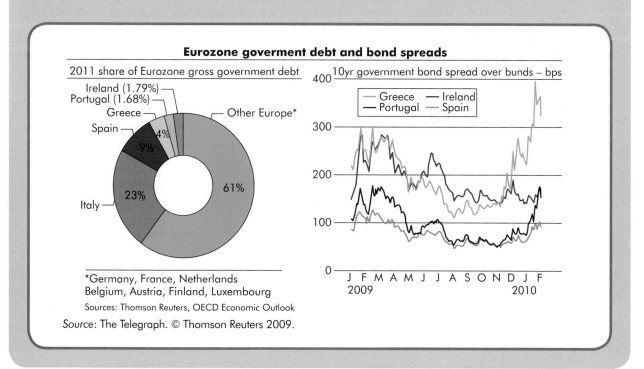

Eurozone goverment debt and bond spreads

2011 share of Eurozone gross government debt

- Ireland (1.79%)
- Portugal (1.68%)
- Greece
- Spain
- Other Europe*
- 4%
- 9%
- Italy 23%
- 61%

10yr government bond spread over bunds – bps

Greece — Ireland
Portugal — Spain

J F M A M J J A S O N D J F
2009   2010

*Germany, France, Netherlands Belgium, Austria, Finland, Luxembourg

Sources: Thomson Reuters, OECD Economic Outlook

Source: The Telegraph. © Thomson Reuters 2009.

Adjustment to shocks

With a fixed exchange rate, how does the economy adjust to a shock when the government takes no monetary or fiscal action to accommodate the shock? Suppose there is a fall in desired consumption spending at each output level. In a closed economy, output would fall, thus reducing inflation. The central bank would reduce interest rates, thus boosting aggregate demand again. Eventually, internal balance is restored.

What happens in an open economy with a fixed nominal exchange rate and high capital mobility? After the adverse demand shock, there is still a domestic slump. However, any fall in interest rates will generate a massive capital outflow. Interest rates cannot be reduced. Since money demand falls because of lower output, the central bank must reduce the domestic money supply, in line with lower money demand, to *prevent* a change in interest rates.

Thus the adoption of a fixed exchange rate precludes the pursuit of a Taylor rule or inflation target. Interest rate policy has to take care of the exchange rate objective. Any attempt to set interest rates at a different level immediately prompts a massive capital inflow or outflow that changes the money supply and restores the equilibrium interest rate to the required level.

With interest rates thus fixed, the adjustment mechanism of a closed economy is blocked. Lower output and falling prices no longer trigger interest rate cuts that boost aggregate demand again. So how does the economy now get back to long-run equilibrium?

Figure 25.3 illustrates. Suppose initially that both the domestic and the foreign country had 2 per cent inflation. With a fixed nominal exchange rate, the real exchange rate was also constant. A domestic slump then reduces domestic inflation. With a fixed nominal exchange rate, the real exchange rate depreciates, thus raising competitiveness and net exports. An initial fall in domestic absorption $(C + I + G)$ eventually induces a sufficient rise in competitiveness to raise net exports $(X - Z)$ to restore internal balance. However, higher net exports imply a current account surplus. External balance is not yet restored.

Current account surpluses raise the country's net foreign assets. By not spending all its foreign income, the country is saving and getting wealthier. Higher wealth raises consumption demand and domestic absorption. The consequent boom raises inflation, reduces competitiveness at the fixed exchange rate and net exports fall again.

Domestic absorption $(C + I + G)$ rises and $(X - Z)$ falls. Eventually, both internal and external balance are restored *without any change in interest rates during the adjustment process*. Instead, in an open economy with a fixed exchange rate, adjustment is achieved through temporary booms and slumps that temporarily affect inflation, with induced effects on the real exchange rate, the balance of payments and changes in external wealth.

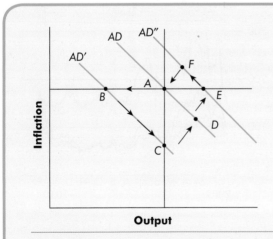

Beginning from internal and external balance at *A*, a fall in domestic demand shifts aggregate demand from *AD* to *AD'*, moving the economy initially to *B*. The recession bids down inflation, moving the economy down *AD'* to *C*. It now has lower inflation than its competitors, and gains competitiveness, eventually shifting aggregate demand back to *AD*. Although point *D* restores internal balance, there is a current account surplus because of the gain in competitiveness. With inflation still below that of competitors, aggregate demand keeps rising, taking the economy to *E*. It then requires a period of above-average inflation, at point *F*, to eliminate the competition and allow eventual return to internal and external balance at *A*.

Figure 25.3 Adjustment under fixed exchange rates

A shock from abroad

Suppose next there is a shock to foreign demand, raising demand for net exports. The current account $(X - Z)$ moves into surplus. Aggregate demand shifts up, and the economy has a boom and a current account surplus. It adds to forex reserves.

In a closed economy, the boom induces a rise in interest rates that eventually returns aggregate demand to potential output. In an open economy with a fixed exchange rate, interest rates remain constant. The boom gradually bids up inflation and reduces competitiveness, reversing the original rise in net exports. When prices rise enough to restore current account balance, aggregate demand reverts to its original level and internal balance is also restored.[1] Thus a temporary period of extra inflation permanently raises the price level, permanently changing the real exchange rate.

CONCEPT 25.1

Sovereignty and monetary union

In 1999 Chicago professor Robert Mundell won the Nobel Prize for helping invent open economy macroeconomics. He was the first to realize that openness in product and factor markets may create powerful pressures for monetary union. He also showed what it would be like for a small country to try to hang on to **monetary sovereignty** when international capital mobility is high.

> Perfect capital mobility undermines **monetary sovereignty**. If interest rates are set to maintain the pegged exchange rate, they cannot be set independently to influence the domestic economy.

The figure below shows a pegged exchange rate. The UK pegged the pound during its short membership of the ERM in 1990–92. IS is the usual relationship between interest rates and output consistent with goods market equilibrium. A small country can peg its exchange rate only by matching the foreign interest rate r^*. We show this as a horizontal line. The money supply adjusts to make sure this is always the domestic interest rate. Initial equilibrium is at A.

As in Figure 25.2, any attempt to change the money supply, and hence interest rates, causes an immediate capital inflow or outflow on the financial account until the money supply and interest rates are restored to r^*. For a small open economy with a pegged exchange rate, monetary policy is powerless.

Picture: The €1 coin
© Jenny Zhou | Dreamstime.com

A fiscal expansion shifts IS to IS'. There is a big short-run effect on output, from Y to Y', since interest rates cannot rise to dampen the expansion. Monetary policy is forced to create additional money supply to accommodate the extra money demand when output rises. We can think of the horizontal line for interest rates as being achieved by a shift in the implicit LM schedule from LM to LM'. In fact, we may as well regard the horizontal line as the LM schedule itself.

Y^* is potential output. If a demand shock shifts IS to IS', potential output is not restored by induced changes in interest rates as in a closed economy. Interest rates remain at r^*. Rather, higher prices

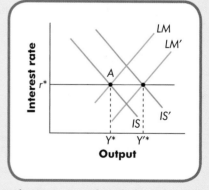

reduce competitiveness and hence shift IS' leftwards. Under a pegged exchange rate, induced changes in IS schedules restore output to full capacity. If this takes too long, fiscal policy must shift IS' back to IS.

---

1   During the boom, the current account surplus adds to foreign assets, which may therefore be a little higher in the new equilibrium than in the original equilibrium. If so, restoring current account balance does not quite restore the original level of the trade balance. For internal balance, potential output equals domestic absorption plus net exports. If net exports have changed a little, so has domestic absorption. Such details belong in a more advanced course. The basic adjustment mechanism remains as described in the text.

So far we have shown that an open economy *can* return to internal and external balance under a fixed exchange rate, without assistance from interest rates. Otherwise, monetary union (a permanently fixed exchange rate between member states) would be a non-starter!

However, the speed with which internal and external balance are restored depends a lot on the flexibility of wages and prices. The faster inflation adjusts, the faster the real exchange rate changes and the less a recession is needed to accomplish the required change in competitiveness.

The founding fathers of the eurozone understood that their monetary union would be more successful if their member states had flexible labour markets, so that domestic wage and price adjustment could act as a substitute for exchange rate changes. There was always a tension between the political desire to include the Club Med countries (Portugal, Italy, Greece and Spain) and the economic concern that their labour markets might find it hard to adjust in a crisis.

Can domestic adjustment be assisted by monetary and fiscal policy?

 ## 25.2 Macroeconomic policy under fixed exchange rates

Monetary policy

Interest rates are dedicated to defending the exchange rate when capital mobility is perfect. The higher is capital mobility, the less is the scope for an independent domestic monetary policy.

Since it would be nice to be able to use monetary policy too, countries sometimes try to reduce the degree of capital mobility. Outlawing capital flows is unlikely to work. Smart bankers find fancy ways to do the same transactions through other means that as yet are unrestricted. Capital controls go against the general trend of financial integration. If monetary policy cannot speed adjustment back to long-run equilibrium, can fiscal policy do better?

Fiscal policy

A fixed exchange rate, plus perfect capital mobility, undermines the scope for monetary policy, but enhances the effectiveness of fiscal policy.

In a closed economy, in the short run a fiscal expansion raises output. The central bank responds by raising interest rates, thus moderating the output increase. In an open economy, monetary policy adjusts passively to keep the interest rate fixed in order to defend the pegged exchange rate. With a constant interest rate, the fiscal expansion no longer crowds out other components of aggregate demand via higher interest rates. Hence, fiscal policy is more powerful under fixed exchange rates than in a closed economy.

Hence, any fall in domestic demand can be offset by a fiscal expansion to help restore internal balance more quickly. If the change in domestic demand was the only reason that the current account departed from external balance, this fiscal expansion will also restore external balance.

Fiscal policy is potentially an important policy weapon under fixed exchange rates. It helps compensate for the fact that monetary policy can no longer be used. Automatic fiscal stabilizers play this role. Discretionary changes in government spending and tax rates are possible only if fiscal policy can respond quickly to temporary shocks. In some political systems, such as in the UK, this is feasible. In others, such as in the US, in which Congress and president may be from different political parties, rapid changes in fiscal policy are harder.

Having analysed the economy with a *given* exchange rate, we now analyse changes in the pegged exchange rate.

25.3 Devaluation

Even where exchange rates are pegged at fixed values, occasional adjustments in these **par values** sometimes occur.

During three decades after 1945 the major countries agreed to fix their exchange rates, with occasional adjustments or realignments of these par values. Sterling was devalued in 1949 and 1967, before finally floating in 1973. The general idea was to keep exchange rates fixed for long periods if possible. We discuss exchange rate regimes more fully in Chapter 29.

Here, we assess the effects of a **devaluation**. A devaluation of sterling against the dollar is of course a revaluation of the dollar against sterling.

> The **par value** is the exchange rate that the government agrees to defend.
>
> A **devaluation (revaluation)** reduces (increases) the par value of the pegged exchange rate.

We distinguish between effects in the short, medium and long run. Initially, we assume that the domestic country begins from internal and external balance. This lets us highlight the effect of the devaluation itself. Then we consider whether devaluation is an appropriate policy response to a shock that has already moved the economy from its long-run equilibrium position.

The short run

When prices and wages adjust slowly, the immediate effect of a devaluation is to reduce the real exchange rate, thus improving the country's competitiveness. Resources are drawn into domestic industries that compete with imports and into export industries that compete in foreign markets.

Although devaluation tends to raise the quantity of net exports $(X - Z)$, the initial response may be slow. Overnight, there are contracts outstanding that were struck at the old exchange rate. It also takes time for buyers to adjust to the new prices they face and for sellers to build up production capacity to supply more.

Hence, in the very short run, devaluation may not improve the trade balance – the value of exports minus imports. Suppose we measure the current account in pounds. If domestic prices of export goods are unchanged and the quantity of exports has yet to rise much, export revenues rise only a little in the short run. Import quantities have not yet fallen much. If their foreign prices are unchanged, their price in pounds rises by the amount of the devaluation. Hence, the value of imports in pounds may rise substantially. In *value* terms, the current account initially gets worse.[2] However, in the longer run, as quantities adjust, higher export quantities and lower import quantities improve the trade balance.[3]

The medium run

Domestic output Y equals aggregate demand, which is domestic absorption $(C + I + G)$ plus net exports $(X - Z)$. Once quantities begin to adjust, devaluation increases net export demand $(X - Z)$. What happens next depends crucially on aggregate supply.

An economy with Keynesian unemployment has spare resources with which to make extra goods to meet this rise in aggregate demand. But if the economy begins at potential output, it cannot produce many more goods. Higher aggregate demand bids up prices and wages. Competitiveness falls, undoing the gain in

---

2 The famous Marshall–Lerner condition says that devaluation improves the trade balance only if the sum of the price elasticities of demand for imports and exports is more negative than –1. Recall from Chapter 4 that, when demand is elastic, the revenue effect of changes in quantity more than offsets the effect of a change in price. In the short run, when demand is inelastic, devaluation may worsen the current account.

3 Thus a devaluation first worsens then improves the trade balance, a response known as the *J-curve*. As time elapses after the devaluation, the trade balance falls down to the bottom of the *J* but then rises above its initial position.

competitiveness achieved by devaluation. When domestic prices and wages have risen as much as the exchange rate was initially devalued, the real exchange rate and competitiveness return to their original levels. If the economy began from internal and external balance, long-run equilibrium is now restored.

If devaluation is meant to raise net exports for a sustained period, for example to raise more money to service foreign debts, this is compatible with internal balance $[Y^* = (C + I + G) + (X - Z)]$ only if domestic absorption $(C + I + G)$ is permanently cut, for example by tightening fiscal policy.

Thus, beginning at full employment, devaluation *accompanied* by higher taxes will raise the demand for net exports without increasing total aggregate demand. Since there is no upward pressure on domestic prices, higher competitiveness can be sustained in the medium run.

The long run

Can altering the *nominal* exchange rate permanently change the value of *real* variables? Suppose devaluation is accompanied by tighter fiscal policy to allow the economy to meet the higher demand for net exports without any direct upward pressure on prices. Although this takes care of demand-side effects on prices, we must also think about supply-side effects.

Domestic firms importing raw materials want to pass on these cost increases in higher prices. Workers buying imported TVs realize that import prices are higher and demand higher nominal wages to maintain their real wages. These price and wage rises lead other firms and other workers to react in similar fashion.

In the absence of any real change in the economy, the eventual effect of a devaluation is a rise in all other nominal wages and prices in line with the higher import prices, leaving all real variables unchanged. Eventually, devaluation has no real effect. Most empirical evidence suggests that the effect of a devaluation is completely offset by a rise in domestic prices and wages after four or five years.

Figure 25.4 summarizes this discussion. A once-off nominal devaluation leads to an instant real devaluation that is gradually unwound again; to a rise in output that is gradually unwound as the real exchange rate stimulus wears off; and to a complicated response in the current account balance in value terms. Initially, the devaluation is effectively a price cut – until quantities can respond, making exports cheaper actually harms export revenue. In the medium run, the induced quantity rise in exports benefits the current account in value terms, provided quantities respond sufficiently to price incentives. Eventually, since the real exchange rate is restored to its original level, so is the current account.

In September 1992 sterling left the Exchange Rate Mechanism and quickly fell about 15 per cent against other currencies. The UK also had big devaluations in 1949 and 1967. Table 25.1 shows the effect of the sterling devaluation by 15 per cent in 1967. It took two years for the current account to move from deficit into surplus. Devaluation did not improve the current account until quantities of imports and exports had time to respond.

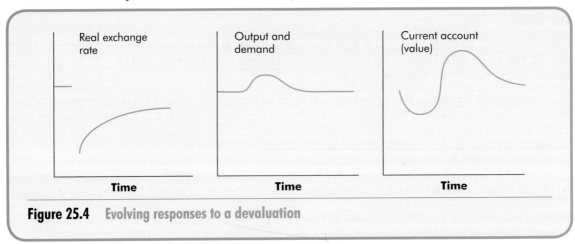

Figure 25.4   Evolving responses to a devaluation

Table 25.1 The 1967 sterling devaluation

	1967	1968	1969	1970
Current account (£bn)	−0.3	−0.2	0.5	0.8
Public sector deficit (% of GDP)	5.3	3.4	−1.2	0
Nominal exchange rate: $/£	2.8	2.4	2.4	2.4
Real exchange rate (1975 = 100)	109	102	102	103

Source: ONS, Economic Trends.

The public sector deficit as a percentage of GDP shows fiscal policy. In 1967 UK unemployment was low. The economy had few spare resources with which to produce extra goods for export or for import substitution. In 1969 fiscal policy was tightened substantially, reducing domestic absorption and allowing an improvement in net exports. The government (*including* the nationalized industries) actually ran a budget surplus in 1969.

The final row of Table 25.1 shows the real exchange rate, the relative price of UK goods to foreign goods when measured in a common currency. Note two things. First, instead of using the 15 per cent devaluation to cut export prices in foreign markets, UK exporters responded in part by raising prices and profit margins. Only half the competitive advantage was passed on to foreign purchasers as lower foreign prices for UK goods. Second, even by 1970, competitiveness was falling again. Domestic wages rose as workers asked for wage increases to meet higher import prices. By 1970, the real exchange rate had begun to rise.

Devaluation and adjustment

To sum up, once quantities begin adjusting, devaluation leads to a temporary but not a permanent rise in competitiveness relative to the path that would have occurred without the devaluation. In the long run, real variables are determined by real forces. Changes in one nominal variable eventually induce offsetting changes in other nominal variables to restore real variables to their equilibrium values.

But devaluation may be the simplest way to change competitiveness *quickly*. It is a useful policy when the alternative adjustment mechanism is a domestic slump and a protracted period of lower inflation until competitiveness is increased.

Suppose there is a permanent fall in export demand. At the original exchange rate, this generates a slump that induces a period of lower inflation, which reduces wages and prices enough to boost competitiveness and restore current account balance. But this takes several years. Devaluation accomplishes an overnight improvement in competitiveness. It speeds up adjustment.

Devaluation may therefore be an appropriate response to a real shock that requires a change in the equilibrium real exchange rate. Conversely, where no real change is required, devaluation eventually generates rises in prices and nominal wages. Chapter 22 discussed inflation expectations and credibility.

Economies can get locked into self-fulfilling prophecies of high inflation. In such circumstances, maintaining a constant real exchange rate requires a steady reduction in the nominal exchange rate. One way to accomplish this is by regular devaluations.

Devaluation has a bad name because it is often associated with periods of high inflation and weak government. This is correct. However, even well-designed macroeconomic policy might choose occasionally to realign the nominal exchange rate. The appropriate circumstance would be a large and sustained shock to the trade balance.

25.4 Floating exchange rates

With floating exchange rates, monetary sovereignty is restored even under perfect capital mobility. The central bank sets the interest rate and accepts the exchange rate determined by market forces.

Having discussed fixed exchange rates, we now turn to the opposite case, freely floating exchange rates. The foreign exchange reserves remain constant, the balance of payments is zero and the government refrains from any intervention in the forex market. In this section we explain how the level of the exchange rate is determined in the short run. The next section uses this analysis to study monetary and fiscal policy in an open economy with floating exchange rates.

The long run

In long-run equilibrium the economy is at both internal and external balance. Chapter 24 analysed determinants of the real exchange rate in long-run equilibrium. Given that output is at potential output, this real exchange rate must achieve current account balance. Anything that tends to create a current account surplus (a resource discovery, a new export industry, income from foreign assets) induces a real exchange rate appreciation to reduce competitiveness. This reduces net exports until external balance is restored.[4]

When exchange rates float freely, there is no official intervention in the forex market and no net monetary transfer between countries since the balance of payments is always zero. Just as in a closed economy, the central bank controls the domestic money supply or sets it to achieve the interest rate it wishes.

The monetary rule, and associated nominal anchor, then determines the domestic price level as explained in Chapter 22. For example, we can think of inflation targeting as pursuing a target path for the price level. In the long run, a Taylor rule has the same result since interest rates are adjusted until output is restored to potential output and inflation is restored to target inflation.

With perfect capital mobility, the central bank can use interest rates to peg the exchange rate, thereby giving up the independent use of interest rates to manipulate the domestic economy, or can set interest rates to manipulate the domestic economy but must then accept the level to which the exchange rate floats.

Our theory of floating exchange rates in the long run is thus easily summarized. Real forces determine the long-run equilibrium *real* exchange rate necessary for external balance. Domestic, sovereign, monetary policy determines the path of the domestic price level. Given the path of foreign prices, there is then only one path of the *nominal* exchange rate that achieves the appropriate real exchange rate in the long run.

If domestic and foreign monetary policies generate the same inflation rates, a constant real exchange rate in the long run is compatible with a constant nominal exchange rate in the long run. However, if domestic and foreign inflation rates differ permanently, the nominal exchange rate must change steadily to keep the real exchange rate at its equilibrium level.

Two examples may help reinforce this argument. Suppose first that there is no inflation anywhere. A once-and-for-all change in domestic monetary policy leads to a doubling of the domestic price level. Thereafter prices are constant. To maintain the real exchange rate, there is a once-and-for-all depreciation of the nominal exchange rate by 50 per cent, say from $2/£ to $1/£.

Although domestic prices have doubled, the dollar price of UK exports is unaffected in the long run. A £10 shirt used to sell for $20 at an exchange rate of $2/£. Now it costs £20 to make the shirt but it still sells for $20 since the exchange rate is now $1/£. Similarly, a US baseball bat costing $40 used to sell for £20 in the

---

4   Economists usually use devaluation (revaluation) to describe discrete falls (rises) in pegged exchange rates, but depreciation (appreciation) to describe falls (rises) in floating exchange rates.

UK. After the exchange rate falls to $1/£, it still costs $40 to make but now sells for £40 in the UK. The price of UK imports doubles because the exchange rate falls by 50 per cent. Import prices rise in line with domestic prices in the UK. Whether we compare the relative price of UK and US goods in dollars or in pounds, their relative price is unaltered. Competitiveness does not change.

How about continuous inflation? Suppose US inflation is zero but annual UK inflation is permanently 10 per cent. A steady depreciation of the $/£ exchange rate, by 10 per cent a year, leaves the real exchange rate and competitiveness constant. The dollar price of UK goods is constant, like US prices, and the pound price of imports from the US rises annually at 10 per cent, just like UK goods.

Hence, in the long run, floating exchange rates adjust to achieve the unique real exchange rate compatible with internal and external balance. Knowing monetary policy and the price level, we know the required path for the nominal exchange rate. In the absence of real shocks, the nominal exchange rate follows the PPP path to achieve the equilibrium real exchange rate. Any real shocks that are not accommodated by changes in monetary policy and the price level will eventually induce changes in the nominal exchange rate to achieve the required change in the real exchange rate.

> **Purchasing power parity (PPP)** is the path of the nominal exchange rate that offsets differential inflation rates across countries, maintaining a constant real exchange rate.

However, in the short run, the real exchange rate can fluctuate a lot. The stock of internationally mobile funds is now vast. If those funds were all to move in a short period, say an hour, between two currencies, this massive flow on the financial account could not possibly be offset by the small net flows that occur on the current account during that hour. Under freely floating exchange rates there is no government intervention and no official financing. The forex market could not clear.

But clear it does, hour by hour, and indeed minute by minute. Short-run equilibrium in the forex market is achieved because the exchange rate is capable of jumping at any instant to the level necessary to *prevent* one-way capital flows of large magnitude. To examine this process in more detail, we need to think more about capital flows.

The short run

When international capital mobility is perfect, interest parity must hold. If assets in different currencies offer different expected returns, there will be massive one-way traffic in capital flows, which is inconsistent with forex market equilibrium. Hence, expected returns are equated to *prevent* massive one-way capital flows.

Expected returns include capital gains and losses as exchange rates change while foreign assets are held temporarily. The current level of the exchange rate affects this capital gain between now and the next period. Hence floating exchange rates can always be set at a level that makes expected capital gains just offset interest rate differentials across currencies, for example between UK bonds in sterling and US bonds in dollars, as interest parity requires.

Suppose UK interest rates are 2 per cent higher than US interest rates. Why do holders of funds not move all their funds into sterling? If speculators expect the pound to depreciate by 2 per cent a year against the dollar, investors in pounds get 2 per cent extra interest but lose 2 per cent a year on the exchange rate, relative to the alternative strategy of lending in dollars. The extra interest just compensates for the expected loss and most speculators will not mind where they hold their funds. Without massive flows between currencies, the forex market can be in equilibrium.

What happens if UK interest rates rise and are now 4 per cent above US interest rates? If people still think that the UK exchange rate will fall at 2 per cent a year, the extra UK interest rate more than compensates for capital losses on sterling. Everyone tries to move into pounds. Almost instantly, this bids up the $/£ exchange rate. By how much? Until it reaches such a high level that people expect the pound then to fall by 4 per cent a year thereafter. Only then are the capital losses expected on funds lent in pounds sufficient to offset the 4 per cent interest differential. This restores interest parity and ends one-way traffic.

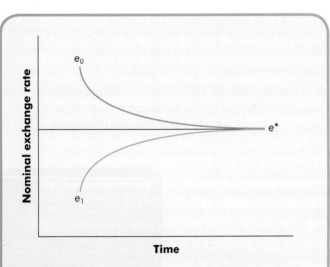

Suppose e* is the equilibrium nominal exchange rate in the long run. To be constant, this requires that there is no inflation differential across countries. The Fisher hypothesis then means that interest differentials are also eliminated eventually. For a country with temporarily high interest rates, the exchange rate begins at e_0 and moves along e_0e^*. For a country with temporarily low interest rates, the exchange rate begins at e_1 and moves along e_1e^*. In either case, expected exchange rate changes offset interest differentials.

Figure 25.5 Floating exchange rates

Why does a higher value of the pound today make people expect the UK exchange rate to fall in the future? Because smart speculators figure out that eventually the exchange rate has to return to the level that achieves external balance long-run equilibrium. With the end point anchored, a higher initial value means a faster rate of subsequent fall.

Figure 25.5 sums up our theory of floating exchange rate determination. For simplicity, suppose domestic and foreign monetary policies generate similar eventual inflation rates. The constant equilibrium real exchange rate in the long run then implies a constant nominal exchange rate e^* to achieve external balance. In the short run the nominal exchange rate can depart a lot from e^* and can change rapidly.

A country with high (low) interest rates in the short run must have a currency expected to depreciate (appreciate) if it is not to generate one-way capital flows in or out of the currency. Figure 25.5 shows two possible paths for the nominal exchange rate. If interest rates are expected to be high by world standards, the exchange rate begins at e_0 and depreciates steadily until long-run equilibrium is reached at e^*.

At every point along e_0e^*, the slope of this schedule reflects the interest differential, and the capital loss is just offsetting the interest differential.

> **Floating exchange rates are volatile** because they are asset prices that reflect beliefs about the entire future. Such beliefs can change a lot.

In the long run, the nominal exchange rate can be constant only if the interest rate differential is eliminated. Recall from Chapter 22 the Fisher hypothesis which says that nominal interest rates largely adjust in line with inflation, since real interest rates are fairly constant. Figure 25.5 assumes the inflation differential is eventually zero, so that the nominal exchange rate can be constant. This is quite consistent with assuming that eventually monetary policies converge and the interest rate differential disappears.[5]

Conversely, if a country is expected to have abnormally low interest rates for a while, its exchange rate will begin at e_1 in Figure 25.5. The foreseen exchange rate appreciation along e_1e^* provides expected capital gains on the exchange rate to compensate for the low interest rate on sterling-denominated assets.

From time to time, financial markets change their view about the likely future path the economy will follow. This can lead to a dramatic reassessment of the current exchange rate needed to prevent massive capital flows.

Suppose financial markets revise their expectations about the future of interest differentials. Formerly, they believed a country would have high interest rates for a while; now they believe that interest rates will be low by world standards. In terms of Figure 25.5, the appropriate path switches from e_0e^* to e_1e^* and the initial exchange rate therefore jumps from e_0 to e_1.

> **When new information becomes available, asset prices jump** to the level that now properly reflects the new information.

Any jump in an asset price is unexpected. If people had expected the exchange rate to jump from e_0 to e_1, they would already have moved out of sterling assets. People holding an asset when its **price jumps** up or down are either lucky or unlucky.

---

5 A different assumption about monetary policy would imply a permanently changing nominal exchange rate.

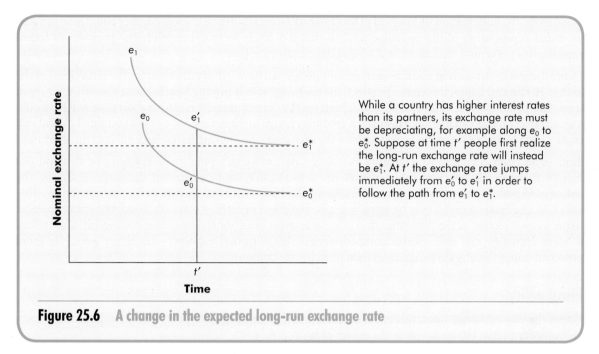

Figure 25.6   A change in the expected long-run exchange rate

While a country has higher interest rates than its partners, its exchange rate must be depreciating, for example along e_0 to e_0^*. Suppose at time t' people first realize the long-run exchange rate will instead be e_1^*. At t' the exchange rate jumps immediately from e_0' to e_1' in order to follow the path from e_1' to e_1^*.

One reason exchange rates may jump is because of new information about the future of interest rates. Another reason is because of new information about the long-run equilibrium exchange rate. Figure 25.6 shows a country with temporarily high interest rates that was initially expected to have a long-run equilibrium exchange rate e_0^*. Its exchange rate was expected to move along $e_0 e_0^*$ as time elapsed.

At time t' the financial markets get information that the long-run equilibrium exchange rate will in fact be e_1^*. Had they known this all along, the exchange rate would have begun at e_1 and moved along $e_1 e_1^*$. When this is first realized at time t_1, the forex market immediately jumps the exchange rate to e_1' so that the exchange rate is appropriate from now on.

Along the path $e_1' e_1^*$ the expected capital loss on the exchange rate continues to offset the interest differential. And the path is expected to end up in the right place; namely at the long-run equilibrium exchange rate.

25.5   Monetary and fiscal policy under floating exchange rates

In a closed economy with slow wage and price adjustment, changes in monetary and fiscal policy have real effects in the short run, although the economy eventually returns to internal balance. In an open economy with fixed exchange rates, almost perfect capital mobility makes monetary policy almost powerless in the short run; however, the power of fiscal policy is enhanced since fiscal expansion no longer bids up interest rates. Under floating exchange rates the converse is true: monetary policy is powerful in the short run, but the effectiveness of fiscal policy is reduced.

Monetary policy

Figure 25.5 has already displayed the power of monetary policy to affect the real economy in the short run under floating exchange rates. Given the exchange rate expected in the long run, the anticipation of higher interest rates in the short to medium run causes an immediate appreciation of the exchange rate so it is then likely to fall thereafter. Anticipated capital losses from now on are what choke off the capital inflow that high interest rates would otherwise cause.

Conversely, the anticipation of a period of low interest rates (relative to trading partner countries) induces an initial depreciation of the exchange rate, so that it is likely to rise thereafter. The prospect of future capital gains prevents a capital outflow when interest rates are low.

Hence, beliefs about current and future monetary policy can have a dramatic effect on the initial level of the exchange rate and competitiveness. In effect, the exchange rate is pricing beliefs about the entire future of monetary policy, both at home and abroad. Changing the current interest rate for a short time will have only a small effect on this calculation. However, a credible change in monetary policy for a sustained period will cause a large re-evaluation of the correct path for the exchange rate. This can have a large effect in the short run.

Thus in an open economy with floating exchange rates, monetary policy affects aggregate demand not merely through the effect of interest rates on consumption and investment demand. Changing the anticipated path of interest rates can have a large effect on the exchange rate and competitiveness. This effect on aggregate demand may be large. Because the effect of interest rates on competitiveness operates in the same direction as the domestic effect – lower interest rates boost domestic spending, but also induce a lower exchange rate and greater competitiveness, boosting net exports – monetary policy is more powerful under floating exchange rates than in a closed economy.

Fiscal policy

Under floating exchange rates, this effect of interest rate changes on competitiveness *reinforces* the power of monetary policy, but *undermines* the power of fiscal policy.

Suppose the government undertakes a fiscal expansion, raising government spending. This increases aggregate demand. Whether monetary policy follows an inflation target, a Taylor rule or a nominal money target, the boom induces the central bank to raise interest rates. The higher interest rate induces an immediate appreciation of the nominal exchange rate to choke off a capital inflow: if the exchange rate is high enough, people will believe it will fall from now on.

In a closed economy, higher interest rates partially crowd out private expenditure by reducing consumption and investment demand. But in an open economy with floating exchange rates, the induced exchange rate appreciation also reduces competitiveness and the demand for net exports, further dampening the power of fiscal expansion to stimulate aggregate demand in the short run.

ACTIVITY 25.1

A 30-year look at sterling

The figure on the right shows the nominal and real sterling exchange rates since 1980. We show the nominal effective exchange rate (eer) against a basket of the currencies most important for the UK's international trade, weighted by their importance in UK trade. We also show the real effective exchange rate (rer), adjusting the nominal exchange rate for movements of relative prices at home and abroad (using the same weights as used to construct the nominal effective exchange rate).

Notice the high correlation between movements in the nominal exchange rate and real exchange rate. In the short run, most changes in the real exchange rate are caused by changes in the nominal exchange rate, not by changes in domestic and foreign prices.

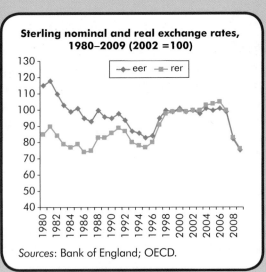

Sterling nominal and real exchange rates, 1980–2009 (2002 =100)

Sources: Bank of England; OECD.

The nominal exchange rate is more volatile than the price of goods or the price of labour. This correlation got much stronger after the mid-1990s, when all the major countries adopted inflation targeting with similar inflation targets, largely eliminating differential price trends as sources of real exchange rate movements. We can use this figure to discuss UK exchange rate behaviour during the last 30 years.

In 1980 a tight monetary policy had been introduced to fight inflation. The prospect of high interest rates for some time had led to a sharp appreciation in the nominal exchange rate, precisely so that it fell thereafter, thus generating expected capital losses on holding sterling that would offset the high UK interest rates and prevent a one-way flow of financial capital into the UK. At the same time, the UK had found oil and the rise in oil prices made this oil more valuable. Figure 25.3 showed that a substantial resource discovery raises the equilibrium exchange rate in the long run. In anticipation of this, capital inflows begin immediately. Hence the exchange rate appreciates as soon as the discovery is made.

Together, tight money and North Sea oil explain why the real value of sterling was high in 1980. Competitiveness was therefore low and exports of non-oil products, particularly manufactured goods, were badly hit. After 1981, competitiveness improved for a while as the real exchange rate depreciated. By 1988 the real exchange rate index had depreciated by about 12 per cent, from 85 to 75.

By the late 1980s, Chancellor of the Exchequer Nigel Lawson was 'shadowing' the monetary policy of the likely eurozone countries, partly to see if the UK would be suitable as a potential eurozone member. As it happened, German interest rates were quite low at the time; too low for what was good for the UK. The ensuing boom caused the UK economy to overheat. As inflation took off again, the UK was forced to raise interest rates sharply in the late 1980s. As you would expect, the figure shows that this induced a new exchange rate appreciation, of both nominal and real exchange rates, after 1987.

In 1990 the UK joined the Exchange Rate Mechanism – the prelude to the eurozone – and pegged its nominal exchange rate to other EU countries.* To sustain the peg, the UK had to match interest rates in other ERM countries. The timing was lousy. 1990 was the year of German reunification. Soon Germany was giving big budget subsidies to support East Germans until their productivity caught up to West German levels. Given this fiscal expansion in Germany, it took very high interest rates in the ERM to restrain inflation in Germany.

Like many other ERM members, the UK was crippled trying to match these huge interest rates that were fine medicine for Germany but not for its partners. By 1992 the UK problem was no longer overheating but a deepening recession caused by very tight monetary policy. Since most of the UK's trade partners also had high interest rates, the pound did not appreciate much during 1990–92.

In September 1992 the UK left the ERM, floated the exchange rate, and announced that it was cutting interest rates to end recession. The figure shows the consequent and substantial depreciation of nominal and real UK exchange rates in late 1992. Unlike the UK, most ERM members stayed in the system and staggered on under high interest rates for several years more.

Greater competitiveness gave the UK an export boom during 1993–95 that helped pull it out of recession. However, the figure shows that by 1997 the real exchange rate was back above its level of 1992 when the UK had left the ERM. Sterling continued to appreciate thereafter. Most EU countries were now tightening fiscal policy to meet the Maastricht criteria for monetary union. With tighter fiscal policy, their monetary policy no longer had to be so tight. As their exchange rates depreciated, the pound appreciated.

In addition, Labour looked likely to be the party of government for several years to come. Independence for the Bank of England guaranteed that interest rates would rise if required to keep inflation under control. Despite the Code for Fiscal Stability and the Chancellor's emphasis on prudence, financial markets were

⏵ never convinced about Labour's commitment to tight fiscal policy. Markets were already wondering when higher future interest rates woud become necessary.

UK exchange rates are not of course the result only of UK policy. In particular, the data in the figure also reflect a major weakening of the US dollar after 2000: a low dollar means a high pound and a high euro. Global investors woke up to the fact that the US had been living beyond its means. It took a depreciation of the dollar to begin to restore US competitiveness. One side effect was the rise in the pound.

Although the government continued to describe the UK economy as sustainable – 'you've never had it so prudent' – the figure shows just how much sterling had appreciated in real terms before the financial crash of 2007–09. This helps explain why the UK current account was in substantial deficit – financial services apart, most of the UK economy had become quite uncompetitive at the high real exchange rate, which could be sustained only as long as global investors remained happy to pile into London, creating capital inflows on the financial account to offset the current account deficit.

The financial crisis pricked international confidence in the UK economy, which was unusually exposed to the financial sector. As capital inflows abated, it became evident that a lower real exchange rate was needed in order to boost the international competitiveness of other sectors of the UK economy. The ensuing real depreciation, by over 25 per cent, is the largest change in competitiveness experienced by the UK economy during the last 30 years.

What should we expect its effect to be? First, increased competitiveness will have a significant effect on the trade balance – higher exports and lower imports – but this will take one to two years to feed through. Depreciation takes time to affect behaviour. The size of this stimulus will also depend on the growth rate of UK export markets. If export markets are weak, competitors may cut prices to defend their market share, thus reducing the impact of the exchange rate change; if export markets are strong, the stimulus is likely to be larger and be experienced more quickly. In this context, it is helpful to the UK that China and India are booming again, but very unhelpful that its largest trading partner, the eurozone, is still stagnating.

Since, following the reduction in aggregate demand, the UK has spare capacity, there is little danger of an increase in exports crowding out other categories of aggregate demand.

To the extent that higher competitivness implies output and income are higher than they would otherwise have been, tax revenue will also be higher than it would otherwise have been. Thus, following the financial crash and considerable increase in government indebtedness, the real depreciation of sterling is welcome from a fiscal viewpoint as well as an employment viewpoint.

* A different assumption about monetary policy would imply a permanently changing nominal exchange rate.

Questions

(a) Why are there considerable differences between the evolution of nominal and real exchange rates before 1996 but such a close correlation thereafter?

(b) The real exchange rate was systematically and substantially higher during 1998–2006 than at any other time. If markets had concluded that a higher sterling real exchange rate was permanently sustainable, what underlying factors could have led to such a conclusion?

(c) Suppose the UK had been a member of the eurozone after 2000. How would the response of the UK economy to the financial crisis have differed? Would the UK have experienced more or fewer problems? What would have been the alternative to an exchange rate depreciation?

To check your answers to these questions, go to page 687.

Summary

- With a **fixed exchange rate** and **perfect capital mobility**, the domestic interest rate must match foreign interest rates to prevent massive capital flows and allow equilibrium in the forex market. **Monetary sovereignty is then lost.** Monetary policy cannot be used independently to control the domestic economy.

- A **fall in domestic demand** causes a fall in output and a decline in prices. Unlike a closed economy, monetary policy cannot respond by cutting interest rates. Rather, the fall in prices boosts competitiveness and raises aggregate demand. When internal balance is restored, there is now a current account surplus. This generates greater wealth, thus raising domestic demand again. After a temporary boom to raise prices and reduce excess competitiveness, internal and external balance can be restored.

- A **fall in export demand** generates a slump, lower prices and higher competitiveness that restores internal and external balance. No subsequent boom is then required.

- In the short run, fiscal policy is a powerful tool under fixed exchange rates. Fiscal expansion no longer bids up domestic interest rates in the short run. Output expansion is accompanied by a rise in the money supply to maintain interest rates at the world level.

- A **devaluation** is a fall in the value of the fixed exchange rate. With sluggish price adjustment, it raises competitiveness and aggregate demand. With spare resources, output rises. But at potential output, net exports can rise only if domestic absorption is cut by tighter fiscal policy.

- In the long run, devaluation is unlikely to have much effect. Changing one nominal variable merely leads to offsetting changes in other nominal variables. In passing on higher import prices and seeking cost-of-living wage increases, firms and workers offset the competitive advantage of devaluation. But devaluation may speed up adjustment to a shock that requires a permanent change in competitiveness to restore internal and external balance.

- Under **floating exchange rates**, the long-run level of the nominal exchange rate achieves external balance, given prices at home and abroad. In the short run, the exchange rate adjusts to prevent massive flows on the capital account.

- The exchange rate must begin at a level from which the anticipated convergent path to its long-run equilibrium continuously provides capital gains or losses to offset expected interest rate differentials, thus equating the expected return on lending at home and abroad.

- Under floating exchange rates, monetary policy is a powerful short-term tool. The belief that interest rates will be higher for some time induces a sharp appreciation of the exchange rate, so that it can then credibly promise capital losses to offset high interest rates. With sluggish price adjustment, the initial appreciation of the nominal exchange rate causes a sharp fall in competitiveness. This reduction in demand for net exports reinforces other effects of high interest rates in reducing aggregate demand.

- Fiscal policy is a weaker tool under floating exchange rates. Fiscal expansion induces a boom and higher interest rates. The latter induce an exchange rate appreciation that crowds out some net exports, reinforcing domestic crowding out of consumption and investment.

- The actual path of the UK nominal exchange rate reflects changing beliefs about the future course of domestic and foreign interest rates, and about the eventual level of the exchange rate in long-run equilibrium. The latter depends on beliefs about the eventual price level at home and abroad, but also on supply shocks such as resource discoveries.

Review questions   connect

1 Rank the following three situations according to the ability of monetary policy to affect real output in the short run: (a) a closed economy; (b) an open economy with fixed exchange rates; (c) an open economy with floating exchange rates. Explain.

2 Beginning at internal and external balance, an economy devalues its fixed exchange rate. (a) What happens to its interest rate? (b) What happens to output? (c) What happens to inflation? (d) How are internal and external balance restored?

3 Suppose in Question 2 that the nominal exchange rate is devalued by 30 per cent. (a) What is the eventual change in the price level? In nominal wages? In the nominal money supply? (b) What is the nominal anchor in this economy?

4 A country faces a permanent fall in export demand. Would devaluation help? How else might internal and external balance be restored.

5 A country discovers a new technology that will add significantly to its export capacity in five years' time. (a) What must happen to its real exchange rate in the long run? (b) Why does the exchange rate react immediately to the news rather than wait until the new export supply comes on stream?

6 Common fallacies   Why are these statements wrong? (a) Collectively, global speculators have more money than central banks. Hence, central banks can no longer defend fixed exchange rates. (b) Floating exchange rates are volatile because imports and exports fluctuate a lot. (c) Exchange rate policy is really monetary policy, so it makes no difference to the impact of fiscal policy.

7 Which is correct? Devaluation is most effective: (a) when a country has a small export and import sector, since higher import prices then have little effect; (b) when domestic wages and prices are very flexible; (c) when nominal wages and prices are slow to change; or (d) when the country is already at potential output.

8 Manchester has a local government but a fixed exchange rate with the rest of the UK. How powerful are the monetary and fiscal policies of the local government in Manchester?

9 Because of the strength of long-run Asian demand for its mineral exports, markets conclude that the Australian real exchange rate will have to be permanently higher. Since Asia also emerged from recession more quickly than Europe and the US, Australian monetary policy is already much tighter. Draw a diagram showing the likely evolution over time of the exchange rate of the Australian dollar against sterling.

10 Suppose Australia now discovers vast new mineral deposits that will take five years to begin to exploit. What further effect, if any, will this have on the evolution of Australia's exchange rate? Illustrate with a diagram.

11 The following table shows the evolution of an index of the $/£ nominal exchange rate, and the behaviour of prices in each of two countries. In the initial years, monetary policy is very different; in the last three years both countries succeed in achieving inflation targeting at a low level. For simplicity, we assume that the inflation target is zero. (a) Calculate the evolution of the implied real exchange rate, setting the index initially at 100. (b) Graph the nominal and real exchange rates. (c) What happens to the correlation between nominal and real exchange rates once inflation convergence is achieved?

	Different inflation			Inflation convergence		
Period	1	2	3	4	5	6
Nominal $/£ index (period 1 = 100)	100	110	90	80	70	90
UK price index (period 1 = 100)	100	110	120	120	120	120
US price index (period 1= 100)	100	100	90	90	90	90
Real $/£ index (period 1 = 100)						

12 Because of China's sustained export success, many people in the West call for China's fixed exchange rate against the dollar to be revalued or for its currency to be floated in the expectation that it will then appreciate. (a) At its current stage of development, should China be running a deficit or surplus on the financial account of its balance of payments? (b) Given that its trade surplus in 2006 exceeded $170 billion, was China running a balance of payments surplus or deficit? (c) With such large monetary inflows, what was happening to China's foreign exchange reserves? And to the Chinese money supply? Must this be inflationary, or could the demand for money increase just as quickly?

13 'Once the central bank is made independent, with a specified inflation target, the principal role of macroeconomic policy is to determine the real interest rate and hence the exchange rate.' Explain.

14 **Essay question** What do you see as the relative advantages and disadvantages of fixed and floating exchange rates?

HARD

For solutions to these questions contact your lecturer.

Economic growth

Learning Outcomes

By the end of this chapter, you should understand:

1. growth in potential output

2. Malthus' forecast of eventual starvation

3. how technical progress and capital accumulation made the forecast wrong

4. the neoclassical model of economic growth

5. the convergence hypothesis

6. the growth performance of rich and poor countries

7. whether policy can affect growth

8. whether growth must stop to save the environment

During 1870–2009 real GDP grew 11-fold and real income per person more than 5-fold. On average, we are richer than our grandparents, but less rich than our grandchildren will be. Table 26.1 shows that these long-term trends were even more dramatic elsewhere. During 1870–2009 real GDP in Japan rose 100-fold and real income per person 27-fold.

Table 26.1 prompts three questions. What is long-run economic growth? What causes it? And can economic policies affect it? We mainly focus on industrial countries that have grown a lot already.

Economists were always fascinated by the theory of economic growth. In 1798 Thomas Malthus' *First Essay on Population* predicted that output growth would be far outstripped by population growth, causing starvation and an end to population growth – the origin of the notion of economics as the 'dismal science'. Some countries are still stuck in a Malthusian trap; others broke through to sustained growth and prosperity. We examine how they did it.

As Table 26.1 shows, an extra 0.5 per cent on the annual growth rate makes a vast difference to potential output after a few decades. By the end of the 1960s, economists had worked out a theory of economic growth. It yielded many insights but had one central failing. It predicted that government policy made no difference to the long-run growth rate.

Table 26.1 Real GDP and per capita real GDP, 1870–2009

	Real GDP		Per capita real GDP	
	Ratio of 2009 to 1870	Annual growth (%)	Ratio of 2009 to 1870	Annual growth (%)
Japan	98	3.5	27	2.6
US	73	3.4	11	1.8
Australia	52	3.1	4.5	1.2
Sweden	35	2.8	15	2.2
France	16	2.2	10.5	1.9
UK	11	2.0	5.5	1.3

Sources: Maddison, A. (1979) Phases of capitalist development, in R. C. O. Matthews (ed.), *Economic Growth and Resources*, vol. 2, Macmillan; updated from IMF, *International Financial Statistics*.

In the mid-1980s, a simple insight spawned a new approach in which long-run growth is affected by private behaviour and government policy. We briefly explain this new approach to economic growth.

Finally, we consider whether growth is good. Might it be better to grow more slowly? Can the costs of growth outweigh its benefits?

26.1 Economic growth

The growth rate of a variable is its percentage rise per annum. To define economic growth, we must specify both the variable to measure and the period over which to measure it. Table 26.1 uses real GDP. We get similar results using real GNP or national income.

> **Economic growth** is the rate of change of real income or real output.

GDP and GNP measure the total output and total income of an economy. Even so, they are very incomplete measures of *economic* output and income. Moreover, it is hard to account for the introduction of new products. Nor does more GDP guarantee more happiness.

GDP and economic output

GDP measures the net output or value added in an economy by measuring goods and services bought with money. It omits output not bought and sold and therefore unmeasured. Two big omissions are leisure and externalities such as pollution or congestion.

In most industrial countries, average hours of work have fallen at least ten hours a week since 1900. In choosing to work fewer hours, people reveal that the extra leisure is worth at least as much as the extra goods that could have been bought by working longer. When people decide to swap washing machines for extra leisure, recorded GDP falls. GDP understates the true economic output of the economy. Conversely, the output of pollution reduces the net economic welfare that the economy is producing, and ideally should be subtracted from GDP.

Including leisure in GDP would have raised recorded GDP in both 1870 and 2006. Since the value of leisure probably rose less quickly than measured output, which rose 11-fold in the UK and 98-fold in Japan, a more comprehensive output measure might show a slower growth rate.

Conversely, pollution and congestion have increased rapidly. Allowing for them would also reduce true growth rates below the measured growth rates in Table 26.1. A measure of true economic output each year would have to allow for environmental depreciation – everything from the true cost of global warming to the reduction in genetic diversity and the loss of amenities as grasslands are replaced with urban sprawl.

New products

In 1870 people had no TVs, cars or computers. Statisticians do their best to compare the value of real GDP in different years, but new products make it hard to compare across time. We can estimate how much people's real income rises when a new product does an old task more cheaply. The calculation is harder when the new product allows a new activity not previously possible. A small amount of what we think of as inflation probably reflects real price increases justified by better quality or completely new products.

GDP and happiness

Even with an accurate and comprehensive measure of GDP, two problems remain. First, do we care about total GDP or GDP per capita? This depends on the question we wish to ask. Total GDP shows the size of an economy. However, if we care about the welfare of a typical individual in an economy, it is better to look at GDP per capita. Table 26.1 tells us that, although real GDP grew more quickly in Australia than in France or Sweden during 1870–2009, in part this reflected rapid population growth, largely through immigration. Sweden and France had faster growth in GDP per person over the period.

Even so, real GDP per person is an imperfect indicator of the happiness of a typical citizen. When income is shared equally between citizens, a country's per capita real GDP tells us what every person gets. But some countries have very unequal income distributions. A few people earn a lot, and a lot of people earn only a little. Such countries may have fairly high per capita real income but many citizens still live in poverty.

Finally, even when GDP is adjusted to measure leisure, pollution and so on, higher per capita GDP need not lead to greater happiness. Material goods are not everything. But they help. Movements in which people return to 'the simple life' have not had much success. Most of the poorer countries are trying to increase their GDP as quickly as possible.

A recent phenomenon?

Table 26.1 makes a final point. Even an annual growth rate of only 1.3 per cent in per capita GDP led to a 5.5-fold rise in UK per capita real GDP between 1870 and 2009. In 1870 UK per capita income was about £1900 in 2000 prices. If its annual growth rate had always been 1.3 per cent, per capita real income would have been £370 in 1750, £75 in 1630 and £16 in 1510. This is implausible. Hence, it is only in the last 250 years that per capita real income has risen steadily.

In the long run, output fluctuations around potential output are swamped by the growth of potential output itself. If potential output rises 2 per cent a year, it will increase seven-fold in less than a century. To explain growth, we must think about changes in potential output.

26.2 Growth: an overview

For simplicity, we assume that the economy is always at potential output. The **production function** tells us that higher potential output can be traced to more inputs of land, labour, capital and raw materials, or to technical advances that let given inputs make more output.

In the long run, population growth may be affected by per capita output, which affects the number of children people decide to have, and the health care and nutrition people then get. Nevertheless, we simplify by assuming that the rate of population growth is independent of economic factors. Thus we assume that anything that raises output also raises per capita output.

> The **production function** shows the maximum output obtainable from specified quantities of inputs, given the existing technical knowledge.

Capital

Productive capital is the stock of machinery, buildings and inventories with which other inputs combine to make output. For a given labour input, more capital raises output. However, capital depreciates over time. Some new investment is needed just to stop the existing capital stock from shrinking. And with a growing labour force, even more investment is needed if capital per worker is to be maintained. With yet faster investment, capital per worker rises over time, increasing the output each worker can produce. Higher capital per worker is a key means of raising output per worker and per capita income.

Labour

Employment can rise for two reasons. There may be population growth, or a larger fraction of a given population may have jobs. Labour input also depends on hours worked per person. For a given number of workers, more hours worked raises effective labour input, thus raising output.

Weekly hours worked have fallen a lot since 1870. The rise in per capita real output in Table 26.1 does not reflect longer hours. Since 1945, labour input has risen mainly because more women have joined the labour force.

Human capital

Human capital is the skill and knowledge embodied in the minds and hands of workers. Education, training and experience allow workers to make more output. For example, much of Germany's physical capital was devastated during the Second World War but the human capital of its labour force survived. Given these skills, Germany recovered rapidly after 1945. Without this human capital, there would have been no post-war German economic miracle.

Land

Land is especially important in an agricultural economy. If each worker has more land, agricultural output is higher. Land is less important in highly industrialized economies. Hong Kong and Singapore have grown rapidly despite overcrowding and a scarcity of land. Even so, more land would help.

Increases in the supply of land are pretty unimportant to growth. In theory, land is the input whose total supply to the economy is fixed. In practice, the distinction between land and capital is blurred. By applying more fertilizer per acre, the effective quantity of farming land can be increased. With investment in drainage or irrigation, marshes and deserts can be made productive. Dubai built superstar homes, hotels, and even a new airport, on land reclaimed from the sea.

Raw materials

Given the quantity of other inputs, more input of raw materials allows more output. When raw materials are scarce and expensive, workers take time and care not to waste them. With more plentiful raw materials, workers work more quickly.

When a barrel of oil has been extracted from the ground and used to fuel a machine, the world has one less barrel of oil reserves – it is a **depletable resource**. If the world has a finite stock of oil reserves, it will eventually run out of oil, though perhaps not for centuries.

> **Depletable resources** can be used only once.

> **Renewable resources** can be used again if not over-exploited.

In contrast, timber and fish, if harvested in moderation, are replaced by nature and can be used as production inputs for ever – they are **renewable resources**. However, if over-harvested they become extinct. With only a few whales left, whales find it hard to find partners with whom to breed. The stock of whales falls.

Factor contributions and scale economies

The marginal product of a factor is extra output when that input rises by a unit but all other inputs are held constant. Microeconomics tells us that marginal products eventually decline as the input increases. With two workers already on each machine, another worker does little to raise output.

Economies of scale

Instead of increasing an input in isolation, suppose all inputs are doubled together. If output exactly doubles, there are *constant returns to scale*; if output more (less) than doubles, there are *increasing (decreasing) returns to scale*.

Scale economies reinforce growth. Any rise in inputs gets an extra bonus in higher output. There may be engineering reasons for scale economies. Simple mathematics shows that it takes less than twice the steel input to build an oil tanker of twice the capacity. On the other hand, many developing countries regret that their resources are tied up in huge steel mills that are now inefficient. Bigger is not always better. In practice, economists often assume constant returns to scale.

Having discussed the different production inputs, we turn now to the role of technical knowledge.

 26.3 ## Technical knowledge

At any given time, a society has a stock of technical knowledge about ways in which goods can be produced. Some of this knowledge is written down in books and blueprints, but much is reflected in working practices learned by hard experience.

> Technical advances in productivity come through **invention**, the discovery of new knowledge, and **innovation**, the incorporation of new knowledge into actual production techniques.

Invention

Major inventions can lead to spectacular increases in technical knowledge. The wheel, the steam engine and the modern computer are examples. Technical progress in agriculture has also been dramatic. Industrial societies began only when productivity improvements in agriculture freed some of the workforce to produce industrial goods without leaving people short of food. Before then, everyone had to work the land merely to get enough food to survive. The replacement of animal power by machines, the development of fertilizer, drainage and irrigation, and new hybrid seeds, all played a large part in improving agricultural production and enabling economic growth.

Embodiment of knowledge in capital

To introduce new ideas to actual production, innovation often requires investment in new machines. Without investment, bullocks cannot be transformed into tractors even once the know-how for building tractors is available. Major new inventions thus lead to waves of investment and innovation as the ideas are put into practice. The mid-nineteenth century was the age of the train, and mid-twentieth century the age of the car. We are now in the age of the microchip.

Learning by doing

Human capital can matter as much as physical capital. With practice, workers get better at doing a particular job. The most famous example is known as the Horndal effect, after a Swedish steelworks built during 1835–36 and kept in the same condition for the next 15 years. With no change in the plant or the size of the labour force, output per worker-hour nevertheless rose by 2 per cent a year. Eventually, however, as skills become mastered, further productivity increases are harder to attain.

CASE 26.1 Growth and competition

For centuries, per capita income growth was tiny. Most people were close to starvation. Now we take growth for granted. After 1750, industrialization changed everything. Capital and knowledge, accumulated by one generation, were inherited and augmented by the next generation. Why 1750? Partly because mathematical and scientific ideas reached a critical mass, allowing an explosion of practical spin-offs. Yet many pioneers of the industrial revolution were commonsense artisans with little scientific training. Conversely, the ancient Greece of Pythagoras and Archimedes achieved scientific learning but not economic prosperity.

By the start of the fifteenth century, China understood hydraulic engineering, artificial fertilizers and veterinary medicine. It had blast furnaces in 200 BC, 1500 years before Europe. It had paper 1000 years before Europe, and invented printing 400 years before Gutenberg. Yet by 1600 China had been overtaken by Western Europe, and by 1800 had been left far behind.

Economic historians continue to debate the root causes of progress, but three ingredients seem crucial: values, politics and economic institutions. Growth entails a willingness to embrace change. China's rulers liked social order, stability and isolation from foreign ideas: fine attitudes when progress was slow and domestic but a disaster when the world experienced a profusion of new technologies and applications.

Powerful Chinese rulers could enforce bans and block change in their huge empire. Even when individual European rulers tried to do the same, competition between small European states undermined this sovereignty and offered opportunities for growth and change. Economic competition helped separate markets from political control. Rights of merchants led to laws of contract, patent, company law and property. Competition between forms of institution allowed more effective solutions to emerge and evolve. Arbitrary intervention by heads of state was reduced. Opportunities for business, trade, invention and innovation flourished.

The making of Western Europe

Date	Per capita income (1990 prices)	Inventions
1000	400	Watermill
1100	430	Padded horse collar
1200	480	Windmill
1300	510	Compass
1400	600	Blast furnace
1500	660	Gutenberg printing press
1600	780	Telescope
1700	880	Pendulum clock, canals
1800	1280	Steam engine, spinning and weaving machines, cast iron, electric battery
1900	3400	Telegraph, telephone, electric light, wireless
2000	17 400	Steel, cars, planes, computers, nuclear energy

Source: Adapted from *The Economist*, 31 December 1999. © The Economist Newspaper Limited 2010.

Research and development

What determines the amount of invention and innovation? Some new ideas are the product of intellectual curiosity or frustration ('There must be a better way to do this!'). But, like most activities, the output of new ideas depends to a large extent on the resources devoted to looking for them, which in turn depends on the cost of tying up resources in this way and the prospective benefits from success. Some research activities take place in university departments, usually funded at least in part by the government, but a lot of research is privately funded through the money firms devote to research and development (R&D).

The outcome of research is risky. Research workers never know whether or not they will find anything useful. Research is like a risky investment project. The funds are committed before the benefits (if any) start to accrue, but there is one important difference. Suppose you spend a lot of money developing a better mousetrap. When you succeed, everyone copies your new mousetrap: the price is bid down, and you never recoup your initial investment. In such a world, there would be little incentive to undertake R&D.

If the invention becomes widely available, society gets the benefit but the original developer does not: there is an *externality*. Private and social gains do not coincide and the price mechanism does not provide the correct incentives. Society tries to get round this *market failure* in two ways. First, it grants *patents* to private inventors and innovators – legal monopolies for a fixed period of time that allow successful research projects to repay investments in R&D by temporarily charging higher prices than the cost of production alone. Second, the government subsidizes a good deal of basic research in universities, in its own laboratories and in private industry.

26.4 Growth and accumulation

In this section we explore the links between output growth, factor accumulation and technical progress. We organize our discussion around a simple production function:

$$Y = A \times f(K, L) \tag{1}$$

Variable inputs capital K and labour L combine to produce a given output $f(K, L)$. The function f tells us how much we get out of particular amounts of inputs K and L. This function f never changes. We capture technical progress separately through A, which measures the extent of technical knowledge at any date. As technical progress takes place, we get more output from given inputs: a rise in A. For simplicity, we assume that land is fixed.

Malthus, land and population

Writing in 1798 and living in a largely agricultural society, Malthus worried about the fixed supply of land. As a growing population worked a fixed supply of land, the marginal product of labour would fall. Agricultural output would grow less quickly than population. The per capita food supply would fall until starvation reduced the population to the level that could be fed from the given supply of agricultural land.

In terms of equation (1), starving people consume all their income. Without savings, society cannot invest in capital, so K is zero. The production function then has diminishing returns to labour: adding more workers drives down productivity. Figure 26.1 illustrates.

Some poor countries today face this *Malthusian trap*. Agricultural productivity is so low that everyone must work the land to produce food. As the population grows and agricultural output fails to keep pace, famine sets in and people die. If better fertilizers or irrigation improve agricultural output, the population quickly expands as nutrition improves, and people are driven back to starvation levels again.

Yet Malthus' prediction was not correct for all countries. Today's rich countries broke out of the Malthusian trap. How did they do it? First, they raised agricultural productivity (without an immediate population increase) so that some workers could be switched to industrial production. The capital goods then produced included better ploughs, machinery to pump water and drain fields, and transport to distribute food more effectively. As capital was applied in agriculture, output per worker rose further, releasing more workers to industry while maintaining enough food production to feed the growing population.

Second, the rapid technical progress in agricultural production led to large and persistent productivity increases, reinforcing the effect of moving to more capital-intensive agricultural production. In terms of equation (1), rises in A and in K let output grow faster than labour, causing a *rise* in living standards.

Thus, even the existence of a factor in fixed supply need not make sustained growth impossible. If capital can be accumulated, more and more capital can be substituted for fixed land, allowing output to grow at least as rapidly as population. Similarly, continuing technical progress allows continuing output growth even if one factor is not increasing.

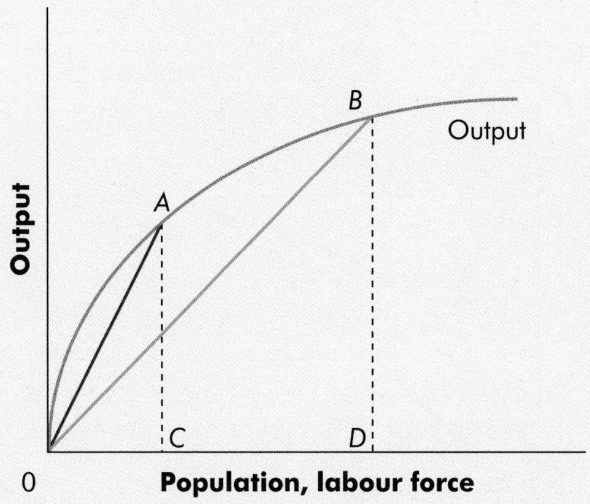

The price mechanism provides the correct incentives for these processes to occur. With a given supply of land, higher agricultural production raises the price of land and the rental paid for land. This provides an incentive to switch to less land-intensive production methods (heavy fertilizer usage, battery chickens) and an incentive to focus on technical progress that lets the economy get by with less land. A similar argument applies to any natural resource in finite supply.

The labour force grows with population, but there are diminishing returns to output. At labour force C, output is AC and output per head is given by the slope of OA. At population D, output is higher at DB but output per head has fallen from the slope OA to the slope OB. When output per head falls to starvation levels growth cannot continue.

Figure 26.1 The Malthusian trap

Capital accumulation

Post-war theories of economic growth date back to work in the 1940s by Roy Harrod in England and Evsey Domar in the US. In the late 1950s, Bob Solow of MIT assembled the nuts and bolts of the neoclassical growth theory – the basis of empirical work ever since.[1]

The theory is *neoclassical* because it does not ask how actual output gets to potential output. Over a long enough period, the only question of interest is what is happening to potential output itself. Neoclassical growth theory simply assumes that actual and potential output are equal.

In this long run, labour and capital grow. Usually, equilibrium means that things are not changing. Now we apply equilibrium not to levels but to growth rates and ratios. The **steady state** is the long-run equilibrium in growth theory.

Assume that labour grows at a constant rate n. To keep things simple, we also assume a constant fraction s of income is saved; the rest is consumed. Aggregate capital formation (public and private) is the part of output not consumed (by both public and private sectors). Investment first **widens** and then perhaps **deepens** capital.

> Along the **steady-state path**, output, capital and labour grow at the same rate. Hence output per worker and capital per worker are constant.
>
> In a growing economy, **capital widening** extends the existing capital per worker to new extra workers.
>
> **Capital deepening** raises capital per worker for all workers.

---

1 Solow won a Nobel Prize for his work on long-run growth. He is also famous for his one-liners. Since, in short-run analysis, he is an unrepentant Keynesian, many of his famous barbs are aimed at those who believe that prices clear markets quickly: 'Will the olive, unassisted, always settle half way up the martini?'

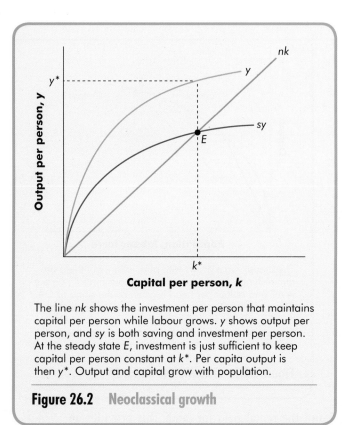

The line *nk* shows the investment per person that maintains capital per person while labour grows. *y* shows output per person, and *sy* is both saving and investment per person. At the steady state *E*, investment is just sufficient to keep capital per person constant at *k**. Per capita output is then *y**. Output and capital grow with population.

Figure 26.2 Neoclassical growth

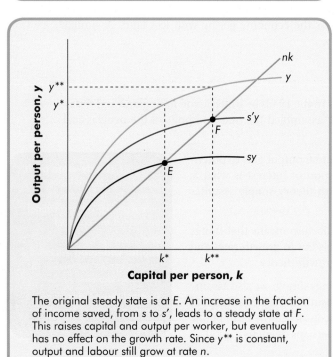

The original steady state is at *E*. An increase in the fraction of income saved, from *s* to *s*′, leads to a steady state at *F*. This raises capital and output per worker, but eventually has no effect on the growth rate. Since *y*** is constant, output and labour still grow at rate *n*.

Figure 26.3 A higher saving rate

To keep capital per person constant, we need more investment per person the faster is population growth *n* (extra workers for whom capital must be provided), and the more capital per person *k* that has to be provided. Figure 26.2 plots the line *nk* along which capital per person is constant.

Adding more capital per worker *k* increases output per worker *y*, but with diminishing returns: hence the curve *y* in Figure 26.1. Since a constant amount of output is saved, *sy* shows the saving per person. Since saving and investment are equal, it also shows investment per person.

In the steady state, capital per person is constant. Hence investment per person *sy* must equal *nk*, the investment per person needed to keep *k* constant by making capital grow as fast as labour. *k** is the steady-state capital per person and *y** the steady-state output per person. Capital, output and labour all grow at the same rate *n* along this steady-state path.

Figure 26.2 also shows what happens away from the steady state. If capital per worker is low, the economy is left of the steady state. Per capita saving and investment *sy* exceed *nk*, the per capita investment required to keep capital in line with growing labour. So capital per person rises. Conversely, to the right of the steady state, *sy* lies below *nk* and capital per person falls. Figure 26.2 says that, from whatever level of capital the economy begins, it gradually converges to the (unique) steady state.

A higher saving rate

Suppose people permanently increase the fraction of income saved, from *s* to *s*′. We get more saving, more investment and hence a faster rate of output growth. Oh no, we don't! Figure 26.3 explains why not.

There is no change in the production function relating output to inputs. At the original saving rate *s*, the steady state is at *E*. At the higher saving rate, *s*′*y* shows saving and investment per person. At *F* it equals *nk*, the per capita investment needed to stop *k* rising or falling. Thus *F* is the new steady state.

F has more capital per worker than *E*. Productivity and output per worker are higher. That is the permanent effect of a higher saving rate. It affects levels, not growth rates. In *any* steady state, *L*, *K* and *Y* all grow at the same rate *n*, and that rate is determined 'outside the model': it is the rate of growth of labour and population. We return to this issue shortly.

In Figure 26.3, the higher saving rate raises output and capital per worker. To make the transition from E to F, there must be a temporary period in which capital grows faster than labour; only then can capital per worker rise as required. A higher saving rate, if successfully translated into higher investment to keep the economy at full employment, causes faster output growth for a while, but not for ever. Once capital per worker rises sufficiently, higher rates of saving and investment go entirely in capital widening, which is now more demanding than before. Further capital deepening, the basis of productivity growth, cannot continue without bound.

MATHS 26.1

Neoclassical growth theory

Output per head is $f(k)$. With a constant saving rate s, saving per head is $sf(k)$.

In a simple economy with no government or foreign sector, at full capacity this must equal investment per head, which comprises replacement investment per head nk and capital deepening that adds to k. If $\dot{k}$ denotes the rate of growth of k,

$$\dot{k} + nk = sf(k) \tag{1}$$

In the steady state k^*, the growth of k is zero, hence $nk^* = sf(k^*)$. Elsewhere,

$$\dot{k} = sf(k) - nk \tag{2}$$

Thus,

$$\dot{k} > 0 \quad \text{if} \quad f(k)/k > n/s \quad \text{and} \quad \dot{k} < 0 \quad \text{if} \quad f(k)/k < n/s$$

With diminishing returns to adding extra units of k, $f(k)$ increases less quickly than k itself. Hence, for $k > k^*$ it must be the case that $f(k)/k$ is less than n/s. Conversely, for $k < k^*$, $f(k)/k$ must exceed n/s. Thus, capital deepending is positive whenever k is less than its steady-state value k^*, and is negative whenever k exceeds its steady-state value k^*, confirming that the neoclassical economy converges to its unique steady state whatever level of k it begins with.

In this steady state, $nk^* = sf(k^*)$. Hence, for given n, an exogenous increase in the saving rate s, must increase $k^*/f(k^*)$. Because the function $f(k)$ has diminishing returns to increasing k, it requires a higher value of k^* to increase $k^*/f(k^*)$ when s increases. Higher saving leads to a rise in the steady-state level of capital per head.

26.5 Growth through technical progress

We have made a lot of progress, but still have some problems. First, the theory does not fit *all* the facts. So far, the theory says output, labour and capital all grow at rate n. Although capital and output do grow at similar rates, in practice both grow more rapidly than labour. That is why we are better off than our great-grandparents.

The answer may lie in technical progress, which we ignored in trying to explain output growth entirely through growth in factor supplies (population growth and the accumulation of capital). It turns out that **labour-augmenting technical progress** would do the trick.

Labour-augmenting technical progress increases the effective labour supply.

Population growth might eventually double the number of workers. Imagine instead that the number of workers is constant but that new knowledge allows the same workers to do the work of twice as many as before, as if the population had grown.

Suppose this progress occurs at rate t. Effective labour input grows at rate $(t + n)$ because of technical progress and population growth. Now go back to Figure 26.1 and simply put $(t + n)k$ instead of nk. To make this valid, we have to measure capital and output not per worker but per worker-equivalent. Worker-equivalents are created by population growth or technical progress. Otherwise the diagram is identical.

E remains the steady state. Output per worker-equivalent and capital per worker-equivalent are constant. Since worker-equivalents grow at rate $t + n$, so must capital and output. Since actual workers increase at rate n, output and capital per actual worker each increase at rate t. Now our growth theory fits all the facts. Living standards grow over time at rate t.

It is uncomfortable that the two key growth rates, n and t, are determined outside the model. For that reason, for the next 30 years the main use of this growth theory was in growth accounting: showing how to decompose actual output behaviour into the parts explained by changes in various inputs and the part residually explained by technical progress. We next examine the results of accounting for growth.

26.6 Growth in the OECD

The Organization for Economic Cooperation and Development is a club of the world's richest countries, from industrial giants like the US and Japan to smaller economies like New Zealand, Ireland and Turkey. Table 26.2 shows labour productivity growth of selected OECD countries since 1950.

During the post-war boom years 1950–73, productivity grew strongly in a climate of rapid trade expansion, investment and recovery. These happy days ended in 1973 in all OECD countries. Several explanations were put forward. Some stressed the rise in trade union power, resulting in their enjoying greater legal protection in the 1970s. If this explanation had been correct, the supply-side reforms of the late 1980s and 1990s should have led to high productivity growth in the 1990s. There is little evidence that it did.

The first OPEC oil price shock, when real oil prices quadrupled, also occurred in 1973. This had two effects. First, it diverted R&D to long-term efforts to find alternative energy-saving technologies. These efforts take decades to pay off and raise actual productivity. Second, higher energy prices made much of the capital stock economically obsolete overnight. Energy-guzzling factories were closed. The world lost part of its capital stock, which reduced output per head. In practice, scrapping took a long time, and was given renewed impetus by another sharp rise in oil prices in 1980/81. That is why its effects were drawn out over such a long period, lasting for much of the 1980s.

Table 26.2 Average annual growth in real output per person employed (%)

	OECD	Japan	Germany	Italy	France	Sweden	UK	US
1950–73	3.6	8.0	5.6	5.8	4.5	3.4	3.6	2.2
1973–90	1.4	2.9	2.3	2.4	2.8	1.6	1.8	0.4
1990–2007	1.5	1.2	2.4	1.1	1.4	2.1	1.6	1.6
2008–09	−0.5	−2.0	−2.6	−2.7	−0.7	−1.9	−1.4	1.1

Sources: Dowrick, S. and Nguyen, D. (1989) OECD comparative economic growth 1950–85, *American Economic Review*, 79: 1010–1030; OECD, *Economic Outlook*.

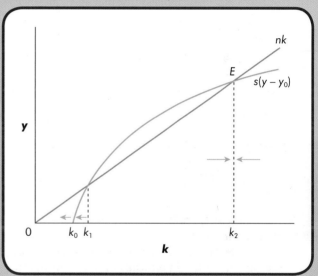

ACTIVITY 26.1

Aborted take-offs on the growth runway

We assume people save a constant fraction s of their income. Even poor people earning only y save sy and consume $(1 - s)y$. But if y is low enough, $(1 - s)y$ is too low to stop starvation. So they consume all their income and save none. Below a critical income level y_0, saving is zero. What does the Solow diagram look like now? See diagram below. Suppose k_0 is the capital per person that just generates the critical income y_0. Higher capital generates saving as in previous diagrams, and nk is still the gross investment needed to maintain a given capital–labour ratio in the face of growing population. There are now three steady states!

If capital begins above k_1 the economy converges to the steady state at E. Between k_1 and k_2, saving and investment exceed the amount needed for capital widening: capital-deepening also occurs and the economy grows. Above k_2, saving and investment are insufficient to maintain the capital–labour ratio, and the economy shrinks. Either way it ends at E. This is the case analysed in Figures 26.2 and 26.3. Suppose, next, the economy begins at exactly k_1. Saving and investment just maintain the capital–labour ratio. So this is a steady state, but an unstable one.

A little above k_1 the economy begins converging on E. And below k_1 there is insufficient saving and investment to provide for the growing population. Capital per person shrinks and keeps shrinking until the economy reaches $k = 0$.

In this model, countries beginning with capital below k_1 are stuck in a poverty trap. They cannot break out. All output is consumed to prevent starvation. There is never a surplus to begin accumulation and growth. This model can also explain why convergence seems to occur within the OECD (countries already above k_1), but why simultaneously many countries are stuck in poverty. Modern growth in the last two centuries began when some key events first generated the surplus to allow saving and accumulation to begin.

Questions

(a) Why is there no poverty trap when saving is proportional to income?

(b) When a poverty trap exists, is the payoff to overseas aid from rich countries greater if it is concentrated on helping poor countries break out of the poverty trap?

(c) The poverty trap shown above is based on there being a minimum level of per capita consumption. Could we get a poverty trap based on different population growth rates above and below some critical threshold of living standards? Is this plausible?

To check your answers to these questions, go to page 688.

Neither the internet boom nor supply-side reforms restored the productivity growth rates that the rich countries enjoyed prior to 1973. Emerging market economies, such as China, India, Brazil and Russia, are now where the action is. We turn to their story in Part Five. For rich mature economies, Table 26.2 confirms that underlying productivity growth showed a modest improvement after 1990, until it was dramatically interrupted by recession after the financial crash.

Why was productivity growth negative during 2008–09? OECD countries did not mysteriously forget the skills they had learned over previous decades, nor did their capital explode. Table 26.2 is alerting us to a short-term effect that is a normal feature of business cycles. We discuss this more fully in the next chapter. If normal output growth is resumed, we expect to see productivity growth return to normal levels again.

Having discussed differences in growth across periods, we now examine differences across countries. The one sheds light on the other. The fact that OECD countries move together across sub-periods shows that many aspects of growth are outside a country's own control. Technical progress diffuses across countries quite quickly, wherever it originates. Countries are increasingly dependent on the same global economy.

Even so, growth rates differ markedly across countries. Can growth theory explain why? First, it suggests that, if countries have access to the same technology, differences in output growth should reflect differences in labour force growth. Table 26.1 provides some degree of corroborating evidence: differences in per capita output growth are less marked than differences in output growth.

Second, we need to know how long it takes to get to the steady state, a question to which Figures 26.2 and 26.3 provide no direct answer. Is output growth over two or three decades an adjustment *towards* the steady state, or can we assume that an economy has reached it within that time?

The convergence hypothesis

Figure 26.2 has a unique steady state at E and, whatever the level of capital per worker with which an economy begins, the figure implies that it will eventually converge to E. Poor countries with a low inheritance of capital grow extra rapidly until they reach the steady-state growth rate of output and capital; rich countries with a very high inheritance of capital grow at below-average rates until capital per worker falls back to its steady-state level k^*.

> The **convergence hypothesis** asserts that poor countries grow more quickly than average, but rich countries grow more slowly than average.

When capital per worker is low, it doesn't take much investment to equip new workers with capital (capital-widening), so the rest of investment can go on raising capital per worker (capital-deepening). When capital per worker is already high, it takes a lot of saving and investment just to maintain capital-widening, let alone to deepen capital. This is one reason for the convergence hypothesis.

This explanation for convergence relies purely on the effect of capital accumulation. A second explanation for convergence or 'catch-up' operates through a different channel. Technical progress no longer falls out of the sky at a fixed rate. Suppose instead we have to invest real resources (universities, research labs, R&D) in trying to make technical improvements. It is rich countries that have the human and physical capital to undertake these activities, and it is in rich countries that technical progress is made. However, once discovered, new ideas are soon disseminated to other countries.

Since poorer countries do not have to use their own resources to make technical breakthroughs, they can devote their scarce investment resources to other uses, such as building machines. By slipstreaming the richer countries, they can temporarily grow faster.

CASE 26.2

Does convergence occur in practice?

The table below shows World Bank estimates of per capita income in 1987, 2008 and the ratio of 2008 to 1987. East Asian economies such as China and South Korea grew very quickly during the last 30 years. India (not shown below) is also now growing strongly. Yet convergence cannot be a powerful force in the world or the very poorest countries would all be growing very rapidly. In reality, many poor countries stay poor and sometimes even decline in absolute terms.

Within the rich OECD countries, convergence is much more reliable. The richest OECD countries tend to grow less quickly than the poorer OECD countries.

Why did the East Asian 'tigers' grow so quickly in the post-war period? What was their secret? Professor Alwyn Young* of MIT has shown that there is little mystery about their rapid growth, even though they did sustain dramatic rates. These economies managed rapid growth in measured inputs – labour (via increases in participation rates), capital (via high saving and investment rates) and human capital (via substantial expenditure on education). Once we allow for the rapid growth of these inputs, Young showed that the growth of output in the tigers was not very different from what standard estimates, based on OECD and Latin American countries, would have led us to expect.

Generally, growth seems to be fostered by two conditions: absence of internal strife and openness to the world economy. Once China put insularity and the Cultural Revolution behind it, the potential for catching up was enormous. India had less internal strife, but took off only after it embraced the world economy and relaxed its more bureaucratic controls. Civil war held back Nigeria despite its oil wealth. Indeed, there is considerable evidence that mineral-rich countries without a long tradition of stable government suffer disproportionate incidence of civil war – fighting for the spoils – to the detriment of economic growth and higher living standards.

Note finally that Switzerland, with much the highest living standard, has one of the slowest rates of growth of per capita GNP. The Swiss are rich today because they were rich yesterday, a secret that they discovered long ago.

Per capita GNP (thousands of 1997 US$)

	Initially	1987	2008	Ratio of 2008/1987
Bangladesh	Poor	0.30	0.50	1.67
Nigeria	Poor	0.42	0.70	1.68
China	Poor	0.35	2.17	6.22
Indonesia	Poor	0.78	1.35	1.72
Turkey	Middle income	3.28	5.71	1.71
South Korea	Middle income	6.23	16.80	2.70
Portugal	Middle income	9.92	17.40	1.75
Spain	Rich	14.84	26.90	1.81
Ireland	Rich	15.27	40.9	2.68
Italy	Rich	21.83	31.5	1.42
UK	Rich	21.23	39.9	1.88
France	Rich	27.13	38.2	1.39
US	Rich	29.92	45.2	1.61
Switzerland	Rich	46.17	59.4	1.29

Source: World Bank, *World Development Report*, various issues.

The figure below plots the final column, the ratio of per capita income in 2008 relative to 1987, on the horizontal axis, and on the vertical axis plots 1987 per capita income in ten-thousands of US dollars, obtained by dividing the third column of the table by ten in order to keep the two scales comparable. The figure conveys two messages. First, on average countries that have become rich then grow more slowly. Second, individual country performance can depart significantly from this underlying relationship.

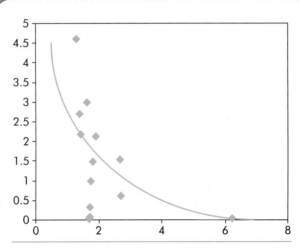

With this understanding, what should we expect for the next 40 years, long after the consequences of the financial crash have worked themselves out? Global consultancy PricewaterhouseCoopers make brave projections for the future, based largely on the framework we have set out. They estimate population growth, the evolution of skills and human capital, investment in physical capital, and rates of technical progress and its dissemination across countries. From this information, they make estimates of future growth in GDP.

The chart below, drawn from their 2008 report, refers to the projected evolution of aggregate GDP.† Their first important conclusion assesses who will be the economic superpowers in 2050. At present, US GDP significantly exceeds that of the second largest economy, Japan. By 2025, China will have overhauled the US, and by 2050 will have a significant economic lead. With its much larger population, catch-up in productivity is all that is

The convergence hypothesis, 1987–2008

Note: Vertical axis = 1987 per capita income $0000; Horizontal axis = Ratio of 2008 to 1987 per capita income.

Source: World Bank, *World Development Report*, various issues.

required. With an aged population, Japan will fail to keep up: old people consume but do not produce, and so attract resources away from investment and accumulation. After a slower beginning, India becomes the most exciting story of all. With the fastest population growth and the second-largest population to start with, India should start to narrow the gap on China and will overtake the US eventually, but not before 2050.

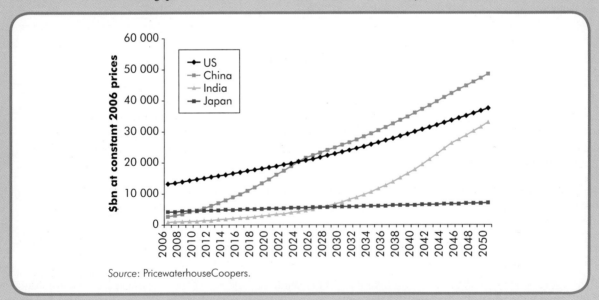

Source: PricewaterhouseCoopers.

The table overleaf shows Pricewaterhouse Cooper's estimates for a variety of emerging markets during 2007–50, isolating the effect of population growth as well as the general catch-up in productivity levels implied by more rapid productivity growth in poorer countries.

	Annual real growth (%)		
	GDP	Per capita GDP	Population
Vietnam	6 .8	6.0	0.8
India	5.8	5.0	0.8
Bangladesh	5.1	3.9	1.2
China	4.7	4.6	0.1
Malaysia	4.3	3.3	1.0
Turkey	4.1	3.4	0.7
Mexico	3.7	3.2	0.5
Russia	2.5	3.2	−0.6
Poland	2.1	2.7	−0.5

Source: World Bank, *World Development Report*, various issues. © 2010 The World Bank Group. All rights reserved.

The poorer countries have more rapid GDP growth not merely because they have opportunities for productivity catch-up but also because they often have more rapid population growth, except in China with its one-child per family policy. Whether this will continue until 2050, as assumed in the table, is hard to assess at this juncture. The middle-income countries (Malaysia through to Poland) are expected to have fewer opportunities for rapid productivity growth, and in the case of Eastern Europe and Russia, may actually experience falling populations. This helps their per capita growth – capital widening is less of a burden – but not their aggregate GDP growth.

* Young, A. (1995) The tyranny of numbers: confronting the statistical realities of the East Asian growth experience, *Quarterly Journal of Economics*, 110: 641–80.

† Hawsworth, J. and Cookson, G. (2008) *The World in 2050*, PricewaterhouseCoopers.

In a pathbreaking empirical study over 50 years ago, Professor Bob Solow compared growth rates across countries and across time, documented how much growth could be traced to growth of inputs of labour and capital via a standard production function, and attributed the unexplained part of economic growth to unmeasured technical progress.

Case 26.2 already provides two alarm bells. First, countries do not immediately share the same technical knowledge, providing scope for catch-up by poorer countries. Second, even allowing for this, different countries behave differently.

The **Solow residual** measured our initial ignorance about economic growth, and economists have spent the last 50 years trying to explain more and more of it. Two useful approaches have been to keep explict track of more inputs – such as energy and knowledge capital – and to elaborate a dynamic model of technical progress in which some countries get new information before others.

> The part of output growth not explained by the growth of measured inputs is known as the **Solow residual**.

One early attempt, by Professor Nick Crafts of Warwick University, took the Solow residuals and tried to see how much of them could then be explained by catch-up. The lower a country's per capita GDP relative to that of the US (the assumed technical leader), the larger should be the potential for catch-up.

Crafts discovered that there is a systematic role for catch-up, as we would have expected from Case 26.2, but also that, after allowing for 'average catch-up' for a country of that living standard, big differences remain across countries. These may reflect the social and political framework in which the economy must operate. Change usually helps the majority but has very adverse effects on a few people whose skills are made obsolete or whose power is suddenly removed. The large number of winners should club together to buy off the few big losers, allowing change to proceed. Some societies are much better than others at organizing the deals that allow catch-up to be achieved more rapidly.

Increasingly, the effort of research economists is now focused on analysing and measuring the accumulation of knowledge capital. Amazingly, recent estimates suggest that investment in knowledge creation is even more important than investment in physical capital in generating high levels of GDP. With around 80 per cent of GDP now comprising the supply of services rather than the production of goods, perhaps this should come as no surprise. Know-how matters a lot.

This also helps explain some historical puzzles, such as why Germany and Japan grew so quickly after the Second World War. Part of the modern answer is that their advanced knowledge survived intact even if the bombs had destroyed their buildings. Conversely, if foreign aid is to help some of the world's poorest countries, supplying food and shelter may not be enough. Education and training are hugely important.

 ## 26.7 Endogenous growth

Endogenous growth implies that the steady-state growth rate is affected by economic behaviour and economic policy.

In its simplest form, Solow's theory makes economic growth depend on population growth and technical progress. Both proceed at given rates. The subsequent literature on catch-up makes technical progress respond to economic circumstances and the political and cultural environment. It would be nice to have a stronger link between economic behaviour and the rate of economic growth. We want to make growth *endogenous*, or determined within our theory.

The original insight is due to Professor Paul Romer of Chicago University. Saving, investment and capital accumulation lie at the heart of growth. In Solow's theory, applying more and more capital to a given path for population runs into the diminishing marginal product of capital. It cannot be the source of permanent growth in productivity.

We know there must be diminishing returns to capital alone at the level of individual firms; otherwise one firm would get more and more capital, become steadily more productive and gradually take over the entire world! Because diminishing returns to capital hold at the level of the firm, economists had assumed they held also at the level of the economy.

Romer's insight was the possibility (likelihood?) that there are significant externalities to capital. Higher capital in one firm increases productivity in *other* firms. When BT invests in better equipment, other firms can do things previously impossible. The insight also applies to human capital. Training by one firm has beneficial externalities for others.

Thus the production function of each individual firm exhibits diminishing returns to its own capital input, but also depends on the capital of other firms. No firm, acting in isolation, would wish to raise its capital without limit. But when all firms expand together, the economy as a whole may face constant returns to aggregate capital.

Consider the following simple example of the aggregate economy. Per capita output y is proportional to capital per person k. To isolate the role of accumulation, suppose there is no technical progress. Thus $y = Ak$, where A is constant, and there are constant returns to accumulating more capital. Given a constant saving rate s and population growth at rate n, is there a steady state in which capital per person grows at rate g? If so, investment for capital deepening is gk and investment for capital widening, to keep up with population growth, is nk. Hence, in per capita terms:

$$\textbf{Gross investment} = (g + n)k = sy = sAk = \textbf{gross saving}$$

Hence $gk = (sA - n)k$ and the steady-state growth rate g is

$$g = (sA - n) \tag{2}$$

Why does this confirm the possibility of *endogenous* growth? Because it depends on parameters that could be influenced by private behaviour or public policy. In the Solow model, without technical progress, steady-state growth is always n, whatever the saving rate s or the level of productivity A. Equation (2) says that any policy that succeeded in raising the saving rate s would *permanently* increase the *growth rate g*. Similarly, any policy achieving a once-off rise in the *level* of A, for example greater workplace efficiency, would permanently increase the growth rate of k. Since $y = Ak$, this means permanently faster output growth.

Not only can government policy affect growth in this framework, government intervention may increase efficiency. In the simple Romer model outlined above, there are externalities in capital accumulation: individual firms neglect the fact that, in raising their own capital, they also increase the productivity of *other* firms' capital. Government subsidies to investment might offset this externality.

Since Romer's original work there has been huge interest in endogenous growth. Sustaining small additions to annual growth rates eventually makes a big difference to living standards. As a result of this research we now have many potential channels of endogenous growth. For example, instead of assuming that the rate of technical progress is given, we can model the industry that undertakes R&D to produce technical progress. Constant returns in this industry will generate endogenous growth. In fact, constant returns to aggregate production of any *accumulable* factor (knowledge, capital and so on) will suffice.

Note, too, that endogenous growth models explain why growth rates in different countries might permanently be different. This might explain why convergence does not take place and why some countries remain poor indefinitely. Different countries have different growth rates g.

While endogenous growth theory is an exciting development, it also has its critics. Most criticisms boil down to a key point. Whatever the relevant accumulatible factor, why should there be *exactly* constant returns in the aggregate? With diminishing returns, we are back in the Solow model where long-run growth is exogenous. With increasing returns, the economy would settle not on steady growth but on ever more rapid expansion of output and capital. We know this is not occurring. So for endogenous growth theory to be the answer, only constant returns to accumulation will do. Some people think this seems just too good to be true.

 ## 26.8 The costs of growth

Can the benefits of economic growth be outweighed by its costs? Pollution, climate change, congestion and a hectic lifestyle are a high price to pay for more cars, washing machines and video games.

Since GNP is an imperfect measure of the true economic value of the goods and services produced by the economy, there is no presumption we should want to maximize the growth of measured GNP. We discussed issues such as pollution in Part Three. Without government intervention, a free market economy produces too much pollution. But complete elimination of pollution is also wasteful. Society should undertake activities accompanied by pollution up to the point at which the net marginal benefit of the goods produced equals the marginal pollution cost imposed on society. Government intervention, through pollution taxes or regulation of environmental standards, can move the economy towards an efficient allocation of resources in which marginal social costs and benefits are equalized.

> The **zero-growth proposal** argues that, because higher measured GNP imposes environmental costs, it is best to aim for zero growth of measured GNP.

The full implementation of such a policy would (optimally) reduce the growth of measured GNP below the rate where there is no restriction on activities such as pollution and congestion. And this is the most sensible way in which to approach the problem. It tackles the issue directly. In contrast, the **zero-growth** solution is a blunt instrument.

The zero-growth approach fails to distinguish between measured outputs accompanied by social costs and measured outputs without additional social costs. It does not provide the correct incentives. The principle of targeting, a key insight of the welfare economics discussed in Part Three, suggests that it is more efficient to tackle a problem directly than to adopt an indirect approach that distorts other aspects of production or consumption. Thus, when there is too much pollution, congestion, environmental damage or stress, the best solution is to provide incentives that directly reduce these phenomena. Restricting growth in measured output is a crude alternative, distinctly second best.

Some problems might evaporate if economists and statisticians could measure true GNP more accurately, including the 'quality of life' activities (clean air, environmental beauty, sustainable climate and so on) that yield consumption benefits but at present are omitted from measured GNP. Voters and commentators assess government performance against measurable statistics. A better measure of GNP might remove perceived conflicts between measured output and the quality of life.

This is also a good way to address 'sustainable growth'. At present, Mediterranean beauty spots become concrete jungles of hotels and bars; once the environment is spoiled, upmarket tourists move on to somewhere else. An economist's advice, however, is not to abandon being a tourist destination, but to keep track of environmental depreciation and only engage in activities that show a clear return after proper costing of environmental and other damage. Embodying these costings in actual charges also provides the market incentive to look after the environment.

This also provides the answer to those who argue that tackling climate change will hamper economic growth. Growth of what? The subset of outputs that are traded anyway, and hence easily measured? Just as we want congestion charging to *reduce* some outputs (rush-hour traffic), we want environmental pricing to *reduce* some activities (greenhouse gas emissions, lax building insulation). In both cases, the objective is to get aggregate output, *properly measured*, to increase!

No matter how complete the framework, the assessment of the desirable growth rate will always be a normative question hinging on the value judgements of the assessor. Switching resources from consumption, however defined, to investment will nearly always reduce the welfare of people today but allow greater welfare for people tomorrow. Nowhere is this clearer than in the speed with which we try to deal with climate change. More sacrifice today will make life easier tomorrow; less sacrifice today will compound the problems for our children's children. The priority attached to satisfying wants of people at different points in time is always a value judgement.

Summary

- **Economic growth** is the percentage annual increase in real GNP or per capita real GNP in the long run. It is an imperfect measure of the rate of increase of economic well-being.

- Measured GNP omits the value of leisure and of untraded goods and bads that have an impact on the quality of life. Differences in income distribution make per capita real GNP a shaky basis for comparisons of the welfare of the typical individual in different countries.

- Significant rates of **growth of per capita GNP** occurred only in the last two centuries in the advanced economies. In other countries persistent growth is even more recent.

- Potential output can be increased either by increasing the inputs of land, labour, capital and raw materials, or by increasing the output obtained from given input quantities. **Technical advances** are an important source of productivity gains.

- An apparently **fixed supply of a production input**, such as a particular raw material, need not make growth impossible in the long run. As the input becomes scarce, its price rises. This makes producers substitute other inputs, increases incentives to discover new supplies and encourages inventions that economize on the use of that resource.

- The simplest theory of growth has a **steady state** in which capital, output and labour all grow at the same rate. Whatever its initial level of capital, the economy converges on this steady-state path. This theory can explain output growth but not productivity growth.

- **Labour-augmenting technical progress** allows permanent growth of labour productivity and enables the simple growth theory to fit many of the facts.

- There is a **tendency of economies to converge**, both because **capital deepening** is easier when capital per worker is low and because of **catch-up in technology**. Implementing technical change may depend on how well society is organized to buy off (or defeat) the losers.

- Thatcherism did induce an identifiable rise in UK productivity growth, even after controlling for factor accumulation and catch-up opportunities. It is difficult to be sure whether Thatcherism changed the growth rate for ever.

- Theories of **endogenous growth** are built on constant returns to accumulation. If aggregate investment does not encounter diminishing returns to capital, choices about saving and investment can affect the long-run growth rate of productivity. An externality on a giant scale provides a powerful rationale for government intervention to encourage education, training and physical capital formation.

- Nevertheless, endogenous growth rests on the presence of constant returns to accumulation. Nobody has yet explained why this should hold.

Review questions   connect

1 What is the distinction between total output and per capita output? Which grows more rapidly? Why? Always?

2 'Britain produces too many scientists, too few engineers.' What kind of evidence might help you decide if this is true? Will a free market lead people to choose the career that most benefits society?

3 Name two economic bads. Suggest feasible ways in which they might be measured. Should they be included in GNP? Could they be?

4 'If the convergence hypothesis is correct, the poor African countries should have grown long ago!' Is this correct? Do newer approaches to economic growth help explain why some countries remain so poor?

5 'Because we know Malthus got it wrong, we are relaxed about the fact that some minerals are in finite supply.' Is there a connection? Explain.

EASY

6 **Common fallacies** Why are these statements wrong? (a) Since the earth's resources are limited, growth cannot continue for ever. (b) If we save more, we'd definitely grow faster.

7 Which is correct? Countries that isolate themselves from the world economy tend to grow slowly because: (a) they fail to learn about technical progress elsewhere; (b) without competition, they have insufficient incentive to invest; (c) there are other adverse consequences of the political regime that took such a decision; (d) all of the above; (e) none of the above.

8 Which is correct? The empirical correlation between countries that possess extreme mineral wealth and the prevalence of civil wars suggests: (a) wars raise the demand for resources and encourage exploration for minerals; (b) when easy wealth is available it increases the incentive to fight over the spoils provided by nature rather than co-operate to produce goods and services; (c) mineral wealth attracts foreign predators.

MEDIUM

9 Several decades ago, China adopted a policy of allowing only one child per family. Using the analysis of this chapter, explain what the purpose of this might have been. Illustrate in a diagram.

10 Suppose the private secor has a given saving rate out of disposable income, but that the public sector levies taxes and utilizes all of this revenue for investment by the public sector. If the private and public sector are equally efficient, what happens to the long-run growth rate? What happens to per capita incomes eventually?

11 Consider an economy in which there is constant population. Each firm's production function exhibits diminishing returns to its own capital accumulation. However, each firm creates beneficial production externalities for other firms. In the aggregate, the economy faces constant returns to capital accumulation, so that $y = 2k$. If the saving rate is 0.2, what is the permanent rate of growth of capital and output?

12 Consider a planet on which population grows at the constant rate n and people save a constant fraction s of their per capita output. Output is produced by environmental capital k, which depreciates at a constant d. Gross investment is used only to improve environmental capital, and $y = f(k)$ so that output depends on environmental capital and there are diminishing returns to environmental capital. (a) Draw a figure similar to, but different from, Figure 26.1. (b) Suppose the rate of environmental depreciation rises. What happens to the steady-state level of output per person y? (c) Is it true that if recycling were to reduce environmental depreciation it would therefore raise output per person in the long run?

13 Can technical progress be negative?

HARD

14 **Essay question** Is growth good?

For solutions to these questions contact your lecturer.

Business cycles

Learning Outcomes

By the end of this chapter, you should be able to:

1. distinguish trend growth and economic cycles around this path

2. discuss why business cycles occur

3. analyse why output gaps may fluctuate

4. discuss whether potential output also fluctuates

5. assess whether national business cycles are now more correlated

6. apply these principles to UK business cycles

After a deep recession during 1990–92, the UK left the Exchange Rate Mechanism, cut interest rates and let the pound depreciate. Prime Minister Major delayed the next general election until May 1997, in the hope that recovery would increase the 'feel-good factor' and allow a Conservative victory. It did not. Tony Blair won by a landslide.

The incoming Labour government then made the Bank of England independent, to try to take some of the politics out of economic policy making. Gordon Brown also emphasized fiscal prudence to keep inflation expectations in check. Yet, as the 2001 election approached, Labour came under pressure to spend more money to improve the public services. Transforming the public services became the principal domestic policy of the Labour government after 2001. Fiscal policy became imprudently loose.

However, fiscal loosening after 2001 did not lead to inflation. With an independent Bank of England, committed to an inflation target, markets expected interest rates to be increased to whatever level maintained inflation stability. This expectation of high UK interest rates helped maintain the UK real exchange rate at high levels prior to the financial crisis.

In the aftermath of the financial crisis, interest rates were slashed nearly to zero and fiscal policy was loosened dramatically, both to bail out the financial system and to avert a catastrophic fall in aggregate demand whose effects would be more prolonged the more hysteresis was a key feature of the labour market.

Gordon Brown had often claimed that making the Bank of England independent had abolished boom and bust. Certainly, the setting of interest rates by independent central banks appeared to have reduced the extent of cyclical fluctuations. In so doing, private banks, the property market and policy makers themselves were lulled into a false sense of security. With credit overextended and risk under-recognized, economies became more vulnerable to a financial crash when it came.

These episodes illustrate many of the issues that we examine in this chapter. First, is there a business cycle? Output fluctuates a lot in the short run, but a cycle does not mean merely temporary departures from trend: it also requires a degree of regularity. Can we see it in the data? Can monetary and fiscal policy insulate economies from business cycles? If so, should the Monetary Policy Committee or the Treasury get the credit?

We also explore the international dimension. Can a single country display cycles that are out of phase with those in its trading partners? What does this have to do with whether the UK might ever be able to adopt the euro? Is globalization making business cycles more correlated across countries? If they are, might a single monetary policy become increasingly appropriate?

  Trend and cycle: statistics or economics?

> The **trend path of output** is the smooth path of long-run output once its short-term fluctuations are averaged out.
>
> The **business cycle** is the short-term fluctuation of total output around its trend path.

In practice, aggregate output and productivity do not grow smoothly. In some years they grow very rapidly but in others they actually fall. Actual output fluctuates around this hypothetical **trend path**.

Figure 27.1 shows a stylized picture of the business cycle. The blue curve is the steady growth in trend output over time. Actual output follows the orange curve. Point *A* represents a *slump*, the bottom of a **business cycle**. At *B*, the economy has entered the *recovery* phase of the cycle. As recovery proceeds, output climbs above its trend path, reaching point *C*, which we call a *boom*. Then the economy enters a period in which output is growing less quickly than trend output, and is possibly even falling. When output is falling for at least two successive quarters, we call this a *recession*. Point *E* shows a *slump*, after which recovery begins and the cycle starts again.

Figure 27.2 shows the annual percentage growth of real GDP and of real output per employed worker in the UK during the period 1975–2009. Output and productivity grew most rapidly during 1986–88 and fell in 1975, 1980–81, 1990–92 and 2008–09. The figure makes four basic points.

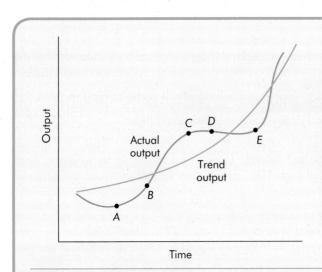

Trend output grows steadily over time as productive potential increases. Actual output fluctuates around this trend. Point A shows a slump, the trough of a cycle. At B recovery has begun and it continues until the peak of the cycle is reached at C. At C there is a boom. Then a period of recession follows until the next slump is reached at E. It takes roughly five years to move from one point in the cycle to an equivalent point in the next cycle, for example from A to E.

Figure 27.1   The business cycle

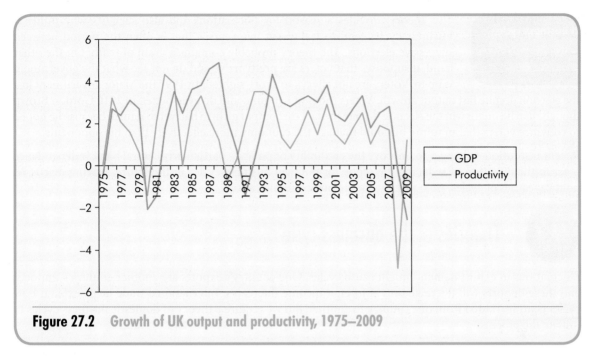

Figure 27.2 Growth of UK output and productivity, 1975–2009

First, the growth of output and productivity fluctuates in the short run. Second, although cycles are not perfectly regular, there is evidence of a pattern of slump, recovery, boom and recession, with a complete cycle lasting around five or six years. Third, output and output per person are closely correlated in the short run. Typically, output fluctuations used to precede fluctuations in productivity by about a year, but since the mid-1990s this gap has been reduced. Fourth, during 1995–2007 it appeared that cycles had become less pronounced than in previous decades – hence the optimism that boom and bust had been partly put behind us – but the output fall of 2009 then turned out to be the worst single year of the post-war period. The rest of the chapter seeks to explain these facts.

Any series of points may be decomposed statistically into an average trend and fluctuations around that trend. We initially assume that potential output grows smoothly. Later we consider whether potential output itself can fluctuate significantly in the short run.

Thus, we start by assuming that business cycles reflect fluctuations in the **output gap**. The data in Figure 27.2 show that cycles are too regular to be a complete coincidence. What causes business cycles?

> The **output gap** is the deviation of actual output from potential output.

Since we associate potential output with aggregate supply in the long run, it seems natural to think first about aggregate demand shocks as the source of cyclical deviations of actual output from potential output. We know what shifts demand: changes in export demand, in the desire to save, in expected future profits and incomes, and in monetary and fiscal policy.

We could argue that demand shocks just happen to be cyclical, generating cycles in output gaps and actual output. However, that is not an *explanation* of the business cycle: it does not tell us why demand shocks have this cyclical pattern. One version of this approach does at least claim to be a theory.

Suppose voters, having short memories, are heavily influenced by how the economy is doing immediately prior to the election. Knowing this, the government uses monetary and fiscal policy to manipulate aggregate demand. Policy is tight just after a government is elected, creating a slump and spare capacity. As the next election date approaches, expansionary policy can then create unsustainably rapid growth by mopping up the spare capacity again. Voters misinterpret this as permanently faster growth of potential output and gratefully re-elect the government.

A **political business cycle** arises if politicians manipulate the economy for electoral advantage.

This theory provides a reason for fluctuations and also suggests why **political business cycles** tend to last about five years – that is often the period between successive elections. The theory probably contains a grain of truth. On the other hand, it supposes that voters are pretty naive and do not see what the government is up to. Voters are not always so short-sighted. In 1997 the Major government lost the election despite fast output growth. Voters thought Labour could do even better. In 2010 Gordon Brown thought that he might win the election despite the fact that output growth had yet to return, because he hoped to convince voters that in future he could manage the economy more effectively than his opponents.

Recent institutional changes to improve the credibility of policy – particularly central bank independence – act in the direction of reducing the scope for political business cycles in the future. Having discussed political causes of cycles, we now concentrate on economic causes.

27.2 Theories of the business cycle

Fluctuations in export demand might cause cycles. One country's exports are another country's imports, and these imports will fluctuate only if foreign income fluctuates. International trade helps explain how cycles get transmitted from one country to another, but we require a theory of domestic business cycles to initiate the process.

Sluggish adjustment is necessary but not sufficient to generate cycles caused by demand shocks. It is necessary because rapid adjustment would quickly eliminate output gaps and restore output to potential output. It is not sufficient because sluggishness only explains why the return to potential output takes time. An oil tanker moves sluggishly but it does not oscillate its way into port. Cycles require a mechanism by which deviations in one direction then set up forces that cause output to overshoot potential output on its return.

Having ruled out the government, a theory of domestic cycles must be based on consumption or investment spending. Investment spending is the most likely candidate, since it is more likely to take time to assess and adjust. Firms do not rush into major and irreversible investment projects, nor are new factories built overnight.

ACTIVITY 27.1 The cyclical behaviour of wages

In a recession, firms employ fewer workers. A competitive firm would pay workers the real value of their marginal product. Given a diminishing marginal product of labour, cutting back on workers should raise labour's marginal product. Fewer workers have the same capital as before to work with. Real wages should rise in a slump. But they don't. They fall. This is the *real-wage puzzle* over the business cycle.

Real business cycle theorists suggest that a temporarily adverse shock may make it advisable to engage in some intertemporal labour substitution. When times are tough, you don't sacrifice much by taking time off; lifetime earnings can be rebuilt when conditions are easier. So recessions, caused by temporarily low productivity, make firms offer temporarily low wages, and households temporarily reduce their labour supply. We get low employment *and* low wages.

A second possibility is that recessions wipe out plants that were anyway teetering on the edge, often those with outdated capital stock. For example, in early 2010 Indian multinational Tata, which had recently acquired Corus (formerly British Steel), announced plans to close the large steelworks in Middlesbrough. This scraps capital as well as workers. Although employment may fall in a recession in a highly visible way, it is harder to keep track of what is happening to the capital stock. But this may shrink at least as much as employment. Real wages may fail to rise in a recession because the smaller number of workers actually have a significantly smaller quantity of capital with which to work.

A third possibility is labour hoarding by firms. Given the cost of firing workers, only to rehire most again when recovery takes place, firms that expect a recession to be relatively short may find it cheaper to hang on to most of their workers despite a reduction in demand and output. In such circumstances, labour is not fully utilized and output per worker falls.

The figures below, taken from the OECD's *Economic Outlook* of November 2009, confirm that this phenomenon is pervasive. Hours worked per worker (bottom panel) fell sharply in 2008, just before employment turned down (middle panel) and unemployment turned up (top panel).

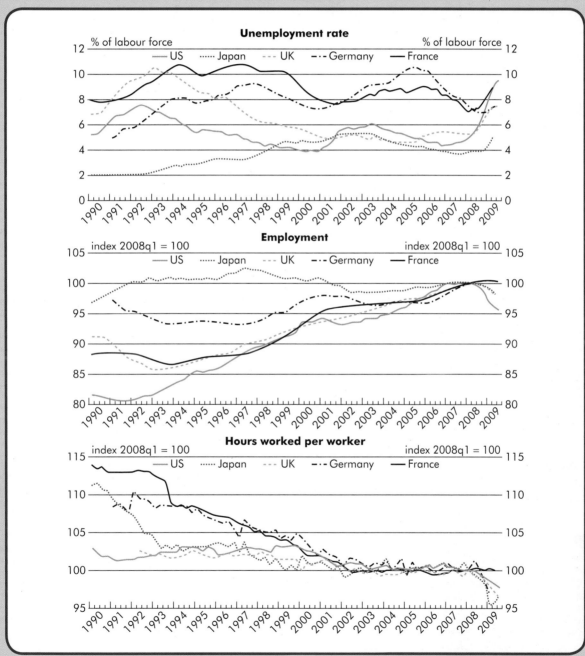

> ## Questions
>
> (a) If the labour demand curve does not alter, should lower employment be associated with higher or lower real wages?
>
> (b) In whch direction might labour demand curves shift during a recession? What would you then expect the correlation to be between changes in wages and changes in employment?
>
> (c) Would it matter whether the recession was caused by an adverse demand shock or an adverse supply shock?
>
> (d) When it is expensive to hire and fire workers, how are firms likely to react to a recession that is perceived as temporary?
>
> (e) If firms then become pessimistic about the persistence of the recession, what is likely to happen to their demand for labour?
>
> *To check your answers to these questions, go to page 688.*

The multiplier–accelerator model of the business cycle

The multiplier–accelerator model distinguishes between the consequences and the causes of a change in investment spending. The consequence is straightforward. In the simplest Keynesian model, higher investment leads to a larger rise in income and output in the short run. Higher investment not only adds directly to aggregate demand but, by increasing incomes, it adds indirectly to consumption demand. Chapters 16 and 17 examined the multiplier effect on output.

What about the cause of a change in investment spending? Firms invest when their existing capital stock is smaller than the capital stock they would like to hold. When firms are holding the optimal capital stock, the marginal cost of another unit of capital just equals its marginal benefit – the present value of future operating profits to which it is expected to give rise over its lifetime. This present value can be increased either by a fall in the interest rate at which the stream of expected future profits is discounted or by an increase in the future profits expected.

Thus far we have focused on the role of changing interest rates in changes in investment demand. However, although nominal interest rates change a lot, real interest rates change a lot less. The simplest way to calculate the present value of a new capital good is to assess the likely stream of *real* operating profits (by valuing future profits at *constant prices*) and then to discount them at the *real* interest rate.

In practice, changes in interest rates may *not* be the most important source of changes in investment spending. Almost certainly, changes in expectations about future profits are more important. The dotcom bubble collapsed not because of high real interest rates but because people realized they had been too optimistic about the future profits to be made.

> The **accelerator model of investment** assumes that firms guess future output and profits by extrapolating past output growth. Constant output growth leads to a constant level of investment. It takes *accelerating* output growth to *raise* desired investment.

More generally, if real interest rates and real wages change slowly, the main source of short-term changes in beliefs about future profits is beliefs about future levels of sales and output. Other things equal, higher expected future output raises expected future profits and raises demand for investment in new capacity. This is the insight of the **accelerator model of investment**.

The accelerator is only a simplification. A complete model of investment would examine changes in expected future profits and changes in (real) interest rates. Even so, many empirical studies confirm that the accelerator is a useful simplification.

Table 27.1   The multiplier–accelerator model of the business cycle

Period	Change in last period's output $(Y_{t-1} - Y_{t-2})$	Investment I_t	Output Y_t
$t = 1$	0	10	100
$t = 2$	0	10	120
$t = 3$	20	20	140
$t = 4$	20	20	140
$t = 5$	0	10	120
$t = 6$	−20	0	100
$t = 7$	−20	0	100
$t = 8$	0	10	120
$t = 9$	20	20	140

How firms respond to changes in output depends on two things: first, the extent to which firms believe that current output growth will be sustained in the future; second, the cost of quickly adjusting investment plans, capital installation and the production techniques thus embodied. The more costly it is to adjust *quickly*, the more firms spread investment over a longer period.

This simple multiplier–accelerator model can lead to a business cycle. In Table 27.1 we make two specific assumptions, although the argument holds much more generally. First, we assume that the value of the multiplier is 2. An extra unit of investment raises income and output by 2 units. Second, we assume that current investment responds to the growth in output *last* period. If last period's income grew by 2 units, we assume that firms raise current investment by 1 unit.

In period 1, the economy is in equilibrium with output $Y_1 = 100$. Since output is constant, last period's output change was zero. Investment $I_1 = 10$, which we can think of as the investment needed to offset depreciation and keep the capital stock intact.

Suppose in period 2 that some component of aggregate demand rises by 20 units. Output increases from 100 to 120. Since we have assumed that a growth of 2 units in the previous period's output leads to a unit increase in current investment, the table shows that in period 3 there is a 10-unit increase in investment in response to the 20-unit output increase during the previous period. Since the assumed value of the multiplier is 2, the 10-unit increase in investment in period 3 leads to a further increase of 20 units in output, which increases from 120 to 140.

In period 4 investment remains at 20 since the output growth in the previous period was 20. Thus output in period 4 remains at 140. But in period 5 investment reverts to its original level of 10, since there was no output growth in the previous period. This fall of 10 units in investment leads to a multiplied fall of 20 units in output in period 5. In turn, this induces a further fall of 10 units of investment in period 6 and a further fall of 20 units in output.

Since the rate of output change is not accelerating, investment in period 7 remains at its period 6 level. Output is stabilized at 100 in period 7. With no output change in the previous period, investment in period 8 returns to 10 units and the multiplier implies that output rises to 120. In period 9 the 20-unit increase in output in the previous period increases investment from 10 to 20 units and the cycle begins all over again.

The multiplier–accelerator model explains business cycles by the dynamic interaction of consumption and investment demand. The insight of the model is that it takes accelerating output growth to increase investment. Once output growth stabilizes, so does investment. In the following period, investment must fall, since output growth has been reduced. The economy moves into a period of recession, but once the rate of output fall stops accelerating, investment starts to pick up again.

This simple model is not the definitive model of a business cycle. If output keeps cycling, surely firms stop extrapolating past output growth to form assessments of future profits? Firms, like economists, recognize that there is a business cycle. The less investment decisions respond to the most recent change in past output, the less pronounced will be the cycle.

> **MATHS 27.1**
>
> # The multiplier–accelerator model of cycles
>
> Suppose I denotes current investment, I_{-1} denotes investment in the previous period, Y denotes output and ΔY denotes $(Y - Y_{-1})$, the increase in output between last period and the current period. Output Y is related to current investment I by the multiplier $Y = I/(1 - c)$, where c is the marginal propensity to consume. Investment depends on output growth, so $I = a \, \Delta Y$. Hence,
>
> $$I = a \, \Delta Y = [a/(1 - c)][I - I_{-1}]$$
>
> Hence
>
> $$I = -\{a/[1 - c - a]\}I_{-1}$$
>
> This equation is of the general form $I = bI_{-1}$. If b is a positive fraction, I is always smaller than the period before and gradually converges on zero. If b exceeds unity, I gets larger and larger for ever. Negative values of b imply I becomes negative every second period, either converging to zero or becoming ever larger. None of this generates things like business cycles.
>
> Cycles emerge however with small changes to these formulae. Table 27.1 offers one example. Here is another. Suppose the consumption function depends not on current income but on income the previous period so that $C = A + cY_{-1}$ and current investment depends on output growth in the previous period, so that $I = a[Y_{-1} - Y_{-2}]$. Since $Y = C + I$ in this simple economy,
>
> $$Y = A + cY_{-1} + a[Y_{-1} - Y_{-2}] \qquad (1)$$
>
> If the economy is in long-run equilibrium, output is constant, the final term is zero, and equilibrium output Y^* is given by $Y^* = A/(1 - c)$. Using y to denote $Y - Y^*$, the deviation of output from its long-run level, we can subtract Y^* from both sides of equation (1) to yield
>
> $$y = cy_{-1} + a[y_{-1} - y_{-2}] \qquad (2)$$
>
> Depending on the values of c and a, equation (2) can yield constant cycles, damped cycles that gradually get smaller and smaller, or explosive cycles that get larger and larger. When $c = a$, we simply get
>
> $$(y - y_{-1}) = -(y_{-1} - y_{-2})$$
>
> so that positive and negative growth of similar size alternate for ever.

Ceilings and floors

The multiplier–accelerator model can generate cycles even without any physical limits on the extent of fluctuations. Cycles are even more likely when we recognize the limits imposed by supply and demand. Aggregate supply provides a *ceiling* in practice. Although it is possible temporarily to meet high aggregate demand by working overtime and running down stocks of finished goods, output cannot expand indefinitely.

This tends to slow down growth as the economy reaches a boom. Having overstretched itself, the economy has to bounce back off the ceiling and begin a downturn. Conversely, there is a *floor*, below which aggregate demand cannot fall. Gross investment (including replacement investment) cannot be negative unless, for the economy as a whole, machines are unbolted and shipped abroad for sale to foreigners. Falling investment is an important component of a downswing, but investment cannot fall indefinitely, whatever our model of investment behaviour.

Fluctuations in stockbuilding

Having examined investment in fixed capital, we now look at inventory investment in working capital. Firms hold stocks of goods despite the cost, namely the interest payments on the funds tied up in producing the goods for which no revenue from sales has yet been received. What is the corresponding benefit of holding stocks? If output could be instantly and costlessly varied, it would always be possible to meet sales and demand by varying current production. Holding stocks makes sense because it is expensive to adjust production *quickly*. Output expansion may involve heavy overtime payments and costs of recruiting new workers. Cutting output may involve expensive redundancy payments. Holding stocks allows firms to meet short-term fluctuations in demand without incurring the expense of short-run fluctuations in output.

How do firms respond to a fall in aggregate demand? Since rapid output adjustment is expensive, in the short run firms undertake the adjustments that can be made more cheaply. They reduce hours of overtime and possibly even move on to short-time working. If demand has fallen substantially, this still leaves firms producing a larger output than they can sell. Firms build up stocks of unsold finished output.

If aggregate demand remains low, firms gradually reduce their workforce, partly through natural wastage and partly because it becomes cheaper to sack some workers than to meet the interest payments on ever-larger volumes of stock. Once aggregate demand recovers again, firms are still holding all the extra stocks built up during recession. Only by increasing output *more slowly* than the increase in aggregate demand can firms eventually sell off these stocks and get back to their long-run equilibrium position.

Costs of employment adjustment explain both the pattern of inventories over the business cycle and the pattern of labour productivity in Figure 27.2. Output per worker rises in a boom and falls in a slump. In other words, output adjusts more quickly than employment. This is what we expect, given the costs of adjusting employment rapidly.

A fall in demand is met initially by cutting hours and increasing stocks. With a shorter working week, output per worker falls. Only as the recession intensifies do firms undertake the costlier process of sacking workers and restoring hours to their normal level. Conversely, a boom is the time when output and overtime are high and productivity per worker peaks.

Figure 27.3 confirms this clearly in response to the fall in aggregate demand that began in 2008. During 2006–07, the level of stocks fluctuated from quarter to quarter without any particular trend. In the first quarter of 2008, aggregate demand fell and firms were left with unsold goods. Their stocks rose unexpectedly. Foreseeing

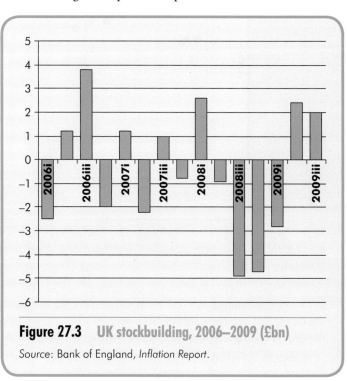

Figure 27.3   UK stockbuilding, 2006–2009 (£bn)

Source: Bank of England, Inflation Report.

that demand would be weak for some time, firms began to cut back production, reducing stocks of work in progress. When production had fallen more than demand, stocks of unsold finished goods also fell. Figure 27.3 shows substantial destocking during the rest of 2008 and early 2009. Once production had fallen more than demand, stocks started to increase again.

Competitiveness

Chapter 24 identified another potential mechanism that could generate cycles. An economy on a fixed exchange rate experiences a downward domestic demand shock. Interest rates, fixed at world levels to peg the exchange rate, cannot be used to restore aggregate demand.

Recession eventually bids down wages and prices, thus raising competitiveness and restoring internal balance by raising the demand for net exports. However this is not external balance, since net exports are now positive. With a current account surplus, the country gets richer, and additional wealth gradually boosts consumption demand. The economy now has a boom, which bids up prices and reduces competitiveness. Long-run equilibrium is restored when the current account falls back to zero.

This is a proper story about cycles. Output gaps induce changes in the price level that restore internal balance only by destroying external balance. This sets off a movement in the opposite direction that gradually reverses all these effects. Adjustment entails necessary overshooting of the final equilibrium.

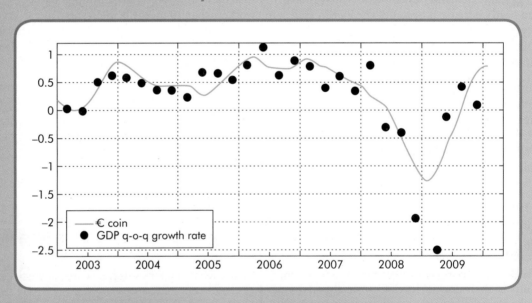

CASE 27.1

Eurozone business cycles

EuroCOIN, the monthly coincident indicator of the eurozone business cycle, is published by the Centre for Economic Policy Research based in London. The figure shows values of the indicator (in blue) and the quarterly growth rate of the eurozone GDP (in black) during 2003-10.

Why not use changes in GDP itself to measure the business cycle? Mainly because initial estimates of GDP are unreliable and the data are often revised a lot as time elapses. The *EuroCOIN* indicator not only estimates the cyclical component of GDP more accurately but is also available monthly, whereas GDP estimates appear only quarterly. By examining past correlations of GDP growth with data that do appear monthly, the indicator provides a more frequent and more reliable picture of the eurozone business cycle – helpful information for the monthly meetings of the European Central Bank at which interest rate decisions are made.

The figure shows that, like other independent central banks, the European Central Bank had been fairly successful up to 2007 in stabilizing output. There was not much of a business cycle. The monthly *EuroCOIN* indicator shows a slowdown beginning to happen even during 2007 and then rapidly during 2008. The indicator dates early 2009 as the cyclical bottom for output growth, even though the growth indicator did not climb above zero until later in 2009, and did not deliver two successive quarters of positive growth – the official definition of the end of the recession – until the end of 2009.

Source: http://www.cepr.org/Data/eurocoin.

27.3 Real business cycles

So far our analysis of business cycles focuses on demand shocks and cyclical movements in output gaps. This is compatible with our earlier analysis of sluggish wage adjustment in the short run. This view of cycles is consistent with a model that is Keynesian in the short run, but classical or monetarist in the long run.

Not all economists share our assessment of how the economy works. In particular, there is an influential school, known as the New Classical economists, whose intellectual leader is the Nobel Laureate Robert Lucas of the University of Chicago. Although we discuss competing views of macroeconomics more fully in the next chapter, one implication of the New Classical view should be discussed immediately.

A key assumption of the New Classical school is that all markets clear almost instantaneously. Effectively, output is almost always at its full-employment level.[1]

Proponents of the theory argue that macroeconomics should base theories of firms and households in a microeconomic analysis of choice between the present and the future. For example, this approach would view each household as making a plan to supply labour and demand goods both now and in the future in such a way that lifetime spending was financed out of lifetime income plus any initial assets. Such plans would then be aggregated to get total consumption spending and total labour supply. An equivalently complex story would apply to firms and investment.

> **Real business cycle theories** explain cycles as fluctuations in potential output itself.

One implication of this approach is that it is no longer helpful to distinguish between supply and demand. If labour supply and consumption demand are part of the same household decision, things that induce the household to change its consumption demand also induce it to change its labour supply.

For this reason, real business cycle theorists simply discuss what happens to actual output, which reflects both supply and demand and, by assumption, equates the two at potential output. In this view, the economy is then bombarded with shocks (for example, breakthroughs in technology, changes in government policy), which alter these complicated plans and give rise to equilibrium behaviour that looks like a business cycle.

Why is this approach called the *real* business cycle approach? In the classical model, nominal money only affects other nominal variables. Output and employment depend only on real variables. Since real business cycle theorists believe in the classical model, they take it for granted that the source of business cycles must be in real shocks. Fancy dynamics can then explain why shocks last and have convoluted effects.

---

1 For an accessible introduction to these issues, see the lively exchange between Charles Plosser and Greg Mankiw in 'Real business cycles: a new Keynesian perspective', *Journal of Economic Perspectives*, 3 (3): 79–90.

Intertemporal substitution: a key to persistence

Real business cycle theories need to combine rapid market adjustment to equilibrium with sluggish behaviour of aggregate output over the business cycle. Intertemporal substitution means making trade-offs over time, postponing or bringing forward actions in the sophisticated long-run plans of households and firms. This behaviour can cause effects to persist and look like part of a business cycle.

Suppose the productivity genie visits while we are all asleep. When we wake up, our productivity has doubled. But only for a year. We know that by next year our productivity will have returned to normal. We face a temporary productivity shock, a blip in our technology. What should we do?

We are definitely wealthier after the genie's visit. We are pleased it happened. We could simply behave as before, working just as hard and investing just as much. In that case, our extra productivity would make extra output this year, but it is output that we would blow entirely on consumption this year. We would get little extra utility out of the hundredth bottle of champagne, and we would be making no provision for the future. There must be a better way.

We could put in a temporary spurt of extra work while we are superproductive, but in itself that would only exacerbate the problem: even more champagne today, still nothing extra for tomorrow. In fact, because leisure is a luxury and because we are better off than before, we may feel like taking it easy and doing less work.

We need a way of transferring some of our windfall benefit into future consumption. The solution is investment. A sharp rise in the share of output going to investment will provide more capital for the future, thereby allowing higher future consumption even after our productivity bonus has evaporated. Once we get to the future, being then richer than we would have been without the genie, we may in consequence work less hard than we would have done, since leisure is a luxury.

The point of this example is to show that even a temporary shock can have effects that persist well into the future. Persistence occurs both through investment (in human as well as physical capital) and through intertemporal labour substitution – deciding when in one's life to put in the effort.

Real business cycle theories still need to be worked out fully. Apart from optimism about the speed of adjustment, they have been criticized on two grounds. First, they are usually theories of persistence not cycles. Shocks have long drawn out effects, but rarely are these cyclical. To 'explain' business cycles, so far real business cycle theorists have had to assume a cyclical pattern to the shocks themselves. The theory is therefore incomplete.

Second, and related, since the most widely researched example involves shocks to technology, a cyclical pattern of shocks implies that in some years technical knowledge actually diminishes: we forget how to do things. Not just once, but regularly every few years. This may be a bit hard to swallow.

However, this can be given a more plausible interpretation. In the dotcom bubble of the late 1990s, investors made extravagant projections about future productivity growth and associated profits from the new technologies. By 2000 evidence was accumulating that previous estimates, necessarily guesses in a new situation, were too optimistic. In 2001 investment collapsed, particularly in the US where dotcom optimism had been greatest.

Thus, the adverse shock was not a fall in existing technology – which is indeed implausible – but in estimates of future technology, which affects current behaviour since firms, households and governments all make long-term plans.

Policy implications

Research on real business cycles has much still to accomplish, but it does have a vital message for macro-economic policy. If the theory is right, it destroys the case for trying to stabilize output over the business cycle. Fluctuations in output are fluctuations in an *equilibrium* output that efficiently reconciles people's desires.

For example, in the parable of the genie, the induced effects on investment, labour supply, output and consumption implement people's preferred way to take advantage of the beneficial opportunity. Trying to prevent these ripples is misguided policy.

Although important, this caveat undermines the case for stabilization policy only if we buy totally the assumptions of complete and instant market-clearing and the absence of any externalities. For most economists these assumptions are too extreme to reflect the real world, which continues to exhibit Keynesian features in the short run. Valid reasons for stabilization policy then remain.

Even so, real business cycle theories force us all to acknowledge that there is no reason why potential output should grow as smoothly as trend output. The latter is a statistical artefact whose construction, averaging, forces it to be smooth.

Credit constraints and aggregate supply

The financial crash provided a huge adverse shock to aggregate demand, as people watched their wealth evaporate. But it would be wrong to assume the crash had no direct effect on aggregate supply. Firms need to borrow to finance the costs of production before this output can be sold.

When banks became insolvent, or people feared that banks were close to being insolvent, this had two effects. First, banks had inadequate reserves to take their normal business risks. Second, banks and all other financial market participants suddenly raised their estimate of the likely riskiness of borrowers. The result, as we saw in Chapter 18, was that interest rate spreads became huge and banks stopped lending almost completely.

This meant that many businesses found it impossible to finance production and had to cut back. Aggregate supply fell, independently of what was happening to aggregate demand.

27.4 Towards a consensus: supply-side effects of the financial crash

We began this chapter by exploring mechanisms through which we might generate cycles in aggregate demand. These include the multiplier–accelerator, the effects of stockbuilding, the consequences of fixed exchange rates, political cycles in the policy stimulus, and simple effects of floors and ceilings. Within such frameworks, fluctuations in aggregate demand lead to similar fluctuations in output gaps, since the trend behaviour of potential output is unaffected.

Fluctuations in aggregate demand could in principle be completely offset by an independent central bank with perfect foresight. Eliminating fluctuations in output gaps would eliminate a key source of inflationary pressure and help stabilize inflation. The fact that there is substantial evidence that business cycles were much less marked during 1995–2007, when independent central banks were explicitly asked to conduct this task, is prima facie evidence that demand fluctuations had been the most frequent source of business cycle fluctuations. Since central banks do not have perfect foresight, and since interest rate changes take time to affect aggregate demand, even excellent central banks could never have been expected to eliminate cycles completely.

Demand is very important, but it is not the whole story, for four reasons. First, real business cycle theories provide a healthy antidote to an exclusive focus on demand. Sometimes, supply-side factors will cause uneven growth of potential output, and may even reduce potential output for a while. Nobody promised that technological progress would occur at an even rate.

Second, hysteresis matters, especially for large shocks. In Chapter 25, we explored how temporary shocks to demand could have lingering, even permanent, effects on supply, through induced effects on the capital stock, skill base and union power. Third, credit rationing by banks and other lenders directly curtailed the ability of firms to finance production.

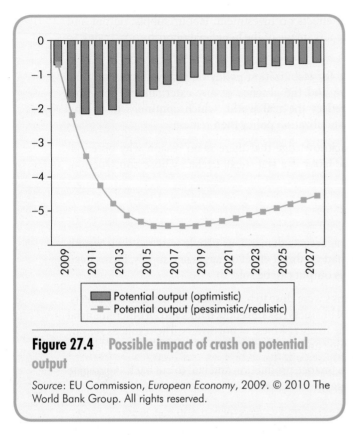

Figure 27.4 Possible impact of crash on potential output

Source: EU Commission, *European Economy*, 2009. © 2010 The World Bank Group. All rights reserved.

Finally, in Chapter 26 we introduced the concept of endogenous growth. Although it is possible that nature obeys the simplicity of the neoclassical growth model, in which the economy inevitably reverts to its unique long-run growth rate, it will require decades if not centuries of evidence to be certain that this is correct. Allowing for endogenous growth – in which changes, for example in saving rates, permanently affect the growth rate of potential output – introduces a third channel by which potential output could be affected by the financial crash.

Research for the EU Commission has tried to model how large these four effects might be.[2] Since we do not have enough evidence to give a definitive estimate, the Commission economists have produced an 'optimistic' and 'pessimistic' scenario, shown in Figure 27.4. In the optimistic scenario, the crisis leads to a fall in EU potential output by about 2 per cent in 2011, after which potential output gradually reverts to the path it would anyway have followed. However, even in the optimistic scenario, the financial crisis and subsequent recession is still casting a shadow on potential output as late as 2025. Since output cannot remain above potential output indefinitely, anything that reduces potential output for 15 years entails sacrificing considerable output cumulatively, even after the immediate crisis has been overcome.

In the pessimistic scenario, the induced effects on potential output are much, much larger and last much longer. Potential output gets worse until 2017 and is still 5 per cent worse than it would have been as late as 2025. From the perspective of a practical politician, this is as bad as a permanent reduction in potential output.

In order to fully understand business cycles, and hence to assess the consequences of the financial crash, we need to be quite sophisticated. Aggregate demand fluctuates (unless stabilized by monetary policy), but this should probably be superimposed on a path of potential output that is also capable of fluctuations. Although it is an empirical question which is larger, in normal circumstances the possible fluctuations in aggregate demand are probably more important.

In more extreme circumstances, and particularly where a financial crash is involved, aggregate supply is also capable of falling sharply for two reasons: the credit impact on the ability to finance production, and the various hysteresis effects that demand falls then induce as supply falls.

 27.5 An international business cycle?

National politicians want all the credit when output is high but produce a cast-iron alibi when the economy turns sour. They say domestic difficulties were caused by a world recession. How good is their alibi?

Figure 27.5 plots data during 1996–2009 for the US, Japan, the UK, Germany, France and Italy. Although there were differences in the 1990s – for example, Japan continued to stagnate – it is striking how similar

2 'Impact of the current economic and financial crisis on potential output', *European Economy*, Occasional Paper 49, June 2009.

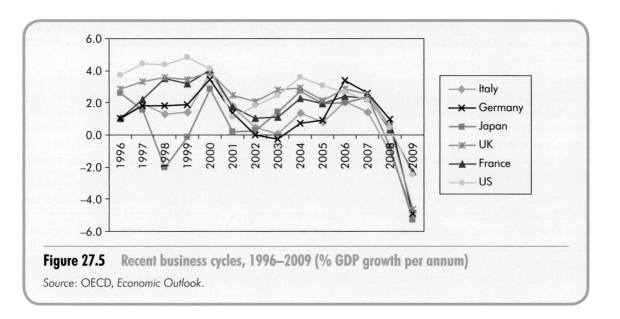

Figure 27.5 Recent business cycles, 1996–2009 (% GDP growth per annum)

Source: OECD, Economic Outlook.

output growth has been across countries since 2000. Largely this reflects the fact that both the dotcom bust and the financial crisis were global events. In addition, independent central banks have pursued rather similar monetary policies, eliminating one important source of differences in national policy shocks.

These patterns warn us how interdependent the leading countries have become in the modern world. Economies are becoming more open. In product markets, protectionist policies are being removed, through global institutions like the World Trade Organization and through regional integration, as in the creation of a Single European Market.

Improvements in transport and telecommunications also favour greater integration of product markets. When R&D costs are large, producers need a global market if they are to recover their overheads. Product market integration provides an international transmission mechanism through exports and imports. Increasingly, we have a global financial market. Closer financial integration increases the likelihood that different countries pursue similar monetary policies.

The business cycle is transmitted from one country to another not just through private sector decisions about imports and exports (and induced effects on labour supply, investment and consumption), but also, sometimes, through induced changes in the economic policy of other governments.

The considerable integration of advanced economies prompts a second question: are the leading emerging market economies, particularly China and India, on the way towards similar integration with their longer-established partners? Figure 27.6 shows the most recent part of the answer. Prior to

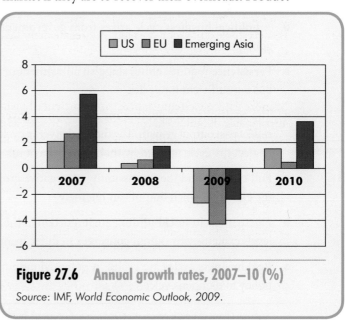

Figure 27.6 Annual growth rates, 2007–10 (%)

Source: IMF, World Economic Outlook, 2009.

the crisis, Asian economies had been growing much more quickly as they caught up with the OECD. The cyclical pattern in response to the global crisis was very similar to OECD countries, albeit from a higher baseline rate of growth.

Making the same point in another way, Chinese and Indian markets were not sheltered from the effects of the US sub-prime mortgage crisis. Either the financial impact was felt directly, because Asian lenders had invested in companies such as Lehman Brothers or been induced to buy securitized products that were subsequently exposed as worthless, or the impact was a second-round effect – as Western economies contracted, exports from India and China suffered. Whatever the channel, Figure 27.6 confirms that most of the important parts of the world are now sufficiently connected that national policy makers cannot expect to escape unscathed.

This is not to say that all shocks will create identical ripples. In mid-January the *Financial Times* reported that Chinese house prices were growing at 1.5 per cent a month, or around 20 per cent a year, prompting fears that the Chinese economy might soon be growing too quickly again.[3] An expansionary demand shock specific to China might be expected to bid up prices of raw materials, from oil to copper, that China imports as raw materials. Whereas, in China, rising raw material prices would be the consequence of the local demand shock, in Europe and Japan these rising global materials prices might appear as an adverse supply shock. In such circumstances, international transmission would transmit shocks differentially.

The key message, therefore, is that some shocks are experienced in common, but others are not. For most countries, globalization increases the probability that the shocks with which its policy makers have to deal are not emanating from the domestic economy but from abroad. Most of the time, only countries as large as the US, China and soon India will be big enough, acting alone, to have a major effect on the rest of the global economy.

Summary

- The **trend path of output** is the long-run path after short-run fluctuations are ironed out. The **business cycle** describes fluctuations in output around this trend. Cycles last about five years but are not perfectly regular.

- A **political business cycle** arises from government manipulation of the economy to make things look good just before an election.

- **Persistence** requires either sluggish adjustment or intertemporal substitution. Persistence is necessary but not sufficient for cycles.

- The **multiplier–accelerator model** assumes investment depends on expected future profits, which reflect past output growth. The model delivers a cycle but assumes that firms are stupid: their expectations neglect the cycle implied by their own behaviour.

- Full capacity and the impossibility of negative gross investment provide **ceilings and floors** that limit the extent to which output can fluctuate.

- Fluctuations in **stockbuilding** are important in the business cycle. The need to restore stocks to original levels explains why output continues to differ from demand even during the recovery phase.

- **Real business cycles** are cycles in potential output itself. In such circumstances, it is not desirable for policy to dampen cycles.

---

3 'Soaring Chinese house prices increase fears of property bubble', *Financial Times*, 15 January 2010.

● Some swings in potential output do occur, but many short-run fluctuations probably reflect Keynesian departures from potential output. Aggregate demand and aggregate supply both contribute to the business cycle.

● Increasing integration of world financial and product markets has made most countries heavily dependent on the wider world. Business cycles in the rich countries are closely correlated.

● In 2001 central banks cut interest rates to prevent recession from spiralling. Japan's difficulty escaping from the deflation trap suggests that dampening business cycles remains an important aim for other countries.

Review questions

1 'If firms could forecast future output and profits accurately, there could not be a business cycle.' Is this true?

EASY

2 Heavily dependent on output of oil and fishing, Norway's business cycle goes in the opposite direction from those in other European countries. Why?

3 Why might voters care more about the direction in which the economy is heading than about the absolute level of its position at election time?

4 Would it help the world economy if all the largest countries elected governments on the same day? Why, or why not?

5 What is real about a business cycle?

6 Common fallacies   Why are these statements wrong? (a) Closer integration of national economies will abolish business cycles. (b) The more we expect cycles, the more we get them. (c) Because output and labour productivity are closely correlated, fluctuations in productivity are the main cause of business cycles.

7 Which is correct? (a) Business cycles imply that people are stupid: if they could see a cycle coming they would already be taking action to abolish it. (b) It is easy to explain why it takes a while to return to long-run equilibrium but hard to explain why this return then overshoots and has to come back again. (c) Economic dynamics are slow and complicated. There are many models in which cycles result.

8 Greece, Spain, Portugal, Ireland and Italy have emerged as weak members of the eurozone. Do you think this is because their business cycles are less correlated with France and Germany or because their political institutions are weak?

9 Consider an economy with a fixed exchange rate. Beginning from internal and external balance, the economy experiences an adverse domestic demand shock that is not fully offset by a policy response. Draw a diagram to illustrate subsequent adjustment. Why does the requirement to get back to *both* internal and external balance generate a cyclical response?

MEDIUM

10 Plot the data of Table 27.1 and confirm that both output and investment exhibit cyclical behaviour. Which is causing which?

11 Suppose $Y = C + I$, $C = A + 0.6Y$ and $I = 0.1(\Delta Y)$. Does this economy converge to long-run equilibrium, explode away from long-run equilibrium or cycle for ever?

12 (a) Since central banks became independent, do you expect to see more or less evidence of a political business cycle? (b) Might there be an interest rate cycle instead? Why, or why not?

13 If the multiplier–accelerator model still fits the data quite well, does this imply that people are stupid?

HARD

14 Essay question 'The business cycle ought to last for different lengths of time depending on whether the original shocks were supply shocks or demand shocks.' Is this true?

For solutions to these questions contact your lecturer.

PART FIVE: The world economy

Part Five focuses on the world as a whole. What determines the pattern of international trade and the tariff policies pursued by individual countries? Can free trade benefit everyone? How on earth can Europe compete with China and India? What difference does the international monetary system make? Can the IMF prevent financial crises?

Chapter 28 analyses why international trade takes place, studies the gains from trade and considers what this implies for trade policy of nation states. Chapter 29 examines the international monetary system through which trade is financed and discusses different types of exchange rate regime.

Contents

International trade

Learning Outcomes

By the end of this chapter, you should understand:

1. patterns of international trade

2. comparative advantage and the gains from trade

3. determinants of comparative advantage

4. why two-way trade occurs for the same product

5. trade policy

6. the principle of targeting

7. motives for tariffs

International trade is part of daily life. Britons drink French wine, Americans drive Japanese cars and Russians eat American wheat. China makes European clothes but buys up raw materials that Europeans would otherwise have bought. There are three reasons why trade between the UK and Japan is different from trade between London and Birmingham.

First, because international trade crosses national frontiers, governments can monitor this trade and treat it differently. It is hard to tax or regulate goods moving from London to Birmingham but much easier to impose taxes or quota restrictions on goods imported from Taiwan or Japan. Governments have to decide whether or not such policies are desirable.

Second, if trade between London and Birmingham redistributes income between residents of these two cities, the UK government can, if it wishes, use the national tax system to offset this effect. If trade between the UK and China leaves the UK worse off, UK fiscal policy cannot compensate in the same way.

Third, international trade may involve the use of different national currencies. A British buyer of American wine pays in sterling but the American vineyard worker is paid in dollars. International trade involves international payments. We examine the system of international payments more fully in the next chapter.

This chapter concentrates on trade flows and trade policy. Who trades with whom and in what commodities? Why does international trade take place? Countries trade with one another because they can buy foreign goods at a lower price than it costs to make the same goods at home.

Is this possible for all countries? International trade reflects *exchange* and *specialization*. International differences in the availability of raw materials and other factors of production lead to international differences in production costs and goods prices. Through international exchange, countries supply the world economy with the commodities that they produce relatively cheaply and demand from the world economy the goods made relatively cheaply elsewhere.

These benefits from trade are reinforced if there are scale economies in production. Instead of each country having a lot of small producers, different countries concentrate on different things and everyone can benefit from the cost reductions that ensue.

We discuss the benefits from international trade and examine whether our analysis can explain the trade flows that actually take place. There are many circumstances in which international trade can make countries better off, but trade can also carry costs, especially in the short run. Cheap foreign cars are great for UK consumers but less good for unemployed UK car workers.

Because foreign competition makes life difficult for some voters, governments are frequently under pressure to restrict imports. We conclude the chapter by discussing trade or commercial policy and whether it is a good idea to restrict imports.

 ## 28.1   Trade patterns

Every international transaction has both a buyer and a seller. One country's imports are another country's exports. To measure how much trade occurs, we can measure the total value of exports by all countries or the total value of imports. Table 28.1 shows the value of world exports and, as a benchmark, the value relative to GNP in the world's largest single economy, the US.

World trade has grown rapidly since 1950, at an average annual rate of 8 per cent. International trade becomes ever more important to national economies. Between 1960 and 2009, UK exports as a fraction of GNP rose from 18 per cent to 27 per cent. Details for selected countries are shown in Table 28.2. World exports are now around 20 per cent of world GNP.

The Great Depression of the 1930s and the Second World War virtually destroyed international trade. Measured relative to US GDP, it was not until the 1960s that world trade regained its level of 1928.

As trade has grown, both in absolute terms and relative to the size of national economies, the interdependence of national economies has increased. Like many of the countries in Table 28.2, the UK is now a very open economy. Smaller countries are usually more open. Trade between Paris and Brussels is *international* trade, but trade between New York and California is not. Events in other countries affect our daily lives much more than they did 20 years ago. We now look at the facts about who trades with whom.

Table 28.1   The value of world exports

	1928	1935	1950	1973	2009
World exports (2005 £bn)	388	164	246	1303	6200
(% of US GNP)	57	27	20	40	85

Sources: League of Nations, *Europe's Trade*, Geneva, 1941; IMF, *International Financial Statistics*; National Income Accounts of the United States, 1928–49.

Table 28.2 Exports as a percentage of GDP

	1967	2009
Belgium	36	74
Netherlands	43	73
UK	18	27
France	14	30
Italy	17	25
US	5	14
Japan	10	10

Source: OECD, *Economic Outlook*.

Table 28.3 Trade patterns, 1980–2008 (% of world exports)

	Destination of exports			
	1980		2008	
Origin of exports	Developed	Other	Developed	Other
Developed countries	50	21	41	16
Other	21	8	24	19

Source: UNCTAD, *Handbook of Statistics*, 2009 (www.unctad.org).

World trade patterns

Table 28.3 shows the pattern of trade, which is dominated by the rich countries of Europe and North America, and Japan. As late as 1980, the developed countries were the origin of and destination for 71 per cent of world exports, most of this trade being among themselves. Trade between other countries – the poor and middle-income countries, and the former communist economies – accounted for only 8 per cent of world trade.

The rapid growth of emerging market economies – particularly China, India and Brazil, but also the Asian 'tigers' (including Singapore, Thailand, South Korea and the Phillipines) – and the economic liberalization of the former Soviet Union and Eastern Europe has led to rapid growth in their international trade. As a result, by 2008, the picture had changed substantially. Trade among the developed countries, although absolutely much larger, had fallen from 50 per cent to 41 per cent of total world trade, whereas trade among the other countries had risen from 8 per cent to 19 per cent of world trade. This rapid improvement in some countries obscures the fact that other countries remain stuck at the bottom. The **less-developed countries** (LDCs) as a whole range from the very poor such, as Bangladesh, to the nearly rich, such as Brazil. Having enjoyed per capita income growth of nearly 10 per cent a year for 25 years, China is breaking all records in making the transition from very poor to nearly rich.

Less-developed countries (LDCs) have low per capita incomes.

Table 28.4 The composition of world exports

% share of	1955	2008
Primary commodities	50.5	31
Food, agriculture	22.3	8.5
Fuels and mining	15.0	22.5
Manufactures	49.5	66.5

Sources: GATT, *Networks of World Trade, 1955–76*; www.wto.org.

Table 28.5 Merchandise trade patterns, 2008 (% of region's exports)

	Agriculture	Fuels, minerals	Manufactures
World	**8.5**	**22.5**	**66.5**
North America	10.4	17	68
Europe	9.3	11.9	76.8
CIS	6.8	66.8	24.9
Africa	6.8	70.6	17.9
Middle East	2.4	74.1	21.6
Asia	6	12.4	79.2

Source: www.wto.org.

The commodity composition of trade

In rich countries, services are most of value added or GDP. International trade in services is growing rapidly, but from a small baseline. Trade in goods – or merchandise trade – remains important because many countries import goods, add a little value and then re-export them. The value added makes a small contribution to GDP but gross flows of imports and exports of goods are large. By importing goods, adding a little value and re-exporting, it is even possible that the value of exports exceeds the value of GDP itself.

Table 28.4 distinguishes between *primary commodities* (agricultural commodities, minerals and fuels) and manufactured or processed commodities (chemicals, steel and cars). Primary products fell from 50.5 per cent of world merchandise trade in 1955 to below 25 per cent in 2000; but by 2008 had risen to 31 per cent as China scoured the world for metals and fuel to sustain its industrial boom. However, over the 50-year period, the big story is the fall in primary commodity trade and the huge rise in trade in manufactures.

Table 28.5 shows again the commodity shares of world exports, and shows commodity composition by region for merchandise trade excluding services. The mature economies of Europe and North America and the Asian economies (whether rapidly growing or mature Japan) export mainly manufactures, whereas the Commonwealth of Independent States (the ex-Soviet Union), Africa and the Middle East mainly export oil and other minerals.

World trade: the issues

Tables 28.1 to 28.5 set out the facts. World trade has grown faster than world income, and is increasingly important. Forty per cent of all international trade is between rich industrial countries, which are also the main export markets for emerging market economies. A third of world trade is in primary products, the rest in manufactures. These facts help explain some of the key issues in world trade.

Raw material prices

LDCs claim that industrial countries exploit them by buying raw materials at a low price and returning manufactured goods at a much higher price. Producers of coffee, sugar, copper and many other products would like to be able to copy OPEC and triple the price of their primary products without suffering a significant reduction in the quantities demanded.

Agricultural protection

Farmers in rich countries not only receive agricultural subsidies, such as those through the EU Common Agricultural Policy, but also enjoy protection behind high tariffs on imported farm goods. LDCs complain that exclusion of their exports from the richest markets not only reduces the quantity of what they can sell but also forces down the price when all their supply must be absorbed in the remaining world markets to which they have access.

Manufactured exports from emerging market economies

These countries want to make their own manufactured goods and export them to the industrial countries. Brazil, Mexico and South Korea already have major manufacturing industries, China is now a powerhouse, and Indian companies such as Tata are now moving into Western markets. But exports to industrial countries have led to complaints in industrial countries that jobs are being threatened by competition from cheap foreign labour. Should Asian exports be restricted to prevent massive job losses in Western Europe and North America or should rich countries take advantage of low costs in Asia?

Globalization

Lower transport costs and better information technology are gradually breaking down the segmentation of national markets and increasing competition between countries. This trend has been reinforced by reductions in tariffs as a matter of policy. Sometimes the pace of change has been rapid.

However, poor countries feel that the process is largely dictated by rich countries according to their own self-interest. Poorer countries feel pressurized to dismantle their own tariffs and allow in foreign investors, while rich countries remain reluctant to pay attention to concerns of poor countries. By raising the demand for LDC exports, reducing agricultural protection in rich countries might do more to help LDCs than the entire programme of foreign aid.

Before examining these issues, we explain why international trade takes place at all.

28.2 Comparative advantage

Trade is beneficial when there are international differences in the **opportunity cost** of goods.

Suppose a closed economy with given resources can make DVD recorders or shirts. The more resources used to make DVD recorders, the fewer resources can be used to make shirts. The opportunity cost of DVD recorders is the quantity of shirts sacrificed by using resources to make DVD recorders not shirts.

> The **opportunity cost** of a good is the quantity of other goods sacrificed to make another unit of that good.

The **law of comparative advantage** states that countries specialize in producing and exporting the goods that they produce at a lower *relative cost* than other countries.

Opportunity costs tell us about the *relative* costs of producing different goods. We now develop a model in which international differences in relative production costs determine the pattern of international trade. The model demonstrates the law of comparative advantage.[1]

Opportunity costs or relative costs may differ in different countries. We begin with a very simple model in which different technology explains the cost difference. Suppose two countries, the US and the UK, produce two goods, DVD recorders and shirts. Labour is the only input and there are constant returns to scale. Table 28.6 shows the assumed production costs. It takes 30 hours of US labour to make a DVD recorder and 5 hours to make a shirt. UK labour is less productive. It takes 60 hours of UK labour to make a DVD recorder and 6 hours to make a shirt.

Costs and prices

For simplicity, assume there is perfect competition. Hence the price of each good equals its marginal cost. Since there are constant returns to scale, marginal costs equal average costs. Thus, prices equal average costs of production. Because labour is the only factor of production, average cost is the value of labour input per unit of output – the unit labour cost.

Assume US workers earn $6 an hour and UK workers £2 an hour. The last two rows of Table 28.6 show unit labour costs of the two goods in each country. With no international trade, each country makes both goods. The unit labour costs are the domestic prices for which the goods are sold. Perfect competition means price equals marginal cost, and constant returns to scale means marginal cost equals average cost.

US unit labour requirements are *absolutely* lower for *both* goods than those in the UK. But US labour is *relatively* more productive in DVD recorders than in shirts. It takes twice as many labour hours to make a DVD recorder in the UK as it does in the US but only 6/5 times as many hours to make a shirt. These relative productivity differences are the basis for international trade.

Allowing international trade

Now the countries trade with each other. This section makes two key points. First, if each country concentrates on producing the good that it makes *relatively* cheaply, the two countries together make more

Table 28.6 Production techniques and costs

	US	UK
Unit labour requirement (hours/output unit)		
DVD recorders	30	60
Shirts	5	6
Wage per hour	$6	£2
Unit labour cost		
DVD recorders	$180	£120
Shirts	$30	£12

---

1 This law was formulated by the great English economist David Ricardo (1772–1823), a successful stockbroker before retiring at the age of 40 to become a Member of Parliament and an economist. Ricardo's arguments have a modern ring to them because he used models, clearly stating their assumptions and implications.

Table 28.7 Costs, prices and the range of equilibrium exchange rates

	Domestic price		$2.50/£		$2/£		$1.50/£	
	DVD recorders	Shirts	DVD recorders	Shirts	DVD recorders	Shirts	DVD recorders	Shirts
US goods	$180	$30	£72	£12	£90	£15	£120	£20
UK goods	£120	£12	£120	£12	£120	£12	£120	£12

of *both* goods. Trade leads to a pure gain: extra output to be shared between the two countries. Second, the free market provides the right incentives for this beneficial trade to occur.

The countries now trade. Since they use different currencies, a foreign exchange market is set up and an equilibrium exchange rate established. A country's current account must be zero in long-run equilibrium. For simplicity, we ignore foreign debts and assets, and assume that eventually the equilibrium exchange rate adjusts to make the value of imports equal to the value of exports, thus balancing the trade account in the long run.

Table 28.7 shows the unit labour cost and price of DVD recorders and shirts in different currencies and then shows their price in pounds at three possible exchange rates: $2.50/£, $2/£ and $1.50/£. The domestic prices reflect the unit cost data in Table 28.6. The price in pounds of UK goods is unaffected by the exchange rate, but the UK price of US goods depends on the exchange rate. The more dollars to the pound, the cheaper are both US goods when valued in pounds.

At the exchange rate of $2.50/£, US DVD recorders are cheaper in pounds than UK DVD recorders, but the price of UK and US shirts is the same. If the exchange rate exceeds $2.50/£, even US shirts cost less in pounds. The equilibrium exchange rate cannot lie above $2.50/£, for then nobody would buy UK goods.[2] A one-way flow in trade and foreign exchange is not an equilibrium.

Conversely, at $1.50/£ US shirts are dearer than UK shirts, but UK and US DVD recorder prices are the same. If the exchange rate is lower than $1.50/£, both US goods are dearer than UK goods when valued in the same currency. At $1/£, US DVD players cost £180 and US shirts cost £30. At any exchange rate below £1.50/£ there is a one-way flow of trade and foreign exchange, though it is now UK goods everyone wants to buy.

The foreign exchange market is in equilibrium only if the value of UK imports, and hence the demand for dollars with which to purchase them, equals the value of UK exports, and hence the supply of dollars as UK exporters convert their revenues back into pounds. Hence the highest possible equilibrium exchange rate is $2.50/£, the exchange rate at which one UK good (shirts) is still just competitive with US shirts; and the lowest possible equilibrium exchange rate is $1.50/£, the exchange rate at which one US good (DVD recorders) is still just competitive with UK goods.

Comparative advantage

Table 28.7 shows an intermediate exchange rate, $2/£. The exact position of the equilibrium exchange rate depends on the demand for DVD recorders and shirts. Regardless of a country's **absolute advantage** in making goods more cheaply, there

> **Absolute advantage** means a country is the lowest-cost producer of that good.

---

2   If both US goods are cheaper than UK goods when valued in pounds, they must also be cheaper when valued in dollars. We simply multiply all prices in pounds by the same exchange rate to get the corresponding dollar prices.

Comparative advantage means the country makes the good relatively more cheaply than it makes other goods, whether or not it has an absolute advantage.

is always an exchange rate that lets the country make at least one good more cheaply than other countries when all goods are valued in a common currency. At the equilibrium exchange rate, the country has a **comparative advantage** in the production of at least one good which it can then export to pay for its imports.

Although the US has a lower absolute labour requirement for both goods, the relative cost of DVD recorders is lower in the US, and the relative cost of shirts higher, than in the UK. In the US, where DVD recorders cost $180 and shirts $30, the former cost six times as much as the latter. In the UK, where shirts cost £12 and DVD recorders £120, the latter cost ten times as much as the former. Making DVD recorders costs less relative to shirts in the US than in the UK. The *opportunity cost* of DVD recorders is lower in the US, which must give up six shirts to make another DVD recorder.

Conversely, the opportunity cost of shirts is lower in the UK than in the US. The UK must give up only one-tenth of a DVD recorder to make another shirt, compared with one-sixth in the US. The law of comparative advantage says that the UK will specialize in shirts, which have a low opportunity cost for UK producers, and the US will specialize in DVD recorders, which have a low opportunity cost for US producers. We discuss the **law of comparative advantage** further in Concept 28.1.

The **law of comparative advantage** says countries specialize in producing the goods they make relatively cheaply.

Production and trade patterns depend on *comparative* advantage and *relative* costs because the level of the equilibrium exchange rate takes care of differences in absolute advantage. Even if US producers have lower unit labour requirements for both goods, a sufficiently low $/£ exchange rate makes US goods dear in the UK and UK goods cheap in the US. Beginning from a high $/£ exchange rate at which no UK goods can compete with US goods, which of the UK goods first becomes competitive as the exchange rate falls? The good in which the UK has a comparative advantage or lower opportunity costs.

The principle of comparative advantage has many applications in everyday life. Suppose two students share a flat. One is faster both at making the dinner *and* at vacuuming the carpet. If tasks are allocated according to absolute advantage, the other student does nothing. The jobs get done fastest if each student does the task at which he is relatively good.

CONCEPT 28.1 Comparative advantage and the gains from trade

The table below summarizes earlier data on unit labour requirements (ULR) in labour hours per unit of output, unit labour cost (ULC) in domestic currency, and opportunity cost (OC) in domestic goods forgone. With lower ULRs, the US has an *absolute advantage* in both goods. One way to calculate *comparative advantage* is to compare ULRs across countries. Relative to the UK, the US needs less labour to produce DVD recorders than shirts. The US has a comparative advantage in DVD recorders, the UK in shirts.

Alternatively, we can compare opportunity costs, OC. By sacrificing six shirts, the US gets 30 labour hours that make an extra DVD recorder. More simply, six shirts cost $180, the price of one DVD recorder. The opportunity cost of a DVD recorder is six shirts in the US and ten shirts in the UK. But the opportunity cost of a shirt in the UK (one-tenth of a DVD recorder) is less than in the US (one-sixth of a DVD recorder). Again, the US has a comparative advantage in DVD recorders and the UK in shirts. When there are many factor inputs, this method of calculating comparative advantage is simpler.

The gains from trade

To make 60 shirts, the UK gives up output of 6 DVD recorders. To make 6 DVD recorders, the US gives up only 36 shirts. Trade and international specialization let the world economy have an extra 24 shirts with no loss of DVD recorders. Or if the US makes another 10 DVD recorders, giving up 60 shirts, the world economy has four more DVD recorders with no loss of shirts. These are the *gains from trade*. Only when opportunity costs are the *same* in both countries are there no gains to exploit.

	ULR	ULC	OC
US			
DVD recorders	30	\$180	6 shirts
Shirts	5	\$30	1/6 DVD recorder
UK			
DVD recorders	60	£120	10 shirts
Shirts	6	£12	1/10 DVD recorder

Comparative advantage explains why Europe ought to be able to benefit by opening up trade with Asia, even if Asian producers are very low cost. Europeans can enjoy cheaper goods than before and redeploy resources to more productive alternatives. Of course, this has two implications.

First, even if both trading countries benefit on average, there is no guarantee that each and every individual will benefit. For example, those who specialized in producing the products or services now outcompeted by cheaper imports may be individually worse off. Whether they are actually worse off depends on what the country as a whole does with the gains from trade. It could redistribute some of this gain to the particular individuals who had lost out, thereby ensuring that everybody wins. In practice, it is hard to accomplish complete compensation even if it is attempted.

Second, the gains are largest after the redundant resources have been redeployed to a better use. At best, this takes time. At worst, it may lead to prolonged inactivity and political unrest.

Governments are often driven to make political commitments – 'No export of British jobs!' – but in practice these are both impossible to deliver – the market finds a way – and undesirable to deliver – the whole point of finding a cheaper supplier is to make the switch and allow the purchasing power of consumer incomes to increase. Precluding the switch entails throwing away the potential gains from trade.

We study gainers and losers more fully in Case 28.1.

Many goods

The principle of comparative advantage still holds with many goods. Table 28.8 shows a range of commodities. The first two rows show unit labour requirements to make each good in the US and the UK. The third row shows unit labour requirements in the US relative to the UK.

Rank the commodities in order. Beginning at the left, the US has the largest comparative advantage in computers, where its relative unit labour requirement is only one-sixth that of the UK. Next is cars, where the US relative unit labour requirement is half that in the UK; then TVs, textiles, glass and finally shoes. The comparative advantage of the US falls as we move to the right in the table.

Table 28.8 Unit labour requirements and comparative advantage: many goods (hours of labour input per unit output)

	Computers	Cars	TVs	Textiles	Glass	Shoes
US goods	200	300	50	5	7	15
UK goods	1200	600	90	8	6	10
US/UK relative ULR	1/6	1/2	5/9	5/8	7/6	3/2

Conversely, the UK has the largest comparative advantage in making shoes, the good in which UK producers are most efficient relative to US producers. As we move to the left, the comparative advantage of the UK declines; US producers become increasingly efficient relative to UK producers.

The US has an absolute advantage in producing computers, cars, TVs and textiles. The UK has an absolute advantage in producing glass and shoes. Nevertheless, absolute advantage plays no direct part in the analysis. Comparative advantage is what counts.

The equilibrium exchange rate occurs at some intermediate level that just balances the value of trade between the two countries. Essentially, the level of the exchange rate takes care of the overall level of absolute advantage, leaving comparative advantage to determine trade patterns.

Different capital–labour ratios

Comparative advantage need not depend on technology differences. It may also reflect different factor supplies. Consider the UK and China. The UK has more capital per worker than China. Even though China's vast size may mean that it has absolutely more capital than the UK, the UK has *relatively* more capital than China.

What does this imply about the relative price of hiring labour and capital in the two countries? With more capital per worker, the marginal product of labour is higher in the UK. This makes real wages higher in the UK than in China. Conversely, the number of workers per unit of capital is lower in the UK than in China. The marginal product of capital and the rental of capital will tend to be lower in the UK, where machinery is relatively plentiful, than in China, where machinery is relatively scarce. Because the UK is endowed with more capital relative to labour than China, the cost of using labour relative to capital is higher in the UK than in China.

Relative costs of using inputs affect the relative price of the goods they produce. Goods made by labour-intensive methods cost relatively more to make in the UK than in China. Suppose car production is capital intensive with sophisticated assembly lines, but textile production is labour intensive with detailed tasks best done by hand. The price of cars relative to textiles is lower in the UK than in China.

Hence, a *relatively* abundant supply or endowment of one factor of production tends to make the cost of renting that factor relatively cheap. Goods that use that factor relatively intensively are thus relatively cheap. In these goods the country has a comparative advantage. Thus the UK, relatively generously supplied with capital relative to labour, exports capital-intensive cars to China. China, relatively well endowed with labour, should export labour-intensive textiles to the UK. Differences in relative factor supply are an important explanation for comparative advantage and the pattern of international trade.

Figure 28.1 supports this analysis. It emphasizes skills, or human capital, rather than physical capital, although the two are usually correlated. Countries with scarce land but abundant skills have high shares of manufactures in their exports. Countries with lots of land but few skills typically export raw materials. The figure also shows regional averages. Africa lies at one end, the industrial countries at the other.

We now have two explanations for comparative advantage or international differences in relative production costs. The first is the Ricardian explanation – international differences in technology that cause differences in relative physical productivity and relative unit labour requirements. Second, even if countries have access to the same technology, the domestic relative price of goods may differ across countries because the relative cost of renting factor inputs differs across countries. Where a factor is in relatively abundant supply, goods that use that factor relatively intensively are likely to be relatively cheaper than in other countries.[3]

---

3 Strictly speaking, this explains differences in relative prices before countries start trading. Export demand may bid up the relative price of the good until relative prices are equalized across countries. This explains why trade is not infinite. Nevertheless, beginning from no trade, comparative advantage explains which goods the country then exports and which it imports.

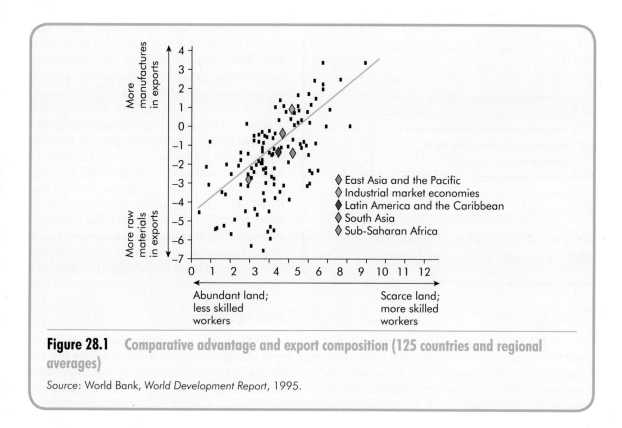

Figure 28.1 Comparative advantage and export composition (125 countries and regional averages)

Source: World Bank, *World Development Report*, 1995.

28.3 Intra-industry trade

Different countries have a comparative advantage in different goods and specialize in producing these goods for the world economy. This explains why the UK exports cars to China but imports textiles from China. It does not explain why the UK exports cars (Jaguar, Aston Martin, Mini) to Germany while simultaneously importing cars (Mercedes, BMW, VW) from Germany.

> **Intra-industry trade** is two-way trade in goods made within the same industry.

A Jaguar is not exactly the same commodity as a Mercedes, nor is Carlsberg exactly the same as Stella. Cars and beer are industries each making a range of different, but highly substitutable, products which enjoy brand allegiance.

Intra-industry trade reflects three factors. First, consumers like a wide choice of brands. They do not want exactly the same car as everyone else. Second, there are important economies of scale. Instead of each country making small quantities of each brand in each industry, it makes sense for the UK to make Jaguars, Germany to make Mercedes and Sweden to make Volvos and then to swap them around in international trade. Third, the tendency to specialize in a particular brand, to which the demand for diversity and the possibility of scale economies give rise, is limited by transport costs. Intra-industry trade between Germany and France is larger than intra-industry trade between Germany and Japan.

To measure the importance of intra-industry trade, we define an index as zero when trade in a particular commodity is entirely one-way: a country either exports or imports the good, but not both.

At the opposite extreme, the index equals 1 when there is a complete two-way trade in a commodity: a country imports as much of the commodity as it exports. Figure 28.2 shows the index for trade by a typical developed economy.

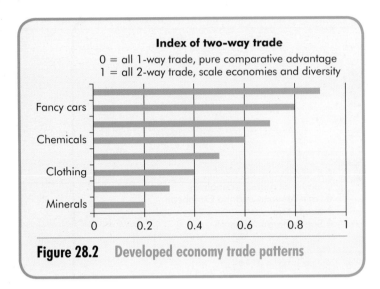

Figure 28.2 Developed economy trade patterns

At one extreme, in clothing there is little two-way trade. The US imports clothing but exports very little. This trade obeys the principle of comparative advantage. Similarly, Africa largely exports minerals but does not import them. At the other extreme is banking. Here, trade is almost completely two-way. There are French banks in London and British banks in Paris. As a general principle, the more commodities are undifferentiated goods (fuel, steel, oil), the more trade patterns reflect comparative advantage based on relative resource abundance. As we move towards finished manufactures, product differentiation becomes dominant and comparative advantage loses some of its overriding role. Intra-industry trade is more significant in cars, banking, and indeed universities – where French students study in the UK and UK students study in France.

The more closely markets are integrated, and the lower the obstacles to trade – in terms of both distance and tariffs – the more intra-industry trade we expect. Japan, geographically isolated from the US and Europe, engages in quite a lot of one-way trade with these markets. In contrast, the EU has a more diversified resource endowment and a more integrated market, in which distance, information barriers and tariffs are now small. Intra-industry trade is extensive. The gain from trade is not the exploitation of differences in relative prices across countries but greater diversity and the lower unit costs that scale economies allow.

CASE 28.1

Historical gainers and losers from trade

Countries trade because they have a comparative advantage (based either on a relative advantage in technology or on relative factor abundance) or because different countries specialize in making different brands when scale economies exist. Either way, countries buy goods more cheaply than they could have done without international trade.

Although trade is beneficial in the aggregate, this is no guarantee that trade makes *everyone* better off. Current concerns about globalization arise because there are losers too. Here are some historical examples of the conflicts to which international trade gave rise.

Refrigeration
At the end of the nineteenth century, the invention of refrigeration enabled Argentina to supply frozen meat to the world market. Argentina's meat exports, non-existent in 1900, rose to 400 000 tonnes a year by 1913. The US, with beef exports of 150 000 tonnes in 1900, had virtually stopped exporting beef by 1913.

Who gained and who lost in this early example of globalization? Argentina's economy was transformed. Owners of cattle and land gained; other land users lost out because higher demand bid up land rents. Argentinian consumers found their steaks becoming dearer as meat was shipped abroad. Argentina's GNP rose a lot, but the gain from trade was not equally distributed. Some people in Argentina were worse off. Similarly, in Europe and the US, cheaper beef made consumers better off. But beef producers lost out because beef prices fell. Landowners experienced an overall drop in the demand for land, and had to reallocate it to other, less profitable uses.

Refrigeration opened up the world to Argentinian beef. As a whole, the world economy gained. In principle, the gainers could have compensated the losers and still had something left over. In practice, gainers rarely compensate losers. So some people lost out. In this example the biggest losers were beef producers elsewhere in the world and other users of land in Argentina.

The UK car industry

A second example is the UK car industry. As recently as 1971, imports of cars were only 15 per cent of the domestic UK market, while 35 per cent of UK car output was exported. The UK was a net exporter of cars. Since 1971 UK car makers have lost market share to foreign imports. Imports now exceed 60 per cent of the UK market. Exports recovered in the 1990s, in part because companies like Nissan, Honda and Toyota established UK plants to produce for the EU market.

UK car buyers and foreign car exporters benefited from the rise in UK imports of cheaper foreign cars. But UK car producers like Rover had a very tough time; Rover was eventually sold off to Nanjing Automobile of China in 2005.

Restricting car imports to the UK helps the UK car industry but raises car prices for UK car buyers. Should the government please producers or consumers? More generally, how should we decide whether to restrict imports or have free trade in all goods? In the next section we analyse the costs and benefits of tariffs or other types of trade restriction. In so doing, we move from *positive economics*, why trade exists and what form it takes, to *normative economics*, what trade policy the government should adopt.

The steel industry

As the workshop of the world in the nineteenth century, the UK pioneered industries such as steelmaking. An early technological lead, and convenient deposits of raw materials, provided an initial comparative advantage. As the industry prospered, the UK acquired skills – human capital – that further consolidated its comparative advantage.

Gradually, of course, other countries learned the technology and trained their workers. Britain lost its unique lead, and was then overhauled by countries that had more easily mined deposits of coal and iron, cheaper wages, or less crowded locations in which low-cost modern factories were more easily assembled.

Initially, this additional global capacity was built in Europe and the US, then in Japan. By the 1970s many global sources of cheaper steel were making European steel less competitive. European governments were drawn into state subsidies and an exit game among themselves – if some countries sharply contracted their steel industry, world prices would rise and other European steel producers might survive for a while longer. But no country wanted to take the pain of cutbacks that would largely benefit its neighbours.

Within the UK, British Steel was nationalized in 1967 and privatized again in 1988, seeking a global niche as a producer of high-quality and high-priced steel. Unable to succeed on its own, it then merged with a Dutch company in 1999 to form Corus, which in turn was taken over in 2007 by Tata Steel, part of the Indian conglomerate Tata Sons. In 2010 Tata Steel announced plans to mothball indefinitely its Middlesbrough steel plant, an iconic symbol of heavy industry in the north-east of England.

Like the UK coal industry, the UK steel industry is well on the way to disappearing, as comparative advantage evolves over time. If evolution did not occur, the UK would still be a land of handloom weavers, indeed of hunter gatherers. Against these costs of global competition we have to weigh: (a) the consumer benefits of obtaining similar or better products more cheaply through imports, and (b) the productivity gains of diverting the labour force out of old industries into the industries of the future.

28.4   The economics of tariffs

> **Trade policy** affects international trade through taxes or subsidies, or by direct restrictions on imports and exports.
>
> An **tariff** is a tax on imports.

We now turn from the determinants of international trade to international trade policy.

The most common type of trade restriction is a **tariff** or import duty.

If t is the tariff rate as a decimal fraction (for example, 0.2), the domestic price of an imported good is $(1 + t)$ times its world price. By raising the domestic price of imports, a tariff helps domestic producers but hurts domestic consumers.

The free trade equilibrium

Figure 28.3 shows the domestic market for cars. The UK faces a given world price of cars, say £10 000 a car, shown by the solid horizontal line. Schedules *DD* and *SS* show the demand for cars by UK consumers and the supply of cars by UK producers. For simplicity, we assume that domestic and foreign cars are perfect substitutes. Consumers buy the cheaper one.

At a price of £10 000, UK consumers wish to buy Q_d cars, at point *G* on their demand curve. Domestic firms wish to make Q_s cars at this price. The gap between domestic supply Q_s and domestic demand Q_d is imported.

Equilibrium with a tariff

Suppose that the government levies a 20 per cent tariff on imported cars. Car importers charge £12 000 to cover their costs, inclusive of the tariff. The broken horizontal line at this price shows that importers will sell any number of cars in the domestic market at a price of £12 000. The tariff raises the domestic tariff-inclusive price above the world price.

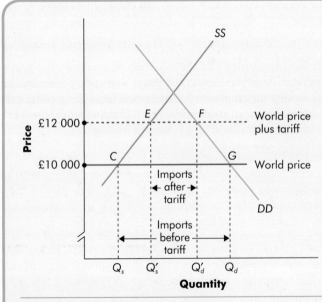

DD and SS show the domestic demand and supply for cars. In the absence of a tariff, consumers can import cars at a price of £10 000. In free trade equilibrium, domestic producers produce at C and domestic consumers consume at G. The quantity of imported cars is CG. Q_d is the total quantity demanded. Domestic production Q_s is supplemented by imports ($Q_d - Q_s$). A 20 per cent tariff raises the domestic price of imports to £12 000. Domestic output is now at E and consumers consume at F. Imports fall from CG to EF.

Figure 28.3   The effects of a tariff

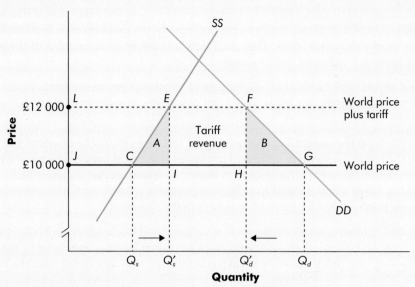

The tariff leads to both transfers and to net social losses. The tariff raises the domestic price from £10 000 to £12 000. *LFHJ* shows extra consumer payments of the Q'_d cars they now buy. But *EFHI* is a transfer to the government and *ECJL* is a transfer to extra profits of producers. Areas *A* and *B* are pure waste and net social losses. Triangle *A* is the extra that society spends by producing cars domestically instead of importing them at the world price. Triangle *B* is the excess of consumer benefits over social marginal cost that society sacrifices by reducing its consumption of cars from Q_d to Q'_d.

Figure 28.4   **The welfare costs of a tariff**

By raising domestic car prices, the tariff boosts domestic car production from Q_s to Q'_s. The tariff protects domestic producers by raising the domestic price at which imports become competitive. In moving up the supply curve from *C* to *E*, domestic producers with marginal costs between £10 000 and £12 000 can now survive at the higher domestic price of cars.

The higher price also moves consumers up their demand curve from *G* to *F*. The quantity of cars demanded falls from Q_d to Q'_d. For consumers, the tariff is like a tax. Cars cost more.

Figure 28.3 shows the combined effect of higher domestic production but lower domestic consumption. Imports fall because domestic production rises *and* because domestic consumption falls. The more elastic are these supply and demand schedules, the more a given tariff reduces imports. If both schedules are very steep, the quantity of imports hardly changes.

Costs and benefits of a tariff

Figure 28.4 shows the costs and benefits of imposing a tariff. We distinguish *net costs to society* from *transfers* between one part of the economy and another.

After the tariff is imposed, consumers buy the quantity Q'_d. Since the consumer price rises by £2000, consumers spend (£2000 × Q'_d) *more* than before to buy the quantity Q'_d. Who gets these extra payments – the area *LFHJ* in Figure 28.4?

Some of the extra consumer payments go to the government, whose revenue from the tariff is the rectangle *EFHI*, the tariff of £2000 per imported car times ($Q_d - Q'_s$) the number of imported cars. This transfer *EFHI* from consumers to government is *not* a net cost to society. For example, the government can use the tariff revenue to reduce income tax rates.

Higher consumer payments also go in part to firms as extra profits. Firms get a higher domestic price for their output. The supply curve shows how much firms need to cover the extra cost of making Q'_s not Q_s. Hence the remaining area *ECJL* shows the extra profits; namely, the extra revenue from higher prices not required to cover extra production costs. Thus *ECJL* is a transfer from consumers to the pure profit or economic rent of firms. It is *not* a net cost to society.

The shaded area *A* is part of the area *LFHJ* showing extra consumer payments, but is neither revenue for the government nor extra profits for firms. It is a net cost to society: the cost of supporting inefficient domestic firms.

The supply curve *SS* shows the marginal cost of making the last car in the home economy. But society *could* import cars from the rest of the world in unlimited quantities at the world price, which is the true marginal cost of cars to the domestic economy. The triangle *A* shows the resources that society wastes by making the quantity $(Q'_s - Q_s)$ at home when it could have been imported at a lower cost. The resources drawn into domestic car production could be better used elsewhere in the economy.

Triangle *B* is a second net loss to society. If the tariff is scrapped and free trade restored, the quantity of cars demanded rises to Q_d. The triangle *B* shows the excess of consumer benefits, measured by the height of the demand curve showing how much consumers will pay for the last unit demanded, over the marginal costs of expanding from Q'_d to Q_d, the world price at which imports can be purchased. Conversely, by imposing the tariff, society incurs a net loss shown by triangle *B*. It is the net benefit society gives up when fewer cars are bought by consumers.

To sum up, when we begin from free trade equilibrium and then impose a tariff, the rise in the domestic price leads both to transfers and to pure waste. Money is transferred from consumers to the government and to producers. The net social cost of these transfers is zero.

A tariff also involves pure waste. Society can always import cars at the world price. Efficiency requires that this marginal cost is equal both to the marginal benefit to consumers and to the marginal cost of domestic production. By raising the domestic price, to which domestic producers equate marginal cost and domestic consumers equate marginal benefit, a tariff leads to domestic overproduction and domestic under-consumption of the good. Triangles *A* and *B* measure this waste that the tariff distortion creates. Society does better to use fewer resources in the car industry and to transfer these resources to an export industry which could earn enough foreign exchange to import cars at the cheaper world price. This is the *case for free trade*.

Should tariffs never be imposed? We now examine common arguments in favour of tariffs.

28.5 Good and bad arguments for tariffs

Table 28.9 lists some of these arguments. We group them under several headings. The *first-best* argument is a case where a tariff is *the* best way to achieve a given objective. *Second-best* arguments are cases where a tariff is better than nothing, but where another policy is better still if it can be implemented. Non-arguments are partly or completely fallacious.

The optimal tariff: the first-best argument for tariffs

> When imports affect the world price, the **optimal tariff** reduces imports to the level at which social marginal cost equals social marginal benefit.

In presenting the case for free trade, we were careful to assume that the domestic economy can import as many cars as it wished without bidding up the world price of cars. For a small economy this is a reasonable assumption. However, imports by a large country may be large relative to the world market and bid up the world price of those commodities.

Table 28.9   Arguments for tariffs

Type	Example
First-best	Foreign trade monopoly
Second-best	Way of life, anti-luxury, infant industry, defence, revenue
Strategic	Games against foreigners
Non-argument	Cheap foreign labour

In this case, the world price of the last unit imported is *lower* than the true cost of the last unit to the importing economy. In demanding another unit of imports, the economy raises the price it has to pay on the quantity already being imported. But in a free trade world without tariffs, each individual thinks only about the price he pays. No single individual bids up the price, but collectively they bid up the price of imports.

Under free trade, each individual buys imports until the benefit to that individual equals the world price he pays. Since the collective cost of the last import exceeds its world price, the social cost of that import exceeds its benefit. There are too many imports. Society gains by restricting imports until the benefit of the last import equals its social cost.

A small country's imports have no effect on the world price of its imports. The marginal social cost of imports then equals the world price. Then, and only then, is the optimal tariff zero. Free trade is then first-best.

The optimal tariff is a straightforward application of the principles of efficient resource allocation discussed in Part Three.

Second-best arguments for tariffs

We now introduce the **principle of targeting**.

The optimal tariff is a first-best application of the principle of targeting precisely because the source of the problem is a divergence between social and private marginal costs in trade itself. A tariff on trade is the most efficient solution. The arguments for tariffs that we now examine are all second-best arguments because the original source of the problem does not directly lie in trade. The principle of targeting assures us that there are ways to solve these problems at a lower net social cost.

> The **principle of targeting** says that the most efficient way to attain a given objective is to use a policy influencing that activity directly.

Way of life

Suppose society wishes to help inefficient farmers or craft industries. It believes that the old way of life, or sense of community, should be preserved. It levies tariffs to protect such groups from foreign competition.

There is a cheaper way to attain this objective. A tariff helps domestic producers but hurts domestic consumers through higher prices. A production subsidy would still keep farmers in business and, by tackling the problem directly, would avoid hurting consumers. In terms of Figure 28.4, triangle A shows the net social cost of subsidizing domestic producers so they can produce Q'_s rather than Q_s. But a tariff, the second-best solution, also involves the social cost given by the triangle B.

Suppressing luxuries

Some poor countries believe it is wrong to allow their few rich citizens to buy Rolls-Royces or luxury yachts when society needs its resources to stop people starving. A tariff on imports of luxuries reduces their consumption but, by raising the domestic price, may also provide an incentive for domestic producers to use scarce resources to produce them. A consumption tax tackles the problem directly, and is more efficient.

Infant industries

A common argument for a tariff is that it allows infant industries to get started. Suppose there is *learning by doing*. Only by actually being in business do firms learn how to reduce costs and become as efficient as foreign competitors. A tariff provides protection to infant industries until they master the business and can compete on equal terms with more experienced foreign suppliers.

Society should invest in new industries only if they are socially profitable in the long run. The long-run benefits must outweigh the initial losses during the period when the infant industry is producing at a higher cost than the goods could have been obtained at through imports. But in the absence of any divergence between private and social costs or benefits, an industry will be socially profitable only if it is privately profitable.

If the industry is such a good idea in the long run, society should begin by asking why private firms cannot borrow the money to see them through the early period when they are losing out to more efficient foreign firms. If private lenders are not prepared to risk their money, society should ask whether the industry is such a good idea after all. And if the industry does make sense but there is a problem in the market for lending, the principle of targeting says that the government should intervene by lending money to private firms.

Failing this, a production subsidy during the initial years is still better than a tariff, which also penalizes consumers. The worst outcome of all is the imposition of a *permanent* tariff, which allows the industry to remain sheltered and less efficient than its foreign competitors long after the benefits of learning by doing are supposed to have been achieved.

Defence

Some countries believe that, in case there is a war, it is important to preserve domestic industries that produce food or jet fighters. Again, a production subsidy, not an import tariff, is the most efficient way to meet this objective.

Revenue

In the eighteenth century, most government revenue came from tariffs. Administratively, it was the simplest tax to collect. Today, this is still true in some developing countries. But in modern economies with sophisticated systems of accounting and administration, the administrative costs of raising revenue through tariffs are not lower than the costs of raising revenue through income taxes or taxes on expenditure. The balance of tax collection should be determined chiefly by the extent to which taxes induce distortions, inefficiency and waste, and the extent to which they bring about the distribution of income and wealth desired by the government. The need to raise revenue is not a justification for tariffs themselves.

Strategic trade policy

In Part Two we argued that game theory is useful in analysing strategic conflict between oligopolists. In international trade, strategic rivalry may exist either between the giant firms or 'national champions' of different countries, or between governments acting on their behalf.

Strategic international competition may justify industrial policy. Initial government subsidies to the European aircraft producer Airbus Industrie was a pre-commitment to deter Boeing from trying to force Airbus out of the industry.

Similar considerations arise in trade policy. Levying a tariff on imports, thereby protecting domestic producers, may deter foreigners from attempting a price war to force the domestic producers out of the industry, and may prevent foreign producers from entering the industry.

This sounds like a very general and robust argument for tariffs, but it should be viewed with considerable caution. If it is attractive for one country to impose tariffs for this purpose, it may be as attractive for foreigners to retaliate with tariffs of their own. We then reach an equilibrium in which little trade takes place, domestic giants have huge monopoly power since they no longer face effective competition from foreigners, and all countries suffer.

In fact, this game has the structure of that of the Prisoner's Dilemma, which we introduced in Part Two. All countries may be led to impose tariffs even though all would be better off if tariffs were abolished. This suggests there is a role for international co-operation to agree on, and subsequently enforce, low tariffs. We take up this theme shortly.

Dumping

> **Dumping** occurs when foreign producers sell at prices below their marginal production cost, either by making losses or with the assistance of government subsidies.

Although the preceding discussion relates to tariffs, it can also be applied to trade subsidies.

Domestic producers say this is unfair and demand a tariff to protect them from foreign competition. If we knew foreign suppliers would supply cheap goods indefinitely, we should say thank you, close down our more expensive industry and put our resources to work elsewhere. To this extent, dumping is a non-argument for a tariff.

However, foreign producers may be engaged in predatory pricing meant to drive our producers out of the industry. Once the foreigners achieve monopoly power in world markets, they raise prices and make big profits. If so, it may be wise for our government to resist. Even so, a production subsidy is the efficient way to insulate our producers from this threat. A tariff has the undesirable side effect of distorting consumer prices.

Non-arguments for tariffs

Cheap foreign labour

Home producers frequently argue that tariffs are needed to protect them from cheap foreign labour. Yet the whole point of trade is to exploit international differences in the relative prices of different goods. If the domestic economy is relatively well endowed with capital, it benefits from trade precisely because its exports of capital-intensive goods allow it to purchase *more* labour-intensive goods from abroad than would have been obtained by diverting domestic resources to production of labour-intensive goods.

As technology and relative factor endowments change over time, countries' comparative advantage alters. In the nineteenth century Britain exported Lancashire textiles all over the world. But textile production is relatively labour intensive. Once the countries of Southeast Asia acquired the technology, it was inevitable that their relatively abundant labour endowment would give them a comparative advantage in producing textiles.

New technology frequently gives a country a temporary comparative advantage in particular products. As time elapses, other countries acquire the technology, and relative factor endowments and relative factor costs become a more important determinant of comparative advantage. Inevitably, the domestic producers who have lost their comparative advantage start complaining about competition from imports using cheap foreign labour.

In the long run the country as a whole will benefit by facing facts, recognizing that its comparative advantage has changed and transferring production to the industries in which it now has a comparative advantage. And our analysis of comparative advantage promises us that there *must* be some industry in which each country has a comparative advantage. In the long run, trying to use tariffs to prop up industries that have lost their comparative advantage is futile and costly.

Of course, in the short run the adjustment may be painful. Workers lose their jobs and must start afresh in industries in which they do not have years of experience and acquired skills. But the principle of targeting tells us that, if society wants to smooth this transition, some kind of retraining or relocation subsidy is more efficient than a tariff.

Why do we have tariffs?

Aside from the optimal tariff argument, there is little to be said in favour of tariffs. Economists have been arguing against them for well over a century. Why are tariffs still so popular?

ACTIVITY 28.1

The EU Single Market

The European Community was founded in 1957 as a free trade area – abolishing tariffs and quotas on trade between member states. Over the next 50 years, the EC was enlarged. The original six – West Germany, France, Italy, Netherlands, Belgium and Luxembourg – were joined by Denmark, Ireland and the UK in the 1970s, by Spain, Portugal and Greece in the 1980s, and by Austria, Finland and Sweden in the 1990s. The European Community (EC) became the European Union (EU). In 2004 the EU admitted the Baltic republics (Estonia, Latvia, Lithuania), the countries of central Europe (Hungary, Poland, Czech Republic, Slovakia, Slovenia) and the Mediterranean islands of Malta and the Greek part of Cyprus. Bulgaria and Romania were admitted in 2007.

EU enlargement was not initially accompanied by any change in its fundamental structure. Member states still set national policies. Harmonization was usually thwarted for two reasons. First, since each country did things differently, it was hard to find a single set of regulations for all member states. Second, it was political dynamite. No country wanted to adopt the policies of others.

In the 1980s, the member states set a deadline of 1992 for establishing a single EU market among member states, in particular involving: (a) free capital flows between members; (b) removal of all non-tariff barriers to trade in the EU (different trademarks, patent laws, safety standards that made it hard for imports to compete with domestic goods even when tariffs were zero; (c) ending of the bias in public sector purchasing to favour domestic producers; (d) removal of frontier controls (delays); and (e) progress in harmonizing tax rates. Examining the effect of these measures is of interest because it reminds us that tariffs and quotas are not the only form of trade protection.

Non-tariff barriers are different national regulations or practices that prevent free movement of goods, services and factors between countries.

By removing **non-tariff barriers**, the Single Market aimed to allow countries to exploit their comparative advantage more fully.

A second inefficiency in small and segmented national markets is that firms cannot fully exploit economies of scale. As barriers came down, firms got larger and costs fell. Two-way trade in the same industry increased, not just in goods but also in services such as banking.

The Single Market intensified competition in two ways. First, competition between forms of regulation led on average to lower levels of regulation. For many continental European countries, the Single Market led to substantial deregulation from initial levels that had been very high. Second, a larger market enabled large firms to enjoy scale economies *without* the high market share and potential monopoly power that this would have meant in small, segmented economies.

Quantifying the gains

How large were the gains in practice? In 2002 the European Commission estimated that during 1992–2002 the first decade of the Single Market had raised members' GDP by 1.8 per cent above what it otherwise would have been (a gain of €5700 per household, which is quite substantial), and had also raised employment by 1.46 per cent.

In general, small countries gained more than large countries, but gains also reflected the pattern of trade. The largest gains came as the most protected activities were opened up. Not only was the Single Market good for the EU, it also turned out to boost trade with the outside world. Fears of fortress Europe were unfounded.

The Single Market: a vision for the twenty-first century
In January 2007 the Department of Trade and Industry, together with HM Treasury, issued a report, *The Single Market: a vision for the 21st century*, outlining the challenges that the Single Market faces – globalization, climate change, demographic change – and the principles needed to ensure that the Single Market continues to deliver for Europe's consumers and businesses.

The free movement of goods, persons, services and capital is a fundamental principle of the European Union. It is these four freedoms as set out in the EC Treaty, which form the basis of the Single Market. The government believes that the Single European Market benefits the economy of each member state, and that the removal of trade barriers leads to a reduction in business costs as well as increasing competition and stimulating efficiency, benefiting consumers and encouraging the creation of jobs and wealth.

Benefits of the Single Market
The Single Market is a *wider market* for UK goods comprising nearly 380 million consumers and making up almost 40 per cent of world trade. Such a huge market gives consumers greater choice.

The greater *competition and liberalization* the Single Market has helped to bring about has led to *lower prices*. Take air fares, for example: cheap airlines such as easyJet would not have been possible without the Single Market. Airlines can now fly where they want, without national restrictions. BA has become the second-largest domestic airline in France.

The Single Market provides for better *consumer protection*; for example, the Toy Directive means that all toys sold in the EU must be safe for children. Another example is the Fourth Motor Insurance Directive on which political agreement was reached by member states in December 1998. This Directive will make it easier for those involved in motor accidents in other member states to make an insurance claim when returning to their state of residence.

The Single Market principle of mutual recognition of standards means UK manufacturers can sell their products all over Europe without expensive retesting in every country. For business, there has been a significant reduction in export bureaucracy. The Single Market is in effect a domestic market for European business.

UK citizens have the *right to work, study or retire* in all the other member states – there are around three-quarters of a million Britons living in other countries.

Questions

(a) Gains from trade arise either from exploiting comparative advantage and engaging in more one-way trade, or from achieving greater scale economies and diversity by engaging in more two-way trade in the same commodities or services. Did the largest gains from the EU Single Market programme arise from one-way or two-way trade in the product? Why do you think this?

(b) If trade also leads to greater competition, which of the above two channels are gains from trade arising through?

(c) Could the removal of non-tariff barriers lead to greater one-way trade? Could Figure 28.4 be amended to display this?

To check your answers to these questions, go to page 688.

Concentrated benefits, diffuse costs

A tariff on a particular commodity helps a particular industry. It is easy for firms and workers in an industry to organize effective political pressure, for they can all agree that this single issue is central to their livelihood, at least in the short run. But if the tariff is imposed, the cost in higher consumer prices is borne by a much larger and more diverse group of people whom it is much harder to organize politically. Hence, politicians heed the vociferous, well-organized group lobbying *for* tariffs, especially if they are geographically concentrated in an area where, by voting together, they have a significant effect on the outcome of the next election.

Tariffs vs subsidies

Why does government assistance often take the form of tariffs rather than production subsidies, which are frequently more appropriate? First, because if domestic industry is suffering from imports of Japanese goods, the solution seems to be to do something that hurts Japan directly. Second, because the government would have to raise taxes to finance a production subsidy. A tariff is often politically easier because it seems to augment government revenues (raising hopes of an income tax cut), whereas a subsidy seems to deplete government revenues (raising fears of higher tax rates). You now know that a tariff hits consumers directly by raising the domestic price of the good, but the government may be able to invoke impersonal 'market forces'. Tariffs cause the government less political hassle.

 ## 28.6　Tariff levels: not so bad?

In the nineteenth century world trade grew rapidly, in part because the leading country, the UK, pursued a vigorous policy of free trade. In contrast, US tariffs averaged about 50 per cent, although they had fallen to around 30 per cent by the early 1920s. As the industrial economies were hit by the Great Depression of the late 1920s and 1930s, there was pressure to protect domestic jobs by keeping out imports. Tariffs in the US returned to around 50 per cent, and the UK abandoned the policy of free trade that had been pursued for nearly a century.

Table 28.1 showed that the combination of world recession and increasing tariffs led to a disastrous slump in the volume of world trade, further exacerbated by the Second World War.

The World Trade Organization

After the war there was a collective determination to see world trade restored. Bodies such as the International Monetary Fund and the World Bank were set up and many countries signed the General Agreement on Tariffs and Trade (GATT) – a commitment to reduce tariffs successively and dismantle trade restrictions.

Under successive rounds of GATT, tariffs fell steadily. By 1960 US tariffs were only about one-fifth of their level at the outbreak of the Second World War. In the UK the system of wartime quotas on imports had been dismantled by the mid-1950s, after which tariffs were reduced by nearly half in the ensuing 25 years. Europe as a whole has moved towards an enlarged European Union in which tariffs between member countries have been abolished.

The GATT Secretariat, now called the World Trade Organization (WTO), began the latest round of negotiations – the Doha Development Round, named after the meeting in Doha in the Middle Eastern state of Qatar in 2001. Chinese membership of the WTO has now been agreed. The WTO is increasingly associated with pressure not only to dismantle substantial protection that severely reduces efficiency but also to extend trade liberalization to more and more countries. Tariff levels throughout the world are probably as low as they have ever been. Trade liberalization has been an engine of growth. World trade has seen four decades of rapid growth.

Neverthless, the Doha round has not yet been a success. As emerging market economies become more successful, they become more powerful in negotiation in trade issues. The most significant differences are between developed nations – led by the US, EU and Japan – and the major emerging market countries led by India, Brazil, China and South Africa. There is also considerable contention against and between the EU and the US over their maintenance of agricultural subsidies, which are seen to operate effectively as trade barriers.

Nor can we expect trade negotiations to solve other problems. Fears about globalization often have less to do with change itself than with other distortions that it may then exacerbate. For example, when environmental protection is inadequate and corporate accountability weak, it is legitimate to draw attention to the fact that globalization may allow environmental exploitation.

The principle of targeting also tells us that the best solution may not be to hinder trade but rather to attack the problems at source. For example, strengthening environmental protection may be a more effective response than perpetuating trade restrictions.

28.7 Other trade policies

Tariffs are not the only form of trade policy. We now examine three other policy instruments: **quotas, non-tariff barriers** and **export subsidies**.

For example, the EU has a ceiling on imports of steel from Eastern Europe. Although quotas restrict the *quantity* of imports, this does not mean they have no effect on domestic prices of the restricted goods. With a lower supply, the equilibrium price is higher than under free trade.

Thus quotas are rather like tariffs. The domestic price to the consumer rises. It is this higher price that allows inefficient domestic producers to produce a higher output than under free trade. Quotas lead to social waste for exactly the same reasons as tariffs.

> **Quotas** are restrictions on the maximum quantity of imports.
>
> **Non-tariff barriers** are administrative regulations that discriminate against foreign goods.
>
> **Export subsidies** are government assistance to domestic firms in competing with foreign firms.

Because quotas raise the domestic price of the restricted good, the lucky foreign suppliers who succeed in getting some of their goods sold make large profits on these sales. In terms of Figure 28.4, the rectangle *EFHI*, which would have accrued to the government as revenue from a tariff, now accrues to foreign suppliers or domestic importers. It is the difference between domestic and world prices on the goods that are imported, multiplied by the quantity of imports allowed.

If these profits accrue to foreigners they are a social cost of quotas over and above the cost of an equivalent tariff. However, the government could always auction licences to import and so recoup this revenue. Private importers or foreign suppliers would bid up to this amount to acquire an import licence.

Non-tariff barriers include delaying imports at the frontier, a home-goods bias in purchases for the government and contracts that specify standards with which domestic producers are familiar but foreign producers are not. In Chapter 29 we examine how the EU Single Market tried to end non-tariff barriers inside the EU.

So far, we have looked at restrictions on imports. Countries also use trade policy to boost exports. This can vary from outright subsidy to cheap credit or exemption from certain domestic taxes.

Figure 28.5 shows the economics of an export subsidy. Suppose the world price of a computer is £5000. Under free trade, domestic consumers buy a quantity Q_d at point G on their demand curve, producers make a quantity Q_s at point E on their supply curve and a quantity GE is exported.

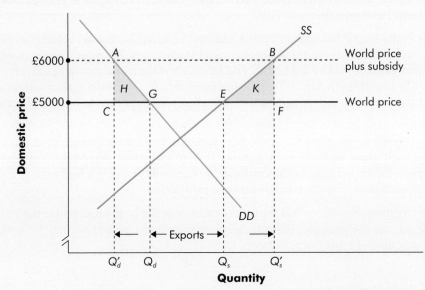

Under free trade, consumers demand Q_d, production is Q_s, and exports are GE. With a subsidy on exports alone, domestic producers will restrict supply to the home market to Q_d' so that home consumers pay £6000, the same as producers can earn by exporting. Total output is Q_s' and exports AB. K shows the social cost of producing goods whose marginal cost exceeds the world price for which they are sold. H shows the social cost of restricting consumption when marginal benefits exceed the world price of the good.

Figure 28.5 **An export subsidy**

To help the computer industry, the government offers a 20 per cent *export subsidy* on all exported computers, on which domestic producers now earn £6000. No firm sells at home for £5000 when it can sell abroad for £6000. The supply to the domestic market is reduced to Q_d' so that domestic consumers also pay £6000. Total domestic output rises to Q_s' and exports are AB.

Although the subsidy increases exports, it entails a social cost given by the shaded triangles H and K. Triangle H is the social cost of reducing domestic consumption from Q_d to Q_d'. The consumer benefits of the extra consumption would have exceeded the world price, the social marginal cost at which the economy can obtain computers. Triangle K is the social cost of increasing output from Q_s to Q_s' when the marginal domestic cost exceeds the world price at which computers could have been imported.

Just as with a tariff, an export subsidy is usually a second-best policy. Even if a country wants to raise its output of computers, it is cheaper to use a production subsidy, incurring the cost of the triangle K, but avoiding the cost of the triangle H.

Summary

- World trade grew rapidly over the past 40 years, and is dominated by the **developed countries**. Primary commodities are 25 per cent of world trade; the rest is trade in manufactures.

- Countries trade because they can buy goods more cheaply abroad. Differences in costs reflect differences in technology and factor endowments. Scale economies also lead to international specialization.

- Countries make the goods in which they have a **comparative advantage** or can produce relatively cheaply. By exploiting international differences in opportunity costs, trade leads to a pure gain.

- When technology diffuses quickly to other countries, **relative factor endowments** are the main cause of different relative costs. Countries produce and export goods that use intensively the factors with which the country is relatively well endowed.

- **Intra-industry trade** occurs because of scale economies and consumer demand for diversity. The gain from this trade is cost reduction and greater diversity of products.

- If trade is to balance, and the forex market is to be in equilibrium, each country must have a comparative advantage in at least one good. The level of the equilibrium exchange rate offsets international differences in **absolute advantage**.

- Although international trade can benefit the world as a whole, trade usually hurts some groups of people, unless the gainers compensate the losers.

- By raising the domestic price, a **tariff** reduces consumption but raises domestic output. Hence imports fall.

- A tariff leads to two distortions that are social costs: overproduction by domestic firms whose marginal cost exceeds the world price, and under-consumption by consumers whose marginal benefit exceeds the world price.

- When a country affects the price of its imports, the world price is less than the social marginal cost of importing. This is the case for the **optimal tariff**. Otherwise, arguments for tariffs are usually second-best solutions. A production subsidy or consumption tax achieves the aim at lower social cost.

- **Export subsidies** raise domestic prices, reducing consumption but raising output and exports. They involve waste. Goods are exported for less than society's marginal production costs and for less than the marginal benefit to domestic consumers.

- Tariffs and other non-tariff barriers fell a lot in the last 40 years.

- Trade protection is usually costly to society. Yet governments often adopt it as an easy option politically.

Review questions   connect

1 (a) Why does composition of African and Asian trade differ in Table 28.5? (b) Which pattern do you expect in the UK? Why?

EASY

2 'A country with uniformly low productivity should prevent foreign competition.' Discuss.

3 Wine, cars, steel sheeting: which have a high index of intra-industry trade? Why?

4 Making TVs has scale economies. Is this an argument for a tariff on TV imports?

5 To preserve its heritage, a country bans exports of works of art. (a) Is this better than an export tax? (b) Who gains and loses from the ban? (c) Does it encourage young domestic artists?

6 **Common fallacies** Why are these statements wrong? (a) British producers are becoming uncompetitive in everything. (b) Buy British and help Britain.

7 Which is correct? (a) Now that services account for over 80 per cent of GDP in most developed countries, trade in goods cannot be the major part of international trade; (b) international trade in services is not possible; (c) the only reason that trade in goods remains so important is that countries import goods, add a bit and then re-export them.

8 A small country has no effect on the price of any of the goods that it trades. What is the optimum tariff level on its imports?

9 How can an export subsidy, which promotes international trade, be protectionist? Illustrate your answer with a diagram.

10 Give two examples of non-tariff barriers. Draw a diagram to illustrate their effect on domestic producers and consumers.

11 A perfectly competitive industry faces domestic demand $q_D = 100 - p$ and has the industry supply curve $q_S = 40 + p$. (a) If the world price is 50, what is the value of net exports? (b) If the world price is 20, what is the value of net exports? (c) In the absence of trade, what is the equilibrium domestic price? (d) With a world price of 20, suppose the government levies a tariff of 5 per unit. Calculate the value of tariff revenue and the total value of the two deadweight loss triangles.

12 'Large countries gain proportionately less from world trade than small countries.' True or false? Why?

13 Usually, participating in the world economy leaves a country better off, even though there may be winners and losers within the country. (a) Will workers with skills useful to the export industries be better or worse off when a country opens up to international trade? (b) What about workers in industries whose output is now displaced by imports? (c) Could technical progress in the export industry then ever leave a country worse off? Why, or why not?

14 Essay question   Over the last 60 years, international trade has grown much more quickly than world output. How can this occur? Can it go on indefinitely?

For solutions to these questions contact your lecturer.

Exchange rate regimes

Learning Outcomes

By the end of this chapter, you should be able to:

1. contrast different exchange rate regimes

2. describe the gold standard

3. discuss an adjustable peg

4. explain the impossible triad

5. examine speculative attacks

6. analyse floating exchange rates

7. explain the Exchange Rate Mechanism and the Maastricht criteria

8. discuss how the eurozone operates

Having studied international trade between different countries, we now examine the corresponding system of international payments. In a closed economy, money is the medium of exchange that reduces transaction costs. An efficient **international monetary system** promotes trade in goods, services and assets by reducing transaction costs and avoiding unnecessary uncertainty.

> The **international monetary system** provides a medium of exchange for international transactions.

The exchange rate is the price at which two national currencies exchange. Chapters 24 and 25 discussed fixed and floating exchange rates, analysing how the exchange rate regime affects domestic monetary and fiscal policies in a single country. Now we are interested in how an exchange rate regime affects the world economy as a whole.

We review different **exchange rate regimes**, then analyse their relative merits. Finally, we examine whether interdependence of nation states creates a motive to co-ordinate national economic policies. Table 29.1 identifies five regimes – the gold standard, a currency board, an adjustable peg, managed floating and free floating – according to the intervention obligations on the central bank. Any exchange rate involves two countries. Most regimes require that the two governments agree on which regime is in force.

> An **exchange rate regime** is a policy rule for intervening (or not) in the forex market.

Table 29.1 Exchange rate regimes

| | Exchange rate | |
Forex intervention	Fixed	Flexible
None	–	Free float
Automatic	Gold standard, Currency board	–
Some discretion	Adjustable peg	Managed float

29.1 The gold standard

The gold standard was in force for most of the nineteenth century, though some countries like the UK had adopted it much earlier. It had three key rules.

First, each government fixed the price of gold in its domestic currency. Second, gold was convertible domestic currency, at this fixed price, in whatever quantities people wanted to transact. Third, domestic money creation was linked to the government's stock of gold. Each pound in circulation was backed by an equivalent value of gold in the vault of the central bank. Cash could not be created unless the central bank could acquire gold.

The US gold price was $20.67 an ounce, the UK's was £4.25 an ounce. The $/£ exchange rate was thus fixed at $4.86/£, or $20.67 divided by £4.25. At any other exchange rate, people could sell gold in one country and buy gold in the other country, making a profit with certainty. In the forex market, the flow between currencies would be entirely one way, not an equilibrium. The equilibrium exchange rate was the relative gold price in the two currencies.

> A **monetary union** of different countries is a commitment to permanently fixed exchange rates.

The gold standard was a **monetary union** based on fixed gold prices, convertible currencies, and complete gold backing for the money supply. Because monetary union is a live issue today, it is interesting to ask how the gold standard worked.

Balance of payments adjustment

In long-run equilibrium, each country has internal and external balance. Each country also has a constant money supply, a given level of gold in the central bank vault, a given price level and a constant interest rate.

Suppose Americans now spend more on imports from the UK. The UK has a trade surplus. If domestic prices and wages are slow to adjust, the UK has an export-led boom in the short run. Aggregate demand for UK output rises. Conversely, the US has a recession and a trade deficit.

This provides an *automatic* adjustment mechanism. Initially, the UK has a balance of payments surplus. This causes a rise in the foreign exchange reserves. Under the gold standard, these reserves were gold. A UK trade surplus leads to more gold at the Bank of England, and a matching increase in the domestic money supply. This augments the UK boom.

As prices rise, the UK becomes less competitive: the nominal exchange rate remains fixed but the real exchange rate appreciates. This gradually eliminates the trade surplus, eventually restoring external balance.

The opposite happens in the US. With a payments deficit, the US stock of gold and money falls, raising US interest rates and reducing aggregate demand yet further. Gradually US prices and wages fall and competitiveness rises. The trade deficit is gradually eliminated and external balance restored.

The gold standard provided an automatic mechanism for adjusting imbalances in trade and payments. However, adjustment was slow. Since it depended on changes in domestic wages and prices to adjust competitiveness, the speed of adjustment reflected the speed with which domestic prices and wages adjusted to excess supply or excess demand.

CONCEPT 29.1 The gold standard and capital flows

Our discussion of the adjustment mechanism under the gold standard ignored capital flows. By treating the trade balance and the balance of payments as the same thing, our discussion made the automatic adjustment mechanism seem more effective than it really was. Capital flows frustrated adjustment in two ways.

First, countries with a trade deficit sometimes raised domestic interest rates to encourage a capital inflow. A trade deficit no longer necessarily implied a payments deficit and monetary outflow. Recession and downward pressure on domestic wages and prices could be avoided. A trade deficit could persist longer than the idealized account of automatic adjustment suggests.

Picture: Gold bullion © Jgroup | Dreamstime.com

Second, capital flows explain much of UK economic performance in the nineteenth century. The industrial revolution and access to markets in a worldwide empire caused a huge UK trade surplus, offset by a huge capital outflow, partly because of heavy investment abroad. However, investment gradually earns interest and profits. Eventually, UK foreign assets became so large that the current account inflow of interest, profits and dividends exceeded the rate at which profitable opportunities for new capital outflows could be found.

This net inflow of money started to raise domestic prices and wages and make UK producers uncompetitive. External balance now meant a big trade deficit plus large net inflows of property income. The monetary adjustment mechanism of the gold standard made inevitable a UK trade deficit in the late nineteenth century. It was not necessarily the result of laziness or decadence, as Victorians believed at the time. A clearer understanding of international monetary economics would have reduced some of the angst experienced in late Victorian Britain.

The gold standard in action

The UK was on the gold standard from 1816 until 1931, apart from a gap around the First World War. The gold standard had a big benefit and a big drawback. By tying the domestic money supply to gold, it ruled out persistent large-scale money creation, and hence ruled out persistently high inflation. The UK price level in 1914 was the same as in 1816. In between, in some decades the price level rose by 20 per cent and in others it fell by 20 per cent.

However, since monetary policy was dictated by the flow of gold implied by the balance of payments, interest rates could not be set independently for domestic purposes to counter an anticipated boom or slump. Instead, monetary policy had to wait for flows of gold to change the money supply and thus change domestic prices and wages. It could take years to adjust fully to a large fall in aggregate demand. During the gold standard, individual economies were vulnerable to long and deep recessions, as well as sustained booms.

We discuss the eurozone later in the chapter. Our look at the gold standard already gives three helpful hints. First, permanently fixing nominal exchange rates does not permanently fix real exchange rates. Eventually, competitiveness can change because domestic prices can adjust relative to foreign prices. Second, by curtailing the role of monetary policy, a monetary union raises the significance of fiscal policy for individual member countries that wish to manage aggregate demand independently of the rest of the monetary union. Third, monetary union is therefore easier when wage flexibility in member states is greater.

29.2 An adjustable peg

> An **adjustable peg** is a fixed exchange rate, the value of which may occasionally be changed.

In operation during 1945–73, the most famous example of an adjustable peg was called the Bretton Woods system, after the small American town where US and UK officials met in 1944 to agree its details. Because countries agreed to use dollars as well as gold as foreign reserves, the system was also called the dollar standard.

Each country fixed its exchange rate against the dollar. The price of gold was fixed in dollars. Currencies were convertible against dollars or gold, which together were foreign exchange reserves. At the fixed exchange rate, central banks were committed to buy or sell domestic currency for foreign exchange reserves. They intervened in the forex market to defend the exchange rate against the dollar.

Unlike the gold standard, the dollar standard did not require 100 per cent forex reserve backing for domestic currency. Governments could print as much money as they wished. The designers of the Bretton Woods system feared that the world gold supply could not increase quickly enough to keep up with the rising demand for money that they hoped would accompany post-war prosperity.

Giving governments the discretion to print money solved that problem but created two others. First, it inhibited the adjustment mechanism built into the gold standard, in which countries with a balance of payments deficit lost gold and their domestic money supply fell, thereby bidding down their prices and boosting their competitiveness. Under the dollar standard, countries with a payments deficit lost money, but the government could print more money again. This prevented higher unemployment in the short run, but also prevented long-run adjustment by stopping the fall in prices that raised competitiveness.

Such policies were not feasible for ever. If the balance of payments deficit persisted, the country ran out of foreign exchange reserves. Then it had to devalue its exchange rate to raise competitiveness and remove the underlying imbalance in international payments.

Speculators faced a one-way bet. When a country was in payment difficulties, either the exchange rate would stay the same a bit longer or it would be devalued at once. Speculators might as well bet on devaluation, since the exchange rate was unlikely to appreciate. Sometimes speculative pressure made devaluation happen earlier because countries lost reserves not only from a current account deficit but also because of a financial account outflow. Foreseeing this difficulty, the architects of the Bretton Woods system decided to solve the problem of speculative capital flows by making private capital flows illegal.

Perfect capital mobility implies interest parity. Interest differentials must be offset by expected exchange rate changes to equate expected returns in different currencies. Fixed exchange rates imply expected exchange rate changes are zero. Hence, interest rates have to be equal. Countries cannot retain the sovereignty to set interest rates.

> Fixed exchange rates, perfect capital mobility and monetary sovereignty are the **impossible triad**. All three cannot co-exist at the same time.

In 1944 the architects of Bretton Woods decided that fixed exchange rates were important, but that countries were not ready to surrender monetary sovereignty. Hence, capital mobility had to be suspended. Capital flow controls were severe until 1960, when controls on long-term capital flows were relaxed. After the adjustable peg was abandoned in 1973, the need for capital controls diminished. Capital controls were gradually dismantled and integration of global financial markets intensified.

The dollar standard had a second drawback. It led to a world of sustained inflation. Dollars had become the world's medium of exchange. A US payments deficit could be financed by printing more dollars. In the mid-1960s US payments deficits increased, partly because of heavy military spending in Vietnam. The supply of dollars rose rapidly. Raising the world's money supply led to inflation throughout the trading world.

Under the gold standard, national and international money supplies had risen only as quickly as new gold could be mined. This system wasted real resources. Why use scarce workers to dig up gold for use as money when money can be printed using almost no real resources? But the difficulty of augmenting the gold supply had ensured that the world money supply grew slowly. It was a commitment to low inflation.

29.3 Floating exchange rates

Pure floating implies that forex markets are in continuous equilibrium without government intervention using the forex reserves. The reserves stay constant and there is no external mechanism to change domestic money supply. The balance of payments is exactly in balance.

Chapter 24 explained how floating exchange rates are determined. In the long run, exchange rates adjust to achieve external balance. This determines the real exchange rate that has to prevail in the long run. Domestic and foreign monetary supplies determine the domestic and foreign price levels. Given these, there is only the path of the nominal exchange rate that delivers the real exchange rate required for external balance when domestic economies are also at internal balance.

In long-run equilibrium, nominal exchange rates then obey **purchasing power parity**.

When capital mobility is high, neither external balance nor purchasing power parity need hold in the short run. Chapters 24 and 25 discussed how exchange rates adjust to achieve interest parity and prevent massive one-way capital flows. In the short run, what matters is not balancing current account flows but the need to balance the potentially much larger financial account flows that might occur when international capital is highly mobile.

> The **purchasing power parity** path of the nominal exchange rate is the path that keeps the real exchange rate constant. Nominal exchange rates offset inflation differentials between countries.

In the long run, there is no conflict. Once real interest rates return to their long-run equilibrium level, nominal interest differentials reflect inflation differentials; PPP and interest parity can be satisfied simultaneously.

Hence, a floating exchange rate does not provide continuous short-run insulation against large changes in competitiveness. Sharp changes in the expected path of interest rates, or in the eventual real exchange rate that will achieve external balance, have big effects on the real exchange rate.

However, floating exchange rates offer no one-way bet to speculators, since new information can make exchange rates jump up or jump down. Floating helps prevent massive capital flows that cause acute problems for macroeconomic management. Floating exchange rates are also the fallback exchange rate regime when countries cannot agree what other regime to adopt.

A managed float

Under a free float there is no central bank intervention in the forex market. The forex reserves are constant, the balance of payments is zero and the net monetary inflow from abroad is also zero.

> In a **managed float**, central banks intervene in the forex market to try to smooth out fluctuations and nudge the exchange rate in the desired direction.

In practice, exchange rates have rarely floated absolutely freely since 1973, when the Bretton Woods adjustable peg was replaced by a floating exchange rate regime.

Intervention may smooth day-to-day exchange rate fluctuations; in the long run it probably makes little difference to the path the exchange rate follows. Central banks have large stocks of foreign exchange reserves which they could dump on the foreign exchange market to try to alter the equilibrium exchange rate. But nowadays speculators have even larger funds at their disposal.

29.4 Speculative attacks on fixed exchange rates

National policy makers hate to admit that national sovereignty is being eroded. Capital mobility rose sharply in the last two decades of the twentieth century. Under floating exchange rates, the influence of capital flows and speculative opinion is immediately evident. Under fixed exchange rates, policy makers sometimes deluded themselves that their sovereignty was unaffected. Often, it took a crisis to convince them otherwise.

In 1990 the UK pegged its exchange rate against EU currencies in the Exchange Rate Mechanism (ERM), the precursor to the euro. In 1992 the UK was forced to abandon this exchange rate peg against its European neighbours. By leaving the European Monetary System (EMS), and floating its exchange rate, the UK regained the ability to set its own interest rates. Lower UK interest rates brought an end to its recession, but led to sharply lower levels of the sterling exchange rate.

More recently, supposedly pegged exchange rates were successfully attacked in Mexico (1994), many Asian countries (1997), Brazil (1999) and Argentina (2002). When the speculators have more money than the central bank, the peg does not always survive.

Now that capital mobility is high, modern crises are not caused directly by trade deficits but by financial account outflows. These usually reflect a perception that some aspect of current policy is unsustainable. Raising interest rates to defend the currency against capital outflows may be unconvincing if the domestic economy obviously cannot stand the pain of high interest rates for long. Speculators understand that if they push hard enough, the government has to cave in.

> A **speculative attack** is a large capital outflow. If successful, it causes a devaluation. Attacks are sometimes resisted, by raising interest rates and tightening fiscal policy. This works only if it can credibly be sustained.

There are several interpretations of a **speculative attack**. One is that it corrects a policy mistake. If a country has such a large budget deficit that it needs to finance by creating money, it is bound to have inflation. Promising to peg the nominal exchange rate then makes little sense. A speculative attack merely forces policy makers to switch to a more realistic exchange rate regime; namely, floating. This is a good description of the Russian crisis in 1998, and partly explains speculation against Greece in 2010; but it does not explain attacks against Asian economies, such as South Korea and the Philippines, in 1997, or the attack on the UK in 1992.

A second interpretation is that there are two possible equilibrium exchange rates. Without any attack, the original peg survives. The exchange rate is a little overvalued, but the cost of devaluing (which is likely to raise inflation expectations) outweighs the cost of a little uncompetitiveness. However, once attacked, the cost of repelling the attack must be added to the scales. It may tip the balance, making it optimal now to accept defeat and take the (temporary) advantage of higher competitiveness that the devaluation achieves. Whether the peg survives or not depends entirely on whether speculators decide to attack.

Successful attacks may do a lot of damage. When domestic banks have borrowed in foreign currency, the domestic value of their debts rises when the exchange rate falls. This may bankrupt the banks and cause a widespread loss of confidence. If a country wants to be less vulnerable to attack, what can it do?

Repelling boarders

> **Capital controls** prohibit, restrict or tax the flow of private capital across currencies.

Three responses have been adopted. First, try to reduce capital mobility, making it easier to defend fixed but adjustable exchange rate pegs. This was the solution adopted by those designing the Bretton Woods system after the Second World War. Private capital flows were outlawed by **capital controls**.

Capital controls make it easier to defend pegged exchange rates. However, from the 1970s onwards, controls were progressively dismantled as a global financial system was created. It became harder and harder to enforce controls – smart bankers found offshore ways to do the same business.

One form of control that may work is a tiny tax on financial transactions, proposed many years ago by Nobel Prize winner James Tobin. Paying a tiny tax on a ten-year investment is trivial, the same tax on holding a foreign asset for two hours takes away all the profits. A Tobin tax mainly hits short-term 'hot money'.

Capital controls have been used quite successfully in Chile, and were introduced by Malaysia in 1997 after its currency was attacked. Whether the global economy is consistent with widespread controls is doubtful. Small emerging markets can probably use them. The more highly integrated a country is with the world's financial markets, the harder it is to use capital controls.

If capital controls are not to be the answer, the exchange rate regime has to become more robust. Pegged exchange rates are an uncomfortable halfway house: usually pegged, sometimes adjustable. While they are pegged, the central bank has to defend them, even when a one-way bet is emerging. But because they are not completely pegged, the speculators can win in the end.

If this is the diagnosis, the solution is to retreat to one of the safer extremes: float or peg completely. Thus, a second solution for repelling boarders and avoiding spectacular exchange rate crashes is simply to float. Let the speculators punch thin air. They can take the currency down, but, if it was for no good reason, the currency will probably come up again. Most Asian exchange rates recovered rapidly after the 1997 crisis.

The alternative is to make the peg much more credible, akin to the old gold standard. A popular device is a currency board.

A **currency board** removes the ability of the central bank to create money. Balance of payments surpluses (deficits) are the only source of expansion (contraction) of the monetary base. Suppose a country has a deficit because it imports too much. Importers take domestic money to the currency board to get the foreign exchange they need; the board simply keeps the domestic money, which is retired from circulation. Countries using currency boards at some point within the last two decades include Estonia, Bulgaria and Argentina.

> A **currency board** is a constitutional commitment to peg the exchange rate by giving up monetary independence.

Like all commitments, it hurts when it has to take the strain. Since a country loses monetary independence, it cannot use interest rates for domestic reasons. To live comfortably with a fixed nominal exchange rate, it needs to avoid higher inflation than its trading partners. If it has a fiscally irresponsible government, it will require money creation and inflation that will eventually get it into trouble. Argentina's crisis in 2001/02, and Greece's crisis in 2010, reflected such a trend deterioration in competitiveness. In other cases, knowledge of the monetary commitment may induce the fiscal authorities to behave responsibly, as for example in Estonia prior to its entry into the EU.

Similarly, if the country's banks get into trouble, a currency board prevents easier monetary conditions to help the banks during the crisis. If people worry that, in these circumstances, the country might find a way to give up the currency board, speculators may foresee this possibility and attack the currency anyway. Currency boards are more likely to work the better the public finances are under control and the more evident it is that the country has a sound system of bank regulation that prevents banks taking risks that may get them into trouble.

No solution is ideal. If one solution were perfect, it would have been adopted everywhere long ago. We now consider other issues in choosing between fixed and floating exchange rates.

 ## 29.5   Fixed vs floating

In this section we consider robustness, volatility and financial discipline.

Robustness

How do different regimes cope with major strains? Nominal strains arise when different countries have very different domestic inflation rates. Real strains occur when the world economy suffers a major real shock, such as a quadrupling of real oil prices.

With fixed nominal exchange rates, countries with higher inflation than their competitors become less competitive in international markets. Unless countries pursue domestic monetary policies that lead to roughly equal inflation rates, a fixed exchange rate system simply cannot cope. If frequent devaluations are required to restore competitiveness, credibility evaporates and the country may as well float. In the long run, floating exchange rates can depreciate gently along the PPP path and 'cope' with inflation differences.

How about strains caused by real shocks? Imagine how the OPEC oil price shocks would have hit a fixed exchange rate regime. Overnight, countries that were big oil importers would have faced enormous trade deficits and speculators would have bet on these currencies being devalued. Under a fixed exchange rate regime, the OPEC oil price shock would have led to consultations, tentative exchange rate adjustments, and further consultations to determine whether adjustments already undertaken were sufficient to achieve the adjustments required. In practice, floating exchange rates coped better.

Volatility

Floating exchange rates can be volatile. Under the adjustable peg, between 1949 and 1967 the $/£ exchange rate was rarely more than 1 cent either side of $2.80/£, and between 1967 and 1972 rarely more than 1 cent either side of $2.40/£. In contrast, Figure 29.1 shows the volatility of the $/£ exchange rate since 1975 under floating exchange rates. Not only did it fluctuate between $2.50/£ and $1.05/£, it sometimes moved very rapidly. Such volatility, it is argued, leads to great uncertainty, reducing both trade and foreign investment.

The volatility of floating exchange rates cannot be disputed. Is it always bad? First, it is not obvious that a system with usually fixed nominal exchange rates but occasional large crises is less uncertain than a system in which nominal exchange rates change every day.

Second, what would have happened if the exchange rate had not adjusted so much? To keep the exchange rate more stable in the face of shocks, perhaps interest rates or tax rates would have had to adjust to these shocks. Is uncertainty about competitiveness under floating exchange rates necessarily worse than uncertainty about interest rates or tax rates under a fixed exchange rate regime? British business was pleased when high interest rates were abandoned after the pound fell out of the Exchange Rate Mechanism in 1992.

The volatility argument may not go decisively against floating exchange rates. However, this argument also comes in a more sophisticated form. The shocks with which the world international monetary system has to deal may not be independent of the exchange rate regime in force. By their very flexibility and robustness, floating exchange rates may make shocks more likely. The most important version of this argument relates to inflation shocks and financial discipline.

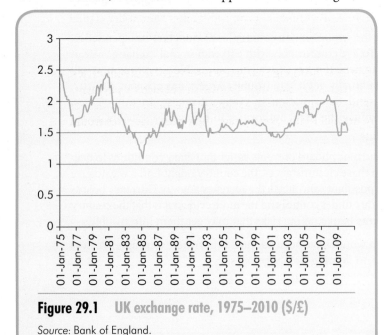

Figure 29.1 UK exchange rate, 1975–2010 ($/£)

Source: Bank of England.

Financial discipline

Floating exchange rates let different countries pursue different inflation rates indefinitely. Exchange rates of high-inflation countries depreciate to maintain purchasing power parity and constant competitiveness. Critics of floating exchange rates argue that they do not provide any financial discipline.

In contrast, with a fixed exchange rate, countries become uncompetitive if they have above-average inflation. Unless allowed to devalue, they eventually have no choice but to adopt more restrictive domestic policies to get their inflation rates back in line with the rest of the world.

Fixed exchange rates, however, are not the only route to financial discipline. Instead, the government can make domestic commitments about monetary policy. In recent years, many countries have made their central banks operationally independent of government, giving them freedom to decide interest rates in pursuit of low-inflation targets laid down by the government.

Domestic commitments are not always foolproof. But exchange rate commitments are no certainty either. The weaker EMS currencies (sterling, the lira, the peseta, the escudo) could not maintain previous fixed exchange rate commitments in September 1992, and by 2010 financial markets were beginning to wonder whether the PIGS could survive inside the eurozone.

There is now mounting pressure on China to abandon its peg to the US dollar, which has been maintained at a level that has left China supercompetitive. If China is running a vast current account surplus, only two outcomes are possible. The first is that its balance of payments is broadly in balance, in which case it is experiencing a capital outflow of similar size to its current account surplus; but it is paradoxical that rich countries such as the US are therefore borrowing from China whose standard of living is so much lower. The other possible outcome is that China does not have a massive capital account outflow, in which case its current account surplus will imply an overall balance of payments surplus, and a huge monetary inflow into the country which, sooner or later, will cause domestic inflation that gradually erodes Chinese competitiveness again.

Table 29.2 shows the recent balance of payments performance of emerging Asian economies as a whole, a group that includes China and India. The group has been running a current account surplus of between $400 billion and $500 billion per annum. The combination of private sector capital flows and other capital flows has also contributed to an inflow. Hence, the combined balance of payments of this group of countries has exceeded $500 billion a year.

What is happening to this monetary inflow? It is adding to the foreign exchange reserves of these countries. Are they floating or fixing their exchange rates? If they were floating, the overall balance of payments would be zero. They are fixing, and the level of the peg is below the exchange rate that would deliver external balance. Putting it differently, if they were now all to float, on average their exchange rates would appreciate and their competitiveness would decline.

Table 29.2 Emerging Asia, balance of payments, 2008–10 ($bn)

	2008	2009	2010
Current account	+420	+481	+469
Capital account	+214	+34	+57
Balance of payments	+634	+515	+526
Growth in forex reserves	+634	+515	+526

Source: IMF.

It is the massive size of this imbalance that prompts Western governments to press for a change of exchange rate policy, particularly by China. The counterpart to Chinese trade surpluses is trade deficits in the US and Europe, whose domestic trade unions protest that jobs are being exported to Asia. Comparative advantage implies that many manufacturing jobs are bound to disappear from the US and Europe, but the current exchange rate configuration is artificially accelerating the process. If hysteresis matters, jobs that go now may never return, even if there is a subsequent exchange rate correction.

CASE 29.1 World economy in a cul de sac?

After the slump of 2008/09, the world economy recovered in 2009/10 after the largest monetary and fiscal expansion in peacetime. Fiscal stimulus cannot be sustained at this level. What happens when fiscal policy has to tighten again?

While governments were spending so much, the private sector had been taking the opportunity to save like crazy to rebuild its balance sheet. The OECD forecast a private sector surplus of around 7 per cent of GDP, both for the eurozone and for the OECD as a whole. Given that private saving had previously fallen to tiny levels during the borrow-to-spend boom, by both firms and households, this represented a significant rise in the private sector saving rate. Equivalently, it represented a dramatic fall in private sector spending, which lowered aggregate demand. Without the aggregate demand rescue by governments across the world, output and employment would have fallen much more dramatically still. And without the simultaneous and drastic easing of monetary policy, private spending would also have fallen further.

If governments are to tighten fiscal policy, as they must, without causing the very collapse of aggregate demand that fiscal expansion was originally designed to prevent, private spending must somehow be jump-started again. This cannot be achieved by further monetary loosening since interest rates are already near zero.

In the optimistic scenario, credit growth is somehow restored in the rich countries: both firms and households, anticipating future economic growth, are prepared to start borrowing and spending again. In the pessimistic scenario, the private sector and its potential creditors remain scared of the economic future once fiscal policy cuts back. Private saving remains high, consumption and investment demand remain low, and the paradox of thrift (see Chapter 16) stifles economic recovery.

The rich but now highly indebted OECD countries can 'solve' their debt problem either by reducing their debt or by increasing their income. The latter is much less painful if it can be achieved. One possible source of higher aggregate demand is export demand from emerging markets such as China; since emerging markets have recovered much more quickly, they have not accumulated nearly so much government debt during the crash. This is why OECD politicians are so concerned about the undervaluation of the exchange rates of emerging market economies – and corresponding overvaluation of exchange rates of OECD countries. This reduces the scope for the US, Europe and Japan to enjoy substantial export booms to emerging markets as these latter economies resume rapid growth.

If the mature economies do not experience this export-led growth, the next-best bet is probably a resurgence of private and public investment. Although this would require further borrowing today, it would not only add to aggregate demand in the short run but also boost aggregate supply in the longer run as this new capital stock became available for production.

Such thinking underlay the New Deal pursued by the US in the 1930s, with extensive government support. Whether national economies in a globalized economy can credibly co-ordinate and sustain the financing required must be an open question. For example, if competitive emerging markets are continuing to peg exchange rates and run trade surpluses, it might require a mechanism, such as the IMF, to channel surplus funds from emerging markets to the US, Europe and Japan.

If neither of these can be accomplished, we run the risk of ending up in a cul de sac: OECD governments forced to tighten fiscal policy before they go bankrupt, their private sectors still unwilling to spend, and a protracted slump becoming a greater possibility.

Source: Adapted from Wolf, M. (2010) The world economy has no easy way out of the mire, *Financial Times*, 23 February. © The Financial Times Limited 2010.

Where the government is weak at home, invoking external pressures may be a useful tactic. But a tough government may be able to institute domestic forms of commitment (appointing a tough governor of the central bank or giving that bank greater independence from government control) which still leave the choice of exchange rate regime determined by other factors.

29.6 Antecedents of the eurozone

Small, open economies that trade a lot with one another dislike exchange rate volatility between them. In 1979 the members of the European Community set up the European Monetary System (EMS), a system of monetary and exchange rate co-operation in Western Europe. Its most important aspect was the **Exchange Rate Mechanism (ERM)**.

> In the **Exchange Rate Mechanism (ERM)**, each country fixed a nominal exchange rate against each other ERM participant. Collectively, the group floated against the rest of the world.

Each country in the ERM could let its exchange rate fluctuate within a band of $\pm 2\frac{1}{4}$ per cent of the parities it had agreed to defend.[1] When the currency hit the edge of a band, all central banks in the ERM countries were supposed to intervene to try to defend the parity. Realignments of the fixed exchange rates against partner countries were possible but had to be unanimously agreed by participants of the ERM.

Table 29.3 shows the realignments of the major ERM currencies during 1979–91 (the UK did not join until 1990 and left in 1992.) Realignments largely restored purchasing power parity. High-inflation countries (initially Italy and France) were allowed nominal exchange rate devaluations. Notice that there was a realignment every six months between 1979 and 1983, but after 1983 realignments were much less frequent. Between 1987 and 1991 there was no realignment at all.

Did the ERM exert financial discipline? Were France and Italy forced to converge to low German inflation? Not initially. The old policies continued and regular exchange rate realignments fixed up competitiveness again. However, realignments did not *fully* restore competitiveness, so a little discipline was exerted. After 1983 discipline was much stricter.

Since high-inflation countries needed regular devaluations, which required the consent of other ERM members, by withholding consent it was possible to put pressure on the high-inflation countries. Monetary policies steadily converged, especially after 1983.

The role of Germany was crucial. German hyperinflation in 1923 had been a disaster. Germans now hate inflation and are determined to prevent it. The Bundesbank (Buba) has a constitution mandating it to achieve price stability as its overriding objective. The Buba was never prepared to set interest rates at a level that endangered price stability in Germany.[2]

---

1 Italy, an especially high-inflation country in 1979, was allowed a band of 6 per cent. By the mid-1980s, it was a matter of honour for Italy not to use this wider band. Spain and the UK also joined the ERM with a wider band.

2 In 1978, during the negotiations to establish the EMS, the Buba obtained its own 'opt out' deal. The German government privately assured the Bundesbank that it had the option to not support other currencies if doing so threatened German price stability.

Table 29.3 EMS realignments, 1979–91 (date and percentage realignment)

Date	German mark	French franc	Dutch guilder	Italian lira	Belgian franc	Danish kroner	Luxem-bourg franc	Irish punt
Sept. 79	+2.0					−2.9		
Nov. 80						−4.8		
Mar. 81				−6.0				
Oct. 81	+5.5	−3.0	+5.5	−3.0				
Feb. 82					−8.5	−3.0	−8.5	
June 83	+4.3	−5.8	+4.3	−2.8				
Mar. 84	+5.5	−2.5	+3.5	−2.5	+1.5	+2.5	+1.5	−3.5
July 85	+2.0	+2.0	+2.0	−6.0	+2.0	+2.0	+2.0	+2.0
Apr. 86								−8.0
Jan. 87	+3.0		+3.0		+2.0			
Cumulative	+23.7	−9.3	+18.8	−20.3	−3.3	−6.2	−5.0	−9.5

In the mid-1980s, Germany made it harder for high-inflation countries to get regular devaluations. Without them, high-inflation countries had to reduce inflation or face trend deterioration in competitiveness. They chose austerity and disinflation.

By the mid-1980s the implicit deal in the ERM was simple. Germany set interest rates according to what was good for Germany alone. Other ERM members adopted German interest rates in order to keep exchange rates pegged within the ERM. In return, the other members 'borrowed' German credibility. Low inflation was expected in Spain and Italy not because their own policies were suddenly more credible but because Germany might block the devaluations that would be needed if inflationary policies ever re-emerged.

Why the ERM survived

After 1983 the success of the ERM reflected policy convergence on low inflation. Before 1983 little policy convergence had taken place. Two things explain the early survival of the ERM.

First, with a band of ±2¼ per cent, there were periods when countries were effectively floating. High-inflation countries had exchange rates that started off near the top of the band and gradually depreciated, just as they would have done under floating. When they got near the bottom of the band, a devaluation soon followed. The early ERM was largely cosmetic.

Second, most countries initially had controls preventing big financial account flows. Despite differences in interest rates, fixed nominal parities survived because capital flows were prevented. Only occasionally was the prospect of a realignment so imminent that capital controls had trouble stemming the speculative tide. However, to create a single market in the EU, in 1987 countries committed themselves to the removal of capital controls within a few years.

When capital mobility is high, to peg the exchange rate between two countries both countries need to have the same interest rate. The key issue is who chooses the common interest rate. Because of the role of Germany in ERM disinflation in the mid-1980s, Germany set the single interest rate thereafter.

Table 29.4 ERM devaluations, 1992–98

Date	Punt	Peseta	Escudo	Lira	Pound
Sept. 92		−5		left ERM	left ERM
Nov. 92		−6	−6		
Feb. 93	−10				
May 93		−8	−6.5		
Mar. 95		−7			
Dec. 96				rejoined ERM	

After five years without any realignment during 1987–92, by mid-1992 several exchange rates appeared overvalued. Germany proposed a general ERM realignment in August, but this was declined by other countries. As speculative pressure continued, the Buba intervened heavily to support weaker currencies, as did other central banks.

Speculation persisted. Sterling and the lira were forced out of the ERM and depreciated substantially. The peseta, escudo and Irish punt were devalued but remained in the ERM. Table 29.4 shows ERM realignments during 1992–97.

A new attack on the French franc in August 1993 led to a face-saving 'redesign' of the ERM to allow the franc to survive within it. Previous narrow bands ($2\frac{1}{4}$ per cent each side of the parity) were replaced by very wide bands (15 per cent each side of the parity). With such wide bands, the ERM survived thereafter.

CASE 29.2 Capital controls and the ERM

Initially, the ERM allowed high-inflation countries regular devaluations that largely shadowed the nominal exchange rate depreciation they would have had under floating. After 1983 discipline increased, and realignments got less frequent. During 1983–85 inflation rates converged substantially to the low German inflation rate.

In 1986 the Single European Act, a commitment to a single market, signalled the end of controls on capital flows. Yet capital controls had underpinned the early ERM. For a high-inflation country, figure (a) shows the path $ABDE$ of nominal exchange rate depreciation to maintain real competitiveness. Initially, the exchange rate is pegged within a band around central parity e_0. When the exchange rate hits the bottom of the band at B, central banks intervene to try to defend the band. As time elapses, the exchange rate moves along BC. With continuing inflation, competitiveness is now being eroded. Eventually this prompts a devaluation of the central parity from e_0 to e_1, so the whole band shifts down. The actual exchange rate jumps from C to D on the day of the realignment.

This is a one-way bet. As the exchange rate moves along BC nobody is expecting a sharp appreciation! Only capital controls prevent a massive outflow on the financial account to avoid the imminent capital loss on holding the currency. If capital controls had been removed in the early 1980s, there would have been an immediate crisis. Figure (b) explains why this did not occur after 1986.

By the mid-1980s, inflation convergence within the ERM meant even Italian inflation was nearly down to German levels. Slow depreciation of the lira could offset extra Italian inflation. The line is flatter in figure (b)

671

▶ than in (a). In figure (b) when the parity is devalued from e_0 to e_1, the actual exchange rate at B is inside both the old band and the new band. No jump is required in the exchange rate, and there is no one-way bet for speculators. A small interest differential will compensate them for the gradual depreciation.

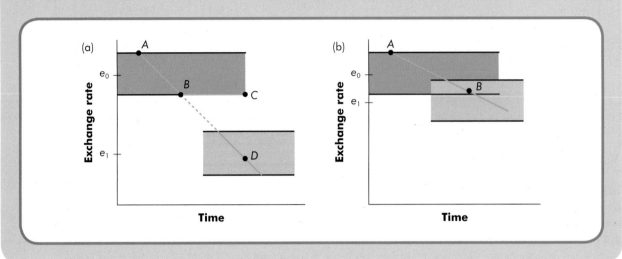

From ERM to EMU

> A **monetary union** has permanently fixed exchange rates within the union, an integrated financial market and a single central bank setting the single interest rate for the union.

By 1988 capital controls were largely gone as part of the Single Market reforms. It was only a matter of time before speculators attacked the pegged exchange rates of the Exchange Rate Mechanism that was then in place. One solution was to go forward rapidly to completely fixed exchange rates.

A monetary union need not have a single currency. English and Scottish currencies circulate side by side in Edinburgh. What matters is that the exchange rate is certain and that a single authority (the Bank of England) sets the interest rate for both.

In 1988 the European heads of state established the Delors Committee to recommend how to get to European monetary union. Interestingly, the Committee was not asked to discuss whether EMU was a good idea. Small, highly integrated European economies needed to avoid large exchange rate fluctuations. With capital controls gone, there was no guarantee that the ERM could deliver. In any case, since ERM members had already given up monetary sovereignty by letting Germany set the single interest rate in the ERM, formal ratification of a monetary union did not seem such a big step.

The Delors Committee recommendations became the basis of the Treaty of Maastricht in 1991. Monetary union was to be achieved in three stages. In Stage 1, which began in 1990, any remaining capital controls were abolished, and the UK was encouraged to join the ERM (it joined in 1990). Realignments were possible but discouraged. In Stage 2, which began in January 1994, a new European Monetary Institute prepared the ground for EMU, realignments were even harder to obtain and excessive budget deficits were to be discouraged but not outlawed.

> The **Maastricht criteria** for joining EMU said that a country must already have achieved low inflation and sound fiscal policy.

Stage 3, in which exchange rates were irreversibly fixed and the single monetary policy began, was to start in 1997 if a majority of potential entrants fulfilled the Maastricht criteria (in the event, they did not). Otherwise, EMU was to begin in January 1999 with whatever number of countries then met the criteria. Monetary policy in EMU was to be set by an independent central bank, mandated to achieve price stability as its principal goal.

There were two sets of criteria, one for monetary policy and nominal variables and one for fiscal policy.

The monetary criteria said that, to be eligible, a potential entrant had to have low inflation, low nominal interest rates (market confirmation of low inflation expectations) and two prior years in the ERM without any devaluation. This last requirement was to prevent competitive devaluations or 'last realignments' as EMU approached.

The fiscal criteria said budget deficits must not be excessive, interpreted to mean that budget deficits should be less than 3 per cent of GDP and that the debt/GDP ratio should not be over 60 per cent. Tight fiscal policy would mean there was little pressure on the central bank to print money to bail out fiscal authorities. In 2009 Greece admitted that its previous national statistics had been inaccurate and that its budget deficit was much larger than had previously been reported. This immediately led to speculative pressure against an EMU member state, precisely what the Maastricht Treaty had sought to avoid.

At the time, many economists complained that the Maastricht criteria were caution taken to extremes. An independent central bank with a tough constitution was an adequate commitment to low inflation. It was unnecessary to constrain fiscal policy as well. Indeed, since national governments would no longer have a national interest rate or national exchange rate policy to deal with purely national circumstances, leaving them fiscal room for manoeuvre might be a good idea.

The Maastricht deal reflected the balance of power in the negotiations. At the time, Germany ran the EMS and trusted itself to do so in its own interests. Why would Germany give up such a good position? Only if EMU was going to be super-safe. The Maastricht criteria were the price of getting Germany on board.

Sterling and UK membership

Why was the UK reluctant to join both the ERM and EMU? First, until the late 1980s, North Sea oil made sterling behave differently from other European currencies. As UK oil production slowed down, this objection evaporated.

Second, whereas the core countries of Europe are now very integrated with one another, offshore UK is less integrated with the rest of Europe. A common policy may be less suitable. Table 29.5 shows the composition of UK trade and how it has changed since the UK joined the EU in 1973. The trend is clear. The UK is becoming more integrated with continental Europe all the time, even if from a lower baseline than some other European countries. If this trend continues, the issue is eventually not whether the UK should join but when.

Third, the UK has greater macroeconomic sovereignty: it seems to have more to lose. Whereas ERM countries had already allowed the 'single' interest rate to be set by Germany alone, sterling floated during the entire period except for the two years of its ERM membership during 1990–92.

However, the absence of capital controls and the power of the speculators limit monetary sovereignty whatever the exchange rate regime. The Bank of England has often wished to raise interest rates for domestic reasons, to cool down a housing boom, but been unprepared to do so because higher interest rates would bid up further the value of the floating pound, exacerbating the woes of UK exporters. The Bank has often found itself hoping for interest rate rises in Frankfurt and Washington that would allow it to raise sterling interest rates without causing a further appreciation of sterling.

Finally, Black Wednesday (16 September 1992) made it hard for UK politicians to enthuse about EMU. While Chancellor, John Major took the UK into the ERM in 1990 to combat rising inflation at

Table 29.5 UK trade patterns (%)

	EU	North America	Rest of world
1970	34	17	49
2005	62	11	27

Sources: UN, *International Trade Statistics*; www.statistics.gov.uk.

the end of the Lawson boom. Unfortunately, this coincided with German reunification. Big subsidies to East Germany caused German overheating. When Chancellor Kohl refused to raise taxes, the Bundesbank raised interest rates to cool down the German economy. Interest rates high enough to do this job were far too high for Germany's partners in the ERM. This provoked the crisis of 1992–93. The UK and Italy left the ERM, slashed interest rates and depreciated their currencies. Other countries struggled on inside the ERM, though many had devaluations (see Chapter 28).

German reunification was the biggest country-specific economic shock in post-war Europe. It was not a good guide to how EMU would subsequently fare. Indeed, the mandate of the European Central Bank to take an EU-wide view prevents it reacting in such extreme fashion to the needs of one country. But UK voters remember the UK flirtation with a single European interest rate as an unhappy experience.

During 1996–98 EU countries scrambled frantically to get their budget deficits below the 3 per cent Maastricht limit to be eligible for EMU. There was fiscal tightening in continental Europe. Since the UK was enjoying the effects of looser policy after 1992 – the whole point of leaving the ERM had been to reduce interest rates and stimulate the economy – the UK business cycle got out of phase with the rest of Europe. This had little to do with any structural difference. It simply reflected the fact that, while the UK had its foot on the accelerator, its EU partners still had the brakes on tight.

Membership of a common currency is easier the more the different members want to do the same thing. The financial crash of 2007–09 placed huge strains upon the eurozone. Different countries wished for differing degrees of fiscal expansion to offset the crash, and were left with different sizes of debt problem as a result.

Germany, always the most prudent as well as most powerful member, resisted pressure to depreciate the euro to stimulate aggregate demand, fearing this would also lead to inflation. Countries such as Ireland, Greece and Portugal became trapped in a position involving an uncompetitive exchange rate, a substantial fiscal debt, and no possibility of either creating money or depreciating the exchange rate to help resolve the problem.

Whatever its previous view, the UK enjoyed more flexibility. Although more exposed to the banking crisis than other European countries, the UK also possessed the ability to allow sterling to depreciate, making exports more competitive, and/or to allow domestic inflation that would erode the real value of government debt denominated in nominal terms. As of 2010, sterling had been allowed to depreciate a bit, but inflation had yet to materialize. Although Lord Mandelson took the opportunity to restate the eventual benefits of UK membership of the eurozone, most policicians, and most voters, reinforced their view that the crisis had increased the likelihood of the UK remaining outside the eurozone for some time to come.

29.7 The economics of the euro

> An **optimal currency area** is a group of countries better off with a common currency than keeping separate national currencies.

In 1999 Professor Robert Mundell won the Nobel Prize for Economics, in part for his pioneering work on **optimal currency areas**.

Mundell, and the economists who came after him, identified three attributes that might make countries suitable for a currency area. First, countries that trade a lot with each other may have little ability to affect their equilibrium real exchange rate against their partners in the long run, but they may face temptations to devalue to gain a temporary advantage. A fixed exchange rate rules out such behaviour and allows gains from trade to be enjoyed.

Second, the more similar the economic and industrial structure of potential partners, the more likely it is that they face common shocks, which can be dealt with by a common monetary policy. It is country-specific shocks that pose difficulties for a single monetary policy.

Third, the more flexible are the labour markets within the currency area, the more easily any necessary changes in competitiveness and real exchange rates can be accomplished by (different) changes in the price level in different member countries.

Conversely, countries gain most by keeping their monetary sovereignty when they are not that integrated with potential partners, have a different structure, and hence are likely to face different shocks, and cannot rely on domestic wage and price flexibility as a substitute for exchange rate changes.

To these purely economic arguments, we should add an important political argument. Currency areas are more likely to work when countries within the area are prepared to make at least some fiscal transfers to partner countries. In practice, this cultural and political identity may be at least as important as any narrow economic criteria for success.

Is Europe an optimal currency area?

Those who have studied the structure of national economies, and the correlation of shocks across countries, generally reach the following conclusions. First, Europe is quite, but not very, integrated. Second, there is a clear inner core of countries – France, Germany, Netherlands, Belgium, Luxembourg, and perhaps Austria – more closely integrated than the rest.

However, the act of joining the EMU changes the degree of integration, possibly quite substantially. A common currency, by eliminating a source of segmentation into national markets, will increase integration. Moreover, there is evidence that countries that trade a lot have more correlated business cycles. And countries which belong to currency unions tend historically to trade much more with each other than can be explained simply by the fact that their exchange rates are fixed.

These bits of evidence imply that it may be possible to start a currency union before the microeconomic preconditions are fully in place. The act of starting speeds up the process. Even so, a decade of the eurozone was not sufficient to prepare all its members for the severe strain that would be imparted by the financial crash and its fiscal aftermath.

The Stability Pact

The Stability Pact, ratified by the Treaty of Amsterdam in 1997, confirmed that the Maastricht fiscal criteria would not merely be entry conditions for EMU but would continue to apply after countries joined the monetary union. Some EMU members had debt/GDP ratios of close to 100 per cent. Reducing these towards 60 per cent might take decades. The focus was on the 3 per cent ceiling for budget deficits.

In principle, countries exceeding the limit had to pay fines unless their economy was in evident recession. Thus countries had to wait for output to fall before they were allowed to expand fiscal policy by having deficits above the ceiling of 3 per cent of GDP.

The pact did not preclude countries from using fiscal policies more vigorously, as they most certainly did in 2008/09 when they were clearly in recession. The corollary is that, ideally, they should aim for something more like budget balance in normal times, and for budget surplus during periods of boom. Then they still have room to increase deficits in times of trouble without exceeding the 3 per cent ceiling.

Note that if budgets are roughly in balance over the business cycle, but output grows for ever, debt/GDP ratios should exhibit trend decline, whatever their cyclical behaviour. This may eventually lead to the tough conditions of the Stability Pact being eased.

The European Central Bank

The single monetary policy is now set in Frankfurt by the European Central Bank (ECB). National central banks have not been abolished, but the board of the ECB sets the interest rate on the euro.

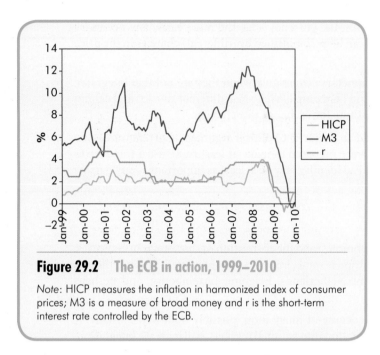

Figure 29.2 The ECB in action, 1999–2010

Note: HICP measures the inflation in harmonized index of consumer prices; M3 is a measure of broad money and r is the short-term interest rate controlled by the ECB.

The ECB mandate says its first duty is to ensure price stability, but it can take other aims into account provided price stability is not in doubt. In press conferences, officials of the ECB have emphasized that their interest rate decisions should be interpreted largely as the pursuit of price stability. Neither the financial markets nor academic economists are entirely convinced. ECB behaviour looks as if they pay some attention to output gaps as well as inflation. Empirically, a Taylor rule explains their behaviour quite well: interest rates are changes to reflect deviations of both inflation and output from their underlying target levels.

Empirically, it is always difficult to distinguish between a central bank that actually cares about output as well as inflation (however much it says its only concern is inflation) and a central bank that cares about current and future inflation, and uses output gaps as one means of forecasting future inflation. For whichever reason, a Taylor rule works well in capturing empirically how central banks actually behave in setting interest rates.

Despite the fact that its behaviour is largely explained empirically by a Taylor rule, the ECB describes its monetary strategy as pursuing two intermediate targets – the 'twin pillars'. The first pillar is a monetary target, the growth rate of the M3 measure of nominal money. The second pillar is expected inflation. The ECB insists that it takes both pillars into account in setting interest rates in the eurozone.

Figure 29.2 shows the interest rate decisions of the ECB, the evolution of inflation and the rate of nominal money growth. It is easy to see how the rise and fall of actual and expected inflation led to the rise and fall of interest rates in the eurozone. It is very hard to detect any clear correlation between nominal money growth and interest rate decisions.

It is precisely the volatility in both money demand and the money supply behaviour of banks that has made most central banks abandon monetary targeting in favour of flexible inflation targets or Taylor rules. The ECB continues to insist that monetary targets have an important role because it wants to emphasize continuity with the Bundesbank, which uses monetary targets.

Fiscal federalism?

> A **federal fiscal system** has a central government setting taxes and expenditure rules that apply in its constituent states or countries.

One reason for the survival of the monetary union that we call the US is its **federal fiscal** structure. When a particular state has a slump, it pays less income tax revenue to Washington and gets more social security money from Washington, without any decisions having to be taken. Automatic stabilizers are at work, courtesy of federal tax rates and federal rates of social security payments. Conversely, a booming state pays more tax revenue to Washington and gets less social security money back.

When state income rises by $1, the state pays an extra 30 cents in income tax and gets 10 cents less in social security. Conversely, when state income falls by $1, the state pays 30 cents less in federal taxes and gets an extra 10 cents in social security. Originally, economists thought that this meant each state was effectively insured by up to about 40 cents in the dollar. The eurozone has no federal fiscal structure on anything like this scale. The pessimists concluded that the EMU would come under pressure from country-specific shocks.

The idea was correct but the sums were wrong. The original US calculations are relevant to a world in which state incomes are uncorrelated with each other. In practice, the correlation is quite high.

Hence, when one state slumps and gets help from Washington, many other states are slumping and also getting help. But this increases US government debt and means *every* state has to pay higher future taxes.

But an individual state could have done that on its own, without membership of the federal 'mutual insurance' club. It could have borrowed in the slump to boost its own fiscal spending, and paid it back later when times were better. Making allowance for this, US states are probably insured by nearer to 10 cents in the dollar than 40 cents.

However, the Stability Pact may have *prevented* individual EMU countries behaving in this way, by restricting their ability to borrow in bad times. In fact, over time the Stability Pact was interpreted more flexibly, having greater regard for the effect of temporary cycles in temporarily reducing tax revenue.

Even before the financial crash, the most powerful eurozone members, Germany and France, were not penalized for exceeding the 3 per cent ceiling. Once the crash took place, and the world followed the lead of the UK and US in opting for huge fiscal deficits to stave off even worse reduction in aggregate demand, budget deficits soared in the eurozone as elsewhere.

By the start of 2010, the eurozone therefore faced a number of fiscal challenges. First, to what extent could the reputation for fiscal prudence be restored? Second, how could acute differences in the outcomes of different member states be resolved without having a common fiscal policy? Third, could the possible bankruptcy of individual member states be prevented? As in all questions of redistribution, the fortunate have to be willing to pay for the unfortunate. In part, the definition of a workable nation state is a grouping of citizens across whom the common bond is sufficiently large that the rich agree to be taxed (a bit) to pay for the poor. During 2010 German voters made it pretty clear they were not excited about paying for Greece or Portugal. The less fiscal support such countries obtain, the more they may be driven to restore their monetary autonomy by leaving the eurozone altogether.

ACTIVITY 29.1 Irish deflation

Irish unions agree to link pay rises to efficiency, reported John Murray Brown in the *Financial Times* (30 March 2010), following a deal between the government and public sector trade unions. In exchange for the avoidance of compulsory redundancies, unions agreed to flexible work practices and possible pay cuts as well.

The objective of the policy was two-fold. The direct effect was to tighten fiscal policy by shrinking public spending. During 2008–10 Irish fiscal policy was tightened by 6 per cent of GDP. Ireland aims to have reduced its budget deficit from 12 per cent in 2008 back to the Stability Pact target of 3 per cent of GDP by 2014.

The second effect of the policy is to reduce the price level in Ireland. If nominal wages are reduced, and prices then fall, Ireland's competitiveness will increase even within the eurozone. Domestic wage and price reduction is a substitute for nominal exchange rate depreciation.

In the December 2009 budget, public sector workers took pay cuts from 5 per cent for people earning below €30 000 to 10 per cent for those on higher incomes. This was on top of a pension levy in February 2009 that reduced take-home pay by 5 per cent.

Suppose Irish prices and wages each fall by 10 per cent. How much poorer have Irish people become? The answer depends on the openness of the Irish economy. If imports were only 10 per cent of the size of GDP, real wages would be reduced only a little since most goods are produced domestically and their prices have fallen by the same percentage as nominal wages. Conversely, if imports are 90 per cent of the size of GDP, then the nominal wage cut is matched by a price cut on only the 10 per cent of goods produced and consumed in Ireland, and

Irish residents are worse of by around 9 per cent in real terms. For exactly the same reason, Irish competitiveness has increased substantially.

Since we know Ireland is a small, open economy, the answer in practice is closer to the latter example than the former. Annual consumer price deflation bottomed out in Ireland at −6.4 per cent in October 2009, but was still −4 per cent as late as January 2010.

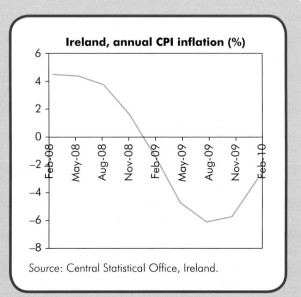

Source: Central Statistical Office, Ireland.

Questions

(a) Opponents of monetary union argue that it prevents adjustments in competitiveness when required. In each of the following cases, label this problem as important or less important:

(i) an economy with flexible labour markets

(ii) an economy that trades only a little with the rest of the world

(iii) an economy with powerful trade unions

(iv) an economy that is extremely open to trade with its near neighbours

(v) an economy with similar industries to its major trading partners

(vi) an economy whose government always pursues fiscal prudence

(b) Suppose everyone in the economy simultaneously took a 20 per cent reduction in income, and firms passed on lower costs as lower prices:

(i) Would people's living standards have fallen?

(ii) Does this depend on how open the economy is?

(iii) Would it always be better to have the option to depreciate the exchange rate?

To check your answers to these questions, go to page 688.

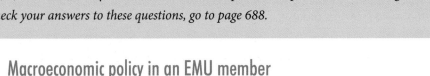

Macroeconomic policy in an EMU member

Figure 29.3 shows what life is like for an EMU member. Interest rates are set by the ECB in Frankfurt. From an individual country's viewpoint, it is as if the *LM* curve is horizontal at r_0. Suppose the initial level of the *IS* curve allows equilibrium at *A*. Aggregate demand equals potential output.

Now the country faces a shock that shifts the *IS* curve down to IS_1. With full monetary sovereignty, the country might have cut its interest rate to restore full-employment output at *C*. This might still happen in EMU if the country is highly correlated with other EMU countries. The ECB will react to what is happening throughout the eurozone and cut interest rates for everybody.

However, if no other countries face the *IS* curve shock and the country is too small to influence eurozone data to which the ECB reacts, interest rates will remain at r_0. The country now faces two choices. Provided it does not infringe the Stability Pact, it can use fiscal policy to shift IS_1 to the right or it can wait for its labour market to do the same thing.

How does this work? At *B*, the country is facing a slump. This gradually reduces inflation. At the fixed nominal exchange rate against its partners, this makes the country more competitive. Higher exports and lower imports shift the IS_1 curve to the right. If wage and price flexibility is high enough, there may be no need for fiscal policy. However, many European labour markets are quite sluggish. Sensible use of fiscal policy may speed up the process.

One final point. If there is no discretionary change in tax rates and spending levels, fiscal relaxation in a recession is limited to the automatic stabilizers. However, these cannot see into the future. Only after income falls is revenue from income tax reduced. In 2001 Europe was hit by two demand shocks: the US recession as the dotcom bubble burst and the confidence collapse after 11 September.

Because the real economy is sluggish, it took time for these to feed through into lower output, lower employment and lower inflation. But by 12 September everyone knew these were coming. Ideally, demand policies should have been eased to offset these demand shocks. If fiscal policy is largely confined to backward-looking automatic stabilizers, the only channel for a forward-looking policy response is through interest rate cuts.

Hence, the fiscal framework in the EMU raises the burden on monetary policy to react to shocks even before they have fed fully through into output and inflation.

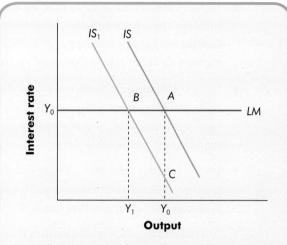

A small EMU member faces a horizontal *LM* curve at the interest rate set by the ECB. If the *IS* curve shifts to IS_1, interest rates will be reduced only if the whole of EMU is affected by the shock. Otherwise, the country faces a slump that gradually reduces its prices and wages, boosting competitiveness and shifting IS_1 to the right. A fiscal expansion could induce this shift more quickly.

Figure 29.3 **A member of the eurozone**

Summary

- Under the **gold standard**, each country fixed the **par value of its currency** against gold, maintained the **convertibility** of its currency into gold at this price and linked the domestic money supply to gold stocks at the central bank. It was a fixed exchange rate regime.

- Without capital flows, countries with a trade deficit faced a payments deficit, lower gold stocks and a lower money supply. Domestic recession then bid down wages and prices, raising competitiveness – an automatic adjustment mechanism. Trade surplus countries faced a monetary inflow, higher prices and lower competitiveness. In practice, this adjustment mechanism was hampered by capital flows.

- The post-war **Bretton Woods system** was an **adjustable peg** in which fixed exchange rates were sometimes adjusted. It was a dollar standard. But domestic money supplies were no longer linked to forex reserves, so the adjustment mechanism of the gold standard was weakened.

- **Purchasing power parity (PPP)** is the path of the nominal exchange rate that would maintain constant competitiveness by offsetting differential inflation across countries. In the long run, floating exchange rates return to the PPP path if no real shocks occur.

- In the short run, the level of **floating exchange rates** is determined largely by speculation. Exchange rates adjust to ensure interest differentials are offset by expected exchange rate changes. This chokes off large speculative flows. In the short run, exchange rates can depart significantly from their long-run level.

- Unlike fixed exchange rates, floating exchange rates can cope with permanent differences in national inflation rates. High-inflation countries have a depreciating exchange rate in the long run. In practice, floating exchange rates also coped with the severe real shocks of the 1970s. Floating exchange rate regimes are more robust than fixed exchange rate regimes.

- Critics of floating exchange rates claim they are volatile in the short run, which discourages international trade and investment. However, they are volatile because the world is uncertain. Under fixed exchange rates the uncertainty would show up somewhere else, possibly in volatile domestic interest rates to maintain the fixed exchange rate.

- Fixed exchange rates impose financial discipline by preventing a country having permanently higher inflation than the rest of the world. However, there are other ways to commit to low inflation. And fixed exchange rates do not always survive!

- International policy co-ordination is hard to implement but allows policy makers to take account of the externalities they impose on each other. It may allow individual governments to commit themselves to policies that would otherwise not be credible.

- The UK was always a member of the European Monetary System but belonged to its key feature, the Exchange Rate Mechanism, only during 1990–92. The early survival of the ERM arose only partly from greater co-ordination of monetary policy by ERM participants. Foreign exchange controls and exchange rate bands were also important. After 1983 devaluations became harder to obtain and monetary policies had to converge on the low inflation rate in Germany.

- In abolishing capital controls before 1992, the ERM had already harmonized monetary policy, under German leadership. The UK became an ERM member in 1990, but left in 1992.

- A monetary union means permanently fixed exchange rates, free capital movements and a single interest rate.

- The Maastricht criteria say that EMU entrants, including future ones, must have shown low inflation, low interest rates and stable nominal exchange rates before entry; and must have budget deficits and government debt under control.

- EMU members must continue to obey the Stability Pact, which fines countries for excessive budget deficits, except if they are in recession, as in 2009/10.

- In the EMU, a country's competitiveness can change through the slow process of domestic wage and price adjustment. Without a federal fiscal system, individual member states may want to keep control of fiscal policy to deal with crises.

Review questions

connect

1 During the First World War the gold standard was suspended. To pay for the war, Britain printed money and sold off its foreign assets. What do you think happened in 1925 when Britain tried to rejoin the gold standard at the old nominal exchange rate?

2 Contrast the dollar standard and the gold standard in terms of: (a) the automatic adjustment mechanism, and (b) financial discipline.

3 What are the advantages and disadvantages of a currency board?

4 If floating is so great, why did most EU countries join a monetary union in 1999?

5 When the UK left the ERM in 1992, the UK stock market and the UK bond market reacted very differently. Which market rose strongly? What was worrying the other market?

6 Common fallacies   Why are these statements wrong? (a) Floating exchange rates make sure that exports and imports always balance. (b) Fixed exchange rate regimes prevent necessary changes in competitiveness.

7 Which are correct? Some countries in the eurozone have suffered speculative attack in 2010 because: (a) interest rates have been unnecessarily high; (b) they have been unable to devalue to boost growth and tax revenues; (c) they can put pressure on richer eurozone countries to bail them out; (d) they cannot use inflation as a weapon of last resort for deflating away government debt.

8 'What has not flowed in cannot then flow out.' Which exchange rate regime would best insulate a country from capital inflows? What would be the cost of this policy?

9 Use an *IS–LM* diagram to show the consequences of negative inflation in Ireland.

10 Use a similar diagram to illustrate what happened to the UK in 1992 after it left the Exchange Rate Mechanism.

MEDIUM

11 A Mediterranean eurozone country's government has borrowed entirely in Berlin and London. It owes each £5 billion. On the total £10 billion, it is supposed to pay £500 million a year, a return of 5 per cent to creditors, matching the going rate of return elsewhere. But the country is bust and can only raise enough tax revenue to pay £100 million a year. Recognizing this, each bond worth £100 is trading for only £20 in the secondary market. People buying those bonds second-hand realize that they will only get a fifth of what they should. (a) The IMF writes off £5 billion of the country's debt. What is the maximum the country can pay in interest now? What do remaining creditors insist on? What happens to the price of its debt in secondary markets? (b) Who benefits from this capital gain? (c) Should the UK and Germany contribute to a further bail out?

12 You are Finance Minister of Cuba in the new government that has decided to abandon five decades of communism and move as rapidly as possible to a free market. (a) Should Cuban citizens expect rising or falling incomes in the long run? (b) If they implement life-cycle or permanent income approaches to consumption, will they wish to borrow or to lend during this transition? (c) What do you expect to happen to Cuba's international trade balance?

13 (a) Continuing from Question 12, from now on, will Cuba offer unusually good or unusually bad investment opportunities? (b) What will happen if Cuba pursues a fixed exchange rate policy during this period? (c) What will happen if Cuba follows a floating exchange rate policy? (d) Which of the two would you recommend?

14 Essay question   'Small open economies need fixed exchange rates; large economies need floating exchange rates.' Is this broad generalization correct? Explain why, or why not.

HARD

For solutions to these questions contact your lecturer.

Answers to activity questions

Activity 1.1

(a) Health care was largely rationed by price – if you could not afford it, you could not buy it.

(b) NHS still rationed health care via (i) waiting lists, and (ii) not making some procedures available.

Activity 2.1

(a) 3.5.

(b) 2.33.

(c) Samantha.

(d) Possible explanations include: Samantha is cleverer, concentrates more effectively and has a better memory; David's mind is always on politics no matter how hard he studies.

Activity 3.1

(a) As European and Chinese labour markets are unified, the huge addition of Chinese labour makes the labour supply schedule shift to the right, reducing equilibrium wages.

(b) With the Chinese economy growing rapidly, the demand for raw materials such as coal is enhanced worldwide. The demand curve shifts up.

(c) The demand curve for Bentleys shifts down.

Maths 4.1

(a)

	B	D	E
(1) Initial P and Q	P = 2	P = 4	P = 5
	Q = 8	Q = 4	Q = 2
(2) New P and Q	P = 3	P = 3	P = 6
	Q = 6	Q = 6	Q = 1
(3) % change in P	100 * (3 − 2)/2 = 50	100 * (3 − 4)/4 = −25	100 * (6 − 5)/5 = 20
(4) % change in Q thus induced	100 * (6 − 8)/8 = −25	100 * (6 − 4)/4 = 50	100 * (1 − 2)/2 = −50
(5) PED = (4)/(3)	−0.5	−2	−2.5

(b)

	B	D	E
(1) Initial P and Q	$P = 2$	$P = 4$	$P = 5$
	$Q = 8$	$Q = 4$	$Q = 2$
(2) New P and Q	$P = 3$	$P = 3$	$P = 6$
	$Q = 6$	$Q = 6$	$Q = 1$
(3) % change in P	$100 * (3 - 2)/$ $((3 + 2)/2) = 40$	$100 * (3 - 4)/$ $((3 + 4)/2) = -28.6$	$100 * (6 - 5)/$ $((6 + 5)/2) = 18.2$
(4) % change in Q thus induced	$100 * (6 - 8)/$ $((6 + 8)/2) = -28.6$	$100 * (6 - 4)/$ $((6 + 4)/2) = 40$	$100 * (1 - 2)/$ $((1 + 2)/2) = -66.7$
(5) PED = (4)/(3)	-0.7	-1.4	-3.7

Activity 7.1

(a) In period 2, the cost of the machine is a sunk cost and should not enter calculation of marginal cost. Since the machine ties the two periods together, the smart way for the firm to think in period 1 is to not make a single-period decision but to make a decision over the two-period horizon, foreseeing how it will itself behave once period 2 arrives and it then has a low MC schedule because the machine is by then a sunk cost. Forecasting its own period-2 behaviour, it can decide in period 1 what the marginal benefit of the machine is over the two periods and choose output and investment accordingly in period 1. Tough question!

(b) Sunk costs are sunk. From now on, if you think you are going to lose, ignore what you have bet and quit!

Activity 12.1

(a)

	Asset price			Portfolio value		
Outcome	(a) FTSE index	(b) Low beta asset	(c) High beta asset	A ½ of (a) + ½ of (b)	B ⅓ of (a) + ⅔ of (b)	C ½% of (a) + ½ of (c)
Boom	120	90	150	105	100	135
Normal	100	100	100	100	100	100
Slump	80	110	50	95	100	65

Activity 13.1

(a) Use a zero discount rate on future utility.

(b) A unit of additional future consumption yields less benefit than a unit of current consumption; using a positive discount rate for future consumption reflects this. Conversely, if the burden of global warming reduces the utility of future generations below that of current generations, the consumption of future generations should then carry more weight than current generations (a negative discount rate!).

(c) At least as high a rate of return on environmental investments as investment in physical or human capital.

Activity 14.1

(a) Party leaders prefer the prospect of power to the adoption of a political position that they happen to think correct (and party members have elected leaders with these attributes).

(b) Smart politicians will each locate in the centre.

(c) Now locating too centrally risks losing some extremists, who will abstain from voting. How close a party should move to the centre depends on how many votes it loses by occupying an extreme position versus how many it gains by being closer to the centre. Political equilibrium should now have some clear blue water between the two parties, with neither contesting the exact centre ground. And of course all this presumes voter opinions are equally spread. If there is a big cluster of voters a third of the way from left to right, this is where the median voter will be. Parties will be trying to position themselves near here, even though it is not halfway from left to right.

Activity 15.1

(a) It does not – that is why it is *gross* domestic product.

(b) Net domestic product or net national income would include a deduction for capital depreciation.

(c) Fairly rough and ready – assuming, for example, a lifetime of five years for a TV, ten years for a car, 25 years for a factory, and writing the initial value off steadily over the period.

(d) You would need to estimate the value of the stock of environmental capital – green fields, fresh air, temperate climate, and so on – and then decide each year whether reduction caused by humans (pollution, etc.) was more or less than investment made by humans (land improvement, lower emissions, etc.).

(e) In practice, the best way to estimate the capital value would probably be to estimate the annual consumer benefit (e.g. of green fields) and then work out the present value using a suitable discount rate.

Activity 16.1

(a) and (c) are shifts in *AD*, but (b) is a movement along a given *AD* schedule.

Activity 17.1

(a) Because fluctuations in income alter tax revenue.

(b) An independent report could be useful, although regular IMF reports on individual countries perform some of the same function.

(c) Bond markets would experience price falls and long-term interest rates would rise.

(d) Government investment today adds to output and potential tax revenue tomorrow, and hence is close to self-financing from a long-run government perspective.

(e) (i) Raise taxes and cut spending. (ii) Reduces aggregate demand unless has sufficiently beneficial effect on confidence and autonomous demand to offset these effects; (iii) to the extent output falls, tax revenue will be lower than it would have been if output had not fallen; (iv) even so, the deficit will be reduced relative to what it would have been; (v) autonomous investment could go either way – depends on whether confidence effect outweighs the short-term pessimism on immediate course of output and growth.

Activity 18.1

(a) Because cash is liquid and can be used to make transactions; it is also riskless and hence may be valuable as an asset.

(b) The key difference between debt and equity is that equity never has to be repaid and firms can vary the level of dividends that they pay each year – in a bad year the firm can make zero dividend payments. If all its financing was debt, it might (often) be unable to meet the required interest payments and have to declare bankruptcy.

(c) In exchange for absorbing this degree of risk, investors in equities demand a rate of return that on average exceeds the return on debt by several percentage points a year, though because of capital gains and losses of volatile share prices, this is only true on average – particular years can be much better or much worse.

(d) Liquidity crisis. If it was a solvency crisis, the Treasury would have to be involved since taxpayers' money would then be at risk.

Activity 19.1

(a) Interest rate changes will not take effect until people next recalculate their optimal behaviour – for example, it may affect new car purchases but only when people have decided that their current car is no longer appropriate.

(b) Yes. As with monetary policy, it is important to distinguish changes that have immediate effect (mortgage payments, VAT changes) on disposable income, which must affect behaviour somehow, and those which operate through behavioural incentives once decision makers have recognized the effect of the new incentives.

(c) People would wait to see if interest rate changes were temporary or persistent before changing big decisions such as car or house purchase.

Activity 20.1

(a) 1998, 2000 and 2007.

(b) Expected future inflation.

(c) Lewis Hamilton does not mind turning left and then turning right shortly afterwards; however, his performance is very transparent and his skill easily assessed. Central banks need people to trust their competence, and may worry a bit more about the impact rapid reversals have on their perceived credibility. If so, they will deliberately err on the side of changing interest rates by small amounts so that the next change is likely to be in the same direction, appearing to add to their credibility. The better established their credibility, the more they might be prepared to change interest rates by a larger amount or to reverse a previous decision more quickly.

(d) With zero nominal interest rate and negative inflation, real interest rate is positive, reducing aggregate demand, causing yet more negative inflation, yet higher real interest rates, and yet lower aggregate demand. A death spiral to be avoided at all costs.

Activity 21.1

(a) Statistical extrapolation of past trends and cycles requires only the macroeconomic data on output itself, is quickly implemented and easily conducted for many countries. An economist would think it a crude approximation. If there was a serious shock to the level of potential output, past extrapolation would stop working, but a statistician could always start a new extrapolation recognizing that other things were no longer equal.

(b) A direct economic approach might try to use the level and rate of change of inflation to make inferences about the level of excess demand or supply, or might try to build up a more detailed model of aggregate supply based on inputs of capital, labour, technology etc.

(c) Actual output was at, or already above, potential output.

Activity 22.1

(a) An Asian policy boost from monetary and fiscal policy.

(b) Little.

(c) The sooner Asian countries run out of spare capacity, the sooner they will have to tighten monetary policy.

(d) Either Australia was more prudent more quickly, or its economic concentration on minerals made demand for its output rise more quickly once Asia recovered.

(e) They will face an adverse supply shock while demand is still low; the former will start to cause inflation and interest rates may have to rise even before output recovery is well established.

Activity 23.1

(a) If you are a mathematician, try answering Review Question 11 at the end of the chapter. Otherwise, try Question 9, which will provide a diagrammatic answer. If you struggle with this, the solutions will be available to your lecturer on the OLC.

(b) It does not make any difference who pays the tax. Either way, it drives the same wedge between the cost of labour to the firm and the take-home pay of the worker.

(c) If there is Keynesian unemployment in the labour market, the balanced budget multiplier implies that the demand effect of extra spending on nurses outweighs the demand effect of higher taxation. If there is only equilibrium unemployment, the extra tax drives a wedge and creates extra equilibrium unemployment. Since the labour supply and job acceptances schedules are closer together at higher levels of wages and demand, adding to overall demand would in itself tend to reduce equilibrium unemployment by a small amount. On balance, the former effect might be larger, but the net result might not be large.

Activity 24.1

(a) Yes.

(b) Switzerland, Italy, Greece, China. Switzerland, being already richest, may have least scope for future productivity growth.

(c) What matters for the Balassa–Samuelson (BS) effect is traded versus non-traded. Technical progress in services makes more of these tradeable: if that was the only effect, it might not affect BS much. However, if it generally raises wages and productivity in non-tradeds, it erodes the distinction on which BS is based. As yet, we are not near that point in practice.

Activity 25.1

(a) Try answering Review Question 11 at the end of the chapter. Inflation convergence took place once different countries adopted inflation targeting with similar targets.

(b) Don't forget that this could also be a judgement on the weakness of UK trading partners. Optimism regarding the strength of London's financial services could also have been significant.

(c) On interest rates, not much difference. On quantitative easing, the Bank of England is more aggressive than the European Central Bank, so the UK would have suffered more. Sterling has fallen substantially, and the greater competitiveness has helped mitigate the UK recession relative to what it might have been. Without this, fears about future UK growth would have been greater, and concerns about tax revenue exacerbated.

Activity 26.1

(a) In Figure 26.1, if k and y are low, even a small amount of saving is sufficient for capital deepening, this improving the future position.

(b) If aid to countries in a poverty trap allows them to break out completely, the present value of the extra output and welfare is huge compared with aid that merely speeds up slightly what would have happened anyway.

(c) In Figure 26.2 suppose the line nk has a larger n whenever k is below a critical amount. There are then two possible equilibria – a high-n low-k equilibrium and a low-n high-k equilibrium. Aid would be very valuable if it allowed the economy to increase k enough to move into the more benign regime. It might be plausible if children were seen as insurance against old age, and poor countries feared more for life in old age.

Activity 27.1

(a) Wages and employment are inversely related as the economy moves along a given labour demand curve.

(b) Labour demand curves shift down, which tends to mean lower wages and lower employment. If the shift is large enough, this dominates the effect in (a).

(c) A supply shock leaves the demand curve unaltered and restores the answer in (a).

(d) It is not worth firing to rehire in the near future. If the recession is temporary, it would be better to hang on to labour.

(e) They are likely to shed labour if they become pessimistic about the length of recession.

Activity 28.1

(a) Probably from two-way trade since the countries are rather similar to one another in economic structure – hence the benefits probably result more from greater competition and scale economies than from more comparative advantage. There are exceptions – for example, the agricultural Mediterranean regions probably traded different goods with northern Europe.

(b) Imperfect competition often reflects the presence of scale economies. Therefore if trade enhances market size and competition, it is probably the two-way-trade channel rather than comparative advantage that is generating gains from trade.

(c) Yes, in the same way as removal of tariffs allows greater exploitation of comparative advantage. Instead of adding a tariff, we are removing a barrier. The only difference is that tariffs create a revenue rectangle for government, whereas non-tariff barriers create a profit rectangle for domestic producers.

Activity 29.1

(a) (i) less, (ii) less, (iii) important, (iv) less, (v) less, (vi) less.

(b) Domestically, if all wages and prices fall together, no real incomes change. In a closed economy, the only remaining effect is that nominal debts increase in real value unless their nominal value can be adjusted too. In an open economy, cutting domestic wages and prices makes foreign goods and services more expensive – that is precisely the competitiveness gain achieved either by devaluation or by domestic price and wage cuts – in effect it is a fall in the international value of the domestic wage. Depreciation co-ordinates the international value of wage and price falls – trying to do so through domestic recession is messy and takes much longer. In itself, this is an advantage of the ability to depreciate, but may be offset by other benefits of fixed exchange rates or monetary union if other conditions are right.

THE LIBRARY
TOWER HAMLETS COLLEGE
POPLAR HIGH STREET
LONDON E14 0AF
Tel: 0207 510 7763

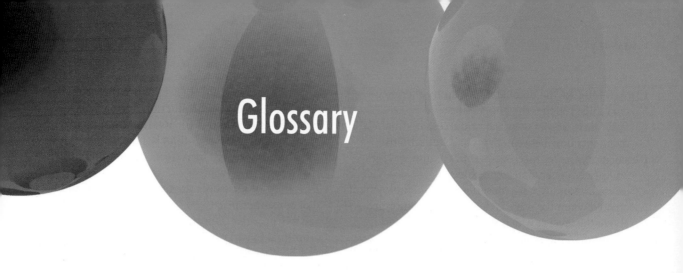

Glossary

Absolute advantage an individual, company or country is the lowest-cost producer of a good.

Accelerator model of investment assumes that firms guess future output and profits by extrapolating past output growth. Constant output growth leads to a constant level of investment. It takes accelerating output growth to raise desired investment.

Adjustable peg a fixed exchange rate, the value of which may occasionally be changed.

Aggregate demand the amount firms and households plan to spend at each level of income.

Aggregate price level measures the average price of goods and services.

Aggregate supply schedule shows the output that firms wish to supply at each inflation rate.

Appreciation (of the exchange rate) a rise in the international value of a currency.

Asset motive this motive for holding money reflects dislike of risk. People sacrifice a high average rate of return to obtain a portfolio with a lower but safer rate of return.

Automatic stabilizers reduce the multiplier and thus output response to demand shocks.

Average tax rate the fraction of total income paid in tax.

Balance of payments records transactions between residents of one country and the rest of the world; it is the sum of current account, capital and financial account items.

Balanced budget multiplier a rise in government spending plus an equal rise in taxes leads to higher output.

Bank deposit multiplier the ratio of broad money to bank reserves.

Bank reserves the money that the bank has available to meet possible withdrawals by depositors.

Barter economy an economy in which there is no medium of exchange; goods are swapped for other goods.

Behavioural law a sensible theoretical relationship not rejected by evidence over a long period.

Benefits principle the belief that people getting most benefit from public spending should pay most for it.

Bertrand model each firm treats the prices of rivals as given.

Beta measures how much an asset's return moves with the return on the whole stock market.

Broad money includes all assets fulfilling the functions of money, and is principally bank deposits.

Budget the spending and revenue plans of an individual, company or government.

Budget constraint the different bundles that the consumer can afford.

Budget deficit the excess of government spending over government receipts.

Budget share the price of a good times its price times the quantity demanded, divided by total consumer spending or income.

Budget surplus the excess of government spending over government revenue.

Business cycle the short-term fluctuation of total output around its trend path.

Capital adequacy ratio a required minimum value of bank capital relative to its outstanding loans and investments.

Capital controls regulations preventing private sector capital flows between different currencies.

Capital deepening raises capital per worker for all workers.

Capital gain the rise in a share's price while it is held.

Capital widening extends the existing capital per worker to new extra workers.

Cash flow the net amount of money actually received during a period.

Central bank banker to the government and to the banks. It also conducts monetary policy.

Glossary

Chosen bundle the point at which an indifference curve just touches the budget line.

Circular flow shows how real resources and financial payments flow between firms and households.

Classical model of macroeconomics assumes wages and prices are completely flexible.

Classical unemployment describes the unemployment created when the wage is deliberately maintained above the level at which the labour supply and labour demand schedules intersect.

Closed shop an agreement that all a firm's workers will be members of a trade union.

Collusion an explicit or implicit agreement to avoid competition.

Command economy a government planning office decides what will be produced, how it will be produced, and for whom it will be produced. Detailed instructions are then issued to households, firms and workers.

Commercial banks financial intermediaries licensed to make loans and issue deposits, including deposits against which cheques can be written.

Commitment an arrangement, entered into voluntarily, that restricts future actions.

Company an organization legally allowed to produce and trade.

Comparative advantage an individual, company or country has a comparative advantage compared to another in the production of a good if they/it have (has) a lower opportunity cost in producing it.

Comparative static analysis changes one of the 'other things equal' and examines the effect on equilibrium price and quantity.

Complements goods which accompany a chosen good; a price increase for one good reduces the demand for these complements.

Constant returns to scale long-run average costs are constant as output rises.

Consumer price index (CPI) inflation measures the rate of growth of an index of consumer prices.

Consumption function shows aggregate consumption demand at each level of personal disposable income.

Contestable market has free entry and free exit.

Convergence hypothesis asserts that poor countries grow more quickly than average, but rich countries grow more slowly than average.

Convertible a currency is convertible if the central bank will buy or sell as much of the currency as people wish to trade at the fixed exchange rate.

Corporate control who controls the firm in different situations.

Corporate finance how firms finance their activities.

Cost what is spent on production during a period.

Cost of holding money the interest given up by holding money rather than bonds.

Cournot model each firm treats the output of the other firm as given.

CPI inflation measures the rate of growth of an index of consumer prices.

Credible promise a promise about the future that is optimal to carry out when the future arrives.

Credible threat one that, after the fact, is still optimal to carry out.

Cross-price elasticity of demand the percentage change in the quantity of a good demanded, divided by the corresponding percentage change in the price of that good.

Cross-section data record, at a point in time, the way an economic variable differs across different individuals or groups of individuals.

Crowding out a fiscal stimulus to aggregate demand crowds out some private spending. Higher output induces a rise in interest rates that dampens the expansionary effect on demand by reducing some components of private spending.

Currency board a constitutional commitment to peg the exchange rate by giving up monetary independence.

Current account of the balance of payments records international flows of goods, services and current transfers.

Current transfers transfer payments paid across borders.

Data pieces of evidence about economic behaviour.

Deadweight loss lost social surplus by producing the wrong output level.

Deflation negative inflation, when the price level is falling.

Demand the quantity that buyers wish to purchase at each conceivable price.

Demand curve shows the relationship between price and quantity demanded, other things equal.

Demand-deficient unemployment occurs when output is below full capacity.

Demand-determined output since markets trade the smaller of supply and demand, output is demand-determined when there is excess supply and wages and prices have yet to adjust to restore long-run equilibrium. Output then depends only on aggregate demand.

Demand elasticity demand is elastic if the price elasticity is more negative than −1.

Demand for money a demand for real money balances.

Demand inelasticity demand is inelastic if the price elasticity lies between −1 and 0.

Demand management uses monetary and fiscal policy to stabilize output near potential output.

Depletable resources resources that can be used only once.

Depreciation the loss in value of a capital good during a period.

Depreciation (of the exchange rate) a fall in the international value of a currency.

Derived demand the demand for inputs reflects demand for a firm's output.

Devaluation (revaluation) reduces (increases) the par value of the pegged exchange rate.

Diminishing marginal rate of substitution tastes exhibit this when, to hold utility constant, diminishing quantities of one good must be sacrificed to get successive equal increases in the quantity of the other good.

Diminishing marginal utility each extra unit consumed, holding constant consumption of other goods, adds successively less to total utility.

Direct taxes taxes on income and wealth.

Discount rate the interest rate that the Bank charges when banks want to borrow cash.

Discouraged workers people pessimistic about finding a job who leave the labour force as a result.

Discretion free choice without restrictions imposed by prior commitments.

Discretionary fiscal policy decisions about tax rates and levels of government spending.

Discriminating monopoly one which charges different prices to different people.

Diseconomies of scale (or decreasing returns to scale) long-run average cost rises as output rises.

Distortion exists if society's marginal cost of producing a good does not equal society's marginal benefit from consuming that good.

Diversification pools risk across several assets whose individual returns behave differently from one another.

Dividends the regular payments of profit to shareholders.

Domestic price of foreign exchange quantity of domestic currency per unit of foreign currency.

Dominant strategy a player's best strategy *whatever* the strategies adopted by rivals.

Dumping occurs when foreign producers sell at prices below their marginal production cost, either by making losses or with the assistance of government subsidies.

Econometrics uses mathematical statistics to measure relationships in economic data.

Economic growth a rise in real GNP.

Economic rent (not to be confused with income from renting out property) the payment a factor receives in excess of the transfer earnings needed to induce it to supply its services in that use.

Economic sovereignty the power of national governments to make decisions independently of those made by other governments.

Economics the study of how society decides what, how and for whom to produce.

Economies of scale (or increasing returns to scale) long-run average cost falls as output rises.

Effective exchange rate an average of a country's exchange rate against all its trade partners, weighted by the relative size of trade with each country.

Efficiency wages high wages that raise productivity through their incentive effect.

Efficient asset market already incorporates existing information properly in asset prices.

Endogenous growth implies that the steady-state growth rate is affected by economic behaviour and economic policy.

Endogenous variables those variables which a model delivers as outputs, conditional on the values of the exogenous inputs.

Entry when new firms join an industry.

E-product a product that can be digitally encoded, then transmitted rapidly, accurately and cheaply.

Equilibrium output is independent of inflation.

Equilibrium price the price at which the quantity supplied equals the quantity demanded.

Equilibrium unemployment (also called the natural rate of unemployment) the unemployment rate when the labour market is in equilibrium.

Excess demand exists when the quantity demanded exceeds the quantity supplied at the ruling price.

Excess supply exists when the quantity supplied exceeds the quantity demanded at the ruling price.

Exchange rate the price at which two currencies exchange.

Exchange Rate Mechanism (ERM) part of the EMS. Each country fixed a nominal exchange rate against each other ERM participant. Collectively, the group floated against the rest of the world.

Exchange rate regime describes how governments allow exchange rates to be determined.

Exit when existing firms leave an industry.

Glossary

Exogenous variables those variables fed into a model as inputs.

Experience good or service one that must be sampled before the user knows its value.

Export subsidies government assistance to domestic firms in competing with foreign firms.

Exports domestically produced goods that are sold abroad.

External balance a zero current account balance.

Externality arises if one person's production or consumption physically affects the production or consumption of others.

Fair gamble a bet which, on average, yields zero monetary profit.

Fallacy of composition what is true for the individual may not be true for everyone together, and what is true for everyone together may not hold for the individual.

Fan chart indicates the probability of different outcomes.

Federal fiscal system has a central government setting taxes and expenditure rules that apply in its constituent states or countries.

Final goods goods purchased by the ultimate user, either households buying consumer goods or firms buying capital goods such as machinery.

Financial account of the balance of payments records international purchases and sales of financial assets.

Financial intermediary specializes in bringing lenders and borrowers together.

Financial panic a self-fulfilling prophecy in which, believing a bank will be unable to pay, people rush to get their money out. But doing so makes the bank bankrupt.

First-best allocation is fully efficient; it removes all distortions.

First-mover advantage the player moving first achieves higher payoffs than when decisions are simultaneous.

Fiscal drag the rise in real tax revenue when inflation raises nominal incomes, pushing people into higher tax brackets in a progressive income tax system.

Fiscal policy government policy on spending and taxes.

Fiscal stance shows the effect of fiscal policy on demand and output.

Fisher hypothesis says higher inflation leads to similarly higher nominal interest rates.

Fixed costs total costs do not vary with output.

Fixed exchange rate regime governments maintain the convertibility of their currency at a fixed exchange rate. A currency is convertible if the central bank will buy or sell as much of the currency as people wish to trade at the fixed exchange rate.

Fixed factor of production an input that cannot be varied.

Flexible inflation targeting commits a central bank to hit inflation targets in the medium run, but gives it some discretion about how quickly to hit its inflation target.

Flight from cash the collapse in the demand for real cash when high inflation and high nominal interest rates make it very expensive to hold cash.

Floating exchange rates the exchange rate is allowed to find its equilibrium level without central bank intervention using the forex reserves.

Flow the stream of accounts measured over a period of time.

Foreign direct investment (FDI) the purchase of foreign firms or the establishment of foreign subsidiaries.

Foreign exchange (forex) market exchanges one national currency for another.

Foreign exchange reserves foreign currency held by a domestic central bank.

Forward market deals in contracts made today for delivery of goods at a specified future date at a price agreed today.

Free markets markets in which governments do not intervene.

Free rider a person who, unable to be excluded from consuming a good, has no incentive to buy it.

Frictional unemployment the irreducible minimum unemployment in a dynamic society.

Functional income distribution the division of national income among different factors of production.

Game a situation in which intelligent decisions are necessarily interdependent.

GDP at basic prices measures domestic output exclusive of indirect taxes on goods and services.

GDP at market prices measures domestic output inclusive of indirect taxes on goods and services.

Globalization the increasing integration of national markets that were previously much more segmented from one another.

GNP deflator the ratio of nominal GNP to real GNP expressed as an index.

Government solvency requires that the present value of the current and future tax revenue equals the present value of current and future spending plus any initial net debts.

Gross domestic product (GDP) the value of total output of an economy in a given period.

Gross investment the production of new capital goods and the improvement of existing capital goods.

Gross national product (GNP) measures the income of an economy; the quantity of goods and services the economy can afford to purchase.

Growth rate the percentage change per period (usually a year).

Headline inflation actual inflation reflected by growth in the retail price index.

Hedging the use of forward markets to shift risk on to somebody else.

Higher government spending on goods and services increases equilibrium output.

Horizontal equity the identical treatment of identical people.

Horizontal *LM* schedule implies the money supply is adjusted to keep interest rates constant.

Hyperinflation a period of very high inflation.

Hysteresis when a particular long-run equilibrium depends on the path any economy follows in the short run.

***ii* schedule** shows that at higher inflation rates the central bank will wish to have higher real interest rates.

Imperfectly competitive firm a firm that faces a down-sloping demand curve. Its output price reflects the quantity of goods it makes and sells.

Import tariff a tax on imports.

Imports goods produced abroad but purchased for use in the domestic economy.

Impossible triad fixed exchange rates, perfect capital mobility and monetary sovereignty. All three cannot co-exist at the same time.

Income distribution tells us how total income is divided between different groups or individuals (in a country or in the world).

Income effect the income effect of a price change is the adjustment of demand to the change in real income alone.

Income elasticity of demand the percentage change in quantity demanded of a good divided by the corresponding percentage change in income.

Income expansion path how the chosen bundle of goods varies with consumer income levels, keeping constant everything else.

Incomes policy the direct control of wages and other incomes.

Index number expresses data relative to a given base value.

Indifference curve shows all the consumption bundles yielding a particular level of utility.

Indirect taxes taxes on spending and output.

Inferior good a good for which demand falls when incomes rise; it has a negative income elasticity of demand.

Inflation a rise in the price level.

Inflation accounting uses fully inflation-adjusted definitions of costs, income and profit.

Inflation illusion confusing nominal and real changes. People's welfare depends on real variables, not nominal variables.

Inflation rate the percentage increase in the average price of goods and services.

Inflation target the central bank adjusts interest rates to try to keep inflation close to the target inflation rate.

Inflation tax the effect of inflation in raising real revenue by reducing the real value of the government's nominal debt.

Inflation-adjusted budget uses real not nominal interest rates to calculate government spending on debt interest.

Information overload arises when the volume of available information is large but the cost of processing it is high. Screening devices are then very valuable.

Injection money that flows to firms without being recycled through households.

Innocent entry barrier one not deliberately erected by incumbent firms.

Innovation the incorporation of new knowledge into actual production techniques.

Input (or factor of production) a good or service used to produce output.

Insider those with jobs, represented in wage bargaining.

Interest parity means that expected exchange rate changes offset the interest differential between domestic and foreign currency assets.

Interest rate spread the excess of a loan interest rate over a deposit interest rate.

Intermediate goods goods that are partly finished and form inputs to a subsequent production process that then uses them up.

Intermediate target a key indicator used to guide interest rate decisions.

Internal balance aggregate demand equals potential output.

International monetary system provides a medium of exchange for international transactions.

Glossary

International value of the domestic currency quantity of foreign currency per unit of domestic currency.

Intra-industry trade two-way trade in goods made within the same industry.

Invention the discovery of new knowledge.

Inventories goods held in stock by the firm for future sales.

Investment the purchase of new capital goods by firms.

Investment demand firms' desired or planned additions to physical capital (factories and machines) and to inventories.

Investment demand schedule shows desired investment at each interest rate.

Invisible hand the assertion that the individual pursuit of self-interest within free markets may allocate resources efficiently from society's viewpoint.

Involuntary unemployment when workers want to work at the going wage but cannot find jobs.

IOU money a medium of exchange based on the debt of a private firm or individual.

IS **schedule** shows combinations of income and interest rates at which aggregate demand equals actual output.

Isoquant shows minimum combinations of inputs to make a given output. Different points on an isoquant reflect different production techniques.

Labour-augmenting technical progress increases the effective labour supply.

Labour force all individuals in work or looking for work.

Laffer curve shows how much tax revenue is raised at each possible tax rate.

Land the factor of production that nature supplies.

Law of comparative advantage countries specialize in producing and exporting the goods that they produce at a lower relative cost compared to other countries.

Law of diminishing marginal returns further increases in a variable input lead to steadily decreasing marginal product of that input.

Law of diminishing returns says each extra worker adds less to output than the previous extra worker added.

Leakage leakage from the circular flow is money no longer recycled from households to firms.

Lender of last resort the central bank: it lends to banks when financial panic threatens the financial system.

Less-developed countries (LDCs) countries with low per capita incomes.

Life-cycle hypothesis assumes people make a lifetime consumption plan (including bequests to their children) that is just affordable out of lifetime income (plus any initial wealth inherited).

Limited liability shareholders of a company cannot lose more than they have already invested in the business.

Liquidity the cheapness, speed and certainty with which asset values can be converted back into money.

Liquidity crisis an institution is temporarily unable to meet immediate requests for payment even though its underlying assets exceed its liabilities.

LM **schedule** shows combinations of interest rates and income-yielding money market equilibrium when the central bank pursues a given target for the nominal money supply.

Log-rolling a vote for another person's preferred outcome on one issue in order to exchange for their vote your preferred outcome on another issue.

Long run the period needed for complete adjustment to a price change; its length depends on the type of adjustments consumers wish to make.

Long-run average cost the total cost (*LTC*) divided by level of output.

Long-run equilibrium when the price equates the quantity demanded to the total quantity supplied by the number of firms in the industry when each firm is on its long-run supply curve and firms can freely enter or exit the industry.

Long-run marginal cost the rise in long-run total cost if output rises permanently by one unit.

Long-run supply curve how price affects desired output; hence, the part of a firm's *LMC* curve above its *LAC* curve.

Long-run total cost the minimum cost of producing each output level when a firm can adjust all inputs.

Luxury good a good with an income elasticity above unity.

Maastricht criteria for joining EMU said that a country must already have achieved low inflation and sound fiscal policy.

Macroeconomics the study of the economy as a system.

Managed float central banks intervene in the forex market to try to smooth out fluctuations and nudge the exchange rate in the desired direction.

Marginal cost the rise in total cost when output rises 1 unit.

Marginal firm the last firm to enter in the market, which makes zero long-run profits.

Marginal product the marginal product of a variable factor is the extra output from an extra unit of that input, holding constant all other inputs.

Marginal product of labour is the extra total output when an extra worker is added, with other input quantities unaltered.

Marginal propensity to consume the fraction of each extra pound of disposable income that households wish to consume.

Marginal propensity to import (*MPZ*) the fraction of each extra pound of national income that domestic residents wish to spend on extra imports.

Marginal propensity to save the fraction of each extra unit of income that households wish to save.

Marginal rate of substitution the quantity of a good a consumer must sacrifice to increase the quantity of another good by one unit without changing total utility.

Marginal revenue the rise in total revenue when output rises 1 unit.

Marginal revenue product of labour the change in total output revenue when a firm sells the extra goods that an extra unit of labour input allows it to produce.

Marginal tax rate the fraction of the last pound of income paid in tax.

Marginal utility of a good is the increase in total utility obtained by consuming one more unit of that good, for a given consumption of other goods.

Marginal value product of capital the extra value of the firm's output when another unit of capital services is used, all other inputs being held fixed.

Marginal value product of labour the extra revenue from selling the output made by an extra worker.

Market a process by which households' decisions about consumption of alternative goods, firms' decisions about what and how to produce, and workers' decisions about how much and for whom to work are all reconciled by adjustment of prices.

Market demand curve the sum of the demand curves of all individuals in that market.

Median voter the person whose opinion represents the middle position on an issue.

Medium of exchange something accepted as payment only to be subsequently reused to pay for something else.

Menu costs of inflation the physical resources needed for adjustments to keep real things constant when inflation occurs.

Merit (demerit) goods goods that society thinks everyone should have (not have) regardless of whether an individual wants them.

Microeconomics offers a detailed treatment of individual decisions about particular commodities.

Minimum efficient scale (*MES*) the lowest output at which a firm's *LAC* curve stops falling.

Mismatch occurs if the skills that firms demand differ from the skills the labour force possesses.

Mixed economy a system in which the government and private sector jointly solve economic problems. The government influences decisions through taxation, subsidies and provision of free services such as defence and the police. It also regulates the extent to which individuals may pursue their own self-interest.

Model or theory makes assumptions from which it deduces how people will behave. It is a deliberate simplification of reality.

Monetary base (or **narrow money**) the quantity of notes and coins in private circulation plus the quantity of reserves held by commercial banks.

Monetary instrument the variable over which the central bank makes day-to-day choices.

Monetary policy a relationship between the state of the economy and the interest rate chosen by the central bank.

Monetary sovereignty a country's monetary independence. It is undermined if interest rates are set to maintain the pegged exchange rate because they cannot be set independently to influence the domestic economy.

Monetary target adjusting interest rates to maintain the quantity of money demanded in line with a given target for money supply.

Monetary union a commitment to permanently fixed exchange rates, an integrated financial market and a single central bank setting the single interest rate for a union.

Money any generally accepted means of payment for delivery of goods or settlement of debt.

Money illusion exists if people confuse nominal and real variables.

Money market equilibrium a situation in which the quantity of real balances demanded and supplied is equal.

Money multiplier the ratio of broad money to the monetary base.

Money supply currency in circulation outside the banking system, plus deposits of commercial banks and building societies.

Monopolist the only seller or potential seller in the industry.

Glossary

Monopolistic competition an industry with many sellers of products that are close substitutes for one another. Each firm has only a limited ability to affect its output price.

Monopoly power power exhibited by the excess of price over marginal cost.

Monopsony power with an upward-sloping factor supply curve, a firm must offer a higher factor price to attract more factors. The marginal cost of the input exceeds the factor price, since the firm bids up the price paid on all inputs already employed.

Multinationals firms operating in many countries simultaneously.

Multiplier the ratio of a change in equilibrium output to a change in autonomous spending that caused the change.

Nash equilibrium each player chooses the best strategy, *given* the strategies being followed by other players.

National debt the government's debts.

Natural level of output the level of output in long-run equilibrium.

Natural monopoly has falling average cost no matter how high its output rises. It undercuts all smaller competitors and fears no entrant.

Natural rate of unemployment the level of unemployment in long-run equilibrium.

Necessity a good with an income elasticity below unity.

Net investment gross investment minus depreciation of the existing capital stock.

Net taxes taxes minus transfers.

Net worth assets a firm owns minus liabilities it owes.

Network externality arises when an additional network member conveys benefits to those already on the network.

N-firm concentration ratio the market share of the largest N firms in the industry.

Nominal anchor determines the level of other nominal variables. Market forces determine real variables.

Nominal GNP measures GNP at the prices prevailing when income was earned.

Nominal interest rate how many actual pounds are earned by lending £1 for a year.

Nominal values are measured in the prices ruling at the time of measurement.

Non-tariff barriers different national regulations or practices that prevent free movement of goods, services and factors between countries.

Normal good a good for which demand increases when incomes rise; it has a positive income elasticity of demand.

Normal profits accounting profits which just cover the opportunity cost of an owner's money and time.

Normative economics offers recommendations based on personal value judgements.

Oligopoly an industry with few producers, each recognizing their interdependence.

Open economy macroeconomics examines how the economy is affected by links with other countries through trade, the exchange rate and capital flows.

Open economy an economy with important trade and financial links with other countries.

Open market operation occurs when the central bank alters the monetary base by buying or selling financial securities in the open market.

Opportunity cost the amount lost by not using a resource (labour, capital) in its best alternative use.

Optimal currency area a group of countries that is better off with a common currency than keeping to separate national currencies.

Optimal tariff a tariff to reduce imports to the level at which social marginal cost equals social marginal benefit.

Other things equal a device for looking at the relationship between two variables, but remembering other variables also matter.

Output gap the deviation of actual output from potential output.

Outsiders those without jobs, who are unrepresented in wage bargaining.

Panel data record observations over multiple time periods for the same individuals or groups of individuals.

Par value the exchange rate that the government agrees to defend.

Paradox of thrift a change in the amount households wish to save at each income leads to a change in equilibrium income, but no change in equilibrium saving, which must still equal planned investment.

Pareto efficiency for given tastes, resources and technology, an allocation is efficient if there is no other feasible allocation that makes some people better off and nobody worse off.

Participation rate the fraction of the population of working age who join the labour force.

Partnership a business jointly owned by two or more people, sharing the profits and being jointly responsible for any losses.

Per capita real GNP real GNP divided by the total population. It is real GNP per head.

Percentage change the absolute change divided by the original number, then multiplied by 100.

Perfect capital mobility means that a vast quantity of funds flow from one currency to another if the expected return on assets differs across currencies.

Perfect competition a market in which both buyers and sellers believe that their own actions have no effect on the market price.

Permanent income hypothesis a belief that consumption reflects long-run or permanent income.

Permanent supply shock changes potential output.

Personal disposable income the income households receive from firms, plus transfer payments received from the government, minus direct taxes paid to the government. It is the net income households can spend or save.

Personal income distribution the division of national income across individuals, regardless of the factor services from which these individuals earn their income.

Phillips curve shows that a higher inflation rate is accompanied by a lower unemployment rate. It suggests we can trade off more inflation for less unemployment or vice versa.

Physical capital machinery, equipment and buildings used in production.

Policy co-ordination the decision to set policies jointly when two interdependent areas have big cross-border spillovers.

Political business cycle arises if politicians manipulate the economy for electoral advantage.

Political economy the study of how governments make decisions.

Positive economics studies objective or scientific explanations of how the economy works.

Potential output the economy's output when inputs are fully employed.

Precautionary motive holding money to meet contingencies that we cannot yet foresee.

Present value the present value of a future £1 is the sum that, if lent today, would cumulate to £1 by that date.

Price controls government rules or laws setting price floors or ceilings that forbid the adjustment of prices to clear markets.

Price elasticity of demand (PED) the percentage change in the quantity demanded divided by the corresponding percentage change in its price. PED = (% change in quantity)/(% change in price).

Price of an asset the sum for which an asset can be purchased outright. The owner of a capital asset gets the future stream of capital services from that asset.

Principal–agent problem difficulties of a principal or owner in monitoring an agent to whom decisions have been delegated.

Principle of targeting the most efficient way to attain a given objective is to use a policy influencing that activity directly.

Private good a good that, if consumed by one person, cannot be consumed by others.

Production efficiency means more output of one good can be obtained only by sacrificing output of other goods.

Production function the maximum output obtainable from specified quantities of inputs, given existing technical knowledge.

Production possibility frontier (PPF) shows, for each output of one good, the maximum amount of the other good that can be produced.

Profit revenue minus cost.

Property rights the power of residual control, including the right to be compensated for externalities.

Public good a good that, if consumed by one person, must be consumed by others in exactly the same quantity.

Purchasing power of money an index of the quantity of goods that can be bought for £1.

Purchasing power parity (PPP) the path of the nominal exchange rate that would maintain a constant real exchange rate. Nominal exchange rate changes offset inflation differentials between countries.

Pure inflation prices of goods and inputs rise at the same rate.

Quantitative easing the creation of substantial quantities of bank reserves in order to offset a fall in the bank deposit multiplier and prevent large falls in bank lending and broad money.

Quantity theory of money changes in nominal money lead to equivalent changes in the price level (and money wages), but have no effect on output and employment.

Quotas restrictions on the maximum quantity of imports.

Reaction function how optimal actions by one player vary with the assumed actions of the other player.

Real business cycle theories explain cycles as fluctuations in potential output itself.

Real exchange rate the relative price of goods from different countries when measured in a common currency.

Glossary

Real GNP adjusts for inflation by measuring GNP in different years at the prices prevailing at some particular date known as the base year.

Real interest rate the return on a loan, adjusted for inflation, which shows as the extra quantity of goods earned by postponing consumption.

Real money supply the nominal money supply M divided by the price level P.

Real values adjust nominal values for changes in the price level.

Regulatory capture the regulator gradually comes to identify with the interests of the firm it regulates, becoming its champion not its watchdog.

Renewable resources resources that can be used again if not over-exploited.

Rental rate (for capital) the cost of using capital services.

Replacement rate the level of benefits relative to wages in work.

Repo the sale of an asset with a simultaneous agreement to repurchase later.

Required rental on capital an amount which just covers the opportunity cost of owning the asset.

Required reserve ratio a minimum ratio of cash reserves to deposits that banks are required to hold.

Reserve ratio the ratio of reserves to deposits.

Resource allocation a complete description of who does what and who gets what.

Retained earnings the part of after-tax profits ploughed back into a business.

Revenue what the firm earns from selling goods or services in a given period.

Reverse repo a purchase with a simultaneous agreement to resell later.

Ricardian equivalence says that it does not matter when a government finances a given spending programme. Tax cuts today do not affect private spending if, in present value terms, future taxes rise to match.

Risk-averse a person who will refuse a fair gamble.

Risk-lover a person who bets even when the odds are unfavourable.

Risk-neutral a person who is interested only in whether the odds yield a profit on average.

Risk pooling aggregates independent risks to make the aggregate more certain.

Risk sharing works by reducing the stake.

Rule a commitment describing how behaviour changes when circumstances change.

Saving the part of income not spent buying goods and services.

Saving function shows desired saving at each income level.

Scarce resource a resource is scarce if the demand of that resource at a zero price would exceed the available supply.

Scatter diagram plots pairs of values simultaneously observed for two different variables.

Second-best the most efficient outcome that can be achieved conditional on being unable to remove some distortions.

Seigniorage real revenue acquired by the government through its ability to print money.

Self-fulfilling prophecy an expectation that creates the incentive to make it come true.

Shoe-leather costs of inflation the extra time and effort in transacting when we economize on holding real money.

Short run the period after prices change but before quantity adjustment can occur.

Short-run average fixed cost (SAFC) short-run fixed cost (SFC) divided by output.

Short-run average total cost (SATC) short-run total cost (STC) divided by output.

Short-run average variable cost (SAVC) short-run variable cost (SVC) divided by output.

Short-run equilibrium when the price equates the quantity demanded to the total quantity supplied by the given number of firms in the industry when each firm is on its short-run supply curve.

Short-run equilibrium output the output at which aggregate demand or planned spending equals the output actually produced.

Short-run marginal cost the extra cost of making an extra unit of output in the short run while some inputs remain fixed.

Short-run output decision the firm supplies the output at which $MR = SMC$, if the price covers average variable cost $SAVC_1$ at that output. If not, the firm supplies zero.

Short-run Phillips curve higher unemployment is associated with lower inflation. The height of the short-run Phillips curve reflects expected inflation.

Short-run supply curve (SAS) shows how desired output varies with inflation, for a given inherited growth of nominal wages.

Shutdown price the price below which the firm cuts its losses by making no output.

Sight deposits money that can be withdrawn 'on sight' without prior notice.

Social cost of monopoly the failure to maximize social surplus.

Sole trader a business owned by a single individual.

Solow residual the part of output growth not explained by the growth of measured inputs.

Solvency crisis an institution's assets have become less than its liabilities. The institution is then bankrupt without a rapid new injection of assets from government or shareholders.

Speculation the purchase of an asset for subsequent resale, in the belief that the total return – interest plus capital gain – exceeds the total return on other assets.

Speculative attack a large capital outflow. If successful, it causes a devaluation. Attacks are sometimes resisted, by raising interest rates and tightening fiscal policy. This works only if it can credibly be sustained.

Speculator a person who temporarily holds an asset in the hope of making a capital gain.

Spot market deals in contracts for immediate delivery and payment.

Stabilization policy government action to keep output close to potential output.

Stackelberg model a firm with a first-mover advantage can deduce how its actions induce rivals subsequently to behave.

Stagflation high inflation and high unemployment, caused by an adverse supply shock.

Steady-state path output, capital and labour grow at the same rate. Hence output per worker and capital per worker are constant.

Sterilization an open market operation between domestic money and domestic bonds, to offset the change in domestic money supply that a balance of payments surplus or deficit otherwise induces.

Stock a quantity at a given point in time.

Store of value any asset whose value largely lasts into the next period.

Strategic entry deterrence behaviour by incumbent firms to make entry of other firms less likely.

Strategic move a move that influences the other person's choice, in a manner favourable to oneself, by affecting the other person's expectations of how you will behave.

Strategy a game plan describing how a player acts, or moves, in each possible situation.

Structural budget shows what the budget will be if output is at potential output.

Structural unemployment arises from the mismatch of skills and job opportunities as the pattern of demand and supply changes.

Substitutes alternative goods sought by consumers as a result of a price increase in their original choice of good; a price rise in the chosen good raises the demand for these substitutes.

Substitution effect the substitution effect of a price change is the adjustment of demand to the relative price change alone.

Supernormal profit pure economic profit after measuring all economic costs properly.

Supply the quantity of a good that sellers wish to sell at each possible price.

Supply curve shows the relationship between price and quantity supplied, other things equal.

Supply-determined output output determined by excess demand, as under rationing.

Supply-side economics (1) analyses how taxes and other incentives affect national output when the economy is at full capacity; (2) the use of microeconomic incentives to alter the level of full employment, the level of potential output and equilibrium unemployment.

Switching costs these arise when existing costs are sunk. Changing supplier then incurs extra costs.

Tangency equilibrium in the long run, each firm's demand curve just touches its AC curve at the output level at which MC equals MR. Each firm maximizes profits but just breaks even. There is no more entry or exit.

Tangible wealth capital and land.

Tariff a tax on imports.

Tax incidence describes who eventually bears the burden of that tax.

Tax wedge the gap between the price paid by a buyer and the price received by a seller.

Technical efficiency exists if there is no other way to make a given output using less of one input and no more of the other inputs.

Technical progress a new technique allowing a given output to be made with fewer inputs than before.

Temporary supply shock shifts the short-run aggregate supply schedule, but leaves potential output unaltered.

Time deposits these deposits, paying higher interest rates, require the depositor to give notice before withdrawing money.

Time series a sequence of measurements of the same variable at different points in time.

Tobin tax a small tax on capital flow transactions.

Token money a means of payment whose value or purchasing power as money greatly exceeds its cost of production or value in uses other than as money.

Trade balance the value of net exports.

Trade deficit net exports are negative.

Glossary

Trade policy policy that affects international trade through taxes or subsidies, or by direct restrictions on imports and exports.

Trade surplus net exports are positive.

Trade union power is measured by the ability of unions to co-ordinate lower job acceptances, thereby increasing wages but reducing employment.

Transactions motive the transactions motive for holding money reflects the fact that payments and receipts are not synchronized.

Transfer earnings the minimum payments needed to induce the input to work in that job.

Transfer in kind the gift of a good or service

Transfer payment a payment, usually by the government, for which no corresponding service is provided by the recipient.

Transmission mechanism of monetary policy is the channel through which it affects output and employment.

Trend path of output the smooth path of long-run output once its short-term fluctuations are averaged out.

Two-part tariff a fixed charge for access to a service and then a price per unit that reflects the marginal cost of production.

Underlying inflation growth in the retail price index, after omitting the effect of mortgage interest rates on the cost of living.

Unemployment rate the fraction of the labour force without a job but registered as looking for work.

Unit elasticity demand elasticity is −1.

Unit of account the unit in which prices are quoted and accounts kept.

Unsterilized intervention uses forex reserves to offset balance of payments surpluses or deficits. Since foreign reserves are exchanged for domestic cash, this alters the cash in circulation and the domestic money supply.

Value added the increase in the value of goods as a result of the production process.

Variable costs total costs change with output.

Variable factor an input that can be varied, even in the short run.

Vertical equity the different treatment of different people in order to reduce the consequences of these innate differences.

Voluntary unemployment when, at the given level of wages, a worker wishes to be in the labour force but does not yet wish to accept a job.

Wealth effect the shift in the consumption function when household wealth changes.

Welfare economics deals with normative issues. It does not describe how the economy works but assesses how well it works.

Zero-growth proposal because higher measured GNP imposes environmental costs, it is best to aim for zero growth of measured GNP.

Index

Index

TOWER HAMLETS COLLEGE
Learning Centre
Poplar High Street
LONDON
E14 0AF